IN HEALTH AND IN SICKNESS

PHARMACY, PHARMACISTS, AND THE PHARMACEUTICAL INDUSTRY IN LATE IMPERIAL, EARLY SOVIET RUSSIA

MARY SCHAEFFER CONROY

EAST EUROPEAN MONOGRAPHS, BOULDER
DISTRIBUTED BY COLUMBIA UNIVERSITY PRESS, NEW YORK
1994

EAST EUROPEAN MONOGRAPHS, NO. CCCLXXXVI

Photographs are reprinted courtesy of the following:

Historical photographs of the Ferrein enterprises, except the photograph of workers sorting medicinal plants, from *Apercu historique du developpement general de la Pharmacie en Russie, et en particulier de la "Pharmacie Ferrein," fondee sous le regne de Pierre le Grand en 1901, par Daniel Gourtschin* (Moscow, 1910), no pagination. The photograph of workers sorting medicinal plants from *Opyt istoricheskago ocherka vozniknoveniia i razvitiia vsego aptekarskago dela v Rossii, a v chastnosti Staroi Nikol'skoi Apteki, prinadlezhashchei nine Tovarishchestvu "V. K. Ferrein"* . . . (Moscow, 1911).

Photograph of *signatura* from the Pharmacy Museum, Moscow; Viktor Matveevich Salo, director.

Advertisements from Keler's catalog from *Optovyi preis-kurant tovarov firmennoi zadelki Moskovskago tsentral'nago optovago sklada Fabrichno-torgovago Tovarishchestva "R. Keler i Ko. v Moskve"* (Moscow, July 1914).

Photograph of Antonina Lesnevskaia in her early twenties courtesy of Dr. Andrei Viktorovich Shabunin, St. Petersburg; the older photographs of Antonina Lesnevskaia courtesy of the Lesniewski family, Warsaw.

Photographs of the reception/dispensing area of the First Women's Pharmacy and classrooms of the Women's Pharmacy School from the Warsaw Pharmacy Museum, Dr. Teodor Kikta, director.

Photograph of the preparation room in the First Women's Pharmacy from *Apothekenbilder von Nah und Fern* III, ed. Hans Heger (Vienna, 1905).

ISBN 0-88033-283-2
Library of Congress Catalog Card Number 94-70069

Printed in the United States of America

To the memory of my father, Edward M. Schaeffer,
and to my husband Tom—their enterprise, tenacity, integrity,
and contributions to society are enduring models.

Contents

Acknowledgments

I wish to thank the following for helping me to produce this book: Dr. Glenn Sonnedecker, Professor Emeritus, School of Pharmacy, University of Wisconsin and historian of pharmacy extraordinaire, for encouraging my study of Russian pharmacy and the pharmaceutical industry, and the staff at the American Institute of the History of Pharmacy for unearthing materials relating to this topic; Dr. Viktor Matveevich Salo, Director of the Pharmacy Museum, Moscow, for assisting my research and sharing his voluminous knowledge of Russian pharmacy with me over many years, and wife Lydia Petrovna, son Nikolai and daughter-in-law Tanya (and their son Aleksei) for their generous hospitality during my trips to Moscow; Dr. Viktor Aleksandrovich Kumanev, Institute of History, Academy of Sciences, Moscow, for making possible my research in the TsGA RSFSR (Central State Archive of the RSFSR) in Moscow in the fall of 1990, as well as the excellent staff of that archive, especially Natalia Petrovna Voronovna and her marvelous colleague, who stayed at work during the October Revolution holiday 1990, while the archive was officially closed, so that I could maximize my research time; Dr. Mikhail Pavlovich Iroshnikov, Institute of History, St. Petersburg Academy of Sciences, who helped me gain entree to TsGIA SSSR (Central State Historical Archive of the USSR) in St. Petersburg, and his wife Inna Mikhailovna and daughters Lena and Faina, who, like the Salo family, have extended incredible hospitality to me and my family on several trips to Russia; Galina Alekseevna Ippolitovna, Agnessa Valentinovna Muktanova, and other archivists at TsGIA; the International Research and Exchanges Board for funding my 1990 research trip to Russia, and the University of Colorado, Denver, for assisting in funding other research trips; Dr. Andrei Viktorovich Shabunin, for generously taking time from his own work on history of medicine to send me materials from GIA P (the State Historical Archive of St. Petersburg); librarians at the Saltykov Shchedrin Library, St. Petersburg, the Lenin Library, Moscow, the Central State Scientific Medical Library and Fundamental Library of the Academy of Medical Sciences, Moscow; librarians at the National Library of Medicine, Bethesda, Auraria Library, Interlibrary Loan, and Julia Gauchman and other superb librarians at the Slavic Library at the University of Illinois; Tat'iana Biriukova, Moscow historian, for sharing information on the Ferrein family and for her hospitality; Dr. Jerzy Lesniewski, his wife Dr. Lesniewska, and Drs. Ewa and Andrzej Koryn for their information on Antonina Lesnevskaia and their hospitality in Warsaw; Dr. Teodor Kikta, director of the Pharmacy Museum, Warsaw, for sharing with me his knowledge of Antonina Lesnevskaia, Russian pharmacy, and the Polish pharmaceutical industry; Dr. Krystyna Kuzlik-Jochym and Mgr. Anna Stabrawa, Pharmacy Museum, Krakow; Miroslawa Pabis Braunstein; colleague, friend, and consummate historian Dr. Frederick (Dick) Stetson Allen for reading the manuscript of this book; colleagues, friends, and Russian (and Polish) language specialists Dr. Eugene Kozlowski, Dr. Nicholai Safonov, Regina and Alexander Avrashov, and Dr. Geraldine Kelley; my sister, Dr. Judith Ann Schaeffer, mother Blanche Schaeffer, and daughters Alexandra and Margaret Conroy for reading portions of this manuscript; and most of all my husband Thomas Francis Conroy, without whose insightful suggestions, infinite patience, and unflagging support this book could never have been written.

Vladimir Karlovich Ferrein, circa 1910.

General view of the laboratory and wholesale warehouse in *Krivokolennyi pereulok,* circa 1910. Note that Ferrein's house is attached to one of the buildings in the complex.

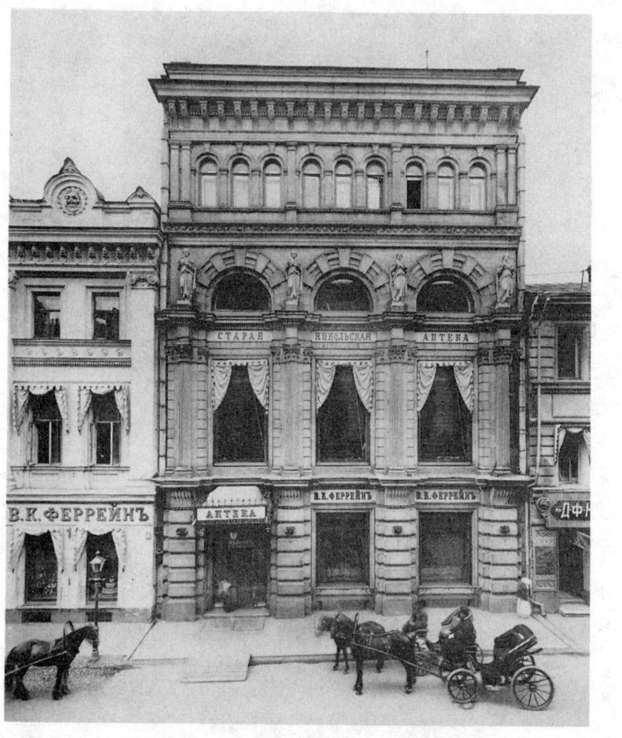

Two views of V. K. Ferrein's pharmacy: *left*, on *Staraia Nikol'skaia* Street, near the Moscow Kremlin, circa 1910, when the pharmacy was the largest in the world; *right*, the pharmacy today, which was nationalized in 1918 and named Pharmacy No. 1; the street was renamed 25th October Street.

Ground-floor department in the *Staraia Nikol'skaia* Pharmacy for *ruchnaia prodazha*–sales of over-the-counter wares–circa 1910.

Second-floor reception/dispensing room in the *Staraia Nikol'skaia* Pharmacy, circa 1910.

One of the rooms for preparing prescriptions, circa 1910. Note the women pharmacists.

One of the basement "materials" rooms in the Ferrein wholesale warehouse, circa 1910.

Partie du laboratoire pharmaceutique.

Une presse hydraulique.

Partie du laboratoire pharmaceutique.

Les percolateurs.

Various electrical apparatus in the Ferrein laboratory, circa 1910.

Interior of Ferrein's *aptekarskii magazin*, or drug store, on *Staraia Nikol'skaia* Street, next door to the pharmacy, circa 1910.

Ferrein's log *dacha* on his medicinal herb plantation at the outskirts of Moscow, 1990. After nationalization, the plantation became a research institute in the Soviet pharmacy administration.

Workers sorting medicinal plants in the *Staraia Nikol'skaia* Pharmacy, circa 1910. The ducts insured clean air for workers and materials.

Packaging and quality-control in the Ferrein wholesale warehouse, circa 1910.

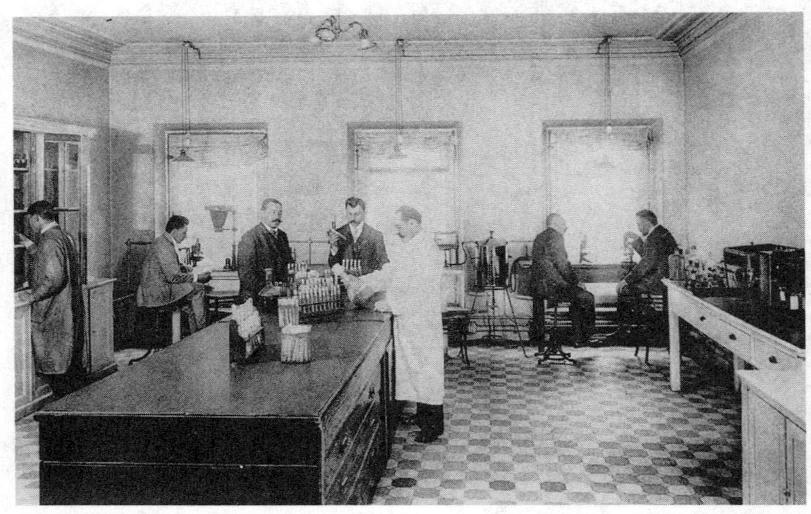

Histological-bacteriological and chemical-analytical laboratory in the Ferrein complex, circa 1910.

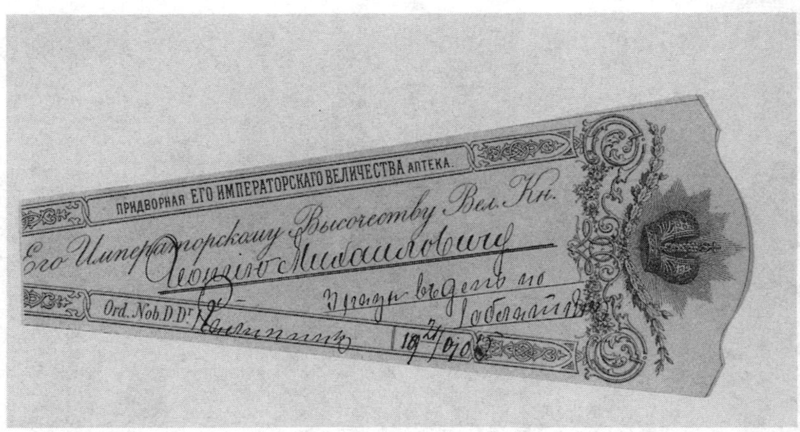

A *signatura,* or stiff cardboard label tied on Russian medicine. This label was from the imperial pharmacy.

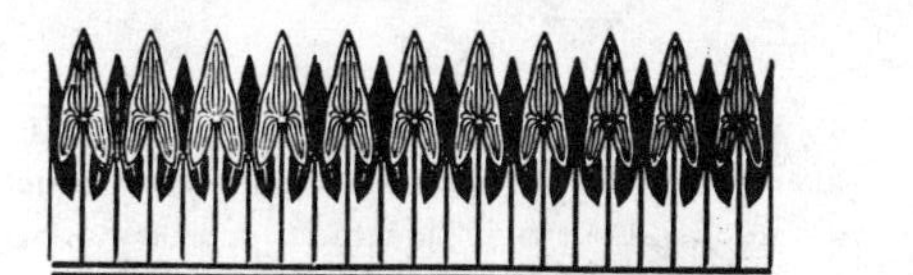

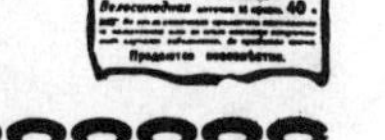

Typcial low-keyed pharmaceutical and consumer advertisements in late imperial Russia. These products, made by the Keler pharmaceutical company in Moscow, were touted in the firm's catalog, or *preis-kurant*, on the eve of World War I; *left*, "Aseptikon" tablets on page 8 were guaranteed to "immediately banish every... toilet . . . garbage . . . or other . . . stench"; *right*, on page 10, cold sufferers were urged "not to cry . . . Keler *Boro-Mentol*, sold everywhere" would banish their symptoms. On the same page, artists and artisans, housewives and children were informed that *Termidora* would gild or silver any item, including plaster, wood, metallic figures, furniture, shoes, eggs, and nuts.

Three views of Antonina Lesnevskaia, born October 16, 1866: *left*, she appears to be in her early 20s, about the time when she embarked on her pharmaceutical career in St. Petersburg; *middle*, probably dates from the turn of the century or the first decade of the twentieth century; *right*, from about the same time, depicts her with Florentina Stankevich, who, as one of the first women Provizors, or fully qualified pharmacists, managed Antonina's *Pervaia Zhenskaia Apteka* (First Women's Pharmacy) in St. Petersburg for many years.

Two views of the building that housed the First Women's Pharmacy, 32 *Nevskii Prospekt,* St. Petersburg: *top,* early twentieth century; *bottom,* 1993. The Medical Council and Medical Department of the Ministry of Internal Affairs waived stringent rules to allow Antonina Lesnevskaia to establish the *normal'naia,* or fully stocked, pharmacy in 1901. It was in a prime location on the main boulevard in St. Petersburg. To the right of the pharmacy is St. Catherine's Catholic Church.

Reception/dispensing area of the First Women's Pharmacy, 1901-1917.

Preparation room in the First Women's Pharmacy, circa 1905.

The first chemistry class in the Women's Pharmacy School, 1903, taught by P. L. Mal'chevskii from the Military Medical Academy. Note the portrait of Tsaritsa Alexandra on the wall.

One of the laboratory classes—perhaps pharmaceutical chemistry—in Antonina Lesnevskaia's women's pharmacy school, early twentieth century.

Provinces and railroads of European Russia, including Finland, Russian Poland, the Caucasus, circa 1900.

Provinces of Central Asia and Siberia, circa 1910. Note the Trans-Siberian Railway.

Introduction

Scholars have looked at late imperial Russia, and to a slightly lesser extent, early Soviet Russia, through many lenses–government institutions and political figures; intellectual and cultural elites; factory workers and peasants; liberals and revolutionaries; popular culture; women; medicine. One subject that has not been adequately studied is pharmacy and the pharmaceutical industry. There is no history of Russian pharmacy and the pharmaceutical industry in English. Soviet studies of pharmacy and the pharmaceutical industry in prerevolutionary and early Soviet Russia are discrete and incomplete. Some may object that there were only somewhat more than 10,000 pharmacists in a total population of approximately 144,000,000 on the eve of World War I. However, pharmacists and pharmaceutical industrialists were as or more numerous than intellectual and cultural leaders. Further, pharmacists' heterogeneity made them a mirror of society. Pharmacists represented national minorities; women; lower-, middle-, and upper-economic strata; students; entrepreneurs and employees; academics and scientific researchers; journalists; revolutionaries. Pharmacists' professional activities–compounding and dispensing medicines, mass producing medicines, pharmacological research, testing foods for adulteration, controlling drug abuse–were crucial to Russia's health and well being. The pharmacists of Russia deserve their day in the sun. This book attempts to portray their world–before, during, and after the Russian revolutions of 1917.

This book presents a picture only of civilian pharmacy. It does not address military pharmacy. Furthermore, the study of civilian pharmacists, pharmacy, and the pharmaceutical industry is by no means complete. Nevertheless, it paints a large canvas. For pharmacy and the pharmaceutical industry were a microcosm of Russian polity and economy in the late imperial, early Soviet period. The Russian government monitored pharmacy and pharmacists from the fifteenth century. In the nineteenth and early twentieth centuries the Ministry of Internal Affairs, through its Medical Council, Medical Department, Chief Medical Inspector, and local medical bodies, supervised pharmacy and the pharmaceutical industry. After October 1917, the Soviet Commissariat of Health, Supreme Economic Council, and assorted other central and local agencies did so. Thus, a study of pharmacy gives added information on how the tsarist and early Soviet governments operated. Such a study enlarges our knowledge of revolutionary activity in the first two decades of the twentieth century. Pharmacy reflected developments in education and science. A review of dispensing and large-scale production of pharmaceuticals depicts entrepreneurship and business in late imperial Russia and the fate of entrepreneurs and businesses in early Soviet Russia. Indeed, the study of pharmacy, pharmacists, and the pharmaceutical industry in late imperial, early Soviet Russia is a tale of two opposing socioeconomic systems.

To illustrate both the continuities and the differences between late imperial and early Soviet Russia, the first eleven chapters of this book are organized topically. They portray pharmacy and the pharmaceutical industry as they were in late imperial Russia. The first chapter sets the stage, showing how, in contrast to *laissez-faire* countries like England and America, the Russian government orchestrated pharmacy and the pharmaceutical industry. Successive chapters explore pharmacy education and training; how different types of pharmacies—private and restricted, public and semisocialist, and unrestricted drugstores—worked and provided medicine to the public; the life of pharmacists on different strata and their economic and political attitudes; how national minorities and women pharmacists fared; positives and negatives of the Russian pharmaceutical industry; pharmacists' contributions to pure food and environment in prerevolutionary Russia; drug use and abuse in prerevolutionary Russia.

Chapters 12 through 20 move into a kinetic, dramatic mode. They narrate how tsarist pharmacy and the pharmaceutical industry metamorphosed into the Soviet pharmacy system. We witness pharmacists forming self-help and pension societies; radical socialist pharmacists gradually taking them over; militant socialist pharmacists beginning to undermine private pharmacy through fomenting strikes and organizing rank-and-file pharmacists; government bureaucrats eroding the vitality of private pharmacy and the pharmaceutical industry in the two decades before 1917; the medicaments crisis of World War I; socialism overtaking private pharmacy and private enterprise in the pharmaceutical industry during the war; the role of pharmacists in the revolutions of 1917; and finally the construction of the Soviet pharmacy system.

Quite obviously, the story of pharmacy, pharmacists, and the pharmaceutical industry in late imperial, early Soviet Russia transcends health and medicine. And the telling of it has relevance beyond academia and, in fact, beyond Russia. The fate of Russian pharmacy and the pharmaceutical industry emphasizes that the Soviet government retained the political institutions and management style of the tsarist government but altered—indeed distorted—Russia's economic system. Under the old regime the government dominated the economy. Socialism also was deep and widespread. But private enterprise thrived as well. The Soviet government amplified big government and socialism and eliminated private enterprise, thus throwing the Russian economy off balance. A clearer picture of how the economy of pre-Soviet Russia functioned, how the Russian government traditionally operated may help outsiders to better understand post-Soviet Russia and post-Soviet Russians to better understand themselves. Additionally, a study of pharmacy and the pharmaceutical industry in late imperial, early Soviet Russia begins to tackle the specific problem of how the Soviet pharmaceutical industry got into the straits in which it is today and how to get the industry back on track. The findings may apply to other Soviet industries. And finally, and most importantly, the story of pharmacy and the pharmaceutical industry in late imperial, early Soviet Russia provides a case study of how excessive government interference strangles economic vitality, how large-scale socialism drains a country's coffers, how well-intentioned but misguided theorists can ruin a healthy economy. Such a lesson has universal significance.

The pathology of the Soviet political, economic, and social systems emerges when we compare these sectors to their pre-Soviet Russian counterparts. Soviet historians have distorted or clouded the picture of late imperial Russia. Until recently, archival sources were largely off-limits. Nevertheless, a mosaic of the polity, economy, society, and culture of this period has been painstakingly assembled. However, there are lacunae. Western works that display the complexity and capability as well as weaknesses of the late imperial government abound.[1] Yet old notions die hard. Otherwise excellent Western studies still depict the tsarist government, particularly that of Nicholas II, as both oppressive and inept.[2] Russians have their own sophisticated studies of the late imperial government on both the central[3] and local level.[4] Nevertheless, countering Soviet histories that denigrated or were ambivalent toward tsarist Russia there is now a trend toward mythologizing Nicholas, the Imperial family, and the pre-Soviet era. Additionally, although there are a handful of works that emphasize the connections between the *modus operandi* and personnel of the late tsarist and early Soviet government,[5] Western media reports on post-Soviet Russia still exhibit ignorance of and confusion about the type of government organic to and therefore most probably appropriate for Russia.

The picture of pre-Soviet economy and society is fuzzier still. In the West and particularly in Russia, there is popular consensus that entrepreneurship and business acumen were lacking in pre-Soviet Russia, a recent spate of books to the contrary notwithstanding.[6] The notion that peasants, workers, and ordinary people in Russia languished in penury is pervasive, despite revisionist Western works.[7] And there is a whole school that portrays strikes and strikers, revolutionaries, and the revolutions of 1905 and 1917 as both necessary and justified.[8]

A review of pharmacy and the pharmaceutical industry gives added dimension to government and politics in pre-Soviet Russia. Since the Ministry of Internal Affairs controlled pharmacy and the pharmaceutical industry, a look at this sector particularly highlights the *modus operandi* of that ministry and, more specifically, controversial ministers like P. A. Stolypin. The behavior of central medical officials underscores the paternalism, legalism, and sluggishness of the tsarist government. But it also emphasizes that the Russian political system, like any other, had trade offs. Government control ensured high-quality pharmaceutical education and protected public health. Early on, the government spurred the pharmaceutical industry. Overprotectiveness stunted the growth of the pharmaceutical industry and made some pharmacists dependent. Still, the dialogue between central medical bureaucrats, local medical officials, and pharmacists shows that pharmacists often were far from quiescent. They routinely complained to, lobbied, and asked for handouts from governmental bodies. Their requests were sometimes denied and sometimes granted. On the other side the pharmacy policies of several late imperial ministers of Internal Affairs, including Stolypin, reveal them as far more innovative than hitherto depicted. Additionally, the evolution of pharmacy policy suggests that a balance was emerging between parliament and government in late imperial Russia. As for revolutionary pharmacists, their activities highlight the variations among Russian revolutionaries, their legalism, which mimicked that of the tsarist government, their excessive idealism, their lack of touch with reality. Further, rank-and-file pharmacists' tepid responses to revolutionary pharmacist leaders raises doubts as to the depth of commitment on the part of the masses for the revolutions of 1905 and 1917, particularly the economic focus of these revolutions. On the other hand, the zeal with which many pharmacists, including nonpolitically motivated reformers, supported the Bolsheviks, indicates how that regime got a foothold in Russia.

In the economic arena, a review of pharmacy and the pharmaceutical industry emphasizes that three engines ran the pre-Soviet Russian economy. The tsarist government zealously regulated the economy–for good and ill. Pharmacies operated by zemstvos, or locally elected councils, from the 1870s were trial runs of socialized pharmacy and they manifested the problems in that type of pharmacy. Additionally, they underscored the attraction to socialism that pervaded imperial Russia. This tendency was to grow, within the government as well as among socialist pharmacists, in the decades before 1917. Finally, however, ambitious pharmacists who spread high-quality dispensing to the farthest corners of the empire, owners of drugstores and pharmaceutical factories, and pharmacy self-help societies, particularly the National Pharmacists Pension Fund, testify to the healthy current of entrepreneurship, competitiveness, and talent for self-management that coursed through imperial Russia and tempered big government and socialism.

In the social sector, a look at pharmacists shows that women and national minorities had opportunities in pre-Soviet Russia. Further, the lot of staff pharmacists was not so bleak as to warrant strikes and an overturn of the pharmacy system. Pharmacists contributed to raising the quality of life in Russia as well as supplying remedies to the sick. From the perspective of pharmacy, pharmacists, and the pharmaceutical industry, life was good in prerevolutionary Russia. To be sure, there were annoyances and defects. But there also were signs of progress, even during World War I. Judging from pharmacy and the pharmaceutical industry, Russia might have enjoyed economic expansion and political maturity and stability if revolutions had not intervened in 1917.

Unfortunately there were revolutions in 1917. The February-March revolution was largely political but had economic overtones. The October Revolution preserved the government of Russia but greatly changed the economic structure. Explanations for these revolutions have focused on the inadequacy of the tsarist government; a flawed economic and social system; economic and political tensions; World War I, which accentuated Russia's supposed long-standing, intrinsic problems, finally causing her to disintegrate; and Lenin's tactical genius.[9]

From the point of view of pharmacy and pharmacists there were no intrinsic reasons for economic revolution–for eliminating private enterprise in pharmacy and the pharmaceutical industry.[10] Additionally, as noted, socialist pharmacist leaders and labor organizers had great difficulty in rousing rank-and-file pharmacists to strikes and hostility toward pharmacist entrepreneurs.

Pharmacy and the pharmaceutical industry in prerevolutionary Russia did not need much fixing. Yet theorists in the government, who were not pharmacists, and pharmacist ideologues, who were not actively engaged in dispensing or the pharmaceutical industry, were determined to make improvements anyway. Their tinkering, their assaults finally destroyed the system.

During 1917 socialist pharmacists goaded staff pharmacists to demand salaries and concessions from owners of pharmacies and pharmaceutical enterprises that were economically infeasible. After October 1917, socialists of various hues (mainly Mensheviks) began implementing their policy of "municipalization"–transferring private pharmacies to city councils dominated by socialists, to councils of workers or other local bodies. The new Soviet (basically Bolshevik) government soon attempted to bring pharmacies and pharmaceutical enterprises more firmly under control of the central government and its branches and to centralize supply and funding. Both sets of socialist policies crushed private enterprise. But the Bolshevik pharmacy system was particularly ruinous because it exaggerated the negative and problematical features of the previous tripartite system–an interfering and dominating government and socialized dispensing–and was extremely expensive.

Because it was cumbersome, eliminated the initiative that gives an economy vitality, and ignored economic verities, the Soviet economic system never worked. It was altered slightly during the "New Economic Policy" of the 1920s but then reapplied with vengeance from the beginning of state planning in the late 1920s and early 1930s. Pharmacy and the pharmaceutical industry, thus, document socialism gone awry and the danger of the few–specifically government bureaucrats–making economic choices for the many, without proper information, practical experience, or attending to economic reality.

Is there any need to belabor the bankruptcy of the Soviet economic system when even textbooks scream "'War Communism': An Economic Disaster"?[11] Reams have been written on the genesis of early Bolshevik economic policy, on Lenin's economic theories, on the connection between them and his political theory and praxis, on the economic theories of his socialist competitors, on popular support for Bolshevik economic theory, on the evolution of Bolshevik economic policy during the Civil War of 1917/1918-1920, the period of so-called War Communism.[12] A very accessible adumbration of Soviet economic policies, Alec Nove's *An Economic History of the USSR*,[13] documents the Russian economy's downward spiral following Bolshevik takeover in 1917. Paul Gregory's *Russian National Income, 1885-1913*,[14] utilizes econometrics to compare the economy of tsarist Russia with that of Soviet Russia. The comparison is not favorable for the Soviet period. Charles Ruud's recent monograph, *Russian Entrepreneur*, portrays the tragic denouement of Ivan Sytin's publishing enterprise in the Soviet era.[15] Larry Holmes' recent *The Kremlin and the*

Schoolhouse relates how tangled bureaucracy, pedagogical utopianism, and lack of money felled Soviet education reform.[16] Denise Youngblood's *Movies for the Masses* describes the vacuousness of Soviet film policies.[17]

Nevertheless, scrutinizing one sector of the Russian economy–pharmacy and the pharmaceutical industry–before and after the revolutions of 1917 graphically demonstrates how much healthier economy and society were before the revolutions than after. Moreover, such a study explains *why.* Detailing pharmacy and the pharmaceutical industry before the revolutions of 1917 highlights the productive elements as well as the flaws in tsarist government and economy. Viewing pharmacy and the pharmaceutical industry after 1917 spells out the misconceptions underlying Bolshevik economic premises, and the structural defects in the system as implemented, that would ultimately cause the Soviet economy to collapse.

For, as stated, while the Bolsheviks replicated the tsarist government institutions and management style they exaggerated those features in the previous system–big government and socialism–that were least productive and braked the economy. Bolshevik government was similar but far more intrusive than tsarist, Bolshevik ministers' economic precepts were more extreme than those of tsarist ministers. Bolshevik officials not only controlled pharmacies and pharmaceutical enterprises, they actually ran them. A review of pharmacy and the pharmaceutical industry in the early Soviet era depicts out how disastrous this was–not only for the expropriated proprietors but for dispensing, medicaments production, the health of society, and ultimately the Russian economy.

Additionally, it appears necessary to emphasize the systemic weaknesses in early Soviet economic policy and the devastating effect of this policy on the common weal in the light of apologists who insist that the Bolshevik economic program was validated by its social component, namely, transferring the property of haves to have-nots.[18] Juxtaposing pharmacy, pharmacists, and the pharmaceutical industry in imperial Russia with this sector in Soviet Russia leaves no doubt that polity, economy, and society were better before the Bolsheviks and assorted socialists took over. Paralleling the disintegrating pharmacy system of early Soviet Russia with the viable pharmacy system of the Ukraine in 1918, where the old order still prevailed, sharpens the contrast.

As the catalog of errors that the Bolsheviks and their supporters imposed upon pharmacy and the pharmaceutical industry unfolds, the reader is increasingly prodded to ask how so many people could have been so deluded as to believe that such a destructive economic experiment was necessary and beneficial.

Russia is on the threshold of a new era. A profile of the government and economy *sui generis* for Russia can assist Russians in getting a foothold and outsiders in grappling with the new Russia. Pharmacy, pharmacists, and the pharmaceutical industry remind us that a domineering, paternalistic central government and tripartite economy are traditional to Russia. The achievements of pre-Soviet entrepreneurs, including women pharmacists, can inspire Russians today.

Additionally, the fate of pharmacy and the pharmaceutical industry has implications beyond the boundaries of Russia. It offers a handbook, step-by-step procedures, on how theorists destroyed a fairly healthy sector of the Russian economy. In so doing, it confirms the perils of socialized pharmacy in particular and excessive government control and social engineering in general. How much better to trust in "the invisible hand."

1

Rules and Regulations

Debates among ministers, personnel and policy changes, altercations between local and central authorities, and regional variations gave the activities of the nineteenth- and early twentieth-century Russian government color and chiaroscuro. Nevertheless the overwhelming impression of the tsarist government—most specifically the Ministry of Internal Affairs—in the realm of pharmacy and the pharmaceutical industry was that of a quintessential bureaucracy, operating with meticulous but ponderous legalism.

The difference between *laissez-faire* British and American pharmacy[1] and highly regulated Russian pharmacy prompted Prosper H. Marsden, Lecturer on Pharmacy at the University of Liverpool, to exclaim in exasperation, after on-site observation in 1905 that

> The first thing that strikes you on entering Russia is that you have at length discovered the habitat of the official. The longer you reside in the country, I understand, the more certain do you become that Russia principally consists of uniformed officials and persons of no consequence, who exist for the convenience of the former class. . . . The regulations relating to pharmacy deal with its very inception and enter into every detail of its daily routine.[2]

Russia's government-dominated, procedure-oriented pharmacy system dated to the formation of the nation-state in the fifteenth century.[3] Congruent with the centralizing tendencies of that era, this system also reflected the conscious German orientation that marked so many Russian policies. English pharmacists helped organize Russian pharmacy in the sixteenth century[4] and the accoutrement of the first court pharmacy came from England.[5] But Russian tsars imitated pharmacy models common in many German states,[6] rather than those of England, Italy, or France, which were decentralized and managed by guilds.[7]

The agencies and regulations that monitored Russian pharmacy until the end of the empire, rechristened, modified, and amplified in intervening years, were in place by the seventeenth century. The Pharmacy Department (*Aptekarskii prikaz*)[8] of that era managed both pharmacy and medicine.[9] It certified pharmacists, purchased medicines, managed a factory that produced pharmaceutical implements and vessels, undertook antiepidemic measures, conducted forensic analysis, developed pharmaceutical texts, and served as a teaching institution.[10]

In 1672 the government opened a pharmacy to dispense to Moscow citizenry.[11] The pharmacy department duly formulated regulations for its operation. Virtually identical to those governing Russian pharmacies in the nineteenth, early twentieth centuries, these regulations were meant to provide quality dispensing and protect pharmacists' incomes. They established fixed prices for medicines, specified the layout of the pharmacy–kitchen, room for drying herbs, room for storing bottles and medicines, quarters for assistants, and so on.[12] Simultaneously, a governmental edict of 1673 forbade chandleries and groceries to sell medicinal herbs and restricted this trade to pharmacies.[13]

The Russian government never relinquished its control over pharmacy. Peter the Great chartered the first private pharmacy in Moscow in 1701.[14] Henceforth, these pharmacies were called *vol'naia*—enfranchised or unrestricted. But this appellation—in use until 1917—did not mean that the pharmacies were independent. Rather, it referred to the fact that such pharmacies were owned by private individuals or groups rather than the state treasury. The government strictly controlled their establishment and operation.[15]

The first herbal in Russia, *Blagoprokhladnyi vertograd*, was independently translated from Latin into Polish in 1534. In 1661 the Pharmacy Prikaz officially sanctioned it.[16] The government mandated national pharmacopoeias from the eighteenth century. In 1762, Catherine the Great ordered the Medical College to compose a national pharmacopoeia emphasizing native herbs. The resulting first Military Pharmacopoeia appeared in 1765.[17]

Since the rules on dispensing especially made sense and meshed with cameralist theories of the time,[18] government regulations on the establishment and operation of pharmacies became the norm in continental Europe—although not in England—by the 1770s. Thus, the Russian pharmacy system was in the mainstream. However, at the same time, its administrative apparatus became more complex. Additionally, pharmacists increasingly came under domination of bureaucrats and physicians, a matter that would pique them until 1917.

The Pharmacy Department metamorphosed into the Medical Chancellery in 1721 and the Medical College in 1763. This central governmental agency was composed of eight individuals; only one was a pharmacist.

Similarly, on the local level, following Catherine the Great's reorganization of provincial administration in the 1780s, pharmacists and pharmacies in the fifty-some provinces of European Russia, the district of the Don army in the Southeastern Ukraine, and the twelve provinces and regions of Siberia and Central Asia came under the jurisdiction of the medical department (*Vrachebnoe otdelenie*) of the governor's or military governor's provincial board (*Gubernskoe pravlenie*).[19]

By the nineteenth century the bureaucracy governing pharmacy had become a lumbering leviathan.[20] Worse still, pharmacists were virtually excluded from policy-making.

Until 1917 the chief authorities for pharmacies, pharmacists, and pharmaceutical matters at the central level were the twin institutions of the Medical Council (*Meditsinskii sovet*) and Medical Department (*Meditsinskii departament*) in the Ministry of Internal Affairs. The Medical Council was the supreme policy-making body; the Medical Department was the body that implemented regulations. A physician chaired the Medical Council. The council comprised directors of the Medical Department and the Military Medical Administration, Chief Medical Inspector of the Navy, Inspectors of the Institutions of the Empress Marie and Imperial Court, and representatives from the ministries of Public Enlightenment and Finance. Pharmacists were gratuitous; when the council dealt with matters pertaining to pharmacy two deputies, elected for three-year terms from the St. Petersburg Pharmacy Society, participated in deliberations. However, their input was merely consultative.[21]

On the provincial level a provincial medical inspector (*vrachebnyi inspektor*) supervised pharmaceutical establishments. He was assisted by district medical inspectors in the ten or so districts into which each province was divided.[22] The medical inspectors sometimes were assisted by pharmacy assessors.[23] For supervision of pharmaceutical products, particularly those that were imported, the medical inspectors enlisted the excise supervisor (*aktsiznyi nadzor*), a representative of the Ministry of Finance. None of these officials were pharmacists.

The link between the provinces and the center was the Chief Medical Inspector (*Glavnyi vrachebnyi inspektor*), located in the Ministry of Internal Affairs, and his administrative apparatus (*Upravlenie*). Decisions, regulations, and orders from the Medical Council or Medical Department—and sometimes from the Ministry of Internal Affairs, directly—flowed downward to the Chief Medical Inspector, who then dutifully passed them on to the governors and medical division of the governor's provincial board. These agents, in turn, informed owners or would-be owners of pharmacies or pharmaceutical establishments. Correspondence flowed upward from the owner or would-be owner of a pharmacy or pharmaceutical establishment to the medical department of the provincial board through the governor to the administration of the Chief Medical Inspector. The Chief Medical Inspector, in turn, forwarded petitions or missives to the Medical Department or Medical Council.

The entire apparatus was governed by a plethora of rules. There was no one, comprehensive compilation of these pharmacy regulations. They were contained in a number of statutes: the Pharmacy Statute (*Aptekarskii ustav*), the Medical Statute (*Vrachebnyi ustav*), and the Statute on Punishments (*Ulozhenie nakazaniia*). Periodical updates were published in pharmacy journals. They were supplemented by circulars and orders dispatched from the Medical Department or Medical Council–and sometimes from the Ministry of Internal Affairs directly.

The regulations touched every aspect of pharmacy: the number, type, ownership, and operation of pharmacies; parapharmaceutical establishments; prices for medicines; the national pharmacopoeia; importing of medicines; factory production of medicines; training and education of pharmacists. These rules impacted the various sectors of pharmacy differently. Their economic effect, on the growth of pharmacies and the pharmaceutical industry, was mainly negative. But, as the rules concerned public health, they had a positive effect on pharmacy education, the operation of pharmacies, and drug use and abuse.

The legalism of the Russian government and the cumbersomeness of the Russian pharmacy system was most noticeable in the establishment of pharmacies. The government methodically classified civilian pharmacies in four categories. Normal pharmacies (*normal'naia apteka*) predominated, comprising 2,181 out of 3,518 pharmacies in 1901.[24] They were fully stocked, contained over 800 medical essences, and dispensed 3 sorts of medicines–simples (crude animal and vegetable products), chemical compounds (mixed according to an exactly prepared formula), and so-called galenical preparations (tinctures, mixtures, decoctions, solutions, and the like). Only full-fledged pharmacists or Provizors could manage normal pharmacies.[25] Normal pharmacies could be owned by private individuals (most were owned by pharmacists), groups, societies, or public institutions–cities and so-called zemstvos. The second type of pharmacies–rural or village (*sel'skaia*)–were to be established, according to a circular of the Medical Department of November 19, 1881, in place of government or treasury pharmacies (*aptechnoe otdelenie*) and branch pharmacies (*filial'naia apteka*) in "small towns, settlements, villages, localities, and the countryside." In the 1890s village pharmacies were required to have about 280 medicaments and 8 types of utensils. Assistant Pharmacists (*Aptek-*

arskii pomoshchnik) of at least twenty-five years of age were allowed to manage them.[26] In 1901 village pharmacies amounted to 1,173 or about one third the total number.[27] Homeopathic pharmacies amounted to only 31 in 1901. Eight were located in St. Petersburg.[28] Pharmacies of the fourth type came under the rubric *aptechnoe delo.* Numbering only 133 in 1901, these pharmacies were located in institutions maintained by the government. They included hospital pharmacies, which chiefly supplied medicine to patients but at times dispensed to the general populace. Finally, in areas with a shortage of pharmacies, the Medical Council permitted small-scale pharmacies (*domashnaia aptechka*) suitable for first aid in schools or private residences.[29]

The Medical Council determined the number of pharmacies according to mathematical formulae–population and prescriptions dispensed annually in any given area. According to a circular of May 25, 1873, each new pharmacy in St. Petersburg and Moscow required 12,000 inhabitants and 30,000 new and repeat prescriptions. In the capital cities of each province each new pharmacy required 10,000 inhabitants and 15,000 prescriptions. In district towns the figures were 7,000 and 6,000.[30] The population norms were based on data gathered by the Provincial Statistical Commissions.[31] Additionally, normal pharmacies could be no closer than 15 versts (a verst is about 2/3 mile) from each other. Distance determined the number of village pharmacies. Each was required to be 7 versts from the next. Privately owned normal pharmacies were bound by these rules until 1917; public, or zemstvo and city, pharmacies were confined by them until a regulation of February 12, 1912, removed restrictions.[32]

The population figures were comparable to those used by the Hapsburg government in northern Italy, the Austrian Empire proper,[33] and many German states.[34] However, the Russian government applied the rules with special zeal and, in order to protect pharmacies from "superfluous competition,"[35] added further precautions. The owner of a private pharmacy was not allowed to have a branch in the same district.[36] The establishment of new pharmacies required the approval of owners of already-existing pharmacies. The individual wishing to establish a pharmacy had to have the wherewithal–in districts and rural areas for much of the nineteenth and early twentieth century this amount was 1,500 rubles.[37] Finally, requests to open pharmacies had to be accompanied by a stamp tax (*gerbovyi sbor*) of 60 kopeks per sheet, according to a regulation of 1902. The actual certificates of permission cost 1 ruble per sheet.[38]

Persons wishing to establish a pharmacy applied to the local medical inspector. He forwarded the request to the provincial medical board and governor.[39] If all was in order the local authorities sent the request to the

Chief Medical Inspector. Ultimate approval came from the Medical Department or Medical Council.

The Chief Medical Inspector and Medical Council assiduously totaled up the numbers. The paper trail was voluminous, the triviality of information stupefying. For example, in 1906 Provizor Ivan Petrovich Rozenburg petitioned the Minister of Internal Affairs directly to permit him to open a fourth normal pharmacy in the city of Pskov. His chosen location was a "cluster of settlements, thickly populated," near the St. Petersburg-Warsaw Railway. There was a branch pharmacy in the vicinity but the nearest normal pharmacies were 2 versts away, and transportation was difficult. The Chief Medical Inspector ruled that according to a law of 1892 this request had to be channeled through the local authority. Ignoring his advice, in February 1909, Rozenberg again requested the right to open the pharmacy. He admitted that according to the Provincial Statistical Committee, the population in Pskov was only 32,452–not enough for a fourth pharmacy. However, according to police data the population was 41,998–which fulfilled the legal norm. Throughout 1909 the issue was tossed back and forth between local and central authorities. The Chief Medical Inspector averred that a fourth pharmacy appeared necessary for the population but asked the Pskov governor for his opinion. The governor agreed the new pharmacy was necessary and included a report of the medical department of his provincial board. This body opined that according to updated rules of February 25, 1906, there must be 10,000 people to warrant a pharmacy in a provincial city and there was discrepancy between Statistical Committee and Police population figures (students at the local school and domestic servants being counted in the general population, when they should not be). However, since the three existing pharmacies did not fully serve the needs of the population in the area, the provincial medical department sanctioned the request for the fourth pharmacy. The Medical Council balked; they had not received information on truly extraordinary conditions justifying opening a pharmacy outside the rules, such as lack of bridges or epidemics. In the summer of 1909 the medical division of the Pskov governor increased its ammunition. Twelve years had passed since the first petition for the new pharmacy; in that time 360 new homes had been built housing about 7,000 new inhabitants; the distance to the city was 1½ versts; the people of the locality were chiefly poor; their need for medicine was not satisfied by the branch pharmacy with one manager and an assistant. The governor and provincial medical inspector strongly advocated the pharmacy. In a meeting in September 1909, the Medical Council held to the rule that statistical data did not support the opening of the fourth pharmacy. However, other factors–the new homes, distance from the city, and poverty of the people—indicated a pharmacy was necessary for the health of the population. Consequently, through the chain of command, the Chief Medical Inspector permitted Rozenberg to open his pharmacy.[40] This case was replicated by thousands of others.

In rural areas, the central authorities steadfastly applied the rule that normal pharmacies must be 15 versts from one another. For example, in Moscow province in 1912 Vladimir Alekseevich Sokolov requested permission to establish a normal pharmacy in the hamlet of Tomlino. His justification was that although the population amounted to only 200 in the winter it swelled to 2,000 in the summer. Nevertheless, the Chief Medical Inspector's administration rejected the request because the population norm of 7,000 not been reached and because the nearest normal pharmacy was less than 15 versts away.[41]

On the other hand, normal pharmacies could not be downgraded to village status even when circumstances warranted. For example, in May 1905, the Chief Medical Inspector informed the Kursk provincial medical inspector that reclassifying a normal pharmacy in the village of Mikhailovsk, Dimitrievsk district, which had lost customers and had few new and repeat prescriptions, contradicted an 1885 circular of the Medical Department.[42]

Pharmacists who disagreed with decisions on new pharmacies, either would-be owners of new pharmacies or owners of existing pharmacies trying to block competition, could appeal to the Senate, highest court of the land. However, the procedure, as Prosper Marsden remarked in 1905, required

> YEARS OF RED TAPE: If the already established pharmacies do a business in prescriptions and repeats so much in excess of their legitimate allowance, defined as above by law, as to allow of the new place being opened without detriment to their own trade, and the increase of population has been shown to be sufficient, the petition goes through various hands until it reaches the governor of the province. The most surely based petition may be delayed at any one of its stages for years of perfectly legitimate means, and so one can understand that a qualified man may waste a deal of his life in getting into his own place of business.[43]

Case studies bore him out. In 1906, one Rabinovich, owner of a pharmacy in Semipalatinsk province in Central Asia, appealed to the Senate, protesting establishment of a third pharmacy in the area. The Senate supported him, reversing the Temporary Governor General's permission for a third pharmacy—but only in 1913—seven years after the initial decision had been taken by the local authority. Further, in 1913, Rabinovich complained that he had received no response on the Senate decision from the governor-general.[44] The Semipalatinsk governor was still corresponding with the Chief Medical Inspector on the issue and Rabinovich was still writing letters of complaint in 1914.[45] Similarly, in December 1906, Provizor Ivan Leopol'dovich Rodovich protested to the Senate that the Minister of Internal Affairs was permitting a second normal pharmacy, outside the rules of 1873, in the city of Rogachev in Mogilev province.[46] The Medical Council found the population was 14,475–1,778 less than the norm. However, the city had spread in the direction of the railway station and it was difficult for people to get medicine. On these grounds, and following a precedent of an 1898 State Council opinion, the Medical Council proposed that Rodovich's objection be dismissed and the new pharmacy be allowed outside the rules of May 25, 1873. The Senate endorsed the proposal of the Medical Council–but two years later, in 1909.[47]

Restrictions on pharmacies paved the way for drug emporia, or drug stores (*aptekarskie magaziny*). They were allowed to sell prepared medicaments received from pharmaceutical factories,[48] but were not supposed to prepare medicine. Yet in some instances they did so.[49] Local authorities sometimes emphasized the drug stores' potential danger to public health to prod the Medical Council into allowing new pharmacies. Usually, this tactic had little result. For example, the governor and provincial medical division of Grodno began their quest for second normal pharmacies in two towns–Korbin and Volkovsk–neither of which met population or prescription requirements, in 1905. Noting that in one town troops and a new railway line had pushed the population close to the required norm, the Grodno governor complained that delays in granting permission for bona fide pharmacies in regions that did not exactly meet the population norms had led to the proliferation of the drug stores, which were dispensing medicaments of dubious quality. Two new drug stores had been established in one town in Grodno province since the first petition for a new pharmacy, bringing the total number of these establishments in that town to six and, although they were prohibited by law from doing so, the drug stores were secretly preparing medicine. The Medical Council was unmoved and rejected new pharmacies in both towns in 1906, on the grounds that neither population nor number of prescriptions warranted them. The Medical Council dismissed the governor's warning about the dangers of the drug stores as an invalid reason for a new pharmacy "outside" the rules advising that such violation of the Pharmacy Statute should be stopped not by a new pharmacy but by better control over the drug stores on the part of the governor.[50] Nevertheless, during 1907 and

1908 the governor and provincial medical division continued their struggle to prove the need for a second normal pharmacy in the town of Volkovsk. Finally, three years after the initial request, the Medical Council agreed that the population met the requirements.[51]

In any case, drug store owners, like would-be pharmacy owners, had to wait for the official wheels to turn. In 1905, Rosa Sinai, wife of a Provizor, and owner of a drug store, complained to the Senate that the governor of Kaluga province would not allow her to trade certain medicinal substances. The Senate ruled in her favor; she could sell prepared medicaments, as received from the factory. However, the decision was handed down in 1907, two years after her petition.[52]

Establishing a pharmacy was only the first step. The Fundamental Laws of the Empire, edition 1836, contained rules for operating pharmacies. It described rooms, laboratories, cold or dry storage rooms for preserving medicaments; weights, measures, equipment and how "strong-acting [*sil'nodeistvuiushchie*] and poisonous medicines were to be kept"; pharmacopoeias; books of various sorts—for certified physicians, taxes, prescription records; proper labeling of medicaments, penalties for falsification, error, uncleanliness, and so forth.[53]

Circulars, the Medical Council's *Collection of Laws for Pharmacists, Owners of Pharmacies and Druggists* edited by P. N. Bulatov and published in St. Petersburg in 1897, I. Kal'ning's *Short University Pharmacy Course* published in Moscow in 1899, and various pharmacy journals kept pharmacists current on the rules for operating normal and rural pharmacies.

As the Pharmacy Department did earlier, the *Short University Pharmacy Course* detailed the layout of the normal pharmacy—a reception or prescription room for dispensing medicaments, storage room for dry substances in which the temperature was to be preserved and an ice room for perishable products; a decoctorium (preparation) room; and laboratory—as well as the components for each room. The prescription room was to include Russian, German, and military pharmacopoeias; a list of all licensed medical practitioners; records of all prescriptions filled during the last three years; various weights, jars, vessels, pill- and capsule-making machines. The laboratories were to include stoves, extracting cupboards, distilleries, presses, sieves, and other equipment. The book provided illustrations of all these apparatus.[54]

The Medical Council was especially concerned about the storage and dispensing of poisonous, narcotic, and so-called strong-acting, or heroic, medicaments. It designated about 300 items in this category. In 1898 there were 90 items on list A, in 1905, 82. The list included many vegetable alkaloids, such as codeine and morphine, aconite, arsenic, nitric acid, nitroglycerin, amyl nitrite, and anesthetics such as chloroform.[55] List B contained 36 items in 1898 and 47 in 1905. Here were to be found mineral acids, oxalic acid, iodine, bichromate of potassium, cyanide of potassium, and ammonium.[56] List V included 150 items in 1898, including opium. The 1905 list contained 144 items, according to Prosper Marsden, "the commoner hypnotics, colocynth, and many poisonous crude drugs, as calabar bean, belladonna root and herb, ipecacuanha, savin oil, and cantharides."[57] In 1898 the fourth list G had 23 items, including belladonna and digitalis. In 1905 this list "contained chiefly poisons of very active herbs and roots."[58] These items could be dispensed only upon prescription of a physician. They were to be kept in a locked cupboard, the key of which was to remain at all times with the manager. Special balances were to be used for weighing poisons.[59]

To prevent accidental poisonings, the pharmacist was required to affix a special label (*signatura*). These long, stiff, triangular pieces of paper listed the number of the prescription, name of the patient, name of the physician, date, directions, and price. "On the right side at the wide end was printed the Russian eagle and the name of the pharmacy. On the other" was rewritten the entire prescription. They were color-coded.[60] The pharmacist was required to retain the original of all prescriptions for three years. The patient received a copy, and a second copy was put into the pharmacy's sealed record book. A special book, supplementing the regular prescription book, listed poisons, narcotics, and strong-acting substances that had been dispensed.[61]

Regulations without supervision and enforcement were meaningless. Pharmacies made annual reports that were filtered through district and provincial medical authorities to the Chief Medical Inspector's office in the Ministry of Internal Affairs. The reports included the name of the pharmacy, number of pharmacists employed, number of students, number of prescriptions dispensed, pharmacy income—from prescriptions and over-the-counter sales.[62] Sometimes the reports included additional information, such as pharmaceutical houses supplying medicines and materials to the pharmacy.[63] Pharmacy records were amalgamated with those on other local medical activities—diseases, number of clinics, maternity homes, insane asylums, and so forth—to provide a profile of the health of each district and province for the year. The Chief Medical Inspector compiled the provincial reports.[64] They were subsequently published, providing an annual collage of the empire's health, entitled: "Report on the State of National Health and the Organization of Medical Care in Russia."[65]

Additionally, local medical authorities made spot checks (*revizii*) of pharmacies. The Medical Statute of 1856, subsequently updated, required provincial medical administrations to inspect private pharmacies in provincial cities not less than three times per year. District physicians were responsible for inspecting pharmacies at the district level. If violations were discovered a more formal investigation was to ensue.[66] An instructional handbook devoted twelve pages to pharmacy matters that inspectors were to investigate.[67]

There is no categorical information on the frequency or thoroughness of inspections. They definitely were carried out. In its maiden-Russian-language edition in 1879, for example, *Farmatsevticheskii zhurnal* announced that "the great part of pharmacies were inspected in the report year [1878] by the provincial medical inspector, his assistants, and district doctors, and the following important disorders were quickly corrected." In one case, "The Medical Council, on the basis of article 152 of the Statute on Punishments, severely reprimanded [*vygovor*] a pharmacy owner for . . . not writing all prescriptions in the . . . book, dispensing one medicine in place of another, although it caused no harm" and "refilling prescriptions of a strong-acting medicine" when "on that prescription the doctor had not written 'repetatur.'"[68] Inspections continued until the end of the empire. The minutiae were overwhelming. In 1905, the medical department of Akmolinsk region fulminated to the military governor of the region that one Provizor Ebert, was "ignoring legal requirements about order in the pharmacy he managed" in Petropavlovsk. Further, "correspondence with him had not been fruitful." Inspection in March 1905 revealed that Ebert considered the pharmacy "his domestic economy–one could not tell where one stops and the other starts–the kitchen and laboratory are one institution . . . preservation of strong-acting and poisonous medicines is haphazard and according to the personal taste of the owner, no lawful system exists–lists A and V are ignored. After three months there was a second inspection but, aside from separating the laboratory and kitchen, all remained without change."[69]

The local medical authorities advocated closing the pharmacy. The Medical Council, however, disagreed, pointing out that this could be done only if articles 885 and 890 of the Statute on Punishments had been violated, which had not occurred.[70] Ignoring the order of lists A and V was not specifically prohibited and, moreover, was a small infraction. The fact that Ebert lived in a drunken state (*netrezvyi*) was not a criminal offense nor was absence of a book for correspondence coming from the medical department of the provincial board, as there was no requirement in the regulations about such a book. Further, Ebert had a book to record dispensation of poisonous medicaments.[71]

In the spring of 1906 the Orenburg provincial administration reported to the administration of the Chief Medical Inspector that Assistant Pharmacist Nirenberg, manager of a village pharmacy in the village of Isaev, had given a potion composed, in addition to spirits and mint oil, of an alkaloid (brutsin) to a sick woman who died soon after. The woman's death apparently was not connected with the medicine but the alkaloid in it was a strong-acting substance that, by law, could not be dispensed without a doctor's prescription. Fairly quickly, early in 1907, the Medical Council got statements from witnesses, had the medicine analyzed by a chemical expert, A. P. Dianin, and authorized the Orenburg governor to have Nirenberg brought to court.[72]

In December 1908, inspection of L. A. Levitskii's pharmacy revealed "damp dishes, dirty walls, dirty towels. The label on the glass of *Liquor arsenicalis Fowler* was unclear. The cupboard was not in order." Narcotic substances–*Tinctura Opii simple* and *Tinctura opii crocat.*–did not pass tests. The owner/manager was notified that "if the disorders were not rectified the pharmacy would not be permitted to dispense medicine."[73]

In 1909 the medical department of the St. Petersburg Provincial Administration informed the administration of the Chief Medical Inspector about the dispensation of a poor quality iron-protein preparation from Provizor Moskovskii's pharmacy, located at a station on the St. Petersburg-Warsaw Railway line. The pharmacist was to write a written refutation of the charge. Additionally, the Chief Medical Inspector queried why the pharmacy in question was said to be the property of Provizor Moskovskii when in the annual medical register it was listed as *belonging* to Meshchanin (Citizen) Rogalev and only under the *management* of Moskovskii.[74] The same year the Warsaw medical administration informed the administration of the Chief Medical Inspector of a case of mistaken dispensing involving the wife of a factory worker.[75]

In May 1911, the medical department of Grodno province reported to the administration of the Chief Medical Inspector that the provincial inspector had descended upon a pharmacy at 7 o'clock in the evening and found strong-acting medicines kept in an unlocked cupboard. An attached hand-penned letter from the manager explained he had accidentally left the cupboard unlocked for only half an hour. The Medical Council absolved him but determined he should be given severe notice (*zamechanie*) for insufficiency of weights and pharmaceutical vessels of various kinds.[76]

Even World War I did not stop pharmacy inspections. In January 1917, the Medical Council reviewed the case of one Shliom-Khaim Davidov Gurevich. The previous November 1916, the procurator of the Appellate Court had found Gurevich guilty of violating articles 885 and 892 of the Statute on Punishments. According to the report of the Petrograd medical inspector of December 1915, inspection of Gurevich's pharmacy in October 1915, revealed that "medicaments were carelessly kept in the prescription or reception room ... the vessels for the medicaments were dirty ... their labels were stained ... in cupboard A there were old advertisements ... in the materials room some labels were unclear ... the vessels in which the medicaments were preserved were covered with dust. The wash basin was dirty, there were no soap or towels. In the office of the manager was dirty madeira. Poisonous materials on list A, like morphia, were in an unlocked cupboard . . . the laboratory was cold, the vessels for pharmaceutical operation few."[77]

On these grounds Provizor Gurevich had been indicted for violating six articles of the Statute on Punishments.[78] Provizor Gurevich's defense focused on the fact that his experienced workers had been called into the army; additionally he maintained that he had always had soap and towels, kept strong-acting substances in a locked cupboard, and rectified such disorders as there were–substances in list A were now locked away.[79]

One factor that might have affected the objectivity of the inspection was that, in some cases, the inspection fee was paid by the pharmacy owner. For example, in 1878 the provincial medical inspector complained to the Medical Department that one owner had not paid his 20-ruble fee to the pharmacy assessors. The Chief Medical Inspector criticized this practice, noting that in 1879 the provincial inspector had a budget of over 200 rubles per year and the inspection must be done properly.[80]

Foreign observers gave inspections and adherence to pharmacy rules in general mixed reviews. D. A. Ruffman, director of Parke, Davis and Company opined that the "number of assistants employed in a pharmacy is very small indeed in comparison to the work to be got done; the preparations are consequently got up in a hurry, and the exactness of the dose is very doubtful indeed; the quality of the drug leaves much to be desired; the general cleanliness that ought to reign in the pharmacy does not strike one when making close inspection of things."[81]

Prosper Marsden, on the other hand, insisted that "The greatest care is observed with regard to poisons.... I may say that into whatever pharmacy

I went in Russia, I observed the greatest care being exercised in this particular part of the business. One would see the dispenser take a key from the *provizor*'s desk, go into the rooms set apart for poisons and *medicamenta heroica*, and return with the drug weighed in his scales. . . . The dispenser takes them to the bottle of powder to be weighed, and not the bottle to the scales, as is our custom." If rules on poisons and *Medicamenta heroica* were not observed, Marsden noted, "the responsible person is liable to loss of his right to control for all time; if in addition . . . he be the owner, he likewise loses his right to own a pharmacy."[82]

H. M. Gordin, reporting to the School of Pharmacy at the University of Michigan in 1899, took a middle path. He allowed that

> A very important feature of Russian pharmacy is the occasional inspection . . . by a commission appointed by the medical department. This commission generally consists of the director of the medical department, a chemist, also an official of this department, and some prominent druggist of the city. The commission often swoops down quite unexpectedly and . . . scrutinizes the purity of the chemicals, the cleanliness with which they are kept, and often even quizzes the junior clerks about pharmaceutical matters. The chemist accompanying the commission carries with him a small outfit of reagents and utensils and also makes use of these reagents, of which, indeed every drug store [*sic*] is obliged to keep on hand a full list. The chemist takes the specific gravity of the more important tinctures, tests quinine and morphine salts for adulterants, estimates the strength of tincture of iodine, examines crude drugs for foreign substances, and drawers, bottles and other containers for general care and cleanliness with which things are kept. Of drugs that cannot be assayed quickly he takes along small quantities for subsequent examination.[83]

Gordin advocated official inspections for the United States. However, he was skeptical about Russian pharmacists' adherence to the rules on dispensing and inspectors' thoroughness. He implied bribes were handed out.

> The proprietors of pharmacies generally try to keep on good terms with the lower officials of the medical department, who for the sake of a small present often inform the druggist beforehand of an intended inspection of his shop and so give him a chance to give his store a thorough scrubbing before the appearance of the inspectors . . . where, owing to the lack of integrity among officials, the commission often spend their time with the proprietor at a game of whist and tasting his champagne instead of testing his drugs.[84]

The penalties for violating the rules on dispensing varied from severe—

barring the individual from owning or managing a pharmacy temporarily or permanently—to exceedingly mild. In 1884 a pharmacy owner was prohibited from managing it for six months. Disorders had caused such distrust in the local populace that they used a pharmacy in another town. Consequently, the governor also requested that a second pharmacy be opened in the district city despite the fact that prescriptions did not meet the norm.[85] In 1915 Provizor Al'fons Kazimirovich Martsinkevich was fined 5 rubles and deprived forever of the right to manage a pharmacy.[86] On the other hand, strong censure was merely imposed in other cases. Additionally, there apparently was some loosening of the rules on dispensing during World War I. In May 1916, a circular of the Ministry of Internal Affairs ruled that strong-acting though nonnarcotic substances in list B could be dispensed in small amounts without a physician's prescription.[87]

In addition to regulating the establishment and operation of pharmacies, the Russian government published a price list, the Pharmacy Tax (*Aptekarskaia taksa*), for which medicines were to be sold. The concept had originated in medieval Germany and in 1905 the German *Arzneitaxe* set drug prices and fees for pharmacy labor in the empire.[88]

The Russian Pharmacy Tax would become very contentious, socialists claiming it set prices too high, enabling pharmacy owners to make exorbitant profits, pharmacy owners claiming prices were set too low, barely allowing them to make a living. Isaiah Ginzburg, an aspiring pharmacist at the turn of the century, recalled neutrally, "To compute the price of prescriptions, we used a price chart, and there was no guess-work about it. Nor could one pharmacy's charge be a great deal different from that of another, for the Tsar's government sent a price chart showing what could be charged for the various drugs, the containers, and the labor, and we had to figure according to that."[89] An English observer commented that because of the official tax "privileged pharmacies are not allowed to advertise . . . Even if somebody dispenses below the official prices, which is permissible, he is not allowed to call the attention of the public to it in any way."[90] Prosper Marsden affirmed of the "tariff to control the prices charged" that "These prices are marked upon every single article purchased in plain figures, and no overcharge is allowed."[91]

The Pharmacy Tax was adjusted upward or downward about every five years in the nineteenth and early twentieth century. For example, in January 1891, a circular of the Ministry of Internal Affairs lowered the price of 74 items.[92] During World War I, the Pharmacy Tax was adjusted every few months.

The Russian government regulated pharmacy education and training. The Medical Council first established ranks and requirements for pharmacists in 1810. The rules were updated in 1819, 1835, and several times thereafter.

The government kept control over pharmacists through passbooks (*konduitnyi spisok*). These passbooks included vital statistics–date of birth; rank; information on education and time of service; police testimonials on conduct; and records on fines or court summons.[93] Managers of pharmacies were to notify the local medical department each time a pharmacist entered or left the employ of a pharmacy.[94] Pharmacy students and staff pharmacists were to receive their passbooks when they transferred to another pharmacy but, in some cases, they had to pay a small stamp fee for it.[95] Local medical inspectors examined the passbooks in their periodical inspections of pharmacies and, like other pharmacy regulations, those on passbooks were periodically updated; the Chief Medical Inspector issued new instructions in 1909.[96]

Finally, the Medical Council's tentacles stretched to the pharmaceutical industry. The council approved all pharmaceutical factory start-ups.[97] It essayed and approved all mass-produced medicines, whether imported or domestic, "patented," "proprietary," or in the public domain. Decisions were published in official compendia, such as the 1897 *Collection of Laws for Pharmacists*, which listed several hundred "prepared" and "patent" medicaments permissible for sale,[98] and in pharmacy,[99] dental, and medical journals. The government also impounded dangerous preparations, such as an iron remedy that caused the death of one patient.[100] The pharmaceutical press thundered against the "charlatanism" of proprietary medicines that eluded the Medical Council's scrutiny and advertised outlandish cures.[101] These cautionary measures protected public health but curtailed research, development, and entrepreneurship necessary for a healthy pharmaceutical industry.

In sum, the rules and regulations governing Russian pharmacy were weighty. They bogged down government officials and pharmacists alike in a morass of technicalities.[102] In contrast, Italy and France discarded limitations on establishing pharmacies during the nineteenth century.[103] Denmark, Germany, and Austria-Hungary retained the concession system,[104] but many German states applied the rules with greater elasticity and some, notably Prussia and Saxony, allowed pharmacists a greater role in policymaking[105] and more leeway in pharmaceutical research and development. America and Britain, of course, wielded precious little control over pharmacy.

The Russian pharmacy system was not only sluggish. Because theorists who were not pharmacists formulated policies, they were not always in the best interests of pharmacy or the general public. They braked the establishment of pharmacies. They slowed the growth of the pharmaceutical industry. They engendered a protectionist mind-set in pharmacists.

Nevertheless, as we will see in the chapters following, the Russian pharmacy system had trade-offs, like any other. It provided good pharmacy education. It insulated consumers from the nostrums that freely circulated in America and England at the time. It did not entirely curb initiative and entrepreneurship. It did not prevent professionalization. Further, the government was forced to bend, if not capitulate, to the force of free trade. Drug stores sprang up in the gaps left by restricted pharmacies. The Medical Council was forced to permit the drug stores although it tried its best to exert a modicum of control. Additionally, in the first decades of the twentieth century the Medical Council belatedly realized that excessive regulation strangled the pharmaceutical industry. It tried to boost the industry and finally began to dismantle some restrictions during World War I.

What would finally topple private pharmacy and the pharmaceutical industry was not simply bureaucratic meddling but the attraction to socialism, which grew ever stronger in the pharmacy corporation and in the government.

2

Becoming a Pharmacist: Pharmacy Education

Until the end of the Russian empire one became a pharmacist by completing a modicum of secondary-school education, serving a three-year apprenticeship in a fully stocked pharmacy, and passing an examination. This conferred on one the title Assistant Pharmacist. Although Assistant Pharmacists were only partially qualified, they could dispense at any pharmacy and manage a partially stocked village pharmacy; many remained at this level until the end of their career. Those wishing to advance to the level of Provizor, or fully qualified pharmacist, served a second apprenticeship and then attended two years of university-level courses. Those desiring the rarefied degree Master of Pharmacy had to complete four years of university study, do original research, and write a thesis. The Russian government established requirements for all levels of pharmacist and outlined curricula for Provizor and Master courses in the early nineteenth century and periodically updated them. While onerous and restrictive, the rules unquestionably benefited Russian pharmacy training. The examination in pharmacognosy, pharmaceutical chemistry, and chemical-pharmaceutical preparations required of the Assistant Pharmacist covered three densely packed pages in the government regulation book of 1907. Additional information on mineralogy, geology, botany, zoology, physics, chemistry, pharmacology, pharmacognosy, and pharmaceutical preparations required of Provizors and Masters of Pharmacy amounted to a staggering twenty-four pages in the 1907 government regulation book.[1]

Russian pharmacy education and training may have lagged behind that of France, which established examinations as early as the thirteenth century, required university lectures for apprentice pharmacists in some regions from the sixteenth century, had a university chair of pharmacy in the seventeenth century, and six higher schools of pharmacy from the early nineteenth century. However, Russian pharmacy education, particularly on the level of Provizor and Master, was comparable to that of Germany. In Prussia, first-class pharmacists were required to take courses at the medical college in Berlin and from 1808 Bavaria required university education for pharmacists.[2] Yet, not all German universities had chairs of pharmacology by the 1880s, whereas this subject was part of the university curriculum for Russian Provizors.[3]

Russian pharmacy education and training was superior to the *laissez-faire* preparation most British and American pharmacists received. In England, the Society of Apothecaries offered lectures on botany and *materia medica* from 1830, but there was no pharmacy school until 1841. Examinations for pharmacists became compulsory in 1868,[4] but this gave rise to the so-called cram schools with scanty sixteen-week courses.[5] American pharmacy societies established pharmacy schools in five cities before 1865; these were supplemented by scattered proprietary pharmacy colleges. But the curriculum of the schools was neither uniform nor certified by state or federal authorities. Enterprising pharmacists created pharmacy schools in several Midwest land-grant universities in the late nineteenth century. Nevertheless, apprenticeship remained an important component of American pharmacy training until the 1920s. Further, certification for American pharmacists continued to differ from state to state through the early twentieth century.[6]

In 1910, Alexander Semenovich Ginzberg, harsh critic of Russian pharmacy education, disparaged British and American pharmacy education after on-site inspection. He rated pharmacy education superb in Sweden—"a country of high culture" requiring "full gymnasium education" and good in Switzerland, Germany (which had recently increased specialized education to two years), and Austria ("with its learned degrees of Master and Doctor of Pharmacy"). But despite the "talented character" of pharmacists in "both Anglo-Saxon countries . . . full absence of norms" and "weak pharmacy education" put "both England and American pharmacies on a low level"; Russian pharmacy could "learn nothing" from them.[7]

Nevertheless, Russian pharmacy training and education also had flaws, particularly on the lower level of Assistant Pharmacist. And the dependency that government control generated in many pharmacists as well as a penchant for endless discussion meant that Russian pharmacy education and training were not reformed before the revolution. Lack of progress would prompt frustrated pharmacist reformers like Ginzberg to move increasingly leftward and finally support the Bolshevik regime because it seemed to offer greater autonomy and an opportunity to improve pharmacy education.

Russian pharmacy education on the highest levels steadily improved from the seventeenth through the mid-nineteenth centuries. Early Russian pharmacists trained exclusively in pharmacies.[8] Relatively well-equipped pharmacy laboratories sometimes spawned major chemists and pharmacologists.[9]

Formal education entered pharmacy training with the founding of teaching hospitals in the eighteenth century. From 1707 one Eikhler taught botany, *materia medica*, and pharmacy in the Moscow teaching hospital. From 1733 one Shreiber taught these subjects in the St. Petersburg-Kronstadt teaching hospitals. Pharmacy students apprenticed in pharmacies connected with these hospitals.[10] In 1798 the teaching hospitals were transformed into medical-surgical academies. They admitted pharmacists. The school in Kronstadt closed but a pharmacy department opened in the Medical-Surgical Academy in St. Petersburg in 1808.[11] Courses were taught in German.[12]

Pharmacy became part of the university curriculum from the founding of Moscow University in 1755. The medical faculty delivered lectures on "chemistry with application of pharmaceutical chemistry."[13] Professor I. Kh. Kershtens, a physician from Leipzig, taught mineralogy, experimental chemistry, and *materia medica* from the late 1750s.[14] In the 1790s Moscow University was mandated to give examinations and certify pharmacists at all levels.[15] Those who wished to become fully qualified pharmacists were admitted to lectures, along with medical students.[16] Native pharmacy specialists began to emerge by the middle of the eighteenth century. John G. Model, "the first pharmaceutical [and] chemical authority in Russia . . . whose periodical 'Chemishce Nebenstunden' [Chemical Leisure Hours] was translated into French," rose to prominence in the 1740s.[17] P. D. Venimanov and S. G. Zybelin, educated in Konigsberg and Berlin, began to teach at Moscow University in 1765. Venimanov became the first professor of botany; his field was the native flora of central Russia. Zybelin, extraordinary professor of theoretical medicine, taught a practical course in pharmaceutical-chemical preparation, which used Russian rather than Latin as the language of instruction.[18]

The government organized ranks, requirements, and examinations for pharmacists in 1810, there being 400. The rungs on the pharmacy ladder were apprentice (*aptekarskii uchenik*), *gezel*, Provizor, and Pharmacist (*Aptekar'*). No formal preparation was offered for the *gezel* exam but it was administered by the Medical-Surgical Academy in St. Petersburg or the universities. In 1819 the Medical Department authorized universities and the medical-surgical academies to give "external" students (studying on their own) examinations for medical and pharmaceutical titles, a practice which ceased in 1838. A *gezel* stood at eleventh place in the Table of Ranks, a Provizor at tenth place, and the highest level, Pharmacist, at ninth place, the rank just below that conferring nobility, at that time.[19] An imperial edict of December 28, 1838, rechristened the three pharmaceutical degrees Assistant Pharmacist (*Aptekarskii pomoshchnik*), Provizor, and Pharmacist and more thoroughly defined the qualifications for each.[20] In 1845 the degree Master (*Magistr*) of Pharmacy superseded that of Pharmacist.[21] The titles Assistant Pharmacist, Provizor, and Master lasted until 1917.

On paper, requirements for each title were impressive. In 1840 the Assistant Pharmacist examination was held at the Military Medical Academy or one of the six universities, in a full meeting of the Faculty of Medicine. Candidates were to demonstrate proficiency in mineralogy, botany, physics, chemistry, pharmacognosy, general pharmacy (sight translations from the Latin Pharmacopoeia), and pharmacology, including familiarity with acceptable doses of strong or heroic medicines. Further, candidates prepared four medicines under supervision of the examiners.[22]

To become a Provizor, the newly minted Assistant Pharmacist served in a treasury or private pharmacy for an additional two or three years and audited courses at the Military Medical Academy or one of the universities. The Provizor examination required knowledge of mineralogy, botany, zoology, physics, chemistry, and pharmacognosy. Candidates also were required to prepare two pharmaceutical and two chemical preparations and remedies for "first aid."[23]

To acquire the title Pharmacist, Provizors were required to do chemical research, prepare three chemical preparations under supervision of examiners, and have knowledge of commerce and bookkeeping.[24] The Master of Pharmacy degree demanded completion of the full program of university study and a dissertation.

University education kept pace with these requirements. In 1804 Moscow University introduced pharmacology and animal experiments into the curriculum of the Faculty of Medicine. Professor S. G. Shchegolev, whose dissertation dealt with the cultivation and use of medicinal plants, taught *materia medica*. In 1835 the medical course was increased from four to five years; second-year students studied pharmacy and pharmacology; third-year students studied pharmacology, toxicology, mineral waters, and the writing of prescriptions. Professor Alexander A. Povskii, who occupied the chair of *materia medica* in the 1830s, published more than forty articles on analytical chemistry, pharmacology, general therapy, and pharmacy. He edited a journal and published three texts on pharmacology and pharmacy.[25] Physician I. E. D"iadkovskii, whose dissertation concerned the activity of medicines on humans, taught botany and pharmacology at the Medical-Surgical Academy in Moscow in the early nineteenth century. His student

K. B. Lebedev taught a course on pharmacology and prescriptions, and published a text on practical pharmacology in the 1840s.[26] A. F. Filomatskii, professor at the Medical-Surgical Academy, pioneered the use of anesthesia in the 1840s.[27] Moscow University established Provizor courses in the medical faculty in 1839. Assistant Pharmacists were allowed to audit although they were not considered full-fledged students.[28]

In the early nineteenth century seven universities supplemented the University of Moscow. Six included medical faculties with pharmaceutical courses. Kazan, Khar'kov, and Vil'na opened in 1804, Warsaw University in 1816, Dorpat (later Iur'ev) University in 1832, and in the University of Kiev in 1834.[29]

The course of study in the Pharmacy Department of St. Petersburg Medical-Surgical Academy lasted five years. First-year students studied mathematics, physics, mineralogy, and zoology; the second-, third-, and fourth-year students studied chemistry, botany, pharmacology, and pharmacy. Fifth-year students practiced pharmacy. Some of the texts were authored by Russians–V. M. Severgin, N. M. Ambodik, and N. K. Karpinskii. In 1835 the academy shortened the pharmacy program to four years, with pharmacy practice in the fourth year. Students were required to have completed middle school and apprenticed three years in a pharmacy. Forty students enrolled in the Pharmacy Department of the St. Petersburg Military Medical Academy during the first three years. In Moscow the Medical-Surgical Academy merged with the medical faculty of Moscow University.[30]

Pharmacist Gebel, who occupied the chair of pharmacy at the University of Dorpat in Estland, modern Estonia, made a major contribution to pharmaceutical education by founding a pharmacy institute there in 1844. A later critic of Russian pharmacy education praised this institute as the first true pharmacy school in Russia, providing solid pharmaceutical education for a large contingent of Russian pharmacists.[31] In the 1850s, Professor Claus of Dorpat sagely attributed the excellence of the pharmacy program not only to the presence of "celebrated pharmacists," one of whom, "Scherer was the editor of the Northern Journal for Chemistry, and the first president of the Pharmaceutical Society of St. Petersburg . . ." but to the fact that "from the beginning at this University the professorship of the pharmaceutical branches has been entrusted to practical men of this profession, which was never compelled to take a subordinate rank, as is too often the case in the hands of men otherwise too much engaged professionally."[32] Claus tactfully ignored the Germanic origins of high-quality pharmacy in the Baltic States. The first pharmacy had been established there in 1422,[33] long before Peter the Great acquired the territory in the eighteenth-century Great Northern War with Sweden.

Moscow University awarded the first Master of Pharmacy degree in 1847, Dorpat and the Military Medical Academy in St. Petersburg granted their first Master degrees in 1848. Twelve pharmacists had received the Master degree by 1864.[34]

Specialists gave Russian pharmacy education good marks in the middle of the nineteenth century. In 1840, an anonymous contributor to the *American Journal of Pharmacy* claimed that the Russian pharmacist was afforded "the fullest guarantee of knowledge . . . a price worthy of his services, a distinguished place in the social circle, and the consideration [due] everyone who exercises a liberal profession."[35] A few years later, Professor Claus of Dorpat assured readers of the same journal that "in regard to education the mass of Russian apothecaries compare favorably with those of other countries, the ignorant are by far in the minority."[36]

Curricula for Russian Provizors and Masters remained on a high level throughout the nineteenth century.[37] However, as the century progressed, basic pharmacy training increasingly appeared in need of overhauling. Pharmacist intellectuals would be preoccupied with reform of lower pharmacy education until the end of the empire.

Their first concern was that male pharmacy apprentices embarked upon their career without a school-leaving certificate.[38] Additionally, preliminary education for male pharmacy students was deficient in the sciences. Requirements for those entering pharmacy included several options: completing four years of the classical gymnasium (*gimnaziia*); before 1871, completing the fourth or even third class of the district school (*progimnaziia*), with addition of Latin; after 1871, finishing the entire course of the district school or completion of the primary schools run by the Orthodox Church.[39] Later in the nineteenth century, partial completion of the "real" school, established in 1871, allowed one to enter pharmacy.[40]

None of these options, save the last, provided an adequate foundation. The *gimnaziia* had a seven-year program before 1871 and an eight-year program thereafter. The curriculum included five to six hours of Latin, four to five hours of Greek, three to four hours of mathematics, and two hours of physics per week. However, there were no courses in botany or zoology as in the real schools.[41]

Basic education options for prospective pharmacists expanded in the late nineteenth and early twentieth centuries but scientific preparation did not increase. In May 1872, those finishing district or city schools could become pharmacy students. After 1872 the curriculum in these schools included elementary geometry and Russian history; prior to entering the pharmacy, graduates were required to study Latin and, of the modern foreign languages, either German or French.[42] The Orthodox Church school curriculum included Latin but not geometry.[43] In 1901, graduates of the new commercial schools were allowed to become pharmacy students, following courses in Latin.[44] In 1900, graduates of teacher training schools and the private commercial school of Faig in Odessa were allowed to become pharmacy students.[45]

The next problem came with apprenticeship. The aspiring pharmacist began his or her career with a three-year stint in a normal pharmacy.[46] That the pharmacy be normal or fully stocked was mandatory. Further, according to the medical statute of 1905 there were to be no more than two students for each normal and branch pharmacy.[47] Pharmacies sometimes ignored this rule. For example, in 1907, the Viatka Medical Department noted that there were four male students and twelve female students in a normal pharmacy in the city of Viatka, operated by the provincial zemstvo. Although the number of students exceeded the norm, the Viatka medical inspector pronounced their training "fully satisfactory" and a model for other pharmacies.[48]

But, even in pharmacies with the proper ratio of apprentices to managers, even where the manager-mentor was helpful, pharmacy students frequently received little formal education during the formative stage of their career. Students were supposed to prepare for the Assistant Pharmacist examination during their initial three-year apprenticeship. Few formal courses were available. Pharmacists in St. Petersburg established a school in 1817. The school was run by the St. Petersburg Pharmacy Society, chartered the following year. In the 1840s professors from the Medical-Surgical Academy in St. Petersburg taught pharmacy, pharmacognosy, chemistry, botany, mineralogy, and zoology at the school.[49] The school continued to operate throughout the nineteenth century.[50] Initially, classes were free. Members of the pharmacy society, owners and lessees of pharmacies in the capital, donated 1 ruble, 50 kopeks from each 1,000 prescriptions to support the school.[51] Later, students paid some tuition.[52]

The St. Petersburg Pharmacy School was not adequate even for apprentices in the capital. In the third quarter of the nineteenth century students at the St. Petersburg Pharmacy Society school studied translation of prescriptions from the Latin, pharmacognosy, botany, pharmaceutical chemistry, nomenclatura, doses of strong-acting substances, basic physics—weights, areometer, hydraulic press, barometer, electrical and mechanical instruments.[53] However, there were only about ten students enrolled in 1883.[54] And, although the curriculum was laudable, classroom time was minimal. In 1901 sessions lasted several months but students attended class only two hours, from 10 to 12 in the morning, two days per week, Tuesdays and

Fridays.[55] In 1904 the St. Petersburg Society proposed that the sessions be lengthened to seven months (from September 21 until May) and class time lengthened to three hours, but students still were to attend only two days each week.[56]

In most other cities of the empire, pharmacy students acquired knowledge for the Assistant Pharmacist examinations as best they could. In the 1870s the St. Petersburg Pharmacy Society lamely recommended correspondence courses.[57] By the turn of the century, some pharmacy students were able to attend special preparatory courses. By 1906 pharmacy societies in Moscow, Riga, Tiflis, and Odessa (in addition to the St. Petersburg Pharmacy Society) operated free schools for pharmacy students.[58] But most pharmacy students studied on their own, sometimes with supplementary tutoring. For example, in 1907 Provizor F. I. Geilig, no. 10 Kreshchatik Street, Kiev, announced he "prepared students for the Assistant Pharmacist examination. The text, the same used at Kiev University, cost 2 rubles."[59] In 1909, Provizor Sheikman offered courses in Kovno to student-members of the Southwest Union of Pharmacists to prepare them for the Assistant Pharmacist examination. The course cost 10 rubles, with the right to use laboratories in a nearby chemical-bacteriological institute.[60]

Pharmacy students came to the Assistant Pharmacist examination armed with documents testifying to their education, apprenticeship, and character and, to thwart cheating, photographs proving their identity.[61] Students who failed the examination the first time were allowed to retake it after six months.[62] Though travel to a university town to take the Assistant Pharmacy examination posed an expense, apparently it did not usually cause undue hardship. Isaiah Ginzburg, a pharmacy student in the 1890s, recalled that "after I had been an apprentice for three years I went to the city of Kazan where about twenty of us young fellows passed examinations as Assistant of Pharmacy in the medical university [*sic*] which had a college of pharmacy. We had lovely spring weather, and the trip along the great river Volga in a big steamboat with all modern conveniences of those days was delightful."[63]

However, in some cases, the crush of students attempting to take the Assistant Pharmacist examination caused problems. In October 1902, for example, 200 pharmacy students arrived in Kazan for the Assistant Pharmacist examination. According to a new and rather arbitrary rule, the Kazan university examiners gave the examinations only two days per week to groups of 20 to 25 persons. Therefore, only 120 of the 200 completed the examination. The rest were scheduled for the January examination. They complained to the Minister of Public Enlightenment.[64]

Passing the Assistant Pharmacist examination did not make one a fully qualified pharmacist, although for some the title was terminal. Those wishing to advance to the level of Provizor or fully qualified pharmacist were required to serve another three-year apprenticeship, audit two years of lectures at the St. Petersburg Academy or one of eight Russian universities,[65] and pass the Provizor examination. Pharmacist intellectuals contended that there were numerous problems in reaching this plateau.

By 1879 the Provizor examination had been enlarged to demonstrate more knowledge of science and scientific apparatus.[66] Pharmacy texts kept pace. They were comprehensive and up-to-date.[67] But Assistant Pharmacists faced hurdles in obtaining the university education necessary for the Provizor title. Those wishing to attend lectures in the medical faculty or in the natural history section of the physico-mathematical faculty sent a request to the rector before the beginning of each semester (August 10 or January 5) with certification of apprenticeship, the Assistant Pharmacist title, and a police certificate attesting to good conduct. Assistant Pharmacists were required to pay 25 rubles each semester for the Provizor courses. However, the university considered them auditors, not full-fledged students.[68] Additionally, because Assistant Pharmacists had an inadequate background in science, they sometimes required tutoring to pass their courses.[69]

Further, Provizor courses were not uniform. The Medical-Surgical Academy in St. Petersburg permitted Assistant Pharmacists to audit courses until 1869. Then the academy stipulated that students have a seven-year secondary education. This disqualified Assistant Pharmacists. They dwindled from fifty to sixty to two or three. In 1880 the first two courses were closed and soon after the entire veterinary and pharmacy departments were eliminated.[70] Closure of the Medical-Surgical Academy courses forced Assistant Pharmacists in St. Petersburg to move to distant universities—Dorpat, Moscow, Kazan, Khar'kov, Kiev—to audit Provizor courses.[71]

There, their experiences varied. Before 1879 Provizor courses at the University of Kiev lasted one year. Those at Dorpat University originally lasted three semesters. At Moscow University the council of the Medical Faculty established two-year Provizor courses in 1866. First-year students took mineralogy, botany, zoology, physics, and inorganic chemistry. Second-year students took botany, organic chemistry, pharmacognosy, pharmacy, and pharmacology. Courses included practice in chemistry and pharmacy laboratories, although, according to Professor Givartovskii, Professor of Pharmacognosy and Pharmacy at the University of Moscow in 1877, there were insufficient places in the laboratories.[72] Students could stay at the universities for additional study if they wished[73] but, obviously, this entailed some expense. Finally, Assistant Pharmacists had to fulfill their military service. They frequently did so before taking the Provizor examination, which was disruptive.[74]

The career of Nikolai Mikhailovich Mart'ianov confirmed that it was possible for persons of modest background to complete apprenticeships, pass examinations, and acquire the higher education necessary to become a Provizor. Part Jewish, although listed in the 1895 medical register as "Orthodox, *meshchanstvo,*" Mart'ianov's father was a former under-officer who served as a forest warden in Vil'na province. Mart'ianov attended *gimnaziia* and apprenticed at a pharmacy in Minsk, passed his Assistant Pharmacist examination at the Medical-Surgical Academy in St. Petersburg, then worked four years at a pharmacy in Tsarskoe Selo. Although he received only 20 rubles a month he managed to audit Provizor courses at the Military Surgical Academy. Simultaneously, he attended lectures on ores and minerals at the Mining Institute in St. Petersburg. In his off-hours Mart'ianov browsed in markets, studied and purchased stones, and collected plants in Tsarskoe Selo.[75] Eventually, he became "very knowledgeable about botany and minerals." He supported his sister's *gimnaziia* education and subsidized his own move to Moscow by selling six groups of minerals from his collection to St. Petersburg University for 50 rubles. He also received help from a patron in St. Petersburg. Mart'ianov studied in Moscow two years, receiving his Provizor degree there. In 1873 he took employment in a pharmacy in Kazan. The following year he moved to a pharmacy in Minusinsk, in Yenisei province, central Siberia.[76] Minusinsk, where Lenin was exiled in the late 1890s, was a rich archeological site.[77] Mart'ianov made excursions in the area, gathering materials and exhibiting his finds at the local school. In 1877 he persuaded the Minusinsk town council, or duma, to establish a museum in a two-story stone building at a cost of 25,000 rubles. Mart'ianov worked in the museum in his off-hours from the pharmacy. By 1902 the museum included 56,500 botanical, mineralogical, geological, and archeological items. Its Bronze period collection was unique, not only in Siberia and the Russian Empire, but in the world. The museum included a meteorological station and a warehouse of agricultural implements. Mart'ianov also established a public library related to the museum. The library, housed in a separate building, had 16,000 titles and 20,000 volumes. Both the museum and the library ran on a shoestring for the first twenty-four years; each received a small annual subsidy of 100 rubles from the city and only in 1901 did the museum receive a 1,500-ruble annual subsidy from the central government.[78] Mart'ianov received a number of awards in the 1880s and 1890s—a gold medal for service to the local school, the Honored Citizen title, the Anna medal, and the order of St. Stanislav. In 1891 he displayed his archeology collection to tsarevich

Nicholas (soon to become Nicholas II). In 1901, Mart'ianov was awarded a pension of 600 rubles[79] but began suffering "attacks with loss of consciousness." Rest in the Crimea was not helpful, and he died in November 1904.[80]

The careers of Masters of Pharmacy, even more than that of Provizor Mart'ianov, testify that determined individuals could acquire a good pharmaceutical education despite the incomplete secondary education required of the pharmacy student and lack of systematic courses available to most Assistant Pharmacists.

Three hundred individuals received the Master of Pharmacy degree between 1845 and 1901. The universities of Iur'ev (as Dorpat was renamed) and Moscow, and the Military Medical Academy in St. Petersburg, awarded the overwhelming majority. Iur'ev led with seventy, Moscow awarded forty-nine, and the Military Medical academy, forty-one.[81] In 1910 there were ninety-four Masters of Pharmacy.[82] Their program of study was very comprehensive. Courses used both Russian and foreign textbooks.[83]

Many Masters of Pharmacy received gold medals at their examinations, successfully completed foreign programs, and published prodigiously. Ivan Khristoforovich Gertel provides a random example. Born in Kurland in 1858, Gertel completed real school in Mitau, studying Latin at the Riga *gimnaziia*. He apprenticed in a pharmacy in Vladimir. Following his Assistant Pharmacy examination, he apprenticed in two St. Petersburg pharmacies and prepared for the Provizor examination at Dorpat University, receiving that title with a gold medal. After defending his thesis and receiving his Master's degree in 1881, Gertel served as assistant in the Dorpat Pharmacy Institute Faculty of Pharmacy and managed a pharmacy in St. Petersburg, a pharmacy in Kurland, and held a post as pharmacist in the Kurland Medical Administration. Fortified with the standard pharmacy education, Gertel studied at the Hygienic Institute in Berlin, under Koch, studied "synthesizing" chemistry in the organic chemistry laboratory of A. W. Hoffman, and acquired the Ph.D. degree in Germany. He returned for a time to Kurland where he resumed his post of pharmacist in the Kurland Medical Administration and acquired a pharmacy in Mitau; in 1890, the government again sent Gertel to study the latest information on tuberculosis under Koch and to the Pasteur Institute in Paris.[84]

Gertel and other Masters of Pharmacy could not have been admitted to foreign institutes and could not have published significant research without a sound, preliminary pharmacy education. Certainly, if lower pharmacy education provided a good foundation for those who achieved the Master title, it should have done so for all pharmacists.

Nevertheless, from 1879 when their first Russian-language journal appeared, pharmacist-intellectuals anguished over the defects in basic pharmacy preparation and training. The St. Petersburg Pharmacy Society attacked "one-sided exploitation of [pharmacy] students . . . in violation of the law," unsystematic learning–"the student was to learn by watching, directed by books which casually fell into his hands," and insufficient preliminary education–"the student of the fifth-year class in an eight-year school has a certificate but does not possess knowledge." The Pharmacy Society emphasized that it was not easy for pharmacy owners and managers to act as teachers and mentors for pharmacy students. They suggested suitable compensation.[85]

Pharmacists debated four issues in the last decades of the nineteenth century: raising entrance requirements for pharmacy students, decreasing apprenticeship and increasing formal pharmacy education, whether special pharmacy schools ought to be established, and if so, the nature of these schools. But, despite exhaustive deliberation and reams of projects, reform never materialized.

Elimination of apprenticeship proved to be a major stumbling block. Some pharmacists insisted it provided hands-on experience and financial assistance to students from poor families. Pharmacy students also were deemed necessary to supplement pharmacy staffs.[86] This argument was increasingly used after double shifts became common in the early twentieth century.

The issue of special institutes versus university education to prepare Assistant Pharmacists for the Provizor examination was equally contentious. In the 1870s, Russian pharmacy societies rejected special institutes, emphasizing that Provizor courses were best taught in a university. They would repeat this decision time and again.[87]

By the turn of the century, pharmacists in most European countries were calling for higher entrance qualifications and more formal education for pharmacists.[88] Russian reformers now urged completion of the real school, four-year university Provizor courses, and to prepare for the Assistant Pharmacist examination, special schools akin to feldsher, or paramedical, schools.[89] The special schools, in turn, generated a new debate–whether they ought to be proprietary or government-sponsored.

A few private pharmacy schools already existed in Russia. The Chemico-Bacteriological Institute of Dr. F. M. Bliumental', established about 1897, offered courses in microscope techniques and the latest findings on bacteriology. In 1907 there were 40 auditors, "predominantly pharmacists."[90]

Some pharmacists welcomed more private education. In 1902 Provizor M. V. Polumordvinov proposed that he be allowed to organize courses on pharmaceutical accounting.[91] At the same time Pharmacist A. Purve chided pharmacists and pharmacy societies for not establishing institutes for Assistant Pharmacists. He proposed that pharmacists in each provincial city elect a committee to ascertain how strongly pharmacists desired pharmacy institutes, then follow the example of merchants who had established commercial schools supported by self-imposed tax. A central committee in Moscow and St. Petersburg would coordinate and disseminate the information.[92] Two years later he advocated a network of short-term proprietary schools on an American model. Purve was especially intrigued with a New York pharmacy school founded by one Dr. Robinson. Students in Dr. Robinson's school prepared for the pharmacy examination in twice-a-week, three- to four-month sessions, paying the "rather high" tuition of $75 to $100. They were "almost always more successful" than those who studied at Colleges of Pharmacy, with a two-year program and tuition of $90 to $100. Purve opined that "the secret was in the method of teaching . . . textbooks were important. Students in Doctor Robinson's school read five to six textbooks of 300 to 400 pages each and wrote in three notebooks of 30 to 35 pages each." Many Russian pharmacy students paid 120 to 150 rubles to private tutors to help them prepare for the Assistant Pharmacist examination. Instead, schools like Dr. Robinson's ought to be instituted in Russia.[93] Despite Purve's enthusiasm, however, Dr. Robinson's school appeared analogous to the "cram schools" that operated in Britain in the nineteenth century. In any case, most pharmacists in Russia vehemently rejected proprietary schools.

Thus, pharmacy education, as so much else in Russian pharmacy, had both pluses and minuses. At the highest levels it was equal to European pharmacy education. At the lower levels it held its own. Additionally, as later chapters will show, pharmacy training and education offered opportunities to non-Russian minorities and women.

Nevertheless, as we shall see, the flaws in lower-level pharmacy training and education continued to trouble reform-minded pharmacists. Further, in the two decades before 1917 the government finally began to grapple with the problems in pharmacy education. It particularly tried to address lack of ties between academic pharmacists and the pharmaceutical industry during World War I. But conflicts over apprenticeship and proprietary schools within the pharmacy corporation, coupled with bureaucratic foot-dragging, prevented real reform. And frustration with these issues would eventually drive a number of reformist pharmacists leftward and into the arms of the Bolsheviks.

3

Privately Owned Pharmacies

Every system has pluses and minuses. The duality of the Russian pharmacy system is particularly evident when we examine pharmacies (*apteki*) in late imperial Russia. Government regulations on *operating* pharmacies were beneficial because they imposed a fair amount of standardization. They also prevented access to poisons and narcotics. Regulations on *establishing* pharmacies, on the other hand, predictably stunted their growth. Additionally, these restrictions led to the establishment of drug stores (*aptekarskie magaziny*) and other quasi-pharmaceutical emporia. Their operation was regulated, but not as stringently as pharmacies. They soon became far more numerous than pharmacies and a headache to pharmacists (although some bowed to the inevitable and operated drug stores themselves).

Drug emporia will be discussed in the following chapter, pharmacists' reactions to them and drug abuse in subsequent chapters. Here we explore how the rules on establishing pharmacies affected pharmacies, pharmacist owners or would-be owners of pharmacies, and the general populace. We will see that the availability of pharmacies was not as dire as might have been expected. Further, while government paternalism made some pharmacists complacent, other pharmacists and provincial governors proved to be a feisty lot. They stubbornly confronted and sometimes flaunted the rules on establishing pharmacies. Their refusal to accept the restraints imposed upon them highlights the nuances in the dialogue between the central government, the local government, and the public in late imperial Russia.

The uniformity in Russian pharmacies, particularly fully outfitted normal (*normal'naia*) pharmacies, was praised by Russian and foreign specialists alike. In 1853 Professor C. Claus of the pharmacy faculty of Dorpat University conceded that "Model pharmaceutical establishments . . . are more frequently found in the interior [European Russia], particularly in the provincial capitals . . . the fixtures of some stores in the principal cities have cost as high as 10,000 rubels [*sic*] (about $7,000)." But he stressed that "In all establishments may be found good sets of pharmaceutical and chemical apparatus, mostly with the latest improvements, and their business is purely pharmaceutical without the addition of the grocery, hardware, liquor, or other business, as is sometimes met with in other countries."[1]

Some fifty years later, H. M. Gordin, from the University of Michigan Pharmacy School found Russian pharmacies superior to American. Russian pharmacies, he noted approvingly, differ "considerably from that of an American drug store. The Russian pharmacy is often situated not on the ground floor, but in the second story and looks more like a physician's office connected with a pharmaceutical laboratory than a retail shop. The windows are used for the simple purpose of admitting light, not for displaying gold fish, flower seeds, pictures of foolish, bald-headed men who could never be persuaded to try X's Hair Tonic. . . ."[2]

Both Gordin and British pharmacist Prosper Marsden admired the professional ambience of the Russian pharmacy and Russian pharmacists' professional demeanor, noting multiple special-purpose rooms and wide variety of apparatus. "In the first room, which often resembles a physician's waiting room, the prescriptions are received and priced by the so-called 'receptuarius' and then carried to the next room containing a row of small tables or a long counter with several assistants waiting to compound them. The assistant, after filling the prescription, delivers it to the receptarius without tying and sealing it. The receptarius" subjected "the medicine to as much scrutiny as possible before tying, sealing and delivering it to the customer."[3] Beyond the prescription room was the "material room . . . where the stock and larger containers are kept." Behind that was a laboratory "fitted out with a boiler having several compartments for infusion vessels and a still for distilled and aromatic waters and . . . a drying chamber; an oil press, a tincture press and a lot of other apparatus. . . ." The laboratory "generally was connected with a cellar for salves, syrups, etc." and, finally there was an "attic for drying fresh roots and herbs."[4] Gordin was particularly impressed that "Prescriptions containing substances easily affected by light are always put up in amber colored bottles, and odoriferous or hygroscopic powders in wax paper. . . ."[5]

Indeed, some turn-of-the-century Russian pharmacies were grand establishments. Perhaps the epitome of the normal pharmacy was the Ferrein pharmacy in Moscow, located on Staraia Nikolskaia Street (now 25th October Street), near Red Square. Peter the Great had chartered the pharmacy in 1701. In 1832, Karl Ivanovich Ferrein, a Prussian, awarded the title "Pharmacist [*Aptekar'*] first class" from Moscow University, acquired it and began to enlarge its scope. Housed in a four-story Renaissance-style building, the Ferrein pharmacy was the largest in the world in the early twentieth century and surely one of the most elegant and up-to-date. To the right of the entrance was a room that dispensed over-the-counter medicines. A marble staircase with a wrought iron and brass art-nouveau banister led to the immense, second-floor reception room. Customers waited for their prescriptions in this twenty-foot-high reception room, graced with Corinthian columns, a gilded, coffered ceiling, and electrified globe chandeliers. Neoclassical busts of medical and pharmaceutical giants gazed from the upper walls, polished wooden and brass cases and counters lined the lower. Pharmacists prepared the medicines in rooms beyond and on the upper floors; the preparation rooms were equipped with all manner of apparatus, some of it electrically driven. As did smaller pharmacies, the Ferrein pharmacy had drying rooms for herbs and underground storage rooms. A bacteriological and chemical laboratory employing fourteen was situated in an adjacent building. There was a warehouse for packaging and distribution; a fleet of horse-drawn buggies delivered prescriptions around the city.

By 1910 the Ferrein pharmacy employed over 300 people, including 43 Provizors and 121 Assistant Pharmacists. Twenty-two women typed the *signatury,* or labels, that accompanied each prescription. The number of prescriptions dispensed annually climbed from 27,359 in 1832 to 717,901 in 1910. Like other Russian pharmacies Ferrein was open twenty-four hours a day; at times it dispensed almost three thousand prescriptions in twenty-four hours.[6] By 1910 employees enjoyed a seven-hour day with a half hour for rest. Pharmacists on the night shift (*dezhurstvo*) were free the next day. There was an employee dining hall. A ventilation system and specially constructed chambers admitting only the pharmacists' hands protected them from harmful gases and fumes when working with poisons and strong-acting materials. There was an outpatient clinic for employees.[7] There were a number of pharmacies similar to the Ferrein establishment in Moscow, St. Petersburg and other major cities.[8]

Normal pharmacies in small towns were simpler, but adequate. In 1894, as a seventeen-year-old, Isaiah Ginzburg apprenticed at a pharmacy in a small town some 150 miles from Moscow.[9] The pharmacy was located in "a two-story frame building" surrounded by a "yard in which the former owner still kept cows and horses." It complied with the rules on layout—"In the back of the pharmacy was a large laboratory, stock rooms, cellar filled with tinctures, liquid extracts, salves, and wines. The dry herbs were all in separate wooden boxes and kept high on the second floor of the barn, high and dry. Shipments of drug merchandise . . . had to be stocked in bulk for months ahead. . . . The prescription desk had all the necessary clean bottles, jars, pills, suppository machines, scales, boxes, bags, etc. There were closets with drugs in small packages, such as narcotics and poisons."[10]

The pharmacy conscientiously followed the rules on dispensing. "A customer was never allowed to venture into" the closets with narcotics and poisons," although the doctors walked freely into this sacred sanctum of the pharmacy and felt at home . . . prescriptions were taken by the assistant pharmacist, who worked in the second room of the pharmacy. It was a big two-windowed room, with walls lined from floor to ceiling with prescription drugs. The boss's private desk and pharmacy library were there. . . ."[11]

Remedies in late nineteenth- and early twentieth-century Russia included time-honored products made from natural ingredients. However, Russian pharmacies also dispensed the newest coal-tar febrifuges and pain killers.

Traditional plant remedies included citric acid, grape juice for bronchial catarrh, bronchitis, and urinary disorders; vinegar acid for fever, scarlatina, and eczema.[12] *Fructus Foeniculi* was used as an expectorant, for digestive problems in newborns, in small doses to increase breast milk (4 grams), and in larger doses (8 to 16 grams) in hemorrhaging from the womb and (spontaneous) abortion. *Herba origani*, "grown all over Russia," was used for toothache, despite its bitter taste.[13] Camphor was dispensed in cases of typhus, cholera, and heart diseases. The oil and acid of valerian root, grown all over Russia, was one of the most frequently used remedies. It was dispensed for nervous diseases, including "hysteria in women," in typhus, and to kill worms. *Artimisiae* root, also grown all over Russia, was used in contractions of the womb. Kumiss, the fermented mares' milk, was a common remedy. However, pharmacists were warned that strong kumiss increased the pulse and made breathing difficult.[14] Siberian castor was used in *Tincture Castorei sibirici s. russici, s. moscovitchi*, for problems of the womb. Tannin was dispensed for digestive diseases, kidney problems, and diarrhea. Tannic acid was used as an antidote for morphine poisoning.[15] Russian pharmacies dispensed several worm and parasite remedies. These included "santonin" and other vermifuges.[16]

Traditional mineral-based remedies included carbolic acid, used from 1864 to kill trichinae in the digestive tract, and skin parasites. One fourth to one drop of creosote, covered with gelatin, was dispensed for stomach disorders; creosote also was used for toothache. Phenol was dispensed for lung problems but pharmacists were warned that it was "more dangerous than carbolic acid." Phenol also was used as an antiseptic in surgery. The effects of carbolic phenol ether were described by the Russian Vasil'ev in a 1881 dissertation. This substance was used to counter diphtheria.[17] Chloroform was used in diseases of the lungs and asthma. Pharmacists were warned of the dangers of too large doses of both chloroform and chloral hydrate. The latter, used as an antidote for strychnine poisoning, as an anesthetic, in nervous diseases like choreae, and in obstetrics could also be dangerous, pharmacists were advised, causing breathing problems and delirium tremens.[18]

Newer mineral products in the arsenal of late nineteenth-century Russian medicines included salicylic acid, a coal-tar product synthesized by French chemists in 1838.[19] Russians used the product in cases of rheumatism and arthritis, and as a febrifuge. However, pharmacists were warned that salicylic acid did not work as well as quinine in fevers caused by malaria,[20] which was Russia's main communicable disease at the time.[21] One remedy pioneered by Russians was *naftalin.*[22] One of its uses was for "catarrh" of the bladder. Bromal and iodal were used in epilepsy.[23]

Turn-of-the-century Russian pharmacies received some medicines from factories, both Russian and foreign, in prepared form. But many remedies were prepared from scratch in the pharmacy. Russian pharmacists' continued reliance on in-house production was due as much to their desire to protect their monopoly status as to the state of the Russian pharmaceutical industry, subjects that will be dealt with in future chapters. In any case, by law pharmacies were required to have on hand a wealth of materials–herbs, powders, pills, capsules, oils, gelatin, sweeteners, extracts, tinctures, solutions, suppositories–and apparatus–metal and glass stoves, Bunsen burners, distilling globes and pipes, weights, areometers, papers for powders, pill machines, wafer holders, tablet presses, and bandage machines.[24]

In the pharmacies that Gordin visited "All galenicals and pharmaceuticals that can be made on an ordinary scale, like solid and powdered extracts, salves, aromatic waters, etc. are manufactured in the drug store [*sic*]. The laboratory is under the care of a special pharmacist called 'laborant,' who has under his direction one or two common laborers . . . to do the hard work, like powdering drugs, working the press, etc."[25]

Similarly Ginzburg's small-town pharmacy was both primitive and modern. It dispensed beeswax, strained through cheesecloth and poured into paper boxes made in the pharmacy; tincture of *Convallaria Majalis,* made from the tops of lily-of-the-valley and used as a heart stimulant; and a powder made of dried beetles. These items were purchased from local peasants.[26] But the pharmacy also had on hand "plasters, cotton, ointments, quinine, sodium bromide, potassium, iodide, and other drugs. . . ."[27] It strove to be self sufficient, making "wax paper, paper bags, folded filter papers, and paper boxes."[28] It supplied oxygen to hospitals and homebound patients and sold other hospital supplies.[29] But it made up medicine the old-fashioned way. Mercury ointment took ten days to prepare.[30]

Of course, many people treated themselves at home. Gordin informed the University of Michigan Pharmacy School in 1899 that "For ordinary ailments, where the advice of a physician is not considered imperative, the [Russian] public use simple remedies like black draught, volatile ointment, etc. A few other remedies are put up by every druggist, like corn salve, diarrhoea drops, and so on."[31]

Despite restrictions the network of pharmacies gradually expanded. In 1851 there were only 743 privately owned pharmacies in the empire. Some twenty-five years later, in 1877, enfranchised (*vol'naia*) pharmacies, owned by private individuals or groups, had more than doubled to 1,621.[32] Ten years later, in 1877, there were half again as many pharmacies for a total of 2,616.[33] By 1901 there were 3,518 pharmacies,[34] in 1905–3,919.[35] By 1911 there were almost 1,000 more, for a total of 4,804 pharmacies.[36] Thirty-one were homeopathic–8 of which were located in St. Petersburg[37]–2,845 were normal pharmacies, 1,825 were partially stocked village or rural (*sel'skaia*) pharmacies, and 102 in government institutions or hospitals referred to as *aptechnoe delo.*[38]

Thus, cumbersome as it was, the Russian pharmacy system worked–and more efficiently than in Austria where private pharmacies numbered only 1,820 in 1913.[39] However, the unfettered system in France clearly worked far better. In 1907 there were over 10,000 pharmacies in France; in Paris alone there were 1,200 pharmacies–one for every 3,000 to 3,500 inhabitants.[40] Nor did the Russian system function as well as the German system, which it copied. In 1905 Prussia had 3,258 pharmacies; Bavaria, 726 ; and Germany, as a whole, 5,703. Undoubtedly this was partly due to fairly elastic rules for buying and selling pharmacies. In Germany approximately 25 percent of pharmacies were "privileged," which meant the owner was "quite free" to dispose of them; and 58.6 percent were "sold on concession," which meant that operation rights could be sold with government approval–usually forthcoming; the remainder were not sold on concession. In addition there were 165 branch pharmacies in Prussia in 1905, 202 hospital pharmacies, and 305 small "home" pharmacies. In 1905 one pharmacy in Prussia served 11,515 people; in Bavaria the ratio was better still: there, one pharmacy served 8,942 inhabitants.[41]

In 1905 Russia, in contrast, one pharmacy served, on average: 20,000 in the "Polish provinces," 29,500 inhabitants in the twelve "nonzemstvo" provinces, 48,700 people in the thirty-four zemstvo provinces, 33,500 in the Caucasus, 33,900 in the region of the Don army, 85,700 inhabitants in Siberia, and 185,200 people in Central Asia.[42]

Turn-of-the-century inhabitants of the Russian Empire flagellated themselves with these statistics. However, as with any statistics, one must look beneath the surface, for Russian pharmacies were very unevenly distributed. Rural dwellers of the Russian Empire had limited access to pharmacies, except in the Baltic provinces. The zemstvo provinces had the worst record. In 1905, one pharmacy served 101,200 rural inhabitants. Siberia was worse still; one pharmacy served 276,200. (No data were given in 1905 for rural areas in Central Asia.) One pharmacy served 39,800 rural dwellers in the twelve nonzemstvo provinces. The ratio was slightly better in the Polish provinces where one village pharmacy served 27,200 rural dwellers. Best off were the rural dwellers of the Baltic provinces; there one pharmacy served 8,500—better than the ratio for urbanites in both nonzemstvo and zemstvo provinces![43] Probably many rural dwellers were forced to rely largely on home remedies and self-appointed healers, commonly called *znakhari* (wise men) or *babki* (grannies).[44]

Urbanites, on the other hand, had quite good access to pharmacies, no matter in what region of the empire they lived. In 1905, in the twelve nonzemstvo provinces there was, on average, one pharmacy for every 9,400 city dwellers. The ratio of pharmacies to urban dwellers in the Polish provinces of the empire was 1:10,100. Warsaw had more pharmacies per inhabitant than St. Petersburg and Moscow; the ratios were 1:13,000, 1:16,600, 1:22,800, respectively. The ratio of pharmacies to urban dwellers was phenomenally good in the Baltic provinces—1:7,300 and the region of the Don army—1:7,600; the ratio was acceptable in the Caucasus—1:11,900. Cities in the western provinces of Vil'na, Kovno, and Kiev also had many pharmacies, although Arkhangel'sk, in the north, and Astrakhan, at the mouth of the Volga, had few. In Siberian cities and towns there was one pharmacy for every 10,100 inhabitants—a slightly *better* ratio than for the thirty-four zemstvo provinces of European Russia where one pharmacy served, on average, 10,300 urban dwellers. In the nine regions (*oblast'*) of Central Asia there were only half as many pharmacies per town dwellers as in Siberia or European Russia, but the ratio was still five times better than that for rural dwellers in European Russia—1: 20,300.[45]

Even in areas where the number of pharmacies was unremarkable, the number of prescriptions dispensed increased significantly. For instance, in the Volga province of Simbirsk there were twenty-three pharmacies in 1905; during the next eight years only six more pharmacies were founded. They were located in cities or district towns. Nevertheless, the number of prescriptions dispensed in Simbirsk province virtually doubled between 1895 and 1907—from 13,308 to 26,130.[46] The man on the street noted progress. In 1909 an inhabitant of a small town in Khar'kov province, in eastern Ukraine, informed the Social Democratic journal *Zhizn' farmatsevta* that "our town is small—30,000; two-thirds of the population are peasants . . ." While he asserted that "pharmacy [*aptechnoe delo*] is weakly developed . . . if the local pharmacy owners work well it is only thanks to . . .

grannies and wise men [self healers]," he also proudly announced that the town had "three pharmacies. The boulevard pharmacy belonging to Skiiar works especially well. It is located in the very center of the city not far from the bazaar and on Sundays and holidays it becomes a market."[47]

The march of pharmacies into the towns of European Russia and the vast reaches of Siberia and Asia was due to the persistence of provincial governors and pharmacists, who with their families owned the vast majority of pharmacies.[48]

Governors began their attempts to increase dispensing from the early nineteenth century.[49] The governor of Tomsk established a pharmacy in that western Siberian town in 1809; a pharmacist was hired from Berlin to manage the pharmacy and organize a medical garden.[50] The governor and Board of Public Welfare in Perm province, in the Urals, established a pharmacy in 1813.[51] In Simbirsk province, on the middle Volga, there were seven pharmacies by 1851.[52] Professor Claus recounted in 1853 that the Siberian cities of Orenburg, Ufa, Ekaterinburg, Tobol'sk, and Irkutsk also had one pharmacy each, although he admitted that "The furniture and interior arrangements" of Siberian pharmacies were "generally unexceptionable."[53] Kostroma, a province in northeastern European Russia had fifteen pharmacies by 1868.[54]

Governors continued their efforts to improve dispensing in the early twentieth century. Time and again they bombarded the Medical Council and the Chief Medical Inspector with tales of woe and elaborate computations to convince these authorities new pharmacies were justified. In 1906 the governor of Vladimir province, just northeast of Moscow, petitioned for a third normal pharmacy in the capital city, "outside the rules of 1873, modified in 1903," asserting it had been needed for nine years but the ministry of Internal Affairs had permitted only a branch. The populace had "no faith" in this branch and trekked to normal pharmacies some distance away. Ten thousand people now dwelled in the region; a regiment was quartered nearby as was a "suburban settlement" with 2,000 souls. According to the Provincial Statistical Committee, the city population was 33,071, the requisite number for a third normal pharmacy.[55] In 1910 the governor of Chernigov province, in Ukraine, petitioned the Medical Council for a second normal pharmacy in his provincial capital. He reasoned that the city was spread out and some of the population lived 3 versts (about 2 miles) away from the existing normal pharmacy. Epidemics of scarlatina, diphtheria, and cholera in 1911 prompted the Medical Council to grant the request.[56] In 1911, both the Warsaw governor and his medical inspector emphasized to the Medical Council the plight of two small towns near Warsaw, Mokotov and Volia. Thriving factory towns, their populations had nearly doubled in the last ten years and they desperately needed additional fully stocked pharmacies.[57]

In December 1912, the medical division of Sedletsk province, Russian Poland, presented seven pages meticulously documenting population growth and decrease in the town of Vlodav between 1899 and 1911, to prove the current population of 14,738 which would entitle the town to a second normal pharmacy.[58] A few months later, in April 1913, the Sedletsk provincial administration sent a follow-up report, insisting that "one pharmacy in the city of Sedletsk does not serve the city and its surroundings and also the 17th Artillery brigade, quartered in the city."[59]

Limitations on pharmacy franchises engendered a protectionist mindset in established pharmacy owners. They invoked the restrictive laws to block new pharmacies. But governors and would-be owners were unflagging in their efforts and frequently won their cases. For example, in 1905 two Provizors applied for a franchise to open a fourth normal pharmacy in the town of Borisoglebsk, Tambov province. Managers of existing zemstvo and private pharmacies opposed the new pharmacy. The local medical inspector, on the other hand, insisted that a fourth pharmacy was "desirable." He dismissed the fact that the population was 1,672 short of the norm—"an insignificant number"—and assured authorities that the new pharmacy would not compete with existing ones.[60] Similarly, in the Pacific port city of Vladivostok, owners of existing normal pharmacies attempted to block a new fourth pharmacy in 1906 and a new eighth pharmacy in 1908 and 1909 on the basis that Japanese, Chinese, and Koreans living in the city could not be counted in the total population as they did not use Russian physicians or pharmacies.[61] The Primorskii governor, the medical division of his provincial board, and the Medical Council rejected their argument and gave permission for the new pharmacies.[62] In 1906 owners of two pharmacies in Semipalatinsk, Central Asia, protested to the Chief Medical Inspector the local medical inspector's approval for a franchise for a third pharmacy. In part their opposition stemmed from the fact that the new owner was a feldsher rather than a pharmacist. However, they also complained that the medical inspector had included in his population count people who lived beyond the Irtysh River, which, due to lack of a bridge, was not linked to the rest of the city; further, half the population of the city of Semipalatinsk consisted of Tatar and Kirghiz who rarely turned to Russian physicians or Russian pharmacies for medical help.[63] In 1916, Eva Grabskaia, wife of a Provizor and owner of a pharmacy in Novogeorgievsk, Kherson province, protested the impending establishment of a second normal pharmacy. However, her objection was found invalid for several reasons: the population of both sexes had reached 15,801; the wait to fill prescriptions at her pharmacy was long; infectious diseases had become more prevalent during the last three years; finally, with prohibition of alcohol and increase in wages due to the war, the population had become "significantly richer."[64]

Sometimes impatient local authorities and would-be pharmacy owners ignored the laws and did not wait for approval from the center to establish pharmacies. Such was the case in Ekaterinoslav province, just north of the Crimean peninsula. In 1908 and 1909 two Provizors and an Assistant Pharmacist requested the provincial board to allow them to open a second normal pharmacy in the village of Kamenskoe. This sparked complaint from the wife of the owner of the existing pharmacy. Five years later, in 1913, the provincial medical department petitioned the Minister of Internal Affairs for a *third* pharmacy in the village of Kamenskoe, claiming "lively trade-industrial activity due to the Dneprovsk South Russian Metallurgical Factory" made it necessary. The astonished Chief Medical Inspector reminded the Ekaterinoslav governor that "we have your request about opening a third normal pharmacy... we bring to your attention that the Administration of the Chief Medical Inspector still has not resolved the ... question permitting the opening of the *second* normal pharmacy." He asked the governor to quickly send information justifying it. The governor then confessed that the second pharmacy had been "factually" existing since 1909,[65] an admission reminiscent of the mayor's wife in Gogol's *Revizor* who was "in a way... married."[66]

Pharmacists' energy and determination in establishing pharmacies were particularly evident in Central Asia and Siberia. The population in both areas increased markedly in the two decades before World War I.[67] Though meager in absolute terms, the number of pharmacies in Asiatic Russia–the Caucasus, Central Asia, and Siberia–kept pace, increasing at a faster rate than in European Russia. In 1901 there were 367 pharmacies in Asiatic Russia, or 10.4 percent of the total number in the empire. Ten years later pharmacies in Asiatic Russia had nearly doubled to 676, or 14.1 percent of the total. Pharmacies in the Caucasus increased from 264 to 464, pharmacies in Central Asia (the regions of Akmolinsk, Samarkand, Semipalatinsk, Turgaisk, Fergana) from 30 to 74, and pharmacies in Siberia from 73 to 148.[68] Most of the pharmacies in Asiatic Russia were normal, fully stocked pharmacies. In 1901 44.9 percent of the pharmacies in Asiatic Russia were normal as compared with 51.8 percent village. In 1911 the percentage of normal and rural pharmacies were nearly the same.[69]

The Russian press paid tribute to "The private initiative of pharmacists in opening and organizing pharmacies . . . most of all . . . in Siberia." In 1900 "only 57.5 percent of pharmacies there belonged to pharmacists" whereas "at the beginning of 1911–71 percent, i.e., 13.5 percent more did." In the region of the Don army pharmacists owned 88.2 percent of the pharmacies, in the Central Asian region they owned 82.4 percent.[70]

Perhaps pharmacists established pharmacies in Siberia and Central Asia so enthusiastically because restrictions drove up prices in the cities of European Russia. In any case, gaining a franchise and establishing a pharmacy in Siberia and Central Asia was a feat, given the legalism of the central medical bureaucracy, established owners' hostility to competition, and the remoteness of the area.[71] The voluminous correspondence between would-be pharmacy owners and local officials, on the one hand, and central authorities on the other, regarding the establishment of pharmacies in Siberia and Central Asia provides a fascinating glimpse of life in those areas in the early twentieth century. The missives underscore the intransigence of established pharmacy owners and the determination of would-be owners, but profile both camps as risk-takers, reveal conduits for ordering and distributing medicines and pharmaceutical supplies in outlying areas, and explain how the sizable non-Russian native population–which rejected "Western" pharmacy–alleviated the disproportion of pharmacies to inhabitants in Siberia and Central Asia.

Krasnoiarsk was situated on the Yenisei River in central Siberia. It also was a station on the Trans-Siberian Railway. By January 1907, troops moving to and from the Pacific for the war with Japan had pushed the population to 47,577.[72] The city boasted of several pharmacies. A normal pharmacy near the eastern border of the old city dispensed over 13,000 prescriptions at a profit of almost 8,000 rubles per year. The Society of Doctors in the western part of the old city dispensed over 35,000 prescriptions per year, realizing income of over 19,700 rubles.[73] The society ordered medicines from catalogs and dispensed them at 10 percent over cost.[74] A Provizor managed the pharmacy in the city hospital, maintained by the government. It sported its own laboratory and dispensed 40,000 prescriptions annually.[75] The city hospital and rural clinics bypassed local pharmacies, ordering medicines and supplies through catalogs of the local branch of the Russian Society of Trade in Pharmaceutical Wares. Goods were sold at the current market rate.[76]

However, despite the fairly good set-up, Krasnoiarsk needed more pharmacies. The governor of Yeniseisk had requested a third normal pharmacy in 1905 and petitioned for a fourth shortly thereafter.[77] In 1907 the Yenisei Provincial Medical Department petitioned for pharmacies in the western part of the city to serve railway workers and vacationers who lived there.[78] The owners of two existing pharmacies in Krasnoiarsk complained. Nevertheless, two Provizors received permission to open a third and fourth normal pharmacy in 1907. Unfortunately, the opening was delayed because troops flooding the city made it impossible to find premises.[79] Continuing the quest for improved dispensing, at the end of 1907, the Irkutsk governor-general petitioned that the Krasnoiarsk City Hospital pharmacy be allowed private sale of medicines. The provincial Statistical Committee noted that it would not have precise information until March 1908, but estimated the population at 51,846, underscoring how every *i* had to be dotted and every *t* crossed when petitioning for new pharmacies. Meanwhile, the council of the city hospital announced plans to establish a central warehouse so that it could supply medicines, bandages, and surgical instruments to all district hospitals and rural clinics in the province.[80] The medical inspector[81] and the Medical Council rejected the petition for the hospital pharmacy to sell medicine privately.[82]

Vladivostok and Khabarovsk, located in Eastern Siberia, were a thousand miles away from Krasnoiarsk and a good distance from each other. The Russo-Japanese War similarly boosted their populations. That of Vladivostok was 31,000 before the Russo-Japanese War and 43,600 in 1907. As noted, the city was multiracial. Russians predominated at over 22,000. There were 15,700 Chinese, 3,500 Koreans, and a handful (883) of Japanese. In 1907 the owner of one normal pharmacy in Vladivostok filled over 33,000 prescriptions, the equivalent, in the opinion of a contemporary commentator, of a pharmacy in St. Petersburg. As a result of this, the military governor of the region (Primorskii Oblast') petitioned the Chief Medical Inspector to permit the opening of a fourth normal pharmacy. During 1907 and 1908 local authorities insisted that four more pharmacies were needed, despite denials from owners of existing pharmacies. The population of Khabarovsk also grew precipitously during the Russo-Japanese War, reaching almost 40,000. Three new pharmacies were opened in 1906, 1907, and 1908, bringing the total to five. However, although local authorities wanted a sixth pharmacy and the Medical Council concurred that medical care and dispensing were inadequate, the Medical Council held fast to the rule regarding the number of pharmacies in district towns and rejected the request. Khabarovsk's population must expand to the 60,000 required for a sixth normal pharmacy.[83] The population of Vladivostok continued to rise after 1908. By 1912 it was twice that of 1907 with over 91,000 inhabitants, exclusive of the troops stationed there. As a result, both a Provizor and the committee of the Vladivostok Charitable Society requested that they be granted permission to open a ninth normal pharmacy. Owners of the eight existing pharmacies protested that the city could not support another pharmacy but the candidates for the new pharmacy insisted that one was needed in outlying districts of the city, inhabited by needy people (one of the areas was called the "Worker," or *Rabochaia Slobodka*). In November 1913 the Medical Council approved the ninth pharmacy.[84]

The hamlet of Stretenskaia, also a station on the Trans-Siberian Railway line, was located hundreds of miles from Krasnoiarsk, Vladivostok, and Khabarovsk, near Lake Baikal in eastern Siberia. Although the permanent population–most of whom were Cossacks–did not meet the norms for a second pharmacy, the outpost was an important trading center, and when the rivers Shilk and Amur were navigable, traders, manufacturers, and working people swelled its population. In 1906 this prompted the military governor of Baikal region to petition for a new pharmacy "outside the rules of May 25, 1873."[85] The owner of the existing pharmacy, a merchant, and the managing Provizor protested. The Assistant Minister of Internal Affairs rejected their complaint on formal grounds–the Senate was still discussing the institution of the second pharmacy in 1909.[86]

Tomsk, in western Siberia, had boasted a pharmacy from the early nineteenth century. In 1904 there was a pharmacy in the city outpatient clinic, which had a good laboratory and dispensed a significant amount of medicine.[87]

The city of Semipalatinsk in the south central Siberian steppe, near western China, had just over 25,000 inhabitants in 1906. There were only two normal pharmacies but this was sufficient because the Tatar and Kirghiz, who comprised half the population, rarely used the pharmacy. Additionally, over 3,400 Cossacks dwelled in a nearby suburb with their own doctor and pharmacy. Some 4,500 people lived in a settlement beyond the River Irtysh. There was no bridge to link them with the city of Semipalatinsk. In the summer when the river was navigable a one- to two-hour barge trip gave these people access to the city but during the remaining three-fourths of the year the journey took two weeks to one month. Because of the isolation of the settlement, a doctor and veterinarian lived there and served the inhabitants. Some of the dwellers in the settlement "Beyond the Irtysh" (*zarechnaia slobodka*) were able to get prescriptions filled in the two city pharmacies.[88]

As a result of the fact that "foreigners in the steppe regions and Central Asian region rarely turned to pharmacies for help" in the Central Asian city of Tashkent, capital of modern-day Uzbekistan, three normal pharmacies with seven pharmacists served 156,400 people. In the nearby city of Kokand, one pharmacy and several one-pharmacist branches for different regions of the city easily served 82,000 people. In neighboring Samarkand, two pharmacies with five pharmacists sufficed for 54,900 people.[89]

Ekaterinburg, a city in Perm province, in the Ural mountains, was well-served by seven pharmacies in 1912. Nevertheless, two Assistant Pharmacists, a physician, and three Provizors petitioned the provincial board for permission to open an eighth pharmacy. The owners of the existing pharmacies claimed Ekaterinburg already had a sufficient number of pharmacies, well-distributed in the city and outlying areas. Additionally, dispensing was augmented by a city pharmacy, a normal pharmacy at one of the factories, and an outpatient clinic with a pharmacy in the zemstvo school. Further, pharmacy owners asserted they were being squeezed by over-the-counter trade, concentrated in the wholesale Society for Trade in Pharmacy Wares. The governor of Perm province agreed they would be hurt financially by an eighth pharmacy and asked the Medical Council to reject the petition for it.[90]

Thus, the network of normal pharmacies slowly but consistently expanded in Siberia and Central Asia, as well as European Russia. Moreover, owners of private pharmacies displayed generosity toward the poor. On average, the cost of filling a prescription at a private pharmacy was fairly high. In 1905 prescriptions from private pharmacies averaged from 20 to 40 kopeks in zemstvo provinces. In Moscow, St. Petersburg, Odessa, and Sevastopol', the cost of prescriptions averaged 50 to 55 kopeks.[91] In 1913, according to one source, the average prescription cost 51.9 kopeks.[92]

However, in many cities provision was made for low-cost or even free distribution of medicaments to the poor or to specific groups. In 1903 the American *Druggists Circular and Chemical Gazette* noted that "For poor people . . . there exist many gratis dispensaries, as, for instance, the government, town, and benefactory hospitals."[93] As early as 1863, physicians and inhabitants in many district towns in the far northern Arkhangel'sk province collected funds for pharmacies. Pharmacies were established by subscription in Kemi, Kholmogorakh, Shekyrsk, Peneg, and Mezeni. Management was entrusted to district doctors, who had the right to use profits from the pharmacies.[94] In 1891 in Saratov, following a request by the local medical inspector, all pharmacy owners except one expressed readiness to dispense to the poor free of charge (*bezvozmezdno*) 200 rubles' worth of medicine from each pharmacy. Pharmacy owners in Kazan also approved free dispensing to the poor. One pharmacy owner agreed to dispense 300 rubles' worth and eight others agreed to dispense 2 percent of their medicines free, on condition that the cost of each prescription would not be higher than 50 kopeks.[95] In the small-town pharmacy where he apprenticed in the 1890s, Isaiah Ginzburg recalled that "If the doctor wrote *pro paupero* ['for the poor'], we wrote the regular price as usual, then a reduced price on the bottom."[96] In the Central Asian region of Semipalatinsk in

1906, the two existing private pharmacies dispensed medicines to the poor at half the regular cost and gave medicine completely free to indigents.[97]

Further, philanthropic organizations provided free or low-cost medicaments to their constituents. In 1894, "Moscow Followers of Homeopathy" organized a charitable society with the dual function of promoting homeopathy and providing free medical help and dispensing to members. The society's charter entitled it to open hospitals, sanitoria, and pharmacies and, additionally, to found a school of homeopathy and a library, give public lectures, and publish popular treatment manuals and journals. Persons of either sex, any title, and place of residence who paid at least three rubles annually were welcomed as members.[98] In 1898 a "self-help" society in Tomsk, which raised 6,400 rubles from the sale of 640 shares, opened a private pharmacy in Omsk.[99] In April 1901 the Moscow clinic of military doctors offered free medical care to over 5,000 poor and dispensed over 6,000 free medicines from its pharmacy.[100] A zemstvo-like organization in the Polish provinces of Russia provided medicine at 10 kopeks and waived even this nominal fee for the poor.[101] In November 1904 an imperial order instructed the trustees of the Imperial Philanthropic Society to dispense medicines to the poor from pharmacies in city hospitals in St. Petersburg, Moscow, Ufa, Kamanets-Podolsk, and Odessa at a price reduction of 30 to 40 percent or entirely free.[102] In Grodno in 1906 the Jewish hospital dispensed free medicines to poor Jews.[103] In Krasnoiarsk in 1907, the Society of Doctors dispensed medicine free (*bezplatno*) upon prescription of a physician; the pharmacy of the city clinic also supplied the population of the region.[104] In the Zabaikal hamlet (*stanitsa*) of Stretensk in 1906, 4,210 Cossacks (out of a the total population of 5,273) received free medicine from the Sheopuginskii Cossack hospital.[105] In 1911, eight Provizors in Warsaw opposed the opening of additional pharmacies in three industrial villages near the city. The Provizors claimed that the workers lived only 2 or 2½ versts from Warsaw and could easily travel there to obtain medicines. Further, two pharmacies already existed in one village. Additionally, according to the Provizors, poor *batraki* (indentured workers) and other workers who lived in the villages received medical help and medicines for themselves and their families from pharmacies in the Lil'pon Rau & Levinshtein and Gerlakh & Pul'st factories where they worked. Poor workers also got medicine from a paralytic outpatient clinic, from the outpatient clinic of the city of Warsaw, and from the outpatient clinic of the Red Cross. The Red Cross apparently dispensed annually 50,000 medicines at 5 kopeks each and also dispensed medicines entirely free.[106] In 1912 there was a pharmacy in the town of Vlodav, Sedletsk province, Russian Poland, and a pharmacy in the invalid home in the colony of Aleksandov, 3 versts from the town.[107] Railroads frequently provided medicines for their workers. In 1906 the railway station in Grodno dispensed free medicine to the railway workers although the latter were not numerous.[108] In 1912, the railway station located 4 versts from Vlodav dispensed medicine to railroad personnel.[109]

An interesting experiment in cooperative purchase of medicines was inaugurated in Tiflis, Georgia, in 1901. A joint-stock association (*tovarishchestvo*) "Narodnoe Zdravie" (Public Health) was launched to provide its members with cheaper medicine. Sixteen hundred shares were floated at 50 rubles per share. The price was hefty, indicating that members would come from the middle class; however, it was payable over a three-and-a-half-year period. The association was to have its own pharmacy, laboratory, and factory for producing mineral water and fruit juice. The founders included physicians, Masters of Pharmacy, Provizors, and some "local capitalists."[110]

But, while pharmacies increased in cities and towns, even in the hinterlands, the real difficulty lay in providing adequate dispensing for people in the countryside. It was not that there was no activity here. Quite the contrary, in the second half of the nineteenth century pharmacies in villages increased at a faster rate than in towns, as Table 3.1 shows, discrepancies in statistics notwithstanding (see Table 3.1).

TABLE 3.1 Increase in Pharmacies in Villages and Towns, 1877–1911

Year	Pharmacies in Capitals and Provincial Cities	Pharmacies in Districts, Villages, Rural Areas	
1877	387	1,234[111]	
1890	500	1,500	small towns, villages
(one account)		700–800	district towns[112]
1890	1,952	741	village
(second account)		69	*aptechnoe otdelenie*
		41	branch
		20	military
		11	homeopathic
		40	various
		922	
1900	2,148	1,132[113]	
1901	2,181	1,173	*normal'naia apteka*[114]
1905	2,407	1,337[115]	
1911		1,826[116]	

Thus, while pharmacies in cities continued to outnumber rural pharmacies, the latter increased 34 times between 1876 and 1877 whereas the number of pharmacies in capital and provincial cities increased only 7 times. Between 1890 and 1900 village pharmacies increased 39 percent; normal pharmacies increased only 19 percent. Put another way, in 1901 village pharmacies in European Russia amounted to 31.4 percent of the total number of pharmacies; normal pharmacies amounted to 64.0 percent.[117] In that year the Governing Senate, the Russian supreme court, "made easier the establishment of pharmacies in settlements, villages, and the country side."[118] By 1905 village or rural pharmacies amounted to 34.1 percent of all pharmacies, and pharmacies in the capitals and provincial cities had shrunk to 61.4 percent of all pharmacies. By 1911 village pharmacies amounted to about 36 percent of the total and normal pharmacies had decreased to 61.2 percent of the total.[119]

In sum, village pharmacies increased 55.7 percent between 1901 and 1911; normal increased only 30.4 percent.[120] In some areas the pharmacies were predominantly of the village type. In 1905, in Kurland, for example, 50 of 90 pharmacies were village pharmacies.[121]

But the overwhelming majority of the population, at least in European Russia, lived in villages. Therefore, although a modicum of professional pharmacy had penetrated the countryside, there simply were not enough pharmacies to serve rural areas. Further, village pharmacies did not offer the range of medicines dispensed in normal pharmacies; nor were they managed by fully qualified Provizors. Unfortunately, we have only snippets of information about village pharmacies. One 1905 photograph depicts the outside of a solid-looking "typical country apteka" in Velikoe Selo, Yaroslavl' province.[122] In 1901 a village pharmacy in the trading-factory village of Mikhailov, Tula province, was advertised for sale at 3,500 rubles, with 1,000 rubles down. The village was located 7 versts from the railroad. There were two practicing physicians and a zemstvo "point" in an 18-verst radius. The turnover of the pharmacy amounted to a paltry 2,500 rubles a year.[123]

Hospital and clinic pharmacies supplemented village pharmacies. Additionally, small pharmacies (*domashniia aptechki*), allowed by the Governing Senate from 1879 where no other types of pharmacies existed,[124] supplied essential medicines, made up according to the Russian pharmacopoeia, and first-aid materials.[125]

Most probably, dearth of pharmacies in the countryside occurred because of poor infrastructure and because pharmacists did not want to live there. But restrictive rules contributed to some extent. Doctors were not allowed to work outside their district, even if it bordered on another district, and rural medical points sometimes were established where they were least needed. In 1902 in Yenisei province, the doctor and feldsher, the village pharmacy, and hospital were concentrated 1½ versts from the district town of Kansk, where there was a town hospital with five doctors and a private pharmacy. The remainder of the district was nearly bereft of medical help. A similar situation obtained in Tomsk province. In Bogotol' medical district the doctor, hospital, and feldsher all were in the village of Bogotol' where there existed a hospital belonging to the Migration Commission, a doctor, two feldshers, a railroad hospital, midwife, and private pharmacy near to the city of Achinsk (today both dreary stations on the Trans-Siberian Railway). The periphery of the medical district lacked medical help. As a result, self-appointed healers worked in the outlying areas.[126]

Lack of adequate dispensing in the countryside, coupled with governmental concern for the needy, led to the experiment in socialized pharmacy. Meanwhile, strictures on pharmacies led to the proliferation of drug stores and drug emporia. As might be expected, owners of private pharmacies bitterly resented the government's greater leniency toward drug stores and low-cost or free public dispensing.

4

Drug Stores and Socialized Public Pharmacy

The Russian government was neither oppressive nor capricious when dealing with pharmacy owners, but rather irritatingly legalistic. Nevertheless, the government required pharmacy owners to play by one set of rules (and stringent ones at that) while allowing their competitors–drug stores (*aptekarskie magaziny*), and pharmacies established by publicly funded bodies, zemstvos and municipal councils–to play by different, more lenient rules.

The growth of drug stores emphasizes the entrepreneurship that existed in prerevolutionary Russia, the strength of free trade, and the government's ambivalence toward both private enterprise and market principles. The story of public pharmacies, on the other hand, illustrates the strong current of support for socialized pharmacy in prerevolutionary Russia, not only on the part of radical and revolutionary pharmacists but within the Russian government on both central and local levels. It also underscores the defects inherent in socialized pharmacy.

Drug stores were considered trading establishments. As such they were not bound by the rules that governed the establishment and operation of pharmacies (*apteki*). Drug stores filled the gap that pharmacies, limited by the government, were powerless to fill. As a result, by 1904 there were more than 3,500 drug stores and 2,200 chandleries (*moskatel'nye i krasil'nye lavki*) in the empire[1] compared with some 3,919 pharmacies.[2]

From the beginning–in instituting the first government pharmacy for the public in 1672 and then chartering the first private pharmacy in 1701–the Russian government had attempted to limit the sale and dispensation of medicaments to bona fide pharmacies operated by qualified pharmacists. This policy was based on a desire to protect public health and, additionally, to ensure sufficient income for pharmacy owners, managers, and staff.[3] In 1756 the government imposed fines for practicing medicine without a license and sale of medicaments outside official or chartered pharmacies.

However, restrictions on selling and dispensing medicaments backfired. "Outside pharmacy" trade went on anyway–to a large extent because pharmacies *were* limited–and the government was forced to permit them. Indeed, drug stores expanded at a more rapid pace than pharmacies. The government only halfheartedly attempted to exercise control over them, thus sending mixed messages about free trade throughout the nineteenth, early twentieth centuries.

In 1814, the newly instituted State Council issued a regulation, "On the Sale of Pharmacy Materials," which permitted chandlers and grocers to trade freely in medicaments that were not strong-acting, while curbing their sales of strong-acting and poisonous medicines. As guidelines, the government published two catalogs, one listing seventy-four strong-acting substances, the second, fifty-nine poisonous substances. These items were to be sold only in wholesale quantities and in raw form.[4]

Some pharmacists themselves became owners of drug stores. In other cases owners of these stores (*drogisty* or *materialisty*) had no pharmaceutical training. Regardless, pharmacy owners protested that the drug stores infringed on their monopoly. In 1830, to clarify matters, the government reworked the lists of substances that grocers and chandlers were allowed to sell. List A now included twenty-seven poisonous items–two times less than in the earlier catalog. All vegetable poisons had been excluded. Those remaining were medicinal substances and also items used in industrial production. List B, on the other hand, included seventy-seven strong-acting, or "heroic," substances. These were basically newly discovered alkaloids–morphine, atropine, narcotine, strychnine, and others. Items in list A could be sold only to a fixed group of people–artists, artisans, and workers in industrial enterprises. Druggists could sell the items in list B, but only in wholesale quantities and raw form, to pharmacy owners or hospitals through special catalogs.

In 1852 the two lists were subdivided into four. They were entered into the Code of Laws of the Empire in 1857. The third group, list V, included substances prepared in pharmaceutical factories and pharmacies and having only pharmaceutical significance. These could be dispensed only in a pharmacy or hospital, by a doctor's prescription. The fourth list, G, pertained to medicinal herbs, poisonous and strong-acting substances, derived from domestic flora. In rural areas these items could be sold freely. However, in cities or localities where pharmacies or chandlery-groceries existed, they could be sold only through these institutions.[5]

The development of the pharmaceutical industry in the nineteenth century gave druggists wider scope. Article 31 of the Pharmacy Statute of 1836 allowed them to sell factory-prepared medicines and sundries over the counter in drug stores or chandleries if they were sold "in the form they had been received from the factory."[6]

Despite attempts to clarify the status and operation of drug stores, the laws continued to be ambiguous and contradictory. On the one hand, the Medical Statute of 1857 forbade druggists to store medicinal herbs that could be turned into medicines. However, in exceptional cases they were permitted to sell such items to pharmacies.[7] The Criminal Laws published in 1866 imposed a punishment of imprisonment from two to four months or a fine up to 100 rubles for trade in poisonous or strong-acting materials without proper permission. Supervision over proper application of the rules was entrusted to the medical section of the provincial administration or to district police who were to periodically inspect the drug stores.[8]

Since the laws pertained to sales of *wholesale* quantities of medicinal items outside the pharmacy, pharmacy owners demanded that the government prohibit small-scale drug stores. They sometimes sued, claiming that medicines were secretly prepared in drug stores, despite the fact that this was forbidden by law.[9]

Suits and lobbying did not solve the problem. The Russian government continued to preserve the pharmacy monopoly while allowing competitors to it to function quite freely. In 1887 the Senate officially sanctioned drug stores, issuing an opinion that all persons had the right to sell medicaments "in the form that they were received from the factory." Pharmacy owners then mounted a stronger campaign against the drug stores, asserting that lack of restrictions permitted them to sell strong-acting and poisonous substances, thus endangering public health.[10]

As a result, the Medical Department of the Ministry of Internal Affairs and the Ministry of Finance further limited the drug stores–but in no way eliminated their existence. In May 1891, the two ministries published a list of 93 medicinal substances that could not be sold in drug stores or chandleries.[11] In March 1892, the Ministry of Internal Affairs enlarged the list of items that could not be sold in drug stores and chandleries to 177 items.[12] A law of May 11, 1898, reiterated that drug stores, chandleries, and groceries could sell complex pharmaceutical preparations received in ready form from factories and laboratories over the counter without a doctor's prescription, but reiterated that the substances *had to be sold in the exact form received.*[13]

In 1902 the Senate somewhat relaxed its stand regarding the sale of prepared medicines by drug stores, stating that it would "prosecute only sale of complex prepared medicine received from factories, laboratories, and pharmaceutical factories which could not be dispensed from a pharmacy without a doctor's prescription."[14] The Senate clarified this regulation in

1903.[15] Pharmaceutical factories were permitted to sell complex medicines—that is, those containing more than one substance—only to pharmacies. To drug stores they could sell only simple medicaments.[16]

This did not iron out the ambiguous position of the drug stores. It did, however, restrict the pharmaceutical industry. Pharmacies, even those employing sixteen workers, had more freedom to produce and sell complex medicines than factories.[17]

There were numerous reports of drug stores violating the regulations on keeping medicines and sundries separate. In 1901 Provizor Mendel Grossman in Odessa was cited for selling "wares of the first class"—"pharmaceutical wares, such as sweet water, Aleksandrye leaves, English salt, Kuzmich herbs, ointment"—alongside "wares of the third class"—sundries—despite the fact that this was forbidden by article 3 of the "Regulations on Industrial Trade, Code of Laws, 1898."[18]

Worse, there were numerous allegations that drug stores prepared and sold medicines. In 1903, in *The Druggists Circular and Chemical Record* averred that:

> As even a qualified pharmacist is not allowed to dispense prescriptions but from a privileged pharmacy, the drug stores are as well not allowed to do it. They have no permission even to sell divided powders, cut or mixed herbs, or any kind of worked drugs, or to make any mixture. Owing to insufficient control over the drug stores they are practicing everything like a privileged pharmacy, and often they take more liberty than the latter, because they do not run so great a risk as a pharmacy. For instance, if anybody is unable to get a poisonous prescription repeated at a pharmacy, he may be sure to get it at a drug store, and often with the old copy-label of the pharmacy! Sometimes they are prosecuted but, as it is generally difficult to find any evidence against them, without result.[19]

In 1905, the governor of Grodno province informed the Ministry of Internal Affairs that "four drug stores in the city serve the population with secret preparation of medicine. . . ." As a result the governor asked permission for a second normal pharmacy in the city of Grodno.[20] In 1905 192 drug stores were taken to court,[21] although this is not an inordinately large number considering there were about 5,500 drug stores.

Scholars have noted the frequently conflicting policies of Ministers of Finance and Ministers of Internal Affairs.[22] This was the case with regard to drug stores. The Medical Council of the Ministry of Internal Affairs was concerned only about adherence to the regulation that they sell factory-prepared medicaments *exactly as received*. The Ministry of Finance, on the other hand, imposed additional regulations on drug stores, requiring them *to stock and purvey medicaments and sundries separately.* Ministerial confusion worked to the advantage of the drug stores.

The Ministry of Internal Affairs did not chastise transgressions unless they were against its own regulations. In 1905 the governor of Kurland informed the Chief Medical Inspector that, while inspecting a tobacco shop, the local excise inspector, a representative of the Ministry of Finance, had noticed that medicines were being sold alongside sundries such as photographic equipment and manufactured wares. He admitted that such violations occurred widely, but that supervision of pharmaceuticals, including poisonous and strong-acting medicines, was difficult in these conditions of "mixed trade."[23] The vice-governor and local medical inspector emphasized that in cases of mixed storage it was difficult to keep medicines free from "dust and extraneous substances" and that drug stores were not needed in Kurland because pharmacies were plentiful—there were ninety pharmacies in Kurland, fifty of which were located in villages.[24] However, none of these arguments affected the ministry. In March 1907, the Medical Council stated that, against the objections of the Kurland authorities and the Ministry of Finance rules, it found no objection to drug stores selling prepared medicines alongside tobacco products as long as the medicines were sold *as received.*[25] In 1905 and 1906 the Chancellery of the Medical Council prohibited drug stores to dispense antidiphtheria vaccine.[26] However, it allowed grocers to sell galenical preparations in prepared form, over the counter and without a doctor's prescription, *if done so in the exact form received.*[27]

The tangle of regulations regarding drug stores was underscored by the prosecution of the manager of the Keler and Company Drug Store in 1910. The case was at the appellate level of the Justice-of-the-Peace courts in Moscow. The manager had been found guilty of selling complex preparations, forbidden to drug stores by a regulation of January 8, 1909. However, his "defenders" skillfully appealed that the regulations pertaining to drug stores were unclear. As a result the case went up to the cassation department of the Senate.[28]

Neither pharmacy owners nor authorities were able to block the drug stores. First and foremost, they filled a public need. A 1903 article in *The Druggists Circular and Chemical Record* commented that: "By the public they are known as 'cheap pharmacies.'"[29] In 1912 the governor of Warsaw informed the Chief Medical Inspector that an insufficient number of pharmacies in a village near Warsaw led not only to the establishing of drug stores but to their owners and managers establishing warehouses that sold pharmaceutical wares and dyes. Although the governor warned that this situation was not "beneficial for good quality dispensing . . . warehouses, permitted by the 'Statute for Materialists,'" proliferated because they were not subject to restrictions, as were pharmacies, and the public flocked to them "to receive medicine at a cheap price."[30]

Additionally, the drug stores were attractive, judging from the smart exteriors of the Keler Drug Store in Moscow[31] and three drug stores belonging to Ludwig Speiss and Son in Warsaw[32] as well as the inviting interiors of the three Ferrein drug stores on Staraia Nikol'skaia, Tverskaia and Arbatskaia streets. The Staraia Nikol'skaia Drug Store, located next door to the huge Ferrein pharmacy, and the Tverskaia and Serpukhovskaia drug stores belonging to Ferrein are still in existence. Though small, the Tverskaia store still displays its beautiful polished cabinetry with mosaic inserts. The larger Serpukhovskaia store had more simple cabinetry. In 1910 and 1911 these emporia beckoned patrons with bentwood chairs and tables bearing stoppered carafes. The Staraia Nikol'skaia Drug Store displayed sandals and athletic shoes. Clean and with the professional atmosphere of a pharmacy,[33] they offered good service and popular wares. In 1905, for example, the Moscow pharmaceutical firm Keler and Co. advertised the "Korset Karess," "sold in the Women's department of its drug stores on Nikol'skaia street, the Arbat, and in Smoleshinskov *pereulok*."[34]

As a result, drug stores became a third more numerous than pharmacies. For example, in Khar'kov in 1900 there were only 5 drug stores. By 1910, there were 150 drug stores as opposed to 25 pharmacies.[35] More significant, from 1904, it appeared that the new Pharmacy Statute anticipated widening so-called outside pharmacy trade.[36]

The same phenomenon occurred, even more dramatically, in Prussia, where pharmacies were controlled, albeit more loosely than in Russia. In 1905 there were 3,237 pharmacies in Prussia; in 1908 there were 23,122 *Drogerien* selling factory-prepared medicines and sundries.[37] In France competition between pharmacies and drug stores was neatly solved. By 1907 pharmacies turned themselves into "drug stores," selling commercially prepared patent medicines. The message for Russia was clear: she should increase factory production of medicines and open the door to competition.

The Russian government's vacillation toward drug stores was writ small in the case of small pharmacies, literally "domestic" pharmacies, or *domashniia aptechki*. Early in the second half of the nineteenth century, the Minister of Internal Affairs permitted the selling of these small pharmacies to zemstvo doctors, railroads and other administrative institutions, and the public. They contained tinctures, powders, pills, and other ready-made medicaments, prepared according to the Russian pharmacopoeia. No doctor's prescription was needed for dispensing their contents. The small pharmacies were intended for use in situations requiring first aid in areas with no nearby doctors and regular pharmacies. The Medical Council was unable to come to agreement on their appropriateness since, although their contents were prepared according to the pharmacopoeia, a doctor's prescription was not involved. The State Council, the supreme legislative body in the empire, got involved in the discussion but its main concern was whether purchasers of the small pharmacies would have to pay for the boxes or containers in which the medicaments were packed. The State Council finally approved small pharmacies with two caveats: that the medicines be prepared according to the Russian pharmacopoeia and that the price of the medicines not be higher than that set in the Pharmacy Tax. The test case for legality of the small pharmacies came before the Russian supreme court, the Governing Senate, in the 1870s when the owner of a St. Petersburg pharmacy asked the Medical Council to allow him to advertise and sell "domestic pharmacies" wholesale, with a complete stock of ready-made medicines and a handbook, "Immediate First-aid Measures for Those Becoming Ill" (translated from the German) at an additional price of 12 rubles. In 1879 the Senate sanctioned the small pharmacies as useful in cases of emergency first aid in areas where there were no regular pharmacies or doctors.[38]

The small pharmacies filled a need, as did drug stores, that restricted pharmacies could not address. In 1901 the diocese of Penza allocated 250,000 rubles for the establishment of small pharmacies in church schools located far from feldsher points. One D. Mal'tsev published a companion brochure for teachers to guide their dispensing first aid from the school pharmacy. The brochure provided basic information about eighty-six illnesses and forty-six medicines.[39] Count Avgust Zamoyskii likewise established a small pharmacy on his estate in Sedletsk province, Russian Poland, where, in 1912 a feldsher dispensed medicines to family members and estate workers.[40]

The growth of drug stores spoke to the vitality of free trade, halfhearted commitment toward it on the part of the Russian government, and enthusiasm for it on the part of those pharmacists who owned and managed drug stores. But curiously–and this emphasizes the complexity of the Russian economy in the late imperial period–a contradictory trend could be observed. That was increasing attraction to socialized pharmacy–free or discounted dispensing of medicines from pharmacies owned by municipalities or local councils, the so-called zemstvos.

City-owned pharmacies were minuscule. Only seventeen pharmacies, or 0.5 percent of the total, belonged to city institutions in 1901.[41] There was only one city pharmacy in all the nonzemstvo provinces, one in the Don military region, and five in zemstvo provinces. Two cities in the Caucasus owned pharmacies, two in the Central Asian region, and six in Siberia.[42] By 1901 a city pharmacy operated in Taganrog.[43] The St. Petersburg city duma spent 150,000 rubles on a city hospital, and the city sanitary commission began to build a city pharmacy.[44] The St. Petersburg city duma also discussed opening a central warehouse for medicines and pharmaceutical wares.[45] By 1904 the Moscow city pharmacy was still in the discussion stages as was a city warehouse, which purportedly could purchase medicines and supplies "12 percent" cheaper than those sold by the Ferrein firm.[46] However, the St. Petersburg city duma was moving closer toward the establishment of a city warehouse,[47] as was the city of Baku.[48] Nevertheless, the socialist journal *Farmatsevticheskii vestnik* lamented that "in practice, building public pharmacies has met with great difficulty." By 1910, thirty-nine, or 0.8 percent of the total number of pharmacies, belonged to city administrations. There were three city pharmacies in nonzemstvo provinces, two in the Don region, nine in zemstvo provinces, ten in the Caucasus, four in Central Asia, and eleven in Siberia.[49]

Experiences of cities in Arkhangel'sk province may have been typical in accounting for the delay. Following a mandate from the Medical Council of December 17, 1863, approved by the Ministry of Internal Affairs and reported by the Medical Department to the Arkhangel'sk Medical Department January 4, 1864, public pharmacies were instituted in four cities of the province–Komi, Kholmogorakh, Shenkursk, and Pzhneg. But in the early twentieth century the Medical Council of the Ministry of Internal Affairs noted that "only pharmacies in Komi and Kholmogorakh could truly be called public." In Mezeni public pharmacies continued to operate under the old Board of Public Welfare. The inhabitants of Onega, furthermore, refused to support a public pharmacy in 1864 and, as a consequence, local doctors took responsibility for establishing one in the Society of Onega Forestry Trade.[50]

Zemstvo-owned pharmacies were only slightly more numerous than municipal pharmacies. In 1864 the Russian government established zemstvos, or councils, in thirty-four European provinces. Curiae of communal peasants (often ex-serfs), local landowners, and owners of immovable property (usually town dwellers) elected representatives to the district zemstvo; this body chose delegates to the provincial zemstvo; although zemstvos periodically met in plenary sessions, a permanent executive committee made policy. Zemstvos levied local taxes to boost educational, medical, and other services, primarily in rural areas, although their tax base was limited.

Zemstvos inherited some pharmacies from the Boards of Welfare, established for free classes in the eighteenth century. Additionally, zemstvos established pharmacies in zemstvo hospitals and as independent entities from the late 1860s. The first new zemstvo pharmacy opened in Nizhegorod, or Nizhi Novgorod, province, on the middle Volga, in 1868.[51] However, no network of zemstvo-owned pharmacies developed as envisioned in 1867.[52]

By 1871, there were only 20 zemstvo pharmacies in the empire.[53] By 1877, 1,183 of the 1,621 pharmacies in the empire were owned by pharmacists, 376 were owned by private persons who were not pharmacists, and only 62 were owned by public institutions, including zemstvos.[54] In 1878 36 new pharmacies opened–only one under the auspices of a zemstvo.[55] By 1901 the number of zemstvo pharmacies had doubled to 138; however, zemstvo pharmacies amounted to only 3.9 percent of the 3,518 in the empire.

Zemstvo pharmacies grew at a slow pace during the next ten years. By 1910 only 165 of 4,804 pharmacies belonged to zemstvos –a mere 3.4 percent.[56] By 1916 there were only 201 zemstvo pharmacies.[57]

There were not only far fewer zemstvo pharmacies than privately owned pharmacies, but zemstvo provinces had fewer pharmacies per inhabitant than nonzemstvo provinces. As noted, the ratio of pharmacies to inhabitants in the towns of zemstvo provinces was only a little worse than that in the nonzemstvo provinces. But in rural areas, where the zemstvos particularly were to operate, there was on average only one pharmacy for every 101,200 rural dwellers. The far northern provinces of Perm, Vologda, and Viatka were worst off; also faring poorly were the central provinces Voronezh, Vladimir, Kazan, Pskov, Novgorod, Samara, Riazan, and Simbirsk.[58] According to a Soviet historian there were only two zemstvo pharmacies in Chernigov province and three in Moscow provinces.[59] The best situated of the zemstvo provinces were those in the south–Tavrida, Kherson, Bessarabia, and the city of Odessa.

Zemstvo pharmacies developed slowly for several reasons. First, zemstvos were not permitted to establish pharmacies until 1868, four years after the zemstvos had been instituted.[60] Additionally, from 1868 until 1912, the government restricted zemstvo pharmacies as it did privately owned, normal pharmacies, linking their franchises to population and prescription turnover.[61]

In the early stages of zemstvo activity, the Medical Council rather rigorously enforced the rules limiting the establishment of their pharmacies. For example, in 1878 the Medical Council rejected requests from several zemstvos to open pharmacies. In February, the council rejected the request of the Bakhmut district zemstvo, in Ekaterinoslav province, the Don region of the Ukraine[62] to open in the zemstvo hospital in the city of Bakhmut, a pharmacy with right of unrestricted (*vol'naia*) sale of medicine. The council denied the request because, on the basis of a Senate decision of 1868 and the regulation of the Committee of Ministers of 1872, the number of new and repeated prescriptions in the city of Bakhmut did not warrant a second pharmacy.[63] In April the council rejected the request of the Shuisk district zemstvo assembly to establish in the zemstvo hospital in the city of She a pharmacy with right of unrestricted sale because the amount of prescriptions filled by the existing pharmacy did not warrant a second pharmacy.[64] In May the Medical Council rejected the request of the Iaransk district zemstvo for unrestricted sale of all medicines from the zemstvo hospital pharmacy. However, the rejection resulted from the fact that the medicines, *including strong-acting ones*, were to be prepared by feldshers, rather than pharmacists.[65]

But, although there were only some two hundred zemstvo pharmacies operating in the empire by World War I, they proved to be an ongoing headache to owners of private pharmacies. A major bone of contention was that zemstvo pharmacies dispensed medicine free or at a discount.

The principle of free dispensing by zemstvo pharmacies was worked out through trial and error. In 1876 the Ministry of Internal Affairs approved the zemstvo's right to dispense medicines free (*bezplatno*) to sick persons whose poverty was certified by the police and the zemstvo doctor.[66] In September 1877, in response to the protest of the governor of Vladimir province, regarding the Aleksandrovsk district zemstvo's resolution to dispense free medicine, the Governing Senate ruled that zemstvos were obliged to dispense free medicine to all sick who could document their poverty.[67] In July 1877, the principle of free dispensing to *all* zemstvo taxpayers was raised. Another district zemstvo resolved to dispense medicine free, from its pharmacy (duly managed by a Provizor), to all persons without regard to station, upon prescription of a zemstvo doctor, since all owners of immovable property, without regard to station, paid zemstvo taxes. The local governor opposed this resolution. The zemstvo, in turn, contested, and both appealed to the Senate for clarification of the matter. The Senate admitted that there was nothing in the law to forbid the zemstvo from distributing free medicine to all taxpayers. However, restrictions on the establishment of pharmacies were intended to prevent harmful competition. If the zemstvo pharmacy gave out free medicine to all–rich as well as poor, outsiders as well as hospital patients–it would destroy privately owned pharmacies in the district, for "it is not in the order of things to buy for money what is given as a gift." Therefore, the Senate reiterated that, according to volume 13 of the Fundamental Laws, zemstvo pharmacies could dispense medicine free only to those who had a police certificate of their poverty.[68]

This ruling notwithstanding, in June 1879, Assistant Pharmacist Tsipkin, owner of a private pharmacy in the city of Petrovsk, Yaroslavl' province, alleged that the Rostov zemstvo pharmacy incorrectly dispensed medicines. Thereupon, the Medical Department reminded the Yaroslavl' governor that when dispensing from their own pharmacies, zemstvos were to charge 10 to 20 kopeks for each prescription. Only to hospital patients could medicine be dispensed without distinction to class (*soslovie*) or station (*sostoianie*).[69]

Ten years later, in 1889, there was still no uniformity on whether zemstvos should dispense medicine free or for payment and, if for payment, at what price. A minority of district zemstvos charged varying amounts for medicines. Maloarkhangel'skoe district zemstvo in Orlov province and Muromskoe district zemstvo in Vladimir province charged the full price, stipulated in the Pharmacy Tax, for medicines. Oboianskoe district zemstvo in Kursk province dispensed medicine at a 26 percent discount from the price in the Pharmacy Tax. The majority of those district zemstvos that required payment for medicines did so at a nominal cost of from 5 to 20 kopeks, sometimes allowing doctors, at their discretion, to dispense free to poor patients. The average cost of a prescription at the pharmacy in the Voronezh zemstvo hospital was 7 kopeks; in Kursk, 9 kopeks; in Tsezarevskii, Khorol'sk district, 7 kopeks; in Moscow district, 8 kopeks; in Tver, 7½ kopeks.[70] Zemstvos that charged for medicines defended the practice for a multitude of reasons. Free dispensing would drain zemstvo coffers; "demoralize people"; result in waste–people often wished to receive medicine not just for a specific ailment but to store at home for later use; payment limited patients–the zemstvo having been instituted primarily for dealing with epidemics, extremely poor could always be exempted from payment; and, finally, peasants were accustomed to pay for medicine they received from self-appointed healers and from private pharmacies.[71]

In 1889 the Senate issued new regulations on zemstvo dispensing. The Senate ruled that a zemstvo pharmacy or warehouse had no right to dispense prescriptions for complicated medicines based upon a doctor's prescription.[72] However, all people living in the vicinity, independent of their station and class, and whether or not they had paid the zemstvo tax, had the right to receive medicine from the zemstvo pharmacy. In localities where no private pharmacy existed the zemstvo could dispense medicine free to all who it judged were needy. To the remainder it should dispense for money. However, in the latter case, the zemstvo pharmacy could not charge more than the Pharmacy Tax. In localities where a privately owned pharmacy already existed, the zemstvo could dispense medicine free by prescription of a doctor, *exclusively to poor people.* Police, doctors, or the zemstvo had to certify the poverty of the people requesting free medicine. With regard to dispensing prepared medicines over-the-counter, in regions where a private pharmacy operated, the Senate placed the zemstvos on the same basis as pharmacy warehouses, drug stores, and chandleries. While granting the zemstvos these fairly liberal rights, particularly with regard to over-the-counter medicines, the Senate piously expressed the hope that zemstvo pharmacies would not harm private pharmacies.[73] Thus, although the Senate interpretation was supposed to "clarify" the issue of free dispensing, it only led to further confusion.

The Medical Council of the Ministry of Internal Affairs added to the confusion by sometimes granting franchises to zemstvos denied to private persons. For example, in 1878 the Medical Council admitted that population norms in the city of Lukhe, Iur'ev district, did not warrant opening a new normal pharmacy. Nevertheless, it permitted the Iur'ev zemstvo to establish a central warehouse in Lukhe. The warehouse, managed by a Provizor and Assistant Provizor, not only was permitted to acquire medicine for the zemstvo hospital but also could dispense it free to local poor people. The Medical Council stipulated only that the warehouse could not *prepare* the medicine and, additionally, that the medicines dispensed free must exclude those that were poisonous or strong-acting. The latter, denoted in list II with a plus sign, had to be kept under lock and key and could only be dispensed from the hospital pharmacy and feldsher points upon a doctor's prescription.[74]

In 1891, frustrated pharmacy owner A. Liven emphasized that because rules for zemstvo dispensing were muddled they were being applied with too great elasticity,[75] thus causing problems for owners of private pharmacies. *Farmatsevticheskii zhurnal* agreed with him, noting in November of that year that "unlawful sale of medicine by the zemstvos, frequently encountered . . . harms to a great degree the lawful interests of private pharmacy owners. . . ."[76]

Some free dispensation was obviously dubious. For example, in 1901, the Khar'kov provincial zemstvo assembly decided to dispense free medicine to all serving in the provincial zemstvo with salaries less than 1,000 rubles per year and their families. Zemstvo employees with salaries above 1,000 rubles paid the full price.[77] The ceiling was embarrassing as some Provizors and many Assistant Pharmacists made less. In the same year, the Kursk zemstvo debated a request to build a special zemstvo hospital for persons of privileged "class" in the city of Kursk so they could be isolated from patients of other classes.[78] Also in that year the Nizhegorod zemstvo discussed the problems of middle-class patients who could not afford to purchase medicines from privately owned pharmacies and debated whether to offer these people medicines at a 50 percent discount.[79]

In 1903 the American journal *The Druggists Circular and Chemical Gazette* alleged that zemstvos benefited from advantages not given private pharmacies and thus presented stiff competition to the latter:

> There exist two kinds of semstvo [*sic*] pharmacies, both impossible to compete with for a private pharmacy. The first is the pharmacy with the right of selling prescriptions, perfumery, etc. and is managed by a provizor; the second kind a pharmacy of a semstvo hospital. This latter kind is managed by an assistant, and has only to supply the hospital and its ambulance with medicines. What makes it impossible to meet this competition is that everybody paying taxes to the semtsvo is entitled to get the advice of a physician without fee and to get every prescription of the latter for 5 copeks = 1/1/4 d. All other citizens of the same place get everything for half price compared with the official pharmacy tax. The semstvo system not being fully developed, it may happen to any provincial pharmacist that in his neighborhood will be opened a semstvo pharmacy, making his existence impossible. For several diseases the semstvo is obliged to dispense gratis, but where a private pharmacy exists the law provides certain restrictions on the gratis dispensing, though these are not enough to secure to the pharmacist his income.[80]

In addition to the issue of free dispensing, some owners of private pharmacies claimed zemstvo personnel were harassing them. For example, Provizor Lapin, owner of a normal pharmacy in the city of Onega, Arkhangel'sk province, complained to the provincial medical inspector that a district doctor was trying to ruin him, not only by dispensing free medicine from the hospital pharmacy, but by publicly labeling him an "exploiter." The pharmacy owner also criticized the fact that a feldsher, rather than a pharmacist, ran the city pharmacy. Lapin claimed that he was now in financial distress–in the last five months he had filled only sixty-three prescriptions–and he requested the Chief Medical Inspector in St. Petersburg to muzzle the district doctor.[81]

Zemstvo purchase of private pharmacies fueled pharmacy owners' resentment. By 1904 zemstvos in the capital cities of several provinces had franchises for all or a majority of normal pharmacies in those provinces. This was the case in Vologda, Olonets–only one pharmacy did not belong to the zemstvo, Viatka–of seventeen pharmacies, twelve belonged to the zemstvo, and Kazan–nine of fourteen pharmacies belonged to the zemstvo. In other provinces zemstvos owned significant numbers of pharmacies.

These provinces included Kursk, Nizhegorod, Novgorod, Orlov, Penza, Perm, Riazan, and Ufa.[82] In the villages of Kursk province in 1904 there were 116 public pharmacies, supplemented with 14 factory and treasury pharmacies. Only 14 of the pharmacies in the cities of Kursk province were privately owned.[83] In 1908, the socialist pharmacy journal, *Russkii farmatsevt,* noted increasing transfer of privately owned pharmacies to zemstvos. This trend predominated among district zemstvos that bought partially stocked village pharmacies.[84] Obviously, transfer of private pharmacies to zemstvos, through purchase or lease, did not increase the *absolute number* of pharmacies and solve the dearth of pharmacies in the countryside.

But, even as zemstvos attempted to squeeze out private pharmacies, there were indications that socialized pharmacy was problematical. Some zemstvo pharmacies were profitable enterprises. Cherepovets district provided an example of a viable zemstvo pharmacy. The pharmacy had right of unrestricted (*vol'naia*) sale. In 1897 it dispensed 9,111 paid prescriptions at a 20 percent discount for a sum of 4,016 rubles, 45 kopeks. Over-the-counter sales brought in 3,338 rubles, 66 kopeks. Profits from total turnover amounted to 7,355 rubles, 51 kopeks. The pharmacy also dispensed 5,198 prescriptions free of charge. Expenditures neatly balanced income.[85] Similarly, although Kursk province spent a sizable amount on purchase of medicines, its pharmacy system–consisting of 116 public pharmacies and 14 factory and treasury pharmacies–was deemed to be in a "healthy state" in 1904.[86] Kursk pharmacies dispensed up to 1,800,000 prescriptions annually, private pharmacies accounting for only one-tenth of the total. Provizors managed all pharmacies and warehouses. The zemstvo purchased more than 100,000 rubles worth of medicine annually and, in an attempt to economize, acquired medicines, if possible, firsthand and from "world-famous" factories and firms.[87] The Perm zemstvo pharmacy celebrated its successful centennial in 1913 (it included the period it had been under the pre-zemstvo Board of Welfare) by discussing total elimination of payment for medicines and offering two stipends of 120 rubles each for staff Provizors and Assistants.[88]

In contrast to these success stories, Sir Donald Mackenzie Wallace, raconteur of nineteenth-, early twentieth-century Russian life, remarked on ever mounting increase in zemstvo tax rates and sizable zemstvo spending on public health. He opined that, while zemstvo rates were not inordinate as compared with France and Austria, zemstvo preoccupation with public health–and to a lesser extent education–led to neglect of the infrastructure, another important purview of the zemstvo.[89] Historians such as

Thomas Pearson and John Hutchinson have documented zemstvos' irresponsible spending in the medical sector.[90] A study of zemstvo pharmacy enlarges the picture of zemstvo prodigality and provides food for thought on the feasibility of socialized medicine in general.

In the 1880s, Russian physician M. Ia. Kapustin warmly supported zemstvo medicine in general and free dispensing by zemstvo pharmacies in particular.[91] However, honest as well as socially aware, he also admitted that many zemstvos were wasteful. He provided copious examples of zemstvo pharmacies that failed to pay their own way, despite the fact that some had purchased private pharmacies that were profitable entities at the time of their purchase.[92] He especially criticized "feldsher points" as unproductive and inefficient,[93] zemstvos periodically dispensing medicines free to well-off landowners,[94] and liberal use of expensive quinine in cases where it was totally ineffectual.[95] He suggested that zemstvos save money by ordering medicines carefully,[96] through wholesale channels. With assistance from university professors V. A. Tikhomirov and N. F. Mikhailov, Kapustin developed a catalog of the most essential medicines for zemstvo pharmacies.[97] Kapustin also advised zemstvos to consider the most practical form for dispensing medicine.[98]

A few zemstvos attempted to cut expenditures by establishing warehouses and ordering medicaments and pharmaceutical supplies directly from pharmaceutical factories, foreign as well as domestic. The Tver provincial zemstvo began ordering medicaments from the "best German firm Merck" in 1888.[99] In 1898 the Moscow provincial zemstvo asked the Ministry of Finance to waive import duties for medicaments that it and the Moscow municipal administration ordered from abroad. (The Ministry reminded the zemstvo that tax exemptions applied only to charitable institutions but agreed that zemstvo orders of disinfecting solutions would be exempt from the tariff.)[100] In 1897 the Kherson zemstvo ordered 721 rubles' worth of instruments from abroad "at a price 25 percent cheaper than from Shvab in Moscow."[101] In 1898 Nizhni Novgorod sent the Medical Council its proposal for a pharmaceutical warehouse to be managed by an Assistant Provizor.[102] In 1900 the Simbirsk province sanitary doctors ordered medicines from large factories and claimed they saved 10,000 rubles on a 60,000-ruble order, compared with prices of Moscow druggists.[103] In 1904 the Commission on Pharmaceutical Matters noted that after setting up a warehouse, the Elizavetgrad zemstvo was able to purchase medicines 7,153 rubles cheaper than from the Lemme pharmaceutical firm, 15,000 rubles or 40 percent cheaper than from the Ferrein firm, and 19 to 22 percent cheaper than from the Russian Society of Private

Pharmacy Owners.[104] In 1908, the socialist journal *Russkii farmatsevt* publicized zemstvos' attempts to establish warehouses and order medicines directly from pharmaceutical firms.[105]

Some zemstvos also tried to shave costs by hiring pharmacists at low salaries[106] or by employing feldshers in their stead. Both socialist and non-socialist pharmacists vehemently opposed these cost-cutting measures.

In 1907, for example, the Social Democratic *Farmatsevticheskii Trud*, inclined to support zemstvo, or public, pharmacy in theory, railed against the Kherson zemstvo hospital. Only 15 percent of the budget was devoted to pharmacy and the hospital refused to increase pharmacists' salaries. The journal noted that "in such a situation, there was no hope of cooperating with the zemstvo."[107]

Pharmacists particularly criticized feldshers managing zemstvo pharmacies. They were not entirely justified in this. There were two types of feldshers in nineteenth-century Russia, *rotnye* and *shkol'nye*. The former were military paramedics and only perfunctorily trained.[108] School feldshers were more numerous by the 1890s and had a modicum of education. In 1905 there were forty-four civilian feldsher schools–seventeen male, sixteen female, and eleven mixed.[109] In that year over six hundred students completed courses. Most probably the curriculum was similar to that of the military feldsher schools. These schools offered a four-year program including zoology, botany, physics, anatomy, bandaging, the management of fractures and dislocations, first aid, pharmacy, pharmacognosy, pharmacology, hygiene, and surgery.[110] Dr. N. Shchepotev's ninety-seven-page *Textbook of Pharmacology for Feldshers and Student Feldshers*, published in Kazan in 1886, appeared thorough.[111] Feldshers' education, thus, appeared adequate for managing a pharmacy. Additionally, the Medical Department issued a circular August 22, 1873, forbidding feldshers to dispense strong-acting materials, marked in the Apothecary Tax with a plus sign; these were the exclusive purview of physicians.

Nevertheless, pharmacists alleged that feldshers violated regulations on dispensing. A typical example was the claim of a pharmacist in Zhitomir in 1901 that a feldsher had attempted to procure strong-acting medicines for a patient.[112] Some local officials and even some zemstvos joined pharmacists in disparaging feldshers. On occasion, it was claimed that mere pharmacy students were more capable of managing zemstvo pharmacies than feldshers. For example, in 1898, Griazovets district zemstvo, in Vologda province, approved replacing the feldsher currently managing the zemstvo pharmacy with two pharmacy apprentices at annual salaries of 240 rubles each. The zemstvo executive council claimed the hospital feldsher "did not satisfy the requirements for pharmacy."[113] According to a report by V. P. Uspenskii in 1904, "pharmacy in the proper sense of the word did not exist in the districts of Riazan province" because in most of the districts perfunctorily trained, ex-military feldshers were in charge of pharmacies; only in Sapozhkovskii district did proper pharmacists manage city pharmacies and two rural pharmacies.[114]

Somewhat hypocritically, pharmacists did not resent feldshers staffing small pharmacies in isolated, insignificant areas. In the second decade of the twentieth century there were 2,500 subdistrict (*uchastkovye*) "feldsher points" with pharmacies.[115] Characteristic of these tiny pharmacies was that of "Birzh. district, Luginsk subdistrict, Volhynia province." During 1898 only 25 rubles' worth of medicine had been dispensed in the subdistrict, containing fifteen to twenty villages, and the feldsher received a petty salary.[116]

In any case, despite cost-cutting measures, by the early twentieth century there was mounting evidence that free or low-cost dispensing was an economic burden for many zemstvos, that much zemstvo pharmacy was wasteful, and that many zemstvo pharmacies and warehouses were poorly managed.[117] These defects in zemstvo pharmacy were noted by the government, conservative pharmacy journals, and socialist pharmacy journals alike.

In 1901 the Department of Taxes in the Ministry of Finance issued a report on zemstvo budgets for the thirty-four provinces in 1900 that showed that zemstvo expenditures for medical care in general and free or low-cost medicaments were spiraling out of control. Expenditures for the medical sector had risen faster than all other zemstvo expenditures during the preceding five years from 17,673,000 rubles to 24,322,000 rubles and, in 1900, in all the provinces amounted to one fourth the total budget. Salaries for medical personnel constituted 28 percent of total expenditures; maintenance of city, provincial, and district hospitals, 21 percent of the budget; and maintenance of pharmacies and purchase of medicaments, 3,931,000 rubles, or 16 percent of the budget.[118]

In 1901 the socialist journal *Farmatsevticheskii vestnik* admitted that zemstvo budgets nearing 4 million rubles were a consequence of distribution of medicaments free or at low cost.[119] The more conservative *Farmatsevticheskii zhurnal* published a breakdown on zemstvo expenditures according to region. This revealed a further problem—great disparity in zemstvo expenditures on medicine from province to province.[120]

In 1902 *Farmatsevt* published a report on Gorbatovsk district zemstvo. An investigation criticized lavish dispensing of medicines causing expenditure of 12,000 rubles for the year as against 9,000 rubles allotted.[121]

In 1904, investigations showed that some district zemstvos in Riazan and Simbirsk province were in poor financial shape. For example, Alatyr district pharmacy in Simbirsk province liberally dispensed medicines. As a result its expenditures of 1,073 rubles 81 kopeks for pharmaceutical stores in 1903 far exceeded its budget allotment of 173 rubles 81 kopeks.[122] In 1904 *Farmatsevticheskii vestnik* emphasized that, if the new Pharmacy Statute, which allowed more liberal rules for establishing zemstvo pharmacies, were implemented, zemstvo budgets would have to be increased.[123]

Direct ordering of medicines by provincial zemstvos for their district zemstvos and the establishment of warehouses proved economical in some cases. However, they foundered in others. Tver province presented a flagrant example. The American authority on zemstvos, Charles Timberlake, has praised the Tver provincial zemstvo's contributions to education and public health.[124] Unfortunately the Tver provincial zemstvo pharmacy warehouse experienced financial distress throughout most of its existence. The warehouse claimed it profited by directly ordering medicines–for example during the course of the first four years the gross profit amounted to 13,854 rubles, 15 kopeks. However, payments from the district zemstvos to the provincial zemstvo were irregular. The Tver zemstvo warehouse asserted that it was not interested in profit, for with realization of too much profit, it would lose its "zemstvo physiognomy."[125] There was little danger of that. The Tver provincial zemstvo first extended noninterest credit to its district zemstvos for medicines that they purchased from the provincial warehouse.[126] In 1892 the provincial zemstvo established tighter financial terms. In 1904, inspection of Bezhensk district zemstvo pharmacy in Tver province revealed outdated and insufficient medicaments, insufficient storage space and equipment, and prodigal dispensing. Inspectors suggested a catalog to facilitate more economical purchase of medicines, better accounting, and in order to cut costs, that the zemstvo eliminate "free dispensing of prescriptions written by privately practicing physicians, since the latter were not within the purview of zemstvo interests . . . such dispensing amounted to subsidy of private [medical] practice."[127] By 1905 and 1906 many district zemstvo coffers in Tver province were empty and the district zemstvos could not pay for schools, hospitals and medicines. In succeeding years Tver provincial zemstvo was forced to extend credit to the district zemstvos for purchase of medicines.[128] In 1907, realizing that it was impossible to enforce the rule that stipulated credit would be shut off in cases of nonpayment, the Tver warehouse again became more lenient with its districts. As a result, the Tver zemstvo was forced to give credit to the district zemstvos during most of the twenty years of its existence.[129] Moreover, the Tver provincial zemstvo itself suffered financial problems, partly because its accounting procedures were poorly organized for a number of years.[130]

Zemstvo pharmacies in Moscow province experienced similar problems. Before 1896 district zemstvos in Moscow province ordered medicines independently. The provincial zemstvo congress of 1896 resolved to centralize ordering and, from 1898 through 1907, district zemstvos ordered supplies through the sanitary bureau of the provincial zemstvo. This system proved untenable. By 1907 district zemstvos had piled up 51,000 rubles' worth of debts. To trim costs, the Moscow provincial zemstvo again ordered district zemstvos to order independently; three district zemstvos continued to place orders through the provincial sanitary bureau. This changeover created disorder. As a consequence, the old system was restored and by 1910 Moscow province was spending 170,000 rubles on medicines.[131]

By 1907 socialist, even more than conservative, journals criticized zemstvo pharmacies for their financial excesses. Social Democratic *Farmatsevticheskii trud* remarked on the high expenditures of the Kherson zemstvo hospital.[132]

In 1908 the socialist journal *Russkii farmatsevt* publicized accounts of many zemstvo pharmacies and warehouses with "disordered finances."[133] The journal hurled its most scathing indictment at the Moscow provincial zemstvo warehouse and its manager B. N. Saltykov. Saltykov was editor of *Farmatsevticheskii trud* and erstwhile colleague of L. Ia. Zimin and S. K. Lintser, editors of *Russkii farmatsevt*. In 1905 Saltykov had been arrested by the Russian political police, the Okhrana, for revolutionary agitation in the zemstvos.[134] In 1908 his socialist comrades attacked him for financial ineptitude. A government inspection detailed Saltykov's mismanagement of the Moscow pharmacy warehouse. Although zemstvo orders of medicines from Merck, Ferrein, Iakovlev, and other foreign and domestic pharmaceutical firms totaled 129,914 rubles in 1905 and 125,826 rubles in 1906, there were no books, contracts, or budgets for district zemstvos that purchased from the Moscow provincial warehouse. Saltykov's orders for the Moscow warehouse, in turn, had never been audited. The accounting was sloppy, there were unpaid bills, and retail prices of items sold in hospitals and clinics under the zemstvo fluctuated wildly.[135] And this was the Saltykov who wanted all pharmacy in Russia socialized and who implemented wide-scale socialized pharmacy as Chief Executive of a Soviet Pharmacy Department in 1919![136]

Changes in zemstvo hiring practices further contributed to the zemstvos' financial burdens. Some zemstvos reversed their earlier cost-cutting practices of hiring feldshers at low salaries and began to hire pharmacists at high salaries. For example, in 1910 Khar'kov zemstvo paid the manager Provizor 1,500 rubles; his two assistants made less at 800 and 600 rubles, respectively, but their salaries were supplemented by apartment allowances of 120 rubles.[137]

Municipal pharmacies also ran into financial problems. In 1916, the one privately owned normal pharmacy in the city of Novogeorgievsk, Kherson province, could not satisfy the population of 15,801. In the face of rampant disease, people had to wait hours for the prescriptions to be filled. The city executive council petitioned the provincial Medical Department for the right to establish a normal pharmacy but it acknowledged that it had no means at its disposal to establish one. Admittedly, this was at the height of World War I.[138]

The problems experienced by zemstvo and city pharmacies should have flagged the Russian government. They did not and in the two decades before 1917 a contingent of the Russian public, radical pharmacists, and the government itself increasingly supported socialized pharmacy. Thus, three contradictory and confrontational camps were forming. The first consisted of pharmacists who espoused maintaining the old order of things–restrictions on establishing pharmacies. The second included progressive pharmacists who advocated abolishing these controls. And the third–and strangest–coalition was formed of disparate elements who desired more socialized pharmacy. This last group advocated abolishing restrictions on establishing pharmacies, but only for municipalities and zemstvos. Conversely, they proposed transferring private pharmacies to public institutions. The escalating conflicts between these various groups will be examined in succeeding chapters. First, a look at the issues of class, nationality, and gender among pharmacists.

5

Class: Life and Work in the Pharmacy

Pharmacists' status and income were related to several variables: whether they owned or worked in a pharmacy; if they owned the pharmacy, its type—a fully stocked, elegantly outfitted normal pharmacy in a sizable town or big city or a partially stocked, modest or humble village pharmacy; and, if they were employed, whether they managed the pharmacy or merely staffed it. Management of pharmacies, in turn, was tied to educational level. Provizors and Masters of Pharmacy were allowed to manage normal, fully stocked pharmacies. Assistant Pharmacists were permitted to manage only village pharmacies.

Nevertheless, socioeconomic advancement was possible. Assistant Pharmacists could become Provizors. And any individual or group could *own* a pharmacy. Thus the Russian pharmacy system admitted a certain amount of upward mobility.

However, the Russian system also blocked pharmacists. Since the establishment of new pharmacies was linked to population, prescriptions, and other rules, the number of pharmacies was limited. Profitable pharmacies commanded high prices when they went on the market. The ceiling thus imposed denied many pharmacists the possibility of reward for grueling years of training and work. It provided grist for socialist propaganda. The obvious solution was to abolish restrictions and allow pharmacists to freely establish pharmacies. However, cushioned and conditioned by the pharmacy monopoly most pharmacists resisted change and clung to the security of government control.

In 1902 some 3,000 pharmacists owned or managed pharmacies. About twice as many pharmacists worked in them.[1] In 1905 a total of 11,551 persons were said to be "occupied with pharmacy," a 2.4 percent increase over 1904.[2] By 1911 there were about 11,205 pharmacists and student pharmacists working in pharmacies;[3] 2,731 Provizors managed pharmacies.[4]

Of the six thousand or so pharmacists in the Russian Empire at the turn of the century, approximately ninety had reached the pinnacle of

Master of Pharmacy.[5] Some Masters of Pharmacy taught and served in the civil or military service, sixty-two owned pharmacies in 1900, sixty-one did so in 1908. Sixty Masters managed pharmacies and twenty-three worked in them in 1900; the figures for 1908 were fifty-seven and fifteen respectively.[6] Obviously, there was overlap in ownership and management.

About one-third of pharmacists were Provizors—fully qualified pharmacists with at least two years of higher education. The vast majority of Provizors either owned or managed pharmacies. In 1900, 1,984 Provizors owned pharmacies and 2,731 managed them. Most managed their own. Only 893 Provizors worked in pharmacies owned by others. In 1908, 2,078 Provizors owned pharmacies, 2,836 managed them, and the percent working in others' pharmacies declined—to 731 in absolute numbers.[7]

By 1910 there were 4,724 male Provizors and 85 female Provizors.[8] Over 51 percent—2,419 in absolute numbers—owned pharmacies. Most—1,769, or 73.1 percent—were high-status normal pharmacies; only 576, or 23.8 percent, were village pharmacies. Over 34 percent of Provizors—1,645—managed pharmacies; 1,458 of these were normal pharmacies, 148 were village pharmacies, and 39 were homeopathic pharmacies.[9]

Most Provizors in 1910 were young. Three-fourths were below fifty. Two-thirds had received their degree in the last twenty years.[10] Among respondents to a questionnaire in 1911, 86 percent had received their Provizor degree before their twelfth year of pharmacy practice.[11] However, as the respondents represented only 27 percent of pharmacists, these individuals obviously were conscientious as well as ambitious.

In the thirty-four zemstvo provinces in 1910, more Provizors lived in provincial cities rather than district towns. In the Baltic regions, the nonzemstvo provinces, and Poland the situation was reversed. Significantly more Provizors lived in rural areas than in provincial or district cities.[12] Pharmacists, chiefly Provizors, also actively established pharmacies in the towns of Siberia and Central Asia in the first decade of the twentieth century.[13]

Assistant Pharmacists, unlike Provizors, were not fully qualified. As such, although they could own or lease normal pharmacies, they could manage only village, public, or homeopathic pharmacies.[14] Some Assistant Pharmacists would advance to the Provizor level. Others remained assistants all their lives. Most Assistant Pharmacists worked in pharmacies owned by others. In 1902, of 5,966 persons staffing pharmacies, 2,120 were Assistant Pharmacists.[15] A 1911 study of pharmacists predicted that only 15 percent of pharmacists serving in pharmacies would become owners.[16]

Nevertheless, Assistant Pharmacists were not layabouts. In 1900, 387 owned pharmacies. One year later 420, or 12 percent of the total number of pharmacies owned by pharmacists, were in the hands of Assistant Pharmacists.[17] By 1908, 605 Assistant Pharmacists owned pharmacies. By 1910, pharmacies owned by Assistant Pharmacists had increased to 857, or 17.8 percent of the total number of pharmacies owned by pharmacists.[18]

The number of Assistant Pharmacists who *managed* pharmacies also climbed. In 1900 only 607 did so. By 1908 this figure had nearly doubled to 1,133. Further, the number of Assistant Pharmacists working in pharmacies rose markedly between 1900 and 1908, from 1,837 to 3,175,[19] indicating that many were willing to bank on pharmacy as a career.

The number of those beginning pharmacy–pharmacy students or apprentices–also mounted each year, with a slight decrease around 1908. In 1900 there were 1,772 pharmacy students, both male and female.[20] In 1902 there were 4,647 men and women Assistant Pharmacists and pharmacy students.[21] In 1904 the number of student pharmacists alone had risen to 4,483, by 1905, to 4,662.[22] By 1908 the number of pharmacy students had dropped slightly to 4,338,[23] but the total number of "persons occupied with pharmacy" showed steady gains.

The quality of life of these different categories of pharmacists became topics of heated debate from the second half of the nineteenth century. Some pharmacists focused on the financial problems of pharmacy owners (*aptekaria*). Others were preoccupied with staff pharmacists (*sluzhashchie*). Not only did each group depict the other as its nemesis but the pharmacy systems proposed by each camp as most conducive to the betterment of its constituents appeared polar opposites. Those concerned about pharmacy owners proposed a tighter version of the status quo—eliminating competition from drug stores (*aptekarskie magaziny*) and public pharmacies (zemstvo and city pharmacies), and in some cases increasing limitations on the establishment of new private pharmacies. They reasoned that fewer pharmacies would mean a greater slice of the pie for pharmacy owners. They also lobbied for a higher scale of prices in the Pharmacy Tax to enable owners to increase gross income. Those sympathetic to staff pharmacists had minimum and maximum programs, which appeared antithetical to those of pharmacy owners. The minimum program attempted to force owners to improve conditions and raise salaries. The maximum program envisaged transferring all private pharmacies to the pharmacy corporation (*soslovie*) or to public ownership. Thus, the owners' camp advocated a more stringent version of the pharmacy monopoly then existing whereas the staff pharmacists' camp advocated collective, socialized pharmacy.

Nevertheless, a common thread underlay the two proposals. Both camps invoked government intervention and more regulation to achieve their agendas. Only a small contingent of pharmacists advocated free trade—

removing restrictions on establishing pharmacies, thereby widening the pool of pharmacy owners and increasing pharmacists' opportunities for upward mobility.

Pharmacy Owners

In the 1850s, Professor C. Claus, of the Pharmacy Faculty of Dorpat University, sensibly observed that "The amount of trade of the Russian drug stores [*sic*] is of course very unequal. There may be 2 with an income of 40,000 rubels [*sic*], 5 with about 25,000 r., about 50 with from 10 to 15,000 r., while the majority have a gross revenue of 3 to 5,000 r., and in the small interior towns between 1,000 and 2,500 r.; the smallest business amounting to but 300 r. annually, is done in Zaryzin, a town with 4,426 inhabitants."[24]

Archival records support his contention. For example, in 1908, annual income of pharmacies in the city of Kiev ranged from over 16,000 rubles to over 32,000 rubles. Income from village pharmacies in the districts of Kiev province, on the other hand, hovered at less than one-fourth to one-tenth of that–3,600 rubles. Some village pharmacies reported a paltry annual income of 100 rubles![25]

Both socialists and lobbyists for pharmacy owners dismissed these facts. Those of socialist bent alleged that pharmacy owners reaped fantastic profits. In 1864, Ia. Chistovich, editor of a physicians' journal sometimes hostile to pharmacists, asserted that the system of restricting pharmacies and the Pharmacy Tax allowed owners to mark up medicines from 50 to 100 percent; profits sometimes amounted to 2,000 percent. He documented his claims with a chart of sixty-eight medicinal substances, prices paid by owners for civilian weights of these substances on the world market, prices for the medicinal (smaller) weights at which they sold these substances, and the percentage of profit in each case.[26] This indictment would resurface time and again.

On the opposite side of the ledger, from its maiden Russian-language issue in 1879, one of the chief pharmacy journals, *Farmatsevticheskii zhurnal*, was flooded with letters and articles claiming that pharmacy owners could scarcely make ends meet. On the one hand, they were squeezed by the Pharmacy Tax, which prevented them from raising prescription prices to adequately cover expenses; on the other, they were undercut by zemstvo pharmacies and drug stores.[27]

The Pharmacy Tax was the target of many complaints. In 1879 "Shul'ts," a pharmacy owner in Moscow, claimed that turnover in Russian pharmacies had increased 50 percent in the last fifteen years but "one cannot conclude owners are well off" since during the same period expenditures had increased 75 percent. He contended that salaries and maintenance of staff pharmacists had doubled, and rent payments for pharmacy premises had more than doubled. However, price increases permitted by 1869 Pharmacy Tax had not kept pace.[28] A. V. Pel', owner of one the largest pharmacies in St. Petersburg, advocated increasing the Labor Tax (*Taxae laborum*) in the proposed revision of the Pharmacy Tax "in view of additional expense for all animal products, significant increase in salaries of personnel, and a fall in the value of our currency [*valiuta*]."[29] Naum Zaidman, pharmacy owner from Odessa, charged that the tariff on foreign pharmaceutical products in gold had nearly doubled. Additionally, the previous Pharmacy Tax, attempting to protect the poor, had put a higher tariff on cheap, frequently used medicines and a lower tariff on expensive medicines. Since that tax had been issued eight years ago, a number of cheap items had been replaced by more expensive medicines, such as quinine and alkaloids. Thus, the old tax impacted pharmacy owners negatively. Zaidman recommended increasing the Labor Tax to 25 kopeks and separating the tax on medicines that required preparation and items sold over-the-counter.[30] (The average cost of a prescription to a consumer was 34 kopeks in 1879.)[31]

Many pharmacists blamed zemstvo pharmacies and drug stores for their plight. In 1879 "Ia. F." dramatically announced that "pharmacies at the present time are in a very unfortunate position and might be closed soon." He warned "that if conditions are not changed in the very near future, pharmacies will become objects of speculation and will be managed by feldshers, who will take the place of pharmacists, since few wish to become pharmacists. Students are found only in pharmacies in the capital and provincial cities; district pharmacies often lack Assistant Pharmacists and, in all cases, if there is an assistant there is no student. The Medical Department can verify this from its annual reports." "Ia. F." asserted that as "the condition of pharmacy owners is not much to look at," pharmacists were leaving the profession for other occupations; "not long ago four Assistant Pharmacists finished the course at the junker school and became officers; it is understandable that they would want to attend school for one and a half to two years and come out an officer, which is more prestigious than a pharmacist." "Ia. F." castigated zemstvo pharmacies that "dispensed to all and each; in Vichansk, Khar'kov province they even have labels [*signatury*] like private pharmacies" and "city administrations which can open their own pharmacies." He emphasized that "the pharmacy owner also suffers from drug stores" and "feldshers–in zemstvos they give out medicine liberally."[32]

Owners of village pharmacies sent pitiful accounts of their straitened circumstances. One from 1879 lamented that "If pharmacy owners in large cities get insignificant return for their labor and medical materials, what of those in the villages? Life there is as dear as in the cities." In the vicinity where the author resided, "a *funt* of *axungia* cost 40 kopeks, meat 12 to 15 kopeks per *funt* . . . an apartment 200 rubles per year, heat and lighting of the pharmacy. . . . True, in the city it is more expensive but the income of the pharmacy is greater." The village pharmacy also faced competition from nonpharmacists: "In all the localities and villages of Novorossiisk and the southwest region there is the 'backward feldsher' who is both doctor and pharmacist; he spreads rumors about the pharmacist. . . . Further, the great part of the people of the villages are simple people; they have their zemstvo doctor, assistant feldsher, various women healers [*babki*]." Additionally, villagers treated themselves. The author provided a fascinating catalog of home remedies: "in all markets of the village one can get sulfuric acid, muriatic nitrate, cinnabar, sublimate corrosive, arsenic, aloes, sulfur, quinine, liquid ammonia, magnesium sulfate, oil ricini, hoffmans drops, guttae Botkin, *inozemstzoff*, tincture menthe, and also 'red drops.' The simple people go to the market–not the pharmacy–thereby lessening the income of the pharmacist." Finally, the village pharmacist was undercut by discounts for the poor: "What of the surchage [*nadbavka*] of 25 percent based on the philanthropic purpose of giving poor people medicine? This does not attain its purpose. Simple people cannot use the medicine acquired as a gift. Despite the surcharge of 25 percent the simple people pay dearly for mang. sulfate [40 to 60 kopeks per *funt*], radix galangae . . . and pay only the grocer [*lavochnik*] . . . pharmacy income is more than insignificant; pharmacy trade turnover consists mainly of over-the-counter sales [*ruchnaia prodazha*] [of prepared medicines]."[33]

Pharmacy owners' complaints did not cease. In 1884 *Farmatsevticheskii zhurnal* related that many pharmacy owners "from internal provinces" (the thirty-four provinces that had zemstvos) had complained to the St. Petersburg Pharmacy Society about "the state of their business . . . and competition from zemstvos."[34]

In 1891 Naum Zaidman asserted that "pharmacy here is going through a crisis [*krizis*]; pharmacists are in a state of ruin [*gibeli*]. Cases of bankruptcy by pharmacy owners are not rare and many would have gone bankrupt if not for lease or sale of their pharmacy." This situation was due to drug stores and zemstvo pharmacies: "in localities where there could be one or two pharmacies the number of such has doubled because of drug emporia or more truly secret pharmacies . . . in Odessa where there were 15 to 20 pharmacies now there are more than 30 pharmacies and more than

60 secret pharmacies!!! [exclamation points in the original] The same is true over the entire Empire, especially in the South and Southwest." He argued that drug emporia had lower expenses than pharmacies because they had "no staff or preparation and no wares, except for cosmetics where they use general substances—benzine, glycerin, soda, etc.; medicine by prescription is dispensed from one bottle." Zemstvo pharmacies also engaged in unfair competition. They spared "no pains to spite [*nasolit'*] the pharmacist. The zemstvo has public money and can sell cheaper than the pharmacist—each prescription costs in all 6½ kopeks. How can the private pharmacy compete with the zemstvo when his expenses in small turnover amount to 60 or more kopeks per prescription?" He fumed against home remedies and patent medicines purveyed by physicians: "methods of treatment now often consist of diet and mineral water, sold outside the pharmacy. Specialists for various illnesses treat with their own medicines. Cosmetics and other material for home use now have their own department. In such conditions pharmacy income has significantly deteriorated."[35]

Pharmacy owners' complaints continued in the twentieth century. In 1901, Robert Idel'son from Taganrog cited several pathetic letters from pharmacists laid low by competition.[36] At the same time, Naum Zaidman, tireless advocate for pharmacy owners,[37] insisted that, although some pharmacies in provincial cities realized income of 15,000 rubles and some in the capitals 25,000 rubles, the vast majority had paltry incomes. Their average turnover in 1901 was 4,000 rubles. Of 3,000 pharmacies, 500 had a turnover of up to 1,000 rubles, 500 of 3,000 rubles, and 1,000 of 5,000 rubles.[38]

In 1906, D. A. Ruffman, director of the American pharmaceutical firm Parke, Davis and Company,[39] agreed that Russian pharmacy owners were in a bad way. He cited the rapacious creditor as a major factor in the Russian pharmacists' impoverishment, painting a picture of Marxian doom for his American readers.

> The actual proprietor of the pharmacy is thus in reality not the man who has purchased the license, but the one who has loaned the money; the former works like a slave for the latter, and many, many years pass before he is able to pay off the debt with its high interest. Nowadays, when chemistry, pharmacy, and medicine have far more products than was the case 40 or 50 years ago, a Russian pharmacy that is expected to concoct and mix up all the preparations prescribed by physicians cannot cope with the task without having large premises, an ample stock of drugs, and large staff of trained pharmacists. This fact our pharmacists lose sight of and blindly pay anything that is demanded for a license. Experience, however, soon shows them that their expenses in keeping up the establishment and paying off the

debts with interest are enormous in comparison with the profits, and in consequence they are slowly reaching the end, the beginning of which has already commenced in Russia.[40]

In fact, lobbyists for pharmacy owners overstated their case. Pharmacy owners were heterogeneous. While some pharmacy owners were having a hard time, others–probably the majority–were making a decent living. One indication of the relative prosperity of pharmacy owners is that, among respondents to a questionnaire in 1911, 82.19 percent of pharmacy owners were married as opposed to 64.27 percent of staff pharmacists,[41] indicating a sufficient income among the former.

Nevertheless, most pharmacy owners, conditioned to believe they were a favored monopoly, saw the solution to their problems in squelching competition. Established pharmacists like Naum Zaidman were willing to sacrifice colleagues to benefit themselves. In 1891, he recommended that the government: "1. limit expansion of . . . pharmacies–that is, increase the norms for opening new pharmacies and 2. limit competition–that is, grant exclusively to pharmacies the right to sell and prepare medicine in all forms and amounts."[42]

Protectionist pharmacy owners generally trained their ammunition on zemstvo pharmacies and drug stores. In 1884 the St. Petersburg Pharmacy Society lobbied against zemstvo pharmacies through its representative to the Medical Council of the Ministry of Internal Affairs and provided pharmacy owners with legal counseling on how to combat zemstvos.[43]

Most arguments wielded by pharmacy owners emphasized the higher quality and cost effectiveness of private dispensing as compared with socialized pharmacy. In 1904, the Kazan Pharmacy Society petitioned the Ministry of Internal Affairs to eliminate the clauses in the proposed new Pharmacy Statute making it easier for zemstvos to open pharmacies. The society emphasized that "the initiative and personal work of the pharmacist" made private pharmacies more efficient and qualitatively better than public pharmacies, "which work through hired hands; they spend great amounts on establishing pharmacies, paying for personnel, outfitting the laboratory–then–in the end, in zemstvo districts, management of medicines is under a feldsher, for whom control in monetary matters, is absolutely unthinkable."[44]

Owners of private pharmacies particularly castigated feldshers managing zemstvo pharmacies. They claimed that feldshers "dispensed mechanically, lowered the trust of the public in pharmacy" and dissipated the "economy, achieved through personal management. . . ." Feldshers did not make zemstvo "medicine cheaper" but did lessen pharmacists' chances to become managers or owners: "on the contrary it [the practice of using feldshers to manage zemstvo pharmacies] takes rights from us pharmacists. Pharmacists, who all their life study pharmacy, will be deprived of their dream—to acquire a pharmacy."[45]

Owners of private pharmacies stressed that they offered a range of public services. They contributed to public health through sanitary, hygienic, and bacteriological research, subjecting each preparation from abroad to careful chemical and microscopic analysis, and analyzing food and other products. Such services naturally entailed greater expenditure for personnel and equipment.[46] Thus they had to charge higher prices for filling prescriptions and needed commensurate income.

Still, protectionist pharmacists argued that medicine in Russia was cheaper than in countries with less restricted or *laissez-faire* pharmacy systems. Time and again those who advocated tightening the "pharmacy monopoly" argued that "the poor are now guaranteed not only cheap but also free medicines from zemstvos and charitable organizations; as for making medicines cheaper for the middle class and rich, statistics show that in Russia, by comparison with other European states, medicine is very cheap, although we receive all chemical preparations and masses of dried products from the West and consequently bear expenses for import, tariff, and spoiling."[47] In 1913 E. K. Khrzhanovskii, the pharmacists' representative to the Medical Council, provided a chart compiled by Warsaw pharmacy owner E. Gessner, which compared the price of 143 similar units of pharmaceutical wares and medicines in Russia, England, Denmark, Germany, Italy, France, Austria, Sweden, and Switzerland. While the medicines listed were usually cheaper in Denmark, sometimes cheaper in Sweden and Germany, at times cheaper in France and Austria, in England, the home of *laissez-faire* pharmacy, medicines were usually more expensive than medicines in Russia; often they were twice the price.[48]

Radical socialist pharmacists, of course, portrayed pharmacy owners in the opposite light—as exploiters—and staff pharmacists as victims. They began publicizing the plight of staff pharmacists in the 1890s. Labor laws in the 1880s had regulated work for juveniles and women. Hours and conditions of work for artisans and apprentices were not regulated.[49] This situation provided grist for socialist journalists.

Staff Pharmacists

Staff pharmacists included fully qualified Provizors as well as pharmacy students and partially qualified Assistant Pharmacists. Additionally, as noted, some Assistant Pharmacists owned pharmacies. However, statistics at the turn of the century showed declining numbers of *qualified* pharmacists, despite rising numbers of *student* pharmacists. In 1896 there were

1,160 pharmacy students; in 1897, 1,162; in 1898, 1,208; and in 1899, 1,488. The figures for male Assistant Pharmacists, on the other hand, diminished from 2,584 in 1897 to 2,391 in 1898 to 2,171 in 1899.[50] Radical pharmacists seized on these statistics to substantiate their claim that the pharmacy corporation was shrinking because the staff pharmacist's life style was unendurable. They began a crusade for shorter hours and increased pay.

Most spokesmen for staff pharmacists were not themselves serving in pharmacies nor were they connected with dispensing. Rather, the vanguard for staff pharmacists were mainly journalists, like the editor of *Farmatsevticheskii vestnik*, B. N. Saltykov and his colleagues S. K. Lintser, E. Basilaia, and L. Ia. Zimin. They belonged to the political left; many were Marxists.

The advocates for staff pharmacists served up somber pictures of work in the pharmacy–long hours, night duty, low pay, and payment that included room and board. For example, in 1904 *Farmatsevticheskii vestnik* described two pharmacies in Mogilev. One dispensed two hundred prescriptions daily, but was staffed with only four student-pharmacists and two Assistant Pharmacists. The assistants received only 35 rubles per month, the students were not paid at all the first year, then they received only 8 to 10 rubles per month. The "assistant" Provizor was allowed only a half hour for lunch; the staff performed night duty fifteen to sixteen nights each month. The pharmacy was open from 9 A.M. until midnight; assistants worked fifteen hours in twenty-four, *standing*. In the second pharmacy students lived in a small, dirty room; they drank tea with no sugar; during their sixty-minute rest period they were forced to do errands like going to the post office.[51] In a pharmacy in Odessa, the local branch of the Russian Society for the Protection of Public Health found that pharmacists worked fourteen to eighteen hours in twenty-four and performed night duty fifteen times a month, after which they had only "a few minutes of rest." "They had no special room for night duty. They slept in the so-called materials room, breathing poisonous gases."[52]

Pharmacists inclined to socialism made night duty (*dezhurstvo*) a cause célèbre. In 1901 *Farmatsevticheskii vestnik* announced that in 1900 the workday in St. Petersburg pharmacies ranged from seven and a half to fifteen hours. In forty-seven of seventy-five pharmacies the workday was thirteen hours; in seven it was fourteen hours. Twenty-nine pharmacies required seven and a half nights on duty per month; twenty-four required ten nights.[53] Elimination of night duty was to become one of the rallying cries of radical pharmacists in 1905.

Yet, long hours, particularly for staff pharmacists, resulted mainly from the government regulations that pharmacies must remain open twenty-four hours. In 1898 a group of doctors instituted the practice of night duty at St. Petersburg pharmacies in order to give immediate help to the sick; Moscow doctors soon imitated the experiment. This night duty began at 3 P.M. and ended at the same hour the following day.[54] Indeed, in 1904, while *Farmatsevticheskii vestnik* termed staff pharmacists "white slaves," who toiled from 9 A.M. to 11 P.M., with night duty every third night, the journal simultaneously published a Gogolesque letter from one "Alexander B.," which explained the logic of night duty:

> A St. Petersburg winter, damp winds, with fog . . . in the city there are many kinds of disease. In the pharmacy there is a mass of work. In the evening—this picture: a full room of the most varied people with only one wish—to soon receive medicine and hurry home to relieve their sickness. Behind the counter are two or three people, draining their strength. The public does not realize that people work without rest until 10 P.M.; they do not realize the difficulty when they are asked to hurry . . .[55]

Some pharmacists did not regard night duty as terribly onerous. In 1885 a Russian pharmacist informed his American colleagues that

> In the large pharmacies they have both day and night clerks. In the smaller ones the clerks alternate in day and night duty. Two full days in each week are allowed for recreation. The [drug] stores [*sic*] are always open, but the regular business day begins at half-past 8 and lasts until 9 P.M., during which each clerk makes an average of from 100 to 150 prescriptions.[56]

The American observer H. M. Gordin praised some characteristics of Russian pharmacy practice and criticized others. However, he did not depict Russian pharmacists' hours or night duty as particularly burdensome in his address to students at the University of Michigan Pharmacy School in 1899:

> All galenicals and pharmaceuticals that can be made on an ordinary scale, like solid and powdered extracts, salves, aromatic waters, etc., are manufactured in the drug store [*sic*]. The laboratory is under the care of a special pharmacist called a "laborant," who has under his direction one or two common laborers (*mujik*) to do the hard work, like powdering drugs, working the press, etc. . . . The [drug] store is opened at about 8:30 A.M. and closed at about 10 P.M. but there is always an assistant sleeping in the store to answer night calls. When the night bell rings, one of the common laborers mentioned above, with whose sleeping place the bell is connected, goes down and lets in the customer and then wakes up the assistant.[57]

Regarding night duty, Isaiah Ginzburg said simply some fifty years later "In those days the pharmacy was open all night, and we all took turns working."[58]

Socialist-pharmacists regarded low remuneration for staff pharmacists coupled with pay in room and board to be a second major problem. Nevertheless, the idea that pharmacists' salaries were abysmally low appears to have been more perception than reality, judging from comparison with salaries of other semiprofessionals, workers, and professionals. Pharmacists' salaries were lower than those of full-fledged professionals but nowhere near as low as the salaries of hapless, semiprofessional rural primary teachers.

In the 1890s, Assistant Pharmacists averaged 600 rubles per year.[59] In 1901 an advertisement for an Assistant Pharmacist to serve as laborant in a zemstvo pharmacy promised a salary of 600 rubles per year if the individual served not less than one year.[60] In contrast, one chemist's position in a sugar refinery in southern Russia paid 840 rubles a year in 1896; a second chemist's position paid 1,200 rubles.[61] Unskilled laborers, on the other hand, received average wages of 150 rubles per year; skilled laborers could make 400 rubles or more.[62] By 1906 miners, observed by American traveler Kellogg Durland, made about 400 rubles per year.[63] Full-fledged health professionals such as district physicians received salaries of 950 to 1,225 rubles per year in the early twentieth century. Provincial medical inspectors received 2,500 rubles at that time.[64] But teachers in zemstvo schools in the 1880s made only 200 to 300 rubles per year; in the early twentieth century, in southern provinces, where higher salaries prevailed, rural primary teachers received only 350 to 400 rubles per year.[65] Pharmacists' pay frequently was supplemented by room and board. Militant pharmacists at the turn of the century and their latter-day partisans contended that this *pansion* system coupled with night duty virtually enslaved serving pharmacists.[66] But their view was not shared by all pharmacists. In reminiscences, written a half-century after the events, Isaiah Ginzburg's enthusiasm for his work as a student pharmacist and assistant is palpable. Undoubtedly his memories were affected by nostalgia but he recalled:

> Looking back, I can say that these years were a happy time—physically, mentally, and spiritually. I was doing the kind of work I preferred. I had young friends I enjoyed at the pharmacy and hospital. The food in the house was of the best. I had one day off a week, wore good clothes, even sported a cane. . . . [After passing the Assistant Pharmacist examination] I came back to the pharmacy and now I drew a salary of $15 per month due to my higher rank and the passing of the exam. After working six more months I left for a better position in one of the largest and most modern pharmacies

in Moscow as a prescription clerk, a dream of mine from the beginning of my career.[67]

The Russian pharmacist Zewalthoff, writing in 1885, found neither pharmacists' pay nor the boarding system objectionable:

> The salaries of students and clerks vary according to their standing. Generally, they are paid as follows: Students, from 10 to 40 roubles per month. After receiving diploma to second diploma, from 45 to 100 roubles monthly. On receiving the third and last diploma, their salary becomes from 100 to 150 and 200 per month. It is to be remembered that from the beginning (as students), and afterwards as full graduates and clerks, they are also provided with rooms and board, and all possible comforts.[68]

The American observer Gordin, in 1899, was more critical of Russian pharmacy apprentices' pay and work conditions. However, he regarded the boarding system with equanimity:

> The first year of apprenticeship the would-be pharmacist is pretty much knocked about, as he has to cut and paste labels, fill bottles and drawers and help everybody else in the store without having any well defined sphere of occupation. He generally gets board and lodging and only a few "roubles" for pocket money. The second year his pay is increased and he is allowed to put up prescriptions under the strict supervision of an assistant. The third year apprentice divides his time between work in the laboratory and putting up prescriptions. . . . The drug store [*sic*] is in most cases connected with a dining room and several sleeping apartments, as the clerks are generally lodged and boarded with the proprietor.[69]

All this is not to say that the Russian system needed no improvement. Russian pharmacies might have adopted the French system. Night duty was "nearly nonexistent" in France by 1907. French pharmacies kept regular hours like other trading establishments. Large pharmacies (which were in the minority) hired special pharmacists for night duty. Those needing emergency medical aid between 10 at night and 6 in the morning could go to physicians on duty in district police stations. Additionally, some pharmacy owners remained open at night by special agreement. Most pharmacies also were closed on Sunday, posting locations of the few pharmacies which did dispense.[70]

Russian pharmacies did not modernize their schedules wholesale. However, some pharmacies introduced shorter hours and more free days by the turn of the century. For example, in 1898, *Farmatsevticheskii vestnik*, which scrupulously kept watch on conditions for staff pharmacists, noted improvements in pharmacies located in the Georgian port city of Batum. In Petkevich and Bialusskii's pharmacy staff had a free day after every three days of work; whereas formerly they had 91 free days per year they now had 122. In L. F. Damrof's pharmacy pharmacists had night duty for two days and the third day was free. The workday was fourteen hours with one free day each week. "Such a system satisfies the staff pharmacist."[71] In 1904, *Farmatsevticheskii vestnik* reported that some pharmacy owners in southern provinces, returning from a Congress in Moscow, introduced double shifts for their workers. Unfortunately, the majority did not. In Elizavetgrad, the life of staff pharmacists was "very hard," but three pharmacies had introduced the double shift.[72] In February 1905, even before strikes erupted in pharmacies, the Chief Medical Inspector V. Anrep and Assistant Minister P. Durnovo issued a circular to governors and municipal police chiefs demanding information on the work hours, amount of night duty, pay, and work environment for staff pharmacists and student pharmacist-apprentices. Point 2 of the eleven-point list inquired as to whether the pharmacy practiced a two-shift system. This indicated that some pharmacies did so. Indeed, a response in the national archives from one "Naval Pharmacy" duly signed by its manager and six-person staff (five were apprentices) announced that the regimen consisted of double-shifts of seven hours each. (Pay ranged from 15 to 45 rubles per month plus a 10-ruble per month rent allowance.)[73]

Double shifts, frequently of seven hours per shift, were widely implemented during 1905, generally in response to strikes, of which more will be said in a later chapter. In March of that year, for example, the Kiev Provincial Administration notified the Chief Medical Inspector that "some managers of normal pharmacies in Kiev have requested the Medical Division of the Kiev Administration to allow pharmacy students above the norm established by the regulation of 28 December 1901, that is more than one student for every 3,000 prescriptions, in view of the introduction now of the double shift system for staff."[74] In June 1905, the Tomsk Provincial Medical Administration informed the Chief Medical Inspector that, as a result of staff pharmacists' and pharmacy students' demands for shorter work time and improved conditions, "work hours both for pharmacists and students are established now at *six hours* [italics mine] in twenty-four in nearly all pharmacies in Tomsk."[75] The Tomsk Provincial Medical Department was concerned that the shortened workday might affect the three-year apprenticeship requirement for pharmacy students and assistant pharmacists, but the Medical Council assured them laconically that "until change by legislative means the existing regulations about time spent in the pharmacy by students and assistants remains in force."[76]

In 1906 the Khar'kov Society of Pharmacy Owners reported that "nearly all pharmacies in the Russian empire at the present time have introduced a double shift." Five thousand prescriptions per year merited two students; pharmacies with higher than 5,000 prescriptions per year were to employ one student for each 5,000 prescriptions.[77] That double shifts did increase expenditures for pharmacy owners is evident from a report of a pharmacy owner in the city of Kursk. He announced that he was forced to hire five students in addition to four qualified pharmacists after he introduced the double shift for his staff.[78]

In the normal pharmacy operated by the Viatka provincial zemstvo in 1906 the four male and twelve female students were occupied daily from 9 A.M. until 6 P.M. They had an hour break for lunch. The students had night duty in shifts of four (the sexes were separated). Night duty began at 6 P.M.; students remained on duty until morning under supervision of an Assistant Pharmacist. Assistant Pharmacists had one free day after two days' work; students were free after three days' work.[79]

Radical pharmacists could claim that, in part, double shifts were due to the strikes they had fomented. However, they did not cease pressure for higher pay, summer vacations, and so on in addition to shorter hours in the years after 1905 and 1906. Further, they never analyzed the economic feasibility of their demands, a topic which shall be explored further in a later chapter.

In 1910 the government entered staff-management relations and began to regulate the hours and conditions of work for staff pharmacists with its usual methodical thoroughness. One Pliushevskii Pliushchik (his name reminiscent of a character in Gogol's *Inspector General*) chaired a special commission that "drafted norms for staff pharmacists." The Chief Medical Inspector conceded that work in the pharmacy had a certain educational component for apprentices, and the system should be preserved until specialized pharmacy schools and institutes were established. At the same time, he acknowledged that much of the work of pharmacy students and Assistant Pharmacists was "not of scientific character." Consequently, the commission, formed of two representatives from owners and two from staff, determined that staff were to work a maximum of 230 hours per month, enjoy double shifts or rest after two days in three, and two hours for dinner daily. Pharmacies that dispensed 10,000 or fewer prescriptions annually were to employ two to three pharmacists in addition to the manager. In pharmacies that filled a greater number of prescriptions annually one additional pharmacist was to be hired for each 5,000 additional prescriptions. The number of students allowed each pharmacy depended upon the staff and number of prescriptions filled: there were to be no more than two students for each Provizor and one student for every 10,000 prescriptions filled.[80] Late in 1910 the Medical Council reviewed the work of this commission and applied norms to St. Petersburg pharmacies.[81]

And thus, another layer of regulations was imposed upon Russian pharmacies.

Meanwhile, conditions for staff pharmacists continued to improve without outside interference. In 1910, there were 11,205 staff pharmacists, including students. In 1911 a questionnaire was sent to pharmacists. Only 27.2 percent of those polled responded; however, some trends were visible. Seventy-one percent of pharmacists responding received their salary entirely in rubles, rather than room and board. Average monthly wages were 165 rubles for Masters of Pharmacy, 107 for Provizors, 64 for Assistant Pharmacists, and 26 for students.[82]

By 1913, according to E. K. Khrzhanovskii, representative to the Medical Council from the St. Petersburg Pharmacy Society, the average annual salary for the manager of a pharmacy was 1,200 rubles; salaries for staff were less but still respectable–senior assistants made 800 rubles per year; junior assistants made 720.[83] Radical pharmacists disparaged Khrzhanovskii as the pharmacy owners' spokesman. Additionally, the average he produced meant that while some pharmacists received high salaries, some also received meager ones. Further, whether real wages had improved depended upon prices.[84]

Nevertheless, that salaries had increased by the eve of World War I is corroborated by a random sample–salaries at the Tomsk city pharmacy in 1914. The manager of the Tomsk city pharmacy, Vasilii Vasil'evich Nikitin, received 2,000 rubles per year plus an apartment. The assistant manager, Provizor Grigorii Mikhailovich Zorokhovich, received 100 rubles per month or 1,200 rubles per year. The two male pharmacist-receptionists and the female laboratory assistant all received 80 rubles per month, or 960 rubles per year. The female pharmacy assistant, Liubov' Ippolitovna Gorinovich-Vershinina, who had just received her Assistant Pharmacist title, received 60 rubles per month, or 720 rubles per year; the male pharmacy assistant, Viacheslav Kornilievich Suzdal'tsev, who was merely a pharmacy student, received 50 rubles per month or 600 rubles per year. Both "pharmacist-assistants" had been in service for less than a year.[85]

Many aspects of pharmacy training and work were ripe for improvement in the early twentieth century.[86] But there were a number of indications that the pharmacist's life was far from intolerable. Pharmacy continued to attract eager aspirants. In August 1905, the St. Petersburg chief of police informed the Chief Medical Inspector that as of January 1, 1905, 15 Masters of Pharmacy, 179 Provizors, 293 Assistant Pharmacists, and 242 pharmacy students were serving in St. Petersburg pharmacies. He noted that the "Number of pharmacy students had increased from year to year and, as a consequence, pharmacy owners had stated that it was necessary to limit the number of pharmacy students and replace them with pharmacists who had 'been examined.'"[87] In 1907, the Viatka provincial medical inspector informed the Chief Medical Inspector that the greater numbers of pharmacy students serving in a local zemstvo pharmacy was "explained by the many proposals for work on the part of people wishing to be occupied in the pharmacy."[88] Additionally, in 1907 the St. Petersburg Pharmaceutical Society reported to the Chief Medical Inspector that there were 4,326 pharmacy students in the entire empire. This was a significant increase compared with turn-of-the-century figures of 2,525, even if the students were unevenly distributed.[89]

Attrition in the ranks proved to be a temporary phenomenon. In 1902, according to rough figures, there were 2,525 pharmacy students of both sexes. This was not significantly higher than the 2,120 Assistant Pharmacists of both sexes.[90] Furthermore, some of the disparity between pharmacy students and Assistant Pharmacists was due to Jews enrolling as pharmacy students. As Jewish pharmacy students were allowed to live outside the Pale, many Jewish pharmacy students had no intention of remaining in the profession and left when it was convenient.[91]

As for life style, during World War I radical pharmacists looked back with nostalgia to the prewar era, when staff pharmacists' tables were graced with "white bread, meat, and milk."[92]

Two other phenomena testified to the fairly decent position of staff pharmacists: the emergence of *praktikanty*–untrained persons–eager to work in pharmacies and school feldshers filling pharmacy positions and demanding to take the pharmacist examinations.

Reference to *praktikanty* appeared in the 1880s. In 1884, I. A. Gershtein of Yalta informed the readers of *Farmatsevticheskii zhurnal* that "The number of '*praktikanty*,' or people taking the title pharmacist, without lawful right, in recent times has increased (especially here in the south)." Gershtein claimed that *praktikanty* "occupied" the places of Assistant Pharmacists in pharmacies. Somewhat inaccurately, he continued, "pharmacy students with *gimnaziia* certificates" and "Assistant Pharmacists with university diplomas cannot find vacancies in pharmacies." In Yalta there were two pharmacies that employed *praktikanty*. They spent long hours at work, "sort of" learned the names of medicines, and in red shirts and pantaloons, worked their way up to assistants and laboratory assistants, working for five to ten rubles per month. One old and one young *praktikant* worked in a provincial pharmacy, acquiring the place of "sub-receptionist-dispenser" (*retseptar'*).[93] In 1904 *Farmatsevticheskii vestnik* contended that some pharmacists used in the capacity of *praktikanty* people who had no educational qualifications. This "did not conform to the law, for only pharmacy students, Assistant Pharmacists, or managers should be doing more or less responsible work in a pharmacy."[94] In 1904 the Ministry of Internal Affairs forbade pharmacies to hire *praktikanty* or persons having insufficient educational qualifications as pharmacy students.[95]

From 1902,[96] but particularly from 1906 and 1907, school feldshers agitated to take the Assistant Pharmacist examination. Many feldshers served as pharmacists in zemstvo pharmacies or those belonging to industrial establishments. They adduced many reasons why they should be allowed to take the Assistant Pharmacist exam. There were 20,000 feldshers in Russia. In the thirty-four zemstvo provinces there were 5,635 male and female feldshers and only 157 pharmacists; likewise 1,453 feldshers served in railroad establishments, compared to only 45 pharmacists. Feldshers' education included pharmacology, pharmacognosy, pharmacy, and pharmaceutical chemistry. Doctors were satisfied with feldshers' pharmacy practice. In 1893 and 1897 the Medical Department allowed feldshers to perform small surgical operations and other independent medical work in the absence of physicians; some universities, notably Warsaw, Khar'kov, and Moscow, allowed feldshers finishing the course at the Moscow Golitsyn School and all military feldsher schools to take the Assistant Pharmacist examination. On the basis of these arguments feldshers requested the Ministry of Internal Affairs, through the Medical Council, that they be allowed to take the examination. They also discussed the question at length in the First Feldsher Congress held in Moscow in 1907. Pharmacists, of course, opposed this movement. B. N. Saltykov, the Marxist, pharmacist-editor, was particularly negative toward the notion of feldshers becoming pharmacists.[97]

Solutions

Both advocates for pharmacy owners and staff pharmacists exaggerated their cases. Further, neither group considered opening up the system—allowing more pharmacies and competition and, concomitantly, more opportunity for proprietorship and upward mobility—as a solution to their problems.

The impressions of socialist pharmacists to the contrary, neither the gulf between Provizors and Assistant pharmacists nor between owners and staff was permanent. Upward mobility was possible. Assistant Pharmacists who became owner-managers multiplied dramatically; Provizors managed to move into the rarified world of the Master of Pharmacy. Nevertheless, it also was true that, while the vast majority of Provizors managed pharmacies, only a little more than half owned them. One analyst questioned the validity of even this figure.[98] Further, very few Assistant Pharmacists owned pharmacies. The reason for this was that limitations on pharmacy franchises drove up prices. One historian contended that because new pharmacies were limited, fifteen of thirty-five pharmacies operating in Moscow in the second half of the nineteenth century were leased and speculation was rife, some pharmacies going for eight to ten times their worth.[99] It is impossible to say whether or not this was true for all pharmacies.

To observers from England and America, who operated in a *laissez-faire* system, the solution seemed obvious—Russia should allow unfettered establishment of pharmacies. Perhaps the best exposition on this subject was contained in H. M. Gordin's address to the University of Michigan Pharmacy School in 1899. He stressed that students and Assistant Pharmacists could endure hardships if they could look forward to reward at the end.

> The Russian pharmacist, like his American colleague, works much more and gets much less for his work than most other professional people of the community. The inability sufficiently to appreciate the value of the services which the pharmacist renders to society, seems to be common to all nations and in this respect the pharmacists of all countries are placed on the same footing. But an American drug clerk has that advantage over his Russian confrere, that it is always possible, if only he has the ability, to work himself up to a higher position in life and become the owner of a pharmacy. True, such a pharmacy will often be not much more than a small insect powder shop, but it is at any rate a beginning, and many a small beginning can be brought to a fine success by energy, skill and economy. Unfortunately there are no such chances for the Russian pharmacist. The Russian drug clerk that enters upon his toilsome career with empty pockets is doomed to remain clerking all his life long, as no amount of ability, perseverance and economy can enable him ever to accumulate sufficient means to buy an established pharmacy. As to starting a new one, that is almost impossible. The reason for this state of things is that pharmacy, like most other professional occupations in Russia, is under strict regulation of the government. The number of pharmacies in the empire is limited by law.[100]

Gordin praised Russian regulations on dispensing, which curtailed the circulation of patent nostrums, then flooding America.[101] However, he emphasized that the Russian system limited upward mobility for the pharmacist.

> . . . those that happen to own a pharmacy in Russia know very well that they have a gold mine in possession and are very seldom willing to sell out. If once in a while a druggist, *apres fortune faite*, desires to retire, his business commands such a high price in the market that a poor drug clerk would have to work as long as Methusalem lived and spend as little as a Chinaman in order to save up half of it. Of course, there is plenty of room for new drug stores in the peasant districts of the vast Russia empire; but if country life is pretty dull in all countries, life among the Russian peasants with their poverty and dense ignorance offers little attraction indeed for an educated pharmacist.[102]

The Russian system also hurt consumers:

> in St. Petersburg, with about a million inhabitants, there are less than a hundred drug stores, whereas in San Francisco for a population of less than three hundred thousand there are over two hundred drug stores. As to the contrary, an American traveler who is used to meet the sign of a drug store in every little village, where streets, avenues and even most of the buildings exist as yet only in the imagination of the real estate agent, would be surprised to pass dozens of Russian villages never missing the sign of a saloon but hardly ever noticing a drug store.[103]

In 1903 an American pharmaceutical journal presented a more sanguine view of the Russian system, asserting that "A new vacancy for a pharmacy in a town is considered as existing when the population has increased by a certain amount and prescriptions made up already by the existing pharmacies exceed a certain average. Generally, people desirous to establish themselves buy the business from another, which in recent times is very easy to do owing to the hard conditions of the business."[104]

However, in 1906, D. A. Ruffman, director of Parke, Davis and Company, concurred with Gordin that limiting pharmacies was detrimental to consumers[105] and pharmacists alike.

> The obtaining of a license for opening a pharmacy is naturally very difficult on account of the law which prescribes that it can be opened only for every 7,000 to 12,000 inhabitants. The inhabitants in a city do not increase as fast as the number of qualified pharmacists, and therefore the pharmacist who succeeds in getting the license prefers to sell it right out to someone else for a very high amount (50,000 to 100,000 roubles) instead of opening the pharmacy himself. You will seldom find a qualified pharmacist in Russia with such an amount of cash; consequently the money is borrowed and a high interest rate is paid for it in the hope that the pharmacy will bring in a good return.[106]

But, although outside observers pointed out the benefits of free trade and competition, most Russian pharmacists resisted the idea. Centuries of restriction and regulation created a dependent mentality in the majority of Russian pharmacists.

Only a handful appeared to perceive how limiting pharmacies restricted ownership. In 1879 Moscow and St. Petersburg pharmacists lamented the difficulty of acquiring a pharmacy of one's own.

> The insufficiency of pharmacy students at the present time can be explained first of all by the fact that of the number of pharmacists achieving the degree of Provizor, a very small part acquire or manage their own pharmacy because pharmacy is the preserve of poor people—acquisition of a pharmacy requires, nearly without exception, credit, which the poor cannot receive. If one wants to establish a new pharmacy it demands significant outlay on the basis of the new law.[107]

An equally small number conceded that competition was beneficial. In 1879 one pharmacy owner, Glezar, or Glaser, from Velikii Ustiug, enthusiastically described how he turned competition from a neighboring zemstvo pharmacy into cooperation. The result was improved dispensing all around.[108]

From the success story of the drug stores it would seem that more rather than less competition would benefit pharmacists. G. Zeskov, from the town of Krettingen, Kovno province, argued along these lines in 1891. He contradicted Zaidman's contention that pharmacy owners were in financial distress. His argument included socialist buzzwords, such as "capitalists" and "giving productive force as a gift" but he also endorsed free trade which would help the public and increase upward mobility for pharmacists, particularly partially qualified pharmacists. His sensible observations deserve quoting at length:

> . . . Zaidman suggests stopping further increase of pharmacies and granting pharmacy owners the exclusive right to sell and prepare medicine and all substances used for medicine (all chemical-pharmaceutical preparations).
>
> Why? The first measure would be beneficial only to some pharmacists and for some capitalists, but the majority of pharmacists only would be hurt by it and many conditionals [partially qualified pharmacists] would complain. A limited number of pharmacies would only raise the price of them and pharmacists would not be able to accumulate the capital to purchase a pharmacy. Therefore this measure would not be useful for pharmacists but only for capitalists. I hold that rational increase of pharmacies

> cannot be harmful to pharmacists. In district cities a pharmacy with turnover of about 5 thousand rubles can exist very suitably. In provincial cities turnover of 8,000 or 9,000 rubles would be sufficient. . . . What is sensible about the fact that in the provinces there are pharmacies with 20,000 to 30,000 turnover, enjoyed by a few owners, when on the other hand much productive force is given as a gift and leads to competition among conditional [pharmacists] to an impossible degree. Rational increase of pharmacies limits capital but to the benefit of pharmacists . . . and if the abnormal growth of pharmacists is preliminarily checked by raising requirements on the education of pharmacy students, for example, by requiring the complete *gimnaziia* course, it would benefit pharmacists and their stature would rise in the eyes of society.
>
> As for the second proposal of Zaidman—to grant to pharmacies a monopoly to prepare and sell all medical preparations, I must turn attention to the absolute infeasibility of this measure. We live in a century which requires free growth of . . . competition. Implementation of such a demand would ignore the interests of the public. Eliminating factory preparation of medicine would eliminate cheaper medicines—make medicine more expensive since the factory can make medicine more cheaply than the pharmacy laboratory. We cannot put our personal and corporate interests above those of suffering humanity! Drug stores are far from dangerous for pharmacies, if they follow the laws. Unfortunately, control over them is exceptionally weak and this is one source of the evil![109]

In 1891, V. A. Sokolov, owner of a pharmacy, and its Provizor-manager Epifan similarly denied that competition hurt pharmacy owners. They noted that pharmacies already had a monopoly on preparing and selling medicines and that secret (*tainye*) "pharmacies" and markets (*lavki*) always had existed and would continue to exist. They blamed pharmacy owners' problems on delay of the new Pharmacy Statute. Touted at the Pharmacy Congress of 1889, "not one of the projects had appeared." In their view, the chief challenges confronting the pharmacy corporation were, first, to provide cheaper medicine for the public—this meant *more* not fewer pharmacies—and second, improving communication among pharmacists. The authors particularly criticized pharmacists' lack of participation in government policy-making. Pharmacists were reactive rather than proactive and only learned of government policy from published circulars. They urged "collective activity on the part of pharmacy owners." Since this was "nowhere visible . . . it is not surprising that no changes in the personal position of pharmacists have come about."[110]

Critics of the pharmacy monopoly grew more vociferous in the first decade of the twentieth century.[111] Radical pharmacists continued to advocate socialized pharmacy, either buying out private pharmacies and making them available to all pharmacists or *municipalization*—transferring all pharmacies to democratically elected zemstvos and municipal dumas. On the other side, proponents of free trade began to gain a few more adherents. In 1906, Russians were granted a parliament and, in 1907 progressives in the lower chamber, the State Duma, began tendering proposals for the right to establish pharmacies without prior government permission (*iavochnyi poriadok*).

Both movements began to influence the Russian government, and the Minister of Internal Affairs began to alter the pharmacy monopoly. However, as we shall see in chapter 15, by 1910, the movements fused, and free trade became subordinate to socialism. Progressives or radicals in the Duma introduced a bill granting municipal dumas and zemstvos the right to establish pharmacies freely. Individuals had been forgotten. As a consequence the Ministry of Internal Affairs created a strange hybrid of socialism and free trade. The Medical Council allowed public institutions, zemstvos, and municipal dumas, who could dispense medicine free or at low cost, to establish pharmacies, *where there were none,* freely, without government permission or fulfilling population and prescription requirements.

Before reviewing the escalating conflict between advocates of restricted pharmacy, free trade, and socialized pharmacy, let us look at nationality and gender issues among pharmacists, pharmacist industrialists, and pharmacists' contributions to public health.

6

Pharmacists and Nationality

In 1864 Ia. Chistovich, editor of *Meditsinskii vestnik*, asserted that because pharmacy had difficult requirements, an arduous path of training, and few rewards, few Russians would want to embark on such a path. Additionally, since most German pharmacy owners in major cities would not take on Russians, pharmacy in Russia was and would remain a career for foreigners.[1] He was right–but only if one considers national minorities "foreign." One of the most noticeable characteristics of "Russian" pharmacists in the late imperial period was that they largely belonged to non-Russian nationalities of the empire. In 1904, out of a population of approximately 144,000,000,[2] there were 6,815 pharmacists and 4,483 pharmacy students.[3] Jews constituted only about 4 percent of Russia's population, but in 1910, 32.7 percent of Provizors were Jewish, 29.4 percent were Polish, and 12.9 were German. Only 13.2 percent were Russian.[4]

A second striking characteristic of pharmacists–particularly in their training period–was that they were incredibly peripatetic. Did they, as one historian contends, consider "their constant job-hopping in the pursuit of practical training 'a six year obligatory *batrachestvo* [indentured servitude]'"?[5] Or did they regard moving about as a given and the vastness of the Russian empire as an asset?[6]

It is impossible, on the basis of information at hand, to definitively discern pharmacists' views on the subject of nationalism. However, random biographies of Masters of Pharmacy suggest that many who reached the apex of their profession considered the entire empire their home.

Eduard Iakovlevich Abol', who figures prominently in these pages, was born in Kurland province, apprenticed in Riazan, took his Assistant Pharmacist examination at Moscow University, performed his second stint of apprenticeship at Ferrein's *Staraia Nikol'skaia* pharmacy and worked as assistant accountant in a state treasury office while writing his Master's thesis. Pharmacy students from Kherson province took the Assistant Pharmacist examination at Kiev University, the Provizor examination at Dorpat, and the Master degree from Moscow University; pharmacy students from Georgia studied and took their exams in Moscow; Poles from

Kaluga province apprenticed in Odessa, took Assistant Pharmacist examinations at the University of Kiev, Provizor courses at Dorpat, and Master examinations at the St. Petersburg Military Academy. Pharmacy students from Moscow might apprentice there, take a Master degree at Dorpat, and manage a pharmacy in Tiflis, Georgia. A student from Vil'na might apprentice in Yaroslavl' and Tver provinces north of Moscow, take the Provizor examination at Kiev University, the Master examination at the Military Medical Academy in St. Petersburg, and work as a laboratory assistant in Nizhni Novgorod, on the Volga. A Master from Dorpat might manage a pharmacy in the White Sea port of Arkhangel'sk and then take a post as a chemist in a factory there. A lad from Grodno province in the northwest might receive preliminary education at a cadet school in St. Petersburg, the Assistant Pharmacist title at Dorpat, do research for the Master degree in the Caucasus, and serve as pharmacist in a military hospital in Brest-Litovsk, Western Russia. Oscar Rudolfovich Brashe apprenticed in his father's Reval pharmacy, received the Provizor title at Dorpat, worked for a chemist in a soap factory in Warsaw, became owner of a pharmacy in Estland, and began his political career in the local court and city council. He was elected to the national parliament, the Fourth State Duma, in 1912 and became a major political voice in 1913.[7]

What of Jewish pharmacists? In 1910 1,546 of 4,724 registered Provizors were Jews.[8] The lot of Jews in Russia had worsened in the nineteenth century. From 1804 they had been confined largely to the so-called Pale of Settlement–the western provinces of the empire–although they were able to attend school in all parts of the empire. From the 1880s Jews were subject to a number of disabilities. They were limited by quotas at classical *gimnazii* and universities–10 percent of the student body within the Pale, 5 percent outside the Pale, and 3 percent in Moscow and St. Petersburg. Jews were not admitted to the Bar and the number of Jews entering medicine was limited to 5 percent.

The status of Jewish pharmacists was both unclear and uneven.[9] Indefiniteness gave rise to tragedy but also allowed for opportunity. The rights of Jewish pharmacists to live outside the Pale fluctuated. Before 1879, the Imperial Code of Laws did not permit Jewish pharmacists to live in all areas of the empire.[10] However, Jewish pharmacy students could live outside the Pale during their apprenticeship. Additionally, the Medical Statute allowed Jews to own and manage pharmacies. This implied the right to live where the pharmacy was located. Nevertheless, Jews were allowed to reside in cities outside the Pale for only two months and only with approval of the police and provincial administration. To live outside the Pale for a prolonged time, Jews needed the approval of the "highest authority"–the

Medical Department of the Ministry of Internal Affairs or Governing Senate, the supreme court of Russia.[11] In 1879, some categories of Jews were permitted to reside in all areas of the empire. These included Jews finishing higher educational institutions and Jews "studying pharmacy." In 1884 and 1886 the Governing Senate emphasized that Jews studying pharmacy as well as "feldsher and midwifery arts," but not dentistry could live outside the Pale.[12]

The capriciousness of the laws on residency, as well as their stringency, sometimes created hardships for Jewish pharmacists. The cases of Jewish Assistant Pharmacist Begermeister and Provizor Soloveichik provide sobering examples. Begermeister owned a pharmacy in Khar'kov province, in the eastern Ukraine. In January 1876, the Khar'kov Medical Inspector asked the Medical Department for a decision on whether this was legal.[13] The Department of Police in the Ministry of Internal Affairs averred that according to "existing legislation" Begermeister could not own a pharmacy nor live in Khar'kov province. As a consequence, in June 1876 the Khar'kov Provincial Medical Administration asked the Medical Department whether the pharmacy should be closed.[14] The Medical Council and then the supreme court, the Governing Senate, reviewed the case. Two years later the Medical Division of the Khar'kov Provincial Administration phlegmatically informed the Medical Department that Begermeister "had sold his pharmacy."[15] Provizor Lazar Soloveichik was luckier in part because of "clerical error" and because regulations on residence changed in 1880. In 1876 the Medical Division of the Khar'kov Provincial Administration ordered Soloveichik to "quickly sell" his pharmacy in the city of Khar'kov "on the basis that as a person of Jewish belief" he "did not have the right to live and own a pharmacy in that city."[16] However, the Medical Surgical Academy had not noted "his Jewishness"[17] and an Imperial Regulation of January 19, 1880, gave "Jewish pharmacists the right of residence in the empire equal with pharmacists of other creeds."[18] Therefore, although the Governing Senate did not support Provizor Soloveichik's complaint against the Khar'kov Medical Inspector, he nonetheless petitioned the Medical Department on October 25, 1880, that on the basis of the revised legislation he be allowed "to retain ownership of my pharmacy in the city of Khar'kov."[19]

Residency laws continued to be quirksome. In 1894 St. Petersburg police were ordered to approve both temporary and permanent residence permits for Jews. According to article 788 of the 1899 edition of the Code of Laws, Jews could live in St. Petersburg to take examinations for admission to higher educational institutions. They were allowed to live in the capital during the four times each year examinations were held. Jews who stayed in St. Petersburg after or without taking examinations, were "subject to removal from the capital to the Pale."[20] On the other hand, in 1901 the Senate ruled that widows of Jewish Provizors could live outside the Pale.[21] In 1903 an official commission debated the right of Jewish Provizors to practice outside the Pale.[22] However, early in 1906, *Russkie vedomosti* announced that the governor general of St. Petersburg forbade Jewish pharmacists to live on the island of Kronstadt. The paper did not note whether the reason was because the island harbored a major naval base or because of recent revolutionary upheavals. In any case, it noted that many Jews had already left and the remainder had been given dates for departure.[23] Additionally, Jews sometimes met discrimination in finding positions.[24]

On the other side of the ledger, Jews aspiring to become pharmacists were not as heavily impacted by educational quotas as Jews entering careers that were more thoroughly professionalized. While Jews' attendance at the *gimnaziia* was limited, requirements for pharmacy students in the late nineteenth, early twentieth century included other secondary school options, such as the real school, the private commercial school of Faig in Odessa, and, from 1872, district and city schools, supplemented by study of Latin.[25] From 1901, Jews finishing the Jewish Vilensk Teacher's Institute could become pharmacy students with additional study of Latin, necessary to read the pharmacopoeia.[26]

It sometimes was difficult for Jews to get places in pharmacies so they could begin the initial three-year apprenticeship. Sometimes they were paid less than gentile apprentices. But, because there were no formal schools for pharmacy students preparing for the Assistant Pharmacist examination, it was impossible to impose quotas on Jews in this category.[27]

Further, Jews used the regulations allowing Jewish pharmacy students to live outside the Pale to their advantage. In January 1907, the Minsk Medical Department reported that there were 210 pharmacy students in the 52 normal pharmacies in Minsk province. Some pharmacies had as many as 15 students of "Jewish nationality; such a number was explained . . . by the attempt of Jews to acquire the degree of Assistant Pharmacist and with it the right to live outside the Jewish Pale. Many of the students were occupied with another profession and only used the pharmacy as a place to study." Further the medical inspector was "unable to verify the number of students in the pharmacy because they disappeared during the time of the inspection."[28] To combat such violations the medical inspector insisted that pharmacies adhere to the norm of one student for each 1,000 or 2,000 prescriptions. Pharmacies that dispensed more than 20,000 prescriptions were limited to 10 students.[29] Additionally, two new circulars on pharmacy students appeared in 1907. The first stipulated that each Master and Provizor was to take on no more than two students. The second prohibited Jewish pharmacy students from apprenticing in tsarist Poland.[30]

The position of Jewish Assistant Pharmacists attending Provizor courses varied from university to university. At Iur'ev-Dorpat University in the 1890s, Jewish Assistant Pharmacists were limited to 5 percent of the student body. At Warsaw University they were limited to 20 percent.[31] Khar'kov University authorities ignored quotas for Jews before 1901, with the apparent sanction of Minister of Public Enlightenment Delianov. Convinced that in certain cases the fixed percentage for Jews was not appropriate, Delianov allowed trustees of the Khar'kov educational district to waive the quotas for Jews in pharmacy courses at the university. His successors reversed the policy, with predictable hardship for Jewish auditors. In 1901, 100 of the 120 applicants for Provizor courses at the Khar'kov University were Jews. According to the rules only two could be accepted. The Khar'kov Pharmacy Society protested, arguing that "insufficiency of pharmacists due to the diminution of people choosing pharmacy as their profession," necessitated that as in former years Jewish Assistant Pharmacists be considered auditors and quotas be ignored.[32]

Jewish Assistant Pharmacists at Moscow University were bound by percentage norms affecting regular Jewish university students. Additionally, in 1904, in contradistinction to other university cities where Jews in Provizor courses could live outside the pharmacy, Moscow officials determined that the passport designation "persons studying pharmacy," which permitted residence within the city, applied exclusively to Jews registered and *living in* a pharmacy. A. B. Solonouts protested this ruling, emphasizing that according to law, attendance at university guaranteed living in a university city. Further, Jewish Assistant Pharmacists would have to combine work in a pharmacy with university lectures or be forced to leave Moscow within twenty-four hours if no pharmacy position was available. He petitioned the Senate to waive the rule imposed in Moscow. The Senate agreed to his specific request but did not authorize a general waiver.[33] The problem was still in evidence in 1906.[34]

At the same time, Novorossiisk University in Odessa ignored quotas for Jews auditing Provizor courses in 1904. Apparently the Assistant Minister of Public Enlightenment concurred. However, there were only six Jewish Assistant Pharmacists in the university Provizor courses in 1904.[35]

In 1906 the new Minister of Internal Affairs and Chairman of the Council of Ministers, P. A. Stolypin, proposed removing some disabilities on Jews. Nicholas II vetoed the proposal. In ensuing years Stolypin and the ministry discussed partial improvements in the position of Jews, such as slightly increased quotas for secondary schools and institutions of higher learning and allowing merchants' sons to live in Moscow. But the Russian government never entertained a proposal for inclusive reforms for Jews.[36]

Nevertheless, Jews continued to flock to pharmacy, for quotas remained higher than those in other disciplines. In 1907, Jewish quotas at Moscow University were 3 percent–for pharmacists in Provizor courses they were 6 percent; in Kiev, Kazan, and Khar'kov universities quotas for Jews were 5 percent–for pharmacists they were 20 percent; at Tomsk University quotas were 5 percent–for pharmacists, 15 percent; at Odessa and Warsaw universities, which were within the Pale, quotas for Jewish students were 10 percent–for pharmacy students, 25 percent.[37]

Some problems with residency remained after 1906. The Ministry of Trade and Industry imposed new limitations on Jews with regard to opening factories. The Ministry of Internal Affairs "confined Jews' right to open pharmacies . . . to the Pale."[38] As a result, according to a contemporary newspaper, more Jewish pharmacists emigrated to America.[39] In 1907 Assistant Minister of Internal Affairs Kryzhanovskii announced that Jewish auditors were not allowed to live in St. Petersburg.[40] In 1909 the authorities in Moscow reiterated that Jewish Assistant Pharmacists (and dentists and midwives) living in the city must be "occupied with their profession."[41] Jewish Provizors were expelled from Moscow in 1910. They appealed to the city police chief in light of the fact that a recent Senate ruling had included Provizors among Jews with a higher education who had special rights to live outside the Pale. However, the police chief refused to take action without official permission.[42] Later that year the Department of General Affairs in the Ministry of Internal Affairs issued a circular confirming that Jewish pharmacy students could live temporarily in university towns outside the Pale for the purpose of preparing for and taking their examinations only if they were engaged in pharmacy practice in a normal–fully stocked–pharmacy.[43] At the same time new impediments to Provizor courses were imposed. The quota for Jews in Provizor courses at St. Vladimir University in Kiev was 20 percent. In September 1910, because no Christians enrolled in the courses, the Minister of Public Enlightenment closed them.[44] The local pharmacy corporation expressed "surprise" and "disbelief," acknowledging solidarity with Jewish colleagues.[45] At Khar'kov only 40 Christians applied for Provizor courses. Although 146 Jews applied officials steadfastly held to the 10 percent quota for Jews. As a result only 4 Jews were accepted![46]

In 1911, replies to a questionnaire revealed that Jewish pharmacists in the Pale received less pay than their colleagues.[47]

Jewish pharmacy owners suffered from pogroms. For example, in

November 1905, the Chief Medical Inspector notified the Medical Section of the Tavrida Provincial Administration that it had received a request, forwarded by the provincial administration, from a Jewish pharmacy owner in the city of Chernigovke, Berdiansk district to temporarily close his pharmacy because of an expected pogrom. (Pharmacies were not ordinarily allowed to close.) The administration of the Chief Medical Inspector, in turn, informed the Tavrida Provincial Administration that if the local authorities in the village of Chernigovke could not prevent danger to the pharmacy owner and provide him with defense, he had the right to close his pharmacy—all the more because a zemstvo point existed in the village and, thus, the inhabitants would not be deprived of medicine.[48] During 1906 one Jewish owner was able to rebuild his pharmacy, damaged by a pogrom, through aid from relatives, the Committee for Aid to Jews, and his creditors.[49]

Nastiness on the part of officials was sometimes blatant. In November 1913, Privy Councillor and member of the Council of the Ministry of Internal Affairs Zaiochkovskii (the more reformist Stolypin having been assassinated in September 1911) noted approvingly in a report of his survey of pharmacies in Kherson province that "Zemstvos in a majority of provinces have sufficiently developed a network of medical 'points' and village pharmacies." But, he continued ominously, these advances in public pharmacy were being obstructed by the machinations of Jews. "Private [*chastnaia*] zemstvo [*zemliia*] pharmacies are being opened in zemstvo provinces nearly exclusively by Jews, not for satisfying the needs of the population, as the zemstvos themselves testify, whose every new request to open village pharmacies is forbidden by the provincial [medical] administration. . . . There has been created a Jewish nest. Jewish pharmacy owners . . . attract peasants to their pharmacies with artifice: they suggest to the ignorant [*temnyi*] peasant mass that they should not use grants of [free] medicine from the Medical Council . . . the zemstvo doctor and zemstvo pharmacy, that they should take medicine only from them; they treat the sick with the occult and give them medicines from Jewish factories."[50] In a postscript of December 1913, the clerk (*deloproizvodstvo*) in the Ministry of Internal Affairs questioned the accuracy of some of Zaiochkovskii's information, remarking that a private person could not open a zemstvo pharmacy; the author evidently was referring to a village (*sel'skaia*) pharmacy. In Kherson province there were twenty-three village pharmacies. Only in a few medical points, with more population, were there normal pharmacies. However, nit-picking aside, the commentator supported the anti-Jewish bias of the report: "If the author means that the pharmacies established by Jews are village [pharmacies], then one must conclude that the Kherson administration has . . . poorly used its right to permit the opening of village pharmacies only by people having the full trust of the population through their experience in pharmacy matters and *their moral qualities* [italics in original] as stated in the Circular of the Ministry of Internal Affairs to the Medical Department, 31 January 1892, no. 145 . . ."[51] In June 1915, the Chief Medical Inspector commented in his turn that, "In the report of Privy Councillor Zaiochkovskii . . . it was concluded that allowing Jews to found pharmacies in rural localities was undesirable, because of the negative character of the Jewish pharmacy owners' activity. . . . I ask you not to refrain from exercising your authority to permit only people having full knowledge of pharmacy to open pharmacies . . . and not allowing any kind of abuse."[52]

To his credit the governor of Kherson province, Kamerger, defended both himself and Jewish pharmacists. In July 1915, he informed the Chief Medical Inspector that

> I have the honor to inform you that in the past 4 years there have been only two cases where I refused to allow the opening of village pharmacies to persons, on the basis of article 572 of the Medical Statute, vol. XIII, 1892, because I did not have full confidence in their moral qualities—namely, the refusal to Assistant Pharmacists Brodskii and Iaff to open village pharmacies.[53]

Quotas continued to be imposed during wartime. For example, in the fall of 1916 only thirty auditors were admitted to new pharmacy courses at Saratov University. Jews were limited to 10 percent, or three students.[54]

Nevertheless, Jewish pharmacists were not so easily cowed. Jewish owners of drug stores in the city and suburbs of Vil'na were particularly aggressive and professional, requesting the governor of Vilensk province in 1910 to allow them to remain open until 10 P.M. instead of 9, to better serve their customers.[55]

Despite hindrance and injustice, Jews continued to regard pharmacy as a suitable career and some fared well.

In 1891, 2,782 pharmacists managed pharmacies. Thirty-nine percent, or 1,086, were Poles. Next came Jews at 616, or 22.14 percent. They were followed by 547 Germans, 327 "Orthodox"—presumably Russians and Ukrainians, and other nationalities in small numbers.[56] By 1901 the number of Jews managing pharmacies rose to 26.83 percent. By 1908 the number of pharmacies managed by Jews stood at 31.32 percent. Meanwhile, the number of pharmacies managed by Catholics (presumably Poles) dropped from over 39 percent in 1900 to 36.17 percent, the number managed by Lutherans dropped from 19.62 percent to 17.34 percent.[57]

A number of Masters of Pharmacy were Jews. Many achieved material success and distinction, although it must also be noted that they were fairly assimilated. Ol'ga Evgen'evna Gabrilovich, the first woman Master of Pharmacy, was Jewish but very much part of the St. Petersburg establishment.[58]

Gustav Osipovich Gabrilovich may have been Jewish. Owner of pharmacies in Kovno and Minsk in the 1870s and 1880s, he was prominent in civic and philanthropic affairs. The only clue to a possible Jewish affiliation was his position as trustee of the Jewish Hospital in Minsk.[59] In 1906 Gustav Osipovich was elected to a special branch of the Moscow Pharmacy Society.[60]

Gustav Osipovich's son Osip Gustavovich became a famous radical pharmacist. The only clue to his possible Jewish identity was that he attended the Gurevich *gimnaziia* in St. Petersburg. The founder, noted pedagogue Iakov Grigor'evich Gurevich, was Jewish.[61]

Savelii Abramovich Ginzburg studied outside the Pale and contributed to the "pure food" movement. Born in Mogilev in 1873, he attended the Simferopol' *gimnaziia,* took the Assistant Pharmacist examination at Khar'kov University, and then audited courses at Iur'ev University where he received his Master degree in 1896. His dissertation dealt with "Chemical-Sanitary Research on the Sale of Milk in the city of Iur'ev." He published eleven works on food and drug products–on saccharin, the falsification of food products and so on.[62]

Alexander Semenovich Ginzberg loomed large in pharmacy education reform. He published seventeen works on terpinhydrate, chloral hydrate acid.[63] His Jewish affiliation, however, was in very low profile.[64] Isaakh Moiseevich Normanson also was very much part of the "establishment," receiving the title "Honored Citizen" in 1893.[65]

In any case, whatever the defects of pharmacy in late imperial Russia, non-Russian minorities were attracted to the profession. Their motives appear variegated. Pharmacy offered non-Russian minorities, particularly Jews, opportunities for social and physical mobility and advancement. For those who reached the level of Master, pharmacy was intellectually satisfying. Conversely, through the medium of pharmacy many non-Russians, including Jews, made contributions to the profession, to the economy, and to society.

But the status quo in pharmacy and in the empire was soon to undergo enormous changes. Some pharmacists, including Jews and members of other national minorities, were instrumental in making these changes. Other pharmacists, including Jews and members of national minorities, were to suffer from them.

7

Gender: Women Pharmacists in Late Imperial Russia

Men dominated the pharmacy profession in Russia. However, women began to play a role in the late nineteenth century. The strides made by women pharmacists testified to their own enterprise and also to a surprisingly sizable amount of assistance from the imperial government and male pharmacists.

In 1886, Anton Chekhov published the "Aptekarsha." In the story, the *aptekarsha*, unhappy wife of a Provizor, or fully qualified pharmacist, in a small provincial town, is brooding at a window above the pharmacy in the middle of the night. Two officers, a doctor and a lieutenant, come to the pharmacy to purchase seltzer water and medicinal wine, confident that the pharmacist will answer the bell since "pharmacists are obliged to trade at night." The pharmacist is not roused so his wife waits on the two men. When the doctor expresses amazement, never having seen a woman serving in a pharmacy, the pharmacist's wife informs them that she always helps her husband as he has no assistant.[1]

Two years later the Russian government opened the field of pharmacy to women. Women had been allowed to practice as pharmacists in *women*'s medical facilities from 1871.[2] They also had been able to own pharmacies.[3] In 1901, of 3,518 pharmacies in the Russian Empire, wives of pharmacists owned 110 in European Russia and 20 in Asiatic Russia.[4] But they were allowed to become pharmacists with right of general practice only in 1888. This made pharmacy one of the last medically related fields in Russia accessible to women,[5] and put Russia behind the United States,[6] Canada,[7] Great Britain,[8] the Netherlands,[9] and Belgium[10] but in advance of Germany,[11] Austria-Hungary,[12] the Scandinavian countries,[13] Spain,[14] and France.[15]

Sometime after 1871 women petitioned the Ministry of Internal Affairs to allow them to become pharmacists with right of general practice.[16] In 1882, Tsar Alexander III, despite having a conservative reputation and closing most courses for women physicians in that year, approved the request and instructed government agencies to work out procedures.[17] But only in

1888–emphasizing both the thoroughness and dilatoriness of the tsarist government–did the Medical Department of the Ministry of Internal Affairs issue a circular announcing that women could become pharmacy students and take exams for the title Assistant Pharmacist and Provizor. By 1903, women were eligible for the highest degree, Master of Pharmacy.[18] Finnish women were allowed to practice pharmacy in 1902.[19]

Male pharmacists reacted both positively and negatively to the admission of women to their fraternity. At the Second Congress of Pharmacists in 1888, noted pharmacologist A. B. Tikhomirov opposed women in the field.[20] Conversely, other pharmacists immediately took on female apprentices[21] and, in 1892, A. M. Semenov published a pamphlet supporting women pharmacists.[22] In 1889 the physician V. S. Bogoslovskii stressed that the women pharmacists would be competent and were needed because of the great increase in pharmacies, particularly village pharmacies, between 1878 and 1886.[23] Finally, even reluctant male pharmacists were forced to acquiesce to female colleagues because they believed (falsely as it turned out) that pharmacists' numbers were dwindling.[24]

Four leitmotifs surfaced in the saga of women pharmacists in late imperial Russia. First, *determined* women were able to succeed in the field. Second, women pharmacists were virtually equal to their male counterparts. Third, women pharmacists were sympathetic to their female colleagues but feminism was subordinate to economic and class considerations. Fourth, although many women came from non-Russian national minorities, nationalism was not a key factor until World War I.

It took three years' apprenticeship and an examination to become an Assistant Pharmacist. Three years more apprenticeship, two years' university courses, and a second examination were required to become a Provizor. Many Assistant Pharmacists never progressed to this stage. Workdays in turn-of-the-century Russian pharmacies were frequently long. Salaries were adequate but not high. Pharmacists faced night duty several times per month. Since pharmacies were regulated, it was difficult to establish new ones, and prices for existing pharmacies were high. Pharmacy owners faced competition from unregulated drug stores. Pharmacy was in the throes of professionalization.[25] Thus, women could expect that parity would entail burdens as well as rewards.

Nowhere was this more evident that in the arena of pharmaceutical education where reformers bewailed excessive apprenticeship and inadequate formal instruction. Educational requirements for women entering pharmacy were identical to those for men–completion of the equivalent of four years of the eight-year *gimnaziia*. After passing a Latin language examination women certified as governesses could become pharmacy students.[26] Indeed, women enjoyed a slight advantage over male candidates by the first decade of the twentieth century. Whereas in the 1890s there were three times as many boys "in school" as girls,[27] by 1910 there were 958 girls' *gimnazii* compared to 657 boys' *gimnazii* and in 1912 303,690 female *gimnaziia* students compared to 142,935 male *gimnaziia* students.[28] In 1899 both women and men pharmacy students who had finished the full eight years of the *gimnaziia* were allowed to reduce their period of initial apprenticeship from three to two years.[29] In 1900 women graduates of church schools were allowed to become pharmacy students if they took examinations in supplementary subjects.[30]

An apparently confining proviso in the circular of 1888, which forbade pharmacists who hired female apprentices to hire males,[31] was intended to protect women, since pharmacy students often boarded in the pharmacy.[32] In any case it was rescinded in 1892, although women were to live outside the pharmacy and work in daytime if males were employed simultaneously.[33] The circular of 1888 also stipulated that women obtain private pharmaceutical instruction[34] but, in fact, circumstances forced many men to do this as well. Preparatory courses for the Assistant Pharmacist examination were offered in large cities but men typically studied on their own or with tutors during their apprenticeship. Thus, both men and women lacked adequate formal instruction for the Assistant Pharmacist exam.

Women moving to the level of Provizor, or fully fledged pharmacist,[35] initially were more disadvantaged than men as this title required two years' university education. The university was inaccessible to many male pharmacists; those who attended were labeled auditors and denied access to laboratories if places were scarce.[36] However, Russian universities did not even admit women until 1906, and then only for two years. Consequently, the Imperial Military Medical Academy authorized private instruction for the first two women who took the Provizor's exam in 1898.[37]

Nevertheless, the circular of 1888, which admitted women to pharmacy, intended the establishment of their formal instruction, and courses to prepare women for the Assistant Pharmacist and Provizor examinations gradually appeared. In February 1891, St. Petersburg newspapers announced the opening of special courses in pharmacology, botany, and chemistry in the City Aleksandrovskii Barrack hospital to prepare women pharmacy students (*aptekarskie uchenitsy*) for the Assistant Pharmacist examination. Professors from the Military Medical Academy were to lecture.[38] In March 1891, it was reported that special courses for women were to open in universities. Women between seventeen and forty years of age were eligible. After three years they would be able to take the Assistant Pharmacist examination and could serve in a pharmacy. They were not required to complete a preliminary three-year apprenticeship.[39] These courses did not fully materialize. However, the Women's Medical Institute, which opened in St. Petersburg in 1897, was empowered by its statute to prepare women "for pharmaceutical activity."[40] In 1899 the St. Petersburg "Municipal Barrack Hospital in Memory of S. N. Botkin" began to offer courses to prepare women for the degree of Provizor.[41] In Moscow in 1898 the Society of Russian Doctors received permission from the Ministry of Internal Affairs to open special pharmaceutical courses to prepare women for the degrees of Assistant Pharmacist and Provizor.[42] By 1902, the Iur'ev-Dorpat Pharmaceutical Institute in Estland was open to women.[43] In the same year, Antonina Boleslavna Lesnevskaia, one of the first women pharmacists, established a pharmacy school in St. Petersburg to prepare women Assistants and Provizors. Special pharmaceutical courses appeared in other cities[44] although, according to an announcement in *Farmatsevticheskii vestnik* for November 1902, the opening of pharmaceutical courses by the Society of Women Doctors in Warsaw had been deferred indefinitely because of lack of a suitable place.[45] The Russian government also honored foreign degrees.[46] In 1898 a Russian woman, Luisa Tendler, received a doctorate from the New York College of Pharmacy.[47] Thus, by the early twentieth century a modicum of university-level education was available to women aspiring to the degree of Provizor.[48] By February 1905 women were admitted to laboratories at Novorossiisk University in Odessa.[49] In May of that year the Siberian Pharmaceutical Society petitioned the rector of Tomsk University to allow women to attend.[50]

A small band of women immediately entered the field. Anna Mikhailovna Makarova apparently passed the exam for Assistant Pharmacist at Kiev University, March 11, 1892. Antonina Boleslavna Lesnevskaia, qualified as a governess in 1886 and became a pharmacy student in 1889, just before her twenty-third birthday.[51] She received the Assistant Pharmacist title after passing the examination at the Military Medical Academy in October 1893,[52] and received the Provizor degree in April, 1898.[53] Z. (Zinaida) I. Akker studied with her and was awarded the Provizor degree at the same time.[54] Beating them to the finish line by a hair was Stanislavna Frantsevna Doviaglo, who was cited in *Farmatsevticheskii zhurnal*, January 15, 1898, as the first woman to pass the exam for degree of Provizor. The journal noted that the Ministry of Public Enlightenment had permitted two other women to take the Provizor examination.[55] The two, who did so in the fall of 1898, were A. I. Levitan and A. P. Gal'perin-Vogava.[56] Antonina Lesnevskaia (she rarely used her patronymic) was the first to take the examination for the degree Master of Pharmacy at the Military Medical Academy in February 1900.[57] However, Ol'ga Evgen'evna Gabrilovich was the first to actually receive the Master's degree. She took the Master examination at Moscow University in 1904 and defended her thesis, requisite for the title, at the Military Medical Academy in December 1906.[58] Apparently, she was the second woman to receive a learned degree in a Russian educational institution, a woman having received the degree Doctor of Medicine in 1876.[59]

Although figures vary due to inexact terminology, the number of women pharmacy students, Assistant Pharmacists and Provizors increased slowly but steadily in the last two decades of the nineteenth century, indicating women's attraction to pharmacy as a career. According to the 1897 Russian census there were 8,723 pharmacists in the empire, excluding apprentices; 245 pharmacists were women.[60] In 1902 a German pharmacy journal mentioned 500 women "assistants" in Russian pharmacies.[61] In contrast, an 1898 article in *Farmatsevticheskii zhurnal* alluded to about 100 student pharmacists and 29 women pharmacists (26 Assistant Pharmacists and 3 Provizors) in Russia.[62] A 1901 article in *Farmatsevt* provided a breakdown on women pharmacists in the last years of the twentieth century. In 1896, according to this source 60 women students were apprenticing in all the pharmacies in the empire, in 1897 the number "had increased insignificantly" to 62, but the next year, 1898, witnessed a phenomenal leap to 101 women students.[63] For women Assistant Pharmacists this article gave figures of 13 in 1895, 22 in 1896, 28 in 1897, and 47 in 1898. Inexplicably only 41 women Assistant Pharmacists were recorded for 1899.[64] In 1902, J. Schindelmeiser, privatdocent at the Iur'ev-Dorpat Pharmaceutical Institute provided nearly identical statistics, adding 123 women student pharmacists and 56 Assistant Pharmacists in 1900.[65] In 1902, 5 women pharmacists were working in the Caucasus.[66]

Women physicians outnumbered women pharmacists, an understandable phenomenon, in view of the fact that the former profession had at least a ten-year lead. There were over 470 Russian women medical students in 1878 and almost 1,400 by 1903.[67] Also, the number of women pharmacists was meager when compared to men pharmacists. By 1905, official statistics reported a total of 6,800 pharmacists and 4,600 pharmacy students.[68] Nevertheless, the ratio of women pharmacists to men pharmacists in early twentieth-century Russia was comparable with that in the United States. In 1870 there were 34 women out of 17,335 "Traders and Dealers in Medicine" in the United States; in 1900 American women constituted 1,178 "Traders and Dealers in Medicine," compared with 56,168 men in the same category.[69]

Women entered pharmacy for a variety of reasons—emulation of their fathers, desire for intellectual fulfillment, economic security, social advancement, physical mobility, and the fact that there were openings in pharmacy.

Two early pharmacists, Lesnevskaia and Gabrilovich, had physician fathers.[70] Lesnevskaia dreamed of assisting her father, who practiced in a Volga town. She also was determined to have a career and believed pharmacy would be interesting.[71] Eva Broido, who later became a Menshevik, asserted that she entered pharmacy because of "an unquenchable desire for learning but also for escape . . . from the depressing, inactive life at home and in our little town. . . ."[72] Further, Broido's family, comfortably well-off when she was a small child, suffered a reversal of fortune when she was ten, stimulating her to strive for economic security.[73]

Whereas women physicians were predominantly Orthodox, and thus, by implication, Russian, pharmacy was a magnet for minority women in the empire, as for men.[74] Several of the first women pharmacists in the Russian Empire were Poles. Stanislavna Doviaglo (Polish spelling, Stanislawa Dowgiallo), possibly the first woman Provizor in Russia, was born in 1865 in Livonia, graduated from secondary school in Riga in 1889, and took her examination for the Assistant Pharmacist degree at Warsaw University. She audited university courses required for the Provizor degree at the University of Krakow in Austrian Poland, between 1894 and 1897, and passed the Provizor examination at Moscow University late in 1897.[75] Antonina Lesnevskaia was born to a Polish family living in Kostroma province.[76] Her sister Zhosefa (Josepha) Boleslavna, five years her junior, received the Provizor degree in 1910; the Polish woman Provizor Florentina Florian Stankevich, friend of Antonina Lesnevskaia, managed the latter's pharmacy from 1908.[77] Ol'ga Gabrilovich and Eva Broido were Jewish, as were thirteen of eighteen women studying pharmacy at the Iur'ev-Dorpat Pharmaceutical Institute in 1902. Two of the eighteen were Poles; one was a Baltic German.[78] By 1910, there were eighty-five women Provizors, fifty-eight of whom were Jewish and seven Polish; only sixteen were Russian.[79]

However, nationalism was not paramount to these women; rather it appeared their objectives were assimilation and financial and social advancement. The Lesnevskaia sisters' maternal grandparents had participated in the Polish uprising of 1830 and been exiled to Siberia.[80] But like many other cosmopolitan Poles who lived in cities throughout the Russian provinces of the empire,[81] the Polish sympathies of Antonina and Zhosefa Lesnevskaia, Florentina Stankevich, and Doviaglo were in low profile, at least until World War I.[82] Doviaglo worked in Antonina's St. Petersburg pharmacy during 1904; she became active in the Polish School Society only in 1918.[83] Antonina Lesnevskaia received her primary education at the

Roman Catholic school at St. Catherine's Church in St. Petersburg.[84] She established her women's pharmacy adjacent to the neoclassical St. Catherine's Church, in a building, according to one source, owned by the Polish Benevolent Society.[85] The society had been founded in St. Petersburg in 1884.[86] However, this was after four attempts to establish the pharmacy in other locations, described more at length below.[87] Lesnevskaia also published a Polish-language pamphlet on women pharmacists in Warsaw in 1908 (*Nowa dziedzina pracy kobiet*).[88] Yet her other writings were in Russian. Further, Lesnevskaia did not appear to routinely participate in Polish functions in St. Petersburg. Between 1905 and 1909 *Kraj*, the journal that detailed the Polish activities in various Russian cities of the empire, mentioned three times that Polish meetings were held in the building which housed Lesnevskaia's pharmacy but cited her directly only once in contrast to prolific mention of other Poles in St. Petersburg.[89]

Similarly, Eva Broido desired to "escape from the Pale;" she took her Assistant Pharmacist examination at Kazan University and served for a time in a pharmacy in St. Petersburg.[90] Gabrilovich, the first woman Master of Pharmacy, also was Jewish, but was very much a part of the pharmacy establishment and academic community in the capital.[91] Born in St. Petersburg in 1879, she finished the sixth class of the St. Anna *gimnaziia*, apprenticed at the pharmacy in the Aleksandrovsk City Hospital in St. Petersburg, and took the Assistant Pharmacist examination in 1897 and her Provizor examination in 1901 at the Military Medical Academy in St. Petersburg. During 1902 and 1903 she was invited to serve in the Pharmacy Department of the Women's Medical Institute in St. Petersburg. During 1903 and 1904 she took courses for the Master degree at Moscow University.[92] She performed the chemical experiments for her Master's thesis, described further in this chapter, in the laboratory of A. Ia. Danilevskii, at the Military Medical Academy. Since the botanical laboratory of the Military Medical Academy was closed in summer, she conducted her botanical experiments at the St. Petersburg Botanical Gardens under the direction of St. Petersburg University privatdocent I. L. Serbinov.[93]

Another factor propelling women into pharmacy was simply availability of positions. The number of pharmacies continued to expand in the early twentieth century.[94] Conscription of male pharmacists during the Russo-Japanese War of 1904–1905 accentuated the diminution of male Assistant Pharmacists evident at the turn of the century. World War I created further openings for women.[95]

It must be noted that mature women, as well as teen-aged girls, were willing to commit themselves to three to six years' apprenticeship, one to two demanding examinations, special courses, and a considerable outlay of money to become pharmacists. The eighteen women students at the Iur'ev-Dorpat Pharmacy Institute ranged in age from twenty-two to over forty years. One student had graduated from a trade school in Berlin; another had graduated from a conservatory in Leipzig.[96] The first class of twenty-four students at Lesnevskaia's St. Petersburg pharmacy school ranged in age from sixteen to twenty-six. All the women in the school, as well as six on a waiting list, had completed secondary education. This meant that their families had paid the tuition fees, which amounted to half the total support of girls' schools,[97] and that the women or their families were willing to pay the 300 rubles' tuition for the two-year program at Lesnevskaia's school.[98]

Historians have emphasized the difficulties of two of the first women pharmacists, Eva Broido and Antonina Lesnevskaia.[99] However, the women's own reminiscences and, in the case of Lesnevskaia, archival material, provide a more nuanced picture. Following an official announcement in the early 1890s, Broido "took the apothecary's diploma for my target" and although six years' apprenticeship, two years of university courses, and two examinations were daunting, she calculated that "I would be able to earn my living during my apprenticeship and saw nothing further to dismay me. I threw myself into study immediately."[100] She became a pharmacy student at the age of fifteen in Dvinsk. The hours were long—"nine in the morning to nine at night, and often to ten or eleven." But Broido considered the work "only as a means to an end . . . study and more study." Though the work was "dull" and "monotonous" it was also "exacting." She frequently studied until "four o'clock in the morning." Her pay as apprentice was meager—"eight rubles a month (plus free lunch and dinner)" and "out of this" she paid "five rubles for bed and breakfast," sharing a room with her cousin. However, she "usually met for picnics and other gay occasions" with the youths with whom she studied.[101] A male pharmacist colleague loaned her money to travel to Kazan for the Assistant Pharmacist examination and another male helped her find communal lodgings. University life for Broido was "a particularly bright and happy time"; she enjoyed rowing on the river and "nightly gatherings with song and dance."[102] She had no difficulty passing her examinations or getting a position as Assistant Pharmacist. "Having successfully passed my examination, I at once got a job, and that at a salary that made me feel a Croesus—full board and thirty-five rubles a month!"[103] She also quickly got a job when she left her first husband and moved to St. Petersburg in 1899. "I needed a better paid job. Ten days after my arrival I was working in a big chemist's shop [*sic*] on the Vassilyevsky Ostrov."[104] In general, while she recalled life with her first husband as "three years in private hell,"[105] her recollections of her work as a pharmacist exude ebullience.

Antonina Lesnevskaia met some obstacles in her pharmacy career that were gender related. One mentor or "principal's" wife was jealous, she had to teach his children[106] (a fate which also befell other women apprentices).[107] To some inquiries for positions she was asked to send her photograph and received marriage proposals.[108]

But other problems she faced were common to male pharmacists and, indeed, her career as she recounted it in her autobiography, was identical to those of males as they climbed the pharmacy ladder. Her family and friends disapproved her finishing a long education to stand behind a counter rolling pills, preparing powders and pouring castor oil.[109] She was readily accepted as an apprentice numerous times but in two instances was dissatisfied with her training and left of her own accord.[110] Her pay was low and living conditions uncomfortable.[111] On the other hand she developed camaraderie with several principals and they gave her good training.[112] Studying for the Assistant Pharmacist exam in St. Petersburg, as the only woman in a class of forty, she became friends with her classmates.[113] She met no difficulty in getting permission to take or in passing the Assistant Pharmacist, Provizor, and Master exams, although by the time she prepared for the last she was weary.[114] At all stages government officials and professors were helpful.[115] She also had no problems in finding Assistant Pharmacist positions[116] although, in one case, she became exhausted from fourteen-hour days.[117]

Lesnevskaia's record book (*konduitnyi spisok*) substantiates these reminiscences. Her periods of apprenticeship (*stazh*) seem not much more checkered than those for males; the timetable for her Assistant Pharmacist, Provizor, and Master examinations appears similar to that for male pharmacists.[118] She became a pharmacy student in September 1889, following completion of the required study of Latin in the Tver *gimnaziia*. She served "with great success" in the normal pharmacy of Provizor Brzhozovskii (apparently a Pole) from October 1889 till May 1890. From January, 1891 through August 1891, she served in the private pharmacy of Provizor Edreitol'd. The next two years–August 1891 through August 1893–she served in the private pharmacy of Zhanevich.[119] Passing her Assistant Pharmacy examination at the Military Medical Academy October 16, 1893, she served a nearly two-year period of apprenticeship in Zhanevich's pharmacy–from November 1, 1893, through September 1,

1895. This was followed by five months' service (from September 5, 1895, through February 1, 1896) in the private pharmacy of Kosinskii (apparently another Pole); a short stint (from March 1, 1896, to April 25, 1896) in a private pharmacy belonging to one Zhukovskii; and a six-month period of apprenticeship (from October 20, 1896, to April 26, 1897) in the St. Petersburg Rozhdestvenskii Barracks Clinic pharmacy.[120] Passing her Provizor examination April 21, 1898, in the Military Medical Academy, she served as Provizor from July 15 of that year through February 15, 1899, in the Naval Pharmacy in St. Petersburg.[121] She attempted to establish her own pharmacy during this time and studied for her Master's examination, which she passed February 11, 1900.[122]

The experiences of other women aspiring to become pharmacists varied. In 1904, Bertha Aizenshtadt was more negative than Broido or Lesnevskaia, asserting that women encountered special prejudice. However, she also criticized the apprentice system, which prevented adequate training for males as well as females entering pharmacy.[123] In early 1905, Anna Roget, from the Ural region, bitterly described her low pay as a student pharmacist (5 rubles per month) and the burden of caring for the pharmacy owner's children (at 4 rubles per month).[124] But Liubov' Lavrova struck an optimistic note. She emphasized that more women were entering pharmacy each year and with higher qualifications than men since most completed secondary school. She also recommended eliminating the apprentice system.[125]

The feminist commitment of women pharmacists also varied. Antonina Lesnevskaia was sympathetic to aspiring women pharmacists. After receiving her Provizor degree, Lesnevskaia invited her "sisters" to write her for advice on becoming pharmacists and practicing pharmacy.[126] In 1900, she spoke about organizing a society of women pharmacists.[127] In 1901 she established a clearinghouse for women pharmacy students and assistants seeking positions, inviting them, on the one hand, and doctors and pharmacists needing employees, on the other, to contact her.[128]

However, Lesnevskaia was not solely or even predominantly a feminist. She recognized that excessive apprenticeship and lack of educational opportunity was a flaw in turn-of-the-century Russian pharmacy affecting men as well as women, and all her public utterances put women pharmacists' problems in a general context.

In a November 17, 1904, report to the Minister of Internal Affairs, Lesnevskaia criticized the superficial pharmacy education acquired by pharmacy students. "After finishing apprenticeship, the student acquires offhand [*na skoruiu ruku*], outside the pharmacy, from 2 to 8 weeks of scanty, compressed, theoretical information and in universities or the academy takes the exam for the first pharmaceutical degree and again [undergoes] 3 years' unsystematic physical labor in a pharmacy."[129] She emphasized difficulties for women wishing to study for the Provizor examination: "While for men there are two-year courses in the university . . . women . . . must prepare privately.[130] However, she urged the ministry to undertake reform of general as well as women's pharmacy education, namely to: "1) raise the educational qualification for those entering the pharmacy to the 6th–7th classes [of middle school]; 2) *retain artisanal training in pharmacies* for 2-3 years; and 3) after finishing practice [require pharmacists] to begin scientific preparation in higher pharmaceutical institutions, institutes, and faculties, about the opening of which the government has solicited opinions."[131]

A week later she added: "in view of the proposed draft by the Minister of Internal Affairs of a new law on pharmacy education it is necessary to turn serious attention to the full absence of all special scientific preparation of pharmacists."[132] She reiterated the flaws in lower-level pharmacy education as then constituted: ". . . the pharmacy owner . . . has no interest in engaging the student and wastes his time, he pays him a salary of 5 rubles per month and demands that he work . . . for the owner . . . for this money. He is the proprietor and the student serves as a cheap work force." Additionally, "not every pharmacy owner has sufficient knowledge, pedagogical ability, and if he does possess all these, he does not feel obliged to spend time on the student, whom he must utilize."[133] Lesnevskaia emphasized that the pharmacy "does not give and cannot give scientific systematic preparation" and the student gives "only minimal answers to the examiners' stereotyped questions. As a result it is very easy to take the formal examination and the student becomes an Assistant Pharmacist, although in essence he is scarcely different from a student." She called for "basic school preparation," to enable Russia to "preserve public health," "prepare enlightened pharmacists," "compete with foreign pharmacists," "struggle with falsification of pharmaceutical substances," and "finally . . . become competitive in the world market."[134] She urged "all measures to abolish apprenticeship in the pharmacy and artisanal training" and "to institute special pharmacy schools . . . reform of pharmacy education in Russia."[135]

At about the same time, speaking before the Third Congress of Technologists, Lesnevskaia emphasized special difficulties women faced in becoming pharmacists. It was hard for women to begin apprenticeship and complete additional practical work in pharmacies. Most pharmacists wanted cheap labor; pharmacy apprentices and assistants worked fourteen-hour days. Women were often hidden from the public; fifteen women in one Moscow pharmacy worked behind opaque glass. But Lesnevskaia also admitted that men had trouble acquiring the formal education required for the Assistant Pharmacist exam; they could hear university lectures only as auditors and not full-fledged students. In fact, the thrust of this report was that pharmacy education as a whole needed overhauling. Nevertheless, ignoring the university-level courses available to women, she claimed that women were more disadvantaged than men in acquiring formal pharmacy education because they were not admitted to universities at all. She confirmed that professors at the Military Medical Academy had cooperated with her and the other women who first prepared for the Provizor exam but this was not repeated for successive women. Some women took formal courses but many struggled to prepare for the exam for three to six months without laboratories. The full five pages of Lesnevskaia's criticism and suggestions were printed in the February 1, 1904, issue of *Farmatsevticheskii zhurnal.*[136]

Lesnevskaia similarly emphasized both women's problems in becoming pharmacists and inadequate education for all entry-level pharmacists in her address to the First All-Russian Women's Congress, held in St. Petersburg in December 1908. She admitted that women pharmacy students were often forced to double as unpaid governesses. She now alluded to twenty women working in the Moscow pharmacy behind an opaque glass partition. But she also related that professors at the Military Medical Academy had greatly helped her and the other first women pharmacists, decried poor educational facilities for male pharmacy students and Assistant Pharmacists, and affirmed that once women had their degree they received the same pay as men.[137]

In 1912 Lesnevskaia again balanced women pharmacists' problems with those of male pharmacists. She asserted that women had difficulty getting pharmacists to accept them as students, sometimes having to pay as much as 100 rubles to the proprietor. She emphasized that, once accepted, because of owners' fears that they would drive away customers, women often had to work out of the public eye–in late night shifts and as *fasovshchiki* (packers of pharmacy vessels and implements–or were allowed to only sell medicaments, artists' wares and the like over the counter. However, she also contended that women students were more easily accepted in small pharmacies and got more hands-on experience there. Further, more and more often, pharmacies located in the capitals of St. Petersburg and Moscow, while shunning women pharmacy students, invited women to positions of Assistant Pharmacist and Provizor. Some pharmacy owners had begun to send their daughters to special pharmacy courses before putting them to work in their pharmacies.[138]

Lesnevskaia attempted to solve both the problem of women's pharmacy education and that of inadequate early pharmacy education with her "First Women's Pharmacy" and Women's Pharmacy Institute. The pharmacy was to help subsidize the school as well as serve as a training facility. In addition, Lesnevskaia hoped the school and institute would serve as prototypes for upgrading pharmacy education in general.[139]

She petitioned the Medical Department of the Ministry of Internal Affairs to open a women's pharmacy in August 1898, immediately after receiving her Provizor degree, again in May 1899, and, a third time, in January 1900.[140] A German pharmacist observed that Lesnevskaia obtained permission to open her pharmacy only after "difficult battles with the Russian authorities." However, he noted as well that the Minister of Internal Affairs personally intervened and waived the ordinary rules for establishing new normal pharmacies, when he permitted Lesnevskaia to open her pharmacy.[141]

His qualification was important, for although Lesnevskaia had to struggle three years to open her pharmacy, it must be emphasized that she was asking for permission to open a normal (*normal'naia*) pharmacy "outside the rules of May 1873," that is, without the requisite population or prescription norms established by the government. This being the case, as chapters 1 and 3 of this work relate, three years was not an inordinate period in which to acquire permission. Further, the Russian government was very legalistic and, according to an 1893 regulation of the Medical Council of the Ministry of Internal Affairs, women pharmacists were permitted to manage only village (*sel'skie*) pharmacies.[142] Lesnevskaia's biggest problems came not from government officials but from fellow pharmacists. But even here, while some opposition resulted from Lesnevskaia's gender, much of it resulted from established pharmacy owners' dislike of competition. Male prospective pharmacy owners faced the same hurdle.

When Lesnevskaia's petition for a new pharmacy became known, some three letters of opposition were printed in pharmacy journals. One relayed supposed complaints from a former male student. The other two lamented that women would be forced to spend long days at menial labor, such as cutting the labels required for medicaments, filling capsules, and so on.

Lesnevskaia's response revealed the strong personality and the political savvy that enabled her to achieve her goals. She vehemently assailed the criticism of her teaching ability, dismissing her opponent Levitan's statements as "lies." She stoutly insisted that she had twenty-four students, not eight as Levitan had stated, and that her income from them was 700 rubles, not a paltry 240 as he had claimed. She asserted that her students had done very well at their exams and that not one of them had complained about her.[143] She rebutted the general question of women's suitability for pharmacy by noting that male pharmacy students also were forced to perform mundane tasks. The solution was not to prevent women from becoming apprentices but to reform the apprentice system. She advocated shortening the workday in private pharmacies.[144]

But Lesnevskaia also took care to cultivate the pharmaceutical community and undoubtedly this strategy, coupled with her indomitable drive, accounted for the success that characterized her career. At the Third All-Russian Pharmaceutical Congress in 1899 she "expressed her heartfelt . . . hope in the name of all women pharmacists that with general comradeship we would resolve effectively all problems for the general good of science and our society. Women pharmacists have entrusted me to express to all the honorable members the hope that the congress will be successful."[145] This got her high marks from the journal *Farmatsevt,* which described the opening of her First Women's Pharmacy, emphasizing that Lesnevskaia was known to many readers for her energetic support of raising women's pharmacy education at the Third All-Russian Pharmaceutical Congress. The anonymous author averred that this had earned her "the sympathy of her comrades."[146]

Local and central governmental medical officials generally supported Lesnevskaia. Her main problem was getting established pharmacy owners to agree to a new pharmacy in their vicinity. Yet one pharmacy owner generously did so. In May 1900, after debate on the issue of whether women could manage other than village pharmacies, the St. Petersburg Medical Board "suggested that it was possible to approve her request."[147] Lesnevskaia found premises, but the Medical Council disapproved of the address.[148] She found a second place but two nearby owners, A. A. Vagner and M. S. Volkovskii, protested.[149] A third owner, Vestberg, on the other hand, opined that although another normal pharmacy might cause "significant material loss to the normal pharmacies in the locality . . . nevertheless . . . I consider it superfluous and useless to speak about such material losses . . . [and] I personally can support the opening of the pharmacy of Ms. [*gospozha*] Lesnevskaia." He applauded the purpose of her pharmacy.[150] Nevertheless, receiving no decision on the location from the Medical Board, Lesnevskaia found another. On November 30 the St. Petersburg Medical Board rejected it. Instead they offered her a choice of three other locations.[151] Lesnevskaia found premises in one. Two nearby pharmacy owners protested; the third did not answer. This time (January 21, 1901), despite the pharmacy owners' opposition, the St. Petersburg Medical Board approved her choice.[152] Unfortunately, the owner leased the premises to another tenant.[153] However, by mid-February Lesnevskaia found premises in a building adjacent to St. Catherine's Church, 32 Nevskii Prospekt. The medical authorities sanctioned her location within the week.[154]

Lesnevskaia's First Women's Pharmacy (*Pervaia Zhenskaia Apteka*) was ready three months later. It opened with fanfare June 5, 1901.[155] The pharmacy was situated in one of the choicest sections of St. Petersburg, across from the city duma, and near the arcade of shops called the "Gostinnyi Dvor," the Passage women's store, the Singer Sewing Machine Building, and Our Lady of Kazan Cathedral. According to a 1902 account the First Women's Pharmacy had an elegant layout—all white and gold, costing 22,000 rubles. Like all normal pharmacies, whose floor plans the government dictated, the pharmacy had a cash register, a section for over-the-counter items, a prescription area, a "nicely furnished waiting room," and a laboratory. Laboratory equipment was state-of-the-art, including a steam apparatus from Wolff and Sons.[156] Women between sixteen and twenty-six were employed, exclusively. Contemporary photographs portrayed them, attired in white smocks, attentively inspecting lavishly stocked shelves and apparatus.[157]

In her 1901 autobiography, Lesnevskaia blamed both pharmacy owners and staff pharmacists for the class conflict that was rending the pharmaceutical corporation.[158] She herself was a progressive pharmacy owner, instituting double shifts and a seven-hour workday.[159] The women pharmacists she employed handled the night shift but, according to a contemporary observer, no improprieties had occurred during the first six months of operation. Lesnevskaia also provided a lodging house where, the contemporary observer noted that, "incoming girls from the provinces, who would have been exposed to dangers of the capital without shelter, can find food, lodging, and supervision."[160]

The Russian and international press acclaimed Lesnevskaia as a pioneer. She acknowledged that the all-women's pharmacy put Russia in the avant-garde.[161] Reaction of pharmacists and the general public was mixed. Some members of the Society of Russian Pharmacists and Physicians were sympathetic. The public was both curious and skeptical. In some cases patrons took prescriptions filled at the women's pharmacy to neighboring pharmacies, claiming that the original medicine was too weak. Some people were convinced there were male pharmacists working behind the scenes who actually prepared the medicine. Others believed the female pharmacy students were sisters of mercy because they wore white uniforms. About a month after the Women's Pharmacy opened a summer theater performance satirized it. Lesnevskaia asked the St. Petersburg police chief to stop the performance, but the performance induced young drunkards to come to the pharmacy at night for the purpose of harassment.[162]

Still, Lesnevskaia told representatives to the First All-Russian Women's Congress that most often *women* exhibited hostility toward or lack of confidence in her Women's Pharmacy. In one case a physician asked that a prescription for a seriously sick infant be filled at the Women's Pharmacy since it was closest; the mother insisted that the prescription be filled at a pharmacy managed by males. In other instances women bought sundries such as glycerine and cold cream at the Women's Pharmacy but refused to have their prescriptions filled there.[163]

Nevertheless, the First Women's Pharmacy remained healthy until 1918.[164] Woman-Provizor Zinaida I. Akker was the first manager; she was followed by one Bulatava, and in 1908 by Florentina Stankevich.[165] In 1916 two Provizors, ten Assistant Pharmacists and two students staffed the pharmacy.[166]

In the summer of 1901, a month and a half after her pharmacy opened, Lesnevskaia petitioned the Medical Council to open a women's pharmacy school.[167] In January 1902, not having received permission to open the school, she informed medical authorities that she had accepted eleven pharmacy students.[168] The Ministry of Internal Affairs finally approved the statutes for the pharmacy school in January 1903.[169]

Entrance requirements at the Women's Pharmacy school were higher than normal–completion of the full eight years of the female *gimnaziia.*[170] The faculty had good credentials. In 1903 P. L. Mal'chevskii, from the Military Medical Academy, taught chemistry; V. M. Artsikhovskii from the Women's Medical Academy taught botany; S. V. Gol'dberg, Doctor of Medicine, taught anatomy and physiology; V. V. Redikortsev, Doctor of zoology [*sic*] taught that subject; Woman (Medical) Doctor T. P. Sebriakova-Zhitkova taught hygiene and first aid; Lesnevskaia herself taught pharmacognosy, and her friend Zinaida Ivanovna Akker taught pharmaceutical chemistry; one N. A. Orlov taught physics; and N. I. Prokhorov, teacher at the Tenishevskii school taught geology.[171]

Thirty young women applied for the first class although only twenty-four were accepted due to space constraints.[172] The curriculum, which was two years or four semesters in length, appeared to provide excellent preparation for pharmacy. Lesnevskaia considered it nearly equal to the full university course demanded for Provizor; certainly it was more thorough than the six- to eight-week courses she claimed most pharmacists took with Provizors in university cities in order to pass the Assistant Pharmacist exam.[173] Liubov' Lavrova, one of the successful graduates, claimed in 1904 that the program at Lesnevskaia's school "included all that was necessary for a Provizor degree (in other words equal to the first two years of university)" and "all the subjects of the first two courses of the Women's Medical Institute with wider requirements in chemistry and pharmaceutical sciences."[174] It also is interesting to note that the program in Lesnevskaia's Women's Pharmacy School was very similar to the program for new Soviet pharmacy schools which I. Levinshtein, Director of the State Pharmacy Administration, advocated in November 1921.[175]

Women in the first year of Lesnevskaia's women's pharmacy school studied–weekly–three hours of chemistry, two hours of zoology, two hours of physics, two hours of botany with practical application, and one hour of mathematics. The second year lectures, per week, consisted of two hours of organic chemistry, two hours of analytical chemistry, two hours of pharmaceutical chemistry, one hour of pharmacognosy, two hours of mineralogy and geology, three hours of botany, one hour of hygiene, one hour of pharmacology, two hours of physics, and a half hour of jurisprudence. All chemistry courses included laboratory work with quantitative and qualitative analysis and use of microscopes where appropriate. One contemporary photograph recorded such a class–twenty-four serious women seated in a rococo room adorned with a portrait of Tsarina Alexandra, waiting expectantly for chemistry professor Mal'chevskii, standing before a table laden with vessels and apparatus, to begin his lecture. The curriculum paid special attention to preparation of prescriptions and first aid. In the first year, students performed practical work for three to four hours weekly in a special pharmacy connected with the school. During the fourteen-week summer vacation, students were required to work at least six weeks in a zemstvo, village, or normal pharmacy. During their second year, students worked four hours per day in the Women's Pharmacy. Students finishing the program were then eligible to take the Assistant Pharmacist exam.[176]

The government granted graduates of Lesnevskaia's school preferential treatment in admitting them to the Assistant Pharmacist examinations. Normally the Military Medical Academy allowed only three-fifths of the pharmacy students who applied each semester to take the examination; the remainder had to work not less than one year in St. Petersburg pharmacies–obviously a disappointment, if not an outright hardship. Authorities waived this limitation for Lesnevskaia's students, admitting the entire class.[177]

The happy symbiosis between Lesnevskaia and the pharmacy establishment prevailed until the collapse of the tsarist government. However, the solidarity between Lesnevskaia and her feminist and socialist "sisters" became strained in 1904 and 1905. Some women pharmacists exhibited radical tendencies. Eva Broido became a revolutionary, married a fellow revolutionary, and was exiled to Siberia. There she periodically worked as a pharmacist, once in a municipal dispensary in Yakutsk.[178] Some women pharmacists participated in strikes in 1905. A few women pharmacists became prominent in male-dominated socialist organizations. F. Lapitskaia was elected secretary of the Southwest Union of Staff Pharmacists in 1911[179]; one Rubasheva and S. Lapitskaia were elected officers in the Menshevik-oriented St. Petersburg Society of Staff Pharmacists in 1914. Other feminist-socialist women pharmacists repudiated male-dominated organizations. In Moscow, contending that pharmacy owners willingly hired women pharmacists only because they "pay them a lower salary and get more work. In other words, women appear an element which can be exploited," some women pharmacists rejected the Russian Pharmacy Society and decided to form "their own circles, where women can freely attend to their own needs."[180]

Antonina Lesnevskaia and her colleagues, on the contrary, identified with the establishment. Lesnevskaia owned a pharmacy; Zinaida Akker and Florentina Stankevich managed it; Zhosefa Lesnevskaia worked in it. Stanislavna Doviaglo managed her own pharmacy in Livonia from 1897 to 1900. Ol'ga Gabrilovich, Liubov' Nikolaevna Lavrova, and L. A. Kovaleva, whose contributions are reviewed below, became respected, published pharmacologists. There is no evidence that Lesnevskaia supported the suffragist movement. She was sympathetic to pharmacist workers and established a model regimen for the women working in her own pharmacy. In 1905 it was rumored that she was connected with a new Women's Pharmacy Society in St. Petersburg.[181] However, her individualism and entrepreneurial instincts ill-disposed her to the militant feminism and socialism espoused by some women.[182]

In 1904 and 1905 two incidents occurred that showed the gulf between Lesnevskaia and her feminist, socialist "sisters." Lesnevskaia did not initiate either conflict. The first underscored her professionalism and competency, the lack of these traits on the part of her sisters, and their unscrupulousness as well. The second showed Lesnevskaia to be a pharmacist first and a feminist second. Her commitment to pharmacy and the solvency of her pharmacy and proprietary pharmacy school superseded her commitment to feminism.

The first fissure between Lesnevskaia and her "sisters" involved the establishment of a Second Women's Pharmacy and pharmacy school. In May 1904, Princess Evgeniia Maksimilianovna Ol'denburgskaia asked Minister of Internal Affairs Pleve to permit the Society for Preservation of Women's Health, of which she was sponsor, to open in St. Petersburg "a pharmacy and pharmacy courses for women." Ol'denburgskaia enthused that the proposed manager: "The chairman of Administration of the Society, Woman Doctor Volkova, is personally known to me as knowledgeable, wise, and serious."[183] The Society for Preservation of Women's Health obviously copied Lesnevskaia's prototype. The society proposed to open a pharmacy with right of private dispensation. The pharmacy was to have two functions. First, it would make medicine available to poor women at a 50 percent discount. Second, as in Lesnevskaia's operation, the pharmacy would support students at the pharmacy school and give students practical training. The courses were to prepare women for the Assistant Pharmacist and Provizor titles.[184]

The Chief Medical Inspector was sympathetic. He recommended that the Committee of Ministers approve the society's proposal, noting that "On 17 January 1903 a Decision the Committee of Ministers permitted in the First Women's Pharmacy of A. B. Lesnevskaia the institution of a pharmacy school for women. . . . Now, her Imperial Highness Princess Evgeniia Maksimilianovna Ol'denburgskaia has sent me a proposal in the name of the Society for Preservation of Women's Health about permitting the Society to open a pharmacy . . . and pharmacy courses. . . . The academic preparation of women wishing to enter pharmacy is fully desirable and correct . . . I suggest approval . . . on the same basis as the request of *Grazhdanina* Lesnevskaia . . . to open outside the rules."[185]

Not only did Princess Ol'denburgskaia and her group imitate Lesnevskaia but their pharmacy and school was to be located at no. 65, Nevskii Prospekt,[186] just down the street from Lesnevskaia's pharmacy and school at no. 32 Nevskii. This would have resulted in strong competition for Lesnevskaia, for the Women's Society Pharmacy was to dispense medicine at a 50 percent discount. Additionally, the society had sizable capital at its disposal. One pharmacy journal alleged that the society contributed 20,000 rubles to the project and sold 700 shares of stock at 50 rubles a share to raise the total 35,000 rubles estimated as necessary for establishing the pharmacy.[187]

Princess Ol'denburgskaia spared no efforts to get her pharmacy and school implemented, regardless of the impact they would make on Lesnevskaia's institutions. She periodically dashed off letters to high officials such as P. D. Sviatopolk-Mirskii, who occupied the post of Minister of Internal Affairs in 1904.[188]

To their credit, the medical authorities in St. Petersburg opposed the plan. Princess Ol'denburgskaia complained, with considerable chutzpah, to Minister of Internal Affairs Bulygin, who succeeded the assassinated Sviatopolk-Mirskii, that "the Capital Medical Administration will not allow the Society to open the pharmacy in that place, in view of the proximity of . . . [other] pharmacies, although not long ago, as much as is known to me, there was permitted the opening of a pharmacy, in nearly the same conditions, by the woman doctor [*sic*] Lisnevskoi [*sic*]." Ol'denburgskaia insisted that "I have spent a lot of time and the society will have great difficulty in locating another place within the allotted yearly date for the opening." She asked Bulygin to override the objections of the St. Petersburg Medical Administration and ranted on about Woman Doctor Volkova's sterling qualifications.[189] Next, Ol'denburgskaia trained her guns on Chief Medical Inspector Vasilii Konstantinovich fon Anrep, lamenting that the "St. Petersburg Medical Inspector would not allow the Society to open their pharmacy next door to the pharmacies of other people." She urged him not to refuse the Society's request since "the successful activity . . . depends upon the growth of organizing the hygienic courses."[190]

Although initially, the pharmacy and school of the "Society for Preservation of Women's Health" presented formidable competition for Lesnevskaia, the project eventually collapsed. The society did not open its pharmacy on Nevskii Prospekt, but rather "in the Liteinyi region, Znamenskaia Street, no. 15." The society claimed to have "accumulated capital of 14,700 rubles . . . of private persons . . . on a stock basis."[191] However, the enterprise was a financial disaster. By 1909 the society was pleading with the authorities to allow them to sell their pharmacy.

> Unfortunately, the enterprise of the society not only did not bring the expected income, but three-year operation of it finished with sad results: the society made expenditures of more than 5,000 rubles not counting expenditures for the premises and management of the pharmacy and, above this, spent for wares 8,000 rubles, for payment of which it did not have means.
>
> Following the impossibility to continue business because of loss of credit and absence of means, and recognizing the necessity to satisfy creditors, for loans of money to the society to open the pharmacy and for medicaments, the members of the society in a general meeting of April 3, 1909, came to the conclusion to quickly liquidate the business of the pharmacy and sell it for a price not lower than 35,000 rubles.[192]

The problem, however, was that special privilege to open the pharmacy "outside the rules," for which Ol'denburgskaia had agitated, precluded selling it. "Titular Councillor Provizor Kiril Nikolaevich Granat agreed to buy the pharmacy for the desired sum, but, realizing that Imperial approval to the Society did not involve selling the pharmacy, the Society requested the Minister of Internal Affairs to allow them to do so."[193] When no dispensation from the rules was forthcoming, Woman Doctor Volkova wrote to Emperor Nicholas himself relating the financial problems of the society and asking permission to sell the pharmacy.[194]

The matter dragged on through 1910. The Chief Medical Inspector and Minister of Internal Affairs Stolypin did not "recognize it possible to satisfy the [Society's] request."[195] Maria Volkova again begged permission to sell the pharmacy to Kiril Granat; State Secretary Baron Budbeg became her advocate. At last, in October 1910, His Imperial Highness Nicholas II directed the Minister of Internal Affairs to allow the society to sell the pharmacy to Granat.[196]

A more positive imitation of Lesnevskaia's pharmacy and school occurred in 1906 in Kiev. There, two women Provizors requested permission to open a pharmacy staffed exclusively by women.[197]

On the heels of the Second Women's Pharmacy embroglio, strikes broke out in St. Petersburg pharmacies in September 1905[198] and engulfed Lesnevskaia's pharmacy. Through late 1904, all had been well. In December of that year, pharmacy journals carried announcements that applications for Lesnevskaia's school spring 1905 term should be sent before December 15.[199] That the women in Lesnevskaia's First Women's Pharmacy joined the strike, despite the fact that the pharmacy was run on progressive lines, is one of the strongest proofs that agitators rather than real grievances had fanned if not fomented strikes in 1905.

The strikers' chief demands–a seven-hour day and two shifts–had already been met at Lesnevskaia's pharmacy. Thus, her instinct as a responsible owner dictated her reaction to the upheaval. On October 10, 1905 (perhaps to protect herself from legal problems, perhaps to combat the strike in the pharmacy), she turned over management of her school to Woman Doctor I. I. Charnomskaia.[200] On November 3, she purportedly announced to a meeting of pharmacists in St. Petersburg that she was sympathetic to the strike. However, on November 9 she gave notice to her women pharmacists that they would be fired unless they stopped striking. Additionally, she forbade them to participate either in further strikes or even in meetings of staff pharmacists.[201] When the strikers resisted Lesnevskaia proposed to the students of the pharmacy school that they take over the responsibilities of the striking pharmacists. The students refused and Lesnevskaia retaliated by declaring the school closed until September 1, 1906. The students, in turn, protested, noting that having paid 150 rubles per year they were entitled to the courses. However, Lesnevskaia refused to revoke her decision and the students threatened a lawsuit.[202]

Lesnevskaia reopened the women's pharmacy school October 20, 1906. The faculty included three women teachers–A. A. Kasuskaia for anatomy and physiology; Lidia Aleksandrovna Ergunova for pharmacology, "optotherapy," and "serotherapy"; and Vera Vladimirovna Berezina, for physics.[203] But the upheavals of 1905 cost Lesnevskaia as other proprietors. In 1906 she informed the government that the school was expensive and asked to be freed from taxes (probably city property or turnover taxes). The authorities granted her request.[204]

Lesnevskaia subsequently mended her fences with feminists and socialists. In 1907, the Social Democratic journal, *Farmatsevticheskii trud* announced that "the pharmacy women's courses established by the founder of the First Women's Pharmacy, A. B. Lesnevskaia, have begun acceptance of those wishing to enter the [spring] courses."[205] In 1908 Lesnevskaia participated in the All-Russian Women's Congress, as described above, and in April 1909 hosted a meeting of the women's section of the St. Petersburg Polish *kolo,* which was establishing training courses for practical work, such as furrier, for the winter season.[206]

Minister of Public Enlightenment A. N. Schwarts forbade women to attend university in 1908.[207] However, opportunities for women's pharmaceutical education enlarged slightly. E. Ia. Abol', whose rocky path to founding a private pharmacy school will be recounted in a later chapter, finally opened "the first women's pharmacy courses in Moscow," September 1910.[208] For some years–according to one newspaper as a result of the "emancipation movement"–women Assistant Pharmacists in Kiev audited courses at St. Vladimir University in the capacity of private auditors. In 1910, when the Minister of Public Enlightenment closed Provizor courses at the university because only Jews had applied, these women "turned to the Dean of the medical faculty requesting permission to take the Provizor examination as "externs." Their request, which contested two policies of the Minister of Education–one against Jews, the other against women–was "satisfied."[209]

The major contribution to pharmacy education for women and a major contribution to the reform of pharmacy education in general came from Antonina Lesnevskaia's school. In 1910 her school added a third year to prepare women Assistant Pharmacists for the Provizor title. Tuition was 200 rubles.[210] Enrollment leapt from 23 and 22 in 1903 and 1904, to 62 in 1905, dropped to 40 in 1906, shot to 54 in 1907, and averaged at 40 in 1908, 1909, 1910, falling to 25 in 1911.[211] By 1913, 387 women had attended the school[212] and 199 had graduated, one (Liubov' Lavrova) dying an untimely death in 1908.[213] Fourteen graduates took the Provizor's exam; 184 received the Assistant title.[214] Two of those receiving Provizor degrees, N. F. Kasperovich and Zhosefa Lesnevskaia, Antonina's sister, remained as assistants in Lesnevskaia's pharmacy school.[215] In the 1908 First All-Russian Women's Congress Lesnevskaia asserted that thirty-nine of those who had graduated from her school by that time worked in St. Petersburg pharmacies–predominantly in city pharmacies and those owned by societies; three worked in private pharmacies. The majority of graduates had received places in the provinces.[216] In 1912 Lesnevskaia reported a reverse trend–nearly 100 of the 198 living graduates worked in St. Petersburg. Many of those graduates who had become Provizors managed zemstvo and railroad pharmacies or those owned by societies.[217] In 1913 two former students managed their own pharmacies.[218] Two former students, Liubov' Nikolaevna Lavrova and L. A. Kovaleva, discussed below, did research at the Institute of Experimental Medicine.[219]

The Russian government acknowledged Lesnevskaia's achievements. In 1912 the Ministry of Internal Affairs and the Ministry of Public Enlightenment recognized her school as the exclusive institution for training women pharmacists, stating that they planned to upgrade the school to a scientific institute of pharmacy in 1913.[220] While the Medical Council announced in 1913 that the Women's Medical Institute in St. Petersburg would also establish a Pharmacy Department to provide higher education courses for women pharmacists,[221] Assistant Chief Medical Inspector P. N. Bulatov praised Antonina's school at its tenth anniversary celebration January 29, 1913.[222]

Lesnevskaia's determination and political skills never wavered. In 1914 Bulatov was chair of the Pedagogical Council of the school.[223] And, in May of that year she requested of Minister of Finance Peter Bark an annual 3,000 ruble subsidy for the next five years because tuition and income from the Women's Pharmacy were not adequate to maintain the school. He and Minister of Internal Affairs N. A. Maklakov acceded to her request.[224]

During World War I a fourth year was added to the curriculum and Lesnevskaia's school was finally upgraded to a Pharmacy Institute. In 1916, *Farmatsevticheskii zhurnal* noted that

> on the basis of a rule of 1 July, 1916, on private educational institutions, A. B. Lesnevskaia, founder of the First Women's Pharmacy and Pharmacy School, received permission . . . to open women's pharmaceutical courses. The courses will be four years with two departments. The first two years will involve preparation for the degree Assistant, the second two for the degree Provizor. . . . This year only the first department for degree of Assistant will begin in September. Applicants are limited to those who have a school-leaving certificate from a middle educational institution and have taken the examination for Latin for the fourth class of the male *gimnaziia*.[225]

Some of Lesnevskaia's male colleagues generously applauded her educational experiments and her success. Others spitefully ignored her. The socialist journal *Farmatsevticheskii vestnik* (ironically) lauded her achievement. In 1904 the journal noted that "If one private pharmacy in St. Petersburg can establish a school for women assistant pharmacists it should not be difficult for the Government to build five or even ten."[226] V. V. Rumiantsev praised Lesnevskaia's school in 1912.[227] On the other hand, T. I. Lonachevskii-Petruniak, professor at St. Vladimir University in Kiev, did not mention Lesnevskaia's school in his 1905 plea for pharmacy institutes.[228] And influential St. Petersburg pharmacist Alexander Semenovich Ginzberg[229] ignored Lesnevskaia's school in his 1913, twelve-page pamphlet on pharmaceutical education.[230]

The emerging network of medical and pharmaceutical facilities for women[231] began to bear fruit by the early twentieth century. A handful of women Master Pharmacists made serious scientific contributions. Ol'ga Evgen'evna Gabrilovich, contemporary of Lesnevskaia, wrote her Master of Pharmacy thesis on "The Cause of [so-called] Intoxicating Bread." At her defense in the Military Medical Academy, December 21, 1906, her "opponents" Academician A. Ia. Danilevskii, Professor V. K. Varlikh and privatdocent M. D. Il'in, termed it a "colossal work, which had taken two years–the first, according to Danilevskii, to find a simple method of separating healthy flour from harmful–very important for practical life."[232]

Gabrilovich's thesis responded to a disease which occurred a few hours after eating rye bread. Symptoms included throat ache, dizziness, deterioration of vision, and vomiting. The disease attacked animals as well as humans and usually ended in twenty-four hours. Since the symptoms were similar to those resulting from drinking too much vodka the bread had been nicknamed "intoxicating bread."[233] This disease occurred in dry regions during rainy years[234] but was distinct from ergotism.[235] The disease had appeared in Sweden, Germany, and France. In Russia it was especially prevalent in the dry localities of the southern Ukraine but had been noted in 1904 in the northern part of Tikhvinsk district, Novgorod province, Vologda, Novoladoga, and Shlissel'burg. It had pernicious repercussions in Belozersk in early 1905.[236] In order to combat the disease several district zemstvo executive committees requested that the St. Petersburg Society for Preservation of Public Health investigate both rye kernels and flour.[237] In 1905 the Russian Society for the Preservation of Public Health sponsored research on the problem and the Medical Academy offered a prize for papers on the subject.[238]

According to Gabrilovich, there was little literature on the disease caused by "intoxicating bread." In 1883 a Swedish physician, Erikson, described the disease in Sweden; a more detailed work of 1888 described the disease in the Ussuri region of southeastern Siberia. The disease sometimes affected kernels of millet, oatmeal, and hemp. The main clue was that kernels milled into the flour that caused intoxication were rosy or darkened. A number of scientists had attempted to determine the substance that affected the kernels but their results had not been definitive.[239] There were three possible culprits. Through laborious chemical experiments and tests of both kernels and flour on frogs, Gabrilovich concluded that the most likely cause of the disease was the fungus *Fusarium roseum link*, a glucoside whose nitrous content was formed at the expense of protein in the rye kernel, thus depriving the rye of nutrition.[240] Gabrilovich's work appeared extremely careful and thorough. Unfortunately, in the course of her experiments she noted the coexistence of penicillin and bacteria in her petri dishes but did not note penicillin's effect on bacteria.[241]

The audience applauded Gabrilovich at her defense, and the pharmaceutical press hailed her thesis as "especially important, being the first case of a major independent work of a woman pharmacist in Russia, attaining the degree of Master of Pharmacy, and because of the major significance of the topic in the contemporary life of our peasantry"; the press saluted Gabrilovich as a "pioneer in the matter of attaining the highest pharmacy degree."[242]

Liubov' Nikolaevna Lavrova, graduate of Lesnevskaia's women's pharmacy school, did seminal research on a method of preventing arteriosclerosis resulting from massive injections of adrenalin. This research, necessitated by the therapeutics of the early twentieth century, was crucial, and it appears that Lavrova's findings may have preempted those of a German scientist. Unfortunately Lavrova died in 1908.

Scientists had isolated adrenalin in the early twentieth century. They injected massive amounts into patients to combat enlarged, obtrusive red veins, particularly those on the face. For example, in 1909 Khar'kov physician E. A. Rothmann informed the British medical journal *The Lancet* that he had successfully injected adrenalin, one of the strongest "vaso-constrictors," into two patients in 1907 to cure the condition known as "red nose" or "erythematous taches."[243] Unfortunately, this treatment frequently also enlarged the walls of the blood vessels and affected the heart with fatal results.[244]

Lavrova thoroughly reviewed previous methods of combating pernicious effects of massive injections of adrenalin. During 1906 she conducted numerous experiments on rabbits and dogs and concluded that iodine and iodine salts were the substances that could successfully counter vascular changes leading to arteriosclerosis resulting from injections of adrenalin.[245]

Lavrova's work, "O deistvii ioda na patologicheskiia izmeneniia v sosudakh, obuslovlivaemyia vvedeniem zhivotnym adrenalina," was published early in 1908.[246] In November 1908, *The Lancet* announced that a German scientist, Dr. Mansfield, had successfully conducted experiments showing that one grain of cholin subcutaneously injected prevented serious disease of the aorta in rabbits who had been injected with two and a half grains of adrenalin.[247] Allowing for a time lag in the German researcher's reporting and publication, it appears that Lavrova's experiments preceded his.

L. A. Kovaleva graduated from Lesnevskaia's school in 1908. She then did research in the Institute of Experimental Medicine, receiving her Provizor degree in 1912. Kovaleva published two articles. One detailed her research on the effect of *fotin* on the oxidization and breathing ability of humans. A second, published in 1912, reported her research on the effect of preparations of phosphorous–most specifically lecithin–on the oxidization processes of animals. After testing a number of phosphorous compounds on rabbits, Kovaleva concluded that only lecithin raised both breathing coefficients and the ability to oxidize.[248]

In the years immediately preceding World War I, women pharmacists did not achieve complete equality with men but their position was respectable. Women pharmacists continued to be outnumbered by men. By 1910 there were 85 women Provizors as compared with 4,724 men Provizors. Women Provizors, therefore, amounted to only 1.8 percent of the total number of Provizors. The majority of women Provizors received their degrees at Moscow and Khar'kov universities between 1907 and 1910.[249] There were only a handful of women Masters of Pharmacy. The Russian Medical Register for 1916 recorded only three–Ol'ga Evgen'evna Gabrilovich, Kaz. [*sic*] Vladislavna Zaluska, and Konstant. [*sic*] Tsomaia.[250] But on the credit side of the ledger, women Provizors owned three rural and five normal, or fully stocked, pharmacies in their own right and almost one-third of women Provizors managed normal pharmacies. Interestingly, the majority of women pharmacists were single.[251]

In 1913 a woman, E. S. Morshiner, owned a warehouse of pharmaceutical and cosmetic wares in Mogilev. She petitioned the supervisor of the postal-telegraph district to allow her to have a post office in her enterprise. He was agreeable.[252]

Women pharmacists' salaries varied. Lesnevskaia had reported to the First All-Russian Women's Congress in 1908 that women pharmacists' pay was commensurate with men's. She asserted that women Assistant Pharmacists received between 50 and 90 rubles per month–600 to 1,080 per year; women Provizors' salaries ranged from 100 to 150 rubles per month–1,200 to 1,800 per year.[253]

No doubt women pharmacists sometimes received less pay than men.[254]

However, random data supported Lesnevskaia's contentions. In 1913 *Farmatsevticheskii zhurnal* claimed that "Assistant Provizors" made 50 to 75 rubles per month and that Provizors made between 75 to 150 rubles per month.[255] In 1913, Provizors at an average pharmacy in a provincial city received 1,200 rubles per year, senior Assistant Pharmacists received 800 rubles, and junior Assistant Pharmacists received 720 rubles.[256] Undoubtedly there had been some inflation between 1908 and 1913. In 1914 in the First City Pharmacy in Tomsk, women pharmacists did not occupy high positions but their pay was nearly equivalent to that of their male counterparts. The male manager of the pharmacy received a salary of 2,000 rubles per year including an apartment, light, and heat. The assistant manager, a male Provizor, received 100 rubles per month. The female laboratory technician and two male pharmacist-receptionist-dispensers received 80 rubles per month; the only inequality apparent was that the female had worked at the pharmacy since 1907 whereas the male receptionist-dispensers had worked there only from 1913, the previous year. But the pay of the female Assistant Pharmacist was higher than that of the male Assistant Pharmacist—the woman being paid 60 rubles per month and the man 50 rubles per month. Both had worked at the pharmacy the same length of time—since the summer of the previous year, 1913. The male "accountant" in charge of the pharmacy's material needs and prescription records also was paid 60 rubles per month. The two male pharmacy students, one in service at the pharmacy from 1910, the other from 1914, received only 35 and 30 rubles per month, respectively. The two female cashiers, who had both worked at the pharmacy from the previous year, 1913, earned 25 rubles per month.[257]

Although some pharmacies had introduced double shifts as early as 1904,[258] double shifts and seven-hour days were fairly common in large cities by 1910, and women pharmacists undoubtedly benefited.[259] The woman Assistant Pharmacist at the Tomsk City Pharmacy worked the same hours and fulfilled the same responsibilities as her male associates. The pharmacy personnel, excluding the manager, laboratory technician, cashiers, and menials or cleaning help, worked six-hour shifts, alternating between day shifts, which began at nine and ended at three, and evening shifts, which began at three and ended at nine in the evening. In addition, all pharmacists, including students, had night duty every five days. At these times pharmacists, including the female Assistant Pharmacist, and students worked twenty-four hours straight—from three in the afternoon through the nine in the evening, followed by the day shift. The night shift personnel worked in pairs composed of a pharmacist and a student. Obviously, the woman Assistant Pharmacist worked alongside a male student when on night duty. The female cashiers alternated seven-hour shifts, one day from eight until three, the next day from three in the afternoon to ten at night.[260]

Despite these hopeful signs, in the spring of 1914 there were also hints of trouble brewing—omens that the 1905 clashes between "establishment" women pharmacists like Antonina Lesnevskaia and her socialist sisters might recur. On February 23, International Women's Day, one hundred members attended a general meeting of the Menshevik-oriented[261] Professional Union of Pharmacy Workers in the city of St. Petersburg and elected a Women's Presidium. One Rubasheva was elected chair, one Kaminskaia, associate chair, and one Akselrod, secretary.[262] S. Lapitskaia[263] presented the first report. She emphasized that despite the existence of a proletarian holiday, women workers needed a special day. She averred that women workers were subordinate to men, machines had had an adverse affect on the family, and although the numbers of women in industry had increased they received lower pay than men. In a second report Rubasheva presented a bleak picture of women pharmacists prior to 1905–1906, when they competed against men and were compelled to teach pharmacy owners' children, but she stated that after 1906 conditions for women pharmacy workers had improved with higher pay and decreased night duty and that women in pharmacies already were an independent force. Unfortunately, in her opinion, only an insignificant part of women—20 percent of St. Petersburg staff—were members of the professional union. In conclusion, a resolution was adopted that "only friendly struggle together with their male comrades could better the difficult position of women pharmacy workers."[264] Lapitskaia also wrote an article terming unemployment a capitalist device and praising her union's St. Petersburg Labor Bureau, which had found jobs for twenty-seven of thirty-two registered in two and a half months.[265]

Indeed, much would change for Russian pharmacists, both male and female, during the turmoil of World War I and the revolutions of 1917.[266] But on the eve of these upheavals pharmacy provided an interesting and obtainable career for *determined* women. Women were able to enter pharmacy and were accepted on fairly equal terms with men because pharmaceutical practice was in flux. Women choosing pharmacy had to share with their male colleagues various problems and the drive for professionalization. This, in turn, presented women with opportunities, which a few seized, making contributions to pharmacy, pharmacology, and the advancement of women in Russia.

8

The Russian Pharmaceutical Industry Before World War I: Signs of Health

Well into the twentieth century, Russian pharmacists compounded medicines in pharmacy laboratories. This is still the case in Russia today. However, during the nineteenth century a pharmaceutical industry emerged in Russia. As in Western Europe,[1] its rise was due to a constellation of factors. In Russia these included government programs for collecting and cultivating medicinal plants; development of a chemical industry; large-scale manufacture and sale of cosmetics; pharmacists' discoveries; increasing interest in public health; and entrepreneurial energy.

Thus, some impetus for the pharmaceutical industry came from above, from the government. Some came from pharmacist researchers. And some came from entrepreneurs–mainly pharmacists–who responded to public needs and market forces. Indeed, the story of the pharmaceutical industry particularly highlights the complexity of the pre-Soviet Russian economy–the entrepreneurship that percolated through prerevolutionary Russia but also the political, economic, and cultural factors that thwarted Russian industry and business.

The Russian government, more accurately progressive rulers, inaugurated large-scale production of medicines in Russia. Ivan III established a medical garden in Moscow in the second half of the fifteenth century. In the mid-seventeenth century Tsar Alexei Romanov established a second medical garden. The government mandated collection of medicinal plants, sending out skilled persons (*travniki*) to locate wild medicinal plants and ordering local authorities to purchase medicinal plants from the populace.[2] The government controlled the rhubarb trade and supervised the quality of this purgative.[3]

Progressive rulers continued to promote large-scale production of medicines in the eighteenth and early nineteenth centuries. In 1716 Peter the

Great established a pharmaceutical garden on Apothecary Island in his new capital St. Petersburg. He also encouraged chemical factories, issuing the first two concessions (to foreigners) to produce the corrosive vitriol and sulfur from pyrites in 1718. Although they were short-lived, other vitriol enterprises were established in the eighteenth century in Yaroslavl', Tambov, and other provinces. Catherine the Great followed in his footsteps. By the 1760s there were twenty-five vitriol and sixteen dye factories.[4] The government allowed a modicum of free enterprise in the rhubarb trade in the early eighteenth century, although it subsequently took back control.[5]

The Russian chemical and dye industry laid the foundation for the pharmaceutical industry. And while the government forced the industry at first, entrepreneurs–Russian as well as foreign–quickly expanded it. Between 1825 and 1830 ten chemical and dye factories sprouted in Moscow province alone. By the 1830s factories in twenty cities of the empire produced a total of 100,000 *pud*s of sulfuric acid.[6] Chemical factories grew markedly between 1830 and the Crimean War. In 1832 there were 57; in 1842, 98; and in 1850, 111.[7] They produced substances such as sulfuric acid, carbolic magnesia, and salts of copper, zinc, and boric acid for pharmacies.[8]

The government assisted the chemical industry by establishing courses on factory technology at Moscow, Kazan, and Khar'kov universities in 1804 and at St. Petersburg University in 1819.[9] The government also protected the industry with high tariffs in the first half of the nineteenth century. But Russian factory owners competed with foreign firms on their own. Many enterprises used steam power and, in the first half of the nineteenth century, produced twenty-six chemicals as cheap or cheaper than British factories.[10]

Large-scale production of cosmetics stimulated the development of a Russian pharmaceutical industry. Cosmetics factories sprang up in the seventeenth century, apparently completely under the auspices of private entrepreneurs. By the last quarter of the eighteenth century, a white cosmetic (*belila*) was a familiar substance in the countryside as well as towns. By the beginning of the nineteenth century large quantities of powder, pomade, and other cosmetic substances were hawked in Russia. By 1843 there were fourteen cosmetic factories in Moscow province alone. The largest, the Musatov concern, employed thirty-eight workers and made twenty products, at an annual income of 126,000 rubles.[11]

By the nineteenth century, private enterprise also began to assume a leading role in the collection and cultivation of medicinal plants. For example, in Poltava province in the Ukraine, a treasury pharmacy was established in 1730 and a pharmaceutical garden and two plantations soon after. In the early nineteenth century, Frants Del' established a private pharmacy and began to assume control over cultivation and export of medicinal plants. This province, particularly Lubiansk district, remained a thriving center of medicinal plant cultivation and export through World War I.[12]

A number of pharmacist researchers would contribute to the pharmaceutical industry in the nineteenth century. Only one, a russified German at that, did so in the eighteenth. Nevertheless, his findings were milestones and they were made in the context of Russian pharmacy. Tobias Egorovich Lovits, born in Gottingen, in 1757, migrated to Russia in 1768 with his cartographer father, who died while on a five-year expedition for the Academy of Sciences in the Caspian steppes. Completing his *gimnaziia* education in 1777, Lovits apprenticed two years in the Court Pharmacy in St. Petersburg, passed his examination for *gezel*, as Assistant Pharmacists were called at that time, and attended lectures at the University in Gottingen. Upon his return to Russia in 1784 he again entered service in the Court Pharmacy in St. Petersburg.[13] Lovits's major discovery was that charcoal had decolorizing and deodorizing properties.[14] In 1785 he discovered a simple, quick method of using charcoal to purify a solution of cream of tartar acid. He applied this method to obtain the crystallization of acetate potash and studied the effects of charcoal on vegetable and mineral acids, oils, and solutions. In 1791, using charcoal for cleansing a solution of acetic acid, with the help of distillation, Lovits obtained crystallized acetic acid. The Russian government applied his findings to make potable water for the army and navy.[15] Lovits also discovered mono- and trichloroacetic acids in 1793 and was the first to prepare absolute alcohol and pure ether in 1796.[16]

The first factories producing pharmaceuticals were created by private entrepreneurs in the early nineteenth century, only slightly after the first German pharmaceutical houses and contemporaneous with the first American factories,[17] in Russian Poland, the western periphery of the empire. In 1823 Ludwig Hirschman and Jan C. Kijewski established the first pharmaceutical factory in Poland, Fabryka Plodow Chemicznych. In 1848 Assistant Pharmacist Ludwig Speiss and his partner founded a pharmaceutical factory in Warsaw. In 1869 Speiss bought the Hirschmann-Kijewski factory. The factory produced galenical preparations until 1879.[18]

Large-scale pharmaceutical production in Great Russia began only in the 1860s. However, Russian pharmacists such as A. P. Neliubin prepared the ground for factory production of medicines by making significant discoveries in their pharmacy laboratories and publishing information on new pharmaceutical products. Born in Viatka in 1785, Neliubin received the Provizor title in 1806. Subsequently he acquired the medical degree of *lekar'* (lowest rank of physician) in 1817 and served as city obstetrician for thirteen years. However, he continued his connection to pharmacy and research in pharmacology. The government sent him to the Caucasus to study mineral waters, he helped formulate the Pharmacy Tax of 1829, and was a member of the committee that analyzed foreign pharmaceutical wares. From 1831 to 1851, Neliubin was secretary in the Medical Council; from 1831, vice-director of the Medical Department; and in 1838, 1839 and 1851, president of the St. Petersburg Pharmacy Society, which had been founded in 1818. Neliubin established a method of deriving salts of quinine and created apparatus for making ether and analyzing arsenic. One of his texts, *Farmakografiia*, was published in five editions between 1827 and his death in 1858; it included the nomenclature and description of new medical substances. Neliubin's *The Dispensing of Secret, Specific, Universal, and Patented Substances* appeared in 1831 and analyzed patent or proprietary medicines received from abroad or produced in Russia. For example, he declared of one antipyretic that "the universal remedy contained in it is *macilaginem gummi Tragacanthae* and sugar and therefore nothing can be expected from its use."[19] A contemporary of Neliubin, A. M. Butlerov, discovered two alkaloids. He derived urotropine in 1859 and, studying the structure of quinine, discovered "khinoline." He also synthesized saccharin from formaldehyde.[20]

Although these advances were small-scale, a British journal noted them approvingly in 1842. Reviewing Russian, Danish, British, and American pharmacopoeias, the author gave high marks to the Russian military pharmacopoeia for "accuracy of research, generally . . . sound therapeutic views, and . . . an acquaintance with modern discoveries in medical science." He specifically praised several pharmaceutical procedures developed by Russians: a method of obtaining hydrocyanic acid and, "being more alive to modern discoveries in medicine," a formula for potassium bromide. The British reviewer was "gratified" that the Russian (as well as the Edinburgh pharmacopoeia) included a process for the preparation of hydrated sesquioxide of iron, which was an antidote for the poisonous effects of arsenious acid.[21]

The pharmaceutical industry in Russia and the Ukraine took off after the mid-century Crimean War, propelled by four factors: increased interest in public health, expanding production of and a market for disinfectants, pharmacists' further discoveries in chemistry and pharmacology, and entrepreneurial energy.

Increased concern for public health was partly a response to the cholera epidemics of the early nineteenth century[22] and partly a worldwide phenomenon.[23] Both the embryonic public health movement and the pharmaceutical industry were stimulated by production of disinfectants during the Crimean War. Two engineers–the brothers Zhdanov–began making disinfecting liquids. By the 1860s, according to a contemporary chronicler, they acquired "significant usage" as "attention in Russia began to be turned to the question of healthy air in dwellings."[24] Carbolic acid continued to be imported but by the mid-1880s domestic manufacture of "carbolic acid . . . achieved some significance."[25]

Russian pharmacists' and physicians' research on medicinal plants and minerals and synthesis of key chemical-based medicaments bolstered the nascent Russian pharmaceutical industry. Much of this pharmacological work involved quinine and febrifuges, as had the earlier work of Neliubin and Butlerov–probably because malaria was Russia's most prevalent communicable disease.[26]

One of the most important Russian pharmacologists in the second half of the nineteenth century was Georg Dragendorff. Born in Rostok in 1836, Dragendorff apprenticed in a pharmacy, took the *gezel* examination in 1856, the Provizor examination in 1858, and then studied two years at Heidelburg University. Following his classroom studies he worked in the chemical laboratory of Rostok University. His Ph.D. dissertation from Rostok analyzed the influence of phosphorous on carbonic acid and boric acid salts. Dragendorff briefly managed the laboratory of the St. Petersburg Pharmacy Society, then, following his Master of Pharmacy degree from Dorpat University in Estland in 1864 (his research dealt with the chemical composition of mushrooms), he was appointed ordinary professor and director of the Pharmacy Institute at the university. Dragendorff's own research and that which he directed in the 1860s and 1870s focused on alkaloids. He and his students analyzed quinine, ptomaines, salicylic acid, and ether oil.[27] An American historian has contended that Dragendorff contributed "importantly to plant chemistry by developing a systematic process of plant analysis, based largely on solvent extraction procedures."[28]

Dragendorff, like Lovits, owed much to his German training. Yet, both men did their major work in Russia, although Dragendorff's was done in a university with German traditions. But Neliubin and Butlerov had shown that Russian pharmaceutical education produced capable and creative researchers. They were followed by a number of Russian pharmacists in the second half of the nineteenth century. V. A. Tikhomirov, professor of pharmacy and pharmacognosy at the University of Moscow, did research on the acclimation of foreign herbs and tea to Russia. A. V. Pel', who received a Master of Pharmacy degree from the Military Medical Academy in St. Petersburg in 1873, investigated atropine and other alkaloids, rational methods of preparing galenical mixtures, and antiseptic and aseptic medical procedures. Pel' published 132 scientific studies.[29] He was the first to extract spermine in pure form, a product he sold under his name. P. P. Kravkov experimented with preserving organs in nutrient media. He isolated pancreotoxin, an "effective insulin preparation" and obtained "endocrine extracts by perfusion with blood."[30] A. A. Voskresenskii and N. N. Zinin, both of whom died in 1880, isolated the alkaloid theobromine and conducted research on the chemical structure of quinine. In 1880 the physician N. I. Lunin researched protein, fats, sugar, and discovered substances later termed vitamins. In 1889 Master of Pharmacy E. A. Shatskii published *Studies on Vegetable Alkaloids, Glucosides, and Ptomaines.* In 1885 Iu. K. Trapp published one of his first textbooks on pharmaceutical chemistry.[31] In 1896, Professor E. A. Leman of Tomsk University isolated a glucoside, which he called periplotsin, from the root of *Periploca graeca L.* In the same year P. V. Burzhinskii caused ripples of interest from physicians by discovering that the substance had a beneficial effect on heart problems.[32]

Entrepreneurial energy, mainly on the part of pharmacists, was an essential ingredient in the development of the Russian pharmaceutical industry.[33] A. A. Andreev established a steam-powered laboratory for pharmaceutical preparations in Moscow in 1862.[34] In line with general economic expansion, pharmaceutical workshops and factories proliferated in the 1870s and early 1880s. Long a center of herb growing and exporting, the Ukraine became a key arena of pharmaceutical production. The laboratory of I. Zinger was established in 1874. In 1875 the factory of P. Legran and Company was set up in Odessa, and P. I. Gruzdev founded the "Khar'kov Chemical Laboratory." M. Krivitskii and F. G. Leviton established a factory in Odessa in 1884. In the early nineteenth century Del"s pharmacy in Lubniakh, Poltava province, began large-scale growing and gathering of medicinal herbs; in the early 1880s the pharmacy laboratory and factory prepared plant extracts and ether oil. In 1878 S. N. Snapir in Kremenchug established a special warehouse for medicinal herbs. This was the beginning of the firm "S. N. Snapir and Sons," which worked up and packaged raw pharmaceuticals from medicinal herbs. Other such warehouses and firms later were established in Kremenchug, Lubniakh, Pereiaslav, and other cities. In the 1880s, I. M. Isaevich in Lubenshchina, began to cultivate mint and produce mint oil. In Kiev A. A. Martsinchik prepared galenical preparations in his pharmacy laboratory. In 1881, in Kiev, the joint-stock company "South Russian Society of Trade in Pharmacy Wares" was founded; it was known by the acronym IUROTAT. In 1883 Lintvarev in Odessa opened a smallpox vaccination center. By the mid-

1880s there were ten or so laboratories, workshops, and factories mass-producing pharmaceuticals in the Ukraine.[35]

Moscow became the hub of the Russian pharmaceutical industry by the turn of the century. Oskar Getling established a wholesale pharmaceutical warehouse in the city in 1875.[36] Roman Romanovich Keler established "Keler and Co." in Moscow in 1882. The Russian Chemical Factory Association produced narcotic ether, tannin, colloids, and other preparations by 1888.[37]

St. Petersburg was second to Moscow in production of pharmaceuticals. One of the pioneers in the capital was the pharmacologist A. V. Pel'. In addition to his work on spermine, in 1885, Pel' developed a method of making special sterile solutions and glass ampules, or tubes, in which to package them. He quickly began to mass-produce these items.[38] Organized as a family stock company, "Association Pel' and Sons" flourished through the early twentieth century.[39]

By 1885 "in St. Petersburg alone there were 5 enterprises, preparing 100,000 rubles worth of disinfecting and pharmaceutical substances, in Moscow there were 4 enterprises making pharmaceutical substances worth 60,000 rubles, and additional enterprises operated in Odessa, Yaroslavl', Ekaterinburg, and Mogilev provinces, with production worth 20,000 to 25,000 rubles."[40]

Russian Poland continued to be a vital center of pharmaceutical production. Ferdinand Werner began making medicinal tablets in Warsaw in 1860. Werner's son Emil, a Master of Pharmacy, took over the business in 1868. With the death of his father in 1868, Emil Werner rechristened the enterprise "Factory Przetworow Chemicznych" and enlarged its scope to include production of pharmaceuticals, photographic materials, and technical items. The factory increased its pharmaceutical output after the establishment of a warehouse in 1872, producing opium-based substances, belladona, digitalis, collodium, and ammonia. By 1885 the factory employed fifty workers; by 1905, its name enlarged to "Fabryka Chemiczna: Setzer Jan i Werner Emil, Warszwa, Solec," the factory employed ninety workers and produced 110,900 rubles worth of materials.[41]

By 1885, in addition to the Speiss and Werner factories, there were seven establishments in Warsaw producing pharmaceutical wares. One made bandages; six produced medicines. The new businesses were small, operating out of pharmacy laboratories. In 1887, four new pharmacy laboratories appeared. Additionally, in 1887 one institute, producing mineral water, and one free-standing laboratory appeared. Despite their small scale, the pharmacies cum laboratories were innovative and produced vital medicines. That of Franciszka Kusmierski was the first to make gelatin capsules;

that of Provizor Jan Dabrowski also produced gelatin tablets. One pharmacy laboratory made chloroform, that of Jan Rutkowski made syrups, and that of I. Hoser made salicylic acid. The pharmacy laboratory of Edward Gessner, in particular, enjoyed wide-scale distribution; in 1905, Gessner developed a new preparation called Haematogen, which he sold in tablet form.[42] A pharmaceutical warehouse was organized in Warsaw in 1870.[43]

In the 1890s, some of the pharmaceutical concerns in Warsaw were reorganized as joint-stock companies. In 1893 Ludwig Speiss linked his factory with the pharmaceutical warehouse. Speiss died in 1896; in 1899 his firm was reorganized as a joint-stock association, the "Warszawskie Towarzystow Aptekarze i Ludwik Speiss i Syn." From 1907 to 1922 the substances that this company produced—oil, tablets, boromenthol, glycerophosphate granules, baby powder—carried the name "Speiss" in their titles.[44] The name "Speiss" was the first Polish specific, analogous to the term "Bayer" in German pharmaceuticals. A 1906 photograph displayed fourteen proud employees and a horse-drawn conveyance before the two-story Speiss factory-warehouse; three posh drug stores in different parts of Warsaw purveyed Speiss products.[45] In 1898, Provizor Teodor Tafilowski, director of the institute producing mineral water, and Provizor Jan Rutkowski, owner of the pharmacy and laboratory producing syrups, merged and formed a second joint-stock company called "Motor." One thousand shares were sold at 250 rubles a share for founding capital of 250,000 rubles. There were thirteen shareholders, including Rutkowski and Edward Gessner. "Motor" produced mineral water, chemicals, microscopes, and pharmaceutical preparations. The third joint-stock company, that of Karpinski, was organized in 1910.[46]

Medical Societies and zemstvos also began producing medicines in the 1880s and 1890s.[47] The Poltava zemstvo began to make antismallpox vaccine in 1885, the Chernigov zemstvo followed in 1886, the Khar'kov and Kherson zemstvos in 1889. In 1886, I. I. Mechnikov, N. F. Gamaleia, and other scientists organized a bacteriological station to produce antirabies vaccine in Odessa. This was the first such station in Russia and the second in the world. The following year the Khar'kov medical society established a Pasteur Institute and bacteriological station, subsequently reorganized into a bacteriological institute.[48] The Khar'kov Medical Society, which performed diagnostic bacteriological research, also prepared serums, tuberculin, and vaccines. Other bacteriological stations for producing antirabies vaccine were established in Samara, Moscow, and St. Petersburg.[49] In Kiev, in 1894, the "Society for Struggle with Infectious Diseases," organized by the initiative of A. D. Pavlovskii and V. V. Podvysotskii, and other scientists, established an antidiphtheria station; in 1896 these scientists established a Pasteur station and united the stations with the Kiev Bacteriological Institute.[50] The bacteriological stations also prepared scarlatina-streptococcus vaccines and antiscarlatina serum.[51] In 1894 the Zolotonosh zemstvo founded a laboratory for galenical preparations; in 1898 the Aleksandriiskaia chemical pharmaceutical laboratory was established; a laboratory was established in Elizavetgrad in 1900, in Lebedin in 1909, and in Khorol in 1910. Bacteriological stations were established in Feodoskaia in 1909 and in Elizavetgrad in 1911; Pasteur stations, bacteriological institutes, and smallpox vaccination centers were established in Chernigov and Ekaterinoslav in 1912; galenical laboratories in Akhtyrk, Ekaterinoslav, Kupiansk, and Melitopol' in the Ukraine.[52]

The Russian army had its own pharmaceutical factory. Between 1895 and 1903 the Military Medical Factory produced twenty-six forms of tablets, in addition to other items. The Military Medical Academy, the medical school in the capital, produced sixty-four forms of tablets, as well as other pharmaceuticals.[53]

Yet, private entrepreneurs continued to dominate the pharmaceutical industry. Additionally, they adopted more progressive forms of organization. As in Poland, a number of pharmaceutical enterprises in Russia and the Ukraine were reorganized as joint-stock companies, either publicly held concerns (*Aktsionernoe Obshchestvo*) or more intimate partnerships and associations (*Tovarishchestvo*) under partial or full control of a family.[54]

Keler's Moscow firm became the "Association Keler and Co." in 1893. Ferrein established his factory in 1894. In Odessa, P. S. Razumov established a factory to produce disinfecting materials in 1893; other factories operated in the city at the end of the nineteenth century supplying talcum, cream of tartar acid, purifying benzine, *naftalin*, phenol (carbolic acid), paraffin, vaseline oil, borax, and other products.[55] In Nikolaev in 1894 the chemical factory "Astra" began to make galenicals. In the same year K. I. Debu founded a mint factory in Poltava province. In 1896 a factory opened in Kiev to produce medical soap, disinfectants, glycerine, and other products. In 1897 an "Association for making mint oil" was established in Poltava province; five factories for producing mint oil opened in succeeding years. In 1895 a factory for producing anise oil was established on a *khutor,* or separate farmstead, in Pavlovsk, Kupiansk district, Poltava province. In 1897 two factories to produce anise oil were established in Podolia province.[56]

Several pharmaceutical corporations were established in the first decade of the twentieth century. In 1903 the Council of Ministers approved the enterprise "Shibaev and Co.," for producing mineral oil. Shibaev was organized as a joint-stock company, selling 3,000 shares at 1,000 rubles each.[57] In 1903 the Association "S. N. Snapir and Sons" in Kremenchug founded a factory to work up raw medicinal herbs; in 1912 the association established a factory named "Labor" to produce galenical preparations. In 1905 the "Society K. Shmidt and Co." in Kiev opened a laboratory of pharmaceutical capsules.[58]

In 1906 pharmacist B. M. Shaskol'skii established the Borzhom mineral water factory. Shaskol'skii had received the Provizor title from the Military Medical Academy in 1867. In 1870 he purchased one of oldest pharmacies in St. Petersburg–the Samson'evskaia. In 1884 he founded a drug store cum warehouse at one of the choicest spots in St. Petersburg–the Kazan bridge on the Nevskii Prospekt. The store "offered good quality, fresh, cheap wares and good service"; it spawned a branch on the island of Kronstadt. In its first year the Borzhom factory exported two million bottles of mineral water; by 1910 the factory exported five million bottles.[59]

In 1907 the "First Factory of Pharmaceutical and Galenical Preparations" was organized in Khar'kov; it later became the "Galenika Joint-Stock Company."[60] The "Joint-Stock Company Karbonik" was organized in Kiev in 1907 in order to raise capital to establish a 50,000 cubic meter oxygen-producing factory.[61] The factory "Sanitas" opened in Khar'kov in 1909. In 1908 the society IUROTAT acquired the Martsinchik enterprise and united the latter with its own laboratory in a chemical-pharmaceutical factory. In 1911 a French joint-stock company laboratory, "Stella," opened in Odessa to produce galenicals.[62] At the end of 1910 the pharmaceutical conglomerate of the "Brothers' Stolkind" merged with the firm of Ermans. I. Ia. Stolkind produced perfume, chemicals, and organic-therapeutic wares at his factories in Moscow, Ivano-Voznesensk, and Kishinev, the province of Bessarabia. M. Ia. Stolkind supplied these commodities to pharmacies and hospitals in Russia and abroad. The basic capital of the merged Association, 250,000 rubles, was realized from sale of 250 shares of stock at 1,000 rubles each.[63] The Association I. B. Segal founded a chemical-pharmaceutical factory "Ars" in Vil'na in 1911.[64]

By the early twentieth century almost a hundred Russian pharmaceutical enterprises supplied a substantial amount of materials to the internal market.

Geographically, they were scattered over the European part of the empire.[65] Seven were located in Warsaw.[66] Seven enterprises were located in the Baltic region.[67] There were three pharmaceutical enterprises in Kremenchug, in the Ukraine.[68] Seven enterprises were located in Tver or

Tver province.[69] Two enterprises were situated east of Moscow in the old Tatar city of Kazan,[70] two were located in northeastern Kostroma province,[71] two were located in the Volga-river trading city of Nizhni Novgorod,[72] and one in the province of Nizhni Novgorod.[73] The provinces of Olonets, Dvinsk, the Caucasus, Kiev, Saratov, Minsk, Grodno, and Khar'kov had at least one enterprise each.[74] Some twelve enterprises were located in St. Petersburg.[75] Moscow was the hub of the pharmaceutical industry with some twenty enterprises.[76]

The ownership and structure of these pharmaceutical enterprises continued to run the gamut from individually owned pharmacies and laboratories, laboratories operated by zemstvos and chemical societies, family-owned stock partnerships, and large, publicly held, joint-stock companies.[77]

Branches of foreign pharmaceutical firms also operated in Russia. These included the German "Shtol' and Shmidt" and the American "Parke, Davis and Company" in St. Petersburg. "Shering" was probably a branch of the Shering AG organized in Berlin in 1851. In 1905 E. Merck had a branch factory in Moscow and distributors in St. Petersburg, Poland, Kiev, Podolsk, the Kuban, Terek, in the Caucasus, Daghestan and Stavropol, in the Black Sea area, and Kishinev.[78] Multinational pharmaceutical enterprises likewise operated in Western Europe and the United States at the time. For example, Merck established a branch in New Jersey in 1899.[79] The presence of multinationals in Russia benefited consumers and signaled the fact that Russia was integrated into the world market.

Increased use of prepared medicaments and synthetic and chemical compounds in Russia impacted the official pharmacopoeia. The first civilian pharmacopoeia, *Pharmacopoea Rossica,* had appeared in 1778; it was reissued in 1798. First published in Latin, it was translated into Russian in 1802. The Medical College issued the first state pharmacopoeia in Russian, the *Rossiiskaia Farmakopeia* in 1866. It was revised and reissued in 1870, 1880, 1893–1895, 1902, and 1910.[80] The first pharmacopoeia included about 120 prepared medicaments, or 24–25 percent of the total. In the 1866 pharmacopoeia prepared items amounted to 427 items, or 46 percent of total medicaments. Mineral-based medicines amounted to 35 percent. In the pharmacopoeia of the 1890s, 80 percent of medicines were prepared and mineral based.[81]

How did the Russian pharmaceutical industry operate? What was the caliber of its preparations? How did they compare with foreign products? In some ways the industry was very modern. But it also had serious defects. In fact, the Russian pharmaceutical industry, with its pluses and minuses mirrored Russian industry as a whole in the nineteenth and early twentieth century.

Soviet pharmacists did not disdain using the nationalized factories of their predecessors. However, in the late 1920s, when the First Five Year Plan ground into action, they began to disparage the pharmaceutical industry which had existed under the old regime. The Keler factory, known for years after nationalization under the name of the former owner, but subsequently renamed the N. A. Semashko Factory, was particularly ridiculed as primitive.[82] Some latter-day Soviet historians perpetuated this notion.[83]

Many Russian pharmaceutical enterprises were, indeed, small-scale workshops. However, this was not necessarily a detriment. Most pharmaceutical enterprises in France in the nineteenth and early twentieth century were small and specialized in "one or two remedies." As late as the 1920s "fully 50 percent of the licensed pharmacists in France" were "engaged in this business, most of them in a small way."[84] True, France also boasted of the *Pharmacie Centrale*. Organized in the middle of the nineteenth century, this stock association coordinated the production of alkaloids, chemicals, and pharmaceutical products; the shareholders were pharmacists. In 1907 the cooperative had capital of ten million francs and supplied the majority of French pharmacies with prepared medicaments.[85]

Imperial Russia had no such organization. Nevertheless, in aggregate Russian pharmaceutical enterprises produced a large quantity of medicines and supplies.[86] In 1898 the City Hospital of Nizhni Novgorod debated whether to order medicines from abroad or from Russian firms,[87] testifying to the fact that domestic firms had ample supplies. In Simbirsk province in 1896 the zemstvo sanitary bureau purchased medicines and supplies from nineteen Russian and four foreign firms.[88] Between 1889 and 1910 the Tver Zemstvo Warehouse bought 140,000 rubles' worth of medicines and wares from foreign firms compared with 193,000 rubles' worth from domestic enterprises. In 1910 the Tver Zemstvo Warehouse procured pharmaceuticals from thirty-seven foreign firms and ninety-five domestic enterprises.[89] In Mogilev province, medical authorities reported that zemstvos did not order medicine and supplies from abroad during 1913.[90] Oskar Getling's Wholesale Warehouse in Moscow stocked and sold a myriad of products before World War I. His 122-page catalog listed hundreds of simple and compound medical substances and prepared medicines; oils; powders; bandaging materials; apparatus and equipment for pharmacies; food products such as decaffeinated coffee, cocoa, and flavorings; household items such as soaps, perfumes, toothpastes, toilet paper, fly paper, cleaning fluids; cigarettes; mineral water. The origin of most medicinal substances was not noted. Some suppliers were foreign—Parke, Davis, Merck. The catalog listed two pages of trademarked tablets, powders, and other medicinal items from Burroughs, Wellcome. Shering's Pepzin-Ezzenz, Chesebrough's vaseline, and Colgate's Cashmere Bouquet Soap, toothpaste, and Bay Rum after shave were noted. A good many perfumes were foreign. But Getling also sourced domestically. The warehouse carried nonmedicinal items such as soaps, powders, and creams from A. A. Rubanovskii in Moscow and A. Englud in St. Petersburg. And, the firm also sold thirty-two organic medical preparations from Pel' and Sons.[91]

Several Russian pharmaceutical enterprises were, in fact, quite large. In 1909 Ferrein employed 425 workers and produced 403,000 rubles' worth of galenical[92] and chemical products. Keler and Company employed 394 workers; output in 1909 amounted to 1,204,000 rubles. Shering, which made sulfuric ether, colloids, iodide salts, and iron chloride (*khlornoe zhelezo*), employed 83 workers and produced 208,000 rubles' worth of goods in 1909. Ermans and Company, which produced "galenical preparations," "technochemical preparations," and "perfumes" was smaller with 25 workers, but produced 76,000 rubles' worth of wares.[93] In 1897 IUROTAT cleared a net profit of 39,491 rubles.[94] In 1909 the company, producing both pharmaceuticals and perfumes, employed 92 workers and had an income of 512,000 rubles. Pel' and Sons in St. Petersburg was the third largest pharmaceutical enterprise in Russia in terms of workers, employing 121, but produced 223,000 rubles' worth of pharmaceuticals in 1909–less than IUROTAT. Two other enterprises in St. Petersburg, the cooperative FARMAKON, and Association Miller, were small with 38 and 20 workers, respectively. However, the first produced 173,000 rubles' worth of pharmaceutical preparations and drying oil; the second produced only 50,000 rubles' worth of pharmaceutical preparations and perfumes. The Association Snapir in Kremenchug was small, producing only 36,000 rubles' worth of pharmaceuticals and perfume and employing only 35 workers. Association Galenika in Khar'kov also was small, employing only 25 workers but produced 69,000 rubles' worth of perfumes and pharmaceutical wares.[95]

Additionally, although the government's hand was very visible in the Russian pharmaceutical industry, native business acumen also was strikingly evident. Russian pharmaceutical firms such as Keler and Company, Ferrein, and Pel' and Sons were progressive, efficient, and diversified.

Roman Romanovich Keler was born in Reval in 1837. He apprenticed in a pharmacy. When his father, chair of the criminal court in Reval for many years, died, Roman Romanovich came to Moscow "to seek his fortune," reputedly with only 40 kopeks in his pocket. He worked for a time at Ferrein's Nikol'skaia Street pharmacy and briefly for another Moscow pharmacy. In 1862 Keler opened his own business, a pharmacy, then a factory and drug store (*aptekarskii magazin*) at the Rogozhsk gates. According to a 1907 Social-Democratic publication, both his factory and drug store were so successful that he aroused the enmity of other pharmacy owners. They accused his drug store of improperly dispensing poison; as a result authorities closed the store and factory for one year. However, Keler fought and won the right to reopen, transforming his company into a joint-stock association in 1893, as noted above.[96]

The Keler factory produced a wide variety of items: sulfuric ether; galenical medicines–twenty kinds of drops, including valerian and mint drops, cough syrups, quinine, salicylic preparations, vaseline, menthol, boric acid, various oils–mercury, zinc, sulfur, arsenic, cod liver and fish oils; antiseptics; cotton and bandaging materials; all manner of soaps for humans and animals; toothpaste, powder and other dental hygiene products; food supplements, essences and materials used in food preparation—acorn coffee, cocoa, malt, bouillon, tapioca, salts, gelatin, egg dye; various cleaning products for clothes, dishes, floors, bathtubs; toilet paper; perfumes; products to combat household pests, and photographic film. The association also sold pressed tablets of quinine and aspirin but the provenance of these medicines was not indicated. The Keler Association made up small "household pharmacies." Further, it provided quick photograph and slide processing through its "Electra-Ekspress."[97]

Keler attempted to be self-sufficient, making its own cartons and operating its own printing press. The firm also had a branch in the village of Khoroshovo, outside Moscow, where it produced narcotic ether and table salt.[98] It received both Russian and foreign awards (three silver vases, the Anna medal, the 1900 Paris Prize) for its high-quality wares.[99]

Keler was a forthright, canny businessman. He offered credit to customers with solid references, but they were advised that prices could change and invoices must be paid within a month after delivery. The firm was not responsible for spoilage en route. Returns could be made only with approval of the company. Dangerous or flammable items were delivered in special railroad cars at higher rates.[100] In 1914 Keler's production grossed 1,473,311 rubles.[101]

The enterprises of Vladimir Karlovich Ferrein were particularly impressive. Born in 1834, Ferrein apprenticed in his family pharmacy on Staraia Nikol'skaia Street, passed examinations at Moscow University for his Assistant Pharmacist and Provizor degrees, studied chemistry at the University of Munich with Professor Beuchner, and received the Master of Pharmacy degree in 1869 at the University of Moscow.[102] Ferrein expanded his pharmacy into a veritable empire.[103] By the turn of the nineteenth century it included the pharmacy, which annually dispensed more than 400,000 prescriptions and employed 250 pharmacists and 150 workers, four drug stores, a wholesale warehouse, an analytical laboratory, a research institute, and a factory for producing galenical preparations, chemical preparations, and medicines (tablets, pills, capsules, and plasters) all located in the city of Moscow; a plantation on the outskirts of Moscow; and a pharmaceutical factory in the city of Mologa, Yaroslavl' province.[104] In 1902 the Ferrein complex of pharmacy, drug stores, and factories was transformed into a family-held joint-stock company.[105]

Like All-Russian pharmacies, Staraia-Nikol'skaia originally included laboratories, which produced large quantities of medicines and engaged in experimental research. In 1894 Ferrein moved the bacteriological and chemical-analytical laboratory to a neighboring building in order to provide more reception room in the pharmacy.

This laboratory, also situated on Nikol'skaia street, continued to perform medical-diagnostic, chemical-hygienic, and technical analysis—tests on urine, tissue, food products, and water. It was under the direction of three physicians and employed fourteen people, including two chemists and three Provizors.[106] The bacteriological-chemical laboratory served as both a research and teaching institution. From 1893 to 1896 noted Master of Pharmacy Arkadii Moiseevich Semenov managed the laboratory, reading lectures, and training pharmacy students and Ferrein workers in the use of microscopic techniques.[107]

The factory in Mologa was established in the mid-1890s. In 1910 it employed 104 people and the following year, 112, including a physician, a chemist, 2 Masters of Pharmacy, and 10 Provizors.[108] In 1912 the factory was moved to Moscow.[109] In that year the Ferrein complex realized 7 million rubles turnover and employed more than 600 specialists and 1,000 "workers."[110]

The wholesale warehouse for pharmacy products employed 348 people in 1911—23 Provizors; 35 Assistant Pharmacists; 53 male and female clerks; and 237 male and female "workers."[111]

The Ferrein enterprises produced mineral-based pharmaceuticals—terpinhydrate, amygdalin, calcium carbonate, sulfuric barium, calcium chloride;[112] plant-based lozenges of arsenic, morphine, and quinine; bandages and powders; and sundries such as soaps, perfumes, and cosmetics. The firm produced its own glassware.[113] The Yaroslavl' factory concentrated on benzoin preparations.[114]

Ferrein practiced a hands-on management style. The factory cum laboratory was connected with his Moscow residence on Krivokolennyi *pereulok*. Production rooms were spacious, spotlessly clean, and equipped with state-of-the-art apparatus, most of it electrically powered.[115] The firm engaged in research and development, testing new products on animals in a physiological laboratory.[116] It practiced quality control.[117] Men attired in aprons and women in smocks and veiled headdresses checked each outgoing product in the wholesale warehouse. Aproned men packaged cartons in the factory's own distribution center. The Ferrein firm sold medicines both retail and wholesale. Horse-drawn wagons distributed medicines and supplies locally and the firm also sold wares to pharmacies and drug stores around the country.[118]

Ferrein was socially aware as well as a savvy businessman. He offered a profit-sharing plan to employees in his pharmacy and drug stores as early as 1881. Employees also could apply for noninterest aid and loans at 6 percent interest.[119] By 1910 workers' health was protected by ventilation systems and devices to shield them from harmful gases. They also enjoyed amenities, such as a canteen.[120]

One of the last factories founded before World War I was "Ars" in Vil'na. The factory opened in 1911, after "careful supervision of a mixed commission composed of the local medical inspector and his assistant, the senior factory inspector." According to a contemporary, thanks to "the energy and initiative of Directors Zaidele Mushkatu and Gol'dberg and foreign chiefs of the B. I. Segal firm," Ars represented the first attempt in the region "to prepare pharmaceutical preparations by factory methods." It used "the last word in pharmaceutical techniques," was "equipped with the newest apparatus, vacuum and electric." Master of Pharmacy Zal'kind managed the factory.[121]

Throughout the world many medicines in the nineteenth and early twentieth centuries were derived from plants. This was particularly true in Russia.[122] Ferrein imported plant materials and prepared alkaloids from pharmaceutical firms in France, England, and Holland, such as cocaine from the Nederlansche Cocainefabriek in Amsterdam.[123] However, both Ferrein and Pel' and Sons cultivated and did research on plants used in their medicaments. In 1890, on his estate on the outskirts of Moscow Vladimir Karlovich Ferrein established a large botanical garden. This experimental plantation, now part of the Russian state pharmacy organization, still exists, crowned by Ferrein's log house, with its carved veranda and window surrounds.[124] In 1904, Pel' and Sons established their "Experimental Field" in the town of Tsarskoe Selo, some fifteen miles outside of St. Petersburg,[125] for cultivation of medicinal plants.

Russian pharmaceutical firms also purchased plants from private growers.[126] Ferrein's factory and Staraia Nikol'skaia pharmacy included large rooms for drying and storing herbs.[127]

This preserved and encouraged popular collection and cultivation of medicinal plants and additionally stimulated scientific interest in time-honored remedies. In 1901 *Farmatsevticheskii zhurnal* carried a series of articles on the cultivation of medicinal plants in Russia as far north as the 62nd parallel;[128] in 1902 *Farmatsevt* reported on popularly used plants grown near the town of Bogotol', Tomsk province, in western Siberia.[129] Some peasant entrepreneurs established profitable businesses as suppliers to pharmacies and pharmaceutical firms. For example, turn-of-the-century peasants in Perm province, in the Urals, developed a new industry, the production of disinfectants made of fir-tree oil. The pine oil was made on a small-scale, *kustar*, basis. Peasant families received from 200 to 350 rubles per winter (not a small sum) for selling the oil, used as a disinfectant, to pharmacies and city dwellers.[130] In 1901 Dr. P. F. Merkul'ev reported to the Russian Society for the Protection of Public Health on his research in Poltava province in the Ukraine. One of the chief remedies in that region, in use for at least twenty-five years, was *gadiachskiia griazi*, or mud containing "a small amount of iodine mixed with various organic materials. Local inhabitants used this to treat rheumatism, neuralgia," and other maladies.[131] The peasants of Poltava province also had a thriving cottage industry in the production of mint oil. In 1914, some 800 dessiatines were sown to mint.[132] Mint oil, or menthol, was widely used in medical practice to treat stomach disorders by increasing the acidity of the digestive juices.[133]

Books on the use of herbs, such as the *Household Treatment*, for the Urals region, published by Sputnik Zdorov'ia at a price of 4 rubles,[134] were part of the medical lexicon. However, as there was no comprehensive work on flora in the empire in the early twentieth century, Nicholas II allocated 24,000 rubles for an official compilation in 1900. Members of the Academy of Sciences undertook the project, which was scheduled to last four years.[135]

In contrast to the extravagant claims made by purveyors of American medicines during the eighteenth, nineteenth, and early twentieth centuries,[136] Russian firms soberly stressed quality and customer satisfaction. In 1907, Ferrein advertised that it sold "chemical and galenical preparations . . . wholesale and retail sale of pharmacy wares and all [supplies] needed for the establishment of a pharmacy" and also consumer items such as "condensed milk (55 kopeks per tin), coffee with milk at 80 kopeks per tin, and chocolate with milk at 85 kopeks per tin to pharmacies and drug stores at the usual discount."[137] The Bandaging Materials Factory of N. Iakovlev advertised "moderate prices" and an "illustrated price-list upon request." Iakovlev touted the fact that it was distributor of bandaging materials "for the Red Cross and other public institutions" as well as "for pharmacies and drug stores."[138] Ermans and Company on Tverskaia street, Moscow, promised of one of its products "no more rats and mice."[139] Dr. Ia. M. Bliumental', located on Malaia Liubianka street in Moscow, advertised "Production of all kinds of disinfectants, disinfecting chamber, and equipment and apparatus" and "the first private Disinfecting Institute."[140] The Tallow and Oil Factory of V. A. Lepskii promised "lard, Russian vaseline and green soap–best quality * prices reduced."[141] A cherub alerted readers that Keler's fish oil was "incomparable"; frequent doses would banish worry about children's health.[142] "Karbonic" in Kiev vowed to produce "technically, chemically, and medically pure oxygen at the lowest possible price. Those having oxygen cylinders can send them to be filled."[143] The advertisements in the Keler and Company Wholesale Catalog were simple and straightforward. They promised basic results, such as supplementing children's diets, curing headaches, ridding the household of pests, cleaning one's clothes, or polishing one's bathtub.[144]

Very few patent medicines were advertised in Russia. One was the nostrum "Skavulin," made by Shtol' and Shmidt and distributed by the Russian Society for Trade in Pharmaceutical Wares. The advertisement portrayed a pensive woman, accompanied by the words "Mother, do you know?" Readers were informed that Skavulin was "preferred to pills–it has no taste, no smell" and "children take it as easily as candy"; it did not "harm the intestines" but acted "smoothly." The remedy appeared to be a laxative–"Take Skavulin at night, before sleep and action will take place the following morning"–but the advertisement also claimed that "it improves the color of the face, eliminates mouth odors, and strengthens the stomach." Skavulin was "sold in all pharmacies, upon a physician's prescription." One bottle, containing "numerous doses," cost a ruble.[145] But such advertisements were the exception rather than the rule.

The marketing techniques of large Russian pharmaceutical firms were efficient and adapted to the vastness of the empire. They sold medicaments and other wares to pharmacies through catalogs (*preis-kuranty*). Sometimes these were illustrated, sometimes not.[146]

Oskar Getling's warehouse in Moscow distributed medicines, cosmetics, and pharmaceutical equipment throughout the empire. Getling required payment within thirty days. Shipments were sent upon receipt of half the purchase price; the balance was due within fourteen days after receiving orders. A 2 percent discount was offered for orders above 25 rubles, and lower prices for bulk shipments. Railroad shipments to various provinces were scheduled throughout the week.[147]

Some large Moscow pharmaceutical firms established their own branches or agents in provincial cities. The Keler firm had a branch in Saratov. The Wholesale Association Provizor M. V. Polumordvinov advertised an Agent-Inquiry office (*Komissionnerno-Spravochnoe biuro*) in 1907, where foreign and domestic medicines and medical, pharmaceutical supplies (medicaments, bandages, and surgical items) could be ordered. The enterprise noted that it specialized in outfitting public (zemstvo and city) clinics and offered service as well as goods—it consulted with zemstvo, city, and factory institutions. The firm (as did many others) offered two telephone numbers for the convenience of clients.[148] The St. Petersburg cooperative FARMAKON had branches in Khar'kov and Ekaterinburg, and agents in Moscow, Odessa, Warsaw, Saratov, and Gomel in 1910. Advertisements proclaimed that these outlets sold "pharmaceutical wares, patented substances, mineral water, bandages, surgical instruments, and corsets" and that "from February 1, prices in the wholesale catalog were to be lowered. Prices of Cocaine, Oil of Cocoa, Opium, Extract opii, Tincture opii, and Dover's Powders were to be raised."[149]

On the consumer end in the early twentieth century, owners of pharmacies and drug stores in some areas formed purchasing cooperatives. St. Petersburg pharmacy owners and druggists formed a cooperative in 1906. Shares were sold for 10 rubles per share; members were required to purchase at least ten shares. The government approved the society's charter in 1907 and it duly elected an administrative board. By 1908 this cooperative included fifty members.[150] In 1909 owners of the largest drug stores in Kazan established an Association for Trade in Pharmaceutical Wares. The new joint-stock association offered shares to staff pharmacists in drug stores.[151]

Zemstvo pharmacy procurement practices in the early twentieth century illustrate more fully the methods by which pharmaceutical producers supplied customers in the hinterlands, how the producers responded to market forces and foreign, mainly German, competition, and how Russians viewed domestic pharmaceutical products.

The Tver zemstvo warehouse was established in 1887 under the leadership of senior physician M. I. Petrunkevich in order to circumvent the heavy tariffs and high prices of Moscow druggists;[152] Provizor D. S. Ginzburg, manager of the pharmacy in the provincial hospital, ordered many medicines directly from abroad[153] as well as from Russian firms. The Tver provincial zemstvo bought large quantities of medicaments—for example, a total of 29,790 rubles' worth in 1888; the zemstvo then resold the medicaments not only to its district zemstvos and to neighboring zemstvos but also to zemstvos in Pskov and Saratov provinces.[154] The tsarist government itself organized a warehouse for medical and pharmaceutical supplies in St. Petersburg in the 1890s; in 1906 the Red Cross established a warehouse in the capital, and some Siberian cities established warehouses for medicines and medical supplies.[155] The Moscow municipal government established a warehouse in 1896. Between 1897 and 1905 the warehouse's annual net profit fluctuated between 1,889 and 8,000 rubles. The warehouse ordered from the wholesale catalog of Ferrein, purchasing medicines at a 17 percent discount.[156]

However, the Tver zemstvo warehouse claimed the prices of the Moscow "druggists," particularly Keler and Ferrein, were too high. The zemstvo alleged that Russian "druggists" engaged in "speculation"[157] and emphasized that public institutions could realize great savings by ordering drugs directly from foreign firms.[158] The Tver zemstvo also asserted that in 1899 and again in 1903, unnamed Moscow "druggists" pressured foreign pharmaceutical firms "Shering" and "Tsimer and Hartman" to stop dealing with zemstvos.[159]

German firms may have been able to offer their wares at cheaper prices for various reasons. They may have been more efficient. They may have benefited from economies of scale–German firms formed syndicates and set prices for key pharmaceuticals such as morphine, codeine and salicylic acid.[160] Or they may have engaged in price-cutting to undermine Russian firms.

Russian firms tried to squelch foreign competition but they also attempted to compete in terms of prices, service, and quality. As noted above, Ferrein offered discounts. In an 1898 pamphlet, *The Truth About One Public Issue,* Keler criticized zemstvos for directly ordering medicines and supplies from abroad. He lambasted physicians for encouraging them, pointing out that this practice hurt the domestic pharmaceutical industry. But Keler also provided figures to show that, while Ferrein may have been more expensive than E. Merck, his own prices were cheaper, when one took into account customs and transportation fees, and the quality of his wares was as high or higher than those of the German firm.[161] Pel' and Sons was known for its high-caliber wares. Prices in 1914 appeared reasonable. The firm also offered 25 percent discounts for "quick payment" (*pri nemedlennoi uplate*) and 20 percent for an "open account" (*po otkrytomu schetu*).[162]

Nevertheless, while the Tver zemstvo acknowledged that Russian firms competed with German by offering more discounts and easier credit,[163] it continued to maintain that Moscow druggists charged inordinately high prices compared with those of foreign firms, labeling Ferrein the most expensive.[164]

Zemstvos in Saratov province, on the other hand, ordered a substantial percentage of their wares from Russian pharmaceutical enterprises, although they sometimes considered foreign quality higher. Zemstvo executive boards in Saratov, both at the provincial and district levels, ordered pharmaceutical wares for their pharmacies usually once or twice each year. Some ordered wares directly from Russian firms, others directly from foreign firms. Orders were placed through branches of the firms, through buying trips by zemstvo doctors, and through intermediary warehouses, such as that established by the Tver zemstvo.

Kamyshinsk district zemstvo in Saratov province ordered part of its wares for 1906 from Merck through Merck's Moscow branch and through the Keler Association; it purchased other foreign wares from the Society of Trade in Pharmaceutical Wares. However, wares needed between the regular six-month orders were purchased from local pharmacies, from Ferrein, and from the Keler branch in Saratov. The zemstvo had also tried to purchase medicaments from the Tver provincial zemstvo warehouse but that zemstvo, finding itself in financial straits, stopped credit for a year. Serdobskii district zemstvo in Saratov province placed orders each October and April directly from Ferrein, who had supplied the district since 1902. Atkarsk district zemstvo ordered various items directly from different firms. Vaseline and salts came from Oswald (Osval'd), ointment from the Fabrikant Marakin, and cotton from the Laboratory of Bandaging Materials of N. Iakovlev, in Moscow. Atkarsk zemstvo ordered all medicaments from Merck. However, when Merck shut off credit to zemstvos in 1905, Ermans in Moscow offered medicaments to the Atkarsk zemstvo at a discount of 5 percent plus two months' free credit, and after that, at an 8 percent discount.[165] Thus, Atkarsk zemstvo began purchasing all medicaments from Ermans in Moscow. Petrovskii district zemstvo ordered wares once each year; additional items were purchased from Keler in Saratov or from Moscow. This zemstvo also divided its orders. It purchased all herbs, flowers, fruits, seeds, and galenicals from Keler in Moscow and all chemical preparations and alkaloids from Merck. Keler offered the Petrovsk zemstvo a discount of 10 percent,[166] but the zemstvo found that despite discounts Keler's wares were more expensive than Merck's.

Kurzhensk district zemstvo likewise split its orders. In 1896 the zemstvo ordered the great part of its medicines (at wholesale prices) through the Moscow branch of Merck, galenical preparations through the Tver warehouse, and bandages largely from Ventsel and Martens. Tsaritsynsk district zemstvo did the same. It originally ordered all alkaloids from Merck abroad at a 12 percent discount and other materials from Ermans in Moscow. From 1905, for reasons of economy, the zemstvo switched from

Ermans to the Tver zemstvo warehouse. Balashov district zemstvo ordered medicaments through a catalog from the Moscow branch of Merck. The zemstvo sent zemstvo doctors on special trips to Moscow to acquire "pharmaceutical wares" and bandages. The firm chose those suppliers that offered the best credit terms. The Saratov district zemstvo ordered "more valuable" medicaments from Merck and "less valuable" from Keler. When Merck closed off credit to zemstvos, the zemstvo ordered from Keler, which offered good credit terms. However, determining that it "spent more" but received "goods of inferior quality," the zemstvo returned to Merck in 1908.[167]

Despite the preference of the majority of district zemstvos in Saratov province for German firms, two district zemstvos ordered predominantly or exclusively from Russian firms. Vol'skoe district zemstvo established its own warehouse. Orders were placed directly by pharmacy managers to Bruns, Medler, Ferrein, and other Russian firms. The zemstvo only rarely ordered from abroad. Khvalynsk district zemstvo also had its own warehouse, managed by a Provizor. It ordered wares, according to catalogs developed by physicians, twice per year. The zemstvo purchased wares exclusively from Russian firms at wholesale prices, because these firms offered the most convenient conditions.[168] Additionally, these zemstvos spent less on medicaments annually–9,000-plus to 15,000-plus rubles–than Saratov district zemstvos, which ordered from both foreign and Russian firms. The latter spent from 12,000-plus rubles to 24,000 rubles annually, although their districts may have been more populous.[169]

The Saratov provincial zemstvo split its orders between domestic and foreign suppliers. During 1906 and 1907 the Saratov provincial zemstvo ordered medicaments chiefly from Keler in Saratov and also from Merck. In 1908 it placed orders through Merck and Ferrein. The zemstvo chose firms that offered the best credit.[170]

It was easier for Russian firms to compete with foreign in terms of price and service. Quality was more problematical. Although customers such as the district zemstvos in Saratov gave Russian firms mixed reviews on both quality and the price of their products, neutral observers gave a number of Russian pharmaceutical products high marks for quality. In 1914, D. M. Shcherbachev, privatdocent at the University of Moscow, cited a factory in Riga for "high quality preparations" and asserted that the generic or "identical" preparations made by the Ferrein, Rozenberg, and other factories were "fully the same as German patented products."[171] K. I. Kresling, of the St. Petersburg Pharmacy Society, termed the narcotic or anesthetic ether made by the Tentelevskii Chemical Factory in St. Petersburg as "fully satisfactory."[172] Academic pharmacists periodically compared the quality of

Russian medicaments with foreign, publishing their findings in books and pharmacy journals. In 1915, a review of pressed quinine tablets found that "in exactness of dose" Russian tablets "did not yield to the tablets of the best foreign firms and in some cases were significantly superior."[173]

Additionally, Russia pioneered the use of some plants and minerals for therapeutic purposes. In an 1898 report on the pharmaceutical industry, E. Merck-Darmstadt credited the Russian pharmaceutical industry with a number of advances in the use of both medicinal plants and chemical pharmaceuticals. These included the use of *Acidum picronitricum* for wounds and in surgery, experiments with a controversial *Extractum chelidonii aquosum spiss.* for cancer, and experiments with *Chistotela*, a paralyzing drug. Merck duly acknowledged Leman and Burzhinskii's discovery and use of the glucoside *Extractum periplocae graecae fluidum*, made from a plant found in the vicinity of the Black Sea. Additionally, according to Merck, Russians also were among the first to use *Iodterpin*, a powder for dusting wounds. The physician V. Ia Danilevskii reported in 1895 that subcutaneous injections of lecithin markedly increased the weight of young animals. Russians pioneered the use of *naftalin,* or as Merck called it, *naftalan*, found in the Caucasus as a byproduct of oil extraction, for burns. They experimented with leprosy serum and with injections of adrenal gland and its effects on raising blood pressure. Original, if somewhat dubious, experiments by Russians were termed "optotherapy." Reminiscent of Paracelsus's use of plants and herbs, some Russians promoted injections or other application of extracts from certain animal parts to cure similar diseased human organs. For example, injections derived from portions of animal thyroid glands were thought to help obesity, psoriasis, and eczema; red marrow was thought to help pernicious anemia; portions of animal liver were thought to be beneficial for cirrhosis of the liver; portions of spleen for malaria; portions of kidney for chronic nephritis; and so on.[174]

In addition to competing for customers, Russian pharmaceutical firms attempted to achieve balance between exports and imports of medical substances. Major exports were licorice root (*Solodkovyi koren'*), a special fungus (*Sporyn'ia*), and club moss (*Likopodii*). Licorice root was used to treat chronic constipation and also in a preparation to treat bronchial asthma in children. A powder made from licorice root was used to improve the taste and smell of pills.[175] An alkaloid of *Sporyn'ia* or *Claviceps purpurea, Tulasne*, was used in obstetrical practice.[176] Poltava province in the Ukraine was the chief producer and exporter of these substances. In 1910, total exports of *Sporyn'ia* amounted to 5,765 *puds* and brought in over 23,000 rubles. Exports of the substance reached a peak in 1912 when 8,433 *puds* were exported at a hefty sum of 35,383 rubles. Exports dropped before the war although the substance continued to be exported. Club moss was more profitable. Russia exported from 10,565 to 12,518 *puds* between 1910 and 1912 for sums between 292,919 and 366,929 rubles. Licorice root was more plentiful and thus brought in still larger sums of money. Prewar exports rose from 809,973 *puds* in 1910 for a return of 879,701 rubles to a peak of 1,722,032 *puds* in 1913 for a return of 1,875,108 rubles.[177]

Russian pharmaceutical firms particularly tried to reverse the trend of exporting medicinal plant materials and importing finished medicines. The Russian government was wont to export raw materials such as turpentine, acetic acid, calcite, and sulfuric ammonia for low prices–in 1901 prices for these items were lower in the countries to which they were exported than in Russia[178]–and to import finished products made from these items at high prices. This policy obviously harmed the native pharmaceutical industry, and Russian pharmaceutical industrialists fought it, making concerted efforts not only to source domestically but to export Russian medicines made from native medicinal plants. They were particularly successful with "santonin," a poisonous, bitter crystalline compound derived from the unopened heads of several varieties of artemesias flowers and used as a vermifuge. Originally the raw substance was exported and the refined substance imported. However, santonin began to be produced within the empire, in Chimkent, the southern region of Turkestan, 900 *puds* were produced in 1885 and 1,200 in 1886. In the 1890s the factories of Pfaff and Nikitin successfully produced santonin; amounts fluctuated between 257 and 758 *puds* between 1890 and 1896 but reached an impressive 2,268 *puds* in 1897, leveling to 900 *puds* in 1898 and 887 in 1899.[179] Santonin became one of Russia's important pharmaceutical exports. Between 1900 and 1917, 189.7 tons of this product were sold; the price fluctuated from 9,000 rubles per ton in 1908 to 180,000 rubles per ton in 1917. In that year Russia sold 1,566,000 rubles' worth of santonin.[180]

By the turn of the century the Russian pharmaceutical industry was self-sufficient or nearly so in production of some wares. In 1901 Russia was in fourth place internationally in production of mercury, a key pharmaceutical substance at that time.[181] By World War I Russia produced a sufficiency of hygroscopic gauze "of the very best quality"[182] and unrefined or nonnarcotic chloroform. The Tentelevskii Chemical Factory, Shering, Keler, and other firms produced sufficient amounts of ether.[183] Production of formalin was well-established in Russia; it was made by the firms Formoza and Shering. Shering, Keler, Ferrein, and Tentelevskii made hydrogen peroxide but this product also was imported from Germany.

Russia produced sublimate but in small amounts and of poor quality; Russia also produced small amounts of calomel. Ferrein and Keler produced carbolic acid; however quantities were insufficient for domestic use and the strength was only 40 percent, whereas that imported from Germany was 60 to 100 proof. Russia produced sufficient quantities of turpentine for her use.[184] Unrefined sulfuric acid was produced in large amounts although sulfuric acid of chemical cleanliness was imported from abroad.[185] By World War I the Russian pharmaceutical industry further produced sufficient amounts of potassium chlorate, cotton batting, fitin, lanolin, amygdalin, tannalbin, calomel, adrenaline, terpinhydrate, sulfo-carbolic zinc, and "many other small chemical products."[186]

Put another way, by World War I Russian pharmaceutical enterprises produced some seven million rubles' worth of wares in comparison with three million rubles' worth of imported products.[187] Thirty-nine crucial medicaments and disinfectants were produced in Russia and forty-eight were imported.[188]

Nevertheless, despite these signs of progress, at the outset of World War I, it was alleged that 64 percent of Russian pharmaceuticals came from abroad. Crucial plant substances such as iodine and alkaloids like morphine, cocaine, quinine, codeine, and atropine as well as mineral-based salicylic preparations and febrifuges, such as phenacetin, antipyrine, piramidon, and *salol*, were imported.[189] Reputedly, between 1909 and 1913, imports of iodine and bromine almost doubled from 3,564 *puds* in 1909 to 6,964 *puds* in 1911.[190] Further, Russia imported iodine almost exclusively from Germany, which produced 90 percent of the world's supply.[191] Imports of salicylic preparations ranged from 6,100 *puds* in 1909 to 8,800 *puds* in 1913. Imports of arsenic and its acids increased from 15,000 *puds* to 22,000 *puds* in 1913 with a dip to 17,000 *puds* in 1912. The amount of imported opium doubled from 500 *puds* in 1909 to 1,000 in 1913 although there was a cutback to 400 in 1910. Russia imported from 3,300 *puds* to 4,300 *puds* of quinine and its salts each year. In aggregate, imports of morphine, codeine, atropine, and cocaine remained at a steady 200 *puds* between 1909 and 1913 except for a cutback to 50 *puds* in 1910. Russia also did not produce chlorine, chloric acid, carbon, and phosphorous.[192] This foreign dependency was to be traumatic at the outset of World War I. How had it come about?

9

The Russian Pharmaceutical Industry: In Need of a Cure

Notwithstanding the strides taken by the pharmaceutical industry, Russian pharmacist-theorists–and in one case a foreigner–periodically sounded alarms that the country was overly dependent on foreign pharmaceuticals. Most were couched in terms of the drain on national coffers. In 1885, V. I. Kozlov complained that total imports of chemicals and dyes during 1879 cost forty-one million rubles–nearly seven times more than the sum of domestic production.[1] In 1900, one Eugene Shatskii, privatdocent at the University of Kazan, vituperated that: "Our great and able country annually pays a 10,000,000- to 15,000,000-ruble 'tribute' to foreigners [for medicines]."[2] In 1906 D. A. Ruffman, director of Parke, Davis and Company, noted accusingly: "Notwithstanding the fact that the laboratory is turning out so many home-made products, the firm of Ferrein is still buying enormous quantities of foreign pharmaceuticals and chemicals, which, together with their own wares, they are selling at wholesale and retail to jobbers, pharmacists, druggists, and the public direct."[3] In 1906, pharmacists at a Congress in St. Petersburg fretted: "Medicinal herbs are cultivated in the southern provinces . . . pharmacists must create pharmaceutical factories which abolish dependence of our factories and pharmacies on foreign firms such as Merck, Shering, Shimpel, Parke, Davis, etc."[4] In 1911, the organizing committee of the Society of Representatives of the Chemical Industry and Trade alleged that because government policies favored foreign pharmaceutical firms, imports of foreign medicines had risen 50 percent from 1906, from 7,000 *puds* to 11,500 *puds*.[5] In 1913, E. K. Khrzhanovskii, the St. Petersburg Pharmacy Society's representative to the Medical Council, implied that Russia was virtually bereft of domestic medicines and would be in a dangerous position should war occur:

> The increase in the scientific qualifications of our pharmacists provides the possibility for the rise of the chemical industry in Russia. Now Russia is in such a position that decisively she receives all medicines from abroad and in case, for example, of war and the cessation of foreign imports in Russia

> at the most in two or three months there would be a medicaments shortage [*lekarstvennyi golod*], since in this area we do not produce anything of our own.[6]

All these criticisms were exaggerations in one way or another and for one reason or another. Kozlov can be forgiven in that he was discussing the chemical and dye industry as well as the pharmaceutical industry, and the latter in his time was incipient. Shatskii was publishing in a Social-Democratic pharmacy journal, which typically portrayed the existing pharmacy system negatively. Ruffman visited pharmacies but may not have been familiar with all aspects of the Russian pharmaceutical industry. The same may have been true for pharmacists at the Pharmacy Congress. The Society of Representatives of the Chemical Industry and Trade were industrialists. Thus, their statement had stronger credibility although it left a lot unsaid. Nevertheless, as lobbyists, the society overstated the hardships that the industry faced. But Khrzhanovskii, pharmacy corporation representative to the Ministry of Internal Affairs, was so inaccurate in characterizing the industry and so prescient in his prediction of the so-called *lekarstvennyi golod,* or medicaments crisis, which occurred a year later at the outbreak of World War I, that one wonders both about his competency and about collusion with those hostile to pharmaceutical industrialists.

The Russian pharmaceutical industry did have flaws. However, these were not so much related to balance of payments. Rather, the main defect of Russia's pharmaceutical industry was that it did not produce adequate supplies of or did not produce altogether key medicines, principally opiates such as morphine and heroin; other plant-based medicines like cocaine, iodine, and quinine; and chemical-based medicines, particularly the coal-tar derivatives salicylic acid, aspirin and similar preparations.

The inadequate production of, or in some cases lack of production of, essential medicines resulted, in turn, from several factors: lack of certain crucial plants and minerals, feeble ties between pharmaceutical chemists and the pharmaceutical industry, preference for foreign-made products. But the biggest single factor was misguided government economic policy—excessive government interference in pharmaceutical production and tariffs that favored foreign firms at the expense of domestic.

A major problem for the Russian pharmaceutical industry was lack of crucial plant materials. In part this was due to the fact that no one bothered to cultivate them. In 1898, A. G. Kling, editor of *Farmatsevticheskii vestnik,* urged Russians to increase domestic cultivation of medicinal plants.[7] In 1915, V. G. Varzar, an official in the Ministry of Trade and Industry, attributed failure to cultivate crucial medicinal plants to absence of an internal market.[8] Pharmaceutical firms themselves placed a large measure of blame on the Ministry of Agriculture, asserting it had made no effort to encourage growing or collecting crucial plants, such as opium poppies and seaweed for iodine.[9]

But lack of crucial medical plants also resulted from Russia's geography and climate. Her northern latitude and short growing season made cultivation of some medicinal plants difficult, although the "white nights" partly compensated.[10] Additionally, medicinal plants that were available often were of poor quality. In particular, they had low alkaloid content. The Russian government spent millions of rubles on the culture of Chavinsk tea, but the tea was mediocre. Attempts to cultivate rhubarb in Minsk by one private enterprise continued for fifteen years, but rhubarb suitable for medicine was obtained only in the seventh year.[11] Similarly, Vladimir Karlovich Ferrein did not get good results from cultivating certain medicinal plants, although application of a phosphorous-nitrate-potassium compound raised the alkaloid content of some. He achieved particular success with *Hydrastis Canadensis,*[12] the goldenseal plant whose root stalk produced a bitter, crystalline alkaloid used in treating constipation.

Poor alkaloid content especially affected Russian production of opiates. Russia imported raw opium, chiefly from Turkey[13] but also from Persia,[14] because her own opium had a low morphine content. The Russian Civilian Pharmacopoeia required opium with a morphine content of 10 percent.[15] Caucasian opium contained a minuscule amount of morphine–only 1.58 to 1.74 percent.[16] Opium from Russian poppies generally had a morphine content of only 8.17 to 8.23 percent. The conquest of Central Asia in the 1860s and 1870s presented Russia with a golden opportunity for domestic opium production. However, the government prohibited the growing of opium poppies there.[17] In 1910, two types of poppies were cultivated in the Iur'ev-Dorpat botanical garden. One yielded 12.20 percent morphia.[18] Unfortunately, production was arduous and still in the experimental stage.

Although the Russian government banned the growing of opium poppies in Semirech'e in the Turkestan region of Central Asia, *Dungane*–Chinese Mohammedans who had migrated to Semirech'e to flee Chinese persecution in the early eighteenth century–grew opium poppies anyway. Local authorities periodically confiscated and burned the illegal opium–reputedly 200,000 rubles' worth at the time of World War I. Stores that escaped this vigilance were sent to China for smoking. However, the opium sold for very low prices and analysis of confiscated opium showed it to be of little medicinal value.[19] Shortage of opium at the outset of World War I finally compelled the Russian government to reverse its position and encourage cultivation of the opium poppy in Semirech'e. More than 5,000 dessiatines were sown to the opium poppy in 1916. The center of cultivation was Pishpek, especially the Dungan villages of Aleksandrovsk, Tokmak, Przheval'sk, and Dzharkent. In Przheval'sk Russians as well as Dungan, Kirghiz, and other natives participated in growing the opium poppy; the Dungan acted as instructors. Late in 1916, it was reported that these experiments had yielded high-quality opium, especially from Dzharkent, and while railroads were inadequate, it was hoped that after the war pharmacists in the area would develop a Russian opiate industry.[20] Opium gathered from other "southern regions" (apparently the Caucasus) sown to opium poppies in World War I–despite worry that opium poppy cultivation would lead to opium smoking[21]–had to be sent to special laboratories to extract the maximum amount of meager alkaloid content.[22] Opium confiscated by the Ministry of Finance in Vladivostok in 1915 yielded not more than 1 percent morphia.[23] And in 1916, an article in *Farmatsevticheskii zhurnal* confirmed that "The opium poppy is not raised in Russia because attempts to cultivate it have not given good results. In the Caucasus around Derbent is the Aliev farm, where from one fourth of a dessiatine [a little over ½ acre] is gathered up to 12 *funt* of opium, which sells for 5 rubles per *funt*."[24]

The attempt to domestically source iodine also proved difficult. According to pharmacist-industrialists V. I. Pokhitonov and P. B. Shaklovskii, and F. G. (A.) Ferrein, scion of the Ferrein pharmaceutical family, the type of seaweed from which iodine could be derived was found only at great depth in the northern waters of Russia.[25] Shtol' and Shmidt, in St. Petersburg, spent a significant amount searching Russia's far eastern waters for seaweed adequate for producing iodine. The firm's efforts came to naught.[26]

Nevertheless, other countries, most specifically Russia's rival Germany, were forced to import medicinal plants. Sound economic principles, in fact, endorsed importing items that were too costly or infeasible to produce at home. Unfortunately Russia's attempts to import crucial raw materials ran into roadblocks. In the case of iodine, a syndicate controlled supply. Ninety percent of the world's iodine, about 100,000 kilograms a year, came from the brine of Chilean saltpeter. The rest–about 10,000 kilograms–were extracted from seaweed predominantly found off the coast of Norway. To prevent a glut of iodine and consequent lowering of prices, the syndicate reputedly destroyed excess supplies.[27]

Far more pernicious were the Russian government's export and tariff policies. It was alleged that Russia exported raw materials for some alkaloids and glucosides that, in turn, she imported from Western European countries.[28] In any case, Russia's tariffs worked against her pharmaceutical companies.

Tariffs protected domestic pharmaceutical production until the 1880s.

In the decades following, tariffs discouraged importation of raw materials necessary for Russian production and encouraged importation of prepared medicines.[29] The Russian-German tariff treaty of 1904 particularly favored German pharmaceuticals over domestic.[30] It was claimed that Germany took advantage of Russia during the Russo-Japanese War. Following the war, pharmacist entrepreneur Roman Romanovich Keler served as consultant to the tariff commission in the Ministry of Finance. He strove to erect a tariff that would protect the Russian pharmaceutical industry.[31] In 1909 *Russkiia vedomosti* announced that "in the near future the import tariff on manufactured pharmaceutical wares was to be raised."[32]

Unfortunately, this did not happen. Examples abounded of heavy tariffs on raw materials and light tariffs on prepared items. Quinine required thirty-three *puds* of cinchona bark. Customs duty for the bark amounted to 28 rubles, 5 kopeks. Meanwhile, the tariff for a *pud* of prepared quinine was a mere 2 rubles, 25 kopeks.[33] Fifty *puds* of tea were needed to make one *pud* of caffeine. Tariffs on a *pud* of caffeine cost a paltry 2 rubles, but the tariff on fifty *puds* of tea equaled 562 rubles.[34] Similarly, the difference between a *pud* of raw cotton and a *pud* of foreign hygroscopic cotton was one ruble.[35] The same obtained with opium and its alkaloids. Since Russian opium was deficient in morphine content Russia needed to import opium. Yet the rates for morphine and other finished opiate-based products were lower than for crude opium. The tariff on a *pud* of opium was 22 rubles and 50 kopeks while the morphine derived from it was subject to duties of 80 rubles per *pud*. Much opium contained only 10 percent morphine; therefore, one needed ten *puds* of opium to produce a *pud* of morphine. This drove up the import tax for enough opium to make a *pud* of morphine 220 rubles. German pharmaceutical firms undercut Russian morphine by selling this substance at 145 rubles a *pud*. Tariffs also were higher on salicylic acid than its product, aspirin. The import tax on a *pud* of aspirin was 4 rubles. The tax on the amount of salicylic acid needed to make a *pud* of aspirin was 11 rubles.[36] In 1924, F. G. (A.) Ferrein, by this time an official in the Soviet government agency in charge of pharmaceutical production, still railed about how illogical tsarist tariffs had retarded Russia's prewar pharmaceutical industry.[37]

Russia lacked minerals as well as medicinal plants for key medicaments. She imported salicylic preparations from Germany, in part because she did not produce sufficient amounts of benzol, phenol (carbolic acid), and toluol, key components of these preparations.[38] Sulfuric and hydrochloric acid of chemical purity also were imported from Germany before World War I.[39] Further, unrefined sulfuric acid was not produced in Russia in sufficient quantities.[40] Inadequate production of cheap sulfuric acid was criticized as early as 1885. At that time, to produce the amount of soda imported from abroad, Russian industry needed 1 and 2/3 million *puds* of sulfuric acid. However, she produced only 1 and 1/3 million *puds* of sulfuric acid and only 100,000 *puds* of hydrochloric acid. Insufficient production of primary chemicals retarded production of other chemicals. In 1879, Russia produced only six million rubles' worth of chemicals and dye products and imported forty-one million rubles' worth.

In 1885 Kozlov astutely attributed this situation to three factors: poor tariff policy, lack of capital, and lack of ties between industry and chemist-pharmacists. Tariffs were lowered in the 1870s and early 1880s on several chemicals to make them more affordable for the cloth printing and dyeing industry.[41] Too easy access to foreign chemicals obviously inhibited Russia's domestic chemical industry. As for cooperation between industry and chemists, Germans cornered the dye market from the 1860s and the aspirin market from the 1890s by tying research to industrial production.[42]

In 1915, Russia still had not properly integrated pharmacists-chemists into her pharmaceutical industry.[43] True, some Russian pharmacologists made important breakthroughs in their laboratories, some pharmacists-pharmacologists founded their own pharmaceutical concerns, and large firms such as Ferrein employed pharmacist-chemists. However, in 1915, V. I. Pokhitonov, member of the Society for Developing the Chemical Industry and Trade, particularly criticized Russia's poor use of coal-tar byproducts, essential ingredients for dyes, carbolic acid, and salicylic preparations.[44]

Of course, by the early twentieth century, German control of patents for coal-tar products put Russia at a disadvantage.[45] In this vein, it must be noted that before World War I America also failed to produce sufficient amounts of benzol and toluol (toluene). In 1918, Grinnell Jones, chemist to the United States Tariff, acknowledged that "In 1914 our production of crude light oil would have been sufficient for the production of only about 4,500,000 gallons of benzol and of about 1,500,000 gallons of toluol . . . only a part of which was distilled. . . . In 1917 our output of benzol was 40,200,000 gallons and of toluol 10,200,000 gallons . . . the war we had no synthetic phenol industry."[46]

Nevertheless, areas of research were still open to Russians, although those which Russian pharmacists specifically cited appeared minor. P. B. Shaskol'skii, reporting on the state of Russian mineral water production in 1915, criticized lack of a chair of balneology at Russian universities and the Military Medical Academy. He called for systematic study of Russian waters to increase and improve domestic mineral water output.[47] M. I. Sosaar, who sat on the administrative board of Pel' and Sons, asserted that the Russian match syndicate had quashed production of phosphorous some years earlier when it decided to order phosphorous from abroad at the very time that electrical methods of production were introduced.[48] In 1916, *Farmatsevticheskii zhurnal* emphasized that there were no chairs, courses, or even specialists for producing chemicals and pharmaceuticals in any higher technical educational institution in Russia. Russia imported millions of rubles' worth of organic dyes from Germany each year despite the fact that a Russian chemist Zinin had obtained the basic aniline material for pigments from benzol. In 1913, Russia prepared 150 million *puds* of portland cement, in 1915, 300 million *puds*. Yet there were no specialists on silicates, particularly cement.[49]

Those distressed by Russia's lagging pharmaceutical industry alleged further that private individuals and firms had concentrated on unearthing valuable minerals such as gold, copper, and lead. They had neglected to search for minerals crucial to pharmaceutical production such as bromine, bismuth, boron, and mercury, used in making sublimate. The tendency of Russians, pharmacists included, to rely on the government was underscored by the suggestion that the government order the Geology Committee to search for valuable minerals.[50]

Preference on the part of some physicians and consumers for foreign-made medicines hurt the Russian pharmaceutical industry. During World War I, K. I. Kresling, of the St. Petersburg Pharmacy Society, claimed that "doctors always prefer preparations by . . . Merck, Shering, Gee. . . ."[51] D. M. Shcherbachev, privatdocent at Moscow University, noted that while "Many doctors and zemstvos–Tver, Ekaterinoslav, and others refused to use patented medicines because they were too expensive and fully replaced them with 'identical' preparations, in general German druggists have hypnotised us." However, he admitted that "druggists of the South" eroded confidence by selling poor-quality wares.[52] And, indeed, if pharmaceutical firms had routinely used pharmacist-chemists and practiced adequate quality control, foreign competition should have spurred Russian production.

Thus, it appeared that an essential, perhaps *the* most essential, debilitating influence on the Russian pharmaceutical industry was excessive government regulation and interference. The Medical Council was mandated to approve production of all medicines and pharmaceutical wares. It zealously carried out its mission, scrutinizing and essaying every product in minute detail.

In just one month, April 1891, the Medical Council rejected the request of an Assistant Pharmacist in Kazan to prepare and sell Santiago balsam for toothaches, headaches, rheumatism, and other ills; the request of a *meshchanin*, or "citizen," in Rostov-on-Don to sell Santiago balsam drops for toothaches; and the petition of a Provizor to prepare and market Santiago balsam as tooth drops, elixir, and powder. Additionally, the Medical Council rejected a dentist's request of a patent for his rheumatism- and tooth-pain remedy on the grounds that dentists did not have the right to treat or prepare and sell medicines, and also because his preparation did not contain anything new. The Medical Council approved two petitions—that of a Provizor in Warsaw to prepare and sell a corn plaster that contained nothing harmful to the health, and that of a dentist in Yaroslavl' to prepare and sell a tooth elixir that was not harmful to tooth enamel.[53] Similarly, in one month in 1900, the Medical Council approved Provizor Gesner's preparing a complex camphor essence for over-the-counter sale. At the same time the Medical Council denied the petition of "Maria Ye." to prepare the liquid "Naturanie" as a cure for various diseases, and the council also rejected the petition of Provizor Gesner to make cough syrup and headache drops.[54]

An 1898 law "On Factory production of complex pharmaceutical preparations" was touted as a stimulus for factory production of medicine because it permitted "Masters of Pharmacy and persons with a higher chemical education to organize production of medicinal substances in special factories, laboratories and sections of chemical enterprises."[55] Unfortunately, any shot in the arm that this law provided was neutralized by the Medical Council's continued restrictions on factory production and trade.

For example, in 1905 Israil Zakovich, a Provizor who had received a Ph.D. from the University of Zurich, penned a letter to the Medical Department requesting permission to open a factory for production of chemical, pharmaceutical, and galenical preparations. As Zakovich had adequate credentials, the Medical Department approved this request.[56] In 1909, however, Peasant Aleksei Dmitrievich Makarov sent a hand-penned request, duly bearing two 75-kopek stamps, to the Chief Medical Inspector, asking permission to make and sell a "Universal Remedy to treat colds, tumors, fevers, cholera, and stomach catarrh." The Medical Council rejected his petition on the grounds that the substance could not cure the diseases mentioned.[57] In 1913 the Medical Council rejected Ivan Karnovich Eknadsiosov's request to "produce mineral water from sulfuric water found on the land belonging to him in the . . . region of the Don army" because "there was no guarantee that the source was not subject to dirty water."[58] The council likewise rejected two proposals from I. N. Ivanov and Z. N. Ivanov, owners of "a laboratory of complex pharmaceutical and galenical preparations," because analytical analysis had shown that the contents and recipe of one product "did not correspond" and the second preparation had "irrational composition." However, it approved two other products for preparation and sale and published their recipes.[59] Although such impeccable scrutiny benefited the Russian consumer, they throttled the pharmaceutical industry. The lengthy process of petitioning the government and the latter's detailed debates over every trivial aspect of the proposed manufacture of medicaments stifled initiative and output.

Government regulations on the sale of factory-prepared medicines to drug stores also worked against the pharmaceutical industry. For example, in 1879 the Samara provincial medical administration rejected local Provizor Ivan Iakovlev Rekk's petition to open wholesale and retail trade in pharmaceutical wares and substances. The determined Provizor repeatedly petitioned the provincial medical department.[60]

Sometimes, local medical authorities gave the laws a little more elasticity. In 1905, the Kiev provincial medical department informed the Chief Medical Inspector that, on the basis of a Ministry of Internal Affairs Circular of 1883, no. 219, it had permitted a dentist to prepare and sell a tooth elixir.[61] In 1905, the Orlov provincial medical department similarly gave a local pharmacy owner the right to sell cosmetic substances on the condition that they did not contain anything harmful to the health.[62] But only ambiguity in the regulations allowed this latitude.

One indication of the deleterious effect of government regulations on the pharmaceutical industry was the dearth of entries between 1905 and 1917 in the large government registry: *Russian Preparations . . . following Requests About Pharmacy Production.*[63]

In 1911, the organizing committee of the Society of Representatives of Chemical Industry and Trade lashed out at government controls, asserting that the "unsatisfactory position of Russian pharmaceutical factories resulted" from the fact that they "cannot make new preparations without the decision of the Chief Medical Inspector's Administration . . . lists of permitted preparations slow production."[64]

Four years later, during World War I, F. G. (A.) Ferrein lambasted the restrictions on production and trade. He stressed that for the industry to grow, the stipulation that industrialists receive prior approval for production must be done away with. Pharmaceutical enterprises must have the freedom to produce and tailor medicaments to their customers.[65]

Worse still, not only did the Russian government confine domestic pharmaceutical manufacturers, but frustrated pharmaceutical entrepreneurs alleged that the government was unduly lenient in permitting foreign products to enter Russia.

The Medical Council did deny requests from foreigners to import or produce products as evinced by published records in pharmacy journals[66] and the archival files of the Medical Council. Nevertheless, a number of foreign nostrums circulated. Dover's Powders was commonly used.[67] In 1879, F. D. Iordana, a deputy to the Medical Council, sarcastically noted that "Curious foreigners, predominantly French and English–and recently German–charlatans concerned about the public health in Russia, attempt to bring in their patented medicines to this poor state." He alerted pharmacists to sixteen foreign proprietary nostrums that he considered pernicious or worthless.[68] In the 1890s the Medical Council permitted the importation of 139 foreign prepared medicines and additional homeopathic substances.[69] More "permissions" were doled out in succeeding years, for example, to a German chemical company[70] and to an Austrian firm to import medicinal wine.[71] Equally significant were government "privileges" to foreign firms to develop Russian resources, such as that in 1901 to the joint-stock company "Berlin" to produce protein.[72] The number of patents granted to foreigners appeared to outnumber those granted to Russians.[73] In 1913, pharmacists claimed that suspicious foreign laboratories, such as the "New York Institute of Knowledge," staffed with nonexistent professors and physicians, were still advertising proprietary medicines that, "after years of research and a long series of clinical tests" would accomplish health miracles.[74]

In 1907, the Medical Council itself acknowledged that it was not as strict toward foreign proprietary medicines as toward domestic. Although it analyzed both foreign and domestic proprietary medicines, it published the ingredients of domestic patent medicines in *Vestnik obshchestvennoi gigieny, sudebnoi i prakticheskoi meditsiny* but did not do so in the case of foreign remedies. As a result, foreign medicines were advertising specious health claims for their products. Consequently, the Medical Council determined to publish the ingredients of these product.[75] In succeeding years the Medical Council did publish "recipes" and methods of making foreign medicines, including patent or proprietary medicines, which it permitted to be imported from abroad both in the official *Vestnik obshchestvennoi gigieny, sudebnoi i prakticheskoi meditsiny* and the journals of pharmaceutical societies, such as *Farmatsevticheskii zhurnal.*[76] This practice, in conjunction with article 198 of the Statute on Industry, 1906 edition, which forbade the granting of "privileges" for chemical substances and medicines,[77] led to a forceful, if belated, attempt on the part of the ministry of Internal Affairs to boost the domestic pharmaceutical industry on the eve of World War I.[78] However, little was actually achieved from this attempt, which will be discussed in a later chapter. In 1915, an angry F. G. (A.) Ferrein went so far as to call for a ban on foreign galenical preparations.[79]

Restrictions and regulations on manufacture kept the Russian pharmaceutical industry in leading strings. However, in fairness, it must be noted that restrictions on pharmaceutical factories and internal trade were partly, perhaps even largely, the result of lobbying, which pharmacy owners had engaged in for decades against both drug stores and pharmaceutical enterprises. Many pharmacy owners, bred in a climate of protectionism, could not think in other terms and demanded more, not less protection.

From 1882, according to a 1915 account, pharmacy owners viewed increasing factory production as "undesirable competition." They feared that the greater accuracy,[80] convenience and eventual cheapness of prepackaged medicines, particularly if sold in drug stores, would make pharmacy laboratories obsolete. The Commission for Composition of the Pharmacy Tax, chaired by Privy Councillor Ragozin, raised the issue of factory production of pharmaceuticals in Russia in 1891 and successive years—1893, 1894, and 1895. The Medical Council discussed factory production of medicine in 1895. But, in 1898, the twenty-two members of the St. Petersburg Pharmaceutical Society (including Shaskol'skii[81] and Kling) went so far as to reject "in principle" the need for special pharmaceutical factories. They claimed that production of medicaments in the pharmacy was sufficient. However, when they discovered it was impossible to buck the trend and stop the rise of pharmaceutical factories, the St. Petersburg Pharmacy Society grudgingly accepted the proposal, which became the Law of May 11, 1898, on creation of factories. The society managed to insert the stipulation that Masters of Pharmacy and Provizors must manage these factories to provide a modicum of protection for pharmacists.[82] The 1898 provision was included in the new Pharmacy Statute, which was being drafted in 1904. The draft statute mandated that managers of "pharmaceutical factories and special departments of chemical factories must be pharmacists, with not less than two years service . . . the [new] provincial pharmacy inspector must be informed of the acceptance and firing of the manager."[83]

In 1906, D. A. Ruffman, Parke, Davis and Company executive, accused pharmacy owners of "constantly pleading before the Medical Council (through the two delegates who represent the pharmacists of Russia at the sittings of the Medical Council) to 'shut out' the foreign pharmaceuticals and to wrench from the 'drug stores' that bit of limited right which they are possessing now in selling household and other prepared medicaments."[84]

Unfortunately, many pharmacists resisted Ruffman's argument that "Nowadays, when chemistry, pharmacy, and medicine have far more products than was the case 40 or 50 years ago, a Russian *apteka* [pharmacy] that is expected to concoct and mix up all the preparations prescribed by physicians cannot cope with such a task without having large premises, an ample stock of drugs, and a large staff of trained pharmacists . . ." although doctors realized that "the Russian *apteka* does not answer the present requirements, and that the nation is paying far more for a badly prepared medicine in the *apteka* than for a correctly made-up article that hails from an up-to-date laboratory."[85]

Nevertheless, some pharmacy owners themselves became large-scale producers of pharmaceuticals. These entrepreneurs advocated some protection from foreign pharmaceuticals but free internal trade. Marxist pharmacists, in particular, urged development of a pharmaceutical industry, perhaps partly for reasons of common sense, but also because Marxist ideology canonized industrial progress.

S. K. Lintser, a socialist when staff pharmacists were concerned, followed Adam Smith in the area of pharmaceutical production and trade. Sometime editor of *Farmatsevticheskii vestnik* until its demise in 1906 and editor of *Russkii farmatsevt* from 1908, Lintser vociferously criticized all aspects of the "pharmaceutical monopoly" (restrictions on establishing pharmacies and dispensing medicines). In 1904 he particularly castigated the rule that managers of chemical factories must be Masters of Pharmacy.[86]

The Social Democratic journal *Farmatsevticheskii trud* lauded pharmacy owner and industrialist Roman Romanovich Keler for advocating development of the Russian pharmaceutical industry and fighting pharmacy owners' opposition to prepared pharmaceuticals. The socialist journal portrayed Keler as something of a maverick for daring to publish his pamphlets, "A Truthful Word to Authorities, Society, and the People" in 1894; "The Truth About One Social Issue" in 1898 (adumbrated in the previous chapter); and his newest work from 1906, "Under the Protection of Orders and Circulars," claiming that the last emphasized how the "pharmacy monopoly" stifled factory-production of medicines and caused a medicaments shortage in rural areas.[87]

The Russian pharmaceutical industry provides insight into why business did not flourish as it should have in late imperial Russia. Entrepreneurs did forge a pharmaceutical industry. Some of their wares were of high quality. They successfully competed with foreign pharmaceutical firms in terms of goods as well as services. However, excessive government interference hobbled development. Inadequate government control over the pharmaceutical sector was harmful to the American consumer in the nineteenth-, early twentieth-century. But unfavorable tariffs and too much government control stifled the Russian pharmaceutical industry. The Russian pharmaceutical industry presented a classic case of the negative effects of big government and ill-conceived government policy.

In the decade before World War I the Ministry of Internal Affairs would attempt to boost the domestic pharmaceutical industry. World War I, so cataclysmic for the Russian Empire, would prove a major catalyst for the Russian pharmaceutical industry. Unfortunately, antibusiness sentiment would also increase during the war.

10

Pharmacists and Public Health

Milestones in the English public health movement, such as John Snow's linking the spread of cholera to the Broad Street Pump, are enshrined in the annals of medical history. Generations have become familiar with the American "Pure Food and Drug" movement from Upton Sinclair's *The Jungle.* It is popularly assumed that obsession with ecology and diet are contemporary phenomena. Few realize that nineteenth, early twentieth-century Russians were concerned about adulteration of food and pollution of the environment. If not in the vanguard, or even in the mainstream, Russia at least participated in the world public health movement. And pharmacists were among the leading players.

The tsarist government, traditional guardian of public health, led the crusade against falsification and pollution of food and drink.[1] In the late sixteenth and early seventeenth centuries, in line with other European states, which displayed a "connection between sixteenth- and seventeenth-century state building and 'social disciplining,'"[2] the Russian government turned its attention to food, regulating the quality and price of bread.[3] The Russian government also licensed production and sale of spirits from the seventeenth century, although this legislation was inaugurated by budgetary concerns rather than public health.[4] In the eighteenth century the Governing Senate encouraged the growing of potatoes and in 1782 prohibited the selling of spoiled foodstuffs.[5] In the early nineteenth century the Russian government focused on the quality of tea and alcohol sold in the country. In 1816 the newly formed Committee of Ministers issued a regulation (*Vysochaishe utverzhdennoe polozhenie*) forbidding the substitution of inferior tea for Chinese tea.[6] This regulation "strictly prohibited gathering the herb from which was made *kaporskii* tea [sometimes spelled *koporskii*] or Ivan-tea" and the sale of such herb in place of real Chinese tea.[7] The herb in question was *kipreia,* or *Epibolium angustifolium.* According to Master of Pharmacy A. V. Pel', the leaves of *Epibolium angustifolium* were not harmful to the health–consequently, sale of them constituted "economic harm" rather than "sanitary harm."[8] Since the term "Ivan" was slang for peasant, it may be inferred that this tea was used by peasants.[9] In

1819 the Committee of Ministers forbade adding "lead sugar" to drink, specifically to *vino*–a term which may have referred to wine or "common drinks based on spirits."[10]

The individuals responsible for drafting this legislation and their motivation have not been determined.[11] However, by the middle of the nineteenth century, pharmacists and other health professionals began assisting the government in promoting pure food and environment.[12] What is more interesting, these specialists began to educate the public about the importance of pure food and environment, underscoring both growing literacy and increasing medical sophistication in imperial Russia.[13]

As early as 1848 Professor-Akademician Pavel Gorianinov directed his book on mushrooms to both the medical police and the general public. He noted that mushrooms were commonly eaten with bread in the western provinces of the Russian Empire. Although mushroom poisoning was rare in Russia, his book was intended to forestall tragedies such as the recent death of eight peasants in Podolia, announced the previous year by the St. Petersburg city police.[14]

In 1859, Doctor of Chemistry and Physics A. N. Khodnev, infused with cameralist sentiments–"the wealth of the government lies in the health of its people, especially the poorer classes"–addressed a 276-page book on analyzing food and drink to "all sorts of educated homeowners." Khodnev claimed that Russia's medical police, in contrast to those in Western Europe, neglected foodstuffs sold in the marketplace; medical statutes focused only on cases of death from immediate poisoning. Meanwhile, adulteration was prevalent, in some cases because tradesmen received food in this state. His book was designed to enable homeowners to protect themselves. Khodnev reviewed instruments and chemicals required for analyzing food and drink, recommending thirty-two apparatus and vessels including thermometers, weights, areometer, microscope, "spirtometer," vessels, and fifty-six chemicals including distilled water, alcohol, nitric acid, muriatic acid, sulfuric acid, reactive paper. Appearing somewhat self-serving, Khodnev advised his readers to purchase these items from The Trading Firm C. Strugovshchikh, G. Pokhitonov, P. Vodov and Company, who had published the book.[15] In his introduction and the chapters devoted to flour and bread; sugar, candy and sweeteners; meat; seasonings; tea, coffee, and cocoa; and spirits, Khodnev provided numerous illustrations of apparatus and microscopes. He discussed both tests that could be used at the market–smelling, examining physical properties of the substance–and more thorough chemical tests to be done at home,[16] assuming both a sophisticated and well-fed readership.

In his *Outlines of the Bases of Sanitary Activity*, A. Dobroslavin, Professor-Akademician at the Medical-Surgical Academy in St. Petersburg, claimed that in Russia the "business of public health had made few strides forward, despite progress in some provinces in recent years." However, Russia still lagged behind England, where "attention to sanitary matters" was ahead of continental countries. Dobroslavin, therefore, decided to publish a short handbook for the use of zemstvo physicians on the order of E. Smith's *Manuel* [*sic*] *for medical officers of health*, in its second edition, and Hart's 1874 *Manuel* [*sic*] *of public health.*[17] Far more technical than Khodnev's work, Dobroslavin discussed pure air in dwellings, heating, water supply, and food, comparing foreign and Russian legislation on these subjects.[18]

One Tikhomirov published a second book on edible and poisonous mushrooms in Moscow in 1879.

Further, translations of English, French, and German books on food appeared in Russia in the 1860s and 1870s. *Issues of Nutrition* was translated from the English by A. S. Ermolov and published in St. Petersburg in 1872. *On Nutrition in a Physiological, Pathological, and Therapeutic Sense* was translated from the French by A. N. Morigerovsky and appeared in St. Petersburg the same year. Another work on a similar subject, *Studies about Nutrition in Physiological and Therapeutic Relations,* was translated from its second English edition by M. Manassein and published in St. Petersburg in 1876.[19]

Despite Dobroslavin's accusation, the Russian government's interest in pure food, drink, and environment did not wane but, in fact, escalated in the second half of the nineteenth century. This resulted from both international[20] and internal factors.[21] In 1868 the Medical Council of the Russian Ministry of Internal Affairs recommended a simple method of testing wallpaper for dangerous dyes–particularly green dyes, which contained arsenic. This involved putting a teaspoon of ammonia on the green color for five to ten minutes and watching the reaction.[22] In 1878 and 1885, after publication of Dobroslavin's work, the Ministry of Internal Affairs issued circulars prohibiting the use of lead sheets and lead vessels for storing food including tea, chocolate, cheese, sausage, tinned or preserved meat, and cigarettes.[23]

Local governments also began to take a more active part in insuring pure food and environment. Finland, though part of the Russian Empire, enjoyed a separate legal system.[24] In 1888 Finland passed a law forbidding the preparation, storage or sale of wallpaper dyed with arsenic.[25]

In addition, the government transferred some jurisdiction over sales of food and drink to municipalities and Justice-of-the-Peace courts through regulations in new editions of the Statute on Rural and Urban Economy, the Statute on Industry, the Medical Statute, and the Statute on Punishments to be Imposed by Justice-of-the-Peace Courts, all of which appeared in the mid-1860s. Four articles from 1866, amendments to the Statute on Urban and Rural Economy, the Statute on Industry, and the Medical Statute, focused on falsification of *vino,* or wine.[26] The first article decreed punishment for the sale of Russian or artificial wine in place of foreign or real wine. The second article ordained that on the bottles of wine prepared in Russia there must be labels with the firm or name of the seller (*vinotorgovets*). The third article forbade the importing of foreign corks, stamped with brands of foreign trading houses, separately from importing bottles. The fourth article, appended to the statute of the medical police, prohibited including in *vino* or other drinks substances harmful to the health, especially metallic or "strong-acting" substances.[27] As noted, the Medical Council of the Ministry of Internal Affairs published and periodically updated a list of 300 "strong-acting substances, including narcotics and poisons, which pharmacists were to keep in locked cabinets and dispense only upon a doctor's prescription.[28]

The 1866 statutes on "Punishments to be Imposed by the Justice-of-the-Peace Courts," instituted in 1864,[29] targeted the use of false weights and measures and other fraud affecting sale of wares and also forbade the "preparation for sale or sale of edibles or drinks which were harmful to the health or spoiled."[30]

Penalties for disregarding these laws varied. Originally the punishment for fraud in sale was limited to three months' incarceration if the value of the falsified item was less than 300 rubles.[31] Imprisonment increased to six months in attenuating circumstances–if several people were involved, when the perpetrators engaged in special preparation, or when the fraud affected minors, the blind, or the deaf.[32] If the value of the falsified item was under 300 rubles but the perpetrators were noble, monk, priest, or "honored citizen," these persons forfeited all special rights and privileges.[33] If deception involved an item worth more than 300 rubles, the swindler was liable to deprivation of rights and possible exile to Siberia.[34] Originally the penalty for preparation for sale or sale of food that was spoiled or harmful to the health amounted to imprisonment up to one month or a fine no higher than 100 rubles. However, if death resulted from the sale, the perpetrator permanently lost the right to engage in trade or preparation of food and drink and, if Christian, also was subject to punishment imposed by the Orthodox church.[35]

The medical and pharmaceutical profession did not consider this legislation entirely satisfactory. In 1887, Professor A. P. Dobroslavin, recently returned from an official fact-finding trip to Western Europe, asserted that

Russian laws on food adulteration were commensurate with those in England, Germany, and France and adequate in their own right.[36] In contrast to his earlier commendation of England, Dobroslavin now painted a dismal picture of that country. There had been only three hundred analyses of food in England in twelve years. Despite parliamentary investigations and tighter laws, during 1880, in forty-one cities, there had been not one investigation into the quality of food sold.[37] Laboratories in Paris made many more investigations than those in London.[38] Germany admitted there were flaws in her laws on food adulteration and was addressing them in the 1880s.[39] But while Dobroslavin now felt more comfortable with Russian legislation he believed more laboratories were needed to test foodstuffs.[40]

Master of Pharmacy A. V. Pel' was not as generous as Dobroslavin. In 1889 he dismissed Russian legislation on falsification as totally inadequate. He cited three main flaws: there was no "exactly established legislation regarding separate food products and items of use, . . . no special organs whose responsibility it was to observe and supervise the good quality of products sold, and finally, . . . no government-instituted laboratories in which scientific analysis could be conducted."[41]

F. F. Erisman, zemstvo doctor, specialist on eye diseases, and director of the Moscow City Sanitary Station, located in the University of Moscow, was a perennial critic of the Russian government. In the report of the first year's activity of the sanitary station in 1892, he lamented that Russian laws against adulteration and falsification lacked quantitative norms on fat or weight, specific punishments, institutions to enforce the laws in stores and bazaars, and that the public was "strangely indifferent" to the subject.[42]

V. M. Iakimov, member of the Voronezh Branch of the Russian Society for the Preservation of Public Health,[43] also was a severe critic, alleging in 1898 that Russian legislation on falsification of foodstuffs lagged behind that of the "West," notably England, Germany, and the Swiss cantons.[44] Iakimov specifically castigated existing legislation for not being specific enough, for focusing on falsification in sales rather than manufacture, and for imposing too-lenient penalties, and he also lamented the lack of laboratories for determining falsification and adulteration.[45]

How accurate were these criticisms? How did Russian legislation on falsification and adulteration compare with foreign? Although Iakimov claimed that Russian laws did not refer to manufacture, from the 1860s they included the clause "preparing for sale" as well as the simple term "sale," implying manufacture of the item sold.[46] As regards penalties, Russian legislation was similar to French and German. For example, a French law of 1851 prohibiting sales of "adulterated wares, foodstuffs, and medicaments," imposed a fine of 50 to 500 francs or imprisonment from three months to two years. Use of false weights incurred lighter punishment.

Pel', Erisman, and Iakimov stood on stronger ground when they asserted foreign laws had greater specificity; in addition, French and German laws gave police greater enforcement power. A French law of 1862 on the use of dyes in sweets and food products specifically excluded "Berlin blue, ultramarine, ochre, and chalk" from the rubric of dangerous dyes, specified that sweets or candy bear the label of the factory, required that syrups containing glucose bear labels enumerating the contents, and forbade adding starch, flour, and "other substances" to milk. This law instructed the Paris police and village police, with the help of "scientists," to examine workshops, stores, factory outlets, sales booths to verify their conformity with the law of 1851. The police could confiscate drinks and foodstuffs that appeared to be falsified; the case would then be decided by a court.[47]

A lengthy German law of 1879 did not enumerate specific dangerous substances but was exact in its own way and gave police inspectors a fair amount of authority. For example, foodstuffs, toys, wallpaper, dyes, mineral oil, and cooking vessels were subject to supervision. Police had "the right and the responsibility" to investigate places where these wares were made, stored, and sold in order to analyze them. Further, the German law ordained that "in order to preserve health, by order of the emperor," it was prohibited to "include harmful ingredients" in wares produced and sold; sell meat from diseased animals; use "some substances and dyes" in clothes, toys, wallpaper, tableware and cooking vessels, which were forbidden; and sell mineral oil lacking determined quality. Punishment was severe—a fine of 150 marks, deprivation of freedom or, if death resulted, imprisonment in a mental asylum up to five years[48]—but no more stringent than the Russian punishment of deprivation of right to trade and possible exile to Siberia in case fatality occurred.

A Belgian law of 1891 itemized prohibited harmful dyes.[49] An Italian law was late on the scene, having been published in 1890, but had separate articles for twenty-four items of food and drink, as well as pharmaceutical wares, tableware and cooking vessels, perfume, cosmetics, and petrol! Each article was very detailed. For example, each village or town of over six thousand inhabitants was required to have a public slaughterhouse.[50]

In addition to lack of specificity, Russian legislation was somewhat inconsistent. In 1874 Dobroslavin noted that according to article 52 of the Justice-of-the-Peace Court Statute, polluting canals and rivers warranted a fine of 10 rubles; according to article 53, polluting underground water pipes was punished by a fine not higher than 100 rubles; and according to article 111, urinating or polluting water sources not used for internal purposes netted a fine of not more than 25 rubles or detention for not more than seven days.[51]

Thus, Pel''s, Erisman's, and Iakimov's criticisms had some validity. But even as they voiced them the Russian government tightened legislation on pure food and household items and, more significantly, municipalities and Justice-of-the-Peace courts attempted to enforce these rules.

Pel' himself noted that two commissions were meeting in the Ministry of State Domains in the late 1880s. One was chaired by Professor Ivan Pavlovich Arkhipov. Arkhipov was a specialist on the falsification of wine, having published a work on this subject in 1887.[52] Arkhipov's commission was preparing legislation for the establishment of "state scientific institutions," which were to combat and prevent falsification. Simultaneously, a second commission was meeting under the chairmanship of Professor S. I. Botkin.[53]

In the 1890s, the Russian government imposed stricter penalties for violation of existing regulations and extended their purview. Where the mid-1860 laws had stipulated imprisonment up to one month or a fine no higher than 100 rubles, laws of 1899 designated imprisonment up to three months or a fine up to 300 rubles. Furthermore, food products sold in the marketplace were now to bear official stamps testifying to their healthfulness. If foods bore no such mark but were harmless, sellers were liable to imprisonment up to one month or a 100-ruble fine. If foodstuffs sold without the mark were harmful, the purveyor could be fined up to 300 rubles or imprisoned for up to three months.[54] Probably inflation somewhat lessened the onerousness of the higher fines. Nevertheless, it was obvious that progress was being made.

A regulation of 1891 addressed the manufacture and sale of margarine.[55] In addition, on July 19, 1895, the Ministry of Internal Affairs restricted meat sales with a circular that amplified articles 631 and 633 of the Medical Statute. These articles forbade the sale of meat from animals or birds suffering from Siberian plague (bubonic plague), glanders, smallpox, tuberculosis, trichinosis, and other diseases. The new regulations stipulated that animals known to be diseased could not be slaughtered. Meat from animals suffering from the aforementioned diseases and others could not be sold as food except in certain cases—for example, when the tuberculosis was localized, when tapeworms were few and could be destroyed by cooking at high temperatures, if the animal with worms did not appear to be wasted. Police and city officials were to observe whether meat or other edibles were not fresh or were harmful to the health.[56] In 1899, the government clamped down on harmful dyes. Imitating Finland, which passed a similar law in 1888, the Russian Medical Statute in 1899 forbade the preparation, storage, or sale of wallpaper dyed with arsenic; excluded was wallpaper displaying only minuscule amounts of green such as leaves in a floral pattern. This statute also prohibited the use of green dyes in children's toys.[57]

In addition to updating legislation, the Russian government took specific measures to prevent harm from adulteration and substitution. For example, in 1899 Pel' alerted the Medical Department of the Ministry of Internal Affairs to the fact that a poisonous anise substitute was being sold in the markets of St. Petersburg, Odessa, and Nizhni Novgorod. The Medical Department ordered local authorities to confiscate the substitute.[58]

Furthermore, in line with its traditional paternalism, the Russian government sponsored research on additives in food. In March 1900, it announced a competition for research on the use of dyes and aromatic essences, or "bouquets." Two prizes of 1,500 rubles were offered. One was to be awarded to a paper on essences, the other to research on dyes. Requirements were stringent. Winning papers were to be published.[59] Fifteen hundred rubles was more than the annual income of most pharmacists but less than that of university professors.[60] One wonders how many applied.

One of the most interesting aspects of the pure food and environment movement in Russia was public outreach. Since pharmacists and physicians continued to find Russian legislation wanting in the last decades of the nineteenth century, they increased their efforts to make the public more aware of adulteration and pollution. Further, they stimulated municipal governments in Moscow, St. Petersburg, Kiev, and Odessa to take greater responsibility for the purity of food and other products. A number of laboratories were established in these cities by municipal governments and pharmacy societies. Thus, the onus for pure food and environment was put in the proper place, on the shoulders of local government and the public—the constituencies most intimately involved. The last decades of the nineteenth century saw greater devolution and decentralization in the pure food and environment movement.

A spate of articles, pamphlets, and books were published during the 1880s and 1890s on harmful additives in food, food-borne diseases, harmful components of household items, and the evils of water and air pollution.[61] Some of these treatises were highly technical, intended for members of the health professions. However, a number were intended for the public. Unfortunately, there are no hard data on the numbers of people who actually purchased and read these books. However, in a market economy they would not have been published without estimated or intended readership; thus we can assume a fair amount were purchased and read.[62] They vividly capture the life-style and diets of various classes and groups at the turn of the century.

Russian translations, mainly of German works, continued to appear in the 1880s. Original Russian texts included Faerman's *Falsification of the Most Important Foodstuffs* (Odessa, 1881) and Geidenrikh's *Methods of Researching Lower Organisms* (St. Petersburg–first edition 1885, second, 1887).[63]

Works intended for the health professions included I. I. Kanonnikov's *Handbook of Chemical Research of Foodstuffs,* published in St. Petersburg in 1891, an 1890 article by S. N. Iakovlev, and a series of articles by A. S. Shcherbakov published in 1891. Kanonnikov was a professor of technical chemistry at Kazan University. His weighty tome of over 450 pages appeared to be a text for specialists; the foreword noted that the students in Kanonnikov's course had used the methods of analysis that the book described. Endpapers advertised books on healthy dwellings and dangerous heating systems, published in 1882, and on maintaining the health of factory workers, published in 1891. Written by engineers, these works sold for 2 and 3½ rubles, respectively–substantial sums for the general public.[64]

Kanonnikov devoted chapters to vegetables, bread, starch and dextrine, beer and *kvas,* spirits and strong drink, wine (Crimean, Caucasian, Bessarabian, and Don), eggs and mushrooms, spices, tea, coffee and chocolate, tobacco, sugar and honey, milk and milk products, animal and vegetable oil, water, and meat and meat products. He described the components of these foods and drinks, giving percentages and chemical formulae, ingredients used to preserve them, hundreds of methods by which international and Russian specialists analyzed them, and illustrations of the modern types of apparatus for this purpose. In the case of meat, for example, Kanonnikov discussed both fresh and preserved meat. He reviewed diseases found in meat, including parasites. He described meat parts used in sausages and preservatives for meat products. These included salicylic acid, flour, and dyes. However, he approached the subject from the point of view of the laboratory technician rather than the housewife, offering information but no practical remedies for flaws in the product.[65]

Very interesting was the chapter on tobacco, which revealed that Russia produced almost seventy-two million kilograms of tobacco annually, more than any other European country, and imported additional amounts from

America and other sources. Kanonnikov discussed the amount of nicotine in various types of tobacco, provided chemical formulae, and warned that nicotine was a "cardiac poison and the most harmful of tobacco's properties."[66]

Another work for specialists, that of S. N. Iakovlev, reviewed the newest methods of analyzing water, wine, vodka, and selected food.[67] The 1891 articles of A. S. Shcherbakov described the most accurate chemical tests to ascertain the wholesomeness of flour, meat, bread, milk products, mushrooms, sauces, and marinades.[68] Most of these tests had been developed by Western scientists but some were Russian contributions. In the section dealing with bread, Shcherbakov included frightful pictures of flour ticks.[69] He claimed spoiled meat "very often" was used for sausage but provided no substantiation for this statement.[70] Although Shcherbakov's articles appeared in a publication whose subtitle billed it a "journal of popular medicine and hygiene," his work seemed too technical to be truly accessible to people at large.

A number of books aimed at popular audiences. Doctor S. Notkin's *Falsification of Food Products and Domestic Methods of Discerning This,* which appeared in 1889, warned the public in its introduction that deception occurred daily in the marketplace; governments had been concerned with the problem since the time of Hammurabi. However, according to the author, in former times the buyer was able to judge the quality of the item by its physical characteristics. Now, factory production and chemical additives made it difficult for the public to readily ascertain the wholesomeness of the product. Notkin discussed tea, coffee, milk, sour cream, oil and butter, bread, flour, and meat. Although he included instructions for simple chemical tests, he urged the consumer to rely on scrutiny of the physical properties of food. The text was short–the book totaled only sixty-six pages–and simply written but informative, nonetheless. For example, Notkin warned readers that sometimes lead and graphite were used to color what was sold for "black" tea. He reassured them that they could "easily" ascertain this "dangerous substitution"; they were to put some leaves on a white paper where, "residue, as from a pencil, would show the presence of the aforementioned substances." But to ascertain other artificial dyes he recommended three tests; one used a small amount of chloroform.[71] In the section on bread, Notkin alerted readers to the fact that sometimes bakers used alum and even sulfuric acid of copper (copper vitriol) to make bread made from spoiled flour appear attractive. Notkin provided a "simple" test for ascertaining the first substance. Readers were to wet part of a piece of bread with poison of campeachy wood; if in one-quarter of an hour the moistened half appeared a dirty violet color at least one percent of alum was present. For determining sulfuric acid readers were to wet a piece of bread with a solution of "yellow blood salts," and if the bread became stained a rosy color the dangerous additive was present; if not, the bread would be stained a yellow color.[72] Because of government control over pharmacies it may have been difficult for readers to procure chemicals needed for Notkin's tests. But the fact that he labeled them "simple," as well as the format and title of the work, distinguished it from the more scientific texts cited earlier. That the book was intended for a literate, middle-class audience was underscored by the endpaper advertisements of works by Mayne-Reed and other adventure novels.[73]

Alexander Al'medingen's 1890 *Home Handbook on Falsification of Food, Flavoring, and Also Other Substances* sold for only 60 kopeks, an indication that it targeted a wider public than did Notkin's work. The *Home Handbook* was part of a series of the "Library of Useful Knowledge"; F. Pavlenkov was the series editor. Al'medingen noted in the foreword that he had tried to describe methods to essay food and other substances that could be done at home, without a special laboratory.[74] He ambitiously addressed common household items and medicine as well as food and drink, reviewing a multitude of foods, drink, and in addition, kerosene, soap, and commonly used medicines, such as quinine.[75] The latter was very prevalent because malaria was the chief communicable disease in Russia at this time, and quinine also was used as a general prophylactic.[76] Items were arranged alphabetically and short paragraphs were devoted to each. This permitted presentation of only the most basic facts to the reader. For example, under "Canned Foods" (*Konservy*) Al'medingen warned of the use of salicylic acid, glycerin, tannin, salts, zinc, copper, and even lead used to preserve tinned meats. He also warned of the bacteria that invaded the product once the tin was opened and exposed to air.[77] Another section alerted readers to the fact that yellow macaroni, sold in Odessa, was colored with a harmful dye.[78]

Al'medingen thoroughly reviewed wines–red and white, table, Crimean, and Caucasian wine.[79] The author assured readers that "Russian red and white wine *in the majority of cases was pure.*" He had made over three hundred investigations of Russian grape wine in the past six years and had found saccharin only in one sample of white Bessarabian wine; he had never personally found lead sugar.[80]

Especially interesting were Al'medingen's comments on vodka. He observed that "The purity of vodka played [*sic*] great significance for the health, especially when one pays attention to the colossal amount of vodka, poured into the stomachs of the Russian people." Vodka could be adulterated with fusel oil.[81] Al'medingen warned his readers not to drink alcohol with even an insignificant amount of fusel oil. He recommended a test to insure safety. Readers were to pour vodka into a wine glass, add three drops of concentrated hydrochloric acid, and mix well with a wooden or, preferably, glass wand. Then they were to put ten drops of colorless aniline oil, "which could be obtained from any store selling pharmaceutical wares," into the glass containing vodka and hydrochloric acid. If the vodka acquired a bright red color this meant it contained the fusel oil.[82]

Despite brevity, the book was practical and up-to-date and a bonus was the portion that contained laws on adulteration, which had been published in Russia, France, Italy, Belgium, and Germany.[83]

Two works, one from 1889, the second from 1890, were midway between the highly technical and the popular. Both were written in lively style and included illustrations of bacteria, fungi, and parasites lurking in food, water, and other substances.

The shorter of the two works was that by A. V. Pel'. In addition to owning a large pharmacy and pharmaceutical factory in St. Petersburg, Pel' had researched atropine and alkaloids, galenical preparations, and antiseptic medical procedures. He became internationally known as the first to extract spermine in pure form.[84] He also devoted much time and energy to the proper water filtration for St. Petersburg.[85]

Pel' originally presented the contents of his pamphlet on pure food, *Falsifications and Methods of Combatting Them,* which was published in 1889, as two public lectures to students of the Military Medical Academy in St. Petersburg. The pamphlet was terse but enlightening and practical; it cost only 75 kopeks. Very helpful were the drawings of leaves of plants sometimes substituted for tea, and drawings and photographs of microscopic slides depicting bacteria in water, parasites in meat, bacteria in milk, and ersatz coffee, chocolate, cake flour, and other products.[86] In the introduction Pel' reviewed inadvertent adulteration such as lead poisoning due to bakers' use of lead vessels or fuel which contained lead, the use of arsenic in cosmetics and mineral water, and deliberate use of additives to disguise spoiled food.[87] With regard to meat, Pel' discussed trichinosis and other parasites in meat, proper cooking temperatures to destroy these pests, and a chemical test to discern whether meat was fresh or diseased. Pel' claimed that often poor quality meat was used for sausage or the weight of sausage was increased with starch.[88] It ought to be noted that Pel' urged readers to boycott an *American* brand of lard, Armour and Company's "Family Refined Lard," because it was adulterated, being a mixture of pork lard, stearin, and cottonseed oil.[89] With regard to flour, Pel' revealed the practice of adding large amounts of white clay and sometimes poisonous salts to flour to make it whiter. He warned that wet rye could cause fungus in rye flour. This, in turn, caused ergot convulsions. According to Pel', who was a specialist on ergotism, the disease still was a problem in Germany, England and other European countries; in Russia, it was most prevalent in the northern Volga provinces, especially Viatka, Kazan, and Kostroma. He noted that a Russian chemist, Zinin, had developed a stain to detect simple spores in flour; another Russian, Rakovich, had developed a simple apparatus to ascertain the presence of worms and certain minerals.[90] Adulteration of milk included the age-old practice of adding water. New practices included using starch and soda. According to Pel', in St. Petersburg milk sellers commonly put live frogs in milk to prevent spoiling. Pel' reminded readers that tuberculosis could be spread from cows to humans; he claimed that not only typhoid fever but also smallpox, scarlatina, and diphtheria could be spread through milk. According to Pel', the last had occurred on Vasilevskii Island in St. Petersburg in 1888. Pel' informed readers of stains he used to ascertain the presence of bacteria in milk and urged sterilization of milk. Pel' further cautioned readers to store milk in cold temperature.[91]

P. O. Smolenskii's *The Simplest Methods of Investigating and Evaluating the Good Quality of Foodstuffs, Drinks, Air, Water, Dwellings, Etc.* was first published in 1890. The third edition appeared in 1899. Smolenskii was a Doctor of Medicine. The title page noted that the Educational Committee of the Ministry of Public Enlightenment recommended the book for libraries of secondary schools, both male and female, for adults, and also for teachers' institutes and pedagogical courses.[92] However, Smolenskii also intended his work for the literate consumer. In the preface to the second edition, he emphasized that the chemicals he suggested for determining the wholesomeness of food could be acquired in any pharmacy or drug store (*aptechnyi magazin*) that purveyed sundries as well as medicines (chiefly factory-manufactured and sold over-the-counter).[93] In addition, Smolenskii published four inexpensive pamphlets (properly approved by the censor) in 1898. These included one on margarine at 60 kopeks and an historical overview of food at 40 kopeks.[94]

In his massive tome of 526 pages, Smolenskii discussed a plethora of common foods and drinks, dyes, dinnerware and cooking utensils, lighting, and so on. The book was exceedingly thorough. The chapter on meat discussed types of cattle and other animals used for meat in Russia, and the nutritional content of various meats. There were illustrations of cuts of meat, review of sausages, instructions on storing and cooking meat, with proper temperatures to prevent trichinosis, tuberculosis, and other diseases. As mentioned, there also were illustrations of the parasites and bacteria found in meat. Smolenskii claimed that poor quality and sometimes spoiled or diseased meat was canned. He enumerated easily detected physical characteristics that indicated fresh, healthy meat, but in addition, discussed chemical tests and depicted apparatus that laboratories used to analyze meat. As did Pel' and other authors, Smolenskii confirmed that Russian scientists had developed some of the tests that were employed worldwide.[95] The chapter on dyes discussed the harmful, even poisonous, components in commonly used dyes: white dyes frequently contained lead and mercury; green dyes, arsenic; and so on.[96] The chapter on tinned food stressed the harmful chemicals, such as salicylic acid, and metals, such as copper and lead, used to preserve food.[97] At the end of each chapter Smolenskii included recent Russian antiadulteration and antipollution legislation.

Three pages at the end of the book listed instruments and implements for testing various kinds of foods.[98] Some of the implements were cheap enough to be accessible to the layman—1 to 6 rubles. Others at 40, 50, even 110 rubles were obviously designed for specialized laboratories.

Smolenskii's work not only provides insight into the state of Russian public health but a glimpse into turn-of-the-century diets. Ten pages of charts compared the diets of workers and peasants in various parts of Russia with workers and other groups in Western Europe, the United States, and Japan in the 1880s and 1890s.[99] They showed that in intake of calories, protein, fats, and carbohydrates, Russian workers and peasants compared favorably with their American counterparts.[100] The amount of protein in the diets of poor Russian was less than the norm. However, their diets included as many calories as German nutritionist Voit recommended for minimum requirement.[101] Diets of Russian workers and peasants, as well as of Western Europeans and Americans, were higher in calories and protein than those of Japanese.[102] However, experts at that time believed animal protein was more valuable than that from vegetables and therefore suggested the diet include at least one-third animal protein. According to this criterion, Russian workers did not come off so well. Smolenskii stated that basically Russian peasants and workers had a vegetarian diet. Russian workers derived one-third to two-thirds of their protein from bread (as compared with the well-off who derived one-fifth to one-tenth of their protein from bread); Moscow workers received as much as three-fourths to nine-tenths of their protein and carbohydrates from vegetable products, chiefly black bread. Smolenskii also emphasized the importance of affordable prices for essential, nourishing foods, citing one study by I. Skvortsov, which concluded that adequate daily food for an adult worker in Khar'kov cost 13 kopeks.[103]

Smolenskii's second chapter provided a window on middle- and upper-class diets. He asserted that of Russian cattle, Kirghiz and Kalmyk beef was the most flavorful but American beef was tastiest of all because cattle were slaughtered by age two whereas Russian cattle were slaughtered at closer to six years of age. He provided drawings showing that the cuts of beef were more selective in St. Petersburg than in Moscow and other Russian cities, but he noted (sensibly) that studies had shown that poorer (and cheaper) cuts of meat could be good from a nutritional standpoint. According to Smolenskii, pork was second to beef as a source of meat in Russia, lamb was favored in the Caucasus, the Don, Turgaisk region, as well as Tavrida province (the Crimea), Bessarabia, Ekaterinoslav, and Saratov. Smolenskii claimed that although the urban poor in Western Europe ate horse meat, only Tatars did so in Russia.[104]

Master of Pharmacy A. Bukovskii, on the staff of the laboratory of Professor D. L. Davydov, detailed the falsification of tea in Warsaw in his 1896 work, *Izsledovanie chaia i fal'sifikatiia ego v Varshave.* The 102-page work had anti-Semitic passages. Bukovskii alleged that police data showed that falsified tea in Warsaw was made and sold exclusively by Jews. The adulterated tea was sold either by itself or in a mixture of real tea. The police raided apartments and confiscated the ersatz tea, taking the perpetrators to court.[105]

In 1898 Master of Pharmacy Savelii Abramovich Ginzburg wrote an article for the "Northern Caucasus" newspaper detailing his "Chemical-Sanitary Research on Stavropol' Milk–Bakers and Sold [to the Public]." He also wrote "part scientific, part popular" "Conversations on the Falsification of Food Products" and an article on saccharin for *Farmatsevticheskii vestnik* in 1899.[106]

Turn-of-the-century Russian pharmacy journals–*Farmatsevticheskii zhurnal, Farmatsevticheskii vestnik,* and *Farmatsevt*–devoted many pages to combating adulteration and pollution. The substance that elicited most concern was saccharin, a substance made of coal tar and petroleum, discovered in 1879 and, though considered harmful, still used today. In February 1900, *Farmatsevticheskii vestnik* announced that the physiological institute of Moscow University was just beginning research regarding saccharin's effect on the human organism.[107] In June, the journal noted that the Minister of Finance was examining more stringent ways to combat the sale and use of saccharin.[108] From August to October 1900, the journal ran two sets of long, thorough articles on the physical composition of saccharin and other artificial sweeteners, Russian and foreign scientists' opinions on the pros and cons of saccharin, and its usage in Western Europe. The author included several processes for making saccharin and provided many chemical formulae.[109]

❖❖❖

Crucial to the success of the "pure food movement" was implementation and enforcement of government regulations by municipal governments[110] and the Justice-of-the-Peace courts.

Historians have given low marks to municipal sanitation, public health, and public services in late nineteenth-, early twentieth-century Russia. They emphasize that only a handful of major cities in late tsarist Russia provided public health services and that even these cities were hampered by budget constraints.[111] These latter-day opinions are supported by contemporary accounts such as that of Charles Marvin, an Englishman traveling by train in 1888, who lamented the squalor of towns in Russian Poland compared to the neatness of the towns in Austrian and German Poland.[112]

Definitive studies of hygiene in late tsarist Russia remain to be done. Geographical and chronological factors must be taken into consideration, for not only did the vastness of the empire cause wide variation from city to city, between urban and rural areas, and between various regions of the empire, but disease and mortality statistics fluctuated considerably from year to year.[113] Further, while Russia lagged behind the West, especially Germany,[114] public health also was uneven in Western countries. For example, in 1880 the English medical journal *The Lancet* admitted that sanitation in mining and manufacturing towns was inferior to that of London.[115] Additionally, in 1885 *The Lancet* stated that only 276 of 2,328 houses occupied by Jews in the city of London had water closets[116] and in 1887 reported that eels had been found in the London water supply.[117]

In any case, although the Russian public health movement had a long way to go, major cities at least were taking steps forward in grappling with falsification and adulteration of food by the late nineteenth, early twentieth centuries.

Municipal authorities in St. Petersburg began inspecting pork and ham for trichinosis in 1881. Four years later, *The Lancet* claimed that during the first half of that year only "five carcasses and 133 hams were offered for inspection, notwithstanding the smallness of the fees charged and the certainty of an indemnity in case trichinae were found."[118] However, by 1882 the system became successful. During that year two veterinary surgeons and some dozen assistants made 30,000 examinations. Further, "branch institutions were established, some of them by the traders themselves, and microscopic examinations systematically carried out." In 1884 "30,650 carcasses, 2,362 hams, 18 portions, and 31 wild boars" were examined. "Those free from trichinae" were "marked, all infected meat is destroyed."[119] As a result, in 1885 *The Lancet* asserted that there had been only one case of trichinosis in St. Petersburg "for some years past."[120] The main city slaughterhouse in St. Petersburg was obliged to put a red stamp on diseased meat. No doubt diseased meat was sold in many Russian cities. However, statistics show that the St. Petersburg slaughterhouses rejected diseased meat for human consumption. In 1886 the slaughterhouses rejected 5,979 carcasses out of 343,629. Three hundred fifty-three were rejected because of disease, such as plague, 58 because of trichinosis, and 5,568 because of "worms" in general. At the same time, slaughterhouses in Berlin rejected only 3,978 carcasses out of 640,655. One thousand, two hundred forty-eight had various diseases such as plague, 143 contained trichinosis, and 2,587 were found to have worms.[121] These data implied either that the St. Petersburg slaughterhouses were more selective or that Russian meat was more defective.

Laboratories established by major cities were very important in insuring purity in food, drink, and household items. The Moscow city sanitary station was established in 1889. The organization of this laboratory illustrates both local initiative and also the dilatoriness that plagued Russian government on all levels. Moscow governor-general Prince Vladimir Andreevich Dolgorukii suggested the laboratory to the mayor of Moscow as early as 1880. The latter appointed a subcommittee of the city sanitary commission to study the matter. The subcommittee recommended to the executive board of the city duma that the laboratory be linked with the Hygienic Institute at the University of Moscow for practical reasons.[122] By 1886 a municipal laboratory existed in St. Petersburg,[123] by 1893 a sanitary station was operating in Kiev,[124] and by the early twentieth century there were laboratories in major university cities such as Odessa, Iur'ev (or Dorpat, in Estonia), and Lodz (Russian Poland).[125] The Perm zemstvo had established a sanitary station by 1889.[126] The Samara provincial zemstvo operated a bacteriological lab and Pasteur station in 1900.[127]

V. M. Iakimov, member of the Voronezh province branch of the Russian Society for the Preservation of Public Health, criticized giving local government responsibility for enforcing pure food regulations. He complained that the Moscow city laboratory fell short of the Paris municipal laboratory because the Moscow lab had a lower budget.[128] In his 1895 dissertation for the Doctor of Medicine degree, M. P. Zakharbekov concluded that milk sold in St. Petersburg had a high concentration of disease-causing microorganisms–about 17.5 percent.[129] Nevertheless, municipal laboratories were investigating food products, drinks, and household items.[130]

In 1896 the St. Petersburg municipal laboratory made 2,069 analyses of milk, water, ice, meat and meat products, flour, bread, sour cream, oil, and miscellaneous household items. The sanitary station sponsored about 60 percent of the tests, private persons about 40 percent. However, only about 10 percent of the products were of poor quality and only 2.2 percent were found to be falsified.[131]

The Moscow city sanitary station was not as active as that in the capital. For example, in 1891 the station made 498 investigations of food and household items;[132] in 1896, only 467;[133] and in 1897, only 373.[134] However, by 1898 the number of analyses rose to 616.[135] During 1896 it became possible for private persons to pay for investigations, but the bulk of these continued to be initiated by the Moscow city executive committee or by the sanitary station itself.[136] In 1897, the sanitary station began a systematic analysis of olive oil, grape juice, "gaseous" milk, and formaldehyde for disinfecting.[137] The subjects essayed at the Moscow station varied. In 1892 about half involved wallpaper and kerosene and the rest, food.[138] In 1897, sour cream and olive oil (no doubt due to the above practice) accounted for about two thirds of the investigations.[139] In 1898, one third of the investigations involved *kvas* and another third, olive oil and pepper.[140] In 1900 the Moscow laboratory condemned lozenges made by a St. Petersburg firm because they contained an aniline dye forbidden by a law of 1898.[141] Aniline is a colorless, poisonous, oily liquid, derived from coal-tar products. In 1901 the Moscow city sanitary station decried the substitution of mineral oil for animal oil. It reported that during the last six years it had made 101 tests on oil; 19 were natural, the rest were substitutes.[142] In 1902, in the months of May and June alone, the Moscow city station made 144 chemical analyses. Fifty-two investigations involved candy. The majority dealt with dangerous dyes.[143]

In 1902 the Odessa municipal laboratory discovered fruit *kvas* sweetened with saccharin.[144] In Lodz, Russian Poland, in June 1901, the city laboratory made 71 analyses of syrups and found that 50 contained saccharin; 100 analyses of candy, 43 of which revealed substances harmful to the health; 34 analyses of milk, 14 of which showed the use of dirty water, soda, and disease-causing microbes; 6 probes of sour cream; and tests of *pirogi,* flour, and one investigation of sausage that revealed botulism.[145] From 1896 the Iur'ev city duma investigated milk sold in the city;[146] in 1902 the Iur'ev city laboratory investigated 79 loaves of bread.[147]

Pharmaceutical and medical societies and individual pharmacists established laboratories to complement those founded by municipal administrations. The St. Petersburg Pharmaceutical Society made examinations at the behest of municipal authorities and private individuals.[148] According to its report for 1900, during that year the lab had made 536 tests on urine, 56 on fecal material, and 103 on food products. Of the latter it had found 36 cases of falsification of flour, 15 of wine, and 26 of milk. During 1900, the lab also made 886 bacteriological tests, including 165 on milk. The lab controlled the sale of sterilized milk in St. Petersburg for the firm of Rozentov; fortunately of its 165 tests on this milk it had found 160 fully sterilized and only 5 with microorganisms.[149] In 1901, a society of physicians, formed for the purpose of combating falsification of foodstuffs in St. Petersburg, opened a special laboratory in the capital for the study of milk products.[150] The Russian (Socialist) Pharmacy Society in Moscow also operated an analytical laboratory in the early twentieth century.[151]

Laboratories of individual pharmacists–in out-of-the-way towns as well as major cities–contributed to the pure food movement. In 1898 Provizor A. Valiashko informed the Khar'kov Pharmacy Society that during the past fifteen years he had come to know many old Khar'kov pharmacy owners. One, the owner of a small pharmacy in small district town, was lucky if he made 5,000 rubles' turnover a year. Nevertheless, this old pharmacist performed many analyses on food, such as flour, and water. He also was a member of the local sanitary commission and helped research food sold in bazaars.[152] In 1901, decrying the falsification of animal fats, Master of Pharmacy El'mar Gol'berg reported that he had made 130 tests of oil in his Moscow laboratory during the past year.[153] In 1900, the Medical Council of the Ministry of Internal Affairs ruled that one Moise Matis, a Doctor of Physical Science from Geneva, could set up a laboratory in Kovno.[154] One N. N. Kostiamin managed a hygienic laboratory in Vil'na military district.[155] As noted in a previous chapter, the Ferrein pharmacy in Moscow included a laboratory for inspecting food.

By 1905, according to the Annual Report on the Nation's Health, issued by the government, there were forty-three laboratories for researching food products in the Russian Empire. During 1904 they had made 15,000 investigations.[156] Admittedly, these data meant that some provinces lacked even one laboratory. Nevertheless, progress was being made in combating adulteration.

It is difficult to ascertain how well cities used the information obtained from laboratories to police sales of food and drink. However, a case study of saccharin indicates that, after a low point in 1900, progress was being made in the first years of the twentieth century. Despite the fact that the Russian government permitted the sale of saccharin only in pharmacies, for medical purposes, and upon a doctor's prescription,[157] these regulations were ignored frequently during 1900. According to one article in *Farmatsevticheskii vestnik,* manufacturers of beer, wine, *kvas,* lemonade and other fruit drinks, and candy and other food products used saccharin because it was cheap. They then distributed these products in major Russian cities.[158] Another article claimed that in Moscow, *kvas* manufacturers substituted bottles of *kvas* made with sugar when inspectors from the executive committee of the city council arrived. The manufacturers then sold the *kvas* containing saccharin at railway stations.[159] A third article noted that peasants in Kurland used saccharin.[160] A fourth article emphasized the abuse of saccharin in soft drinks. It seems that, when the government reinstituted the vodka monopoly in 1893, in order to combat inordinate use of vodka the government also issued "compulsory regulations" (*obiazatel'nye postanovleniia*) ordering the establishment of gaseous water and soft drink factories in place of former taverns. The soft drink factories proliferated markedly from 1895; in one district in the Caucasus, for example, there now functioned six soft-drink factories for local miners—each little village had a factory. However, though the compulsory regulations stated that the soft drinks were intended for the workers' well-being, a new problem had arisen. The factories chiefly produced a lemonade called *fialka*, made of nonfiltered water, gas, fruit dye, drops of fruit essence, *and saccharin*. The factories used saccharin because it was cheap and enabled them to compete with one another. The factories sold 100 bottles of *fialka* for 3 rubles, 50 kopeks to 4 rubles—that is each bottle cost no more than 4 kopeks. The article claimed that workers consumed millions of bottles of fruit drinks annually. "All" knew that these drinks contained saccharin, which was harmful for the health, but there were only "prohibitions on paper to prevent this evil." The article opined that saccharin probably also was used in beer-making and urged the city sanitary station to instigate medical supervision and periodical analysis of fruit drinks and beer to eliminate the use of saccharin.[161]

In 1901, control over the use of saccharin tightened. Due to reported abuse of saccharin in Moscow, the executive committee of the city council ordered its bazaar and trade inspectors to systematically take samples from purveyors of mineral drinks, *kvas*, etc. for analysis in the city sanitary station.[162] At the same time, in St. Petersburg, the executive committee introduced into the city council a proposal from the local medical inspector about publishing obligatory regulations regarding the production and trade of sweetened drinks in St. Petersburg. The proposal was approved, and it was determined that regulations would be posted in kiosks.[163] An article in *Farmatsevt* in 1902 claimed that each year there were more factories producing artificial fruit drinks but chemical analyses were keeping pace.[164] Early in 1904, in the city of Minsk, police confiscated twenty-one barrels of contraband saccharin.[165] In 1904, St. Petersburg police investigated a food-oil factory in St. Petersburg. Four chemical analyses revealed some adulteration. Names and addresses of stores and markets carrying the oil were published but unfortunately the factory also supplied markets in

Moscow, Tiumen, Ekaterinburg, Kurgan, Vologda, and villages in Tomsk province.[166]

A *sine qua non* for combating falsification was prosecution. The Justice-of-the-Peace courts, largely abolished in the countryside with the institution of Land Captains in 1889, continued to operate in cities. They were instrumental in prosecuting violations of the pure food laws.

Falsifiers and swindlers were definitely prosecuted although sentences varied considerably. During 1904, according to a government report, more than 12,600 people were brought to court for trading in poor quality or adulterated food. More than 200 of the 3,712 managers of artificial mineral water factories had been brought to court for violations of sanitary regulations.[167]

Surveys of individual cases reveal some heavy fines. In Moscow, in 1898, the Justice-of-the-Peace court levied fines on nine peasant manufacturers of *kvas* who had used saccharin. One fine was 200 rubles, a second–100, a third–50, a fourth–40, and a fifth–30 rubles. Three fines amounted to 15 rubles and one–10 rubles.[168] In 1899, the Justice-of-the-Peace court in St. Petersburg discussed the case of the merchant N. N. Nikitin, accused of using saccharin to sweeten *kvas*. Nikitin claimed the substance was harmless. Various medical witnesses testified that saccharin was forbidden in most Western European cities, that it could be purchased only in pharmacies upon a doctor's prescription, and that German medical literature did not recommend it even for diabetics. Nikitin was incarcerated for two months and fined 40 rubles.[169] In 1899 a wine and spirits merchant in Odessa was fined 150 rubles by a Justice-of-the-Peace court for selling wares in which there appeared saccharin and coal-based dyes. Because the merchant was bankrupt the sentence was commuted to one and a half months' imprisonment.[170] In Odessa at the end of 1900, despite the fact that sale of saccharin was illegal without prescription of a physician, the court of the Land Captain noted that although saccharin was not in the Ministry of Internal Affairs' list of "strong-acting substances," use of it had been limited by a subsequent circular from the ministry. Therefore, the court sentenced the defendant to one month's imprisonment.[171] Also in Odessa, in 1901, ten traders were prosecuted for selling saccharin and coal tar dyes. The Justice-of-the-Peace court sentenced each of the ten to incarceration for fifteen days without substitution by a fine.[172]

On the other hand, there were instances in which the accused were exonerated or suffered only nominal sentences. In another Odessa case of 1899, the Justice-of-the-Peace court convicted a candy factory owner, one Nechaev, for using dyes that contained arsenic. He was sentenced to imprisonment for four days. However, the appellate level of the Justice-of-the-Peace court reversed the decision and acquitted Nechaev.[173] In yet another instance the penalty was ridiculously mild. The April 2, 1900, issue of *Farmatsevticheskii vestnik* decried the use of coal-tar to dye candy in major candy factories in St. Petersburg and Moscow. It reported that a candy factory owner had been convicted of this. However, he was subject to imprisonment only for one day and fined 3 rubles![174]

It is hard to say how much impact the crusade of the central government, municipalities, and health professionals for pure food, drink, and environment had on the public. In imitation of major Western European cities, a few citizens in St. Petersburg established a Society for the Preservation of Public Health in 1878. By 1880 the Society had 296 members and an income of 1,875 rubles. The Minister of Internal Affairs had contributed 2,000 rubles, part of which had been spent on rent. In 1880 the central government approved the establishment of branches in Odessa, Kazan, and Theodosia.[175] In succeeding years, branches sprouted in sixteen more cities of the empire.

The Society for the Preservation of Public Health sponsored research in biology, chemistry, physics; epidemiology, and statistics; school and general hygiene; children's health; climatology and balneology.[176] Nevertheless, membership was small and few pharmacists were involved.[177] But membership in the society was only one indicator of the popular impact of the "pure food movement." No doubt the brochures and books on pure food as well as the exhibits and activities of the society had widespread influence. In 1901 *Farmatsevticheskii zhurnal* reported that "large-scale commercial groups" in St. Petersburg had founded a society specifically for the purpose of combating falsification of foodstuffs and that branches were being opened in other cities.[178] A further sign of progress was A. N. Al'medingen's establishment of a private evening school in 1907 in St. Petersburg to train youths of both sexes to prepare chemical analyses in factory laboratories. The school, under the jurisdiction of the Ministry of Trade and Industry, accepted students who had finished the fourth class of middle school. The course of instruction lasted two years. First semester studies consisted of mathematics, mechanics, physics, chemistry, mineralogy, aereometry; in the second semester, bacteriology, microscopic analysis, chemistry, and selling wares. The third and fourth semesters focused on practical analysis of specific substances. Students attended class from 6 to 10 P.M. six evenings a week; there were eight teachers including Al'medingen. The school very practically included a job placement bureau.[179]

The tsarist government continued to address the issue of pure food in the early twentieth century. In 1902, the central government specifically addressed the production of mineral water and various kinds of fruit drinks. It prohibited use of lead or copper storage containers, use of aniline dyes, artificial fruit essences for smell and taste, and preservatives of salicylic and boric acid.[180]

In 1909 the Ministry of Trade and Industry formed in St. Petersburg a "Committee for the Struggle with Falsification of Food Products." The committee's charge was very broad and indicated that struggle with falsification still was needed.[181] Members of the committee included representatives of central governmental departments; zemstvos and city government; academia;[182] business and financial sectors;[183] rural-agricultural societies; unions, trade and industrial organizations and enterprises; and private persons.[184] The statute provided for regular and emergency meetings, regular audits, and an annual financial report.[185]

Immediately upon its inception in 1909, the committee, composed of representatives from the ministries of Internal Affairs, Trade and Industry, and Agriculture, as well as "public" figures, developed a legislative project "guaranteeing good quality food and drink." Like earlier laws, this legislative project focused on the preparation, sale, and preservation of food and drink. It targeted food and drink harmful for the health, falsification or substitution of ingredients of lesser quality, and spoiled food. The project contained some innovations, however. First, it established *maximum* punishments higher than those in previous laws. Fines for a first offense ranged from 10 to 10,000 rubles with concomitant imprisonment from one week to three months. An alternate penalty, imprisonment without fine, was set from one month to a year and a half. In especially important cases the individual was subject to deprivation of rights and imprisonment from two and a half to three and a half years. Court convictions of a second offense resulted in deprivation of the right to trade from one to five years. The courts could publish these sentences and the Ministry of Internal Affairs could establish government publications for this purpose.[186]

A second innovation was that not just major cities but zemstvos and towns or cities of 25,000 inhabitants or more were to establish laboratories and hire special sanitary doctors. The medical administration nearest to city or zemstvo self-government was to supervise the sale of food and drink. The central treasury was to subsidize half the cost of the laboratories and inspectors; zemstvos and city governments were to defray the remainder of the costs through levying a tax. The Ministry of Internal Affairs, with agreement of the Ministry of Trade and Industry, was to issue the regulations by which the laboratories conducted their research; the ministries could issue further regulations on the preparation and preservation of food and drink, lists of prohibited dyes and preservatives, supervision of food and drink sales, and so on.[187]

One S. Igumnov scathingly criticized this legislative proposal in the journal of the radical Pirogov Society of Russian doctors. Igumnov believed the proposed law was too vague in describing falsification and, thus, there would be controversy when the courts tried to interpret it. He also faulted the proposal because it took a punitive approach toward sales of adulterated or spoiled food rather than stipulating positive measures to improve transport and preservation of food, particularly on the part of small-scale producers and tradesmen.[188] But his chief criticisms were, first, that the proposed law did not grapple with *fundamental* food and drink problems in Russia and, second, that the proposal violated local "self government." Obviously a socialist, in Igumnov's opinion, the main food problem in Russia was not *sale* of adulterated or spoiled food but the fact that peasants, workers, and poorer urban classes had to eat inadequate food because they either had no access to or could not afford better quality food. In line with his worldview, Igumnov asserted that the current legislative proposal might *harm* the poor because higher-quality food might result in higher prices. He perversely insisted that legislative-judicial measures could not achieve better diets for the poor and would only benefit richer classes of the population.[189] Furthermore, Igumnov contended that the regulation made "*nonsens*"[190] of "self government." It forced municipal governments and zemstvos to establish laboratories and hire a cadre of inspectors for which they would have to pay with a new tax and also moved jurisdiction for public health from zemstvos and municipal governments to the central government.[191] Accordingly, Igunmov thundered "implementation of this proposed law would spell death for public sanitation . . . in essence . . . it was detrimental to public self-government . . . to replace it with bureaucratic administration."[192]

Igumnov's criticism that the legislative proposal reflected an authoritarian and patriarchal attitude on the part of the central government had validity. On the other hand, his dismissal of the legislative proposal because it did not address larger social issues was ridiculous. The government's establishment of a committee including representatives from trade and industry, central government, and local self-government and another legislative proposal against adulteration and falsification, underscores its bureaucratic nature but also cooperation with public forces.

The "struggle against falsification" in Russia, was embryonic and minuscule. It affected only a fraction of the populace–those living in a few major cities. Peasants, who in total amounted to about 80 percent of the population in the beginning of the twentieth century, appear to have had poor hygiene. Their food may have been tainted. Nevertheless, the struggle against falsification marked some progress. It emphasized the Russian government's commitment to the health of its citizenry. More interesting, it showed pharmacists' versatility and familiarity with modern bacteriological research and cities' and Justice-of-the-Peace courts' vigor and competency. Considering that additives and preservatives in food and drink, adulteration, and pollution are still pervasive in the 1990s, imperial Russia made respectable efforts to grapple with these problems.

11

Drug Use and Abuse in Tsarist Russia

Restrictions on establishing and operating pharmacies and pharmaceutical factories thwarted expansion, hurting pharmacist and the public alike. On the other hand they also protected public health.

William S. Burroughs and David T. Courtwright have asserted that "Addiction . . . is an illness of exposure. By and large those who have access to junk become addicts. . . . There is no pre-addict personality any more than there is a pre-malarial personality."[1] Similarly, historian of pharmacy Glenn Sonnedecker contends that "efficient, large-scale production and marketing of opium derivates in industrialized Western nations . . .[led to] total production of opium derivates far in excess of the world's medical needs. . . ."[2]

The Russian Empire was located just north of major opium and hashish producing and using countries.[3] Yet, while a plethora of tracts fulminated against alcoholism and tobacco smoking in the nineteenth and early twentieth centuries,[4] dependency on opiates, hashish, and cocaine were rare in nineteenth-, early twentieth-century Russia, judging from the paucity of medical literature on this subject. While other factors contributed, there is no question that the nature of the Russian pharmacy system lessened public access to opiates and cocaine and thus to use and abuse of these drugs.

The fact that alcohol was the drug of choice in imperial Russia certainly played a major role in the low incidence of opiate and cocaine abuse.

The Russian pharmacopoeia also impacted use and abuse of drugs, particularly opiates. Foreign specialists gave Russian pharmacopoeias high marks for accuracy.[5] Although a 1900 article in *Farmatsevticheskii vestnik* complained that the pharmacopoeia did not establish exact norms for all drugs—for example, doses of drugs like belladonna were left to the physician's discretion—it did stress that the pharmacopoeia established strict doses for opium and its extracts.[6] The morphine content stipulated by the Russian civilian pharmacopoeia was on a par with that of other Western European countries—10 percent. However, it was lower than that in the United States pharmacopoeia, which authorized opium with a morphine content of from 13 to 15 percent.[7] Opium poppies were not officially cultivated within the Russian Empire before World War I, in part because the morphine content of local species did not meet the requirements of the Russian Civilian Pharmacopoeia. The opium derived from the Caucasus had particularly low morphine content. Chinese migrants to Russian Central Asia surreptitiously cultivated opium poppies, selling it to kin in China for smoking. However this opium fetched low prices.[8] Russia imported opium from Turkish poppies, in dry form, predominantly through the medium of Western European trading firms. In fact, concern about supplies prompted the journal *Farmatsevticheskii vestnik* in 1901 to advocate that Russia cultivate the opium poppy for medicinal purposes.[9] Coca was not native to Russia.

Conservative prescribing might have lessened narcotic abuse in Russia. Russian medical literature consistently cautioned against indiscriminate use of opiates and cocaine. The first reports of the clinical effects of opium on guinea pigs and rabbits appeared in 1868; this research had been done in Berlin.[10] Russian medical journals continued to publish reports of foreign research on morphine addiction and on cocaine addiction immediately after the latter appeared.[11] In addition, and perhaps of greater significance, was the fact that from the mid-1880s standard Russian texts on pharmacology discussed the dangers of drug addiction.[12] In 1886 Doctor N. Shchepot'ev's handbook on pharmacology for feldshers, or paramedics, warned of addiction to opium and informed the student feldshers (who theoretically could prescribe narcotics only under physicians' supervision) that large doses of opium or morphine could result in death and should not be given to children or should be administered only in small doses.[13] Dr. Bogoliubov's 1889 *Practical Pharmacology . . . for Doctors and Students* noted that, when writing prescriptions, it was currently advised to replace morphine with codeine because the latter was not so dangerous.[14] F. A. Ioganson's 1889 textbook on pharmacology warned of morphine addiction. The victim desired ever-increasing doses; the drug affected the nervous system, then sexual activity; morphine was more potent when injected into the bloodstream.[15] The text also warned of cocaine addiction. "The organism is addicted to cocaine . . . thus, they now are speaking about a special disease–'cocainism,' which is as dangerous as morphinism."[16] It was advisable to use cocaine only as a local anesthetic in eye disease. The dental journal *Zubovrachebnyi vestnik* had reported on the use of cocaine as an anesthetic since American dentists began the practice in the mid-1880s.[17] However, in 1892, the journal cautioned that "acquired use or misuse of cocaine can result in chronic poisoning with psychological deterioration. . . ."[18]

Russian physicians writing at the turn of the century, soon after heroin entered therapeutics, stressed the dangers of this narcotic. In 1899 Dr. Vantser described a case of poisoning by heroin, and in 1900 Dr. Chigaev observed attraction to heroin resulting from a quickly increased dose.[19] In 1902 M. A. Ladyzhenskii, of the Iur'ev-Dorpat Pharmaceutical Institute, published his research on heroin. He announced that in small doses heroin acted as a narcotic but in medium and larger doses acted as a stimulant, resulting in convulsions, loss of consciousness, depressed reflexes, slowing movement. Heroin also acted on the heart, lowering blood pressure in small doses and raising it in large doses.[20] Dr. A. S. Isaev, author of a pharmacology text published in 1912, regarded heroin as a weaker narcotic than morphine, but cautioned that prolonged use of heroin led to "chronic poisoning–heroinism. The latter was much more severe than morphinism, and therefore heroin should not be used in treatment of the latter."[21] Isaev further disapproved of cocaine in treatment of morphine addiction calling "cocainism" more ruinous to the organism than morphinism.[22]

Physicians attempted to alert the citizenry to the dangers of addiction. In 1894 Dr. S. N. Danillo presented a public lecture, which was duly published in a brochure. The author described the mental deterioration resulting from the use of opium, hashish, and alcohol. Imitating de Quincy, the author cited the influence on himself of an internal dose of 0.50 grams of hashish, which he had acquired from Algeria. After half an hour he suffered dizziness; it was difficult to stand and to think. However, the author was able to write fluently and correctly in French and mistook the St. Petersburg bridges for those in Paris. After two and a half hours the author was subject to auditory hallucinations–he heard the march from Tannhauser. The next day he suffered general depression but no headache.[23]

There appear to have been only three instances in Russian medical literature advocating the substitution of one addictive substance for another, a common practice at the time. In 1899, *Farmatsevticheskii vestnik*, contained Dr. G. Nickell's article on the new preparation "Dionin." The article fully informed the readers that Dionin was composed from morphine. Providing the chemical composition of Dionin or hydrochloride ethylmorphine, the author stated that Dionin had successfully replaced morphine in treating coughs, bronchial asthma, and so on, and that there was only limited evidence of its possible bad effect on the stomach. The author noted that Dionin "can show important service in treating morphinism."[24] Nickell's article was informational rather than an endorsement of Dionin; the article contained information on other new preparations. Nevertheless, the fact that the article appeared in one of Russia's major pharmaceutical journals gave a degree of sanction to the product, which was used to treat morphine addiction in the United States at the end of the nineteenth century.[25] In 1901 Dr. Artemov stated that heroin was not addictive and could, thus, replace morphia.[26] Dr. Isaev, in 1912, recommended codeine–a weaker opiate than morphine–to treat morphinism.[27]

Danillo's and other contemporary works such as "Towards a therapy for poisoning by opium and morphia," published in 1895, were filled with references to American, British, and Western European medical literature. In addition, "Therapy" critically noted that opium was a household substance in America.[28] Several complete foreign works on addiction were available in Russian such as *Morphinism and its Treatment*, 1900, translated from German.[29] Of course, Russian physicians continued to report on usage of drugs in therapeutics. For example, an 1887 article described injecting cocaine to anesthetize the joint when correcting a dislocation.[30]

All these factors minimized use and abuse of narcotics and cocaine in late imperial Russia. But the Russian pharmacy system–specifically the medicines produced by the pharmaceutical industry, government control over production, import and sale of medicines, and regulations on dispensing–prevented easy access to opiates and cocaine.

Russian pharmaceutical manufacturers did not have patents on the processes for making alkaloids like morphine, heroin, and cocaine. Further, the Medical Council controlled pharmaceutical imports, analyzing ingredients in so-called patent or proprietary drugs, both foreign and domestic, and sanctioning or prohibiting manufacture and sale in each specific case.[31] Dentists, as well as pharmacists and pharmaceutical industrialists, were curtailed in their use of narcotics. In 1909 a St. Petersburg dentist petitioned the Medical Council to abolish the circular of 18 July 1908, which forbade dentists to use cocaine and other strong-acting substances for painless extraction of teeth.[32]

Russian dispensing was crucial in preventing misuse of narcotics. British pharmacist Prosper Marsden opined that

> The manner of dealing with the prescription in Russia is an excellent one. . . . This document is rightly understood by all to be an order from the medical man to the pharmacist to dispense or supply certain medicaments. The original is obtained by the *aptekar* [pharmacist] . . . for three years, the patient is supplied with a *signatura* [label], the prescription being copied upon the back of this and directions for the patient on the front. In addition the prescription is copied into the sealed book previously mentioned. . . . In case of the prescription containing any of the *medicamenta heroica*, a repeat may only be obtained upon the doctor giving a fresh signature each time, and this fact is before the public at the time of the first filling of

the prescription by means of a rubber stamp upon the reverse of the *signatura.*[33]

Though exasperated at some aspects of Russian pharmacy Marsden acknowledged that a "regulation of this kind is badly required in our own country" and waxed enthusiastic at Russian rules that classed "Even antipyrine, antifebrin and phenacetine . . . as *medicamenta heroica,* and animal preparations such as spermine, special mention being made in the [Russian] code to the preparations of Poehl [Pel'] and Parke, Davis and Co. These are absolutely forbidden to be sold at retail. . . ."[34]

Of course, he acknowledged "In order that trades requiring to use poisons for manufacturing purposes may not be unduly hampered by rigid restrictions there are special regulations for chemists, artists, mill owners and craftsmen. The most important of these is that the persons mentioned must have a certificate either from the police or from their immediate chief, ere they can be supplied with poison."[35] Nevertheless, Marsden noted approvingly, "There is none of the loose way of supplying mineral acid in beer bottles, which is not unknown here, nor can one buy cyanide and perchloride at the photographer's in Russia. . . . The list of articles of foreign manufacture occupies many pages of the code, most of the foreign proprietaries being forbidden, and all plant extracts manufactured abroad. . . . Another instructive list is that of medicaments which may not be sold in the *aptekarski magazin* [drug store]–that is to say, which one must go to a *apteka* [pharmacy] for." Marsden also emphasized that, in contrast to the English practice, in Russia only pharmacists–and not physicians–could dispense drugs.[36]

In England and America in the nineteenth, early twentieth century, in contrast, the *laissez-faire* pharmacy system matched the fairly democratic political system. American physicians liberally prescribed opiates.[37] Reputedly, some American pharmacists made large profits on illegal sales of narcotics. Furthermore, patent medicines that contained opiates and cocaine circulated widely.[38] Cocaine usage also rose in late nineteenth-, early twentieth-century America.[39]

In June 1902, Joseph L. Lemberger informed the Pennsylvania Pharmaceutical Association that from a poll of thirty-eight states regarding their laws on dispensing poisons, "most give some attention to this very important subject. Some States, however, have no poison law."[40] The states that did have such laws generally classed drugs according to two schedules, "A" and "B," as was the case in Russia.[41] The American lists, however, were much shorter. Further, as befitting a country with a federal form of government and "states' rights," they varied from state to state. Most state laws regulated the dispensation of poisons and/or narcotics, stipulating special wrappers and labels for the poison, registration in a special book, sale of cocaine only to physicians and dentists, and no refills on prescriptions except by physician. There also were penalties for violating the rules on dispensing poisons and narcotics. Usually the minimum fine was $25.00 and the maximum, $100.00 Sometimes the laws included an alternative punishment of fifty days' imprisonment.[42] However, there was no uniformity from one state to another. Additionally, state laws were often vague. Lemberger noted that Indiana "allows merchants to sell Paris green, white hellebore, London purple, and any chemicals used as insecticides, and has a special Act forbidding sale, gift or barter of opium, morphine or cocaine to any persons addicted to the habitual use of that same. Penalties for violation: Minimum $10 and maximum $50 for each offense."[43] Lemberger did not reveal how the druggist would ascertain whether the customer was addicted, whether state or local authorities performed regular inspections, or how violations would be discovered. Further, New Mexican authorities lamented that although the state had schedules "A" and "B" and provided for the register of sales of all poisons:

> We believe our own statute to be weak in not requiring an age condition similar to the thought expressed in the Ohio, Virginia and Nebraska law. There is no plainer law, nor one more easily comprehended than our own, but we realize how readily persons can obtain anything they want in person or by proxy—the latter may be a child or an idiot. A note written by the party desiring a poison can have it if the dealer wants to sell it.[44]

Although the concept is anathema to political liberals of today, Lemberger emphasized that consideration for personal freedom and resistance to government control, while laudable, also had pitfalls—particularly with regard to narcotics.

> We know that from peer to peasant, from the most cultured to the most ignorant, danger threatens their existence by voluntary resort to the use or abuse of poisons, the sale of which may not be sufficiently guarded by law. All of us who have been active in the drug business have met with the habitual user of opium or morphia or cocaine, and would gladly have taken refuge from responsibility on a rigid law, and have helped our fellow mortals as they gratified an abnormal desire which must hasten physical wreck. It may be considered a deprivation of personal liberty to offer this suggestion, but in the writer's judgment, after years of observation and the knowledge of misery entailed by the abusive use of poisonous drugs, he feels persuaded that a more stringent law making the indiscriminate purchase less easy, would, in a large measure, serve as a protection against their too free use.[45]

Free access to drugs in America had predictable consequences. While David Courtwright has emphasized that in no Western country did drug abuse[46] affect a large percentage of the population in the nineteenth and early twentieth centuries, he estimates that there were perhaps 313,000 opiate addicts in America before 1914.[47]

As for England, while data are available on deaths from opiates in the nineteenth, early twentieth century[48] statistics on drug abusers are harder to come by.[49] According to authorities like Virginia Berridge, opiate abuse in nineteenth-, early twentieth-century England has been overrated. Nevertheless, before the enactment of the Pharmacy Act of 1868 British pharmacists and physicians were unfettered in prescribing and dispensing opiates. After passage of the Pharmacy Act, opiate-based patent medicines remained exempt and circulated widely. The British government tried to limit them only in the late nineteenth and early twentieth century; the government established no thorough controls over narcotics and cocaine until the 1920s. Britain produced most of the world's morphine in the second half of the nineteenth century. Physicians were incautious in prescribing and pharmacists in dispensing narcotics.[50] Until the 1920s, in Berridge's words, "prescriptions were . . . still the property of the patient, and could be redispensed at will."[51]

In Russia, on the contrary, because poisons were "so rigidly guarded," would-be suicides had to resort to other means. Marsden claimed that in "90 percent" of suicides "ammonia" was "the agent employed."[52] Indeed, in Moscow in 1908, of 594 attempted cases of suicide, 342 used spirits and iodine. Others used revolvers, threw themselves under trains, or, in two cases, leapt from windows.[53] Additionally, individual pharmacists sometimes went to heroic lengths to prevent access to harmful medicaments. For example, in January 1900, a pharmacist in Simferopol' refused to sell a young woman 10 kopeks worth of carbolic acid when she hysterically announced she was going to use it to commit suicide. Apparently, the St. Petersburg Women's Medical Institute had rejected her. The kindly pharmacist collected 40 rubles to send her back to her family in Rostov.[54]

Unfortunately, the Russian system was not entirely foolproof. Thus, some accidental poisonings and drug abuse did occur in the imperial period.

Foreign patent medicines particularly filtered through the barriers and escaped the Medical Council's scrutiny. In 1907, *Farmatsevticheskii trud* noted that medicines or raw materials had been imported from abroad "for illegal purposes," prompting the Ministry of Internal Affairs and the Minister of Finance to "commandeer" to the customs border special doctors and chemists and to increase tariff duties.[55] The Medical Council admitted, according to the Social Democratic journal, that "At the present time in the daily press and special advertisements there are a mass of advertisements about various substances not only not approved by the Medical Administration but not examined by them . . . these nostrums dupe the poorly educated."[56] In 1913 *Farmatsevticheskii zhurnal*, not usually given to sensationalism, claimed that although the Medical Council analyzed the contents of patent medicines, there was insufficient supervision over their sale. The journal noted that, beginning in 1905, a gang had been selling fraudulent patent medicines.[57]

Not all Russian physicians heeded the warnings in medical texts and the press. As a result, addiction could originate with the physician's prescription. For example, in Leo Tolstoy's *Anna Karenina*, a reflection of the 1870s in which it was written, Anna tells her sister-in-law Dolly that she takes drops of morphia to help her sleep and that she cannot sleep without them.[58] Lamenting the inadequate attention to dentistry in Russia, an 1885 article in *Zubovrachebnyi vestnik* implied that doctors routinely prescribed drops of opium for toothaches.[59] An 1893 article related the violent reaction of a woman to the morphia prescribed for her bronchitis. In recounting her medical history the author noted she had taken opium or morphine only on three occasions; in one case a gynecologist had prescribed drops of opium for "some sort of women's disease."[60] Although admittedly isolated, such instances indicate that Russian physicians sometimes incautiously prescribed opiates and that women may have been particularly vulnerable to this practice.

Most interesting was the possibility of drug abuse in the imperial family. The imperial pharmacy trunks are stashed under a staircase in the pharmacy museum in Moscow. Director of the museum, pharmacist and historian of pharmacy V. M. Salo claims they contain an inordinate number of vials of morphine and cocaine.[61] In a letter of September 20, 1914, to Nicholas, Alexandra informed her "own beloved One" that she "lay down and smoked to get myself into order."[62] Might the substance which calmed her nerves have been hashish?[63] Of Tsar Nicholas, French Ambassador Maurice Paleologue commented Sunday, November 19, 1916, that

> During recent months the Emperor has frequently suffered from nervous maladies which betray themselves in unhealthy excitement, anxiety, loss of appetite, depression and insomnia.
>
> The empress would not rest until he had consulted the quack Badmaiev. . . . The charlatan soon discovered in his pharmacopoeia the remedy appropriate to the case of his august patient: it is an elixir compounded of "Tibetan herbs" according to a magic formula and has to be prescribed very strictly.

> Every time the Tsar has used this drug, his baneful symptoms have vanished in a twinkling. He has not only recovered sleep and appetite, but experienced a general feeling of well-being, a delightful sense of increased vigour and a curious euphoria.
>
> Judging by its effects, the elixir must be a mixture of henbane and hashish, and the Emperor should be careful not to take too much.[64]

In addition to prescriptions by dubious or misguided physicians, cracks in controls on dispensing and distribution allowed of some drug misuse and adulteration. Master of Pharmacy A. V. Pel', famous researcher and founder of a pharmaceutical firm in St. Petersburg, also was a crusader against pollution and adulteration of water, food, and other products. In an 1899 pamphlet he discussed the substitution of mineral oil for castor and cod-liver oil, and the dilution of quinine. Pel' claimed he had discovered a substance sold as cod-liver oil which actually contained 45 percent petroleum oil although by appearance, taste, and smell it could not be distinguished from true fish oil. Concomitantly, he discovered that in some cases quinine had been diluted by 20 percent milk sugar, a practice which could not be readily discerned.[65] In 1907 the police in St. Petersburg discovered a cache of adulterated cocaine and codeine. The cocaine was actually antifebrin, the codeine, bromide salts. A racket had been at work. Five people were arrested, including a nobleman, peasant, and three wholesale drug traders (*komissionery*). They had packaged the false drugs and labeled them with the name of the German pharmaceutical firm Merck in Darmstadt.[66]

At times accidental poisonings or overdoses occurred. In 1899 *Pravitel'stvennyi vestnik* reported five cases of accidental poisoning due to improper storage or dispensing. Most of the cases were prosecuted. For example, in February, a feldsher in a zemstvo hospital mistakenly gave a peasant girl powder of strychnine in place of the cough medicine *kashlia.* Court proceedings followed. Pharmacists had long been haranguing against feldshers dispensing medicine. Thus, this case gave pharmacists additional ammunition to insist that only qualified members of their *soslovie,* or corporation, be allowed to dispense poisonous or strong-acting medicine.[67] In April a circuit court ordered the medical institute in St. Petersburg to pay a peasant family 3,600 rubles because a member of the family, employed at the institute, drank a poisonous liquid that had been improperly stored there.[68] In Moscow there was legal investigation into the case of a peasant who had to be admitted to Sheremet'ev hospital when he became unconscious after drinking eighteen drops of a medicine.[69] In 1900 a case of great notoriety involved an Odessa pharmacist's mistaken dispensing of poison instead of heart medicine.[70] A case in 1901 highlighted the extraordinarily long hours pharmacists sometimes had to work; a St. Petersburg pharmacist dispensed the wrong medicine after working sixty hours at a stretch.[71]

Pharmacists, of course, having access to drugs, also could abuse them. In 1907, *Farmatsevticheskii trud* carried the story of an Assistant Pharmacist who had lost his position and, in desperation, decided to poison himself and his two-year-old child with morphia.[72]

Apparently, one means of easy access to poisonous or dangerous substances was through the so-called *aptekarskie magaziny* (drug stores) or chandleries. Proprietors and managers usually were not pharmacists; thus, by law they could not prepare medicine on the premises. The drug stores could, however, purvey commercially prepared medicaments in an area separate from where sundries were sold.[73] Since pharmacies were restricted–the number of pharmacies being dependent upon population, geographical ratio, and prescription turnover–the drug stores filled a need and proliferated. As noted in a previous chapter, by the first decade of the twentieth century there were nearly twice as many drug stores and "groceries" where medicines were sold.[74] Drug stores were forbidden by law to prepare complex medicines and were required by law to sell prepared medicines exactly in the form they had been received. Apparently, the managers of the drug stores did not always adhere to government regulations. In May 1899, *Farmatsevticheskii vestnik* disclosed that "many" drug stores sold heroic or poisonous medicines; furthermore, these were not kept in a special locked cupboard nor were sales recorded for the medical inspector. In addition the journal claimed that the drug stores sold patent medicines.[75] In January 1900, the journal reported that there were fourteen drug stores in Astrakhan; only four were managed by pharmacists. Although the drug stores were forbidden to dispense poisons, not long before one had dispensed sublimate in place of quinine, thus poisoning a teacher from Nizhni Novgorod.[76] In June 1900, a Justice-of-the-Peace court fined the owner of a drug store 100 rubles for trading in so-called galenical, or complex preparations, made on the premises. However, the appellate court reduced the fine to 50 rubles.[77] *Farmatsevticheskii vestnik* cited other cases of mistaken dispensing in 1900.[78] In 1902, an Odessa court investigated a death from poisoning; the medicine had come from a drug store.[79] Since pharmacists were campaigning mightily for prohibition of the drug stores, they welcomed evidence of such wrongdoing.

Danger also lurked in officially approved patent medicines. The medicine *kashlia*, cited above, was morphine and codeine-based. Another commonly used medicine, potentially dangerous, was Dover's Powders. In existence since the eighteenth century, Dover's Powders was composed of ipecacuanha and opium.[80] In late nineteenth-, early twentieth-century Russia at least three published cases of overdoses were attributed to this officially approved "patent medicine." An 1886 account related that a nurse in a foundling home mistakenly gave an eight-month-old child 5 grains of Dover's Powders. A physician successfully brought the comatose child round with atropine.[81] According to an 1894 article a feldsher gave a child of one year, four months three ¼-grain doses of Dover's Powders over a two-hour period. Convulsions resulted. After three days the physician whom the family frantically consulted was able to counteract the opium with a catheter and doses of strong black coffee. The physician warned readers that the ¾-grain dose for an infant was the equivalent of 15 grains for an adult and reminded colleagues of "the necessity of caution in prescribing opium in pediatric practice." Although he often had heard that "children over one year can take Dover's Powders in doses of one grain . . . our case can serve as a warning about how dangerous it is to give opiates to children."[82] In any case, by law feldshers were forbidden to prescribe narcotics or strong-acting medicine.[83] A 1902 article described an incident in which five grams of Dover's Powders were mistakenly given to a three-and-a-half-month-old infant. The doctor tried to induce vomiting and finally brought the child round with repeated doses of strong black coffee and then an injection of potassium per manganate. The doctor echoed the injunction that opium must be prescribed for children with great care; one sixtieth of a grain was appropriate.[84]

Rural pharmaceutical practice was fraught with special problems. One was insuring proper doses–it was difficult for peasants to measure liquids; powders for decoctions or infusions were only slightly more accurate.[85] Containers for medicaments presented potential hazards. Zemstvo and rural pharmacies had only a limited supply. In some cases peasants brought old containers for new prescriptions; if these had been used to store poisons fatalities could result.[86] In 1902, the pharmacy journal *Farmatsevt* complained that feldshers could get opium preparations from pharmacies on demand of the zemstvo although arsenic required a physician's prescription.[87]

Peasants also used home remedies and turned to unlicensed, self-appointed healers. Samuel Ramer's recent interesting study of peasant remedies emphasizes their medical relevance.[88] However, sometimes peasant remedies had disastrous results. In 1899, the press reported that a young woman died from poison she had received from a self-appointed healer.[89] In 1900 *Farmatsevticheskii vestnik* reported two cases of poison administered by self-appointed healers. Also, in that year a court trial sentenced a peasant woman in Nizhni Novgorod province to eight years' hard labor for poisoning her husband. The case brought to light illegal trading in poisons and medicaments–arsenic, *kashlia* (the morphine and codeine-based cough preparation), strong vodka, sublimate, and others. Peasants in nearby villages apparently knew about and took advantage of such trading.[90]

Finally, in the 1850s and 1860s Russia expanded into the Ussuri and Amur regions of the Far East; from 1868, particularly in the 1880s and 1890s, into Central Asia; and from the mid-1890s into Manchuria. Russian troops stationed in these areas and colonists who migrated there were exposed to hashish- and opium-using natives.[91]

All of this meant that there was a certain amount of drug addiction in tsarist Russia. Unfortunately, no statistics appear to be available; evidence must be gathered from scattered accounts. Some reports discussed drug use in general; others gave information on use of specific drugs.

Polynarcotism

Polynarcotism, or simultaneous use of more than one drug, was reported from time to time. On November 20, 1899, an article in *Farmatsevticheskii vestnik* related that in Krasnoiarsk and Yeniseisk, despite the fact that local apothecaries could not sell morphia and cocaine without a doctor's prescription, there had appeared special dealers (*prodavets*) of these "poisons." They supplied "morphinists" and "cocainists" (*morfinisty, kokainisty*). Thanks to this, these "maniacs" (*maniik*) had the possibility of injecting themselves daily, according to their own statements, with up to 100 grains of these and other "poisons."[92] In 1904, Dr. Bereznitskii provided case studies on eight morphine addicts to the Society of Ekaterinoslav Doctors. Three addicts used cocaine in addition to morphine; one of these three also used opium as did a another addict.[93]

Opium Usage

It appears that there was very little addiction to opium in European Russia. For example, a pharmacist in Tsarskoe Selo killed himself with a Derringer in 1900. His suicide note referred to doses of opium, morphia, and cocaine.[94] As noted above, two of Dr. Bereznitskii's patients took opium.

On the other hand, there was a fair amount of opium smoking in the Caucasus, Russian Central Asia, and eastern Siberia. An opium pipe used around the turn of the century is on display in the Varetskii museum in Tbilisi. No further information on opium smoking in Georgia has been forthcoming. However, by the early twentieth century opium smoking had penetrated the Amur and Ussuri regions in eastern Siberia, which Russia had acquired in late 1858 and 1860. In 1903 the Military Medical Study Committee established a commission on opium. The report discussed opium use in Persia–the upper classes took small doses of opium their entire lives, infants being given opium to accustom them to future use–but only the poor became addicts; it emphasized that England had fostered opium trade in China to increase revenue from her Indian colony. Claiming that opium affected 60 to 70 percent of China's population, the report presented lurid descriptions of opium smoking and addiction. The Military Medical Study Committee confirmed that Russia imported opium for medicinal uses from Turkey.[95]

But the primary thrust of the 1903 Military Medical report was that Russia should prevent free importation of opium into Russia and into the Kvantunskaia region in Manchuria, which was "leased" by Russia. Such a policy would protect Russian citizens living there and would prevent opium circulating in the Amur and other eastern provinces of Siberia. The commission opposed government-regulated sale of opium and legal opium dens. It stressed that the Russian government must prohibit secret sales and use tariffs to keep opium out of Kvantunskaia, Amur, and other eastern Siberian provinces.[96]

From a publication which appeared three years later it appeared this warning was too late. In 1906, I. S. Levitov informed the State Duma, the newly instituted Russian parliament, and the Russian government that contraband opium was being imported into the far eastern provinces of Siberia. Levitov noted that there were no laws in Russia prohibiting opium smoking; however, there were regulations regarding the importation of opium. According to Levitov, the local police were ignoring these import laws; as a consequence, opium smoking had quickly spread among the Russian inhabitants of the Ussuri region (*oblast'*). Interestingly, Levitov traced the source of much of the opium in eastern Siberia to the cultivation of the opium poppy in Manchuria, which had begun in 1901 and 1902 during the Russian "occupation." Levitov accused the government and Duma of ignoring the importation of opium. To stop the practice he urged that an excise tax be imposed on opium.[97] In a 1909 pamphlet devoted to hashish smoking, described below, Levitov highlighted opium smoking in Russian Central Asia. Apparently, Persians moving into Fergana and Kokand brought opium with them.[98] Russia participated in The Hague Convention of 1911-1912 which sought to regulate the international opium trade.[99]

Hashish

Hashish usage, during the tsarist period, also seems to have been confined mainly to border provinces, in this case to Russian Central Asia. In 1909 Levitov published a pamphlet on hashish usage in Central Asia based on studies he had undertaken in 1907. Levitov stressed that the Moslems of Central Asia, amounting at the time to some twenty million, had drunk *buza*, an alcoholic or rice beverage and smoked hashish for some six centuries. From them, Russian and Cossack colonists had adopted the habit. Levitov did not provide hard data but he claimed that twenty-five out of every one hundred Cossacks smoked and of every fifty Cossacks in Semirech'e who smoked, two smoked hashish.[100]

Levitov related that the hashish trade was in the hands of Kirghiz tribesmen; whole villages participated. Nonsmoking Chinese Kirghiz from the western Chinese province of Kashgar sold hashish to their Russian tribesmen across the border. Imports had risen for a number of reasons. First, Great Britain raised import duties on hashish imported into India, causing hashish to be diverted to the nearby Russian provinces. Instead of destroying contraband hashish, local police colluded with smugglers in return for a share of the profits. Finally, local officials curtailed vodka sales, turning colonists and troops to buza and hashish. In 1886, in a misguided attempt to quell drunkenness, the military governor of the Sir Daria region forbade the sale of vodka in localities with exclusively native population and in Russian rural settlements. After 1887, authorities no longer gave permission to open drinking establishments in these localities.[101]

Levitov peppered his pamphlet with racist innuendo. He asserted that "the quick spread to Russia of narcotics . . . was the dirty influence of Asia . . . narcotics were the first advance guard of the yellow race in Russia."[102] Just as the French colonial service who had served in Indochina had brought drug usage back to Paris, so too, drug usage was filtering into Russia from her colonial areas. But the problem was potentially more worrisome for Russia because her colonies were contiguous. In fact, Levitov saw Russia as a buffer, protecting Europe from Asia.[103] However, despite his chauvinism, Levitov's explanation for the greater impact of hashish-smoking on Russians and Cossacks, as compared to Moslems, had nothing to do with racial differences but with the type of hashish smoked by each group. According to Levitov, Moslems smoked hashish that had been cured for at least two and in some cases four years. Russians and Cossacks, on the other hand, smoked fresh hashish. This caused headaches, dizziness, vomiting, and greater intoxication.[104]

A 1975 Soviet text has credited Dr. A. L. Kamaev with being the first to recognize the addictive nature of hashish.[105] Kamaev's work dealing with hashish smoking in Samara was published in 1931.[106] However, it would seem that I. S. Levitov was eligible for this distinction. Levitov noted that there was controversy as to whether hashish smoking was harmful to Moslems, but he implied that hashish smoking was addictive. He referred to hashish as a narcotic and noted that Tamerlane had attempted to eliminate hashish usage–without success–in the fourteenth century. Levitov emphasized that prolonged smoking of hashish led to mental and physical deterioration. People who had smoked hashish for ten years became living corpses.[107]

Since Levitov estimated that there were one thousand hashish smokers in Turkestan, he did not believe hashish smoking could be entirely prohibited.[108] Furthermore, he admitted that hashish had medicinal qualities; Indians used it as a febrifuge and antispasmodic.[109] However, Levitov was concerned with abuse of the substance by Russians and importation of contraband hashish into European Russia. He emphasized that hashish was more valuable in Russian Turkestan than in China because it was scarcer. The hashish trade was lucrative; a *pud* of hashish cost 12 or 15 rubles in China but sold for as much as 240 rubles in Russia.[110] Therefore, to stop the smuggling of hashish into Russia, Levitov recommended legalizing the sale of hashish to Moslems. He advocated only that Russian authorities essay the quality of hashish in especially constructed laboratories. High-quality hashish would command a higher price.[111] Levitov also suggested that the Anti-Alcohol Commission, then meeting in St. Petersburg, coordinate its activity with the local Buzo-Hashish Commission. Levitov believed that prohibition of vodka in Central Asia had led to hashish smoking. Thus, he opposed empire-wide prohibition on the grounds that it would increase addiction to drugs other than the banned alcohol.[112]

Morphine

In early twentieth-century Russia morphine was sold on the streets, if we can judge from the 1899 account on "morphinists" in Krasnoiarsk related above. However, as in the West, morphine usage also was medically related and physicians and pharmacists were particularly vulnerable. In 1900, *Farmatsevticheskii vestnik* related the case of a pharmacy student admitted to a hospital with signs of morphia poisoning.[113] The pharmacist in Tsarskoe Selo who committed suicide took morphia and cocaine as well as opium.[114]

In 1904, M. I. Bereznitskii read a paper to the Society of Ekaterinoslav

Doctors on the treatment of morphine addiction, as well as alcoholism and smoking, by hypnosis. Bereznitskii presented case studies of four patients, three men and one woman morphinist, whose treatment had proven successful. He also alluded to other morphine addicts whose treatment had not succeeded.

Bereznitskii analyzed the stages of addiction–prolonged usage and increased dosage, physical and psychic sensation (*oshchushchenie*) in the interval after the last injection, and heavy attacks called morphia craving (*golodanie*), the symptoms of which were nervousness, vomiting, diarrhea, and other ills. Modern specialists labeled this the "abstinence syndrome."[115]

Bereznitskii's patients ranged from lower-middle to upper class. One was a landowner (*pomeshchik*); one, a machinist; one, a medical student; and the fourth, the wife of an engineer. They turned to morphia because of physical pain and mental distress. The landowner had begun taking morphia because of psychic problems following the death of his young daughter. The medical student had taken the drug to heighten his mental ability for examinations and because of physical pain. Both these morphine addicts also used cocaine. In addition, the landowner smoked opium and the medical student drank vodka and took chloral. The machinist and the engineer's wife began taking morphia to alleviate physical pain. The former was a paraplegic who suffered severe pain in his legs and spine; the latter had stomach colic.[116]

Bereznitskii's information on how his patients obtained morphine confirms that medical and pharmaceutical practice did not always adhere to the strict regulations regarding prescribing and dispensing of narcotics. Doctors originally had prescribed morphia for two of the patients to whom Bereznitskii applied his hypnotherapy. In addition, although the woman patient's physician belatedly warned her that morphia was addictive, he gave her a needle and syringe so that she could inject herself while on a vacation trip.[117] The landowner stole the morphia. Bereznitskii did not reveal where the landowner and medical student acquired their cocaine. However, he commented that while it was difficult to get even a small amount of morphia from a pharmacy without a doctor's prescription, it was easy to get morphia from the proprietors of the drug stores. According to Bereznitskii, the addict could receive morphine from these "drug stores" upon presenting a "little piece of paper signed by the morphinist himself."[118]

During the course of their treatment, addicts lived at Bereznitskii's home. In some cases, he put them into a deep sleep twice daily, in others every other day. Treatment lasted from fifteen to twenty-five days. Bereznitskii believed hypnotherapy was beneficial because it did not require special closed treatment centers and enabled the patient to continue his occupation during treatment. It also shortened the time of treatment. However, though not new, Bereznitskii complained that doctors did not commonly use hypnotherapy because of a lack of trained practitioners and the medical profession's general distrust of hypnosis. Also, to succeed, patients had to be strongly motivated.[119]

Morphine abuse continued in the second decade of the twentieth century. A Soviet account told of a patient who had abused morphine from 1911, through *gimnaziia* and university in the prewar and early war years. Although the individual began to take two tablets of morphia per day in his final year in the *gimnaziia*, he began injecting morphine as a student in the medical faculty of the University of Warsaw.[120] Dr. S. A. Isaev claimed, in his 1912 pharmacology text, that 40 percent of morphine addicts were physicians and pharmacists.[121] In 1914 the journal *Sibirskii vrach* stated that in Blagoveschensk and the Amur region, morphine abuse was widespread, chiefly among the proletariat, in addition to smoking opium and abusing cocaine.[122]

Heroin

Heroin addiction was basically a street affliction in early twentieth-century America.[123] In Russia heroin addiction was very rare and seems to have been the result of medical prescriptions. According to Dr. S. I. Kagan, Russian medical literature cited only two cases of chronic heroinism. One, published in 1913, claimed the victim had become an addict for three years as a result of a prescription for neuralgia. The second, a case study by Dr. Kutanin, published in 1914, claimed a woman became addicted to heroin for ten years when her feldsher husband advocated the drug for toothache.[124] The Soviet account, above, of the student morphine addict also related that the patient had used heroin for six months in 1911. It did not indicate the source of the heroin.[125]

Cocaine

Although the 1899 article, cited above, referred to "cocainists," they were located in the Russian Far East. Cocaine addiction seems to have become noticeable in the center of European Russia only in the years immediately preceding World War I. Apparently, cocaine could easily be acquired from drug stores, from authentic pharmacies, and from physicians. In 1913 *Farmatsevticheskii zhurnal* carried an article that originally had appeared in *Rannee utro*. The article began dramatically:

In Moscow there rages a new "plague"—
chronic passion for cocaine.
The "import" of this evil into Russia
increases with each year.
Cocaine has become modish.

The article went on to say that surgeons and dentists used the substance as a local anesthetic in small operations. But "lovers of 'stimulating' their tired nerves" also were using cocaine to a great degree. Although cocaine could be sold in pharmacies only with a doctor's prescription, the article claimed the practice of falsifying prescriptions was widespread—even doctors' signatures were being falsified. Furthermore, in "apothecary stores" (the drug stores, called in this article *aptekarskie lavochki*) cocaine could be purchased without any prescription. According to the article the use of cocaine was strongly established among the Muscovite intelligentsia.[126] In 1915 the Moscow physician M. P. Kutanin, the specialist on heroin addiction, related the case of a patient who suffered cocaine "intoxication" in the winter of 1911-1912. He had acquired 5 to 6 grams daily from a pharmacy.[127] Kutanin considered cocaine addiction more difficult to cure than morphinism; he claimed that when deprived of cocaine, addicts turned to opium. Kutanin also stated that cocaine circulated among singers and artists in Moscow in 1914.[128]

Drug Abuse during World War I

The balance sheet on drug addiction in tsarist Russia, prior to World War I, reveals that addiction to opiates, hashish, and cocaine was minuscule. Drug abuse apparently was smaller than in England and the United States at that time. Unfortunately this balance was upset during World War I. Exposure to drugs other than alcohol increased markedly during the war for a number of reasons. Prohibition on alcohol turned people to substitutes—home-brewed liquor (*samogon*), denatured alcohol, narcotics, and cocaine.[129] Prescriptions for morphia and cocaine increased due to wounds suffered in the war.[130] The price of medicaments escalated precipitously during the war. Speculation in drugs occurred and quantities of drugs began reaching the street in major cities, particularly St. Petersburg. Early in 1916 the police chief of Petrograd, as the capital was named during the war, announced that an apothecary stock market (*aptekarskii birzh*) had been organized in the cafe "Kontsert" on Ekaterinoslav Street. The police raided the place, arrested twenty people, and found "significant" quantities of opium, cocaine, and other medicaments. Some of the "speculators" lived in Petrograd but many lacked permission to live in the capital. A search of one apartment revealed 600 rubles' worth of various pharmaceutical wares. Speculation in drugs was going on in other cafes on the main boulevard, the Nevskii Prospekt. After the arrests the action moved to the railway station.[131]

Use and abuse of narcotics and cocaine spiraled during the Civil War of 1918 to 1921. Drug addiction continued to be a major problem for the new Soviet government through the 1920s and the 1930s.[132] The trauma of World War I and the Civil War were largely responsible for the rise of drug use and abuse.

Pharmacy practice in tsarist Russia cannot be credited with preventing this scourge. However, it did help to limit the supply of drugs on the street.

12

Professionalization

One of the defects in the Russian pharmacy system was that bureaucrats and physicians dominated and made policy for pharmacists, pharmacy, and pharmaceutical education. Pharmacists did not make serious noises about emancipating themselves until 1906.[1] In 1910 they bitterly contended that the "reason for the abnormal position in which pharmacy finds itself is that physicians manage pharmacy."[2] They railed against the Pirogov Medical Congress for refusing to admit Provizors along with other medical specialists.[3]

Nevertheless, from the early nineteenth century, pharmacists managed their own internal affairs and expended considerable energy on professionalizing their corporation (*soslovie*). They founded societies, convened congresses, launched journals, established assistance (*vspomogatel'naia kassa*) and mutual aid funds (*vzaimo-vspomogatel'naia kassa*), and a National Pension Fund (*Pensionno-Vspomogatel'naia Kassa*).

Such efforts, which paralleled pharmacists' activities in the United States and Western European countries, indicated pharmacists' dynamism and initiative, ability to manage their own destiny, and concern for their less fortunate brethren. Additionally they emphasized the existence of an embryonic civil society in imperial Russia. However, pharmacists' professionalization in Russia was to have a more dramatic denouement than in the United States and Western Europe. The movement begat revolutionary pharmacists who worked to overturn the pharmacy system existing in Russia by eliminating privately owned pharmacies and pharmaceutical enterprises.

The pharmacy corporation's first step in self-management and increasing professionalism was the St. Petersburg Pharmaceutical Society organized in 1818.[4] The first pharmacy journal appeared in 1820. From 1839 until 1843 one Siller published *Nordische Centralblatt fur Pharmacie* and from 1839 until 1848 one Gauger published *Repertorium*. Russian pharmacists published original research in both journals.[5]

The great push toward professionalization began in the second half of the nineteenth century, during the period of the "Great Reforms" following the Crimean War. Pharmacy societies opened in eleven more cities: Riga, Kiev, Moscow, Poltava, Pskov, Warsaw, Odessa, Lublin, Khar'kov, Kazan, and Tiflis. In May 1863, pharmacy societies were founded in Riga and Kiev.[6] Moscow pharmacists established the Moscow Pharmacy Society in 1864.[7] In 1869 societies combining "Doctors, Veterinarians, and Pharmacists" were established in Poltava and Pskov, respectively. During the 1870s three more societies appeared–the Warsaw Pharmacy Society in 1870, the Odessa Society of Pharmacists in 1873, and the Lublin Society of Doctors and Pharmacists in 1874. The Khar'kov Pharmacy Society was established in 1881 and the Kazan Pharmacy Society in 1887. Pharmacy owners in Odessa organized a special society in 1885. A Caucasian Society of Pharmacists was established in Tiflis in 1890.[8] At least eighteen pharmacy societies operated in Russia in 1913.[9]

Membership and functions of pharmacy societies varied. By 1884 the St. Petersburg Pharmacy Society had 343 members, 209 of which were "actual" members, although members lamented that new pharmacy owners did not join the society as expected.[10] One of the objectives of the society was to protect pharmacy owners from the competition of zemstvo and city pharmacies.[11] Additionally, the society assisted in writing the new national pharmacopoeia (members tested new medicaments) and continued the pharmacy school, instituted by the society in 1817. (In 1883 there were four to ten students, six receiving stipends.) The society was particularly pleased with its chemistry laboratory. The lab contributed to public health by essaying foodstuffs sold in the marketplace and performing diagnostic analyses, many of which were increasingly requested by private citizens.[12]

Working capital for the society and capital for pensions came from the 10 ruble annual dues of members–owners and lessees of pharmacies in the capital. By 1907 the Audit Commission complained about "irregularities in dues" although the fund appeared healthy, as discussed below. Members additionally paid 1 ruble, 50 kopeks from each 1,000 prescriptions to support the school of the society.[13]

The Dorpat Pharmacy Society had 84 members in the summer of 1884.[14] In 1901 the Caucasian Pharmacy Society library included a number of textbooks and subscribed to one Polish and three Russian pharmacy journals and the English-language *Journal of Analytical Chemistry.*[15] The 151 members of the Warsaw Pharmacy Society in 1904 included all levels of pharmacist: 2 Masters, 112 Provizors, 30 Assistant Pharmacists, and 7 pharmacy students. The society was proud of its reading room with seven journals and forty-eight books. However, members lamented that only a minority of the 276 staff pharmacists (*sluzhashchie*), who included 102 Provizors, 122 Assistants, and 52 students, employed in Warsaw considered it their duty to join the society.[16] Kiev,[17] Warsaw,[18] Khar'kov,[19] and Kazan had pharmacy societies by the late nineteenth century.[20]

Pharmacists' growing sense of professionalism was reflected in and shaped by a number of pharmacy congresses that met from the second half of the nineteenth century. Early congresses were convened by the St. Petersburg Pharmacy Society.[21] The first Russian Pharmacy Congress was held in 1864; successive congresses were held in 1889, 1900, 1902, 1906, 1907, and 1913.[22]

Until 1906 these congresses were comprised of fully qualified pharmacists—Provizors and Masters—and many delegates owned or rented pharmacies. A. N. Popovskii, delegate to the 1913 Pharmaceutical Congress, defended the practice of permitting only fully qualified pharmacists to attend, noting that physicians banned second- and third-year medical students from their Pirogov Congresses.[23] But, their background notwithstanding, delegates discussed issues common to the whole corporation—raising the level of pharmaceutical education, improving pharmacy practice (*aptechnoe delo*), regularizing trade in "patent," or proprietary, medical substances, and revising the Pharmacy Tax.[24] Further, progressive pharmacists in the 1906 and the 1913 congresses advocated liberal, even radical, solutions to problems confronting "conditional" pharmacists. They proposed buying out private pharmacies (*samovykup*), by the corporation, the government, or other means, and turning them over to zemstvos and municipal dumas. In fact, two delegates to these congresses—Professor Alexander Semenovich Ginzberg and Magister of Pharmacy O. G. Gabrilovich—became administrators of the Bolshevik pharmacy organization in 1919 and 1920.[25]

In addition to the proliferation of congresses and societies, the pharmaceutical press expanded in the period between the Crimean War and World War I. In 1867 the St. Petersburg Pharmacy Society began to publish identical German- and Russian-language journals—*Pharmazeutische Zeitschrift fur Russland* and *Farmatsevticheskii zhurnal.* Publication of the Russian-language edition ceased for about a decade because of lack of subscribers. Then, in 1878, subscriptions to the German-language edition declined. Meanwhile, the number of Russian-language speaking pharmacists had risen, necessitating *Pharmazeutische Zeitschrift* to publish "official regulations [*postanovlie*] and information from various parts of Russia" in the Russian language. As a consequence, although the St. Petersburg Pharmacy Society deemed a German-language journal necessary because "while all Russian pharmacists knew Russian, many had received their higher education in German and also the German scientific language was richer," after polling members and receiving "permission from the government," the Russian-language *Farmatsevticheskii zhurnal* resumed publication in 1879.[26] Active until 1916, *Farmatsevticheskii zhurnal* was the most comprehensive of Russian pharmacy journals. It published articles on scientific developments, social topics, government reports, history of pharmacy, and pharmacy abroad. Although it represented the St. Petersburg Pharmacy Society, which counted only fully qualified pharmacists among its members, the journal presented solid and objective commentary on issues of interest to the entire corporation.

Among the most interesting developments of pharmacists' professionalization were their mutual assistance funds and the National Pension Fund. The latter generated the great Pension Fund war between radical and mainstream pharmacists in the two decades before the revolutions of 1917. It ought to be noted that other service and white collar groups also had mutual assistance funds; some, like those for salesclerks, originated earlier than those for pharmacists.[27]

The first pharmacy insurance funds were government-sponsored. In 1833 the Russian government established a medical-pharmaceutical trusteeship (*Mediko-farmatsevticheskoe popechitel'stvo*) in the department of the Institutions of the Empress Marie. The trusteeship still existed in 1909. Between 1904 and 1909 it had disbursed small pensions to sixty-three persons (for a total of 6,045 rubles), one-time grants to thirteen people for a sum of 5,790 rubles, three stipends to the Aleksandrovsk Institute, and full board in a charitable home for thirty to thirty-three people (they each received 194 rubles and 55 kopeks). The Charity Home had capital of 59,500 to maintain it. The trust had capital of 68,000 rubles, a percentage of which was distributed to children of needy members of the trust, and two stipends to Moscow University. The total pension capital was 67,000 rubles; 7,000 rubles were available for 1909.[28]

Pharmacists began founding their own mutual aid and insurance organizations at the middle of the nineteenth century. They reflect pharmacists' social consciousness and ability to organize. A number included job bureaus. They also provide insight into investment procedures and methods of financing private philanthropy in late imperial Russia.

Mutual aid funds for pharmacists and their dependents sprang up in Riga, St. Petersburg, Moscow, Warsaw, and Kiev. Special assistance funds also were organized in Khar'kov and Tiflis. As with other aspects of pharmacy, the government regulated mutual aid societies. The Ministry of Internal Affairs issued charters to each society.[29]

The Assistance Fund for Widows and Orphans of Pharmacy Owners in the city of Riga was established in 1854, before the Riga Pharmacy Society. The Assistance Fund of Riga Pharmacists was established in 1860. The St. Petersburg Pharmacy Society may have organized an assistance fund as early as December 1846.[30] However, a late nineteenth-century register of Mutual Aid and Insurance Societies dated the statute of the St. Petersburg Pharmacists' Assistance Fund with Labor Bureau to 21 June 1863.[31] Perhaps the first fund metamorphosed into the latter.[32]

In April 1867, the Moscow Pharmacy Society, founded in 1864, established the Assistance Fund for Conditional Pharmacists in Moscow.[33] Conditional pharmacists were not fully qualified. Most served in pharmacies and the term came to refer to all pharmacists who did not own pharmacies. The St. Petersburg Pharmacy Society chartered the Widows and Orphans Fund in 1869.[34] During the 1870s mutual aid societies were established in Warsaw and Kiev. The Fund of Assistance to Impoverished Pharmacists, Their Widows, and Orphans was established in Warsaw in 1870. The Kiev Pharmacy Society of Reciprocal Assistance was chartered in Kiev in 1874.[35] A Society for Student Pharmacists existed at the University of Dorpat (Iur'ev) in Estonia in 1879.[36] The Warsaw Pharmacy Society opened a savings and pension fund May 1, 1897.[37]

These assistance or mutual aid funds varied in size. Most were fairly modest. In March 1879, the auditing commission of the St. Petersburg Society reviewed the society's six funds. The Fund for Widows and Orphans, founded ten years earlier, amounted to 37,659 rubles. In the ten years between 1869 and 1879 it had disbursed grants to seventeen widows, amounting to more than 35,000 rubles.[38] Thus, average grants to widows were about 2,000 rubles, about three times the annual salary of the average Provizor. The main Assistance Fund for Staff Pharmacists Serving in Private Pharmacies in St. Petersburg was smaller. Its fundamental capital totaled 9,963 rubles, 58 kopeks in January 1878, including 5 certificates of deposit from the State Bank at 4,100 and an account in the St. Petersburg credit society of 2,200. During 1879, to its basic capital, members contributed 595 rubles, 15 kopeks and interest added 182 rubles, 50 kopeks.[39] Expenditures included books and various stipends.[40] The St. Petersburg Pharmacy Society also sponsored four other funds, which gave out endowed stipends to pharmacists auditing courses at the university for the Provizor degree.[41]

By 1891 the St. Petersburg Fund for Widows and Orphans was in trouble. For some years new members had not joined and old members had died, leaving the fund "very limited." The annual report called on "younger comrades" to join in order to preserve the "existence of this philanthropic institution."[42]

The St. Petersburg Mutual Assistance Fund for Pharmacists, meanwhile, remained healthy. By January 1891 its fundamental capital had swelled to 19,700 rubles.[43] During 1890, according to the annual report, two Masters of Pharmacy, forty-five Provizors, eighty-two Assistant Pharmacists, and twenty-one students had registered at the fund's job-finding bureau; pharmacy owners had turned to the bureau forty-five times to hire staff. They were urged to continue the practice. Those who had found places were asked to notify the bureau and those who had received loans from the fund were requested to repay so monies could be recycled for other members. During 1890 the fund distributed about 1,300 rubles.[44] It had disbursed two stipends, 200 rubles and 150, respectively, "on the basis of paragraph 2" for a total of 350 rubles. Total expenditures for 1890 amounted to 2,997 rubles. This included maintenance of the chancellery at 206 rubles and purchase of 6 bank certificates of deposit worth 627 rubles and 1 mortgage from the Noble Land Bank at 213 rubles. Total income balanced out expenditures at 2,997 rubles. This sum included 1,481 from members' dues, 892 rubles from dividends, and 311 rubles in loans repaid to the fund.[45]

Nine years later, in 1901, the St. Petersburg Mutual Assistance Fund had basic capital of 30,000 rubles, including 100 rubles in the Noble Land Bank, 25 government securities worth 28,000 rubles, and 3 government securities worth 900 rubles. The fund's operating income of 3,223 rubles for 1900 was derived from members' dues, interest on investments, profits, loans repaid to the fund, and special events such as a concert which brought in 898 rubles. Expenditures for the fund during 1901 amounted to 3,223 rubles. This figure included 240 rubles for overhead—a hall, office, salaries for secretary and other staff, and 12 rubles for insurance. The fund had disbursed four mutual assistance grants of 50 rubles for four persons, including one to a V. Broido, who was arrested January 1900. (It is tempting to think that this individual was related to the Menshevik woman pharmacist Eva Broido.) The fund also gave out two loans at 50 rubles each, a stipend of 75 rubles and grants to widows of 140 rubles, 160 rubles, 180 rubles and six at 120 rubles. Two grants of 50 rubles were spent for burials.[46]

By 1905, the capital of the St. Petersburg Mutual Assistance Fund had risen to 33,205.[47] During 1905 it spent a total of 3,031 including 390 rubles, 19 kopeks for overhead; a total of 120 rubles for mutual assistance, a total of 250 for reciprocal assistance, and payment for one funeral at 50 rubles. Nonreturnable aid included a total of 1,305—grants to widows, stipends, purchase of state securities, and a 410-ruble loan. As before, the fund derived income from member contributions—544 rubles, 1,268 rubles from interest, 253 rubles from a concert, 94 rubles profit from the inquiry or job-finding bureau, and 377 rubles returned from debtors, including Broido.[48]

By January 1907, the capital of the St. Petersburg Fund amounted to 34,100 rubles. The operating capital of the fund was 2,554 rubles, 40 kopeks. During 1906 the fund spent only 338 rubles, 87 kopeks for administration. The fund distributed various types of grants: reciprocal aid in amounts of 25, 50, and 100 rubles; 1,084 rubles of "nonreturnable" aid to thirteen people in amounts of 60, 90, and 120 rubles; and 225 rubles in stipends. The largest part of the fund's income came from interest on investments–1,288 rubles, 73 kopeks; member contributions amounted to only 493 rubles; seven people returned 137 rubles from their reciprocal grants; 269 rubles came from a concert fund; the job-finding bureau netted only 11 rubles.[49]

Contemporary radical socialist (probably Marxist) pharmacists disparaged the St. Petersburg Pharmacy Pension Fund, asserting it paid only 400 or 500 rubles per pension after twenty-five years of contributions.[50] It is difficult to ascertain the truth of this contention without data on those eligible for pensions. However, disbursements were small. For example, in 1913 interest-bearing securities amounted to 36,000 rubles but the fund spent only 2,500 rubles plus 611 for the apartment fund.[51] The funds often received bequests from pharmacists. For example, in 1913, the widow of L. S. Braunshtein gave 3,500 rubles to the St. Petersburg Pharmacy Society; interest on the grant was to help "poor, sick pharmacists, without regard to nationality or creed."[52]

Funds in other cities ranged from modest to minute. However, they all performed some useful functions and afforded experience in self-government. The Dorpat Society of Student Pharmacists Fund was tiny, as one would expect from a group of apprentices or interns with limited income. In 1878 it included 32 actual members, 107 correspondents, and 5 honorary members. During 1879, 8 members left. All 5 members of the society's executive council, or *sovet* (soviet, in the English), were Germans, underscoring the predominance of Germans in Estonia and the prevalence of Baltic Germans among pharmacists in the empire. Despite its meager size, the fund managed to support some small projects. In 1879, after paying an insurance premium of 12 rubles, the fund spent 133 rubles on improving the pharmacy library, disbursed two stipends at 25 rubles each, and doled out small sums to members–one amounted to 50 rubles, one to 42 rubles, but most equaled 5, 10, or 15 rubles.[53]

The Kiev Pharmacy Society of Mutual Aid also was small, providing token support for local pharmacists and their families. A general assembly supervised grants; 15 rubles could be given out without approval of the general assembly in cases of "emergency." The family of a deceased pharmacist could request up to 25 rubles. Income during 1897 amounted to 50 rubles from members' dues, 5 rubles from "private" persons, and 94 rubles from an exhibit. The fund had 237 rubles on hand in January 1898. During 1897 the fund spent only 16 rubles on clerical needs, paid 112 rubles for state taxes and other requirements, and disbursed a total of 95 rubles in aid.[54] Grants had gone to a widow of a Provizor, mother of a Provizor, and daughter of a Provizor, as well as a blind Assistant Pharmacist.[55] According to Soviet historian Rodionova, during twenty-five years of its existence–to 1901–the fund gave out 168 long-term loans for a total of 11,044 rubles; 243 short-term loans for a total of 11,432 rubles; and 144 travel advances for a total of 1,190 rubles. The long-term loans, therefore amounted to only about 65 rubles per loan and the short term-loans to about half that amount. Monies went to help pharmacists living in university cities in order to audit lectures or take examinations, and to help sick and invalid members. The fund also built an apartment for members and a library. Perhaps the most useful function of the Kiev mutual assistance fund was its job-finding bureau. In twenty-five years it found work for 831 staff pharmacists.[56]

The Khar'kov Pharmacy Society did not have a mutual aid fund. However, in 1898 members held an evening function to raise money for "needy pharmacists to audit lectures at the university," preventing circumstances that had forced "60 student pharmacists" and "6 pharmacists in Warsaw" to "drop out of lectures at the university because they did not have enough money."[57]

Despite this oblique criticism of Warsaw colleagues, an assistance fund had operated in Warsaw since 1870. The Warsaw Pharmacy Society opened an additional Savings and Pension Fund May 1, 1897. At the outset the fund comprised 135 members, including thirty-five pharmacy owners. Members mainly resided in Warsaw. The fund's capital was small. On January 1, 1898, it amounted to only 3,361 rubles, 1,700 of which was basic, as opposed to operating, capital.[58]

The Caucasian Mutual Aid Society in Tiflis was minuscule. In 1901 it had only fifteen actual and fifteen corresponding members. One of its good deeds that year was to disburse 25 rubles to a widow with three minor children. That this was an inconsequential amount was obvious to members, who "decided that this sum was insignificant and took up a collection" receiving "100 more rubles." The administrative board of the fund included a German, a Russian, and a Georgian, I. G. Tsereteli. One wonders whether the latter was related to the Menshevik of that name.[59]

The Moscow Assistance Fund for Conditional Pharmacists particularly came under fire. Between 1867 to 1892 the Moscow Assistance Fund allegedly spent only 9,619 rubles, 83 kopeks to help those out of work; 1,696 rubles were dispensed for costs associated with burials; 4,473 rubles were given out in the form of loans. The Moscow Assistance Fund was based on a 1 percent deduction from the salaries of pharmacists. In total it disbursed only 15,000 rubles—an average of 631 rubles per year. Further, it was asserted that, because the Moscow Assistance Fund was dominated by owners, they summarily rejected requests from staff pharmacist members.[60]

E. A. Al'tgauzen, moderate editor of an early twentieth-century pharmacy journal, did not see a sinister plot on the part of owners in the organization. However, he did criticize the fund for being too conservative in its fiscal policies. He noted that "the fund did not cover the masses of urgent needs of the conditional pharmacists" both because of lack of funds—"the diminutive 1 percent inputs from the insignificant salaries of conditional pharmacists" and because of conservative fiscal policies of the directors of the fund—"while the fund had amassed 40,000 rubles by the beginning of the 1890s, the directors focused on future rather than present needs."[61]

Nevertheless, the mutual aid funds, particularly those with job bureaus, were of some benefit to pharmacists. In 1907 Provizor A. B. Potkov established a more modern job bureau, the "Central Recommendation Office." This enterprise, billed as "the first in Russia," located positions for pharmacists, who paid the bureau a percentage of their salary, and assisted pharmacists in purchasing and leasing pharmacies.[62]

Finally, several new pharmacy societies and journals were founded in the late nineteenth, early twentieth century. Master of Pharmacy A. V. Pel' published the scientific and technically oriented *Zhurnal meditsinskoi khimii i farmatsii* in St. Petersburg from 1892 to 1898. E. A. Al'tgauzen, Master of Pharmacy, published *Farmatsevt* from 1893 until 1907, when he unexpectedly died.[63] *Farmatsevt* reflected Al'tgauzen's humanity and integrity. It was catholic in content and balanced in tone. Radical pharmacists admitted that *Farmatsevt* was "the most popular, and widely subscribed organ of the pharmaceutical press."[64] *Farmatsevt-praktik*, under the editorship of Master of Pharmacy I. I. Zakharevich and Professor M. D. Sherbachev, appeared irregularly between 1907 and 1909. *Vrachebno-farmatsevticheskii posrednik* appeared in 1910, and *Vserossiiskii farmatsevticheskii posrednik*, under the editorship of V. S. Kobrinets, appeared twice a month from 1909 to 1914 and then monthly from 1914 to 1916. *Khimik i farmatsevt* was published between 1910 and 1912.[65]

But, in addition to these scientific and truly professional societies and journals, there also emerged pharmacy societies and journals that called themselves "professional" but were, in fact, radical and revolutionary. Radical and revolutionary pharmacists split the pharmacy corporation into exploiters and exploited. They burrowed into pharmacists' mutual assistance funds and attempted to take over the National Pharmacists' Pension Fund. They helped precipitate the revolutions of 1905 and 1917.

13

Radical Pharmacists and the Pharmacy Pension Fund

During the late 1880s and 1890s, whether sincerely concerned about staff pharmacists, distressed by the inadequacy of existing pharmacy insurance societies, or for other reasons, some pharmacists embraced Marxism or at least a strident, aggressive brand of socialism. In 1902, J. Schindelmeiser, Private Docent at the Pharmacy Institute in Iur'ev-Dorpat University, dated the appearance of radical pharmacists to the second Pharmacy Congress of 1889. He recalled obliquely that "a movement began among pharmacy personnel which threatened to become dangerous to the pharmaceutical establishment. . . . Without going into detail about the struggle . . . it can be said that this caused the profession to be turned upside down."[1]

By 1914, as we shall see, a number of leading radical pharmacists appeared to be affiliated with the Menshevik branch of the Marxist Russian Social Democratic Labor Party. Since party affiliation was not clear before that time, for convenience sake theorist-pharmacists who wanted radical reform of the pharmacy system will, for the most part, be called radical pharmacists in this and the following chapter.

The short-term goal of radical socialist pharmacists was to improve the living and working conditions of staff pharmacists (*sluzhashchie*). Their long-term goal was to overturn pharmacy practice in Russia and ultimately the entire economic system. These ambitions required diverse and constantly shifting tactics, some confrontational, some more subtle. Radical pharmacists organized strikes–one of the first occurred in 1892 at the Ferrein pharmacy complex in Moscow[2]–founded journals to disseminate revolutionary propaganda, organized unions, convened congresses of staff pharmacists, and took control of the Mutual Aid Society for Staff Pharmacists in Moscow. Their most audacious endeavor was to take over the National Pharmacists Pension Fund.

Radical pharmacists established their first society in Moscow in 1895. They did not form a wholly new society but reorganized and used the funds of the Moscow Assistance Fund for Conditional Pharmacists in Moscow, founded in 1867. Renamed the Russian Pharmaceutical Society of Mutual Assistance and duly confirmed by the Minister of Internal Affairs,[3] the Russian Pharmacy Society became as much a vehicle for socialist propaganda as a mutual benefit organization.

A similar society, the Northern Pharmacy Society, emerged in St. Petersburg in 1901. According to its statutes, this society's purpose was to succor needy members–those out of work, old pharmacists, and families of deceased pharmacists. The Northern Society in St. Petersburg included pharmacists of both sexes, pharmacy students through Masters. Members paid a one-time fee of 5 rubles and annual dues of 6 rubles.[4] The Northern Society also provided a forum for radical pharmacists.[5]

The official organ of the Russian Pharmacy Society in Moscow was *Farmatsevticheskii vestnik.* Editors of the journal between 1897 and 1902 were Assistant Pharmacist B. N. Saltykov and S. O. Chirvinskii, professor at Iur'ev (formerly Dorpat) University. Provizor S. K. Lintser, along with other "participants," contributed articles. From 1904 to 1906 Saltykov was the sole editor, but the 1904 masthead noted that he worked "in close connection with S. K. Lintser and I. M. Kal'ning." E(vsenii) Basilaia wrote articles and "op-ed" pieces between 1904 and 1906.[6] As the mouthpiece of the Russian Pharmacy Society, *Farmatsevticheskii vestnik* discussed social issues–the problems of staff pharmacists and measures for eliminating the "pharmacy monopoly" (limitations on establishing pharmacies).[7] However, the journal also ran sophisticated articles on scientific developments in pharmacy and the pharmaceutical industry, in the format of its "establishment" rival, *Farmatsevticheskii zhurnal.*

The journals founded by radical pharmacists in the early twentieth century more obviously preached Social Democracy and attempted to mold the political consciousness of staff pharmacists. In 1907, following *Farmatsevticheskii vestnik*'s demise, B. N. Saltykov launched *Farmatsevticheskii trud.* This journal, the offices of which were located at no. 10 Malaia Lubianka, was published through 1909. It billed itself the "official organ" of the Russian Pharmacy Society and claimed to be "non-Party." *Farmatsevticheskii trud* had a Social Democratic orientation, but was neither Bolshevik nor Menshevik. It spouted Marxist slogans, sententiously informing its readers: "Staff pharmacists like all other proletariat are deprived of the means of production"[8] and "Women's, as men's slavery began with the rise of private property and can end only with its abolition."[9] The journal quoted Karl Kautsky, heaped praise on "Vladimir Il'yich's [Lenin's] *Development of Capitalism In Russia,*"[10] advocated strikes and boycotts to better conditions of staff pharmacists, opposed the pharmacy monopoly or "pharmacy privilege," and advocated both "municipalization" (ownership of pharmacies by zemstvos and cities–generally regarded as a Menshevik idea) and nationalization (this became a Bolshevik policy). As progressives and Marxists, the journal championed the development of the pharmaceutical industry in Russia.[11] It chronicled the "working class movement" in other sectors of Russia and abroad.

Nevertheless, *Farmatsevticheskii trud* was not so antibourgeois as to reject advertising to supplement subscriptions. Many advertisements concerned pharmacy products but others portrayed consumer items suitable for middle-class families. These goods implied a modestly well-off readership and, additionally, confirm how integrated into the world market prerevolutionary Russia was. Readers were proffered "Happy Family" gramophones (fourteen dealers in Moscow and in sixteen "provincial cities"),[12] men's suits ("M. I. Mandl on Tverskaia Street has received material from all the best English firms and offers new designs for autumn"),[13] Russian-made washing machines ("at 25 rubles more than 185,000 sold"),[14] and "Zinger" sewing machines. The Warsaw Singer dealer particularly used modern merchandizing techniques: sales ("a rare occasion" at 2 rubles, 50 kopeks, down from their normal price of 4 rubles, 50 kopeks and 6 rubles, 50 kopeks), illustrated price lists, and for purchasers–"a screw-driver, thread, needles, oil, and handbook . . . entirely free."[15]

Additionally, editor Saltykov supported the Pension Fund, the investments of which (if not the concept) were very "bourgeois" indeed.[16] Furthermore, *Farmatsevticheskii trud*'s socialistic inclination did not extend to fellow-exploited feldshers. The journal vehemently opposed feldshers taking the examination for assistant pharmacist or acting as pharmacists in zemstvo pharmacies.[17]

In 1908, two years after *Farmatsevticheskii vestnik* ceased publication, S. K. Lintser, erstwhile colleague of B. N. Saltykov, that journal's editor, and L. Ia. Zimin began *Russkii farmatsevt*. E. Basilaia contributed articles. *Russkii farmatsevt* contained scattered references to "peasants and workers" and "the proletarian army,"[18] termed the six-year apprenticeship "*batrachistvo*," or indentured servitude,[19] and claimed pharmacy owners promoted foreign pharmaceutical firms while opposing the Russian pharmaceutical industry.[20] However, the ideology of the journal was fairly neutral. Lintser's *Russkii farmatsevt* seemed less militant than Saltykov's *Farmatsevticheskii trud*. Additionally, it posited some sensible economic ideas. *Russkii farmatsevt* stressed that the press should not represent one pharmacy faction,[21] opposed lack of competition–specifically the "pharmacy monopoly"–for making medicine more expensive for consumers, asserted that excessive government regulations and circulars stifled the Russian pharmaceutical industry,[22] and criticized drug stores (*aptekarskie magaziny*) for evading regulations on dispensing.[23] *Russkii farmatsevt* was not the official journal of the Russian Pharmacy Society; *Farmatsevticheskii trud*, which did represent the Society, derided *Russkii farmatsevt* for being "middle-of-the-road."[24] Indeed, the advertisements in *Russkii farmatsevt* were as "bourgeois" as those in *Farmatsevticheskii trud.* They depicted pianos, women's cosmetics (Mme. Flora of Vienna's soap and powder), false teeth, cocoa, and typewriters.[25]

A fourth early-twentieth century journal, *Farmatsevt praktik,* was dismissed by *Farmatsevticheskii trud* as a mouthpiece of pharmacy owners.[26] But other radical journals sprouted. *Sluzhashchii farmatsevt* was published for a few months in St. Petersburg in 1907,[27] *Iuzhnyi farmatsevt* appeared briefly in Kiev in 1908, and *Zhizn' farmatsevta* was published in Kiev from 1909 to 1911. A second *Zhizn' farmatsevta* was published in Petrograd from 1914 to 1916.[28] These last will be examined more fully in the following chapter.

While radical pharmacists realized the power of the media, a greater concern was funding their movement. They tried to raise money locally and, in some cases, took over local mutual assistance funds. But their major focus was the National Pharmacists' Pension Fund.

In his magnum opus, *St. Petersburg between the Revolutions*, Robert B. McKean described how the Mensheviks regarded labor-union funds "a weapon of working class organization" and how the Bolsheviks attempted to take over individual funds and an incipient national insurance fund, between 1912 and 1914, in order to use their organization (and capital) for revolutionary purposes.[29] So it was with the National Pharmacists' Pension Fund.

However, the assault on the Pharmacists' Pension Fund appeared over a decade earlier than those McKean discusses and it is difficult to ascertain whether, at the outset, the opposition leaders were Mensheviks, intent on preserving the Pension Fund to benefit staff pharmacists, or Bolsheviks, keen on siphoning money for revolution. In any case the struggle for the National Pension Fund is interesting in and of itself for it provides insight into the tactics and character of radical socialists, mainly Mensheviks. The fund's original managers employed interesting investment procedures to build it up. Radical pharmacists employed a wide variety of "legal" strategies to take it over—public relations gambits, court suits, and lobbying ministers. Radical pharmacists were not homogenous—in time some became committed to maintaining the fund; others to destroying it. In general, however, the radical pharmacists displayed financial ineptitude as well as ruthlessness and disregard for the constituency they claimed to represent.

The proposal for the Pharmacists Pension Fund surfaced at the Second Pharmacy Congress in 1889. Soviet historian Rodionova claimed that "In creating such an organization pharmacy owners saw the possibility of blunting the sharpness of the struggle on the part of workers in pharmaceutical establishments."[30] An early twentieth-century account stated more matter-of-factly that St. Petersburg pharmacists "believed" such a fund was "necessary." Moscow pharmacists moved the proposal forward. Master of Pharmacy Vladimir Karlovich Ferrein suggested pharmacy owners donate 1/4 kopek from each prescription. The two hundred representatives to the congress (pharmacy owners and Provizors) agreed. Pharmacy magnate Ferrein became chair of the commission to draft a statute.[31] I. I. Keller, no relation to the Moscow pharmacy magnate, chaired the Moscow Pharmacy Society at the time. By 1891 the draft statute was ready and was distributed to all pharmacy societies in the empire for preview. According to the draft statute five hundred pharmacy owners had to voluntarily join during the course of six months. But after deliberations this clause was revised.[32] The Pension Fund received its government charter in 1894. It was headquartered in Moscow.[33]

Radical pharmacists had already displayed lack of business acumen. They dissipated the funds of the local Moscow Pharmacy Society for Aid to Conditional Pharmacists, which provided the capital for their Russian Pharmacy Society. Emanuil Adol'fovich Al'tgauzen, editor of *Farmatsevt*, accused them of "prodigal spending of a great part of the capital of the former mutual aid fund" in the first year of the new society's existence.[34]

Next, they ran aground the finances of their journal, *Farmatsevticheskii vestnik*. In 1901 A. Vinogradov, chair of the Russian Pharmacy Society, B. N. Saltykov, vice-chairman and editor of *Farmatsevticheskii vestnik*, and secretary of the society K. Lenkovskii admitted that *Farmatsevticheskii vestnik* was in financial straits.[35] The three explained that the journal, founded in 1897 with a view toward "bettering the living conditions of staff pharmacists. . . . In its first year" incurred "a deficit of 2500 rubles." But, despite the deficit, the editors lavishly "decided to expand the journal, publish reports from the second pharmacy congress in appendices, and publish the Bulletin of the Congress. They expected that the "pharmacy corporation would help" defray these expenses. Instead the editors met "apathy" on the part of pharmacists "toward our society business."

Thus, *Farmatsevticheskii vestnik* appeared irregularly during 1901. Nevertheless, editors hoped "to emerge from this difficult situation" with outside contributions, insisting that "if the corporation" considered "the journal independent and important" they would not let it fail." Dismissing their record of financial ineptitude, the editors vowed that "the Russian Pharmacy Society" would "do all necessary to improve the position of the pharmacy corporation. . . ." They assured readers that "a special commission" would be established "to discuss questions about publication of the journal" and again asked "all comrades" to assist, noting that "some Moscow pharmacies have organized a collection to help cover the deficit."[36] The finances of the Russian Pharmacy Society for Mutual Assistance remained in a muddle. Late in 1904 at a meeting of the General Assembly of the society, S. K. Lintser lamented that a good part of the members of the Supervisory Commission were in the Far East and therefore could not present their report. L. Ia. Zimin suggested inviting paid (outside) accountants to "correct" the ledgers of the society." An "inspection Commission" was then elected by secret ballot.[37]

The inability to handle money evinced by the board of the Pharmacy Society of Mutual Assistance and editors of *Farmatsevticheskii vestnik* was ominous when, in the late 1890s, these selfsame individuals put their hand to the tiller of the National Pharmacists' Pension Fund.

According to its statute the National Pharmacists' Pension-Assistance Fund was primarily intended to provide pensions and assistance to pharmacists serving in privately owned normal (*normal'naia*) pharmacies.[38] Other pharmacists were eligible to participate, such as owners of rural or village (*sel'skaia*) pharmacies, renters of pharmacies, owners or renters of pharmaceutical laboratories, managers of mineral water factories, and societies for trade in pharmaceutical wares, as well as pharmacists serving in these establishments. Likewise all pharmacists in government service, whether civilian or military, in charitable and private medical institutions, in city and zemstvo pharmacies, or even employed by the pharmaceutical, chemical, or natural history presses could become members. Pharmacy students and Assistant Pharmacists could participate in the fund upon reaching their majority. Owners of private normal pharmacies could join the Pension Fund. In other words, all pharmacists could be members of the Pension Fund. However, staff pharmacists, working in privately owned normal pharmacies, were *required* to join the fund.[39]

Both staff pharmacists in privately owned normal pharmacies and owners of these pharmacies were responsible for generating money for the pension assistance fund. Each obligatory staff member was to contribute 5 percent from his or her salary,[40] women pharmacists being equated with men in the statute.[41] Pharmacists in privately owned normal pharmacies who had reached the age of forty when the fund opened were exempt from the obligatory contribution.[42] Similarly, each pharmacy owner was *obligated* to contribute ¼ kopek from each prescription and renewal of a prescription filled in his pharmacy.[43] Regulations prohibited pharmacy owners from funding this contribution at consumers' expense.[44]

Additional provisions were made for "nonobligatory" participants, those who wanted to contribute more, for additional contributions, how the monies in the fund were to be allocated, and so on.[45]

Eighty-five percent of the fund was to be devoted to pensions for members, on the basis of "statistical data." Pensions were to be given out ten years after the fund opened.[46] Five percent of the remainder of the fund was dedicated to relief for invalids or those who had lost their capacity for work, 5 percent for grants to widows and orphans, and 5 percent for administration of the fund. Pharmacists entering the fund at age forty were to receive a one-time grant rather than a pension. One-time grants for invalids and widows and orphans were to be disbursed not later than three weeks from the death or onset of debilitating illness.[47]

The fund had an elaborate organization, as was typical of Russian institutions, whether governmental, public, or private. There was an administrative board and a supervisory committee with an audit commission. The administration was comprised of a chairman, cashier, and six members, elected for three-year terms by a general assembly comprised of staff pharmacists and pharmacy owners. The chair, cashier, and two members were to represent pharmacy owners; staff could hold the other four posts.[48]

Honorary members and owners of private normal pharmacies had the right to vote and be elected to the administration and supervisory-audit committee and any other committees deemed necessary. The supervisory-audit committee was supposed to play a crucial role. It was to make preliminary review of the annual budget and prepare an annual report, verify the books of the fund at least two times a year, audit the fund at least two times a year, and resolve any arguments between members of the fund.[49] A meeting of the general assembly was mandated each year, no later than March 1. The date, time, place, and other particulars of the general assembly meeting were to be published in *Pravitel'stvennyi vestnik*, the government newspaper, *Farmatsevticheskii zhurnal*, and two other newspapers in St. Petersburg and Moscow.

All members of the fund–owners of private normal pharmacies, pharmacists serving in these pharmacies, honorary members, and other pharmacists who had made contributions to the fund–had the right to vote in the general assembly session. Members of the fund who could not personally attend could delegate representatives. A quorum amounted to one-fifth of the members. The general assembly was to review and approve the annual budget, review the conclusions of the audit committee, elect the chair and members of the administration, chair and members of the supervisory committee, and other committees deemed necessary, determine the staff and expenditures of the chancellery, make requests to the Minister of Internal Affairs about changes in the statutes, review all proposals of the administration, elect members of the audit commission for the following year.[50] Extraordinary sessions of the general assembly could be called by the administration for its own reasons, upon demand of the supervisory committee, by written declaration of not less that twenty actual staff-pharmacist and pharmacy-owner members. Invitations to the extraordinary meetings were to be publicized in the same manner as the regular annual session.[51]

The fund was guaranteed by the State Bank.[52] It was under ultimate supervision of the Ministry of Internal Affairs.[53] In the event of "disorders" or if "existence of fund became impossible" the charter provided for its "liquidation" to be decided at an "extraordinary session" of the general assembly. The Ministry of Internal Affairs had to approve liquidation. The local police chief was empowered to close down the fund in the event of disorders. He then was to inform the Ministry of Internal Affairs.[54] These provisions were to prove especially significant for the fate of the Pension Fund.

The capital of the Pension Fund mushroomed during its first eleven years under the aegis of V. K. Ferrein, chairman of the administrative board of the fund from 1894 through 1905.[55] Owner of the largest pharmacy in the world, four drug stores and a pharmaceutical firm, Ferrein had proven himself to be a successful businessman and the fund steadily increased under his direction. In 1906 it was alleged that the core of the Pension Fund had been constituted from 40,000 rubles belonging to the Mutual Assistance Fund of Staff Pharmacists. The increase in the capital of the Pension Fund was due partly to the annual 5 percent contributions from the salaries of working pharmacists, as Social Democratic pharmacists claimed.[56] However, it also resulted from the matching ¼ kopek per prescription contributed by pharmacy owners and, even more importantly, from sound investments. Therefore, the Pharmacists' Pension Fund was not merely the fruit of staff pharmacists' labor as socialist pharmacists asserted.

In 1898, a short financial statement reported income and expenditures from 1895 to 1898 (see Table 13.1).

TABLE 13.1 National Pharmacists Pension Fund Balance Sheet (in rubles), 1895 to 1898[57]

	Income	Expenditures	
Jan. 1, 1895 to Jan. 1, 1898	197,837	178,869	for securities (*tsennye bumagi*)
		18,869	other expenses
Jan. 1, 1898 to	33,976	29,359	for securities
May 1, 1898		2,240	other expenses
Total	231,813	229,337	
On hand		3,105	

At the end of 1898 the total income and expenditures of the fund amounted to 258,194 rubles and 58 kopeks, including 234,194 rubles' worth of securities. There were only slightly more than 1,000 rubles on hand.[58]

By November 1901, total income and expenditures of the Pension Fund had climbed to over half a million rubles.[59] In 1904, when the Pension Fund was scheduled to begin its operation there were 6,815 pharmacists "occupied in private pharmacies" and 4,483 pharmacy students.[60] (There were no figures on how many pharmacists were due to retire and receive a pension.)

By the spring of 1906 there were 6,000 to 7,000 members of the Pension Fund.[61] At that time the capital of the fund amounted to over one million rubles. According to its financial report, the fund had disbursed 124,044 rubles in grants between 1895 and May 1906. It had spent a total of 898,746 for securities. The capital of the fund was distributed among the State Bank, banks in Moscow, and other banks; the report listed numbers of all accounts.[62]

Despite the impressive performance of the fund it encountered three persistent problems. First, not all pharmacists joined the fund and paid their dues as required. Second, some claimed the fund was poorly managed. The third and most crucial problem faced by the Pension Fund was factional struggle perpetrated by a group of radical socialist pharmacists who had a hidden agenda—taking over the fund for their own purposes, toppling the pharmacy corporation as constituted, and eventually destroying the political and socioeconomic system in Russia as then constituted.

The first problem—pharmacists balking at making contributions to the fund—plagued the fund from the beginning. Riga pharmacists, who had founded their own mutual assistance fund in 1860, refused to join the

Pension Fund. In May 1898, they petitioned the Ministry of Internal Affairs to "waive their obligatory participation in the Pension Fund." The tsar refused to accede to their request.[63] Other pharmacists balked as well. In 1901 *Farmatsevticheskii zhurnal* noted that the fund, in its eighth year, had had a "difficult and uncertain existence," in part because there were "not enough members." Riga pharmacists had attempted to extricate themselves, "complaining to the Minister of Internal Affairs and to the State Council." In addition, only a portion of the "3,600 pharmacy owners in the Russian Empire" had made contributions during "the present budget year."[64]

Members continued to evade their dues-paying responsibilities during 1904 and 1905. In 1904 several pharmacy owners tried to avoid making contributions to the fund. One claimed his pharmacy had burned leaving him without means.[65] The Mosal'skoi district zemstvo executive board reported that "payment to the Fund of 286 rubles, 81 kopeks, representing ¼ kopek contribution from prescriptions, was not forthcoming." A pharmacy owner in Odessa, one Shtern, requested that he be allowed to pay his dues to the fund in installments. The administration refused his request.[66] In 1905 the administration–Ferrein, Director of the Fund I. Ia. Samgin, and Cashier V. Vagner–began to crack down on recalcitrant owners. While contributions from those in the military were waived, an owner who claimed to be in arrears because he dispensed many free prescriptions was not excused from his contribution and an owner's widow who claimed to be without means was similarly not excused.[67] In December 1904, the Ministry of Internal Affairs sent a circular to "all Governors, military governors, police chiefs and *oberpolitsmeisters* obliging them to inform the Medical Administration and the Administration of the Pension-Mutual Assistance Fund about newly opened pharmacies and transfer of pharmacies from one owner to another in order to verify ¼ kopek per prescription contributions to the Fund. However, some months later the Administration of the Fund complained that it had not received the information."[68] In 1906 two members of the Pension Fund claimed that the head of the St. Petersburg Pharmacy Society, the famous pharmacist, K. I. Kresling, had "contributed only 5 rubles over an eleven-year period of time."[69] During 1905 and 1906, members withholding contributions or clamoring to withhold contributions swelled, as a result of takeover struggles and real or alleged mismanagement.

The second problem, accusations that the fund was poorly managed, must be grouped into two periods. The first period was that of Ferrein's administration, 1894 to 1905. His opponents criticized him both for not issuing detailed financial reports and not holding regular meetings. For example, in 1901, *Farmatsevticheskii zhurnal* claimed the fund was in a shaky position because of "internal causes–lack of order [*neuriaditsa*]."[70] The second period pertained to the administration that succeeded Ferrein, that of his former critics. When Ferrein's opponents finally wrested control over the fund from him they, in turn, were accused of sloppy accounting and spending an inordinate amount on the administration. For example, in 1911, I. I. Korol'kov accused the Pension Fund administration of "full absence of any kind of report tables; participants were denied proper management."[71]

Since Ferrein's opponents alleged that their takeover was justified by his mismanagement, the state of the fund under his administration deserves attention. Admittedly, Ferrein set himself up for criticism because the financial statements of the Pension Fund, periodically published in pharmacy journals such as *Farmatsevticheskii zhurnal*, were very concise and did not fully itemize expenditures. In particular the reports lumped together "grants and administration." Nevertheless, not only did the Pension Fund grow markedly during Ferrein's administration, but it appears that the bulk of the Pension Fund's expenditures went for purchase of securities that would enlarge the money available for future pensions, rather than for administration and grants. For example, expenditures for grants and administration combined from 1895 to June 1901 amounted to 37,258 rubles; purchase of securities during these five years amounted to 435,510 rubles for a total of 477,784 rubles.[72] In the early part of 1901 out of 442,770 expended, 326,698 had gone for securities and 78,790 for "grants and maintenance of the administration" combined. There were only 31 rubles, 77 kopeks on hand at this point,[73] although in August 1901, there were 2,459 rubles on hand.[74] Thus, the attacks on Ferrein's administration appear to have been largely fabricated by his opponents on the political Left. Further, they were motivated by political, rather than financial considerations. They justified the hostile takeover, the "boring from within" of Social Democratic pharmacists.

Radical pharmacists began their struggle for the Pharmacists' Pension Fund in 1898. This date is significant because it followed on the heels of the founding of the Russian Social Democratic Labor Party in 1897. In 1898, B. N. Saltykov, founder of the Russian Pharmacy Society of Mutual Assistance in Moscow and one of the editors of *Farmatsevticheskii vestnik*, became a member of the supervisory committee of the Pension Fund. Socialist pharmacists began attacking the administration of the Pension Fund at the same time. On February 28, 1898, a meeting of the general assembly was held in a building owned by V. K. Ferrein. Only members as of October 1, 1897, and personally in attendance had the right to vote.

Out-of-town members who could not attend were permitted to send a proxy with their signature on the envelope. Saltykov presented the report of the supervisory committee. The audit commission read its report, the 1897 report was approved, and officers elected. V. K. Ferrein was elected chair of the administration.[75] Then disruption broke out.

While some criticism might have been warranted, an account published in *Farmatsevticheskii zhurnal* in 1898, implied that the unrest had been orchestrated:

> For a week before the meeting among Moscow pharmacists there circulated rumors that pharmacy owners wanted to keep the Pension Fund in their hands and possibly transfer it to St. Petersburg. However, the observer continued, "many of those who could not attend the meeting gave their entry ticket to others who were not even members of the Fund. Two-hundred, seventy people attended the meeting; nine were from out of town. The meeting did not begin on time. Ferrein opened the meeting. From the beginning it was obvious that the major part of the attendees were not "normal" and would not be quiet. After the proposal to elect the chair of the Assembly . . . loud cries shouted the name Kil'chevskii. Kil'chevskii refused . . . he insisted that Ferrein must be chair of the assembly. There was loud applause; cries of "V. K. Ferrein, V. K." filled the hall. Then instead of discussion of the draft rules, cries and applause went on until recess. After half an hour, Ferrein again opened the meeting. The cries and applauding began again. No suggestion about closing could quiet the crowd. The Chair finally closed the meeting.[76]

The author of this account believed there was little reason to criticize the administration, as the capital of the Pension Fund had doubled since the previous year. He averred that

> On Monday I again was in the Fund. A large provincial crowd expressed full confidence in the Administration for development and growth of the Fund. The capital of the Fund has risen to a colossal figure—220,000 rubles. From 1 January 1896 to 1 January 1897 there were only 118,000 rubles in the Fund. In the course of that period the Fund gave out 445 rubles to 5 people as non-returnable grants, even though they had contributed only 300 rubles. Instead of heartfelt thanks, because of unfortunate circumstances in the operation of the Fund the representatives in the city of Moscow had another response.[77]

One might question the wisdom of allocating grants to members in access of their contributions. Nevertheless, the Pension Fund was unquestionably a financial success. Furthermore, it appeared suspicious that radical founder of the Russian Pharmacy Society and editor of *Farmatsev-*

ticheskii vestnik B. N. Saltykov, who was a member of the supervisory committee that contained the audit commission, did not note the irregularities which his group castigated.[78]

Unrest quieted down for a time, a contemporary observer remarking that "the majority of pharmacists have entered into a normal condition. The usual circle of activists has become clear . . . the first signs of reaction."[79]

However disorder erupted again in the fall of 1901. *Farmatsevticheskii zhurnal* accused radical Moscow pharmacists of instigating friction "between the Administration of the Fund on the one hand and a so-called 'opposition group' of Moscow pharmacists on the other."[80]

Lack of contributions from members coupled with criticism of his management of the fund prompted V. K. Ferrein to propose turning the Pension Fund over to the Treasury. Vladimir Andreevich Tikhomirov, honorary member of the fund and noted pharmacist-researcher, strongly supported him. "Pressured with a senseless struggle, the Administration decided it was best to put the Pension Fund in the hands of the Treasury in order to escape from attacks and criticism."[81]

Farmatsevticheskii zhurnal–supposedly the organ of nefarious and exploiting pharmacy owners–opposed turning the fund over to the government. It wryly editorialized that the pharmacists' appeal to the government was tantamount to ninth-century Slavic tribes appealing to Varangians or Vikings to "Come and Rule over us."[82] The inconsistency in the claims of radical socialist pharmacists (probably members of the Russian Social Democratic Labor Party) testifies to their speciousness. One of the chief early critics of Ferrein's management was S. K. Lintser,[83] one of the founders of the Russian Pharmacy Society of Mutual Assistance, and collaborator of B. N. Saltykov, editor of *Farmatsevticheskii vestnik.* In 1901, when the administration of the Pension Fund publicized its intent to transfer the fund to the government,[84] the Russian Pharmacy Society of Mutual Assistance in Moscow, headquarters of Lintser and other radicals, came out *against* the move, although this would have restored the order which the fund ostensibly lacked.

> On Monday, 8 October, was held a stormy meeting of the members of the Russian Pharmacists' Assistance Fund. They discussed the question about accepting or not the proposal of turning the treasury [of the Pension Fund] over to management of the government. There were present about 200 pharmacists. Before the time of voting a majority of pharmacists–about 150–left the meeting, thanks to which the ballot was decided affirmatively.[85]

Radical pharmacists disguised their policies by linking them with those of nonpolitically motivated members and pharmacy owners who opposed transferring the Pension Fund to the government. In October 1901, some one hundred pharmacists in Moscow presented a collective protest to the fund administration, demanding that they call an extraordinary session to discuss transferring the fund to the State Treasury. The St. Petersburg members sent a similar protest.[86]

Despite Lintser and the Russian Pharmacy Society's objection to moving the Pension Fund to government management—which would surely have restored the order they asserted was needed in the fund—*Farmatsevticheskii vestnik*, the organ of the radical Russian Pharmacy Society, continued to criticize management of the fund.

Early in 1902, "Pharmacist Uleveli" analyzed the situation in the Pharmacists' Pension Fund in Marxist terms. He railed that "abuse of position for personal and party interests cannot be tolerated and must be exposed." The Pension Mutual Assistance Fund had been "established for the purpose of aid to members. The capital was up to half a million." Considerably distorting the facts, the author asserted that "The chief source of increase in the Fund was the 5 percent collection from the wages of pharmacists." He dismissed the "¼ kopek from prescriptions" paid by pharmacy owners as "absolutely and comparatively a lower sum than contributions from the conditional pharmacists." The author did not even mention that the fund's investments swelled its capital. Instead he harangued that 5 percent taken from the meager salaries of staff pharmacists was a "heavy" exaction and asserted that the proposal to transfer the fund to the Treasury was a thinly veiled plan to relieve pharmacy owners of their contributions. He queried—emotionally as well as rhetorically—whether owners were "morally responsible to make contributions" and whether the "development of the Fund is useful for the entire group of owners," then insisted in Marxist fashion that "The welfare of pharmacy owners is created only by the difficult life of 'conditionals.' No high tax, no privilege, no raw materials can create one atom of profit without movement of the pharmacy mechanism—uninterrupted work of conditional pharmacists."[87]

Ignoring the fact that specific funds in a number of cities offered help to pharmacists attending Provizor courses, Uleveli further faulted the Pension Fund because "it did not give stipends to poor pharmacists to audit lectures." He predicted that the fund "must change its physiognomy" and claimed "the majority of members left the hall [the previous October] to protest abuse of power by the administration. . . . The majority of members present demanded that the question [whether to transfer the Fund to the

State Treasury] be discussed further." Uleveli ended on a Marxist note: "each kopek of the half a million is a crystal of human labor."[88]

Between 1903 and 1905, L. Ia. Zimin and E. G. Basilaia were elected to the administration of the Pension Fund. This generated the great election conflict that continued over a decade. It involved much acrimony, appeals to local authorities, court suits, and finally, intervention from the Ministry of Internal Affairs.

At a general meeting of the fund December 20, 1903, seven persons were nominated for the administrative board of the Pension Fund, including L. Ia. Zimin, E. G. Basilaia, and E. A. Al'tgauzen. A coterie of members protested irregularities in the process. They claimed that persons who were not members of the fund had been allowed into the meeting, although they did not have the right to vote, and had elected Basilaia and Zimin to a commission "of the Fund." All persons elected to the fund, including Basilaia and Zimin, "remained in the meeting . . . took part in the debate and balloting."[89]

An additional problem was that Evsevii Basilaia was not eligible to stand for election because, not having contributed to the fund, he was not technically a member. Nevertheless, he protested, alleging that he should be considered eligible because he came under the rubric of advisory specialist; he could be invited to assist the fund, in this case, with drafting rules for giving out pensions.[90] His candidacy was put on hold for a year.

However, by 1904, S. K. Lintser and B. N. Saltykov were firmly ensconced in the administration of the Pension Fund, which these radical pharmacists had heretofore labeled the bastion of pharmacy owners. The Left was strengthening its presence. Meanwhile, Ferrein remained as chair of the administration. Privatdocent Peter Vasil'evich Preobrazhenskii, recommended by the Ministry of Internal Affairs, reworked the statutes of the fund, and was paid 1,500 rubles for his trouble.[91]

But, Ferrein and his associates realized that a hostile takeover was in process and tried to save the Pension Fund from radical socialist pharmacists. They again requested that the government take over the fund and introduce several changes. The Pension Fund was to remain in Moscow. However, its administrative staff was to be cut and the supervisory committee was to include two representatives from the Ministry of Internal Affairs. The Minister of Internal Affairs was to appoint the chair of the administration, his assistant and "introduce order into the electoral process." Members of the Fund were to be limited to those 25 years of age and older. Contributions ought to be increased from 5 to 10 percent. Basilaia and the leftist pharmacists, of course, rejected these suggestions. Instead, they called loudly for "reorganization of the Fund" but also "struggle against the Administration running it." The fund must be reorganized on "strictly democratic lines." This was to be "the task of the conscious masses of staff pharmacists and their organizations."[92]

The radical pharmacists' takeover of the administration of the Pension Fund exemplified the tendency of Russian revolutionaries to rely on theory to the exclusion of common sense, their expediency, and their lack of real concern about the disadvantaged they claimed to represent. Given the increase of capital that had occurred under Ferrein's administration, as well as their own lack of business acumen, there were no economic reasons for radical pharmacists to seize management of the Pension Fund. Their incessant agitation to wrest control of its over one million rubles in fact wreaked havoc on the fund. Under their management expenditures for fund administration skyrocketed. The entire pharmacy corporation was weakened by the struggle.

Saltykov had misused the finances of the Russian Pharmacy Society Mutual Assistance Fund and its journal, *Farmatsevticheskii vestnik*. After he and Lintser joined the administration of the Pension Fund they dissipated its working capital, either as a result of a tendency toward prodigality or for more devious purposes—to destroy the Pension Fund, divert its monies to themselves, and undermine the pharmacy corporation. Early in 1905 I. R. Zakharevich criticized the fund's expenditures and Lintser's lack of a detailed budget.[93] Following a meeting of 230 members of the fund (20 percent owners and 80 percent staff pharmacists) early in 1905, E. A. Al'tgauzen noted ominously that "the leaders of the staff pharmacists," who have opposed "the Administration of the Fund for the past ten years," B. N. Saltykov and S. K. Lintser . . . have now taken over the Administration."[94] He asserted that "the people attending the meeting had no confidence in the figures cited in the [financial] report. There were many inaccuracies and inconsistencies. It was impossible to figure out the balance." Director of the fund, Samgin, "blamed the inaccuracies on typographical errors." Nevertheless, the fund clearly overspent on administrative overhead. "Instead of the 5 percent specified in Paragraph 24, the administration spent 14.6 percent. There was discussion on reducing expenditures but, thanks to the 'new group' and extremist speeches of Lintser and Saltykov," the general assembly approved "not the 18,163 rubles" requested for administrative costs, "but 27,623 rubles—21 percent of the Fund's income!"[95] The administration's addition was haphazard: "7,000 rubles plus 13,000 rubles equals 20,000 rubles, not the 27,000 rubles which the Administration requested."[96]

D. S. Podrazhanskii, a Bolshevik, attended the 1905 general meeting. Unaware of Podrazhanskii's political affiliation, Al'tgauzen disagreed with his views but nonetheless praised "the young, talented comrade's oratorical skill." But, Al'tgauzen found nothing redeeming in Lintser's performance.[97]

Elections to the administrative board and committees of the Pension Fund occurred at the early 1905 general meeting. Balloting began in the wee morning hours (as was typical with meetings in Russia), finishing at 7 o'clock in the morning. Basilaia was elected to the administration. Master of Pharmacy Tkeshelashvili was elected to the supervisory committee and three other individuals were elected to the audit commission. The new draft statute was discussed; two hundred members of the fund from St. Petersburg asked to defer ratification for one month as they had received the draft too late. Lintser and the administration were at odds. But as only sixty-six members remained in the hall—less than a quorum—business was deferred until May 1905.[98]

Fund members soon began to criticize the rise in the fund's administrative costs compared with its social expenditures. From a modest 4,959 rubles in 1895 administrative costs had risen to the outlandish figure of 22,721 rubles in 1905—20 percent of total expenditures. Meanwhile the fund had disbursed only 5,614 rubles, 83 kopeks for invalids during the eleven years of its existence (about 500 rubles per year) and 10,918 rubles to orphans (about 1,100 rubles per year).[99]

In 1905 the administration of the fund still included V. K. Ferrein as chair, F. L. Vagner as treasurer, A. A. Geilig, N A Glezar, and I. Ia. Samgin as representative of the fund.[100]

However, during the summer of 1905 *Farmatsevt* argued that not only had the new administrative board been illegally elected, but the board was behaving irresponsibly. The chancellery was "in severe disorder . . . part of the workers did not appear . . . the staff of the administration did not exist . . . the chair went abroad."[101]

In September 1905, because the administration was in disarray, the fund's supervisory committee decided to call a general meeting on "its own authority." However, this was the height of the 1905 revolution and the "Okhrana [the security police organization] not only did not permit . . . the meeting but forbade going out on the street in the evening . . . therefore the extraordinary general meeting was not convened."[102]

The turmoil caused by allegations of mismanagement and by the machinations of radical and revolutionary pharmacists eroded members' confidence. In the report for 1906 there were 7,556 contributions but "nearly 780, more than 10 percent, for whom no contributions were noted."[103] Membership fluctuated from 2,554 in 1895 to over 3,000 in 1896 to a low of 2,435 in 1901, climbing to just over 3,000 in 1904. Five hundred eighty members withdrew in 1905. A contemporary attributed the decline to "disorders in the Fund." People not duly elected by the general assembly served on the administration. As a result, "many members, though it was illegal, withheld their contributions."[104] One Vladislav Ippolitovich Sokulovskii, who leased a pharmacy in Vil'na, summed up the feeling of many pharmacists when he announced that he had been a member of the Pension Fund from the beginning and contributed until 1905 but when he heard rumors that the fund was not doing well, he temporarily "refrained from further contributions." He asserted that contributions, including his own for the rather sizable sum of 203 rubles, 38 kopeks, had not been correctly recorded.[105] Early in 1906 a number of pharmacy owners and staff pharmacists called for a cut in their contributions.[106] Shortly thereafter the radical Moscow Pharmacy Union urged staff pharmacists to cancel their contributions. Al'tgauzen opined that "the Union wanted the millions in the fund" for themselves.[107]

Whether this was true or not, the controversy over the Pension Fund heated up and became more complicated in 1906 and 1907. Fissures now appeared among radical pharmacists. Moscow radicals in the fund's administration found themselves assailed by radicals in St. Petersburg, Moscow, and elsewhere who were not part of the administration. The government and courts were brought into the fray.

Early in 1906, St. Petersburg radicals urged that the Pension Fund be liquidated. "The St. Petersburg Union of Working Pharmacists [established in 1905] . . . recommended both to St. Petersburg and provincial workers that they withhold their 5 percent contribution until the Fund was reorganized. They further requested that representatives of the Government Insurance Department in the Ministry of Internal Affairs audit the Fund."[108]

The government responded with alacrity. In February 1906, Minister of Internal Affairs P. N. Durnovo dispatched government auditors to Moscow.[109] Their office, open from 10 A.M. to 3 P.M., invited members to personally submit complaints. Two representatives from the St. Petersburg and Moscow Pharmacy Societies were also invited to report to the Ministry of Internal Affairs.[110]

Although one would have surmised radical critics would welcome the audit, the executive committee of the Moscow Pharmacy Workers' Union, established in 1905, protested it because staff pharmacists were not represented. According to *Farmatsevt*, representatives of "staff [pharmacists] . . . claimed the audit had been done at the beckoning of pharmacy owners cooperating with the autocracy." In actuality, staff pharmacists had originally demanded the audit, as reported by *Farmatsevt* in 1905.[111]

Government auditors found the fund's account books inadequate. Allegedly, they used the term "plunder" to characterize the actions of the administration and recommended that members make no more contributions. Al'tgauzen challenged their findings, asserting that the problems in the Pension Fund were "not the result of outright plunder but disorganization." He suggested that Ferrein call a general meeting and reorganize.[112] The radical Moscow Union of Pharmacists, on the other hand, called on all pharmacists to withhold their required payments to the fund until its irregularities were corrected.[113]

Indeed there was evidence that, although Ferrein had built up the fund, members of the administration–and not just new radical members–were behaving irresponsibly. I. S. Tkeshelashvili, Master of Pharmacy and secretary of the supervisory committee, concurred that the Pension Fund was in bad shape. He blamed an "illegal" administration for firing the assistant director of the fund, Count Shenhof, and bringing the fund to such an "unhappy state." He recounted that Chairman Ferrein had called a special meeting in which "several external people participated" and proposed a follow-up meeting of the administration, supervisory committee, audit commission, and representatives from both the Moscow Pharmacy Society (pharmacy owners) and fifteen delegates from the Union of Working Pharmacists to iron out problems. Yet, in the face of these serious issues, Tkeshelashvili airily announced he was going to the Caucasus for the summer and could not fulfill his duties as secretary for the supervisory committee. He recommended that the one million rubles in the fund be "transferred to some sort of Insurance Society."[114]

A meeting was held on May 8, 1906, to discuss whether or not the fund should be transferred to the Treasury. It opened at the typically late hour of 10 o'clock in the evening. The proceedings were chaotic. Radical leaders of various persuasions tried to manipulate rank-and-file pharmacists. The latter refused to be cowed.

According to one account, the meeting drew "Only one-tenth of the members . . . only about 50 people gathered–the majority were Jewish traders . . . the rest apparently were so annoyed they did not wish to discuss further measures . . . provincial pharmacists were absent. . . ." Obstructionist tactics were used. "All sorts of obstacles were put to the people in opposition–not allowing them to speak until the end, etc. . . ." There were "speeches about the critical situation of the Fund, disorders, abuses uncovered by the Government audit." Some "speakers stated they were against closing the Fund." They proposed that it "be reorganized and a new administration elected" from "15 staff pharmacists and 10 pharmacy owners. . . ." Others rejected this suggestion, insisting that "the Fund must be boycotted; it was necessary to quickly close" it "in order to be spared the 5 percent obligatory contribution." This group noted that "in Russia there exist not a few insurance societies where those who wished could be insured in more secure conditions. Others spoke about continuing the Fund, electing a commission, reorganizing, using acquired money for insurance or scientific, cultural needs." One "very eloquent orator stated that liquidating the Fund was not possible because pharmacy owners would then receive *our* money. . . ." Debate "continued until 2 A.M. It was proposed to vote on closing the Fund but the Chair and Company would not allow this . . . they decided in favor of Moscow staff pharmacists" to elect "15 members of the commission. Since there remained in the hall at the time 20 to 25 people they decided that even people absent could vote."[115]

Another group of five pharmacists confirmed that a "small group of people ran the May 8 meeting at Ferrein's—local pharmacists were not invited and learned of it later."[116]

Al'tgauzen, editor of *Farmatsevt*, tried to smooth the troubled waters. He disagreed that the old administration of the Pension Fund had squandered its assets—"Government inspection had revealed no large waste in the Fund and no petty theft." However, he urged the administration to make a clear report of the fund's finances at a general meeting, as required by paragraphs 63 and 64 of the statutes. He welcomed the convening of a joint commission of pharmacy owners and staff, elected by a general assembly of members to revise the fund statute. In this way all disorders could be eliminated peacefully without resorting to prosecution and court proceedings.[117] He stressed that the Pension Fund and localized mutual assistance funds were symbols of pharmacists' independence and ability to manage themselves: "Local Pharmacy Assistance Funds in St. Petersburg, Warsaw, Riga, and other places—yes and the former Assistance Fund in Moscow, before transfer of its monies to the Russian Pharmacy society—showed that pharmacists if they want can work for social purposes" and thus, "must not be liquidated but reorganized."[118] Additionally, Al'tgauzen recommended more detailed financial reports.[119]

In August, in a spirit of "glasnost'," Al'tgauzen printed varied letters about the fund and the May 8 meeting.[120] He personally blamed Saltykov for the Pension Fund's deterioration. "The basis of the Pension Fund was 40,000 rubles from the Mutual Assistance Fund of Working Moscow Pharmacists. B. N. Saltykov got his hands on this money and used it for his own purposes."[121] Al'tgauzen claimed that Saltykov took advantage of V. K. Ferrein's frequent trips abroad during the summer of 1906 to create chaos in the fund. One-hundred twenty pharmacists protested that the administration had been illegally elected. Samgin, director of the fund, had served as Assistant Pharmacist in Ferrein's pharmacy. This plus his insubordination had triggered the irregular elections.[122] An anonymous pharmacist supported these contentions, noting that Saltykov now favored preserving the fund, although while he "was Director of the Russian Pharmacy Assistance Fund it diminished by nearly a half."[123]

But Moscow radicals who had joined the fund's administration and had access to its monies, adamantly refused to close it or transfer it to the government. Basilaia and Zimin insisted that "a state insurance society was the best form of guarantee in old age and invalidism. To maintain the fund, *obligatory* contributions of all pharmacists were a necessity."[124] Basilaia claimed "dark forces" had been operating at the May 8 meeting.[125] He further claimed that a "large majority" of rank-and-file pharmacists also rejected the proposal to close the fund. They decided to elect fifteen delegates from staff pharmacists to participate in a reorganizing commission.[126] Seven representatives were to be chosen from Moscow staff pharmacists at large; the remaining eight would include five representatives from the Union of Working Pharmacists, and one each from the Russian Pharmacy Society, Organization of Ferrein Workers, and Corporation of Moscow City Pharmacists.[127]

By the fall of 1906, claims and counter claims became vituperative. Al'tgauzen asserted that "the '[Opposition] Group of Pharmacists' is directed by Jews."[128] His opponents, meanwhile, accused him of being "in collusion with the illegal administration of the Fund."[129] Although he was on record as favoring preservation of the fund, an "Open Letter by a Member of the Fund," alleged that Al'tgauzen had encouraged pharmacy owners to "struggle against the despised ¼ kopek contribution." The anonymous author further claimed that "pharmacy owners had fomented discord," calling staff pharmacists "propertyless elements" and "revolutionaries," who "would use the Pension Fund's capital to purchase weapons for a revolutionary uprising."[130]

There were further revelations about the administration's ineptitude. It was alleged that the government audit uncovered many instances of poor bookkeeping. For three years after 1900 there were no proper records. Director of the fund, Samgin, "kept books according to his own system; he entered income not at the time it was received but significantly later; stocks were not bought in the State Bank but in private offices with falsified accounts; contributions lay in the pockets of the Administration for three to four months [without being invested], and so on."[131] The Table of Contributions was criticized for "not designating obligatory and nonobligatory members."[132]

In the fall of 1906 and early 1907 the various opposition groups began to sue in court. Following calls for the courts to decide the fate of the Pension Fund,[133] the procurator of the Moscow district court was requested to investigate the fund.[134] Meanwhile, the administration of the fund, through their lawyers, sued Moscow pharmacy owners who had not contributed the ¼ kopek from each prescription to the fund. The suits took place in Justice-of-the-Peace courts. Isaac Osipovich Finn was sued for owing the Pension Fund 151 rubles, 89 kopeks. Finn countered that he had formerly contributed but had recently refused because the fund administration was not legal and did not satisfy the existing statute. Interestingly, the Justice-of-the-Peace court ruled against the administration.[135] In 1907, the Moscow Justice-of-the-Peace court heard a suit brought by the fund administration (dating from 1904) demanding a ¼ kopek per prescription contribution from the Romanovo-Borisoglebsk district zemstvo board in Yaroslavl' province. This court also ruled against the administration on the grounds a new administration had been installed and sanctioned by the Ministry of Internal Affairs.[136] In 1907 Pharmacist Chaikovskii sued in a Justice-of-the-Peace court to withdraw from the fund; additionally, he wanted his contributions returned. His suit, however, was rejected.[137]

The acrimony did not abate. Moscow pharmacists *in* the fund administration attacked St. Petersburg pharmacists for suggesting the fund be closed. They asserted that only Moscow pharmacists truly represented staff pharmacists and their pension interests.[138]

However, some staff pharmacists in Moscow continued to advocate boycotting the fund.[139] The "organized staff of the Ferrein pharmacy on Nikol'skaia street" demanded their full wages and cessation of contributions from their salaries to the fund, "in view of incorrect management and disorders in it."[140] Basilaia and *Farmatsevticheskii trud* tried to convince them that "boycott would be directed against the pharmacists themselves, against the weakest members of our corporation, against the very idea of mutual aid. . . ."[141] The Southwestern Conference of Pharmacy Unions supported Basilaia but demanded broad concessions: members of the Pension Fund were to be only staff pharmacists, contributions were to be voluntary, the administration was to be "democratic" and "decentralized" and "professional unions of pharmacists" (who represented radical socialists) were to exercise "control."[142]

In the spring of 1907, perhaps to further public relations, *Farmatsevticheskii trud* published a report from the Pension Fund administration. This report meticulously listed contributions, according to various paragraphs of the charter, made during 1906. Pharmacies in various cities and an alphabetical list of contributions were published in successive issues of *Farmatsevticheskii trud* during 1907.[143]

Nevertheless, in the summer of 1907, clashes again erupted over the legality of new administration and their control over the assets of the fund. The clashes and claims became ever more tangled, gradually assuming the dimensions of a Feydeau farce. There were two sets of elections; appeals to the Moscow chief of police; deputations to the Insurance Department of the Ministry of Internal Affairs and the new Minister of Internal Affairs, P. A. Stolypin; and, finally, more court suits.

Pharmacy owner Feodor Alekseevich Plotnikov was first elected chairman of the fund in June 1907,[144] after claiming "he could quickly help put the Fund on the correct path." Pharmacy owners P. B. Lifshits and P. A. Glezer were elected assistant and cashier, respectively. E. G. Basilaia, L. Ia. Zimin and two others were re-elected members of the administration.[145] The candidate members were all staff pharmacists. As they had earlier, out-of-town members of the fund protested the election. Plotnikov dispatched Geilig to the Moscow chief of police and then to the Insurance Department of the Ministry of Internal Affairs to get official approval for the new administration. The Insurance Department approved the new administration but a group of pharmacists brought suit in the Moscow district court, claiming that the June 1 meeting was illegal. During the next months the pharmacy owners were thrown off the administrative board, leaving E. G. Basilaia, chair, L. Ia. Zimin, secretary, and five staff members of the administration.[146]

T. H. Rigby has emphasized how committee-oriented the Bolsheviks were after they took over in 1917.[147] Radical officers in the Pharmacists' Pension Fund likewise were methodical and used "legal" measures to acquire the monies in the fund. They held daily meetings in the second half of September 1907. They lobbied government officials to counter the old administration and get control over the assets of the fund. Locked out of fund headquarters, despite repeated phone calls to the old administration, and denied papers, checkbook, and access to the fund's bank account, all of which remained under control of the old administration (these items testifying to the sophisticated financial organization of Russia before 1917), the new administration of Basilaia and Zimin fired Samgin,[148] found other meeting places, and appealed to the Moscow police chief to secure for them the fund headquarters and property. The police chief rejected their appeal, suggesting they bring suit in the Justice-of-the-Peace court. Basilaia, Zimin, and the "new administration" further consulted with the *jurisconsult* of the State Bank in Moscow, carefully copying all correspondence to Geilig, erstwhile head of the fund administration, and brought suit against Geilig and Samgin for control of the "million-ruble capital" of the fund.[149]

Finally, both the new administration (represented by Lintser) and the old (represented by V. K. Ferrein) appealed to the Insurance Department of the Ministry of Internal Affairs. According to an account in *Farmatsevticheskii trud*, Ferrein argued that the new administration was illegal and, as it was composed of the proletariat, it could not manage the million-ruble fund properly. *Farmatsevticheskii trud* probably took artistic license with Ferrein's words; he had little confidence in the managerial and fiscal competence of Basilaia and Zimin but it is doubtful that he would label them "proletariat." In any case, to put a halt to the controversy the government took a decisive stand and ruled in favor of the new administration. *Farmatsevticheskii trud* reported gleefully that the representative of the Ministry of Internal Affairs "decided in favor of the New Administration, declaring that the Old had discredited itself with disorders . . . in the Fund account books."[150]

The government ruling went into effect in 1908. On January 14, 1908, the Ministry of Internal Affairs acceded to the request of the new administration for control over the assets of the fund. The Moscow office of the State Bank agreed to turn over the million-ruble capital of the Pension Fund to the new administration. The Moscow chief of police was charged with implementing the transfer of property and documents.[151] The old administration, represented by a committee from the St. Petersburg Pharmacy Society, proposed review of the fund's statute. They sent out a questionnaire to determine whether members wanted the fund liquidated and a general assembly convened, as the statutes required.[152] The new administration also proposed a general assembly. The Insurance Department of the Ministry of Internal Affairs discussed the matter. Then representatives of the ministries of Justice, Finance, Trade, and Industry, the Chief Medical Inspector, and the Insurance Department met to debate the Pharmacists' Pension Fund.[153]

Opponents continued to criticize the new administration.[154] Proposals to "liquidate" the fund continued to surface, causing *Farmatsevticheskii trud* to announce shrilly that "struggle for liquidation of the fund is one form of class struggle . . . struggle for cheaper purchase of staff labor, for raising the level of exploitation of the proletariat."[155] The new administration finally received all pertinent materials from the old administration through the auspices of the Moscow mayor in July 1908.[156]

In March 1910, the general assembly of the fund decided to preserve it. Additionally, the assembly established a commission comprised of pharmacy owners, an equal number of staff pharmacists, and a neutral chair to revise the Pension Fund statutes. Because statistical data were lacking, a questionnaire was sent to all pharmacists with a request to return the information by December 1, 1910. The data provided interesting information on the living and working conditions of pharmacists.[157] The special commission for working out a new draft statute of the Pension Fund was in place by June. The "curia of pharmacy owners" included E. K. Khrzhanovskii, K. I. Kresling, and A. N. Popovskii. Alternate representatives from this "curia" included G. O. Gabrilovich (no doubt the father of the radical O. G. Gabrilovich). Full members of the commission representing staff pharmacists included I. I. Levinshtein, B. N. Saltykov (both later members of the Soviet pharmacy organization; Levinshtein probably was a Menshevik), and L. Ia. Zimin. Additionally, the general assembly resolved that the existing fund be considered "temporarily stopped" and that both administrations be "deprived of authority." The general meeting then entrusted B. N. Saltykov and G. O. Gabrilovich to meet with "zemstvo activist" (and member of the middle-of-the-road Octobrist Party) D. N. Shipov and two others to persuade one of them to chair the commission. D. N. Shipov finally accepted the responsibilities of chair in August. But, despite reorganization and temporary cessation, debates about whether the fund should exist as an independent institution or be transferred to the State Insurance Fund, whether membership should be obligatory, whether funds should apply to pensions or insurance continued during 1910. Strong sentiment was expressed for using fund monies for insurance and turning the fund over to the State Insurance Department.[158]

In 1914 the Menshevik-oriented pharmacy journal, *Zhizn' farmatsevta*, newly established in St. Petersburg, claimed that in 1910 the government called a general meeting of the fund under chairmanship of the Moscow Police Chief Petrov and temporarily closed the fund. Then a compromise commission of pharmacy owners and staff under chairmanship of Octobrist D. Shipov worked on a new statute. In 1911 a second congress of members of the fund discussed whether or not the fund ought to be autonomous or transferred to management of the State Insurance Funds. According to *Zhizn' farmatsevta*, pharmacy owners wanted the fund transferred to the government. Their "tactic" was to liquidate it, in order to eliminate their 1/4 kopek contribution from each prescription. Staff pharmacists left the congress in protest.[159]

Radical pharmacists considered acquisition of the National Pension Fund a step forward in the class struggle. On January 10, 1911, the Social Democratc journal *Zhizn' farmatsevta*, located in Kiev, wished "comrades a Happy New Year," praised the workers' "teacher K. Marks," and exulted that "The bourgeoisie, standing in power is powerless . . . the proletariat have begun to stand up . . . the bourgeoisie cannot be eliminated from pharmacy matters but we have special interests . . . we have deftly taken over an insurance institution of semi-class character . . . we have turned it into a purely class institution . . . this is the *reformed* [italics in the original] Pension Fund."[160]

Nevertheless, in 1913 deputies from the radical professional societies of pharmacists claimed that the new State Insurance Law of June 28, 1912, touched only a "small part of the Russian proletariat" and requested the Fourth State Duma to extend state insurance to staff pharmacists, whose work was "intensive" and whose salary was "lower than ten years ago."[161]

The National Pharmacists' Pension Fund continued to be important to radical pharmacists. But, whereas, St. Petersburg radicals advocated closing the fund in 1906 and 1907, in 1914 radical pharmacists there steadfastly protected it.

In 1914 Ia. L. Kanevskii, Iu. Kuperman, and A. Sh. Aluf led the St. Petersburg Professional Society of Staff Pharmacists. They were Menshevik or Menshevik Internationalist. They advocated municipalization, a traditional plank of the Menshevik platform, and criticized *Pravda* for its "fractional position."[162] In December 1917, A. Sh. Aluf proclaimed his adherence to Menshevik Internationalism.[163]

The St. Petersburg Mensheviks attempted to save the Pension Fund, corroborating McKean's picture of Menshevik approach to other worker insurance funds in St. Petersburg before World War I.[164]

In 1914 the Insurance Department of the Ministry of Internal Affairs decided to liquidate the Pension Fund. Despite the fact that the fund statutes provided for this in the event of "disorders," Menshevik pharmacists insisted that this "violated" their rights. On May 20, 1914, a meeting of staff pharmacists was convened in St. Petersburg. The main topic was "liquidation" of the Pension Fund. Aluf asserted that the fund had been in limbo for two and a half years. Pharmacy owners had voted to turn it over to the State Savings Bank. Their real goal was to liquidate the fund. Woman pharmacist Rubasheva gave a short review of the fund. She asserted that it had originated as a response to the worker movement and worker demands for guarantees in their old age or in times of illness. Her history was somewhat distorted. She alleged that the Pension Fund began as a device for pharmacy owners to control workers and that staff pharmacists had wanted to close it in 1907 and use its capital to establish government insurance. But the fund now was important for staff pharmacists. The bottom line was that it must be preserved.[165]

Aluf, who later was to play a role in the *Farmotdel*, a pharmacy organization established by the Bolsheviks after they took over in 1917, also promoted better insurance for pharmacists. He claimed the new law on insurance was inadequate and urged that it be improved.[166]

The St. Petersburg Mensheviks used legal methods to save the Pension Fund in 1914 as the Moscow radicals had in 1907 and 1908. A general meeting of staff pharmacists resolved to "petition the Ministry of Internal Affairs to convene a General Meeting of the Fund and protest violation of the rights of staff pharmacists"–proposed transfer of the fund to the Treasury.[167] The St. Petersburg Mensheviks also lobbied the Duma and Ministry of Internal Affairs to maintain the Pension Fund and correct abuses in it. Further, *mirabile dictu,* unlike their predecessors, these Marxists displayed keen interest in finances and insurance, even to the point of establishing a finance commission in the Society of Staff Pharmacists.[168]

Additionally, a new society was established in St. Petersburg–the Society of Practicing Pharmacists–which claimed its purpose was to "struggle with abusers of the Pharmacists' Pension Fund." Masters of Pharmacy, Provizors, and Assistant Pharmacists with at least three years' experience were eligible to join the society, which aimed to unite pharmacy owners and staff. One of the founders reputedly was a "well-known pharmacy owner" by the name of Granat.[169]

Controversy over the Pension Fund swirled even during World War I. As late as 1917, according to Soviet historian V. M. Salo, an All-Russian Congress of Staff Pharmacists meeting from August 25 to 28, 1917, discussed the status of the Pension Fund. They resolved to transfer it to a central (government) fund.[170]

The Pension Fund saga had and has significance beyond the pharmacy world. The behavior of radical pharmacists in the matter typified that of Russian revolutionaries and adumbrated the *modus operandi* of those who would run Russian pharmacy–and Russian polity, economy, and society–after the revolutions of 1917. The behavior of the Russian government in the Pension Fund controversy forces us to reevaluate the government's relationship with socialists, who were not involved in strikes or other disruptive behavior, and its broader attitude toward socialism in the last decades of the imperial period.

Radical pharmacy journals, seen in this chapter and the next, were candid, even audacious, belying the oppressiveness attributed to the tsarist government between 1908 and 1912. That the government and, more specifically, reputedly reactionary Minister of Internal Affairs P. A. Stolypin sided with radical pharmacists in the National Pension Fund controversy is more than curious. It tallies with the sympathetic policies of Stolypin and other Ministers of Internal Affairs toward labor norms for staff pharmacists and toward socialized pharmacy, discussed in subsequent chapters. The elaborateness of the Pharmacists' Pension Fund and radical pharmacists' organizations, replete as they were with executive boards, secretariats, recruiting, and editorial offices, emphasizes that these features of Lenin's revolutionary praxis–traditionally touted as manifestations of his organizational genius–were traditional to Russia. Radical pharmacists' behavior in the Pension Fund drama emphasizes that they were as contentious as other Russian revolutionaries and harbored more and less militant members. They also wielded a variety of tactics–aboveboard as well as subversive–to achieve their ends. The profile of the most militant pharmacists is not attractive. Their financial irresponsibility and cavalier treatment of their constituents, strikingly exhibited in the Pension Fund debacle, predicted what was in store for Russia after 1917.

14

Pharmacists and Revolution: 1905 to World War I

Radical pharmacists' minimum goal was to improve the working and living conditions of staff pharmacists. Their maximum objective was to abolish privately owned pharmacies. Liberal reformers also wanted to replace the existing system. However, they advocated the establishment of pharmacies without government permission (*iavochnyi poriadok*)–a measure that would retain, in fact, reinforce, private ownership. Radical pharmacists, on the other hand, strove for collective or socialized pharmacy. Their proposals involved buying out private pharmacies (*samovykup*)–with pharmacy corporation funds or, more likely, with government funds–then permitting all qualified pharmacists to lease the pharmacies. A more radical variant envisioned transferring private pharmacies to public bodies–zemstvos and city dumas–after democratic elections in these institutions. This last program, called "municipalization," became identified with the Menshevik branch of the Social Democratic Labor Party.

Radical pharmacists hoped to achieve both their minimum and maximum goals with strikes, organizing professional unions and societies, and consciousness-raising and publicity. In their organizing they were a mirror image of the government–procedure-oriented and legalistic.

However, because they desired to overturn as well as mitigate the system, they frequently pushed strike demands beyond the realm of financial feasibility. Their unions and societies promoted revolution as well as solidarity. The fact that radical leaders were far in advance of the needs and desires of their constituents is indicated by a growing gulf between them and rank-and-file pharmacists who were satisfied with bread and butter improvements.

Radical pharmacists were not all of a piece. Some were more extreme than others; some mellowed over time. Some saw municipalization as immediately attainable; others regarded it as a future possibility. Most radical pharmacists were prodigal but others were businesslike. The many strains within the radical pharmacist community, in fact, reflected the many strains within the general revolutionary movement.

Nevertheless, radical pharmacists shared common characteristics. They were elitist and imbued with an excess of theory over practicality. They disregarded both the rights of their propertied colleagues and the desires and views of their constituents, staff pharmacists. They were entranced with dismantling a pharmacy system that worked—albeit imperfectly—and replacing it with visionary schemes that, because they ignored economic realities, had strong possibilities for failure.

The policies of radical pharmacists—strikes, labor organization, and furthering municipalization—had parallel progression but different growth spurts. Pharmacy strikes erupted fitfully in the 1890s. In 1898, *Farmatsevticheskii vestnik*, organ of the newly organized Russian Pharmacy Society, tentatively broached the concept of municipalization, noting, for example, that increased population in Mogilev-Podolsk, particularly from poorer classes, necessitated opening city pharmacies to provide medicine at low prices.[1] The journal also reported on a "self-help" society in Tomsk that accumulated 6,400 rubles from the sale of 640 shares to open a private pharmacy.[2]

The pendulum continued to swing in the early twentieth century. Strikes occurred sporadically in 1901 and 1902 in Moscow and two or three major cities. Strikers demanded a double shift and abolition of room and board. Most of these strikes were unsuccessful, the owners often replacing strikers. However, a few pharmacies introduced double shifts and remuneration in money in lieu of room and board, some even without strikes.[3] The Northern Pharmacy Society appeared in St. Petersburg in 1901.[4]

From 1903, the Marxist Russian Social Democratic Labor Party reputedly resolved to organize professionals. Pharmacists were among those targeted. In 1903 in Kishinev, scene of a massive pogrom, "eight to ten pharmacists connected with the Kishinev Russian Social Democratic Labor Party organization" purportedly formed a circle to study "scientific socialism." In early 1903 a "St. Petersburg Committee of Social Democratic Organization of Pharmacists" was allegedly established.[5]

Municipalization took low profile at this time. By municipalization, radical pharmacists did not mean that city and zemstvo governments, as then constituted, should operate pharmacies. A chief criterion was that city dumas and zemstvos be democratically elected. Nor was low-cost or free dispensing to the poor of paramount concern to radical pharmacists. They were preoccupied with who ran pharmacies rather than who received medicine. As a result, while *Farmatsevticheskii zhurnal*, the organ of the St. Petersburg Pharmacy Society (of pharmacy owners), publicized the growth of municipal pharmacies and charity dispensing, the leftist *Farmatsevticheskii vestnik* largely ignored these developments.[6]

By 1904 *Farmatsevticheskii vestnik* began more forcefully to advocate municipalization. Early in 1904 S. K. Lintser railed to the Pirogov Society that "The monopoly system artificially keeps the growth of pharmaceutical practice in the hands of private people, depriving the great majority of public masses of pharmaceutical help and is a serious brake on the zemstvo; the 'pharmacy question' is connected with free distribution of medicine; the [pharmacy monopoly] brakes free distribution of medicine . . . and preserves the Pharmacy Tax."[7] The journal publicized city and zemstvo purchase of private pharmacies,[8] lamenting that "in practice, establishing public pharmacies has met with great difficulty."[9] Two articles discussed the benefits that accrued to inhabitants of German cities when the pharmacy monopoly was broken, implying that the same would be true for Russia.[10] Finally, at a meeting of the Northern Pharmacists' Society in late December 1904, S. K. Lintser again attacked the pharmacy monopoly, exhorting public and zemstvo pharmacies to show more initiative. The more extreme S. G. Tsereteli insisted, according to Marxist canons, that pharmacists were divided into polar opposites–staff pharmacists and pharmacy owner-capitalists.[11]

1905

Nineteen-five was a chaotic year for Russia. Revolutionary councils sprang up. Mutinies, peasant upheavals and strikes swept the empire, culminating in a general strike in October that compelled the government to enlarge civil rights, institute a parliament, and offer other concessions as well as suppress the disorders.

In 1905 radical pharmacists began to tender the notion of "ransoming" pharmacies–purchasing private pharmacies for staff pharmacists.[12] Additionally, they stepped up the strike movement both to erode private ownership of pharmacies as well as to improve working conditions for staff pharmacists.

Some historians still depict the strikes of 1905 and the years following as elemental, spontaneous upheavals to redress fundamental grievances that could be resolved in no other way. However, in 1930 I. Zil'berg emphasized the role Social Democrats played in organizing pharmacists and fomenting pharmacy strikes in 1905.[13] A latter-day historian, Jonathan Sanders, considers the January 1905 pharmacy strike in St. Petersburg spontaneous, but he amply demonstrates how radical pharmacists forged subsequent strikes and imposed a political agenda on rank-and-file pharmacists who were content with economic improvements. Nevertheless, Sanders considers it axiomatic that strikers' economic and political demands were warranted and several other current American labor historians agree with him.[14]

There were certifiable flaws in pharmacy practice and the living and working conditions of pharmacist employees. But E. A. Al'tgauzen, editor of *Farmatsevt* from the 1890s until his untimely death in 1907, brought much-needed perspective to pharmacy conflicts. He conceded that pharmacists had been called "white slaves" because of "day and night work, work on holidays, demanding mental and physical work, only one day of rest each week and one additional Sunday every two or three weeks, miserly pay, and room and board in the pharmacy."[15] However, he emphasized that these conditions resulted from the nature of the profession. By law pharmacies had to serve the public at any hour. He acknowledged that "New studies about work and capital, having an extremely utopian tendency which go beyond Marx, find reception not only among pharmacists with incomplete scientific education but even among not a few Provizors." But, he asserted, "to include pharmacists with incomplete education in the working class in general and in the proletariat in particular, has no foundation."[16] He inveighed against those who brandished inflammatory slogans, "Pharmacists of all ranks unite" and "To honest work you have a right." Al'tgauzen believed that one of the main causes of dissatisfaction among staff pharmacists was the apprentice system of pharmacy training. He particularly criticized inordinate use of student-apprentices, a practice that crowded out Assistant Pharmacists and did not instill professionalism and a love of pharmacy in student pharmacists.[17]

In any case, while individual demands of radical pharmacists had validity, as a package they were economically infeasible. In addition to double shifts and sick leave with pay, which were reasonable, the Russian Pharmacy Society pressed for seven-hour days,[18] a minimum wage significantly higher than existing salaries, two weeks' vacation with pay, pay for strike time, and staff pharmacists' approval in hiring and firing.[19] Along with sensible concessions, St. Petersburg radicals demanded a month's vacation with pay and *double* the existing wages.[20] While this may not have ruined pharmacy owners and left cities bereft of "rational dispensing" as Al'tgauzen claimed,[21] it was obvious that the double shift would require increased hiring and that additional staff coupled with higher salaries would strain pharmacy payrolls.

In part, the excessive demands of the Russian Pharmacy Society in Moscow, the Northern Pharmacy Society in St. Petersburg, and subsequent societies in the south, resulted from lack of business experience. However, one radical pharmacist, O. G. Gabrilovich, was knowledgeable about accounting.[22] In fact, the extremism and intransigence of the radical leaders stemmed from their maximalist aim to abolish private pharmacy and replace it with socialized pharmacy. Al'tgauzen noted that radical pharmacists divided pharmacists into two hostile camps and worked to "prepare the conditional pharmacists for their role as strikers . . . in place of uniting pharmacists . . . the Russian Pharmacists' Society [took on the] role of preparing, then executing strikes."[23]

Indeed, the Pharmacy Union, which was established in 1905 under the protective wing of the legal Russian Pharmacy Society[24] and included 760 members (160 from St. Petersburg, 200 from Moscow, and 400 from various provinces),[25] admitted that its goals were not only to improve the life and work conditions of staff pharmacists, but also "fundamental change in pharmacy practice . . . , raising class consciousness, and organizing strikes as the only means for struggle against the existing pharmaceutical order and regime."[26]

A review of the pharmacy strikes that broke out in many parts of the empire in 1905–St. Petersburg, Moscow, Kiev, Odessa, Saratov, Tiflis, Minsk, Vil'na, Simferopol', Tula, Nizhni Novgorod, and Voronezh–shows that some, particularly those that occurred at the beginning of the year, were warranted. But others were questionable and many were unwarranted.

A strike in Minsk in January 1905 appeared legitimate. Provizors, Assistant Pharmacists, and pharmacy students banded together to petition owners for double shifts, limiting students who crowded out Assistant Pharmacists, and minimal increase in student salaries. The owners refused and the pharmacists struck. They did not strike three pharmacies that had implemented reforms.[27] On the contrary, in January 1905, staff demanding a double shift struck one St. Petersburg pharmacy that had instituted this regimen three years previously. The owner noted that "staff left his pharmacy at the first invitation of demonstrators." Some St. Petersburg owners were willing to grant a double shift although they stipulated that staff who worked only seven hours would have to accept reduced salaries, as owners could not immediately double payroll costs.[28]

In February and March, strikes erupted in Kiev, Odessa, Khar'kov, and Moscow.[29] Some pharmacies in Moscow implemented the double shift.[30] Conditions in Kiev pharmacies varied greatly. Boris Puzis, who observed a February 8 strike in Kiev, was sympathetic to the strikers, half of whom, he claimed, worked for below-subsistence remuneration. In one pharmacy staff worked in "unpleasant conditions" and received only 30 rubles per month without board, room, or tea. Nevertheless, their workday was short–seven hours with about ten stints of night duty per month–which compensated for the low pay.[31] In another pharmacy an assistant pharmacist made 65 rubles per month–10 rubles less than what the Russian Pharmacy Society called for. In some pharmacies, workdays lasted thirteen or fourteen hours. Only one had a room for night duty; in another, pharmacists on night duty slept on lab tables. Puzis claimed that workers struck only after owners rejected peaceful discussion, that only three strikers were "careerists" who initiated the strikes, and that there was "no influence from outside." However, he also indulged in Marxist hyperbole: "Kiev pharmacy owners had systematically exploited the labor of staff pharmacists" and blamed the government for "the poverty of staff pharmacists."[32]

In contradiction to Puzis' accusations, Kiev pharmacy owners announced that they considered strikers' demands modest (*skromnyia*) and were willing to concede.[33] Owners of large pharmacies (12,000 and more prescriptions) in Odessa also agreed to a double shift early in 1905.[34]

Many radical pharmacists advocated ultimately turning pharmacies over to public bodies. However, in 1905 they criticized conditions in public pharmacies as worse than in private.[35] S. G. Tsereteli of the Russian Pharmacists' Society organized pharmacists serving in Moscow city institutions–pharmacies in city hospitals and the city pharmaceutical warehouse. In March 1905, he declared that there had been "significant improvement in private pharmacies in recent times" but the "existing legal position of pharmacists in Moscow city public institutions was not normal; their material position was untenable causing them to leave at the first possibility."[36] The general meeting that he chaired adopted a resolution calling for more autonomy for pharmacists managing city pharmacies and for a pharmacy commission of the city executive council, that vacant management positions in the city pharmaceutical warehouse and city hospital pharmacies be filled by elections among their staff pharmacists, and that the staffs sanction firing.[37]

Radical pharmacists also continued to fan controversy between staff pharmacists and owners of private pharmacies. On April 2, 1905, the Russian Pharmacy Society called for creation of a union to "alleviate the struggle against exploiting pharmacy owners." Additionally, the society also called not only for equal rights for Jews and women, but for inviolability of person and dwelling.[38]

On May 24 pharmacists in Yaroslavl', feuding with one of four local owners about the introduction of a double shift, urged the public to boycott his pharmacy. Staff worked 9 A.M. to 10 P.M. with two hours off for breakfast, lunch, and tea–about 11 hours–which was not inordinate if work was not heavy. They were free every third day.[39]

Pharmacy owners were not oblivious to the problems of working pharmacists. Furthermore, they made a number of conciliatory gestures toward staff pharmacists. In early April 1905, the Odessa Pharmacy Society formed a commission on "reform of pharmaceutical matters." They reiterated the standard reform agenda–improving pharmacy education and decreasing of apprenticeship, freeing pharmacists from the tutelage of physicians, prohibiting nonpharmacists, especially feldshers, from staffing pharmacies–but also advanced more progressive, even radical proposals–abolition of the pharmacy monopoly to allow all pharmacists on the Provizor level to open pharmacies; "improving the economic position of staff pharmacists; equal rights for Jewish pharmacists in entering universities, civilian, and military service; equal rights for women pharmacists."[40] E. A. Al'tgauzen, whom some radicals labeled a tool of reactionaries, published this program in his journal, *Farmatsevt*. He criticized only decreasing apprenticeship.[41]

In May the St. Petersburg Pharmacy Society (of fully qualified pharmacists) proposed to the Northern Society (which included staff pharmacists and was radical in nature) that the two societies work jointly to solve problems in the pharmacy corporation. The capital police chief approved the St. Petersburg Society's request to host a pharmaceutical congress in the fall. All provincial societies were invited to send delegates. Items on the agenda included bettering conditions for pharmacists and regulating work in the pharmacy, discussion of the draft legislation on reform of the pharmaceutical sector being prepared in the Ministry of Internal Affairs, improving pharmacy education, and pharmacies' relation to drug stores (*aptekarskie magaziny*).[42]

In Moscow a group of pharmacists proposed an All-Russian Union of Pharmacists to discuss fundamental reforms in pharmacy, such as curtailing imports of German pharmaceuticals to encourage growth of the Russian pharmaceutical industry, a mandatory school-leaving certificate for pharmacy students, pharmacy faculties in universities, and regulating relations between staff pharmacists and owners. Al'tgauzen welcomed their proposal, stressing only that, in his opinion, the most crucial reform was to emancipate pharmacists from physicians' "guardianship."[43]

Radical pharmacists shared many of these reformist goals but they refused to cooperate. *Farmatsevticheskii vestnik* published letters alleging that the union proposed by the St. Petersburg Society was formed exclusively of "pharmacy owners . . . for struggle with staff pharmacists."[44] Similarly, although the Northern Pharmacy Society claimed to approve the congress sponsored by the St. Petersburg Pharmacy society,[45] the council (*sovet*) of the Northern Society announced that it preferred to present a report on the conditions of working pharmacists to the Tenth Pirogov Medical Congress (a radical medical, as opposed to pharmacy, group) in 1906.[46] Actually, the St. Petersburg Society included teaching and research pharmacists as well as pharmacy owners. Further, as Al'tgauzen countered, the Northern Pharmacy Society was itself exclusionary, since it was organizing a union composed of staff pharmacists to struggle with pharmacy owners. Similar unions were being organized in Moscow and other cities. The union proposed by the St. Petersburg Society, on the other hand, was to include both pharmacy owners and staff pharmacists. Its stated purpose was to further pharmaceutical science and generally improve the entire pharmacy corporation. Al'tgauzen pointed out that the editors of *Farmatsevticheskii vestnik* used "we," "us," and "our" to imply solidarity with staff pharmacists but in reality they had never served in pharmacies; 75 percent of owners who worked in their own pharmacies could with more justification call themselves staff.[47]

The radical pharmacist vanguard continued to stir the pot. In July 1905, orators at a Congress of Staff Pharmacists peppered their speeches with Marxist terms, which sounded stilted when applied to the realities of pharmacy service. One A. Brodskii merely called for institution of an independent department in the Ministry of Internal Affairs to regulate all matters touching pharmacy, including relations between owners and staff, norms for work hours, and improvements in education. But A. Zaidman—apparently no relation to Naum Zaidman, who had chronicled pharmacy owners' hardships—attributed problems in pharmacy to "capitalist production." He was joined by M. E. Linetskii, who claimed the pharmacy monopoly resulted from "the evolution of capitalism" and declared the strike "a weapon of self-defense." He advocated the cooperative pharmacies replace private ownership. D. S. Podrazhanskii, a covert Bolshevik,[48] insisted that pharmaceutical practice was "a means of production," that staff pharmacists were "proletariat," and railed against the "economic differentiation of pharmacy production—pharmacy owners and large druggists versus the army of working pharmacists" and "the class conflict between pharmacist buyers and pharmacist sellers of labor." He called for the nationalization of pharmacies and the establishment of staff unions. But, typical of many radicals, he looked to "big government" to fund his proposals.[49] In this case he proposed that the government support unemployed pharmacists. Podrazhanskii concluded with the Marxist rallying cry, "We, as all proletariat, sell our work strength."[50] On the evening of August 2 the Northern Pharmacy Society held a meeting that, according to the district police officer, barred owners and nonmembers.[51] In response, Al'tgauzen soberly remarked that pharmacy ought to be freed from "outside influences and pressure."[52]

The general strike of pharmacy workers in St. Petersburg in September 1905 was both orchestrated and forced. Observers noted that "rumors about it had circulated since the end of August although it was fully organized only the 6th of September." Over forty-six pharmacies went on strike. "Not all conditionals [staff pharmacists] joined the strike at the outset" but "striking pharmacists . . . went along Gorokhovoi street with the purpose of stopping work in pharmacies on this street." At Pel' 's pharmacy "the crowd . . . demanded staff stop work, threatening force if they did not comply." Fearing "defeat," the manager Friedrikhson complied and "went out with the crowd on the street."[53]

Officials and owners attempted to resolve the conflict by meeting with staff. Additionally, they proposed that a court of arbitration resolve the conflict. Militant pharmacists rejected these conciliatory gestures and escalated their demands. In addition to night-duty rooms with bedding and wages in lieu of room and board, concessions owners were willing to make, strike leaders demanded two seven-hour shifts (which required doubling the amount of workers), reducing night duty, providing a free day after night duty, a month's vacation with pay (!), continued employment of sick pharmacists for three months at full salary, and full salary for the time of the strike. Further, strikers called for *double* existing average wages.[54]

Pharmacy owners logically retorted that "To increase remuneration while establishing twice the personnel is unthinkable" and offered to show strikers their account books to prove their point. Owners also rejected a clause forbidding them to show preference for sex or nationality when hiring (i.e., refusing to hire women or Jews)–as too binding for management.[55]

Strikers initially refused the arbitration court. Then, after two weeks, they abruptly changed tack and clamored for arbitration.[56] At this stage, owners granted some demands–two to four hours' rest following night duty and two weeks' vacation with pay. Thirty-two pharmacies instituted double shifts. The rest established ad hoc contracts between owners and employees. Strikers returned to work after three weeks.[57]

Nevertheless, a month later, in October 1905, a general strike virtually paralyzed the empire. Strike committees in Moscow and Saratov targeted specific institutions. In Moscow they struck chemical-bacteriological labs, in Saratov private pharmacies (public and hospital pharmacies were left alone). The Russian Pharmacy Society urged strikers in both cities to prolong the strike.[58] "Orators" convened staff pharmacists, emphasized unsatisfactory conditions of work, and encouraged them to unite as had other professional groups. The pharmacy workers then resolved to form a professional union.[59] In St. Petersburg, the bureau of the Staff Pharmacists' Union published a blacklist of pharmacies that had fired striking workers and urged pharmacists not to work in them. The Executive Committee of the Soviet of Workers' deputies ordered managers to take back striking workers in pharmacies and drug stores.[60]

Strikers' demands grew more extravagant. On October 11, 1905, nearly all pharmacies in Moscow stopped work.[61] Moscow strikers not only called for shorter workdays, increased wages, and two weeks' vacation with pay but political reform—a constitutional system, abolition of the death penalty, and amnesty for political criminals.[62] On October 13 drug stores in Moscow closed.[63] Strikers advanced one constructive proposal in November. That was to abolish general night duty while designating selected pharmacies in certain regions of the city to remain open at night to serve consumers,[64] a system practiced in France.

In St. Petersburg strikers turned violent, breaking windows in those pharmacies that owners and managers attempted to keep open.[65] In November, the Society of Hospital Pharmacists in St. Petersburg demanded a staff council in each pharmacy, extravagant salary increases, a month's vacation each year, pensions equal to those of physicians, 400-ruble stipend for pharmacists preparing for the Provizor title, insurance, and free education for the children of city pharmacy workers.[66]

Staff pharmacists in private pharmacies and drug stores also began to form unions in St. Petersburg and Moscow in the fall of 1905.[67] The St. Petersburg Union of Drug-Store Pharmacists demanded two months' notice before firing or one month severance pay (the worker also was obliged to inform his employer), comrades' courts to settle differences, two weeks' vacation after one year, six month's salary during times of illness.[68]

In Perm, staff in one pharmacy went on strike, demanding double shifts and full monetary remuneration rather than part room and board. These demands were appropriate. However, some strikers also engaged in vandalism and harassment. Four Assistant Pharmacists and two student-apprentices climbed the roof of another pharmacy, cut telephone wires, sent fictitious prescriptions, and finally helped arm a crowd. Although the local medical inspector and a group of physicians tried to settle the conflict, pharmacy strikers escalated their demands to include salary increases, sick pay and *six-and-a-half-hour* days. Owners accepted these demands after four days, including the last—which was extreme, in view of the fact that pharmacies were required to be open 24 hours—and the strike ended. However, when owners received the official protocol to which they had acceded, they found an addendum, approved by physician witnesses, requiring that a comrades' court sanction any firing. Owners refused to adhere to this demand and strikers resumed their offensive. But the upheaval fizzled. Pharmacists who had returned to work rejected a new strike.[69]

In Moscow, as before, owners were not unwilling to compromise. Some "expressed full solidarity" with the political aims of striking pharmacists, in return, asking cooperation to close drug stores. Ermans, Ferrein, and some other "druggists" did close temporarily.[70] In November, Moscow pharmacy owners finally agreed to higher salaries (although not as high as strikers demanded). However, they refused to abolish night duty and permit serving pharmacists to interfere in hiring and firing. A latter-day historian derided their stand as "intransigent"[71] although these stipulations clearly would have limited owners' and managers' autonomy and decision-making.

That radical leaders were prodding staff pharmacists and that the latter considered their leaders' demands extreme became increasingly evident. In St. Petersburg, a group of staff defied radical leaders and accepted a pharmacy owner's proposal for a joint owner-employee All-Russian Union of Pharmacists. The Union was dedicated to general improvement of pharmacy—better work conditions, arbitration courts, reciprocal aid, a labor bureau, improving pharmacy education, extricating the pharmacy corporation from the tutelage of medical authorities, making easier the establishment of pharmacies, and eliminating the arbitrariness (*proizvol*) of officials. The union also had a political manifesto, which echoed that of the newly founded Constitutional Democratic Party (Kadets) or possibly the more moderate Octobrist Party—civil rights and "a constitutional order based on general elective rights."[72]

When staff were invited to join the union, self-appointed staff spokesmen L. Kliachko and Kal'varskii "categorically" refused, unconvincingly claiming that owners and staff were too far apart. The clause that particularly offended the militant leaders was that the pharmacy monopoly was to be retained. However, "many" rank-and-file pharmacists rejected their advice and "privately" joined the union.[73] The executive bureau included six full and two candidate members from both owners and staff. In November, the All-Russian Pharmacists' Union resolved to set up provincial branches and to convene a Pharmacy Congress.[74] Additionally, staff pharmacists repudiated the demand made by the nascent St. Petersburg Soviet of Workers' Deputies that owners take back fired strikers and labeled "immoral" the Soviet's proposal to blacklist pharmacies that did not comply. Further, although staff may have been pressured by threats to bring in new personnel, the majority returned to work November 7.[75]

In early December, radical pharmacists again fomented strikes in both Moscow and St. Petersburg to wring concessions on night duty and staff participation in hiring. The strikes gradually acquired political overtones. To a latter-day labor historian the strikers were noble (they asked city hospitals to take over their dispensing) and their cause (political rebellion) justified. However, the Moscow Owners and Pharmacists' Union's characterization of the strikers as "selfish extremists" and not "worker proletarians" seems more apt.[76]

Most St. Petersburg pharmacies were back to normal schedules by December 13, 1905. A few younger radical pharmacists attempted to hold out. Owners threatened to fire them unless they returned to work.[77] In Iur'ev-Dorpat pharmacy students replaced strikers so the pharmacies could function.[78] Some large pharmacies in Moscow finally broke the strike with police assistance in mid-December 1905. The Moscow firm of R. Keler fired one-fifth of its staff.[79] As a means of self-defense "Moscow Pharmacy Owners and Pharmacists" formed their own union. Gustav Osipovich Gabrilovich, ostensibly the father of Osip Gustavovich, was elected to the managing board.[80]

Flushed with achieving the double shift and other concessions, radical pharmacists did not push for abolition of private pharmacy or municipalization in 1905. However, a practical move in this direction occurred in Kiev in October. Staff pharmacists there received permission to open their own pharmacy. The charter that they submitted to the authorities was reminiscent of Antonina Lesnevskaia's All-Women's Pharmacy in St. Petersburg. The Kiev staff pharmacy was to serve as a training school for student pharmacists; pharmacists were to pool their monies to operate the pharmacy and share profits; founding and operating capital were strictly demarcated.[81]

Nineteen-five was a turning point within the radical pharmacist movement as it was for newly formed political parties. By the end of the year radical pharmacists splintered into several different subgroups. One wing continued to be confrontational and demanded further concessions. Another wing began to concentrate on the maximalist aim of taking over pharmacies for staff pharmacists and public institutions. However, they employed minimalist tactics. A third group of radicals mellowed, content with the concessions staff pharmacists had achieved in 1905.

1906

The divergent aims of radical pharmacists were displayed in three congresses held during 1906. The first, the Congress of Delegates of All-Russian Pharmaceutical Societies, was convened under the auspices of the St. Petersburg Pharmacy Society in the capital from January 16 to 21.[82] The second, the Congress of the All-Russian Pharmaceutical Union, opened January 21 in St. Petersburg. It elected its central committee February 4. The central committee included both fully qualified and "conditional" pharmacists.[83] Both these congresses were more moderate than the third, the All-Russian Delegates of Pharmaceutical Societies and Unions, planned by Moscow pharmacists to be held in that city in August 1906.

The elected officers of the Congress of Delegates of All-Russian Pharmaceutical Societies included Alexander Semenovich Ginzberg, crusader for reform of pharmaceutical education and later a major figure in the Soviet pharmacy sector, and I(osif). R(omaul'dovich). Zakharevich. The radical Russian Pharmacists' Society of Moscow and Northern Pharmacists' Society of St. Petersburg boycotted the congress, alleging that joint discussion of pharmacy issues could produce no results because there was no solidarity among members of various societies. However, delegates from pharmacy societies in Moscow, the Caucasus, Kiev, Khar'kov, Warsaw, Riga, Reval, Mitau, and Vil'na appeared anyway,[84] so the congress reflected a spectrum from right to left among reformers. Some of those present expressed constructive–in some cases audacious–solutions for many problems confronting the pharmacy corporation.[85]

The congress first discussed extricating the pharmacy corporation from the tutelage of physicians. Delegates agreed that pharmacists should manage pharmacy matters and that a permanent "pharmacy council" rather than the existing Medical Council of the Ministry of Internal Affairs should oversee pharmacy. However delegates differed on whether the pharmacy council should be elective or appointive.[86]

Debate on night duty emphasized that many pharmacists were in favor of lightening burdens on staff pharmacists. A report from the Caucasian Pharmacy Society's "Commission on Pharmacy Reform" recommended a surcharge of 5 to 25 kopeks for prescriptions dispensed at night and eliminating night dispensing of cosmetics and nonessentials. The Caucasian Society also favored double shifts–"where possible"–and annual vacations of up to two weeks. If double shifts were *impossible* they recommended an eight-hour workday.[87] The Congress of Pharmacy Societies seconded these motions and, additionally, recommended councils to resolve conflicts between pharmacy owners and staff.[88]

The Caucasian Society further recommended that posts in chemical and sanitary research occupied by physicians, chemists, and naturalists be exclusively occupied by pharmacists, that Masters of Pharmacy chair pharmacy departments in higher educational institutions, and that Provizors have the right to teach in mid-level educational institutions. The Congress of All-Russian Pharmaceutical Societies adopted these resolutions,[89] stressing pharmacists' growing sense of professionalism.

However, debate on the existing system of establishing pharmacies showed fissures between moderate reformers and their more radical brethren. E. A. Al'tgauzen took a conservative stance. He suggested temporarily retaining the existing "concession" system—that is continuing to tie the opening of normal pharmacies to population, prescription, and geographical radius. Rozenburg and Tkeshelashvili urged that the question be put to the new imperial parliament, the State Duma. Other delegates suggested retaining the basic system but eliminating population and distance norms in favor of prescription turnover. Interestingly, this proposal revealed that the poor acquired medicines from public clinics and hospitals, that many workers in factories and lower military received medicines from their own pharmacies and clinics, and that in orphanages and private clinics doctors themselves supplied patients with medicines.

More progressive delegates, who formed a majority, urged that the existing system be abolished and replaced by a *iavochnyi* system—which would allow the establishment of pharmacies without prior permission from local or central government authorities. The liberal pharmacies argued that a "free-market" system would allow all pharmacists with means to lease or to buy pharmacies. An increase in pharmacies would depress prices, thus making them more affordable.

Reformers to the left of this group, such as those from the Kazan delegation, proposed *samovykup*—buying out privately owned pharmacies by staff pharmacists. One G. Natsiokovskii proposed that artels of staff pharmacists run the pharmacies.

A still more radical group heatedly asserted that it was time to move from private to state ownership of pharmacies. However, they admitted that pharmacy owners' expenditures had recently increased due to strikes, introduction of two and sometimes three shifts, and competition from zemstvo pharmacies and drug stores. Therefore, they insisted that pharmacy owners must be compensated for their investment.[90]

Osip Gustavovich Gabrilovich was one of this contingent and one of the most interesting radical pharmacists. He later would play a major role in the early Soviet pharmacy administration. Gabrilovich had received a Master of Pharmacy degree from Moscow University in 1895. In 1906 he owned a pharmacy in Voronezh. He had a penchant for accounting and published an article on the benefits that pharmacy owners could reap from double-entry bookkeeping.[91] At the Congress of All-Russian Pharmaceutical Societies in January 1906, Gabrilovich described the "ransom" system operating in Sweden.[92] He also published a lengthy article on the financial details of how the pharmaceutical corporation could buy up private pharmacies and lease them to Provizors and Masters with lower-level pharmacists sharing in the profits.[93]

Gabrilovich's proposal, a variant on the concept of municipalization, was socialistic. However, his realism and sense of fairness compelled him to insist on reimbursement for pharmacy owners whose pharmacies were expropriated. Additionally, he recommended that only fully qualified pharmacists manage pharmacies.

Gabrilovich believed that pharmacies must be "extricated from private hands and transferred to the entire pharmaceutical corporation. Such a procedure would create the 'collective pharmacy.'"[94] Nevertheless, in view of the fact that a down payment and 10 percent interest on four- to fifteen-year purchase loans ate up a sizable portion of pharmacy income, Gabrilovich carefully worked out compensation for owners whose pharmacies were put into the common pool. He suggested transforming the existing Pharmacists' Pension Fund (which, in his opinion had not worked well in its eleven-year existence) into a buy-out fund as well as a fund for insurance and loans.[95]

In Gabrilovich's scheme, all pharmacists would become members of a new self-purchase organization. Universal membership was crucial, for lack of membership had emasculated the Pension Fund. Members would contribute 10 percent from their salaries. Students would pay an average of 36 rubles annually, Assistant Pharmacists 80 rubles, and Provizors or Masters 120 rubles. All pharmacy owners–private, zemstvo, city, and philanthropic organizations–would contribute ¼ kopek from each prescription dispensed by them.

One function of the new society would be to dispense loans to any pharmacist three years after entering the organization. Needy students could apply for 100-ruble, nonrepayable loans to enable them to take Assistant Pharmacist exams. Assistant Pharmacists could get interest-free loans of 25 rubles per month for two years to a total of 600 rubles. They were to repay their loans during the next eight years. Provizors or Masters could borrow money from the fund at 6 percent interest. Those unable to work could receive 50 rubles per month but not more than 150 rubles per year. In case of permanent disability or death the society would pay 600 rubles annually. Death benefits would be based on age and premiums.

But the chief purpose of the society was to facilitate full-fledged pharmacists to become lessees or managers of pharmacies, laboratories, and factories. A buy-out fund was to be compiled from the first three years of premia, available capital from the existing Pension Fund (which at that time equaled about one million rubles), a ¼ kopek contribution from prescriptions, and profits from pharmacies.[96] Provizors or Masters were to be eligible to lease and manage pharmacies purchased by the society, after three years of membership.[97] In return they were to pay the society an annual sum equal to 10 percent of the cost of the pharmacy and to share 25 percent of the turnover with their staff pharmacists. The lessee or manager was forbidden to transfer "exploitation" of the pharmacy to another person. After five years of serving in any kind of private pharmacy, lab, or chemical or pharmaceutical factory, Provizors or Masters also had the right to manage the lab or factory, if the society approved and the individual served the "collective pharmacy." The lessee was to pay the society a certain percentage for the capital it had expended.

The administration that Gabrilovich suggested for the society included a central bureau, located in one of the provincial cities, and bureaus in other provincial cities. The bureau was to be elected by a general assembly of delegates from provincial committees, who had been elected on the primary level by regional committees. Members of the bureau and provincial committees were to serve three years. They were to evaluate and supervise pharmacies purchased by the society.[98].

E. A. Al'tgauzen praised Gabrilovich's proposal in his journal *Farmatsevt.* He appeared sincere, thus belying the reactionary label attributed to him by radical pharmacists. He allowed that Gabrilovich's plan was "pharmacy for pharmacists" and would abolish "the Chinese wall now existing between pharmacy owners and staff pharmacists." However, before one could be "for" or "against" the proposal some hard questions must be answered. Was buying out private pharmacies acceptable to the majority of the corporation? Could the procedure be undertaken contractually or was legislation needed? What should be done about "the sale of medicines" in drug stores? Was there enough buy-out capital?[99]

While the Congress of All-Russian Pharmaceutical Societies successfully debated these innovative proposals, the general meeting of the newly organized Union of Pharmacists, which convened at the end of January 1906 in the Free Economic Society in St. Petersburg, was dispersed by police, despite adhering to "all the formalities of the law of December 12 [allowing assemblies]."[100]

However, the Union of Staff in Wholesale and Retail Drug Stores did meet in Moscow at the beginning of May 1906. The union reputedly had five hundred members but only fifty appeared to hear speakers agitate for an eight-hour day and harangue for the necessity to "struggle" against "bourgeois capitalism," then move beyond economic to political struggle. Delegates agreed to remain "nonparty."[101]

Additionally, the "First Congress of the All-Russian Pharmacy Union" not only met in St. Petersburg but enjoyed an audience with the newly appointed Minister of Internal Affairs P. A. Stolypin. This second assembly of moderates discussed reforming the concession system, insurance, gathering information on conditions in pharmacies, and ending the "enslavement" of pharmacy to medicine. Its brochures stated that the union also was committed to uniting owners and staff pharmacists, elevating pharmacists' educational level, and establishing an employment bureau. On May 20 two Provizors and one Assistant Pharmacist, elected from the union, called on Stolypin, presenting him with "a short report about the necessity of reforming pharmacy practice." According to *Farmatsevt* "the Minister received them very courteously . . . and promised to study pharmacy practices, especially the Swedish system."[102]

More radical Moscow pharmacists planned a congress for their own professional unions in August 1906, asserting that the previous two congresses and All-Russian Pharmacy Union represented only "establishment" pharmacists. Al'tgauzen scorned them as "an extremely small . . . clique of Moscow pharmacists" who did not represent most Moscow pharmacists.[103]

Thus, the differences rending the pharmacy corporation now seemed to have a geographical component. Moscow appeared to harbor more militant radicals. However, the times and the pharmacy corporation were complex. The traditional Moscow Pharmacy Society included liberals such as Al'tgauzen, who in 1906 advertised the new journal *Pravda* in his journal *Farmatsevt*. *Pravda* was concerned with "art, literature, and public life." But "its stated mission" also "was to express the interests of the working class and champion its ideology."[104] And the St. Petersburg Pharmacy Society was visited by progressives like A. S. Ginzberg.

Strikes and unrest continued to assault pharmacies and pharmaceutical enterprises during 1906, as they did other sectors of the economy. One hundred twenty bombs were reportedly found in one St. Petersburg pharmacy.[105] Revolvers and illegal literature were found in another.[106] Bombs were found in the apartment of a manager of a St. Petersburg drug store.[107] In Moscow there were strikes in the Ostroumov perfume factory in July[108] and at the Keler Pharmaceutical factory in August.[109] Robberies were reported in pharmacies in Warsaw, Berdichev,[110] and Yalta[111] in the summer of 1906.

But unemployment, resulting from the strikes and upheaval, also absorbed the energy of many pharmacists during 1906. In June, the Union of Pharmacists in Moscow reported staff cuts in both private and public pharmacies. To help the unemployed they suggested that a council (*sovet*) of pharmacists petition the Moscow city administration to increase pharmacy staffs. Additionally they petitioned the National Pharmacists' Pension Fund to assist unemployed pharmacists.[112]

Soviet historians and some Western historians after them have traditionally depicted the period 1907 to 1911 as the "Stolypin reaction." Supposedly, the withering of labor unions was due to government repression, ultimately wielded by that Minister of Internal Affairs.[113]

Pharmacy labor unions did suffer some harassment between 1907 and the outbreak of World War I. However, several Social Democratic pharmacy journals broadcast their message fairly audaciously. In fact, by union leaders' own lights, fall-off in membership appeared as much the result of improved conditions and worker apathy as government repression. Social Democratic pharmacy journals were replete with the term "indifference" (*indifferentnost'*) when referring to rank-and-file pharmacists' attitude toward the unions.

1907

Farmatsevticheskii trud, the new organ of the Russian Pharmacy Society, cited both improved conditions and apathy on the part of rank-and-file pharmacists in its inaugural issue in 1907. Due to "pharmacists' activity of the last two years," the journal acknowledged, "The double shift has been established in a whole range of cities and pay has been significantly raised." As a consequence "Even in large centers comrades' interest in organizing has evaporated."[114] Unemployment in St. Petersburg, which had attained a high of 150–200 had fallen to 20 or 25.[115] In Moscow the Union of Pharmacy Owners opened a pharmacy and clinic for unemployed pharmacists, which gave them service for three months.[116] In Kiev the "unemployed were not so numerous as to warrant discussion" and many comrades were "indifferent" to participation in a union. Only 170 of 350 comrades "organized."[117]

Iu. Kuperman, though heavily involved in revolutionary activities and a leading radical by 1912, worked steadily as a pharmacist during the years of "reaction." Receiving his Assistant Pharmacist title in 1904, he became a representative to the administrative board of a "professional [revolutionary] union" in 1905. Simultaneously he served in a pharmacy in Vil'na and in Yaroslavl' in 1905. Kuperman was laid off early in 1906, ostensibly because the pharmacy owner was cutting back, and fired again later in the year when his affiliation with the union became known. (The union leader was arrested and exiled from Yaroslavl'.) However, Kuperman received 40 rubles' severance pay through a Justice-of-the-Peace court settlement. And, in 1907 he found work in Tula and subsequently in another city.[118]

Some years later Kuperman alleged that pharmacy students were sometimes forced to work twelve to sixteen hours. However, he lived comfortably at home during his apprenticeship. Indeed, his main complaints were the inadequacy of early pharmacy education–he bribed university laboratory workers to study the collections necessary for passing his Assistant Pharmacist examination–and quotas imposed on Jews. Jews were limited to 20 percent of students enrolled in the Provizor courses at the University of Kiev. Kuperman claimed later that as only two or three Jews were admitted annually, he entered the Provizor course only in 1914, ten years after receiving his Assistant Pharmacist degree.[119] So, although Kuperman suffered because he was a Jew, he did not lack work and, apparently, survived his formative years as a pharmacist.

Because staff pharmacists' lives were not intolerable, radical leaders were forced to struggle to maintain the urgency of labor issues. They did so by ferreting out instances of ill treatment and painting as dark as possible a picture of them, by organizing professional pharmacy unions, and by orchestrating and applauding strikes. For example, radical pharmacists publicized a strike in two Riazan pharmacies that erupted because of "lamentable" (*plachevnye*) conditions. The onerous conditions consisted of a "rest day after two 15-hour workdays" and requiring pharmacy students to do work "not connected with pharmacy," namely, going to the post office and carrying water from the railway station."[120] Still, Riazan leaders had a hard time getting worker participation "because of lack of solidarity among pharmacists . . . only in two pharmacies did staff unanimously strike."[121] That this also was due to the fact that conditions were not half bad is evident from demands which had moved from sensible to extreme: two *six-and-a-half*-hour shifts; sizable pay raises; a maximum of eight night-duty shifts per month; two weeks' vacation with pay; an end of outside-pharmacy tasks; two months' sick pay; settlement of disputes by arbitration court. Owners conceded all demands after six days, balking only at the requirement that they could not fire staff without cause or because of the strike.[122]

Similarly, demands in Berdichev implied strikers were casting for straws. In July a strike bureau demanded of one owner twenty days' vacation with salary after one year's work, an end of night duty for students, and hiring staff on recommendation of the bureau.[123] Pharmacists in the

Caucasus also were dulled by apathy–many did not answer strike calls–and were poorly organized, although the Governor General finally agreed to a general meeting of pharmacists in February 1907.[124]

Despite improved conditions in pharmacies, radical leaders zealously established professional unions for staff pharmacists. The Russian Pharmacy Society in Moscow formed a union as early as September 9, 1906. It operated under the wing of the society.[125] The founding meeting of the "Professional Society of Staff Pharmacists of Kiev" was held February 1, 1907.[126] The first meeting was held in March.[127] The Union of Staff Pharmacists in Odessa was in operation by the spring of 1907 and organized a pharmacy March 1 of that year.[128] The St. Petersburg Pharmacy Union was legalized in May under the name "Professional Society of Staff Pharmacists."[129] The Khar'kov "Professional Society of Staff Pharmacists" held its first meeting at the public library on the evening of June 29.[130] A Union of Pharmacists was inaugurated in Vil'na in September.[131]

Three years later, in 1909, General Kurlov, Assistant Minister of Internal Affairs and head of the gendarmerie, branded professional unions fronts for "illegal parties." He claimed that on the basis of Social Democratic documents in his possession sixteen administrative boards of thirty-six professional unions consisted of Social Democrats; only eight were nonparty.[132]

At the time, the Kiev-based *Zhizn' farmatsevta* scoffed at Kurlov's suggestion. But in the 1930s the old activist Zil'berg emphasized the Social Democratic policy of boring into pharmacy unions.[133]

Nevertheless, in 1907, as later, Bolshevik policies differed from Menshevik. The Bolsheviks insisted upon party allegiance, the Mensheviks advocated that unions be "nonparty."[134] However, neither group conceded that professional unions should be devoid of ideological underpinnings. *Farmatsevticheskii trud*, speaking for the Russian Pharmacy Society and its professional union, admitted that while pharmacy unions should be "nonparty"[135] their primary function was to raise consciousness. The upward mobility that pharmacy offered must be downplayed. Staff must be discouraged from believing they could someday be pharmacy owners.

> Owners and staff pharmacists work together day after day. Naturally, between them cannot be the relationship that exists between workers of factories and their administration. They must "get along together." Additionally, workers are reluctant to move and owners can make the situation worse. Therefore, organizations of staff pharmacists more than those of factory workers must struggle on two fronts–to preserve improved conditions and struggle against all petit bourgeois dreams.[136]

Professional pharmacy unions consistently broadcast a Social Democratic message.[137] The council of the Russian Pharmacy Society announced that its new union had been organized to "struggle with representatives of capital" and "develop class consciousness of staff pharmacists" as well as defend their rights, professional and economic interests, and reform pharmacy practice. The new union expressed "its support for the Social Democrats" and announced that "among local comrades has been formed a circle, agitating for support of the electoral bloc of the extreme left."[138] The Kiev Professional Union was composed "nearly exclusively of Jews" because Poles did not have "developed self-consciousness–they did not have the correct understanding of the need to organize... they are inert... rather than unite with proletarian pharmacists they unite with bourgeois capitalist pharmacists."[139] The first meeting of the Kiev Professional Union "called comrades from the Society for Mutual Aid" to a joint "struggle against capitalist pharmacists" but was disappointed that "the great majority" proclaimed "solidarity with owners." Frustrated in its attempt to unite local staff pharmacists, the Kiev Professional Union warned them that "only in a class-conscious organization is struggle possible."[140] The Vil'na Pharmacy Union organized lectures on chemistry and "political questions" although it lamented that "general political and economic themes have little interest for our comrades."[141] The first meeting of the Khar'kov Professional Union announced that "The purpose of the movement of exploited proletarian masses" was "to abolish the order of domination of one group and the slavery of the other... the consciousness of the masses is the true task for success of the movement."[142]

Hidebound by their Marxist convictions, the most militant radical pharmacists ignored evidence of social mobility within the pharmacy corporation. They stubbornly continued to divide pharmacists into exploiting owners and a permanent underclass of staff pharmacists. Practical solutions–setting pharmacists up in business–were feebly applied. Only in Moscow during 1907 did an artel of pharmacists attempt to manage their own pharmacy. On April 1 the Novo-Petrovskaia Pharmacy of Master of Pharmacy I. Ia. Sychev turned over its lease to the "First Moscow Artel of Pharmacists." The artel was incorporated to "open," "purchase," "lease," and "manage" pharmacies, drug stores, pharmaceutical factories, and bacteriological cabinets. Following examples by the woman pharmacist Antonina Lesnevskaia and male pharmacists in Kiev, the artel also determined to open a "school of practical pharmacy." The artel's charter specified that it had the right to acquire, rent, and sell any kind of immovable property and fill orders from private people, the treasury, or public institutions. The artel admitted as members persons of seventeen years of age of both sexes having a pharmacy diploma. All members had the right to share in profits and income of artel enterprises. In case of liquidation, members' contributions would be returned.[143]

At the same time the newly established Moscow journal *Farmatsevticheskii trud* revived the notion of municipalization. The journal approvingly noted that the Medical Council and Senate were frequently siding with public institutions–zemstvos and municipalities–in their conflicts with "private" individuals over the establishment of pharmacies. Desperate owners of "private pharmacies" were lobbying against a growing sympathy for "public" pharmacies in the Medical Council and Senate. *Farmatsevticheskii trud* was sympathetic to the plight of pharmacy owners but noted sanctimoniously that "our journal always expresses how necessary it is to reorganize pharmacy practice on the lines of municipalization."[144] The sooner "pharmacy practice is reorganized, the better for the population and the pharmacy corporation. Delay will only make things worse." The journal was confident that owners would accept expropriation of their pharmacies and adapt to socialized pharmacy. "Pharmacists will go into service in the city and zemstvos as managers. Their work and knowledge will be for the populace. . . ." However they also noted that "pharmacists who feel their rights are violated [by expropriation] can sue."[145]

1908

During 1908 *Farmatsevticheskii trud* valiantly tried to keep up the faith, reminding readers that "We pharmacists, as all workers, live by selling our work strength . . . [we] are objects of exploitation on the part of capital."[146] But despite this disquieting contention, the journal frequently cited favorable conditions in major cities,[147] although conditions in smaller towns lagged. A report from "M. Tanin" emphasized that the double shift, reduced night duty, and increased pay were the norm in large cities but "provincial comrades have not improved their conditions one iota."[148] One "A. N." added that pharmacists in the capitals and provincial cities had achieved a double shift but advocated legislation in the State Duma, to "strengthen and spread" this reform.[149]

Despite the militant pharmacists' contention that their message was needed, particularly in small towns, accounts to the radical press during 1908 depicted rank-and-file pharmacists as dulled with apathy.

A report from Kishinev was representative. Although "decline in professional movements" was attributed to "oppressive political conditions," the main problem faced by union organizers was "indifference by the members of the [pharmacy] society. . . . The Administration's repeated attempts to organize a representative council, or *sovet*, to be an intermediary for the masses" met with "no success." At the end of 1907 the Administrative Board of the Pharmacy Society "brought up the business of a union . . . the first task was to struggle with comrades' indifference." The administrative board urged pharmacy staff to establish "close connection with the masses of pharmacists," that "comrades" cast off their "apathy." Leaders finally succeeded in forming a council but it collected only 13 rubles for the first six months. The union established a "bureau of labor" but "with passage of time the bureau deteriorated because of owners' offensive policy" (they "energetically undertook reforms") and also because of "indifference." The report sagely concluded "perhaps we live too well–a union is not needed."[150]

The situation in Nikolaev was similar. A meeting to develop a statute for a professional organization could not be held due to "insufficiency of professional organizers"[151] In June *Farmatsevticheskii trud* simply noted that "The strike movement in May was very weak and in a large majority of cases unsuccessful for workers."[152]

In St. Petersburg the professional organization sent out a questionnaire to determine the cause of members' failure to pay dues. "One questionnaire showed extreme weakness of interest in organization on the part of the majority of the members" although in another "absence of a professional press" was said to be at fault.[153]

Radical leaders asserted that lack of interest in labor organization caused conditions to worsen. Purportedly, in Belaia Tserkov', Kiev province, "because of the lack of organization and lack of consciousness of local pharmacists . . . there is again . . . exploitation. A female pharmacy student had to pay 300 rubles to be admitted as an apprentice; one pharmacy had only a single shift although another had gone to a double shift."[154] Three pharmacies in Slaviansk, Khar'kov province, had unpleasant regimens–much night duty, "miserly" salaries, and "heavy," "intensive" work. A local report lamented that "We could improve conditions but there is little consciousness on the part of comrades."[155] One article warned that staff pharmacists were entering owner's societies, their vision blurred by bourgeois dreams. "The wide mass of staff pharmacists was inert; into the [owner] society entered predominantly those who considered themselves future owners" although owners dominated the society.[156] Kherson also reported "inertness of local staff pharmacists . . . among us there is complete absence of solidarity."[157]

While efforts to organize staff pharmacists foundered during 1908, the idea of abolishing or modifying the pharmacy monopoly gained greater acceptance.[158] However, the debate on this issue revealed not only continuing diversity of opinion among radical pharmacists but that some had become more radical while others had mellowed. A. G. Strel'tsov emphasized there were "two tendencies" in the Russian Pharmacy Society in Moscow. One supported "municipalization." The other merely recommended free establishment of pharmacies—"opening pharmacies without prior permission [*iavochnyi poriadok*]."[159]

Pharmacists who promoted municipalization claimed this the only way for staff pharmacists to advance.

> The social problem of staff pharmacists and workers in general can be solved only in a social order where there will be no exploitation of man by man, where there will not be private ownership of the means of production, where all will be equal—i.e. collectivism. . . . Abolition of private privilege *under conditions of municipalization of pharmacies* [italics in original].[160]

Alexander S. Ginzberg, as professor in the Women's Medical Courses in Moscow, was distanced from both the desire of staff pharmacists to own a pharmacy and the concerns of pharmacy owners. He opposed the existing, restricted, system but asserted that "the *iavochnyi* system will not better conditions of staff pharmacists . . . only municipalization will decide the question."[161] A. G. Strel'tsov advanced a proposal akin to that which Gabrilovich had suggested in 1906—"ransoming pharmacies according to fair evaluation."[162]

On the contrary, some former radicals in the Russian Pharmacy Society now shrank from such extreme solutions. E. Basilaia, for example, rejected municipalization at that time, regarding it as "an ideal to which we must strive." For the time being, he advocated simply "abolition of privilege, giving the right to open pharmacies to Provizors and Masters, municipalities, unions, and societies."[163] One Erokhin straddled the fence claiming that he was "in favor of municipalization" but also believed "pharmacists must have the possibility of displaying initiative in opening pharmacies."[164] Other radical pharmacists were more cautious. Basilaia's colleague, L. Ia Zimin, formerly an advocate for municipalization, now opposed it as "premature," pointing out that "there is no basis to suppose that municipalities will manage pharmacy practice better than pharmacists themselves . . . our municipalities are not prepared for this." He argued sensibly that "It is necessary to give city and zemstvo self-government wide freedom to open pharmacies but we should not turn over all pharmacy practice to their hands." Zimin wanted fully qualified pharmacists to benefit from free trade: "Besides these institutions the right to open pharmacies must be given . . . to all Provizors and Masters." Sounding every inch the *laissez-faire* economist, he advocated abolishing the pharmacy monopoly and allowing free establishment of pharmaceutical factories as well as pharmacies. ". . . [P]rivilege braked public and personal initiative in the pharmacy industry . . . competition results in a better product."[165] Like Zimin, E. A. Abramson reminded his colleagues that zemstvo pharmacies were riddled with financial problems:

> We recognize zemstvo pharmacies have many defects. Zemstvos cannot now afford free dispensing of medicine, not to mention necessary staff in pharmacies. To turn over pharmacy practice to municipalities . . . is to guarantee to the populace improper medical care.[166]

Another radical pharmacist, S. K. Lintser, echoed Zimin on free trade, arguing that abolishing restrictions on establishing pharmacies would stimulate the pharmaceutical industry. He proposed sending amendments to the Duma and Stolypin, Minister of Internal Affairs, regarding the law they were drafting on abolishing the pharmacy monopoly.[167] One Leibin warned his colleagues that they could not "artificially proletarize the masses. Pharmacists must have free right to open pharmacies."[168]

Russkii farmatsevt, organ of the moderate-reform branch of Moscow pharmacists, was markedly objective in reviewing the record on zemstvo pharmacies. During 1908 the journal published information on zemstvo warehouses, efficient purchases of medicine, and cases of transferring private pharmacies to zemstvos, developments that had occurred mainly in the "north." It also exposed poorly run zemstvo pharmacies.[169] It must be remembered, of course, that radical pharmacists regarded zemstvos, as constituted in 1908, bulwarks of conservative, establishment classes.

The First Conference of Staff Pharmacists' meeting in Ekaterinoslav province in the summer of 1908 included three options on pharmacy reform in their program, indicating that they too were rent by factions. Conference resolutions included "municipalization, underwritten by a special tax on the population"; "forbidding further opening of pharmacies by private persons while conversely allowing cities and zemstvos to open pharmacies with free dispensing"; and "abolishing privilege and granting free right to open pharmacies to all."[170]

A "general meeting" of the Kiev Union of Staff Pharmacists, July 25, 1908, meanwhile, adhered to a radical program. Noting that "private pharmacies do not correspond to the needs of the population" and "private owners do not improve pharmacy practice," Kiev staff pharmacists asserted that "radical change was needed," namely, to "give pharmacies to public self-government." They not only advocated "municipalization"—turning over "all pharmacies to municipalities with right to dispense medicine for payment" but reform of pharmacy administration—establishing "inspection through representatives of staff pharmacists, physicians, and municipal representatives over pharmacies, legislating [minimum] working hours in pharmacies, and a Pharmacy Collegium for administration of the Pharmacy Sector."[171]

1909

Debate on municipalization continued during 1909. The radical pharmacy journal *Zhizn' farmatsevta*, launched in Kiev in that year, promoted itself as a vanguard for municipalization. Its maiden editorial announced that "the organ" had as its "task–struggle for democratization of the entire pharmacy structure, in particular for municipalization of pharmacies." This task was made easier by the fact that "members of the Duma were addressing the issue" and "the government had developed a draft law on abolishing the pharmacy monopoly."[172]

But labor organizing and strikes were not forgotten. *Zhizn' farmatsevta* emphasized that its secondary task was to carry on the mission of its predecessor *Iuzhnyi farmatsevt*–"to defend the interests of working pharmacists and insure correct medical help to the population." Editors reassured readers that they had "close connections with *Farmatsevticheskii trud*."[173] A few issues later they remarked sententiously that "Some comrades want a scientific section. But economic and professional interests of staff pharmacists come first."[174] *Zhizn' farmatsevta* claimed to be nonpartisan and dedicated to establishing "cheaper or free dispensing of medicine for the masses, raising scientific qualifications of pharmacists, and struggle against surrogates." The journal did indeed promote a four-year pharmacy institute after four years of middle-school education[175] and carried information on medicines. However, *Zhizn' farmatsevta*'s avowed dedication to "stand for economic interests of staff pharmacists and the class struggle of the proletariat . . . to preserve the rights of working pharmacists from the 'autocracy' of the pharmacy owner"[176] and its assiduous reporting on strikes in Russia and abroad[177] underscored its Social Democratic orientation.

The South-West Union of Pharmacists also had a Social Democratic, perhaps even a Bolshevik, orientation. In 1909 the bureau of the South-West Union of Pharmacists, established in 1908, coordinated unions in Kiev, Podolia, Volynsk, Poltava, Chernigov, Kherson, and Ekaterinoslav. The bureau alleged that authorities had closed "professional unions of working pharmacists" in Odessa and Khar'kov. The bureau was encouraged that the number of unions was increasing. But as earlier, membership in the local unions was meager. As a result, the South-West umbrella union urged the forming of "small, local groups" through "careful planning."[178] This tactic saw success with new branches in Nikolaev and Elizavetgrad in February 1909. However, though "some members were living in Odessa . . . a branch could not be registered because Odessa comrades did not elect an executive body."[179]

Other instances of Bolshevik influence on local pharmacy unions were apparent in 1909. For example, Smolensk activists characterized their professional union as a "cell." They were unable to get legal status for their organization, although efforts to improve working conditions in pharmacies were successful.[180]

But union organizing was difficult in 1909 as in 1908 and mainly for the same reasons. In some cases, "local police conditions" were to blame.[181] Tiflis reported "this year there was no organization" because of "spying" and "intrigue."[182] Zhitomir stalwarts claimed they had no union because "administrative authorities refused an attempt to create a Volynsk union or South-West division."[183] In a few cases high dues or nationality conflicts destroyed unions. A letter from Gomel' related that after *Farmatsevticheskii trud* stopped there was "no activity in our union for some time. General meetings were rarely held." As a result local pharmacy owners eliminated the double shift for students. Members also considered annual dues too high. When they were lowered "general work increased."[184] In Zhitomir, solidarity disintegrated because the twenty-four staff in seven pharmacies were segregated into groups of Jews and gentiles—"two national groups . . . with no connection between them."[185]

Nevertheless, the main reason for declining interest in pharmacy unions was indifference. "Information from the provinces" *Zhizn' farmatsevta* soberly intoned, "unanimously confirms that lively activity of professional unions and societies stands still [*zamerla*] or is trifling [*svedena k pustiakam*]. From many cities [comes] testimony as to the complete collapse [*pol'nom upadke*] of interest in union matters." In Sumy, Khar'kov province, "comrades were not well-informed" or "serious about professional issues," they themselves did "not try to widen the circle of their knowledge."[186] Kherson suffered from "inertness," "the majority of pharmacists do not know each other." The double shift did not exist but pharmacists had every fourth or fifth day off and had ten to fifteen stints of night duty per month. An Assistant Pharmacist "was invited to work for 40 rubles per month."[187]

The prevailing mood of apathy appeared the natural consequence of "economic improvement observed following the double shift."[188] Reports from the provinces generally, though not universally, revealed tolerable, if not completely acceptable conditions.

Khar'kov radicals accused local authorities of preventing "comrades" from opening a branch of the South-West Union of Staff Pharmacists and alleged that conditions "were getting worse and pay had decreased." At the same time, they affirmed that double shifts were "universal" for pharmacists although students enjoyed a double shift only in three pharmacies. The lower salaries of which the report complained were obviously a trade-off.[189]

Ekaterinoslav pharmacists enjoyed fairly high pay, the double shift, and limited night duty.[190] Reports dredged deep to find abuses. For example, "harshness toward a student pharmacist" consisted of the pharmacy owner staying "in his dacha while the student toiled"; the student had worked "two in three" but "the owner knew he needed money . . . therefore he changed the schedule to three in four and the student left." The Ekaterinoslav Union of Pharmacists had drawn up the questionnaire that supplied information on hours and pay but the union suffered from "indifference" (*indifferentnost'*). "Member contributions . . . do not come . . . if there are general meetings, few people show up." The report blamed the local authorities—"The Administration of the Union is disorganized with arrests and searches"; "1905–06 were years of organization for us . . . we organized the union . . . then repression."[191] However, it seems just as likely that indifference to the Ekaterinoslav Union was due largely to prevailing good conditions and high pay. Despite this, the union decided to dun members for dues.[192] In the city of Bakhtum, Ekaterinoslav province, two pharmacies had double shifts and "acceptable" (*snosnoe*) salaries, in a third, working pharmacists had duty fifteen nights a month, in a fourth, there was no night duty and a six-hour (9 A.M. to 3 P.M.) workday.[193]

A report from Sevastopol' noted laconically that the double shift had been introduced in 1906.[194] A report from the Riga Pharmacy Society was criticized for failing to delineate "the composition of the society, its program of activity . . . the double shift or class consciousness of workers." Pharmacy staff there enjoyed a number of perquisites.[195]

The Kiev Union of Pharmacists was "quiet" and, as in the case of Ekaterinoslav, this appeared to stem from acceptable local conditions. For example, "conflicts arising in pharmacies were resolved in an arbitration court."[196]

In Poltava province one pharmacy reported "more or less acceptable [*snosnye*] conditions of work—correct double shift and norms for pay" until recently when "conditions of work" worsened—the double shift was cut, six-day work weeks became the rule, one Assistant made a miserly 20 rubles per month. However, another received 50 to 60 rubles.[197] Kremenchug, Poltava province, reported some problems: pharmacists suffered "chronic unemployment," even "suicides. . . . Pay for Assistant Pharmacists has fallen to 25-30 rubles." Nevertheless, the double shift had been "preserved" and in one pharmacy an Assistant Pharmacist received 50 rubles *plus* a month's vacation. He was less generous than his employer. When he went on vacation, he proposed that a substitute (an unemployed pharmacist), be paid only 30 rubles.[198]

Voronezh reported that a "Professional Society of Staff Pharmacists" had existed since 1907, hailed the advent of *Zhizn' farmatsevta* because although Voronezh enjoyed "Public libraries, a press, and theaters there was no special organ for pharmacists." Unfortunately, "recently there had been observed a chilling of comrades' interest in the organization." No doubt this was because only one or two pharmacies did not have a double shift and "the society enjoyed not a little authority among pharmacy owners."[199]

According to N. Shatov, conditions in Vologda were "impossible." Fourteen pharmacies existed in the province, nine in districts and five in the city of Vologda. The latter included three private pharmacies, one zemstvo pharmacy with right of private dispensing, and one railroad pharmacy to serve the needs of workers on the Northern railroad. But, despite attempts to paint a dismal picture, Shatov emphasized that conditions varied; on the whole they did not appear totally "difficult." Salaries were particularly high in the zemstvo pharmacy.[200]

Conditions in Smolensk were quite good and pharmacists engaged in collective bargaining although they were not able to establish a union. At one pharmacy, staff or their leaders were able to get two eight-hour shifts plus 18 rubles per month for meals in lieu of board although they (wisely) refrained from pressing for "two-week vacations with pay, a minimum wage, and staff input in firing." At another pharmacy it proved "impossible to introduce the double shift; therefore the workers limited their demand to abolition of '*internat*' [the *pansion* system, or boarding] and one free day in each two or three."[201]

In the seven "comparatively large cities" of the Turkestan Region in Central Asia there were twenty normal or fully stocked pharmacies. The report from Tashkent claimed conditions of work were very difficult but this was due in part to the severe continental climate. The double shift had been preserved in Tashkent and "2 or 3 pharmacies in other cities." In the remaining pharmacies the work pattern was "4 in 5" with 8 to 15 stints of night duty per month. Salaries were quite good, although the report insisted that the expensive cost of living whittled this remuneration. However, there was little unemployment. There also was "nearly full absence of comradely solidarity. We have a union but its work is not satisfactory. There also is a Turkestan Union but the total membership amounts to 20–

all staff in Tashkent pharmacies." The union treasury was richer than that in Kiev, with 800 rubles; the bulk of the money had come from two evening functions. Unfortunately, half the funds had been spent on assistance grants that had not been repaid and "indifference" was rife.[202]

A report from Batum noted that staff pharmacists had achieved a double shift, increased wages, abolition of board, monthly vacations after a year of service, hiring and firing with approval of the staff, and "many other small improvements. But, gradually, conditions began to return to their former state." However, the reversal was not as draconian as the report attempted to portray it. "Owners took away vacations" and "hiring and firing" with staff input. They only "*attempted* [italics mine] to take away the double shift." The worst that could be said on this score was that "One young owner already has taken steps . . . to think up new exploitations. . . ."[203]

Lack of interest in unions on the part of staff pharmacists generated two trends. On the one hand, stalwarts renewed efforts to organize their lagging brethren; on the other, the unions used "buyers' club" advertising to lure the laggards into joining. In both cases union organizers were methodical and creative.

In Vologda, "groups of local pharmacists invited staff of both privileged [private] and zemstvo pharmacies . . . to organize . . . a society. [They were] to send requests to the Vologda Railroad Pharmacy of N. I. Kapeller."

The Kiev "Professional Union of Staff Pharmacists" had a minuscule budget of only about 100 rubles. The union used double-entry bookkeeping. It included an employment bureau which found jobs for a handful of pharmacists in 1909. In September 1909, nineteen pharmacists from Kiev and twenty-two from outside the city were registered with the bureau. Six "local" and four "out-of-town" pharmacists found work.[204] The Kiev Union advertised discounts for members. Two courses to prepare for the Assistant Pharmacist exam were offered to members at only 10 rubles; the Chemical-Bacteriological Institute of Dr. Ben'iash offered books to members at 10 kopeks per month and no tax; subscriptions to the newspaper *Kievskiia Vesmi* were offered at 2 rubles for three months and 70 kopeks for one month; legal advice was a bargain at 25 kopeks. That life was good in Kiev for staff pharmacists was evidenced by the fact that nine businesses, including an art store with enamels and a watch emporium, offered discounts and, in some cases, deferred payments to members of the Kiev Union of Working Pharmacists. The Isaac Shvartsman Company deferred payment for six months and offered deductions of 15 percent; the art store offered discounts of from 10 to 35 percent; the "Warehouse of Watches," discounts of 2 to 5 percent; the photography shop "Modern," discounts of from 10 to 20 percent; G. P. Leonovich deferred payment and offered a 10 percent discount to members for bookkeeping courses; the Biblioteka bookstore canceled taxes for purchases and offered a discount of 20 to 40 percent; and the barber Mendiuk offered services at only 8 kopeks.[205] The Kiev Club of Working Pharmacists, established November 9, 1909, engaged in purely cultural activities, such as lectures on literature, science, and alcoholism; the newly elected administration planned a rather bourgeois "concert-ball" to increase funds.[206]

Moscow pharmacists also formed a literary-musical circle.[207] It might be assumed that announcements of such innocuous activities were sop to the censors, were it not for the fact that the same issue of *Zhizn' farmatsevta* contained an outspoken article on the need to lessen pharmacists' workday[208] and an ode to Shiller—"The Apostle of Beauty and Freedom"—on the one-hundred fiftieth anniversary of his death.[209]

As in Kiev, the Smolensk union of staff pharmacists had a "bureau of labor" to assist the unemployed. Additionally, an agreement between the union and the "society of people's universities" offered lower tuition for lectures to members of the union.[210]

In the same vein the South-West Union requested permission to open preparatory courses for the Assistant Pharmacist and Provizor examinations and gave loans to members. Members did not repay the loans on time and the union requested payment by December 1.[211] The Kiev branch established a library commission, to which it asked comrades to contribute and sold tickets for lectures at the popular university for 5 kopeks.[212] Thus, the unions were either softening their militancy or were pretending to do so for edification of the government.

The St. Petersburg Professional Society of Staff Pharmacists appeared to be mellowing in 1909, perhaps because of the ground swell of support for its ideas in the parliament. Early in January, one Kalinskii familiarized members with the work of a society commission on the new pharmacy statute. The commission met with the K-D, or Kadet (Constitutional Democratic), "fraction, public figures and members of the [Third] State Duma." The commission was pushing the free establishment of pharmacies without permission (*iavochnyi poriadok*) as well as "municipalization." The St. Petersburg Society even toyed with participating in the K-D fraction but this was opposed by some members on the grounds that it "would give the commission a party character."[213]

There also was evidence of increased moderation among members of the Russian Pharmacy Society in Moscow during 1909. An "opposition movement" claimed that the society was becoming irrelevant in the eyes of staff pharmacists and demanded greater attention to labor issues. E. G.

Basilaia, former head of the Russian Pharmacy Society, left or was forced to leave Moscow. In June 1909 the general assembly met to elect a new chair. Basilaia's peregrinations were not disclosed, but the election meeting attacked his performance during the previous year and a half. The critics—"a group of comrades belonging to the so-called opposition"—claimed the society's activity had been "extremely unsystematic." The society had paid "no attention to mutual aid," did "not participate in issues regarding the Pension Fund," "paid no attention to falsification," did "practically" "nothing to remedy unemployment" ("the council [*sovet*] nearly entirely halted the Bureau of Labor"), and did "nothing about literary, musical evenings." "According to the 'Opposition' a group of Moscow pharmacists was bypassing the Russian Pharmacy Society because the council of the Society does not address their interests." Additionally, the society had gone over its budget by 700 rubles—income equaled 2,000 rubles and expenditures, 2,700. The newly elected chair, S. Ia. Isaev, proposed cutting expenditures by renting a hotel room for meetings but many members "energetically" opposed most expenditures. I. M. Erokhin, who had compromised on municipalization the previous year, now averred that the "Society must be brought closer to Moscow comrades."[214]

Interestingly, in the light of Stalin's later activity, the Moscow "Opposition" urged a more significant role for the secretariat of the organization. During the last year and a half one of the members of the council, or soviet, had filled the position of secretary but, according to one E. Abramovich, "The Opposition holds the view that the secretary is the chief nerve of the society. The Secretary should be a comrade experienced in the professional movement of staff pharmacists."[215]

The Russian Pharmacy Society's journal *Farmatsevticheskii trud* valiantly tried to maintain interest in labor issues during 1909. It covered the general worker's movement—strikes in factories and so forth.[216] But articles in this journal underscored the apathy of rank-and-file pharmacists,[217] as did reports in *Zhizn' farmatsevta.* In Baku, in 1908, a small group of pharmacists drafted a statute for a legal union and sent it to authorities for registration. After three-months' scrutiny, the statute was approved. The founders convened a special meeting. Sixty to seventy pharmacists appeared at the first meeting. However, only thirty signed up for active work.[218] In Tiflis, "at one time the Union of Pharmacists operated very well—now—there is indifference in the majority of the comrades." The author blamed "provocation, spies, and hooligans" for this situation but also admitted that conditions were not too bad—"the double shift is unchanged" although "salary, night duty, firing in some pharmacies is subject to radical change and in others has already been changed."[219]

On the issue of "municipalization," the journal brought out the downside of transferring private pharmacies to zemstvos and municipal bodies. It appeared to endorse a buy-out scheme in which all pharmacists would participate, such as that proposed earlier by Gabrilovich. One A. El'shtein reminded readers that municipalization presented a number of dilemmas. First, owners of private pharmacies would have to be compensated when their pharmacies were transferred to zemstvos and cities; this was the only fair way:

> A great number of pharmacists are in favor of municipalization. Municipalization requires great sums to buy pharmacies since to undertake municipalization without purchase would not allow . . . elementary justice.[220]

But buy-outs would rely heavily on government funds. The result would be a sort of state socialism:

> Even to propose that pharmacies would be purchased not for prices quoted on the stock exchange but according to actual cost would necessitate a large amount [of money] which city treasuries could not afford. The State treasury unquestionably would have to grant means. . . . So this would establish the precedent of a mixture of state and private business.
>
> It is necessary to transfer pharmacies to public hands . . . because of falsification [of medicaments]. If falsification serves as a point for demanding municipalization or nationalization of production, why stop at pharmacies? . . .
>
> "Kontrol" in municipalization must be wielded by specialists. . . .[221]

A further problem was that workers did not have a critical mass in city dumas. Thus, "municipalized" pharmacies would not be in workers' hands:

> Comrades—do not forget that power is not in the hands of democratic representatives. To give the ruling class pharmacies established a dangerous precedent. Democratic municipalization is impossible in a state directed by feudal bureaucrats and capitalists. Reform of pharmacy matters at present is impossible . . . municipalization can be recognized only in principle. The idea is desirable—not actual.[222]

While insisting that "It is necessary to transfer all drug stores to pharmacists," El'shtein also emphasized the benefits of free trade: "According to general economic laws competition improves the quality and cheapness of the cost of production. . . ."[223]

1910 and 1911

The fortunes of professional societies and unions varied during 1910 and 1911. In 1910 *Rannee utro* alleged that "professional societies are in an extremely lamentable situation."[224] The South-West Union reported continued "indifference" on the part of the majority of staff pharmacists."[225] The general meeting of working pharmacists in Nizhni Novgorod early in 1911 likewise fretted that 1910 had been a "dead year"; in particular "members' dues did not come in."[226] While a "lively professional movement" existed in Gomel, in Novo-Nikolaevskaia, Tomsk province, indifference (*indifferentizm*) was the order of the day, even in the face of abolition of the double shift.[227]

In 1910 the Russian Pharmacy Society had 321 members and 27,338 rubles 2 kopeks in its treasury. Nevertheless, the report for 1909, read to the annual general meeting of the society, chaired by Sergei Iakovlevich Isaev, claimed that the society's journal *Zhizn' farmatsevta* was "in a critical position"; the society needed means to support it.[228] Early in 1911, the Russian Pharmacy Society lamented the "indifference" of the masses of staff pharmacists. Additionally, some members now criticized *Zhizn' farmatsevta* for being out of touch with its constituency, once again emphasizing the heterogeneity of leading radical pharmacists. The relatively moderate Erokhin claimed *Zhizn' farmatsevta* was espousing "narrow party" views. O. Karpovich implied that staff pharmacists were more interested in actual "professional" matters than in revolution; thus *Zhizn' farmatsevta* ought to establish a section on science. Kagan and Kanevskii staunchly insisted that *Zhizn' farmatsevta* had a "nonparty" character and was a purely "professional organ."[229]

Their assertion seemed disingenuous in the light of their references to Marx,[230] praise of the newly established "class character" of the Pension Fund,[231] the Social Democratic fraction, and strikes. For example, a half page of the first issue for 1911 was devoted to the "SD fraction" in the State Duma, a strike of textile workers in Teikov, which lasted 65 days, strikes among printers in St. Petersburg and so on.[232]

But militancy had little appeal to rank-and-file pharmacists. Chair of the Russian Pharmacy Society, Isaev, while admitting that he could not speak for all comrades, asserted that *Zhizn' farmatsevta* was unpopular among Moscow staff pharmacists because the masses had now shed their militancy. The journal "did not correspond to the desired direction of the masses . . . the masses were indifferent to all [movements] that had a social character."[233] On May 5, 1910, the Ekaterinburg Society of Staff Pharmacists met to "liquidate the business of the society." No reasons were adduced for this move in the press release.[234] The working pharmacists' union in Kutais was closed by administrative order in 1910.[235] And in Odessa only a tiny group of staff pharmacists (nine people) attended the

Odessa Pharmacy Society in 1911 to mourn the closing of their professional union.[236]

In 1910 and 1911, as earlier, fall-off in membership of staff pharmacists' organizations was due as much to complacency on the part of staff pharmacists as repression by the authorities. Further, when these unions and organizations did feel the brunt of repression, it was because of their subversive and questionable activity.

The Voronezh Society of Staff Pharmacists held its own in 1910, electing a new administrative board of five members and discussing subsidization of *Zhizn' farmatsevta*.[237] The Labor Bureau of the Kiev Union of Pharmacists also realized success during 1910. It was able to place twenty unemployed pharmacists, owners having become accustomed to turn to the bureau for staff.[238] However, late in the year, the union was threatened with closure after an official night raid "collected all documents and correspondence."[239]

Throughout 1911 *Zhizn' farmatsevta* made obligatory murmurs about the "worsening situation" of staff pharmacists and the "need for economic struggle."[240] Yet, reports from various cities did not substantiate the journal's claim that conditions in pharmacies were deteriorating. In fact, few examples of pharmacies with poor conditions were presented.[241] The journal's indignation frequently appeared strained. In one instance salaries were cut when the double shift was introduced.[242] In Poltava, conflict erupted in one pharmacy over night duty. The staff went on strike for three days; the owner satisfied their demands.[243] Elizavetpol' reported "absence of staff organization . . . comrade workers did not display great interest in general." This was not surprising when conditions in the three pharmacies in that city appeared good.[244]

The journal gave great publicity to conditions in Lodz, where owners allegedly tried to deprive staff of gains made in 1905. This precipitated a six-week strike in all ten Lodz pharmacies, strikes in seven other cities in Tsarist Poland, and one-day sympathy strikes Ukrainian cities. Although Lodz pharmacists "feverishly organized all pharmacies when the double shift was abolished,"[245] they ultimately went beyond attempts to restore appropriate work conditions and demanded extreme concessions–six-hour shifts, high wages, compulsory owner-sponsored insurance. The police threatened the strikers and the Okhrana ultimately arrested sixty-five. However, that oppressive body proposed a mixed commission from owners and staff to debate strikers' demands and arrive at a peaceful solution. Further, sixty strikers signed the Okhrana agreement, thereby "liquidating" the strike. Perhaps the strikers felt coerced. On the other hand, this might also have indicated lack of militancy on the part of rank-and-file pharmacists. Matters did not end entirely satisfactorily for the strikers. Pharmacy owners submitted four representatives to the mixed commission; the "policemeister" vetoed the four candidates representing staff.[246]

Militant leaders responded to apathy on the part of staff pharmacists by stepping up union organization in 1911. Early in the year there were seven unions of staff pharmacists and other types of staff organizations in sixteen cities. The chief unions were the Russian Pharmacy Society in Moscow, which had existed since the mid 1890s, with representatives Kotliarevskii and S. G. Kagan; the St. Petersburg Union, with representatives N. I. Levinshtein and Sh. Kuperman; the South-West Union of Staff Pharmacists, with representatives L. Kharzhelskaia and S. Lapitskaia; the Lodz Union of Staff Pharmacists; the Odessa Congress Delegation; the Turkestan Union of Staff Pharmacists; and the Voronezh Society of Staff Pharmacists. "Pharmacy Groups" existed in the cities of Vitebsk, Gomel, Ekaterinoslav, Kutais, Kazan, Kremenchug, Lugansk, Nikolaev, Nizhni Novgorod, Poltava, Samara, Stavropol', Saratov, Tiflis, Kherson, and Khar'kov.[247]

The South-West Union particularly focused on attracting "new members" in 1911. The union employed methods typical to union organizers. Its newly elected administrative board (*pravlenie*) included the woman pharmacist F. Lapitskaia as secretary.[248] The board divided members according to region; they were to be sent out to pharmacies "to propose to comrades not yet members of the union to join it."[249] The South-West Union instituted an elaborate admission procedure, which reflected that of revolutionary parties. For example, when Assistant Pharmacist D. Gol'dgor asked to be admitted, the board of the South-West Union "took into account his recent activity to improve the position of staff in Bernshtein's [pharmacy] and expressed itself in favor of accepting him into the union."[250] In Nizhni Novgorod, one Bunin proposed measures to "strengthen the circle"—a concert fund-raiser, registration to get an accurate count of members and dues, and lectures on chemistry and pharmacy.[251]

1912–1914

Officers of the St. Petersburg Union of Staff Pharmacists in 1912 and 1913 included Kh. Sh. Aluf, Iu. Kuperman, Ia. L. Kanevskii, Zalevskii, and Braido. A. S. Aluf, Iu. Kuperman, Ia. L. Kanevskii were elected "by closed ballot" at a general meeting in St. Petersburg of the Professional Society of Staff Pharmacists, 19 December 1912 to the administrative board.[252]

In 1914 a number of Kiev comrades moved to St. Petersburg and began publishing *Zhizn' farmatsevta* there.[253] Ia. L. Kanevskii served as editor of the St. Petersburg *Zhizn' farmatsevta* in 1914.[254]

Iu. A. Kuperman and S. Lapitskaia were prominent among Menshevik pharmacists in St. Petersburg from 1914 through 1918.[255] I. I. Levinshtein organized pharmacy education in 1921 and 1922.[256] Whether the two Levinshteins–N. I. and I. I.–and the two Kupermans–Sh. and Iu. A.–who figured in the radical movement were related or whether their given names were garbled in reports is not clear.

Some of these individuals–Kanevskii, Iu. A. Kuperman, and A. S. Aluf would be members of the Administrative Board of the St. Petersburg Union in 1917 and 1918. They entered into partnership with the Bolsheviks, at first on an uneasy basis.[257] But, ultimately, they reconciled themselves. Ia. F. Kanevskii, A. Aluf, and Iu. A. Kuperman still occupied high posts in the Soviet pharmacy organization in 1928.[258]

Nevertheless, despite all efforts of the radical socialist pharmacists, to all appearances, rank-and-file pharmacists were "little interested" in the St. Petersburg Union of Pharmacists between 1912 and 1914. Thus the union's activities became increasingly tamer. It polled staff pharmacists, "satisfying the needs of local pharmacists–bettering their conditions and filling their cultural needs," and verbally assaulted pharmacy owners.[259] In 1928, Aluf and his colleagues admitted that in 1914 they had had to "struggle against the petit bourgeois tendencies of staff pharmacists" who had three points of view regarding ownership of pharmacies. One group wanted to preserve the "pharmacy monopoly"–restrictions on establishing pharmacies. This group was largely composed of the "highest qualified and best paid staff pharmacists." Some of these, in turn, were managers of pharmacies, the rest were the "highest group of staff pharmacists." A second group of pharmacists, supporting *Zhizn' farmatsevta*, approved of "municipalization." And, finally, a "significant number" of staff pharmacists favored abolition of the pharmacy monopoly and free opening of pharmacies. However, Aluf claimed they did not openly oppose municipalization.[260]

Meanwhile, support for socialized public pharmacy and bias against private pharmacies was not confined to radical pharmacists. This mind-set was growing among government officials and the public in the first decades of the twentieth century.

15

The Turning Point, 1898-1916: The Government Promotes Public Pharmacy, the Pharmaceutical Industry, Pharmacy Education Reform

The decades between 1898 and 1916 were a turning point for Russia. As a consequence of the upheavals of 1905, the tsar, Nicholas II, granted his subjects a parliament. (Parliaments had functioned in Russia in the fifteenth and sixteenth centuries but died out in the seventeenth.) Radical elements dominated the first two sessions of the State Duma, as the lower chamber of the parliament was called. The tsar summarily shut down both the First and the Second Duma, as allowed by the Fundamental Laws of the empire. Thus, the First Duma lasted only a few months, from April 27 to July 9, 1906, and the Second, from February 20 to June 3, 1907. New elections, held under a revised electoral law, promulgated June 3, 1907, returned a preponderance of middle-of-the-road "Octobrists." It lasted its full five-year term. By 1908, although they still clashed, the State Duma and the government began to learn the art of compromise and cooperation.[1] The upper chamber of the parliament, the revamped State Council, was more obstreperous.[2] Nevertheless, between 1908 and 1916, there was the possibility that Russia would evolve into a constitutional monarchy. The economy took an upturn in 1908. Political and economic progress, along with educational advancement and a flourishing of literature, art, and music, augured brightly for Russia's future before World War I. The war cast a shadow over the empire but, as late as the end of 1916, there were indications that Russia would emerge with a strong economy.

The decades between 1898 and 1916 also were a turning point for pharmacy and the pharmaceutical industry. Antipathy toward the pharmacy monopoly, the restricted system of establishing pharmacies, and sympathy for socialized zemstvo pharmacy surged, reaching a crescendo in parliament by 1910. As noted in a previous chapter, concern for public welfare as well as order precipitated the Chief Medical Inspector in the Ministry of Internal Affairs to regulate hours and pay for St. Petersburg staff pharmacists. Additionally, in the period between 1898 and 1916, the Ministry of Internal Affairs tackled three major problems in Russian pharmacy: whether or not to maintain restrictions and franchises on establishing private pharmacies—the so-called pharmacy monopoly—and concomitantly, how to achieve a growth spurt in public pharmacies; how to make the Russian pharmaceutical industry more competitive; and how to improve lower pharmaceutical education.

The policies formulated for these problems, as that on the pharmacy labor issue, showed that individual Ministers of Internal Affairs stamped the policies to some extent but, also, that the ministers, particularly P. A. Stolypin, Minister of Internal Affairs from April 1906 to September 1911, were influenced by public opinion, both within and outside the parliament, both reformist and radical. The government policies also emphasized the three divergent economic trends and philosophies that jostled each other in late imperial Russia: state capitalism, free market principles, and socialism.

And, although the Ministers of Internal Affairs flirted with free trade, ultimately they opted for continued government control and more socialism. Ministers tinkered with the pharmacy monopoly but continued to restrict private pharmacies. Simultaneously they continued to treat drug stores (*aptekarskie magaziny*) permissively. This might have indicated greater acceptance of free trade. However, the Ministry of Internal Affairs also began to promote socialized zemstvo and municipal pharmacies, at the expense of privately owned pharmacies. With regard to the pharmaceutical industry, the Ministry of Internal Affairs (probably under the aegis of Stolypin himself) devised a scheme to boost production but nevertheless maintained tight control over the industry. As for pharmaceutical education, lack of funds drove the ministry to devolve responsibility for reform of lower pharmacy education to the pharmacy corporation while preserving overall government supervision.

These contradictory policies weakened private pharmacy, they did not allow the pharmaceutical industry to flourish, and they did not solve the problems in pharmacy education. On the contrary, they accentuated big government. They revealed a growing attraction to socialism among government officials, intellectuals, and the general public as well as radical pharmacists. Ironically, the government's policies also turned pharmacist-reformers to the left. Frustrated in their attempts to achieve a complete overhaul of pharmacy education, pharmacist reformers increasingly moved away from the existing political and economic system. Some would join hard-core radicals in embracing the Bolsheviks at the end of 1917. The decades between 1898 to 1916, thus, paved the way to 1917.

Growing Support for Public, Socialized Pharmacy

In 1898 a "sensational rumor" began circulating that the Ministry of Internal Affairs was considering abolishing the "pharmacy monopoly." It was alleged that, according to the new Pharmacy Statute that the ministry was formulating, "private persons are deprived of the right to own pharmacies but those having received the degree Provizor can open pharmacies [presumably as managers rather than owners] unhindered without need to acquire special privileges." Private persons were to be allowed to own warehouses but these were to be managed by Provizors.[3] During the next decades, the trend toward free trade–abolishing restrictions on establishing pharmacies–continued to jockey with the trend toward socialized pharmacy–strengthening public pharmacy and management of pharmacies by the entire pharmacy corporation. And the synthesis of these seemingly contradictory principles, as sketched above, continued to evolve.

In the early twentieth century, the Ministry of Internal Affairs very obviously began to encourage public pharmacy. Upon his accession to the ministry in April 1902, V. K. Pleve dispatched a circular to governors stressing the need to revise the Pharmacy Statute.[4] The statute drafted by the ministry in 1904 gave municipal public institutions and zemstvos predominance over private individuals and medical and philanthropic societies in establishing new pharmacies. The statute also simplified free dispensing for zemstvos; henceforth there were to be no more embarrassing questions about poverty. Further, the ministry's draft statute labeled zemstvo pharmacies "second tier," analogous to village pharmacies, and lowered the number of inhabitants required for their establishment. The new population figures were to be reviewed after five years.[5] To compensate pharmacists for possible increased competition from public pharmacies, the draft Pharmacy Statute of 1904 emphasized that Provizors were to manage the new, more freely established public pharmacies.[6]

Perhaps the initial impetus for this policy was to increase pharmacies in rural areas. However, the ministry's support for public pharmacy grew stronger in response to growing demands for abolition of the pharmacy monopoly and parallel support for public pharmacy. In March 1906, P. N. Durnovo, Minister of Internal Affairs, curtly informed the St. Petersburg City Duma that he could not sanction their request to establish fourteen new pharmacies because existing legislation did not give preference to public institutions over private.[7] This policy was to change with Durnovo's replacement by Stolypin the following month.

Russia's first modern parliament, the First State Duma, existed only a few months in the spring of 1906. The Second State Duma, which met in the spring of 1907, vigorously pushed for abolishing restrictions on establishing pharmacies. The result, the Social Democratic *Farmatsevticheskii trud* contended, was that the "Medical Council of the Ministry of Internal Affairs again . . . reviewed the Pharmacy Statute" and "proposed to abolish the pharmacy monopoly. Owners of private pharmacies . . . have prepared a counter project."[8] Article 72 of the new statute, it was claimed, proposed a radical departure from the existing pharmacy system—"Institution of pharmacies with free dispensing of medicines . . . to all who wish, everywhere, and in unlimited number." Establishing a pharmacy was to require only "a declaration of intent to the local inspector for the pharmacy sector."[9] *Farmatsevticheskii trud* predicted that the draft of the new Pharmacy Statute would "probably be introduced into the State Duma through the Octobrist fraction."[10]

This reform fell by the wayside when the Second Duma was disbanded in June 1907. But, the Medical Council moved free trade forward when it proposed, in 1907, that twenty-four new pharmacies be opened in the city of St. Petersburg without soliciting agreement from owners of existing pharmacies, as was the practice.[11]

Then, in 1908, the pendulum swung back in favor of socialized pharmacy. In May of that year, thirty-four members of the State Duma, led by M. K. Safonov, introduced a bill to abolish the pharmacy monopoly. This bill proposed that private individuals and public institutions—zemstvos and cities—be allowed to establish pharmacies without receiving approval from the Ministry of Internal Affairs or nearby owners of pharmacies. Henceforth, establishing a pharmacy would require only a statement of intent to the provincial medical administration and certification by the local physician—district, zemstvo, or city—that all medicines and accoutrements were in order. The bill went to a Duma commission in May 1909. The commission made its report in November 1909.

Ostensibly, the Safonov bill purported to establish free trade and competition. In fact, the accompanying report attacked the concept of privately owned pharmacies and endorsed the principle of socialized pharmacy. The report emphasized pharmacy owners' extraordinary profits and the difficulty poor people faced in acquiring affordable medicines because the Pharmacy Tax mandated prices. Concomitantly, the report sympathetically portrayed zemstvos and municipal bodies as truly concerned about public health and committed to providing the public with medicines at a cheap price, predicting that "only with the possibility of free opening of pharmacies by public, municipal and zemstvo institutions" would public welfare be served.[12]

Even so, logically the Safonov bill should have furthered free trade. Indeed, the Duma proposal and the impending unveiling of the new government Pharmacy Statute did unleash a torrent of media hostility against the pharmacy monopoly. However, most newspapers focused less on the benefits of free trade and competition and more on the greed and "exploitation" of proprietors of private pharmacies.[13]

The Pirogov Medical Congress of 1910 debated all sides of the issue, that is, whether pharmacies should be private, based on a concession system, or municipal, with free dispensing, and whether drug stores should should be run on the same lines as pharmacies. Still, some delegates warned that the *iavochnyi* system—free trade and competition—was not a "panacea" for Russian pharmacy. Further, other delegates advocated that pharmacists and only pharmacists open and manage pharmacies but be restricted from selling them, a sort of state socialism.[14]

More significant, calls for strengthening public—zemstvo and municipal—pharmacy escalated. Several newspapers, such as the *Odesskii listok*, called for radical restructuring of pharmacy and "municipalization" of pharmacies.[15] Opponents of the pharmacy monopoly in the State Council, the parliament's upper chamber, contended that "pharmacy owners held the public in thralldom" and equated "freeing the people from pharmacy owners" to "freeing the serfs."[16]

Cooperatives and municipalities exhibited a flurry of interest in establishing pharmacies during 1910 and 1911. The Yalta Medical Society planned a cooperative pharmacy, Chita was establishing a municipal pharmacy "to save money," the city of Reval planned to open a normal pharmacy (*normal'naia apteka*), and the nationalistic Society of Michael the Archangel was accumulating money to open a "Russian" pharmacy in St. Petersburg.[17] Early in 1911 a Provizor planning to open a municipal pharmacy in Omsk submitted a lavish budget request of almost 20,000 rubles to the city council to outfit the pharmacy. Although he estimated the annual turnover of 26,000 rubles would amply return the investment, nevertheless his request illustrated the high priority on public pharmacies.[18]

Local authorities sided more and more frequently with public pharmacies in their clashes with private pharmacies. For example, in 1910, the Medical Department in the Ukrainian province of Chernigov forwarded a petition from the city administration of Novgorodsk to permit establishment of a city pharmacy. The Novgorodsk city council considered a municipal pharmacy important for the poor and noted that there were also two *gimnazii*, one male, one female, that could benefit. The petition displayed not only zeal to promote public pharmacy but disapproval of drug stores and a dash of anti-Semitism. It noted that because of lack of pharmacies, three drug stores had sprouted in Novgorodsk; their owners, as well as the owner of the existing normal pharmacy, were Jewish. The Jewish pharmacy owner Korshak protested the establishment of a city pharmacy, claiming that while the zemstvo dispensed free medicine it did so only to the poor. Permitting the city pharmacy to dispense medicine free to the seminary, jail, and railroad station would impact his pharmacy negatively. But, the provincial medical department defended the city pharmacy, alleging that Korshak had dispensed 4,822 prescriptions in 1908 and 5,410 in 1909. Provincial authorities maintained Korshak was only thinking of his own interests and not that of the general public in opposing socialized public pharmacy.[19]

In 1911, Provizor Feofil Aleksandrovich Strochinskii, of Yaroslavl' province, dispatched a hand-penned letter to the Medical Department complaining about operations in the district zemstvo hospital pharmacy. The Provizor asserted that the zemstvo hospital gave free medicine not only to sick-poor certified by the police but to students and to sick prisoners in the local jail. As in the above case, the Yaroslavl' governor, vice governor, and medical inspector supported the zemstvo. In this case the Chief Medical Inspector sympathized with the owner of the private pharmacy. In 1912 he asked the provincial authorities to "confine the zemstvo pharmacy to the lawful limits of free dispensing."[20]

But in Poltava, in early 1911, the Senate dismissed the complaint of one Provizor Martynov (proprietor of a private pharmacy) and allowed the city executive council to establish a *fifth* municipal pharmacy.[21]

Government (more specifically, Ministry of Internal Affairs) policy with regard to the pharmacy monopoly and the related issue of public versus private pharmacy was impacted by Duma and public opinion on these matters and also by the relationship between the Minister of Internal Affairs and the Duma.

The Minister of Internal Affairs from 1906 to 1911, Peter Arkad'evich Stolypin, had tried to coopt "public" figures into his government and enjoyed fairly good relations with the Third Duma. However, he never considered it an equal partner and several times used the lower chamber of the parliament as a weapon in his power struggle with his enemies in the upper chamber, the State Council, and his opponents at court. Such was the case in the "Naval General Staff Crisis" of 1909. The most egregious example of Stolypin's "top-down" management style occurred in the spring of 1911 when he forced the tsar to prorogue the Duma for three days, enabling passage of a bill instituting zemstvos in six southwestern provinces. This undercut the State Council, which had blocked the measure.[22]

In 1910, Chief Medical Inspector L. N. Malinovskii proposed to the Medical Council of the Ministry of Internal Affairs that population norms for establishing pharmacies be lowered and that drug stores have wider rights to sell "dosed," or factory-prepared, medicines. Despite the fact that the Medical Council disagreed, Malinovskii's action signaled sentiment within the Ministry of Internal Affairs for relaxing the pharmacy monopoly in favor of free trade.[23]

However, in May 1911, a plenary session of the Duma discussed a revised version of the 1909 Safonov bill. The new bill displayed strong bias against private pharmacies and strong support for public pharmacy. Introduced March 31, the 1911 bill reiterated that the pharmacy monopoly be abolished, that pharmacies be permitted to be freely established, but now this right was accorded *only* to public institutions. The clause on private individuals in the 1909 bill had been eliminated. Safonov's report accompanying the 1911 bill explained how the shift in emphasis from encouraging free trade to promoting socialized pharmacy had occurred. Owners of private pharmacies amassed huge profits at the expense of the public. Public pharmacies on the other hand contributed to the public welfare. In 1906 "the average price of a prescription in Siberia, where there were no public pharmacies, was 58 kopeks, in all of European Russia—49, and in Vologda province, where the majority of pharmacies had been transferred by purchase to zemstvo hands–9 kopeks." Drug stores also had attempted to sell factory-prepared medicines to the public at cheap prices, but they still were enfettered by a list of hundreds of items they could not purvey even though the government and Cassation Department of the Senate had long debated widening their trading rights. Meanwhile the public suffered. The "most sensible and simplest only way out of this undesirable situation was to publish a law" granting public institutions the right to "freely open pharmacies." Therefore, the 1911 Duma pharmacy bill proposed that henceforth, zemstvos and cities were to be allowed to establish normal pharmacies without adhering to articles 353 to 356 of the Medical Statute, that is, without observing population or distance norms and without receiving approval from local pharmacy owners or preliminary sanction from central or local medical and governmental authorities. To establish the pharmacy the zemstvo or municipal duma needed only to make a resolution on this matter, either in commission or in plenary session, and announce the resolution to the local medical administration within a month's time.[24]

The Duma pharmacy bills (or at least Safonov and his thirty-three colleagues, including five priests, who initiated the bills) took a strong stand on public pharmacy. Additionally, the Duma's behavior in conjunction with the 1911 pharmacy bill made a strong statement on the parliament's right to make policy. The bill emerged out of Duma commission and was not submitted to relevant departments of the Ministry of Internal Affairs for prior discussion or comment, as was the custom.[25] Stolypin's and his fellow ministers' response to the Duma pharmacy bills, in turn, indicated that although the parliament was not yet an equal partner with the government, it was a force with which the government had to reckon.

The Ministry of Internal Affairs had been committed for some years to boosting public pharmacy. On the other hand, Stolypin, in particular, did not approve of complete abolition of the pharmacy monopoly or giving carte blanche to zemstvos and cities in establishing pharmacies. Thus, to balance the Duma bill and retain some norms for establishing pharmacies, the Ministry of Internal Affairs incorporated more liberal ideas into its version of the new Pharmacy Statute that was still being drafted. The ministerial version of the statute, in the making for over a decade, now included revised norms for establishing pharmacies and allowed zemstvos and cities to organize pharmacies *iavochnym poriadkom,* that is, without prior permission from medical authorities. However, the caveat was that the public bodies could do this only in areas where no private pharmacies existed.[26]

The slightly left-of-center Kadet (Constitutional Democratic) paper *Rech'* commented shrewdly that "under pressure of public opinion and in view of the negative attitude of the State Duma toward the pharmacy monopoly, the Ministry of Internal Affairs has decided, simultaneously with working out a new Pharmacy Statute, to introduce some changes in the currently existing rule about the order of granting privileges for pharmacies. The Ministry of Internal Affairs has decided to give preference to zemstvos and cities."[27]

Middle-of-the-road *Farmatsevticheskii zhurnal* noted that although the pharmacy monopoly was to be retained, the Minister of Internal Affairs had transferred to the Senate a proposal from the Chief Medical Inspector for changing some portions of the statutes of "1873, 1903, and 1906," which would give preference to zemstvos and cities to establish pharmacies where there were no privately owned pharmacies. The journal's response was low-keyed. But owners of private pharmacies were nervous. In nearly every issue during 1910 and 1911 the journal discussed the new statute, querying whether "zemstvos would have the means" to establish pharmacies,[28] emphasizing the link between personal ownership and quality dispensing, and pointing out that "Not one country of Western Europe, America, or Australia has a system of municipalized pharmacy."[29]

According to the Social Democratic pharmacy journal *Zhizn' farmatsevta*, Stolypin's "explanatory notes" on the proposal, sent to the departments in his ministry in 1910, acknowledged that he considered unrestricted establishment of pharmacies "correct in principle." However, he did not believe it possible to abolish the concession system at once because it might endanger public health. Thus, his proposal "decisively granted" to city and zemstvos wider rights to establish pharmacies with right of full sale and free dispensing of medicine."[30] In giving permission to open pharmacies, "public establishments took precedence before others . . . after them pharmacists . . . then private social organizations."[31] There were to be two grades of pharmacies—those of the first and those of the second rank.[32] Population figures were still to be the main determinant for establishing pharmacies but more elasticity was allowed.[33] Leasing of pharmacies was open to all who wished except those who had been deprived of their rights by a court. In order to lessen speculation, zemstvos and cities, granted easier terms in establishing pharmacies, were forbidden to sell or give them in lease for a period of five years.[34] In other words, while allowing zemstvos and cities more leeway, Stolypin's proposal still included norms and government approval for opening pharmacies and stipulated that drug stores were to be managed by pharmacists.[35]

The ministerial bill was submitted to the State Council. While waiting for the upper chamber of the parliament's decision, the Ministry of Internal Affairs issued a circular to governors and city heads, slightly modifying the more lenient norms for public pharmacies.[36]

The State Council made a few changes in the Duma bill,[37] debated it during 1911,[38] and finally passed it. Signed by Chair of the State Council, M. Akimov, and duly published by the Governing Senate February 12, 1912, the new Law of February 12, 1912, permitted zemstvo and city executive bodies to establish and maintain pharmacies "without observing the rules for opening them as listed in articles 353 to 356 of the Medical Statute, Code of Laws, XVIII, edition 1905." Henceforth, zemstvos and cities could establish pharmacies merely by passing a resolution at a plenary meeting. Zemstvos and cities were compelled only to report the opening of their pharmacy to the local medical inspector within a month. The pharmacies established by the zemstvo or city duma could not be sold, given in lease or in any other way transferred to other ownership or use.[39] The Law of February 12, 1912, thus permitted public bodies to establish pharmacies under more lenient rules than owners of private pharmacies. Equally interesting, it confirmed that the State Council was as much a maverick as it had been during Stolypin's administration.

The executive "branch" of the government included individuals as committed to public pharmacy as the legislature. The Law of February 12 caused a great deal of confusion on the part of local officials and, initially, the central authorities rigidly enforced its provisions. Local authorities from Kursk, Kazan, Minsk, and Tver bombarded the Chief Medical Inspector for clarification on whether the zemstvo could choose any location it wished for new pharmacies, whether zemstvos could establish an unlimited number of pharmacies, whether zemstvos must first receive approval of the local authorities or only inform them after the fact, and so on. In reply to a test case raised in 1912 by one Provizor Margolin, the Chief Medical Inspector assured local authorities that the zemstvo could establish a pharmacy anywhere it deemed convenient—even near the private pharmacy of Provizor Margolin. The Chief Medical Inspector also informed mayors and governors that henceforth only two criteria were necessary to establish zemstvo and city pharmacies: one, a resolution by the zemstvo assembly or city duma and two, a report about the pharmacy not more than one month later to the local medical inspector.[40] Despite the explanations, queries continued from Tomsk and the Kuban as to whether population norms still had to be considered and about the status of private pharmacies in the region[41] and in June 1913 the governor of Orenburg asked the Chief Medical Inspector as to whether the Law of February 12 applied to Cossack settlements.[42]

In time, Stolypin's successors in the Ministry of Internal Affairs—he had been assassinated in September 1911—attempted to modify the Law of February 12, 1912. In its petition to the Senate for clarification of the law, the ministry recommended, for example, that zemstvos and city dumas be allowed to establish only normal pharmacies under the new provisions, as this type of pharmacy offered the best quality dispensing. Further, the ministry suggested that local authorities have some say so over the establishment of public pharmacies in order to prevent "harmful competition" and to ensure that public pharmacies were adequately staffed.[43]

The Law of February 12 allowing public bodies to establish pharmacies under more lenient conditions than private individuals immediately affected some private pharmacy owners adversely. In March 1912, a Provizor from Penza frantically wrote the Chief Medical Inspector. His letter revealed hostile tactics on the part of the local zemstvo and highlighted local authorities' support for public pharmacies.

> . . . for several months I have been subject to anguish and the risk of losing my small position—the difficult work of my twenty-year pharmaceutical practice. The matter is the following. This autumn the Chembarskoe district zemstvo assembly decided to open a second pharmacy with right of unrestricted dispensing in the city, according to the rules of 1912. They tried to find a building for the pharmacy and decided that there was none better than the premises of my pharmacy; their reasoning was that the illiterate [*bezgramotnyi*] townspeople already knew about the place. The zemstvo proposed a price to the owner of the building. Ignoring the price in our contract, the owner proposed that I pay a higher price or he would sell the building to the zemstvo. . . . I would have been happy had the zemstvo not decided to open a second new pharmacy in this small district town where there is no industry for 6,000 inhabitants. . . .
>
> I complained to the medical inspector and governor. They replied that the zemstvo could now do all this according to the new law of February 12, 1912. I then turned to a lawyer who assured me that the zemstvo could not oust me from my premises because of the sense of my contract . . . and I had a notary write the zemstvo. . . .
>
> To clarify my position, I note that my landlord had one yard in which there was a two-story stone building . . . I occupy the lower floor of this building and according to our contract the landlord cannot lease the next building to anyone trading in pharmaceutical wares. Notwithstanding this, the zemstvo proposed that they would buy the building, where I am located, and get a lease on the second building. On the lower floor they would establish a second zemstvo normal pharmacy—2 *sazhens* from mine—and, in five years, when my contract had expired, they would move into my premises. The zemstvo knows that as an organized society they are stronger than me . . . that by the law of February 12, 1912, they have the right to establish a private pharmacy anywhere . . .[44]

Disregarding these cries for help, the Chief Medical Inspector reiterated to the Penza governor that according to the Circular of 1912 the zemstvo could choose any place it wished to establish its pharmacy. However, in May 1913, the Chief Medical Inspector advised that if the zemstvo's choice of a location was harmful to a private pharmacy owner the governor ought to protest the zemstvo resolution. Nevertheless, the Chief Medical Inspector admitted that the Senate had still not issued a ruling on this or other questions relating to the 1912 regulation.[45]

In May 1913, a Pharmacy Congress in St. Petersburg, composed of Provizors and Masters of Pharmacy, claimed that during the year and a half since the law was promulgated "city and zemstvo pharmacies posed serious competition to private pharmacies." Many were opened right next door. For example, in Kutais where there were five private pharmacies, the city had opened two public pharmacies and was opening another three across the street from the private pharmacies.[46]

Early in 1914, "Owner Stochik," proprietor of a pharmacy in the city of Vladimir, Vladimir province, sent a telegram to the Minister of Internal Affairs himself, which bespoke panic: "The City Duma is opening a pharmacy alongside mine / The dirty path [*zagazhivaia put'*] to it threatens to destroy me / I humbly ask your intercession, Excellency."[47] The city administration stubbornly insisted upon its "rights" although the provincial administration—the governor and medical inspector—sided with the pharmacy owner. In June 26, 1914, the vice governor of Vladimir informed the Chief Medical Inspector that "the city pharmacy, instituted according to the Law of February 12, 1912, not only has not been opened but it has not yet begun to be built. In the city of Vladimir at the present time there are three private normal pharmacies, of which two are in the center of the city, one on Bol'shaia, the other on upper Georgievskaia Street . . . the third at the end of the city on 'Studenaia gora' Street." The vice governor acknowledged the pharmacies were close to each other, admitted that if the city council opened its pharmacy in the building which it owned on Bol'shaia Street, not far from the pharmacy owned by Stochik on George Street, it would "undoubtedly constitute competition for Stochik," and concluded that "Although the population at the borders of the city are not deprived of the possibility of receiving timely medical help, all the same I find that building a municipal or any other pharmacy would be more desirable in one of the borders of the city but, apparently, in this case the City Administration does not agree."[48]

Conservative pharmacy societies lobbied against the more lenient conditions permitted zemstvo pharmacies according to the Law of February 12, 1912. In January 1912, "even before the Law of February 12 received imperial sanction," a deputation from the St. Petersburg Pharmacy Society complained to "Prime-Minister" Kokovtsov that it would destroy the lawful property rights of pharmacy owners. According to Edmund Ksaverevich Khrzhanovskii, pharmacy delegate to the Medical Council of the Ministry of Internal Affairs and one of the deputation, Kokovtsov stated the government "had not even considered who would suffer following the publication of the law and that the request to annul the law was premature. If," however, "it appeared that the law violated the property rights of pharmacy owners and if a concrete proposal for compensating them were developed, they could count on the support of the Chairman of the Council of Ministers" (himself). But, this Minister of Finance and protector of balanced budgets sternly warned the deputation that they could not expect treasury money for reimbursing pharmacy owners but must look to zemstvo and city coffers for reimbursement.[49]

Progressive St. Petersburg pharmacists, on the contrary, welcomed the shift to public pharmacy. Late in 1912, a group of these pharmacists–most of whom not owners of pharmacies themselves–formed a "National Committee" within the St. Petersburg Pharmacy Society. The committee included O. R. Brashe, Master of Pharmacy and delegate to the Fourth State Duma, E. K. Khrzhanovskii, Alexander Il'yich Abramson, and Professor A. S. Ginzberg. The committee endorsed the principle of buying out private pharmacies (*samovykup*), tendered by radical pharmacists in 1906. The 1912 proposal for buying out private pharmacies called for treasury or bank buy-outs, with subsequent transfer of private pharmacies to the government–central, zemstvos, or municipal dumas.[50] The "National Committee" presented their proposal to a Congress of Pharmacists, which it convened in May 1913.

The sponsors of buying out private pharmacies insisted that their plan was similar to a procedure underway in Sweden.[51] S. Zhitomirskii, from the Don Pharmacy Society, on the other hand, pointed out that the Swedish procedure really did involve *samovykup,* or self-purchase, since a corporation of pharmacists bought up pharmacies, whereas in Russia the purchasing was to be done mainly through banks.[52]

However, buying out private pharmacies met a lot of resistance from pharmacists. The editors of *Farmatsevticheskii zhurnal* termed the buy-out concept a necessary evil, a "marriage of convenience" rather than a "marriage of love," a way out of the "difficult crisis through which Russian pharmacy practice was living." Whereas the liberal paper *Rech'* promoted municipalization, insisting that "all cultivated countries of Europe" were moving in this direction," *Farmatsevticheskii zhurnal* regarded the *iavochnyi* system as "anarchism" and claimed that experience with municipalization as embodied in the Law of February 12, 1912, was "deplorable." Criticizing the "zigzags" of government legislation regarding private pharmacy, the journal reminded readers how much buying out private pharmacies would cost. In Sweden there were only 193 pharmacies, in Russia there were 4,000; buying them out, even at three-fourths of their value, would require perhaps 100 million rubles, and for this pharmacists would need to float 10 million rubles' worth of stocks.[53]

Provincial pharmacists were more conservative than the progressive pharmacists in the capital. They opposed the National Committee and their plans for buying out private pharmacies, berating the National Committee for not keeping them informed or getting their input on the issue.[54] The majority of delegates to the May 1913, Pharmacy Congress spoke against the Law of February 12. Most "Russian" pharmacists and pharmacy owners came from the non-Russian minorities of the empire. One delegate spoke to this issue when he asserted that the February 12 law had been passed by a "nationalistic" Duma to thwart non-Russians (*inorodtsy*) who owned "85 percent of pharmacies." The congress opined that small pharmacies were most threatened by the Law of February 12. Pharmacists must lobby and inform legislators about pharmacy practice. They must convene another congress of provincial pharmacy owners. The dissenting majority firmly rejected buying out private pharmacies, terming it an "extreme measure," "suicide for pharmacies," "not a serious solution to loss of property rights," and "premature." "The most effective compensation would be to preserve the status quo for 20 years . . . pharmacies could be opened only where there was extreme need, that is where there were no pharmacies and in villages of 10,000." A majority of the congress resolved that "municipal" pharmacies did not answer the interests of the populace nor the correctly understood mandate of zemstvos and cities" and that it was "necessary to abolish the Law of February 12, 1912." In the meantime they called upon zemstvos and cities to "cease using rights given them" by this law.[55]

Thus, it was clear that there was a gulf between the rank and file, who, as owners or would-be owners of pharmacies, favored retention of private property and resisted competition and progressive St. Petersburg pharmacists, who advocated competition and, further, state-supported socialized pharmacy.

But, whether or not pharmacy owners and the rank and file liked it, a climate for state-supported, socialized pharmacy was growing in late imperial Russia. In 1913, Boris Puzis, sympathizer with staff pharmacists against owners in 1905, showed how the concept of abolishing the pharmacy monopoly could metamorphose into state-subsidized pharmacy. Puzis emphasized that competition resulted in "cheaper," "more accurate wares." However, private pharmacy owners faced a dilemma, for it was difficult for them to adopt the tradesman's practice of selling more cheaply. *Samo-*

vykup, buying out private pharmacies, therefore, was a way out of the dilemma—a recourse against competition from drug stores and municipal pharmacies, which discounted prices on medicines from 20 to 30 percent. Puzis supported complete abolition of the pharmacy monopoly but he approved adequate reimbursement for pharmacy owners.[56]

Fortunately for owners of private pharmacies the wheels of the Russian government ground slowly. The new rule was still in the process of being implemented in 1916 and a new Pharmacy Statute, incorporating the regulations on private pharmacies, was introduced into the Duma only late in 1915.

However, as we shall see, World War I accelerated the public movement toward state-supported socialized pharmacy and in 1915, the Minister of Internal Affairs actually proposed nationalizing pharmacies. In 1916, Dr. M. Ia. Kapustin, authority on zemstvo medicine, chair of a special committee in the Medical Council drafting an instruction on establishing private pharmacies, emphasized that they could be established only with government permission whereas public pharmacies could be established *iavochnym*—without permission.[57]

Thus, the seeds of the socialized pharmacy system, established after the Bolshevik Revolution in 1917, were sown in the late imperial period.

The Pharmaceutical Industry

The second major issue confronting Russian pharmacy was advancement of the pharmaceutical industry. This issue was crucial in and of itself. Additionally, growth of factory-prepared medicines was closely connected with the issues of more liberal establishment of pharmacies, promoting socialized pharmacy, and the role and destiny of drug stores.

After promoting the native pharmaceutical industry in its embryonic stages, the government increasingly restricted the industry as the nineteenth century wore on. In the first decade of the twentieth century, however, the government again began to take active interest in developing and expanding the pharmaceutical industry. Peter Arkad'vich Stolypin made a dramatic effort to boost the industry in 1911, the last year of his administration as Minister of the Council of Ministers.

As noted, Stolypin was embroiled in political turmoil during that year. He had alienated former centrist supporters in the Duma and, it was rumored, the tsar himself in the "Zemstvo Crisis."[58] The clumsy stubbornness Stolypin exhibited in this embroglio long has prompted speculation that exhaustion and stress caused his considerable political skills, indeed his very judgment, to atrophy by 1911. His policies in the sphere of pharmacy give some credence to that interpretation. His 1910 bill giving zemstvos and cities precedence over individuals and private groups in establishing pharmacies where none existed distressed pharmacists but still revealed political finesse for it held off total abolition of the "pharmacy monopoly." However, the Ministry of Internal Affairs' circular to governors and city heads of February 28, 1911, number 363, was cavalier toward foreign pharmaceutical firms and evinced a certain desperation.

There is little doubt that Stolypin was behind the policy. The February circular emanated from the Chief Medical Inspector but this individual was subordinate to Stolypin; the circular was signed "for the Minister of Internal Affairs, Assistant Minister Senator Kryzhanovskii";[59] and correspondence on the matter was addressed to two successive Assistant Ministers of Internal Affairs and, in one case, to Stolypin himself.[60]

The Circular of February 28, 1911, no. 363, originally allowed "all normal pharmacies to prepare and sell all 'preparations' identical to those which the Medical Council allowed to be imported from abroad if on the label was stated the firm and place of production of the substance."[61] Perhaps Circular no. 363 and another Ministry of Internal Affairs circular issued at virtually the same time, which encouraged normal pharmacies to mass-produce medicines, were intended to appease pharmacists, angry at the minister's recent support for public pharmacies. However, subsequent correspondence also referred to factories in mass-producing medicaments and, in fact, pharmaceutical factories stood to gain more than pharmacies from Circular no. 363. Pharmacists themselves observed that pharmacies could not duplicate the production of "colossal American firms like Parke, Davis and Company."[62]

Stolypin's circular was based on the fact that only German firms took out pharmaceutical patents. French firms considered patenting medicine "immoral" as this made exclusive remedies that could help humanity; therefore they relied on brand names.[63] Stolypin's circular permitted Russian enterprises to produce and sell "generic" equivalents of foreign brand name medicines. This testified to Russian competency but enraged foreign producers, French firms in particular. As a result, a special committee was formed under the chairmanship of Chief Medical Inspector Malinovskii, which included advisory member of the Medical Council, S. A. Przhibytek, a delegate from the Ministry of Foreign Affairs, and K. I. Kresling from the St. Petersburg Pharmacy Society.[64]

The Medical Council agreed in the main with Stolypin's circular, but, in a meeting of June 3, 1911, tried to make it more palatable to foreign firms (and prevent foreign counterfeits) by stipulating, first, that the label of the Russian-made product "must be entirely different in form, color and script" from the label of the foreign substance; second, that "above the name of the product must be stated the words 'prepared according to the composition and methods of . . .'"; third, that "all fundamental parts of the label, i.e., the name of the substance, firm, and place of preparation must be in the Russian language"; and, finally, that although the Russian product might be known under the identical name as the foreign product, there must be stated on the label "Russian preparation."[65]

Minister of Finance V. N. Kokovtsov,[66] the ministers of Foreign Affairs[67] and Trade and Industry[68] agreed with the legality of the Ministry of Internal Affairs Circular no. 363. Minister of Justice Shcheglovitov adjudged that making products identical with those foreign products allowed to be imported into Russia was legal and even use of identical names was legal, if these were not registered trade names or marks. However, Shcheglovitov was the only official to emphasize that use of foreign trademarks by Russian pharmaceutical manufacturers violated agreements between Russia and a number of Western European states as well as several foreign conventions.[69]

The amendments to Circular no. 363 did not satisfy foreign firms. Chief Medical Inspector Leonid Nikolaevich Malinovskii continued to defend the circular after Stolypin's assassination in early September 1911,[70] justifying it, for example, in a lengthy report to the Governing Senate, in December 1912.[71] Nevertheless, both in the spring of 1911 and late in 1913, Paul Lefort of the Union des Fabricants pour la Protection Internationale de la Proprieté Industrielle and Artistique fired off complaints to the "Vice-Minister of Internal Affairs" emphasizing that Ministry of Internal Affairs Circular no. 363 violated copyright laws, harmed French industrialists and the Russian consumer, and discredited the Russian pharmaceutical corporation.[72]

In any case, expropriation of foreign brand names was not the most appropriate therapy for what ailed the Russian pharmaceutical industry. Much more constructive would have been freeing Russian enterprises from government domination, an idea bandied about, but not implemented, in the years before World War I. At the end of 1910 and the spring of 1911, a subcommittee formed in the Medical Council under the chairmanship of B. A. Efron, and including assistant Medical Inspector I. N. Bulatov, representatives of the chemical and pharmaceutical industry, and professors such as N. Fedot'ev of the St. Petersburg Polytechnical Institute, proposed that the new Russian Pharmacy Statute give pharmaceutical factories greater leeway, such as being allowed to produce all preparations without asking specific permission from the Medical Council.[73] The impending pharmacy statute did propose that "all permitted to open pharmacies be permitted to open pharmaceutical factories and laboratories." However, as was its wont, the Medical Council and Ministry of Internal Affairs enfettered this provision with another stipulating that the factories "must be under the management of pharmacists, not lower than Provizor, who had spent not less than two years in pharmacies of the first rank."[74]

Further, in practice, the pharmaceutical industry continued to be hidebound, and foreign manufacturers continued to receive preference. In 1913 pharmacists asserted that, despite a Senate ruling which declared that importation of foreign medicines harmed the Russian pharmaceutical industry,[75] the Medical Council liberally allowed importation of foreign patent nostrums because duties on these items filled treasury coffers. Not only did this hurt the pharmaceutical industry but, the entrepreneurs alleged, several foreign products were sold at a higher prices than their Russian-made equivalents, thus penalizing consumers. For example, a 70-capsule box of "Alkola," composed of bromide natron, milk, and sugar, cost 1 ruble 82 kopeks to produce–counting the box; the foreign version sold for 10 rubles. A similar example was to be found in "Moto." *Farmatsevticheskii zhurnal* railed that "The poor were being exploited thanks to prohibitions on production of these items in Russia. . . . We should allow the young Russian pharmaceutical industry to make these items and abolish monopoly and privilege of foreign medicinal substances in our market."[76] In 1915, pharmacists still asserted that the Medical Council's regulations on patent medicines allowed foreign products to circulate more freely than Russian ones. Chief Medical Inspector Malinovskii, serving as chair of the wartime Interdepartmental Committee on the Needs of the Pharmaceutical Industry, acknowledged that Russian patent medicines were at a disadvantage. Foreign "secret" medicines had only to prove they did not contain harmful or poisonous ingredients in order to be imported; on the other hand Russians were forced to prove that their "secret" preparations were "necessary."[77]

As for making tariffs more favorable to the domestic pharmaceutical industry, during World War I, a number of key representatives of the Russian pharmaceutical industry persistently urged the government to revise tariffs.[78] Nevertheless, by 1916 this still had not been done and Provizor D. Ia. Blumental' denounced the government for stifling the growth of Russia's pharmaceutical industry: "The organs which were to develop the pharmaceutical industry have paralyzed initiative. The government publishes circulars forbidding mass production of medicine in pharmacy labs but permits importation into Russia of low-priced foreign prepared substances."[79]

Pharmacy Education

The third major problem confronting pharmacy, that of modernizing lower pharmacy education, was inextricably linked with the operation of pharmacies and advancement of the pharmaceutical industry.

In 1904 government finally began addressing reform of pharmacy education with the Medical Council's draft proposal. The proposal endorsed proprietary pharmacy schools to prepare students for the Assistant Pharmacist examination and courses to prepare Assistant Pharmacists for the Provizor examination. Both sets of educational institutions were to be under the supervision of the Ministry of Internal Affairs, the Chief Medical Inspector, and the local school district but, while the Minister of Public Enlightenment was to have a say in the curriculum, private persons could found the schools and they were to be supported by the founders and by tuition.[80] They could be closed in case of violating regulations. Masters of Pharmacy were to manage the schools. Teachers and instructors were to come from a pool of those who had finished higher educational institutions or pharmacists with the title Provizor. Entering students were to have finished the sixth class of "government general middle education" and passed an education in Latin. Persons receiving the Assistant Pharmacist title were to serve one year in a pharmacy. The curriculum was extensive. There was a two-year program for both lower and higher schools. Consultant-Professor S. A. Przhibytek amended the proposal slightly—for example, Provizors, with incomplete higher education, could instruct only in preparing medicines.[81]

The Chief Medical Inspector and the Ministry of Internal Affairs drafted further projects in 1905 and 1906, assisted by a fleet of experts. All were variations on the 1904 project. Two 1905 proposals on Higher Pharmacy Education stipulated that pharmacists in Provizor courses were to be full-fledged students at the university rather than auditors, their program was extended to three years (from two), apprenticeship was to be reduced to one year (from two periods of three years), and the educational institutions were to be established in university cities and provincial capitals.

These projects envisaged private rather than government-supported pharmacy schools. But this did not indicate unqualified enthusiasm for private education. The main reason for encouraging private pharmacy schools was that the treasury was short of money. Although Chief Medical

Inspector fon Anrep announced he was a "supporter of private pharmacy schools and institutes" and welcomed "private initiative," he warned that one "could not wait for universities to establish the pharmacy institutes." Pharmacy courses "required significant outlay." They "could not be established in every university city at once" and first must be confined to "Moscow, Iur'ev (Dorpat, Estonia) and Novorossiisk (Odessa)."[82]

A bill on Lower Pharmacy Education, intended for debate in the new State Duma, emanated from the Ministry of Internal Affairs April 1, 1906. It proposed a qualifying examination rather than six classes of middle school for the entrant into pharmacy, stipulated that teachers and instructors in the lower schools and institutes were to be *lekari* and Provizors, established one year of apprenticeship for those who had completed the full *gimnaziia* course, and noted that "outside-the-school pharmacy training did not conform to contemporary science"–pharmacy students were "cheap labor." This project reiterated that private pharmacy schools were needed because the government lacked funds. "Contemporary conditions of finances did not permit the possibility of the government or public institutions establishing pharmacy schools . . . hope rested with private initiative." The current system of apprenticeship would be retained until enough schools had been established.[83] Minister of Internal Affairs P. A. Stolypin and Chief Medical Inspector fon Anrep signed a later draft of this proposal November 28, 1906.[84]

From 1904 to 1906, while formulating these draft laws the Medical Council and Ministry of Internal Affairs elicited opinions from pharmacists and pharmacy societies.[85] As before, both the question of apprenticeship and the concept of proprietary schools sparked conflict. But now the influence that geography and economic status played in determining attitudes toward these issues became apparent. In general, owners of large pharmacies in "the two capitals" of St. Petersburg and Moscow and pharmacist intellectuals who did not own pharmacies rejected apprenticeship. Provincial pharmacists and small pharmacy owners took the opposite position. On November 7, 1904, deputies from the St. Petersburg Pharmacy Society proposed to the Minister of Internal Affairs that pharmacy students should finish the full middle school curriculum.[86] The society further criticized reliance on the apprentice system for basic pharmacy education. It did not provide either adequate scientific or practical knowledge; basically pharmacy students were "cheap labor."[87]

Educational reform made strange bedfellows. Although the editors of

Farmatsevticheskii vestnik, representing the radical Russian Pharmacy Society in Moscow, frequently lashed out at the St. Petersburg Pharmacy Society as an "establishment" organization, they opposed the apprentice system and for the same reasons as the St. Petersburg Society. In 1904, editor B. N. Saltykov derided the notion that the pharmacy was a school, contending that pharmacy students merely served as cheap labor for pharmacy owners.[88]

On the other hand, S. Ia. Isaev insisted that apprenticeship was both beneficial and a necessary prerequisite for higher education—"All pharmacy work," Isaev affirmed, "was not unskilled labor."[89] Another pharmacist suggested that prospective pharmacists finish the sixth class of the *gimnaziia*, do a two-year apprenticeship, take the examination for Assistant Pharmacist and then attend university to prepare for the Provizor examination.[90] Provincial pharmacy owners and societies confessed that they were confused about regulations for apprentices; the most common complaint was the need of better guidelines on their numbers. However, generally they justified the apprentice system as an economic necessity. The owner of a private pharmacy in the city of Kursk spoke about the necessity of establishing a minimum date for students to stay in each pharmacy; he suggested six months. His pharmacy dispensed 17,000 new prescriptions, not counting repeats. Upon introduction of the double shift, following the upheavals of 1905, he needed to supplement his four "diplomaed pharmacists" with five student pharmacists; two of the students worked, under his direction, in the laboratory. Pharmacy owners in Minsk claimed that pharmacy owners in their region, the northwestern provinces of the empire, found the work of examined pharmacists too expensive and therefore had to turn to student help. They advocated two students for every 5,000 prescriptions with no more than eight students per pharmacy. The Kiev Pharmacy Society emphasized that students should not merely be a work force. Each staff pharmacist should supervise only two students; there should not be more than four students per pharmacy.[91]

The issue of private versus public pharmacy schools continued to be contentious. A handful of pharmacists took advantage of government sanction of private pharmacy schools. In 1905 Master of Pharmacy E. Ia. Abol', privatdocent at the Kazan Veterinary Institute, proposed to the Moscow School District that he be allowed to open a pharmacy school in Moscow. The Ministry of Public Enlightenment pronounced such a school, to prepare pharmacy students for the Assistant Pharmacist title, desirable.[92] Two gynecologists in Warsaw also petitioned the governor-general of Warsaw to open a private pharmacy school in 1905. But the Warsaw Medical Department and Pharmacy Assessor opposed their school because the doctors' specialties had no relation to pharmacy. Additionally, the Warsaw authorities believed that the training time to be offered by the school was too short. Provizors were required by law to have eight years' total training; the school provided only four. For the title Assistant Pharmacist the school required only two years' formal classes plus work in the school pharmacy. Further, the local authorities worried that the school would not have a fully stocked normal pharmacy. The request to open a normal pharmacy, in turn, would have to proceed through proper channels. On the basis of these objections, the Medical Council turned down the proposal in April 1906.[93]

In contrast to the practical and independent-minded Purve, Abol', and Warsaw gynecologists, the majority of pharmacists looked to the government for pharmacy schools. In 1904, the Lifland provincial director of public schools noted with relief that the Ministry of Education or monies designated for special needs of public education in Lifland province were funding pharmacy departments in ministry and government schools.[94]

Private pharmacy institutes for Assistant Pharmacists preparing for the Provizor degree especially provoked opposition. Although one pharmacist queried *Farmatsevticheskii vestnik* in 1904 about when pharmacists would get pharmacy institutes similar to the proprietary dental institutes that the Ministry of Internal Affairs had just approved,[95] other pharmacists clung to the notion that auditing university courses was more valuable for Assistant Pharmacists aspiring to become Provizors than attending special institutes. They did accept university-affiliated institutes. The Pharmacy Institute at Iur'ev University continued to operate and, in 1904, an analogous institute was organized at Novorossiisk University in Odessa. This university-affiliated institute received high praise. It provided pharmacist auditors with two semesters of analytical chemistry, prescription writing, a special colloquium in the principles of "rational pharmacy–rational dispensing of medicine, the latest research on medicines, sterilization." Even those who had taken the Assistant Pharmacist exam "six, seven, or more years ago and . . . living in the provinces, unable to follow scientific developments" benefited.[96]

In 1905 T. I. Lonachevskii-Petruniak, professor at St. Vladimir University in Kiev, published a short pamphlet on pharmacy education. He criticized the varied nature of Provizor courses and urged the institution of pharmacy institutes. However, he stressed these institutes must be departments of universities rather than independent entities. There should be a sizable complement of professors–two or three in chemistry and one each in pharmacy, physics, mineralogy, botany, zoology, pharmacology, and "technology or technological chemistry." Thus salaries and operating costs for all the institutes would amount to "somewhat more than two-hundred thousand rubles per year."[97] Obviously, he assumed that the institute budgets would be incorporated into those of the universities and, consequently, subsidized by the government.

The Kazan Pharmacy Society vehemently opposed both lower-level private pharmacy schools and pharmacy institutes and urged the Minister of Internal Affairs not to sanction the new Pharmacy Statute, particularly the clauses "transferring pharmacy education to private teachers." State universities were superior to private pharmacy institutes. Further, although it advocated complete secondary education for those entering pharmacy, the society advocated retaining the apprentice system, maintaining that pharmacies were suitable media for training pharmacists and that special lower pharmacy schools would deprive the poor of an opportunity to become pharmacists:

> In their congresses pharmacists fully agreed that pharmacy education must be reformed . . . that the full course of the middle school be finished and that there be higher, specialized education. . . . However, pharmacists never expected that the government would give pharmacy education to private hands. How good can it be to give pharmacy education to private hands when pharmacists can acquire scientific knowledge in the universities, served by professors, working under experienced direction in university laboratories—especially if there would be special chairs of pharmacy in the universities, as is found in Novorossiisk University. . . . Also there are practical problems in giving pharmacy education to private hands. Schools and courses for pharmacists can be founded only in large centers; for the masses who cannot get to large centers, the doors of pharmacy will be closed. Meanwhile, in the situation now existing, each pharmacy is a school for pharmacists entering it, a school which, besides practical and pharmaceutical knowledge, allows them material guarantees. Transferring pharmacy education to private hands will allow only well-off classes to enter pharmacy.[98]

In 1906 the Congress of Pharmacy Societies meeting in St. Petersburg came out strongly against any "*private* pharmacy courses and schools . . . since they entirely do not answer the needs of the corporation and least of all the public." The congress did approve "free schools in the Pharmacy societies for *praktikanty* [untrained persons working in pharmacies] such as exist in St. Petersburg, Moscow, Riga, Tiflis, and Odessa." For special education of Pharmacists the Congress demanded establishment of "*government* [sponsored] *higher educational institutions* . . . the full university program (not two years)—if not four years at least three—with wide practical application." The congress affirmed that "Higher Special Education of Pharmacists cannot be served by *private courses* but only by a government higher education institution."[99] The congress stressed the importance of practical work in the pharmacy; approving new titles of "Kandidat" or "Doktor" of Philosophy, even these august souls wishing to manage a pharmacy had to "*serve in a pharmacy for not less than two years.*"[100]

Russian pharmacists were perhaps justified in rejecting proprietary schools. These had served a purpose but had become outmoded in the United States by the third quarter of the nineteenth century and were gradually superseded by pharmacy schools in the midwestern land-grant universities.[101] Yet, in light of the fact that the government and universities were not founding a network of lower-level pharmacies schools, private schools might have been better than nothing.

But, although topics for study and examination for the three levels of Assistant, Provizors, and Master, amounted to almost fifty pages in the government regulations for pharmacists, published in 1907,[102] no network of pharmacy schools, public or private, higher or lower, was established in Russia before the revolutions of 1917.

There were small signs of improvement in male pharmacy education. In 1904, the term of initial apprenticeship was cut from three to two years for pharmacy students who had finished the real school.[103] Abol"s June 1905 request to open a pharmacy school in Moscow received ministerial sanction surprisingly quickly. The Medical Faculty at Moscow University rejected the courses but the Ministry of Public Enlightenment, while criticizing the request for several reasons–"the 'school' should more accurately be labeled courses since students prepared for only four months . . . there was no evidence as to the university Abol' had attended"–finally approved the school to "train male and female students for the degree of Assistant Pharmacist."[104] In June 1905 the Medical Council stated that it had no objection to Abol"s establishing the lower pharmacy school.[105] In 1907 the St. Petersburg Pharmacy Society planned to increase its classes in its school from two to three days. This required students to pay 10 to 15 rubles more at the beginning of the school year.[106] Polumordvinov's correspondence courses finally materialized in 1907. They were established in his wholesale drug firm in Moscow. The courses focused on twenty-two items and lasted two to three months. Tuition was 25 rubles.[107]

Nevertheless, interminable government debate helped stymie real reform.[108] In December 1906, Assistant Minister Sergei Efimovich Kryzhanovskii presented yet another draft law on reform of pharmacy education, particularly the establishment of lower pharmacy schools. The bill was to be discussed in the Council of Ministers prior to introducing it into the

Second Duma.[109] The Council of Ministers discussed some fine points in December.[110] The Ministry of Trade and Industry slowed the process further, prompting the Chief Medical Inspector to urge them to "hurry and give a decision so the draft could be introduced to the legislature" in January 1907.[111] In February 1907, the Ministry of Trade and Industry finally responded with a list of details it wanted explained: whether the pharmacy was a trade establishment (in this case graduates of city and commercial schools should be recruited for the lower pharmacy schools, which, in turn, should stress bookkeeping and commercial subjects) or a scientific establishment (in this case high-level chemistry courses should be taught); why the proposal addressed provincial and regional cities but not district cities; who should select the teachers–founder or manager.[112] The Second Duma was dissolved in June 1907, and did not consider the project.

Continued wrangling among pharmacists bogged things down further. By 1909 the Medical Council had worked out a proposal for reform of pharmacy education. The reform was part of the revised Pharmacy Statute submitted to the Third Duma. However, pharmacists quibbled with the proposals. Radical pharmacists claimed that "if all staff personnel consist of people with a higher education many small enterprises will not be able to afford them; this will create a cadre of 'illegal' pharmacy workers–'*praktikanty.*'"[113] The St. Petersburg Pharmacy Society, particularly its representative in the Medical Council, also was opposed to Assistant Minister of Internal Affairs Kryzhanovskii's educational reform project. Pharmacists in favor, on the other hand, requested that they be represented in the Medical Council to counter opponents to the project.[114] Educational reform was further complicated by a proposed change in higher pharmacy degrees.[115]

No substantial improvement, not to mention complete overhaul, of lower pharmacy education occurred before World War I. Both government and pharmacists were still discussing lower pharmacy education reform on the eve of the war.

In 1913, "The Minister of Internal Affairs and the Minister of Public Enlightenment, with approval of the Medical Council" published new regulations for male and female pharmacy students. Not only had qualifications not been raised but, if anything, entering pharmacy had been made easier! Those finishing the fourth class of the male *gimnaziia* and the second class of the seminary were admitted "without examination." Those finishing the fourth class of the real school or commercial school, the sixth class of the cadet corps (this said something about military education) and the sixth class of women's *gimnaziia* or institutes were admitted "with an examination in one subject–Latin." Persons finishing the sixth class of the male and female diocesan schools, the fourth class of the women's *gimnaziia* or possessing the title of governess were admitted "with examination in two subjects–Latin and algebra." Finally, those finishing the course in two-class city schools of the southwest region were accepted "with examination in three subjects–Latin, algebra and general history," although it was curious as to how an examination in general history would aid pharmacists. The one bright spot of the new regulations was that "Persons with higher qualifications" could "reduce the three-year apprenticeship in the pharmacy."[116]

In 1913, Alexander Ginzberg, member of the "National Committee" of the St. Petersburg Pharmacy Society, reported on yet another project for educational reform. Those entering pharmacy were to *complete* middle school, enjoy a reduced two-year apprenticeship in a pharmacy, and take three years, rather than two years, of university courses.[117] Lonacharskii-Petruniak presented a variant of this to the All-Russian Pharmacy Congress that met in St. Petersburg in May 1913. The project, developed by a Commission on Pharmacy Education, advocated totally abolishing apprenticeship and establishing pharmacy departments with a four-year course of study in universities. Practice in the pharmacy was to be simultaneous with university study or follow it.[118]

Although pharmacists could blame themselves as well as the ponderousness of the government for failure to resolve the problems in pharmaceutical education, lack of resolution was to have enormous repercussions, which transcended both pharmacy and education. Perhaps pharmacist education reformers were latent radicals. In any case, on the eve of the war, they began to move closer to overt radicals. The "National Committee" of the St. Petersburg Pharmacy Society had political overtones and anticipated the "Progressive Bloc" formed in the Russian parliament, the Fourth Duma, in 1915 which strove for more power for that body.[119] Simultaneously, in 1913, old-time radicals Boris Puzis and Robert Idel'son began to clamor for pharmacists' autonomy and greater participation in government policy-making, or at the least, attaching pharmacists to provincial medical inspectors.[120]

It was the so-called medicaments crisis of World War I, discussed in the following two chapters, that finally forced the Russian government and the pharmacy corporation to implement changes in pharmacy education. But this crisis not only shocked reformers into taking pharmaceutical education into their own hands, it turned them against the tsarist government, or at least predisposed them to alternative governments, including that of the Bolsheviks. Thus the stage was set for 1917.

16

World War I and the Medicaments Crisis

World War I strained the fabric of Russian government, economy, and society. However, the war also stimulated the armaments industry.[1] Similarly, the war energized Russia's pharmaceutical industry. The so-called *lekarstvennyi golod*—shortage of medicines and pharmaceutical supplies and high prices for those available—highlighted defects in the pharmaceutical industry and pharmacy education. Little was done to upgrade pharmacy education, but all sectors of the empire strove to solve the medicaments problem by increasing the quantity and diversity of medicines and pharmaceutical supplies.

A review of the medicaments crisis is interesting for a number of reasons. The strides made in solving the crisis provide additional documentation on the strength of the chemical industry and the Russian economy at the end of 1916, on the eve of the February Revolution.

Second, the medicaments crisis sheds light on the tsarist government's competency during the war. The energy which the Ministry of Internal Affairs, specifically, displayed in dealing with the crisis, the consistency of its operation, the maintenance of traditional connections with provincial officials go far toward belying the dislocation supposedly suffered by the government through frequent changes of ministers—the so-called ministerial leapfrog that occurred during the war[2] and traditionally cited as one of the reasons for the demise of the government and the revolution of February 1917. For the medicaments crisis shows that the Russian government, as most governments, was propelled by the principle of inertia, made possible by the fact that lower level personnel remained at their posts, that policies were in the works, and that operating procedures remained the same.

The medicaments crisis had long-lasting significance for Russia. Although it was to some extent a pseudo-crisis, it tipped the tripartite balance of forces in the Russian economy away from private enterprise and toward its twin antipodes—big government and socialism. By 1916 it appeared that the Russian pharmaceutical industry would emerge from the war stronger than beforehand. However, it was not equally certain that private enterprise would continue to dominate the industry. On the contrary, belief in the efficacy of both big government and socialized pharmacy and pharmaceutical production gained currency during the war. What is more important, the proponents of those belief systems (which, despite apparent antithesis, were actually entwined) emerged into positions of power. Private entrepreneurs would be no match for their combined forces.

On Saturday, August 2, 1914, immediately after Russia entered the war, a worried Medical Council, under the chairmanship of Professor G. E. Rein,[3] met with representatives from the War Ministry, the Red Cross, and major wholesale firms–Shtol' and Shmidt, Shaskol'skii, the Tentelevskii factory, the Russian Society of Trade in Pharmaceutical Wares, Ferrein, Keler, and Parke, Davis–to debate the small stores of crucial pharmaceutical items such as iodine salts, bismuth, and mercury. There were alarming reports that wholesale firms had raised prices astronomically.

In fact, while wholesale prices on some items escalated at the outset of the conflict, level-headed observers averred that retail prices for prescription medicines had risen only about 10 percent.[4] Further, at the beginning of the war, as throughout, conditions varied from place to place. In the Black Sea port of Odessa, estimating that stocks would last for six months, the Society of Pharmacy Owners unanimously agreed not to raise prices for prescription medicines.[5] On the other hand, in Khar'kov, in the eastern Ukraine, foreign patented medicines were in short supply; there were proposals to purchase medicine in Japan, England, and America. Additionally, the Khar'kov Pharmacy Society elected a commission to organize local sourcing, particularly from the nearby Galenika factory.[6] In Moscow prices for cotton rose 30 percent and for gauze 20 percent; there also were severe shortages of soap and rubber.[7] In the Caucasus there was a shortage of medicine although some items were available in pharmacies at very high prices. Aspirin from Germany cost 95 rubles per kilogram, in comparison to 2 rubles, 90 kopeks before the war. Phenacetin cost 80 rubles per kilogram instead of its prewar price of 3 rubles, 90 kopeks. There were allegations that speculation was rife. "Lawyers, engineers," and others "not connected with pharmacy" were "trading in medicines." On the other hand, a recently established factory near Kiev was making aspirin that sold for only 30 rubles per kilogram.[8]

Menshevik pharmacists viewed the medicaments shortage through Marxist lenses. Staff pharmacists meeting in Petrograd in the middle of

October 1914 attributed the medicaments crisis to the pharmacy monopoly, which had blocked growth of the domestic pharmaceutical industry, machinations of syndicates of druggists who controlled medical supplies, policies of the Russian Council of Ministers (such as their rejection of medicines from Denmark because these had allegedly originated in Germany), and the backwardness of the Russian pharmaceutical industry. Ia. L. Kanevskii, editor of *Zhizn' farmatsevta,* emphasized that Russia's pharmaceutical production could develop only with "growth of her productive forces." However, he vehemently rejected the Economic Society's proposal that "industrialists" should create pharmaceutical factories with financial support from the government. Kanevskii contended that the only solution for the medicaments crisis was "municipalization"–transfer of the chemico-pharmaceutical industry to zemstvos and cities.[9]

Menshevik analysis of the medicaments crisis was correct to some extent but both the reasons and solutions for the crisis were more complex. The medicaments shortage resulted, in part, from breakup of international trade links in World War I. All belligerents, not just Russia, suffered a medicine crisis. Although German medicines trickled into France for some time after the outbreak of the war, shortages and disruption of trade prompted France to turn to Britain for pharmaceutical supplies and hastily review measures to improve the domestic pharmaceutical industry.[10] Early in 1916 *Farmatsevticheskii vestnik* noted that Russia got few medicines "from France . . . since she had trouble meeting her own needs."[11] Britain benefited from breakup of syndicates that controlled salts of bismuth from South America and had sufficient supplies of cinchona bark at the outbreak of the war but scurried to find substitutes for bromide, formerly supplied from Germany, eagerly awaited shipments of potash from Canada so as to begin ammonia production, and lacked acetone for chloroform. England was unable to produce salicylic acid for aspirin in acceptable quality or quantity.[12] However, it was claimed she could supply Russia with carbolic acid, an ingredient for aspirin.[13] America did not enter the war until 1917. Nevertheless, from the outset she was cut off from German pharmaceuticals on which she greatly depended.[14] Even Germany, regarded as keeping the rest of the world in thralldom, had medicaments problems. As the war dragged on prices of some items rose astronomically. Late in 1915 a Swiss newspaper compared wartime price increases on fifteen medicinal substances in Germany and Switzerland. The price of yellow vaseline had increased 84 percent in Switzerland but 533 percent in Germany; castor oil had risen 113 percent in Switzerland but 400 percent in Germany; boric acid–imported from Italy–cost 84 percent more in Switzerland and 267 percent more in Germany; tartaric acid had risen 114 percent in Switzerland and 193 percent in Germany; paraffin had risen 175 percent in Germany; borax, 162 percent; benzoic soda, 148 percent; and lanolin, 92 percent.[15]

Requisitioning chemicals for military uses at the beginning of the war limited pharmaceutical production in all countries. Carbolic acid was bought up for defense use. In the spring of 1915 synthetic acid was still not produced in sufficient quantities. The use of benzol was prohibited.[16] At the end of 1915 sulfuric acid, hydrochloric acid, and nitric acid, requisitioned for the war, were still in short supply for civilian use.[17]

But, although the war affected pharmaceutical production among all belligerents, certain factors exacerbated the medicaments crisis in Russia. Supplies were at their lowest ebb in August prior to the final big orders before navigation closed for the winter and representatives of foreign firms, cut off from their factories, stopped accepting orders.[18] The western part of Russia soon came under enemy assault and pharmaceutical factories had to be evacuated to keep them out of German hands. This procedure, anticipating the eastward movement of industry that saved the Soviet Union in World War II, affected the Reval Chemical Factory, which produced ether, the "Brothers Briger" in Riga, which produced green medicinal soap, and factories in Minsk province, which produced turpentine. Domestic production had satisfied orders for all three items before the war but the evacuation disrupted production, causing severe shortages. Only in the case of green medicinal soap were the Brothers Krestovnikov and a factory in Astrakhan able to fill the gap.[19] Poland, one of the key pharmaceutical centers in the empire, was in the midst of the war from the beginning. By 1915 Russian Poland was in German hands.[20]

Depreciation of the ruble increased costs for glassware, raw materials, fuel, labor, and transportation, speculation, and contraction of credit hurt Russia.[21] Transportation was a perennial problem. During the war it was chaotic. Railroads accepted only material directly necessary for the war.[22] Peasants took advantage of the situation and carted goods for steep fees.[23] In early 1916 there still was no railroad connecting Arkhangel'sk with Moscow and Petrograd. In the south, Baku served well as a port, transshipping by railroad and the Volga River. Tiflis, on the other hand, had inadequate railway links and was unable to receive goods from Astrakhan on the mouth of the Volga.[24]

Pharmaceutical firms bombarded the Society for Assistance to the Growth of the Chemical Industry and the Chief Medical Inspector (who forwarded their requests to the Ministry of Ways and Communication and the Department of Military Transport of the General Staff) for permission to ship heavy pharmaceutical wares and carloads of material "outside the normal order"[25] and to send lighter, valuable wares with passenger baggage at premium prices.[26] In November 1915, a Central Committee for Regulating Railway Transportation was finally established,[27] an example of the increasing bureaucracy and centralization that emerged from World War I.[28] In September 1917, this Central Committee still appeared powerful. However, the end of the Provisional Government was fast approaching.[29]

Almost every sector of the empire–government; Red Cross; pharmaceutical, chemical, technical societies; pharmaceutical enterprises; educational institutions and specialists; zemstvos and city governments; ad hoc agencies, such as the War Industries Committee, Union of Zemstvos and Cities, and Evacuation Committee; religious organizations; and citizenry–feverishly devoted their energies to solving the medicaments crisis. Individuals and organizations of both Left and Right orientations contributed. In some cases the participants worked in harmony. However, conflicts also erupted and there was wasteful duplication of effort. The programs and mind-sets that evolved as a result of the medicaments crisis were to have long-lasting impact on dispensing and the pharmaceutical industry.

An immediate solution to the medicaments crisis was to pool available supplies. Many firms and pharmacy owners asked for a raise in the Pharmacy Tax.[30] Moscow firms stopped accepting prior sales contracts.[31] Nevertheless, in a flush of patriotism, large Moscow pharmaceutical wholesalers diverted stocks to the Union of Zemstvos and the Red Cross[32] and pharmacy owners in Yaroslavl', Kiev, and Taganrog contributed money to the Red Cross and public organizations for purchase of supplies.[33]

A second solution to the medicaments crisis was import substitution. City sanitary commissions immediately sent out feelers to the United States,[34] Japan,[35] and Sweden[36] to replace German suppliers.

Japan became one of Russia's chief wartime suppliers.[37] Japanese firms established warehouses in the Far East, supplying Russia with crucial raw materials–camphor, chloral hydrate, agar-agar, iodine, menthol, and iodide potassium and soda.[38] Japan also supplied Russia with ready-made preparations. One of the chief was "Arsaminal," the Japanese equivalent of the antisyphilitic Salvarsan in 1915, as French Salvarsan was difficult to get and Russia did not produce her own until 1916. Japanese Salvarsan was of course very good, as Gata, the head of the Sankio factory in Tokyo that made the product, had been a colleague of Erlich, the creator of Salvarsan.[39] Vladivostok was a chief Russian port for Japanese imports.[40] In September 1917, the tsarist government having fallen and the Provisional Government that had replaced it tottering, the Society for Assistance to the Development of the Chemical Industry requested some thirty wares ordered by Shtol' and Shmidt from a Japanese pharmaceutical firm. These orders provide information on items particularly needed in Russia at that time and sourced by foreign suppliers. Wares included iodine; febrifuges–quinine sulfuric, antipyrine, phenacetin, antifebrin, caustic bromide, caustic iodide, salicylic acid, and aspirin; narcotics–morphine hydrochloric, cocaine, codeine, valerian; disinfecting agents–ammonia, carbolic acid, bismuth, caffeine, silver nitrate, camphor, *naftalin*, oil of wintergreen, and ultramarine blue. These items were to be distributed to Red Cross, zemstvo and factory pharmacies, as well as to private pharmacies.[41]

"No less an important role" was "played by England."[42] The items ordered by Ferrein from six English pharmaceutical firms in September 1916, appeared to be mainly raw materials–herbs, roots (including radix cannabis), flowers, and coffee.[43] From England, Russia also received, "although in limited quantities," aspirin, salicylic acid and soda, *salol*, salipyrine and bromide potassium, quinine, and crystallized carbolic acid.[44] Holland supplied the bulk of Russia's cocaine. Russia had put in orders to the United States for these items but had difficulty getting them.

While France had her own medicaments problem, she was able to supply Russia with arsenobenzol and novarsenobenzol. These two substances to combat syphilis were produced by the Billon factory, Rouen frères in Paris.[45] In August 1917, a Parisian pharmaceutical firm was supplying Russia with barbiturates, atropine, antipyrine, and bismuth salicylicum, caffeine, and calcium.[46]

American supplies, for example to Shtol' and Shmidt in November 1916, included a number of narcotics–Dionin, Alomorphinum, and cocaine–and camphor, Peruvian balsam, and bismuth salicylicum.[47] This underscored how America successfully broke patents during World War I and generated the raw materials necessary for key prepared medicaments.

The Swiss firm Hofman La Roche also supplied Russia. In January 1917, the Society for Assistance to Developing the Chemical Pharmaceutical Industry was asking for help in getting tablets and other prepared pharmaceuticals from Basel.[48]

Unfortunately lack of cooperation from neutral transit countries, primarily Norway and Sweden, hindered imports. Throughout 1915 and 1916 Ferrein, Shtol' and Shmidt, and the Society for Assistance to the Chemical Industry, which became an intermediary for Russian pharmaceutical firms, bombarded the Ministry of Foreign Affairs for help in prying loose shipments.[49] In mid-1915 Sweden prohibited all shipments destined for Russia. Wares then were diverted to Arkhangel'sk.[50]

But most Russians realized that better distribution of materials on hand and import substitution were stop-gap measures. As a consequence, the chief focus was to speed up and expand domestic pharmaceutical production, sourcing domestically as much as possible. The Russian pharmaceutical industry was far from inadequate before the war.[51] However, it also was true that Russia's coal tar byproducts had been little used to produce salicylic acid and other febrifuges. Russia did not grow certain crucial medicinal plants and did not produce certain key chemicals. Russian pharmaceutical research and development had not kept pace with Germany.

Thus, a comprehensive program was undertaken to raise the Russian pharmaceutical industry to a world-competitive level and make Russia more self-sufficient in pharmaceuticals. Measures included intensifying production of key minerals; decoding foreign patented remedies; building pharmaceutical plants; revising the Pharmacy Tax and Civilian Pharmacopoeia; speeding up government approval of formulae for prepared medicaments; cultivating and collecting plants. The government tendered proposals for new pharmaceutical and chemical courses but pharmaceutical education saw little actual improvement.

In his work on public health during World War I, John Hutchinson accused "official Russia"–"the Council of Ministers, the MVD [Ministry of Internal Affairs], Medical Council" of not undertaking measures to combat epidemics.[52] With regard to the medicaments crisis, on the contrary, the Russian government was far from inactive. The Ministry of Internal Affairs and other ministries did a great deal to improve the domestic pharmaceutical industry by prodding and coordinating the work of private and public agencies, by disbursing large sums of money, and by speeding up approval for new medicines, factory start-ups, production, and trade.

At the beginning of the war the Minister of Public Enlightenment L. A. Kasso urged universities and other higher educational institutions to organize production of chemical and pharmaceutical products.[53] In February 1915, the Ministry of Internal Affairs convened an "Interdepartmental Committee on the Pharmaceutical Industry" under chairmanship of Chief Medical Inspector L. N. Malinovskii. The committee met through the spring of 1915. Government representatives predominated but the committee also included representatives from the Red Cross and Zemstvo Union as well as representatives from the pharmaceutical and chemical industries.[54]

In March 1915 the Ministry of Agriculture called an interdepartmental meeting to increase cultivation of medicinal plants.[55] The ministry supplied consultants to educational institutions, botanical gardens, scholars, wholesale and trade firms to help them grow medicinal plants.[56]

The government also allocated respectable sums for developing pharmaceuticals. The imperial treasury gave the Experimental Station (for Research into Obtaining Russian Iodine) at the Ekaterinoslav Mining Institute 50,000 rubles in 1914 to build a factory to produce iodine products.[57] Prince Alexander Ol'denburg, director of the Sanitary and Evacuation Sector, channeled 72,325 rubles during late 1915 and early 1916 to the Sukhum Experimental Agricultural Station, to establish a plantation of medicinal plants on the Black Sea. A Master of Pharmacy managed the plantation. The Sukhum Agricultural Society contributed an additional 10,000 rubles for purchase of seeds.[58] Early in 1916 the government allocated the Migration Administration 60,000 rubles to establish a factory in Tomsk or Vladivostok to derive iodine from seaweed found in Vladivostok, which was shown to have a high iron content.[59]

One of the most important contributions, perhaps *the most important* contribution to domestic pharmaceutical manufacture made by the government, was to loosen its fetters on pharmaceutical manufacturing. Representatives to the 1915 Interdepartmental Committee on the Pharmaceutical Industry unstintingly criticized the Medical Council and the Ministry of Internal Affairs for hamstringing the industry. They urged the government to lower tariffs for crucial raw materials[60] and give the industry more freedom for research, development, and production.[61] The representative from the Society for Developing Chemical Industry and Trade, F. G. (A.) Ferrein, particularly asked that factories be permitted to produce "without lists, all extracts, tinctures, oils, plasters, tablets, pills, including strong-acting" and to sell these to all pharmacies and clinics. He stressed that it was "necessary to introduce individual decision-making for internal production of prepared substances." In other words the government must stop interfering in the pharmaceutical industry. Ferrein also urged that representatives from the industry serve on the Medical Council. Ferrein was not a free-trader, however. He proposed that the government prohibit imports of foreign-made galenicals.[62]

The identity of F. G. (A.) Ferrein is somewhat mysterious.

In the list of members comprising the Interdepartmental Committee he was listed as F. *G.* whereas when he delivered his report on the needs of the pharmaceutical industry, April 10, 1915, he was listed as F. *A.*[63] Were the initials a garbled version of the patronymic Gustavovich/Avgustavovich? The query is important, for an "F. A." Ferrein became a founding member of the Soviet organization "*Farmatsentr.*" In 1918 this institution nationalized former privately owned pharmacies and pharmaceutical enterprises—among them those belonging to the Ferrein Association.[64] Along with radical pharmacists A. Aluf, Ia. Kanevskii, and Iu. Kuperman, F. A. Ferrein also wrote articles (mainly on the pharmaceutical industry) for the Soviet pharmaceutical press during the 1920s.[65]

However, whereas Aluf and Kuperman were longtime radicals and Professor A. E. Chichibabin worked in the public organization, the Union of Cities,[66] during World War I, F. A. Ferrein, on the other hand, achieved distinction in scientific circles and also was closely connected with the tsarist government. He contributed to the draft of a new civilian pharmacopoeia for Russia. Late in 1915 he participated in a Pharmacy/Chemistry Committee at the University of Moscow. The committee discussed replacing patent names with identical or generic products.[67] In the summer of 1916, F. A. Ferrein chaired the Pharmacy/Chemistry Committee of the Moscow Pharmacopoeia Commission, headquartered at the University of Moscow.[68] Russian historian Tat'iana Biriukova considers him a scion of the Ferrein pharmaceutical family.[69]

In any case, in response to F. G./A. Ferrein's indictment, the Medical Council did not relinquish all authority over the pharmaceutical industry, but it did make a concerted effort to approve requests for mass-production more quickly and leniently. Additionally, the Medical Council allowed the Russian pharmaceutical industry to produce generic or identical versions of foreign proprietary medicines with special disclaimers.[70] This policy had been broached by Chairman of the Council of Ministers and Minister of Internal Affairs P. A. Stolypin in 1911.[71] By the spring of 1915 pharmacies in Rostov-on-the-Don were dispensing *identiki* at prices equal to patented medicines.[72]

There still were plenty of instances when the Medical Council moved slowly and proffered the same absurdly trivial objections to factory production as before the war. For example, in June 1915 V. K. Merezhkovskii and Company in Petrograd requested permission to open a factory in Petrograd and to prepare peptone and other medicaments on the premises of the Iur'ev joint-stock Company Canning Factory. The Merezhkovskii firm pursued this with the Petrograd Medical Department throughout 1915 and 1916.[73] The Medical Council finally debated their request a full year and a half later, in January 1917, insisting that "This can be done only after satisfying the local medical administration about fulfilling all sanitary rules for an institution of such kind and in conditions that the Association Merezhkovskii be fully responsible for the good quality of the preparation—Master of Pharmacy Schindel'meiser himself will be responsible."[74] Production of pepsin wine by Smirnov and Pustov was first submitted for approval in 1909 and again in 1913; the Medical Council rejected the proposal in June 1916, because the product included alcohol—port wine—prohibited for sale during the war.[75] Similarly, the Medical Council delayed start-up of cultivation of opium poppies in the southern regions of the empire at the height of the medicaments crisis. The Khar'kov Provincial Medical Administration first sent a proposal on this matter to the Medical Council in July 1915; it amplified the proposal in the summer of 1916 to include participation by one of the district zemstvos. Unfortunately, by January 1917, the council was just beginning to debate both proposals.[76]

However, the Medical Council, inundated with requests from pharmacists to produce medicines, quickly approved many, particularly during late 1916 and early 1917.[77] Applicants were represented by attorneys. The exact ingredients and method of preparation of all approved medicines were published. Most of the applicants had small-scale operations but their recipes were approved for factory as well as pharmacy production. Some remedies were to be sold at drug stores (*aptekarskie magaziny*) without prescription; others were dispensed only upon prescription of physicians.

After the February Revolution of 1917, which ended the tsarist government, the composition of the Medical Council of the Ministry of Internal Affairs was altered. Nevertheless, it was business as usual. The Council and Ministry screened applications as before, often communicating their decisions on stationery from the old regime.

Many of the remedies addressed gonorrhea. For example, two owners of an Odessa pharmacy proposed their gelatin capsule, "Shpanirol," as a remedy for gonorrhea in mid November 1916. The Medical Council approved it early February 1917.[78] An antigonorrheal "Santal-Polsin" submitted by Assistant Pharmacist Fridland in early January 1917 was approved in April 1917.[79] Pharmacist Grigor'evich's antigonorrheal "Santo-Pichilin" was submitted in early February 1917 and approved April 1, 1917.[80] On the other hand, a physician's antigonorrheal medicine, submitted for approval in October 1916, was rejected in February 1917, on the grounds that it was both unoriginal and dangerous.[81] The antigonorrheal preparation "Salamin" took a long time to be approved–it was first proposed in August 1915–but was finally sanctioned in January 1917.[82] An "apparatus" to treat gonorrhea was submitted for the Medical Council's approval in November 1916. The council approved it in June 1917, but forbade advertisements.[83]

Provizor Lev Isiodorovich Fridland submitted for approval a veritable host of remedies, usually in conjunction with a partner. Some of these aimed at gonorrhea, others at other problems. The Medical Council quickly approved them all. Fridland submitted his antigonorrheal remedy "Uropurin" in late December 1916; the Medical Council approved it in early April 1917.[84] Fridland submitted his remedy against gonorrhea "Saginol" in January 1917; the remedy was approved in early April.[85] Fridland submitted his antirheumatism remedy "Elektorin"—a powder—and a remedy for sore throats—"Askola"—in early January 1917. "Elektorin" was rejected as being "Harmful to the health"; "Askola," consisting of capsules containing quinine, aspirin, camphor, and vanilla was approved in early March.[86] Two salicylic products submitted for approval by Fridland in January 1917 were approved in May 1917, although the name of one had to be changed because it was too similar to another remedy.[87] A second antirheumatism product designed by Fridland, "Capsidal," was rejected because it contained a "strong-acting" substance; however, the Medical Council's decision came in less than two weeks![88]

Provizor Zil'berman's cough syrup "Sirolin"—the name apparently attempted to capitalize on the Swiss firm La Roche's cough remedy, "Sironal"—was submitted in July 1916 and approved only in January 1917.[89] However the time lag for approval of most other preparations, such as one Assistant Pharmacist's topical product for rheumatism,[90] averaged about three and a half months. Two remedies of iodine, a crucial antidote for goiter—the liquids "Iodlaktin"[91] and "Pulmonel" (containing medicinal wine)[92]—were speedily approved. Abortifacients were submitted for the Medical Council's approval[93] and also a nourishing "fast food" item or food supplement for children made of flour, malt, cocoa, and protein. A Jewish Provizor requested permission to produce the substance in a Petrograd laboratory in February 1917; the council approved it in June 1917.[94] A radioactive oil, submitted for approval May 1916, was approved by the Medical Council May 1917.[95] Cosmetics also were submitted for approval in 1916 and 1917. Probably one of the strangest late war proposals, submitted in December 1916 by the "Moscow Institute of Medical Cosmetics," was a recipe for reducing tablets! The Council approved the tablets February 21, 1917, three days before the February Revolution broke out.[96]

Existing pharmaceutical industries, as well as start-ups, ultimately benefited from the government's new policy of more quickly approving new pharmaceutical products. But from the very beginning of the war, pharmaceutical industrialists, often in conjunction with the academic community, tried to expand production of medicines and other badly needed wares. It should be noted, however, that the pharmaceutical industrialists had to contend with conservative colleagues within the pharmacy corporation. At the outset of the war, the editors of *Farmatsevticheskii zhurnal* warned, with considerable lack of foresight, that since "capitalistic" pharmaceutical enterprises in Russia were "weak" the "growth of chemical-pharmaceutical industry cannot and must not replace the pharmacy."[97]

Nevertheless, as indicated by the manifold requests from pharmacists to mass-produce medicaments, pharmacist-entrepreneurs forged ahead. In 1914 a professor from the Imperial Therapeutic Society in Moscow, Professor Derevenko, and V. K. Ferrein cooperated to produce chloroform, ether, and urotropin; the Prokhorov factory donated gauze or cheesecloth and hygroscopic cotton, the firm of Shchenkov contributed surgical thread. In the spring of 1915 Moscow Professor N. A. Savel'ev organized an exhibition of Russian-made medicaments, instruments, foodstuffs, and disinfectants to prove that these Russian articles were not inferior to German.[98]

Bacteriological laboratories strove to increase the output of vaccines and other items.[99] The Kiev Bacteriological Institute was particularly successful. By early 1915 it was producing a host of smallpox, gonococcus, cholera, typhus, scarlatina, streptococcus vaccines, antidiphtheria medicines, digestive juice, and gelatin, sugar and potato supplements, the latter costing 15 kopeks.[100]

Enterprises attempted to diversify as well as increase productivity. In Tiflis the large Prokhorov factory, as well as smaller enterprises, which had made ordinary cotton before the war, began manufacturing hygroscopic cotton. Unfortunately, the cotton was not of high quality as key machines were lacking.[101] In 1915 the Tentelevskii factory in St. Petersburg, as well as in Kiev, and the Reinbot-Morozov factory in Perm province produced chloroform. Salicylic natron, caffeine, and aspirin began to be made in Kiev. Ferrein in Moscow began to produce aspirin, piramidon, and *salol.* Shering in Mogilev produced formalin, chloroform, and acetone. Shering in Moscow made sublimate of mercury.[102] In the Caucasus, during 1915, the Borzhom Mineral Water factory and the Zarobednoe estate began making turpentine, formerly imported from the south of France, for the Caucasian market. The production of ammonia increased significantly after the war began.[103] Production of iodide potassium and soda also increased, particularly that made by Shering in Moscow. The Stock Company Farbverke in Moscow began producing ginosulfite; Merezhkovskii in Petrograd began producing the intestinal medicine *tannalbin* and *kollar'gol.*[104] By December 1915, the Keler firm had nearly completed a factory for producing salicylic acid in St. Petersburg; in Moscow morphine had been obtained but with great difficulty.[105] Morphia also was produced in Iur'ev, Estonia, and in Tashkent.[106] Perm and Kostroma in the Ural region produced sulfuric acid and superphosphates.[107] Ammonia was being produced in the Don Basin by the end of 1915. Afanas'ev reported to the Petrograd committee at the end of 1915 that metallic zinc had been obtained in an Alagirsk factory and from October 1915, zinc salts would be produced by the society "El'borus."[108] Early in 1916 the Porokhov factory was obtaining iodine from its stores of Chilean saltpeter and sulfate, *tannalbin, kollar'gol,* and many disinfecting products from wood distillation.[109]

Several new pharmaceutical concerns emerged during the war in different areas of the empire. In Moscow four pharmacists–Filipp Markovich Bliumental', Iakov Markovich Bliumental', who had completed Provizor courses at Moscow University and produced disinfectants in 1907, Master of Pharmacy Aron Oshernovich Kovarskii, and Iosif Gustavovich Gabrilovich (perhaps the progressive pharmacist reformer Osip Gustavovich Gabrilovich?)–established the Chemical-Pharmaceutical Laboratory Bliumental' in 1915. Their Association provided the entire capital of 40,000 rubles.[110] In the spring of 1916 urotropin factory number 3 opened in the treasury wine warehouse in St. Petersburg. Sixty *puds* of bleach were quickly produced. There were plans to enlarge the factory and produce 20 *puds* per day. A factory in Nizhni Novgorod also began to produce urotropin. Reputedly its quality was superior to that imported from America.[111]

By 1917 more than 120 pharmaceutical enterprises–most admittedly small–existed in the Ukraine, which had been a center of pharmaceutical production since the mid-nineteenth century. The new enterprises were located in Kiev, Khar'kov, Ekaterinoslav, Odessa, Zhitomir, Bakhtum, Chernigov, and other cities. In Kiev a chloroform factory began production in January 1915. In May 1915, the Russian Chemical Stock Association was formed in Kiev. In Khar'kov the Polytechnical Institute, under the direction of A. I. Gunder, produced chlorethyl–a topical anesthetic–and sulfate ammonia; the laboratory of the Medical Society under S. A. Sogomonov made lecithin and fitin; K. A. Krasuskii and P. S. Pishchimuk produced salicylate in a laboratory at the university. A chloroform factory was created in Odessa. The chemical-pharmaceutical laboratory "Union" and the "South-Russian Chemical Factory" operated in Poltava. The factory "Farmgalen" (undoubtedly geared to produce galenicals) was organized in the company town of Iuzhovka. A pharmaceutical factory christened Iurasov operated in a town by the same name.[112]

It ought to be noted that while the government subsidized many of these start-ups, investment capital, some of it foreign, circulated in Russia through 1916. In the summer of that year, the Duma approved the request of one Provizor Ivanov to open a factory of medicinal substances in the city of Tashkent. The factory was slated to make a mind-reeling number of items: acetyl-salicylic acid, salts, iodine, bromine, protein, antipyrine, lecithin, tinctures, extracts.[113] Factories in the planning stages for Moscow early in 1916 included a Dye Factory "Russo-Kraska," with fundamental capital of 5,000,000 rubles, and a pharmaceutical factory with a proposed budget of 1,000,000 rubles.[114] In the summer of 1916, a newly capitalized stock company, the Pabiianitskii Stock Company, was finishing the outfitting of a factory in Moscow. The cost of the first stage of outfitting amounted to 300,000 rubles. The company was related to the Society of Chemical Industry in Basle.[115]

Professors at universities and higher educational institutions contributed to solving the medicaments problem.[116] Professor S. Przhibytek served on the Interdepartmental (government) Committee, which met in the spring of 1915,[117] and on the Petrograd City Committee, which met in the winter of 1915/1916. The latter, formed to make the capital self-sufficient in medicines, is discussed below. Przhibytek, along with seasoned radical A. S. Aluf, later served in the Scientific Section of the Soviet Pharmacy Commission.[118]

Other professors struggled to produce pharmaceuticals, heretofore imported, in their university laboratories. They were greatly assisted by government funds. The Moscow Higher Technical School (MVTU) organized the Moscow Committee for the Organization of the Production of Medicinal Substances.[119] The Chair of the Committee was Professor A. E. Chichibabin. From funds allocated from Prince Ol'denburg, head of the government's "Sanitary and Evacuation Sector," Professor Chichibabin established a special factory that began to produce alkaloids such as morphine, codeine, dionin, heroin, atropine, and theobromine.[120] Chichibabin later played a major role in *Farmatsentr,* the Soviet agency that nationalized and ran pharmacies and pharmaceutical enterprises.[121]

The Polytechnical Institute in Kiev allocated funds to faculty member Professor Kashchenko to "acclimatize" and cultivate medicinal plants.[122] In 1915 Professor S. N. Reformatskii of St. Vladimir University, Kiev, developed fifteen medicinal substances not formerly produced in Russia. These included formalin, chloroform, aspirin, caffeine, novocaine, sublimate, atropine, piramidon, salicylic natron, or sodium salicylate.[123] Reformatskii had problems producing chloroform. However, by the spring of 1915 a consortium of the Physico-Chemical Society in the laboratories of St. Vladimir University, the Polytechnic Institute, and higher womens' courses under his direction and that of T. I. Lonachevskii-Petruniak, produced some amounts of novocaine, ether, caffeine, antipyrine, salipyrine, and salicylates.[124]

One Professor Osipov established a factory for galenical preparations in Khar'kov. Less useful was the university's establishment of a museum of medicinal plants. Kuznetsov and Kondakov, professors at Iur'ev University (presumably in the Pharmaceutical Institute), cultivated medicinal plants.[125]

During 1915 professors at Tomsk University produced aspirin, antipyrine, and chloroform. Professor Bogorodskii at Kazan University produced 250 grams of crystallized iodine. Professors at Novorossiisk University in Odessa produced arsenic.[126]

Professional societies lent their talents to manufacturing pharmaceuticals. In Kiev, in the Ukraine, the Physical-Chemical Society organized both production of medicaments and their distribution to clinics and hospitals at the outset of the war. As noted, the society organized a factory for the production of chloroform; I. E. Dushkii, D. K. Martsshevskii, and P. V. Fal'shtinskii directed the factory. In November 1914, the All-Russian Zemstvo Union proclaimed the chloroform equivalent in quality to that of the Shering Pharmaceutical firm. The Committee for Military-Technical Assistance organized a chemical-pharmaceutical section in 1915.[127] In 1915, to counter "the syndicates of druggists and speculators" that had caused "insufficiency of medicine and high prices," the Marxist-oriented Russian Pharmacy Society in Moscow made its contribution to the war effort. It spent 3,000 rubles outfitting a laboratory to produce medicines.[128]

Zemstvos and cities attempted to solve the medicaments crisis. At the outset of the war Mensheviks recommended that public institutions order medicines and pharmaceutical supplies from abroad. They particularly commended the Tver and Moscow zemstvos.[129] Delegates to the "Chief Medical Inspector's Interdepartmental Committee on the Pharmaceutical Industry," which met from February to April 1915, and the members of "The Petrograd Committee for Independent Preparation of Medicines," which met from October 1915 through February 1916, likewise considered zemstvos and cities, and their umbrella organizations The Union of Zemstvos and Zemgor, important players in combating the medicaments crisis.[130] However, in general the Interdepartmental Committee was slightly more sympathetic to the needs of private pharmaceutical enterprises in the growing competition between them and public institutions. As would be expected, the representative to the Interdepartmental Committee from the Union of Zemstvos urged government funding to public institutions. The representative from the Ministry of Ways and Communications agreed and intimated that requisitioning supplies from private enterprises was acceptable. The representative from the Red Cross, on the contrary, rejected requisitioning and the representative from the Ministry of Trade and Industry noted that the Union of Zemstvos and Cities was only a temporary organization and therefore should be relegated to coordinating supply.[131] This support for public pharmacy and pharmaceutical industry that developed during the war and the tensions between private and public enterprise will be discussed in the following chapter.

On the practical front, zemstvos and cities resorted partly to foreign sourcing to increase the supply of medicines. For example, the All-Russian Zemstvo Congress allocated 10 million rubles to a commission for purchase of drugs from friendly countries. By the end of 1916 the All-Russian Zemstvo Union had spent 530,800 pounds sterling on goods from England, 64,000 pounds sterling on wares from France, 52,600 pounds on wares from Holland, 22,700 on wares from America, and 13,900 on wares from Switzerland.[132] English and American goods were routed through Sweden,[133] Arkhangel'sk, and via Japan, although internal transport was still a problem. American wares from Vladivostok reached areas like Tiflis only with difficulty.[134]

But zemstvos, cities, and the All-Zemstvo and City unions also strove to produce chemical pharmaceuticals and to collect and cultivate medicinal plants as well as buy abroad. The All-Russian Zemstvo Union outfitted a factory for the production of salicylic preparations.[135] The Ufa provincial zemstvo organized production of surgical instruments in small factories and workshops.[136] The All-Russian Union of Cities built a small factory in the village of Preobrazhenskoe for the production of phenacetin, chlorethyl, and salicylic preparations.[137] At the end of 1915 a factory built by the Perm zemstvo was producing 1,200,000 *puds* of superphosphates. Production of sulfuric acid in the first eight months of 1914 amounted to 506,000 *puds*. It increased to 693,000 by the fall of 1915.[138]

Native medicinal plants played an important part in solving the medicaments crisis.

Licorice root (*Solodkovyi koren'*), club moss (*Likopodii*), the fungus-based *Sporyn'ia*, and santonin, all of which Russia exported before the war, mainly from Poltava province, continued to be exported during World War I. Club moss brought the greatest return. Exports dropped to a mere 2,000 *puds* in 1915 for a sum of 91,000 rubles but climbed to 3,800 *puds* in 1916 which returned 387,000 rubles. In 1917, 2,400 *puds* were exported for 240,000 rubles. Exports of licorice root dropped to a third or less of their prewar levels but still brought in sizable amounts of rubles. In 1914,

652,231 *puds* were exported for 426,000 rubles; in 1915 only a third of that amount was exported, but ruble income remained the same. Exports dropped to 38,000 *puds* in 1916 for a return of 194,000 rubles, then leapt to 234,000 *puds* in 1917, bringing in 275,000 rubles.[139] Santonin, selling for 180,000 rubles per ton in 1917 brought in 1,566,000 rubles. While the medicaments problem of World War I involved not so much paying for imports of medicine as receiving shipments and increasing domestic production, obviously rubles earned on exports helped to defer import costs and could be channeled to start-ups and production costs.

Additionally, enormous efforts were devoted to gathering and cultivating medicinal plants that Russia did not produce or did not widely produce before the war. Major pharmaceutical firms led the efforts, including Snapir and Kanenbaum in Kremenchug, Shtol' and Shmidt, the Russian Society of Trade in Pharmaceutical Wares, B. Maskol'skii in Petrograd, Ermans and Company in Moscow, IUROTAT in Kiev, Iu. Lemme and Company in Odessa, The Russian Society of Colonial Trade located in Rostov-on-the-Don, and the Caucasian Society of Trade in Pharmaceutical Wares, located in Tiflis.[140] The Experimental Field in the village of Tsarskoe Selo, near Petrograd, which had belonged to the Pel' and Sons Stock Company for ten years, ordered belladonna seeds from Gaare and Shmidt in Erfurt. The plants "grew well." Only their leaves had heretofore been used to extract alkaloids but with wartime exigencies, the stalks were exploited as well.[141]

However, since collection and cultivation of medicinal plants was not so specialized as production of medicines based on chemicals and synthesis, this activity also was the purview of botanical gardens, zemstvos, educational and religious institutions, and the public. But it should be noted that, despite the popular demeanor of these projects, the Russian government supplied much of the funding.

Immediately after Russia's entry into the war, the Russian Physical-Chemical Society convened a special meeting August 12, 1914, to discuss measures to supply medicaments to Petrograd treatment centers and citizens. Concluding that medicines were severely needed because more hospitals had been established and the store of medicines, particularly those imported from Germany, was not large, the society was determined to produce medicine.[142]

The Russian Society for Assisting Development of the Chemical Industry drafted a list of twenty-three medicinal plants, the cultivation of which should be emphasized for producing medicines. The Petrograd Pharmaceutical Society expanded the list to fifty-two and specified amounts needed. The plant materials included flowers and herbs (iris, chamomile, rosemary, crocus, coriander) in varying amounts, from 30 *puds* of aconite roots to 600 *puds* of digatalis leaves to 2,500 *puds* of belladonna leaves and 10,000 *puds* of valerian root.[143] The society also drew up a second list of "wild" medicinal plants that could be collected.[144] The list of "wild" plants was sent to the Chief Medical Inspector in the Ministry of Internal Affairs; that on cultivation was sent to the Minister of Agriculture and Land Use.[145] In November 1914, the Imperial Russian Technical Society sent out questionnaires as to what plants could be cultivated. More practically, the Society of "Public Assistance" organized the culture of cinchona trees, camphor trees, and the opium poppy in the Crimea and Black Sea region, particularly near Sochi. The Moscow Society for Acclimatization received a government subsidy for cultivating medicinal plants.[146]

Botanical Gardens and Agricultural Societies quickly began to cultivate medicinal plants. At the beginning of the war the Imperial Botanical Garden in Petrograd organized a special department under the direction of the chief botanist, appropriately named N. A. Monteverde, to disseminate information on seeds and coordinate the growing of medicinal plants. The department drew up a list of foreign and Russian firms trading in seeds and roots. Of Russian firms there were three in Petrograd, three in the city of Moscow and one in Moscow province, and one each in Riga, Voronezh, Riazan, and Khar'kov.[147] More practically, in Moscow province the workshops for medicaments of Prince Ol'denburg (Supreme Authority of Sanitation and Evacuation) began producing opium-based alkaloids. In 1915 the Tiflis Botanical Garden under A. Kh. Rollov, The Imperial Nikitin Garden near Yalta under N. F. Kuznetsov, the Kiev Polytechnical Institute under Kashchenko, the Odessa Experimental Field under V. G. Rotm(e)istr, the Medicinal Plant Section in the Sukhum Experimental Station under V. V. Markovich, and the Botanical Garden in Khar'kov University under A. G. Zaikevich cultivated medicinal plants.[148] The Society of Agriculture in Turkestan built a nursery of medicinal plants in Tashkent in 1915.[149] The Lubernskoe Agricultural Society of Poltava province in the Ukraine bought up medicinal herbs.[150] Workshops in Poltava prepared mint oil.[151] Cultivation of *kastorka* for castor oil had good results in the Crimea.[152] Cooperatives for the cultivation of medicinal plants stretched across the south–in Turkestan, the Crimea, and the Caucasus.[153] The Migration Station in western Siberia grew English mint.[154]

Many medicinal plants grew wild in Russia, having been part of popular therapeutics though not the official pharmacopoeia for centuries.[155] Great energy was expended on collecting the bulbs and seeds of these plants, in some cases domesticating them, in others, processing them. Collecting was somewhat sporadic. The Turkestan Agricultural Society focused on gathering *durmana* seeds, the base for atropine,[156] and atropine was duly produced in the region.[157] The *kleshcheviny* plant was gathered for castor oil in Simferopol'.[158] During 1915 the Tiflis Botanical Garden, under orders from Prince Alexander Ol'denburg, head of the Sanitation and Evacuation Sector, established a nursery of medicinal plants and also organized collection parties directed by seven specialists. Ol'denburg gave the botanical garden 6,180 rubles to purchase seeds of *durmana* and belladonna, valerian roots, and so forth. In one month Tiflis and Kutais had gathered 3,287 and ¾ *funt* of roots and bulbs and 75,000 stalks.[159]

Organized collecting varied from province to province. Among the southwestern provinces, Kiev and Chernigov had the best-organized programs. One of the chief medicinal plants collected was valerian root. In the remaining southwestern provinces collection was very limited. In the southern provinces (Voronezh, Kursk, Ekaterinoslav, Poltava, Tavrida, and the region of the Don army) thirty kinds of plants were collected. Most were collected in Poltava and Voronezh. The plants often were sold to local pharmacies and through intermediaries to large pharmaceutical firms and warehouses such as Keler, Ferrein, and Snapir, although a report noted that "there should be wider use of these plants in zemstvo warehouses." In the southeastern steppe provinces (Astrakhan, Orenburg, Stavropol' and the Ural, Kuban and Tersk regions) large amounts of five varieties of plants and smaller amounts of other plants were gathered. But, "because of the expense involved in gathering plants" there was "no chance of great development" of this activity. Therefore, it recommended that collectors concentrate on *Atropa belladonna, Adonis vernalis,* and *Valeriana officinalis.* In the Crimea there was no organized collection, except for small-scale collection of belladonna. It was urged that collection be made easier in "treasury" forests. There was no organized collection in the east or west Caucasus (Bakinsk, Elizavetpol'sk, Tiflis, Yerevan, Kutais, Sukhum, Batum regions) although large amounts of medicinal plants were informally collected and worked up in the turpentine factory of His Highness Prince Nikolai Mikhailovich. There also was no organized collection of wild medicinal plants in the western Siberian provinces of Tomsk and Tobol'sk. However, local pharmacies in Tobol'sk province and Turiinsisk district bought small amounts of medicinal plants and local inhabitants collected about twenty kinds of plants for home use. Interestingly, in the eastern Siberian province of Yenisei, particularly Minusinsk and Krasnoiarsk districts, "industrial" collection of medicinal plants had been organized by "foreign agents." Six types of plants were collected. In Primorsk region ginseng was collected and sold through buyers to the Chinese; prices for this item ranged from 40 or 50 to 200 rubles per *funt.* Inhabitants also collected medicinal plants for home use. There was some collecting in Turkestan or Central Asia but cultivation was more prevalent. There was a call for study of medicinal plants native to the region.[160]

Teachers and schoolchildren were drafted to collect medicinal plants such as belladonna[161] and the narcotic *stramonium,* or thorn apple. In Odessa the inspector of the educational district notified all principals that an advance of 5 rubles had been sent for purchase of seeds collected–10 kopeks per *funt*–and proposed organizing collection by students.[162] In Kremenchug, specialists collected wild medicinal plants,[163] which the pharmaceutical firms Snapir and Kanenbaum then purchased. As mentioned above, the Poltava Agricultural Society, the Ekaterinburg district zemstvo, the Tver provincial zemstvo, and pharmaceutical firms purchased medicinal herbs.[164]

Orthodox Church officials lent their support to the cultivation campaign. In the fall of 1916 Archbishops Antonii of Khar'kov and Dmitrii of Tavrida successfully grew medicinal herbs and flowers in the monasteries of their dioceses.[165] Simultaneously, the government department, the Holy Synod, ordered all monasteries to grow medicinal plants.[166]

Courses and books on collecting and cultivation appeared. A course on cultivation of medicinal plants was held at the University of Iur'ev in the spring of 1916. Fifteen people were trained. It was planned to hold the course annually beginning in September 1916.[167] Some courses were targeted for specialists, such as the six-week course offered at the Sukhum Experimental Station, which began May 10, 1916. Thirty people with middle level agricultural or pharmaceutical education were permitted to enroll.[168] Other programs trained specialists for field work. In January 1916 the Department of Agriculture opened a bureau for plant cultivation and courses on the chemistry of medicinal plants. These were to last three months followed by laboratory training. Those completing the course were to be sent to the Caucasus and Central Asia for work "in situ."[169] In the spring of 1916 the Ministry of Education sent one Paskevich to Kiev in the spring of 1916 to organize the collection of medicinal plants, such as valerian root. Rural schools were involved in the collection.[170] In the summer of 1916 an instructor at the Podolia provincial zemstvo, S. A. Zelinskii, published a pamphlet on the "Cultivation of Medicinal Plants," which sold for 1 ruble, 50 kopeks. A more comprehensive tome, *Russian Medicinal Plants,* was advertised at 12 rubles.[171] A brochure on cultivating valerian root in the Caucasus sold out by the fall of 1916; a second edition of 5,000 copies was scheduled to be printed.[172]

❖❖❖

These disparate, sometimes frantic, attempts to increase pharmaceutical production achieved uneven results.[173]

Russians broke a number of patents. Before the war Russia used exclusively German thermometers. By the fall of 1915 a new factory, based on the research of Nechaev and Mal'tsev, had produced the special glass needed for thermometers and production was moving forward.[174] The chemistry laboratory in the Sergeev pharmacy of E. M. Vestberg and Master of Pharmacy V. K. Tomson developed formulae for producing salicylic acid, ammonium salicylicum, lithium, natrium salicylicum, or sodium salicylate, and iodide salts.[175] In March 1916, the Moscow chemist I. I. Ostromyslenskii produced Russian "Salvarsan" in his Moscow University clinic. It was called "Arsol." Although the raw materials necessary for the drug were located in Russia, because of insufficiency of them and lack of wood spirits, Ostromyslenskii was not able to mass-produce the antivenereal preparation. However, tests by other Russian researchers, such as Professor V. V. Ivanov, the Military Medical Academy in Petrograd, and various hospital clinics got good results from "Arsol" and showed the product was equal to "Salvarsan."[176]

Production of coal tar and coal-tar byproducts was particularly successful. Although this source for dyes and salicylic products was plentiful in the Donetsk Basin, before the war Russia imported 2,461 *puds* of coal tar from Germany.[177] A turnaround occurred during 1915. Benzol and toluol, obtained from coking, increased significantly.[178] K. S. Sarkisov informed the chemical sector of the Caucasian Region War Industries Committee in November 1915 that during the first half of 1915, 97,000 *puds* of benzol had been manufactured in the Donetsk Basin; the completion of a new factory in November 1915, increased production even more. In Baku a factory to produce toluol had been proposed.[179] The Kazan city duma outfitted a city gas factory in December 1915, at a cost of 15,453 rubles plus 5,000 rubles for operating costs.[180] A few months later the Kazan gas factory was producing benzol.[181] Production of benzol and toluol in turn stimulated production of important chemicals—phenol, sulfuric dyes, chloroform, salicylic acid, protorgol, *tannalbin*, utropin, lubymin, tannoform.[182] In the spring of 1916 the Kazan War Industries Committee held a small exhibit of phenol, salicylic acid, sodium salicylate obtained from the benzol made by the Kazan gas works.[183] In August 1916, M. I. Sosaar, member of the administration of the Association R. Keler and Company, wrote enthusiastically that "in a short time we will be guaranteed a sufficient amount of our own benzol—a most important product—the base for dyes, explosives, and many medicinal substances. Simultaneously with obtaining benzol we began fabricating phenol (pure carbolic acid) from it.

It is made at present in an amount which will cover with large surplus all our needs in peacetime. Further, we have begun to prepare from phenol salicylic acid and its combinations, salicylic soda, salicylic metal, and aspirin. There exist already a whole range of enterprises, equipped for this purpose. . . ."[184]

Like coal-tar byproducts, most pyrites were imported before the war. Only a few factories near the Ural Mountains used domestic pyrites. Early in 1916 *Kommersant* reported that the "Combined energy of industrialists and the government" during 1915 "achieved significant improvement in the extraction of sulfuric pyrites." As a result, "production of sulfuric acid, so necessary for the needs of government defense, significantly increased. The extraction of mercury had increased "greatly," thereby increasing production of mercury salts–sublimate and calomel; the production of ether, antifebrin, and terpinhydrate also increased.[185]

Cultivating medicinal plants literally bore fruit, as well. By the spring of 1916 the botanical gardens in Tiflis had established an opium poppy plantation. A special knife had been brought from China to obtain opium from the head of the poppy. Experimental stations for cultivating various medicinal plants had been had been established in Sukhum and Odessa.[186]

Collecting medicinal plants also contributed to production of crucial pharmaceuticals. In the fall of 1916 the Estonian Society of Agriculture held an exhibition of items produced by the Iur'ev War Industries Committee, the Iur'ev region All-Russian Union of Cities, and the Baltic Factory of War Supply. The number of medicinal plants collected was impressive.[187] Of course Estonia was soon to leave the empire.

Before the war Russia imported fish oil from Norway. By the end of 1915 she obtained sizable quantities of fish oil in Arkhangel'sk.[188]

Production of iodine, another crucial pharmaceutical substance, which Russia had not heretofore produced, made headway. In 1914 Professor L. V. Pisarevskii of the Ekaterinoslav Mining Institute, Professor A. Zernov, and senior laborant N. D. Averkiev, set up an experimental station to produce iodine. The iodine was derived from "red fillofora," a plant growing in the Black Sea near Odessa. Initial experiments resulted in 3½ *puds* of metallic iodine, the quality of which excelled requirements of the State Pharmacopoeia.[189] Completed in March 1915, by the fall of that year the factory produced more than 10 *funts* daily, or 4 *puds* per month.[190] Between March 1915 and 1918 the factory produced 1,000 kilograms of metallic iodine, 2,500 kilograms of tincture of iodine, 50 kilograms of various iodine preparations, and 3,000 tons of liquid disinfectants.[191]

By the summer of 1916 several other iodine extraction stations were in operation. In Tomsk, western Siberia, the factory established by the Migration Administration extracted 1,000 *puds* of iodine worth 350,000 rubles by mid-1916, although transport to European Russia was very expensive. The Supreme Authority of Sanitation and Evacuation under Prince Ol'denburg conducted tests in Murmansk in 1915. Because summer and fall storms washed up large amounts of seaweed, iodine and potassium salts were cheaper and more accessible than in other locations. Professor V. E. Tishchenko and Arkhangel'sk merchants built an iodine factory in the White Sea area. Subsidized by the Supreme Authority of Sanitation and Evacuation, Professor Tishchenko derived iodine from the ashes of seaweed and sea cabbage. Unfortunately, seaweed decreased due to fewer storms and the ashes had a very low iodine content of only 0.12–0.13 percent. Stations on the Caspian Sea and on the Sea of Okhotsk ultimately produced iodine. By mid-1916 the total production of iodine was 2,000 *puds*, that of potassium salts—75,000 *puds*. Much larger quantities of these items were needed. Therefore the Chief Committee of Zemstvos and Cities debated organizing new factories for producing iodine, chloride potassium, and Bertoletov salts in areas where the soil had high potash content. Research was conducted on extracting iodine from the oily waters and dirt of the Crimea.[192]

A Soviet historian has asserted that the collection and cultivation of medicinal plants was hindered by lack of warehouses.[193] That may be. Nevertheless, the amount of belladonna, atropine, castor oil, and opiates increased to a fair degree. The 1915 crop of the castor oil plant, which grew profusely in the Caucasus and in Turkestan, was not harvested in time. The material had been destined for the Vogau and Keler firms.[194] Happily, during 1916, the castor oil plant, under the direction of Prince Ol'denburg, was cultivated to "a very wide degree" in Turkestan and Novorossiisk region in the Caucasus; 10,000 dessiatines had been planted. Cultivation of the opium poppy in Semirech'e also was "significant" by 1916. The harvest was 50 *funts* per dessiatine at a price of 480 rubles per *funt.*[195] In November 1916, the Supreme Authority of the Sanitation and Evacuation sector, Prince Ol'denburg, sent two wagons of dry belladonna to Petrograd and 400 *puds* of rich starch and castor oil seeds to the Caucasian front to produce castor oil. Ol'denburg sent seeds to experimental stations and eighteen schools: 1,000 *puds* of *durmana* for atropine to the laboratory of Professor Chichibabin in Moscow, and 2,000 *puds* of *lavra* to make vegetables for the army. Other supplies included 6,000 *puds* of bottled fruit juice.[196] Analysis of the dry leaves of belladonna in 1916 showed that they contained a high content of atropine leading to the conclusion that Russia might become self-sufficient in production of this substance.[197]

❖❖❖

The diversity of Russian pharmaceuticals increased each year of the war. In the spring of 1915 F. A. Ferrein informed the Interdepartmental Government Committee that Russia was producing chloroform, potassium chlorate, potassium manganate, carbolic acid, fitin, lecithin, amygdalin, *tannalbin*, mercury preparations, calomel, bismuth salts, adrenaline, terpinhydrate, sulfo-carbolic zinc, and other chemical products.[198] By August 1915, V. Sadikov crowed that "the war has strengthened the productivity of our pharmaceutical factories, thanks to absence of imports and competition, thanks to increased orders and higher prices." He noted that factories first used materials at hand, then began to seek new domestic sources of raw materials.[199] A year later, in August 1916, M. I. Sosaar of Keler and Company, noted that "serious quantities" of formalin, urotropin, albuminate, tannin, and tanoform were being produced. Russia was preparing Salvarsan, adrenaline, chlorethyl, the topical anesthetic, and terpinhydrate. Sosaar praised the achievements made in extracting iodine from seaweed. He also commended one Professor I. A. Kabulkov for deriving bromine from ores of the salt seas in Tavrida province. He admitted that there were still some insufficiencies in the market but this was mainly because many materials had been swallowed up by the military.[200]

Of course, much pharmaceutical production was incipient and small-scale. Additionally, several public and governmental initiatives met dead ends. One of the most conspicuous public failures occurred in Petrograd. During the winter of 1915 and 1916 the city executive council of the Petrograd city duma, the Petrograd City Hospital Commission, and citizenry formed a committee to make the city "self-sufficient" in medicaments.[201] The committee adjudged that Petrograd was in need of sixteen inorganic preparations and five in particular, including *Zincum oxydatum*, *Zincum sulfuricum*, *Plumbum aceticum*, *Ferrum sesquichlorat*, and *Ferrum hydrogen. reductum*. The city needed twenty-one organic preparations and nine of these in particular, including acetic acid (*acidum aceticum puriss*), salicylic acid (*acidum salicylicum*), aspirin, codeine, morphine, and caffeine.[202] Academician N. S. Kurnakov chaired the committee. Public representatives included two town councillors; a member of the St. Petersburg provincial zemstvo executive board; D. Ia. Blumental', assistant manager of the Red Cross Warehouse and a representative from the Red Cross; and Iu. R. Vitman, manager of the Warehouse of the Union of Cities.[203] There were nine physicians,[204] five staff or academic pharmacists,[205] eleven professors,[206] and one engineer.[207] The hospital commission was represented by five individuals.[208] There were only four representatives from industry including three from the pharmaceutical industry: I. A. Merdbitts, chairman of the firm "Shtol' and Shmidt"; B. P. Shaskol'skii, chairman of the trading company "Shaskol'skii and Co."; V. I. Pokhitonov, director of the Tentelevskii Factory; director of the joint-stock company timber-cutting factory, A. A. Tupal'skii.[209] The heavy emphasis on public figures and academics undoubtedly accounted for the bias against private enterprise and toward public institutions in the meetings of the Petrograd Committee, a subject discussed in the following chapter.

The St. Petersburg Committee planned to convert the Vasilievskii Island water treatment plant into a factory for producing medicines and a warehouse. However, although the committee meticulously worked out expenditures and discussed the proposed medicaments plant at length from November 1915 through February 1916,[210] it was more conspicuous for the enthusiasm and good intentions of its members than practical results. In the end, according to a Soviet historian, the project came to naught because of "lack of material means (allocations, equipment, etc.)."[211]

Additionally, some public and governmental projects needlessly duplicated manufacture by private pharmaceutical enterprises, competing with these firms rather than building on their foundations. Some public and government projects were still on the drawing boards in the spring of 1916, despite having been allocated large sums, and some which saw the light of day were unproductive. Before the war chloroform for narcotic purposes was imported. At the beginning of the war Professors Reformatskii and Esorov began making chloroform–of a higher quality than heretofore imported–in their laboratory at St. Vladimir University in Kiev. Unfortunately, the factory that the professors planned to mass-produce chloroform never materialized. Therefore, the Tentelevskii chemical factory began making chloroform; it was sent to pharmacist Karl Ivanovich Kresling for refining.[212]

Although the treasury allocated Prince Ol'denburg 300,000 rubles from the treasury for the building of a factory to prepare technical and chemical products in Moscow, it was still in the planning stage in the spring of 1916.[213] The same was true of a salicylic factory planned for Moscow by the All-Russian Zemstvo Union, which was to be outfitted at a cost of 52,525 rubles.[214] A similar development occurred with a factory to make hygroscopic cotton. Production of this item, 90 percent of which had come from Germany and Austria, was given top priority after the outbreak of the war. The All-Russian Union of Zemstvos built a factory in Moscow for the purpose. However, the factory was closed because of "technological inadequacy and unproductive personnel." In Omsk, western Siberia, the

Migration Administration proposed to the Moscow Society of Rural Economy that it equip a factory for the making of formalin from wood spirits. That factory had not even been begun in early 1916.[215] Despite this, in August 1916 Prince Ol'denburg queried of some zemstvos "whether it would be possible for them to establish chemical factories" to produce distilled products such as formalin. The zemstvos duly requested of Ol'denburg a 258,000 subsidy (*posobie*) to establish the factories and a 335,000-ruble interest-free loan (*bezprotsentnaia ssuda*) for their basic operating capital.[216] While private entrepreneurs had established an iodine processing plant on the shores of the White Sea, a Zemgor committee was only just debating a similar proposal in late 1916 when it asked Prince Ol'denburg for 70,000 rubles for a start-up.[217] Similarly, in 1916, an aspirin factory was only in the process of being established in Turkestan, the factory housing it having been procured with public funds.[218]

Some private initiatives also failed. Output of mercury, sublimate, and calomel did not reach required targets. Ferrein and Keler and Company managed to produce carbolic acid from Donetsk Basin coking, but quantities were insufficient.[219] However, there were fewer failures on the part of private entrepreneurs than with public projects.

The pharmaceutical market was volatile in 1915. But there were signs that the medicaments crisis was abating. Even more hopeful, there were indications that Russian pharmaceutical production was advancing.

In Moscow, in the fall of 1915, prices for aspirin, codeine and some other key items were high, in some cases seventeen times more than before the war. Some proposed importing more of these items from Sweden. Others put faith in domestic production. Moscow professors recommended publishing an official list of medicines produced by Russian firms that could replace imported medicine. One Professor Savel'ev contended that "in the near future" Russia "entirely can do without foreign patented preparations."[220]

In late 1915 *Kommersant* reported that prices of imported products, such as Chilean saltpeter, zinc, lead, Bertoletov salts, and tartaric acid–had risen 300 to 400 percent and prices of several Russian-made substances such as unrefined sulfuric acid, Glauber's salts, and iron vitriol were still high because of scarcities.[221] Salicylic products were scarce in 1915, since imports from France had stopped and shipments from England and America were slow. In some cases prices for salicylic products, such as phenacetin, were twenty times prewar prices and speculation was rife. On the other hand, prices for bismuth and iodine fell during 1915. In part this was due to shipments of bismuth from America and England and imports of iodine from England and Japan. Prices for mercury were very high but there were expectations that mercury preparations and sublimate being made in Moscow would force them down. There were no shortages of disinfectants in 1915.[222] Additionally, the Russian Red Cross shipped 100,000 rubles' worth of medicine to Serbia from its warehouses.[223] Thus, some supplies were plentiful in 1915.

The medicaments situation continued to fluctuate during 1916. Some claimed that both wholesale and retail prices were being kept artificially high. For example, one large firm in the Caucasus that traded in pharmaceutical wares reportedly raised prices of castor oil, fish oil, and pharmacy glass 300 percent because the goods were not transported in its own wagons. Speculation in pharmaceuticals also was noted. There were allegations that inorganic acids, carbolic acid, and *naftalin* had been bought up to induce scarcity. Large druggists were not able to purchase these items, thus causing shortages of alkaloids such as morphine, cocaine, and atropine, benzonaftal and potassium manganate, and even Russian vinegar essence and Russian vaseline for the general public.[224] *Farmatsevticheskii zhurnal*—traditionally the mouthpiece of the pharmaceutical establishment–reported that some Russian chemical and pharmaceutical firms had made huge profits during the first year of the war. The Tentelevskii Stock Company's net profit was 862.7 thousand rubles in 1915, as compared with 237.5 thousand in 1913; the Ferrein Stock Company's net profit was 792 thousand rubles in 1915 compared with 284 thousand in 1913.[225] The journal further claimed that some pharmacies were gouging consumers. A street test revealed that three Petrograd pharmacies had rejected a customer's request for salicylic acid, not because of lack of supplies but because the Pharmacy Tax did not defray the pharmacy's cost. Wholesale prices for a kilo of *salol* had jumped to 140 rubles compared with its prewar cost of 2 rubles, 60 kopeks. A kilo of carbolic acid cost 15 rubles compared to 1 ruble, 10 kopeks before the war. The tax required pharmacies to dispense 10 grains of *tiokol* at 94½ kopeks whereas it cost them 1 ruble, 90 kopeks. Similarly, the tax listed one unit of one type of quinine at 1 ruble, 46 kopeks and another at 1 ruble, 30 kopeks, whereas wholesale prices for these items were 1 ruble, 55 kopeks and 1 ruble 45 kopeks, respectively.[226]

In November 1916 prices for many key medicines were still higher than before the war.[227] Nevertheless, some areas enjoyed ample medicine at fair prices in 1916. *Kommersant* reported that while prices of most chemicals and pharmaceuticals were still high in early 1916, the price of soda had dropped.[228] A Kiev pharmacy owner informed *Farmatsevticheskii zhurnal* that many medicines were plentiful in Kiev and that he was selling them at prices lower than those of IUROTAT, the wholesale drug firm. IUROTAT listed quinine at 150 rubles a kilo in its price list; the pharmacy owner sold it for 125 rubles. IUROTAT listed *salol* at 100 rubles a kilo; the owner sold it for 80 rubles.[229] Encouraged by these developments, *Farmatsevticheskii zhurnal* urged pharmacy owners to "make known the true state of things" to the public.[230]

The drug situation was particularly satisfactory in Odessa by the summer and fall of 1916. In September, the Odessa Society of Pharmacy Owners requested that the Medical Council review the March Pharmacy Tax with a view to *lowering* it on some items.[231] The Odessa pharmacy owners claimed that aspirin, piramidon, bromine, and other preparations "the price of which was raised in March, have now appeared in the market of the [zemstvo and city] unions . . . and are cheaper; therefore the price on them must be significantly lowered." On the other hand, Odessa pharmacy owners recommended that prices for oils, plasters, and other items should remain unchanged or be raised.[232]

In 1916, as in 1915, greater availability of pharmaceutical wares and hence lower prices were partly due to increased foreign imports, chiefly from England. Imports, in turn, were helped by a rise in the value of the ruble.[233] The stronger ruble testified to the beginning of economic recovery.

But Russian pharmaceutical production also contributed to the growing stockpile of medicines and lower prices by 1916. In September 1916, the Petrograd Stock Market Committee announced "lower prices for a whole range of wares. . . ." In particular, "a significant lowering of prices was observed in the market for pharmacy wares . . . prices for pharmacy wares continue to decline at the present time. Some medical and pharmaceutical wares are two to three times cheaper than at the beginning of the year."[234]

In production of certain pharmaceuticals, Russia surpassed England. The last issue of *Farmatsevticheskii zhurnal*, December 15, 1916, noted that England produced phenol, benzol, and salicylic acid only in insignificant quantities and *salol* not at all.[235] The Russian laboratory in the factory of the Union of Cities, meanwhile, had wound up its experiments on the production of phenacetin (also not made in England), had applied for a patent, and was beginning to produce phenacetin on a mass scale. Prices for phenacetin were still "colossal," but it was predicted that Russian production would lead to lower prices. "At the same time prices for salicylic acid and bromide preparations" were "falling" and other medicines were "prepared in Russia in great amounts."[236]

Truncated, smudged editions of pharmacy journals in 1916 testified to the shortage and poor quality of paper in this third year of the war. In the area of pharmaceutical production, there is question as to whether the intense energy that Russians expended on the medicaments crisis could have been maintained after the war, whether the quality, quantity, and diversity of Russian pharmaceuticals would have been competitive on the international market. Nevertheless, insofar as the medicaments crisis was concerned, Russia was seeing some rays of light at the end of the tunnel on the eve of the February Revolution and there is some reason to believe that progress might have continued after the war. The breakthroughs and increased productivity in the pharmaceutical industry that resulted from the struggle with the medicaments shortage might have enabled Russia to enjoy self-sufficiency in pharmaceuticals and additionally, might have strengthened private enterprise.

However, grappling with the medicaments shortage engendered political and social attitudes and policies that ultimately were to overturn pharmacy, the pharmaceutical industry and the entire political and social fabric of the empire. As we shall see in the following chapter, the war reinforced big government and centralization, traditional in Russia. The war also validated socialized pharmacy in many people's minds. Further, the war brought to the fore individuals who were later to play a major role in the Soviet pharmacy organization. These included old-time radicals like A. Aluf, Ia. Kanevskii, and Iu. Kuperman as well as new converts like Professors S. Przhibytek and A. E. Chichibabin, F. A. Ferrein, Alexander Semenovich Ginzberg, E. Ia. Abol', and O. G. Gabrilovich. These developments paved the way for Menshevik and then Bolshevik pharmacy systems and government in 1917 and 1918.

17

World War I: Toward Revolution, Radical Pharmacists, the Public, the Government

World War I and, more specifically, the so-called medicaments crisis polarized the pharmacy world. But this polarization was not the cleavage between masses and privileged, which some historians claim triggered the 1917 revolutions.[1] Rather, the medicaments crisis pitted pharmacist theorists (principally academic and journalist pharmacists) as well as assorted other theorists (principally politicians and bureaucrats) against practical pharmacists (owners and managers of pharmacies and pharmaceutical enterprises) and pharmacists engaged in dispensing or working in these enterprises.

On the one hand, practical pharmacists–pharmaceutical entrepreneurs and the great majority of rank-and-file pharmacists who were would-be entrepreneurs–kept on with their mundane but productive activities. Indeed, the behavior of rank-and-file pharmacists challenges the portrayal of the revolutions of 1917 as *mass* upheavals, generated by hostility of employees and lower classes toward the propertied. Some workers at the bench may have supported economic revolution. The majority of peasants may have supported economic revolution. Many intellectuals–even most men on the street–may have supported political revolution. Yet few pharmacists were inherently alienated and approved wholesale overturn of traditional pharmacy and the existing economic system. But the war and medicaments crisis brought to the forefront numerous theorists. Among pharmacists they included educational reformers and industrial planners as well as old-time pharmacist revolutionaries. The latter had long been committed to, the former increasingly became convinced of, the necessity of radically changing the existing pharmacy system. Unfortunately, these reformers and revolutionaries were visionaries rather than practical pharmacists. With few exceptions the pharmacist contingent had never actively worked in dispensing or been entrepreneurs. Rather, they were academic and journalist pharmacists. Nor were politicians and bureaucrats who opted for severe changes in the pharmacy system familiar with pharmacy or the pharmaceutical industry. As a consequence, the new pharmacy system the theorists devised was impractical. Worse, it would prove ruinous to pharmacy, the pharmaceutical industry and, ultimately, the common weal.

Practical entrepreneurial or would-be entrepreneurial rank-and-file pharmacists would fight hard to maintain not only themselves but a system that, while flawed, still worked. Rank-and-file pharmacists with less ambition were mostly indifferent to talk of radical change. However, they were no match for the combined strength of visionaries and revolutionaries.

The latter converged from three groups during the war: old-time pharmacist labor organizers and radical pharmacist-journalists; pharmacists predominantly concerned with educational reform; individuals involved with strengthening Russia's pharmaceutical industry—academic pharmacists, politicians, and assorted bureaucrats. It should be noted that women pharmacists, as their male counterparts, were included in both the entrepreneurial/practical and the visionary/revolutionary camps.

Old-Time Labor Organizers and Journalists

On the eve of World War I old-time labor organizers and radical journalists moved their headquarters—the editorial board of their newspaper *Zhizn' farmatsevta*—from Kiev to the capital, St. Petersburg.[2] In April 1914, the St. Petersburg Society of Staff Pharmacists (*Sluzhashchie*) began publishing *Zhizn' farmatsevta*, proclaiming that this was necessary because of the demise of *Farmatsevticheskii trud* in Moscow and *Zhizn' farmatsevta* in Kiev.[3]

Farmatsevticheskii zhurnal, the main-line pharmacy journal for the past thirty-five years, labeled the new journal the mouthpiece of socialists and Jews. It sneered that *Zhizn' farmatsevta* provoked antagonism toward pharmacy owners by accusing them of exploiting staff pharmacists and promoted municipalization (transferring privately owned pharmacies to city dumas and zemstvos), despite the fact that Jewish pharmacists could not receive confirmation from governors to work in city and zemstvo pharmacies.[4]

The St. Petersburg Society of Staff Pharmacists and their journal were indeed socialist. That their orientation was, more specifically, to the Menshevik branch of Russian Marxists, is indicated by the fact that while using Marxist buzzwords, they nonetheless criticized the Bolshevik paper *Pravda* for factionalism.[5] In 1916 the Women's Presidium of the Society sent a telegram to Chkheidze, a Menshevik delegate to the Duma.[6] In 1918, A. Aluf, chairman of the St. Petersburg Society, proclaimed his adherence to the principles of Menshevik Internationalism.[7] *Zhizn' farmatsevta* did try to advance "municipalization."[8] It lauded the opening of city pharmacies in Saratov, Kiev, Moscow, Simferopol',[9] in Orel,[10] and plans for opening a city pharmacy in Ekaterinodar[11] and Nizhni Novgorod[12] in the spring of 1914. But, the journal was objective enough to report slovenly dispensing and understaffing in city-owned pharmacies in Tomsk, Baku, and Samara.[13] The St. Petersburg Society of Staff Pharmacists and *Zhizn' farmatsevta* also purported to speak for "professional" (read socialist) pharmacy societies in other cities. In addition to the St. Petersburg Society of Staff Pharmacists five were registered: The Russian Pharmacy Society in Moscow, the Mutual Aid Society of Staff Pharmacists in Odessa, the South-Western Union of Pharmacists and Pharmacists' Mutual Aid Society both located in Kiev, and the Professional Society of Staff Pharmacists in Rostov-on-the-Don.[14] Most of these societies were small. The St. Petersburg Society of Staff Pharmacists had only about 112 members.[15] The Odessa Society had 180 members.[16] Pharmacists in areas without organized societies sent contributions to the journal.[17]

Whether the St. Petersburg Society and *Zhizn' farmatsevta* were predominantly Jewish is harder to tell. Certainly, the journal publicized the plight of Jews, both before[18] and after the war. On the other hand, some of the strikes that the society and *Zhizn' farmatsevta* lauded occurred in pharmacies owned by Jews. And, as will be seen, conflicts occurred amongst St. Petersburg radicals over the issue of helping Jewish refugees through Jewish "bourgeois" organizations.

In the halcyon months before the war the St. Petersburg and other "professional" societies were able to tend to the cultural enrichment of staff pharmacists. In the spring of 1914 the St. Petersburg society's cultural commission organized an excursion for 65 members to an exhibit of paintings by the *peredvizhniki*, nineteenth-century social critic artists,[19] the Pulkovo Astronomy Observatory, and a chemical factory. For the latter trip, members were advised they would need an entire day off.[20] The society also established a library and discussed founding a literary-musical circle.[21] The Odessa pharmacy society likewise conducted lectures and excursions; members visited a gas factory and first aid station.[22]

Their track record in labor organizing was rockier as a result of the fact that conditions for staff pharmacists varied on the eve of the war. In the capital, fifty-four of ninety-two St. Petersburg pharmacies had "correct shifts." Forty-two pharmacies required night duty eight times per month; the rest had ten, twelve, or fifteen; one had thirty.[23] There were isolated instances of abuse–a woman pharmacist was not allowed to take time off to go to the doctor; a staff pharmacist was fired for talking on the phone.[24] In a few pharmacies shifts, particularly for student pharmacists, were inordinately long,[25] in a few pharmacies pay was low.[26]

However, the St. Petersburg Society and *Zhizn' farmatsevta* never flagged in their commitment to organizing staff pharmacists and improving their conditions of work. They managed to call a few strikes in the months before the war. However, they also employed peaceful tactics–bringing suits against violations, lobbying the Duma and ministers, negotiating and bargaining.

Factory workers in several cities struck on May Day 1914.[27] Staff struck in some St. Petersburg pharmacies in July 1914. The staff in the Edelshtein pharmacy demanded the double shift for all staff, annual two weeks' vacation with pay, increase of staff, abolition of unpaid work for student pharmacists, and increase of their pay. One staff pharmacist refused to strike. Therefore the St. Petersburg Society put the pharmacy under boycott and expelled the recalcitrant pharmacist. The strike was resolved when the pharmacy management conceded salary raises.[28]

As earlier, some strikes clearly overstepped sensible bounds. Pharmacy owners had instituted double shifts in Ekaterinodar. Therefore, staff pharmacists pressured owners for two weeks' vacation with pay and subscriptions to *Zhizn' farmatsevta*.[29]

In general, possibly because of such extremism, on the eve of the war, radical pharmacists lamented that rank-and-file pharmacists were cool to their blandishments. The staff pharmacist in the Edelshtein factory who refused to strike provided a notable example.[30] In Rostov-on-the-Don, leaders of the "professional society" were frustrated by lack of "class consciousness" on the part of staff pharmacists. The latter stubbornly continued to regard themselves as future pharmacy owners rather than "one of the branches of the working class."[31] In Batum some staff pharmacists desired to open a "professional" society but others were opposed.[32]

In the face of this apathy, radical pharmacist leaders resorted to a number of practical measures. The Odessa Society opened an employment bureau, which found places for forty pharmacists during one month. An evening fund-raiser produced funds.[33] The Odessa Society reported income of 535 rubles during the first six months of 1914; the employment bureau placed thirty-five pharmacists although eighty-one were still unemployed.[34] The St. Petersburg Society was business-like enough to establish a Finance Commission.[35] Radical pharmacists brought lawsuits and lobbied. There were several suits on behalf of staff pharmacists during 1913 and the spring of 1914.[36] The St. Petersburg Society offered cut-rate legal advice to those who were up to date on dues. Simple legal advice cost 80 kopeks; bringing cases to court cost 3 rubles.[37] The St. Petersburg Society advocated lobbying Duma members, scheduled to discuss the new pharmacy statute, because it did not address night duty.[38] They urged pharmacy unions in St. Petersburg, Rostov, and Odessa to lobby the Duma because pharmacists were excluded from the government-sponsored insurance program.[39] Aluf prodded the St. Petersburg Society to work to get the insurance law improved.[40] A new society was organized to struggle with abuses in the National Pharmacists' Pension Fund.[41] The Odessa Society of radical pharmacists elected a commission to lobby the Duma,[42] although some radicals there asserted such tactics were not forceful enough.[43] In Viatka, the district zemstvo petitioned the provincial zemstvo for better insurance for pharmacists.[44] Khar'kov radicals refused to enter the local pharmacy society to discuss the new Pharmacy Statute because of its "class character,"[45] but staff pharmacists in Rostov elected three representatives to the Don Pharmacy Society (of pharmacy owners and Provizors) to discuss a circular from the Ministry of Internal Affairs on work norms for pharmacies and a "court of honor" to settle labor-management disputes.[46]

World War I ultimately offered opportunities to longtime radical pharmacist labor organizers and journalists. However, the war also challenged their resourcefulness for it impacted their constituents–staff pharmacists–differently and in some cases favorably.

Some pharmacists immediately joined the military, leaving needy families in their wake.[47] However, many pharmacists were deferred.[48] They benefited from the mobilization of their colleagues. The "significant amount of unemployed" vanished in many cities[49] during the first eight months of the war. The Union of Staff Pharmacists in Petrograd (as St. Petersburg was called during the war) closed March 1915, for lack of activity.[50] On the fifteenth of that month, Aluf, Chair of the Petrograd Professional Society of Staff Pharmacists, and Kamenskii, the society secretary, exulted to sixty-five staff pharmacists attending the society's general meeting that unemployment had virtually disappeared and conditions of work were good.[51] The Petrograd labor bureau successfully demanded high wages and good conditions for all working pharmacists whom they placed.[52] Student pharmacists in Petrograd averaged 550 rubles per year, Assistant Pharmacists, 912, and Provizors, 1,380.[53] The Rozhdestvenskaia pharmacy was cited for particularly good relations between management and staff.[54] In May 1915 the main concern of the radical pharmacists in Petrograd was summer vacation with pay.[55] They attacked the Pel' Association pharmacy, the city's largest, because although it had the double shift it refused to grant summer vacations.[56] However, in another Petrograd pharmacy staff were given two weeks' vacation, in yet another, one month, and in a third, the whole summer of 1915.[57]

In Baku the war offered staff pharmacists the opportunity to migrate to pharmacies that offered the best pay. Additionally, the labor shortage resulting from mobilization forced Baku pharmacies to shed discriminatory policies and gratefully hire women and Jews.[58] By May of 1915 pay for Assistant Pharmacists shot up to 50 or 85 rubles per month and, in some cases to 100 rubles per month; students received 20 to 45 rubles. Many pharmacies had double shifts; night duty averaged about ten per month; only one pharmacy required fifteen stints of night duty per month.[59]

There were five pharmacies with seventeen staff pharmacists in Elizavetpol'. In the summer of 1915 staff shortages compelled some pharmacy owners or their children to take on the duties of making up and dispensing medicines. All pharmacies had double shifts and the workday, at six hours, was amazingly short. However, pharmacists complained that with Sunday and night duty, work averaged out at nine or even ten and a half hours. Pay in the city pharmacy was high—70 rubles a month for Assistant Pharmacists and 30-40 rubles for students. Despite these favorable conditions, radical pharmacists were seeking one month's vacation with pay.[60]

There were twenty pharmacies in Vil'na. They were segregated, Christians hiring Christians and Jews hiring only their coreligionists. The double shift predominated but in some pharmacies there was a day off only after the second or third day of work. Pay varied considerably. Since the amount of prescriptions dispensed and other conditions of work were not disclosed, it is difficult to ascertain how fair or unfair salaries were.[61]

That there was little to complain about in Khar'kov in the summer of 1915 was evinced by the fact that radical pharmacists were outraged that the double shift for students (not regular pharmacists) had been preserved in only five or six pharmacies.[62] Samara reported a "heavy" workday—from 9 A.M. to 10 P.M.—but only in one pharmacy.[63]

By the summer of 1915 a few problems were noticeable. Women staff pharmacists frequently made less than their male colleagues. Pharmacists' salaries did not keep pace with the sharply escalating cost of living. Petrograd radicals formed a "tariff" commission to work out minimum wage scales and attempted to recruit new members to increase finances.[64] Tsaritsyn pharmacists had double shifts but miserable pay.[65] In Askhabad there were four privately owned pharmacies and one railroad pharmacy. One pharmacy eliminated the double shift; another cut staff. It was alleged that the cost of living was two times dearer than in Russia but pay remained at prewar levels.[66] In the majority of pharmacies in large cities staff worked two days and a night, with the following day free. In small towns the work shift was longer—three or four days, followed by a free day. Workdays were sometimes nine and a half hours. Radical pharmacists lambasted such schedules as unacceptable for pharmacist "intelligentsia."[67]

Radical Petrograd pharmacists had little sympathy for the war, which they scornfully dismissed as the result of "propertied classes" competing for "new markets."[68] Therefore, from the outset, they urged their colleagues to use the war to strengthen the radical movement. *Zhizn' farmatsevta* proselytized energetically, urging pharmacists to seize the moment to better their position by participating in all "class" activities, supporting *Zhizn' farmatsevta*, and organizing and joining professional societies.[69]

Unfortunately, as before the war, radical pharmacists preached to deaf ears. Khar'kov pharmacists were "quiet and inert."[70] Elizavetpol' pharmacists were "indifferent."[71] Although there were six hundred staff pharmacists in Moscow, the Russian Society had only twenty members and was unable to rouse a quorum for its February 6, 1915, meeting. The society's dream of resurrecting its journal had to remain just that. The rival Petrograd Society gloated about this, asserting that the poor showing was due to lack of class consciousness on the part of Moscow rank and file, who did not realize the seriousness of the struggle between pharmacy owners and proletariat. This failure, in turn, was the result of the do-nothing "parade mentality" of the Russian Society leaders during the last three years.[72] However, Tsaritsyn pharmacists also responded to the call to organize with apathy.[73] Similarly, Tiflis pharmacists were indifferent. They displayed "an absence of all thought about social questions and lived only with their petty personal interests."[74]

By May 1915, the Odessa Society of [Reciprocal Aid to] Staff Pharmacists had "collapsed." Its labor bureau "declined to a minimum," although there were signs of revival."[75] Baku pharmacists were "indifferent"; only one third of staff pharmacists attended a general meeting in early 1915. No student pharmacists attended.[76] Even in Petrograd, only 106 of the 984 staff pharmacists in the city were members of the Petrograd Society of Staff Pharmacists. Income was small. February 1915, brought only about 143 rubles, March, 152, although the total amount of money on hand amounted to some 584 rubles.[77] The Petrograd Society faced "significant" late payment of dues and *Zhizn' farmatsevta* was in dire straits in the spring of 1915. Consequently, the board threatened to apply paragraph 6 of the statutes and expel members who were three months late with dues.[78] By the end of 1915 there were less than 300 rubles in the till. The journal doubled up on the August-September issue, and published the October through December issues in one.[79]

By August 1915, conditions for staff pharmacists deteriorated in certain cities. As the Germans conquered Russia's western provinces a flood of refugees swarmed into Petrograd, causing a glut of pharmacists. In June and July 103 unemployed registered with the labor bureau; 77 found positions but some of these were temporary—for two weeks to two months. There were only 30 positions available for students. It was a bit of an exaggeration to use the term "army of unemployed." However, since the refugees were willing to accept low pay, pharmacists could no longer demand and receive high wages.[80] Many refugees also crowded into Khar'kov. For the refugee pharmacists, lack of documents proved a problem. Those without papers were allowed to work in pharmacies under supervision but were barred from becoming managers.[81]

Jewish pharmacists particularly experienced problems. Those mobilized for military service were not considered "sanitation specialists" and although later they were permitted to apply for this title, each case was judged separately. Only Jewish Provizors were recruited.[82] Most of the refugee pharmacists were Jews, since many Jews lived in Poland and the western Russian provinces comprised the Jewish Pale of Settlement. Although some 155,000 Jewish refugees had received aid by November 1915, some 350,000 more needed help. A thousand or so Jews were sheltered in summer theaters, asylums, and schools, but 40,000 were still on evacuation trains. Thousands lacked clothes and shoes. By November 1915, the Petrograd Jewish Relief Committee gathered 5 million rubles from philanthropists. It spent over 1 million rubles on Jewish refugees from Poland and about 2,600,000 rubles on Jewish refugees from the western provinces. The tsarist government contributed over 1½ million rubles to needy Jews, although I. I. Levinshtein, one of the radical leaders in the Petrograd Society of Staff Pharmacists, denigrated this sum as puny compared with the 11 million rubles the government had given to the Polish refugee committee. The Jewish refugee pharmacists in turn caused cleavage among radical Petrograd pharmacists. During 1915, some members of the Petrograd Society of Staff pharmacists voted to tax themselves 2 percent, to raise supplementary funds for Jewish refugees. The money was to be channeled through the Petrograd Jewish Relief Committee. Radical pharmacist leaders, particularly Kanevskii, claimed they approved of the measure but, owing to the "bourgeois" character of the Jewish Relief Committee, resolved to leaven it with representatives from professional unions and other "democratic" groups.[83] Assistance to Jewish refugees through the Jewish Relief Committee, euphemistically referred to as the "nationality" question, became very acrimonious amongst radical pharmacists during 1916.

Strikes were illegal during the war. As a consequence, there were virtually no pharmacy strikes during the fall of 1914 and 1915. One did erupt at a pharmacy in Petrograd in early February. The five Assistant Pharmacist strikers were fined 100 rubles each.[84]

Deprived of confrontational means, radical pharmacists relied on peaceful methods to settle conflicts. For the most part they were successful. Staff in the largest pharmacy in Khar'kov were able to convince the manager to raise their salaries.[85] In Rostov, following directives from the Minister of Internal Affairs, staff and owners established a "court of honor" for resolving differences. Pharmacy owners and staff pharmacists also jointly established a fund to help staff pharmacists in cases of illness. Owners contributed 50 kopeks monthly for each staff pharmacist; staff pharmacists themselves contributed 25 kopeks apiece.[86] Pharmacists resorted to arbitration courts to settle differences between labor and management.[87] According to data gathered by the Tariff Commission of the Petrograd Society of Staff Pharmacists, salaries were not commensurate with the cost of living. To remedy the situation the society decided to work through the city administration or War Industries Committee to establish a mediation board. Mediation boards, including pharmacy owners and staff, operated in Tiflis and other cities.[88] Additionally, on October 21, 1915, Tiflis staff pharmacists established norms for salaries.[89] They concluded agreements with a consortium of five pharmacy owners for pay raises for students and Assistant Pharmacists.[90]

The Petrograd Society of Staff Pharmacists continued to lobby for pharmacists' entry into the government insurance program, insisting (in a rather garbled version of Marxist economics) that "like factory workers and commercial staff pharmacists lived only from the sale of their labor power" but had less recourse for betterment, and the Pharmacists' Pension Fund was inadequate for wages lost during illness.[91]

During the fall of 1914 and 1915, the Petrograd Society of Staff Pharmacists agitated for "municipalization" of pharmacies[92] and "a network of municipal enterprises–bakeries, meat markets, and so forth," to help pharmacists cope with the high cost of living and counter "speculation."

Apparently about twelve to fifteen such municipal enterprises were operating by the spring of 1915. There were bakeries in Moscow and Odessa, warehouses in Petrograd and Warsaw, and a meat market in Tiflis.[93] However, as before the war, *Zhizn' farmatsevta* retained enough objectivity to criticize poor conditions in zemstvo and municipal pharmacies. The journal particularly noted poor conditions in the city pharmacy in Sukhum.[94] The journal also criticized the poor financial condition of district zemstvo pharmacies in Tavrida province, the Crimea; one had not made a profit in twenty years.[95] During 1916, some radical pharmacists also focused on improving pharmacy education, discussed in greater detail below.

Nevertheless, radical pharmacists' greatest concern was raising the consciousness of the rank and file and mobilizing them for pay raises. Despite apathy on the part of the rank and file and fissures amongst the leadership over too much conciliation toward pharmacy owners and aid to Jewish refugees, these objectives remained top priorities for radical pharmacist leaders. Indeed organization and pay raises became their battle cry by the end of 1916.

In the early part of 1916 conditions in Petrograd pharmacies were still relatively good. In some pharmacies staff worked only six hours a day, average pay was 120 rubles a month, and management was "democratic."[96] The Tariff Commission of the Petrograd Society for Staff Pharmacists worked out minimum wage scales, which it presented to pharmacy management. A number of pharmacies paid minimum wages and granted paid summer vacations.[97] Several owners were particularly cooperative. Upon receiving the wage norms, the owner of the Pel' pharmacy convened managers and staff and announced salary raises.[98] That conditions in Petrograd pharmacies were tolerable during the first half of 1916 was evinced by the fact that the radicals' sole objective in early summer was vacation with pay.[99]

The position of women staff pharmacists was mixed through most of 1916, as before. On February 23, 1916, International Women's Day, according to the Julian Calendar then used in Russia, a Plenary Meeting of the Petrograd Society of Staff Pharmacists discussed the "women's question" and elected a presidium, which was to focus on women workers in general and women pharmacists in particular. The presidium conceded that hiring difficulties women had formerly faced had evaporated. In Petrograd there was not one pharmacy that did not employ women. However, S. Lapitskaia, who had been active in the St. Petersburg Society of Staff Pharmacists since its founding, asserted that women were paid significantly less than men. In light of this, she advocated that women pharmacists concern themselves about their future. However, she categorically opposed *separate* organizations, insisting that women pharmacists join "professional unions."[100]

During World War I, Antonina Lesnevskaia reputedly became a Polish patriot. She allegedly left her pharmacy in the hands of Florentina Stankevich and went to Siberia to help Polish prisoners of war.[101] She raised a great deal of money for the Society for Assistance to Polish Officers.[102] Nevertheless, her First Women's Pharmacy operated as before. Further, relations between staff and management appeared harmonious. The radical pharmacy press implied this was due to the fact that a majority of "old" staff were "on sabbatical" and current staff did "not find it comfortable to demand salary increases." But reluctance to press for higher wages might have been due to the fact that women assistant pharmacists in Lesnevskaia's pharmacy received 150 rubles per month "and more."[103] Likewise, in the autumn of 1916, woman pharmacist Liza Ol'khoba informed *Zhizn' farmatsevta* that conditions at the Mariinskaia Pharmacy in Petrograd had been misrepresented and were far better than depicted. Senior male Assistant Pharmacists made 150 rubles and senior women pharmacists, 125 rubles per month; junior Assistant Pharmacists and students with two and a half years experience made 100 rubles per month.[104] In Kiev, the shortage of pharmacists caused barriers to dissolve. Pharmacists were able to transfer from pharmacies where conditions were poor to "the aristocracy," owners "forgot" about nationality, and "the door was open to women"–some women even participated in night duty.[105] But radical women pharmacists worried that their position would worsen after the war.[106]

Conditions in privately owned pharmacies were generally acceptable in the Caucasus and Ukraine in early 1916. Large pharmacies in Tiflis implemented minimum-wage scales—40 to 55 rubles a month for students and 80–100 rubles for Assistant Pharmacists, depending on years of service, as well as 150 rubles minimum for Provizors. Small pharmacies, however, had not given raises.[107]

In Kiev, radical leaders still were dissatisfied that pay had risen only 10 to 15 percent as compared with the 40 to 50 percent rise in the cost of living, and work was "intensive."[108] In Odessa in the summer of 1916, staff pharmacists, except in two pharmacies, enjoyed summer vacation. Staff in the pharmacy in the Jewish hospital, however, asked for pay raises in addition.[109] In Rostov-on-the-Don, in the summer of 1916, radical pharmacists demanded an increase in wages for students to 70 rubles, for Assistant Pharmacists to 120 rubles, and for Provizors from 200 to 225 rubles per month. Additionally, radicals there planned to lobby the State Duma for an eight-hour day and annual summer vacations.[110]

Some radicals asserted that salaries were poor in district zemstvo pharmacies. One in Riazan province offered 600 rubles a year plus an apartment for an Assistant Pharmacist; a zemstvo in Viatka province offered 510 rubles a year plus 100 extra for the war to an Assistant Pharmacist.[111]

Petrograd pharmacy owners admitted that staff pharmacists' salaries often did not match the high cost of living and their work was heavy.[112] However, owners were having a hard time of it too in this third year of the war. Although pharmacists were frequently deferred and pharmacist refugees in some cities caused a surplus of pharmacists, other pharmacies were short-staffed. In normal times, shortage of labor might have forced higher salaries, but wartime costs for fuel and supplies cut pharmacy owners' income.[113]

Further, some objective radical pharmacists denied that staff pharmacists had grievous problems. One Mirlin, a member of the Petrograd Society of Staff Pharmacists, asserted that conditions in Petrograd were "not so sad." He pointed out that "there was not one pharmacy where the owner had rejected [wage] demands" and "some pharmacies were close to the norms." Pharmacy owners also had expressed willingness to organize a mediation chamber with staff representatives.[114]

Nevertheless, radical pharmacist leaders in Petrograd began to campaign for higher salaries in May and June. At this time their assault may have genuinely represented a desire to help staff pharmacists. However, gradually the campaign took on the dimensions of an all-out class struggle. Even in the early summer of 1916 the pay raise issue assumed larger significance. Radical leaders denied that owners were financially unable to raise salaries—"They pay low because we do not *force* them to pay more" [italics mine]. They emphasized that "conditions for the struggle" (*bor'ba*) (read "class struggle") were favorable because of a shortage of labor." They determined to "agitate among staff." Replicating tsarist government methodology, they planned to "send special circulars to all staff in Petrograd" to gather data.[115] They alluded to possible strikes.[116]

But staff pharmacists would not cooperate with their radical leaders. The editors of *Zhizn' farmatsevta* repeatedly wrung their hands over staff pharmacists' "indifference." The journal had only 1,000 subscriptions early in 1916. This, despite the fact that editors labored mightily to convince staff that "the large mass of pharmacists will never become pharmacy owners but will always remain staff."[117] To the anguish of most radical leaders "Peaceful cooperation was observed in Petrograd pharmacies." Petrograd union organizer Comrade Gonikberg, could not "succeed in interesting and attracting the masses to the pharmacy union." Consequently, members of the Petrograd Society of Staff Pharmacists recommended "more attention to political education of the pharmacy masses"; they specifically suggested that staff representatives be elected in all pharmacies in order to "attract the inert masses."[118] At May and June meetings of the society, I. I. Levinshtein noted that "the idea of raising salaries was not popular to a sufficient degree . . . it is necessary all the time to push staff pharmacists or they will forget. In many pharmacies staff did not realize the necessity of putting forth demands."[119]

Worse still, the radical leadership was rent by defection. Comrades Zil'bershmidt and Mirlin were too conciliatory toward pharmacy owners. Zil'bershmidt heretically suggested turning to Popovskii, the pharmacy owners' representative, to request joint establishment of a mediation chamber. Mirlin also spoke in favor of a mediation chamber.[120]

Radical stalwart Levinshtein "categorically" rejected any "proposal for cooperating with pharmacy owners." He stressed that "the worst evil was amicable relations with pharmacy owners. . . . This precluded the possibility of demanding concessions. Such kind of abnormal relations must always end." Another hard-liner, Comrade Isaevich, insisted that the society could not make concessions.[121] Nevertheless, it was obvious that some radicals doubted the wisdom of using force, particularly in wartime.

Apathy on the part of the rank and file and disagreement within the leadership were not confined to Petrograd. The meeting to found a Mutual Aid Society for Staff Pharmacists in Poltava, in the Ukraine, January 8, 1916, "attracted few participants," probably less than half the staff pharmacists in the city. Additionally, radical stalwarts (who spent much time drafting a statute for the society) faced mutiny, as in Petrograd. Some members would not support the stalwarts' attempt to stress the "severe difference between staff pharmacists and owners" and prohibit owners from participating in the society. Assistant Pharmacist A. S. Rozenfel'd, on the contrary, "spoke warmly in defense of the rights of pharmacy owners" and, deviating from his radical leaders, claimed that both staff and owners were "members of one family."[122] Tiflis staff pharmacists were "indifferent" to *Zhizn' farmatsevta*, their official organ. Staff made only one subscription to the journal and paid not one kopek to the journal fund. Tiflis staff were "inert" insofar as organizing a union was concerned, despite the fact that thirty Tiflis pharmacy owners had their own society.[123] In Odessa there were "too few members present" at the January 19 meeting of the Society of Reciprocal Aid for Staff Pharmacists to vote on sending 100 rubles to *Zhizn' farmatsevta*. The administration of the society was "not of united opinion"; it "did not keep accurate account of members' dues" and as members did not keep their appointed hours of service in the bureau of labor, it was not always open.[124]

At the end of the summer of 1916 militant leaders saw heartening signs of renewed "energy" on the part of staff pharmacists. Nevertheless, even the most committed activists could see that staff pharmacists did not embrace the radical movement with unqualified enthusiasm. In one Petrograd pharmacy, staff showed "activity after a long sleep." They decided to struggle for the double shift and elected representatives to discuss the matter with the owner. However, when the owner refused the staff backed off.[125] In Odessa, in the summer of 1916, staff pharmacists cooperated with pharmacy owners. Both camps elected delegates to a mixed commission to discuss pay raises.[126] Radical leaders found it gratifying to note that two hundred turned out for a meeting of the Odessa Society of Reciprocal Aid to Staff Pharmacists August 31. Nevertheless, radical stalwart Ia. A. Kuperman lamented that the organization counted only forty to fifty regular members and "among the masses increased pay has not become the issue of the day."[127] Khar'kov radicals prepared to set up a tariff commission in imitation of Petrograd but staff pharmacists shrank from confrontation with pharmacy owners. As almost all commercial establishments in Khar'kov enjoyed increased wages, staff pharmacists were "convinced that their request" for higher wages would be met with "sympathetically by local owners and that they would not have to resort to any kind of excesses."[128] In Ekaterinoslav pharmacy owners were also conciliatory, "granting 30 percent raises without a reconciliation commission" thus dooming hopes for class struggle.[129]

Reports of the revival in certain areas, replete with campaigns for wage increases, indicated fairly high wages and underscored how radical organizations mirrored the bureaucracy of the Russian government. In late August 1916, Rostov-on-the-Don Professional Society of Staff Pharmacists followed Petrograd's example and established a tariff commission to investigate wages. The Staff Society requested of the Don Pharmacy Society (of owners) 60 to 15 percent raises for wages between 60 and 100 rubles per month, the double shift, no more than ten stints of night duty per month, and 1 ruble, 50 kopeks per hour of overtime. The Staff Society also established a Library Commission.[130] In Nizhni Novgorod staff pharmacists created a "circle after two years of inactivity." The local tariff commission asked for 60 to 20 percent raises. They demanded that pharmacy students with a half year's experience be paid 30 rubles per month, 40 rubles after one year, 60 rubles after two years, and 75 rubles for more than two years. Assistant Pharmacists were to be paid 100 rubles per month after one year of practice, 130 rubles after two years, and 150 rubles after three years. Provizors were to receive 175 rubles per month.[131]

Moscow radicals were buoyed by renewed interest on the part of rank-and-file pharmacists in September and October 1916. Membership in the Russian Pharmacy Society increased to two hundred, more than one half of Moscow pharmacies sending representatives. Four hundred attended one meeting. The old gadfly B. N. Saltykov resumed his starring role, demanding wage increases to 50 rubles per month for male and female students with one year of experience and 225 rubles per month for Provizors. Women Assistants and Provizors were to receive equal pay. The Moscow Pharmacy Society (of owners) agreed to establish a Reconciliation Commission (*Soglasitel'naia komissiia*) to settle wage and other disputes but rejected Saltykov and a second member of the Russian Pharmacy Society as delegates because the two did not practice in a private pharmacy.[132]

The "dead sea of the Baku pharmacy world" also showed signs of awakening by the fall of 1916. One hundred gathered to organize a professional organization, subscribe to *Zhizn' farmatsevta*, form a tariff commission, and develop a questionnaire to provide data on salaries.[133] On the other hand, the sixty or so staff pharmacists in the nine pharmacies (including one municipal pharmacy) in Ekaterinburg were accused of lacking "energy" in the late summer of 1916.[134] Tiflis pharmacists were similarly in a "lethargic sleep" (*letargicheskim snom*).[135]

In any case, Petrograd radicals continued to assess the professional movement as "weak" in the early autumn of 1916. Only two cities—Petrograd itself and Rostov-on-the-Don—had bona fide professional societies and of the twenty members of the tariff commission in Petrograd "only 5-6 people actually worked." Petrograd radicals lamented the "disorganization" and the "passivity" of staff pharmacists.[136] Further, the Petrograd organization was top-heavy, a situation which boded ill for the future. To avert a "financial crisis" and cover administrative costs membership had to increase.[137]

By December 1916, a few Petrograd radicals noted a change for the better. In some cases "staff pharmacists were being roused from their sleep . . . tens of thousands of unemployed had opened their eyes to the need for struggle for pay raises."[138]

However, others still characterized the rank and file as "indifferent" and apathetic, pointing out that only two representatives had been elected in two or three of 120 Petrograd pharmacies to launch the struggle for high wages.[139] Aluf, acting as chief editor of *Zhizn' farmatsevta*, admitted that lack of funds was responsible for the journal's irregular appearance.[140]

Further, conflicts amongst the Petrograd radical leadership continued and broadened. Some radicals stubbornly defended the need to cooperate with pharmacy owners and organize a mediation chamber (*primiritel'naia kamera*). Kanevskii vehemently opposed such cooperation.[141] Disagreement on aid to Jewish refugees further rent the leadership. Kanevskii, ever the orthodox Marxist, insisted that giving aid to Jewish refugees through the Jewish Relief Organization was tantamount to aiding and abetting bourgeois nationalists. Several Jewish radicals heatedly criticized this stance. One Levinshtein (I. I. Levinshtein?) contended that it indicated the "editorial collective" was "deaf to the sufferings of the Jewish People" and "did not correspond to the overwhelming feeling of the majority of staff pharmacists." In support of Kanevskii, Mirlin countered that the Petrograd Society could not focus on "nationality issues." Eidel'man, on the contrary, sympathetic with the Jewish contingent, rebutted that "nationality *ipso facto* was not opposed to class understanding" and one Roitman pointed out that the Jewish people were divided into two classes—political fighters (*bortsov*) and political speculators (*spekulantov*). Against them, Paperin took the side of Kanevskii and Mirlin, warning of Serbian-like repercussions if the cause of "Jewish chauvinists" was supported and Gonikberg emphasized that "Jewish democracy could not disguise Jewish barony." Aluf summed up for the orthodox Marxists by claiming that to aid Jewish refugees through the Jewish Relief Organization would "be a crime to the Jewish proletariat." The resolution proposing self-taxation for aid to Jewish pharmacists was voted down. Twenty-five left the hall in protest. Those remaining applied a Leninist approach to the opposition. They barred the protesters from future elections.[142]

Despite sluggish support from the rank and file and opposition within their own ranks, radical pharmacist leaders were determined to use the crusade for higher wages as a step forward in the class struggle.

Educational Reformers

As noted, even before the war Boris Puzis, Robert Idel'son, and a few other pharmacists had urged that the movement to reform pharmacy education incorporate demands for pharmacists' corporate autonomy and greater voice for pharmacists in government policy-making. During the war educational reformers such as Alexander Semenovich Ginzberg and E. Ia. Abol' became increasingly radicalized. Restless at the slow pace of educational reform before the war, as the war progressed they became more disillusioned with the government's ability to eliminate the flaws in pharmacy education.

At the beginning of the war Russian pharmaceutical education was found glaringly wanting compared with Germany's. Particularly lamented was the lack of connection between pharmacist-researchers and the pharmaceutical industry. In September 1914, the editors of the "establishment" *Farmatsevticheskii zhurnal* urged that more chemist pharmacists be quickly produced to boost the pharmaceutical industry.[143] Consultants on the domestic pharmaceutical industry emphasized that "many medicinal substances . . . were either held in secret or expressed in patent literature in vague and unclear form." Private factories in Germany had laboratories where "200 or more scientifically trained chemists labored." They advocated establishing well-equipped factory laboratories in Russia where chemists could work out formulae for medicines in great demand.[144] In April 1915 F. G./A. Ferrein called for "revamping . . . pharmaceutical education."[145]

But, whereas the government frantically attempted to boost production of crucial medicines, it tackled reform of pharmaceutical education in a more leisurely fashion. In 1914 the government urged chemical laboratories in medical faculties of universities and higher technical schools to produce medicines.[146] About a year later, the Ministry of Public Enlightenment issued two circulars, one on June 5, the second on August 26, 1915, acknowledging the inadequacy of Russian chemical-pharmaceutical education and proposing three-year courses in the Physics-Mathematics Departments or Medical Faculties of universities. The courses were to admit those who had finished seven years of real or commercial school as well as Assistant Pharmacists, who had only a partial secondary education.[147] The courses were specifically targeted to produce specialists for the pharmaceutical-chemical industry "to make preparations received until now from Germany."[148] Those desiring to receive the title Provizor were to take an additional one-year apprentice-training period in a pharmacy and pass the Provizor examination.[149] Special pharmacy courses for women were to be opened in the Women's Medical Institute and higher women's courses. The government promised to support the programs with special funds.[150] Unfortunately, implementation of the courses was slow, possibly because the ministry insisted that special buildings be erected for the new chemistry departments.[151]

In any case, radical Petrograd pharmacists opposed the government proposal. *Zhizn' farmatsevta*'s chief caveat—which was rather strange, in view of its commitment to building up the pharmaceutical industry—was that the Ministry of Education proposal would advance the training of pharmaceutical chemists but slight the training of dispensing pharmacists. *Zhian' farmatsevta* proposed instead that the required six years of apprenticeship be abolished and that aspiring pharmacists have a school-leaving certificate, that special pharmacy departments be established in medical faculties of universities, that the university curriculum include a one-year practicum in pharmacy management. They provided no details on courses.[152]

A delegation from the radical Russian Pharmacy Society in Moscow, meanwhile, requested that Minister of Public Enlightenment Ignat'ev demolish barriers to Jews seeking to audit pharmacy courses at Moscow University, claiming that four hundred Jews had been barred during 1915.[153]

Academic response to the government proposals was tepid. The Physics-Mathematics Faculty of Petrograd University discussed the initial proposal on September 4 and elected a committee under Professor Favorskii to plan the courses.[154] But the university accomplished little. An impatient Alexander Ginzberg reported to the Petrograd Pharmacy Society September 22, 1915, that the university's decision to institute a *chair* of pharmaceutical-chemistry delayed the reform. The Petrograd Women's Medical Courses, with which Ginzberg was affiliated and which he later turned into the First Soviet Pharmacy Institute, also "had not proposed anything."[155]

He crowed that the Psycho-Neurological Institute in Petrograd, being "free from routine and aware of the voice of reality" and "in view of the fact that there were no higher pharmacy courses in Petrograd—in the Military Medical Academy or Women's Medical Institute" (a statement that ignored Antonina Lesnevskaia's pharmacy program for women Provizors) had established a commission, chaired by himself, in May 1915, to implement pharmacy education reform. On paper, the project was quite audacious. The commission developed a charter for a new "Private Petrograd University" (*Chastnyi Petrogradskii Universitet*), which included a Department of Pharmacy among its five faculties. Women as well as men were eligible for admission. The three-year pharmacy program was ambitious indeed. In addition to chemistry, physics, mathematics, pharmaceutical chemistry, pharmacognosy, and pharmacology the curriculum required courses in history, philosophy, literature, and art. Courses on sociology, political theory, and law might have been regarded as a cover for propounding radical socialist theories, since Ginzberg and his colleagues were increasingly moving in that direction, but the first-year curriculum also included religion.[156]

In any case, Ginzberg and the Psycho-Neurological Institute were typically deliberative academics. How practical their program would have been for the pharmaceutical industry was anyone's guess. Further, the courses were not slated to open until the spring of 1916. Similarly, the pharmacy program developed by Kazan University was not due to open until August 7, 1916.[157]

Progress was evident in certain provinces. The Odessa Higher Women's Courses planned to establish a three-year pharmacy program for those who had finished the full seven-year program of the women's *gimnaziia.*[158] The University of Saratov reported twenty auditors to the new chemical-pharmaceutical courses in the fall of 1915. The university council planned to admit Jews under the usual quotas. It also entertained the possibility of admitting women.[159]

It should be noted that most of the new pharmaceutical-chemical courses relied heavily on government subsidies. Tomsk University asked for 18,000 rubles from the government for its courses, which enrolled thirty people by the end of 1915.[160]

A few other steps toward pharmacy education reform occurred during 1916. In the spring, male pharmacists asked permission to take their examinations for "Assistant Provizor" at the Women's Medical Institute in Petrograd.[161] At the same time, Minister of Public Enlightenment Count P. N. Ignat'ev sent a memorandum to the Minister of Internal Affairs, urging that zemstvos and cities implement a right granted them June 1, 1914, to open educational institutions of all types. Ignat'ev advocated that the public institutions open two types of pharmacy schools, one for persons who had completed their secondary education and another for persons who had completed only higher city schools. Apprenticeship would accompany the pharmacy courses, not precede it. *Farmatsevticheskii zhurnal*, the organ of the Petrograd Pharmacy Society, opposed the ministry proposal, purportedly on the grounds that these schools would graduate "pharmacist-technicians" rather than qualified pharmacists. More probably, this was another sideswipe at public institutions for the concessions given them to open pharmacies in 1912.[162]

During 1916 the radical pharmacy press carried reports on efforts in Moscow, Kiev, and Odessa to implement chemistry-pharmacy courses proposed by the Minister of Public Enlightenment. Pharmacist auditors fought shortage of laboratory place in Kiev. That Russian science was competitive was underlined by the fact that the chemistry, physics, zoology, botany, and mineralogy texts used in the courses were authored by Russians.[163]

At the end of 1916, the Minister of Public Enlightenment found another quick fix for pharmacy education. He proposed to the Minister of

Internal Affairs that an Imperial Regulation of 1883 and a circular from the Ministry of Internal Affairs in 1888, which allowed women Assistant Pharmacists to take Provizor examinations without auditing university courses, be applied to males, namely, that Assistant Pharmacists who had served eight to ten years in a pharmacy be allowed to take the Provizor examination without auditing Provizor courses in the university.[164]

Finally, in the spring of 1917 special pharmacy courses opened in the Women's Medical Courses in Moscow.[165]

These developments did not satisfy educational reformers like Alexander Ginzberg. In the fall of 1916 he became more aggressive. Further, solidarity developed between Ginzberg and other educational reformers, on the one hand, and out-and-out radicals, on the other.

There were hints–but only hints–that Ginzberg might be becoming more militant during 1915. November 17, 1915, sixty auditors at the Psycho-Neurological Institute turned up to hear him propose that they form a "circle." Ginzberg had been made an honorary member of the Petrograd Pharmacy Society–the establishment society representing fully qualified pharmacists–in October 1915.[166] Nevertheless, the term "circle" usually was a code-word for radical political activity.[167] He may not have had this in mind, but, in light of his entrance into the Bolshevik pharmacy organization two years later it is a possibility.

By the fall of 1916 the struggle for reform of pharmacy education had clearly taken on larger dimensions.

In the summer and fall of 1916 the venerable radical B. N. Saltykov emphasized the "question of pharmacy education in connection with the medicaments crisis" and called for a congress to discuss pharmacy education. However, his behavior was moderate for he petitioned the Minister of Public Enlightenment to convene the congress.[168]

Alexander Ginzberg supported Saltykov in calling for a pharmacy congress in the summer of 1916.[169] N. A. Valiashko, professor at Khar'kov University, and I. N. S. Vysotskii, professor at Kazan University, added to the chorus.[170]

More significantly, Master of Pharmacy E. Ia. Abol', thwarted in his earlier attempts to found a pharmacy school, called for a "special pharmacy institute" outside the universities. He urged Saltykov to start moving on the idea. He proposed that the State Duma and the All-Russian Society of Pharmacists fund the new institute.[171]

A. N. Popovskii, who had been elected the pharmacists' representative in the Medical Council after the death of K. I. Kresling,[172] championed not only reform of pharmacy education with a view to improving Russia's pharmaceutical industry but autonomy for the pharmacy corporation and a greater role for pharmacists' in the pharmaceutical industry. In May 1916, he proposed creating a "Secretariat for Pharmacy Matters."[173] In the spring of 1916 he advanced the Kazan Pharmacy Society's proposal for organizing a bureau to stimulate the Russian pharmaceutical industry. Members would make a one-time contribution of 3 rubles.[174] In 1917, he published a pamphlet on the need to improve pharmacy education on the German model. He stressed the need for creating German-style pharmacist-chemists and special pharmacy faculties in the universities. He criticized the new Pharmacy Statute, recently introduced into the State Duma, because it did not envision independent university pharmacy departments.[175]

Popovskii's proposals were fairly tame. But more radical pharmacists involved in the fall 1916 discussion on pharmacy education went on to suggest the election of delegates from pharmacists in each Moscow pharmacy to work out increased wage rates for staff pharmacists, equal to those in Petrograd.[176] Thus, by the fall of 1916, the agenda of educational reformers had expanded to include an independent pharmacy organization in the government and radical improvement for staff pharmacists.

Within the year reformers like Ginzberg and Abol' would join radicals like Saltykov and with advocates of *samovykup,* or buying out private pharmacies, like O. G. Gabrilovich, would cross the Rubicon and align themselves with the Bolsheviks. In the case of Ginzberg and Abol', it would seem that their decision was not based so much on ideological conviction, but to achieve improvements in pharmacy, which they had long sought.[177]

Pharmacist Academics, Politicians, Bureaucrats

Meanwhile, the concept of socialism began to gain currency in the country at large. It even found supporters within the tsarist government.

As noted in the previous chapter, the Interdepartmental (government) Committee on the Pharmaceutical Industry, meeting in the spring of 1915, discussed requisitioning supplies from private pharmaceutical enterprises for use by public organizations. Professor S. A. Przhibytek, future Soviet pharmacy administrator, sat on that committee[178] and also was a member of the Petrograd Committee for Independent Preparation of Medicines, which met in the fall and winter of 1915/1916.[179] The latter committee fairly bristled with hostility toward private enterprise. Simultaneously, it strongly endorsed both public organizations and big government, averring that public organizations in Petrograd were not independent enough to rely on self-financing. Thus they needed subsidies from the central government to carry out their tasks.

Academician N. S. Kurnakov led the attack, asserting that private industry had failed Russia. Russia received "the majority of chemical-pharmaceutical items from abroad, chiefly from Germany." She produced only "a few substances which could not be called medicaments in the proper sense of the term but were only products necessary for the production of medicaments" such as acids (sulfuric, nitric, hydrochloric), caustic potash, caustic soda, potash, ammonia, and organic combinations such as wood spirits, vinegar acid, formalin, and "some others." Russia lacked major preparations such as bromine and iodine, vegetable alkaloids, and coal tar products–phenol and salicylic preparations.[180] The solution was to establish a *public* pharmaceutical industry.

A committee meeting in the apartment of member of the Petrograd city duma Sazonov took up the theme. It was emphasized that although it was acceptable for the pharmaceutical industry in Germany to be in private hands (no reason was adduced), in Russia pharmacy should be under zemstvos and city governments. Russia had an "historical tradition" of "public organization." "If zemstvos and cities could build schools" and "successfully organize warehouses for seeds, agricultural equipment," "workshops for craftsmen," "for many years sensibly lead the business of public health," "organize insurance for cattle and against fires," and "in time of war successfully undertake various orders connected with defense," then zemstvos and cities could successfully "organize chemical-pharmaceutical factories." However, these should be "staffed only by specialists."[181] The discussants admitted that there were arguments against zemstvo and city-owned chemical-pharmaceutical factories. At the end of the war the Russian chemical-pharmaceutical industry would face "serious competition" from large foreign, particularly German, syndicates. This competition would be "the more dangerous" since German industry was supported by "large capital" and had "great technical and scientific strength," whereas the Russian side would be characterized by "comparatively small enterprises." Nevertheless, "in extreme cases" " city and zemstvo factories could consider material support from the government." Such support would not have the "odious [*odioznyi*] character of handouts [*podachki*] to individuals." Further, "public organizations" had advantages over "private people." They could utilize "vacant lots not bringing in any income" "suitable for building a factory." Many chemical products were absent in the market because of requisitioning but city and zemstvo factories could more easily obtain them than private enterprise. Finally, "representatives of science" "would more likely devote their time and effort to a public enterprise" than "to a private factory."[182]

Comments against private industry became more strident in subsequent meetings. On December 12, 1915, Professor L. A. Chugaev referred darkly to "unhealthy speculation" that "had become more and more widespread" recently. He reported on Khar'kov Professor N. V. Valiashko's proposal for producing chemical-pharmaceutical products on a "public basis." Professor Chugaev reminded his colleagues that "public entities long ago began to play a significant role" particularly the "city self-government of Petrograd." At the end of the war "both public and private industry would meet strong competition from Germany, where there was more capital, organization, and experience," but "public enterprises, especially those united in one purpose," would be firmer in meeting this competition. "One had to remember that private enterprises" were "flourishing . . . thanks to huge profits." "Lowering prices, especially artificially," would "be their downfall," but "city and zemstvos" would "find it much easier to fight this situation [than private industry]."[183] Professor Efimov was only slightly little more conciliatory to private enterprise, advising private-public sector cooperation in the face of strong [postwar] competition from Germany.[184]

Professor Tishchenko noted that the Customs Department had confiscated opium in Vladivostok making possible the preparation of morphia and other opiates, and the Institute of Experimental Medicine had prepared Salvarsan with success. Tishchenko was confident that Petrograd could "outfit a factory . . . to serve the common weal." He castigated private industry with Marxist fervor, maintaining that "we scientists are opposed to going into service to industrialists, exploiters of the people [*ekspluatiruiushchim narod*] . . . we are happy to cooperate with public institutions, serving the people without profit."[185] Town councillor N. N. Afanas'ev supported him, alleging that "Stopping imports of German medicine has caused prices to fluctuate in the internal market, and private industrialists . . . have attempted to seize the moment. It is the responsibility of public organizations to resist this and then "to stop or crush the chemical work of private industrialists."[186] He added that N. V. Valiashko had proposed a system of stock sharing for workers: "in order to create personal interest for all staff and workers in the factory there must be established a certain percent computed from the income of the enterprise as an addition to salaries."[187]

Two representatives of private firms, Pokhitonov and Shaskol'skii, were present. They signed the minutes and did not counter these statements.

Only Professor A. E. Makovetskii spoke in favor of private enterprise. His reasons were practical rather than philosophical. He revealed that in the plenary meeting of the council of the Physico-Chemical Society, October 1915, he had suggested the establishment of a small factory for making chemical-analytical and photographic preparations. But, he emphasized that public organizations "with an absence of material means could not always successfully compete with private industry."[188] At the December 12 meeting of the Petrograd Committee he proposed "a large factory to prepare five or six of the most needed medicaments" and emphasized that "the city" would "not be in condition to accomplish this business as quickly as private enterprise could."[189] He believed that most chemists would be inclined to work in a factory organized on stock company lines, selling shares. But this should be a privately owned factory. "I continue to think that a private group of people, from the number of those who strongly support my proposal, have the most chance of success."[190] Makovetskii reminded his colleagues December 18 that "in Petrograd the construction of the Keler factory for producing salicylic acid" was "nearly finished."[191]

Nevertheless, on December 31, Professor Chugaev reiterated the case for zemstvo and city ownership of pharmaceutical industries, maintaining that to "prepare chemico-pharmaceutical preparations in Russia . . . to secure her from foreign competition . . . can be done if the factory or factories are organized on a public basis [*na obshchestvennykh nachalakh*] [owned by] city and zemstvo self-government." He predicted that production by cities and zemstvos would result in lowering prices on foreign products, which would "hurt German syndicates" and "ruin private entrepreneurs."[192] Chugaev averred that private entrepreneurs would shun public factories. They had vested interests and regarded public institutions as "competition," which lowered "their artificially high prices." He also reiterated that "raw materials, requisitioned by the war departments" would be "given to public organizations rather than to private persons. . . ."[193] Town councillor A. E. Bari supported Chugaev and prophesied that the city duma would sanction his proposal.[194]

Attraction to socialized pharmacy swelled not only among local officials and academics but within the government itself. In the fall of 1915, simultaneous with the Petrograd Committee meetings, the new Minister of Internal Affairs A. N. Khvostov proposed "municipalizing" all pharmacies—transferring private pharmacies to cities and zemstvos.[195]

In February 1916, the Council of Ministers discussed sequestering the property of pharmaceutical enterprises under provision of article 87 of the Fundamental State Laws, which allowed the government to issue regulations, having the force of law, while the Duma was not in session. Enterprises were to provide information on their books and other documents.[196]

There were calls for a centralized purchasing agent for pharmaceuticals "such as had been created in other sectors during the course of the war . . . their significance is very apparent." Ostensibly the authoritarian Supreme Authority of the Sanitation and Evacuation Sector Prince Ol'denburg, as well as the Zemstvo and City Union, approved of this step. "Unfortunately" the proposal "had not met with wide sympathy."[197]

At the end of 1916 at least one pharmaceutical firm, the Odessa Society of Trade in Pharmaceutical Wares A. Iu. Lemme and Co., which had occupied a "very visible position" since December 1895, enjoyed a profit of 2,000,000 during the war, and paid dividends of 14 percent, was forced to liquidate.[198]

The relationship between the pharmacy establishment, on the one hand, and the government, public organizations, and academics, on the other, became increasingly adversarial during 1916.[199] The government, academics, and public institutions ignored and snubbed pharmaceutical experts and industrialists. For example, in March 1916, Prince Alexander Ol'denburg, the Supreme Authority of the Sanitation and Evacuation Sector, established two committees on the "collection, preparation and cultivation of medicinal plants" and on "organizing the chemical-pharmaceutical industry." A representative from the Ministry of Agriculture, Shakhnazarov, headed the first committee. Participants included government officials and specialists from various geographical regions, such as the director of state properties in Samarkand region, director of the Tiflis Botanical Gardens, and manager of the Sukhum Experimental Station. Red Cross representative V. K. fon Anrep was appointed chair of the second committee. Participants included academicians from the Imperial Academy of Sciences, Mining Engineer Kurnakov, members of the Petrograd Committee on Medicaments, professors from the Military Medical Academy and the University of Petrograd, Tishchenko and Chugaev, who had been members of the Petrograd Medicaments Committee, and other engineers. There was only one pharmacist, Tol'stopiatov–a lowly laboratory assistant at Petrograd University. No representatives from the pharmaceutical industry were appointed to either committee, a particularly glaring oversight with regard to the second, whose special mandate was to develop that very industry.[200]

At about the same time, Kazan University requested permission of the Minister of Internal Affairs to hold a Congress on "struggle with the medicaments crisis." Red Cross representative fon Anrep proclaimed with great inaccuracy that "a congress for struggle with the medicaments crisis was timely" but there was a question about how much it could improve the problem of insufficient medicine since heretofore, "medical preparations were not produced in Russia. By autumn it is hoped that we will have our own medical preparations." Professor Chugaev, radical professor at the University of Petrograd, announced sententiously: "I do not know how much a congress is necessary. In Russia there is so much talking–now we must act. It is desirable to implement the business of preparing medicine without a congress. In Russia there are many institutions *like chemical sections of physical chemistry societies or the Organization of Prince Ol'denburg* [italics mine] which can prepare chemical-pharmaceutical preparations for the need of the country." As noted, Master of Pharmacy and Instructor at the Women's Medical Institute Alexander Ginzberg would cross over to the Bolsheviks in 1918 but in 1916, to his credit, he supported the pharmaceutical industry, noting that the proposed "congress will be fruitful only if . . . representatives of industry . . . representative of theoretical chemistry . . . [and] . . . representatives of pharmaceutical chemistry . . . participate in its work. . . . Pharmacy laboratories in the higher educational institutions must be mobilized but the illusion cannot be created that this will satisfy the medical market."[201]

In the late summer of 1916 the Sanitary Section of the War Industries Committee proposed the convening of a congress in Petrograd for struggle with the medicaments crisis in October of that year. The congress was to "enlighten on the position of medicine in Russia . . . and work out plans for development of the Russian chemical-pharmaceutical industry." The War Industries Committee stressed that "Two years of war have shown that Russian industry is capable of developing independently." An agenda for the congress was published. Participants were invited from pharmaceutical societies.[202]

Nevertheless, on the eve of the congress Prince Ol'denburg informed the Assistant Minister of Internal Affairs that the congress was "untimely." The War Industries Committee, in turn, was instructed to "postpone the congress until a better time."[203]

In the fall of 1916 the stage was being set for the revolution of February 23–27, 1917. This upheaval, which toppled the tsarist regime, was precipitated by women and unemployed workers standing in bread lines in Petrograd. Tsuyoshi Hasegawa has emphasized that strikes among workers during the war and in February were not entirely spontaneous.[204] Michael Melancon strongly contends that the events of February 23 were orchestrated.[205] The pages of *Zhizn' farmatsevta* tend to confirm that opinion. From the fall of 1916 reports and discussions hint at a larger agenda than organizing staff pharmacists and campaigning for wage increases. A September 5 meeting of four hundred radicals in Moscow debating the rise in the cost of living referred rather cryptically to "spiritual food" and "essential food."[206] Reports of meetings on September 29 and October 6 stated that radicals decried "endless speeches on old, endless themes. . . ." They asked "when the important question about *bread* would be raised [italics mine]."[207] Reports of meetings of radical pharmacists in Petrograd in November emphasized that "conscious elements in our midst must raise the question about wide participation in the struggle for resolving the procurements crisis . . . but it would be a mistake to wait while pharmacy owners are occupied only with the procurements issue. . . . To solve the procurements crisis the organization of pharmacists, it is hoped, will find a more suitable campaign."[208] In December 1916, *Zhizn' farmatsevta* reminded readers that "the struggle for higher wages has gradually slumped in Petrograd, strengthened in Moscow, and only begun in a range of other areas." The campaign for pay raises was likened to the revolution of 1904–1905: "It ranks with the 1904 struggle for the double shift and the organized struggle for the pension fund. . . ." When the journal informed readers that the Petrograd union began the campaign for higher wages in the spring, when the journal talked about a "struggle," when it emphasized that "contact between organizations and cities must be established," and the "movement had taken on wider form,"[209] one senses that far more than higher wages was at stake. Preparations for a massive upheaval were underway but information had to be relayed in code because of wartime censorship.

18

Pharmacists and the Revolutions of 1917

Background

Russia was rent by revolution in 1917. Crowds of unemployed and striking workers, many of them women, students, and assorted other citizenry, queueing for bread on the streets of Petrograd February 23, 1917, precipitated what became known as the February Revolution. The revolution reached its peak Monday, February 27. Several regiments of soldiers joined the insurgents. The tsar ordered the Fourth Duma prorogued. Policy disagreements among divergent political groups ultimately caused the parliament to implode. Beforehand, an inner core of deputies replaced the tsarist Council of Ministers (who were arrested) with a Temporary, or Provisional, Government (*Vremennoe Pravitel'stvo*) composed mainly of centrist and just left-of-center Kadets. The new ministers had been selected in advance. Two had managed zemstvo and industrial committees formed to prosecute the war. The government included only one socialist, Alexander Kerensky, who took the portfolio of Minister of Justice. Meanwhile, the Petrograd Soviet of Workers and Soldiers' deputies held its first meeting on February 27. The Soviet represented socialists–Mensheviks of various hues, Bolsheviks, Socialist Revolutionaries.[1] On March 2, Nicholas II abdicated at Mogilev for himself and his son. Nicholas' brother Michael abdicated the following day.

The end of the Romanov dynasty set off shock waves of instability, reminiscent of Russia's "Time of Troubles" in the late sixteenth, early seventeenth century. The Provisional Government underwent four changes during the eight months of its existence. By July it included more socialists. Kerensky assumed the chairmanship as well as posts of war and navy.[2]

But for some months, the Provisional Government carried on business as usual. The Ministry of Internal Affairs, for example, often used the stationery of its predecessor while speeding up approval for manufacturing medicines.[3] Additionally, throughout 1917, local pharmacy owners and managers dutifully filled out cards on the ownership, management, and operation of their pharmacies and sent them to the Medical Inspector, who then compiled this information.[4]

Lenin characterized the political situation between February and October 1917 as "Dual Power."[5] Actually, triple, quadruple, quintuple power are more apt terms. Local soviets went their own way. Unions and other worker organizations had their own agendas. The Petrograd municipal duma had become noticeably attracted to socialism during the war. Radical socialists entered the Petrograd duma and dumas in several provincial cities during the summer elections of 1917. Thus, many loci of power existed in Russia.[6]

One group of socialists—Lenin's Bolsheviks—began to come to the fore in the summer of 1917. Upon his return from Zurich in early April, Lenin urged moving beyond the bourgeois revolution, represented by the Provisional Government, to a full-fledged socialist revolution. The extension of the revolution would encompass political and economic change. No support was to be accorded the Provisional Government, for power should pass to the Petrograd Soviet and local soviets of workers and soldiers' deputies (after sufficient infiltration by Bolsheviks). The term *sovet* had meant "council" and was strictly neutral until it acquired a radical connotation for grass-roots government in 1905 and again in 1917. In the economic sphere, the means of production—factories, businesses, shops, estates, and dwellings would be transferred from their owners to workers, peasants and "have-nots." Russia would stop participating in the war.[7] Under Lenin's guidance Bolsheviks radicalized military regiments quartered in Petrograd,[8] encouraged peasants to take over landlord land,[9] and stirred up factory workers. Various elements of the populace moved leftward during the summer.[10] A majority of socialists were elected to the Petrograd city duma in August.[11] By August and September the Bolshevik party counted about a quarter of a million members. The new recruits had been affected by Bolshevik propaganda and were ready for action. Through elections in August and September 1917, Bolsheviks achieved majorities in the soviets of key cities such as Moscow and Saratov.[12] On the night of October 24/25 they took over government buildings and communications in Petrograd. They arrested the Provisional Government, October 26, and took Moscow about a week later.[13]

The Bolsheviks did not have a popular mandate. Although they took over almost all the portfolios in the new Soviet government, the Socialist Revolutionary Party received the majority of votes (twenty-one million out of thirty-six million) in the November elections for the Constituent Assembly, slated to draft a new constitution for Russia in 1918. But the Bolsheviks maintained themselves in power, although they were forced to fight a two-and-a-half-year civil war to do so.

The Bolsheviks replicated the tsarist government's structure and style of management. However they and their supporters greatly altered Russia's economic system and the political and cultural environment. Thus, 1917 was a pivotal year in Russia's history. The Bolshevik victory especially had momentous and long-lasting repercussions for Russia.

Narratives and analyses of 1917 abound. There are studies on non-Bolshevik socialist contenders for the rule of Russia, such as Alexander Kerensky[14] and the Mensheviks.[15] There are studies of the various facets and phases of Bolshevik policy-making and tactics—vis-à-vis the military, peasantry, and workers.[16] There are studies of developments in the provinces,[17] and so on. Two accessible works for college history courses are John Thompson's stimulating *Revolutionary Russia, 1917*[18] and Hans Rogger's thoughtful *Russia in the Age of Modernization and Revolution.*[19] Almost all these works portray the revolutions of 1917, which so profoundly changed the course of Russian polity and economy, as the product of insistent and escalating radicalism amongst various segments of the empire. The authors imply that this surge of radicalism was elemental, the product of deep-seated, irreconcilable grievances. Labor historians like Tsuyoshi Hasegawa,[20] Diane Koenker, and William Rosenberg explain February 1917 by variations on Leopold Haimson's theme that "haves" and "have-nots" were impossibly alienated in late imperial Russia.[21] Of the move to October 1917, John Thompson states that "the growing frustration and resentment the masses felt when the revolution did not at once fulfill their needs and desires drove them to stronger and more forceful demands."[22] Ziva Galili opines that Mensheviks, in the fall of 1916, were guided by "a perception of growing militancy among the workers."[23] She also claims the Mensheviks in the Petrograd Soviet in the spring of 1917 kept radical elements in line for a time and thus stabilized the Provisional Government.[24] In depicting the political situation in late 1916, early 1917, Rogger underestimates the pluralism in the Russian government and the inertia that enabled it to carry on during World War I.[25] With regard to February/March 1917, he avers that the "mood of the masses was so implacably anti-monarchist that the removal of Nicholas became a necessity and his replacement by Michael, either as regent . . . or as tsar in his own right, an impossibility." In depicting the social situation, Rogger alludes to the "workers' impatience" at the end of 1916. Although he acknowledges that "As the strikes and marches gained momentum, they were aided by agitators and organizers of all socialist factions," he depicts the February upheaval in Petrograd as spontaneous, brought on by women and soldiers "exasperated by hours of mostly futile waiting in bread lines."[26]

Further, historians generally portray the strikes and strikers of 1917 in a sympathetic light. Donald Raleigh, for example, stresses that strikes in

Saratov were necessary to help working people cope with the relentless rise in the cost of living.[27] Ronald Grigor Suny regards industrialists as obstinate because they refused to concede to strikers in Baku.[28] Diane Koenker and William Rosenberg are perhaps most uncritically supportive of factory worker strikes, including "offensive" strikes, not for economic gain, but to achieve "dignity" and self-esteem.[29]

Pharmacists played a major role in the events of 1917. And, with the possible exception of their attitude toward the monarchy, none of the above interpretations holds true for them. The majority of rank-and-file pharmacists do not appear to have been motivated by radicalism or desire to realize self-esteem. Militant pharmacist leaders had to struggle to organize them and orchestrate strikes. Despite this, most rank-and-file pharmacists remained lethargic, retained their petit bourgeois mentality (desire to own a pharmacy themselves, adherence to law, order, and custom) or were even conciliatory toward pharmacy owners. Militant pharmacists in the provinces were excited by the establishment of a "Republic" in March 1917. However, they favored political pluralism for some time, supporting the Provisional Government and other central and local contenders for the rule of Russia. Militant Menshevik pharmacist leaders, particularly in the capital of Petrograd, did not help preserve stability or shore up the Provisional Government. Rather they weakened it and added to economic disruption. Pharmacy strike demands were unrealistic and indefensible for wartime. In time, even some militant socialist pharmacist leaders rejected their extremism. If pharmacists thus deviated from the models of mass behavior in 1917 that have been presented to us, one wonders about the validity of the traditional explanations for the two revolutions that swept away the old order in Russia.

But, regardless of the motivations and origins of the strikes of 1916 and 1917, there is no doubt that pharmacy strikes helped the Bolsheviks to come to power. Once they were at the helm, some militant pharmacists (and some moderate reformer pharmacists) joined the new Soviet (Bolshevik) government. Others, on the contrary, began to have second thoughts about the new order. But by then it was too late. Militant pharmacists would suffer the consequences of their captivation with theory and their disregard for economic reality. So would pharmacy, pharmacists, the pharmacy industry, and Russia as a whole.

The Story

Over a thousand people were killed in Petrograd during the February Revolution, among them I. I. Ioffe, treasurer of the Professional Society of

Pharmacists. Nevertheless, the mood of the revolutionaries was ebullient, even festive. Mutinous regiments raised red flags and cried "Hurrah." Regimental bands played marches and the "Marseillaise." Revolutionaries raided arsenals and emptied prisons. Two dress stores opened to provide newly freed women prisoners with clothes.[30]

Radical Petrograd pharmacists—mostly Mensheviks of one kind or another[31]—hailed the February days as the dawn of a new era. On Sunday, March 5, Ia. F. Kanevskii, A. Aluf, and E. V. Bronshtein convened a meeting of staff pharmacists in the headquarters of the district zemstvo executive council. More than six hundred staff pharmacists showed up. The meeting was "long and lively." The leaders saluted deceased comrade I. I. Ioffe, who had been killed in the February upheavals. They cautiously pledged support for the Provisional Government insofar as it "honestly and fully implemented its published program and quickly called a Constituent Assembly."[32] At the same, they informed those assembled that "the main task" was "struggle of the proletariat for a better socialist future" and for a "democratic republic." They urged their comrades to join the Russian Social Democratic Labor Party, pledged 1,000 rubles to the fund of the Soviet of Workers and Soldiers' deputies, and elected I. I. Levinshtein and Kanevskii delegates to the Petrograd Soviet. E. V. Bronshtein and A. Aluf were elected candidates.[33]

Militant Petrograd leaders tried to coordinate events. They were eager for a move leftward. But their colleagues, both in Petrograd and in the provinces, hesitated. Many radical pharmacy societies hedged their bets and supported all centers of authority—the Provisional Government, Petrograd Soviet, local soviets, and local governing bodies held over from the tsarist regime.

In March, radical leaders in Petrograd admitted that many pharmacists did not belong to the Union of Staff Pharmacists.[34] Kanevskii tried to encourage militancy. Power was in the hands of the bourgeoisie, he acknowledged to the audience of staff pharmacists, but the Petrograd Soviet numbered one thousand delegates. Sounding more Leninist than Lenin would in April, he emphasized that the task was to "push the bourgeoisie as far as possible . . . prevent them from . . . establishing a constitutional monarchy" and press for "a democratic republic." I. I. Levinshtein seconded him, opining that the Provisional Government would not fulfill its program. He called for "people power."[35] Ef. Bronshtein and others created a Soviet of Pharmacy Workers, urged municipalization,[36] and planned an All-Russian conference of staff pharmacists for April 10.[37] Kanevskii and Mirlin demanded a shorter workday and forty-eight-hour week for staff pharmacists. Staff pharmacists in several pharmacies called short strikes to achieve these ends.[38]

By late March militant Petrograd pharmacists stepped up their demands for the "minimum program of the Social Democrats"–wide, real self-government, inviolability of person and dwelling, freedom of movement, abolition of corporate ranks, general equality, an eight-hour day and forty-two-hour week, abolition of night work for youths under sixteen, creches, and so forth. (They would threaten a general pharmacy strike April 25 to achieve these goals.) But, additionally, promoting their maximalist agenda, they also predicted that the full "Program of the Russian Social Democratic Labor Party" would soon be realized–international solidarity of the proletariat, downfall of capitalists due to their exploitation of workers and over-production, and "social revolution . . . the establishment of a dictatorship of the proletariat, i.e., seizure of political power by the proletariat, thus ending exploitation."[39] Odessa radicals were more moderate than those in Petrograd. Some four hundred pharmacists and one thousand "others" attended a general meeting March 8. The gathering sent "comradely greetings" to the Petrograd Soviet, reminding them that "the Petrograd proletariat could not lay down its arms when victory was not complete." They elected Kuperman and two others as representatives to the Petrograd Soviet. However, they also saluted the Provisional Government, which they called the "Executive Committee of the State Duma" reminding this body that "staff pharmacists in Odessa" were "ready to support the government in all its campaigns, directed to . . . strengthening freedom."[40] By the end of March militancy in Odessa diminished. Only three hundred attended a general meeting of the Society of Staff Pharmacists March 28. There was resistance to Kuperman's attempt to rally the rank and file to support the Social Democrats (*partiinost'*).[41]

Khar'kov staff pharmacists were slightly more radical than those in Odessa but less so than the leaders in Petrograd. They sent a telegram to "Mikhail Vladimirovich Rodzianko," whom they mistakenly identified as head of the Provisional Government–"Chairman of the Executive Committee of the State Duma." In it they repeated the Petrograd formula of "support for the Provisional Government insofar as it fulfilled its stated political program." They also announced that they considered "control over the Provisional Government on the part of the working masses necessary." Covering all bases, Khar'kov staff pharmacists also sent telegrams to the Petrograd Soviet of Workers and Soldiers' Deputies, to the "Public Executive Committee" in Khar'kov asking this body "to strengthen political freedom," and to the Khar'kov Soviet of Workers and Soldiers' Deputies.[42]

Saratov pharmacists lamented lack of revolutionary fervor among the rank and file. However, before long, "thanks to the agitation of some comrades" the latter realized the necessity of establishing a professional union and sending representatives to the local soviet. The union, steered by a temporary organizing committee of seven, elected two representatives to the Saratov Soviet of Workers and Soldiers' Deputies, and discussed pharmacists' participation in the "general proletarian holiday" March 15, declared by the Saratov Soviet as a "Day of Freedom."[43]

Yaroslavl' militants struggled to prod rank-and-file pharmacists. While pharmacy owners were well-organized, the "mass of staff pharmacists" were "inert." However, as in Saratov, propaganda on the part of militant leaders paid off. Many staff pharmacists "at once saw the need to defend their class interests" and resolved to create a union. Bowing to the reality of multiple loci of power, Yaroslavl' militants elected a delegate to the city duma and to the Soviet of Workers and Soldiers' Deputies. They also discussed establishing a mediation board (*primiritel'naia kamera*) to settle labor-management disputes.[44]

On April 8 the administration of the Tomsk Pharmacy Society convened a general meeting of staff pharmacists in the local stock exchange. The assembly approved two pharmacist delegates to the Commissariat (Ministry) of Health. However, there was no unanimity on whether pharmacy owners and managers should be excluded from the local organization of staff pharmacists. Older staff pharmacists agitated for including managers but excluding owners. But a militant core ignored them and decided to form a union composed only of staff pharmacists.[45] Unfortunately, staff pharmacists' militancy evaporated when pharmacy owners offered them the opportunity of managing local chemical-pharmaceutical enterprises.[46]

Before the war, Moscow militants had been forced to pass the baton of leadership over staff pharmacists to Petrograd. Further, Moscow radicals had been split along more and less militant lines for some years. Pharmacists in the military, those in zemstvo and city organizations, and those employed in the Ferrein enterprises formed their own unions. Some Moscow pharmacists supported militants in Petrograd. Others were more moderate. As a consequence of these divisions, the Russian Pharmacy Society, founded in the 1890s, decided to phase itself out.[47]

In Nizhni Novgorod a "circle" of staff pharmacists evolved into a union in April. But rank-and-file pharmacists responded with "indifference." Only about thirty or forty people, out of a possible one hundred, showed up for meetings before July 1917.[48]

Pharmacists in Ekaterinoslav were roused by their radical brethren in Petrograd. But they were not uniformly or conspicuously militant. Uncertain as to how to relate to "privileged" pharmacists they decided to concentrate on improving their own conditions.[49]

Tver staff pharmacists planned to form a general medical union with doctors, sisters of mercy, and feldshers. Radical Petrograd leaders disapproved of this plan on the grounds that staff pharmacists had nothing in common with these medical personnel and, thus, required their own professional union. In Baku, Odessa, and Petrograd, on the other hand, staff pharmacists successfully formed general unions of pharmacy staff by May 1917.[50]

Tula staff pharmacists established a union shortly after the February Revolution, which admitted pharmacy owners, although they were not permitted to vote. This politically incorrect development was straightened out thanks to a "maneuver" on the part of the more militant. Additionally, an emissary from Moscow urged Tula brethren to demand raises and a minimum wage.[51]

Despite lethargy and indecisiveness on the part of the rank and file, militant Petrograd pharmacists pressed forward. They turned the screws on owners of private pharmacies, threatening a general pharmacy strike April 25. It was called off when pharmacy owners granted concessions April 24.[52] The Petrograd Pharmacy Society and the Professional Union of Pharmacy Staff in Petrograd and Petrograd province signed a Collective Agreement. Owners and managers agreed to hire only through the Bureau of Labor, fire only after approval of a conciliation chamber, granted an eight-hour day, extensively raised salaries, promised to replace sick workers at the owner's expense and pay for medical treatment, promised two-week paid vacations after three months' employment and one month paid vacations after eleven months' employment.[53]

Petrograd militants continued to try to radicalize pharmacists in the provinces. They held a conference of "workers in pharmacies" May 5-7. Response was tepid. Five representatives attended from Moscow and one each from Odessa, Baku, Astrakhan, Saratov, and Ekaterinoslav. The group resolved to unite staff pharmacists and workers in pharmacies. They elected an organizing bureau of five to plan an "All-Russian Congress of Workers in Pharmacies" August 1-15 in Petrograd. The agenda for the congress proposed six-hour work shifts, municipalization, a Central Bureau of Professional Unions.[54]

Petrograd militants were committed to municipalization. However, in the late spring and early summer of 1917, there they still evinced ambivalence about quickly implementing public ownership of all pharmacies, acknowledging that it was "necessary to submit the issue to careful discussion." Kanevskii, in particular, emphasized that the "privilege" to open private pharmacies was "deeply antisocial." He praised the regulation of 1912, claiming, with considerable distortion that it did not originate with the Minister of Internal Affairs but rather that "after a long and fruitless struggle, zemstvos and cities achieved a change in the law and received the right to open pharmacies *iavochnym poriadkom,* without prior permission, without regard to population figures or numbers of prescriptions dispensed, as required for private pharmacies." Unfortunately, he reminded his comrades, the public zemstvo and city pharmacies in existence were only "quasi-municipalized" because the local bodies were still "in the hands of the commanding classes." Still, they were a step forward and their staff pharmacists must strive for further "democratization." Yet, having made this point, Kanevskii concluded, on an odd note, that there were three possible options for Russian pharmacy in the future: nationalization, municipalization, and free trade, that is, allowing all pharmacists on the Provizor and Master level to own pharmacies.[55]

In April and May, 1917, Kadets P. N. Miliukov and Alexander Guchkov resigned from their respective posts of Minister of Foreign Affairs and War over criticism of their determination to continue the war partly to gain Constantinople and the straits. During June and July regiments quartered in Petrograd and radicalized by the Bolsheviks took to the streets on three occasions. The most crucial upheaval occurred July 3 and 4. Soldiers demanded that the Provisional Government resign and hand over power to the Soviets.[56] Kerensky was threatened as he boarded a train for the front, and Chernov, SR Minister of Agriculture, was roughed up although Lenin and the Bolsheviks were frightened because their criteria for revolution—critical party size and control over key soviets—were not yet fulfilled. The July coup attempt was finally thwarted when the Socialist Revolutionary Minister of Justice convinced the rebels that Lenin had received German funds in order to return to Russia.[57]

There was a noticeable turn leftward among Moscow and provincial staff pharmacists during June and July. But rank-and-file pharmacists were not uniformly radical and there were still waverers. In some cases militant leaders had to force party loyalty.

In Moscow, at a general meeting June 21, various "orators" urged staff pharmacists to increase socialist influence in the city duma by participating in coming elections and casting ballots only for members of socialist parties. Kuperman, an emissary from Petrograd, laid down new union rules. To make the pharmacy unions more powerful they must include all pharmacy employees, not merely staff pharmacists. He also broached municipalization. Staff pharmacists did not accept his leadership or proposals willingly. The latter "called forth great differences of opinion on the part of staff pharmacists assembled." Nevertheless, the gathering did sanction "taxing" all staff pharmacists one day's pay for the purposes of establishing an organization bureau, sending delegates to the forthcoming Petrograd pharmacy congress, and use as a strike fund. Overhead was high. One hundred fifty rubles per month went for a "chancery" (*deloproizvodstvo*) and 300 rubles for a secretary.[58] During the summer Moscow militants also determined to fight an increase in the Pharmacy Tax, which pharmacy owners claimed they needed to cover increased expenses.[59]

Militants in Khar'kov founded their union May 20. From the beginning there were "two tendencies." A "small," but "well organized group" desired to maintain friendly relations with local pharmacy owners. This group, which controlled the administration, proposed that staff pharmacists invite members of the Khar'kov Pharmacy Society (of pharmacy owners) into the union. Militants were livid, fretting that the bulk of the rank and file were "not well organized."[60] Nevertheless, at a general meeting of 131 city and provincial pharmacists on May 24, militants, accusing the administration of not "working in pharmacies" and having a "material position no different from pharmacy owners," were able to call an election for a new administration. When the vote went against them—48 voted against changing the administration and 38 in favor—militants used strong-arm tactics and the old administration was ejected anyway.[61]

Ekaterinoslav staff pharmacists also protested raising the Pharmacy Tax, insisting that owners had sufficient funds from a raise two months previously.[62] A July congress debated bread-and-butter issues, such as general insurance for staff pharmacists and labor norms, but also "unanimously" endorsed municipalization.[63]

A province-wide meeting of staff pharmacists was held in Kostroma July 29–30. Representatives from only three districts were able to attend because of communication difficulties. A majority of the assembly refused to amalgamate with *praktikanty* and other pharmacy employees. They did, however, endorse municipalization.[64]

Riazan pharmacists held a province-wide conference July 10. They were mainly concerned with bread-and-butter issues—six-hour shifts, limiting night duty and the number of prescriptions they were required to fill, and a minimum wage. Some of their socioeconomic program, such as abolition of child labor, reflected factory worker demands. Additionally, Kostroma pharmacists called for general pharmacist insurance, using money from the Pharmacist Pension Fund. They endorsed municipalization.[65]

The Tashkent Union of Staff Pharmacists convened about nineteen pharmacists from the Fergana Region. Their chief focus was organizational. They adamantly separated the union of Tashkent pharmacists from the staff pharmacists of Turkestan region. Since the Tashkent professional union had few members, additional members were conscripted from a nearby city.[66]

Gomel pharmacists included a fairly radical contingent by July 10. They gave pharmacy owners three days to respond to demands for norms of work and pay raises. When the owners refused they called a strike. Nevertheless, some staff pharmacists acted as strikebreakers. Additionally, the local Soviet of Workers and Soldiers' Deputies proposed an arbitration chamber to settle the conflict. On July 17 the antagonists agreed to negotiate.[67]

Ural'sk pharmacists presented pharmacy owners with a list of demands to be executed within a two-month time period. The owners conceded some, such as the double shift, but rejected others, such as simultaneously increasing staffs. On June 29, after all but one owner pronounced the new demands unsatisfactory, staff pharmacists went on strike.[68]

Yet, pharmacists in a number of other provinces continued to display lack of militancy. Kursk staff pharmacists merely protested verbally a local pharmacy owner's refusal to hire Jewish pharmacists. Vitebsk pharmacists were solely preoccupied with unemployment.[69] Militants lamented that Odessa pharmacists were hopelessly beset with "zigzags." They did not definitively support "revolutionary democracy." It was not clear whether they possessed a "revolutionary center." One Odessa union was a "yellow" employer-sponsored union.[70] Pharmacists in Belaia Tserkov', Kiev province, established a union in the wake of the February Revolution but the union "counted only 30 members after six months" of existence. A conflict then ensued over whether the union should affiliate with the Kiev union or stand alone. Members readied demands for shorter hours and an end to night duty.[71] In Nizhni Novgorod radical leaders called a strike in July but enthusiasm for the union waned when no palpable results were forthcoming.[72]

During July, Petrograd militants were preoccupied with the abortive revolt in the capital. On July 28 they convened a general meeting of pharmacy workers. A. Aluf criticized the Bolsheviks for their role in the July days. He accused them of widening the chasm between the bourgeoisie and "revolutionary democracy" and labeled their "demagogic tactics dangerous." However, he also asserted that the "July troubles" could not be put entirely on their shoulders. The problem of the war, economic deterioration, and the food crisis had helped generate street demonstrations. Aluf saw the two main foci of power in the country, the Soviet of Workers and Soldiers' Deputies and the Kadets. Still, as the Provisional Government now comprised more socialists, he called upon pharmacists to support it insofar as it upheld promises made on July 8.[73]

Although the state of the country appeared ominous and militants retained their commitment to raising the consciousness of rank-and-file pharmacists, there also were signs of normalcy in the pharmacy world during the summer of 1917. In July, Petrograd militant Epshtein was sufficiently sanguine as to propose an "enlightenment committee," which would establish libraries and encourage literacy amongst pharmacists.[74] May 1, a general meeting of delegates from pharmacy societies and organizations discussed reform of pharmacy education. Alexander Semenovich Ginzberg, former member of the State Duma Master of Pharmacy Brashe, A. I. Zil'berberg, A. N. Popovskii accepted a mandate to move forward reform of pharmacy education. Additionally an All-Russian Pharmacy Congress was planned. Ginzberg was elected to the organizational committee.[75] He worked out an eight-page proposal, "On Reform of Pharmaceutical Education," which detailed the dilatoriness and ineffectualness of the tsarist Minister of Education in establishing "rational" education for pharmacists. No doubt a key reason he later embraced the Bolshevik government was to realize this reform.[76] In July, Ginzberg and several socialist-oriented members of the former Petrograd Committee for Independent Preparation of Medicines petitioned the Committee on Reform of Higher Educational Institutions in the Provisional Government's Ministry of Public Enlightenment to implement changes in pharmacy education, particularly to implement pharmacy departments in university physics-mathematics faculties, as proposed by the tsarist Minister of Education the previous year.[77] In late August, a Congress of Staff Pharmacists in Petrograd listened to a proposal on "fundamental changes in pharmacy education." The lengthy suggestions included special pharmacy institutes with four-year courses, pharmacy faculties in universities or special pharmacy institutes, abolishing the titles of pharmacy student, Assistant Pharmacist, and Provizor and establishing the degree Candidate of Pharmaceutical Sciences, and abolishing apprenticeship.[78] And, in mid-September Petrograd militants were still law-abiding enough to petition the Minister of Internal Affairs to approve statutes for their Pharmacy Soviet. Militant Ia. F. Kanevskii was elected delegate to the Democratic Conference, called by a desperate Kerensky in September to shore up his tottering government.[79]

However, militant pharmacists in Petrograd were not about to become complacent. They still aimed for decisive change. In the fall of 1917, they and militants in Moscow and provincial cities called strikes. These strikes contributed to Russia's economic instability, weakened the authority of the Provisional Government, and facilitated the impending Bolshevik takeover.

On September 20 militant pharmacists in Moscow called strikes in pharmacies, the Ferrein firm, and drug stores.[80] On October 1 militant pharmacists in Petrograd called a strike, which lasted six weeks, ending November 13. Staff pharmacists won "nearly full victory" but their actions, which closely paralleled Bolshevik preparations and periods of decision-making, also enabled the Bolsheviks to take the capital October 25.[81]

Militant pharmacists in Petrograd insisted the strike was necessary because pharmacy owners and managers had not abided by the April 24/25 collective agreement. A mediation chamber had been established in the Ministry of Labor. However, owners and managers reviewed contested cases of hiring and firing before pharmacy staff representatives did so.[82]

Kuperman, one Lapitskii (possibly related to the woman pharmacist Lapitskaia), Bronshtein, and Aluf communicated this grievance to seven hundred members of the new Union of Pharmacy Staff who gathered on October 1. The leaders assured the assembly that the "all democratic organizations" in Petrograd supported the strike as did socialists in the central government. Chief Medical Administrator Bulatov opposed the strike. However, a group within his department lauded militants' commitment to keep forty-five pharmacies open to serve the public during the strike.[83]

The Petrograd city duma sided with the strikers. The duma had become increasingly socialistic during the war. Additionally, as noted, Petrograd pharmacists elected more socialists to the duma in late August.[84] The Petrograd city duma elected a special commission to investigate the conflict. It "came to the conclusion that the fault lay with pharmacy management."[85] Further, socialist members of the Petrograd city duma announced that it was now time to move to municipalization.[86]

Socialists in the central government showed themselves to be more responsible. Skobelev, Menshevik Minister of Labor in Kerensky's beleaguered government, agreed that owners and managers had breached the April contract.[87] However, with the Bolsheviks waiting in the wings, he pleaded with radical pharmacists to cool down, reminding them that pharmacy owners usually lost cases in the mediation chamber and were forced to pay compensation. He urged staff pharmacists to ignore grievances about hiring and firing. Bronshtein dismissed Skobelev's advice as "naive."[88]

Menshevik pharmacists ground into action. Two days before the strike declaration the central executive committee of the Soviet of pharmacy delegates established a central strike committee and strike committees in five regions of the city. When owners and managers refused demands at three o'clock October 2 the strike began. Forty-five pharmacies, twenty-one private and the rest city, public, and hospital, were allowed to continue dispensing.[89] Regional strike committees, to Mensheviks' great satisfaction, functioned smoothly. They established contact with regional dumas and the Petrograd Soviet of Workers and Soldiers' Deputies, now under Bolshevik control. The Vyborg regional soviet called for municipalization. Workers in some factories also clamored for municipalization, after strike committees explained the concept to them.[90]

The pharmacy strikers' timetable paralleled the Bolsheviks' revolutionary timetable. On October 10, from his hide-out in Finland, Lenin urged the Bolsheviks to take over the capital. On the same day, radical pharmacists called a meeting of pharmacy staff. About a thousand people showed up. The city duma now broached the confiscation of pharmacies. The Chief Medical Inspector and leader of the city militia, one Ivanov, tried to counter pharmacists' radicalism by ordering that pharmacists who had signed on to pharmacies to foment the strike be fired. Radical pharmacist leaders condemned Ivanov and lobbied the Provisional Minister of Internal Affairs to take Chief Medical Inspector Bulatov to court.[91]

On October 17, two weeks after the beginning of the Petrograd pharmacy strike and one week before the Bolshevik coup, radical pharmacists called a second meeting of capital pharmacy staff. Fifteen hundred people showed up. But radical leaders admitted that "a majority of strikers did not actively participate." Additionally, some staff pharmacists opposed municipalization. One Bassman had the temerity to announce that confiscating pharmacies "was theft" and pharmacy owners should "not be so cruelly punished." He conceded that pharmacy owners were "our enemy" but "our struggle with them must bear a cultivated character." Lapitskii, Gol'dshtein, Vitenberg, Neiman, and other radicals scoffed at such conciliatory attitudes. Striking and confiscation of private pharmacies were justified. Staff pharmacists were "defending their rights." Resorting to "uncultured measures was acceptable."[92]

About fifteen staff pharmacists also defected at the beginning of the strike. Pharmacy owners desperately tried to defend themselves by increasing the number of such "strikebreakers" and reminding the people of Petrograd that the strike would deprive them of medicine.[93]

Galvanized by strikes in Petrograd and Moscow, Nizhni Novgorod staff pharmacists shed their indifference, and demanded wage increases. Pharmacy owners quickly satisfied their demands except for one.[94] Similarly, a one-month pharmacy strike occurred in Rostov-on-the-Don and a pharmacy strike broke out in Kiev.[95] A strike in Vologda lasted from October 4 to 17. Pharmacy owners had conceded seven-hour shifts and wage increases but "following the example of Petrograd," workers held out for sick pay and a mediation chamber.[96] The Kremenchug Union called a strike October 7. It lasted two weeks—through the Bolshevik takeover of Petrograd. Radical pharmacists demanded six-hour shifts, one-month's vacation after eleven months' service, and other concessions.[97] Odessa militants demanded raises October 25. Their action followed the Bolshevik takeover in Petrograd but preceded the takeover in Moscow and other cities. Odessa pharmacy owners capitulated November 23, offering 40 percent raises for Provizors and Assistant Pharmacists, 50 percent raises for students, and 25, 30, and 60 percent raises for nonpharmacist workers.[98] Pharmacy strikes were called in Lenin's home town of Simbirsk from November 8 to 10, 1917.

Thus, pharmacist stalwarts successfully radicalized the rank and file and forced pharmacy owners to their knees. But staff continued to be obstinately, insufficiently militant. During the fall strikes a number of staff pharmacists in Petrograd, Simferopol', and Kiev leased pharmacies from their owners. Orthodox militants derided their attempt to fulfill "petit bourgeois" dreams of becoming proprietors.[99] And, belatedly, many militant pharmacists realized they had gotten more than they bargained for.

On the morrow of the October Revolution, the Petrograd Soviet of Workers and Soldiers' Deputies threatened pharmacy owners with confiscation of their property unless the strike were settled. But Bolshevik authorities also pressured striking workers, the constituency they claimed to represent, in order to save the new Soviet (Bolshevik) government.[100]

Some members of the union of pharmacy workers refused to cooperate. Others capitulated.[101] Those who did so acknowledged on November 7 that they "regarded the contemporary [Bolshevik] government negatively." However, in light of the fact that there was no other, "if the government opened the pharmacies" they would "go back to work."[102] Five days later Aluf, Lapitskii, and Mirlin worried that pharmacy owners were still powerful and that rank-and-file pharmacists' gains were ephemeral. Further, they viewed the strike as a legitimate "form of class struggle" against owners, who had violated a collective agreement. Nevertheless, the three reluctantly agreed to urge the rank and file to return to work if they were paid for the strike period.[103]

The Petrograd strike finally ended November 12 through the efforts of the mediation chamber. Pharmacy owners did agree to pay strikers for the period they were on strike. At the end of November, however, some pharmacies still were still closed and the Petrograd Soviet threatened to requisition them if they did not immediately open.[104]

The October/November pharmacy strikes helped the Bolsheviks come to power, but like many other white collar and service groups, pharmacists generally were not enthusiastic about the Bolsheviks.[105] Further, staff pharmacists, both in Petrograd and the provinces, displayed a "head in the sand" mentality, preoccupying themselves with corporate reorganization and economic concerns. And, finally, some staff pharmacists continued to be conciliatory toward and cooperate with owners.

In the wake of the October Revolution, Petrograd militants concentrated on organizational affairs. They planned an agenda for the All-Russian Congress of Professional Unions scheduled for January 3, 1918.[106] On November 12 they voted to consolidate with the union of workers in drug stores and laboratories.[107] At the end of 1917 the Union of Pharmacy Workers finally amalgamated with the Union of Workers in Pharmaceutical Enterprises.[108] The Petrograd Union of Pharmacy Workers counted 2,300 members in the spring of 1918.[109]

On January 3, 1918, the Central Soviet of Professional Unions of Workers in Petrograd discussed the unemployment that would result from demobilization. However, attendance at the January 3, 1918, plenary session of the Central Soviet of Professional Unions of Pharmacy Workers was sparse. Only one representative from Moscow showed up. Representatives from Odessa, Kiev, Cheliabinsk, Tiflis notified Petrograd they could not attend. Staff pharmacists in other cities did not reply.[110] Nevertheless, the Central Soviet busily planned a lengthy agenda, which included coordinating the provinces with the center and municipalization.[111]

Moscow militants harangued that capitalists like Ferrein constituted pharmacists' chief enemy[112] and strikers in Baku pharmacies called for "economic gains." But the Simbirsk Union of Staff Pharmacists focused on their union, voting to include all pharmacy workers in it. In Ekaterinburg, staff pharmacists were embroiled in a clash with the director of the zemstvo pharmacy warehouse and appealed to the Union of Staff Pharmacists of Perm province to get him fired from zemstvo service without taking the matter to court. Ekaterinoslav pharmacists were concerned with unemployment. They warned their colleagues there were no places open in city pharmacies. Gomel staff pharmacists were involved in collective bargaining with the local Union of Pharmacy Owners. With help from the local mediation chamber they acquired the right for staff to approve hiring and firing of staff pharmacists. Pharmacy owners did not approve all their demands but did grant sizable raises. Staff pharmacists in Briansk, Orel province, signed a collective agreement with pharmacy owners guaranteeing the double shift and a mediation chamber. Bul'guma pharmacists in Samara province on the Volga concentrated on "starting life anew after the revolution." The zemstvo executive council implemented the double shift and "some other improvements." Pharmacists tried to establish close connections with the provincial pharmacy union but to no avail. They decided to keep on the Provizor-manager of the zemstvo pharmacy because no replacement could be found.[113] By December 7, Briansk pharmacists were overwhelmed with unemployment problems.[114]

Additionally, some militant pharmacist leaders began to express reservations about the new Bolshevik government although they gamely continued to support them. Moscow radicals confessed that the "Proletarian professional unions might not agree with the activities of the party now governing, they might have a negative attitude toward Bolshevik socialism, considering the country not ready for it." Still, they urged colleagues to refrain from strikes in order not to "destroy the entire country."[115]

Petrograd militants also expressed mixed reaction to the Bolsheviks. On December 31, 1917, 130 members of the General Assembly of Petrograd Union of Pharmacy Workers met to discuss the peace talks with Germany inaugurated by the Bolshevik government and Bolshevik economic policies. Because of the small number of those assembled the Bolshevik Iaroslav opposed electing representatives to the Petrograd Soviet. When elections took place anyway, Iaroslav and 20 others stormed out of the meeting in protest.[116] Aluf, the Menshevik Internationalist, approved of the Brest peace talks. But the assembly as a whole condemned the negotiations for "giving away the fruits of the revolution to Germany." They also criticized the form of "worker control" that the Bolsheviks adhered to at that time. Shliapnikov, commissar in the Bolshevik government and a proponent of worker control, maintained that "the organs of worker control have become pushers [*tolkachi*] for orders." The Union of Pharmacy Workers proposed "state control with worker participation." Brushing aside the fact of Bolshevik power, woman pharmacist Lapitskaia urged the pharmacy union to concentrate on important issues like the forthcoming "Constituent Assembly, which alone could give the country democratic peace and settle the land question. . . ." Kanevskii, on the contrary, urged pharmacists to cooperate with the Bolsheviks because the problems facing the country, such as unemployment, required everyone to pull together. However, he also noted that the "proletariat" was "demoralized" and Bolshevik authoritarianism was responsible. They had replaced the "class struggle" with "endless decrees." "Saving the revolution was possible only by establishing a united revolutionary front." Unfortunately, although there were some eighty-four organizations in the All-Russian Central Soviet of Unions of Workers in Pharmacies, they weakly supported their mouthpiece, *Vestnik Aptechnago Truda*, which had replaced *Zhizn' farmatsevta.*[117]

By March 1918, Paperin, a militant pharmacist from Petrograd, labeled the October Revolution a Jacobin coup rather than a proletarian triumph. The Bolsheviks had taken power

> with the help of the Petrograd garrison. The wide masses of workers recognized the takeover after the fact. The original Council of People's Commissars consisted exclusively of Bolsheviks. . . .
>
> For three months the Council of People's Commissars have struggled to strengthen their power, to strengthen the socialist order. The first goal has not been attained. The second is possible only by uprooting remnants of the old, bourgeoisie, capitalist order. . . . But what is more important, until now the new authority has indulged in harsh criticism of all other socialist parties. . . . Parties which had as their purpose the implementation of a socialist order, for which the Social Democrats have worked these many years, regard the overturn of October 25 not as a revolution, but the result of a military conspiracy [*zagovor*], having nothing in common with a revolution.
>
> The implementation of a socialist order in Russia is the most important task before us. All the actions of the Council of People's Commissars and all its policies . . . have not only not achieved this end but threaten the very . . . worker class.[118]

He reminded readers that "Marx had taught" that "revolution consisted in the uprising of a *majority* [italics in original] against . . . the *minority*."[119] The Bolshevik takeover had been the antithesis of that principle. The government did not represent all socialist parties. Bolshevik socialism was not true socialism—"at the last congress of soviets the idealistic leader of the Bolsheviks called socialism—accounting." The Bolsheviks had committed many "mistakes"; they dominated the proletariat, treated the proletariat like a child.[120]

In this distressing political situation, militant pharmacists of orthodox Menshevik persuasion moved to realize their dream of municipalization. Unfortunately, this did not bring hoped-for results. Municipalization did not improve the situation of pharmacists or pharmacy. On the contrary, municipalization was fraught with problems. Furthermore, within a few months, the Bolshevik government began to seize control of pharmacies, pharmacists and the pharmaceutical industry. Their program of nationalization and centralization proved to be even more unworkable.

19

1918: Municipalization and Nationalization

In the early months of 1918, militant pharmacists, the majority Mensheviks, began to implement their dream of municipalization—turning private pharmacies over to public institutions. Although zemstvos had been touted as managers for expropriated private pharmacies, when the program was implemented, city dumas, local "soviets of workers and soldiers' deputies," and other local bodies took over the pharmacies. But almost immediately, the Bolshevik government pulled the rug out from under municipalization. A month or so after the process started, the Bolsheviks embarked upon a program of nationalization—bringing pharmacies and pharmaceutical factories, supply and budgets, pharmacists and their organizations—under control of the central government.

Some Menshevik pharmacists joined the Bolsheviks. Others were outraged at Bolshevik authoritarianism, claiming that the revolution had been betrayed. But it was really Russian pharmacy, the pharmaceutical industry, and the public who were betrayed. For Menshevik as well as Bolshevik economic policies largely ruined Russian pharmacy.

Municipalization

Militant socialist pharmacists began to move toward municipalization even before the Bolshevik Revolution. The Petrograd Soviet of Workers and Soldiers' Deputies proposed municipalization October 3, 1917, the third week of the Petrograd strike.[1] At first, some municipal dumas shied away from taking over private pharmacies.[2] Petrograd mayor Shreiber strongly opposed municipalization.[3]

Nevertheless, although pharmacy owners satisfied strikers' demands after October 25, municipalization gained momentum. As noted in the previous chapter, August elections had increased the socialist component in the Petrograd city duma. In January 1918, socialists in the duma proposed municipalizing private pharmacies. The duma and mayor now approved, on the ground that their owners could no longer be trusted to dispense to the public.[4] The Central Soviet of Professional Unions of Pharmacy Workers in Petrograd received notice in January that municipalization also was to be undertaken in Kazan, Saratov, Kursk, Sevastopol', Kronstadt, and Peterhof.[5]

As befitting citizens of a methodical, legalistic government, municipalization was planned to follow meticulously organized procedures. Pharmacy staffs had dwindled during the fall and winter, but they were encouraged, even if only one or two, to take over their pharmacies. However, municipalization was to be led and supervised by provincial and district committees, control commissions, and a raft of regulations.[6] The actual process varied from province to province and city to city.

In Petrograd, which remained the capital of Russia until March 1918, municipalization began at the end of January. On January 24 the Petrograd city duma forbade pharmacies to dispense medicine and formed "Commissions of Public Control" to insure that the order was carried out.[7] On January 31 the duma formally endorsed municipalizing privately owned pharmacies. A central pharmacy committee and regional committees were established. The central committee consisted of nine members of the city duma, four representatives from the union of workers in pharmacies, and one representative from the professional union of workers in pharmaceutical enterprises.[8] The Petrograd Pharmacy Commission, formed in the city duma, began operating March 23. Upon its inception the Petrograd Soviet of Workers and Soldiers' Deputies had divided the city into thirteen regions and the Pharmacy Commission followed this pattern. An inspector was appointed for each region. The regional inspector promulgated the order for municipalization to owners, renters, and managers of pharmacies. The latter were required to sign the order upon receiving it and list pertinent information about the pharmacy's operation. Local inhabitants were advised that municipalization would put dispensing on a "rational" basis. Pharmacies were closed for three days for inventory. The pharmacy commissions approved new managers. Temporary managers were appointed in cases where no qualified pharmacists were available.[9] Pharmacy owners who tried to hide or dispose of inventories before the transfer of their pharmacies to the city duma were threatened with arrest.[10] Following the confiscation of pharmacies, commissions filled out municipalization forms.[11]

Local authorities agreed that the central government had no funds to assist in the operation. Therefore the Petrograd duma allocated 50,000 rubles to municipalization, although only 10,000 was immediately disbursed.[12] There had been some talk of compensating pharmacy owners but this sum was inadequate for that purpose.[13]

Petrograd pharmacy owners fought back, turning to the government for succor as was their habit, even though this government was now Bolshevik. Owners petitioned the new Commissariat of Internal Affairs, the presidium of the Soviet of Workers and Soldiers' Deputies, and other institutions.[14] On February 14, 1918, Antonina Lesnevskaia sent the required information on her pharmacy to the authorities in charge of municipalization. However, at the same time, in her typical feisty manner, she asked them "not to apply the order on municipalization to her [First Women's] pharmacy."[15] Professor S. Przhibytek, who entered the Soviet (Bolshevik) pharmacy organization, supported her to a certain extent. On February 18 he wrote that as professor of pharmacy and pharmacology at the Military-Medical Academy he had "examined many students of the school of A. B. Lesnevskaia in the First Women's Pharmacy, both for the title Assistant Pharmacist and for the degrees Provizor and Master of Pharmacy. Therefore, I can testify that the students of the aforementioned school distinguished themselves both in theoretical and in practical preparation."[16] Lesnevskaia influenced Soviet officials as she had tsarist. On February 22, the Commissariat of Public Enlightenment went to bat for her, notifying the Petrograd city mayor that "In view of the fact that the pharmacy school in the 1-st Women's Pharmacy of A. B. Lesnevskaia is the sole specialized scientific institution in Russia, preparing women pharmacists for the degree of Assistant and is provided with rational education by professors, the State Commission has decided it necessary to preserve the courses together with the women's pharmacy closely connected with it. . . ."[17]

The fact that Lesnevskaia's pharmacy school was run on "rational" lines was a major compliment in the new order and should have carried weight. Both local and central administrators insisted that in addition to the fact that private proprietors could not be trusted to dispense correctly to the public, the purpose of expropriating private pharmacies was to put dispensing on a rational basis. Whether Lesnevskaia got a stay of execution for a few months is not clear. But, it was claimed that municipalization was completed in Petrograd by July, 1918, 150 private pharmacies having been transferred to the Petrograd "pharmacy authority" (*aptechnoe delo*). The unemployment problem in Petrograd was solved by giving 300 unemployed pharmacists positions in understaffed pharmacies.[18] At a general meeting of the Union of Pharmacy Workers Kuperman enthused that "pharmacy staffs had been equalized as a result of municipalization."[19] And, by the end of 1918, as we shall see, Lesnevskaia's pharmacy had been turned into a "communal" pharmacy.

Militants in Khar'kov, a Bolshevik stronghold in the eastern Ukraine, opted for municipalization even before Petrograd, January 9, following militants' forceful takeover of the local pharmacy union. The Khar'kov Military Revolutionary Committee "decreed municipalization." It then pressured the city executive council (*uprava*) to enforce the decree. The council voted 10 to 7 for municipalization. However, a sizable number of staff pharmacists, particularly in outlying towns, opposed municipalization, viewing it as a "catastrophe."[20]

In Perm province in the Urals, a pharmacy subdepartment arose at the end of January 1918. (These provincial and district pharmacy subdepartments were given various shorthand names, which, in turn, were spelled in various ways, at least at the beginning. In the singular the departments were labeled *pododtdel* or *farpod'otdel*. That in Perm was called *farmpodotdel*.) The purpose of the Perm subdepartment was to supplant the tsarist-era Medical Department of the Perm Provincial Administration, which had functioned from the eighteenth century. The Perm pharmacy subdepartment was loosely under the Department of Health (*otdel zdravookhraneniia*) of the Executive Body of the Perm Soviet of Workers and Soldiers' Deputies. It was composed of a collegium of five pharmacists, members of the executive body of the Perm provincial union of pharmacy staffs, formed during the war, and the new commissar for pharmacy matters. The Perm pharmacy subdepartment would undergo three reorganizations by the midsummer of 1918. Meanwhile, determining that "private pharmacies could not correctly serve the people" it began taking over private pharmacies, laboratories, pharmaceutical warehouses, and drug stores. By the summer of 1918, the Perm pharmacy subdepartment was pleased to announce that no private pharmacies existed.[21]

On the other hand, the pharmacy subdepartment of Yaroslavl' province, north of Moscow, was not established until August 1918, after the central Bolshevik government ordered all provinces to form these bodies.[22] Similarly, Penza did not organize a pharmacy subdepartment until September 1918. Local authorities began taking over private pharmacies after this, but prior to the nationalization decree issued in December 1918.[23] Tambov did not organize a pharmacy subdepartment until October 1918,[24] and local authorities were still seizing private pharmacies in November and the months following.[25] Ivano-Voznesensk did not organize a pharmacy subdepartment until November 1918.[26]

In Saratov province, on the Volga, the executive committee of the local Soviet ordered the expropriation of private pharmacies very early, in February 1918.[27] However, there was no proper provincial pharmacy subdepartment in Saratov until February 1919.[28]

In Kursk in June 1918, the Professional Union of Pharmacy Workers signed a collective agreement with the Union of Pharmacy Owners for six-hour days, three-weeks' vacation after nine months' work, and other idealistic demands.[29] In the city of Lomomna, Moscow province, April 24, three private and one city pharmacy were "nationalized," a term used by local authorities to describe pharmacy takeovers after central authorities attempted to exert more control over the process.[30]

After the first flush of enthusiasm, problems surfaced in municipalized pharmacies. Turf battles ensued. Additionally, economic reality began to set in.

Conflicts flared up between staff and the new management of the municipalized pharmacies. Militant pharmacists in Petrograd insisted that staff initiated municipalization in most cites and provinces where this occurred in early 1918. But they also admitted that city commissions or regional soviets inaugurated municipalization. As a consequence, staff pharmacists exhibited "doubt and distrust" toward the new managers.[31] Groups of disgruntled staff in some municipalized pharmacies elected a special committee to protect themselves.[32] Administrators in the Petrograd Professional Union of Pharmacy Workers censured this lack of cooperation.[33]

Conflicts erupted between various levels of local pharmacy organizations. In Ivano-Voznesensk in February 1918 the new city pharmacy section clashed with the new provincial pharmacy section.[34]

By the summer of 1918, instead of unemployment, Petrograd and a number of other cities faced severe shortages of pharmacists. Apprenticeship had been abolished in January. However, due to lack of pharmacists, in June 1918, the administration of the Petrograd Union of Pharmacy Workers requested the Pharmacy Section of the Petrograd Commissariat of Health to permit students to serve in pharmacies.[35]

Staff pharmacists' position deteriorated. One problem that they confronted was a holdover from the old regime. Some pharmacy owners had withheld pay from staff before municipalization. The Pharmacy Commission promised to pay them.[36] But other vicissitudes suffered by staff pharmacists were the result of municipalization and the exigencies besetting the new regime. Unemployed pharmacists were forced to accept assignments in pharmacies given them by the local Bureau of Labor.[37] By the summer of 1918, staff pharmacists complained that local soviets did not honor the norms for pay and work hours that they had achieved during the strikes of 1917.[38] A cholera epidemic flared up in July. Pharmacists on hand were forced to work longer hours. Their night duty hours were increased. Prices escalated and pharmacists found their pay eaten up by inflation as it had been during the war. Strikes broke out along railways in the Ukraine and in Odessa.[39]

Militant pharmacists grumbled about the lack of democracy, noting for example that only Bolsheviks and left Socialist Revolutionaries were elected to a Proletkult (Proletarian Culture) Conference in the spring of 1918.[40]

In any case, municipalization was short-lived. In the spring of 1918 the new Bolshevik government began to supplant municipalization with nationalization.

Nationalization and Centralization

Officials manning the new Soviet government had been bred in a paternalistic, procedure-oriented pharmacy system. Additionally, they passionately believed that more thorough organization and careful direction of pharmacy and the pharmaceutical industry at the center and in the localities would produce superlative dispensing and pharmaceutical production in the new "Republic." In a manifesto accompanying their plans for reorganizing the pharmacy system, they proclaimed that "the old bureaucratic order had led not only individuals but entire professions, among them pharmacists, into oblivion. Now we are building a new life on new foundations. And the building of this new life must call each professional organization to manifest their potential strength for the good of the proletariat."[41]

The new order called for pharmacies to be transferred from private hands to more capable government administrators. Additionally these administrators must be closely tied to central authorities: "private pharmacies have never stood at a proper level and in recent years [there has been] speculation... nationalization will supply the populace with medicines."[42]

The new order also was to emancipate pharmacists from the tutelage of physicians–the Chief Medical Inspector, Medical Council and Medical Department of the tsarist Ministry of Internal Affairs, and the provincial medical boards and medical inspectors. The pharmacy corporation had striven to extricate themselves for decades. That goal was now to be realized, liberating pharmacists' full potential. "Until now," central authorities declared, "20,000 pharmacists have filled only a passive, executive role, not having the possibility to show any kind of initiative, since direction and management . . . have been in the hands of doctors. This kind of guardianship over pharmacists is entirely without basis, since doctors do not have knowledge or experience in pharmacy matters."[43]

The new bureaucrats responsible for pharmacy expressed no concern that some of their coterie were chemistry professors rather than pharmacists and that those who were pharmacists had never owned or managed a pharmacy or pharmaceutical factory but rather had spent their entire career as journalists, labor organizers, or in academia.

The first step was to properly organize the central pharmacy administration. The Soviet (Bolshevik) government replicated the tsarist government.[44] But, because the Soviet government had a more ambitious agenda than its predecessor, because government officials were to replace private entrepreneurs, because as many decisions as possible were to be made at the center, the number of Soviet pharmacy agencies and bureaucrats increased geometrically compared with the tsarist period.[45]

New pharmacy agencies began to sprout immediately. By the spring of 1918 there were three chief pharmacy departments at the central level. A Pharmacy Department (*Farmatsevticheskii otdel*) located in the new Commissariat of Health (*Narkomzdrav*) was declared the "chief authority for pharmacy." Its three subdepartments–Organization, Control, and Administration; Medical Supply, Accounting, and Distribution; and Scientific and Statistical–were to enable the Pharmacy Department to manage the network of pharmacies, distribute medicines and supplies, and finance these manifold operations.[46] On the local level the Central Pharmacy Department was to be assisted by provincial and district pharmacy subdepartments (*gubfarpod'otdely* and *ufarpod'otdely*). By 1919 A. Aluf was manager of *Farmotdel*, as the Pharmacy Department was familiarly called.[47]

A Pharmacy Center or *Farmatsentr*, as it shall be called, housed in the Supreme Council of National Economy (VSNKh) particularly managed the pharmaceutical industry.[48] Rykov, Chair of the Supreme Council, proposed this agency, whose official name was the "Chief Committee on the Chemical-Pharmaceutical Industry," in February 1918. *Farmatsentr*'s mandate was to nationalize existing pharmaceutical enterprises, expand and develop the Soviet pharmaceutical industry, work out a plan to purchase raw materials, see to quality control of medicines, set prices, distribute medicines to pharmacies.[49] With nice attention to democracy, Rykov allowed possible dissenters a week to protest the new body. If there were no objections the agency was to materialize. Apparently there were none, because *Farmatsentr* held its initial organizational meeting August 20, 1918. Members included F. A. Ferrein, a scion of the famous pharmaceutical family; O. G. Gabrilovich, the radical pharmacist accounting specialist; Professor A. E. Chichibabin who had developed medicines at his University of Moscow laboratory during the war; and N. A. El'kind, said to be a "workers' representative."[50]

The Commissariat of Internal Affairs, successor to the Ministry of

Internal Affairs, locus of the Medical Council and Medical Department, which had supervised pharmacy under the old regime, also kept its hand in pharmacy matters, at least for a time, through its Pharmacy Department.[51] On top of this, a Pharmacy Commission was proposed for the Commissariat of Health. This body was to include representatives from government and "public" pharmacy organizations: the All-Russian Central Union of Professional Unions of Pharmacy Workers, the Moscow and Petrograd Professional Unions of Pharmacy Workers, the Central Committee of Workers in Chemical-Pharmaceutical Factories, *Farmatsentr*, the Department of Civilian Medicine and Department of Procurement and Supply in the Commissariat of Health, the Pharmacy Department of the Petrograd Work Commune, local pharmacy subdepartments (as yet not all formed), the Pharmacy Bureau of Moscow Province, and the Scientific Pharmacy Section. The new body was to have umbrella authority: legislative, executive, and scientific-medicinal. It was mandated to draft pharmacy legislation, instructions for pharmacy subdepartments in the provinces, oversee nationalization of pharmacy enterprises, and handle financing and "scientific and medical issues."[52] By August of 1918, the Scientific Section included A. S. Aluf, and Professors S. Przhibytek and L. F. Il'in, who had served on the Petrograd Medicaments Committee during the winter of 1915/16.[53] The committee debated reform of pharmacy education, fully discussed below.

Other ad hoc subcommissions of these agencies were established when the new bureaucrats decided they were needed. For instance, at its April 19 meeting, 1918, the Medical College of the Commissariat of Internal Affairs proposed a "special commission for budgeting and distributing medicines and medical supplies" for the Pharmacy Department of the same Commissariat.[54]

The new bureaucrats intended to streamline pharmacy administration. Instead, the plethora of central agencies overlapped in function. The Pharmacy Commission particularly engendered confusion, forcing central officials to confirm that the Pharmacy Department in the Commissariat of Health was an autonomous entity, responsible for all pharmacy in the Russian Republic. The Pharmacy Commission was only an advisory organ.[55]

Jurisdiction over the pharmaceutical industry likewise was tangled. *Farmatsentr* was established as the chief managing authority. But the Commissariats of Production and Health and the Department of Chemical Industry in the Supreme Council of the National Economy also supervised the pharmaceutical industry, a matter about which *Farmatsentr* complained.[56]

The next step was to bring pharmacies and pharmaceutical enterprises, local pharmacy officials, and organizations under control of the central authorities and to centralize supply, financing, and distribution of medicines. This task became urgent with the onset of Civil War.

The Bolsheviks' refusal to share authority with other socialist parties, their use of terror,[57] the treaty they signed with Germany at Brest-Litovsk in March 1918, which took Russia out of World War I and turned over the western periphery of the former empire to the central powers, unleashed a Civil War. Though connected with the new government's commitment to making pharmacy more efficient and rational, the Civil War made nationalization of pharmacies and pharmaceutical enterprises and centralization of supply and production a necessity. In the summer of 1917, before taking power, Lenin had advocated worker management or at least worker supervision of the Russian economy and government.[58] This populist program was jettisoned to enable the new Soviet government to win the Civil War. In its place the government instituted "War Communism." The new economic program included both sensible policies (one-man management, use of bourgeois specialists, competitive salaries, enforcement of labor discipline) and draconian measures (seizure of private property, confiscation of peasant grain, suppression of private trade, terror).[59]

The new government began imposing "War Communism" on the pharmacy world–nationalization of pharmacies and pharmaceutical enterprises; centralization of production, financing, and distribution; accounting and control; long hours and night duty for staff pharmacists–at the beginning of 1918.

On February 3 the Supreme Council of the National Economy discussed the formation of the Soviet pharmaceutical industry. They specifically debated the establishment of a phenol-salicylic factory in the city of Kazan. Material and workers were to come from the confiscated Brothers Krestovnikov factory, and other recently confiscated factories in the vicinity. Pharmacists had fought for decades for the principle that specially trained pharmacists were to manage pharmaceutical enterprises. The new regime ignored this principle. Management of the Kazan factory was entrusted to a teacher from the local pedagogical institute and a chemistry professor from the University of Kazan.[60]

Pharmacies came next. In March 1918, the Soviet government announced that municipalization was "too chaotic." This seems strange in view of the thoroughness of the procedure in Petrograd. Nevertheless, the government ordered municipalization to cease until a plan could be worked out for nationalization and central pharmaceutical supply.[61] That local entities did not obey is evident from the government's reiteration in

August that, while soviets had municipalized pharmacies and drug stores in a number of areas–Petrograd, Tula, Kaluga, Nizhni-Novgorod, Orel, Kazan, Riazan, Tomsk, Irkutsk, Perm, and Ekaterinburg–"chaos" and "speculation" had attended the process. Thus a plan for nationalizing pharmacies and pharmaceutical enterprises and central supply was to be promulgated in the near future.[62]

Local pharmacy organization was tightened up in July 1918, presumably because the Civil War was heating up. Central authorities ordered the formation of pharmacy subdepartments in all Medical-Sanitary Sections of provincial, district, and regional Soviets of Workers, Soldiers, and Peasants' Deputies.[63]

Nationalization of pharmacies and tighter lines of communication between central and local government bodies went hand in hand. The order on nationalization from the Commissariat of Health stressed that: "I. General direction, control over activity of nationalized pharmacies belongs to the Pharmacy Department of the Commissariat of Health. II. Direction, control of nationalized pharmacies in the localities belongs to the pharmacy subdepartment in capitals, provinces, and district medical-sanitary departments." Additionally, the provinces were to create Pharmacy Commissions composed of three representatives from the pharmacy subdepartment and two representatives from the provincial union of staff pharmacists. Districts were to create their own pharmacy commissions composed of two representatives from the district pharmacy subdepartment and one from the union of staff pharmacists.[64]

The localities began to come to heel. For example, Yaroslavl' province formed a pharmacy subdepartment August 7, 1918. Pharmacies were turned over to committees of staff pharmacists. Owners resisted, but, of course, to no avail. In several cases, Provizor managers "sided with the owners." They were fired and Assistant Pharmacists, elected by staff pharmacists, were appointed to run the pharmacy, under supervision of the subdepartment. The expropriated owners were thrown the sop of a half thousand rubles as compensation.[65]

Tambov informed central authorities that its pharmacy subdepartment had "nationalized" normal pharmacies November 1918 and undertaken to supply medicine to all pharmacies, handle their finances, and supervise staff, in such matters as transfer from one pharmacy to another, and so on. The subdepartment reported that it now was moving to nationalize village pharmacies, organize their supply, and form unions of pharmacists.[66]

On August 16, 1918, clinics and other facilities of the zemstvo and city unions were transferred to the Commissariat of Public Health.[67] At the same time pharmaceutical factories in Moscow began to be brought under government control. As with pharmacies, the process was very methodical. Firms were ordered to report on their inventory, staff, and other pertinent details. Questionnaires were distributed to all firms. Accustomed to obeying the government (and threatened with coercion if they did not obey), the enterprises promptly reported back, some on company stationery.[68]

By the fall of 1918, pharmacies, factories, and laboratories in some areas—particularly in Petrograd and Moscow—were under control of central authorities. For example, in the *Farmatsentr* meeting of October 29, F. A. Ferrein, O. G. Gabrilovich, and A. E. Chichibabin discussed supplying former zemstvo warehouses, laboratories, and hospital pharmacies.[69] On December 3, 1918, Ferrein, Gabrilovich, and four other members of *Farmatsentr* discussed Professor Chichibabin's report about the management of nationalized chemical-pharmaceutical enterprises by the Scientific-Technical Center of the Supreme Council of the National Economy and began nationalizing giant enterprises like V. K. Ferrein and B. Bliumental.[70]

However, nationalization continued during 1919. Sovnarkom, the cabinet or Council of People's Commissars, issued a general decree on nationalization December 1918.[71] As we shall see in the following chapter, pharmaceutical enterprises and warehouses were mostly nationalized during 1919. And, in addition to further nationalizing pharmacies in the Russian provinces, pharmacies and enterprises in the Ukraine were brought under the new Soviet system during 1919.

The Soviet government's management style was similar to that of the tsarist government, though more domineering and restrictive. As had the Medical Council in tsarist Ministry of Internal Affairs, from the summer of 1918 central authorities issued a flood of regulations dealing with all aspects of pharmacy operation. Some were identical to those issued in the tsarist period. Others related to the Soviet economic program which banned private enterprise and free trade. As under the tsarist regime, Soviet pharmacy rules were published in an official journal, in this case the newly founded *News of the Pharmacy Commission* (*Izvestiia aptechnoi komissii*).

There were many harsh and limiting regulations. On July 27, allegedly to counter speculation and falsification, as well as shortage of medicine, the Bolshevik government stipulated that pharmaceutical firms must get official permission to sell wares. They forbade drug stores (*aptekarskie magaziny*) to sell medicine.[72] A circular prohibited all advertisements of medicine.[73] On August 6 a Pharmaceutical Bureau was empowered to take medicines and other medical and pharmaceutical items from stores of the

Military Department, Red Cross, former zemstvo and city unions, other local bodies, private wholesale firms, and private individuals, and channel these items where needed.[74] A central supply organ *Tsentro-snabzhenie* was established.[75] Central authorities controlled trade. They forbade pharmacies to sell soap, cosmetics, toothpaste, and the like. Tooth elixir, containing spirits, could be sold only upon prescription of a physician.[76] At the end of November 1918, medicines containing sugar were regulated, indicating this item was in short supply.[77]

Other regulations had a familiar air. As had the Medical Council in the previous Ministry of Internal Affairs, *Farmatsentr* established a schedule of wholesale and retail prices (*preis kurant*) at which medicine could be sold, and regulated import and export of medicines, with procedures for applying for permission for the last.[78] Also in the tradition of the tsarist pharmacy system, Soviet authorities approved production of various items. For example, *Farmatsentr* ruled on the production of toothpaste.[79] As under the old regime, some requests were approved; others were denied.[80]

Some petitions were even holdovers from the previous period. The petition of Vasilii Nikolaevich Luchich fell into this category. Luchich, a Serb, had a "Private Analytical Institute" in Moscow, which performed various "chemical-diagnostic, bacteriological, and industrial-technical" tests.[81] Eager to keep his business, he sent a three-page, typed letter to the Commissariat of Health asking permission to turn the institute into a "Central-Suppository Factory" which would produce suppositories containing narcotics.[82] Luchich had begun his campaign to produce the suppositories in 1916, during World War I. At that time an official in the Chief Military-Sanitary Administration of the tsarist Ministry of War had thwarted his proposal, contending that the suppositories "could not replace subcutaneous injections, since the latter was a quicker, stronger therapy."[83] In December 1918, Soviet authorities reproved Luchich for hiding some of his supplies.[84] And in February 1919, they turned down his request, for the same reasons as tsarist authorities.[85]

A third group of Soviet pharmacy regulations blended old and new. The Commissariat of Health promulgated rules on dispensing and preparing mixtures and tablets. Rules on aspirin appeared first. Instructions on *salol*, quinine, urotropin, and other substances followed. The recipes were dictated by whether there were sufficient stocks in pharmacy warehouses. Pharmacies were given numbers instead of names—first communal, second communal, and so on. And "Central" issued instructions on how they were to formulate their budgets and enforce work discipline as well as procedures for accepting pharmacy apprentices. As in tsarist times there were to be periodical inspections of pharmacies, but it was claimed that these would be more thorough.[86] For pharmacists serving in pharmacies, hours of work, including the old bugbear night duty, was regulated and supervised by local authorities.[87]

One of the subdepartments of the Pharmacy Department in the Commissariat of Health was enjoined to gather statistics. Central authorities were scrupulous about gathering data. The questionnaires they used were similar to those used by tsarist authorities. Both provincial and district pharmacy organizations were required to fill out reports on their staffs and operation, the degree to which private pharmacies, drug stores, warehouses, and factories had been "municipalized" or "nationalized," and other pertinent matters. The questionnaires returned to Moscow in August revealed continuing great regional variations. With careful penmanship on a 5-by-7-inch sheet of paper, Rostov province reported that it had a pharmacy subdepartment.[88] Zvenigorod district in Moscow province sent word that it did not have a pharmacy subdepartment.[89] A district in Smolensk province sent back a neatly typed sheet stating that it did not have a provincial pharmacy subdepartment and had not municipalized or nationalized pharmacies. The district had two private pharmacies and one (zemstvo) public pharmacy. It had no wholesale warehouse of pharmacy wares.[90] Similarly, Volokolamsk district in Moscow province reported in August that it had no pharmacy subdepartment, it had not nationalized private pharmacies, there were eight hospital pharmacies and eight private pharmacies, there was no wholesale warehouse.[91] Also Danilovsk district in Yaroslavl' province admitted to having no pharmacy subdepartment. It had not nationalized any pharmacies, having one former zemstvo pharmacy, two private pharmacies, and one private pharmacy warehouse.[92]

The questionnaires further revealed that generous access to dispensing had existed in many regions under the old, private system thus raising the question of whether either municipalization or nationalization was rational or justified. One district, for example, which had properly formed a pharmacy subdepartment in April but had left pharmacies in private hands, reported that there were three normal pharmacies in the district town, one village pharmacy, one hospital pharmacy in the district hospital, no private warehouses, but two private drug stores. There also was a public warehouse serving the city hospital, a city outpatient clinic, dental office, and obstetrical clinic, veterinary clinic, and in the district, three medical "points" with hospitals, one medical point without, one feldsher point, and four veterinary feldsher points.[93] A similar situation obtained in Yaroslavl' province. The questionnaire reported twenty-three private pharmacies, seventeen public pharmacies, and twelve drug stores. Nevertheless, in August, zealous socialists organized pharmacy subdepartments in eight of ten districts as well as on the provincial level. They "transferred all pharmacies from the hands of owners to committees of staff." In some cases "pharmacy managers who sided with owners" "braked" the process. The Provizor managers were, of course, fired and replaced with Assistant Pharmacists.[94] Penza also appeared to have had an adequate pharmacy system under the old regime. A former zemstvo warehouse, drug stores, perfumeries, and a cosmetic factory had been nationalized by the summer of 1918. However, the nine private pharmacies in the provincial city, a pharmacy in the city hospital, and the eight hospital pharmacies, six private normal pharmacies, and twelve village pharmacies in the eleven districts of the province had not been nationalized. In this case, provincial authorities themselves asserted that nationalization would be "premature."[95]

The negative repercussions of the new centralized system were manifold and immediately discernible. Over and over it was claimed that nationalization was to make all aspects of pharmacy—dispensing, pharmacy education, and the pharmaceutical industry more rational.[96] It did nothing of the sort.

On the contrary, minutes of central agency meetings and reports from the provinces for 1918 and 1919 spoke of confusion, preoccupation with minutiae, insufficiency of pharmacists but profusion of administrative personnel, inadequate direction from the center but lack of decision-making and room to maneuver for provincial authorities and pharmacists, hamstringing of pharmacy unions, and, finally, dwindling supplies of materials, medicines, and money. Advocates of the new experiment could claim these were temporary wrinkles that would be ironed out in time. It also might be asserted that provincial records presented a skewed picture in that local officials would not have complained to central authorities if matters were going smoothly. Nevertheless, the problems reported from some fifty provinces and regions were so similar, pervasive, and serious it must be acknowledged that they indicated systemic flaws in Bolshevik pharmacy policy and, by extrapolation, Bolshevik economic policy. From the outset the Bolshevik pharmacy program appeared not only dysfunctional but fundamentally illogical. And it was detrimental to pharmacists, government bodies, public health, the state budget, and the national economy.

The autonomy promised to pharmacists was largely cosmetic. As pharmacies came under the Bolshevik wing, staff pharmacists[97] and militant pharmacy organizations were shorn of their independence. Professional associations struggled to maintain their autonomy. In some cases, staff pharmacists tried to stall for time. One group refused to pay dues to their local union, organized by the Commissar for Health. The three members of the union administration dwindled to one, the secretary.[98] But, with the Civil War raging, pharmacists were forced to accept the Bolshevik government's control. The second All-Russian Conference of Unions of Pharmacy Workers gathered in Moscow October 20–24, 1918. The Menshevik Internationalist A. S. Aluf along with Kuperman, Epshtein, Bronshtein, Kagan, and others, were in the "presidium." Rapoport argued that the pharmacy departments in the central government and pharmacy subdepartments in the provinces "must be autonomous organs." Although professional unions could directly administer pharmacy, nevertheless they must "closely and actively participate in the correct organization of pharmacy administration."[99] Mirlin, Epshtein, and Zalesskii endorsed this resolution at a meeting of the Professional Union of Pharmacy Workers in Petrograd October 13, 1918.[100]

Aluf too announced that "professional unions must be strengthened as autonomous, powerful, fighting organizations of the proletariat."[101] However, he and many militant pharmacists bowed to necessity. The dictatorship of the proletariat was being threatened. There was no choice but to support Soviet power. Aluf informed the general meeting of the members of the Petrograd Union of Pharmacy Workers November 3, 1918, that in the precarious political situation facing the country "we must all support Soviet power." A majority decided to participate in the anniversary of the October Revolution four days later (Russia having switched from the Julian to the Gregorian calendar). Kuperman reported that the administration of the union had decided to send 2,000 rubles to the Red Army.[102]

Aluf, of course, had a vested interest in preserving the new system. He and a number of other key militants and moderate reform pharmacists not only made peace with the Bolshevik government but entered the Soviet pharmacy bureaucracy. Aluf joined a provincial pharmacy subdepartment in the fall of 1918[103] and, as mentioned, served in the scientific section of the Pharmacy Commission during 1918 and was manager of the Pharmacy Department by 1919. Aluf, along with Ia. Kamenskii, had joined the Communist Party, as the Bolsheviks called themselves from 1918. Kuperman was still a "Menshevik Internationalist" in the spring of 1919; Mirlin and Zalesskii were still Mensheviks.[104] Nevertheless, in 1919, Mirlin, along with Zalesskii and nine others, were regional managers of Petrograd pharmacies.[105] By July 1919, Ia. Iaroslav was manager of the Pharmacy Department in the Commissariat of Health. Ef. Bronshtein was manager of the Finance-Budget Committee in the Pharmacy Department of the Commissariat.[106] I. I. Levinshtein zealously tabulated pharmacists' salaries and would ultimately organize pharmacy education.[107] A. S. Ginzberg did the same. As noted, F. A. Ferrein, Professor A. E. Chichibabin, and O. G. Gabrilovich managed the nationalized pharmaceutical industry.

Other militant pharmacists, less supportive of the Bolshevik order, ruefully admitted in early 1919 that "With the transfer of pharmacies to the jurisdiction of the Commissariat of Health, the Pharmacy Commissions continue to be de facto independent organs (with their own funds and departments) but de jure they are already under the subdepartments of the Pharmacy Department of the Commissariat of Health and, consequently, are dependent upon the latter."[108]

For pharmacist entrepreneurs the Soviet pharmacy system was completely untenable. The decree on nationalization issued by Sovnarkom or the Council of People's Commissars was stern and offered no room for compromise. It announced that "all pharmacies, normal and rural, laboratories, warehouses, and so forth, were the property of the Russian Socialist Federative Soviet Republic." The nationalized pharmacies were to be transferred to the local pharmacy subdepartment. The Commissariat of Health was to exert general direction and control. "From the moment the order was promulgated by the local soviet, owners and lessees of pharmacies were obligated to stay in the locality and take measures for the correct functioning of the pharmacy. Those who acted against the order and those who hid or sent away their wares were subject to a revolutionary court."[109]

With the proverbial stroke of a pen, Soviet authorities deprived pharmacist proprietors of the fruits of many years of sacrifice and labor. By the end of 1918, Antonina Lesnevskaia's First Women's Pharmacy was a "communal" pharmacy, owned by the state. In November, day shifts and night duty for her former pharmacy and others in Petrograd were determined by local authorities.[110] In Moscow Ferrein's Staraia Nikol'skaia pharmacy was designated communal pharmacy No. 1–there were 82 others.[111] Ferrein's pharmaceutical factory became factory no. 8, Keler's, factory no. 12, the Association Bliumental', factory no. 9, and so on.[112]

A number of pharmacists were roughed up and arrested. In October 1918, for example, "Citizenness" Frukshtein, Tula province, pleaded with Narkomzdrav to release her husband, manager of a pharmacy, who had been arrested by local authorities. She asserted that he had committed no crime and his pharmacy could not function without him.[113] In Tver both the Union of Pharmacy Owners and the Union of Pharmacy Workers complained to the local representative of the Commissariat of Health that "repressive measures used against pharmacy owners," including "depriving them of freedom," had adversely affected the functioning of pharmacies and threatened public health. On this basis both groups asked that "managers of pharmacies not be deprived of freedom even if they were pharmacy owners."[114]

Some proprietors stayed on, some even managing local pharmacy departments and pharmacies.[115] However, many pharmacy owners and managing Provizors fled Russia. Lesnevskaia was among them. Following confiscation of her property, disease, hunger and terror stalked Petrograd. Cholera was rampant in the summer of 1919. Scores of Poles were rounded up and killed.[116] Lesnevskaia, with her friend and colleague Florentina Stankevich, wended her way southward toward the Polish border. August 1919 found them in Dunaburg district, Vitebsk province, an emigration point for Poles wishing to return to Poland. Lesnevskaia worked among the refugees encamped there. She and Stankevich were given legal documents by the Red Cross. In August 1919, Lesnevskaia learned she was about to be arrested by local Bolshevik authorities. Pskov was under German control. Therefore, Lesnevskaia and Stankevich detoured to Polotsk and, in October, escaped by train to Warsaw.[117]

Lesnevskaia's entrepreneurial skills did not dissipate in Poland. She devoted her energies into helping refugees in Warsaw during the 1920s and operated a pharmacy in Warsaw from 1932 until her death in 1937.[118] But Russia was the poorer for losing pharmacist entrepreneurs like Lesnevskaia.

In addition, there were not enough pharmacists to adequately staff pharmacies, warehouses or manage pharmaceutical enterprises. The new Soviet government encountered difficulties in attracting pharmacists to serve in its institutions "because salaries were lower than those established by collective agreements between staff and pharmacy owners." In Moscow, salaries achieved through collective bargaining ranged from 560 rubles for Assistant Pharmacists with one year of practice, 640 rubles for one to three years' practice, 715 rubles for three to five years' practice, 765 rubles for Provizors or those with more than five years of practice, and 900 rubles for managers. Meanwhile, the Pharmacy Commission of the Commissariat of Health set salaries at 600 rubles for those with up to three years' practice, 650 rubles for pharmacists with more than three years' practice, 750 rubles for managers of "medium-sized" pharmacies, and 850 rubles for managers of large pharmacies. As a consequence, I. I. Levinshtein, Manager of a Pharmacy Budget Bureau, requested raises of 25 to 40 percent.[119] In Tambov in October and November 1918, an epidemic of Spanish flu led to work in pharmacies being "nearly doubled." Authorities complained of "insufficiency of pharmacists" with the result that the manager of the pharmacy subdepartment had to work overtime. They also bewailed lack of direction from the center.[120] General calls were issued for "persons with knowledge of Latin."[121] Administrators admitted that "severe insufficiency of pharmaceutical workers" incapacitated the pharmaceutical industry in Moscow.[122] The Vishevolotsk Soviet of Peasants and Workers' Deputies was forced to keep on the manager of the pharmaceutical warehouse belonging to the former Union of Cities because its "invitation for [another] specialist to fill the vacancy was unsuccessful."[123]

Because of depletion of pharmacists through death, departure, or conscription into the Red Army, and because authorities arbitrarily decided some pharmacies were superfluous, the number of pharmacies declined. At the end of 1918 it was claimed that there were 1,633 pharmacies in "30 provinces of the current Soviet Russia."[124] There had been over 4,000 pharmacies in the former Russian empire. Admittedly the empire was larger in territory and population than the Russian Republic. However, extrapolating from local statistics, there were fewer pharmacies to serve the public in Soviet Russia than under the old regime. Nineteen pharmacies out of 150 were closed in Petrograd between March 23 and October 1, 1918.[125] Eleven pharmacies were closed in Moscow.[126] Pharmacies were closed in other cities. In the city of Kolomna, Moscow province, former owners were allowed to manage nationalized pharmacies because of lack of qualified managers. The nationalized pharmacies "were nearly without wares and without funds because all monies were funneled into a central treasury of other 'nationalized enterprises'–groceries, city gardens, movie theaters, etc."[127]

Centralized supply was cumbersome.[128] Central authorities were not simply burdened with deciding what medicines could be produced, as had the tsarist Medical Council, although at least one agency did attend to that.[129] They now had to draw up budgets and allocate funds and materials to pharmacies, laboratories, and pharmaceutical enterprises. *Farmatsentr* and related committees met frequently (sometimes every other day) in the fall of 1918 debating all manner of issues relating to budgets and supply. For example, on October 18, A. E. Chichibabin, O. G. Gabrilovich, F. A. Ferrein, and four others discussed a fairly short (in comparison to most) agenda dealing with the proper distribution of 2 million rubles per month for the purchase of pharmaceutical wares (according to the government price list). This meeting also stipulated precise hours and days for a future meeting, which would compile the text of a new "obligatory regulation" (*obiazatel'noe postanovlenie*).[130] On another occasion that fall, *Farmatsentr* discussed the allocation of 513,934 rubles to Keler and Company for the past half-year for purchase of some materials.[131] While a meeting of October 22 outlined distribution of raw and semifinished materials in general,[132] on December 3, F. A. Ferrein, O. G. Gabrilovich, and four other members of *Farmatsentr* held a plenary meeting to decide the allocation of twenty specific items, including 500 *vedra* (a *vedro* was equal to 21 pints) of "rectified" spirits to V. K. Ferrein for production of galenical wares, 25 *vedra* of "metallic spirits" to another concern, 75 *vedra* of rectified spirits to the Hofman laboratory, 200 *vedra* of rectified spirits to Ermans and Company, and so on.[133] The inconvenience to nationalized pharmaceutical firms, reduced to begging for supplies, is obvious. Obvious too is the debilitating effect on government policy-making of attending to such trivialities.

One of the most ridiculous examples of Bolshevik insistence on centralized supply occurred in Bukhara in Central Asia during 1919. Stores of medicine acquired through municipalization in 1918 dissipated there by July 1919. With the Spanish flu raging, local personnel went to Persia, Afghanistan, and Tashkent to purchase quinine, aspirin, and other supplies. Private suppliers offered them as much as they needed at prices that compared very favorably with the inflated prices in Bukhara. However, local authorities squelched this sensible initiative and forbade private purchases. Purchasers who had gone to Tashkent were actually arrested. Meanwhile adulterated medicines flooded the market at high prices and people died from lack of medicines.[134]

As would be expected, multiplying committees did not mitigate turf battles in the local arena. In Moscow, during the summer of 1918, the local Soviet of Workers and Peasants' Deputies had closed pharmaceutical warehouses and requisitioned their supplies. In September the "Department of Supply of the Union of Hospital Funds [*kassa*] of the Moscow region" wrote the Pharmacy Department in the Commissariat of Health asking for a share in the requisitioned wares to distribute to institutions under its jurisdiction.[135] Central authorities promised to look into the matter.[136] In Ivano-Voznesensk in November 1918, zealots complained to central authorities that a local official had appointed expropriated owners as managers of the new socialized pharmacies.[137]

The old pharmacy system had kept a tight rein on the dispensing of narcotics. With closure of pharmacies, interruption of supply lines, lack of pharmacists, changes in medical organization, and general lawlessness, stimulants and narcotics began to spill out of pharmacies into the streets. By May 1918 the Bolshevik government began to express concern about illegal sales and speculation in narcotics–cocaine, morphine, opium.[138] The Cheka–acronym for the Bolshevik agency to combat crime and counterrevolution–was asked to take "exceptional measures" to stop this speculation.[139] The government, the Council of Peoples' Commissars, issued a decree forbidding imports and sales in morphia, cocaine, and opium. Violations were punishable with up to three months' deprivation of freedom.[140] Drug abuse burgeoned in 1919 and 1920.[141] In 1921 Educational reformer Izrail Ionasovich Levinshtein, Osip Gustavovich Gabrilovich, member of *Farmatsentr*, Alexander Samonov Aluf, and Eduard Iakovlevich Abol', another former education specialist, were among forty-four selected by the Pharmacy Department of the Commissariat of Health to help the Cheka ferret out and punish trafficking in narcotics.[142]

On the other hand, medicines available for therapeutic use, decreased. Proposals for education reform noted that the "Republic was experiencing a medicaments shortage [*lekarstvennyi golod*]."[143] Tsarist Russia had been emerging from such a medicaments shortage in 1916. In June 1918, the People's Production Committee, housed in the Medical Department of the Commissariat of Internal Affairs, reported "severe shortages of medicines and other pharmaceutical materials . . . for the [Russian] Republic."[144] The [Moscow] Regional Production Committee desperately asked its parent body to immediately send supplies.[145] On August 8, Commissar Michurin from "Poshekhonsk district" sent a frantic telegram to the People's Commissariat of Internal Affairs informing them: "epidemic of cholera/other diseases,/extreme need of spirits . . . quickly inform, where such can be acquired, how much, what conditions/Yaroslavl', Vologda none."[146] In December 1918, authorities in Tambov panicked over the fact that "expenditure of medicines" was "very great" while "stores" were "insignificant . . . in the near future pharmacies are threatened with a catastrophic absence of all medicinal substances."[147]

The shortage of pharmacists did not allow educational reformers the luxury of upgrading pharmacy study. There were no lack of visionary proposals as in general education.[148] Most of these projects were retreads of proposals that had been discussed for years by pharmacist reformers and the tsarist Minister of Education. They all repeated the buzzword "rational." For example, not only were there to be lower pharmacy schools but pharmacy institutes were to produce chemist-pharmacist experts for the new "rational" pharmaceutical industry.[149] The new educational system was to produce pharmacy inspectors.[150] However, shortage of pharmacists and economic reality tempered actual pharmacy education in the Soviet period. Even on paper the quality of Soviet pharmacy education was not noticeably higher than that which had been in place previously. In fact, pharmacy education and training deteriorated. Additionally, precious time was wasted on curricular reorganization.

In November 1918 the Scientific Section discussed pharmacy schools and chemico-pharmaceutical faculties in higher educational institutions. The proposed curriculum of the four-year pharmacy schools included mathematics, general sciences, pharmaceutical sciences. However, the schools admitted fifteen-year-olds. Although Professors S. Przhibytek and L. F. Il'in were members of the Scientific Section, the "manager of the organizing department" was A. S. Aluf, who had no scholarly credentials or pedagogical expertise.[151]

Proposals continued to be ground out. In 1919 a new three-tier pharmacy education system was proposed. The first-level pharmacy school envisioned four summer courses, a two-year program of general subjects, and a two-year program of specialized subjects. However, preliminary requirements were no higher than–if as high as–those for male pharmacy students under the old regime, for "persons not younger than 14, having finished the first level of the newly proposed 'united labor school'" were eligible for admittance. The second tier, "pharmacy technicum," was to have a three-year course but admitted "persons having finished the first pharmacy school or having the second degree of the united labor school." Moreover, it appeared that reformers were willing to compromise on pharmacy training in the interests of churning out desperately needed pharmacists, for the proposal noted that "After [only] two years in the technicum students received the right to be appointed to posts of laboratory assistant, people who took or dispensed prescriptions [*retseptar', subretseptar'*], and administrative posts in small and medium pharmacies." The third and highest level pharmacy school was grandly slated to be a "Chemical-Pharmaceutical Institute." But the institute was to have only a two-year course and would accept persons who had finished as little as the "third summer course of the pharmacy technicum," the caliber of whose training was questionable. The institute was to prepare specialists–managers of chemical-pharmaceutical factories, laboratories, and large pharmacies, and teachers for the lower pharmacy schools.[152]

Out of necessity much of the old system remained in place. Ia. Kanevskii reported in the summer of 1919 that although apprenticeship had been abolished in March 1918, old rules for pharmacy students moving to the Assistant Pharmacist level were to remain in place until January 1922. University Provizor courses for Assistant Pharmacists, however, were canceled for the fall semester of 1919.[153]

The demand for pharmacists led to proposals for crash courses for preparing feldshers, druggists, *praktikanty*, and even dentists to be pharmaceutical assistants.[154] The Scientific Section reviewed these quickie courses at the end of December 1918.[155] Three- and four-month training courses were soon established in eight cities. By 1920 there were thirty-seven such courses.[156]

Pharmacy education ultimately plummeted. Although reformer I. I. Levinshtein continued to perfect a draft curriculum for pharmacy schools, reality dictated retaining "Short six-month courses to train pharmacy workers and pharmacy personnel." Training included 80 hours of Latin, 96 hours of mathematics, 64 hours of physics, 64 hours each of botany and pharmacognosy, 160 hours of chemistry, 24 hours of general hygiene, 8 hours of history of pharmacy, 32 hours of political theory(!) and a whopping 368 hours of practice in the school pharmacy and 132 hours of practice in a Soviet pharmacy—thinly disguised apprenticeship.[157]

By 1921 the situation was not much improved. Levinshtein proposed a first-level pharmacy school to produce "pharmacy workers." The school accepted students as young as sixteen with only two years' general school preparation. A great deal was to be crammed into two years. There were to be three semesters in each year so students could attend year round. The prospective curriculum included a total of 84 hours of human anatomy and physiology, 192 hours of botany, 72 hours of introduction to zoology, 72 hours of Latin, 180 hours of mathematics, 144 hours of inorganic chemistry, and 168 hours of Russian, taught mainly or exclusively in the first year of trimesters. Two hundred and four total hours of organic chemistry, 240 hours of pharmaceutical chemistry, 216 hours of physics, 108 hours of pharmacognosy, 72 hours of pharmacology, and 60 hours of hygiene spanned both years or were relegated to the second. Thirty-six hours of the history of the workers' movement replaced religion; 72 hours of general history also were included in the curriculum. Four hundred and eight total hours of "Pharmacy technique," spanning both years, coyly replaced the abolished apprenticeship. The school was to be financed by a 1 percent turnover tax on pharmacy preparations.[158]

Worst of all the new Soviet pharmacy system did not pay for itself and the country could not afford it. When planning nationalization, the new administrators estimated that the income from all pharmacies in the empire equaled 360,000,000 rubles and expenditures for wares, salaries, and rent and maintenance amounted to 307,000,000. They confidently predicted that the new system would be more efficient and less costly, enthusiastically citing the savings from provincial warehouses and wholesale purchase under the tsarist pharmacy system.[159]

The opposite was true. Managers, statisticians, journalists, assistants of all sorts appeared. They received salaries equal to or larger than pharmacists working in pharmacies. While assistant managers received 500 rubles, managers and clerks (*deloproizvoditeli*) of provincial pharmacy subdepartments received 750 rubles, statisticians received the same, staff of the Pharmacy Bureau received between 750 and 900 rubles, clerks of the first class, 650 rubles.[160] These administrators greatly exceeded the pharmacist owners and managers and tsarist bureaucrats whom they supplanted. As a consequence, large sums of money went for overhead on both the central and provincial levels.[161]

The budget for the Pharmacy Department of the Commissariat of Health for the second half of 1918–in the embryonic stages of nationalization–amounted to 3,350,340 rubles.[162] Administrative salaries for that period amounted to 1¼ million rubles.[163] Expenditures for the Pharmacy Commission in the Commissariat of Health for the month of November 1918 alone, amounted to over 1,800,000 rubles. Salaries for staff of the Pharmacy Commission were over 350,000 rubles, salaries for Regional Subdepartment personnel and the "Organizing Department," another 100,000 rubles.[164]

Without any need to balance expenditure against income, provincial pharmacy subdepartments spent lavishly. For example, Ekaterinburg, in the Urals, bought 900,000 rubles' worth of supplies from Moscow in the late summer of 1918 and purchased other wares from Tomsk–in all 3,000,000 rubles' worth.[165] At the end of 1918 the Yaroslavl' province pharmacy organization submitted a budget for its first nine months of operation–that is until July 1, 1919–of 6½ million rubles.[166] Saratov spent a total of 3,750, 000 rubles to maintain and staff pharmacies, laboratories, and the pharmacy department between February 1918 and January 1919.[167]

Of course inflation pushed up operating costs. However, in any case, income and funds on hand did not cover expenditures. By late 1918 local pharmacy agencies had run out of funds and began bombarding Moscow for subsidies and advances to cover their costs. Authorities in Tambov province worked out a budget in November 1918, following nationalization. It requested 500,000 rubles for the first two months of 1919 for maintaining nationalized pharmacies and purchase of medicines to be dispensed for free.[168] In December a city in Smolensk province requested an advance of 50,000 rubles to tide it over until the municipal budget for 1918 was approved. A district medico-sanitary department in Yaroslavl' province asked for 45,000 rubles to pay pharmacy workers until their budget for the second half of 1918 was approved.[169] The Military Medical Academy clamored for subsidies.[170] The Rubinsk district medical-sanitary department asked for a 35,000-ruble advance for purchase of medicines.[171] In February 1919, Murom district in Smolensk province informed central authorities that before nationalizing local pharmacies, introducing free dispensing of all medicines prescribed by doctors, and stopping over-the-counter sales, the "two normal pharmacies which had served the people of the district were maintained by their property and over-the-counter sales of medicine and other wares . . . this covered salaries of staff and maintenance of the pharmacies–13,300 rubles per month and purchases of medicine up to 30,000 rubles . . . per year 519,000 rubles." After "stopping the dispensing of medicines for money . . . expenditures fell on the district Medico-Sanitary department, which does not have means . . . and [thus] pharmacies will very possibly be closed."[172] Central authorities coldly advised Murom in March to turn to their parent, the Smolensk provincial pharmacy organization, for money.[173] Turkestan region reported that it had spent almost all the 25,000,000 rubles allocated to it after the nationalization of local pharmacies, including 2,350,000 for salaries and 11,750,000 for light, heat, and maintenance of pharmacies. The Turkestan pharmacy department therefore asked for 319,000,000 rubles for the first half of 1919.[174]

Centralization and salaries, a good many of them administrative, began to drain the state treasury. In a meeting of the Commissariat of Health, December 21, 1918, N. A. Semashko admitted that "it was extremely difficult to direct the more than 1,600 [nationalized] pharmacies in the Republic [Russia] from the center."[175] Oddly enough Vinokurov, Representative from the Commissariat of State Control, urged the "immediate centralization of all matters of nationalized pharmacies," i.e., financing pharmacies from the center and depositing all incomes from pharmacies in the State Treasury. But Semashko and some others emphasized that "in view of financial considerations, it is desirable to empower local organs to implement nationalization of pharmacies, with grants of government subsidies in cases of necessity. Later . . . there might be the possibility of centralizing the administration of nationalized pharmacies."[176] By January 10, 1919, Semashko, his colleague, and a representative from the Pharmacy Department in the Commissariat of Health admitted that "the financial situation in provincial clinics was very bad . . . in some provinces medical institutions are closed because of lack of money and medical personnel, not receiving salaries for a whole half year, have stopped work . . . extraordinary measures–searching for local monies for salaries . . . and fighting epidemics . . . are called for."[177] The next day the department asked for a 5-million-ruble advance from the 1919 budget.[178]

As Soviet pharmacy and the pharmaceutical industry disintegrated, mainly as a result of government policies, the new Soviet pharmacy authorities never ceased to believe that reorganization and additional government agencies would solve staff, supply, and money problems. At the end of 1918, for example, *Farmatsentr* proposed a Bureau of Accounting, widening the chancellery, and a new scientific pharmacy institute which would plan production of medicines (better than in the past), create a pharmacy museum, and so forth.[179]

❖❖❖

The contrast between the situation of pharmacy and the pharmaceutical industry in Russia, where the utopia had been implemented, and that of the Ukraine, where the old order still prevailed, was striking.

During 1919 and 1920 the Ukraine became embroiled in the Russian Civil War. Bolsheviks, anarchists, White supporters of the Provisional Government, Cossacks, and various nationalist groups tore the Ukraine apart. However, in the second half of 1918, Khar'kov, Odessa, Kremenchug, and other Ukrainian cities were oases of civilization. The Germans, entering the Ukraine following the Russian-German-Ukrainian Peace of Brest-Litovsk, kept private property and maintained order. In April 1918, Skoropadsky's "Hetmanate" replaced the Ukrainian nationalist Rada, or parliament, the government, and the president, historian Khrushevsky, who had established themselves in December 1917. There were upheavals as Russians fleeing the Bolsheviks swarmed into the Ukraine.[180] Some "cultured" Ukrainian pharmacy owners abandoned their pharmacies. Radical socialist pharmacists complained about hours and conditions in privately owned pharmacies. They demanded a six-hour workday, in addition to other concessions.[181] Nevertheless, pharmacies, many of them run by Jewish pharmacists, continued to operate.[182] Radical socialists complained about retail prices for medicines. The Pharmacy Tax was still in force and it stipulated that aspirin was to sell at 45 kopeks a gram and antipyrine at 80 kopeks. Socialists complained that "market prices" for these items were 12 kopeks and 17 kopeks.[183] Nevertheless, pharmaceutical supplies–from "the best German and Austrian firms"–were ample.[184] Wholesale prices ranged from reasonable to fairly high in the summer of 1918.[185] By early August prices for medicines from Merck, Bayer, Reidel, and other German firms had "significantly fallen" in Khar'kov.[186] By September, the stock market formally listed wholesale prices at hundreds of rubles per kilo lower for aceto-salicylic acid, Bayer aspirin, and other items, and at a thousand rubles per kilo lower for codeine, cocaine, morphia, and quinine than in August.[187] Supplies came from Ukrainian workshops and firms as well as from German, Austrian and Hungarian, and French pharmaceutical houses.[188] Unions, labor bureaus, and the radical socialist press continued to operate,[189] although a union presidium in Kremenchug was arrested for fomenting a strike in June[190] and, in general, strikes were squelched. This policy, however, prevented disruption of the economy. In any case, conflicts between staff pharmacists and management over hours, night duty, hiring and firing were settled in a rational manner. Jurisconsults from the Commissariat of Labor and Medical Inspectors hammered out compromises on hours, pay, and work conditions.[191] Pharmacists still took examinations.[192] Their pay had climbed to 180 rubles per month for a second-year pharmacy student, 210 for a third-year student, 410 for an Assistant Pharmacist, and 520 for a Provizor manager and, as a result, membership in some unions collapsed.[193]

In 1918, the socialist pharmacy system, implemented by Mensheviks and Bolsheviks in Russia, replete with defects and unable to deliver, starkly contrasted with the pharmacy system in the Ukraine, which preserved the amalgam of government orchestration and private enterprise traditional to the tsarist empire. The pharmacy system in the Ukraine—the pharmacy system of the old regime—was not perfect. But it was superior to that existing in Soviet Russia. Additionally, it worked.

Both the Menshevik and Bolshevik pharmacy systems, on the other hand, were problematical. Further, the foundering pharmacy systems of both socialist parties emphasized that neither the Menshevik nor the Bolshevik economic programs were viable. Both Mensheviks and Bolsheviks eliminated private entrepreneurs. Mensheviks allowed for a modicum of local decision-making. Bolsheviks attempted to concentrate decision-making and financing at the center, thus squelching private initiative as well as private property. But both Mensheviks and Bolsheviks were excessively legalistic and bureaucratic. They were both convinced that public organizations could better manage pharmacy and the pharmaceutical industry than private entrepreneurs. Both groups replaced pharmacist specialists and productive pharmacists with an ever-expanding army of bureaucrats and supervisors. The Menshevik experiment was short-lived. Bolshevik policies, on the other hand, modified in the early twenties and imposed again in the late twenties, wreaked havoc on Russian pharmacy and the pharmaceutical industry.

The stock explanation for the dismal state of the Russian economy in 1921 is that the Russian economy was ruined due to the Civil War which racked Russia from 1918 to 1920. Leaving aside the fact that the Bolshevik behavior precipitated the war, the fate of pharmacy and the pharmaceutical industry underscores the fact that, while the Civil War indeed devastated the Russian economy, the Russian economy collapsed in 1919 and 1920 mainly because of defective Bolshevik economic policy.

Even without the war the Bolshevik pharmacy system would eventually have self-destructed. It was inefficient and costly. After wresting control of pharmacies—private, zemstvos, and hospital—and pharmaceutical factories from their former owners and managers, the new government erected a multitude of committees and agencies to run them. Although decision-making, supply, and financing could not be centralized immediately, the labyrinth of administrative agencies caused confusion. In any case, the new administrators, on both local and central levels, had no experience in running a pharmacy or pharmaceutical factory. Thus, they lacked management skills as well as entrepreneurial instincts. Nevertheless, these administrators expanded at a geometrical rate. All of them needed to be paid. Their productivity was not great enough, nor was the income generated by the nationalized pharmacies and pharmaceutical factories great enough, to cover their salaries and the purchase and free dispensing of medicine. Within a few months, local pharmacy agencies had amassed huge debts and were beseeching the center for sums that were astronomical, even taking inflation into account. In sum, examination of Bolshevik pharmacy policies during 1917 and 1918 shows that the Soviet economic system was unworkable from the beginning, primarily because of internal contradictions.

A look at the Bolshevik pharmacy system highlights the similarities between the Bolshevik style of governance and that of the tsarist government. The agencies and procedures created to manage pharmacies and the pharmaceutical industry, the regulations issued for dispensing, pharmaceutical production, imports and exports, and pharmaceutical education replicated those of tsarist Russia.

However, although the Bolshevik *modus operandi* was similar to tsarist, there was a difference in degree, because Bolshevik economic premises were more extreme than tsarist. Bolshevik pharmaceutical administration was far more authoritarian and intrusive than its tsarist predecessor. The Bolsheviks not only dominated private pharmacies, drug stores and pharmaceutical enterprises, they ran them. The consequences were disastrous for pharmacists, society, and, ultimately, for state finances and the economy. The system of state socialism implemented under the Bolsheviks would amply demonstrate its bankruptcy in 1919 and the years to follow.

20

The End and the Beginning: 1919, 1920

The Civil War reached a crescendo in 1919 and had its denouement in 1920. The border areas of the former Russian empire—Poland, Finland, the Baltic States—extricated themselves from the Soviet Russian empire. On the other hand, the Red Army, forged by Trotsky, solidified Bolshevik control over Russia, expanded control in Siberia, and took back the Ukraine and the Caucasian states of Armenia, Azerbaijan and, in early 1921, Georgia.

In the pharmacy world three trends prevailed. First, rules and regulations for dispensing, production of medicines, training pharmacists, inspecting pharmacies, and so on, continued to pour forth as they had in tsarist times. These regulations emanated mainly from the Pharmacy Department of the new Commissariat of Health, which, following in the footsteps of the Medical Council and the Medical Department of the Ministry of Internal Affairs, had supervision over the establishment and operation of pharmacies, dispensing, the staffing of pharmacies and local government pharmacy posts. The Pharmacy Department also authorized purchase and distribution of medicines, a matter that had not been handled by central medical authorities in the tsarist government. As in 1918, many pharmacy rules and regulations issued in 1919 and 1920 were similar to if not identical with those of the tsarist period. From the vantage point of these regulations it appeared that the previous pharmacy system was reincarnate, though larger and more insistent. However, the regulations also hinted of systemic problems in the new Soviet pharmacy system. The operation of central pharmacy agencies in Moscow and in Kiev, in the Ukraine, when the Red Army seized this territory, revealed a second trend. Bureaucrats in *Farmatsentr*, the agency in the Supreme Council of the National Economy (VSNKh), whose jurisdiction focused on the pharmaceutical industry and pharmaceutical trade, as well as authorities in the Pharmacy Department of the Commissariat of Health, and other central pharmacy officials continued to operate under the assumption that proper policy and management would solve the problems surfacing in the pharmacy world. The frequent, almost daily meetings of these central bureaucrats were hectic, sometimes frantic. But the bureaucrats exuded ambition and optimism as they busily furthered nationalization, drafted plans, and fine-tuned the administrative mechanism in the center and the provinces. Their activities produced massive expenditures and budgets. Unfortunately all this effort and spending had a less than beneficent effect on the real pharmacy world. For there–in the cities, provinces, and districts–a third trend was visible. Chaos, shortages of medicines, pharmacists, and money, and closures of pharmacies were the order of the day. In part these problems resulted from the Civil War (which the Soviet government had precipitated). In part, however, the problems in the real pharmacy world resulted from the flaws in the new pharmacy system. The policies devised by the new Soviet pharmacy administrators were illogical, disruptive, and destructive. Nationalization–abolition of private ownership of pharmacies, drug stores, warehouses and pharmaceutical factories; bureaucratization–the growth of officials and committees; centralization of financing and supply did not make sense in wartime or at any time. The new pharmacy system was heavy on theory and short on practicality. It was needlessly cumbersome, thwarted initiative, destroyed or wasted the most capable, productive pharmacists, was not wanted by many rank-and-file pharmacists, and was expensive. Though Soviet authorities intended otherwise, in the real pharmacy world, the availability and quality of dispensing declined and the populace suffered.

Rules and Regulations

Pharmacy regulations were the purview of A. Aluf, Manager of the Pharmacy Department in Narkomzdrav, the Commissariat of Health, and I. Levinshtein, Manager of the Scientific Subdepartment of the Pharmacy Department. These agencies issued sheaves of circulars to provincial medical departments and their pharmacy subdepartments during 1919 and 1920. N. Semashko, Commissar for Health, cosigned the most important. A selection of their orders and instructions amounted to 169 pages in a compilation published by Penza province in 1921.[1] With regard to whether they had any linkage with the pharmacy system of old or whether they broke radically with the past, Soviet regulations from 1919 and 1920 fell into four categories.

One group of regulations was almost identical to those of the tsarist regime. For example, Circular No. 1 issued by the Pharmacy Department December 30, 1919, stipulated that aspirin, bismuth, salicylic acid, urotropin, quinine, and a few other medicines, received from the factory in "dosed tablets" could be dispensed over-the-counter. A doctor's prescription was required for powdered versions of these items made up in the pharmacy in tablets or gelatin capsules. Additionally, pharmacies were required to dispense medicines containing specified percentages of caffeine, cocaine, ergotin, arsenic, and novocaine in sterile ampules obtained from government warehouses.[2] By the summer of 1920 the list of ready-made tablets permitted to be dispensed over-the-counter had been enlarged to fifty-six items, including aspirin, antipyrine, saccharin, codeine, morphia, heroin, santonin, potassium iodide, quinine. The circular also noted that it was desirable that pills be coated with sugar or chocolate.[3] (It might be assumed that this indicated economic recovery in general and adequate supplies of medicines in particular, were it not that circulars 13, 14, 17, and 20, also issued in the summer of 1920 and described below, spoke of severe shortages of medicines.) Several regulations spelled out procedures for making up medicines in the pharmacy. One detailed preparation of camphor oil.[4] Another listed specific doses for sixteen medicines to be dispensed in ampules, twelve to be dispensed in gelatin capsules, one for pills to be covered with saccharin, one for tablets of extract cannabis, and one for a remedy to be dispensed in glass tubes.[5] In imitation of the tsarist provincial medical inspectors of old, a Soviet regulation established "controller-instructors" who were to make periodical visits to institutions subordinate to the provincial pharmacy subdepartment, such as laboratories, warehouses, and pharmacies, and visit "not less than once in two months" each district subdepartment and its subordinate institutions. The instructional function of the "controller-instructors" involved disseminating circulars and protocols from central authorities. Their investigative duties were to cover staffs, methods of preparing and dispensing prescriptions, supplies, general condition of the warehouse or pharmacy, and account books.[6] Pharmacy Department Circular No. 37/137 of November 1920 reviewed procedures for storing poisons and strong-acting preparations in the pharmacy. As in tsarist times these were to be kept under lock and key according to the rules of the sixth edition of the Pharmacopoeia. There then followed a list of 56 poisonous and strong-acting medicines, including heroin, morphine, nicotine, digitalis, and strychnine.[7] And, as tsarist officials stipulated items to be carried by fully stocked normal pharmacies (*normal'naia apteka*), so Soviet authorities ordained, in November 1920, a list of 324 medicines for pharmacies of "The First Class."[8] A circular of November 1920 replicated tsarist procedures in ordering that all medicine must be dispensed upon the original doctor's prescription, within a month after its issuance. Copies of the prescription were to be retained in the pharmacy. If the physician deemed it necessary to refill the prescription, he was to make specific note of this.[9]

A second group of Soviet pharmacy regulations not only implicitly reflected earlier ones, but explicitly referred to and incorporated tsarist ordinances. For example, Pharmacy Department Circular No. 6 inveighed against "the sale of various medical substances no where permitted and not investigated with regard to the rationality of their composition." Prohibited by a circular of October 18, 1918, the Pharmacy Department of the Soviet Commissariat of Health reiterated that pharmacies, drug stores, and chandleries were to sell "only those substances which in their time were permitted by the Medical Council [of the tsarist Ministry of Internal Affairs.]"[10] Similarly, while Circular No. 14, June 1920, resulted from circumstances peculiar to the Soviet era—"limited supplies of spirits and absence of raw materials" restricted tinctures that pharmacies and laboratories were allowed to prepare to a short list of 28, including belladonna, digitalis, opium, and strychnine—nevertheless, this circular hearkened back to the tsarist regime by stipulating that preparation of certain tinctures was to follow the 1910 edition of the Russian Pharmacopoeia and tinctures of the emetic ipecacuanha were to be prepared according to the 1913 edition of the Russian Military Pharmacopoeia.[11]

The Soviet Pharmacy Tax in particular was a variation on a tsarist theme and as contentious as its predecessor. The tsarist Pharmacy Tax, which set payments for prescriptions, had been the subject of much controversy. Pre-Soviet socialist pharmacists had criticized the tax as a vehicle for pharmacy owners to maximize profits. Owners of private pharmacies, on the other hand, had claimed the tax did not take into account their costs for medicines and supplies, maintenance of the pharmacy, and salaries. Soviet pharmacy officials instituted their own Pharmacy Tax. And, it generated the same complaints. For example, after the Red Army conquered the Ukraine and local authorities imposed the new Russian pharmacy system, at the end of 1919, a manager of a district pharmacy subdepartment in the Ukraine typed a three-page letter to the Commissariat of Health claiming that prices for materials from the Commissariat "had significantly risen above the tax . . . published in July 1919 . . . firm prices for medicines, given out by the All-Ukrainian Commissariat of Health in many cases are higher than the tax by 300–500 percent." In view of this, he wondered whether it were possible to make the "prices agree with the introduction of a local tax" worked out by a local commission with representatives from the district pharmacy subdepartment, the branch of the Workers and Peasants' Inspectorate (Stalin headed the main commissariat at that time), the district revolutionary committee, and the district finance department.[12]

A third set of Soviet pharmacy regulations from 1919 and 1920 was similar to previous tsarist regulations, yet slightly different as they were dictated by specific problems peculiar to the new regime. A Pharmacy Department regulation "on dispensing medicine for payment and for free in pharmacies of the Republic" was reminiscent of the debates regarding zemstvo dispensing for free or for payment that had taken place in tsarist times. However, the Soviet regulation also reflected the realities of the new order, for medicine was to be dispensed free in nationalized pharmacies if prescribed by doctors in Soviet service. Medicine prescribed by private doctors was subject to payment according to the Pharmacy Tax.[13] A circular of September 1920 was in the spirit of tsarist regulations but raised doubts about the competency of personnel in the new Soviet pharmacies. It warned that pharmacies did not always prepare mixtures correctly. To correct this, in each pharmacy one of the most experienced workers on the shift was to be appointed controller to verify preparation of medicines by assistants; the controller was to sign each prescription; those guilty of incorrectly preparing medicines must be brought to a comrades' "disciplinarian court" or people's court. Inspectors were to investigate pharmacies not less than every three months.[14]

To win the Civil War, as noted in the previous chapter, the Soviet government embarked upon a program that has been called "War Communism." This combined harshness and terror with sensible businesslike procedures and order in the economy. Several Soviet pharmacy regulations exemplified the businesslike side of "War Communism." For example, Pharmacy Department Circular No. 9, promulgated March 25, 1919, and a variation on the theme of requisite prescription books and books for poisons and strong-acting medicines, stipulated that 248 medicines were subject to cost accounting and required to be entered in a special "Book of Wares." The forms for registering each medicine included columns where there were to be noted (from left to right) the month and date of arrival, account number, source, name of medicines, amount received, price, sum, and application.[15] Similarly, a circular of 1920, ordered inspections of pharmacies every three months. However, the inspectors were to see that "labor discipline" was being enforced and, in addition to verifying cleanliness and correct storage and dispensing of medicines, inspectors were to insure that prices matched the pharmacy tax, that account books balanced, and that the local controller audited the pharmacy frequently.[16] A circular on establishing provincial warehouses for vessels and medicines and one ordering warehouses to distribute supplies to districts likewise had businesslike demeanors. These regulations called for strict quality control of vessels and medicines. Medicine was to be distributed from the provincial warehouse not later than six weeks after the order was received. District distribution points were to send out wares within seven days.[17]

A fourth group of regulations promulgated by Soviet pharmacy authorities had no antecedents in tsarist times. They addressed severe shortages that had surfaced only in the Soviet era and, additionally, reflected the demise of private enterprise and the emergence of state-run, bureaucratic, socialized pharmacy.

Many Pharmacy Department circulars alluded to shortages of medicines and apparatus. The "insufficiency of various kinds of pharmacy glass [vessels]" prompted a circular (undated) encouraging the recycling of pharmacy glass. Provincial and district cities were to "organize the reception and cleaning" of the glass with a 1:1,000 solution of sublimate. Those returning old glass to the provincial warehouse and district medical points received 50 percent of the cost of glass as set in the Pharmacy Tax. Patients who brought old vessels in which to receive their prescriptions paid tax only on the medicine and labor involved.[18] A similar directive resulted from insufficiency of medicines as well as efforts to institute orderly supply channels. Circular No. 7, undated, warned that district clinics could not obtain medicines directly from the central government and forbade district pharmacy departments to make "independent trips" (*samostoiatel'nosti komandirovok*) to Moscow for medicines. The circular warned that such trips, which circumvented mandated channels of distribution, were occurring because of "insufficiency of medicines due to growth of epidemics" and also because provincial pharmacy departments distributed medicines "incorrectly."[19] A circular of March 8, 1920, urged the establishment of provincial warehouses, to combat the "medicaments crisis" (*lekarstvennyi krizis*),[20] a problem reminiscent of World War I. At that time, as discussed in chapter 16, radical socialist pharmacists had blamed the crisis on rapacious capitalists who had largely been eliminated from the Soviet economic system. Circular No. 17 advised local authorities on substitutes that they could use in making up medicines when faced by shortages of key ingredients. Sugar was specifically mentioned as a scarce item.[21] Circulars, such as No. 13, May 16, 1920, reiterated that creating provincial warehouses "was all the more important" because of "extremely limited stores of medicines."[22] Circular No. 20, August 10, 1920, announced that because of shortages provincial warehouses would not distribute wares to individual institutions but to the whole district and then to "the best-equipped pharmacies in the district city, the staff of which was not to be larger than three persons."[23] A circular on the culture and collection of medicinal plants, reminiscent of efforts made during World War I, further testified to shortages of medicines.[24] Circular No. 30, apparently from the late summer or early fall of 1920, advised that because of scarcity, pharmacists must replace distilled water with boiled water in making up prescriptions.[25] A circular of November 1920 declared that "In view of insufficient supplies of camphor and the extreme importance of its significance in typhoid fever and other epidemic diseases, it is proposed temporarily to prepare and dispense it upon a doctor's prescription. . . ."[26]

This fourth category of Soviet regulations also concerned shortages of pharmacists. A Pharmacy Department circular of February 1920 spoke of "the insufficiency of Provizors." As a consequence, "Assistant Pharmacists could be appointed as managers of pharmacy subdepartments and managers of pharmacies."[27] A circular of August 1920 dealt with transferring pharmacists mobilized for military service to civilian service.[28] A related regulation apportioned pharmacy staffs according to meticulous quotas of prescriptions and other work. Indicating its importance, this order was signed by People's Commissar for Health N. Semashko in addition to his subordinate A. Aluf.[29]

Soviet regulations did not stint on administrators, however. The Pharmacy Department in the Commissariat of Health dictated that provincial pharmacy subdepartments (*gubfarpod*) were to consist of nineteen staff members—manager, assistant manager, secretary, and controller-instructor, four accountants, three individuals connected with supply, and four clerks. The salaries of these administrators ranged from 1,380 rubles per month to 3,000 rubles. District subdepartments (*ufarpod*) were to have truncated staffs of seven. City pharmacy subdepartments in cities with a population of 200,000 were to have staffs of thirteen. Cities with populations up to 200,000 were to have staffs of ten. These subdepartments included managers, accountants, instructor-controllers, couriers, machinists, clerks, and so forth. As the Bolsheviks were committed to equality, the lesser officials salaries were in the same range as their provincial overseers.[30]

Soviet pharmacy regulations attended to establishing pharmacy museums with sequestered property from private pharmacies.[31] And Pharmacy Department Circular No. 24 claimed that "homeopathic pharmacies had no place in the medical-sanitary organization of the country because they were not subject to nationalization and . . . received no state subsidies." However, the Scientific Medical Council did not consider it possible to close them.[32]

Central authorities also assiduously collected information. Questionnaires (*anketnyi blank*) were zealously distributed to pharmacies. Some forms were holdovers from the tsarist period. For instance, a questionnaire distributed in Nizhegorodskaia province in 1920 asked whether the pharmacy was located in a freestanding or leased building, whether the owner was a private person or institution, what type of pharmacy it was–normal, hospital, clinic, or mixed, what kind of personnel the pharmacy had (this particular pharmacy had a manager, no controller, two dispensers, four assistants, one laborant, two packers, two cashiers, and five workers.)[33] The questions on the pharmacy budget were strictly Soviet. The space for the date was stated "in 192_" and this section asked for information on "nationalized pharmacies and enterprises," as well as "various others."[34]

Central Agencies at Work

The picture of central pharmacy agencies during 1919 and 1920 was one of self-confident, purposeful labor with strict attention to orderly procedures and careful recording.

Farmatsentr's chief jurisdiction was the pharmaceutical industry but its agendas were catholic. Of necessity, the agency interacted with other agencies managing pharmacy, pharmaceutical and chemical production, and trade and distribution. *Farmatsentr*'s schedule was strenuous. Members met in committees or in a plenary session twice a week or oftener. A survey of their meetings at the end of 1918 and in the early months of 1919 gives a sample of the early Soviet government's thorough, legalistic management style.

At a plenary session toward the end of December 1918, O. G. Gabrilovich and F. A. Ferrein, among others, discussed the nationalization of pharmacies, dispensing of spirits, and procedures for ordering the Ferrein Association to begin to quickly transfer its stock to *Farmatsentr* who in turn would transfer materials to the Chief Administration for State Chemical and Pharmaceutical Factories.[35] A week later the agency discussed the nationalization of the Ferrein Association wholesale warehouse, medical supplies for the Commissariat of Health, and cooperation of *Farmatsentr* with the Chemical Department of VSNKh.[36] On January 3, 1919, *Farmatsentr* debated management of the branches of the Ferrein Association and formed a subcommission of three members, one of whom was O. G. Gabrilovich, to draft a plan for nationalizing wholesale pharmacy warehouses.[37] A week later, *Farmatsentr* elected Professor A. E. Chichibabin its delegate to the Central Executive Committee [of the All-Russian Congress of Soviets–a quasi-Soviet parliament] to iron out "conflict between the Presidium of VSNKh and the Moscow Soviet of Workers and Soldiers' Deputies arising from the nationalization of the Bliumental' and Ferrein enterprises." Meanwhile, the three-person subcommission on nationalization had worked quickly, for its report was presented at the same meeting.

The subcommittee recommended that local management of nationalized enterprises continue on but control over the enterprises reside in *Farmatsentr.*[38] At the end of January, an inner bureau of *Farmatsentr* discussed nationalizing large pharmaceutical enterprises of national significance, specifically the Keler laboratories (spelled with two "l's" in the stenographic report) and Ars laboratory.[39] This must have been the Ars laboratory in Moscow because Vil'na, where an Ars factory had been located, was lost to Russia during the Civil War. A week later, in early February, a "plenum" of *Farmatsentr* reviewed the nationalization of the Keler (still noted as Keller), Ars, and four other major pharmaceutical factories. The fate of small-scale pharmaceutical factories was to be decided separately.[40] At the same time, in conjunction with several other government bodies, *Farmatsentr* debated "the further existence of the Military-Medical Factory of [Pharmaceutical] Preparations" and tackled the "transfer of the Bliumental' Factory" to its own jurisdiction. A representative from the factory administration was present at the meeting.[41]

Farmatsentr had a branch in Petrograd, the former Russian capital. Nationalization of large pharmaceutical enterprises there was discussed in early March.[42] But although *Farmatsentr* administrators formulated major policies, as in 1918, meetings sometimes were consumed with trivialities. On March 14, 1919, in addition to reviewing administrative organization for nationalized perfume enterprises and necessity of delegating one of the Keler employees to a production union, a bureau of *Farmatsentr* busied itself with the distribution of twenty-six medical substances–various *puds* of Vaseline, castor oil, carbolic acid, sugar, two kilos of aspirin, and so forth.[43]

The Commissariat of Health and its departments likewise toiled energetically, extending nationalization and the network of Soviet pharmacy agencies throughout the Soviet state. The Commissariat had issued a general order nationalizing pharmacies in the Russian Republic at the end of December 1918. In 1919, as the Red Army conquered the Ukraine the new pharmacy system was applied there. At this time, before ratification of the constitution of 1924, which established the Union of Soviet Socialist Republics, Moscow treated or pretended to treat break-away states as autonomous. Thus, the decrees of mid-May 1919, nationalizing pharmacies and other pharmaceutical enterprises in the Ukraine, while very similar to earlier Russian decrees, were issued by the Ukrainian Commissariat of Health and the Ukrainian Council of People's Commissars, headquartered in Kiev.

On May 13 the Ukrainian Council of People's Commissars ordered that inventories be taken in all pharmacies and warehouses in the territory of the Ukraine, all private trade in medicines was forbidden, and provincial and district soviets were to begin nationalizing, following instructions from the Ukrainian Commissariat of Health.[44] On May 16, 1919, nationalization began in Kiev. Mirroring municipalization and nationalization in Russia, the procedures were methodical and stern. The Ukrainian Commissariat of Health announced that "all private owners of pharmacy wares, medicines . . . warehouses, labs, workshops, offices, temporary quarters, private apartments in the city of Kiev" were "obliged in the three-day period following publication of this regulation" to present lists to the pharmacy department of the commissariat with information on the owner's full name, exact address where pharmacy wares were located, names and amounts of the substances, their cost–including whether they were bought on account, the date, and signature of the owner. The "House Committee" of the owner's dwelling was to ascertain whether the information on the forms was correct. Those "guilty" of not fulfilling the regulation were subject to the Revolutionary Tribunal, which dispensed summary rulings.[45] Poorly outfitted pharmacies were to be closed. The nationalization of village pharmacies was to follow nationalization of city pharmacies.[46]

Provincial and district pharmacy subdepartments were to manage the nationalized enterprises. These bodies, in turn, were to be subordinate to the main commissariat and to the health departments of local soviets. Financing was to be centralized. Provincial pharmacy departments, assisted by local soviets, were ordered to draw up budgets and send them to the Commissariat of Health. They were advised that until budgets were finalized they could request advances.[47] Forms for personnel, wages, and so on proliferated.[48]

As did local medical authorities in tsarist times, the "Zvenigorod district pharmacy section of the sanitary soviet" asked Moscow for clarification on who should be elected to the local "Pharmacy Commissions" that had been ordered for the Ukraine.[49] And, in the tradition of citizens of tsarist Russia, an "impoverished pharmacist M. Konleim in Berezane, Poltava province," the Ukraine, penned a letter to the Pharmacy Department in Moscow asking for money to journey to Moscow to join his wife, six children, sister, and mother.[50]

The Real Pharmacy World

The pharmacy situation in the provinces–in European Russia and in the Ukraine–was sobering in 1919 and 1920. The Civil War absorbed and decimated pharmacists and supplies. However, anguished reports from provincial pharmacy authorities left no doubt that many of their problems flowed from structural defects in the new pharmacy system: nationalization, centralization, bureaucratization, and lack of cost effectiveness. In Astrakhan, on the Volga, the pharmacy subdepartment of the provincial executive committee of the soviet eagerly moved to nationalize pharmacies December 23, 1918, immediately after hearing about the General Nationalization Decree—even before receiving it.[51]

But matters did not go smoothly in Astrakhan, as limitations on initiative, shortage of pharmacists, reams of paperwork, and shortages set in. In May 1919, the pharmacy subdepartment asked the Commissariat of Health in Moscow for instructions on how to order medicines for hospitals and clinics.[52] Later in the month harassed authorities in Astrakhan admitted that "they had not yet established norms for distributing medicine."[53] In a lengthy report Astrakhan informed Moscow that "it was difficult to administer pharmacies and pharmaceutical enterprises in the whole province in this difficult time. . . ." Problems were partly due to local conditions, partly to the ambitiousness of the new pharmacy structure. ". . . absence of ability [*sposobnost'*] has complicated the work . . ." and "endless differences of opinion" slowed down implementation of the new system. Members of the subdepartments in various areas were "not of the same mind." There were staffing and chancellery problems and inadequate guidance from Moscow. "To concentrate all administration of nationalized pharmacies and pharmaceutical enterprises in the province in the provincial pharmacy subdepartment," the Astrakhan authorities berated Moscow, "this is a great task which demands knowledgeable direction according to a fixed plan."[54] The provincial pharmacy warehouse refused to become subordinate to the provincial pharmacy subdepartment and stopped sending out medicines.[55] Astrakhan was beset with "severe" lack of pharmacists. Due to mobilization, emigration, and death "in the whole province of Astrakhan there were only one-third the experienced workers as there were previously."[56] Many problems were due to the unreasonableness and impracticality of Moscow's plans. Astrakhan minced no words in informing Moscow that its organizational demands and insistence on subordination to the Center were unrealistic and impossible to fulfill. Moscow ordered accountants in the pharmacy; persons with "specialized knowledge of pharmacy accounting" were not available. The proposal by the Center (*Tsentrum*) for "verification" and accounting in all nationalized pharmacies and pharmaceutical enterprises did "not attain its purpose because of its colossal scope in these times when there is not even a little piece of paper, when local printers refuse to undertake most orders." Astrakhan had obeyed in setting up a simplified accounting staff but "due to untrained people" the accounting was minimal. The provincial warehouse could not supply medicines because medical supplies were limited. Underlining for emphasis, local authorities denounced Moscow's prohibition on "deviating from the rule of requesting medicines from the Center."[57] They bewailed conscription of pharmacists into the Red Army, although they admitted that "the bread ration, comparatively large salaries, and minimal amount of work in military pharmacies" induced some pharmacists to leave of their own accord. However, another reason pharmacists joined the military was that they were refused managerial posts in nationalized pharmacies and offered posts they considered inferior, such as that of clerk. In all, Astrakhan authorities asserted that nationalization had led to "stagnation."[58]

By November 1920, the pharmacy situation had improved slightly in Astrakhan province. There was a children's colony, provincial warehouse, and 72 men and 301 women staffing pharmacies. However, pharmacists' ranks revealed erosion of quality and professionalism, for only 6 Provizors and 44 Assistant Pharmacists were cited in the 1920 report compared with 35 students and a whopping 103 *praktikanty*—untrained pharmacy helpers whom socialist pharmacists had disparaged in the tsarist era.[59] Additionally, the 1920 report noted that "measures had been taken to liquidate abuse of narcotic substances on the part of morphinists and cocainists, who presented falsified prescriptions at pharmacies." Also worker discipline was applied with vengeance, for "worker cards had been introduced for staff to keep track of those who are late."[60]

In Arkhangel'sk province in the northeastern part of European Russia, on the White Sea, the main problems were financial. Pharmacy authorities inundated Moscow with requests for money. Their petitions and Moscow's penury in fulfilling them amply demonstrated that the new pharmacy system was expensive and not paying for itself and, further, that centralized financing was not working. The Arkhangel'sk provincial pharmacy subdepartment's budget proposal to the "finance-control department of the provincial soviet" for the first half of 1919 amounted to 1,904,364 rubles and 80 kopeks for salaries and supplies.[61] The budget for Arkhangel'sk Provincial Warehouse for the second half of 1919 zoomed up to 3,342,640 rubles. The acquisition of surgical equipment, apparatus, and medicines amounted to only 800,000 rubles. Personnel amounted to only 126,880 rubles but "preparation of medicines" was an astronomical 1,800,000 rubles and "preparation of bandages" an equally high 500,000 rubles.[62] On April 4, 1919, reflecting scarcity, Arkhangel'sk pharmacy authorities sent a 5-by-7-inch piece of paper to the finance-control section of the soviet asking for an advance until their budget was approved.[63] Conditions deteriorated as the Civil War impacted the northeastern province. Several missives to Moscow were sent on 5-by-7-inch rectangles of tissue paper with the heading "Arkhangel'sk Province" handwritten in ink.[64] In an attempt to light a fire under central authorities, Arkhangel'sk authorities complained that only a "miserly budget sum was disbursed in the first half of the year." They hoped that this would not be repeated because it did not sustain the institutions for which the subdepartment was responsible.[65] However, Moscow did not–or could not–come through. Arkhangel'sk asked for a total sum of 3,342,640 rubles. Moscow sent only 275,080 rubles.[66] This prompted a frantic telegram to the Commissariat of Health March 3, 1920, asking for "credit of one million rubles to hurry [to dole out] to pharmacists."[67] Another telegram later in 1920 bespoke panic: "Staff have not been paid–ask for two millions advance."[68] A request for a 100,000-ruble advance followed shortly thereafter.[69] It might be noted that monthly wages for personnel at the Arkhangel'sk Provincial Warehouse for the second half of 1919 ranged from 600 rubles for cleaning people and 810 rubles for a packer to 1,050 for an "Assistant Provizor" (*Pomoshchnik provizor*), 1,290 for a Pharmacist-Laborant, and 1,510 for a "Laborant-Provizor." The Manager received 1,750 rubles.[70]

However, Arkhangel'sk faced shortages of pharmacists. In September 1919, one district complained there was only one Provizor left; heretofore there had been a "school feldsher" but he had been mobilized; "the situation was critical."[71] A typhus epidemic later in the year made the pharmacy situation precarious. In a note and follow-up telegram the district asked for immediate appointment of two pharmacists–a Provizor and Assistant–and two students.[72] Arkhangel'sk province also had jurisdictional clashes with Vologda province, its neighbor to the south. Vologda "suggested transferring all pharmacy warehouses" to itself. Arkhangel'sk strongly protested.[73]

The problems in Viatka province south of Vologda appeared mainly the result of the Civil War sweeping through the area. Mobilization had created a "severe shortage of pharmacists." The fifty pharmacists in the province were "not sufficient." Medicine could be distributed from the provincial pharmacy warehouse only two days each week.[74]

A good number of the problems in Vitebsk province, in the western part of Russia, on the other hand, were related to the eradication of private entrepreneurs, the proliferation of administrators, centralized financing and supply. Vitebsk beseeched the Central Spirits Supply (*Tsentrospirt*) for spirits. Lack of this substance had created a "critical situation." The local pharmaceutical factory–the "former MIZROKH," now part of the chemical section of the local provincial economic council (*gubsovnarkhoz*), had halted production. Pharmacies were closed because without spirits they could not dispense tinctures and extracts. Local raw materials such as potatoes could not be used because they were needed for food.[75] Many pharmacists were out of work. They were predominantly women pharmacists.[76] Conflicts erupted between the local soviet and local pharmacy subdepartments.[77] The local department of the Commissariat of Health complained that it had not received adequate instructions from the center.[78] There were shortages of medicines.[79] Work in the pharmacies was sloppy. Medicines were carelessly stored, the dispensers (*retseptar'*) refused to give out medicines, particularly over the counter.[80] Pharmacy budgets in Vitebsk province testified to the financial problems with the new system. Overhead and ties to Moscow were expensive and there were no funds to cover these expenses. Provincial administrative personnel were plentiful—controllers, accountants, managers, clerks. They received salaries ranging from 500 to 800 rubles. These were pitiful amounts considering inflation, but in aggregate drained coffers. The controller-instructors traveled around the province fifteen days each month, which necessitated purchasing tickets and renting horses. The manger of the pharmacy subdepartment had to make periodical trips to Moscow.[81] Meanwhile staff (*sluzhashchie*) in the pharmacies, erstwhile constituents of socialist Soviet administrators, had received no pay. Vitebsk officials sent a request for an advance of 350,000 rubles from the Commissariat of Health in Moscow. A week later they dispatched a second request, underlined for emphasis, asking for immediate disbursement of the money.[82]

The problems in Voronezh province, near Ukraine, and Kazan province, due east of Moscow, were partly due to the Civil War and partly to the irrationality of the new system. In Voronezh money and pharmacists were in short supply. A telegram from 1919 pleaded for funds.[83] A typhus epidemic had felled pharmacists. The city subdepartment asked for directions from Moscow.[84] The distribution of medicine had been organized—"the provincial warehouse supplied nationalized pharmacies free."[85] However, Voronezh city pharmacies did not have quinine, aspirin, and other basic medicines. The situation in nationalized pharmacies was "very sad"; many districts did not have enough pharmacists. Some pharmacies and most enterprises had not been nationalized because of lack of funds.[86] By January 1920, pharmacy in Voronezh province was "going through a critical time because of absence of pharmacy workers and severe illness."[87] Kazan railed about a regulation that only the pharmacy cashier could accept money. A typhus epidemic had increased prescriptions by 50 percent but there were not enough pharmacists. Therefore clerical staff who "knew Latin" were filling prescriptions, but "after five months' experience" they could not fully do the work. The regulations on control and verification "were expensive because of lack of paper." There were about thirty pharmacists in Kazan.[88] However, in 1920 the warehouse lacked aspirin, quinine, opium, cocaine, atropine, and other medicines.[89]

A. Khodak, clerk in the public pharmacy in the city of Kostroma, to the northeast of Moscow, was preoccupied during the summer of 1919 with orders from Central to bureaucratize pharmacy. He vented his spleen on the lack of accountants and improper accounting procedures in pharmacies, claiming he had been interested in pharmacy accounting for fifteen years and had developed his own system. He praised American and Italian double-entry bookkeeping and urged the government to establish an Institute of Pharmacy Accounting, asking why this had not been done. He offered to teach a course on American and German bookkeeping.[90]

However, Kostroma province as a whole had larger problems to contend with, mainly resulting from the unwieldiness of centralization and Moscow's orders to increase bureaucracy at the local level. Kostroma was far along in pharmacy organization, which had begun in the summer of 1918, but provincial authorities informed the Commissariat of Health that there was an "extreme insufficiency of pharmacists in the province" and asked the commissariat to send them eleven pharmacists, who had been rounded up for "work duty," to be distributed to five districts "severely needing pharmacists."[91] Despite the shortage of pharmacists, the local provincial pharmacy bureaucracy burgeoned and freely employed pharmacy professionals in administrative tasks. Bureaucracy was evident in the petition itself. It emanated from "the Congress of Managers of the pharmacy subdepartments of the province" and traveled through "the provincial sanitary bureau and the College of the Provincial Executive Committee of Workers and Soldiers' Deputies in the Provincial Department of Health!" Additionally, in four of the five districts short of pharmacists, the only available Provizor managed the mandated pharmacy subdepartments.[92]

Reports on pharmacy from the districts of Kostroma province during 1919 underscored coercion from Moscow to bureaucratize, shortage of pharmacists and misuse of those available, and shortage of money for administrative organization. The decision to nationalize pharmacies in Kostroma province was made in September 1918. The provincial sanitary bureau approved nationalization in October. The college of the provincial pharmacy subdepartment began operating in November and ordered all districts to form pharmacy subdepartments. "All that was in the plan could not be accomplished," however. "The chief reason was shortage of pharmacists free to take on the responsibility of managing the district subdepartments." There also were "communication problems and lack of credits."[93]

Provincial authorities complained that the districts had displayed "inertness" (*inertnost'*) in organizing their subdepartments.[94] It was probably just as well. Membership in the pharmacy union increased from 60 in November 1918 to 220 in 1919. However, only 79 members were pharmacists; 143 were "other pharmacy workers [lumped under the term 'staff pharmacists,' or *sluzhashchie*]." In the first district a pharmacy commission had been organized but it held "no meetings. All decisions were made by the Sanitary bureau . . . in place of five Assistants in the pharmacy there were two. The manager of the pharmacy subdepartment, besides managing the pharmacy did not have the strength to do everything" and in any case he had "received no additional remuneration" for his administrative duties.[95] The second district elected the manager of its subdepartment in December 1918, and soon after organized a Pharmacy Commission. Still the Sanitary bureau made all decisions. There was "great insufficiency of pharmacists" in the district. However, it was evident that those few pharmacists available would be attracted to administrative posts for "the personnel of the pharmacy subdepartment–manager and clerk–received 500 rubles in extra pay."[96] In the third district the pharmacy subdepartment was "established only after pressure from provincial officials."[97] In the fourth district a Pharmacy Commission had been formed December 1918, but had held "only one meeting."[98] In the fifth district a student pharmacist managed the pharmacy warehouse![99]

Still, despite restrictions imposed by centralization Kostroma province pharmacists did show sparks of initiative. Lacking means to establish the mandated provincial warehouse, the pharmacy subdepartment collected money from "interested organizations–provincial, district, and city soviet executive committees, the administration of the hospital," and "in the end, gathered the sum of 975,000 rubles." The chair of the provincial pharmacy subdepartment also made "several trips to Moscow" and finally pried loose needed medicines, enabling the province to open the warehouse April 6, 1919. The medicines were not sufficient for the fifteen normal, eight village, fifty hospital, and nine worker pharmacies and one railroad pharmacy in the province. Thus the province was "preparing to buy medicinal plants from Poltava province [in the Ukraine, a traditional producer and exporter] for the sum of half a million rubles." Kostroma province confidently asserted that "our province was better off than many others." The conclusion of the report did contain a few caveats, however, one of which stressed that "orders from the provincial center must be exact and take into consideration the geography of the province."[100]

Nizhni-Novgorod province, east of Moscow on the Volga, had a stormier relationship with central pharmacy authorities than did Kostroma. Its major problems were financial, and most of its correspondence with Moscow were requests for money. In February, 1919, on a piece of 5-by-7-inch paper, the Nizhegorod provincial health department informed Moscow that "the general situation of pharmacy" was "far from satisfactory." Pharmacies and warehouses were "entirely without medicines" and, as a result, the province asked Moscow for an advance of "not less than 56 thousand rubles." The provincial organization urged Moscow to "show cooperation in quickly filling this request."[101] Subsequent correspondence repeatedly pleaded for funds. Moscow finally sent an advance of 1 million rubles March 1919 to support nationalized pharmacies in the province.[102]

The city of Ekaterinburg in the Ural mountains and districts in Kursk, Penza, and Samara provinces in the southeastern part of Russia and Smolensk, in the west, were swamped with problems resulting from Moscow's demands for organization and accounting.[103] For example, a tiny typed note from Pugashevskii district, Samara province, in March 1920, informed Moscow that "it could not quickly send the information required" because it "had not gathered it." Moscow asked the district to hurry up.[104]

During 1919 Riazan province just south of Moscow had difficulty with accounting and inaccurate prices, was confused about credentials necessary for pharmacy posts, was still in the throes of nationalizing pharmacies, and had "severe need of medical herbs."[105] Not having received the herbs from the designated medical supply organization in the province, pharmacy officials asked for permission to acquire them privately, through the Union of Credit and Loan Savings Association.[106] Contrary to its usual practice, Moscow did not object.[107] Chaos attended Riazan's attempts to get supplies from the center,[108] registering pharmacists and closing rural pharmacies.[109]

Cherepovets was in the throes of nationalizing pharmacies in March 1919. In most cases all went "smoothly." However, in one district a pharmacy owner opposed the process and, additionally, the Union of Staff Pharmacists and pharmacy staffs (the constituency in whose name nationalization was being implemented) did not cooperate with nationalizing the Cherepovets Cooperative Pharmacy.[110] Six pharmacies in the province were nationalized and five were closed for not dispensing medicine to the public.[111] There also were "severe shortages of pharmacists" and shortages of medicines. The first problem prompted a "resolution" to the Professional Union of Pharmacists to organize courses to prepare people to serve as "medicine dispensers to the population"[112] and pay for holidays.[113] The second problem led to a proposal to "elect a commission of three people–agronomist, Provizor, and teacher in the teacher training school–to compose a brochure about collecting medicinal plants in the province.[114]

All pharmacies in the cities of Tambov and Gorodsk were nationalized in 1919, and the pharmacy warehouse in the latter city was nationalized as well. An army of administrators overwhelmed pharmacists involved with dispensing and analyzing.[115]

The Bashkir "Republic" in the Ural region was in dreadful shape in 1919. In a carefully typed letter of several pages, the regional authority informed Moscow that the two normal and two village pharmacies had been nationalized by the middle of 1919. However, there was "absence of medicines and pharmacy personnel." There were only four pharmacists in the "whole republic." There were still "some hospital pharmacies but their equipment was outmoded." The Bashkir pharmacy authority had requested medicines from Moscow and had traveled to Samara province, to the south. To "their shame" the Samara comrades had not helped. "With happiness" the Bashkir republic received their "first order of medicines from Moscow" but this proved to be only an "insignificant amount" and "not the whole catalog," in fact, Moscow sent "what would be stored in one average normal pharmacy [in the tsarist period] for not more than 2–3 months."[116] An epidemic of typhus scourged the region. The hapless regional authority had himself fallen ill. The inspection of the regional pharmacy warehouse that he conducted upon his recovery revealed "sad results." There was only one pharmacist and three packers who worked in "difficult conditions–cold to 30 degrees of frost."[117]

During 1919, Petrograd, the former capital of Russia, moved forward on nationalizing and organizing. The plethora of agencies caused confusion.[118] Additionally, nationalization caused both petty and major problems. Mirlin, Kuperman, and Zalesskii were still manning the College of the Pharmacy subdepartment in Petrograd in 1919.[119] On October 29, 1919, the regional controller was empowered to inspect the wares in Antonina Lesnevskaia's former "First Women's Pharmacy," now the "Communal Former First Women's."[120] G. A. Ginzburg, former owner of Communal Pharmacy no. 3, complained that his overcoat had been confiscated when his pharmacy was nationalized. The subdepartment generously resolved to pay for another for him. A staff pharmacist in a third pharmacy pleaded for his salary for the second half of October because of "extreme need."[121] On a larger scale, a representative from the Petrograd subdepartment went to Moscow to demand 12,000,000 rubles. He received only 8,000,000.[122] In November 1919, Kuperman and Zalesskii requested one million rubles from the Commissariat of Health in Moscow for pay advances for pharmacy workers.[123] The "liquidation" of village pharmacies loomed as a "difficult" project and thus had been put off.[124]

Petrograd pharmacists did not display the alleged hostility toward propertied classes that supposedly motivated Petrograd socialists and "have-nots" to sequester private property, and implement the Dictatorship of the Proletariat.[125] On the contrary, staff pharmacists exhibited concern for expropriated owners. On December 5, 1919, the Petrograd pharmacy subdepartment informed Moscow that "during nationalization–according to the regulation of January, 29, 1919, from the Soviet of Commissars of the Northern Region–trading from wholesale stocks of firms dealing in pharmacy wares to the pharmacy subdepartment had been forbidden on the current account and capital of the aforementioned firms." The subdepartment queried Central as to whether "this capital should be returned to the income of the treasury or remain with the former owners." The Petrograd pharmacy subdepartment acknowledged that it was undecided on the question, as was the People's Bank.[126] A follow-up letter of from the People's Bank of the Northern Region, December 10, 1919, reiterated this query to the Pharmacy Department of the Commissariat of Health (addressed as *Kom. zdrav*), namely whether "current accounts and capital" from Shaskol'skii, The Russian Society in the Trade of Pharmacy Wares, Shtol' and Shmidt, Briuller, and Gofman were "subject to an extraordinary revolutionary tax" and whether the "accounts and capital" should be sent to the treasury or "returned to their former owners."[127] Moscow did not agree that the 7,534,540 rubles in question should be given back, but rather proposed it be kept in Petrograd.[128]

Problems flowing from nationalization continued into 1920. In February of that year it was alleged that some pharmacists were sent to a People's Court for "refusing to work and sabotage."[129] In June 1920, shortage of paper forced pharmacy officials in Petrograd to write reports on the back of order blanks from the former "Shtol' and Shmidt" pharmaceutical house and the enterprise FARMAKON, the latter in German.[130] Local authorities were confused about prices for medicines.[131]

In 1918, despite the Civil War, pharmacy in the Ukraine had been healthy, as the previous chapter disclosed. By 1920, the Soviet pharmacy structure had been imposed and problems were rife. In June of that year one hapless district complained that prices for materials received from the central supply base were 300 to 500 percent higher than the Pharmacy Tax. There were no norms for staffs in pharmacies. Pharmacy accounting was not standardized. District pharmacies lacked qualified workers.[132] Deterioration of pharmacy in the Ukraine was one of the best proofs that systemic problems as well as the Civil War harmed Soviet pharmacy and the pharmaceutical industry.

The government's insistence on controlling medical supplies from the center particularly appeared dysfunctional—and harmful to the people in whose name the revolution had been made. On March 5, 1919, the All-Russian Central Union of Consumer Societies (*Potrebitel'nye Obshchestva*) in Moscow complained to the Commissariat of Health about their "letter of 27 II [1919]" ordering that "medical preparations" could be "distributed only to pharmacies and other medical institutions and forbidding our acquisition of them for proletarian chandleries." The Central Union reminded the Commissariat of Health that "among the rural and . . . city population of Russia" there was "enormous need of medical substances . . . quinine, various drops, and oils." Many cooperatives had approached the Central Union for medicines. "What was the result? Pharmacy bureaucrats' (the Bureau for Ordering and Distributing Medicines) refusal to send medical substances to cooperative chandleries meant that the populace was without them."[133]

Additionally, there were continued signs in 1919 and 1920 that the Soviet pharmacy system was expensive and not paying for itself. In its budget request for the first half of 1919 Petrograd noted that expenditures amounted to 40,438,280 rubles and income was only 21,161,200 rubles. Therefore it asked Moscow for 19,322,080 rubles to make up the difference. The expenditures were explained by the fact that "costs had risen by 50 percent." Outfitting the central warehouse cost 310,000 rubles. Medicines, particularly galenical preparations, and glass were costly and it was expensive to supply pharmacies in the area and also the northern region (as Moscow directed.) The budget was documented with forty-three pages of data. Almost 2 million rubles went for "One-Time Expenditures," mostly to Central Supply, for outfitting laboratories and repairing pharmacies. Over 18 million rubles went for "Ongoing Expenditures," including some 13 million rubles for personnel. Administrators were plentiful. There were staff for "Central Supply"; accountants; staff for the Department for Orders; managers and administrators of the Analytical Laboratory; staff for the warehouse, the chemical-galenical section, the Department of Patented Poisons and Alkaloids, "Central Vessels," Warehouse of Glass, workers' section, Control, pharmacy subdepartment, pharmacy commission, and so on. Over 20 million rubles went for "turnover of substances."[134] A frantic telegram of February 1919, asked Moscow "to quickly send on account 5 millions."[135] Another telegram demanded with obvious panic "I ask you to hurry to transfer 15 millions... no means to pay salaries for the current half month... I sent the budget to Moscow yesterday—Baran sick—We ask you to prepare to transfer the request of 15 millions/ if not—we will not be able to pay salaries."[136] The cumbersomeness of centralization can be seen in a request of February 1919 for 2,200 rubles to purchase a typing machine.[137] And, the inability of the system to pay for itself was again underscored by a May 13, 1920, telegram for "39 millions—extreme need to pay staff."[138]

It has been noted that Lenin was toying with the idea of dismantling the economic provisions of "War Communism" in 1920. Most central pharmacy bureaucrats were sanguine at this time. However, some expressed their dissatisfaction with the pharmacy system as it operated under "War Communism" from early 1919.

Financial and supply problems were a frequent topic of debate in pharmacy administration meetings and the government-sanctioned pharmacy journal. The Chief Committee on the Chemical-Pharmaceutical Industry held a meeting on "disinfecting substances" March 28, 1919. F. A. Ferrein was present for Pharmaceutical Factory Number 8 and O. G. Gabrilovich represented Pharmacy Factory Number 9. Professor Chichibabin, from the *Farmatsentr* Bureau chaired the meeting, which discussed "more rational utilization of raw materials."[139] The April/May 1919 edition of *Vestnik aptechnogo truda* carried a two-page article by A. Aluf, entitled "Three Months of Inactivity," which acknowledged that central supply was not working. Aluf criticized the Central Supply Organization for disorganization, lack of basic medicines, and so forth.[140] By December 1919, the Purchasing Commission in the Department of Medical Supply of the Commissariat of Health planned to buy medicines from Germany. They agreed to pay a 450 to 600 percent price increase over the price list of 1917, and additionally, promised that none of the medicines would be confiscated or requisitioned.[141]

Pharmacy officials and the official journals also disparaged closing pharmacies, shortage of pharmacists, lack of enthusiasm on the part of staff pharmacists for the Pharmacy Union, and clashes between Communist and Menshevik pharmacists. In September 1919, *Vestnik aptechnogo truda* carried an article by I. Levinshtein questioning the policy of shutting pharmacies, which had led to severe deterioration in dispensing in Petrograd and the countryside.[142] Central authorities admitted that the organization of pharmacy subdepartments in provinces, districts, and cities was not working properly because there were not enough pharmacists.[143] In December 1919, central authorities noted that former owners were managing 10 percent of eight hundred pharmacies surveyed because of lack of "prepared worker-proletariat."[144] Worse, pharmacy workers were as cool to the blandishments of their mentors in 1919 as before. Pharmacy workers also eschewed political parties. A survey showed that only 43.7 percent of pharmacy workers (80 percent men and 18 percent women) between the ages of twenty-two and thirty years joined the Pharmacy Workers Union; only 37.5 percent of workers between the ages of thirty and forty-one years (82 percent men and 2 percent women) joined the union, and a paltry 11.1 percent over forty joined. Of these 13.1 percent were members of the Russian Communist Party [Bolsheviks]; 23.2 percent belonged to other socialist parties, and 76.5 percent adhered to no party. The survey also confirmed that administrators were plentiful. Eighty-five administrators balanced out 211 "staff pharmacists."[145] Additionally, central authorities acknowledged that pharmacy workers were undergoing a "crisis" due to hunger and other problems in the fall of 1919 and that Mensheviks competed with Communists [Bolsheviks]. Menshevik pharmacists were still holding out for a coalition government of all parties and independence of professional unions.[146]

By 1921 workers, in whose name the October Revolution had been made, began to revolt against War Communism and the authoritarianism of the Soviet government. Socialist opponents of the Bolsheviks who had been locked out of the government aided and abetted them. Peasants rose up to protest exactions of their produce–sometimes their own food–and prohibitions on trade. Workers struck to protest their conditions–differential pay, harsh discipline, time and motion studies, bourgeois management. Anarchists and rebel sailors on the Kronstadt Naval Base in 1921 forcefully and eloquently exposed the Soviet regime as a distortion of popular revolution.[147]

The story of pharmacy and the pharmaceutical industry after 1917 adds another dimension to these protests against the Bolsheviks, for it raises the larger issue of why overturn and destruction of the previous pharmacy system (and by extension, the old economic and social system) was necessary in the first place. The tsarist government had dominated pharmacy. However, pharmacy education was good, dispensing adequate, and the position of pharmacists tenable under the old system. Pharmacists showed corporate and individual initiative under the old system. Limitations on establishing pharmacies blocked pharmacists' advancement but there was some scope for the ambitious to realize their potential. The tenacity and drive of many women pharmacists brought them success. Misguided government policy hampered the pharmaceutical industry. Nevertheless, the Russian pharmaceutical industry was progressing. The exigencies of World

War I hurt pharmacy and the pharmaceutical industry but this sector of the economy was still viable in 1917.

Theorist-reformers were not satisfied. Their attraction to big government and socialism was deep and strong. These theorists were determined to revamp the pharmacy system in Russia according to their textbook model. They succeeded. And deterioration, rather than betterment of pharmacy, was the result. Pharmacy would make a comeback during the "New Economic Policy" of the 1920s.[148] But Bolshevik-Soviet pharmacy policies from 1917 to 1921 undermined the health of pharmacy and the pharmaceutical industry. The system could never be fully cured, fully restored.

Notes

Spelling and capitalization were inconsistent in the Russian titles cited in these notes. Nevertheless, titles are presented, as much as possible, as they originally appeared. Place names usually are cited according to customary English citation. Russian given names and surnames are cited as in the original except in the case of given names familiar to the English speaker, i.e., Alexander is used in the text in place of Aleksandr.

Introduction

1. For example, Richard G. Robbins, Jr.'s two works, *Famine in Russia, 1891–1892* (New York: Columbia University Press, 1975) and *The Tsar's Viceroys* (Ithaca, NY: Cornell University Press, 1987); Daniel T. Orlovsky's *The Limits of Reform, The Ministry of Internal Affairs in Imperial Russia, 1802–1881* (Cambridge, MA: Harvard University Press, 1981); Thomas S. Pearson's *Russian Officialdom in Crisis: Autocracy and Local Self-Government, 1861–1900* (Cambridge: Cambridge University Press, 1989); Andrew M. Verner, *The Crisis of Russian Autocracy. Nicholas II and the 1905 Revolution* (Princeton: Princeton University Press, 1990); Howard D. Mehlinger & John M. Thompson, *Count Witte and the Tsarist Government in the 1905 Revolution* (Bloomington: Indiana University Press, 1972); Mary Schaeffer Conroy, *Peter Arkad'evich Stolypin: Practical Politics in Late Tsarist Russia* (Boulder, CO: Westview Press, 1977).

2. For example, Richard Abraham, *Alexander Kerensky: The First Love of the Revolution* (New York: Columbia University Press, 1987), is admirably familiar with his subject but bandies the old clichés about Nicholas II and the government, Furthermore, he never satisfactorily explains *why* Kerensky was so opposed to the tsarist government or, indeed, why he was captivated by socialism.

3. For example, Peter A. Zaionchkovsky, *The Russian Autocracy under Alexander III* (reprint, Gulf Breeze, FL: Academic International Press, 1976).

4. V. A. Nardova, *Gorodskoe Samoupravlenie v Rossii v 60-x—nachale 90-x godov XIX* (Leningrad, 1984).

5. M(ikhail). P(avlovich). Iroshnikov, *Predsedatel' Soveta Narodnykh Komissarov* (Leningrad, 1974) uses thousands of questionnaires (*ankety*) to document the continuity in personnel between the government of the old and new regimes. See also T. H. Rigby, *Lenin's Government: Sovnarkom 1917–1922* (Cambridge: Cambridge University Press, 1979).

6. See Olga Crisp, *Studies in the Russian Economy before 1914* (London: Macmillan Press, 1976); Jo Ann Ruckman, *The Moscow Business Elite* (DeKalb, IL: Northern Ilinois University Press, 1984); *Entrepreneurship in Imperial Russia*

and the Soviet Union, ed., Gregory Guroff and Fred V. Carstensen (Princeton: Princeton University Press, 1983); Thomas C. Owen, *The Russian Corporation under Russian Law, 1800-1917* (Cambridge: Cambridge University Press, 1991); Charles A. Ruud, *Russian Entrepreneur Publisher Ivan Sytin of Moscow, 1851-1934* (Montreal: McGill-Queen's University Press, 1990).

7. See, for example, Paul R. Gregory, *Russian National Income, 1885-1913* (Cambridge: Cambridge University Press, 1982); Esther Kingston-Mann, "Peasant Communes and Economic Innovation: A Preliminary Inquiry," pp. 23-51, and Elvira M. Wilbur, "A View from Russia's 'Impoverished Center' at the End of the Nineteenth Century," pp. 101-127 in *Peasant Economy, Culture, and Politics of European Russia, 1800-1921*, eds., Esther Kingston-Mann and Timothy Mixter (Princeton: Princeton University Press, 1991); Joseph Bradley, *Muzhik and Muscovite: Urbanization in Late Imperial Russia* (Berkeley: University of California Press, 1985); Theodore H. Friedgut, *Iuzhovka and Revolution. Vol. I: Life and Work in Russia's Donbass, 1869-1924* (Princeton: Princeton University Press, 1989); Jeffrey Brooks, *When Russia Learned to Read* (Princeton: Princeton University Press, 1985); Ben Eklof, *Russian Peasant Schools* (Berkeley: University of California Press, 1986).

8. See for example, Victoria E. Bonnell, *Roots of Rebellion: Workers' Politics and Organizations in St. Petersburg and Moscow, 1900-1914* (Berkeley: University of California Press, 1983), and more especially, works by Lionel Haimson, Laura Englestein, Diane Koenker, and William Rosenburg, cited in chapter 14 of this work.

9. For easily accessible surveys see, for example, Jerry F. Hough and Merle Fainsod, *How the Soviet Union is Governed* (Cambridge, MA: Harvard University Press, 1979), pp. 71-73, and John M. Thompson, *Revolutionary Russia* (New York: Charles Scribner's Sons, 1981).

10. A look at pharmacy, pharmacists and the pharmaceutical industry suggests that political revolution occurred in Russia in 1917 because the tsarist government's public relations skills were abysmal and that economic revolution occurred because some "have-nots" had a simplistic grasp of how the economy worked and there were revolutionaries to exploit their misconceptions. In 1917/1918 mass hysteria mounted to a crescendo to smash the system. As far as pharmacy was concerned, the revolutionaries were not just the traditional kind–although there were pharmacists who belonged to revolutionary parties–but also revolutionaries in the sense of socioeconomic engineers. The latter type of revolutionaries were to be found among pharmacist reformers, the Russian government, and society at large as well as among militant socialist pharmacists.

11. David MacKenzie and Michael W. Curran, *A History of the Soviet Union* (Belmont, CA: Wadsworth Publishing, second edition, 1991), p. 189.

12. For a handy compendium containing excerpts on revolutionary mentality among peasants, factory workers, soldiers, and so on, see *The Russian Revolution and Bolshevik Victory*, eds., Ronald Suny and Arthur Adams (Lexington, MA and Toronto: D. C. Health and Company, 1990). Additionally, Esther Kingston-Mann, *Lenin and the Problem of Marxist Peasant Revolution* (New York: Oxford Univer-

sity Press, 1985) presents a stimulating view of how Lenin encouraged peasant violence. Ziva Galili, *The Menshevik Leaders in the Russian Revolution: Social Realities and Political Strategies* (Princeton: Princeton University Press, 1989) discusses the Mensheviks in 1917. Donald J. Raleigh, *Revolution on the Volga: 1917 in Saratov* (Ithaca: Cornell University Press, 1986) focuses on Saratov province. Evan Mawdsley, *The Russian Civil War* (Boston: Allen and Unwin, 1987) discusses the economy during the Civil War of 1917–1921.

13. Alec Nove, *An Economic History of the USSR* (London: Penguin Books, 1992).

14. See above, note 7, for full citation.

15. Charles Ruud paints a depressing picture of the Soviet takeover of Ivan Sytin's publishing empire. *Russian Entrepreneur,* pp. 169–200.

16. Larry E. Holmes *The Kremlin and the Schoolhouse: Reforming Education in Soviet Russia, 1917–1931* (Bloomington: Indiana University Press, 1991).

17. Denise J. Youngblood, *Movies for the Masses Popular cinema and Soviet society in the 1920s* (Cambridge: Cambridge University Press, 1992).

18. For example, Mary McAuley's well-wrought *Bread and Justice: State and Society in Petrograd, 1917–1922* (Oxford: Oxford University Press, 1991) argues that although Bolshevik economic policies reduced Petrograd to a wasteland by 1922 they had merit because they fulfilled the social contract that the Bolsheviks made with the masses before their accession. See especially McAuley, *Bread and Justice,* pp. 426–430; also p. 302 and *passim.*

Chapter 1

1. The British Pharmacy Society supervised dispensing, but in loose fashion. For an account of lenient dispensing in nineteenth- and early twentieth-century Britain see Glenn Sonnedecker, *History of Pharmacy* (Philadelphia: J. B. Lippincott Co., 1976), pp. 107–112; see also George Edward Trease, *Pharmacy in History* (London, 1964), pp. 50, 60, 71. In America, regulations on pharmacy practice differed from state to state. See Sonnedecker, ibid., pp. 180–186, 213–219.

2. Prosper H. Marsden, "Pharmacy in Russia," *The Pharmaceutical Era* (February 16, 1905), p. 197. Marsden delivered his paper to the Pharmaceutical Society of Great Britain.

3. Medicinal herbs had been used in Russia from ancient times, and contact with peoples of the Byzantine Empire, Central Asia and the Near East exposed Russians to Arabic and Oriental therapeutics during the Kievan Russian period. However, the organization of pharmacy before the fifteenth century has not been comprehensively portrayed.

For emergence of the national-state of Russia from the Grand Duchy of Muscovy in the fifteenth and sixteenth centuries see Ian Grey, *Ivan III and the Unification of Russia* (New York: Collier Books, 1964); George Vernadsky, *Russia at the Dawn of the Modern Age* (New Haven: Yale University Press, 1959). For development of the bureaucracy in the eighteenth and nineteenth century see George L. Yaney, *The Systematization of Russian Government* (Urbana: University of Illinois Press, 1973).

4. It is generally accepted that James Frencham, emissary of the Elizabeth I of England, organized the first pharmacy in Russia in 1581. I. L. Kondakov, "Kratkii istoricheskii ocherk razvitiia farmatsii i prichiny upadka farmatsevticheskoi shkoly," *Meditsina*, vol. 7, no. 10 (March) 1895, p. 149. A pharmacy was established in Tallinn, Estonia, in 1422, but this did not become part of the Russian Empire until the early eighteenth century. *Soviet Estonia, Land, People, Culture*, ed., L. Valt (Tallinn, 1980), p. 172. Soviet historian of pharmacy V. M. Salo, however, places pharmacists at the Russian court as early as the 1550s and 1560s. V. M. Salo, "Aptechnoe delo v Rossii v XIV–XVII vekakh," pp. 3–4, chapter I of book-length MS, "Istoriia farmatsii v Rossii, XVI-pervaia polovina XIX v. v.," MS in my possession.

5. "The furniture of the first crown stores," Professor Claus of the University of Dorpat (later called Iur'ev) related in the 1850s, "was imported from England and made of costly polished woods, the bottles of cut crystal-glass with covers of massive silver; among the medicines were pearls and precious stones, bezoardicum solare, a powdered gold perfumed with amber, &c" Other medicaments included "Musk . . . Castor . . . Rhubarb." Professor C. Claus, "History of Pharmacy in Russia," *American Journal of Pharmacy*, vol. 31, 1859, pp. 166–167.

6. For pharmacy in the German states see Sonnedecker, *History of Pharmacy*, pp. 85–89.

7. In Italy pharmaceutical guilds regulated pharmacy from the thirteenth century through the 1770s, when the Austrian government brought pharmacy in northern Italy under its control. Sonnedecker, *History of Pharmacy*, pp. 59–60. In France, pharmacy guilds supervised pharmacy from the thirteenth to the sixteenth century. Royal edicts began to regulate pharmacy from the end of the fifteenth century but only in the late eighteenth century did the French government fully control pharmacy. Ibid., pp. 68–72.

8. The Pharmacy Department (*Prikaz*) was established in the sixteenth century, soon after the arrival of the foreign pharmacists, but began to function fully in the seventeenth century. Salo, MS, pp. 8–9, 10–15.

For seventeenth-century government offices or departments (*prikazi*), particularly their sophistication, see Borivoj Plavsic, "Seventeenth-Century Chanceries and Their Staffs," *Russian Officialdom*, eds., Walter McKenzie Pintner and Don Karl Rowney (Chapel Hill: University of North Carolina Press, 1980), pp. 19–45, esp. p. 25.

9. The status of pharmacists vis-à-vis physicians can be seen in their remuneration. The salary of court pharmacists, according to a nineteenth-century Russian pharmacy professor, "was considerable for that time—300 to 360 rubels [*sic*]; it was larger than that of court surgeons, but less than the physicians, which reached 500 or 600 rubels. . . . The Court apothecaries had to be present at the examination of physicians soliciting an appointment, and to sign the diplomas of physicians who had graduated in Russia." Claus, "History of Pharmacy in Russia," p. 167. Professor Claus's address was translated by a Mr. John Maisch of Philadelphia; he obviously spelled transliteration from the Russian idiosyncratically.

10. Salo, MS, translation, pp. 17–26, 31–32.

11. The second Romanov tsar, Alexsei, established the pharmacy. In 1676, his son and successor, Theodore, also permitted the court pharmacy to dispense medicaments to the public. Salo, MS, p. 15.

12. Salo, MS, p. 34.

13. Salo, MS, pp. 35–36.

14. I. S. Tkeshelashvili, "Russkaia farmatsiia do vozniknoveniia pervykh vol'nykh aptek," *Farmatsevt*, vol. 10, 1902, pp. 569, 542.

15. Two more private pharmacies were shortly opened in Moscow; the first private pharmacy in St. Petersburg, the new capital, opened in 1721. (A. S. Ginzberg, "Ocherk razvitiia nauchnoi farmatsii v Rossii za 200-letnii period," *Farmatsevticheskii vestnik* [hereafter cited *F. V.*] vol. 5, no. 16 1902, pp. 185–186. There were 3 treasury pharmacies in Russia at this time.) By 1725 there were 8 pharmacies in Moscow. (Kondakov, "Kratkii istoricheskii ocherk," p. 149; Tkeshevashvili, "Russkaia farmatsiia," p. 542.) By 1776 there were 24 private pharmacies, by 1827, 414, and by 1851, 743. (V. M. Salo, T. B. Grigor'eva, "Peterburgskoe farmatsevticheskoe obshchestvo, *Farmatsiia*, vol. 25, no. 2, 1976, p. 78.) In the city of Moscow there were 30 pharmacies by 1861. (M. Koroleva, "Moskovskie apteki v pervoi polovine XIX veka," *Aptechnoe delo*, vol. 9, no. 3, 1960, p. 77.)

16. This herbal contained an alphabetical listing of herbs and treatment "by knowledge of the pulse" and "by knowledge of urine." It also contained prescriptions such as the application of cool, fresh vegetables—cabbage, flax, hazel nuts—and their juices for surface inflammations. For ulcerating sores the book recommended extracts of onions, garlic, or beets. Skorokhodov, *Kratkii ocherk istorii russkoi meditsiny* (Leningrad, 1926), p. 31. Also, A. G. Natradze, *Russkie i sovetskie farmakopei* (Moscow, 1978), p. 26.

17. For more on private herbals see Natradze, *Russkie i sovetskie farmakopei*, pp. 26–72. Subsequent military and civilian pharmacopoeias appeared, see chapters 8 and 9 of this work on the Russian Pharmaceutical Industry.

18. Cameralism stressed that a healthy populace was a major resource to any government and, hence, that governments must oversee and promote the health of the citizenry.

19. Ginzberg, "Ocherk razvitiia," pp. 186–187; headings on correspondence contained in the Tsentral'nyi Gosudarstvennyi Istoricheskii Arkhiv, St. Petersburg [hereafter cited TsGIA].

For more on the provincial administration see George L. Yaney, *The Systematization of the Russian Government* , pp. 68–74.

20. Nineteenth-century scholars such as Donald MacKenzie Wallace vividly depicted the sluggishness of the Russian bureaucracy. See *Russia*, reprinted from an 1877 edition by AMS Press, New York, 1970, *passim*.

Recent scholarship has emphasized that Russia lacked sufficient bureaucrats to adequately administer her empire. Nevertheless, the centralized system of government was ponderous and domineering as compared with the system in England or the United States. See, for example, W. Bruce Lincoln, *In the Vanguard of Reform Russia's Enlightened Bureaucrats 1825–1861* (DeKalb: Northern Illinois University Press, 1982) and also Daniel T. Orlovsky, *The Limits of Reform: The Ministry of*

Internal Affairs in Impetial Russia, 1802-1881 (Cambridge, MA: Harvard University Press, 1981); Thomas F. Pearson, *Russian Officialdom in Crisis: Autocracy and Local Self-Government, 1861-1900* (Cambridge: Cambridge University Press, 1981). Thomas C. Owen describes the impact of goverment regulations on corporations in *The Corporation under Russian Law, 1800-1917* (Cambridge: Cambridge University Press, 1991).

21. These two pharmacists received no salaries. According to bylaws, the Medical Council met twice a week and oftener if circumstances directed. The Council could call advisory experts when necessary. Svod zakonov, vol. 1, part 2, Uchrezh. Ministerstva, 1892, articles 367-395 cited in *Sbornik Zakonopolozhenii dlia farmatsevtov, soderzhatelei aptek i drogistov* sostavil P. N. Bulatov, zaveduiushchii deloproizvodstvom Kantseliarii Meditsinskago Soveta Ministerstva Vnutrennikh Del (St. Petersburg, 1897), pp. 87-89.

22. Ibid. For more on the medical inspectors of St. Petersburg, Moscow, Warsaw, and Odessa, as well as provincial and district medical inspectors see John F. Hutchinson, *Politics and Public Health in Revolutionary Russia 1890-1918* (Baltimore: John Hopkins University Press, 1990), pp. 16-18. Hutchinson discusses the qualifications of provincial medical inspectors (they were required to have the degree *Doktor meditsiny* and pass additional examinations), their salaries, district medical inspectors, etc.

23. Correspondence of Lomzhinskii gubernator po gubernskomu pravleniiu otdelenie vrachebnago to Ministerstvo Vnutrennikh del. Meditsinskii Departament, Dec. 9, 1878, TsGIA, fond 1297, opis' 155, delo 177, list 1 and 1 oborot [hereafter cited "f.," "op.," "d.," "l" or "ll." in the case of plural; and "ob."].

24. D. I. Toropov, "Dvizhenie i rost aptechnago dela v Imperii za poslednee desiatiletie (1901-1911 g.g.)." *Vestnik obshchestvennoi gigieny, sudebnoi i prakticheskoi meditsiny*, no. 9, 1911, p. 1278.

25. For example, see "Protokol Khersonskago gubernskago pravleniia po vrachebnomu otdeleniiu," July 27, 1916, TsGIA, f. 1298, op. 1, d. 2083, l. 2 and 2 ob.

26. *Tsirkuliary Meditsinskago Departamenta, 19 noiabriia 1881, No. 265 O vvedenii v deistvie pravil o poriadke uchrezhdeniia i ustroistva sel'skikh aptek* as cited in Bulatov, *Sbornik zakonopolozhenii* , pp. 221-226; also Bulatov, ibid., pp. 219-227. If the regulations governing village pharmacies were implemented, these institutions were adequate, contrary to the impression given by Samuel Ramer in his recent chapter "Traditional Healers and Peasant Culture in Russia, 1861-1917" in *Peasant Economy, Culture, and Politics of European Russia, 1800-1921* (Princeton: Princeton University Press, 1991), pp. 207-232. Ramer's comment, "The best of these [peasant] herbal healers were skilled native pharmacists whose armory of medicines in any given case might be every bit as therapeutic as a trained physician could provide," may have been true. However, he does not document his following comment that "This is in part a reflection on how poorly supplied rural pharmacies were in Russia during the nineteenth century (and twentieth century, for that matter)." Ibid., p. 220. Further, he does not define "rural" as to whether this refers to private village pharmacies or zemstvo pharmacies.

27. Toropov, "Dvizhenie i rost," p. 1278.

28. TsGIA, f. 1298, op. 1, d. 1769, l. 1.

Homeopathic pharmacies followed Samuel Hahnemann's principle of applying minute doses of drugs to produce symptoms similar to the disease which they attempted to cure. Sonnedecker, *History of Pharmacy*, pp. 47–48, 176–177.

29. Bulatov, *Sbornik zakonopolozhenii*, pp. 314-316.

30. Bulatov, *Sbornik zakonopolozhenii*, pp. 131–132.

31. "Pravila ob otkrytii aptek, Utverzhdeny G. Upravliaiushchim Ministerstvom Vnutrennikh Del 25 maia 1873 goda, Vtoroe polnoe sobranie zakonov, tom XLVIII, otdel. i, no. 52611, paragraph 1, cited in Bulatov, *Sbornik zakonopolozhenii*, pp. 131–132.

32. See chapter 3, "Privately Owned Pharmacies" and chapter 4, "Drug Stores and Socialized Public Pharmacy" in this work for more information on this subject.

33. In northern Italy there was to be one pharmacy for every 5,000 inhabitants; in some areas pharmacies also were required to be a certain distance from each other. Sonnedecker, *Pharmacy in History*, p. 60. In the Austrian Empire proper in the nineteenth century, the government permitted new pharmacies where the population reached 30,000; in cities with a population of 30,000 to 100,000 there was to be one pharmacy for every 8,000 inhabitants; in cities with a population of over 100,000 inhabitants there was to be one pharmacy for every 10,000 to 12,000 inhabitants. "Proekt reform otnositel'no otkrytiia aptek i vladeniia imi so storony Avstriiskago farmatsevticheskago obshchestva," *Farmatsevticheskii zhurnal* [hereafter cited *F. Zh.*], vol 20, no 43, 1898, p. 611.

34. Sonnedecker, *History of Pharmacy*, pp. 60–61, 85–89, 91.

35. According to a proclamation of the State Council and the Governing Senate, January 5, 1898, "it was necessary to limit pharmacy [*aptechnoe delo*] from superfluous competition . . . new pharmacies could be opened only when the owners of existing pharmacies certified that they would not curtail the existing pharmacies. . . ." Cited in "Zhurnal prisutstviia Sedletskago gubernskago pravleniia," December 18, 1912, TsGIA, f. 1298, op. 1, d. 1932, l. 3 ob.

36. Prosper H. Marsden, "The Practice of Pharmacy in Russia," *American Druggist and Pharmaceutical Record*, 1905, p. 94.

37. Correspondence of MVD to Podol'skomu gubernatoru, Oct. 23, 1878, and MVD, Podol'skago gubernatora, gubernsk. upravlenie otdelenie vrach., May 1879, v Med. Departament, MVD, TsGIA: f. 1297, op. 155, d. 150, ll. 3 and 7. Responding to a governor, forwarding the petition of a Provizor desirous of opening a district pharmacy in Podolia province in 1878, the Medical Department asked whether, in accordance with a circular of the MVD of 16 February 1827, the pharmacist had the means—1500 rubles—to establish a district pharmacy.

The vice-governor assured the Medical Department that the Provizor had this amount.

38. TsGIA, f. 1298, op. 1, d. 1244, l. 18 and l. 61.

39. In 1898 *Farmatsevticheskii zhurnal* printed the approved format: "To His

Excellency . . . Governor of . . . Province. Provizor or Assistant Pharmacist . . . Place of Residence . . . I have the honor to humbly request Your Excellency's permission to establish and open a private . . . pharmacy in (village) in (*volost'*) [subsection of a district], in (district). My papers are attached or my documents will be found in the Office of the Medical Department." Cited in *F. Zh.*, vol 20, no 43, 1898, p. 616.

40. TsGIA, f. 1298, op. 1, d. 1375, ll. 1-18. Ivan Petrovich Rozenberg Ego Vysokoprevoskhoditel'stvu gospodinu ministru VD, February 6, 1906 (l. 1); Ob"iavlenie Glavnago Vrachebnago Inspektora, February 1906 (l. 2); Handwritten letter of Rozenberg to MVD, February 13, 1909 (l. 5); Letter of Pom. Glav. Vracheb. Inspek. to Pskov. Gubernatoru (l. 7); letter from Pskov. Gubernatora po gubernsk. pravleniiu, vracheb. otdeleniia, March 1909 (1. 8); Report of Med. otdelenie, Pskov. gub. pravlen. on population statistics (l. 9); Sovet Meditsinskii, Kantseliariia, April 1909 (l. 11); Letter, Pskov. gub. to Glav. Vracheb. Inspekt., July, 1909 (l. 14); Vypiski iz zhurnala Med. Soveta, September 1, 1909 (l. 17); Upravlenie Glavnago Med. Inspektora, 2nd deloproizvodstvo to Pskov. gubernatoru, September 1909, and Pskov. Gub. and Uprav. Glav. Vracheb. Inspek. to Rozenberg (l. 18).

41. TsGIA, f. 1298, op. 1, d. 1883: Copy, zhurnal Moskov. vrachebnago upravleniia, May 1912 (l. 1); Uprav. Glav. Med. Inspek., Oct. 20, 1912 (l. 4).

42. TsGIA, f. 1298, op. 1, d. 1244, ll. 15 and ob., 16 and ob.

43. Marsden, "Pharmacy in Russia," *The Pharmaceutical Era*, p. 197.

44. TsGIA, f. 1298, op. 1, d. 1420, l. l. 10-11.

45. *Loc. cit.*, l. l. 13, 14-18, 20, 21.

46. TsGIA, f. 1298, op. 1, d. 1275, l. 20.

47. TsGIA, f. 1298, op. 1, d. 1275, ll. 20, 20 ob, 22, 22 ob.

48. The concept of "drug stores" also obtained in Germany in the nineteenth century; as in Russia they became more numerous than pharmacies. Sonnedecker, *History of Pharmacy*, pp. 91-92.

49. "Ukaz Pravitel'stvuiushchago Senata," *F. V.*, vol. 7, no. 41, 1904, pp. 645-647: The Senate ruled that complex, factory-made pharmaceuticals could be sold outside the pharmacy without a doctor's prescription if the pharmaceuticals in question were not forbidden by law. See chapter 4 of this work for more information on drug stores.

50. TsGIA. f. 1298, op. 1, d. 1284, ll. 1-5 Correspondence, 1905, Grodnenskii gubernator, po gubern. pravleniiu Ministru. VD (l. 1), Protokol Vracheb. otdelenie Grod. gubernsk. pravleniia (l. 2) Uprav. Glav. Med. Inspektora Grodnenskomu gubernatoru (l. 3); Grodnensk. gub., po gubernsk pravleniiu to Uprav. Glav. Med. Inspek. (l. 4); Kantseliariia Med. Sov; Vypiski iz zhurnala, January 1906 (l. 5).

See also TsGIA, f. 1298, op. 1, d. 1283, ll. 1-15: Grod. Gub to MVD, May 1905 (l. 1); Protokol vracheb. otdeleniia Grodnenskago gubernskago pravleniia (l. 2); handwritten letter of Upravlenie Glav. Vracheb. Inspektora, June 1905 (l. 3); Grod. Gubernatora, to Uprav. Glav. Vracheb. Inspek., November 1905, (l. 4); Sov. Med. Kants., January 1906 (l. 6); Protokol.

51. TsGIA, f. 1298, op. 1, d. 1283 : Grodnenskii gubernator, December 1907 (l. 11); Sov. Med. Kants., December 1908 (l. 15); Zhurnal vrachebnago otdeleniia (l.

16); Grodnenskii statisticheskii komitet, Kantseliariia, April 1908 (l. 19); Vypiska iz zhurnala, Med. Sov. Kants., May 1908 (l. 21).

52. TsGIA, f. 1298, op. 1, d. 1304, 11. inclusive.

53. *Polnoe Sobranie Zakonov Rossiiskoi Imperii. Sobranie vtoroe.* Tom XI, otdelenie 9494-9821 (St. Petersburg, 1837), article 9808, pp. 312-319.

54. I. Kal'ning, *Kratkaia farmatsiia dlia studentov-medikov i farmatsetov soglosno programme universitetskago kursa* (Moscow, 1899), pp. 3-100. *Sbornik zakonopolozhenii dlia farmatsevtov, soderzhatelei aptek i drogistov,* ed. by P. N. Bulatov (St. Petersburg, 1897) has been cited copiously in this chapter.

55. "Ob utverzhdenii novykh spisov iadovitykh i sil'nodeistvuiushchikh veshchestv," *F. Zh.*, vol. 20, no. 14, 1898, pp. 192-195. Prosper H. Marsden, "The Laws Relating to the Practice of Pharmacy in Russia," *The Pharmaceutical Journal,* vol. 20, January 28, 1905, p. 111.

56. "Ob utverzhdenii," ibid., no. 15, 1898, p. 206 and Marsden, "The Laws," p. 111.

57. "Ob utverzhdenii," ibid., pp. 207-208; Marsden, ibid.

58. "Ob utverzhdenii," *F. Zh.*, vol. 20, no. 16, 1898, p. 222; Marsden, ibid. Bulatov's figures, cited from the 1892 code of Laws match those of Marsden in 1905 . Bulatov, *Sbornik zakonopolozhenii,* pp. 318-325.

59. Prosper H. Marsden, "The Practice of Pharmacy in Russia," *American Druggist and Pharmaceutical Record,* 1905, p. 95.

60. Isaiah Ginzburg, "A Pharmacist in Tsarist Russia—A Reminiscence, 1892-1909," *Pharmacy in History,* vol. 27, no. 3, 1985, p. 145. Marsden noted that a white label (*signatura*) with border printed in green and bearing the grey picture of a building designated internal medicaments, a yellow label with border printed in orange designated external medicaments, a label for mixtures had a simple green border and the stamp of the responsible pharmacist in place of the grey building. Marsden, "The Practice," p. 95. The author has labels for Ol'ga and Anastasia Nikolaevna, the daughters of Nicholas II, in her possession.

61. Kal'ning, *Kratkaia farmatsiia*, pp. 6-7; Bulatov, *Sbornik zakonopolozhenii,* pp. 150, 321-326; Marsden, "The Practice of Pharmacy in Russia," p. 95.

62. For example, TsGIA, f. 1298, op. 1, d. 2680, reports of Kiev province for 1908. ll. 49-51 list medical and pharmaceutical personnel. ll. 51-60 include reports from pharmacies. TsGIA, f. 1298, op. 1, d. 2721, contains the reports for Olonets province for 1908. l. 33 lists medical and pharmacy personnel, ll. 33 ob and 34 provides information on pharmacies. TsGIA, f. 1298, op. 1, d. 2715 provides information for Novgorod province for 1908. Pharmacies are listed in ll. 42 and 42 ob., l. 44 lists hygienic laboratories. TsGIA, f. 1298, op. 1, d. 2799 contains reports for Iakutsk province in Siberia. ll. 30 lists medical and pharmaceutical personnel; l 30 ob. lists information on pharmacies. TsGIA, f. 1298, op. 1, d. 2704, ll. 54 ob-56 ob contains information on pharmacies in Minsk province for 1907.

63. For example, TsGIA, f. 1298, op. 1, d. 2090, ll. 228, 228 ob from Kerch-Eniseisk chief authorities for 1916 (during World War I) noted that 1,000 rubles of foreign medicines were ordered from Merck Darmstadt in previous years. Also, ibid., l. 382 for Kutais province and l. 417 for Mogilev province. (The Russian

Military Headquarters were here during World War I but the list in the 1916 book is from 1913—i.e., prewar.) Kutais province did not order medicines from abroad (l. 382).

64. For example, reports on purchases of medicines by "public institutions" (zemstvos, cities, and the Don army region of the southeast Ukraine), mainly for the year 1916, are contained in a huge book in the national archives in St. Petersburg: TsGIA, f. 1298, op. 1, d. 2090, Upravlenie Glavnago Vrachebnago Inspektora, 2-e D-vo: Svedeniia o godovoi potrebnosti v medikamentakh dlia voiskovykh, zemskikh i gorodskikh uchrezhdenii." Although this was wartime, reports came from the regular local medical authorities—the Oblastnoi vrachebnyi inspektor of the Don; the Minskii gubernator po gubernskomu pravleniiu, otdelenie vracheb.; the Kerch-Eniseisk gradonachal'stvo.

65. For example, Upravlenie Glavnago Vrachebnago Inspektora MVD: *Otchet o sostoianii narodnago zdraviia i organizatsii vrachebnoi pomoshchi v Rossii za 1905 god.* (St. Petersburg: Tipografiia Ministerstva Vnutrennikh Del, 1907).

66. Circular of the Med. Dept to the Gubern. Vracheb. Uprav., Aug. 7, 1856, and Svod. zak., tom XIII, Ust. Vrach., ed. 1892, cited in Bulatov, *Sbornik zakonopolozhenii,* p. 103.

67. "Programma (Protokol) ob osmotre aptek (Utv. Ministerstvom Vnutrennikh Del 25 sentiabria 1863 g," cited in Bulatov, *Sbornik zakonopolozhenii,* pp. 105–109. See also the actual handbook, *Programma (Protokol) ob osmotre aptek,* TsGIA, f. 1298, op. 1, d. 1319, ll. 14-21 (pp. 27-39 in the handbook).

The instructions touched upon personnel; official books (pharmacopoeias, lists of physicians, pharmacy statute, prescription books, etc.); general order, lighting, heating, cupboards, vessels, apparatus, and equipment of each room in the pharmacy, as well as the quality and preservation of all required categories of medical substances. There also were regulations about inspecting drug stores ("Akt osmotra magazinov drogistov," ibid., 21 ob-22), factories ("Akt osmotra v gigienicheskom otnoshenii fabrichnikh . . . zavedenii . . . ," ibid., 22 ob-23, and so forth.

68. "Apteki v Rossii," *F. Zh.*, vol. 1, no. 3, 1879, p. 90. That example was dated February 23; another dated May 20 stated that: "according to the decision of the Medical council and on the basis of art. 898 of the Statute on Punishments, the manager of a pharmacy, Provizor, and pharmacy student in this pharmacy, for mistaken dispensation of medicines, were subject—the first to reprimand (*vygovor*) and the latter to reproof (*zamechaniia*)." The article further noted that on June 23 and September 29 owners of two pharmacies, according to the decision of the Medical Council, were given severe reprimands for dispensing medicine by prescription of people, not having the right of medical practice and, finally, on December 10, according to decision of the Medical Council on the basis of the Statute on Punishments, article 884, a pharmacy owner received severe reprimand for violating the rules on preserving medicines, not observing cleanliness, incorrect notation in the prescription book, and failing to meet the deadline to correct the abuses.

69. TsGIA, f. 1298, op. 1, d. 1319, ll. 1–3.

70. Article 885 stipulated that poisonous materials in the pharmacy and materials room must be kept separately from other substances and under lock and key and nowhere had the local authorities stated that this rule had been violated.

71. Ibid., ll. 4–5.

72. TsGIA, f. 1298, op. 1, d. 1388, ll. 1, 4–6.

73. "V Odesse," *Farmatsevticheskii trud*, vol. 3, no. 21, 1909, p. 26.

74. TsGIA, f. 1298, op. 1, d. 1714, ll. 1 and 2.

75. TsGIA, f. 1298, op. 1, d. 1783. In this case an Assistant Pharmacist had dispensed the medicine during the absence of the Provizor manager of the pharmacy. However, the Warsaw medical administration blamed the owner rather than the manager, for, knowing the manager was ill, the owner had forced the Assistant Pharmacist to substitute.

76. TsGIA, f. 1298, op. 1, d. 1804, ll. 1, 2, and 4.

77. TsGIA, f. 1298, op. 1, d. 2095, ll. 7–8 and 8 ob.

78. TsGIA, f. 1298, op. 1, d. 2095, l. 8 ob. These were articles 173, 884, 885, 892, 1175 and 1176.

79. Ibid., ll. 9–10 and 10. ob.

80. TsGIA, fond 1297, op. 155, d. 177, ll. 1–3 and 3 ob.

81. D. A. Ruffman, "Russian Pharmacy," *Bulletin of Pharmacy*, 1906, p. 17.

82. Marsden, "The Practice of Pharmacy in Russia," pp. 95–96. Marsden further noted that the horn pans were deeper than those used in England.

83. H. M. Gordin, "Pharmacy in Russia," *Pharmaceutical Review*, November 1899, pp. 502–503.

84. Gordin, "Pharmacy in Russia," p. 503.

85. "Zhurnal Med. Soveta," *F. Zh.*, vol. 6, no. 8, 1884, p. 127.

86. TsGIA, f. 1298, op. 1, d. 2098, l. 9; 1. 36.

87. TsGIA, f. 1298, op. 1, d. 2098, l. 36.

88. Sonnedecker, *History of Pharmacy*, pp. 91.

89. Ginzburg, "A Pharmacist in Tsarist Russia," p. 145.

90. Anon., "Pharmacy in Russia," *The Druggists Circular and Chemical Gazette*, October, 1903 p. 203.

91. Prosper H. Marsden, "Pharmacy in Russia," *The Pharmaceutical Record*, February 16, 1905, p. 198.

92. Anon., "Aptekarskaia taksa," *F. Zh.*, vol. 13, no. 6, 1891, p. 94.

93. Bulatov, *Sbornik zakonopolozhenii*, pp. 156–161.

94. TsGIA, fond 1298, op. 1, d. 1376, ll. 10 and 10 ob.

95. The stamp fee varied from 75 kopeks to 1 ruble, 50 kopeks. Some provincial medical inspectors did not demand fees. Varshavskaia vrachebnaia uprava, Aug. 12, 1906, to the Upravlenie Glavnago Vrachebnago Inspektora, TsGIA, f. 1298, op. 1, d. 1376, l. 31. See also, TsGIA, f. 1298, op. 1, d. 1209, ll. 30–32, which seems to indicate a general requirement to pay the stamp tax for the *konduitnyi spisok*, or pharmacist's personal record book.

96. TsGIA, f. 1298, op. 1, d. 1209, ll. 46–48.

97. For example, in 1879 the Samara provincial administration rejected the

request of local Provizor Ivan Iakovlev Rekk to open wholesale and retail trade in pharmaceutical wares and substances. The determined Provizor again requested permission of the medical department of the provincial administration. TsGIA, f. 1297, op. 155, d. 219, l. 2.

98. Bulatov, *Sbornik zakonopolozhenii*, pp. 180-184. The list took up over four pages of this handbook.

99. For example, F-ov, "O patentovykh sredstvakh," *Farmatsevticheskii Vestnik* [hereafter cited *F. V.*], vol. 3, no. 28, 1899, pp. 518-520; "Ofitsial'nyia soobshcheniia: Pravila dlia propuska zagranichenykh lekarstv (Utverzhdeneny, za ministra vnutrennikh del, tovarishchem ministra, 31 iulia, 1899 goda), ibid., no. 40, pp. 729-730; "Ofitsial'nyia soobshcheniia: Tsirkuliar meditsinskago departamenta, 27 avgusta 1899 g. No. 1331, gg. gubernatoram," ibid., no. 41, pp. 745-746. See also *Farmatsevticheskii zhurnal*, 1898 through 1916.

100. "Khronika: Konfiskatsiia preparatov zheleza," *F. Zh.*, vol. 50., no. 17, 1911, p. 204.

101. Some of these did slip past the Medical Council. In 1911 a patent medicine was being sold by the Medico-pharmaceutical Association, or *Tovarishchstvo*, on Artillery Street that claimed to cure sexual weakness. "Neotlozhnyia zadachi," *F. Zh.*, vol. 50, no. 17, 1911, p. 193.

102. Local pharmacists inundated the central medical administration as well as their local medical authorities for information. In 1906 the following were made.

> 1. A Provizor's wife in Tambov province inquired as to whether a private, village pharmacy could be sold to a nonpharmacist whose son was a Provizor, (TsGIA, f. 1298, op. 1, d. 1376, l. 1.) The medical inspector replied that, on the basis of articles 571, 572, 576 *ownership* of a village pharmacy could be transferred, without special permission, whether the new owner was a pharmacist or not. However, the governor had to be notified of change in *management* of a pharmacy, for management of a village pharmacy required a competent person (ibid., l. 2 and 2 ob.).
>
> 2. The military medical inspector of the administration of the Military District of Turkestan requested clarification as to whether a village pharmacy was required to have a special book to note the dispensing of nitric acid and other poisonous substances to artists—allowed without prescription on the basis of article 667 of the Medical Statute—or whether the pharmacy could use the book for recording the dispensing of poisons in general (ibid., l. 29).
>
> 3. The Medical Inspector in Kherson queried as to whether an Assistant Pharmacist, recently freed from prison, could manage the pharmacy that he owned (ibid., ll. 17, 18, 20).
>
> 4. The medical inspector of the Don army inquired as to whether pharmacy owners could be punished for sending tardy information on their staff. See Ispol'niaiushchii iuriskonsul'tskiia obiazannosti po ministerstvu vnutrennikh del Min. Gosudaru Vasiliiu Konstantinovichu Anrepu, March 1906, about the Chief Military Medical Administration opinion regarding

the question of late information from the regional medical inspector of the Don army. TsGIA, f. 1298, op. 1, d. 1376, ll. 10, 11.

The more efficient governor of Kostroma province, on the other hand, requested the Medical Council in 1905 to waive registering job changes for staff pharmacists except when they occurred outside the province and the Medical Council agreed. MVD: Sovet Med. Kants.: Vypiska iz zhurnala. Aug. 24, 1906. TsGIA, f. 1298, op. 1, d. 1209, l. 15.

Sometimes clarification of the rules led to discovery of greater abuses. In 1905, inquiry involving the medical inspector of Poltava province as to whether a certain pharmacy student could be admitted to a pharmacy owned by his mother and managed by his father revealed that the manager of the pharmacy, the student's father, was an Assistant Pharmacist and not a Provizor, required by the law for a normal pharmacy. The Medical Council thus threatened to close the pharmacy. (TsGIA, fond. 1298, op. 1, d. 1244, l. 7.) The hapless Assistant Pharmacist pleaded that he be permitted to run the pharmacy until turnover increased, allowing him to afford a Provizor, or until his son received the title of Provizor—a period of at least eight years. Uncharacteristically, the Medical Council approved his request. Ibid., l. 60, l. 64.

103. See, for example, "Pered S"ezdom," *F. Zh.*, vol. 52, no. 14, 1913, p. 154.

104. For Denmark see "Aptechnoe delo za granitsei za 1912 g.," *F. Zh.*, vol. 52, no. 12, 1913, p. 129.

105. "Aptechnoe delo za granitsei za 1912 g.," *F. Zh.*, vol. 52, no. 12, 1913, p. 129.

Chapter 2

1. "Programma ispytaniia . . . na stepen' aptekarskago pomoshchnika," and "Programma . . . na stepen' provizora i magistra farmatsii," *Ispytaniia na zvaniia i stepeni lekaria, zubnago vracha, povival'noi babki, provizora, aptekarskago pomoshchnika i aptekarskago uchenika.* Sostavil (ed.) N. Malinovskii (St. Petersburg, 1907), pp. 265-293.

2. Glenn Sonnedecker, *History of Pharmacy* (Philadelphia: J. B. Lippincott Company, 1963), pp. 71-72, 82-83.

3. V. O. Podvysotskii, *Farmakologiia veshchestv organicheskoi khimii, rastitel'nykh i zhivotnykh. Po 3-mu izdan. lektsii farmakologii, byvsh. Prof. Kievsk. Univers. Dybkovskago* (Kiev, 1889), pp. i-iii, 6. Professor Dybkovskii lectured on pharmacology in Kiev University in the 1880s; Podvysotskii was a professor at Kazan University and a former assistant in the Pharmaceutical Institute at Dorpat University.

4. George Edward Trease, *Pharmacy in History* (London, 1964), pp. 187-191.

5. P. M. Earles, "The Pharmacy Schools of the Nineteenth Century," *The Evolution of Pharmacy in History*, ed., F. N. L. Poynter (London, 1965), pp. 79-94.

6. The University of Michigan Pharmacy School, organized in 1867, was fol-

lowed by the University of Wisconsin Pharmacy School, established in 1883 and revamped in 1890. Sonnedecker, *History of Pharmacy,* pp. 232–235, 236–238. However, in New York state a supreme court judge awarded Mrs. Anna B. Hummel a pharmacist's diploma because she had worked with her husband, a registered pharmacist, for five years before 1884. "Mrs Anna B. Hummel, Pharmacist," *The New York Times,* June 22, 1896, p. 3, col. 3. In 1912 most states required only grammar school education, two to four years' experience, an examination, and registration with the state pharmaceutical board. Some states permitted pharmacy schools to substitute for practical experience. In any case, pharmacy school was an option. Henry L. Taylor, "Synopsis of the Pharmacy Practice Acts of the United States," *The Pharmaceutical Era,* vol. 45, January 1912, pp. 21–23.

7. "Iz deiatel'nosti S. Peterburgskago Farmatsevticheskago Obshchestva. Protokol sentiabr'skago zasedaniia," *Farmatsevticheskii zhurnal* [hereafter cited *F. Zh.*], vol. 49, no. 41, 1910, p. 438, and A. Ginzberg, "O lekarstvennoi pomoshchi v Anglii i Severo-Amerikanskikh S. Shtatakh," ibid., vol. 50, no. 20, 1911, pp. 230–232. Ginzberg informed the St. Petersburg Pharmacy Society that "pharmacy education was unified for England, Scotland, and Wales under the aegis of the Pharmacy Society of Great Britain and since 1875 for Ireland. The pharmacy was the first school for pharmacists"; they usually worked in the pharmacy three years; they received no pay although they were allotted room and board; on the contrary, British apprentices usually paid the pharmacist under whom they trained "up to the equivalent of 1000 rubles for the entire time." Pharmacists also could enroll in the school of the Pharmaceutical Society in London or Edinburgh as auditors for a year-long course or could study in a private school "of which there were many in various cities." The Pharmaceutical Society School cost the equivalent of 330 rubles; exams were given by the Society in London or Edinburgh. There were two types of exams and titles—"a minor exam" giving the title "Chemist and Druggist" and a "major" examination giving the title "Pharmaceutical Chemist." The examinations cost the equivalent of 100 rubles for the minor and 30 rubles for the major. Ginzberg enthused about the Pharmaceutical Society museum, library, and school with large auditoria, but claimed the "examination program requirements are not high and there are no systematic courses." (ibid., pp. 230–232). Ginzberg also criticized the lack of norms for English pharmacies—England being the "classic country of freedom . . . there is absence of norms and government control" (ibid., p. 230). He presented very negative pictures of London pharmacies—most were basically emporia—and concluded that with "incomplete education . . . the English pharmacy . . . stands much lower than the majority of other European countries" (ibid., pp. 231, 232).

8. A. S. Ginzberg, "Ocherk razvitiia nauchnoi farmatsii v Rossii za 200-letnii period," *Farmatsevticheskii vestnik* [hereafter cited *F.V.*] vol. 5, no. 17, 1902, p. 198, and V. M. Salo, "Aptechnoe delo v Rossii v XVI–XVII vekakh," pp. 21–22, MS in author's possession.

9. Ginzberg, *loc cit.*, and P. M. Luk'ianov, *Istoriia khimicheskikh promyslov i khimicheskoi promyshlennosti Rossii do kontsa XIX veka* (Moscow-Leningrad, 1948), pp. 413–415, 449, 459. See also V. M. Salo, "Ustroistvo i oborudovanie

aptek pervoi poloviny XIX veka," *Farmatsiia*, vol. 23, no. 6, 1974, pp. 45-47.

Alexander Petrovich Neliubin, for example, began his pharmacology career apprenticing in a pharmacy in northern Viatka province in 1798. V. M. Salo, "Vydaiushchiisia deiatel' otechestvennoi farmatsii A. P. Neliubin (k 130-letiiu so dnia smerti)," *Farmatsiia*, vol. 37, no. 2, 1989, p. 73.

10. Ginzberg, "Ocherk razvitiia nauchnoi farmatsii v Rossii za 200-letnii period," no. 16, 1902, p. 186.

11. Ginzberg, "Ocherk razvitiia," *F. V.*, vol. 5, no. 18, 1902, pp. 209-211. More details are given in Mary Schaeffer Conroy, "Pharmacy in Pre-Soviet Russia," *Pharmacy in History*, vol. 27, no. 3, 1985, p. 122.

12. Professor Doctor C. Claus, "History of Pharmacy in Russia," *American Journal of Pharmacy*, vol. 31, 1859, p. 167.

13. Ginzberg, "Ocherk razvitiia," *F. V.*, vol. 5, no. 16, 1902, p. 187. The original charter established three faculties, medicine, law, and philosophy.

14. V. G. Dragurov, A. A. Miazdrikova, "Stanovlenie farmakologii v Moskovskom universitete," *Farmakologiia i Toksikologiia*, vol. 44, no. 6, 1981, pp. 733-734.

15. Alexander Semenovich Ginzberg, privatdocent in the Military Medical Academy in St. Petersburg in 1899 and pharmacy education guru in both late imperial and early Soviet Russia believed that pharmaceutical as well as medical education developed slowly for the first thirty-six years because Moscow University was not entitled to give medical degrees; this was the prerogative of the Medical College. Ginzberg, "Ocherk razvitiia," *F. V.*, vol. 5, no. 17, 1902, p. 197.

16. Claus, "History of Pharmacy in Russia," p. 167.

Neliubin passed his examination for Assistant Pharmacist at Moscow University in 1804. He then took coursework at the university, sitting for his Provizor examination in 1806. Salo, "Vydaiushchiisia deiatel' otechestvennoi farmatsii A. P. Neliubin," p. 74.

17. Claus, "History of Pharmacy in Russia," p. 167. Professor Claus taught at the University of Dorpat in the 1850s.

18. Dragurov and Miazdrikova, "Stanovlenie farmakologii," p. 734.

19. "Aptekar' (Apothecarius, Confectionarius, Medicamentarius, Pharmocopola)," *Entsiklopedicheskii leksikon*, vol. 2 (St. Petersburg, 1835), p. 441. Peter the Great had organized the Table of Ranks; there were fourteen civilian ranks. See also Andrei Mikhalovich Sidorkov, "Issledovanie organizatsionno-metodicheskikh printsipov razvitia farmatsevticheskogo uchenogo dela v SSSR," Unpublished Doctoral Dissertation (Moscow, 1973), pp. 10-12, located in the Tsentral'naia Gosudarstvennaia Nauchnaia Meditsinskaia Biblioteka, Moscow.

20. P. A. C., "Organization of Medicine and Pharmacy in Russia," *American Journal of Pharmacy*, vol. 12, 1840, p. 343.

21. Claus, "History of Pharmacy in Russia," p. 168.

22. P. A. C., "Organization of Medicine and Pharmacy in Russia," pp. 344-345.

23. P. A. C., "Organization of Medicine and Pharmacy in Russia," p. 345.

24. P. A. C., "Organization of Medicine and Pharmacy in Russia," p. 345.

25. Povskii's journal was entitled *Vestnik estestvennykh nauk i meditsiny.* His

texts were *Nachertaniia obshchei farmakologii* (Moscow, 1835), *Pamiatnaia knizhka dlia zanimaiushchikhsia farmakologiei i retsepturoi* (Moscow, 1837), and *Nachertaniia farmatsii* (Moscow, 1838).

26. Lebedev's text was entitled *Prakticheskaia farmakologiia.*

27. His work on this subject was entitled *Fiziologicheskii vzgliad na upotreblenie efirov, khloroforma i benzina kak pritupliaiushchikh nervnuiu deiatel'nost'.* Information on Shchegolev, Povskii, D"iadkovskii, Lebedev, Filomatskii in Dagurov and Miazdrikova, "Stanovlenie farmakologii," pp. 735-736.

28. Sidorkov, "Issledovanie," pp. 12-13.

29. Ginzberg, "Ocherk razvitiia," *F. V.*, vol. 5, no. 17, 1902, p. 198.

30. Sidorkov, "Issledovanie," pp. 10-11.

31. Alexander Ginzberg, "Ocherk razvitiia," *F. V.*, vol. 5, no. 18, 1902, p. 210.

32. Claus, "History of Pharmacy in Russia," p. 168.

33. *Soviet Estonia, Land, People, Culture,* ed., L Valt (Tallinn, 1980), p. 172.

34. Ivan Sofronovich Tkeshelashvili, *Materialy dlia istorii farmatsii v Rossii, biograficheskii slovar' farmatsevtov, poluchivshikh stepen' magistra farmatsii . . . s 1845-1901 god* (Moscow, 1901), p. 6. Warsaw, Khar'kov, Kazan, and Kiev awarded a few degrees. The University of Odessa had no medical faculty in 1901 and Tomsk had been open only a short time.

35. P. A. C., "Organization of Medicine and Pharmacy in Russia," pp. 343-344.

36. Claus, "History of Pharmacy in Russia," p. 168.

37. Strides in higher Russian pharmacy education and pharmacy research paralleled those in mathematics and other branches of science in which Russia excelled. See, for example, Alexander Vucinich, *Science in Russian Culture: A History to 1860* (Stanford: Stanford University Press, 1963).

38. Female students entering the profession in 1888 had a complete secondary education, as chapter 7 relates.

39. *Ispytaniia na zvaniia i stepeni lekaria, zubnago vracha, povival'noi babki, provizora, aptekarskago pomoshchnika i aptekarskago uchenika,* sostavil (ed.) N. Malinovskii, pp. 221 (re: real school), pp. 226-229. On page 227 it was argued that three courses of the *progimnaziia* were allowable whereas the only full four courses of the *gimnaziia* were admissable because the programs in the two types of schools were different.

40. Ibid, p. 221, the term of initial apprenticeship was shortened from three to two years for those finishing the entire course of the real school.

41. For more on *gimnaziia* and real schools, see Patrick L. Alston, *Education and the State in Tsarist Russia* (Stanford: Stanford University Press, 1969), pp. 95-96 and *passim.*

42. "Otkrytaia korrespondentsiia," *F. Zh.*, vol. 40 (23), no. 3, 1901, p. 60; also *Ispytaniia*, pp. 232-233.

43. *Ispytaniia,* p. 233. Apparently, the church schools did not teach a general course of Russian history either (ibid.), but this was not vital for a pharmacist.

44. "Raznyia izvestiia," *F. Zh.*, vol. 23, no. 4, 1901, p. 80.

45. *Ispytaniia*, p. 233.

46. Anon., "Pharmacy in Russia," *The Druggists Circular and Chemical Gazette*, October 1903, p. 202.

47. Upravlenie Glavnago Vrachebnago Inspektora, 2oe deloproizvodstvo, 29 June, 1907 Vrachebnym upravleniem, Tsentral'nyi Gosudarstvennyi Istoricheskii Arkhiv, St. Petersburg [hereafter cited TsGIA], fond 1298, opis' 1, delo 1244, list 4 [hereafter cited "f.," "op.," "d.," "l.," or "ll.," plural].

48. Three assistant pharmacists supervised the students, who were divided into two groups of eight. The first group was designated "staff" and received salaries; the other group of eight did not receive salaries but waited for staff places to open. The latter served as subordinates to the senior students. The senior students, in turn, were supervised by on-duty Assistant Pharmacists and occupied in the pharmacy laboratory controlled by Provizor-managers. The students wrote outpatient prescriptions and labels for prescriptions. Seven were occupied with preparation of medicine, dispensed exclusively by Assistant Pharmacists and Provizors. TsGIA, f. 1298, op. 1, d. 1244, l. 94.

49. Ginzberg, "Ocherk razvitiia," *F. V.*, vol. 5, no. 18, 1902, p. 210.

50. "K voprosu o prepodavanii uchenikam," *F. Zh.*, vol. 1, no. 22, 1879, p. 696.

51. "Obshchee sobranie chlenov S. Peterburgskago farmatsevticheskago obshchestva," *Farmatsevticheskii trud* [hereafter cited *F. T.*], vol. 1, no. 30, 1907, p. 405.

52. In 1907, the St. Petersburg Pharmacy Society discussed increasing class days from two to three days and noted that students would have to pay an *additional* (italics, mine) 10 to 15 rubles at the beginning of the school year. "Obshchee sobranie chlenov S. Peterburgskago farmatsevticheskago obshchestva," *F. T.*, vol. 1, no. 30, pp. 404-405.

53. "K voprosu o prepodavanii uchenikam," *F. Zh.*, vol. 1, no. 22, 1879, pp. 696-700.

54. "Soslovnyia dela: otchet Vysochaishe utverzhdennago S. Peterburgskago farm. obshchestva za 1883," *F. Zh.*, vol. 6, no. 11, 1884, p. 199.

55. In 1901 one session began May 1. "Ot prepodavatelia farmatsevticheskoi shkoly pri Vys. utv. S. Peterburgskom Farmatsevticheskom Obshchestve," *F. Zh.*, vol. 40 (23), no. 17, 1901, p. 350.

56. "Khronika," *F. V.*, vol. 7, no. 32, 1904, p. 508.

57. Pharmacy students and their pharmacist mentors (principals) were urged to follow the curriculum of the St. Petersburg school and use its texts. *Farmatsevticheskii zhurnal* published the curriculum. Especially recommended were Dr. Shul'ts's *Kratkaia latinskaia gramatika*, Elsner's *Rukovodstva k podgotovke dlia ispytaniia na aptekarskago pomoshchnika v Germanii* (this provided information on pharmacognosy, botany, pharmaceutical chemistry), and Dr. Trapp's *Retseptu*. "K voprosu o prepodavanii uchenikam," *F. Zh.*, vol. 1, no. 22, 1879, pp. 696-700.

58. "Reforma vyshago obrazovaniia farmatsevtov," *Farmatsevt*, vol. 14, no. 9, 1906, pp. 246-248.

59. "K eksamenam," *F. T.*, vol. 1, no. 8, 1907, p. 117.

60. "Khronika: Kovno," *F. T.*, vol. 3, no. 3, 1909, p. 42.

61. *Ispytaniia*, p. 221.

62. Ministry of Public Enlightenment Circular of 1886, cited in *Ispytaniia*, p. 230.

63. Isaiah Ginzburg, "A Pharmacist in Tsarist Russia—A Reminiscence, 1892–1909," *Pharmacy in History*, vol. 27, no. 3, 1985, p. 147.

64. "Novye poriadki ispytanii v Kazanskom universitete aptekarskikh uchenikov na zvanie aptekarskago pomoshchnika," *Farmatsevt*, vol. 10, no. 48, 1902, pp. 1583–1584.

65. The eight universities included Dorpat, Moscow, Kazan, Khar'kov, Kiev, Tomsk, and Odessa. St. Petersburg did not have a medical faculty, but, apparently, students could also take courses in the Physico-Mathematical Faculty.

66. The Provizor examination now included pharmacy, pharmacognosy, general chemistry, inorganic and organic chemistry, pharmaceutical and analytical chemistry—with laboratory work, physics, general and pharmaceutical botany—with field work, zoology, mineralogy, research on poisons, familiarity with microscope and spectroscope, algebra, and history of pharmacy. "Farmatsevticheskoe obrazovanie," *F. Zh.*, vol. 1, no. 1, 1879, pp. 7–8.

67. Two such texts were F. A. Ioganson's *Repetitorium po farmakologii. Sostavleno po noveishim istochnikam* (Kiev, 1889, 445 + 32 pp.) and I. Kal'ning's *Kratkaia farmatsiia dlia studentov-medikov i farmatsevtov soglasno programme universitetskago kursa* (Moscow, 1899, 322 pp.). The latter was enlivened by fifty-six drawings of apparatus. I. I. Kal'ning was a member of the radical Russian Pharmacy Society and involved with reform of pharmaceutical education in the early twentieth century. Radical pharmacists are described more fully in chapters 13 and 14 of this work.

Two other texts were P. O. Podvysotskii's *Farmakologiia veshchestv organicheskoi khimii, rastitel'nykh i zhivotnykh. Po 3-mu izdan. Lektskii farmakologii, byvsh. Prof. Kievsk. Univers. Dybkovskago, s pribavleniiami po sovremennomu sostoianiiu farmakologii do 1888 goda* (Kiev, 1889), the third edition of which was a tome of over 400 pages, and M. Bogoliubov's *Prakticheskaia farmakologiia po retseptam sovremennykh klinitsistov dlia Vrachei i Studentov* (Moscow, 1889). Two handbooks were Andrei Chirikov's *Posobie prakticheskikh zaniatiiakh po obshchei farmatsii* (Khar'kov, 1887). [Chirikov was a privatdocent at Khar'kov University] and K. Z. Iatsuta's review, *Povtoritel'nyi kurs (Conspekt) po* Farmatsii i Farmakognozii (St. Petersburg, 1889).

68. "Voprosy i otvety," *F. V.*, vol. 7, no. 33, 1904, p. 525.

69. These were pharmacy, pharmacognosy, pharmacology, organic chemistry, physics, botany, zoology, mineralogy, forensic medicine, and toxicology. K. Butkevich, "Mnenie po povodu predstoiashchago farmatsevticheskago s"ezda," *F. Zh.*, vol. 20, no. 45, 1898, p. 640, and P. V. "Koe-chto ob obrazovanii, " *F. V.*, vol. 2, no. 11, 1898, p. 172.

70. Ginzberg, "Ocherk razvitiia," *F. V.*, vol. 5, no. 18, 1902, pp. 209–210; also "Soslovnyia dela: Farmatsevticheskoe obrazovanie," *F. Zh.*, vol. 1, no. 2, 1879, p.

57; "Obozrenie pravitel'stvennykh mer po delam farmatsevticheskago sosloviia: Slushanie lektsii farmatsevtami v mediko-khirugicheskoi akademii," ibid., no. 5, 1879, p. 149.

71. "Obozrenie pravitel'stvennykh mer," *F. Zh.*, vol. 1, no. 5, 1879, pp. 149-152.

72. Sidorkov, "Issledovanie," pp. 17-18, 22.

73. Sidorkov, "Issledovanie," p. 16.

74. Such, for example, was the case with Karl Gustavovich Gil'bikh. Tkeshelashvili, *Materialy*, p. 23.

75. "Nauchnyi otdel–N. M. Mart'ianov," *Farmatsevt*, vol. 10, no. 8, 1902, pp. 225-228.

76. "Nauchnyi otdel–Mart'ianov," *Farmatsevt*, vol. 10, no. 9, 1902, pp. 256-260, and ibid., no. 10, pp. 293-295.

77. On the Andronovo Bronze Age culture of Minusinsk see Gregoire Frumkin, *Archaeology in Soviet Central Asia* (Leiden/Koln: E. J. Brill, 1970), pp. 14-15; Mikhail P. Griazov, *Ancient Civilization of Southern Siberia* (Cowels Book Co., 1969), *passim*.

Waldemar (Vladimir Il'yich) Jochelson's *Peoples of Asiatic Russia* (American Museum of Natural History, 1928) includes bibliography, on pages 255-259, on Minusinsk and the Yenisei region, which Mart'ianov might have consulted: Gorostchenko, K. I. *Skulls of the Kurgans in the Minusinsk District (Descriptions of the Collections of the Minusinsk Museum), part 2* (Minusinsk, 1900) [in Russian] (p. 253); Krivoshapkin, P. *The Yenisseisk District* (St. Petersburg, 1863) (p. 254); Savenkov, I. T. *The Stone Age in the Minusinsk Country* (Moscow, 1876) [in Russian] (p. 257).

78. "Nauchnyi otdel–Mart'ianov," *Farmatsevt*, vol. 10, no. 9, 1902, pp. 259-260.

79. "Nauchnyi otdel," *Farmatsevt*, vol. 10, no. 10, 1902, pp. 293-294.

80. "Bytovoi otdel," *F.V.*, vol. 7, no. 30, 1904, p. 473 and no. 48, p. 955.

81. Tkeshelashvili, *Materialy*, p. 6.

82. D. I. Toropov, "Dvizhenie i rost aptechnago dela v Imperii za poslednee desiatiletie (1901-1910 g.g.), *Vestnik obshchestvennoi gigieny, sudebnoi i prakticheskoi meditsiny*, no. 9, 1911, p. 1298.

83. The preliminary examination required the following: in the science of pharmacognosy–knowledge of the structure of seventy-three crude drugs (or simples); under the rubric, pharmacy–familiarity with fifty compounds, decoctions and infusions; in inorganic chemistry–knowledge of thirty-five substances; in organic chemistry–knowledge of thirty-one substances; knowledge of physics (thirty-five items required), botany, zoology (sixteen items), mineralogy (twenty items), forensic medicine, pharmacology (the action of drugs), and toxicology. Tkeshelashvili, *Materialy*, pp. 98-114.

84. Tkeshelashvili, *Materialy*, pp. 22-23.

85. "K voprosu o prepodavanii uchenikam," *F. Zh.*, vol. 1, no. 22, 1879, pp. 696-700.

86. Pharmacists who recommended retaining the system looked to Austrian as

well as Russian experience. "Farmatsevticheskoe obrazovanie," *F. Zh.*, vol. 1, no. 1, 1879, pp. 4-7.

87. They buttressed their resolution with a host of reasons: The Third International Pharmacy Congress had recommended pharmacy institutes in countries where pharmacy, pharmacognosy, pharmaceutical chemistry, and botany were not taught by pharmacists, as in Germany; in Russia pharmacists taught these subjects at the universities of Dorpat, Warsaw, and Kiev, and the Medical-Surgical Academy in St. Petersburg; the Fourth International Congress in St. Petersburg in 1874 had also expressed the view that it was not possible for pharmacists to receive a higher education except at a university. Objections to university courses for pharmacists had stemmed from lack of pharmacist-professors and lack of preparedness on the part of Assistant Pharmacists; each year there were more Masters of Pharmacy to teach the courses and the universities of Dorpat, Kiev, and Warsaw certified that Assistant Pharmacists were prepared to audit university lectures. The Moscow Society in particular, noted that it might be advisable for Assistant Pharmacists to take university courses immediately upon finishing their examination for Provizor, as they were better prepared at that time than after the three years additional apprenticeship then required. But Moscow pharmacists did not endorse special pharmacy institutes because they believed education confined to an institute would forfeit the practical training received during the apprenticeship period. They suggested, however, that when the corporation was stronger pharmacy students should be required to finish the entire *gimnaziia* course. "Soslovnyia dela: Farmatsevticheskoe obrazovanie," *F. Zh.*, vol. 1, no. 2, 1879, pp. 53–58.

88. At the International Medical Congress in Moscow in 1898 a professor from Grenoble stressed that students straight from the lycee who practiced pharmacy as *praktikanty* were not well-prepared; they needed advanced scientific subjects. The professor recommended pharmacists spend six years at university. "K voprosu o shkol'nom i prakticheskom obrazovanii farmatsevtov," *F. V.*, vol. 2, no. 11, 1898, pp. 165–167. In Austria reformers advocated for the modern pharmacist six years of *gimnaziia*, two years practical experience in a pharmacy, a one-year course in a special pharmacy school, six half-year courses at the university, and five years' practice before qualifying as a pharmacist. "Reformy farmatsevticheskago obrazovaniia," *F. Zh.*, vol. 20, no. 37, 1898, p. 528. In Holland, at this time, a pharmacist had to have a school-leaving certificate, basic knowledge of physics, chemistry, and Latin, and theoretical and practical knowledge of prescriptions. There were various schools to assist preparation of the first examination, which could not be taken until age eighteen. The examination for the title Provizor included much the same subjects as that for Provizor in Russia. Attendance at university was not mandatory, although candidates usually attended lectures from six to ten semesters. S. Levinson, "Aptechnoe delo za granitsei. III. Gollandiia," *F. V.*, vol. 2, no. 3, 1898, pp. 45–48.

89. For example, Provizor K. Butkevich advocated that potential pharmacists attend the real school in place of the *gimnaziia*. He believed that its six-year curriculum was superior to the full eight-year *gimnaziia* program for would-be pharmacists. The real school offered a total of thirty-one hours of mathematics com-

pared with twenty-nine hours in the eight-year *gimnaziia,* ten hours of physics versus the *gimnaziia*'s seven, nine hours of zoology and botany (none were offered in the *gimnaziia*), and thirty-two hours of German versus nineteen offered in the full *gimnaziia* curriculum. Latin, not available in the real school, could be taken at university level. Following real school, Butkevich proposed that the student pharmacist attend a special school, akin to feldsher schools, established by the government, to qualify for the Assistant Pharmacist title. The four-year curriculum at this school would parallel that of the feldsher school excluding bandaging and management of fractures and dislocations. (Curriculum of feldsher school, Conroy, "Pharmacy in Pre-Soviet Russia," p. 124.) He urged that the last two years of pharmacy school include a practicum in a well-stocked pharmacy. A commission under the chairmanship of the provincial medical inspector was to draw up the Assistant Pharmacist examination. This title as well as that of Provizor was to be upgraded. The Provizor degree was to be awarded the Assistant Pharmacist following four years of university study. The Provizor curriculum was to include anatomy, physiology, pathology, hygiene and sanitology, knowledge of mineral waters, disinfecting, history of pharmacy, general law, and first aid. During the last year there was to be practice at a university pharmacy. The upgraded title of Provizor was to be equal to that of *lekar'*, first medical degree. The degree Master of Pharmacy, in turn, was to be commensurate with that of Doctor of Medicine. Butkevich, "Mnenie po povodu," *F. Zh.*, vol. 20, no. 45, p. 641, and ibid., no. 46, pp. 654–655.

90. "Khimiko-bacteriologicheskie kursy pri institute doktora F. M. Bliumentalia," *F. T.*, vol. 1, no. 28, 1907, p. 385. Bliumental's Institute was located at 10 Malaia Lubianka, seemingly quite close to the offices of the Russian Pharmacy Society and *Farmatsevticheskii trud.*

91. "Storonnee soobshchenie," *F. T.*, vol. 1, no. 30, 1907, pp. 410–411.

92. A. I. Purve, "Farmatsevticheskii institut," *Farmatsevt*, vol. 10, no. 12, 1902, pp. 376–378.

93. A. Purve, "Ekzameny farmatsevtov v Amerike," *F. V.*, vol. 7, no. 10, 1904, pp. 153–156.

Chapter 3

1. Professor C. Claus, "History of Pharmacy in Russia," *American Journal of Pharmacy*, vol. 31, 1859, p. 169.

2. H. M. Gordin, "Pharmacy in Russia," *Pharmaceutical Review*, vol. 17, November 1899, pp. 503–504.

3. Gordin, "Pharmacy in Russia," p. 504. This layout was true of most pharmacies Gordin visited. He added that "In some stores [*sic*] there is a special taster or smeller whose not very enviable duty it is to taste, smell and otherwise examine every prescription before it leaves the pharmacy."

4. Gordin, "Pharmacy in Russia," pp. 504–505. British pharmacist Prosper Marsden added that the "room for storage of materials [must be] so situated that neither damp nor overheating will cause the preparations to deteriorate; [the] coc-

toria . . . and a laboratory . . . may be together . . . a dry cellar, an ice cellar, a drying room for medicinal herbs, and, finally, a suitable dry place for the storage of crude drugs." Prosper H. Marsden, "The Practice of Pharmacy in Russia," *American Druggist and Pharmaceutical Record,* 1905, p. 95.

5. Gordin, *loc. cit.*

6. *Opyt istoricheskago ocherka vozniknoveniia i razvitiia vsego aptekarskago dela v Rossii, a v chastnosti Staroi Nikol'skoi apteki, prinadlezhashchei nyne Tovarishchestvu "V. K. Ferrein"* (Moscow, 1911), pp. 2–4, 5–6, 7–9, 11–18, 21.

7. Ibid., pp. 13, 18, 19.

8. For example, see the description of Antonina Lesnevskaia's pharmacy in St. Petersburg in chapter 7 of this work. Additionally, the author has visited some prerevolutionary pharmacies remaining in Moscow and talked with V. M. Salo, a mine of information on pharmacies in that city.

9. Isaiah Ginzburg, "A Pharmacist in Tsarist Russia—A Reminiscence, 1892–1909," *Pharmacy in History,* vol. 27, no. 3, 1985, pp. 138–159. He estimated the population of the town at 5,000; however, the pharmacy appears to have been a normal pharmacy, for which towns of 7,000 were eligible, rather than a village pharmacy, since pharmacy students could not apprentice in other than normal pharmacies.

10. Ginzburg, ibid., p. 140.

11. Ibid., p. 140. Ginzburg included a charming sketch of the pharmacy, ibid., p. 141.

12. V. O. Podvysotskii, *Farmakologiia veshchestv organicheskoi khimii, rastitel'nykh i zhivotnykh. Po 3-mu izdan. Lektsii farmakologii byvsh. Prof. Kievsk. Univers. Dybkovskago, s pribavleniiami po sovremennomu sostoianiiu farmakologii do 1888 goda* (Kiev, 1889), pp. 21, 23, 26.

13. Podvysotskii, *Farmakologiia,* p. 80.

14. Podvysotskii, ibid., pp. 83, 84–85, 111–114.

15. Ibid., pp. 140–141, 38, 69.

16. Ibid., pp. 161, 169. See chapters 8 and 9 on the Russian pharmaceutical industry, in this work, for information on how Russia became self-sufficient in this product.

17. Ibid., pp. 28, 29, 50, 51, 54.

18. Ibid., pp. 130, 131–139.

19. Charles C. Mann and Mark L. Plummer, *The Aspirin Wars: Money, Medicine, and 100 Years of Rampant Competition* (New York: Alfred A. Knopf, 1991), pp. 21.

20. Podvysotskii, *Farmakologiia,* p. 56. Salicylic acid caused nausea and ringing in the ears.

21. Alas, quinine also had unpleasant side effects. On quinine use and malaria see Mary Schaeffer Conroy, "Malaria in Late Tsarist Russia," *Bulletin of the History of Medicine,* vol. 56, no. 1, 1982, pp. 41–55.

22. See chapter 8 on the Russian pharmaceutical industry in this work.

23. Podvysotskii, *Farmakologiia,* pp. 59, 70, 139.

24. I. Kal'ning, *Kratkaia farmatsiia dlia studentov-medikov i farmatsevtov soglasno programme universitetskago kursa* (Moscow, 1899), pp. 8–148. Russian pharmacies still prepare many medicines in-house today.

25. Gordin, "Pharmacy in Russia," p. 504. There were indications that technologically, small-town town Russian normal pharmacies were beginning to lag behind the typical French pharmacy. Four-fifths of French pharmacies were small establishments, with a manager and two or three assistants. But, by 1908 most French pharmacies had no laboratories; pharmacists mixed factory-prepared, frequently "patent" medicines (*specialialites*). See Glenn Sonnedecker, *History of Pharmacy* (Philadelphia: J. B. Lippincott Company, 1976), pp. 75–76.

26. Ginzburg, "A Pharmacist in Tsarist Russia—A Reminiscence," p. 142. For other traditional remedies used in prerevolutionary Russia see Paul M. Kourenoff, *Russian Folk Medicine*, trans., ed., arranged by George St. George (London, New York: W. H. Allen and Co., Ltd., 1970).

27. Ginzburg, "A Pharmacist in Tsarist Russia," p. 142. The pharmacy sold these items to local doctors as provisions for their clinics.

28. As an apprentice, Ginzburg made up "all the powders such as in two or five grains and Seidlitz powders" and filled up "all the empty pint bottles used up during the day. Ours were made of white china with black and gold decorative lettering." (Ginzburg, "A Pharmacist in Tsarist Russia—A Reminiscence, pp, 140–142.) The apprentice Ginzburg and the pharmacists were were assisted by a peasant helper, named "Big Dmitrii." "Big Dmitrii assigned to us as a helper, was a good-natured peasant about sixty years old, with a big beard. . . . Although he could neither read nor write he was an old hand in the pharmacy and had a knack and instinct for the work that was remarkable. Perhaps if he had had the opportunity early in life he would have made an excellent pharmacist. As it was, Big Dmitrii, as we called him, washed our mortars, bottles, funnels, and pill machines very carefully, and when they left his hands they were spotless. In the laboratory Dmitrii was king. It was his love. And without Dmitrii's assistance even we were helpless." Ginzburg, "A Pharmacist in Tsarist Russia," p. 140.

29. ". . . we were desparate when we got a hurry call for half a dozen big bags of oxygen to be rushed by messenger to a hospital or to a patient's home. As soon as the bag was empty it was rushed back to the pharmacy to be refilled. . . . Our pharmacy was the only one in the city and the countryside around it. . . ." Ginzburg, "A Pharmacist in Tsarist Russia," pp. 140–141, 142.

30. "On a wooden box, a four-legged stool was placed upside down, and into it was put a huge mortar and a pestle rested in a special hole in the ceiling." The peasant helper Dmitrii "then sat down alongside on another box and took hold of the enormous pestle . . . to rub the mercury with lanolin. . . . The pharmacist would come in several times a day, take a sample of it, and rub it between two cardboards to see if the mercury would be noticed." Likewise, distilled water "was manufactured in our laboratory in the winter, because snow was needed to cool the condensing pipes. We had a 'Latin Kitchen' as the laboratory in a pharmacy was called in Russia. There was a huge Russian stove. . . . On the stove was placed

a huge copper boiler, with a hood which had a long narrow spout. This spout formed a pipe that ran right through the wall of the laboratory to a cooler *outside* the building. This cooler contained spiral pipes, which ended up back inside the laboratory. . . . A tremendous amount of distilled water had to be manufactured, for it had to last throughout the warm months in making various drug products used in the pharmacy." Ginzburg, "A Pharmacist in Tsarist Russia," p. 141.

31. Gordin, "Pharmacy in Russia," pp. 502–503.

32. Anon., "Apteki v Rossii," *Farmatsevticheskii Zhurnal* [hereafter cited *F. Zh.*] vol. 1, no. 3, 1879, p. 86.

33. S. Lintser, "Aptekarskii vopros," *Farmatsevticheskii vestnik* [hereafter cited *F. V.*] vol. 2, no. 39, 1898, pp. 619-622. Three years later, in 1890, there were 214 more for a total of 2,230 pharmacies.

Only 44 more pharmacies were established in the next three years but in the succeeding seven 578 were established, giving a total of 3,452 pharmacies in 1900. Gr. Grudinskii, "Bytovoi otdel. Po povodu novago aptekarskago ustava," *F. V.* , vol. 7, no. 38, 1904, p. 599.

34. D. I. Toropov, "Dvizhenie i rost aptechnago dela v Imperii za poslednee desiatiletie (1901–1910 g.g.), *Vestnik obshchestvennoi gigieny, sudebnoi i prakticheskoi meditsiny,* 1911, p. 1278.

35. By 1904 there were 3,795 pharmacies. During the next year 122 more pharmacies were established (a gain of 3.26 percent). De-v, "Aptechnoe delo v Rossii po offitsial'nym statisticheskim dannym," *Russkii farmatsevt*, vol. 1, no. 1, 1908, p. 26.

36. Toropov, "Dvizhenie i rost," p. 1279.

37. Tsentral'nyi Gosudarstvennyi Istoricheskii Arkhiv, St. Petersburg [hereafter cited TsGIA] fond 1298, opis' 1, delo 1769, list 1. [hereafter abbreviated "f.," "op.," "d.," "l.," or "ll." in the plural].

38. Toropov, "Dvizhenie i rost," p. 1279. As described in chapter 1, normal or fully stocked pharmacies had some 800 essences; they required a Provizor or fully qualified manager. Village pharmacies had only some 280 essences; they could be managed by Assistant Pharmacists; homeopathic pharmacies followed the principles of Samuel Hahnemann; pharmacies in the *aptechnoe delo* were usually located in treasury-supported institutions. Public institutions, as well as individuals or private groups could own normal pharmacies.

39. "Aptechnoe delo za granitsei za 1912 g.," *F. Zh.*, vol. 52, no. 12, 1913, pp. 130.

40. "Aptechnoe delo, aptekaria i sluzhashchie vo Frantsii," *Farmatsevticheskii trud* [hereafter cited *F. T.*], vol. 1, no. 20, 1907, pp. 268–272.

Establishment of pharmacies was not limited either in France, Italy, or Switzerland among other countries on the continent. However, in 1913 it was claimed that France, Italy, and the canton of Zurich were considering moving from the right to establish pharmacies without prior government permission to the concession system. "Na temu dnia," *F. Zh.*, vol. 52, no. 11, 1913, p. 115.

41. "Za rubezhom," *F. T.*, vol. 3, no. 2, 1909, pp. 29-30. For additional information on pharmacy practice in Germany, see Sonnedecker, *History of Pharmacy*, p. 87.

Additionally, in Prussia pharmacists managed pharmaceutical affairs; there was a "Pharmacy Council" composed of four owners of pharmacies, four nonowners, and four respresentatives of the medical department of the Ministry of Interior. However, pharmacies did not increase as fast in Prussia as in Russia. By 1911 there were 3,562 normal pharmacies in that German state. This was only 300 more than in 1905. (In Russia, meanwhile, there were about 1,000 more pharmacies in 1911 as compared with 1905.) Of the Prussian pharmacies, 790 were "privileged," 1926 had "real" concessions, 846 "personal" concessions. There were 8,549 pharmacists including students in 1911. "Aptechnoe delo za granitsei za 1912 g.," *F. Zh.*, vol. 52, no. 12, 1913, p. 129.

Pharmacists also were involved in the new central sanitary council established in the German state of Saxony during 1912. *Loc. cit.*

Denmark also had a concession system. It retained the system in its new pharmacy statute. The statute envisioned other improvements, some of which existed in Russia. Branch pharmacies were to be transformed into normal pharmacies by 1920; all pharmacies were to be managed by examined pharmacists; a reciprocal-pension fund was established for staff pharmacists, their wives and children. *Loc. cit.*

42. Upravlenie Glavnago Vrachebnago Inspektora, *Otchet o sostoianii narodnago zdraviia i organizatsii vrachebnoi pomoshchi v Rossii za 1905 god* (St. Petersburg, 1907), pp. vii, 123–126.

The total population of the Russian empire in 1905 was approximately 144,600,000; that of European Russia was approximately 118,900,000.

The zemstvos, or locally elected councils with right of self-taxation, had been organized in the 1860s and 1870s. In the arena of public health their mandate was to counter epidemics and epizootics. However, they were popularly seen as having the responsibility to improve public health in general.

43. *Otchet o sostoianii narodnago zdraviia i organizatsii vrachebnoi pomoshchi v Rossii za 1905 god*, pp. 123–126, and "Aptechnoe delo v Rossii po offitsial'nym statisticheskim dannym," *Russkii farmatsevt*, vol. 1, nol. 1, 1908, p. 27.

It is interesting to compare the ratio of pharmacies to population in the Russian Empire with that in Germany. In all Germany in 1905, one pharmacy served 10,627 people. In Prussia 1 pharmacy served 11,515 inhabitants; in Bavaria, 8,971. "Za rubezhom," *F.T.*, vol. 3, no. 2, 1909, pp. 29–30.

44. See Samuel C. Ramer, "Traditional Healers and Peasant Culture in Russia, 1861–1917," *Peasant Economy, Culture, and Politics of European Russia, 1800–1921*, eds. Esther Kingston-Mann and Timothy Mixter (Princeton: Princeton University Press, 1991), pp. 207-232.

45. De-v, "Aptechnoe delo v Rossii po offitsial'nym statisticheskim dannym," *Russkii farmatsevt*, vol. 1, no. 1, 1908, p. 27.

46. G. A. Vinokurov, "Apteki Simbirskoi gubernii v XIX i nachale XX veka," *Farmatsiia*, no. 19, 1970, p. 52. Soviet historians, of course, were on the horns of a

dilemma. While they frequently displayed pride at advances in tsarist pharmacy, they nevertheless described dispensing during the tsarist era in bleak light.

47. "Korrespondentsii: Akhtyrka, Khar'kovskoi gubernii," *Zhizn' farmatsevta*, vol. 1, no. 3, 1909, pp. 14–15. The author did not rate the other two pharmacies as highly.

48. In 1901 pharmacists owned 69.9 percent of pharmacies, nonpharmacists owned 17.5 percent, pharmacists' wives and descendents owned 12.6 percent. Pharmacists owned fewer pharmacies in 1911 but the difference was partially offset by increased ownership on the part of their wives and children. In 1911, of 4,804 pharmacies, 68.5 percent or 3,291 were owned by pharmacists (Provizors owned 2,382, Assistant Pharmacists owned 857 and Masters of Pharmacy, 52). Another 13.3 percent were owned by pharmacists wives (213) or descendents (421). Toropov, "Dvizhenie i rost," pp. 1293, 1294.

Nineteen percent of pharmacies were owned by various nonpharmacists and institutions. "Public Institutions," that is zemstvos and cities, with publicly elected representatives and powers of self-taxation, owned 204 pharmacies; zemstvos owned 165, and cities only 39. Rural societies owned 10 pharmacies, various societies and institutions owned 42, private persons owned 567, and "others" owned 54. Toropov, "Dvizhenie i rost," p. 1294.

A review of the societies and individuals who owned pharmacies indicates significant public participation in health care in prerevolutionary Russia and a great deal of social mobility on the part of individual owners, as well. The Red Cross owned 13 pharmacies; medical societies, 7; charitable societies, 3; Evangelical Lutherans, 4; Jewish societies, 7; Jewish hospitals, 2; and other hospitals, 7. Clinics of universities, women's societies, nobles and merchants, and the old public health boards dating from the reign of Catherine the Great, each owned two pharmacies in 1911. Toropov, "Dvizhenie i rost," p 1296. Of the 567 "private" persons who owned pharmacies in 1911, the categories of 134 were unknown. The others came from all sections of the social spectrum. Doctors or their wives owned 72 pharmacies, male and female dentists owned 9, feldshers and midwives owned a tidy 35. Ownership of pharmacies by health professionals was not so surprising; nevertheless, the number of pharmacies owned by the paraprofessional feldshers was interesting, as were owners from other social categories. Nobles, male amd female, possessed 79 pharmacies; princes and princesses owned 5; counts, 7; landowners, only 2; merchants or their wives and children owned 53; *meshchanin* and *meshchanka*, "lower class urban dwellers," owned 117; peasants owned 10; soldiers, priests wives and widows, barons, "*kamer-iunkers*," and assorted others owned the rest. Toropov, "Dvizhenie i rost," p 1297.

49. See Robert N. North, *Transport in Western Siberia* (Vancouver: University of British Columbia Press, 1979) and James R. Gibson, *Feeding the Russian Fur Trade* (Madison: University of Wisconsin Press, 1969), and Gibson, *Imperial Russia in Frontier America* (New York: Oxford University Press, 1976) for accounts of Russian colonization in Siberia and Alaska.

For more on governors and their manifold activities see Richard G. Robbins, Jr., *The Tsar's Viceroys: Russian Provincial Governors in the Last Years of the*

Empire (Ithaca, New York: Cornell University Press, 1987). Robbins details governors' attempts to improve sanitation and public health in the late nineteenth, early twentieth centuries, pp. 170-171.

50. N. V. Il'kov, M. I. Zomova, "Pervaia apteka Tomskoi gubernii," *Farmatsiia*, vol. 25, no. 4 (July-August) 1976, pp. 86-87.

51. The manager was Provizor Karl Rummel. "Sessiia Permskago gubernskago zemstva," *F. Zh.*, vol. 52, no.3, 1913, p. 32.

52. Vinokurov, "Apteki Simbirskoi gubernii v XIX i nachale XX veka," pp. 50-52.

53. Claus, "History of Pharmacy in Russia," p. 169.

54. "Predpolozhenie ob ustroistve zemskoi apteki," *Meditsinskii vestnik*, vol. 8, no. 37 (14 September) 1868, p. 348.

55. TsGIA, f. 1298, op. 1, d. 1409, ll. 1 and 1 ob.

56. TsGIA, f. 1298, op. 1, d. 1402, ll. 1, 17.

57. TsGIA, f, 1298, op. 1, d. 1883, ll. 4, 14, 20.

The population of Mokotov had been 9,929 in 1900, that of Volia 14,516; by 1905 the population in Mokotov had climbed to 16,120 and that of Volia to 16,943; by 1910 the population in Mokotov reached 17,155, that of Volia, 26,384. The village of Mokotov was a thriving factory and industrial district. Although the village had one normal pharmacy, the local authorities contended that a second would be convenient for the population, especially at night.

Governors in the provinces of Kherson, Vladimir, Tambov, Samara, Sedletsk, Mogilev provided similar examples of population growth and need for more normal pharmacies.

58. Zhurnal prisutstviia Sedletskago gubernskago pravleniia po vrachebnomu otdeleniu," TsGIA, f. 1298, op. 1, d. 1932, ll. 2, 2 ob, 3, 3 ob, 4 ob, 5.

59. Ibid., ll. 11, 11 ob, 12.

60. TsGIA, f. 1298, op. 1, d. 1260: Tambov. gubernatora po gubernskomu pravleniiu. Otdelenie vracheb. Ministru VD, 1905 (l. 1); Protokol vracheb. otdeleniia Tambovskago gubernskago pravleniia, 1905 (ll. 2, 2 ob.) The new pharmacy would be located far from existing ones and railroad lines, where there existed a settlement of 5,000 people.

61. TsGIA, f.1298, op. 1, d. 1379, ll. 3, 9-11, 24 and ob.

62. *Loc. cit*, l.l. 13, 16-22, 31-32.

63. TsGIA, f. 1298, op. 1, d. 1420, l.l. 1-2, 3-4, and ob.

64. TsGIA, f. 1298. op. 1, d. 2083, ll. 2, 2 ob, 2 a, 2 a ob.

65. TsGIA, f. 1298, op. 1, d. 1838, ll. 2-11.

66. Nikolai Gogol, "The Inspector General," English translation in *A Treasury of Russian Literature*, ed., Bernard Gilbert Guerney (New York: The Vanguard Press, 1943), p. 221.

67. Russell E. Snow, *The Bolsheviks in Siberia, 1917-1918* (Associated University Press, 1977), p. 22.

68. Toropov, "Dvizhenie i rost," p. 1281; statistics on pp. 1278-1279. In 1901 there were 3,148 pharmacies in European Russia or 89 percent of the total. In 1910 there were 4,123 pharmacies in European Russia. *Loc. cit.*

69. Toropov, "Dvizhenie i rost," pp. 1281–1282.

70. Toropov, "Dvizhenie i rost," p 1292. In the Don army region (*oblast'*) the percentage of pharmacies owned by pharmacists increased from 81.9 percent in 1900. In Central Asia increase was less; in 1900 pharmacists had owned 80 percent of pharmacies. In the Polish provinces pharmacists' ownership had increased 1.8 percent, from 95.3 percent to 97.1 percent between 1900 and 1911 and in the Baltic provinces 1.6 percent, from 77.6 percent to 79.2 percent. In the zemstvo provinces the increase was meager—0.6 percent—but pharmacists still owned 80.4 percent of pharmacies compared to 79.8 percent in 1900. However, in some regions pharmacists' ownership of pharmacies *decreased*. In the Caucasus, the number of pharmacies owned by pharmacists decreased by 9.6 percent—from 85.6 percent to 76 percent—and in the non-zemstvo provinces 2.8 percent—from 81.7 percent to 78.9 percent. Toropov, *loc. cit.*

71. Snow describes both the official character and the amenities of Siberian cities in *The Bolsheviks in Siberia, 1917–1918*, pp. 31–33.

72. TsGIA, f. 1298, op. 1, d. 1286, l. 6 and ob. Most were civilians. There were 3,103 troops in the local garrison.

73. Ibid., l. 9 and 9 ob.

74. Ibid., l. 11.

75. Ibid., l. 22.

76. Ibid., l. 9.

77. Ibid., ll. 2, 4.

78. Ibid., l. 9 and 9 ob.

79. As a result, the Provizors requested that the date for them to open the pharmacies be prolonged for six months. TsGIA, f. 1298, op. 1, d. 1286, ll. 1–5.

80. However, dispute arose as to whether the hospital warehouse could make a profit. Ibid., l. 8.

81. Ibid., l. 20.

82. Ibid., l. 24. there were doubts that the city hospital could make a profit and, additionally, the Society of Doctors had made provision for sale of medicaments to the poor, described below.

83. TsGIA, f. 1298, op. 1, d. 1379, ll. 1, 10, 16–22, 28 ob and 29, 31–32.

84. Ibid., ll. 37, 39, 41, 42, 44.

85. TsGIA, f. 1298, op. 1, d. 1424, ll. 1, 8, 10, 18, 19.

86. Ibid., ll. 23, 26.

87. TsGIA, f. 1298, op. 1, d. 1196, ll. 1–2 and ob.

88. TsGIA, f. 1298, op. 1, d. 1420, ll. 1–5. The owners of the two pharmacies in Semipalatinsk estimated they served only 12,000 to 13,000 people, chiefly of Russian extraction.

89. Ibid., l. 4.

90. TsGIA, f. 1298, op. 1, d. 1886, ll. 1, 3, 7–10, 17–18, 26–52.

91. De-v, "Aptechnoe delo v Rossii po offitsial'nym statisticheskim dannym," 1908, p. 28.

92. E. K. Khrzhanovskii, *Polozhenie aptechnago dela v Rossii* (St. Petersburg, 1913), p. 8.

93. Anon., "Pharmacy in Russia," *The Druggists Circular and Chemical Gazette,* October 1903, p. 203.

94. TsGIA, f. 1298, op. 1, d. 1126, l. 2.

95. "Khronika," *F. Zh.*, vol. 13, no. 49, 1891, p. 781.

96. Ginzburg, "A Pharmacist in Tsarist Russia," p. 145.

97. TsGIA, f. 1298, op. 1, d. 1420, l. 4.

98. *Ustav Moskovskago Blagotvoritel'nago Obshchestva Posledovatelei Gomeopatii,* approved April 2, 1894, located in the Tsentral'nyi Gosudarstvennyi Arkhiv [TsGA] RSFSR (Moscow), f. 482, op. 16, d. 3, ll. 38-43 ob. Individuals paying not less than 100 rubles into the coffers of the society on a one-time basis were regarded as honorary members. Doctors, veterinarians, dental doctors, dentists, and pharmacists who joined the society composed a special medical department.

99. Quoted in *F. Zh.*, vol. 20, no. 22, 1898, p. 309. In this case the governor (the governor-general of the steppe) approved.

100. "Raznyia izvestiia," *F. Zh.*, vol. 40 (23), no. 25, 1901, p. 480.

101. "Raznyia izvestiia," *F. Zh.*, vol. 40 (23), no. 20, 1901, p. 398.

102. "Vysochaishiia poveleniia, pred. Pravit. Senatu ministerstvom Iustitsii," *F. V.*, vol. 7, no. 45, 1904, p. 914.

103. TsGIA, f. 1298, op. 1, d. 1283, l. 16.

104. Ibid., ll. 19-20.

105. TsGIA, op. 1, d. 1424, l. 18.

106. TsGIA, f. 1298, op. 1, d. 1803, ll. 1, 2, 4, 4 ob., 14, 16, 17.

107. TsGIA, f. 1298, op. 1, d. 1932, l. 3 ob.

108. TsGIA, f. 1298, op. 1, d. 1283, l. 16. Apparently, there were only a few workers at the station.

109. TsGIA, f. 1298, op. 1, d. 1932, l. 3 ob.

110. "Raznyia izvestiia," *F. Zh.*, vol. 40 (23), no. 47, 1901, p. 860.

111. "Apteki v Rossii," *F. Zh.*, vol. 1, no. 3, 1879, p. 86.

112. S. Lintser, "Aptekarskii vopros," *F. V.*, vol. 2, no. 39, 1898, pp. 619-22. This account claimed there were 2,830 pharmacies in the empire.

113. Grudinskii, "Bytovoi otdel. Po povodu novago aptekarskago ustava," p. 599. This account cited 2,874 pharmacies in the empire. In 1900 there were almost twice as many pharmacies in the government sector (*aptechnoe otdelenie*)—134 as in 1877. Supposedly there were 38 homeopathic pharmacies.

114. Toropov, "Dvizhenie i rost," p. 1278.

115. *Otchet o sostoianii narodnago zdraviia i organizatsii vrachebnoi pomoshchi v Rossii za 1905 god,* p. vii, and "Aptechnoe delo v Rossii po offitsial'nym statisticheskim dannym," *Russkii farmatsevt,* p. 26.

116. Toropov, "Dvizhenie i rost,"p. 1279.

117. "Apteki v Rossii," *F. Zh.*, vol. 40 (23), no. 47, 1901, p. 860, and Toropov, "Dvizhenie i rost," p. 1281.

118. Cited in Protokol Khersonskago Gubernskago Pravleniia po vrachebnomu otdeleniiu, TsGIA, f. 1298, op. 1, d. 2083, l. 2 ob.

119. "Aptechnoe delo v Rossii," p. 26, and Toropov, "Dvizhenie i rost," p. 1281.

120. Toropov, "Dvizhenie i rost," p. 1280.
121. TsGIA, f. 1298, op. 1, d. 1269, ll. 1-10.
122. Marsden, "Pharmacy in Russia," p. 95.
123. Advertisement, *F. Zh.*, vol. 40 (23), no. 23, 1901, p. 451.
124. "Apteki v Rossii," *F. Zh.*, vol. 1, no. 3, 1879, p. 86.
125. "Domashniia aptechki. Ukaz Pravitel'stvuiushchago Senata 18 aprelia 1879 g.," *Sbornik zakonopolozhenii dlia farmatsevtov, soderzhatelei aptek i drogistov.* Sos. P. N. Bulatov (St. Petersburg, 1897), pp. 314-316.
126. Provizor Garber, "Sel'skaia vrachebnaia pomoshch' v Eniseiskoi i Tomskoi guberniiakh," *Farmatsevt*, vol. 10, no. 13, 1902 pp. 400-402.

Chapter 4

1. V. M. Salo, "Vneaptechnaia torgovlia lekarstvennymi sredstvami vo vtoroi polovine XIX veka," *Farmatsiia*, vol. 24, no. 3, 1975, p. 58.
2. Figures for pharmacies date to 1905. Upravlenie Glavnago Vrachebnago Inspektora, *Otchet o sostoianii narodnago zdraviia i organizatsii vrachebnoi pomoshchi v Rossii za 1905 god* (St. Petersburg, 1907), p. VII. The same was true in Germany. For example, in Prussia in 1905 there were 3,237 pharmacies with branches; at the beginning of 1908 there were 23,122 drug stores. "Za rubezhom," *Farmastevticheskii trud* [hereafter cited *F. T.*], vol. 3, no. 2, 1909, pp. 29-30.
3. As late as January 5, 1898, the Governing Senate reiterated that "it was necessary to limit pharmacy (*aptechnoe delo*) from superfluous competition and that new pharmacies could be opened only when the owners of existing pharmacies would not curtail the existing pharmacy. . . ." Cited in "Zhurnal prisutstviia Sedletskago gubernskago pravleniia," December 1912, Tsentral'nyi Gosudarstvennyi Istoricheskii Arkhiv, St. Petersburg [hereafter cited TsGIA], fond 1298, opis' 1, delo 1932, list 3 ob. [hereafter cited "f.," "op.," "d.," "l.," or "ll." in the plural].
4. The 1814 law, "O prodazhe aptekarskikh materialov" is discussed by V. M. Salo, "Vneaptechnaia torgovlia lekarstvennymi sredstvami v XVIII i XIX vekakh," *Farmatsiia*, vol. 34, no. 1, 1985, pp. 88-90.
5. V. M. Salo, "Vneaptechnaia torgovlia..XVIII i XIX vekakh," p. 89.
6. Salo, ibid., p. 90.
7. Salo, ibid., p. 90.
8. Salo, ibid., p. 89.
9. V. M. Salo, Soviet historian of pharmacy, contends that in the majority of cases these suits were dismissed or only a small fine was imposed. Salo, "Vneaptechnaia torgovlia lekarstvennymi sredstvami vo vtoroi polovine XIX veka," *Farmatsiia*, vol. 24, no. 3, 1975, pp. 54-56.
10. Salo, *loc. cit.*
11. "Tsirkuliar Meditsinskago Departamenta, 30 maia, 1891 g., No. 769," *Sbornik zakonopolozhenii dlia farmatsevtov, soderzhatelei aptek i drogistov*, sostavil (ed.) P. N. Bulatov (St. Petersburg, 1897), p. 203; Also, "O lekarstvennykh veshchestvakh kotoryia ne mogut byt' prodaemy v aptekarskikh magazinakh i

lavkakh," *Farmatsevticheskii zhurnal* [hereafter cited *F. Zh.*], vol. 13, no. 26, 1891, pp. 428–430.

12. "O tom zhe 7 marta 1892 g. No. 305," *Sbornik zakonopolozhenii*, pp. 203-204. The combined list of what could not be sold in drug stores ("Spisok lekarstvennykh sredstv, kotoryia ne mogut byt' prodavaemy v aptekarskikh magazinakh i lavkakh," ibid., pp. 204-207), cited items under both their Russian and Latin names and included silver nitrite; most medicinal wines; certain roots and bulbs; cut and pulverized leaves; certain mushrooms; all liniments; certain oils; lichen; all suppositories, infusions and tinctures, and decoctions; powdered opium; most pills, plasters and poweders; all solutions; all medicinal gelatins; most herbs except marjoram and another herb; most flowers except chrysanthemum; extracts, elixirs, emulsions; most syrups; several derivatives of ammonia and iodine; and so on.

13. TsGIA, f. 1298, op. 1, d. 1269, l. 14.

14. "Ukaz Pravitel'stvuiushchago Senata," *Farmatsevticheskii vestnik* [hereafter cited *F. V.*], vol. 7, no. 41, 1904, pp. 645–647.

15. TsGIA, f. 1298, op. 1, d. 1304, ll. 30–31.

16. TsGIA, f. 1298, op. 1, d. 2066a, ll. 103 and 103 ob.

17. *Loc. cit.*

18. TsGIA, f. 1298, op. 1, d. 1261, l. 3 ob.

19. "Pharmacy in Russia," *Druggists Circular and Chemical Gazette*, October 1903, p. 203.

20. TsGIA, f. 1298, op. 1, d. 1284, l. 2.

21. De-v, "Aptechnoe delo v Rossii po offitsial'nym statisticheskim dannym," *Russkii farmatsevt*, vol. 1, no. 1, 1908, p. 28.

22. For example, Thomas S. Pearson, *Russian Officialdom in Crisis. Autocracy and Local Self Government, 1861-1900* (Cambridge; Cambridge University Press, 1989), *passim*, notes conflicts between the Ministry of Finance and the MVD vis-à-vis the zemstvos.

23. TsGIA, f. 1298, op. 1, d. 1261, l. 3.

24. TsGIA, f. 1298, op. 1, d. 1269, ll. 1–10.

25. TsGIA, f. 1298, op. 1, d. 1269, l. 31.

26. Provizor Boris Veisberg, owner of the Aleksandro-polonskii private (*vol'naia*) pharmacy in Bakmut district, had reported to the medical section of the Ekaterinoslav provincial administration in August 1905, that the owner of the local Galantereino drug store dispensed antidiphtheria vaccine prescribed by a local doctor. Veisberg asked the Chief Medical Inspector to clarify whether antidiphtheria vaccine was one of the substances proscribed by the 1891 rules of the Ministry of Internal Affairs. The Chancellery of the Medical Council supported this complaint, verifying in January 1906, that antidiphtheria vaccine could not be dispensed from drug stores. TsGIA, f. 1298, op. 1, d. 1269, l. 10, l. 16.

27. In June 1905, Assistant Pharmacist Iosif Mikhailovich Rozental, manager of the Ul'ianovsk village pharmacy in Zubsovskaia district, complained that the medical department of the Tver provincial administration supported the right of grocers to sell galenical preparations in prepared form. The Medical Council con-

firmed that grocers had the right to sell prepared pharmaceuticals, over the counter, without a doctor's prescription *if done so in the exact form received.* TsGIA, f. 1298, op. 1, d. 1269, l. 14.

28. "Aptekarskie magaziny," *F. Zh.*, vol. 49, no. 18, 1910, p. 212 (here the store was spelled with one "l"); "Delo tovarishcha Keller and Ko," ibid., no. 22, p. 256; "Delo T-va R. Keler i Ko v Moskovsk. stolich. s"ezd Mirovykh Sudei," ibid., no. 37, p. 405-406.

29. "Pharmacy in Russia," *The Druggists Circular and Chemical Gazette,* October 1903, p. 203

30. TsGIA, f. 1298, op. 1, d. 1803, l. 14.

31. Prosper H. Marsden, "Opportunities for Export Trade. The Practice of Pharmacy in Russia," *American Druggist and Pharmaceutical Record,* 1905, p. 95.

32. D. A. Ruffman, "Russian Pharmacy," *Bulletin of Pharmacy,* 1906, pp. 16-17.

33. *Apercu historique du developpement general de la Pharmacie en Russie et en particulier de la "Pharmacie Ferrein"* (Moscow, 1910), no pagination.

34. Advertisement in *Farmatsevticheskii trud* [hereafter cited *F. T.*], vol. 1, 1907, following no. 4.

35. "Farmatsevticheskiia sredstva goroda," *F. Zh.*, vol. 49, no. 19, 1910, p. 224.

36. Gr. Grudinskii, "Bytovoi otdel. Po povodu novago aptekarskago ustava," *F. V.*, vol. 7, no. 40, 1904, p. 629.

37. Za rubezhom," *F. T.*, vol. 3, no. 2, 1909, pp. 29-30.

38. "Domashnyia aptechki. Ukaz Pravitel'stvuiushchago Senata 18 aprelia 1879 g., Bulatov, *Sbornik zakonopolozhenii,* pp. 314-316.

39. The brochure was entitled *Shkol'naia aptechka.* "Raznyia izvestiia," *F. Zh.*, vol. 23, no. 6, 1901, p. 124.

40. TsGIA, f. 1298, op. 1, d. 1932, l. 3 ob.

41. Toropov, "Dvizhenie i rost," p. 1290.

42. Toropov, "Dvizhenie i rost," p. 1293.

43. "Raznyia izvestiia," *F. Zh.*, vol. 40 (23), no. 11, 1901, p. 228.

44. "Po povodu proektiruemoi tsentral'noi gorodskoi apteki," *Farmatsevt,* vol. 9, no. 9, 1901, p. 278.

45. "Raznyia izvestiia," *F. Zh.*, vol. 40 (23), no. 25, 1901, p. 479. The Duma feared this would provide competition for private pharmacies.

46. "Aptechnoe delo v zemstve i gorodskom khoziaistve," *F. V.*, vol. 7, no. 14, 1904, pp. 219-220.

47. "Gorodskoi aptekarskii sklad v Peterburge," *F. V.*, vol. 7, no. 36, 1904, p. 572.

48. "Khronika," *F. V.*, vol. 7, 1904, p. 912.

49. Toropov, "Dvizhenie i rost," p. 1294.

50. Account in TsGIA, f. 1298, op. 1, d. 1126, no *listy* noted on microfilm copy; date of the report circa 1910 or 1911.

51. V. M. Salo, "Razvitie aptechnoi seti," *Farmatsiia,* vol. 25, no. 5, 1974, p. 85.

52. N(ensberg)., "Ob ustroistve zemskikh aptek," *Moskovskaia meditsinskaia gazeta,* 1867, pp. 225-228.

53. Salo, "Razvitie aptechnoi seti," p. 85.

54. "Apteki v Rossii," *F. Zh.*, vol. 1, no. 3, 1879, pp. 86–87. Other public institutions were cities and regional (*oblast'*) organizations.

55. "Apteki v Rossii," p. 87.

56. In contrast, pharmacists owned 69.9 percent of pharmacies in 1901. Their percentage decreased slightly to 68.5 percent in 1911, as noted earlier, but increase in the ownership of pharmacies by pharmacists wives and children made up the decrease in pharmacists' ownership—in 1901 wives and children of pharmacists owned 12.6 percent of pharmacies, they owned 13.3 percent of pharmacies in 1911. Toropov, "Dvizhenie i rost," pp. 1293–1294.

57. Salo, "Razvitie aptechnoi seti," pp. 85–86.

58. *Otchet o sostoianii narodnago zdraviia i organizatsii vrachebnoi pomoshchi v Rossii za 1905 god*, p. vii.

59. Salo, "Razvitie zemskoi seti," p. 86.

60. "Ob aptekakh zemskikh i sel'skikh lechebnits," Bulatov, *Sbornik zakonopolozhenii*, pp. 287–288.

61. "Offitsial'noe pribavlenie k Severnoi Pochte za 1868 g., No. 20," Bulatov, *Sbornik zakonopolozhenii*, p. 289.

62. For more information on Bakmut district, in which John Hughes's mining and metallurgical complex of Iuzhovka was located, see Theodore H. Friedgut, *Iuzhovka and Revolution: Life and Work in Russia's Donbass, 1869–1924* (Princeton: Princeton University Press, 1989), pp. 159–60 and *passim*.

63. "Apteki v Rossii," *F. Zh.*, vol. 1, no. 3, 1879, pp. 87–88.

64. Ibid., p. 88.

65. "Apteki v Rossii," *F. Zh.*, vol. 1, no. 3, 1879, p. 88.

66. "Ukaz Pravitel'stvuiushchago Senata 20 sentiabria 1877 g.," Bulatov, *Sbornik zakonopolozhenii*, pp. 289–290.

67. *Loc. cit.*; also, "Apteki v Rossii, " *F. Zh.*, vol. 1, no. 3, 1879, p. 88.

68. Ukaz of the Governing Senate, no. 32,964 and ukaz of the MVD, Sept. 20, 1876, no. 33243, cited in "Soslovnyia dela," *F. Zh.*, vol. 1, no. 13, 1879, pp. 408–409. Specific articles cited by the Senate were 586 and 587.

69. TsGIA, f. 1297, op. 155, d. 233, ll. 1 and 7.

70. M. Ia. Kapustin, *Osnovnye voprosy zemskoi meditsiny* (St. Petersburg, 1889), pp. 65–66, 77. Also, Mikh. Polumordvinov, "Obshchestvennyia uchrezhdeniia i vol'nyia apteki," *Russkii farmatsevt*, vol. 1, no. 2, 1908, p. 54.

71. Kapustin, *Osnovnye vosprosy* pp. 55–66, 77.

72. "Soslovnyia dela: Ukaz senata kasatel'no otpuska lekarstv iz zemskikh aptek i zemskikh aptechnykh skladov," *F. Zh.*, vol. 13, no. 47, 1891, p. 752.

73. "Soslovnyia dela: Glavnyia polozheniia, izvlechennyia iz Ukaza 1-go departamenta Pravitel'stvuiushchago Senata 1 Marta 1889 g. vosposledovavshago v raz"iasneniia voprosa ob opredelenii prak. zemstv na bezplatnyi otpusk lekarstv iz aptechnykh zavedenii," *F. Zh.*, vol. 13, no. 2, 1891, pp. 28–29.

74. "Apteki v Rossii," *F. Zh.*, vol. 1, no. 3, 1879, pp. 88–89.

75. Ibid.

76. "Soslovnyia dela: Ukaz senata kasatel'no otpuska lekarstv iz zemskikh aptek i zemskikh aptechnykh skladov," *F. Zh.*, vol. 13, no. 47, 1891, p. 752.

The journal also noted that the Ukaz of October 18, 1882, states that the payment for doctor's advice established by the zemstvo "is subject to approval of the Minister of Internal Affairs and . . . all zemstvo income must be stated in the annual zemstvo budget."

77. "Raznyia izvestiia," *F. Zh.*, vol. 40 (23), no. 31, 1901, p. 574.

78. "Raznyia izvestiia," *F. Zh.*, vol. 40 (23), no. 30, 1901, p. 573. For more on the term *soslovie* (corporation) see JoAnn Ruckman, "The Moscow Business Elite (DeKalb, Ill.: Northern Illinois University Press, 1984), pp. 25–31.

79. "Zemskiia dela," *F. Zh.*, vol. 40 (23), no. 3, 1901, p. 56.

80. "Pharmacy in Russia," *The Druggists Circular and Chemical Gazette*, October 1903, p. 203.

81. TsGIA, f. 1298, op. 1, d. 1126, ll. 20, 21 and ob.

82. Gr. Grudinskii, "Po povodu novago aptekarskogo ustava," *F. V.*, vol. 7 , no. 40, 1904, p. 629.

83. "Doklad Kurska gubernskago zemskago sobraniia," *F. V.*, vol. 7, no. 45, 1904, p. 908.

84. Mikh. Polumordvinov, "Obshchestvennyia uchrezhdeniia i vol'nyia apteki," *Russkii farmatsevt*, vol. 1, no. 2, 1908, pp. 51–54.

85. The cost of each prescription–the material plus containers–averaged 7.6 kopeks for a total of about 394 rubles. Meanwhile, the pharmacy cost 5,249 rubles to maintain, including salaries (3,951 rubles), heat (162 rubles), lighting (114 rubles), rent (550 rubles), insurance (60 rubles), trade documents (probably official stamps as well as postage and stationery–92 rubles), miscellaneous expenditures (296 rubles), and contribution to the pharmacists' pension fund–22 rubles, 78 kopeks. "Slukhi i vesti: Cherepovets," *F. V.*, vol. 2, no. 48, 1898, p. 778.

86. In 1901 Belgorodskoe district zemstvo in Kursk province asked permission to close its hospital and to open six feldsher points at 2,700 rubles, to open an additional feldsher point at 600 rubles, and a new hospital. "Raznyia izvestiia," *F. Zh.*,vol. 40 (23), no. 29, 1901, pp. 541–542.

87. "Doklad Kurska gubernskago zemskago sobraniia," *F. V.*, vol. 7, no. 45, 1904, pp. 907–909.

88. The pharmacy had a turnover of 63,000 rubles. "Sessiia Permaskago gubernskago zemstva," *F. Zh.*, vol. 52, no.3, 1913, p. 32.

89. Sir Donald Mackenzie Wallace, *Russia on the Eve of War and Revolution*, reprint, edited and introduced by Cyril E. Black (New York: Vintage Books , 1961), pp. 39–41.

90. Thomas S. Pearson focuses on the relationship of the central bureaucracy and the zemstvos. For his comments on zemstvos' wastefulness see *Russian Officialdom in Crisis*, pp. 89–90. Minister of Finance Vyshnegradskii (1887–1892) warned that zemstvo finances must be kept under control, ibid., p. 133. On this topic see also John F. Hutchinson, *Politics and Public Health in Revolutionary Russia, 1890–1918* (Baltimore: Johns Hopkins University Press, 1990), p. 65.

Charles Timberlake has done extensive research on zemstvos. For a recent work in which he praises zemstvos health care see Charles E. Timberlake, "The Zemstvo and the Development of a Russian Middle Class," *Between Tsar and People*, eds., Edith W. Clowes, Samuel D. Kassow, and James D. West (Princeton: Princeton University Press, 1991), pp. 165–179.

91. Kapustin, *Osnovnye voprosy*, pp. 65, 67. Kapustin was ordinary professor of medicine at Kazan University.

92. The Kursk provincial zemstvo dispensed medicines in its outpatient clinics for 10 kopeks or for paid tickets for the cost of the medicine. In one year—1882—collection from dispensing amounted to 100 rubles but expenditures for medicines amounted to 3,000 rubles. The Riazhskoe district zemstvo bought a private pharmacy, replaced ten Provizors in three years, and finally leased the pharmacy. The Samara provincial zemstvo did the same; the Timnskoe district zemstvo received only a fictitious profit and much real debt from its pharmacy. The Graivoronskoe zemstvo replaced six Provizors in eight years. The Fatezh zemstvo had its pharmacy twelve years; it was very satisfied with the pharmacy but dispensing medicines for 15 kopeks cost the zemstvo 4,000 rubles. The Ranenburg zemstvo was very satisfied with its pharmacy but a well-known pharmacist controlled its business. Kapustin, *Osnovnye voprosy*, pp. 71, 75–76.

93. For example, he presented information on the effects of prodigal spending in a district with twenty independent feldsher points. If the feldsher points dispensed annually 1,000 prescriptions at an average of 7 kopeks per prescription, total expenditures would amount to 1,400 rubles. In Kapustin's opinion this was money "thrown away." Kapustin provided the example of Konotopsk district, Chernigov province, where 48,909 patients were seen annually: 19,046 by doctors and 29,863 by feldshers. On average, one patient received more than two prescriptions, at an average cost per prescription of 5½ kopeks; feldshers dispensed about 3,200 rubles' worth of medicine from the general budget of 6,000 rubles. Kapustin regarded these expenditures as unproductive, because the diagnoses often were inaccurate, feldshers preferred complex medical formulae, and even dispensed medicines mixed with harmful ingredients. Kapustin, *Osnovnye voprosy*, pp. 77–78.

Kapustin also insisted that feldshers should only work under a physician's supervision, as required by law. Ibid., p 95.

94. Kapustin, *Osnovnye voprosy*, pp. 78–79.

95. According to Kapustin, zemstvos should order from local "druggists" only what they could not purchase elsewhere; they should order medicines at the time of year when offers were full so as not to defer payment; they should not order materials such as spirits, linseed oil, pork salt, vaseline, gauze, starch, cotton, cloth, stoppers, and vessels from pharmacies or drug stores when they could be procured more cheaply from special traders; they should not order superfluous medicines. Kapustin advised provincial zemstvos to order medicaments for their district zemstvos, erecting warehouses for the purpose of storage. Second, he recommended that doctors and feldshers prescribe only necessary medicines. He particu-

larly criticized feldshers for the widespread practice of prescribing quinine, which was expensive, for diseases other than malaria. According to Kapustin, in 1879 Bobrovskii district zemstvo, Voronezh province spent 8,000 rubles on quinine, the Kursk provincial zemstvo spent 20,000 rubles on quinine. In 1882 the Konotopskii district zemstvo bought 24 medical funts of quinine; at 4 rubles per ounce this amounted to 1,100 rubles and 20 funts of surrogate sulfuric acid quinidin—in total the zemstvo had spent 1,500 for antimalarial substances. Kapustin, *Osnovnye voprosy*, pp. 80–83.

Malaria was Russia's major communicable disease. Thus, in addition to conserving quinine because it was costly, Kapustin averred that it must be saved to alleviate the symptoms of malaria. For a discussion of malaria in late imperial Russia see Mary Schaeffer Conroy, "Malaria in Late Tsarist Russia," *Bulletin of the History of Medicine*, vol. 56, no. 1, 1982, pp. 41–55.

96. Kapustin claimed that about three-fourths of medicines in the Russian pharmacopoeia were never used by zemstvo physicians. Some zemstvos accumulated stores of unused medicines. Zemstvo doctors varied greatly in the amounts and types of medicines they ordered; medicines from previous zemstvo doctors languished in the zemstvo warehouse after a new doctor's arrival. This was one reason Kapustin disapproved of zemstvos acquiring private pharmacies with full stocks of medicaments. Kapustin, *Osnovnye voprosy*, pp. 84–86, 93.

97. The catalog originally was requested by the Moscow provincial zemstvo assembly at the Seventh Moscow Congress. In his 1889 book on zemstvo medicine Kapustin included the catalog, entitled "Catalog of Medicaments Developed by the Congress of Zemstvo Doctors from Moscow Province for Guiding Zemstvo Doctors when ordering Medicaments for Zemstva Pharmacies." The catalog consisted of 150 medicines and substances. Kapustin also published a list of 58 most necessary items for zemstvo pharmacies, which should be ordered in large quantities. The list included ammonia, distilled water, chloroform, camphor, silver nitrate, morphinum muriaticum, powdered opium, ipecacuanhae root, tincture of valerian, and vaseline. Kapustin, *Osnovnye voprosy*, pp. 86–92.

98. Kapustin noted that it was difficult for peasants to take correct doses of liquids or extracts, powders were better, tablets in exact doses were best. Ointments made of pork lard would decompose. He discussed the need of appropriate vessels and containers in the zemstvo pharmacy, citing Kursk zemstvo. This zemstvo charged patients a small deposit to be returned when the vessel was returned; the patient also could purchase the vessel for a small fee if desired. Kapustin, *Osnovnye voprosy*, pp. 93–95.

99. *Kratkii ocherk deiatel'nosti aptekarskago sklada Tverskogo gubernskago zemstva za istekshie 20 let ego sushchestvovaniia (1889–1909 g.g.)* sostavil M. E. Zaitsev (Tver, 1910), p. 2.

100. "Odnym iz poslednikh zasedanii Moskovskago gubernskago zemstva," *F. Zh.*, vol. 20, no. 20, 1898, p. 279.

101. "Zemskiia dela," *F. Zh.*, vol. 20, no. 43, 1898, pp. 610–611.

102. In zemstvo assembly debates a pharmacy owner, Keizar, and a Dr. Mikh-

alkin agreed on the warehouse but protested that the assistant Provizor [*sic*] would have nothing to do. "Slukhi i vesti," *F. V.*, vol. 2, no. 46, 1898, p. 739.

103. "Zemskiia dela," *F. Zh.*, vol. 40 (23), no. 3, 1901, p. 56.

104. "Zemskaia khronika," *F. V.*, vol. 7, no. 36, 1904, p. 571.

105. For example, Lebedin district and Starobel'sk district, Khar'kov province. The latter district hired an Assistant Pharmacist at 900 rubles a year (this was quite a good salary) to manage the warehouse and order medicines directly at a discount of 10 to 20 percent. *Russkii farmatsevt*, vol. 1, no. 2, 1908, p. 75 and *passim*.

106. In *Farmatsevticheskii zhurnal*, 1898, provincial and district zemstvos advertised for Assistant Pharmacists at annual salaries of 360 to 480 rubles, plus living quarters and, in one case, board and transportation to the job. (Advertisements, *F. Zh.*, vol. 20, no. 27, 1898, p. 385; ibid., no. 31, p. 443; ibid., no. 33, p. 472, ibid., no. 37, p. 530.) In 1901 Meshchovskii district zemstvo advertised for a manager of a village pharmacy at a annual salary of 500 rubles plus apartment and a second position for an Assistant Pharmacist in a zemstvo pharmacy with right of private sale (normal pharmacy) at an annual salary of 500 rubles plus 120 rubles "apartment money." (Advertisement, *F. Zh.*, vol. 40 (23), no. 31, 1901, p. 566.) Also in 1901, a district zemstvo executive council in Novgorod province advertised for an Assistant Pharmacist for service in the city pharmacy at a salary of 600 rubles per year and a Christian helper or *praktikant* at a salary of 20 rubles per month. (Advertisement, *F. Zh.*, vol. 40 (23), no. 23, 1901, p. 451.) In 1902, a district zemstvo executive council in Pskov province advertised for a *Pomoshchnik provizor* [*sic*] to work in the zemstvo hospital pharmacy at a salary of 700 rubles per year sans apartment. The Assistant Pharmacist was to have one day free after five days work. (Advertisement, *Farmatsevt*, vol. 10, no. 16, 1902, p. 523.)

107. "Po povodu konflikta v khersonskoi gubernskoi zemskoi bol'nitse," *F. T.*, vol. 1, no. 25, 1907, 349-350; ibid., no. 27, pp. 372-373.

108. Samuel Ramer, "Who Was the Russian Fel'dsher?" *Bulletin of the History of Medicine*, vol. 50, no. 2, 1976, pp. 215-216.

109. Upravlenie Glavnago Vrachebnago Inspektora, *Otchet o sostoianii narodnago zdraviia . . . za 1905 god*, p. vii.

110. K. Butkevich, "Mnenie po povodu predstoiashchago farmatsevticheskago s"ezda," *F. Zh.*, vol. 20, no. 42, 1898, pp. 600-601.

111. N. Shchepotev, *Uchebnik farmakologii dlia fel'dsherov i fel'dsherskikh uchenikov* (Kazan, 1886). This text is available at the National Library of Medicine, Bethesda, MD.

112. "Raznyia izvestiia," *F. Zh.*, vol. 40 (23), no. 18, 1901, pp. 362-363.

113. "Slukhi i vesti: Griazovets," *F.V.*, vol. 2, no. 41, 1898, p. 659.

114. The zemstvo called upon physicians to economize in prescribing and to exercise control over feldshers and suggested substitution of cheaper medicines for more costly. V. V. S-kii, "Voprosy farmatsii v nekotorykh uezdakh Riazan'skoi gubernii," *F. V.*, vol. 7, no. 28, 1904, pp. 442-443.

115. Salo, "Razvitie zemskoi aptechnoi seti," pp. 85-86.

116. "Slukhi i vesti: Iz Luginskoi volosti," *F. V.*, vol. 2, no. 46, 1898, p. 740.

117. See Pearson, *Russian Officialdom in Crisis*, p 223 and following, for Finance Minister Vyshnegradskii's appreciation that zemstvo finances must be kept under control.

118. "Ofitsial'nye izvestiia, khronika, raznyia soobshcheniia . . . i pr.," *F. V.*, vol. 5, no. 8, 1901, p. 141; "Raskhody zemstv na meditsinskuiu chast' v 1900 godu," *F. Zh.*, vol. 40 (23), no. 39, 1901, pp. 705-706.

119. "Ofitsial'nye izvestiia," *F. V.*, vol. 5, no. 8, 1901, p. 141.

120. The greatest rise in medical expenditures had occurred in the middle industrial provinces—31 percent, or nearly a third of the zemstvo budget, being spent for medical needs. The southern provinces had also seen significant increases in medical expenditures (11 percent) as had "Little Russia," or the Ukraine. Whereas the northern provinces spent the same amount on medicines as the middle industrial provinces in 1895, by 1900 the former were behind, their increase in medical expenditures having risen only 5.4 percent. In the Southern Russian and Ukrainian provinces the average annual expenditure for the medical sector per province was 900,000 rubles but in the northern provinces less than 500,000 rubles. The provinces of Perm, Kherson, Moscow, Kursk, Tambov, Viatka, and Poltava spent more than 1 million rubles on their medical sectors; medical expenditures of these seven provinces amounted to almost one third of the total zemstvo budgets for medical expenditures. Of the remaining provinces, 20 spent from 500,000 to less on their medical budgets. These provinces included Ufa, Tula, St. Petersburg, Pskov, Penza, and Kaluga, the total medical budgets of which amounted to only 13 percent of all zemstvo expenditures for medicine. In general, expenditures for medicines totaled 1,186,000 rubles, or 5 percent of the zemstvos medical budget. However, Kursk province spent 166,000 rubles, or 16 percent of its budget, on purchase of medicines; Vladimir province spent 111,000 rubles, or 17 percent of its budget, on medicines; Orlov province spent 130,000 rubles, or 21 percent of its budget, on medicaments. "Raskhody zemstv na meditsinskuiu chast' v 1900 godu," *F. Zh.*, vol. 40 (23), no. 39, 1901, p. 705-706.

121. "K voprosu ob ekonomii na lekarstvo," *Farmatsevt*, vol. 10, no. 48, 1902, pp. 1581-1582. Generally, *Farmatsevticheskii vestnik* fretted that unrestricted (*vol'naia*) sale of medicines by zemstvo pharmacies would make them "too commercial." "Zemskaia khronika," *F. V.*, vol. 7, no. 36, 1904, pp. 570-571.

122. On the need for district zemstvos in Riazan province to economize in pharmacy matters and more carefully use medicines, see V. V. S-skii, "Letopis' obshchestvennoi farmatsii, voprosy farmatsii v nekotorykh uezdakh Riazan'skoi gubernii," *F. V.*, vol. 7, no. 28, 1904, p. 444. For Alatyr district zemstvo, see V. V. S-skii, "Letopis' obshchestvennoi farmatsii, v nekotorykh uezdakh Simbirskoi guberbnii," ibid., no. 18, 1904, pp. 282-284.

123. "Neskol'ko zamechanii po povodu proekta aptechnago ustava," *F. V.*, vol. 7, no. 43, 1904, pp. 680-681.

124. Timberlake, "The Zemstvo," pp. 171-177.

125. *Kratkii ocherk*, pp. 11, 12.

126. *Kratkii ocherk*, p. 3.

127. Dbz, "Bytovoi otdel. Iz materialov komissii po voprosam obshchestvennoi farmatsii," *F. V.*, vol. 7, no. 35, 1904, pp. 551-552.

128. *Kratkii ocherk deiatel'nosti aptekarskago sklada Tverskogo gubernskago zemstva*, pp. 2, 7, 15-17.

129. *Kratkii ocherk*, pp. 15-16.

130. *Kratkii ocherk*, p. 28.

131. "Khronika: Zemskoe sobranie," *F. Zh.*, vol. 49, no. 37, 1910, p. 404. The three districts were Bogorodsk, Evengorodsk, and Okeinsk.

132. "Po povodu konflikta v Khersonskoi gubernskoi zemskoi bol'nitse," *F. T.*, vol. 1, no. 25, 1907, p. 348. Of course, although socialist pharmacists foresaw zemstvos and cities ultimately taking over private pharmacies, they disparaged the composition of zemstvo and city government at that time as not sufficiently democratic.

133. For example, Zmiev, Kharkov province, and Serpukhov, Moscow province were discussed in "Khronika zemskago i gorodskago aptechnago dela," *Russkii farmatsevt*, vol. 1, no. 2, 1908, pp. 75-76.

134. *Farmatsevt*, vol. 13, nos. 47-48, 1905, p. 1367.

135. "Khronika zemskago i gorodskago aptechnago dela," *Russkii farmatsevt*, vol. 1, no. 3, 1908, pp. 117-118.

136. Tsentral'nyi Gosudarstvennyi Arkhiv RSFSR (Moscow) [hereafter cited TsGA RSFSR], f. 482, op. 5, d. 12, l. 42.

137. Lesser staff received smaller salaries. In 1910 the *praktikant* received 450 rubles and "three staff members" received 576 rubles. In 1911 the cashier was paid 360 rubles and three students were paid 360 rubles. Anon., "V zemstvakh i gorodakh," *Zhizn' farmatsevta*, vol. 3, no. 3, 1911, p. 11.

138. TsGIA, f. 1298, op. 1, d. 2083, l. 2, 2a ob. Two pharmacists, Provizor Vul'f (Vladimir) Berdichevskii and Assistant Pharmacist Anton Robak, had the financial wherewithal and were competing for the privilege of opening a second *private* normal pharmacy. Anton Robak was disqualified since only Provizors could operate normal pharmacies.

Chapter 5

1. An account in 1902 cited 3,610 pharmacists who owned or managed pharmacies and 5,966 pharmacists who worked in them. I. Rubinshtein, "Nemnogo tsyfr," *Farmatsevticheskii vestnik* [hereafter cited *F. V.*], vol. 5. (contains both 1901 and 1902), no. 33, 1902, p. 391.

2. Cited in De-v, "Aptechnoe delo v Rossii po offitsial'nym statisticheskim dannym," *Russkii farmatsevt*, vol. 1, no. 1, 1908, p. 27. Of the total 6,889 were pharmacists—Assistants, Provizors, or Masters.

Russia was not keeping pace with Germany. In Prussia alone there were 7,620 pharmacists. However, in Germany the numbers of pharmacists were declining in the first decade of the twentieth century. The number of pharmacists declined by 142 between 1906 and 1907. The number of Assistant Pharmacists declined by 56 and the number of pharmacy students by 187. Between 1903 and 1904 the number of Assistant Pharmacists decreased by 200 and the number of students by 379. There was actually a shortage of pharmacists; pharmacy owners in rural areas worked without assistants. "Za rubezhom," *Farmatsevticheskii trud* [hereafter cited *F. T.*], vol. 3, no. 2, 1909, p. 30.

3. I. I. Korol'kov, *Farmatsevty Rossii* (Moscow, 1911), p. 7.

4. D. I. Toropov, "Dvizhenie i rost aptechnago dela v Imperii za poslednee desiatiletie (1901–1910 gg.)," *Vestnik obshchestvennoi gigieny, sudebnoi i prakt. meditsiny,* 1911, p. 1300.

5. As noted in a previous chapter, by 1864 there were twelve Masters of Pharmacy. Between 1845 and 1901 three hundred pharmacists received the *Magistr* degree. Ivan Sofronovich Tkeshelashvili, *Materialy dlia istorii farmatsii v Rossii. Biograficheskii slovar' farmatsevtov poluchivshikh stepen' magistra farmatsii . . . s 1845–1901* (Moscow, 1901), p. 6. By 1910 there were ninety-four Masters of Pharmacy. Toropov, "Dvizhenie i rost," p. 1298.

6. F. P., "Statisticheskiia svedeniia," *F. T.*, vol. 3, no. 2, 1909, p. 27. Statistics were based on data from the *Rossiiskii meditsinskii spisok* for 1908.

7. F. P., "Statisticheskiia svedeniia," p. 27.

8. Toropov, "Dvizhenie i rost," p. 1298. Women had been admitted to the profession in the late 1880s. Chapter 7 is devoted to them.

9. Toropov, "Dvizhenie i rost," p. 1300.

10. Toropov, "Dvizhenie i rost," p. 1302.

11. Korol'kov, *Farmatsevty Rossii,* p. 17.

12. Toropov, "Dvizhenie i rost," p. 1300.

13. Toropov, "Dvizhenie i rost," p. 1292.

14. In 1910 there were 4,804 pharmacies in the empire; 2,845 were normal, 1,826 village, 102 "public," and only 31 homeopathic. The German physician Samuel Hahnemann developed homeopathy in the late eighteenth and early nineteenth centuries. Homeopathy is based on the *simile* principle that "disease is cured by remedies that produce symptoms resembling the disease in question. This form of pharmacy also relies on minute doses of tinctures made from fresh crude drugs." Glenn Sonnedecker, *History of Pharmacy* (Philadelphia, 1976), pp. 47–48.

15. Rubinshtein, "Nemnogo tsyfr," p. 391. These statistics cite 1,319 Provizors staffing pharmacies, obviously a contradiction to the figures given above.

16. Korol'kov, *Farmatsevty Rossii,* p. 19.

17. Toropov, "Dvizhenie i rost," p. 1293.

18. Toropov, "Dvizhenie i rost," p. 1294.

19. F. P., "Statisticheskiia svedeniia," p. 27.

20. F. P., ibid., p. 27.

21. Rubinshtein, "Nemnogo tsyfr," p. 391.

22. De-v, "Aptechnoe delo v Rossii po offitsial'nym statisticheskim dannym," *Russkii farmatsevt,* vol. 1, no. 1, 1908, p. 27.

23. F. P., "Statisticheskiia svedeniia," p. 27.

24. Professor C. Claus, "History of Pharmacy in Russia," *American Journal of Pharmacy,* vol. 31, 1859, p. 169. The article, originally delivered as an address at

the University of Dorpat and published in 1853, was translated by a Mr. John M. Maisch of Philadelphia, who used the term "drug store," familiar to an American, in place of the correct *apteka*, or pharmacy; drug store is the literal translation of *aptekarskii magazin*; they were competitors of pharmacies. Maisch also spelled "ruble" as "rubel."

25. Tsentral'nyi Gosudarstvennyi Istoricheskii Arkhiv, St. Petersburg [hereafter cited TsGIA], fond 1298, opis' 1, delo 2680, listy 51-60. [hereafter cited "f.," "op.," "d.," "ll.," or "l." in singular.] Medical and Pharmaceutical Report from Kiev province, 1908.

26. Ia. Chistovich, "Aptechnyi vopros v Rossii," *Meditsinskii vestnik*, vol. 4, 1864, pp. 244-248.

27. Drug stores were accorded privileges not granted to pharmacy owners. According to the Statute for Materialists of 1844 they were allowed to open branches in the same city or different cities if the establishments were under different management. Kantseliariia Varshavskago Generala Gubernatora v Upravlenie Glavnago Vrachebnago Inspektora, 9 Oktiabria 1905 g., TsGIA, f. 1298, op. 1, d. 1244, l. 51 and 51 ob.

By 1913 there were 7,256 "drug stores," nearly twice as many as pharmacies. E. K. Khrzhanovskii, *Polozhenie aptechnago dela v Rossii* (St. Petersburg, 1913), p. 33.

28. The Russian Pharmacy Tax, following calculations for the Prussian Pharmacy Tax of 1863, allowed prices for many powders and pills to rise only a few kopeks. Shul'ts alleged that this did not cover rent, heat and light, personnel salaries, the cost of spoiled substances, and capital spent for purchase of the pharmacy. "Soslovnyia dela: Aptekarskaia Taksa," *Farmatsevticheskii zhurnal* [hereafter cited *F. Zh.*], vol. 1, no. 1, 1879, pp. 21-24.

29. "Soslovnyia dela: Protokol obyknovennago zasedaniia," *F. Zh.*, vol. 1, no. 3, 1879, pp. 83-86.

30. Zaidman argued that the pharmacy owner's expenditures for staff had nearly doubled and other expenditures had risen. Thus, his margin between cost and sale of medicines was negligible.

Zaidman also criticized the underlying rationale for the Pharmacy Tax: It was unlike the tax placed on other consumer items such as meat and bread. With these items lower prices resulted in increased demand and vice-versa. But this economic principle only "weakly applied" to medicines. A tariff on medicines, over and above their actual cost, was justified because of the expenditures of the pharmacy owner—the owner "worked night and day" and the Pharmacy Tax should take into account the percent of capital for building or buying the pharmacy, the percent from turnover of the capital, the price of medicines, expenditures for rent, staff, light, heat, and losses such as spoiling of medicines, breakage of apparatus, etc. But a pharmacy tax that took into account all these items would make medicines prohibitively expensive; as a result the Russian Pharmacy Tax was artificially calculated. He complained that "we are always sentimental about the poor but do not consider how the pharmacy owner can always sacrifice for the truly needy and ignore the fact that in the city and zemstvo hospitals they give medicine as a gift. We must remunerate the pharmacy owner. . . . This would increase the price of prescriptions for the rich by some kopeks." Naum Zaidman, "Soslovnyia dela: 'Aptekarskaia taksa,'" *F. Zh.*, vol. 1, no. 8, 1879, pp. 243–244.

He recommended that the price of medicines that required preparation would increase against the current tax (at a ratio of 2:3); the tax on over-the-counter items would remain or even be lowered by half for uncomplicated, frequently used preparations. *Loc. cit.*

31. "Apteki v Rossii," *F. Zh.*, vol. 1, no. 3, 1879, p. 87.

32. Ia. F., "Soslovnyia dela: O nyneshnem polozhenii aptek v provintsii," *F. Zh.*, vol. 1, no. 6, 1879, pp. 182–185.

33. Z (Zaidman?), "Soslovnyia dela: Ob aptekarskoi takse," *F. Zh.*, vol. 1, no. 7, 1879, pp. 212–215. "Z" further noted of the Pharmacy Tax that the "owner spends a lot of money but unlike trademen, despite higher costs cannot deviate from the tax by law—the tax is revised every six to seven years."

34. "Otchet Vysochaishe utverzhdennago S. Peterburgskago farmatsevticheskago obshchestva za 1883 g.," *F. Zh.*, vol. 6, no. 11, 1884, p. 199.

35. Zaidman ridiculed those who asserted that pharmacy owners made fantastic profits: "The position of our pharmacy owners is very sad, yet it is humorous to read in the papers about exploitation which turns the attention of the public to great profits." N. Zaidman, "Pis'mo v redaktsiiu," *F. Zh.*, vol. 13, no. 35, 1891, pp. 558–559.

36. "Comrade O" owed "druggists" [who supplied him with wares] 16,000 rubles and was burdened with payments for workers. "M. U." asked to be recommended a good *praktikant* as he was "ill and could not work himself" but "was not in a position to hire an assistant." He had enjoyed annual turnover of 4,000 rubles until a pharmacy store (*aptechnaia lavka*) opened in the vicinity and his turnover decreased 60 percent. Another pharmacy owner wrote that a feldsher had opened a drug store (*aptekarskii magazin*) in the village and convinced local peasants to eschew the private pharmacy. A fourth pleaded for "30.0 *chinin muriat*, 1.0 codeine, and 0.5 heroin on credit. God gives. I will pay with gratitude—now I not only have no money but have no bread." He lamented that he "would leave the village, but where would I go . . . my competitor is an Armenian . . . see how he lives." "O-le" claimed that "before the drug store I was well off; with the appearance of the drug store I sold my pharmacy." A pharmacy owner's widow, financially hurt by a zemstvo pharmacy and drug store, had to put her children into service. Robert Idel'son, "Kartiny s natury," *F. Zh.*, vol. 23, no. 10, 1901, pp. 207–208.

37. N. Zaidman, "Glavneishiia prichiny upadka u nas aptechnago dela," *F. Zh.*, vol. 23, no. 16, 1901, p. 328. Also Zaidman, "Russkiia apteki 50 let tomu nazad i teper'," *F. Zh.*, vol. 23, no. 22, 1901, pp. 430–31; ibid., no. 26, p. 494; ibid., no. 28, p. 524. Zaidman reiterated criticism of the Pharmacy Tax, pharmacy owners' constantly rising expenses, unfair competition from zemstvo pharmacies and drug stores in these articles.

38. N. Zaidman, "Russkiia apteki 50 let tomu nazad i teper'," *F. Zh.*, vol. 40 (23), no. 29, 1901, p. 540.

39. Correspondence from MVD, Chief Medical Inspector to the Department of Industry, Ministry of Trade and Industry, June 1911, TsGIA, f. 1298, op. 1, d. 1776, l. 40.

40. D. A. Ruffman, "Russian Pharmacy," *Bulletin of Pharmacy*, 1906, pp. 16-17.

41. Korol'kov, *Farmatsevty Rossii*, p. 13.

42. Zaidman, "Pis'mo v redaktsiiu," p. 559.

43. "Otchet Vysochaish. utverzhden. S. Peterburgsk. obshchestva za 1883," *F. Zh.*, 1884, p. 199.

44. TsGIA, f.1298, op. 1, d. 1111, l. 19

45. TsGIA, f. 1298, op. 1, d. 1111, l. 20.

46. TsGIA, f. 1298, op. 1, d. 1111, l. 20.

47. TsGIA, f. 1298, op. 1, d. 1111, l. 19.

48. Khrzhanovskii, *Polozhenie aptechnago dela v Rossii*, fold out chart, pp. 39 and 40.

49. See Victoria E. Bonnell, *Roots of Rebellion: Worker's Politics and Organizations in St. Petersburg and Moscow, 1900-1914* (Berkeley: University of California Press, 1983), pp. 27-31, 47-52 and *passim*. Bonnell constantly refers to the hard life of the apprentice and worker but she does not adequately illustrate her contention.

50. Vs. Mosal'skii, "Neskol'ko slov o zhenskom trude v aptekakh," *Farmatsevt*, vol. 9, no. 28, 1901, p. 891.

51. "Khronika," *F. V.*, vol. 7, no. 33, 1904, p. 524.

52. "Khronika," *F. V.*, vol. 7, no. 9, 1904, p. 141.

53. L. N. Kliachko and L. Ia. Zimin, "Sovremennoe polozhenie uslovii farmatsevticheskago truda v S. Peterburge 1900 g.," *F. V.*, vol. 5, no. 7, 1901, pp. 123, 126.

54. Untitled announcement, *F. Zh.*, vol. 20, no. 20, 1898, p. 279.

55. "Eshche o polozhenii rabotnikov v Peterburgskikh aptekakh," *F. Zh.*, vol. 6, no. 48, 1884, p. 961.

56. D. Zewalthoff, Russian Pharmacist, "The Origin and Progress of Pharmacy in Russia," *Pharmaceutical Record*, vol. 5, 1885, p. 102.

57. H. M. Gordin, "Pharmacy in Russia" (read before the students of the School of Pharmacy of the University of Michigan), *Pharmaceutical Review*, vol. 17, November 1899, pp. 504-505.

58. Isaiah Ginzburg, "A Pharmacist in Tsarist Russia–A Reminiscence, 1892-1909," *Pharmacy in History*, vol. 27, no. 3, 1985, p. 143.

59. Some pharmacists, of course, made more. In 1884 the St. Petersburg Pharmacy Society decided to raise the wages of the assistant in the chemistry lab of the society from 500 rubles to 800 rubles. "Soslovnyia dela," *F. Zh.*, vol. 6, no. 17, 1884, p. 277.

60. Advertisement, *F. Zh.*, vol. 40 (23), no. 24, 1901, p. 465.

61. *Izvestiia Iuzhno-russkogo obshchestva tekhnologov,* 1896/1897, no. 4, p. 44 quoted in a draft paper by Harley D. Balzar, "Technical Careers in a Modernizing Autocracy," AAASS, Miami, November 22-25, 1991.

62. Chego mozhno trebovat' ot farmatsevtov po voprosu ikh obrazovatel'nago tsenza," *F. Zh.*, vol. 20, no. 22, 1898, pp. 306-307.

63. Kellogg Durland, *The Red Reign in Russia* (New York: The Century Co., 1907), pp. 525-526. Durland also provided prices of basic foods, which were relatively cheap as compared to English or American food. Meat cost 10 kopeks per pound, less than 1/4 the American price; black bread cost 2 kopeks a pound, white bread 3 kopeks; potatoes cost 1½ kopeks per pound; sugar sold at 6 kopeks a pound; tea, 1 ruble, 80 kopeks a pound, coffee, 40 kopeks a pound; milk cost 10 kopeks a "jug"; cabbage and carrots cost 2-7 kopeks per pound.

64. N. P. Iur'ev, *K voprosu o material'nom polozhenii vrachei, sluzhashchikh po vedomstvu Ministerstva Vnutrennikh Del v guberniiakh i oblastiakh Rossii* (St. Petersburg, 1904), pp. 3-4, 5-6, 9-10, 22-23, 38, 41-47, 49-57.

65. Scott J. Seregny, *Russian Teachers and Peasant Revolution: The Politics of Education in 1905* (Bloomington: Indiana University Press, 1989), pp. 34-35. Seregny emphasizes that low teacher salaries plus perceived interference on the part of government officials, turned some teachers to radicalism.

66. Jonathan Sanders, "Drugs and Revolution: Moscow Pharmacists in the First Russian Revolution," *The Russian Review*, vol. 44, 1985, pp. 354-356.

67. Ginzburg, "A Pharmacist in Tsarist Russia–A Reminiscence, 1892-1909," p. 147.

68. Zewalthoff, "The Origin and Progress of Pharmacy in Russia," *Pharmaceutical Record*, p. 102.

69. "Pharmacy in Russia," *Pharmaceutical Review*, p. 505.

70. "Aptechnoe delo, aptekaria i sluzhashchie vo Frantsii," *Farmastevticheskii trud*, vol. 1, no. 20, 1907, pp. 272-273.

71. "Slukhi i vesti," *F. V.*, vol. 2, no. 48, 1898, p. 777.

72. "V pechatleniia," *F. V.*, vol. 7, no. 5, 1904, p. 73.

73. TsGIA, f. 1298, op. 1, d. 1221, ll. 5, 5 ob. The circular (*Tsirkuliarno*) of the Chief Medical Inspector also inquired as to whether a night duty room was provided, and what portion of the gross receipts were spent on salaries, a question that appeared a great invasion of privacy. Response from the Naval Pharmacy, March 10, 1905, ibid., l. 37.

74. TsGIA, f. 1298, op. 1, d. 1244, l. 10.

75. TsGIA, f. 1298, op. 1, d. 1244, l. 30.

76. MVD, Sov. Meditsiny, "Vypiska iz zhurnala," TsGIA, f. 1298, op. 1, d. 1244, l. 40.

77. TsGIA, f. 1298, op. 1, d. 1244, l. 95.

78. TsGIA, f. 1298, op. 1, d. 1244, l. 95.

79. TsGIA, f. 1298, op. 1, d. 1244, l. 94.

80. "Khronika: Novyia normy dlia sluzhashchikh v aptekakh," *F. Zh.*, vol. 49, no. 40, 1910, p. 435.

81. "Khronika: Normirovka truda v Peterburgskikh aptekakh," *F. Zh.*, vol. 50, no. 1, 1911, p. 12.

82. I. I. Korol'kov, *Farmatsevty Rossii*, pp. 7, 24-26.

83. E. K. Khrzhanovskii, *Polozhenie aptechnago dela v Rossii v osveshchenii tsifr i faktov* (St. Petersburg, 1913), p. 16.

84. For example, in 1907, Singer sewing machines cost 2 rubles, 50 kopeks; washing machines cost 25 rubles. See chapter 14 in this work.

85. "Tomsk gor. komissia, Vo Vrachebno-Sanitarnyi Sovet *Doklad komissii po revizii 1-i gorodskoi volnoi apteki* (Tomsk, 1915), p. 2.

86. See the comments of woman pharmacist Antonina Lesnevskaia in chapter 7 of this work.

87. TsGIA, f. 1298, op. 1, d. 1244, l. 39.

88. TsGIA, f. 1298, op. 1, d. 1244, l. 94.

89. There were comparatively few students in central Russia—in Voronezh, Viatka (contradicting information from the Viatka provincial inspector), Samara, Tambov, and Iaroslavl'. In St. Petersburg in 44 pharmacies there were less than three students; in the remaining provinces in 42 pharmacies there were less than 58 students. In seven Novorossiisk and Little Russian provinces, there were 275 pharmacies that employed students; in 63 pharmacies there were fewer than 162 students, or an average of 2.5 students per pharmacy. In the 6 provinces of the northwest region there were 233 pharmacies; in 106 there were fewer than 341 students, or an average of 3 per pharmacy. In the southwest region 3 provinces had a total of 191 pharmacies; in 31 pharmacies there were fewer than 53 students, or about 1.5 per pharmacy. In the Don region there were 15 pharmacies; in 2 pharmacies there were less than three students. In Otseisk region in three provinces there were 86 pharmacies—in 10 there were less than 15 students. TsGIA, f. 1298, op. 1, d. 1244, l. 98 and 98 ob.

90. Rubinshtein, "Nemnogo tsyfr," p. 391.

91. See chapter 6 of this work.

92. "Kooperativ sluzhashchikh farmatsevtov," *Zhizn' farmatsevta*, vol. 3, nos. 1-2, 1916, p. 1.

93. I. A. Gershtein, "Soslovnyia dela: Chto nam delat' za zashchitu ot 'praktikantov,'" *F. Zh.*, vol. 6, no. 21, 1884, pp. 519-520.

94. "Khronika: Aptechnie praktikanty," *F. V.*, vol. 7, no. 32, 1904, p. 509.

95. *Ispytaniia na zvaniia i stepeni lekaria, zubnago vracha, povival'noi babki, provizora, aptekarskago pomoshchnika i aptekarskago uchenika*, sostavil (ed.) N. Malinovskii (St. Petersburg, 1907), pp. 217-218.

96. Zh. B-skii, "Zametki i vpechatleniia," *F. Zh.*, vol. 45, no. 33, 1906, pp. 586-588; ibid., no. 34, p. 597.

97. "Farmatsevticheskii vopros na pervom fel'dsherskom s"ezde v Moskve," *F. T.*, vol. 1, no. 3, 1907, pp. 44-46, and "Aptechnoe delo i fel'dshery," ibid., no. 7, pp. 101-106.

98. Toropov noted that in 1910 supposedly 660 Provizors were occupied in pharmacies, whereas in Warsaw, Moscow, St. Petersburg, and Odessa there were

317 pharmacies and 830 registered Provizors—513 more than the number of pharmacies. Toropov, "Dvizhenie i rost," pp. 1300–1301.

99. M. G. Koroleva, "Moskovskie apteki vo vtoroi polovine XIX i nachale XX vekov," *Aptechnoe delo,* vol. 9, no. 4, 1960, p. 77. Periodical notices for sales of "privilege" or the concession to operate a pharmacy support her claim. For example, in 1901 *Farmatsevticheskii zhurnal* advertised: "Selling privilege for opening a pharmacy in the city of Chimkent, Syr Daria region, for 300 rubles." Advertisement, *F. Zh.,* vol. 40 (23), no. 31, 1901, p. 566.

100. H. M. Gordin, "Pharmacy in Russia," *Pharmaceutical Review,* vol. 17, November 1899, pp. 500–501.

101. Gordin, "Pharmacy in Russia," pp. 502, 503–504.

102. Gordin, "Pharmacy in Russia," p. 501.

Gordin claimed that these difficulties drove pharmacists to seek extreme solutions: "Owing to the difficulty of establishing oneself independently in a large city and to the natural disinclination to remain clerking to the end of their days, a considerable number of Russian pharmacists establish themselves in some God-forsaken corner of the immense empire, others seek salvation in rich marriages and again others try to find refuge in foreign countries where there is more freedom to individual initiative. Most of those that come to this country [America], after overcoming the natural aversion for the unprofessional ways of American pharmacies, turn out very successful men; others who are not able to imbibe the spirit of the land give up the area of a free fight for all and return to the domain of the Czar, completely dissapointed." Gordin, "Pharmacy in Russia," p. 506.

103. Gordin, ibid., p. 501.

104. Anon., "Pharmacy in Russia," *The Druggists Circular and Chemical Gazette,* October 1903, p. 203.

105. See chapters 8 and 9, in this work, on the Russian pharmaceutical industry.

106. Ruffman, "Russian Pharmacy," *Bulletin of Pharmacy,* 1906, p. 16.

107. "Farmatsevticheskoe obrazovanie," *F. Zh.,* vol. 1, no. 1, 1879, p. 6.

108. His account was not complimentary to public pharmacy. He noted, rather sarcastically, that the objective of the zemstvo was to supply free medicine to the poor; the police readily gave the poor certificates testifying to their poverty. However, after purchasing his pharmacy, he became aware that treatment in the zemstvo hospital was unsatisfactory and dispensing in the district was negligible. Since the zemstvo lacked funds to purchase medicines and storage facilities in its hospital, he proposed to its board that he dispense all medicaments to the poor. In return, the zemstvo was to pay him for transporting the medicines plus a 15 percent increment over prices asked in Moscow and St. Petersburg. The zemstvo accepted and, according to Glezar, both he and the zemstvo had benefited. They jointly dispensed free medicines and medical advice to all poor, increased their patients, built a new hospital and 11 feldsher points. Instead of the 350 rubles formerly spent on medicinal substances 3,000 were currently spent; in place of helping 2,000 to 3,000 sick annually the pharmacy owner and zemstvo were help-

ing 25,000. With the increased activity of the zemstvo, his pharmacy turnover and income had not diminished but, on the contrary, had increased by 350 rubles. "O modus vivendi aptekarei s zemstvom," *F. Zh.*, vol. 1, no. 4, 1879, pp. 123-124.

109. Z. Zeskov, "Po povodu aptechnago voprosa," *F. Zh.*, vol. 13, no. 38, 1891, pp. 606-607.

110. A recent example was the list of medicinal substances that could not be sold in drug stores and chandleries markets. V. A. Sokolov, Provizor Epifan, "Soobshcheniia iz sredi nashikh chitatelei," *F. Zh.*, vol. 13, no. 38, 1891, pp. 605-607.

111. For example, I. V. Stavskii opposed "pharmacy privilege" in *Farmatsevticheskii vestnik* in 1904; it was not clear whether he was an owner himself. I. V. Stavskii, "Obshchestvennye obshchesoslovnye interesy i sovremennaia aptechnaia privilegiia," *F. V.*, vol. 7, no. 3, 1904, pp. 39-40. S. K. Lintser, the socialist-inclined editor of the journal criticized the pharmacy monopoly and promoted free trade. Lintser, "Aptechaia monopoliia," ibid., pp. 40-42. He was not an pharmacy owner himself, thus his tolerance was painless.

Chapter 6

1. Ia. Chistovich, "Aptechnyi vopros v Rossii," *Meditsinskii vestnik*, vol. 4, 1864, pp. 238-240.

2. Upravlenie Glavnago Vrachebnago Inspektora MVD: *Otchet o sostoianii vrachebnago zdraviia i organizatsii vrachebnoi pomoshchi v Rossii za 1905 god* (St. Petersburg, 1907), p. 1.

3. De-v, "Aptechnoe delo v Rossii po offitsial'nym statisticheskim dannym," *Russkii farmatsevt*, vol. 1, no. 1, 1908, p. 27.

Pharmacists were far fewer than physicians, who amounted to 23,500 in 1905 (*Otchet o sostoianii narodnago zdraviia i organizatsii vrachebnoi pomoshchi za 1905 god* [St Petersburg, 1907], pp. v-vi) and were minuscule when compared with schoolteachers, there being about 25,000 rural schoolteachers, alone, in 1880 (Scott J Seregny, *Russian Teachers and Peasant Revolution: The Politics of Education in 1905* (Bloomington: Indiana University Press, 1989), p. 9.

For comparison with Western Europe, in 1907 in much smaller Prussia there were 7,620 pharmacists. "Za rubezhom," *Farmatsevticheskii trud* [hereafter cited *F. T.*], vol. 3, no. 2, 1909, p. 30. In France in 1907 there were approximately 15,000 *Pharmacien*. "Aptechnoe delo, aptekaria i sluzhashchie vo Frantsii," *F. T.*, vol. 1, no. 20, 1907, p. 269.

4. D. I. Toropov, "Dvizhenie i rost aptechnago dela v Imperii za poslednee desiatiletie (1901-1910 g.g.)," *Vestnik obshchestvennoi gigieny sudebnoi i prakt. meditsiny*, 1911, p. 1304.

5. Jonathan Sanders, "Drugs and Revolution: Moscow Pharmacists in the First Russian Revolution," *The Russian Review*, vol. 44, 1985, p. 355.

6. The same was true of national minorities who entered the Russian civil service. In "The Evolution of Civil Officialdom, 1755-1855," Walter M. Pintner remarked on how the Russian civil bureaucracy attracted non-nobles and particu-

larly Poles. *Russian Officialdom,* eds., Walter McKenzie Pintner and Don Karl Rowney (Chapel Hill: University of North Carolina Press, 1980), p. 209 and Pintner, "Civil Officialdom and the Nobility in the 1850s," ibid., p. 234.

7. I. S. Tkeshelashvili, *Materialy dlia istorii farmatsii v Rossii. Biograficheskii slovar' farmatsevtov poluchivshikh stepen' magistra farmatsii v Imperatorskikh russkikh Universitetakh i v Imperatorskoi Voenno-Meditsinskoi Akademii s 1845–1901 god* (Moscow, 1901), pp. 9, 13–23.

8. Toropov, "Dvizhenie i rost," p. 1303.

9. Jonathan Sanders does not examine this issue in its complexity in his section on *Jewish Pharmacists* in "Drugs and Revolution: Moscow Pharmacists in the First Russian Revolution," pp. 356–358.

10. Tsentral'nyi Gosudarstvennyi Istoricheskii Arkhiv, St. Petersburg [hereafter cited TsGIA], fond 1297, opis' 155, delo 3, list 4 [hereafter cited "f.," "op.," "d.," "l.," or "ll." in the plural].

11. TsGIA, f. 1297, op. 155, d. 3, ll. 33, 33 ob., 34. The letter regarding the residence of a specific Jewish pharmacist, Assistant Pharmacist Begermeister, mentions only the term "highest authority" but the letters from the provincial medical authorities are addressed to the Medical Department and refer to the Senate.

12. "Svod zakonov, T. XIV, ust. o pasport., izd. 1893 and Uk. Prav. Senata po 1-mu D-tu 5 noiabr. 1886 g. No. 13195, cited in *Sbornik zakonopolozhenii dlia farmatsevtov, soderzhatelei aptek i drogistov,* sostavil (ed.) P. N. Bulatov (St. Petersburg, 1897), p. 83. Bulatov was manager of business of the chancellery of the Medical Council of the Ministry of Internal Affairs.

13. TsGIA, f. 1297, op. 155, d. 3, l. 1.

14. TsGIA, f. 1297, op. 155, d. 3, ll. 4, 7.

15. TsGIA, f. 1297, op. 155, d. 3, ll. 28–31, 32.

16. TsGIA, f. 1297, op. 155, d. 3, l. 36.

17. TsGIA, f. 1297, op. 155, d. 3, l. 24 and ob.

18. TsGIA, f. 1297, op. 155, d. 3, l. 36 and ob. Oddly enough, this regulation was not noted in the *Sbornik zakonopolozhenii dlia farmatsevtov, soderzhatelei aptek i drogistov,* edited by P. N. Bulatov (St. Petersburg, 1897).

19. TsGIA, f. 1297, op. 155, d. 3, l. 36.

20. "Raznyia izvestiia," *F. Zh.*, vol. 23, no. 30, 1901, p. 559.

21. "Khronika," *Farmatsevticheskii vestnik,* [hereafter cited *F. V.*], vol. 2, no. 49, 1898, p. 794.

22. *Mnenie chlenov komiteta I. A. Ivanovskogo* (St. Petersburg, 1903), 13 pp.

23. Cited in *Farmatsevt,* vol. 14, no. 9, 1906, p. 252.

24. Advertisements, such as that in *Farmatsevticheskii zhurnal* in 1901 were sometimes encountered: "Require experienced Provizor (not a Jew), 35–45 years of age, to manage a pharmacy in Tiflis." *F. Zh.*, vol. 23, no. 24, 1901, p. 465.

25. Regulations cited in *Ispytaniia na zvaniia i stepeni lekaria, zubnago vracha, povival'noi babki, provizora, aptekarskago pomoshchnika i aptekarskago uchenika,* sostavil (ed.) N. Malinovskii (St. Petersburg, 1907), pp. 221, 233.

26. Regulations cited in *Ispytaniia na zvaṇiia i stepeni,* p. 234.

27. According to "R. T. S." many advertisements barred Jews and "when a Jew

finally acquired a place as an apprentice, he was paid 5 rubles less [per month] than a gentile," untitled, *F. V.*, vol. 2, no. 49, 1898, pp. 790-791.

28. TsGIA, f. 1298, op. 1, d. 1244, ll. 92-93.

29. TsGIA, f. 1298, op. 1, d. 1244, l. 93.

30. "Novyi Tsirkuliar," *F. T.*, vol. 1, no. 27, 1907, p. 368.

31. *Ispytaniia na zvaniia i stepeni*, pp. 213, 214.

32. Linetskii, "Pis'mo v redaktsiiu," *F. V.*, vol. 5 (1901, 1902), no. 8, 1901, p. 140.

33. A. B. Solonouts, " O slushateliakh farmatsii," *F. V.*, vol. 7, no. 8, 1904, pp. 122-123.

34. Zh. B.-skii, "O prave zhitel'stva," *Farmatsevt*, vol. 14, no. 34, 1906, pp. 997-998.

35. "Khronika: no. 79," *F. V.*, vol. 7, no. 10, 1904, p. 156.

36. See Mary Schaeffer Conroy, *Peter Arkad'evich Stolypin: Practical Politics in Late Tsarist Russia* (Boulder, Colo: Westview Press, 1976), pp. 48-51.

37. "K Novomu uchebnomu godu," *F. T.*, vol. 1, no. 26, 1907, pp. 356-357.

38. Reprinted from *Russkoe Slovo*, *Farmatsevt*, vol. 14, nos. 44-45, 1906, p. 1297.

39. "Pereselenie farmatsevtov evreev v Ameriku," *Farmatsevt*, vol. 14, no. 16, 1906, pp. 461-464.

40. "Khronika," *F. T.*, vol. 1, no. 10, 1907, p. 145.

41. "Khronika," *F. T.*, vol. 3, no. 3, 1909, p. 41.

42. "Pravo zhitel'stva evreev-farmatsevtov," *F. Zh.*, vol. 49, no. 32, 1910, p. 355.

43. "Pravo zhitel'stva aptekarskikh uchenikov," *F. Zh.*, vol. 49, no. 41, p. 446.

44. "Obzor pechati," *F. Zh.*, vol. 49, no. 32, 1910, p. 355.

45. "Korrespondentsiia," *F. Zh.*, vol. 49, no. 33, 1910, p. 366.

46. "Na farmatsevticheskikh kursakh," *F. Zh.*, vol. 49, no. 37, 1910, p. 406.

47. I. I. Korol'kov, *Farmatsevty Rossii* (Moscow, 1911), pp. 26-28.

48. TsGIA, f. 1298, op. 1, d. 1244, ll. 68 and 69.

49. "Khronika," *Farmatsevt*, vol. 14, no. 4, 1906, p. 113; ibid., no. 12, p. 352.

50. TsGIA, f. 1298, op. 1, d. 1959, ll. 1, 2 and ob.

51. TsGIA, f. 1298, op. 1, d. 1959, 1. 3 and ob.

52. TsGIA, f. 1298, op. 1, d. 1959, l. 4.

53. TsGIA, f. 1298, op. 1, d. 1959, l. 5.

54. "Farmatsevticheskie kursy," *F. Zh.*, vol. 55, no. 37, 1916, p. 352.

55. "Pozdniaia torgovlia," *F. Zh.*, vol. 49, no. 31, 1910, p. 346.

56. *Rossiiskii Meditsinskii Spisok*, cited in "Khronika," *F. Zh.*, vol. 13, no. 22, 1891, p. 351. Other nationalities included eighty-seven Lithuanians; twenty-one Belorussians; seventeen Estonians; thirteen Imerintsev; nine Armenians; seven Georgians; four French; three Hungarians; two Finns; two Swedes; two Mingrelians, two Slovaks; one Greek; one Czech; one Karaimov (Crimean Tatar) Jew; and two representatives of tiny minorities.

57. T. P., "Statisticheskiia svedeniia," *F. T.*, vol. 3, no. 2, 1909, p. 27.

58. O. E. Gabrilovich, *Deistvuiushchee nachalo "p'ianago khleba" . . . Disser-*

tatsiia na stepen' magistra farmatsii (St. Petersburg, 1906), p. 59. See also chapter 7 of this work.

59. Tkeshelashvili, *Materialy,* pp. 20–21.

60. "Khronika," *Farmatsevt,* vol. 14, no. 3, 1906, pp. 79–80.

61. Tkeshelashvili, *Materialy,* p. 21. Gurevich is noted in the Jewish Encyclopedia—*Evreiskaia Entsiklopediia* (St. Petersburg, n.d.), vol. 6, p. 850. His school in St. Petersburg, the "Gimnaziia and real school of Gurevich" is described in *Entsiklopedicheskii slovar',* eds. Brokgauz-Efron (St. Petersburg, 1896), vol. 18, p. 911.

62. Tkeshelashvili, *Materialy,* p. 25

63. Tkeshelashvili, ibid., p. 24.

64. Alexander Semenovich Ginzberg's Jewish affiliation is noted in *Evreiskaia Entsiklopediia* (St. Petersburg, n.d.), vol. 6, p. 521.

65. Tkeshleashvili, ibid., p. 56.

Chapter 7

1. A. P. Chekhov, "Aptekarsha," *Sobranie sochinenii,* Tom chetvertyi, *Rasskazy,* 1886 (Moscow, 1961), pp. 220–225.

A shorter version of this chapter appeared in my chapter, "Women pharmacists in Russia before World War I: women's emancipation, feminism, professionalization, nationalism, and class conflict," *Women and society in Russia and the Soviet Union,* ed., Linda Edmondson (Cambridge: Cambridge University Press, 1992), pp. 48–76.

2. "O zhenshchinakh-farmatsevtakh; Vysochaishee povelenie 14 ianvaria 1871 g.," *Sbornik zakonopolozhenii dlia farmatsevtov, soderzhatelei aptek i drogistov, sostavil* (ed.) Dr. of Medicine P. N. Bulatov (Manager of business of the Chancellery of the Medical Council of the Ministry of Internal Affairs) (St. Petersburg, 1897), p. 81.

3. R. B., "Die erste Frauen-Apotheke," *Apothekenbilder von Nah und Fern* III, ed. Hans Heger (Vienna, 1905), p. 3.

4. D. I. Toropov, "Dvizhenie i rost aptechnogo dela v Imperii za poslednee desiatiletie (1901–1910 g.g.), *Vestnik obshchestvennoi gigieny, sudebnoi i prakticheskoi meditsiny,* no. 9, 1911, p. 1293.

5. Women were trained for midwifery from the mid-eighteenth century, studied medicine, albeit irregularly, from the 1860s, became paramedics or feldshers from the 1870s, and comprised two thirds of the students in the first proprietary dental school, which opened in 1881. They continued to comprise one half to three fourths of the students in the nine or so other proprietary dental schools successively founded in Russia. For information on women in other medical specialties see Jeanette E. Tuve, *The First Russian Women Physicians* (Newtonville, MA: Oriental Research Partners, 1984); Richard Stites, *The Women's Liberation Movement in Russia* (Princeton: Princeton University Press, 1961), pp. 31, 84; Samuel Ramer, "Who Was the Russian Feldsher?" *Bulletin of the History of Medi-*

cine, vol. 50, 1976, p. 216; "Khronika i smes'," *Zubovrachebnyi vestnik*, vol. 1, no. 2, 1885, p. 231; and author's MS on dentists in tsarist Russia.

6. Women practiced pharmacy in America from the mid-1770s but state licensing boards, pharmacy schools, and the American Pharmaceutical Association appeared only in the first half of the nineteenth century to regularize the practice of pharmacy. Mary Putnam, later to become famous as a physician under the surname Jacobi, graduated from the New York College of Pharmacy in 1863. Mary Upjohn received a degree from the University of Michigan in 1871; three other women had done so by 1877. One Miss Baker graduated from the Massachusetts College of Pharmacy in 1877, Miss Marian C. Tirrell from Chicago College of Pharmacy in 1878, and Susan Hayhurst (already a physician) from the Philadelphia College of Pharmacy in 1883. Emma Gary Wallace, "Women in Pharmacy," *The Pharmaceutical Era*, vol. 45, no. 1, 1912, p. 102; Glenn Sonnedecker, "Women as Pharmacy Students in 19th-Century America," *Veroffentlichungen der Internationalen Gessellschaft fur Geshichte der Pharmazie*, vol. 40 (Stuttgart, 1973), pp. 136–137. However, in the nineteenth century women, as well as men, could also be licensed as pharmacists after a certain apprenticeship. See "Mrs. Anna B. Hummel, Pharmacist," *The New York Times*, June 22, 1896, p. 3, col. 3 and Sonnedecker, ibid., p. 137.

For the fullest study of women pharmacists in the United States see Teresa Catherine Gallagher, "From Family Helpmeet to Independent Professional: Women in American Pharmacy, 1870–1940," *Pharmacy in History*, vol. 31, no. 2, 1989, pp. 60–77.

7. Canadian women in Ontario began to be licensed between 1868 to 1871. Ernest W. Stieb et al., "Women in Ontario Pharmacy, 1867–1927," *Pharmacy in History*, vol. 28, no. 3, 1986, pp. 125–134.

8. Elizabeth Garret received an apothecary license in 1865; two women had passed pharmaceutical examinations by 1868 when the Pharmacy Act officially admitted women to examinations in Great Britain. However, women were not allowed to prepare for examinations at the lectures or in the laboratory of the British Pharmaceutical Society until 1872. Esther Pohl Lovejoy, *Women Doctors of the World* (New York, 1957), p. 141; W. J. Uglow Woolcock, "Historical Sketch of the Pharmaceutical Society of Great Britain: XXI-Women Pharmacists; Examination Regulations," *The Pharmaceutical Journal*, vol. 75, no. 22, 1906, p. 364.

9. Women were admitted to the practice of pharmacy in the Netherlands in 1872; by 1892 15 Dutch women had received pharmaceutical diplomas. Sonnedecker, "Women as Pharmacy Students in 19th-Century America," p. 135. In 1898 there were 840 "assistant" apothecaries in Holland as compared to 540 men. Martha M. James, "That a Woman Makes as Good a Pharmacist as a Man, Providing They have Equal Advantage," *Procedings of the Wisconsin Pharmaceutical Association* (1898), p. 36.

10. Seventeen Belgian women passed pharmaceutical examinations between 1881 and 1891. Sonnedecker, "Women as Pharmacy Students in 19th-Century America," p. 135.

11. V. Vekhter, "Zhenshchiny v apteke," *Farmatsevticheskii vestnik* [hereafter cited F. V.], vol. 4, no. 32, 1900, p. 580.

12. The Austrian government permitted women to audit university medical courses in 1896; women were allowed to become physicians and pharmacists in 1900. Anon., "Uspekhi zhenshchin na vrachebnom i farmatsevticheskom poprishchakh," *F. V.*, vol. 4, no. 37, 1900, p. 664. To independently manage pharmacies women needed specific approval from the ministry of Internal Affairs. Oddly enough, Hungarian women in the Dual Monarchy were allowed to practice pharmacy "a few years earlier." R. B., "Die erste Frauen-Apotheke," p. 1. The Austrian government permitted women in Austrian-occupied Croatia to enter pharmacy in 1901. R. B., *loc. cit.*

13. Swedish women were allowed to study and practice pharmacy in 1891; the first Norwegian women passed the qualifying examination in 1894. Sonnedecker, "Women as Pharmacy Students in 19th-Century America," p. 135.

14. Spanish women were permitted to study pharmacy in 1892. Sonnedecker, ibid.

15. In France in 1900, 20 women (19 French and 1 foreign) were studying pharmacy in universities; 129 women (29 French) were studying medicine. Anon., "Khronika," *F. V.*, vol. 4, no. 7, 1900, p. 137.

16. "O dopushchenii lits zhenskago pola postupat' v apteki dlia obucheniia (Circular of the M.V.D., Medical Department, 19 May 1898, no. 1886)," Bulatov, *Sbornik zakonopolozhenii,* p. 82. No dates were cited for the arrival of the women's petition at the Ministry of Internal Affairs.

17. According to one version, Alexander III then instructed the Committee of Ministers to discuss the admission of women to pharmacy and they in turn presented a draft law to the Ministry of Internal Affairs in 1883. J. Schindelmeiser, "Nichtamtlicher Teil, Weibliche Pharmazeuten in Russland," *Apothekar-Zeitung,* no. 74, 1902, p. 636. According to another version Alexander III directly ordered the ministries of Internal Affairs, Public Enlightenent and War to work out procedures. "O dopushchenii lits zhenskago pola . . . ," *Sbornik Zakonopolozhenii,* p. 82.

18. Russia: *Ispytaniia na zvaniia i stepeni lekaria, zubnago vracha, povival'noi babki, provizora, aptekarskago pomoshchnika i apterkarskago uchenika.* Svod uzakonenii, razporiazhenii, postanovlenii i raz'iasnenii Pravitel'stva, pravila, trebovaniia, instruktsii, programmy dlia ekzamenatorov i ekzamenuiushchikhsia. Sostavil (ed.) I. Malinovskii (St. Petersburg, 1907), p. 215 [No. 46]. The degree Master of Pharmacy required four years of university education, a qualifying examination, and thesis.

19. "Khronika," *F.V.*, vol. 5, no. 48, 1902, p. 579. Ironically, Russian women were allowed to study medicine (though not pharmacy) at the University of Helsinki in the 1870s. Jeanette E. Tuve, *The First Russian Women Physicians* (Newtonville, MA: Oriental Research Partners, 1984), p. 34.

20. A. M. Semenov, *Zaslugu zhenshchin na vrachebno-farmatsevticheskom poprishche* (Moscow, 1892), pp. 5–6.

21. See stories of Eva Broido and Antonina Lesnevskaia in text, below.

22. Semenov adumbrated the history of women in medicine from ancient times and, curiously, for a Russian, presumably of the Orthodox faith, quoted a letter from the American Catholic Cardinal Gibbon, which acknowledged that, while women could not serve in worship they were eminently qualified for medicine. The Cardinal recalled that obstetrics had been in women's hands until the eighteenth century, women had been professors of medicine at Salerno and Bologna in the Middle Ages, and recommended that contemporary women study medicine. Semenov, *Zaslugu zhenshchin*, pp. 5-6, 9-10, 27, 29-45.

23. As a physician Bogoslovskii had no vested interest in the issue but his reasoning was interesting. He assured the Moscow Society for the Preservation of Public Health that women pharmacists would be competent, having already proven their ability as doctors, feldshers, and sisters of mercy; also, women had satisfactorily worked with expensive machinery performing quality control in a gun factory in Perm. Bogoslovskii appeared condescending in suggesting that women would be particularly suitable for staffing rural (*sel'skie*) and zemstvo pharmacies, but in fact, this is where qualified pharmacists were needed. He also believed women pharmacists could contribute to forensic chemical analysis. However, he stressed that women pharmacists must have pharmacy institutes with fully equipped chemical, botanical, pharmaceutical, and other laboratories. He revealed that Count P. A. Kapnist, trustee of Moscow University, planned to establish a a women's pharmacy institute in Moscow. Bogoslovskii had drawn up the curriculum. However, the institute needed 50,000 rubles. V. S. Bogoslovskii, *O prestoiashchei farmatsevticheskoi deiatel'nosti zhenshchin i neobkhodimosti ustroistva zhenskago farmatsevticheskago instituta* (Moscow, 1889), pp. 4, 6, 7-8, 9.

24. Schindelmeiser, "Nichtamtlicher Teil: Weibliche Pharmazeuten in Russland," p. 636.

Statistics in the late nineteenth century showed numbers of pharmacy students rising but numbers of assistant pharmacists decreasing. In 1896 there were 1,160 students, in 1897, 1,162, in 1898, 1,208, in 1899, 1,488; the number of male assistant pharmacists meanwhile declined from 2,584 in 1897, to 2,391 in 1898, to 2,171 in 1899. Data cited in V. Mosal'skii, "Neskol'ko slov o zhenskom trude v aptekakh," *Farmatsevt*, vol. 9, no. 28, 1901, p. 891.

25. See chapters 2, 5, 12 of this work.

26. "O dopushchenii lits zhenskago pola," p. 82 and *Ispytaniia na zvaniia i stepeni*, p. 231 [no. 83]. In 1881 there were 103 girls' secondary schools—76 girls' *gimnazii* under the Ministry of Public Enlightenment and 27 comparable schools of the Empress Marie. Patrick L. Alston, *Education and the State in Tsarist Russia* (Stanford: Stanford University Press, 1969), p. 70.

27. Richard Stites, *The Women's Liberation Movement in Russia* (Princeton: Princeton University Press, 1978), p. 166.

28. The number of male *gimnaziia* students might have been affected by the 76,971 "real school" students and 162,858 "urban" students; nevertheless, according to education authority Patrick Alston, in 1909 one of every 319 girls received a

secondary education as compared to one of every 423 boys. Alston, *Education and the State in Tsarist Russia,* pp. 70, 204, 286, 289.

29. *Ispytaniia,* p. 223 [No. 68].

30. These were Latin, German, French, history, geometry, and algebra. Anon, "Voprosy i otvety," *F.V.,* vol. 4, no. 1, 1900, p. 15.

31. "O dopushchenii," p. 82.

32. According to a survey of 1900, 89.7 percent of pharmacists were compelled to board in the pharmacy; this was called the *pansion* system. See Jonathan Sanders, "Drugs and Revolution: Moscow Pharmacists in the First Russian Revolution," *The Russian Review,* vol. 44, 1985, p. 357, and chapter 5 in this work.

33. "O razreshenii litsam zhenskago pola zanimat'sia v aptekakh v kachestve aptekarskikh uchenits odnovremenno s litsami muzhskogo pola" (Circular Med. Dept. 24 Feb. 1892, no. 1906) *Sbornik zakonopolozhenii,* pp. 82–83. Also *Ispytaniia,* p. 225.

34. "O dopushchenii," p. 82.

35. Pharmacists with this title were permitted to manage "normal" or fully stocked pharmacies.

36. The required courses included botany, zoology, chemistry, and physics. See Conroy, "Pharmacy in Pre-Soviet Russia," p. 123, and chapter 2 in this work.

37. "Akusherskie, fel'dsherskie, zubovrachebnye i farmatsevticheskie kursy—Zhenshchiny-Farmatsevty," in L. N. Ariian, *Pervyi zhenskii kalendar'* (St. Petersburg, 1899), p. 154.

38. "Farmatsevticheskie kursy dlia zhenshchin," *Farmatsevticheskii zhurnal* [hereafter cited *F. Zh.*], vol. 13, no. 9, 1891, p. 143.

39. "Khronika: Zhenshchiny Farmatsevty," *F. Zh.,* vol. 13, no. 12, 1891, p. 192.

40. *Ispytaniia* [No. 46 (10)], p. 215.

41. "Zhenshchiny-Farmatsevty," *Pervyi zhenskii kalendar',* p. 154.

42. R. T. S., untitled (Editorial), *F. Zh.* vol. 20, no. 1, 1898, p. 8, and Anon., "Melkiia soobshcheniia," ibid., no. 44, 1898, p. 627. The rooms in which the courses were to be held were fully equipped with labs and necessary apparatus.

43. Schindelmeiser, "Weibliche," p. 636.

44. Schindelmeiser, Ibid., p. 636. Unfortunately, Schindelmeiser did not enumerate the cities. According to James McClelland, curriculum in all these special courses was equivalent to that in universities, remarking that: "Although Russian women had still not achieved complete educational equality with men, Russia was clearly a European leader in women's higher education on the eve of World War One." James McClelland, "Diversification in Russian-Soviet Education," in *The Transformation of Higher Learning 1860–1930,* ed., Konrad H. Jarausch (Chicago: University of Chicago Press, 1983),p. 184.

45. "Khronika," *F.V.,* vol. 5, no. 43, 1902, p. 522.

46. Anon., "Uspekhi zhenshchin," p. 664.

47. Untitled announcement, *F. Zh.,* vol. 20. no. 28, 1898, p. 397.

48. By 1906 the State Council ruled that the Women's Medical Institute in St Petersburg could give the Assistant Pharmacist and Provizor exams, heretofore

held in the Military Medical School in St. Petersburg and universities in other areas. *Ispytaniia* [No. 46], 215.

49. "Khronika," *Farmatsevt*, vol. 13, no. 8, 1905, p. 237.

50. "Khronika," *Farmatsevt*, vol. 13, no. 20, 1905, p. 626.

51. "Konduitnyi spisok o farmatsevticheskoi deiatel'nosti A. B. Lesnevskoi," Gosudarstvennyi istoricheskii arkhiv Peterburga [hereafter cited GIAP], fond 212, op. 8, delo 127, list 2 [hereafter cited "f.," "op.," "d.," "l."].

52. Ibid., l. 3.

53. Ibid., l. 4.

54. N. I. Afanas'ev, *Sovremenniki. Al'bom biografii* (St. Petersburg, 1909, pp. 261-262 ("Lesnevskaia Antonina Boleslavna").

55. "Khronika," *F. Zh.*, vol. 20, no. 3, 1898, p. 41. A. M. Sidorkov was obviously mistaken when he stated that Lesnevskaia and Akker were the first to receive the Provizor degree. See "Vozniknovenie i razvitie zhenskogo farmatsevticheskogo obrazovaniia v Rossii," *Aptechnoe delo*, vol. 6, no. 4, 1957, p. 60. Antonia Lesnevskaia recounted her own story but was vague on certain dates. *Po neprotorennoi doroge* (St. Petersburg, 1901—reprinted 1914), pp. 3, 22, 39.

56. Anon., Untitled, *F.Zh.*, vol. 20, no. 41, 1898, p. 584.

57. "Konduitnyi spisok . . . A. B. Lesnevskoi," GIAP, f. 212, op. 8, d. 127, l. 25.

58. For Ol'ga Gabrilovich, see details below in this chapter.

59. S. Iu. Borisovskaia, "Iz istorii nauchnoi farmatsevticheskoi deiatel'nosti zhenshchin," *Farmatsiia*, no. 3, 1947, p. 32; also Sidorkov, "Vozniknovenie i razvitie," pp. 60, 61. The first woman to receive a learned degree, according to Sidorkov, was V. A. Rudneva-Kashevarova.

60. Sanders, "Drugs and Revolution," p. 357. Purportedly, in 1900 there were 2l female pharmacists (and 756 male pharmacists) in St. Petersburg in 1900 and 43 female pharmacists (and 729 male pharmacists) in Moscow in 1902. *Loc. cit.*

61. R. B., "Die erste Frauen-Apotheke," p. 3.

62. "Khronika," *F. Zh.*, vol. 20, no. 1, 1898, p. 14.

63. Mosal'skii, "Neskol'ko slov o zhenskom trude v aptekakh," pp. 859.

64. Mosal'skii, ibid., p. 892.

65. In 1895 there were 77 women student pharmacists; in 1896, 72; in 1897, 60; in 1898, 62; in 1899, 101; and in 1900, 123 The corresponding numbers for women Assistant Pharmacists were 13, 22, 28, 47, 41, and 56. Schindelmeiser, "Weibliche," p. 636.

66. Anon., "Sovremennoe polozhenie uslovii farmatsevticheskago truda v Zakavkaze," *F. V.*, vol. 4, no. 25, 1902, p. 298.

67. Tuve, *The First Russian Women Physicians*, pp. 67-68, 111. This also was the case in the United States. In 1889-1890, 884 American women were studying medicine as compared with 60 studying pharmacy; in 1899-1900, 1,456 American women were enrolled in medical school as compared with 196 in pharmacy school. Wallace, "Women in Pharmacy," pp. 17, 20; Sonnedecker, "Women as Pharmacy Students," p. 139.

68. Upravlenie Glavnago Vrachebnago Inspektora, *Otchet o sostoianii narod-*

nago zdraviia i organizatsii vrachebnoi pomoshchi v Rossii za 1905 god (St. Petersburg, 1907), pp. 123–126.

69. Wallace, "Women in Pharmacy," pp. 17, 20; Sonnedecker, "Women as Pharmacy Students," p. 139; 1900 census in Anon, "Women in Pharmacy," *The Druggists Circular*, vol. 51, January 1907, p. 151.

70. O. E. Gabrilovich, *Deistvuiushchee nachalo "p'ianago khleba" [Materialy dlia ustanovki sposoba vydeleniia ego iz muki i ego khimicheskikh svoistv . . . Dissertatsiia na stepen' magistra farmatsii* (St. Petersburg, 1906), "Curriculum vitae," p. 59.

71. Antonia Lesnevskaia, *Po neprotorennoi doroge*, pp. 3, 5–6. Her father subsequently died. Lesnevskaia does not specify the town where her father practiced but she was born in the city of Makar'ev, Kostroma province, October 16, 1866, and baptized February 12, 1867, in the same town, which was in the Nizhni Novgorod Roman Catholic diocese, so it may be that her father continued to practice here. *Vypiska iz metricheskoi knigi Nizhegorodskoi rimsko-katolicheskoi tserkvi*, GIAP, f. 212, op. 8, d. 127, l. 1.

72. Cited in Sanders, "Drugs and Revolution," p. 357. According to Sanders, Eva Broido commented that this desire for personal fulfillment was the result of "the oppressive shtetl environment." Sanders, *loc. cit.*

73. Eva Broido, *Memoirs of a Revolutionary* (trans., ed., Vera Broido) (London: Oxford University Press, 1967), p. 4 and *passim.*

74. Toropov, "Dvizhenie i rost," p. 1303. Of 4,724 total Provizors in 1911, 32.7 percent were Jewish, 29.4 percent were Polish, 12.9 percent were German, and 13.2 percent were Russian.

75. Miroslawa Pabis-Braunstein, "The First Polish Women Pharmacists," *Pharmacy in History*, vol. 31, no. 1, 1989, pp. 12–13, 15. An appendix to this article states that Doviaglo *graduated* from the University of Warsaw but this is inaccurate as universities in the Russian Empire did not admit women at this time. The universities did administer the examination for Assistant Pharmacist, however, and thus Doviaglo received the assistant pharmacist degree from the University of Warsaw.

76. Pabis-Braunstein, "The First Polish Women Pharmacists," p. 15 stated that Lesnevskaia was born in Warsaw. Information subsequently uncovered at the city archive of St. Petersburg lists her birth (October 16, 1866) and baptism in Kostroma province. *Vypiska iz metricheskoi knigi Nizhegorodskoi rimsko-katolicheskoi tserkvi*, GIAP, f. 212, op. 8, d. 127, l. 1. Lesnevskaia is, however, buried in Warsaw.

77. A. B. Lesnevskaia, "Zhenshchiny-farmatsevty. Pervaia zhenskaia apteka. Zhenskaia farmatsevticheskaia shkola." *I Vserossiiskii zhenskii s"ezd. Trudy 10-16 Dek 1908g* (St. Petersburg, 1909), pp. 688. Also *Rossiiskii meditsinskii spisok na 1916 god*, p. 104; and Pabis-Braunstein, "The First Polish Women Pharmacists," p. 15.

78. Schindelmeiser, "Weibliche," p. 636. Only one student was Russian, which is not surprising for this border area.

79. Toropov, "Dvizhenie i rost" p. 1304. Of eighty-five women Provizors in 1910, Estonians, Germans, Belorussians, and Latvians claimed only one each. While nearly two-thirds of women Provizors were Jews less than a third of men Provizors (32.7 percent) were Jews. *Loc. cit.*

80. These were the Cheliuta branch of the family. Reminiscences of Madam Cheliuta and Dr. Jerzy Lesniewski, Antonina's nephew, Warsaw, March 1990. The transliterated Russian version of Lesnevskaia's maternal grandparents was Sheliuta. As she was born in the Nizhninovgorod diocese, her baptismal certificate (which lists her full name as Antonina-Frantsiska) cites her mother as "Mikhalina, *urozhdennoi* [née] Sheliuta. Her sponsors were *pomeshchik* (landowner) Frants Sheliuta and *pomeshchitsa* (presumably his wife) Mariia Bogurska. GIAP, f. 212, op. 8, d. 127, l. 1.

81. Antonina's father, Boleslav, practiced medicine in a Volga town. A Cheliuta (Sheliuta) relative of Antonina—possibly her cousin—graduated from the Women's *Gimnaziia* of the Empress Marie in Saratov. The family also had a dacha in Finland. Antonina Lesneskaia's younger brother Boleslav possessed religious documents from the Roman Catholic Consistory in Tver. He graduated from the Iaroslavl' Kadet Corps school and served in a Viatka regiment in 1917. *Gimnaziia* certificate in the possession of Madam Cheliuta, Warsaw; Boleslav's documents in the possession of Dr. Jerzy Lesniewski, Warsaw; both examined by the author in March 1990.

82. See chapter 17 of this work for Antonina Lesnevskaia's alleged assistance to Polish refugees during World War I.

83. Pabis-Braunstein, "The First Polish Women Pharmacists," p. 15.

84. "Konduitnyi spisok . . . A. B. Lesnevskoi," GISP, f. 212, op. 8, d. 127, l. 2.

85. Wojciech Roeske, *Antonina Lesniewska, 1866–1937* (Warsaw, 1970), p. 14. *Farmatsevt* ("Otkrytie v S. Peterburge pervoi zhenskoi apteki,"), vol. 9, no. 23, 1901, p. 727, stated that the building housing the pharmacy belonged to St. Catherine's Catholic church. R. B., "Die erste Frauen-Apotheke," p. 3 stated that the pharmacy was housed in the "Catholic church building." The building is still in existence in St. Petersburg next to the (closed) Catholic church.

86. In 1909 the Polish Benevolent Society, which had branches in various cities of the empire, celebrated its twenty-fifth anniversary in St. Petersburg. *Kraj*, no. 17, 1909, p. 9.

87. GIAP, f. 212, op. 8, d. 127, ll. 33, 41, 45, 48, 50, 53, 58, 72, 82, 85.

88. A. Lesniewska, *Nowa Dziedzina pracy kobiet. W zwiazku z reforma zawodu farmaceutycznego.* (Warsaw, 1908) located in the University of Warsaw library.

89. In April 1905, *Kraj* noted that the Polish Philanthropic Society (*Towarzystwa Dobrocznnosci*) in St. Petersburg held a meeting in the library of the church at 32–34 Nevskii Prospekt. (Lesnevskaia's pharmacy was located at No. 32.) *Kraj*, no. 17, 1905, p. 22. During 1909, *Kraj* noted that both the Benevolent Society and a Polish Women's Society held meetings at No. 32, Nevskii. *Kraj*, no. 17, 1909, p. 9 and no. 14, p. 12. In the spring of 1909, *Kraj* informed its readers that the hospital committee of the Polish *kolo* in St. Petersburg planned a performance

of *La Traviata* as a fund-raiser, and that tickets could be purchased, among other places, "at Lesnevskaia's pharmacy, 32 Nevskii Prospekt—telephone 405. "Khronika," *Kraj*, no. 10, 1909, p. 10. Otherwise, *Kraj's* photographs and articles on the many activities of the Polish *kolo* in St. Petersburg did not mention Lesnevskaia, her sister Zhosepha, or Stankevich.

90. Quote cited in Sanders, "Drugs and Revolution," p. 357.

91. In contrast to the high percentage of minority women in pharmacy a much smaller percentage of minority women enrolled in the practical, more obviously "feminine" courses established in Moscow by Privy Councillor Novikov and his wife. Between 1888 and 1912 only 395 Catholic and 152 Jewish women compared to 7,513 Orthodox women took advantage of these classes in sewing, cooking, housekeeping, drawing, stenography, and the like.

Kratkii ocherk deiatel'nosti Obshchestva rasprostraneniia mezhdu obrazovannymi zhenshchinami prakticheskikh znanii (Moscow, 1912), p. 23.

92. Gabrilovich, *Deistvuiushchee nachalo "p'ianago khleba."* "Curriculum vitae," p. 59, and A. Abrahamson, "K zashchite dissertatsii O. E. Gabrilovicha: Pis'mo v redaktsiiu," *Farmatsevt*, vol. 15, no. 1, 1907, pp. 10–11.

93. O. E. Gabrilovich, *Deistvuiushchee nachalo "p'ianago khleba."* cover and p. 5.

94. There were 3,518 pharmacies of all kinds in the empire in 1901 and 4,804 in 1910. Toropov, "Dvizhenie i rost," pp. 1278–1279.

95. The *Peterburgskaia Gazeta* commented in 1916 that the "insufficiency of male pharmacists in recent times significantly increased the number of women pharmacists." Cited in Borisovskaia, "Iz istorii nauchnoi farmatsevticheskoi deiatel'nosti zhenshchin," p. 31. See chapter 17 of this work for further details on the position of pharmacists during World War I.

96. Schindelmeiser, "Weibliche," p. 636. Four regarded their compulsory practicum in the pharmacy as "sport" but the others were very serious.

97. Alston, *Education and the State in Tsarist Russia*, p. 285.

98. R. B., "Die erste Frauen-Apotheke," pp. 3–4.

99. Of Eva Broido, Jonathan Sanders remarked that: "Legislation and practice did not bar women from pharmacy work. However, the apprenticeship system, frequent night duty, the close quarters of the boarding system offered too many opportunities for sexual harassment to make pharmacy an attractive career. Furthermore, curtailment of opportunities for women's high education precluded them from advancing into the *provizor* rank." "Drugs and revolution," p. 357.

Similarly Richard Stites has claimed that "Lesnevskaia has left us a depressing account of her wanderings and her efforts to study and practice pharmacy in the face of every sort of unpleasant obstacle." Stites, *The Women's Liberation Movement in Russia*, p. 175.

100. Broido, *Memoirs of a Revolutionary*, p. 6.

101. Broido, Ibid., pp. 8–9.

102. Ibid., pp. 9–10.

103. Ibid., p. 10.

104. Ibid., p. 14.

105. Ibid., p. 11.

106. In all fairness to her "principal," Lesnevskaia had advertised in pharmacy journals that she had a governess' certificate. *Po neprotorennoi doroge*, p. 6.

107. In 1902, Schindelmeiser, docent at the Iur'ev-Dorpat Pharmaceutical Institute, noted that "a few" of his eighteen female students also had to tutor the children of their principal. Schindelmeiser, "Weibliche Pharmazeuten in Russland," p. 636.

108. Lesnevskaia, *Po neprotorennoi doroge*, p. 28. In her photograph, undated, but judging from the fashions, from the late nineteenth or early twentieth century, Lesnevskaia appears attractive but serious, with a determined jaw. Original photograph sent to me in 1989, by Historian of Medicine Andrei Viktorovich Shabunin, who resides in St. Petersburg.

109. Lesnevskaia specifically recalled a male pharmacist acquaintance who was not held in high esteem. Lesnevskaia, Ibid., pp. 3–4.

110. For example, her second "principal" had told her his pharmacy was fully stocked and had "normal" status, required for pharmacy apprentices. This was not true. Moreover the pharmacy was small and dirty. Lesnevskaia, ibid., pp. 7–13.

111. At one point flies and heat forced her to camp outdoors. Lesnevskaia, Ibid., pp. 3–14.

112. Lesnevskaia was sympathetic with one principal, who was forced to compete with a zemstvo pharmacy that dispensed medicine cheaply, even to the well-off. Ibid., pp. 14–18, 29–30.

113. Ibid., pp. 19–22.

114. Ibid., p.13

115. For example, a government official helped her retrieve her papers from her second principal. Ibid., p. 13. The Master of Pharmacy who helped her prepare for the Assistant Pharmacist exam again helped prepare her for the Provizor exam. Ibid., p. 34.

116. Ibid., p. 28.

117. Ibid., pp. 28–40. Also, Lesnevskaia, "Zhenshchiny-farmatsevty," p. 684.

118. Ivan Sofronovich Tkeshelashvili, *Materialy istorii farmatsii v Rossii. Biograficheskii slovar' farmatsevtov poluchivshikh stepen' magistra farmatsii v Imperatorskikh russkikh Universitetakh i v Imperatorskoi Voenno-Meditsinskoi Akademii s 1845–1901 god* (Moscow, 1901), *passim*.

119. "Konduitnyi spisok . . . A. B. Lesnevskoi," GIAP, f. 212, op. 8, d. 127, l. 2.

120. Ibid., l. 3.

121. Ibid., l. 4.

122. Ibid., l. 25, and below, in this chapter.

123. Bertha Aizenshtadt, "Koe-chto o polozhenii zhenshchiny v apteke," *F. V.*, vol. 7, no. 44, 1904, pp. 698–699.

124. "Ne pora li prekratit' neobosnovannuiu bran' aptekarei v pechati," *Farmatsevt*, vol. 13, no. 5, 1905, pp. 144–147. A pharmacy owner refuted her accusations, "Pis'mo v redaktsiiu," no. 29, ibid., pp. 910–912.

125. L. Lavrova, "K reforme farmatsevticheskago obrazovaniia," *F. V.* vol. 7, no. 49, 1904, p. 971.

126. Lesnevskaia, "Pis'ma v redaktsiiu," *F. Zh.*, vol. 20, no. 45, 1898, p. 643.

127. Lesnevskaia, "Pis'ma v redaktsiiu," *F. V.*, vol. 4, no. 48, 1900, p. 856.

128. Lesnevskaia, "Pis'ma v redaktsiiu," *F. V.*, vol. 5, no. 3, 1901, p. 50, and ibid., no. 12, p. 192. Also A. Lesnevskaia, "Pis'mo v redaktsiiu" (St. Petersburg, January 23, 1901) *Farmatsevt*, vol. 9, no. 5, 1901, p. 144. Lesnevskaia gave her address as St. Petersburg, Maksimilianov per., No. 2, kvartira 29.

129. "Ego siiatel'stvu g-nu Ministru Vnutrennikh Del, uchreditel'nitsi farmatsevticheskoi shkoly dlia zhenshchin Antoniny Lesnevskoi, Dokladnaia Zapiska," Tsentral'nyi Gosudarstvennyi Istoricheskii Arkhiv, St. Petersburg [hereafter cited TsGIA], fond 1298, opis' 1, delo 1111, list 15 (five-page letter, listy 15–18) [hereafter abbreviated as "f.," "op.," "d.," "l." and "ll." in the plural].

130. *Loc. cit.*

131. Ibid., l. 16.

132. TsGIA, f. 1298, op. 1, d. 1111, l. 17.

133. TsGIA, ibid., ll. 17 and 17 ob.

134. TsGIA, ibid., ll. 17 ob. and 18.

135. *Loc. cit.*

136. A. B. Lesnevskaia, "Bytovoi otdel. Doklad tret'emu s"ezdu Russkikh deiatelei po tekhnicheskomu i professional'nomu obrazovaniiu v Rossii, 'O farmatsevticheskom obrazovanii zhenshchin,'" *F. V.*, vol. 7, no. 4, 1904, pp. 55-59.

137. A. Lesnevskaia, "Zhenshchiny-farmatsevty," *I Vserossiiskii zhenskii s"ezd. Trudy pri russkom zhenskom obshchestve v S. Petersburge 10-16 Dek 1908 g.* (St. Petersburg, 1909), pp. 683–687.

138. A. B. Lesnevskaia, *K voprosy o reforme farmatsevticheskago obrazovaniia v Rossii* (St. Petersburg, 1912), pp. 4–5.

139. *Zhurnal SPb Stolichnogo Vrachebnogo Prisutstviia 19 maia 1900 g*, "Slushali: otnoshenie med. departamenta MVD ot 27 marta No. 2455 na imia SPb gradonachal'nika s khodataistvom magistrantki farmatstii A. B. Lesnevskoi o razreshenii ei otkryt' v SPb vne pravil 25 maia 1873 g. normal'nuiu apteku, v kotoroi budet rabotat' zhenskii personal." GIAP, f. 212, op. 8, d. 127, l. 29. Also, Lesnevskaia, "Doklad tret'emu s"ezdu Russkikh deiatelei . . . O farmatsevticheskom obrazovanii," p. 57.

Apparently a "company of several women-doctors requested the authorities to open a "First Women's Pharmacy" in St. Petersburg in 1893. The Pharmacy was to employ exclusively women and the manager was to be a woman. *Peterburgskaia gazeta*, 27 iunia, 1893. But as there were few women qualified as pharmacists at that time it would seem that their project was only a pipe dream. It is not known whether Lesnevskaia was aware of this project.

140. GIAP, f. 212, op. 8, d. 127, l. 33.

141. R. B., "Die erste Frauen-Apotheke," p. 4.

142. The regulation on women managing rural or village pharmacies: "O dopushchenii zhenshchin k upravleniiu sel'skimi aptekami . . . 31 ianvaria, 1892,

no. 145," *Sbornik zakonopolozhenii*, p. 83. Debate on the issue: "'Zhurnal Med. Soveta 17 iulia 1893,' Zhurnal SPb Stolichnogo Vrachebnogo Prisutstviia 19 maia 1900 g.," GIAP, f. 212, op. 8, d. 127, l. 29 ob.

143. A. Lesnevskaia, "Pis'mo v redaktsiiu (24 Dek. 1901)," *Farmatsevt*, vol. 10, no. 1, 1902, p. 11.

144. A. M. Prokof'ev, "Pis'ma v redaktsiiu," *F. V.*, vol. 4, no. 46, 1900, pp. 817–818; A. Lesnevskaia, "Pis'ma v redaktsiiu," ibid., no. 50, pp. 894–895; A. Lesnevskaia, "Pis'ma v redaktsiiu," *F. V.*, vol. 5, no. 1, 1902, p. 11 (volume 5 included 1901 and 1902); A. Lesnevskaia, "Pis'ma v redaktsiiu," ibid., no. 23, 1902, p. 278. Also, A. Lesnevskaia, "Pis'mo v redaktsiiu (Kaliazin, Tversk gub., 24 Dek., 1901," *Farmatsevt*, vol. 10, no. 1, 1902, pp. 10–12.

145. "III Vserossiiskii Farmatsevticheskii S"ezd," *Farmatsevt*, vol. 8, no. 3, 1900, p. 78.

146. On the other hand, the author projected some of the ambivalence undoubtedly felt by many male pharmacists. He opined that establishment of new pharmacies should not be based on whether the managers were men or women but on the basis of "the firm law," which took into account the "needs of the population," and expressed hope that Lesnevskaia's pharmacy would embody "the highest principles of pharmacy" and that "women pharmacists would work in full harmony with men pharmacists."

"Otkrytie v S-Peterburge pervoi zhenskoi apteki," *Farmatsevt*, vol. 9, no. 23, 1901, pp. 728–729.

147. *Zhurnal SPb Stolichnogo Vrachebnogo Prisutsviia 19 maia 1900*, GIAP, f. 212, op. 8, d. 127, l. 33.

148. Ibid., ll. 33, 41.

149. Ibid., li. 48, 53.

150. Ibid., l. 50.

151. Ibid., l. 58.

152. Ibid., l. 72.

153. Ibid., l. 82.

154. Ibid., ll. 85, 90.

155. Notables attending the opening ceremonies included physician N. A. Vel'iaminov; St. Petersburg Medical Inspector Dr. V. I. Skabichevskii; G. Gintsburg, privatdocent at the Military Medical Academy; Professor Shtein, director of a hospital sponsored by a philanthropic society, and Baronness Iskul'-von Hildebrandt. Other physicians and women pharmacists reportedly were in the audience. A Catholic priest offered a Mass and there were telegrams of good will from Moscow Russian Pharmaceutical Society and the Women's Self-Help Society represented by A. I. Shabanova. "Otkrytie v S.-Peterburge pervoi zhenskoi apteki," *Farmatsevt*, vol. 9, no. 23, 1901, pp. 727–728.

156. R. B., "Die erste Frauen-Apotheke," p. 3.

157. Ibid., pp. 3–4.

158. Lesnevskaia criticized pharmacy owners for regarding staff pharmacists

(*sluzhashchie*) as cheap labor. She criticized working pharmacists for their carelessness and lack of attention to the owners' property. *Po neprotorennoi doroge*, p. 21.

159. Afanas'ev, *Sovremenniki. Al'bom biografii*, pp. 261–262.

Cited [incorrectly] in a letter from R. Arbuzov, Assistant Director of the Military Medical Academy imeni S. M. Kirova, Leningrad, 18 November 1987 no. 25-131-331 to Dr. Teodor Kikta, Director of the Museum of Pharmacy, Warsaw, p. 1. Original in possession of Dr. Kikta.

160. R. B., "Die erste Frauen-Apotheke," pp. 3–4.

161. Lesnevskaia, "Doklad tret'emu s"ezdu Russkikh deiatelei . . . o farmatsevticheskom obrazovanii," p. 58.

162. Lesnevskaia, "Zhenshchiny-farmatsevty." *I Vserossiiskii zhenskii s"ezd. Trudy*, pp. 687–688. American, German, French, as well as Russian photographers descended.

Information on the offensive theater performance is included in GIAP, f. 212, op. 8, d. 127, l. 95.

163. Lesnevskaia, "Zhenshchiny-farmatsevty." *I Vserossiiskii zhenskii s"ezd. Trudy* , p. 688.

Similarly, in her early career, she recalled that a female patroness promised a great deal but did not deliver. Lesnevskaia, *Po neprotorennoi doroge*, pp. 37–38.

164. In 1918, socialists in Petrograd, as the capital was called during World War I, expropriated the First Women's Pharmacy. See chapter 19 of this work for details on "municipalization" of Lesnevskaia's pharmacy and its subsequent status as a "communal" pharmacy.

165. Lesnevskaia, "Zhenshchiny-Farmatsevty," *I Vserossiiskii zhenskii s"ezd. Trudy*, p. 688.

166. *Rossiiskii meditsinskii spisok na 1916 god*, p. 104.

167. She petitioned July 19, 1901. GIAP, f. 212, op. 8, d. 127, l. 95. A commission formed of Military Medical Academy professors Przhibytek, Kravkov, Varlikh, and *Magistr* of Pharmacy Ivanov, manager of the pharmacy in the Clinical Military Hospital, reviewed the proposal. "Protokol zasedanii konferentsii Imperatorskoi Voenno-meditsinskoi Akademii za 1901–1902 uch. god.," cited in letter of Arbuzov to Dr. Teodor Kikta, November 18, 1987, p. 1 (original in possession of Dr. Kikta, Warsaw Pharmacy Museum.

168. GIAP, f. 212, op. 8, d. 127, ll. 95, 147.

169. GIAP, f. 212, op. 8, d. 127, l. 95.

A women's pharmacy school existed in the United States in Louisville, Kentucky, from 1883 to 1893. A Louisville pharmacist, Joseph Barnum, established the school to serve women interested in pharmacy (some of whom he employed) when they met opposition upon enrolling in the all-male Louisville college of Pharmacy. Eunice Bonow Bardell, "America's Only School of Pharmacy for Women," *Pharmacy in History*, vol. 26, no. 3, 1984, pp. 127–133. Unfortunately, there is no evidence that Barnum's school influenced Antonia Lesnevskaia.

170. Lesnevskaia, "Zhenshchiny-farmatsevty," *I Vserossiiskii zhenskii s"ezd*, 688; Lesnevskaia, *K voprosu o reforme farmatsevticheskago obrazovaniia v Rossii*, p. 13.

171. GIAP, f. 212, op. 8, d. 127, l. 108.

172. Sidorkov, "Vozniknovenie i razvitie zhenskogo farmatsevticheskogo obrazovaniia v Rossii," p. 60; R. B., "Die Erste Frauen-Apoteke," pp. 3–4.

173. Lesnevskaia, *K voprosu o reforme*, pp. 5, 14. Lesnevskaia claimed that in these short courses pharmacy students basically concentrated on topics to be covered on the examination.

174. Lavrova, "K reforme farmatsevticheskago obrazovaniia," p. 972.

175. I. Levinshtein, *Materialy po farmatsevticheskomu obrazovaniiu* (Moscow, 1922), pp. 3–6, 7 and *passim*. The course of instruction that Levinshtein advocated was two years in length; each year was composed of three twelve-week trimesters. First-year students took one hour of anatomy the first two trimesters and two hours the third, with a one-hour lab each trimester; one hour of pharmacy technique with three to four hours of practical work each trimester; four hours of botany the first two trimesters and two hours the third (plus two hours of lab); three hours of zoology, three hours of Latin, four hours of mathematics the first trimester and six hours the second (with two and three hours of practicum, respectively); five hours of Russian the first two trimesters and four the second; four hours of physics the second and third trimester; four hours of analytical chemistry the third trimester; four hours of inorganic chemistry the first trimester and two hours the second and third, three hours of pharmaceutical chemistry the third trimester (two hours of lab each). Second-year students took six to eight hours of *practical* pharmacy, two to three hours of hygiene; two hours of pharmacognosy the first and second trimester; four hours of physics the first semester; two hours of analytical chemistry, first trimester; two hours of inorganic chemistry, first trimester; three hours of organic chemistry, first trimester and two hours the second; three hours of pharmaceutical chemistry the first two trimesters and two hours the second. Chemistry labs varied from two to six hours. Students worked in pharmacies during the two-month summer vacation. They also took history, including that of worker movements, in their second year. Table, p.8.

See chapter 19 on pharmacy education in the new Soviet state.

176. Sidorkov, "Vozniknovenie i razvitie," pp. 60–61. Also, A. Lesnevskaia, *K voprosu o reforme farmatsevticheskago obrazovaniia v Rossii*, p. 14. Lesnevskaia believed the ideal program in a pharmacy institute should be three years in length. Ibid., pp. 11–12.

177. In the fall of 1904, *Farmatsevticheskii vestnik* noted that "in the last semester it was possible to allow more than three-fifths . . . deviating from the rule in order to examine eighteen students from the First Women's Pharmacy of A. B. Lesnevskaia for the title Assistant Pharmacist." "Ekzamen v voenno-meditsinskoi Akademii," *F. V.*, vol. 7, no. 36, 1904, pp. 571–572. Among the examiners was S. A. Przhibytek, Professor of Pharmacognosy and Pharmacy. Their relationship would be significant in 1918, as related in chapter 19 of this work.

178. Broido, *Memoirs of a Revolutionary*, p. 34.

179. See chapter 13, "Pharmacists and Revolution," in this work.

180. E. D., "Po povodu sobraniia zhenshchin farmatsevtov," *F. T.*, vol. 1, no. 20, 1907, p. 278. See also an editorial on this topic "Zhenskii vopros v apteke," *F. T.*, vol. 1, no. 24, 1907, pp. 327–329.

181. "Raznyia izvestiia," *F. Zh.*, vol. 27, no. 38, 1905, p. 1245.

182. See Linda Harriet Edmondson, *Feminism in Russia, 1900–1917* (London: Heinemann Educational Books Ltd, 1984), pp. 87–101, *passim*.

183. TsGIA, f. 1298, op. 1, d. 1124, l. 1.

184. *Proshenie*, 23 May 1904, TsGIA, f. 1298, op. 1, d. 1124, ll. 2–3; "Ustav farmatsevticheskikh kursov dlia zenshchin pri sostoiashchem pod pokrovitel'stvom eia Imperatorskago Vysochestva Printsessy Evgenii Maksimilianovny Ol'denburgskoi Obshchestve okhraneniia zdorov'ia zhenshchin v S.-Peterburge," ibid., ll. 4–7.

185. TsGIA, f. 1298, op. 1, d. 1124, l. 8.

186. Letter of Princess Ol'denburgskaia to [Minister of Internal Affairs] A. G. Bulygin, 16 September 1905, TsGIA, f. 1298, op. 1, d. 1124, ll. 23–24.

187. "Khronika," *Farmatsevt*, vol. 14, no. 10, 1906, pp. 283–284, and ibid., no. 26, p. 757.

188. Letter of 17 September 1904, TsGIA, f. 1298, op. 1, d. 1124, l. 11.

189. Letter of 16 September 1905, TsGIA, f. 1298, op. 1, d. 1124, ll. 23–24.

190. Letter of 1 December 1906, TsGIA, f. 1298. op. 1, d. 1124, l. 28.

191. TsGIA, f. 1298, op. 1, d. 1124, l. 31.

192. Letter to His Excellency, MVD, 30 May 1909, TsGIA, f. 1298, op. 1, d. 1124, ll. 31, 32.

193. Ibid.

194. TsGIA, f. 1298, op. 1, d. 1124, l. 36.

195. TsGIA, f. 1298, op. 1, d. 1124, ll. 43, 46 and 47.

196. TsGIA, f. 1298, op. 1, d. 1124, ll. 46, 27, 49–52, 57.

197. "Khronika," *F. V.*, vol. 9, no. 8, 1906, p. 93.

198. Sanders, "Drugs and Revolution," pp. 370–371.

199. *F. V.*, vol. 7, no. 46, 1904, p. 930.

200. GIAP, f. 212, op. 8, d. 127, l. 158. She duly reported this to authorities on October 16, 1905.

201. *Nasha zhizn'*, as cited in "Khronika," *Farmatsevt*, vol. 13, nos. 41–42, 1905, pp. 1240–1241.

202. "Khronika," *Farmatsevt*, vol. 14, no. 3, 1906, p. 78.

203. GIAP, f. 212, op. 8, d. 127, l. 144. Ivan L'vovich Serbinov taught botany, Dmitrii Konstantinovich Tret'iakov taught zoology, and Vladimir Iul'evich Eikhval'd taught geology and mineralogy.

204. GIAP, f. 212, op. 8, d. 127, l. 144.

205. "Kursy A. B. Lesnevskoi," *F. T.*, vol. 1, no. 27, 1907, p. 374. Additional courses included clinical hygiene, sanitary analysis, and also special courses for pharmacists preparing for exams.

206. "Z naszej kolonyi," *Kraj*, no. 14, 1909, p. 12.

207. E. P. Braunshtein, *K istorii zhenskogo meditsinskogo obrazovaniia* (Khar'kov, 1911), p. 14.

208. "Zhenskie farmatsevticheskie kursy," *F. Zh.*, vol. 49, no. 38, 1910, p. 416.

209. "Zhenshchiny eksterny v universitete," *F. Zh.*, vol. 49, no. 43, 1910, p. 468.

210. "Ekzameny dlia farmatsevtov," *F. Zh.*, vol. 49, no. 34, 1910, p. 374, and advertisement, "Zhenskaia Farmatsevticheskaia Shkola," ibid., following no. 32. The advertisement noted the address of the school at 32 Nevskii, the phone number as 405, that only women who had finished the full *gimnaziia* course and taken the fourth class of Latin were accepted. The course of preparation for Assistant Pharmacist lasted two years; the academic year began September 1. The course of preparation for Provizor took an additional year. These courses began September 10.

Lesnevskaia had actually asked for *two* additional years, asserting that the Pedagogical Council had recommended this to her. She also wanted the second practicum—for Assistant Pharmacists—cut from three to two years. See three-page letter to the Minister of Internal Affairs, "Ego Vysokoprevoskhoditel'stvu gospodinu Ministry Vnutrennikh Del," TsGIA, d. 1298, op. 1, d. 1111, ll. 5, 5 ob., 6. Accompanying this was a four-page prospectus for the Provizor courses and a five-page "Statute" of the program for the Medical Council of the Ministry of Internal Affairs: "Ustav zhenskikh farmatsevticheskikh kursov pri pervoi zhenskoi apteke A. B. Lesnevskoi v S. Peterburge," and "Polozhenie o farmatsevticheskikh uchebnykh zavedeniiakh i utverzhdenii okonchivshikh v ikh obuchenie lits v stepeni provizora i zvanii apteckarskago pomoshchnika." Ibid., ll. 3, 3 ob., 4, 4 ob., 7, 7 ob., 8, 8 ob., 9.

The proposed Provizor courses included mineralogy with basic geology, bacteriology, study of pharmaceutical preparations (*farmatsevticheskoe tovarovedenie* [*ispytanie aptekarskikh preparatov*]) practical aspects of physics, analytical chemistry, pharmacy, forensic-chemical and chemical-physiology, and also sanitary researches. Ibid., l. 9. It is significant that the statute included the proviso that in case of disorders the Minister of Internal Affairs could close the courses. *Loc. cit.*

211. GIAP, f. 212, op. 8, d. 127, l. 209. In 1908 the enrollment was forty-eight; in 1909, thirty-nine; in 1910, thirty-six; in 1912, six more students were added for thirty-one.

212. Borisovskaia, "Iz istorii nauchnoi farmatsevticheskoi deiatel'nosti zhenshchin," p. 32.

213. Lesnevskaia, *K voprosu o reforme*, pp. 14–15. This student, Liubov Nikolaevna Lavrova will be discussed below.

214. "Desiatiletie shkoly zhenshchin farmatsevtov," *F. Zh.*, vol. 52, no. 5, 1913, pp. 52–53. See also Sidorkov, "Vozniknovenie," p. 61.

215. Lesnevskaia, *K voprosu o reforme*, p. 14. Zhosefa, or Josepha, Boleslavna Lesnevskaia received her Provizor degree in St. Petersburg in 1910. *Rossiiskii meditsinskii spisok na 1916 god*, p. 121.

216. Lesnevskaia, "Zhenshchiny-farmatsevty," *I Vserossiiskii zhenskii s"ezd*, p. 689.

217. Lesnevskaia, *K voprosu o reforme*, p. 14.

218. "Desiatiletie shkoly zhenshchin farmatsevtov," *F. Zh.*, vol. 52, no. 5, 1913, p. 53.

219. The Russian government established the Institute of Experimental Medicine in 1892. It was a premier institution that attracted world attention when I. P. Pavlov, who conducted research on the neurophysiology of digestion, received a Nobel Prize in 1904. The journal of the institute was the renowned *Archives of Biological Sciences*, published in Russian and French. Alexander Vucinich, *Empire of Knowledge. The Academy of Sciences of the USSR (1917–1970)* (Berkeley: University of California Press, 1984), pp. 66–67.

220. Pabis-Braunstein, "The First Polish Women Pharmacists," p. 14, and Roeske, *Women of Polish Pharmacy*, p. 18.

221. "Zhenshchiny farmatsevty," *F. Zh.*, vol. 52, no. 12, 1913, p. 138.

222. "Prazdnik zhenshchin farmatsevtov," *F. Zh.*, vol. 52, no. 6, 1913, p. 65. E. S. Arbuzova, graduate and current manager of a railroad pharmacy, also extended "warm . . . thanks" to Lesnevskaia.

223. GIAP, f. 212, op. 8, d. 127, l. 209. Other members of the Pedagogical Council included P. L. Mal'chevskii, chemistry professor from the Military Medical Academy who had taught at the school from the beginning; F. F. Stankevich; Lesnevskaia herself; and L. L. Kovaleva, graduate of the school and by then a pharmacist researcher.

224. TsGIA, f. 565, op. 6, d. 21652, ll. 1–10 ob. Lesnevskaia claimed enrollment had dropped to eighteen because she demanded full secondary school preparation. She provided a financial statement to prove her need.

As or even more interesting, such requests from private citizens to the Minister of Finance were not unusual. Many wrote asking for from 2,500 to 25,700 rubles for trips abroad, subsidization for manuscripts, supplements to pensions, support for various organizations. TsGIA, f. 565, op. 15, 1080, ll. 96, 97, 124, 175.

225. "Zhenskie farmatsevticheskie kursy," *F. Zh.*, vol. 55, no. 29, 1916, p. 263.

226. "Khronika," *F. V.*, vol. 7, no. 45, 1904, p. 909.

227. In 1912, V. V. Rumiantsev, claimed women enjoyed privileges in their pharmaceutical education that men did not. Women who had finished the full course of middle school had to complete only one year of practical work in a pharmacy compared to the two required from 1903 for those with a school-leaving certificate; furthermore, women did not risk losing their places in the pharmacy because they were not forced to attend university to receive their Provizor degree! However, Rumiantsev admitted that this practice cost women the theoretical knowledge necessary for pharmacy practice. He singled out Lesnevskaia's pharmacy school. He fretted that no women had founded higher pharmacy institutes, but noted that women could now enter the pharmacy division of the Psycho-Neurological Institute in St. Petersburg to prepare for the Provizor examination. V. V. Rumiantsev, *Zhenskoe farmatsevticheskoe obrazovanie* (Moscow, 1912), pp. 3–12.

228. Lonachevskii-Petruniak emphasized the defects in Russian pharmacy education. He referred to various courses to prepare Provizors but lamented lack of pharmacy institutes. Although he mentioned a 1904 report of the St. Petersburg

Pharmaceutical Society School Commission, he did not cite Lesnevskaia's women's pharmacy or school. T. I. Lonachevskii-Petruniak, *Vopros ob obrazovanii russkikh farmatsevtov* (St. Petersburg, 1905), pp. 7, 13, 20, *passim*.

229. Ginzberg was four years younger than Lesnevskaia. Ironically, they both died in 1937 (according to V. M. Salo, Russian pharmaceutical historian, Ginzberg was purged), and Ginzberg did research for a time in Warsaw, Lesnevskaia's final home. While acclaimed for his research, Ginzberg had a checkered career. In 1891 he studied in the pharmacy department at Khar'kov university; he then worked in the pathology laboratory of the Vil'na Medical Society and in the chemistry laboratory of the Warsaw Veterinary Institute of one Professor Vagner. Here he finished his *Magistr* dissertation, which he defended at the Military Medical Academy and which received a prize. Following this, in 1898, Ginzberg became chair of pharmaceutical chemistry at the Women's Medical Courses in St. Petersburg. In 1919, after the Bolshevik revolution, the women's courses were transformed into the Chemico-Medical Institute, a state institution supplanting Lesnevskaia's private school, and Ginzberg became Director of the Institute. Ginzberg was director of the institute for five years; he also occupied the chair of pharmaceutical chemistry until 1923. *Professory 1 Len. Med. In. za 50 let* (Moscow, 1947), p. 21.

230. Instead he mentioned that a pharmacy section was due to be instituted at the Women's Medical Courses in St. Petersburg, where he taught, and that there must be "more initiative in the creation and growth of the technical-chemical industry in Russia." He revealed that "there had been much argument about where higher pharmacy institutes should be established—in medical faculties, in polytechnical institutes or as independent pharmaceutical institutes." Ginzberg emphasized that the issue was not *where* the institutes should be located but *that* they be established.

A. S. Ginzberg, *K voprosu ob obshchem i spetsial'nom obrazovanii farmatsevtov* (St. Petersburg, 1913), pp. 7-9.

231. The Odessa municipal duma, executive board, and mayor began discussing women's medical courses and established an organizing committee for this purpose in 1908. The committee, including nine professors from the University of Odessa, modeled the courses on those in St. Petersburg. The first stumbling block was money; the land alone cost 88,000 rubles. The Odessa Ladies Committee, under the direction of Ol'ga Vasilevna Levatova, held a lottery for this purpose in May 1909, which netted 17,000 rubles; a second lottery in 1910 brought in over 5,000 rubles more. The Pedagogical council began meeting in November 1909 but further delay occurred in refurbishing and properly equipping the classrooms and laboratories. The institute finally opened in the fall of 1910. *Otkrytie Vysshikh Zhenskikh meditsinskikh kursov v g. Odesse* (Odessa, 1911), pp. 18-28.

The Khar'kov Medical Society founded an autonomous women's medical institute; in 1911 there were 980 students. E. P. Braunshtein, *K istorii zhenskogo meditsinskogo obrazovaniia* (Khar'kov, 1911), pp. 1, 14.

232. Abramson, "K zashchite dissertatsii O. E. Gabrilovicha," *Farmatsevt*, vol. 15, no. 1, 1907, p. 9.

233. Gabrilovich, *Deistvuiushchee nachalo "p'ianago khleba,"* [*Materialy dlia ustanovki sposoba vydeleniia ego iz muki i ego khimicheskikh svoistv*], as cited in note 70, above, p. 3.

234. Ibid., p. 4.

235. For a study of the effects of ergotism on population see Mary Kilbourne Matossian, "Climate, Crops, and Natural Increase in Rural Russia, 1861-1913," *Slavic Review*, vol. 45, no. 3, 1986, pp. 457-469.

236. I. R. Zakharevich, "Belozerskii krai," *Farmatsevt*, vol. 13, no. 20, 1905, pp. 629-630.

237. Gabrilovich, *Deistvuiushchee nachalo "p'ianago khleba,"* pp. 4-5. The Russian Society for the Preservation of Public Health was established in St. Petersburg in 1878. Branches were established in nineteen other cities by the end of the nineteenth century.

238. *Farmatsevt*, vol. 13, no. 2, 1905, p. 44, and ibid., no. 14, p. 433.

239. Ibid., pp. 7-13.

240. Ibid., pp. 9-58.

241. Ibid., pp. 18-19.

242. "Khronika," *Farmatsevt*, vol. 14, nos. 47-48, 1906, p. 1365.

243. E. A. Rothman, "The Removal of Erythma from the Face ('Red Nose') by the Prolonged Internal Administration of Adrenalin," *The Lancet*, January 16, 1909, pp. 194-195.

244. "The German Congress of Internal Medicine: Alteration of the Arteries produced by Injections of Adrenalin," *The Lancet*, May 6, 1906, p. 1222.

245. L. N. Lavrova, "O deistvii ioda na patologicheskiia izmeneniia v sosudakh, obuslovlivaemyia vvedeniem zhivotnym adrenalina," *Arkhiv biologicheskikh nauk*, vol. 8, no. 3, 1908, pp. 205-236.

246. *Loc. cit.*

247. "The Prevention of Arterio-sclerosis following the Use of Adrenalin," *The Lancet*, vol. 22, November 28, 1908, p. 1641.

248. L. A. Kovaleva, "O deistvii fotina na okislitel'nyia i dykhatel'nyia sposobnosti cheloveka" and "Vliianie preparatov fosfora na protsessy okisleniia v zhivotnom organizme," *Arkhiv biologicheskikh nauk* (St. Petersburg), vol. 17, no. 3, 1912, pp. 293-320.

249. Toropov, "Dvizhenie i rost," pp. 1298, 1304.

250. *Rossiiskii meditsinskii spisok na 1916 god*, pp. 80-81.

251. Toropov, "Dvizhenie i rost," p. 1305.

252. "Prepriimchivoi drogist," *F. Zh.*, vol. 52, no. 3, 1913, p. 32. This individual may not have been a pharmacist, as women who were not pharmacists had long owned pharmacies. Nevertheless, Morshiner did reflect women's initiative and enterprise.

253. Lesnevskaia, "Zhenshchiny-farmatsevty," *I Vserossiiskii zhenskii s"ezd*, p. 689.

254. For example, according to a latter-day Russian historian, *Farmatsevticheskii zhurnal* stated in 1916 that the average pay for women pharmacists was less than that for men. According to the journal the average Provizor's income was

141 rubles per month, women Provizors received on the average only 86 rubles; men Assistant Pharmacists' salaries averaged 98 rubles per month, women Assistant Pharmacists', 77; male students' pay on the average was 48 rubles per month, female students', 34. Quoted in Borisovskaia, "Iz istorii nauchnoi farmatsevticheskoi deiatel'nosti zhenshchin," p. 31-32.

255. "Desiatiletie shkoly," *F. Zh.*, vol. 52, no. 5, 1913, p. 53.

256. E. K. Khrzhanovskii, *Polozhenie aptechnago dela v Rossii v osveshchenii tsifr i faktov* (St. Petersburg, 1913), p. 16.

257. *Tomsk gor. komissiia. Vo vrachebno-sanitarnyi sovet. Doklad komissii po revizii 1-i gorodskoi vol'noi apteki* (Tomsk, 1915), pp. 1-2. The three boys in charge of the pharmacy ware were paid 30, 25, and 15 rubles per month. There was also an old charwomen and her boy helper. Ibid., p. 3.

258. "Vpechatleniia i zametki," *F. V.* vol. 8, no. 5, 1904, p. 73.

259. By 1910 while there still were cases of long hours and low pay, less pay was remitted in room and board, 86 percent received their Provizor degree before twelve years of pharmacy practice, there was some upward mobility, etc. (*Farmatsevty Rossii,* sostavil I. I. Korol'kov (Moscow, 1911), pp. 25, 17, 20-21 and *passim.*) Pharmacies in large cities had seven-hour workdays by 1910. Khrzhanovskii, *Polozhenie aptechnago dela v Rossii v osveshchenii tsifr i faktov,* p. 10.

260. *Tomsk gor. komissiia,* p. 1.

261. The organ of the union, *Zhizn' farmatsevta,* advocated "municipalization"—taking private pharmacies out of the hands of their owners and transferring them to the people through management by city self-government. The journal also advocated struggle by workers against pharmacy owners. However, it frequently proposed parliamentary methods, such as incluencing worker representatives in parliament, and called *Pravda* a "factional organ." *Zhizn' farmatsevta,* vol. 1, no. 1, 1914, pp. 4-5, 7.

262. "Zhenskii den' v peterb. obshchestve farmatsevtov," *Zhizn' farmatsevta,* vol. 1, no. 1 (April 3), 1914, p. 9.

263. One Lapitskii is cited in *Vestnik aptechnago truda,* vol. 4, nos. 16-17, 1917, p. 11, as participating in the meeting of the Petrograd Union of Working Pharmacists, in the November 12, 1917, debate to decide whether or not to continue the pharmacy workers' strike in St. Petersburg, but it is not clear whether this individual was related to Lapitskaia or whether the masculine form of her name might have been erroneously used.

264. "Zhenskii den' v peterb. obshchestve farmatsevtov," p. 9.

265. S. Lapitskaia, "Voprosy besrabotitsy," *Zhizn' farmatsevta,* vol. 1, no. 2, 1914, pp. 7-8.

266. The fate of Antonina's pharmacy is discussed in chapter 19 of this work, which details "municipalization" and nationalization of Russian pharmacies.

Chapter 8

1. In Western Europe common factors—mass-production of medicaments in pharmacies, chemist-pharmacists' discoveries, particularly of alkaloids, technical

improvements in making pills and tablets, and modern business methods—coalesced to produce a modern pharmaceutical industry. However, timetables and final configurations of the industry varied from one country to another.

For example, large-scale drug manufacture appeared in Venice in the fourteenth century, in Amsterdam and London in the seventeenth century, in France in the mid-1770s, and in German states in the early nineteenth century. In England, The Worshipful Society of Apothecaries founded a joint-stock company to initiate production. French production was dispersed in many small pharmacy workshops. In the German states pharmaceutical production was concentrated in large pharmaceutical houses. For details see David L. Cowen and William H. Helfand, *Pharmacy, An Illustrated History* (New York: Harry N. Abrams, 1990), pp. 123–143, 161–174. For information on the American pharmaceutical industry see Glenn Sonnedecker, *History of Pharmacy* (Philadelphia: J. B. Lippincott Company, 1976), p. 331. The differences in modern pharmaceutical firms are illustrated by the fact that those in France and Basel rejected patents and relied on brand names, whereas German pharmaceutical firms dominated through patents. See Renate A. Riedel, "A Brief History of the Pharmaceutical Industry in Basel," *Pill Peddlers*, eds., Gregory J Higby and Elaine C. Stoud (Madison, Wisconsin: American Institute of the History of Pharmacy, 1990), pp. 50–58, and Michael Robson, "The French Pharmaceutical Industry, 1919–1939," ibid., pp. 108–110.

2. L. Ia. Skorokhodov, *Kratkii ocherk istorii Russkoi meditsiny* (Leningrad, 1926), pp. 31, 33–34, 35, 37–38, 42. Also, V. M. Salo, MS "Aptechnoe delo v Rossii v XVI-XVII vekakh," pp. 52–55.

3. Clifford M. Foust, *Rhubarb, the Wondrous Drug* (Princeton: Princeton University Press, 1992), pp. 56–78.

4. I. V. Kozlov, chapter VIII: "Khimicheskie produkty," in *Istoriko-statisticheskii obzor promyshlennosti Rossii*, vol. III, ed., D. A. Timiriazev (St. Petersburg, 1886), pp. 8–11.

5. Foust, *Rhubarb*, pp. 55–58.

6. Kozlov, "Khimicheskie produkty," in *Istoriko-statisticheskii obzor promyshlennosti Rossii*, pp. 8–12.

For example, in 1805 Prince D. V. Golitsyn founded a chemical factory on one of his estates to produce sulfuric acid, copper vitriol, hydrochloric and nitric acids. Three of the chemical factories established between 1822 and 1830, that of Schlippe (later named the joint-stock company, or *Tovarsichestvo*, of the Chemical Factory Schlippe), Lepeshkin, and Afanas'ev (later the joint-stock compay of Paul Afanas'ev and Sons), were still operating in the mid-1880s.

Karl Ivanovich Schlippe personified the entrepreneurship that helped build Russia's chemical industry. After leaving the University of Berlin early in the century with a degree in chemistry, Schlippe began making wine vinegar (*uksus*) and wine acid (*vinnyi uksus*) in Vepeisk district, Moscow province. At the end of the 1820s Schlippe expanded production to include chromium salts (*khromovye soli*), nitric and hydrochloric acids, and dextrine. In 1834 he enlarged production to factory scale. In 1842 Schlippe was given a "privilege" (franchise) to make sulfuric acid from pyrites. Schlippe's factory produced carbolic magnesia, vitriol, blue potassium, various salts of copper and zinc, alum, boric acid. Kozlov, ibid., pp. 13-14.

A *pud* equals thirty-six pounds.

7. P. M. Luk'ianov, *Istoriia khimicheskikh promyslov i khimicheskoi promyshlennosti Rossii do kontsa XIX veka,* (Moscow-Leningrad, 1948), pp. 136, 139.

8. Kozlov, "Khimicheskie produkty," p. 12.

9. Luk'ianov, *Istoriia khimicheskikh promyslov,* p. 130.

10. Kozlov, "Khimicheskie produkty," p. 11. Kozlov provided a table comparing British-made chemicals with Russian in 1822 and 1830 and the amounts of these chemicals used by Russian industry in 1830. Industry naturally used the cheapest product in most cases. The table was based on data gathered by one Baron Meyendorff. The high tariff was the policy of Finance Minister Count Kankrin. For information on steam engines and the tariff of 1851 see Luk'ianov, *Istoriia khimicheskikh promyslov,* p. 139.

11. Luk'ianov, *Istoriia khimicheskikh promyslov,* p. 141. Entrepreneurship was very evident in the cosmetics industry. For example, in 1802 an *ukaz* promulgated by the Senate gave permission to court distiller Novigrad to make perfume (syrups and liquors). Novigrad was permitted to sell perfume to the public on the condition that he pay the treasury 5 kopeks for each vial (*slianki i banki*). In 1810 this enterprise was transferred to Councillor Kusovikov, who paid an excise tax of 20 kopeks per bottle of perfume. Advertisements in early nineteenth-century newspapers alerted the public to sales of perfumes—"the very best for 225 kopeks, other sorts for 175 kopeks a bottle . . . ," ibid., pp. 160–161. The Parisian perfumerie "Moderne" opened a branch in Moscow in 1907 to spare patrons the "inconvenience of ordering directly from abroad." Advertisement, *Farmatsevticheskii trud* [hereafter cited *F. T.*], vol. 1, no. 12, 1907, p. 179. Russian perfume concerns continued to operate. The Association (Tovarishchestvo) Ostroumov Parfumerie in Moscow advertised its products in the early twentieth century. Ibid., no. 4.

As for the substance *belila,* or "whiting," in the late sixteenth century the Englishman Giles Fletcher described how "The women, to mend the bad hue of their skins, used to paint their faces with white and red colors. . . . This parches the skin, and helps to deform them when their painting is off." *The Russe Commonwealth,* cited in Basil Dmytryshyn, *Medieval Russia: A Source Book, 900–1700* (Hinsdale, IL: The Dryden Press, 1973), p. 252.

12. V. D. Abramov, "Eksport leksyr'ia," *Khimiko-farmatsevticheskii zhurnal,* no volume cited, no. 3-4 (6-7), 1924, pp. 2-3. Written during the NEP when a modicum of private enterprise was allowed to exist, this Soviet article lauded Del' as a pioneer in the collection and cultivation of medicinal plants.

13. V. M. Salo, "Akademik Rossiiskoi Akademii Nauk farmatsevt T. E. Lovits (k 250-letiiu Akademii Nauk SSSR)," *Farmatsiia,* vol. 24, no. 1, 1975, p. 36.

14. Sonnedecker, *History of Pharmacy,* p. 357.

15. Salo, "Akademik Rossiiskoi Akademik . . . Lovits . . . ," p. 37. Lovits studied the effect of charcoal on more than twenty substances.

16. Sonnedecker, *History of Pharmacy*, p. 357.

17. Large-scale pharmaceutical production in the Russian Empire lagged about fifty years behind France, where a pharmaceutical factory developed in 1775. However, the westernmost areas of the empire were only slightly behind some of the German states, where the first pharmaceutical house appeared in 1821. The American "druggist" John K Smith founded Smith, Kline and French in Philadelphia in 1830 and Sharp and Dohme was established in Baltimore in 1845. See Cowen and Helfand, *Pharmacy, An Illustrated History*, p. 174 and Sonnedecker, *History of Pharmacy*, p. 326. For development of the pharmaceutical industry in England, see Sonnedecker, ibid., pp. 119–121; France, ibid., p. 75; Germany, ibid., pp. 369–370.

18. Teodor Kikta, *Przemysl farmaceutyczny w Polsce (1823–1939)* (Warsaw, 1972), pp. 13–14. The "Steam-powered Laboratory of Pharmaceutical and Galenical Preparations, Medical Soaps and Pressed Lozenges (*Parovaia laboratoriia farmatsevticheskikh i galenovykh preparatov, meditsinskikh perezhirennykh i gigienicheskikh myl i pressovannykh lepeshek*), supposedly began production in 1847, in Kiev. Natradze, *Ocherk razvitiia khimiko-farmatsevticheskoi promyshlennosti SSSR* (Moscow, 1977 edition), p. 70. Unfortunately, Natradze does not cite a source for this information. The making of pressed tablets had originated in America in the 1820s and only became common in Europe during the 1850s. "K kharakteristike patentovannykh sredstv s soliami khinina," *Farmatsevticheskii zhurnal* [hereafter cited *F. Zh.*], vol. 54, no. 43, 1915, p. 421.

19. Russian title of A. P. Neliubin's work: *Dispensatoriia sekretnykh, spetsificheskikh, universal'nykh i patentovannykh sredstv* (1831). V. M. Salo, "Vydaiushchiisia deiatel' otechestvennoi farmatsii A. P. Neliubin (k 130 letiiu so dnia smerti)," *Farmatsiia*, no. 2, 1989, pp. 73–74.

20. V. G. Belikov, *Farmatsevticheskaia khimiia* (Moscow, 1985), p. 9. A. G. Natradze, *Ocherk razvitiia khimiko-farmatsevticheskoi promyshlennosti* (Moscow, 1967), p. 45 cites Professor A. A. Iovskii (1796–1857), Vice Director of the Medical Department, for his 1820s and 1830s publications, which accelerated development of the Russian pharmaceutical industry.

21. Anon., "Russian, Danish, British, American Pharmacopoeias," *The British and Foreign Medical Review*, vol. 13, 1842, pp. 58–85.

22. See Roderick E. McGrew, *Russia and the Cholera, 1823–32* (Madison: University of Wisconsin Press, 1965), pp. 135–138.

23. See the chapter on "Pure Food and Environment" in this work.

24. Kozlov, "Khimicheskie produkty," in *Istoriko-statisticheskii obzor promyshlennosti Rossii*, p. 43.

25. In 1885 I. V. Kozlov referred to the production of carbolic acid by one "Kil'vein and a Professor Kittary" but, unfortunately he supplied no details. "Khimicheskie produkty," *Istoriko-statisticheskii obzor promyshlennosti Rossii*, p. 43.

26. For more on malaria in Russia see Mary Schaeffer Conroy, "Malaria in Late Tsarist Russia," *Bulletin of the History of Medicine*, vol. 56, no. 1, 1982, pp. 41–55.

27. V. M. Salo, "Vydaiushchiisia deiatel' otechestvennoi farmatsii Georg Dra-

gendorf, " *Farmatsiia*, 1985, pp. 78–79. Russian title of Ph.D. dissertation from Rostok: "*O vliianii fosfora na nekotorye uglekislye i bornokislye soli.*" Dragendorff's work for the Master of Pharmacy degree was done at Dorpat University. Dragendorff also served briefly–from 1862–1864–as editor of the St. Petersburg Pharmacy Society's German-Russian journal, *Farmatsevticheskii zhurnal.* Ibid, p. 78.

28. Sonnedecker, *History of Pharmacy*, p. 343.

29. Ivan Sofronovich Tkeshelashvili, *Materialy dlia istorii farmatsii v Rossii. Biograficheskii slovar' farmatsevtov poluchivshikh stepen' magistra farmatsii v Imperatorskikh russkikh Universitetakh i v Imperatorskoi Voenno-Meditsinskoi Akademii s 1845–1901 god* (Moscow, 1901), pp. 57–63.

30. Quote in W. Horsely Gantt, *Russian Medicine* (New York, 1937), pp. 124–125; Russian version in Skorokhodov, *Kratkii ocherk istorii russkoi meditsiny*, pp. 151–152; previously cited in Mary Schaeffer Conroy, "Pharmacy in Pre-Soviet Russia," *Pharmacy in History*, vol. 27, no. 3, 1985, p. 127.

31. Belikov, *Farmatsevticheskaia Khimiia*, pp. 9–10. Belikov notes that Kast and Ginzberg synthesized the antipyretic phenacetin in 1887 but apparently this was a foreign rather than Russian discovery. Russian title of E. A. Shatskii's work: *Uchenie o rastitel'nykh alkaloidakh gliukozidakh i ptomainakh.*

32. "Obvoinik grecheskii (Periploca graeca L.)," A. D. Turova and E. N. Sapozhnikova, *Lekarstvennye rasteniia SSSR i ikh primenenie* (Moscow, 1984), pp. 83–84. P. V. Burzhinskii and E. Leman, "Obvoinik (Periploca graeca) kak serdechnoe sredstvo," *Vrach*, no. 22–24, 1986, p. 25 cited in Turova and Sapozhnikova, *Lekarstvennye rasteniia SSSR, loc. cit.*

33. While V. I. Kozlov assessed the Russian chemical industry as "generally weak" in 1885 he conceded that "where the industry has grown it is due to the energy of individual personalities" as well as "local conditions," "temperature," and "accidental circumstances." Kozlov, "Khimicheskie produkty," *Istoriko-statisticheskii obzor*, p. 5. Soviet historian Luk'ianov, writing about the chemical industry some sixty-five years later, asserted that the tariff of 1857 was harmful and caused a number of small enterprises to go out of business. Yet, new ones continued to be founded. By 1868 there were 322 chemical enterprises. In 1860, ten were opened; in 1870, fifteen more; and in 1875, eleven more. Luk'ianov, *Istoriia khimicheskikh promyslov*, pp. 149, 144.

Entrepreneurs also boosted the cosmetic industry. Luk'ianov, *Istoriia khimicheskikh promyslov*, pp. 161–162. In 1894 in Russia there were twenty cosmetic factories. The number of them decreased in Moscow to eight and in St. Petersburg to five but others were established in other provinces. Luk'ianov was particularly impressed with the Eliashev factory, which began in 1875 with only two workers and expanded in the 1890s to sixty (ibid., p. 162).

See Jo Ann Ruckman, *The Moscow Business Elite* (DeKalb: Northern Illinois University Press, 1984) *passim*, for discussion of Moscow entrepreneurs, in related fields.

34. Kozlov, "Khimicheskie produkty," p. 43; Luk'ianov, *Istoriia khimicheskikh promyslov*," p. 162.

35. M. G. Ena, "Khimiko-farmatsevticheskaia promyshlennost'," *Razvitie khimicheskoi tekhnologii na Ukraine* (Kiev, 1976), pp. 260–262. Russian name of company: Aktsionernoe Obshchestvo (Joint-Stock Company) *Iuzhno-russkoe obshchestvo torgovli aptekarskimi tovarami.*

36. *Optovyi Preis-Kurant za nalichnyi raschet sklada aptekarskikh tovarov Oskar Getling v Moskve. Firma sushchestvuet s 1875 goda.* This 122-page brochure is located in the Pharmacy Museum in Moscow. Director, Viktor Matveevich Salo.

37. Ena, "Khimiko-farmastsevticheskaia promyshlennost'," p. 261. Russian name of Chemical Factory Association: *Tovarishchestvo russkogo khimicheskogo zavoda.*

38. Ena, ibid., p. 262.

39. Natradze, *Ocherk razvitiia khimiko-farmatsevticheskoi promyshlennosti SSSR* (1967), p. 65. Pel' and Sons was an Association, or *Tovarishchestvo.*

40. Kozlov, "Khimicheskie produkty," *Istoriko statisticheskii obzor promyshlennosti Rossii,* p. 43.

41. Kikta, *Przemysl,* pp. 19–20.

42. Kikta, *Przemysl,* pp. 21–27. In addition to making kumiss, one pharmacy made extracts and pepsin. Twelve other enterprises in Warsaw in 1885 produced cosmetics, mineral water, and kumiss. Ibid., pp. 23–24.

43. Kikta, ibid., p. 40.

44. Kikta, *Przemysl,* pp. 40–43.

45. Photographs of the four establishments appear in D. A. Ruffman, "Russian Pharmacy," *Bulletin of Pharmacy,* 1906, pp. 16, 17.

46. Kikta, *Przemysl,* pp. 40–45.

47. These institutions began to open bacteriological stations for preparing vaccines. Physicians in charge were especially trained in Paris. These included N. F. Gamaleia (Odessa), N. M. Unkovskii (Moscow), and N. A. Protopopov (Khar'kov), Natradze, *Ocherk,* pp. 73–74.

48. Ena, "Khimiko-farmatsevticheskaia promyshlennost'," p. 262.

49. *Ustroistvo gorodskogo-farmatsevticheskago zavoda. Doklad komissii akademika N. S. Kurnakova* (Petrograd, 1916), p. 86.

50. Ena, "Khimiko-farmatsevticheskaia promyshlennost'," p. 262.

51. Natradze, *Ocherk razvitiia khimiko-farmatsevticheskoi promyshlennosti SSSR,* pp. 73–74.

52. Ena, "Khimiko-farmatsevticheskaia promyshlennost'," p. 263. This Soviet publication alleged that the 1912 law loosening restrictions on zemstvos and cities to establish pharmacies led to the establishment of galenical factories in Akhtyrk, Ekaterinoslav, Kupiansk, Melitopol, and other cities in the Ukraine.

53. "K kharakteristike patentovannykh sredstv," *F. Zh.,* vol. 54, no. 43, 1915, p. 421.

54. See Thomas Owen, "Entrepreneurship and the Structure of Enterprise in Russia, 1800–1880," *Entrepreneurship in Imperial Russia and the Soviet Union,* eds., Gregory Guroff and Fred V. Carstensen (Princeton, 1983), pp. 67–72. Henceforth, the term Joint Stock Company will be used in place of the Russian *Aktsionernoe Obshchestvo,* and the term Association will be used in place of *Tovarishchestvo.*

55. Ena, "Khimiko-farmatsevticheskaia promyshlennost'," p. 260. Ena spells the petroleum product *naftalin* as do several other Russian publications. Merck refers to *naftalan,* see note 174.

56. Ena, ibid., pp. 260-261.

57. "Torgovyia i promyshlennyia svedeniia," *F. Zh.*, vol. 40 (23), no. 11, 1901, p. 231. The same page of the journal noted that a joint-stock company had been formed in Finland to develop a rich vein of magnesium, and a joint-stock factory to manufacture perfume had been opened in Warsaw.

58. Ena, "Khimiko-farmatsevticheskaia promyshlennost'," pp. 261-263.

59. "Chelovek dela: Posviashchaetsia pamiati B. M. Shaskol'skago" and "Nekrolog B. M. Shaskol'skii," *F. Zh.*, vol. 49, no. 39, 1910, pp. 417-418. Shaskol'skii was socially aware; in 1907 he established a mutual aid fund (*kassa vzaimopomoshchi*) and a food cooperative for the eighty staff pharmacists in his employ.

60. Natradze, *Ocherk razvitiia khimiko-farmastevticheskoi promyshlennosti SSSR*, p. 65.

61. "Ob"iavlenie," *F. T.*, vol. 1, no. 12, 1907, p. 180.

62. Ena, "Khimiko-farmatsevticheskaia promyshlennost'," p. 263.

63. "Sliianie predpriiatii," *F. Zh.*, vol. 49, no. 41, 1910, p. 446 and "Moskovskoe tovarishchestvo na paiakh torgovli aptekarskimi tovarami Brat'ia Stolkind and Ko.," ibid., vol. 50, no. 20, 1911, p. 240.

64. "Otkrytie fabriki 'Ars' v Vil'ne," *F. Zh.*, vol. 50, no. 10, 1911, p. 120.

65. Unless specifically noted, the information on enterprises cited in notes 68-78, immediately following, is from *Kratkii ocherk deiatel'nosti aptekarskago sklada Tverskogo gubernskogo zemstva za istekshie 20 let ego sushchestvovaniia* (1889-1909 g.g.) sostavil [ed.], Zemskii vrach M. E. Zaitsev (Tver, 1910), pp. 39-40.

66. These were "The Joint Stock Company Morozov, Krell, Otman and Co.," "Vil'dt," "Radokh," "Valetudo," and "The Warsaw Gas Factory."

67. These included "Apteka (Pharmacy) Antonius" in Lifland province, "The Joint-Stock Company of Trampedakh" and the firms "Gaberkorn" and "Briger" in Riga; the enterprises "Rabinovich," "Brothers Esserlin," and "The Vilensk Chemical Factory" in Vil'na.

68. "Brothers Orlovich," "Brodskii," and "Snapir."

69. These were the "Brothers Dobrovol'skie," "Korovkin," and "Kuznetsov" in Tver province, and in Tver "The Association Prodvodpik," "Misseigevich" and "Mocharskii" as well as the "Tver Office of the Brothers Nobel."

70. "Tsypkin" and "Brothers Krestovnikov."

71. "Morokin" and "Gents."

72. "Bal'trenas" and the "Kustar or Handicraft Museum of the Nizhegorod Zemstvo."

73. This was the "Biuro (Bureau) of the Potrebit Association."

74. "Zeisler" was located in Olonets province, "Plavin" in Dvinsk, "The Association Naftalin" in the Caucasus, "Factory oblatok (tablets) Schmid" in Kiev, "Renman" in Saratov province, the "Association Ekstrakt" in Minsk, "Volakh" in Grodno province, and "Gofman and Deuel" in Khar'kov.

75. These included "The Institute of Experimental Medicine," "Kirshten Genri," "Knip and Verner," the "Russian Society for Trade in Pharmaceutical Wares," "Tentelevskii Chemical Factory," "Shtol' and Shmidt," the "Chemical Laboratory of Dr. Pel'," "The St. Petersburg Hygienic Laboratory," "Likfel'd," "Gandin," the "Society of Russian-American Rubber Wares."

In 1910 a cooperative, the Russian Society of Trade and Pharmacy Wares, or FARMAKON, also operated in St. Petersburg. Advertisement, *F. Zh.*, vol. 49, no. 4, 1910.

76. "Anna Rikhter," "Bever," Bliumental'," "Brokar," the "Bacteriological Institute of Moscow University," "Vinogradov," "Borau and Co.," "Veierbush," "Govard and Co.," "Diutfua," "Epes," "Isaev," the "Kustar or Handicraft Museum of the Moscow Zemstvo," "Kuzmin and Abazaev."

In 1907 the Bandaging Materials Factory of Provizor N. Iakovlev, the Moscow Joint Stock Company K. Ermans and Co., the Steam Tallow-melting and Oil Factory of Provizor V. A. Lepskii operated in Moscow. Advertisements in *Farmatsevticheskii trud*, vol. 1, following no. 4, 1907.

77. *Kratkii ocherk deiatel'nosti aptekarskago sklada Tverskogo gubernskago zemstva*, pp. 39–40. Thomas C. Owen, "Entrepreneurship and the Structure of Enterprise in Russia, 1800–1880," pp. 67–72, claims the *Aktsionernoe obshchestvo* (publicly held Joint Stock Society or Company) was preferred in St. Petersburg, the *Tovarishchestvo* (Stock Association or Partnership, often family-held) were preferred in Moscow. In the pharmaceutical industry it was otherwise. Some of the major St. Petersburg pharmaceutical enterprises were *Tovarishchestva*; some of the key Moscow ones were *Obshchestva*; provincial cities included both types of pharmaceutical enterprises as well as small workshops and pharmacies.

78. Some wares came directly from Germany. Wares also were produced in Moscow. Advertisement, *Farmatsevt*, vol. 13, no. 13, 1905, p. following no. 13.

79. Cowen and Helfand, *Pharmacy, An Illustrated History*, p. 174.

80. Natradze, *Russkie i sovetskie farmakopei*, pp. 39–40, 44, 62–72. Of course the military and naval pharmacopoeias also were revised and reissued. The military pharmacopoeia was reissued in 1799 amd six times thereafter until 1913. The first naval pharmacopoeia was issued in 1786; it was reissued in 1806 and in 1869. Natradze, ibid., pp. 36–39, 43, 45–50. Also, E. A. Toreia, *Sovremennyi vzgliad na russkuiu voennuiu i morskuiu farmakopei* (St. Petersburg, 1888), 32 pp.

Special pharmacopoeias for the poor contained remedies based on cheaper materials. Natradze, *Russkie i sovetskie farmakopei*, pp. 51–55.

81. S. P. Fortunatov, 'O Rossiiskoi farmakopee 1866 g," *Aptechnoe delo*, vol. 6, no. 1, 1957, pp. 54–56.

82. I. Bychkov, "Problema syr'ia po piatiletnemu planu razvitiia farmatsevticheskoi promyshlennosti (1927/28–1931/32 g.g.)," *Khimiko-farmatsevticheskii zhurnal*, vol. 6, no. 2, 1928, pp. 8–10, emphasized that most medicines were made from plants rather than synthesized and that Russia imported opium from Turkey and Persia; in 1924 collection of opium was organized in Kazakhstan and Kirgizistan.

S. N. Khitrik, "Proizvodstvo alkaloidov v SSSR," *Khimiko-farmatsevticheskii zhurnal*, no. 7, 1928, p. 5, emphasized that alkaloids of opium, like morphine and codeine and its salts were exclusively imported before World War I. Professor Chichibabin began producing alkaloids in his Moscow laboratory in 1916.

Professor N. D. Averkiev, "O dobyche ioda v USSR iz vodoroslei Chernogo moria 'krasnaia fillofora,'" ibid., no. 8, p. 10, criticized the fact that before 1914 Russia had not one enterprise making iodine. The iodine station established in 1915 was in ruins by 1919 due to the Civil War.

Ia. Mazover, "Gosudarstvennyi salitsilovyi zavod," ibid., no. 10, p. 7, attacked the importation of salicylic products until the war forced establishment of an experimental factory in 1916/1917. He also cited lack of iodine production until 1915. Ibid., p. 11.

In "Ot Kellerovskoi kulinarii k khimicheskomu i khim.-farm. proizvodstvu," ibid., no. 11, pp. 7–9, "S. Ch." alleged that the Keler factory (often spelled, as here, Keller) produced mainly soap, perfume, cosmetics, household items, and topical remedies rather than important medicines.

83. Natradze, *Ocherk razvitiia khimiko-farmatsevticheskoi promyshlennosti SSSR*, pp. 52–78, 92–93. However, as was the case in the pre-*glasnost'* period, he was torn between praising obvious growth in the pharmaceutical industry and toeing the politically correct line that this industry as the entire economy benefited from the Bolshevik Revolution. But, on p. 93, ibid., he conquered his scruples, categorically stating that "Only the great October socialist revolution opened in our country the path for growth of the chemical-pharmaceutical industry."

84. Sonnedecker, *History of Pharmacy*, p. 76.

85. "Aptechnoe delo, aptekaria i sluzhashchie vo Frantsii," *Farmatsevticheskii trud*, vol. 1, no. 20, 1907, p. 272; Sonnedecker, *History of Pharmacy*, p. 76. As a result, in 1907, few French pharmacies had laboratories. "Aptechnoe delo . . . vo Frantsii," *loc. cit.*

86. Nevertheless, Soviet historians downplayed the Russian pharmaceutical industry. In 1956, S. P. Fortunatov emphasized that many of the prepared medicaments listed in the 1866 pharmacopoeia were imported from Germany [*sic*]. Fortunatov, "O Rossiiskoi farmakopee 1866 g.," p. 53. He also stated that many pharmacists at this time were German. Germany, of course, was not a unified state in 1866. In both the 1967 and 1977 editions of his history of the pharmaceutical industry in Russia and the USSR, Soviet historian Natradze alluded to a number of private pharmacies and laboratories producing pharmaceuticals on a workshop, or *masterskoe*, basis in the late nineteenth and early twentieth century. These included the laboratory of galenical preparations of the Tver zemstvo, the German firm Henrikh Bruns, the Russian society for Trade and Production of Pharmaceutical Wares, belonging to the German firm of R(e)idel, the Laboratory of Plotnikov, Neiburg, and "other small factories and laboratories." He also mentioned the "small firms" of "Merkuze, Mozhenko and Company" in Warsaw, The Joint-Stock Companies of "Bliumental'" and "Radio" in Moscow, the Association of Grining in Riga, the "Motor" factory in Warsaw, the Joint-Stock Society of Trade in Pharmaceutical Wares in Warsaw, and "others." Natradze, *Ocherk razvitiia khimiko-farmatsevticheskoi promyshlennosti SSSR*, pp. 69–70. But he

focused only on some eleven pharmaceutical firms operating in Russia in 1909, information on which was derived from data compiled by the Tsarist Ministry of Trade and Industry. Natradze's short list gave the impression that only a few Russian firms were involved in pharmaceutical production.

87. "Nizhni-Novgorod," *F. Zh.*, vol. 20, no. 46, 1898, p. 740.

88. G. A. Vinokurov, "Apteki Simbirskoi gubernii v XIX i nachale XX veka," *Farmatsiia*, no. 19 (July–August) 1970, p. 52.

89. *Kratkii ocherk deiatel'nosti aptekarskago sklada Tverskogo gubernskago zemstva . . . 1889–1909 g.g.*, pp. 34, 39–40.

90. Tsentral'nyi Gosudarstvennyi Istoricheskii Arkhiv, St. Petersburg [hereafter cited TsGIA], fond 1298, opis' 1, delo 2090, l. 417 [hereafter cited "f.," "op.," "d.," "l.," or "ll."].

91. *Optovyi Preis-Kurant . . . sklada aptekarskikh tovarov Oskar Getling*, 122 pages, *passim*. The two pages for Pel' and Sons under "Organopreparaty," no page numbers visible.

92. Galenical preparations are compounds of simple ingredients that remain in their original state, such as oils, extracts, liquor-based infusions, powders, and mineral salts.

93. Natradze, *Ocherk razvitiia khimiko-farmatsevticheskoi promyshlennosti SSSR*, p. 65.

94. "Iuzhno-russkoe Obshchestvo," *F. Zh.*, vol. 20, no. 14, 1898, p. 196.

95. Natradze, *Ocherk razvitiia khimiko-farmatsevticheskoi promyshlennosti SSSR*, pp. 63–65. Of course, the amount of production in rubles depended upon the value of the items produced and thus was not an accurate indicator of the size of the firm or importance of products.

96. "Nekrolog. R. R. Keler," *F. T.*, vol. 1, no. 15, 1907, pp. 214–215.

97. *Optovyi preis-kurant tovarov firmennoi zadelki Moskovskago tsentral'nago optovago sklada Fabrichno-torgovago Tovarishchestva "R. Keler i Ko v Moskve"* (Moscow, July 1914), pp. 1–140. Pressed tablets and photographic equipment and processing, pp. 92–102.

98. Natradze, *Ocherk razvitiia khimiko-farmatsevticheskoi promyshlennosti SSSR* , p. 64.

99. "Nekrolog. R. R. Keler," *F. T.*, vol. 1, no. 15, 1907, p. 215; *Optovyi preis-kurant*, p. 42.

100. "Usloviia prodazhi," *Optovyi preis-kurant . . . "R. Keler i Ko v Moskve."*

101. S. Ch., "Farmatsevticheskaia promyshlennost': Ot kellerovskoi kulinarii k khimicheskomu i khim.-farm. proizvodstvu," *Khimiko-farmatsevticheskii zhurnal*, vol. 6, no. 11 (59), 1928, p. 6. As its subtitle indicates, this Soviet-era article disparaged Keler's prerevolutionary production. The article also implied that during the war Keler's production doubled. In 1916 the association produced 2,751,270 rubles' worth; in 1918, 5,707,614 rubles' worth, but inflation counted for a great deal of the increase. *Loc. cit.*

102. Ivan Sofronovich Tkeshelashvili, *Materialy dlia istorii farmatsii v Rossii. Biograficheskii slovar' farmatsevtov poluchivshikh stepen' magistra farmatsii . . . s 1845 po 1901* (Moscow, 1901), pp. 78–79.

103. As related in a previous chapter, Ferrein's father, Karl Ivanovich, purchased the eighteenth-century pharmacy in 1832. Vladimir Karlovich was Karl Ivanovich's second son. Karl Ivanovich died in 1887 but even during his lifetime Vladimir Karlovich handled the business. Vladimir Karlovich's older brother, Andrei Karlovich, took up chemistry but merely assisted his younger brother in the Staraia-Nikol'skaia Pharmacy until his death in 1895. *Opyt istoricheskago ocherka vozniknoveniia i razvitiia vsego aptekarskago dela v Rossii, a v chastnosti Staroi Nikol'skoi Apteki, prinadlezhashchei nyne Tovarishchestvu "V. K. Ferrein"* (Moscow, 1911), pp. 2–6.

104. *Opyt istoricheskago ocherka vozniknoveniia i razvitiia . . . Tovarishchestvu "V. K. Ferrein,"* pp. 7–9.

105. Hans Heger, "Die grosste Apotheke der Erde," *Apothekenbilder von Nah und Fern*, pt. 2 (Vienna, 1901), pp. 111, 113, 118, 119. French edition of *Opyt*: *Apercu historique du developpement general de la pharmacie en Russie, et en particulier de la "pharmacie Ferrein," fondee sous le regne Pierre le Grand en 1701 par Daniel Gourtschin* (Moscow, 1910), p. 18.

106. Heger, "Die grosste Apotheke der Erde," p. 119; *Opyt . . . Tovarishchestvu "V. K. Ferrein,"* p. 16; "Iubilei Vladimira Karlovicha Ferrein," *F. Zh.*, vol. 53, no. 18, 1914, p. 202.

107. "Magistr farmatsii Arkadii Moiseevich Semenov," *Farmatsevt*, vol. 14, no. 5, 1906, pp. 133–135.

108. Heger, "Die grosste Apotheke der Erde," p. 119; *Opyt . . . Tovarishchestvu "V. K. Ferrein,"* pp. 17, 21.

109. Viktor Matveeich Salo, Director of the Pharmacy Museum, Moscow, recalled that the factory was moved to Moscow in 1914. Natradze, *Ocherk razvitiia* (1967), pp. 63–64 claims it was established in Moscow in 1912. The author has visited the factory, which still operates today.

110. "Iubilei Vladimira Karlovicha Ferrein," pp. 201–202.

111. *Opyt . . . Tovarishchestvu "V. K. Ferrein,"* p. 21.

112. Natradze, *Ocherk razvitiia khimiko-farmatsevticheskoi promyshlennosti SSSR*, p. 64, and advertisement "Tovarishchestvo Ferrein Proizvodstvo khimicheskikh i galenovykh preparatov," *Farmatsevticheskii trud* [hereafter cited *F. T.*], vol. 1, nos. 23, 29, 1907, no pp.

113. Heger, "Die grosste Apotheke der Erde," p. 122; *Opyt istoricheskago*, p. 9.

114. Natradze, *Ocherk razvitiia*, p. 64.

115. Photographs, Heger, "Die grosste," pp. 11–128, *passim*, and Ferrein brochures, *Apercu*, 1910, and *Opyt istoricheskago*, 1911, *passim*.

116. "Iubilei Vladimira Karlovicha Ferrein," p. 202.

117. The Ferrein Association was awarded a State Stamp of Quality at the All-Russian Exhibition in Nizhni-Novgorod in 1896 and a higher award, the gold medal, at the All-Russian Exhibit of Hygiene in St. Petersburg in 1913. "Iubilei Vladimira Karlovicha Ferrein," p. 202.

118. See chapter 4 of this work on zemstvo pharmacies. Also *passim*.

119. *Pravila ob uchastii sluzhashchikh v Staroi Nikol'skoi Apteke i magazin*

aptekarskikh tovarov V. K. Ferreina, v pribylakh predpriiatiia (Moscow, December 23, 1881), pp. 1-7.

120. *Opyt . . . Tovarishchestvu "V. K. Ferrein,"* pp. 18–19.

121. "Otkrytie fabriki 'Ars' v Vil'ne," *F. Zh.*, vol. 50, no. 10, 1911, p. 120.

122. This is also true today, because the Russian pharmaceutical industry neglected to develop synthetic medicaments in the Soviet period.

123. TsGIA, f. 1298, op. 1, d. 2060, ll. 105, 106.

124. F. G. (A.) Ferrein, "Zhurnal Mezhduvedomstvennago Komiteta po delam farmatsevticheskoi promyshlennosti, 1915," p. 22 in TsGIA, f. 1298, op. 1, d. 2066a, l. 22.

The author visited the estate and log dacha with its carved roof, window surrounds and porches in November 1990. It now is the site of a Pharmaceutical Institute.

125. R. Vaita, "Nauchnyi otdel," *F. Zh.*, vol. 55, no. 20, 1916, p. 169.

126. These included Shtol' and Shmidt, The Russian Society of Trade in Pharmacy Wares, The Central Pharmacy Business of B. Maskol'skii in Petrograd, the Moscow Joint-Stock Society of Ermans and Co., the South Russian Society of Trade in Pharmacy Wares (IUROTAT) in Kiev, the Odessa Society of Trade in Pharmacy Wares Iu. K. Lemme and Co., the Russian Society of Colonial Trade in Rostov-on-the-Don, and the Caucasian Society of Pharmacy Wares in Tiflis. Natradze, *Ocherk razvitiia khimiko-farmatsevticheskoi promyshlennosti SSSR*, p. 84.

127. The Russian edition of the Ferrein brochure of 1911, though not the French edition of 1910, included a photograph of female and male workers, obviously garbed in peasant dress, sorting herbs.

Opyt ... Tovarishchestvu "V. K. Ferrein," no pagination, between pp. 10 and 11.

128. A. K. Ginrikhson, "Kul'tura lekarstvennykh rastenii v Rossii do 62° s. sh.," *F. Zh.*, vol. 40 (23), no. 18, 1901, pp. 356–357; ibid., no. 19, pp. 376–377.

129. I. Garber, "Lekarstva, naibolee upotrebliaemye v narodnoi meditsine v derevniakh bliz Bogotola, Tomskoi gubernii," *Farmatsevt*, vol. 10, no. 8, 1902, pp. 232–234, and Garber, "Flora o krestnosti sela Bogotola Tomskoi gub.," ibid., p. 1183.

130. "Raznyia izvestiia," *F. Zh.*, vol. 40 (23), no. 23, 1901, pp. 447–448.

131. "Raznyia izvestiia: Dr. P. F. Merkul'ev," *F. Zh.*, vol. 40 (23), no. 12, 1901, p. 250.

132. A Shuliatel, "Razvedenie miaty a dobyvanie miatnogo masla na Poltavishchine," *Khimiko-farmatsevicheskii zhurnal*, vol. 5, no. 9 (45), September 1927, p. 26.

A *desiatina* equals approximately 2 and 2/3 acres.

133. "Miata perechnaia (Mentha piperita L.)," Turova and Sapozhnikova, *Lekarstvennye rasteniia SSSR*, pp, 123–124. Mint leaves were used in popular medicine. *Loc. cit.*

134. Advertised in *Farmatsevt*, vol. 9, no. 18, 1901, p. 563. Russian title of herbal: *Kniga zdorov'ia* (*Domashnyi Lechebnik*).

135. "Raznyia izvestiia," *F. Zh.*, vol. 40 (23), no. 19, 1901, pp. 384–85. S. I. Karpinskii was leader of the project; with his premature death in March 1901, the Academy of Sciences was forced to elect his successor. This may have delayed the project.

136. Examples abound in the article by Robert J. Valuck, Suzanne Poirier, and Robert G. Mrtek, "Patent Medicine Muckraking: Influences on American Pharmacy, Social Reform, and Foreign Authors," *Pharmacy in History*, vol. 34, no. 4, 1992, pp. 183–192; George B. Griffenhagen and James Harvey Young, "Old English Patent Medicines in America," ibid., pp. 200–229; Pamela W. Lurito, "The message was electric," *Institute of Electrical and Electronics Engineers Spectrum*, vol. 21, no. 9, 1984, pp. 2–6.

137. Advertisements in *F. T.*, vol. 1, 1907, following nos. 4 and 2.

138. Advertisement in *F. T.*, vol. 1, 1908, following no. 4.

139. Advertisements in *F. T.*, vol. 1, 1907, following nos. 2 and 4.

140. Advertisement, *F. T.*, vol. 1, 1907, following no. 4.

141. Advertisement in *F. T.*, vol. 1, 1907, following no. 4.

142. Advertisement, *F. T.*, vol. 1, no. 10, 1907, p. 149.

143. Advertisement, *F. T.*, vol. 1, no. 12, 1907, p. 180.

144. *Optovyi pries-kurant . . . "R Keler i Ko v Moskve," passim* (there were advertisements on nearly every page; some pages included two or three advertisements).

145. Advertisement, end pages of *F. Zh.*, vol. 49, nos. 17 and 18, 1910.

146. Advertisements, *F. T.*, vol. 1, 1907, *passim.* Keler's *Optovyi preis-kurant* of 1914 included advertisements. Oskar Getling's *Optovyi Preis-Kurant* of the same year did not.

147. "Usloviia prodazhi," *Optovyi Preis-Kurant . . . Oskar Getling*, first two pages.

148. Advertisements, *F. T.*, vol. 1, no. 32, 1907, p. 437, and ibid., no. 37, p. 497.

149. Advertisement, *F. Zh.*, vol. 49, no. 4, 1910. The price rise on cocaine and opiates might have further restricted the use and abuse of narcotics. See chapter 11.

150. "Khronika," *F. T.*, vol. 2, no. 26, 1908, p. 431.

151. "V Kazane," *F. T.*, vol. 3, no. 2, 1909, p. 26.

152. *Kratkii ocherk deiatel'nosti aptekarskago sklada Tverskogo gubernskago zemstva*, p. 1.

153. Ibid., p. 3.

154. Ibid., p. 4.

155. *Ustroistvo gorodskogo-farmatsevticheskago zavoda*, p. 20.

156. "Aptechnoe delo v khoziaistve Moskovskago Obshchestvennago Samoupravleniia," *Russkii farmatsevt*, vol. 1, no. 2, 1908, p. 55.

157. *Kratkii ocherk diatel'nosti aptekarskago sklada Tverskogo gubernskago zemstva*, p. 10.

158. For example, in 1888 the Tver zemstvo warehouse ordered medicaments for the provincial hospital and Burashevskii colony from the Merck firm. The cost

of the medicaments plus transportation, commission, and tariff was 3,587 rubles, 30 kopeks. The zemstvo estimated that if purchased from the Moscow druggist Keler (spelled Keller in the brochure, p. 2) the cost of these materials would have been 4,304 rubles, 12 kopeks; the cost from the druggist Ferrein would have been 4,886 rubles, 34 kopeks. During the first nine months of 1889, the warehouse ordered pharmaceutical wares from forty-three foreign and Russian firms; the wares were from 15 to 20 percent cheaper than the wares formerly bought from "capital drug store owners." In 1892, the Bezhensk district zemstvo bought medicines from Moscow druggists at 2,766 rubles, 24 kopeks; if purchased from the provincial zemstvo warehouse, they would have cost only 2,456 rubles, 55 kopeks. As a result, in 1900 eleven districts ordered medicaments from the provincial warehouse and only one district ordered wares from Moscow druggists; after twelve years all districts received at least some medicines from the warehouse. *Kratkii ocherk*, pp. 1–4, 6, 7, 13.

159. Ibid., p. 5.

160. Ibid., p. 35.

161. R. R. Keler, *Pravda po odnomu obshchestvennomu voprosu* (Moscow, 1898), esp. pp. 3–37.

162. "Organopreparaty," *Optovyi Preis-Kurant . . . Oskar Getling*, no page numbers visible on my copy. It is impossible to fully ascertain how competitive Pel' and Sons' prices were as compared to Burroughs, Wellcome, without calibrating weights, substances, quality, and so forth.

163. *Kratkii ocherk deiatel'nosti aptekarskago sklada Tverskogo gubernskago zemstva*, p. 31.

164. Ibid., p. 30–31.

165. O. Borisovskii, "K voprosu o ratsional'noi postanovke dela vypiski medikamentov zemskimi uchrezhdeniiami," *F. T.*, vol. 3, no. 3, 1909, p. 38.

166. Borisovskii, "K voprosu," p. 38.

167. Ibid., pp. 38–39.

168. Ibid., p. 39.

169. Ibid., pp. 38–39.

170. Ibid., p. 39.

171. "Osvobozhdenie ot nemtsy," *F. Zh.*, vol. 53, no. 35, 1914, p. 400.

172. "Po povodu voprosa o vzdorozhanii medikamentov," *F. Zh.*, vol. 53, no. 33, 1914, p. 374.

173. R. Tal', I. F. Rapchevskii reporting in "K kharakteristike patentovannykh sredstv s soliami khinina," *F. Zh.*, vol. 54, no. 43, 1915, p. 423.

174. *Khimicheskaia fabrika i apteka E. Merk v Darmshtadt (Germaniia). Otchet za 1897 god.*, no. 150 (1898), pp. 24–25, 77–80, 106–107, 111, 115–116, 127, 140–142. In this Merck publication the petroleum product is spelled *naftalan*.

175. "Solodka golia (glycyrrhiza glabra L.)," Turova and Sapozhnikova, *Lekarstvennye rasteniia SSSR*, pp. 146–147.

176. "Sporyn'ia (Claviceps purpurea, Tulasne), ibid., pp. 270–271.

177. Abramov, "Eksport leksyr'ia," pp. 2–3. For licorice root see also A. N. Obukhov, "Solodkovyi koren', kak predmet eksporta," *Khimiko-farmatsevticheskii*

zhurnal, vol. 6, no. 3 (51), 1928, p. 11. Licorice root continued to be exported through the war. Both articles, written in Russia's NEP era, lamented that exports of these medicinal plants plummeted after the Soviet period arrived in the Ukraine. For high prices fetched by Likopodii, or *Lycopodium* (club moss) in the 1890s see "Torgovyi otchet Russkago Obshchestva Torgovli i Aptekarskimi Tovarami. S-Peterburg i Khar'kov," *Zhurnal meditsinskoi khimii i farmatsii*, (1892–93), p. 397.

As mentioned, a *pud* equals 36 pounds.

178. "Torgovyia i promyshlennyia svedeniia," *F. Zh.*, vol. 40 (23), no. 16, 1901, p. 329.

179. For a description of Santonin, see V. O. Podvysotskii, *Farmakologiia veshchestv organicheskoi khimii, rastitel'nykh i zhivotnykh. Po 3-mu izdan. Lektskii farmakologii, byvsh. Prof. Kievsk. Univers. Dybkovskago, s pribavleniiami po sovremennomu sostoianiiu farmakologii do 1888 goda* (Kiev, 1889), pp. 161–162. Podvysotskii states that the substance is "prepared in chemical factories." (p. 161). Natradze, *Ocherk razvitiia khimiko-farmatsevticheskoi promyshlennosti SSSR*, pp. 55–56.

180. Natradze, ibid., p. 85.

181. "Torgovyia i promyshlennyia svedeniia," *F. Zh.*, vol. 40 (23), no. 22, 1901, p. 434.

182. "Po povodu voprosa o vzdorozhanii medikamentov," *F. Zh.*, vol. 53, no. 33, 1914, p. 375.

183. K. S. Sarkisov, "Kratkii obzor polozheniia khimiko-farmatsevticheskikh promyshlennosti i rynka v Rossii, a, v chastnosti v Zakavkaz'e v nastoiashchee vremia," *F. Zh.*, vol. 55, no. 6, 1916, p. 49.

184. Sarkisov, "Kratkii obzor polozheniia khimiko-farmatsevticheskikh promyshlennosti i rynka," p. 50.

185. Sarkisov, "Kratkii obzor, *F. Zh.*, ibid., no. 7, p. 59.

186. "Doklad F. A. Ferreina: Mezhduvedomstvennomu Komitetu: O nuzhdakh farmatsevticheskoi promyshlennosti 10 aprelia 1915 goda," TsGIA SSSR, f. 1298, op. 1, d. 2066a, ll. 102 ob. and 103.

187. "Voina i sostoianie Russkoi promyshlennosti," *F. Zh.*, vol. 54, no. 35, 1915, p. 341. The article cited twenty pharmaceutical factories; this obviously excluded small workshops and laboratories.

188. "Zasedanie Meditsinskago Soveta," *F. Zh.*, vol. 53, no. 35, 1914, pp. 397–398.

189. "Po povodu voprosa o vzdorozhanii medikamentov," *F. Zh.*, vol. 53, no. 33, 1914, pp. 374–375.

190. Natradze, *Ocherk razvitiia khimiko-farmatsevticheskoi promyshlennosti*, p. 72. Soviet historian Natradze reproduced a table, supposedly developed by the Tsarist Commission for Assisting the Development of a Native Chemical-Pharmaceutical and Technological Industry, which illustrated the amount of raw and semifinished materials imported into Russia between 1909 and 1913. He cites exports, ibid., p. 78 but does not make comparisons between imports and exports.

191. Sarkisov, "Kratkii obzor polozheniia khimicheskikh promyshlennosti i rynka," p. 50.

192. M. I. Sosaar, "Po ankete 'chto sdelano nashei promyshlennost'iu za vremia voiny," *F. Zh.*, vol. 55, no. 29, 1916, p. 264.

Chapter 9

1. V. I. Kozlov, Chapter VIII, "Khimicheskie produkty," in *Istoriko statisticheskii obzor promyshlennosti Rossii*, vol. III, ed., D. A. Timiriazev (St. Petersburg, 1886), p. 3.

2. Eugene Shatskii, "Krupnoe nedorazumenie v nashei sovremennoi retsepture," *Farmatsevticheskii vestnik* [hereafter cited *F. V.*], vol. 4, no. 13, 1900, p. 234.

3. D. A. Ruffman, "Russian Pharmacy," *Bulletin of Pharmacy*, 1906, p. 18.

4. Report to the Ministry of Public Enlightenment from the Pharmacy Congress, held in St. Petersburg under the auspices of the St. Petersburg Pharmacy Society, "K reforme vyshago obrazovaniia farmatsevtov," *Farmatsevt*, vol. 14, no. 9, 1906, pp. 249–250.

5. "Khronika," *Farmatsevticheskii zhurnal*, [hereafter cited *F. Zh.*], vol. 50, no. 6, 1911, p. 72. A *pud* amounted to approximately thirty-six pounds.

6. E. K. Khrzhanovskii, *Polozhenie aptechnago dela v Rossii v osveshchenii tsifr i faktov* (St. Petersburg, 1913), p. 37.

7. A. G. Kling, "Kul'tura i obrabotka lekarstvennykh i dushistykh rastenii," *F. Zh.*, vol. 20, no. 6, 1898, pp. 71–74.

8. Tsentral'nyi Gosudarstvennyi Istoricheskii Arkhiv, St. Petersburg [hereafter cited TsGIA], fond 1298, opis' 1, delo 2066, list. 24 [hereafter represented by "f"; "op;" "d;" and "l" or in the case of the plural, "ll."].

9. "Voprosy budushchago," *F. Zh.*, vol. 54, no. 39, 1915, pp. 379–380.

10. V. V. Pashkevich, statement in session of November 7, 1915, "Zhurnal no. 2 komissii po zagotovke gorodom lekarstve," *Ustroistvo gorodskogo khimiko-farmatsevticheskago zavoda* (Petrograd, 1916), p. 62.

11. *Ustroistvo*, p. 79.

12. F. G. (A.) Ferrein, "Zhurnal Mezhduvedomstvennago Komiteta," February 1915, p. 22, TsGIA, f. 1298, op. 1, d. 2066a, l. 22.

13. Master of Pharmacy El'mar Gol'dberg, "O russkom opii i kolichestvennom opredelenii morfina," *Farmatsevt*, vol. 9, no. 37, 1901, pp. 1161–1162.

14. Ibid., and I. Shindel'meizer, "Persidskii opii," *Farmatsevt*, vol. 13, no. 3, 1905, pp. 65–68.

15. Actually the opium imported from Persia also had an inadequate morphia content of only 5 or 6 percent but Russia imported it out of desperation. "K voprosu o vvoze persidskago opiia," *F. Zh.*, vol. 55, no. 2, 1916, p. 19. This article affirmed that the Civilian Pharmacopoeia required a morphine content of 10 to 12 percent.

16. Shindel'meizer, "Persidskii opii," p. 68. Shindel'meizer also mentioned falsification of Caucasian opium and, ibid., p. 67, the use of the German pharmaco-

poeia, because of insufficiencies in the Russian pharmacopoeia. Part of his attraction to the German pharmacopoeia may have resulted from his location in Iur'ev (Dorpat), which had a strong German tradition.

17. Gol'dberg, "O russkom opii i kolichestvennom opredelenii morfina," *Farmatsevt*, vol. 9, no. 38, 1901, p. 1200; ibid., no. 40, pp. 1261–1263.

18. "Nauchnyi otdel," Ia. Ia. Mushcinskii, "O soderzhanii morfiia v opii, sobrannom v Iur'evskom botanicheskom sadu," *F. Zh.*, vol. 50, no. 21, 1911, pp. 246–247. Poppies were, of course, grown for seed in Russia, as in Western Europe. France and Germany had, like Russia, attempted to grow opium poppies. The German experiment yielded opium with a substantial amount of morphine, but the experiment was discontinued because of the vagueries of weather and labor costs. (Ibid., p. 247.)

19. "Proizvodstvo opiia," *F. Zh.*, vol. 54, no. 38, 1915, p. 377, and "Otkrytie persidskoi granitsy," ibid., pp. 377–378. The first article asserted that before the war Russia's morphine (and cocaine) had come exclusively from Germany and Austria. On opium growing in Semirech'e, see also E. Svirlovskii, "Kul'tura maka i dobyvanie opiia v Semirech'i," *F. Zh.*, vol. 55, no. 37, 1916, pp. 350–351.

20. Ibid., p. 351.

21. V. G. Varzar, "Zhurnal Mezhduvedomstvennago Komiteta," February 1915, TsGIA, f. 1298, op. 1, d. 2066, l. 40.

22. TsGIA, f. 1298, op. 1, d. 2095, l. 2 ob.

23. *Ustroistvo*, p. 108.

24. "Rasprostranenie lekarstvennykh rastenii v Rossii," *F. Zh.*, vol. 55, no. 11, 1916, p. 98.

25. TsGIA, f. 1298, op. 1, d. 2066, l. 34.

Their assertions were substantiated by the fact that although iodine was derived from seaweed in the Black Sea during World War I, a second station on the shores of the White Sea, near Arkhangel'sk, which operated from 1916–1917, obtained a meager amount of iodine (0.12-0.13 percent) from the ashes of seaweed and sea cabbage. A. G. Natradze, *Ocherk razvitiia khimiko-farmatsevticheskoi promyshlennosti SSSR* (Moscow, 1967), p. 78.

On the identity of F. G. (A.) Ferrein, see chapter 16 of this work, "World War I and the Medicaments Crisis."

26. fon Anrep, "Zhurnal Mezhduvedomstvennago Komiteta," pp. 32–33 in TsGIA, f. 1298, op. 1, d. 2066a, ll. 32 and 33. This may have been the effort cited by N. D. Averkiev in 1928. He recalled that between 1896 and 1898, "on the shores of the Pacific Ocean near America," there was an attempt to build an iodine-producing plant using "sea cabbage." The project was unsuccessful because sea cabbage was a popular food for the Chinese. They paid high prices for it, making it prohibitively expensive to turn into iodine. N. D. Averkiev, "O dobyche ioda v USSR iz vodoroslei chernogo moria 'Krasnaia fillofora'," *Khimiko-farmatsevticheskii zhurnal*, vol. 6, no. 8 (56), 1928, p. 10.

27. "Zhurnal Mezhduvedomstvennago Komiteta," TsGIA, f. 1298. op. 1, d. 2066, l. 34.

28. Natradze, *Ocherk*, pp. 68–69.

29. Report of F. G. (A.) Ferrein to the Interdepartmental Committee, spring 1915, "Doklad F. A. Ferreina Mezhduvedomstvennomu Komitetu. "O nuzhdakh farmatsevticheskoi promyshlennosti," 10 April 1915, TsGIA, f. 1298, op. 1, d. 2066a, l. 102ob and 105, and N. S. Kurnakov, to the Petrograd Committee on the Pharmaceutical Industry, fall of 1915, *Ustroistvo*, p. 10.

30. TsGIA, f. 1298, op. 1, d. 2066, ll. 36, 37.

31. "Nekrolog. R. R. Keler," *F. T.*, vol. 1, no. 15, 1907, p. 215. Keler died April 1907 in Berlin.

32. Cited in *F. T.*, vol. 3, no. 3, 1909, p. 42.

33. "Osvobozhdenie ot nemtsy," *F. Zh.*, vol. 53, no. 35, 1914, p. 400; also F. G. (A.) Ferrein, "Zhurnal Mezhduvedomstvennago Komiteta," 1915, TsGIA, f. 1298, op. 1, d. 2066, l. 36.

34. "Osvobozhdenie ot nemtsy," *F. Zh.*, vol. 53, no. 35, 1914, p. 400.

35. "Po povodu voprosa o vzdorozhenii medikamentov," *F. Zh.*, vol. 53, no. 33, 1914, p. 375.

36. Kurnakov, Petrograd Committee, fall 1915 in *Ustroistvo*, p. 10.

37. F. Ferrein, "Tamozhennye tarify i ikh znachenie dlia khimiko-farmatsevticheskoi promyshlennosti," *Khimiko-farmatsevticheskii zhurnal*, no. 7 (10), Iiul (July) 1924, pp. 10–11. He, of course, intended to make Soviet tariffs facilitate domestic pharmaceutical production.

38. V. I. Pokhitonov, statement in the meeting of December 12, 1915, "Zhurnal No. 5 komissii o zagotovke gorodom lekarstv," *Ustroistvo gorodskogo-farmatsevticheskago zavoda* (Petrograd, 1916), pp. 78–79. During the war production of benzol shot up. In the meetings of the Petrograd Committee it was stated that benzol and phenol were being produced in sufficient quantities in Russia and that these were among the items of which there would be surplus at the end of the war. *Ustroistvo*, p. 17. However, a wartime problem was that benzol was used for defense purposes. "Doklad F. A. Ferreina Mezhduvedomstvennomu Komitetu," TSGIA, f. 1298, op. 1, d. 2066a, l. 103. Also K. S. Sarkisov, "Kratkii obzor polozheniia khimiko-farmatsevticheskikh promyshlennosti i rynka v Rossii, a v chastnosti v Zakavkaz'e v nastoiashchee vremia," *F. Zh.*, vol. 55, no. 7, 1916, p. 60.

39. K. S. Sarkisov, "Kratkii obzor," *F. Zh.*, vol. 55, no. 7, 1916, p. 59.

40. D. Ia. Blumental', *Ustroistvo*, p. 62. On page 17 of this work it was stated that sulfuric acid either was produced in sufficient qualtities in Russia or that there would be a surplus of this item after the war.

41. Kozlov, "Khimicheskie produkty," in *Istoriko-statisticheskii obzor promyshlennosti Rossii*, pp. 2–4, 6.

42. Charles C. Mann and Mark L Plummer, *The Aspirin Wars: Money, Medicine, and 100 Years of Rampant Competition* (New York: Alfred A. Knopf, 1991), pp. 16–31.

43. N. S. Kurnakov in *Ustroistvo*, pp. 10–11.

44. *Ustroistvo*, p. 63.

45. For example, in June 1905, on stationery embellished with a double-headed eagle, the Ferrein Association inquired of the Medical Department as to whether

pharmacies in Russia had the right to produce "Vasogen." In reply the Chancellery of the Medical Sovet reminded the Ferrein firm that according to a regulation of 1896 Vasogen and its contents belonged to "those chemical substances for which the privilege for production and sale could not be given out." TsGIA, f. 1298, op. 1, d. 1244, l. 24 and l. 28.

46. Grinnell Jones, "War's Effect on Chemical Industries," *The Pharmaceutical Era*, October 1918, p. 273.

47. TsGIA, f. 1298, op. 1, d. 2066a, ll. 124 and 124 ob.

48. M. I. Sosaar, "Po ankete 'chto sdelano nashei promyshlennost'iu za vremia voiny,'" *F. Zh.*, vol. 55, no. 29, 1916, p. 264.

49. "K razvitiiu otechestvennoi khimicheskoi promyshlennosti," *F. Zh*, vol. 55, no. 29, 1916, p. 260. A *pud* equaled thirty-six pounds.

50. "Doklad Mezhduvedomstvennago Komiteta," spring 1915, TsGIA, f. 1298, op. 1, d. 2066, ll. 30, 31.

51. "Po povodu voprosa o vzdorozhanii medikamentov," *F. Zh.*, vol. 53, no. 33, 1914, p. 375.

52. "Osvobozhdenie ot nemtsy," *F. Zh.*, vol. 53, no. 35, 1914, p. 400.

53. "Kronika i smes'," *Zubovrachebnyi vestnik*, 1899, vol. 13, no. 4, p. 166.

54. "Meditsinskim Sovetom Ministerstva Vnutr. Del razresheno," and "Meditsinskim Sovetam Ministerstva Vnutr. Del otkloneno khodataistvo," *F. V.*, vol. 4, no. 39, 1900, p. 693.

55. Russian title of law "*O fabrichnom proizvodstve slozhnykh farmatsevticheskikh preparatov.*" M. G. Ena claimed that "notwithstanding its inadequacies . . . it assisted further development of the chemico-pharmaceutical industry." *Razvitie khimicheskoi tekhnologii na Ukraine* (Kiev, 1976), "Khimiko-farmatsevticheskaia promyshlennost'," pp. 262-263. E. K. Khrzhanovskii, delegate to the Medical Council from the St. Petersburg Pharmacy Society, writing in 1912, closer to the time the law was promulgated, was less sanguine, commenting only that "*the purpose* [italics mine] of this regulation was growth in Russia of the chemico-pharmaceutical industry . . . preparation and wholesale sales of preparations to pharmacies and clinics." Khrzhanovskii, *Polozhenie aptechnago dela v Rossii*, p. 35.

56. For two years Zakovich managed a chemico-bacteriological laboratory in a the Staro-Kazanskaia pharmacy of F. G. Filier in Yaroslavl'. He had done sanitary-hygienic research for the city of Yaroslavl' and had been hired by the Yaroslavl' provincial zemstvo to research mineral sources in the area. TsGIA, f. 1298, op. 1, d. 1309, ll. 1-3.

57. The Russian name of the remedy was *Universal'noe sredstvo ot prostudy, opukholi tela, likhoradka, kholery i katarra zheludka.* TsGIA, f. 1298, op. 1, d. 1722, ll. 1 and 3.

58. "Offitsial'nyia Izvestiia," *F. Zh.*, vol. 52, no. 3, 1913, p. 29.

59. "Offitsial'nyia Izvestiia," *F. Zh.*, vol. 52, no. 3, 1913, p. 29.

60. TsGIA, f. 1297, op. 155, d. 219, l. 2.

61. TsGIA, f. 1298, op. 1, d. 1130, l. 27.

62. TsGIA, f. 1298, op. 1, d. 1130, l. 31.

63. *Alfavit Russkikh preparatov, otnositel'no kotorykh imeetsia perepiska po khodataistvam o razreshenii ikh aptechnago ili fabrichno-laboratorno-zavodskago proizvodstva.* (Upravlenie Glavnago Vrachebnago Inspektora; vtoroe deloproizvodstvo, Chast' II, TsGIA, f. 1298, op. 1, d. 2050, *passim.*

64. "Khronika," *F. Zh.*, vol. 50., no. 6, 1911, p. 72.

65. "Zhurnal Mezhduvedomstvennago Komiteta," TsGIA SSSR, f.1298, op. 1, d. 2066a, ll. 78, 79. The identity of this Ferrein, whose patronymic initial was variously cited in the 1915 meetings of the Interdepartmental Governmental Committtee as "G" and "A" will be discussed in a future chapter.

66. For example, a Bohemian firm was barred from importing a medicinal wine in 1913 at the same time that Parke, Davis and Company was allowed to produce "Elastic Globules santal." "Offitsial'nyia Izvestiia," *F. Zh.*, vol. 52, no. 3, 1913, p. 29.

67. See chapter 11, "Drug Use and Abuse," in this work.

68. These included *De Graves Medical Pencil for Corns and Warts* which Iordana characterized as "little tubes of chloric acid," *Papier fruneau contre Asthma*, derided as "leaves of thick paper," *Capsules vial a l'Huile de Genevrier*—capsules filled with juniper oil and recommended against a whole range of diseases, *Wilhelm's antiarthritischer*, and *Reichelt's Breast Pillen*, made of licorice and anise. F. D. Iordana, "Sharlatanstvo patentovannymi sekretnymi sredstvami," *F. Zh.*, vol. 1, no. 12, 1879, pp. 353–356.

69. "Spisok gotovym meditsinskim sredstvam, dozvolennym Meditsinskim Sovetom k propusku v Rossiiu," cited in *Sbornik zakonopolozhenii dlia farmatsevtov, soderzhatelei aptek i drogistov*, sostavil (ed.) P. N. Bulatov (S- Peterburg, 1897), pp. 180–182; Homeopathic, ibid., pp. 182–184.

70. In 1904, the German chemical factory "Atenshtedt und Redeker" near Bremen petitioned the Medical Council to permit importation into Russia of its *Tincture Ferri Athenshtedt* and, further, to permit advertisement about the substance in newspapers; the Medical Council registered no objection.

TsGIA, f. 1298, op. 1, d. 1159, l. 1, l. 6.

71. In 1909 an Austrian firm asked permission to import red wine from Krakow and to publicize it. Deeming it harmless to the health, the Medical Council accepted the petition. TsGIA, f. 1298, op. 1, d, 1726, ll. 1 and 3.

72. "Privilegii," *F. Zh.*, vol. 40 (23), no. 18, 1901, pp. 365–67.

73. *F. Zh.*, vol. 40 (23), no. 13, 1901, pp. 267–269 recorded eight patents to foreigners and only two to Russians; this was pretty much par for the course that year.

74. "Khronika: Bor'ba s reklamoiu," *F. Zh.*, vol. 52, no. 3, 1913, p. 30.

75. "Iz zhurnalov Meditsinskago Soveta," *F. T.*, vol. 1, no. 30, 1907, p. 409.

76. For example, "Iz farmatsevticheskoi praktiki: Extract Cascarae Sagrodae fluid. examarat" according to "Dr. B. Borner'u," *F. Zh.*, vol. 49, no. 34, 1910, p. 372; "Prigotovlenie rastvorov Erlich-Hata 606 dlia podkozhnago vpryskivaniia," ibid., no. 42, pp. 454–55; a table of tablets of antifebrin, phenacetin, salicylic acid, aspirin, salipyrine, in "Iz farmatsevticheskoi praktiki," ibid., no. 37, p. 401.

77. Communique of the Ministry of Trade and Industry, department of

industry, 29 July, 1911 to the Minister of Internal Affairs, TsGIA, f. 1298, op. 1, d. 1776, l. 28.

78. Vypiska iz zhurnala meditsinskago soveta, 3 Iunia 1911, TsGIA, f. 1298, op. 1, d. 1776, ll. 21 and 21 ob.

79. "Doklad F. A. Ferreina Mezhduvedomstvennomu Komitetu," TsGIA, f. 1298, op. 1, d. 2066a, l. 104.

80. "K kharakteristike patentovannykh sredstv s soliami khinina," *F. Zh.*, vol. 54, no. 43, 1915, pp. 421-422.

81. In the fall of 1915 representing the trading house, Shaskol'skii and Company, in Petrograd, B. P. Shaskol'skii lamented the lack of cooperation between scientists and pharmaceutical firms. See the chapter "World War I and the Medicaments Crisis" in this work.

82. "Protokol zasedaniia Vysochaishe utverzhden. S-Pet. farm.-ago Obshchestva 15 sentiabria 1898 g.," *F. Zh.*, vol. 20, no. 42, 1898, p. 598.

83. "Proekt Ustava Aptekarskago," *F. T.*, vol. 1, no. 26, 1907, p. 352.

84. Ruffman, "Russian Pharmacy, pp. 16-17.

85. Ibid.

86. Lintser, "Aptechnaia monopoliia," *F. V.*, 1904, vol. 7 , no. 4, pp. 59-60.

87. "Nekrolog. R. R. Keler," p. 215. *Farmatsevticheskii trud* used the term *lekarstvennyi golod.* The Russian titles of Keler's pamphlets were: *Pravdivoe slovo vlastiam, obshchestvu i narodu* (1884), *Pravda po odnomy obshchestvennomu voprosu* (1898), and *Pod sen'iu predpisanii i tsirkuliarov.*

Chapter 10

1. In "Policing the Health of London: The College of Physicians and the Early Stuart Monarchy," *Social History of Medicine*, vol. 2, no. 1, 1989, pp. 1-33, Harold J. Cook discusses the linkage between absolutist, "cameralist" governments and the medical police and public health measures.

For background on the Russian government's leading role in medicine and pharmacy see preceeding chapters and I. L. Kondakov, "Kratkii istoricheskii ocherk razvitiia farmatsii i prichiny upadka farmatsevticheskoi shkoly," *Meditsina*, vol. 7, no. 10, 1895, p. 149; I. S. Tkesevashvili, "Russkaia farmatsiia do vozniknoveniia pervykh vol'nykh aptek," *Farmatsevt*, vol. 10, no. 10, 1902, pp. 542, 569; A. Ginzberg, "Ocherk razvitiia nauchnoi farmatsii v Rossii za 200-letnii period," *Farmatsevticheskii vestnik* [herafter cited *F. V.*], vol. 5, no. 16, 1902, pp. 185-187; L. Ia. Skorokhodov, *Kratkii ocherk istorii russkoi meditsiny* (Leningrad, 1926, 31, 33-35, 37-40, 42, 151-152.) For information on the Russian government, the medical profession, and public health in the eighteenth century see John T. Alexander, "Medical developments in Petrine Russia," *Canadian-American Slavic Studies*, vol. 8, no. 2, 1972, pp. 198-221, and "Medical Professionals and Public Health in 'Doldrums' Russia (1725-62)," ibid., vol. 12, no. 1, 1978, pp. 116-35.

2. Cook, "Policing the Health of London," p. 2.

3. The government began controlling bread during the troubled 1580s and 1590s; it regulated the ingredients, size, and price of loaves and rolls sold in Mos-

cow, the capital, from 1619. R. E. F. Smith and David Christian, *Bread and salt. A social and economic history of food and drink in Russia.* (Cambridge University Press, 1984), pp. 129–1330.

4. Ibid., p. 154.

5. Smith and Christian, *Bread and salt,* p. 199. Cook reviews the activities of physicians and pharmacists at the Tudor and Stuart courts. See "Policing the Health of London," pp. 9, 23 and *passim.* See also John T. Alexander, *Catherine the Great: Her Life and Legend* (New York: Oxford University Press, 1989), p. 193. The identities of specific physicians and pharmacists who may have participated in drafting Russian regulations are not known.

6. The American government also prohibited artificially colored tea before the Civil War, indicating that public health and specifically pure food and drink now was the purview of other than absolutist governments. See Robert M. Crunden, *Ministers of Reform. The Progressive Achievement in American Civilization, 1889–1920* (New York: Basic Books, 1982), pp. 176–77.

7. Cited in Aleksandr Al'medingen, *Domashnii opredelitel' poddelok pitatel'-nykh, vkusovykh, i takzhe i drugikh veshchestv* (St. Petersburg, 1892), p. 103.

8. A. V. Pel', *Fal'sifikatsii i mery bor'by s nimi* (St. Petersburg, 1899), p. 19.

9. Cited in Al'medingen, *Domashnii opredelitel' poddelok,* p. 103.

10. Smith and Christian, *Bread and salt,* p. 300, assert that the term *vino* commonly referred to lesser spirits whereas vodka referred to higher-quality spirits. However I believe the term *vino* in these laws applied to wine. See discussion in text, below.

11. See Mary Schaeffer Conroy, "Education of the Blind, Deaf and Mentally Retarded in Late Tsarist Russia," *Slavic and European Education Review,* vol. 9, nos. 1 and 2, 1985, pp. 29–49.

12. This trend was in reverse in the American "pure food movement." Individual states regulated food and drink from the last quarter of the nineteenth century. Crunden, *Ministers of Reform,* pp. 176–177.

Bills for national laws against adulteration of food and drink were introduced into Congress during the 1880s and 1890s but a national "Pure Food and Drug Act" was not passed until 1906. *United States: Index Catalogue of the Library of the Surgeon General's Office,* Second Series, 1900, *V,* p. 924. Prior to 1890 there were federal meat inspection laws for exports. James Harvey Young, "The Pig that Fell into the Privy: Upton Sinclair's *The Jungle* and the Meat Inspection Amendments of 1906," *Bulletin of the History of Medicine,* vol. 59, no. 4, 1985, p. 467–480.

13. For growing literacy of peasants and urban workers see Jeffrey Brooks, *When Russia Learned to Read* (Princeton: Princeton University Press, 1985), and Ben Ekloff, *Russian Peasant Schools* (Berkeley: University of California Press, 1986).

14. Pavel Gorianinov, *Griby, pleseny i pyleviki v mediko-politseiskom i drugom otnosheniiakh* (Sanktpeterburg, 1848), pp. 1–3.

15. A. N. Khodnev, *Khimicheskaia chast' tovarovedeniia. Izsledovanie s"estnykh pripasov i napitkov* (Sanktpeterburg, 1859), foreword (4 pp., no pagination); introduction, pp. i–xxxv.

16. Khodnev, ibid., pp. 1-276.

17. A. Dobroslavin, *Ocherk osnov sanitarnoi deiatel'nosti* (Sanktpeterburg, 1874).

18. Ibid., pp. 7-286.

19. Tikhomirov, *S"edobnye i iadovitye griby* (Moscow, 1879). Russian title of French work, *O pitanii v fiziologicheskom, patologicheskom i terapevticheskom otnosheniiakh* (St. Petersburg, 1872). Russian title of 1876 English translation by Manassein, *Uchenie o pishche v fiziologicheskom i terapevticheskom otnosheniiakh,* cited in P. O. Smolenskii, *Prosteishie sposoby izsledovaniia i otsenki dobrokachestvennosti s"estnykh pripasov, napitkov, vozdukha, vody, zhilishch i proch* (St. Petersburg, 1899), pp. 507, 518, 519.

20. Medical research during the cholera pandemics of 1823–1832 and 1847–1851 did not appear to have influenced the "pure food movement" directly but undoubtedly influenced it indirectly. See Roderick E. McGrew, *Russia and the Cholera, 1823–1832* (Madison: University of Wisconsin Press, 1965), pp. 5, 7–9, 131–138, 150–152. But the publication of numerous foreign language works on public health and pure food that circulated in Russia in the 1860s and 1870s indicated familiarity with the public health awakening that engulfed the western world in the wake of the bacteriological revolutions of the nineteenth century.

21. Government regulations on pure food paralleled the "Great Reforms"—abolition of serfdom, etc., which the Russian government discussed prior to the Crimean War and implemented after its loss. See W. Bruce Lincoln, *In the Vanguard of Reform* (DeKalb, IL: Northern Illinois University Press, 1982) and W. E. Mosse, *Alexander II and the Modernization of Russia* (Collier Books, 1962).

22. *Sposob, rekomendovannyi Meditsinskim sovetom Min. Vn. Del v 1868 g.* (dlia torgovtsev i publiki). "Dlia izsledovaniia oboev, po preimushchestvu zlenenykh i dr., v kotorykh podozrevaetsia mysh'iakovistaia kraska . . ." cited in P. O. Smolenskii, *Prosteishie sposoby izsledovaniia i otsenki dobrokachestvennosti s"estnykh pripasov, napitkov, vozdukha, vody, zhilishch i proch* (St. Petersburg, 1899), pp. 378–79.

23. Circulars of the Ministry of Internal Affairs from 4 April 1878, no. 60, and 6 February 1885, no. 192, cited in Smolenskii, *Prosteishie sposoby izsledovaniia,* p. 383.

24. For Finland's position in the empire and her legislative jurisdiction see Mary Schaeffer Conroy, *Peter Arkad'evich Stolypin. Practical Politics in Late Tsarist Russia* (Boulder: Westview Press, 1976), pp. 123–136.

25. Smolenskii, *Prosteishie sposoby,* p. 375.

26. I believe the term *vino* in these articles applied to wine. R. E. F. Smith and David Christian (*Bread and salt,* note 3, above) contend that in nineteenth-century Russia the term *vino* was commonly applied to lesser quality "vodka," while the term vodka was reserved for spirits with greater alcoholic content. According to this opinion the "metallic" substances prohibited in the 1866 articles may have been residue of copper from the distillation process, thus indicating that the *vino* that the article addressed was lesser spirits or vodka. But there is evidence that counters Smith and Christian's opinion and supports mine. The 1866 articles

appended the terms "foreign" and "Russian" to the *vino* they discussed. (Al'medingen, *Domashnii opredelitel'*, p. 104) This implied that *vino* meant "wine" as Russians would not likely import vodka or lesser spirits. Furthermore there was wine production in the Russian Empire, in Georgia and Prince Golitsyn's wine industry, founded in the Crimea about 1861. (General Count Alexander Grabbe, *The Private World of the Last Tsar*, Boston: Little, Brown and Company, 1984, p. 76. In 1911 Nicholas II visited the winery, which was celebrating its fiftieth anniversary). Smith and Christian themselves refer to wine drinking in eighteenth-century Ukraine (*Bread and salt*, p. 223). Finally, Alexander Al'medingen's 1892 handbook, *Domashnii opredelitel' poddelok pitatel'nykh, vkusovykh, a takzhe i drugikh veshchestv*, which cited the 1866 articles, included separate sections on wine (*vino*) and vodka, which are discussed below.

27. "Aprelia 17-go 1867 goda Vysochaishe utverzhdennoe mnenie Gosudarstvennago Soveta, raspublikovannoe 16-go maia ob izmenenii nekotorykh pravil, kasaiushchikhsia vinodeliia i torgovli vinnom," cited in Al'medingen, *Domashnii opredelitel' poddelok*, p. 104; Articles 152, 153 of the Statute on City and Rural Economy; Article 41 of the Statute on Industry; Article 1349 of the Regulation on Punishments; and Article 873 of the Statute of the Medical Police. Also Articles 115 and 173, 176 of the Statute on Punishments to be applied by the Justice-of-the-Peace courts.

28. See Conroy, "Pharmacy in Pre-Soviet Russia," pp. 122-124, 128-130 and chapter 1 of the present work. For one discussion of the list, drawn up and periodically updated by the Medical Council (Meditsinskii Sovet) of the Ministry of Internal Affairs, in conjunction with the Ministry of Finance, see "Ob utverzhdenii novykh spisov iadovitykh i sil'nodeistvuiushchikh veshchestv," *Farmatsevticheskii zhurnal* [hereafter cited *F. Zh.*], vol. 20, no. 14, 1898, pp. 192-195; ibid., no. 15, pp. 206-208; ibid., no. 16, p. 222.

29. The Justice-of-the-Peace courts were part of the judicial reforms of 1864, which were implemented in thirty-four Russian provinces. The JP courts operated on the district level (each province contained approximately ten districts). The judges in the JP courts were elected; they were to handle smaller cases than the regular courts, with appointed judges, which convened in the capital city of the province.

30. Cited in Al'medingen, *Domashnii*, pp. 104-106. Articles 173, 115 of the Statute on Punishments to be imposed by the Justice-of-the-Peace courts (*Ustav o nakazaniiakh . . . mirovymi sud'iami).*

31. Ibid., p 104. Article 173, *Ustav o nakazaniiakh . . . mirovymi sud'iami.*

32. Article 175, *Ustav o nakazaniiakh . . . mirovymi sud'iami*, Al'medingen, *Domashnii opredelitel'*, p. 105.

33. Article 181, *Ustav o nakazaniiakh*, and 1667, *Ulozhenie o nakazaniiakh (izd. 1866)*, Al'medingen, *Domashnii*, pp. 106-107.

34. Article 1666, ibid., p. 106.

35. Article 865, *loc. cit.*

36. A. P. Dobroslavin, O *zagranichnykh laboratoriiakh dlia izsledovaniia pishchevykh veshchestv* (St. Petersburg, 1887), pp. 2-3.

37. Dobroslavin, ibid., pp. 8–10.

38. Ibid., p. 11.

39. Ibid., pp. 12–13.

40. Dobroslavin, Ibid., p. 2.

41. Pel', *Fal'sifikatsii i mery*, pp. 62–63. The last caveat emphasizes Russians' dependence on the government. Pel' believed that private initiative (and apparently even local authorities) could *assist* the central government but could not adequately prevent falsification; only the central government could insure the purity of food and items of everyday use. Ibid., p. 63.

42. F. F. Erisman, *Pervyi godovoi otchet Moskovskoi gorodskoi sanitarnoi stantsii* (established in the Hygienic Institute of Moscow University, March 1891–March 1892) (Moscow, 1892), pp. 1–7.

43. The Russian Society for the Preservation of Public Health was established in St. Petersburg in 1878. Branches appeared in Odessa, Kazan, and Theodosia in 1880, and in sixteen more Russian cities in succeeding years.

44. V. M. Iakimov, "Fal'sifikatsiia pishchevykh veshchestv i bor'ba s neiu v zakone i zhizni," *Meditsinskaia beseda*, vol. 7, no. 8, 1893, pp. 206.

45. Iakimov, "Fal'sifikatsiia," pp. 207–210.

46. For example, article 115 of the Statute on Punishments to be Imposed by Justice-of-the-Peace courts (1866) states "Za prigotovlenie dlia prodazhi (preparing for sale) ili za prodazhu (sale) of s"estnykh pripasov ili napitkov (foodstuffs or drinks), vrednykh dlia zdorov'ia ili isportivshikhsia (Harmful for the health or spoiled) . . ." cited in Al'medingen, *Domashnii opredelitel'*, p. 106.

47. France: Law 10, 19, and 27, 1851, "affecting various adulterated wares," and "Regulation of 15 June 1862 regarding dyes in sweets and foodstuffs . . ." cited in Al'medingen, *Domashnii opredelitel'*, pp. 109–112. The law of 1889 on wine referred to use of saccharin, discussed at length, below.

48. Germany: Law of 14 May 1879 regarding sale of food . . . and other items of use," cited in Al'medingen, ibid., pp. 136–141.

49. Belgium: Law of 17 June 1891 "regarding artifical dyes in food products," cited in Al'medingen, ibid., pp. 141–143.

50. Italy: Law of 15 August 1890 cited in Al'medingen, ibid., pp. 114–136.

51. Dobroslavin, *Ocherk*, pp. 190–191.

52. In this case, again, *vino* meant wine, not lesser spirits—i.e., Arkhipov definitely was a specialist on wine, not vodka. Pel' provided information on Arkhipov in a section entitled "*Vinogradnoe vino*" or grape wine. A further chapter referred to "*Khlebnoe vino*" or grain spirits. *Fal'sifikatsii i mery*, pp. 55, 52–54.

53. Pel', *Fal'sifikatsii i mery*, p. 63. The objective of this commission was to "lessen mortality."

54. Article 115, Statute on Punishments to be Imposed by Justice-of-the-Peace courts cited in Smolenskii, *Prosteishie sposoby*, p. 119.

55. "O proizvodstve i prodazhe margarina i uskusstvennago masla," Zakon 8 aprelia 1891, cited in Al'medingen, *Domashnii opredelitel'*, pp. 107–108.

56. Article 635 of the Medical Statute, cited in Smolenskii, *Prosteishie sposoby*, pp. 118–119.

57. Articles 654-660 of the Medical Statute cited in Smolenskii, ibid., pp. 379-380.

By the late 1890s, according to the Medical Statute, police were to make sure that streets outside each dwelling were kept clean. The Municipal Statute of 1870 granted cities the power to tax homeowners for general street cleaning. The statute on construction stipulated that slaughterhouses be built outside cities. Building a slaughterhouse where forbidden incurred a 100-ruble fine. Medical Statute, articles 621–629; Statute on Punishments, articles 53–56, 110, 114; Law on Punishments, articles 863, 1075, 1348. Cited in ibid., pp. 408–409. It has not been proven whether or not cities were able to enforce these rules.

58. Pel', *Fal'sifikatsii i mery*, pp. 8–9.

59. "Ot Meditsinskago Soveta Ministerstva Vnutrennikh Del," *F. V.*, vol. 4, no. 12, 1900, pp. 222–223. The Medical Council of the Ministry of Internal Affairs, sponsor of the competition, stated that use of dyes and essences was very widespread. Their purpose was to give food products and drinks attractive appearance, taste, and smell but there had recently surfaced cases in which these substances harmed the health. Underscoring its conviction that governments were responsible for the health of their citizenry, the Medical Council noted that "Unfortunately, science, because of an absence of research on these substances, had not given governmental organs the possibility to undertake measures, with full verification, to limit the use of these harmful products and to order other harmless products."

Papers were to establish which essences or dyes were absolutely harmful, which were toxic in significant amounts, and which were harmless. Authors had a two-year period in which to present exact data and chemical composition of substances in the three categories—harmful, harmful in significant amounts, or harmless—and, in addition, cite relevant medical-chemical literature. Competitors could be of either sex and no degree was required; however, competitors had to be Russian citizens.

60. In 1897 ordinary university professors received annual salaries of 3,000 rubles; extraordinary professors, the next highest grade, received 2,000. "The Twelfth International Medical Congress (Moscow, 1897): Medicine Past and present in Russia," *The Lancet*, August 7, 1898, p. 366. For a discussion of pharmacists' pay see Conroy, "Pharmacy in Pre-Soviet Russia," pp. 125, 135, note 108.

61. Since many of these works appeared before the great cholera epidemic of 1892 they cannot be attributed to this as has been asserted by a number of American scholars.

62. While there were many scholarly American studies on diet, for example those cited in Smolenskii, some popular American works on adulteration, especially those that discussed foreign materials in sausage, were sensationalistic. Russian works for public consumption were sober.

63. Smolenskii, *Prosteishie*, pp. 507, 508. Russian title of Faerman: *Fal'sifikatsiia vazhneishikh pitatel'nykh produktov;* of Geidenrick: *Metody izsledovaniia nizhikh organizmov.*

64. Russian title of book on healthy heating: *Zdorovoe i vrednoe otoplenie i ozdorovlenie zhilykh pomeshchenii* (1882); on factory workers' health: *Zashchita*

zhizni i zdorov'ia rabochikh na fabrikakh i zavodakh (1891). Other works listed in the endpapers dealt with physics, the Morse telegraph, oil and steam heating, and first aid.

65. I. I. Kanonnikov, *Rukovodstvo k khimicheskomu izsledovaniiu pitatel'nykh i vkusovykh veshchestv* (St. Petersburg, 1891), pp. 430-448.

66. Ibid., pp. 288-292.

67. S. N. Iakovlev, "Obzor naibolee vazhnykh uspekhov iz oblasti izsledovaniia pishchevykh veshchestv i otkrytii fal'sifikatsii ikh," *Vestnik obshchestvennoi gigieny, sudebnoi i prakticheskoi meditsiny,* vol. 6, (April-June, 2 sect.), 1890 pp. 40-54.

68. A. S. Shcherbakov, "Kratkiia besedy ob izsledovanii pishchevykh produktov," *Meditsinskaia beseda. Zhurnal populiarnoi meditsiny i gigieny,* vol. 5, 1891, pp. 92-100, 127-134, 191-198, 270-274, 354-364, 503-506.

69. Ibid., p. 128.

70. Ibid., p. 195.

71. S. Notkin, *Fal'sifikatsiia pishchevykh produktov i domashnie sposoby raspoznovaniia eia* (St. Petersburg, 1889), pp. 3-5, 14.

72. Ibid., p. 52.

73. One of these books concerned a journey to India (*Tainy velikoi Indii*), another, life in the wilds of North America (*Uedinennoe zhilishche. Zhizn' . . . odnogo semestva v velikoi pustine Severnoi Ameriki*), and a third, the adventures of a hunter in South Africa–with maps (*Okhota na zveri, Progulka molodykh okhotnikov po Iuzhnoi Afrike. C kartinami*). All these works sold for 1 ruble, 50 kopeks, a modest but not inconsiderable sum, again indicating readership of Notkin's text. Ibid., page following p. 66.

74. Aleksandr Al'medingen, *Domashnii opredelitel' poddelok pitatel'nykh, vkusovykh, a takzhe i drugikh veshchestv* (St. Petersburg, 1892), "Predislovie" (one page, no pagination noted).

75. Al'medingen, ibid., *passim*, pp. 1-102; legislation, pp. 103-143.

76. Mary Schaeffer Conroy, "Malaria in Late Tsarist Russia," *Bulletin of the History of Medicine,* vol. 56, no. 1, 1982, pp. 41-55.

77. Al'medingen, *Domashnii opredelitel' poddelok,* pp. 43-44.

78. Ibid., pp. 59-60.

79. Ibid., pp. 24-25.

80. Others had found the following foreign substances in wine: "salicylic acid [a common food preservative], vegetable dyes, glycerine, saccharin, and in one case, 'lead sugar,' '*fuksin,*' and boric acid." Al'medingen informed readers about one Kazenov's method of determining whether wine contained organic dyes or those made from benzol (aniline or petroleum) as well as a Japanese method of determining adulteration of wine–that developed by one Nakagama. Al'medingen, *Domashnii,* pp. 26-27.

81. Fusel oil is "an oily, acrid poisonous liquid occurring in alcoholic products that have not been distilled sufficiently to separate the ethyl alcohol from other substances with a low boiling point; it consists generally of a mixture of amyl, butyl, propyl, and isoamyl alcohols."

82. Al'medingen, *Domashnii opredelitel' poddelok*, pp. 30-31.
83. Al'medingen, ibid., pp. 103-114.
84. L. Ia. Skorohodov, *Kratkii ocherk istorii russkoi meditsiny* (Leningrad, 1926), pp. 151-152.
85. See A. V. Pel', *Khimicheskiia i bakteriologicheskiia izsledovaniia po voprosam vodosnabzheniia i fil'trovaniia vody* (St. Petersburg, 1887).
86. Pel', *Fal'sifikatsii i mery bor'by s nimi* (St. Petersburg, 1889), pp. 19-20, 11-17, 25-27, 39-40, 21-23.
87. Pel', ibid., pp. 2-6.
88. Ibid., pp. 24-32.
89. Ibid., p. 48.
90. Ibid., pp. 48-52. Pel''s works on ergotism were entitled *Sistematicheskii khode analiza rzhanago i pshenichnago zerna i muki* (St. Petersburg, 1873) and *Khimicheskiia izsledovaniia po voprosu o gnienii rzhanoi muki i o deistvii sporini na muki dlia razzhizheniia ergotizma* (St. Petersburg, 1883). For a fascinating examination of ergotism's impact on Russian demography see Mary Kilbourne Matossian, "Climate, Crops and Natural Increase in Rural Russia, 1861-1913, *Slavic Review*, vol. 45, no. 3, 1986, pp. 457-469.
91. Pel', *Fal'sifikatsii i mery*, pp. 38-44.
92. P. O. Smolenskii, *Prosteishie sposoby izsledovaniia i otsenki dobrokachestvennosti s"estnykh pripasov, napitkov, vozdukha, vody, zhilishch i proch* (St. Petersburg, 1899), p. iv, title page.
93. Smolenskii, p. v. By 1904 there were about 3,500 drug stores and 2,200 groceries which sold commercially prepared medicaments as compared with a little over 3,500 pharmacies. On drug stores see V. M. Salo, "Vneaptechnaia torgovlia lekarstvennymi sredstvami vo vtoroi polovine XIX veka," *Farmatsiia*, vol. 24, no. 3, 1975, p. 57; for data on pharmacies in the empire in 1901 and 1910 see D. I. Toropov, "Dvizhenie i rost aptechnago dela v Imperii za poslednee desiatiletie (1901-1910 gg.), *Vestnik obshchestvennoi gigieny, sudebnoi i prakt. meditsiny*, 1911, pp. 1272-1279. See also chapters 3 and 4 of this work.
94. P. O. Smolenskii, *Ob oleomargarine i iskusstvennom korov'em masle. Sposoby ikh prigotovleniia, sanitarnoe znachenie, sposoby opredeleniia v natural'nom korov'em masle i vyzvannyia imi sanitarnyia i zakonodatel'nyia meropriiatiia zagranitsei i v Rossii* (St. Petersburg, 1898) and *Istoricheskii ocherk ucheniia o pitanii*. These were on sale at the Rikker and Petrov bookshops in St. Petersburg and elsewhere.
95. Smolenskii, *Prosteishie sposoby*, pp. 67-119.
96. Ibid., pp. 361-380.
97. Ibid., pp. 350-360.
98. These were sold at various St. Petersburg stores.
99. Russian data came from the following studies: Kozlovskii on St. Petersburg typographers, Sudakov on Astrakhan workers, Kovalevskii on Penza railway workers, Erisman on Moscow workers, Schmidt on the workers in the Volga fishing industry, Fedorov on workers on the south shore of the White Sea, Tishkov and Ivanov on sailors and workers on Kronstadt, Reumovskii on workers in Tomsk

province, Griaznov on peasants from Novgorod province, Skibnevskii on peasants in Moscow province, Galin on peasants in Akkerman district, Zarin on peasants in Moscow province, Bogdanov on peasants in Tambov province, Savel'ev on peasants in Voronezh province, Faer on peasants in Novgorod province, Khelkhovskii on servants in Plotsk province, Peltyn on peasants in Warsaw and Kaliga provinces, Shchepetov on the Crimean Tatars, Dalinger on Astrakhan Tatars, Zmeev on the population in Samara province, Posadskii on the boarding school of the first Kiev *gimnaziia.* Most of the studies actually dealt with specific districts in the provinces above; for the sake of brevity only the name of the province has been cited. Ibid., pp. 10-13.

100. Ibid., pp. 10-17.

101. Ibid., p. 19.

102. Ibid., pp. 15, 20.

103. Ibid., pp. 43, 44, 46, 48.

104. Ibid., pp. 67-78.

105. A. Bukovskii, *Izsledovanie chaia i fal'sifikatsiia ego v Varshave.* (Moscow, 1896), pp. 35-39 describes the part Jews played in the deception.

106. Russian titles of Ginzburg's work: "*Khimiko-sanitarnoe izsledovanie Stavropol'skago moloka—khlebnago i prodazhnago*" (1898) and "*Besedy . . . o fal'sifikatsii pishchevykh produktov.*" The latter were termed *nauchno-popularnyia.* "Ginzburg, Savelii Abramovich," in Ivan Sofronovich Tkeshelashvili, *Materialy dlia Istorii farmatsii v Rossii Biograficheskii slovar' farmatsevtov poluchivshikh stepen' magistra farmatsii v Imperatorskikh russkikh Universitetakh i v Imperatorskoi Voenno-Meditsinskoi Akademii s 1845-1901 god* (Moscow, 1901), p. 25. See chapter 6 in this work for more information on Ginzburg. His Master's thesis dealt with his investigations into milk sold in the city of Iur'ev (Dorpat).

107. "Khronika," *F. V.*, vol. 4, no. 7, 1900, p. 136.

108. "Khronika," *F. V.*, vol. 4, no. 22, 18 June 1900, p. 400.

109. "O sakharin," in "Variia," *F. V.*, vol. 4, no. 30, 1900, pp. 546-547, and Grigory Dain (Master of Pharmacy), "Sposoby rasproznavaniia sakharin v razlichnykh pishchevykh produktov i izsledovanie prodazhnykh sortov ego fabriki Heyden'a," ibid., no. 30 (13 August), pp. 534-537; ibid., nos. 33-34 (10 September), pp. 686-591; ibid., no. 36 (24 September), pp. 634-637; ibid., no. 37 (1 October), pp. 649-652; ibid., no. 38 (8 October), pp. 665-668. One of the articles noted that most of the saccharin used was sold under the name "Heyden," the firm that produced it.

110. City government in late nineteenth-century Russia consisted of a council, or city duma, elected by property owners and those who paid commercial taxes, the duma's executive board, and a mayor. The 1870 municipal government statute, which affected some four hundred cities, charged cities to attend to public health, including sewerage, water supply and public foodstuffs.

111. Michael Hamm, for example, compared Russian cities on the eve of World War I to those in Germany "which spent five times more per capita than Russia on urban amenities and services in cities under 100,000 and about four times more per capita in all her cities combined." Michael F. Hamm, "The Break-

down of Urban Modernization: A Prelude to the Revolutions of 1917," *The City in Russian History* (Lexington: University Press of Kentucky, 1976), p. 185. Hamm concedes that municipal enterprises like slaughterhouses and bakeries generated income. Furthermore he admits that "the cities of southern Russia (led by Odessa) and the Caucasus" were providing public services in the 1880s and 1890s. However, he contrasts these with the "crowded cities of the western provinces" and over all depicts decline in municipal services after 1892 even in St. Petersburg. Ibid., pp. 183-186. On the whole, Hamm's accusations are vague. For example, he states that "in Moscow's crowded hospitals the sick were sometimes placed in closets" (p. 186). This greatly contrasts with the account of Moscow's clinics and hospitals in *The Lancet*, supplement for 1897, pp. 369-72 ("Medicine Past and Present in Russia"). For other negative views on Russian cities see also Walter Hanchett, "Tsarist Statuatory Regulation of Municipal Government in the Nineteenth Century," *The City*, pp. 106-107; Frederick W. Skinner, "Trends in Planning Practices: The Building of Odessa, 1794-1917, ibid., pp. 148-156.

A further potential problem limiting cities was jurisdiction. Hanchett (p. 106) emphasized the ease with which the provincial governor could squelch municipal regulations. Nancy Mandelker Frieden stressed that the central government and zemstvos (elected provincial and district councils established in thirty-four internal provinces in 1864) clashed over public health jurisdiction. *Russian Physicians in an Era of Reform and Revolution, 1856-1905* (Princeton: Princeton University Press, 1981), pp. 64-74. On the contrary, municipal governments and the central government seem to have cooperated in the "struggle against falsification" or adulteration of food.

Richard Robbins, *The Tsar's Viceroys: Russian Provincial Governors in the Last Years of the Empire* (Ithaca, NY: Cornell University Press, 1987), pp. 170-171, further described the governors' dismay at the state of sanitation in Saratov in 1890, as well as in Riazan and Vil'na in the early twentieth century (pp. 170-171).

Odessa, on the other hand, improved her water supply and plumbing before World War I. This contributed significantly to public health. Patricia Herlihey, *Odessa: A History, 1794-1914* (Cambridge, MA: Harvard University Press, 1986), pp. 238-39.

112. Charles Marvin, *The Region of the Eternal Fire: An Account of a Journey to the Petroleum Region of the Caspian Sea in 1883* (First edition, London, 1888; reprinted Westport, CN: Hyperion, 1976), pp. 3, 20-21. Marvin also criticized the spoilage of wheat standing at the railway stations in the Ukraine (p. 80).

On the other hand, Marvin praised the well-stocked shops and fine hotels of Odessa, Batum, and Baku as well as the Nobel Brothers' workers' town in Baku.

113. Reports from Russia in *The Lancet* that criticized hygiene were balanced by those that related advances in public health. On the former see: *The Lancet*, 1877, p. 215 (health statistics in St. Petersburg); 1880, p. 303 (communicable diseases, famine from locust-destroyed crops in the Caucasus); 1882, p. 883 (lack of proper water filtration in St. Petersburg); 1886, pp. 502-503 (health statistics in Russia); 1887, p. 128 (high child mortality, need of more physicians). But war skewed statistics: *The Lancet*, 1879, p. 384 (typhus spread by troops returning

from the Russo-Turkish war). On advances see: *The Lancet*, 1877, pp. 326–327 (sewerage and water-piping in Odessa); 1885, p. 862 (successful use of antipyrine in St. Petersburg); 1887, p. 191 (successful use of antifebrin for typhoid in Kazan clinic); 1879, p. 845 (teaching of hygiene in schools). Admittedly, this is anecdotal evidence.

Hygiene in Russian schools advanced in the last decades of the nineteenth century. See Mary Schaeffer Conroy, "School Hygiene in Late Tsarist Russia," *Slavic and European Education Review*, no. 2, 1981, pp. 17–26.

The following indicates statistical fluctuation. Russians flagellated themselves for their high death rate. However, during 1904, major Russian cities compared favorably with Western European cities with regard to deaths from certain diseases and less favorably with regard to other diseases. For example, St. Petersburg, Moscow, and Odessa had high incidence of measles in 1904 but so had Glasgow, Scotland. St. Petersburg had high incidence of typhoid in 1904—the highest in twenty years. However, in Moscow and Warsaw this disease was not a problem. Furthermore, deaths from tuberculosis of the lungs were lower in Russian cities than in many European cities. Russia: *Otchet o sostoianii narodnago zdraviia i organizatsii vrachebnoi pomoshchi v Rossii za 1905 god* (St. Petersburg, 1907), pp. 5–11.

114. Russia also lagged behind Germany in care of the handicapped. See Mary Schaeffer Conroy, "Education of the Blind, Deaf and Mentally Retarded in Late Tsarist Russia,"*Slavic and European Education Review*, vol. 9, nos. 1 and 2, 1985, pp. 35–36, 38.

115. *The Lancet*, 13 March 1880, p. 417.

116. *The Lancet*, 18 July 1885, p. 126.

117. *The Lancet*, 10 September 1887, pp. 533–534.

118. "Trichinosis in St. Petersburg," *The Lancet* 9 May 1885, p. 861. In 1879 the district of St. Petersburg was divided into nine subdistricts. A medical officer was appointed to each. Five of these "had other than sanitary functions." The zemstvo appointed three of the medical officers. The two senior medical officers had salaries of 2,300 rubles per year. Junior officers received 1,800 rubles per year. "Medico-Sanitary Organization, Rural District of St. Petersburg," *The Lancet*, 26 November 1879, p. 740.

119. Incidentally, women were prominent in staffing the main St. Petersburg institution. *Loc. cit.*

120. *Loc. cit.*

121. Pel', *Fal'sifikatsii i mery*, p. 33.

122. V. M. Iakimov, "Fal'sifikatsiia pishchevykh veshchestv i bor'ba s neiu v zakone i zhizni," *Meditsinskaia beseda*, vol. 7, no. 7, 1893, p. 176; also F. F. Erisman (ed.), *Pervyi godovoi otchet Moskovskoi gorodskoi sanitarnoi stantsii*, 1892, p. 9.

123. Pel', *Fal'sifikatsii*, p. 33.

124. Iakimov, "Fal'sifikatsiia," p. 171.

125. "Khronika," *F. V.*, vol. 5, no. 21, 1902, p. 256; Anon, "Disput v Iur'evskom universitete," ibid., no. 28, p. 332–333; "Khronika," ibid., p. 340.

126. *Sbornik rabot Permskoi zemskoi sanitarnoi stantsii,* red. H. Rum (Perm, 1889) cited in Smolenskii, *Prosteishie sposoby,* p. 512.

127. "Raznyia izvestiia," *F. Zh.*, vol. 40 (23), no. 28, 1901, p. 525.

128. Iakimov, "Fal'sifikatsiia," pp. 176–177.

129. M. P. Zakharbekov, *K bakteriologii Peterburgskago moloka* (St. Petersburg, 1895), pp. 45, 64 and *passim.*

130. See reports on St. Petersburg, Moscow, Odessa, Lodz, and Iur'ev. Kiev also had a sanitary station: *Otchet Kievskoi gorodksoi ispol'nitel'noi sanitarnoi komissii za 1893 god* (Kiev, 1894); *Otchet . . . za 1894 god* (Kiev, 1895); *Otchet . . . za 1895 god* (Kiev, 1896); *Otchet . . . za 1896 god* (Kiev, 1897).

131. S. A. Przhibytek, *Otchet S.-Petersburgskoi gorodskoi laboratorii za 1896 god* (St. Petersburg, 1897), pp. 3–4.

132. *Pervyi godovoi otchet Moskovskoi gorodskoi sanitarnoi stantsii ustroennoi pri Gigienicheskom Institute Moskovskago Universiteta,* ed. F. F. Erisman (Moscow, 1892), pp. 23–24. The 1896 report lamented that the city sanitary station played a very small role in Moscow, despite the fact that the city had a population of almost one million. *Piatyi godovoi otchet Moskovskoi gorodskoi sanitarnoi stantsii . . .* za 1896 god., ed. Prof. S. F. Bubnov (Moscow, 1897), p. 7.

133. *Piatyi godovoi otchet . . . za 1896 god.*,p. 23.

134. *Shestoi godovoi otchet Moskovskoi gorodskoi sanitarnoi stantsii . . . za 1897 god.*, ed. S. F. Bubnov (Moscow, 1899), pp. 5–6. The Moscow city executive council initiated 108 investigations, private persons, 23, and the station itself, 336.

135. *Sed'moi godovoi otchet Moskovskoi gorodskoi sanitarnoi stantsii . . . za 1898 god,* ed. S. F. Bubnov (Moscow, 1900), pp. 5–6.

136. *Piatyi godovoi otchet . . . za 1896 god,* p. 7; *Shestoi otchet . . . za 1897 god,* p. 6; *Sed'moi otchet . . . za 1898 god,* p. 6 . In 1902 sixty-one were done by order of the city administration, private persons requested fourteen, and the station itself initiated sixty-nine investigations. "Khronika," *F. V.*, vol. 5, no. 31, 1902, pp. 374–75.

137. *Shestoi otchet,* p. 7.

138. *Pervyi godovoi otchet,* p. 24.

139. *Shestoi otchet,* p. 5.

140. *Sed'moi otchet,* p. 5.

141. "Khronika," *F. V.*, vol. 4, no. 20, 1900, pp. 362–363.

142. El'mar Gol'dberg, "O fal'sifikatsii zhirnykh masel s mineral'nymi maslami i otkrytie poslednikh," *F. Zh.*, vol. 40 (23), no. 19, 1901, p. 375.

143. "Khronika," *F. V.*, vol. 5, no. 31, 1902, pp. 374–375. The researchers employed a modern spectroscopic method to investigate dangerous dyes.

144. "Khronika," *F. V.*, vol. 5, no. 28, 1902, p. 340.

145. "Khronika," ibid. no. 21, p. 256.

146. S. A. Ginzburg, "Khimiko-sanitarnoe izsledovanie prodazhnago moloka v gor. Iur'eve," *Zhurnal Russkago obshchestva okhraneniia narodnogo zdraviia,* vol. 7, no. 11, 1897, pp. 611–647. Ginzburg averred that from personal observation he saw milk at the market uncovered, a practice that invited bacteria; peasants

brought their milk to market in small containers, frequently made of zinc; when milk was covered the lids were frequently dirty. Ibid., p. 617.

147. Anon., "Disput v Iur'evskom universitete," *F. V.*, vol. 5, no. 28, 1902, pp. 332-333. See also I. F. Mazing, *Khimiko-sanitarnoe izsledovanie prodazhnago khleba v gorode Iur'eve* (Iur'ev, 1901).

148. In 1901 the St Petersburg Pharmaceutical Society Lab advertised charges of 1 to 5 rubles for urine tests and 3 to 5 rubles for other bacteriological tests. "Torgovyia i promyshlennyia svedeniia," *F. Zh.*, vol. 40 (23), no. 9, 1901, p. 189; also ibid., no. 13, p. 258.

149. "Godovoi otchet Vysochaishe utverzhdennago S. Peterburgskago farmatsevticheskago obshchestva za 1900 god—khimiko-bakteriologicheskaia laboratoriia," *F. Zh.*, vol. 40 (23), no. 14, 1901, pp. 288–289.

150. "Raznyia izvestiia: 109," *F. Zh.*, vol. 40 (23), no. 15, 1901, p. 309, and "Raznyia izvestiia," ibid., no. 27, 1901, p. 510.

151. Advertisement "Khimiko-analiticheskaia i bakteriologicheskaia laboratoriia vysochaishe utverzhdennago Rossiiskago Farmatsevticheskago Obshchestva v Moskve," *F. V.*, vol. 7, no. 39, 1904, p. 622. The lab was "open at all times" but, interestingly, was under the management of a physician and chemist, rather than pharmacists.

152. "Protokol zasedaniia Khar'kovskago Farmatsevticheskago Obshchestva 27 fevralia 1898 goda," *F. Zh.*, vol. 20, no. 21, 1898, p. 334. Valiashko was countering another member of the Khar'kov Society, G. Gein, who complained about the expense of building a laboratory to analyze food and water. Ibid., pp. 305–306. N. A. Valiashko entered the Soviet pharmacy administration. He created a chair of pharmaceutical chemistry at Khar'kov University in 1924. M. G. Ena, "Khimiko-farmatsevticheskaia promyshlennost'," in *Razvitie khimicheskoi tekhnologii na Ukraine* (Kiev, 1976), p. 270.

153. El'mar Gol'dberg, "O fal'sifikatsii zhirnykh masel s mineral'nymi maslami i otkrytie poslednikh," *F. Zh.*, vol. 40 (23), no. 19, 1901, p. 375.

154. Anon., "Meditsinskom Sovetom Ministerstva Vnutr. Del razresheno," *F. V.*, vol. 4, no. 39, 1900, p. 693.

155. "Iz oblasti gigieni i khimii pishchevykh produktov i napitkov," *F. Zh.*, vol. 40 (23), no. 8, 1901, p. 161.

156. Russia, Upravlenie Glavnago Vrachebnago Inspektora. *Otchet o sostoianii narodnago zdraviia i organizatsii vrachebnoi pomoshchi v Rossii za 1905 god* (St. Petersburg, 1907), p. vii.

157. Anon., "Khronika," *F. V.*, vol. 4, no. 3, 1900, pp. 55-56; anon., "Voprosy i otvety," ibid., no. 31, p. 56.

158. The cities included St. Petersburg, Moscow, Odessa, Kiev, Zhitomir, Kishinev, Warsaw. "Khronika," *F. V.*, vol. 4, no. 23, 1900, p. 420.

159. "Khronika," *F. V.*, vol. 4, no. 8, 1900, p. 156.

160. "Khronika," *F. V.*, vol. 4, no. 12, 1900, pp. 225–226.

161. "Variia," *F. V.*, vol. 4, no. 17, 1900, pp. 312-313. This information came from "Bakhmut."

162. "Khronika," *F. V.*, vol. 5, no. 11, 1901, p. 228.

163. *Loc. cit.*

164. "Tsirkuliar Med. Dept. k Gospodam Gubernatoram o produktsii iskusstvennykh mineralnykh vod i shipuchikh prokhladitel'nykh i fruktovykh napitkov," *Farmatsevt,* vol. 10, no. 20, 1902, p. 637.

165. "Konfiskatsiia sakharina," *F. V.,* vol. 9, no. 41, 1904, p. 651.

166. "Fal'sifikatsiia masla," *F. V.,* vol. 7, no. 41, 1904, p. 651.

167. Russia, Upravlenie Glavnago Vrachebnago Inspektora. *Otchet o sostoianii narodnago zdraviia . . . za 1905 god,* pp. vii–viii.

168. *Sed'moi godovoi otchet Moskovskoi sanitarnoi stantsii,* p. 9.

169. "Khronika," *F. V.,* vol. 3, no. 40, 1899, pp. 731–732.

170. Case of *kupchika* A. Titrova (either a woman merchant or merchant's wife), "Khronika," *F. V.,* vol. 3, no. 23, 1899, p. 430.

171. "Raznyia izvestiia," *F. Zh.,* vol. 40 (23), no. 2, 1901, p. 37.

172. "Raznyia izvestiia," *F. Zh.,* vol. 40 (23), no. 31, 1901, p. 575.

173. *Loc. cit.*

174. "Khronika," *F. V.,* vol. 4, no. 13, 1900, p. 243.

175. "The Public Health Society of St. Petersburg," *The Lancet,* 18 December 1880, p. 993.

176. *Zhurnal Russkago Obshchestva okhraneniia narodnago zdraviia,* 1902, 1903, *passim.* According to the imperially approved statutes the society could appeal to the Ministry of Internal Affairs and other central governmental institutions to urge them to take useful hygienic measures. The society held exhibitions and established camps for indigent children. Its journal published many interesting articles on individual and public health and social issues.

177. For example, in 1902 the Khar'kov branch included 116 members including 83 physicians, 5 of whom were women, 6 veterinarians, 5 engineers, 4 naturalists, 4 statisticians, 3 medical students, 16 professors, and 6 persons from other professions. Unfortunately no lower-school teachers or pharmacists were members and an average of only 34 people attended the nine meetings convened in 1900.

Otchet o deiatel'nosti Khar'kovskago Otdela R. Obshchestva Okhraneniia narodnago zdraviia v 1900 godu in *Zhurnal* Russkago Obshchestva (St. Petersburg, 1902), pp. 78–79.

178. "Raznyia izvestiia," *F. Zh.,* vol. 40 (23), no. 29, 1901, 542.

179. "Prakticheskaia khimicheskaia shkola," *Farmatsevticheskii trud,* vol. 1, no. 30, 1907, p. 407.

180. "Tsirkuliar Med. Dept. k Gospodam Gubernatoram o produktsii iskusstvennykh mineralnykh vod i shipuchikh prokhladitel'nykh i fruktovykh napitkov," *Farmatsevt,* vol. 2, no. 20, 1902, pp. 637–638.

181. The committee was to: develop norms for food products circulating in Russia and methods of essaying these products; uncover falsification and develop practical methods for eliminating it; cooperate with zemstvo, city, and other public institutions and also private persons in the struggle against falsification; present petitions about falsification to the government; report conclusions about falsification established by the government, public organizations, and private persons; participate in international congresses on food falsification; collect material, pro-

duce reports, organize courses, and publish books and periodicals on falsification; establish exhibits, museums, and competitions to combat falsification; to establish laboratories to investigate food products. The committee could establish branches, statistical bureaux, laboratories, and libraries in various parts of the empire.

182. Scholars, scholarly institutions and societies, and educational institutions.

183. Private trade and industrial institutions such as the Stock-Exchange Committee and the Committee on Trade and Manufacture.

184. The committee was to elect this last group by closed ballot, upon a two-thirds majority, from candidates recommended by two members of the committee. Other actual members were to be appointed by the institutions that they represented. The committee was to derive its funds from government subsidies, public and private contributions, and annual dues. The plenary session or General Assembly of the Committee elected a steering committee, the council. Council members served three-year terms; representatives from trade and industrial enterprises and private persons could not exceed one-tenth of the members of the council. The council elected the usual officers, chairman, vice chairman, secretary, and treasurer. The council's task was to see to the execution of regulations formulated by the General Assembly, represent the committee before government and public institutions, spend monies within perameters established by the General Assembly, acquire or lease property necessary for fulfilling committee functions, invest free monies, and suggest further action for the committee. The council could invite to its meetings specialists, with advisory voting rights, including managers of laboratories established by the committee.

185. Russia: Ministry of Trade and Industry, *Polozhenie o "Komitete po bor'be s fal'sifikatsiei pishchevykh produktov"* (St. Petersburg, 1909), pp. 3–11.

186. S. Igumnov, "Zakonoproekt otnositel'no fal'sifikatsii pishchevykh produktov," *Obshchestvennyi Vrach. Zhurnal Obshchestva russkikh vrachei v pamiat' N. I. Pirogova. Izdavaemyi Pravleniem Obshchestva.* 1912, no. 9 (November), pp. 1–2.

187. Igumnov, Ibid., p. 2.

188. Igumnov, ibid., pp. 3–4.

189. Igumnov, ibid., pp. 5–6.

190. Igumnov, ibid., p. 6.

191. Igumnov, ibid., p. 6.

192. Igumnov, ibid., p. 7.

Chapter 11

1. David T. Courtwright, Dark Paradise. Opiate Addiction in America before 1940 (Cambridge, Mass.: Harvard University Press, 1982), p. 6.

2. Glenn Sonnedecker, "Emergence of a concept of Opiate Addiction," American Institute of the History of Pharmacy, reprinted from the *Journal mondial de pharmacie*, vol. 1, 1963, pp. 17–18.

3. For excellent background information on the production of opiates see Peter T. White, "The Poppy—For Good and Evil," *National Geographic*, vol. 167,

no. 2, 1985, pp. 143-188. For current information on heroin production and markets see Allan Dodds Frank, "Unwelcome side effects from peace in Afghanistan," *Forbes*, vol. 142, no. 3, 1988, pp. 34-36. "The golden crescent"—countries in which the opium poppy was and still is grown—includes Turkey, Iran, Afghanistan, today's Pakistan, and India. Russia's eastern borders fronted on Manchuria; indeed, in the early twentieth century Russia had a sphere of influence in Manchuria, then part of opium-smoking China.

4. Card catalogs of the Lenin Library, Fundamental Library of the Academy of Medical Sciences and State Central Scientific Medical Library, Moscow. Even Chekhov wrote a satirical one-act play in 1902 entitled "On the Injurious Effects of Tobacco." Contained in *Anton Chekhov's Plays*, trans., ed., Eugene K. Bristow (New York: W. W. Norton, 1977), pp. 251-255.

5. See Conroy, "Pharmacy in Pre-Soviet Russia," *Pharmacy in History*, vol. 27, no. 3, 1985, pp. 116-118, 122-124, 127-129, and earlier chapters in the present work. According to government statistics, in 1905 there were 3,919 pharmacies, 6,809 pharmacists, and 4,662 pharmacy students.

6. D. A. Shestopal', "K voprosu ob izsledovanii narkoticheskikh ekstraktov i kolebaniiakh protsennago soderzhaniia atropina v ekstrakte belladonny," *Farmatsevticheskii vestnik* [hereafter cited *F. V.*], vol. 4, no. 29, 1900, pp. 520-523.

7. El'mar Gol'dberg (Mag. Pharm.), "O Russkom opii i kolichestvennom opredelenii morfina," *Farmatsevt*, vol. 9, no. 38, 1901, p. 1200; ibid., no. 40, pp. 1261-1263. The amount of morphine in opium stipulated by the British pharmacopoeia fluctuated between 7.5 and 10 percent; the German pharmacopoeia demanded opium with a morphine content of not less than 8 percent and not more than 12 percent. Ibid., p. 1262. Opium from poppies grown in Russia had a morphine content of only 8.17-8.23 percent. The author discussed the difficulty of using "homegrown" opium; the Russian pharmacopoeia allowed only Turkish and Near Eastern ["Little Asian"]. Ibid., p. 1162.

8. See chapters 8 and 9 on the Pharmaceutical Industry for more details.

9. "Razvedenie opiinago maka i dobyvanie opiuma," *Farmatsevticheskii zhurnal* [hereafter cited *F. Zh.*], vol. 40 (23), no. 51, 1901, p. 940; ibid., no. 52, pp. 955-956.

10. Vl. Bakst, "O fiziologicheskom deistvii nekotorykh alkaloidov opiia i o terapevticheskom upotreblenii papaverina," *Meditsinskii vestnik*, vol. 8, no. 48, 1868, pp. 451-454; ibid., no 50, pp. 470-477; ibid., no. 51, pp. 483-487; ibid., no. 52, pp. 491-495.

11. For example, a synopsis of Germain See's article appeared in *Meditsinskoe obozrenie*, vol. 28, no. 13, 1887, p. 57. A précis of American authors Ball and Jennings, "Lechenie morfinomanii" (obviously with translated title) appeared in ibid., no. 16, p. 366. G. Pinchon's article, from France, was noted in ibid., no. 20, p. 728, and a précis of Mattison's article, above, appeared in ibid., no. 22, pp. 914-915.

12. A Canadian text of 1919, on the other hand, included no warnings about the narcotics noted within. See V. E. Henderson, *A Text-Book of Materia Medica and Pharmacy for Medical Students* (University of Toronto Press, 1919), pp. 62, 93-96.

13. N. Shchepot'ev, *Uchebnik farmakologii dlia fel'dsherov i fel'dsherskikh*

uchenikov (Kazan, 1886), pp. 11, 77–78. Women could also practice as feldshers. See also Mary Schaeffer Conroy, "Pharmacy in Pre-Soviet Russia," p. 124.

14. M. Bogoliubov, ed. *Prakticheskaia farmakologiia po retseptam sovremennikh klinitsistov dlia vrachei i studentov* (Moscow, 1889), pp. 82–83.

15. F. A. Ioganson, *Dobavlenie k repetitorium po farmakologii. Sostavleno po noveishim istochnikam* (Kiev, 1889), pp. 18–29.

16. Ibid., p. 36.

17. "Kokain v zubovrachebnoi praktike," *Zubovrachebnyi vestnik*, 1885 (new pagination following p. 70), pp. 1–4.

18. "Zubovrachebnaia farmakologiia," *Zubovrachebnyi vestnik*, vol. 14. no. 2, (February) 1892, pp. 44–45.

19. Vantser, *Vrach*, 1899, 25 and Chigaev, *Vrach*, 1900, 4 cited in I. S. Kagan, "Sluchai tiazhelogo geroinizma," *Nevrologiia i psikhiatriia: Trudy gosudarstvennogo meditsinskogo instituta v Moskve*, vol. 1, no. 1, 1923, p. 259.

20. M. A. Ladyzhevskii, *Geroin i kofein i ikh sravnitel'noe farmakologicheskoe deistvie na zhivotnyi organizm.Sbornik rabot Iur'evskogo farmakologicheskogo instituta*, ed., Chirinskii (Iur'ev, 1902) cited in ibid., pp. 257–258.

21. A. S. Isaev, *Kratkoe rukovodstvo po farmakologii*, (St. Petersburg-Kiev, 1912) pp. 105–106.

22. Ibid., pp. 135–138.

23. S. N. Danillo, *O vliianii nekotorykh iadov (spirt, opii, hashish) na soznanie u cheloveka* (St. Petersburg, 1894), pp. 18–20.

24. G. Nickell, "Kriticheskii obzor novykh sredstv predpolozhennykh v poslednee vremia," *F. V.*, vol. 3, no. 20, 1899, p. 373.

25. Courtwright, *Dark Paradise*, p. 196, note 61.

26. Kagan, "Sluchai tiazhelogo geroinizma," p. 259.

27. Isaev, *Kratkoe*, pp. 103–104.

28. Anon., "K terapii otravleniia opiem i morfiem," *Novosti terapii*, vol. 1, nos. 1–6, 1895, p. 412.

29. R. Burkgart, *Morfinizm i ego lechenie*, trans., P. L. Leont'ev (St. Petersburg, 1900).

30. N. I. Grich'ev, "Kokain pri vpravlenii vyvikhov," *Meditsinskoe obozrenie*, vol. 28, 1887, pp. 604–606. There were many other "scientific" articles on drugs, such as one by L. G. Spasski, privatdocent at Khar'kov university, dealing with determining the amount of alkaloids in raw materials and galenical preparations (*F. V.*), vol. 2, no. 30, 1898, pp. 469–474, that by Master of Pharmacy El'ram on separating belladonna extract from certain substances, ibid., pp. 437–440, etc.

31. See chapters 8 and 9 on the pharmaceutical industry in this work. Also, V. F-ov, "O patentovannykh sredstvakh," *F. V.*, vol. 3, no. 28, 1899, pp. 518–520; "Ofitsial'nyia soobshcheniia: Pravila dlia propuska zagranichnykh lekarstv (Utverzhdeny, za Ministra Vnutrennikh Del, tovarishchem ministra, 31 iulia 1899 goda), ibid., no. 40, pp. 729–730; "Ofitsial'nyia soobshcheniia: Tsirkuliar Meditsinskago Departamenta, 27 avgusta 1899 g. No. 1331, gg. gubernatoram," ibid., no. 41, pp. 745–746.

In addition to citations in previous chapters one notes that in 1907 the Medical Council announced that it was recalling from the market the substance of Provizor Pruzhan—called Ekzemantin. "Khronika," *Farmatsevticheskii trud* [hereafter cited *F. T.*], vol. 1, no. 5, 1907, p. 78. In 1907, the Pel' pharmaceutical firm advertised that, although the Medical Council had forbidden over-the-counter sale of generic *spermine* they were not referring to the specific "Spermine Pel'." Advertisement, "K svedeniiu gg aptekarei i drogistov," *F. T.*, vol. 1, no. 37, 1907, p. 495.

32. "Raznyia izvestiia," *F. T.*, vol. 3, no. 3, 1909, p. 42.

33. Prosper H. Marsden, "The Practice of Pharmacy in Russia," *American Druggist and Pharmaceutical Record*, 1905, p. 96.

34. Marsden, ibid., pp. 86–97.

35. Marsden, ibid., p. 97.

36. Marsden, ibid., pp. 96–97.

37. Courtwright, *Dark Paradise*, pp. 36–38, 41; Terry M. Parssinen, *Secret Passions, Secret Remedies. Narcotic Drugs in British Society, 1820–1930* (Philadelphia: ISHI, 1983), pp. 80–84. This occurred despite the fact that historian of pharmacy Glenn Sonnedecker concluded "by the late 1870s the main components of a modern concept of opiate addiction had been put forward." Sonnedecker, "Emergence of a Concept of Opiate Addiction," p. 6, *Journal mondial de pharmacie*, p. 21. On this point, see also Virginia Berridge, "Professionalization and narcotics: the medical and pharmaceutical professions and British narcotic use 1868–1926," *Psychological Medicine*, no. 8, 1978, p. 367.

38. Parssinen, *Secret Passions*, pp. 49, 70–73. According to Parssinen the 1868 Poisons and Pharmacy Act regulated the selling of certain poisons; however, "opium, could be sold to anybody, in any amount, so long as the containers were labeled 'poison' . . . the law [of 1868] was ignored because it was toothless. Any infringement . . . had to be prosecuted at the expense of the Pharmaceutical Society. . . . The President of the Pharmaceutical Society, in 1883, claimed that drugs of all kinds were being sold by 'barbers, booksellers, chandlers, confectioners, . . . grocers. . . .'" A second act of 1908 did not establish a monopoly on dispensing of drugs by pharmacists nor did it securely regulate patent medicines.

See also Courtwright, *Dark Paradise*, pp. 51–52, and John Haller, "A Short History of the Quack's Materia Medica," *New York State Journal of Medicine*, vol. 89, no. 9, pp. 520–525, and John Haller, "Opium Usage in Nineteenth-Century Therapeutics," *Bulletin of the New York Academy of Medicine*, vol. 65, no. 5, pp. 591–607.

39. Courtwright, *Dark Paradise*, pp. 9, 97–98, 101–102. Although cocaine is a stimulant it usually is classed with opium, morphine, and heroin under the rubric "narcotic." Heroin addiction appeared in the early twentieth century, ibid., pp. 98–103.

40. Joseph Lemberger, "Laws Regulating the Sale of Poisons," *American Journal of Pharmacy*, September, 1902, p. 430.

41. In Schedule A were listed: Arsenic and its preparations; corrosive sublimate, chite and red precipitate, nin-iodide of mercury, cyanide of potassium, hydrocyanic acid, strychnia and "all other poisons," vegetable alkaloids and their

salts, essential oil of bitter almonds, opium and its preparations, except paragoric and other preparations of opium with less than two grains to the ounce.

Schedule B covered: Aconite, belladonna, colchicum, comium, nux vomica, henbane, savin, ergot, cotton root, cantharides, creosote, digitalis, and their pharmaceutical preparations, croton oil, chloroform, chloral hydrate, sulfate of zinc, mineral acids, carbolic acid, and oxalic acid. *loc. cit.*

42. Lemberger, "Laws Regulating the Sale of Poisons," pp. 430–437.

43. Lemberger, "Laws," p. 432.

44. Lemberger, "Laws," pp. 434–435.

45. Lemberger, "Laws, p. 428.

46. The term "drug abuse" in this article follows standard terminology—use of narcotics for other than medicinal purposes, over a long period of time or in increasingly larger doses, resulting in heightened tolerance of the drug and physical and psychic discomfort upon its withdrawal.

47. Courtwright, *Dark Paradise*, p. 9.

48. Virginia Berridge and Nigel S. B. Rawson, "Opiate Usage and Legislative Control: A Nineteenth Century Case Study," *Social Science and Medicine*, vol. 13A, 1979, pp. 351–363.

49. Virginia Berridge and Nigel S. B. Rawson, "Opiate Usage and Legislative Control: A Nineteenth-Century Case Study," *loc. cit.*; and Parssinen, *Secret Passions, Secret Remedies, passim.* There was a greater acceptance of opium-smoking and morphine injection in Victorian and Edwardian England. Parssinen, ibid., pp. 64, 81, 91, 103–104.

50. Virginia Berridge, "Professionalization and narcotics: the medical and pharmaceutical professions and British narcotic use 1868–1926, pp. 361–372, and Berridge and Rawson, "Opiate Use and Legislative Control," pp. 351–363.

51. Berridge, "Professionalization and narcotics," p. 365.

52. Marsden, "The Laws Relating to the Practice of Pharmacy in Russia," *The Pharmaceutical Journal,* vol. 20, January 28, 1905, p. 109.

53. "Statistika samoubiistv," *F. T.*, vol. 3, no. 3, 1909, p. 42. Most of the attempted suicides were men; 180 were women. One hundred ninety-four deaths occurred; 35 of these were women. Most of the male suicides were peasants (181). Lower middle-class urban dwellers (*meshchantsy)* accounted for 39, intellectuals for 14, artisans for 13, nobles for 13, workers for 9, and so on.

54. Kr. V., "Slukhi i vesti," *F. V.*, vol. 4, no. 1, 1900, p. 13.

55. "Nadzor v pogranichnykh tamozhniakh," *F. T.*, vol. 1, no. 30, 1907, p. 408.

56. "Ob"iavlenie Meditsinskago Soveta," *F. T.*, vol. 1, no. 29, 1907, p. 396.

57. "Sharlatanstvo v torgovle meditsinskimi preparatami," *F. Zh.*, vol. 52, no. 5, 1913, p. 53. In 1900 Eugene Shatskii, whose criticism of Russia's dependency on foreign pharmaceutical firms was noted above, alluded to a "blind" faith and use of "secret" Western European patent medicines. "Krupnoe nedorazumenie," p. 232. However, this allegation is too vague to use as documentation.

58. L. N. Tolstoy, *Anna Karenina* (Moscow, 1964), vol. 2, ch. 24, pp. 234, 235.

59. "Ot redaktsii: Red. V. Abolenskii, *Zubovrachebnyi vestnik*, vol. 1, no. 4, 1885, p. 95.

60. I. Debogorii-Mokrievich, "Sluchai idiosinkrazii k morfiiu i opiiu," *Russkaia meditsina*, no. 26 (18 July), 1893, pp. 430-431.

61. Discussions with V. M. Salo 1989, 1990.

62. *The Letters of the Tsaritsa to the Tsar 1914-1916* (London, Gerald Duckworth and Co., Ltd., 1923; reprint, Stanford: Hoover Institution Press, 1973), p. 3.

63. It is doubtful that the Tsaritsa would have smoked opium. For Russian and Soviet conviction that hashish was addictive and harmful see below and Mary Schaeffer Conroy, "Abuse of Drugs other than Alcohol and Tobacco in the Soviet Union," *Soviet Studies*, vol. 42, no. 3, 1990, p. 457.

64. Maurice Paleologue, *An Ambassador's Memoirs*, trans., F. A. Holt, O. B. E. (New York: George H. Doran Company, third edition, n.d.), vol. 3, p. 96.

65. A. V. Pel', *Fal'sifikatsii i mery bor'by s nimi* (St. Petersburg, 1889), pp. 6-7.

66. "Obnaruzhenie poddel'nykh kokaina i kodeina," *F. T.*, vol. 1, no. 23, 1907, p. 322.

67. Anon., "Slukhi i vesti," *F. V.*, vol. 3, no. 5, 1899, p. 113.

68. Anon., "Variia," ibid., no. 13, p. 262.

69. Anon., "Khronika," ibid., no. 28, p. 521.

70. T. Vdovskii, "Khronika," *F. V.*, vol. 4, no. 11, 1900, pp. 210-212; V. N. Pisorskii, "Khronika," ibid., no. 12, pp. 224-225; T. Vdovskii, "Khronika," ibid., no. 14, pp. 259-261. T. Vdovskii was a physician and V. N. Pisorskii the pharmacist who dispensed the strong medicine. In his defense Pisorskii provided the chemical structure of the medicine he gave the patient, claimed the medicine "trifinen," prescribed by the physician, was too strong for the patient, reminded readers he had been practicing thirty years, etc. The case went to court because the patient died. In a way the pharmacist was not guilty of wrongdoing. He gave the patient a small dose of the "poison" thinking it would be effective; he claimed the substance had been given to other patients with good results.

71. L. Kliachko, "Kto vinovat," *F. V.*, vol. 5, nos. 19-20, 1901, pp. 279-281. The pharmacist in question worked in Pel"s pharmacy. Representatives from the pharmacy attempted to refute the charge that the pharmacist had worked inordinately long hours.

72. "Otravlenie farmatsvtom svoego rebenka," *F. T.*, vol. 1, no. 32, 1907, p. 431.

73. In the early twentieth century the Ministry of Internal Affairs permitted sale of about two hundred medicinal substances outside the pharmacy. *Tsirkuliar ministra vnutrennykh del gubernatoram ot 27 aprelia 1902 g. No. 1050* "Dopolnenie spiska slozhennykh farmatsevticheskikh preparatov, proizvodstvo i optovaia prodazha koikh razreshaetsia vne aptek," *Farmatsevt*, vol. 10, no. 30, 1902, pp. 964-966.

74. V. M. Salo, "Vneaptechnaia torgovlia lekarstvennymi sredstvami vo vtoroi polovine XIX veka," *Farmatsiia*, vol. 24, no. 3, 1975, pp. 54-58.

By 1917 there were some 4,900 pharmacies and almost twice as many drug stores. V. M. Salo, "Perekhod aptechnogo khoziaistva v gosudarstvennuiu sobstvennost'," *Farmatsiia*, vol. 27, no. 6, 1978, p. 57. See also chapter 4 of this work.

75. V. F-ov, "K normirovaniiu torgovli aptekarskimi tovarami," *F. V.*, vol. 3, no. 20, 1899, p. 373.

76. Anon., "Slukhi i vesti," *F. V.*, vol. 4, no. 1, 1900, p. 12.

77. Anon., "Khronika," *F. V.*, vol. 4, no. 20, 1900, p. 364.

78. Anon., "Slukhi i vesti," *F. V.*, vol. 4, no. 13, 1900, p. 246; anon., "Slukhi i vesti," ibid., no. 21, p. 283.

79. Anon., "Khronika," *F. V.*, vol. 5, no. 14, 1902, p. 273.

80. Parssinen, *Secret Passions*, p. 33.

81. D. G. Semchenko, "Sluchai otravleniia rebenka opiem; primenenie atropina v kachestve fiziologicheskago protivoiadiia," *Vrach*, vol. 7, no. 29, 1886, pp. 529-530.

82. A. O. Zeman, "Redkii sluchai otravleniia opiem," *Voenno-Meditsinskii zhurnal*, vol. 72, 2 sect., 1894, pp. 77-82, esp. 82.

83. "Otvet no. 121," *F. V.*, vol. 2, no. 40, 1898, p. 644. Also Shchepot'ev, *Uchebnik farmakologii*, pp. 5-6.

84. E. I. Kark, "K deistviiu margantsevo-kislago kali. Sluchai otravleniia opiumom, okonchivshiisia vyzdorovleniem. Otravlenie morfiem," *Voenno-Meditsinskii zhurnal*, vol. 80, 1902, pp. 4625-4629, esp. 4627. This article referred to other overdoses of opium, but it was not clear whether these related to Dover's Powders.

85. M. Ia. Kapustin, *Osnovnye voprosy zemskoi meditsiny* (St. Petersburg, 1889), pp. 65-77, 80-95.

86. For example see anon., "Khronika," *F. V.*, vol. 5, no. 25, 1902, p. 304.

87. *Farmatsevt*, vol. 10, no. 17, 1902, p. 582. Often zemstvos did not have their own pharmacies; they leased private pharmacies or purchased medicaments from them. In some cases feldshers, rather than pharmacists, managed zemstvo pharmacies. As feldsher education was adequate this was not necessarily bad despite the fact that it displeased pharmacists. See Conroy, "Pharmacy in Pre-Soviet Russia," pp. 124, 119-120, and chapters 4 and 5 of this work.

88. Samuel C. Ramer, "Traditional Healers and Peasant Culture in Russia, 1861-1917," *Peasant Economy, Culture, and Politics of European Russia, 1800-1921*, eds., Esther Kingston-Mann and Timothy Mixter (Princeton: Princeton University Press, 1991), pp. 208-232. The healers were called *znakhari* or *znakharki.*

89. Anon., "Slukhi i vesti," *F. V.*, vol. 3, no. 14, 1899, p. 273. Technically, the article referred to a *sharlatan*, rather than a *znakhar.*

90. Anon., "Slukhi i vesti: Semenov," *F. V.*, vol. 4, no. 7, 1900, pp. 138-139.

91. For Russians in Central Asia see Semour Becker, *Russia's Protectorates in Central Asia: Bukhara and Khiva, 1865-1924* (Cambridge, MA: Harvard University Press, 1968), pp. 1-236.

92. Anon., "Slukhi i vesti, Krasnoiarsk," *F. V.*, vol. 3, no. 45, 1899, p. 825. This was a very high dosage. According to Terry Parssinen, "Although some morphia addicts kept their daily dosage at six grains or less, 10-13 grains was the average, and 30 to 40 grains per day was not unknown." *Secret Passions*, p. 99. Perhaps the morphine and/or cocaine sold on the streets in Krasnoiarsk was diluted.

93. M. I. Bereznitskii, *Lechenie gipnozom morfinistov, alkogolikov i kuril'shchikhov* (St. Petersburg, 1905).

94. Pronomen (in Latin letters), "Dve smerti," *F. V.*, vol. 4, no. 45, 1900, p. 800.

95. A. Ia. Danilevskii and N. P. Kravkov, "Doklad komissii po voprosu o vvoze opiia v Kvantunskuiu oblast'," *Voenno-meditsinskii zhurnal*, vol. 81, 1903, pp. 278-290.

96. Danilevskii and Kravkov, "Doklad Kommissii po voprosu o vvoze opiia v Kvantunskuiu oblast'," pp. 290-293.

97. I. S. Levitov, *O neobkhodimosti opiinoi reformy na Dal'nem Vostoke* (St. Petersburg, 1906), pp. 1-5, 17, 20-24.

98. Fergana was a region (*oblast'*) in Russian Central Asia; the former emirate of Kokand was included in this area.

99. L. Prozorov, "Narkotizm i bor'ba s nim," *Izvestiia narodnogo komissariata zdravookhraneniia*, nos. 2-3, 1924, p. 22.

100. Il'ia Semenovich Levitov, *Buzo-gashishnyi vopros na nashikh okrainakh* (St. Petersburg, 1909). Semirech'e was the easternmost region of Russian Central Asia.

101. Ibid, pp. 3-4.

102. Ibid., p. 23.

103. Ibid., pp. 23-24.

104. Ibid., p. 7.

105. I. N. Piatnitskaia, *Klinicheskaia narkologiia* (Leningrad, 1975), pp. 126-127.

106. A. L. Kamaev, *Anashizm* (Samara, 1931).

107. Levitov, *Buzo-gashishnyi vopros*, pp. 1, 8-9.

108. Ibid., pp. 20, 21, 26.

109. Ibid., pp. 7-8.

110. Ibid., pp. 25.

111. Ibid., p. 27.

112. Ibid., pp. 27, 24.

113. Anon., "Slukhi i vesti: Nizhninovgorod," *F. V.*, vol. 4, no. 7, 1900, p. 138.

114. See above.

115. While the German scientist Eduard Levinstein described withdrawal symptoms in the 1870s they still were a topic of research in the 1940s through the 1960s. Abraham Wikler, *Opiod Dependence* (New York, 1980), pp. 46-47.

116. Bereznitskii, *Lechenie gipnozom morfinistov, alkogolikov i kuril'shchikov*, pp. 1-22.

117. Ibid., p. 20.

118. Ibid., p. 5.

119. Ibid., pp. 8-9.

120. I. S. Kagan, "Sluchai tiazhelogo geroinizma," *Nevrologiia i psikhiatriia: Trudy gosudarstvennogo meditsinskogo instituta v Moskve*, vol. 1, no. 1, 1923, pp. 261-262.

121. S. A. Isaev, *Kratkoe*, p. 100. Isaev advocated the use of morphine as a pain killer in cases of incurable cancer and T.B., in cases of shortness of breath such as "nervous" asthma, and for some bowel and intestinal problems. He believed

morphine was counter-indicated for respiratory problems since morphine increased the accumulation of mucus in the bronchial tubes, for digestive and bowel problems involving worms, during pregnancy and birth, for children under five or six, and for nervous and hysterical patients (pp. 101-103). He recommended heroin for treatment of bronchial asthma, bronchitis, tuberculosis, and inflammation of the urinary tract (pp. 105-106) but warned against prolonged usage, as cited in the text, above.

122. Cited by V. A. Gorovoi-Shaltan, "Morfinizm, ego rasprostranenie i profilaktika," *Voprosy narkologii*, no. 2, 1928, p. 46.

123. Courtwright, *Dark Paradise*, pp. 87-91, 95-102. Only a small percentage of heroin addiction resulted iatrogenically, or from doctor's prescriptions for heroin-based medicine, ibid., pp. 94-95.

124. Kagan, "Sluchai tiazhelogo geroinizma," p. 260.

125. Kagan, ibid., p. 261.

126. Anon, "Kokainisty," *F. Zh.*, vol. 52, no. 5, 1913, p. 53.

127. Kutanin, "Khronicheskii kokainizm," *Trudy Psikhiatricheskoi kliniki*, vol. 3, 1915, cited in M. P. Kutanin, "Narkomaniia," *Saratovskii Vestnik Zdravookhranenii*, vol. 2, nos. 5-8, 1921, pp. 47-48.

128. M. P. Kutanin, "Narkomaniia," pp. 43.

129. L. S. Minor, "K voprosu o preduprezhdenii toksikomanii i lechenii toksikov," *Voprosy narkologii* (Moscow), vol. 1, 1926, p. 22. P. M. Zinov'ev, "Sovremennoe sostoianie voprosa o toksikomaniiakh i bor'be s nimi," *Klinicheskaia meditsina*, vol. 2, no. 7, 1924, p. 266.

130. Kutanin, "Narkomaniia," p. 38; Prozorov, "Narkotizm i bor'ba s nim," p. 21.

131. "Aspekt uchastnikov 'aptekarskoi birzhi,'" *F. Zh.*, vol. 55, no. 13, 1916, p. 114. Also D. Ia. Blumental', "Khronika," ibid., no. 33, p. 308.

132. According to my analyis there were about 7,000 *official* or *registered* drug addicts. The actual number was probably much greater. See Mary Schaeffer Conroy, "Abuse of Drugs other than Tobacco and Alcohol in the Soviet Union," *Soviet Studies*, vol. 42, no. 3, 1990, pp. 447-480.

Chapter 12

1. For the 1906 effort see "Iz protokola pervago zasedaniia s"ezda delagatov farm.," *Farmatsevt*, vol. 14, no. 6, 1906, pp. 179-180. For 1913 see "Ot Pravleniia S.-Peterburgskago Farmatsevticheskago Obshchestva. K programmnym voprosam," *Farmatsevticheskii zhurnal* [hereafter cited *F. Zh.*], vol. 52, no. 8, 1913, p. 80. This subject also was heatedly discussed in the Pharmacy Congress that met in St. Petersburg in 1913. Citations below.

2. "Pis'mo v redaktsiiu," *F. Zh.*, vol. 49, no. 36, 1910, pp. 393-394.

3. "Iz deiatel'nosti S Peterburgskago obshchestva," *F. Zh.*, vol. 49, no. 38, 1910, p. 408. The Odessa Pharmacy Society insisted that it was necessary for pharmacists to participate in the congress. Although the Moscow Pharmacy Society was

opposed, delegates were elected, including I. I. Belikovskii, G. I. Gabrilovich, K. G. Peters, and G. Glezer. V. I. In'kov and I. S. Kvaskovskii represented the Kiev Pharmacy Society, A. N. Popovskii and Professor Blauberg were chosen delegates from the Odessa Pharmacy Society, V. N. Kizeritskii and K. G. Baum from Riga, Master of Pharmacy Bukovskii from Warsaw, B. N. Glukhovskii from Lodz, Master of Pharmacy I. Kh. Gertel from Mitau, Professor Chirikov and Master of Pharmacy Zil'berg from Khar'kov. *Loc. cit.*

4. A. G. Kling, "Iubilei S. Peterburgskago farmatsevticheskago obshchestva," *F. Zh.*, vol. 20, no. 41, 1898, p. 585; A. Ginzburg, "Ocherk razvitiia nauchnoi farmatsii v Rossii za 200-letnii period," *Farmatsevticheskii vestnik* [hereafter cited *F. V.*], vol. 6, no. 18, 1902, p. 210. See also V. M. Salo and T. V. Grigor'eva, "Peterburgskoe farmatsevticheskoe obshchestvo," *Farmatsiia*, no. 2, 1976, p. 78.

5. "Farmatsiia," in *Rossiia: Entsiklopedicheskii slovar'* (St. Petersburg, 1898; reprinted Lenizdat, 1991), p. 775.

Also, Kling, "Iubilei," p. 585; R. T. S., no title, opening words of article, "Staryi otzhivshii god," dated 1 January 1898, *F. V.*, vol. 2, no. 1, 1898, p. 10. Kling labeled *Nordische Centralblatt* the special organ of the St. Petersburg Pharmacy Society.

6. *Sbornik zakonopolozhenii dlia farmatsevtov, soderzhatelei aptek i drogistov,* sostavil (ed.) P. N. Bulatov (St. Petersburg, 1897), p. 382.

7. Bulatov, *Sbornik*, p. 382, and E. I. Rodionova, *Ocherki istorii professional'nogo dvizheniia meditsinskikh rabotnikov* (Moscow, 1962), p. 25.

8. Bulatov, *Sbornik*, pp. 382-382.

9. "Protokol Rossiiskago farmatsevticheskago s"ezda," *F. Zh.*, vol. 52, no. 21, 1913, p. 238.

10. "Soslovnyia dela: otchet Vysochaishe utverzhdennago S. Peterburgskago farm. obshchestva za 1883," *F. Zh.* , vol. 6, no. 11, 1884, p. 199.

11. See chapter 4 of this work for information on zemstvo and city pharmacies.

12. Private citizens increasingly requested analyses, indicating to the society that they acknowledged pharmacists' scientific capabilities. In 1882 the laboratory conducted 243 analyses; in 1883, 296. These included 49 researches on 164 substances, 211 analyses of urine, and 85 other analyses requested by private persons. "Soslovnyia dela: otchet Vysochaishe utverzhden. S. Pet. farm. Obshchestva za 1883," *F. Zh.*, vol. 6, no. 13, 1884, pp. 209-212. See also chapter 10 of this work.

13. "Obshchee sobranie chlenov S. Peterburgskago farmatsevticheskago obshchestva," *Farmatsevticheskii trud* [hereafter cited *F. T.*], vol. 1, no. 30, 1907, p. 405.

14. "Otchet obshchestva uchatsikhsia farmatsevtov v Derpte 1 sent. 1883," *F. Zh.*, vol. 6, no. 28, 1884, p. 453.

15. "Otchet o deiatel'nosti Kavkazskago Obshchestva Farmatsevtov za 1899-1900 god," *F. Zh.*, vol. 40 (23), no. 11, 1901, p. 230.

16. D. Duda, "Iz deiatel'nosti farmatsevtichestkikh obshchestv. otchet pravleniia obshchestva 'Farmatsiia' (Warsaw), s 3 oktiabria 1903g. po 16 aprelia 1904g.," *F. V.*, vol. 7, no. 39, 1904, p. 616.

17. "Soslovnyia dela: Protokol zasedaniia S. Pet. farm. obshchestva," *F. Zh.*, vol. 6, no. 23, 1884, p. 374.

18. "Otchet novootkrytoi sberegatel'no pensionnoi kassy pri Varshavskom farmatsevticheskom obshchestve," *F. Zh.*, vol. 20, no. 10, 1898, p. 139.

19. "Protokol zasedaniia Khar'kovskago farmatsevticheskago obshchestva 27 fev. 1898," *F. Zh.*, vol. 20, no. 19, 1898, pp. 264–265; ibid., no. 20, pp. 278–279.

20. Tsentral'nyi gosudarstvennyi istoricheskii arkhiv, St. Petersburg [hereafter cited TsGIA], fond 1298, opis' 1, delo 1111, list 20 oborot [hereafter cited "f.," "op.," "d.," "l," or "ll." to indicate the plural].

21. For example, eighteen pharmacy societies initiated the 1913 congress. "Protokol," *F. Zh.*, vol. 52, no. 21, 1913, p. 238.

22. According to the Soviet historian of pharmacy V. M. Salo, the Congress of Russian Pharmacy Societies occurred in 1889, the Russian Congress "in commemoration of the 200th anniversary of the First Russian Private (*vol'naia*) Pharmacy" in 1902, the Congress of Delegates of Pharmacy Societies in 1906 and 1907, the Russian Pharmaceutical Congress of 1913, and the Fourth World Pharmaceutical Congress (August 1874). Salo and Grigor'eva, "Peterburgskoe farmatsevticheskoe obshchestvo," 1976, p. 79. In 1906, the journal *Farmatsevt* claimed the first congress had been held in 1878 and added a congress in 1900. *Farmatsevt*, vol. 14, no. 9, 1906, p. 246. The journal listed the Second Pharmacy Congress in 1889, the Third Congress in 1900, the "First Congress on Scientific Pharmacy" in 1902, and the Fourth Pharmacy Congress in 1906.

23. "Protokoly Rossiiskago farmatsevticheskago s"ezda," *F. Zh.*, vol. 52, no. 21, 1913, p. 238.

24. Salo and Grigor'eva, "Peterburgskoe farmatsevticheskoe obshchestvo, p. 79.

25. "Protokol zasedanii s"ezda delagatov farmatsevticheskikh obshchestvakh v S. Petersburge," *Farmatsevt*, vol. 14, no. 23, 1906, pp. 563–566; "Protokoly Rossiiskago farmatsevticheskago s"ezda," *F. Zh.*, vol. 52, no. 21, 1913, pp. 236–237. L. I. Zil'berberg also was prominent in the Soviet pharmacy system.

For a full account of buying out private pharmacies (*samovykup*) see chapter 14 of the present work.

26. Eduard Rennard (redaktor [editor]), "K uchiteliam," *F. Zh.*, vol. 1, no. 1, 1879, pp. 3–4.

27. See Robert Weinberg, "The Politicization of Labor in 1905: The Case of the Odessa Salesclerks,"*Slavic Review*, vol. 49, no. 3, 1990, pp. 427–445.

28. "Khronika," *F. T.*, vol. 3, no. 2, 1909, p. 26.

29. Bulatov, *Sbornik*, p. 381.

30. Rodionova, *Ocherki istorii*, p. 25. the Russian title of the Riga Society was *Vspomogatel'naia kassa dlia vdov i sirot vladel'tsev aptek;* the Assistance Fund of Riga Pharmacists: *Vspomogatel'naia kassa Rizhskikh farmatsevtov.*

31. Bulatov, *Sbornik*, p. 382. Russian title of the St. Petersburg fund: *Vspomogatel'naia Kassa farmatsevtov s spravochnym farmatsevticheskim biuro.*

32. For some strange reason Bulatov, Manager of Records (*Zaveduiushchii deloproizvodstvo*) in the Ministry of Internal Affairs also cites the charter of the

St. Petersburg Pharmacy Society as having been issued in 1851 (ibid., p. 382), which is clearly in error.

33. Bulatov, *Sbornik*, pp. 382, 398. Rodionova agrees on this date, *Ocherki*, p. 27. Russian title of Moscow fund: *Vspomogatel'naia kassa dlia nakhodshchikhsia v Moskve v konditsiiakh farmatsevtov.*

34. Bulatov, *Sbornik*, p. 382. Russian title of Petersburg fund: *Vdov'ia i Sirotskaia Kassa.*

35. Bulatov, ibid., p. 381. Russian title of Warsaw fund: *Kassa Vspomoshchestvovaniia obedneivshim farmatsevtam, ikh vdovam i sirotam.* Russian title of Kiev society: *Kievskoe farmatsevticheskoe obshchestvo vzaimnago vspomoshchestvovaniia.*

36. "Soslovyia dela: Godovoi otchet 'Obshchestva studentov farmatsevtov v Derpte,'" *F. Zh.*, vol. 1, no. 15, 1879, pp. 471–473.

37. "Otchet novootkrytoi sberagatel'no-pensionnoi kassy v Varshavskago farmatsevticheskago obshchestva," *F. Zh.*, vol. 20, no. 10, 1898, p. 139.

38. "Protokol mesiachnago zasedaniia 6 marta 1879 goda," *F. Zh.*, vol. 1, no. 10, 1879, pp. 313–316.

39. "Otchet Pravleniia Vspomogatel'noi kassy dlia farmatsevtov zanimaiushchikh podchinennuiu dolzhnost' v S Petersburgskikh vol'nykh aptekakh" from 1 July 1877 to 31 December 1877, *F. Zh.*, vol. 1, no. 13, 1879, pp. 412–414.

40. There were 2 stipends at 150 rubles each, 1 two-month stipend of 10 rubles, 5 stipends of 540 rubles; various loans—1 returnable loan of 80 rubles, 1 nonreturnable loan of 22 rubles, loans to 2 members of 75 rubles, reciprocal aid to two members of 100 rubles; and 1 pension at 30 rubles. *Loc. cit.*

41. "Protokol mesiachnago zasedaniia 6 marta 1879 goda," *F. Zh.*, vol. 1, no. 10, 1879, p. 315.

42. "Soslovnyia dela: S-Peterburgskoe farmatsevticheskoe Obshchsetvo:Protokol godichnago zasedaniia 5 marta 1891," *F. Zh.*, vol. 13, no. 15, 1891, pp. 238–239.

43. "Otchet S-Peterburgskoi kassy vspomoshchestvovaniia dlia farmatsevtov za 1890," *F. Zh.*, vol. 13, no. 12, 1891, p. 191. The fundamental capital included 42 and 6 bonds (*obligatsiia*) on 3 different "eastern" projects; the first 42 amounted to 15,000 rubles. There were 4 more "eastern" bonds; 1 note on an internal loan dated from 1863; another from 1866 amounted to 100 rubles; there also were 6 bank notes at 600 rubles, and 1 paid-up mortgage from the State Noble Land Bank.

44. These included 3 reciprocal loans of 50 rubles and 1 of 150 for a total of 300 rubles, 6 reciprocal loans of 50 rubles and 1 of 100 rubles "on the basis of paragraph 31" for a total of 400 rubles; 8 grants of 50 rubles and 1 of 100 "on the basis of paragraph 32" for a total of 500 rubles, and 2 recipocal grants 25 rubles and 50 rubles "on the basis of paragraph 35."

45. "Otchet S-Peterburgskoi kassy vspomoshchestvovaniia dlia farmatsevtov za 1890," *F. Zh.*, vol. 13, no. 12, 1891, pp. 189–191.

46. "Otchet, 1900" in *F. Zh*, vol. 40 (23), no. 11, 1901, pp. 226–227.

47. "Khronika," *Farmatsevt*, vol. 13, no. 11, 1905, pp. 334–336.

48. "Sostoianie S. Pet. Vsopomogatel'noi Kassy dlia Farmatsevtov k 1-mu ianvaria 1906 goda," *Farmatsevt*, vol. 14, nos. 7 and 8, 1906, pp. 214–215.

49. "Otchet S. Peterburgskoi vspomogatel'noi kassy dlia farmatsevtov za 1906 god," *F. T.*, vol. 1, no. 6, 1907, p. 91.

50. "Obshchee sobranie chlenov S. Petersburgskago farmatsevticheskago obshchestva," *F. T.*, vol. 1., no. 30, 1907, p. 405.

51. "Otchet vspomogatel'noi kassy," 1912, *F. Zh.*, vol. 52, no. 13, 1913, pp. 146–147.

52. "Iz deiatel'nosti S. Petersburgskago Farmatsevticheskago Obshchestva," *F. Zh.*, vol. 52, no. 12, 1913, p. 131.

53. "Kassovyi otchet obshchestva studentov farmatsevtov v Derpte," *F. Zh.*, vol. 1, no. 15, 1879, pp. 471–473.

54. "Kievskoe farmatsevticheskoe obshchestvo vzaimnago vspomoshchestvovaniia," *F. Zh.*, vol. 20, no. 14, 1898, p. 195; no. 15, p. 208; no. 16, p. 223.

55. "Kievskoe farmatsevticheskoe obshchestvo . . . ," *F. Zh.*, vol. 20, no. 17 , 1898, p. 236.

56. Rodionova, *Ocherki*, p. 27.

57. "Slukhi i vesti: Khar'kov," *F. V.*, vol. 2, no. 46, 1898, p. 740.

58. "Otchet novootkrytoi sberagatel'no-pensionnoi kassy pri Varshavskom farmatsevticehskom obshchestve," *F. Zh.*, vol. 20, no. 10, 1898, p. 139.

59. "Protokol ocherednago sobraniia Kavkazskago Obshchestva Farmatsevtov ot 29 ianvaria 1901 g.," *F. Zh.*, vol. 40 (23), no. 17, 1901, pp. 345–346.

60. Rodionova, *Ocherki*, pp. 26–27.

61. E. A. Al'tgauzen, "K voprosu o zabastovkakh v aptekakh," *Farmatsevt*, vol. 13, no. 25, 1905, p. 787.

62. The office (*Tsentral'n.* [*sic*] *Rekomedatel'naia Kontora*), located at Tverskaia and Sadovaia in Moscow, provided two telephone numbers for clients. Advertisement, *F. T.*, vol. 1, no. 37, 1907, p. 496.

63. Obituary, front page: "Emanuil Adol'fovich Al'tgauzen," *Farmatsevt*, vol. 15, nos. 9–10, 1907, pp. 249–251.

64. "Nashi zadachi," *Russkii farmatsevt*, vol. 1, no. 1, 1908, p. 18.

65. A. G. Natradze, *Ocherk razvitiia khimiko-farmatsevticheskoi promyshlennosti SSSR* (Moscow, 1967), p. 82. Some of the issues of these journals are in the library of the Pharmacy Museum, Moscow.

Chapter 13

1. Schindelmeiser, "Nichtamtlicher Teil. Weibliche Pharmazeuten in Russland," *Apotheker-Zeitung*, no. 74, 1902, p. 636.

2. Soviet historian Rodionova claimed that the strike resulted from management depriving staff of the percentage of pharmacy income which they had heretofore received. She further asserted, without providing proof, that the most active strike organizers were fired. E. I. Rodionova, *Ocherki istorii professional'nogo dvizheniia meditsinskikh rabotnikov* (Moscow, 1962), p. 32.

3. The Russian title of the society was *Rossiiskoe farmatsevticheskoe Obshchestvo vzaimnago vspomoshchestvovaniia. Sbornik zakonopolozhenii dlia farmatsevtov, soderzhatelei aptek i drogistov,* sostavil (ed.) P. N. Bulatov (St. Petersburg, 1897), pp. 398–399, and Jonathan Sanders, "Drugs and Revolution: Moscow Pharmacists in the First Russian Revolution," *Russian Review,* vol. 44., 1985, p. 358 and *passim.*

4. "Raznyia izvestiia," *Farmatsevticheskii Zhurnal* [hereafter cited *F. Zh.*], vol. 40 (23), no. 12, 1901, p. 250. Before 1901 the journal cited its volumes from the beginning of its Russian-language editions, i.e., 1879. From 1901 the journal cited 2 volume numbers, one from the beginning of the German-Russian editions; the second continued citing from the Russian-only editions.

5. Sanders, "Drugs and Revolution," p. 358. The St. Petersburg society published *Retsept* (*Prescription*) under the editorship of E. A. Shatskii from 1902 to 1903, and during 1905 and 1906, *Golos Farmatsevta,* the editor of which was L. M. Kliachko. A. G. Natradze, *Ocherk razvitiia khimiko-farmatsevticheskoi promyshlennosti* (Moscow, 1967), p.82.

6. Mastheads of *Farmatsevticheskii vestnik,* 1898–1906 [hereafter cited *F. V.*]. Jonathan Sanders mistakenly cites Saltykov and Lintser as co-editors from 1897. "Drugs and Revolution," p. 358.

7. See chapters 5 and 14, respectively, in this work.

8. "O farmatsevte proletarii," *Farmatsevticheskii trud* [hereafter cited *F. T.*]. vol. 1, no. 5, 1907, p. 75.

9. Editorial, A. B. Solonouts, *F. T.*, vol. 1, no. 24, 1907, p. 330.

10. "O farmatsevte proletarii," *F. T.*, vol. 1, no. 5, 1907, pp. 71–74.

11. *F. T., passim.* For example, S. K. Lintser, "Aptechnaia monopoliia," *F. V.*, vol. 7, no. 4, 1904, pp. 59–61 emphasized how pharmacy owners braked factory production of medicines and pleaded for the Pirogov Society to petition the Minister of Internal Affairs to abolish the "pharmacy monopoly."

12. Front page, *F. T.*, vol. 1, no. 24, 1907.

13. Advertisement, *F. T.*, vol. 1, no. 27, 1907.

14. Advertisement of V. Blazhei and Co., *F. T.*, vol. 1, no. 32, 1907, p. 438.

15. Advertisement, *F. T.*, vol. 1, no. 33, 1907, p. 447.

16. "Protokol obshchago sobraniia sluzhashchikh farmatsevtov g. Moskvy," *F. T.*, vol. 1, no. 6, 1907, pp. 89–90.

17. See chapter 5 of the present work.

18. *Russkii farmatsevt,* vol. 1, no. 1, 1908, p. 19.

19. "Nashi zadachi," *Russkii farmatsevt,* vol. 1, no. 1, 1908, p. 13.

20. "Nashi zadachi," p. 15.

21. "Nashi zadachi," p. 9.

22. "Nashi zadachi," pp. 9–12, 14, 19.

23. "Nashi zadachi," p. 12.

24. "1908-oi god. Obzor aptechnoi zhizni," *F. T.*, vol. 3, no. 1, 1909, p. 8.

25. Ads in *Russkii farmatsevt,* vol. 1, no. 2, February 1908, p. 87.

26. "1908-oi god. Obzor aptechnoi zhizni," *F. T.*, vo. 3, no. 1, 1909, p. 8.

27. This was heralded as the organ of the St. Petersburg Union of Staff Pharmacists. It began January 1907 (*F. T.*, vol. 1, no. 2, 1907, p. 31) but folded soon after.

28. Nearly full runs of all the journals cited are housed in the Pharmacy Museum in Moscow under the directorship of V. M. Salo. There also are copies in the Lenin Library and the Saltykov-Shchedrin Library in St. Petersburg.

29. Robert B. McKean, *St. Petersburg between the Revolutions* (New Haven, CN: Yale University Press, 1990), pp. 162–172.

30. Rodionova, *Ocherki istorii*, p. 33.

31. I. R. Zakharevich, "K delam pensionno-vspomogatel'noi kassy," *Farmatsevt*, vol. 13, no. 6, 1905, pp. 164–167; also Tkeshelashvili, *Farmatsevt*, vol. 13, no. 7, 1905, pp. 208–211.

32. E. A. Al'tgauzen, "Ot redaktora," *Farmatsevt*, vol. 13, no. 6, 1905, pp. 167–168.

33. I. I. Korol'kov, *Farmatsevty Rossii* (Moscow, 1911), pp. 4-5. The official Russian title of National Pharmacists Pension Fund: *Pensionno-vspomogatel'naia kassa farmatsevtov*.

34. Al'tgauzen, "K voprosu," *Farmatsevt*, vol. 13, no. 25, 1905, p. 788.

35. As a result, 1901 and 1902 were combined in one volume 5.

36. "Ot upravleniia vysochaishe utverzhdennago Rossiiskago farmatsevticheskogo obshchestva vzaimnogo vspomoshchestvovaniia," *F. V.*, vol. 5, 1901—special addendum, 24 March 1901, at the end of the issues for 1901.

37. "Protokol obshchago sobraniia chlenov Rossiiskago farmatsevticheskago obshchestva," *F. V.*, vol. 7, no. 47, 1904, p. 944.

38. Paragraphs 1 and 10, "Ob uchrezhdenii Rossiiskoi pensionno-vspomogatel'noi kassy farmatsevtov v g. Moskve i ob utverzhdenii ustava sei kassy," in Bulatov, *Sbornik*, pp. 383, 384.

39. Paragraphs 1, 9–12, "Ob uchrezhdenii Rossiiskoi pensionno-vspomogatel'noi kassy farmatsevtov v g. Moskve i ob utverzhdenii ustava sei kassy," (Sbornik. uzak. i rasp. prav. 21 okt. 1894 g. No. 174, st. 1250) in Bulatov, *Sbornik* , pp. 384–385.

40. Paragraph 21, "Ob uchrezhdenii," Bulatov, *Sbornik*, p. 386.

41. Paragraph 17, "Ob uchrezhdenii," Bulatov, *Sbornik*, p. 385.

42. Paragraph 21, "Ob uchrezhdenii," ibid. p. 386.

43. Paragraph 9, "Ob uchrezhdenii," ibid., p. 384.

44. *Addendum, loc. cit.*

45. Obligatory members could contribute over and above the required 5 percent of their salary, up to 100 rubles a year. Owners of pharmacies who desired pensions also could contribute up to this amount. Nonobligatory members could join the fund by contributing *at least* 30 rubles a year.

Paragraphs 21 and 22, "Ob uchrezhdenii," Bulatov, *Sbornik*, p. 386.

46. Paragraphs 1, 10, 19, 24, "Ob uchrezhdenii," Bulatov, *Sbornik*, pp. 384–387.

47. Paragraphs 24–34, "Ob uchrezhdenii," ibid., pp. 387–389.
48. Paragraph 47, "Ob uchrezhdenii," ibid., p. 391.
49. Paragraphs 58–60, "Ob uchrezhdenii," ibid., pp. 393–394.
50. Paragraphs 61–70, "Ob uchrezhdenii," ibid., pp. 394–396.
51. Paragraph 64, "Ob uchrezhdenii," ibid., p. 394.
52. Paragraph 2, "Ob uchrezhdenii," ibid., p. 383.
53. Paragraph 6, "Ob uchrezhdenii," ibid., p. 383.
54. Paragraphs 72–77, "Ob uchrezhdenii," ibid., pp. 396–397.
55. "Protokol ekstrennago zasedaniia upravleniia pensionnoi kassy farmatsevtov 1 iiul. 1904 g.," *F. V.*, vol. 7, no. 35, p. 585 and ibid., no. 41, p. 644.
56. These are standard deductions, used for contemporary pension funds in America.
57. "Izvlechenie iz protokola revizii summ Vysochaishe utverzhdennoi Pensionno-Vspomogatel'noi Kassy Farmatsevtov," *F. Zh.*, vol. 20, no. 27, 1898, p. 381. The chair of the supervisory committee at this time was Gr. Al. Geilig.
58. Statements in *F. Zh.*, vol. 20, no. 31, 1898, p. 441; ibid., no. 42, p. 598; ibid., no. 45, p. 639.
59. Statement, *F. Zh.*, vol. 40 (23), no. 52, 1901, p. 958. The exact total was 509,293 rubles.
60. These figures were taken from the the government report, "Otchet o sostoianii narodnago zdraviia i organizatsii vrachebnoi pomoshchi v Rossii," for 1905. *Russkii farmatsevt*, vol. 1, no. 1, 1908, p. 26.

Mikhail Polumordvinov claimed in *Farmatsevticheskii vestnik* ("Vol'nyia apteki v Imperii," *F. V.*, vol 7, no 2, 1904, p 27) in 1904 that the staff of private normal pharmacies amounted to 1903 but this figure was far too low.

61. Anon., "Pis'mo v redaktsiiu," *Farmatsevt*, vol. 14, no. 19, 1906, p. 547.
62. E. Al'tgauzen, "K delam pensionno-vspomogatel'noi Kassy farmatsevtov," *Farmatsevt*, vol. 14, no. 19, 1906, p. 543.
63. "Vysochaishe utverzhdennaia pensionno-vspomogatel'naia kassa farmatsevtov . . . raz"iasneniia Med. Dep. 22 maia 1898, no. 3892," *F. Zh.*, vol. 20, no. 27, 1898, pp. 382–382.
64. "Gor'koe razdum'e," *F. Zh.*, vol. 45 (23), no. 46, 1901, p. 837.
65. "Protokol zasedaniia pravleniia Rossiiskoi pensionno-vspomogatel'noi kassy," *F. V.*, vol. 7, no. 41, 1904, p. 644.
66. Ibid., p. 645.
67. "Izvlechenie iz protokola zasedaniia pravleniia pens. vsp. kassy farmatsevtov," *Farmatsevt*, vol. 13, no. 4, 1905, p. 115.
68. "Iz zhurnalov Meditsinskogo Soveta," *Farmatsevt*, vol. 13, no. 9, 1905, p. 265.
69. Grigori Aleksandrovich Geilig and [I. R.] Joseph Romualdovich Zakharevich, letter to the editor, *Farmatsevt*, vol. 14, no. 42, 1906, p. 1229.
70. N. G., "Gor'koe razdum'e," *F. Zh.*, vol. 40 (23), no. 47, 1901, p. 857.
71. Korol'kov, *Farmatsevty Rossii*, pp. 4–5.

72. Audited Financial Statement: "Izvlechenie iz protokola revizii summ Vysochaishe utverzhdennoi Rossiiskoi pensionno-vspomogatel'noi kassy farmatsevtov," June, 1901, *F. Zh.*, vol. 40 (23), no. 30, 1901, pp. 556–557.

73. Audited Financial Statement: "Izvlechenie iz protokola revizii summ Vysochaishe utverzhdennoi Rossiiskoi pensionno-vspomogatel'noi kassy farmatsevtov," *F. Zh*, vol. 40 (23), no. 13, 1901, p. 264.

74. Audited Financial Statement, "Izvlechenie . . . ," *F. Zh.*, vol. 40 (23), no. 39, 1901, pp. 704–705.

75. "Obshchee sobranie chlenov Rossiiskoi Pensionno-Vspomogatel'noi kassy farmatsevtov, 28 fevralia 1898," *F. Zh.*, vol. 20, no. 4, 1898, p. 54.

76. "Obshchee sobranie Rossiiskoi Pensionno-Vspomogatel'noi kassy farmatsevtov, 28 fev. 1898," *F. Zh.*, vol. 20, no. 11, 1898, pp. 152–153. Frustratingly, the article is signed "An Observer." *Farmatsevticheskii zhurnal,* however, was quite objective throughout its half century of existence.

77. *Loc. cit.*

78. "Obshchee sobranie chlenov Rossiiskoi Pensionno-Vspomogatel'noi kassy farmatsevtov, 28 fev. 1898," *F. Zh.*, vol. 20, no. 4, 1898, p. 54.

79. *Loc. cit.*

80. N. G., "Gor'koe razdum'e," *F. Zh.*, vol. 40 (23), no. 47, 1901, p. 857.

81. A contemporary asserted that "Ferrein declared it was *absolutely necessary* to transfer the Fund to management of the State Treasury." N. G., "Gor'koe razdum'e," *F. Zh.*, vol. 40 (23), no. 46, 1901, p. 838, and ibid., no. 47, p. 858.

82. N. G., "Gor'koe razdum'e," *F. Zh.*, vol. 40 (23), no. 47, 1901, p. 858.

83. I. S. Tkeshelashvili, "K delam nashei pensionno-vspomog. kassy," *Farmatsevt*, vol. 13, no. 7, 1905, p. 208–211.

84. "Raznyia izvestiia: no. 369," *F. Zh.*, vol. 40 (23), no. 42, 1901, p. 761.

85. A. Pokinuli, "Raznyia izvestiia," *F. Zh.*, vol. 40 (23), no. 43, 1901, p. 780.

86. "Raznyia izvestiia: no. 452," *F. Zh.*, vol. 40 (23), no. 47, 1901, p. 860; also Uleveli, "Eshche o farmatsevticheskoi kasse i eia pravlenii," *F. V.*, vol. 5, no. 8, 1902, pp. 93–94.

87. Pharmacist Uleveli, "Eshche o farmatsevticheskoi kasse i eia pravlenii," *F. V.*, vol. 5, no. 8, 1902, p. 93. He compared the Russian Pension Fund to a worker pension fund in France where "each worker was obliged to contribute 10 centimes per day and the *capitalist* [italics mine] was obliged to contribute a certain percent for the use of workers. The workers protested saying they would die before age 65 when they could use the fund."

88. Uleveli, "Esche," pp. 93-94.

89. I. R. Zakharevich, "Pis'ma iz daleka," *Farmatsevt*, vol. 13, no. 5, 1905, pp. 133–134. Jonathan Sanders claimed that "V. K. Ferrein was the driving force behind the Moscow Pharmacy (owners') Society and its journal *Farmatsevt.*" Sanders, "Drugs and Revolution," p. 360.

90. Evsevii Basilaia, "Pis'ma v redaktsiiu," *Farmatsevt*, vol. 13, no. 8, 1905, p. 238.

91. "Protokol ekstrennago zasedaniia upravleniia pensionnoi kassy farmatsevtov 1 iiulia 1904," *F. V.*, vol. 7, no. 37, 1904, p. 585.

92. "Pensionnaia Kassa," *F. T.*, vol. 1, no. 27, 1907, pp. 284-285.

93. Zakharevich, "Pis'ma iz daleka," *Farmatsevt*, vol. 13, no. 5, 1905, pp. 130-36.

94. E. Al'tgauzen, "Obshchee godichnoe sobranie pensionno-vspomogatel'noi kassy farmstevtov 1905 goda," *Farmatsevt*, vol. 13, no. 9, 1905, p. 269.

95. Al'tgauzen, *loc. cit.*

96. Al'tgauzen, "Obshchee godichnoe sobranie pensionno-vspomogatel'noi kassy farmatsevtov 1905 goda," *Farmatsevt*, vol. 13, no. 10, 1905, pp. 296-297.

97. Al'tgauzen, "Obshchee godichnoe . . . ," *Farmatsevt*, vol. 13, no. 10, 1905, p. 297. Jonathan Sanders identified Podrazhanskii as a Bolshevik in "Drugs and Revolution," p. 360. He had "just arrived from Paris" and was organizing strikes among the Moscow pharmacists early in that revolutionary year of 1905. *loc. cit.*

98. Al'tgauzen, "Obshchee godichnoe . . . ," *Farmatsevt*, vol. 13, no. 10, 1905, pp. 298-300.

99. "K delam pens.vsp. kassy. Tsifry," *Farmatsevt*, vol. 14, nos. 44-45, 1906, pp. 1280-1281.

100. V. Iu Martinsen and V. N. Iakimov were also on the administrative board. "Protokol zasedaniia Pravleniia Rossiiskoi Pensionno-Vspomogatel'noi Kassy farmatsevtov, 16 iiulia 1905 g.," *Farmatsevt*, vol. 13, no. 34, 1905, pp. 1076-1079.

101. G. A. Geilig, "K delam pens.-vspom. kassy," *Farmatsevt*, vol. 14, no. 46, 1906, p. 1319.

In 1905 the chair of the Administration was listed as B. Brashe; the secretary of the Fund was listed as Ivan Samgin. *Farmatsevt*, vol. 13, no. 13, 1905, p. 530.

102. G. A. Geilig, "K delam pens.-vspom. kassy," *Farmatsevt*, vol. 14, no. 46, 1906, p. 1319.

103. "K delam pens-vsp. kassy. Tsifry," *Farmatsevt*, vol. 14, nos. 44-45, 1906, p. 1279.

104. "K delam pens.-vsp. kassy. Tsifry," *Farmatsevt*, vol. 14, nos. 44-45, 1906, p. 1280.

105. Vladislav Ippolitovich Sokulovskii, "Pis'mo v redaktsiiu," *Farmatsevt*, vol. 14, no. 46, 1906, p. 1320. He had leased the pharmacy since August 1905; his name had not been cited among Vil'na pharmacy owners.

106. "K delam pensionno-vspomogatel'noi farmatsevticheskoi kassy," *Farmatsevt*, vol. 14, no. 3, 1906, pp. 81-82.

107. "Nespravedlivyi protest protiv pravitel'stvennoi revizii pens.-vsp. Kassy farmatsevtov," *Farmatsevt*, vol. 14, nos. 7 and 8, 1906, pp. 217-218.

108. Al'tgauzen, "Nashi dela," *Farmatsevt*, vol. 14, no. 32, 1906, p. 936.

109. "Khronika," *Farmatsevt*, vol. 14, no. 5, pp. 143-144.

110. "Pravitel'stvennaia reviziia pensionno-vspomogatel'noi kassy farmatsevtov," *Farmatsevt*, vol. 14, no. 6, 1906, pp. 177-178.

111. (Al'tgauzen) "K delam pensionno-vspomogatel'noi Kassy farmatsevtov," *Farmatsevt*, vol. 14, no. 9, 1906, p. 252.

112. "Rezultaty pravitel'stvennoi revizii pensionno-vspomogatel'noi Kassy farmatsevtov," *Farmatsevt*, vol. 14, no. 13. 1906, pp. 386-387.

113. E. Al'tgauzen, "Nepravyi 'protest' i nespravedlivyi 'boikot,'" *Farmatsevt*, vol. 14, no. 15, 1906, pp. 428-430.

114. Tkeshelashvili, "Pis'mo v redaktsiiu," *Farmatsevt*, vol. 14, no. 17 (May 1), 1906, pp. 494–495.

115. "Pis'mo v redaktsiiu," *Farmatsevt*, vol. 14, no. 19, 1906, pp. 545–546.

116. "Otvet na pis'mo g. E. Basilaia" *Farmatsevt*, vol. 14, no. 30, 1906, pp. 890–891.

117. *Farmatsevt*, vol. 14, no. 17, 1906, pp. 494–496. He suggested that the fund should be "transferred from pharmacists to some other institution."

118. "Pis'mo v redaktsiiu," *Farmatsevt*, vol. 14, no. 19, 1906, p. 547.

119. Al'tgauzen, "K delam pensionno-vspomogatel'noi Kassy farmatsevtov. O revizii summ pensionno-vspomogatel'noi Kassy farmatsevtov 1-go maia 1906 g.," *Farmatsevt*, vol. 14, no. 19, 1906, pp. 543–545.

120. "Otvet na pis'mo g. E. Basilaia," *Farmatsevt*, vol. 14, no. 30, 1906, p. 891.

121. E. Al'tgauzen, "Nashi dela," *Farmatsevt*, vol. 14, no. 32, 1906, pp. 934–935.

122. *Farmatsevt*, vol. 14, no. 33, 1906, pp. 963–964.

123. "Pis'mo v redaktsiiu," *Farmatsevt*, vol. 14, no. 19, 1906, p. 546.

124. E. E. Basilaia, "Neudachnaia vylazka," *Farmatsevt*, vol. 14, no. 27, 1906, pp. 787–788.

125. Basilaia, "Neudachnaia vylazka," p. 790.

126. Basilaia, ibid., pp. 787–788.

127. Basilaia, ibid., p. 789.

128. Al'tgauzen, "Ot redaktsii," *Farmatsevt*, vol. 14, no. 34, 1906, p. 995.

129. "Predlozhenie Pravleniia Pens.-vspom. kassy," *Farmatsevt*, vol. 14, no. 34, 1906, pp. 992–993.

130. ". . . [to] Grigori Aleksandrovich Geilig," Iosif Romualdovich Zakharevich, "Otkrytoe pis'mo ispolniaiushchemy obiazannosti predsedatelia Rossiiskoi Pensionno-vspomogatel'noi kassy farmatsevtov, chleny," *Farmatsevt*, vol. 14, no. 42, 1906, pp. 1229–1232.

131. I. R. Zakharevich, "Nasha pensionno-vspomogatel'naia kassa," *Farmatsevt*, vol. 14, nos. 35–36, 1906, pp. 1017–1020.

132. "K delam pens.-vsp. kassy. Tsifry krasnorechivee slov E. A. Al'tgauzena," *Farmatsevt*, vol. 14, nos. 44–45, 1906, p. 1279.

133. "Otkrytoe pis'mo chlenu pens.-vspom. kassy," *Farmatsevt*, vol. 14, no. 34, 1906, p. 993.

134. "Khronika," *Farmatsevt*, vol. 14, no. 34, 1906, p. 998.

135. "Khronika," *Farmatsevt*, vol. 14, no. 42, 1906, p. 1227.

136. "Prava Pensionnoi Kassy farmatsevtov," *F. T.*, vol. 1, no. 26, 1907, p. 363.

137. "K delam Rossiiskoi Pensionno-vspomogatel'noi kassy farmatsevtov," *F. T.*, vol. 1, no. 5, 1907, p. 78.

138. He claimed that in 1907, "curiously, in the general assembly of 1 to 6 June, 1907, voting for liquidation of the Fund were the majority of representatives from St. Petersburg and some provincial pharmacy owners; voting against liquidation were all representatives from Moscow and [working] pharmacists from the provinces. Basilaia stood firmly for retaining and reorganizing the Fund against

the St. Petersburg contingent." "Likvidatsiia ili reorganizatsiia pensionnoi kassy," *F. T.*, vol. 1, no. 27, 1907, pp. 369-370.

139. "Khronika," *F. T.*, vol. 1, no. 5, 1907, p. 78.

140. "Khronika," *F. T.*, vol. 1, no. 5, 1907, p. 79.

141. Ibid., p. 79.

142. "Oblastnaia konferentsiia soiuzov farmatsevtov," *F. T.*, vol. 1, no. 30, 1907, p. 417.

143. "Ot pravleniia Vysochaishe utverzhden. Rossiiskoi Pensionno-vspomogstel'noi kassy farmatsevtov," *F. T.*, vol. 1, no. 5, 1907, pp. 80-81; ibid., pp. 95-96; ibid., pp. 109-110.

144. The pharmacy owners were known as *chlen sorevnovatel.*

145. "Doklad 'predsedatelia' Pensionnoi Kassy," *F. T.*, vol. 2, no. 28, 1908, pp. 460-461; also, "Pensionnaia kassa," *Russkii farmatsevt*, vol. 1, no. 1, 1908 p. 30. According to the latter, the other members were S. B. Shimanskii, P. D. Uriupin, A. V. Tylkin, and candidate members included I. E. Voitsekovich, M. M. Erlikhman, G. A. Abramson and three others, all "actual members" of the Fund, i.e., staff pharmacists.

146. *Russkii farmatsevt*, vol. 1, no. 1, 1908, pp. 30-31.

147. T. H. Rigby, *Lenin's Government: Sovnarkom 1917-1922* (Cambridge: Cambridge University Press, 1979).

148. Ad, "Pravlenie Vysochaishe utverzhdennoi Rossiiskoi Pensiono-vspomogatel'noi Kassy farmatsevtov—signed by the Chair, E. G. Basilaia and Secretary of the Administrative Board or Pravlenie, L. Ia. Zimin." *F. T.*, vol. 1, no. 32, 1907, p. 428.

149. "Pensionnaia Kassa: Zhurnal," *F. T.*, vol. 1, no. 37, 1907, pp. 490-493. (One of the meeting places was the Building of the Russian Pharmacy Society, Sadovaia, 213); "V Pensionnoi Kasse," *F. T.*, vol. 1, no. 36, 1907, p. 482.

The new administration claimed that even Al'tgauzen, before his death, had altercations with the old administration. He had asked N. A. Glezer, treasurer, to turn over a cupboard and typewriter belonging to Warsaw pharmacy owners but Glezer claimed he was not yet installed as treasurer and so could not fulfill the request. "K delam Pensionnoi Kassy," *F. T.*, vol. 1, no. 30, 1907, p. 406.

150. "V Pensionnoi Kasse," *F. T.*, vol. 1, no. 36, 1907, p. 482. Other articles in *Farmatsevticheskii trud* added further information on the meetings, stating, for example that, L. Ia. Zimin decided to get government sanction for the new administration and control over its assets "against the intrigue of the old administration." He went to St. Petersburg to meet with the Department of Insurance of the Ministry of Internal Affiars, and representatives of that ministry and the Ministry of Finance. The Department of Insurance concluded—rather unfairly, it would seem—that the members of the old administration had "braked the correct course of activity" and sanctioned transfer of the fund's assets to the new administration. They decided, however, to present the matter to the new Minister of Internal Affairs, P. A. Stolypin. "Obshchee sobranie sluzhashchikh farmatsevtov g. Moskvy," *F. T.*, vol. 1, no. 25, 1907, p. 345.

Apparently, the new administration received some sort of verbal approval from

Stolypin in favor of their authorizing transfer of the fund's assets to themselves. Allegedly, the ministry officials also urged the new administration not to "waste a minute of time to regularize the Pension Fund." "K predstoiashchemu vozrozhdeniiu Pensionnoi kassy," *F. T.*, vol. 1, no. 28, 1907, p. 379. This must have been only a *promise* to rule in favor of the new administration. It was uncharacteristic of government to issue a decision "on the spot."

151. L. Ia. Zimin, "Pensionnaia kassa," *Russkii farmatsevt*, vol. 1, no. 1, 1908, p. 31.

152. *Loc. cit.*, *Russkii farmatsevt* considered this proposal "witty" (*ne lisheno ostroumiia*).

153. L. Ia. Z[imin], "K polozheniiu del v Rossiiskoi Pensionno-Vspomogatel'noi Kasse Farmatsevtov," *Russkii farmatsevt*, vol. 1, no. 4, 1908, p. 157.

154. Plotnikov, apparently still around, presented a report to the Russian Pharmacy Society, June 24, 1908. *Farmatsevticheskii trud*, organ of the society, implied that Plotnikov and Lifshits were outsiders. The journal also claimed that Plotnikov and Lifshits wanted to wrest control from the other members of the administration. "Doklad 'Predsedatelia' Pensionnoi Kassy F. Plotnikova," *F. T.*, vol. 2, no. 28, 1908, p. 460.

155. No title, *F. T.*, vol. 2, no. 30, 1908, pp. 491-492.

156. "Khronika," *F. T.*, vol. 2, no. 30, 1908, p. 500.

157. There were in 1910 11,205 staff pharmacists, including students. Seventy-one percent of respondents received their salary entirely in rubles. Twenty-four percent received remuneration in room and board—a vast improvement over 1898. Pharmacists in the Pale received less pay than their colleagues. Average wages per month were 165 rubles for Masters, 107 rubles for Provizors, 64 for Assistant Pharmacists, and 26 for students. Also, five unmarried women pharmacy students owned pharmacies; six married women pharmacists owned pharmacies. Women constituted 1.21 percent of pharmacy owners. Korol'kov, *Farmatsevty Rossii*, pp. 5, 13, 24, 25, 28.

158. Other "owners" included E. E. Rozenberg, P. B. Lipshits, and I. I. Belikovskii. Other alternates from the "owners'" camp included I. M. Butvid, G. A. Andres, R. G. Peters, M. L. Gabrilovich, N. A. Glezus, and G. Grake. Other "staff" representatives included E. A. Remogol'skii, A. G. Strel'tsov, M. V. Nakhimov, and A. V. Tylkin. A. S. Tirkel'taub, S. V. Shirmanskii, P. D. Uriupin, I. M. Grokhin, Ia. V. Livshits, A. A. Levashkevich, and I. O. Vasilevskii were elected candidate "staff" representatives.

"O Pensionnoi kasse," *F. Zh.*, vol. 49, no. 42, 1910, pp. 447-449. Also "D. N. Shipov i farmatsevty," ibid., no. 31, p. 345, and "Na temu dnia," ibid., no. 37, p. 397.

159. "Iz istorii pensionnoi kassy," *Zhizn' farmatsevta* (St. Petersburg), vol. 1, no. 3, 1914, pp. 3-4. See also Ve-zr, "Peterburg," *Zhizn' farmatsevta* (Kiev), vol. 3, no. 1, 1911, pp. 7-8.

160. Editorial for the new year, *Zhizn' farmatsevta* (Kiev), vol. 3, no. 1, 1911, p. 2.

161. "Gosudarstvennoe strakhovanie farmatsevtov," *F. Zh.*, vol. 52, no. 17, 1913, p. 197.

162. *Zhizn' farmartsevta* (St. Petersburg) began publishing April 3, 1914. Municipalization was discussed by K. M., "Novyi farmatsevticheskii ustav," *Zhizn' farmatsevta*, vol. 1, no. 1, 1914, p. 4 and "V Peterburge Obshchee sobranie S. P. B. farmatsevtov," ibid., no. 2, pp. 15 and 16. *Pravda* was attacked, ibid., no. 1, p. 7.

163. "V Petrogradskom Soiuze sluzhashchikh v aptekakh," *Vestnik aptechnago truda*, vol. 5, no. 1, 1918, p. 12.

164. Again, see McKean, *St Petersburg*, pp. 162–172.

165. "Iz istorii pensionnoi kassy," pp. 3–4.

166. "Den' pechati v Spb. obshchestve farmatsevtov. Obshchee sobranie 22 aprelia," *Zhizn' Farmatsevta* (St. Petersburg), vol. 1, no. 3, 1914, p. 16.

167. "Pokushenie na pensionnuiu kassu," *Zhizn' farmatsevta* (St. Petersburg), vol. 1, no. 2, 1914, p. 3.

By 1914, wages had risen in St. Petersburg to 122 rubles per month for a Provizor, 98 for an Assistant Pharmacist, and 28 rubles per student. Of 112 pharmacists in St. Petersburg 43 had wives who worked. "Pobochnyi zarabotok," *Zhizn' farmatsevta*, vol. 1, no. 1, 1914, p. 1.

168. "V O-ve Sluzhashchikh farmatsevtov" (St. Petersburg), vol. 1, no. 3, 1914, p. 16.

169. "Khronika," *Zhizn' farmatsevta* (St. Petersburg), vol. 1, no. 3, 1914, p. 7.

170. V. M. Salo, MS on Pension Fund, in possession of the author, pp. 9–10.

Chapter 14

1. "Slukhi i vesti," *Farmatsevticheskii Vestnik* [hereafter cited *F. V.*], vol. 2, no. 4, 1898, p. 659. The context was an article on the Mogilev-Podolsk governor's refusal to permit operation of a society to provide free medical help for the poor.

2. Quoted in *Farmatsevticheskii zhurnal* [hereafter cited *F. Zh.*], vol. 20, no. 22, 1898, p. 309. The announcement from *F. V.* is untitled. In this case the governor (Governor-General of the Steppe Region) approved.

3. Al'tgauzen, "K voprosu," *Farmatsevt*, vol. 13, no. 25, 1905 p. 790.

4. I. Zil'berg claimed that the first meeting of the Northern Society occurred December 16, 1902. *Professional'noe dvizhenie sluzhashchikh-farmatsevtov* (Moscow, 1930), p. 42, as cited in *Istoriia farmatsevticheskogo dela v Peterburge-Petrograde-Leningrade* (Leningrad, 1960), p. 115. However, *Farmatsevticheskii zhurnal* gave particulars about the society in 1901, as noted in the previous chapter.

5. I. Zil'berg, *Professional'noe dvizhenie sluzhashchikh farmatsevtov* (Moscow, 1930), p. 8.

Resolutions of the Communist Party and articles in *Iskra*, *Golos farmatsevta*, and *Novaia zhizn'* on this subject are also cited in *Istoriia farmatsevticheskogo dela v Peterburge . . .*, pp. 115–116. The dates cited, however, do not synchronize. For example, this book notes that the Second Congress of the RSDLP resolved to infiltrate "professional" workers' organizations and that, accordingly, the St.

Petersburg committee was formed. The Second Congress, however, took place in the *summer* of 1903 and this book states that the committee was formed at the *beginning* of 1903.

6. By 1901, as noted in a previous chapter, the number of city-run pharmacies was negligible—seventeen city executive councils in the Russian empire owned pharmacies. One city pharmacy existed in all the non-zemstvo provinces, one in the Don military region (*oblast'*), and five in zemstvo provinces. Two cities in the Caucasus owned pharmacies, two in the Central Asian region, and six in Siberia. D. I. Toropov, "Dvizhenie i rost aptechnago dela v Imperii za poslednee desiatiletie (1901-1910 g.g.)," *Vestnik obshchestvennoi gigieny, sudebnoi i prakticheskoi meditsiny* (1911), p. 1293. By 1910 there were a total of thirty-nine city pharmacies. Three were in non-zemstvo provinces, two in the Don, nine in zemstvo provinces, ten in the Caucasus, four in Central Asia, eleven in Siberia. Toropov, ibid., p. 1294

For example, in 1901 *Farmatsevticheskii zhurnal* and *Farmatsevt* reported the following: the Moscow clinic of military doctors offered free medical care to over five thousand poor and dispensed over six thousand free medicines from its pharmacy ("Raznyia izvestiia," *F. Zh*, vol. 23, no. 25, 1901, p. 480); a zemstvo-like organization in "Privislinskii krai" (the Russian provinces of Poland) provided medicine for 10 kopeks and waived this nominal fee for the poor ("Raznyia izvestiia," *F. Zh*, ibid., no 20, pp. 398-399); a city pharmacy was operating in Taganrog (*F. Zh*., ibid., no. 11, p. 228);. and Moscow and St. Petersburg established city pharmacies. The St. Petersburg city duma spent 150,000 rubles on a city hospital and the city sanitary commission began to build a city pharmacy. "Po povodu proektiruemoi tsentral'noi gorodskoi apteki," *Farmatsevt*, 1901, vol. 9, no. 9, 1901, p. 278. The St. Petersburg duma also discussed opening a central city warehouse for medicines and pharmaceutical wares. "Raznyia izvestiia," *F. Zh*, vol. 40 (23), no. 25, 1901, p. 480. The duma feared this would provide competition for private pharmacies.

7. S. K. Lintser, "Bytovoi otdel: Aptechnaia monopoliia," *F. V.*, vol. 7, no. 2, 1904, p. 21.

8. For example, the journal noted that the Moscow city pharmacy was still in the discussion stage, as was a city warehouse, which purportedly could purchase medicines and supplies "12 percent" cheaper than those sold by the Ferrein firm. "Aptechnoe delo v zemstve i gorodskom khoziaistve," *F. V.*, vol. 7, no. 14, 1904, pp. 219-220. The St. Petersburg city duma was moving toward the establishment of a city warehouse to purchase medicines more cheaply. "Gorodskoi aptekarskii sklad v Peterburge," *F. V.*, vol. 7, no. 36, 1904, p. 572. The city of Baku was doing the same. "Khronika," *F. V.*, vol. 7, no. 45, 1904, p. 912. The journal also noted approvingly that in June 1904, an imperial order instructed the trustees of the imperial philanthropic society to dispense medicines—in pharmacies of city hospitals in St. Petersburg, Moscow, Ufa, Kamanets-Podolsk, and Odessa—either at a price reduction of 30 to 40 percent or entirely free for the poor "Vysochaishiia poveleniia, predl. Pravit. Senatu ministerstrom iustitii," *F. V.*, vol. 7, no. 45, 1904, pp. 914-915.

9. "Khronika: 151," *F. V.*, vol. 9, no. 19, 1904, p. 300.

10. S. Lintser, "Na rodine aptechnoi monopolii," *F. V.*, vol. 7 , no. 43, 1904, p. 679, and ibid., no. 45, p. 906.

11. Meeting of December 29-31, reported in "Protivuaptechnoe techenie," *Farmatsevt*, vol. 13, no. 2, 1905, pp. 41–42.

12. "Samovykup aptek," *Farmatsevt*, vol. 13, no. 33 (1 September) 1905, pp. 1041-1043.

13. I. Zil'berg, *Professional'noe dvizhenie sluzhashchikh farmatsevtov*, pp. 8-9, 14. Zil'berg specifically mentioned organizing committees in St. Petersburg, Moscow, Vil'na, Libau, and Gomel. The strikes erupted in many more cities, as we shall see.

14. Jonathan E. Sanders, "The Union of Unions: Political, Economic, Civil, and Human Rights Organizations in the 1905 Russian Revolution," Diss., 1985, pp. 374–428; 1001-1015.

See also Jonathan Sanders, "Drugs and Revolution: Moscow Pharmacists in the First Russian Revolution," *The Russian Review*, vol. 44, 1985, pp. 351-377.

See Laura Engelstein for orchestration of strikes in 1905 among workers in general. *Moscow, 1905* (Stanford: Stanford University Press, 1982), pp. 83, 93–94, 105, 115–116, 127, 137. Engelstein, writing before Sanders, states that "Pharmacy clerks" did not "dub themselves 'a part of the great proletarian army' without a great deal of consciousness raising from outside by pharmacist intellectuals." Engelstein, *Moscow, 1905*, p. 122.

Leopold Haimson, Diane Koenker, and William Rosenburg, on the other hand, imply that strikes in Russia from 1905 through 1917 were spontaneous as well as appropriate. See Leopold H. Haimson and Ronald Petrusha, "Two strike waves in Imperial Russia, 1905-1907, 1912-1914," *Strikes, Wars and Revolutions in an International Perspective*, eds. Haimson and Charles Tilly (Cambridge: Cambridge University Press, 1989), pp. 101-166; Diane E. Koenker and William G. Rosenberg, "Strikers in Revolution, 1917," ibid., pp. 167-196. To emphasize the strikes' uniformity, even deterministic quality, they reduce strikers to abstraction. Haimson consistently refers to "labor unrest" and the more "militant strata of workers," Haimson, "Two strike waves," p. 120, for example. Koenker and Rosenburg refer to "the dynamics of proletarian activism," implying that laborers were driven by an inner compulsion. Koenker and Rosenburg, "Strikers in Revolution," p. 168.

15. Al'tgauzen, "K voprosu," *Farmatsevt*, vol. 13, no. 24, 1905, p. 751. The term "white slave" became a banner for *Farmatsevticheskii vestnik* and other radical pharmacists and journals.

16. E. Al'tgauzen, "Po puti progressa," *Farmatsevt*, vol. 14, no. 2, 1906, pp. 50–51.

17. "Otkuda Nabirat'sia farmatsevticheskii proletariat?" *Farmatsevt*, vol. 14, no. 4, 1906, pp. 117-118. Al'tgauzen cited eleven pharmacies in the Western Provinces that employed mostly students. Nevertheless, he argued that pharmacists who worked a seven-hour day in the pharmacy could not be considered proletariat. His solution for the apprenticeship problem was to have those entering pharmacy fully

complete the *gimnaziia*, a resolution which Moscow and St. Petersburg pharmacists were submitting to the forthcoming Congress of Russian Pharmaceutical Societies.

18. Al'tgauzen, "K voprosu," *Farmatsevt*, vol. 13, no. 25, 1905, p. 788.

19. "Raznyia izvestiia," *F. Zh.*, vol. 44 (27), no. 44, 1905, p. 1440. The minimum wage was 25 rubles for first-year students, 50 rubles for second-year students, 55 rubles for third-year students, 75 rubles for Assistant Pharmacists, and 100 rubles for Provizors.

20. See below.

21. Al'tgauzen, "K voprosu," *Farmatsevt*, vol. 13, no. 25, 1905, p. 789.

22. For Gabrilovich's background, see below, note 91.

23. Al'tgauzen, "K voprosu," *Farmatsevt*, vol. 13, no. 25, 1905, p. 788. Jonathan Sanders, in contrast, characterized the Russian Pharmacists' Society as benevolently dedicated to "improving the life, working conditions, and status of pharmacy employees." Sanders, "Drugs and Revolution," p. 358. The Russian Pharmacy Society did provide some desultory funds such as those in 1898 to needy pharmacists auditing lectures at the University of Moscow. "Khronika," *F. V.*, vol. 2, no. 45, 1898, p. 720. However, the agenda of the society was far more ambitious.

24. Engelstein, *Moscow, 1905*, p. 120.

25. "Khronika," *Farmatsevt*, vol. 13, no. 25, 1905, p. 782.

26. *Loc. cit.* Engelstein believes both Social Revolutionaries and Social Democrats influenced the proclamation. *Moscow, 1905*, p. 121.

27. "Khronika: Sev. Zap. Krai," *Farmatsevt*, vol. 13, no. 4, 1905, pp. 111–112. Students were to receive 10 rubles the first year, 15 the second, and 15 to 25 the third.

28. "Raznyia izvestiia," *F. Zh.*, vol. 44 (27), no. 12, 1905, pp. 403-406. A. Iurgens had instituted a double shift in his pharmacy five years previously, for those of his pharmacy personnel wishing to accept a reduction in salary. He also noted that it was difficult to have a "shift" administrator and a "shift" laboratory assistant. Kol. Maizel had instituted a double shift three years previously. Professor A. S. Ginzberg, the liberal crusader for reform of pharmacy education and generally quite liberal, noted that staff could not receive the same salary as when they worked longer hours.

29. I. R. Zakharevich, "Pis'ma iz daleka," *Farmatsevt*, vol. 13, no. 10, 1905, p. 302.

30. Jonathan Sanders, "Drugs and Revolution," p. 361. Sanders considered this a "stunning victory."

31. Boris Puzis, "Memuary k istorii farmatsevticheskoi zabastovki v g. Kieve," *Farmatsevt*, vol. 13, no. 29, 1905, pp. 915–916.

32. Puzis, "Memuary," *Farmatsevt*, vol. 13, no. 29, 1905, pp. 915–916; "Memuary," ibid., no. 30, pp. 945–951. Meanwhile staff pharmacists from an unspecified region wrote the journal *Farmatsevt* to publicly thank the owner of their pharmacy for providing a Christmas tree and inviting them to his home on New Year's Day. "Pis'mo v redaktsiiu," ibid., no. 5, p. 144. A letter from another

reader derided them, commenting that the letter probably was from the Western region where conditions in pharmacies were especially bad and "the noose of the pharmacy owners was stronger" than in his region of Vladimir province. "Pis'mo," ibid., no. 8, p. 240.

33. "Raznyia izvestiia," *F. Zh.*, vol. 44 (27), no. 10, 1905, p. 282.

34. *Loc. cit.*

35. One writer to *Farmatsevt* claimed that zemstvo pharmacies adversely affected serving pharmacists as well as pharmacy owners; zemstvos not only undercut privately owned pharmacies by dispensing free or low-cost medicaments to both the well-to-do and the poor, but they employed feldshers rather than staff pharmacists. "Pis'mo iz daleka," *Farmatsevt*, vol. 13, no. 10, 1905, p. 301.

36. S. G. Tsereteli, "Sobranie farmatsevtov sluzhashchikh po Moskovskomu gorodskomu obshchestvennomu upravleniiu," *Farmatsevt*, vol. 13, no. 13, 1905, p. 399.

37. Tsereteli, ibid., pp. 400-401. Pharmacist-managers of municipal pharmacies should interact directly with the city administration rather than the hospital administration. While the Russian Pharmacists' Society assiduously attended to pharmacy students, the Society for Pharmacists Serving in City Institutions specified that only persons who had passed at least the Assistant Pharmacist examination—not students—constituted the pharmacy staff of public institutions. The city pharmacists' resolution also called for a 10 percent salary increase, four months' sick pay in case of illness, money payments in lieu of board, and a full pension after twenty-five years (or a half pension after fifteen years), and finally, specialized libraries in hospital pharmacies and laboratories.

38. "Rezoliutsii Rossiiskago farmatsevticheskago Obshchestva," *Farmatsevt*, vol. 13, no. 15, 1905, p. 461.

Al'tgauzen contended that such statements set staff pharmacists against owners. Ibid, p 463. A latter-day commentator, Jonathan Sanders, characterized this program as part Social Revolutionary, part Social Democratic, and part "Miliukov's insistent unicameralism." Miliukov was a "liberal" leader and founder of the Kadet, or Constitutional Democratic Party. Sanders, "Drugs and Revolution," p. 365.

39. "Boikotirovanie apteki," *Farmatsevt*, vol. 13, no. 20, 1905, p. 627, and "Khronika," ibid., no. 21, p. 655.

40. D. A. Leibenzon, "Pis'mo v redaktsiiu," *Farmatsevt*, vol. 13, no. 14, 1905, p. 434.

41. Ibid., pp. 434-435.

42. "Khronika," *Farmatsevt*, vol. 13, no. 18, 1905, p. 563, and "Khronika," ibid., no 21, p. 658.

43. E. A. Al'tgauzen, "Pervyi bezpristrastnyi otklik nashei periodicheskoi pechati k istinnym nuzhdam farmatsii i farmatsevtov," *Farmatsevt*, vol. 13, no. 18, 1905, pp. 563-566.

44. Cited in "Sluzhashchemu farmatsevtu S. L. L. (otvet na pis'mo ego, pomeshchennoe v No. 28 "Farm. Vestn." s. g.), *Farmatsevt*, vol. 13, no. 29, 1905, pp. 913-915.

45. "Khronika," *Farmatsevt*, vol. 13, no. 18, 1905, p. 563.

46. "Khronika," *Farmatsevt*, vol. 13, no. 22, 1905, p. 689.

47. "Iz pisem i soobshchenii pomeshchennykh v No. 18 "Farm. Vestnika" s.g.," *Farmatsevt*, vol. 13, no. 20, 1905, pp. 627-629.

48. Sanders, "Drugs and Revolution," p. 360.

49. D. S. Podrazhanskii, (also L. A. Brodskii, P. A. Zaidman, M. E. Linetskii), "Tezisy dokladov predstavlennykh byvshemu v Moskve s"ezdu sluzhashchikh farmatsevtov," *Farmatsevt*, vol. 13, no. 29, 1905, pp. 908-909; Podrazhanskii, p. 909.

Radical pharmacists' reliance on big government would be especially evident during the war. See Deborah Hardy for earlier radicals' views on government sponsorship of producer cooperatives. Deborah Hardy, *Petr Tkachev, the Critic as a Jacobin* (Seattle and London: University of Washington Press, 1977), p. 99.

50. Podrazhanskii," Tezisy," p. 909.

51. "Khronika," *Farmatsevt*, vol. 13, no. 31, 1905, p. 971.

52. "Tezisy: Ot redaktskii," *Farmatsevt*, vol. 13, no. 29, 1905, pp. 909-910. Al'tgauzen firmly rejected the idea of nationalizing pharmacies.

53. "Zabastovka sluzhashchikh farmatsevtov v S. Petersburgskikh aptekakh," *F. Zh.*, vol. 44 (27), no. 38, 1905, pp. 1239-1244.

54. Students were to receive 45 rubles per month, Assistant Pharmacists 90 rubles per month, and Provizors 110 rubles. *Loc. cit.*

55. "Zabastovka," pp. 1239-1244.

56. "Zabastovka," pp. 1239-1244.

57. "K zabastovke sluzhashchikh farmatsevtov v S.-Peterburgskikh aptekakh," *F. Zh.*, vol. 44 (27), no. 39, 1905, p. 1277.

58. Raznyia izvestiia," *F. Zh.*, vol. 44 (27), no. 44, 1905, p.1441. The Moscow police chief shut down the Russian Pharmacy Society for a time because of this.

59. "Raznyia izvestiia," *F. Zh.*, vol. 44 (27), no. 47, 1905, p. 1508.

60. "Po povodu boikota nekotorykh s-peterburgskikh aptek," *F. Zh.*, vol. 44 (27), no. 57, 1905, p. 1507.

61. Sanders, "Drugs and Revolution," p. 361.

62. "Raznyia izvestiia," *F. Zh.*, vol. 44 (27), no. 44, 1905, p. 1440.

63. "Khronika," *Farmatsevt*, nos. 37-38, 1905, p. 1157.

64. "Zabastovka sluzhashchikh farmatsevtov v Moskve," *F. Zh.*, vol. 44 (27), no. 51, 1905, p. 1630.

65. "Raznyia izvestiia," *F. Zh.*, vol. 44 (27), no. 44, 1905, pp. 1439-1442.

66. Obshchestvo farmatsevtov v s-peterburgskikh gorodskikh, bol'nichnykh i bogadelennykh aptekakh, *F. Zh.*, vol. 44 (27), no. 48, 1905, p. 1537. Staff pharmacists' salaries were to be 100 rubles per month with a 10 percent raise every four years; managers and assistant managers were to receive 125 and 156 rubles per month, with an apartment.

67. "Raznyia izvestiia," *F. Zh.*, vol. 44 (27), no. 47, p. 1508. The old activist Zil'berg claimed that "mutual-help" societies were outmoded by the end of 1905; the organizations needed for the time were unions. Zil'berg, *Professional'noe dvizhenie*, p. 12.

68. "Soiuz prikazchikov-drogistov," *F. Zh.*, vol. 44 (27), no. 48, 1905, p. 1538.

69. Pharmacy Owners in the City of Perm, V. Bartlinskii and I. Kononov, "Zabastovka v aptekakh gor. Permi i uchastie v etom vrachei," *Farmatsevt*, vol. 14, no. 4, 1906, p. 103.

The interference of physicians in this case substantiates Al'tgauzen's contention that striking pharmacists were sometimes encouraged by physicians, particularly the journal *Vrach*.

70. "Raznyia izvestiia," *F. Zh.*, vol. 44 (27), no. 44, 1905, p. 1440.

71. Sanders, "Drugs and Revolution," p. 374.

72. "Vseobshchii farmatsevticheskii soiuz," *F. Zh.*, vol. 44 (27), no. 45, 1905, pp. 1459–1462.

73. *Loc. cit.*

74. Minimum dues of the All-Russian Pharmacists' Union were 3 rubles per year. Use of the term *Farmatsevticheskii Otdel* (Pharmacy Department) will return in the Soviet period emphasizing the continuity between the tsarist and Soviet pharmacy administration, "Vseobshchii Rossiiskii Farmatsevticheskii Soiuz," *F. Zh.*, vol. 44 (27), no. 48, 1905, pp. 1534–1535.

75. "Po povodu boikota nekotorykh s-peterburgskikh aptek," *F. Zh.*, vol. 44 (27), no. 47, 1905, p. 1507. During 1905 the term *sovet*—in the English, "soviet"—took on radical connotations.

76. Sanders, "Drugs and Revolution," pp. 374–376.

77. "Khronika," *Farmatsevt*, vol. 13, nos. 47–48, 1905, pp. 1367.

78. "Khronika," *Farmatsevt*, vol. 14, no. 3, 1906, p. 79.

79. "Khronika," *Farmatsevt*, vol. 14, no. 1, 1906, p. 13. Here Keler was spelled "Keller."

Additionally, at least one pharmacy, which was not involved in the strike, was destroyed by artillery fire because it was surrounded by barricades. "Razgrom apteki v Moskve," *Farmatsevt*, vol. 14, no. 1 ,1906, p. 13.

80. "Khronika," *Farmatsevt*, vol. 14, no. 3, 1906, pp. 79–80.

81. "Raznyia izvestiia (Sluzhashchikh farmatsevtov V Kieve)," *F. Zh.*, vol. 44 (27), no. 40, 1905, p. 407. Pharmacists were to elect a *pravlenie*, or administrative body, and a revision or audit committee to run the pharmacy. Fifty percent of the capital was kept in reserve, 5 percent and a fixed sum, not higher than 500 rubles, were to be spent on improvements, part of the net profit went to the school, part to indigent pharmacists, part went to pay the staff, and the remainder was designated for a fund for pharmacists' needs.

82. "Khronika," *Farmatsevt*, vol. 14, no. 3, 1906, p. 80.

83. Ibid., and "Iz deiatel'nosti vseobshchago Rossiiskago farmatsevticheskago s"ezda," *Farmatsevt*, vol. 14, no. 24, 1906, p. 678–682.

84. "S"ezd delegatov farmatsevticheskikh obshchestv v S-Peterburge 17–21 ian. 1906," *Farmatsevt*, vol. 14, no. 5, 1906, pp. 145–146. Delegates from pharmacy societies in the army and navy, from the Don, Kazan, and Odessa did not attend.

Delegates from the Warsaw Pharmacy Society included E. B. Gessner and V. A. Manduk; from the Vilensk Society: K. P. Stefanovskii; from the Moscow Society: Ev. E. Rozenberg, E. A. Al'tgauzen, I. S. Tkeshelashvili, G. O. Gabrilovich, and F. A. Plotnikov; from the Mitau Pharmacy Society, E. A. Gershel; from the Khar'kov

Society: I. P. Lapin and M. B. Shvartsman; from the Kiev Society: A. A. Martsinchik and E. Ks. Khrzhanovskii; from the Caucasus Society: L. I. Iakubovich and F. K. Gein; from the Estland Society: O. R. Brashe and K. P. Lebert; from the Riga Society: P. A. Zeebode.

Members of the St. Petersburg Society comprised the organization bureau: K. I. Kresling, Iu. F. Krangal's, M. B. Trofimov, B. M. Shaskol'skii, V. Birken, E. E. Brezinskii, A. G. Abramson, E. A. Germeier, A. E. Bauman, Professor A. S. Ginzberg, and M. L. Gabrilovich.

"Iz protokola pervago zasedaniia s"ezda delagatov farmatsevticheskikh obshchestv, sostoiavshagosia v chas dnia, 17-go ianvaria 1906 goda, v pomeshchenii S-Peterburgskago Obshchestva," *Farmatsevt*, vol. 14, no. 6, 1906, pp. 179-180.

85. Additionally, existing pharmacy organizations and new national organizations proposed for pharmacists showed an interesting correlation with later Bolshevik organizations.

86. Delegates from the Caucasus Pharmacy Society proposed a central Pharmacy Council comprised of independent local units resembling zemstvos. Local councils were not to be democratic—they were to consist of only Provizors and Masters. However, local councils were to be elected, and they in turn were to elect from their midst delegates to a central council of pharmacists and jurists. The St. Petersburg Pharmacy Society modified the elective principle. The head of the central council—entitled the Chief Pharmacy Inspector—was to be appointed by the government, and the council was to consist of representatives of government departments appointed by the government. On the local level all officials were to be confirmed by mayors and governors. The projects generated "heated discussion" but the St. Petersburg proposal received a majority of votes, ostensibly because it "could more easily be implemented given the present form of governmental structure in Russia." "S"ezd delagatov," p. 145.

87. "Doklad komissii pri Kavkazskom Farmatsevt. Obshchestve po voprosu "O reforme aptechnago stroia Rossii," *Farmatsevt*, vol. 15, no. 6, 1906, pp. 180-182.

"Protokoly zasedanii s"ezda delagatov farmatsevticheskikh obshchestv v S. Peterburge," *Farmatsevt*, vol. 14, no. 23, 1906, pp. 663-664.

88. "Protokoly zasedanii s"ezda," ibid., pp. 662-665.

89. "Doklad komissii," p. 182; "Protokoly zasedanii s'ezda," p. 664.

90. "Protokoly zasedanii s"ezda delagatov farmatsevticheskikh obshchestv v S-Peterburge ot 17-22 ianvaria 1906 g.," *Farmatsevt*, vol. 14, no. 19, 1906, pp. 563-566. Those advocating state ownership included Trofimov, Shaskol'skii, Kresling, Brezinski, Iakubovich, Martsinskii, Khrzhanovskii, Lapin, Shvartsman, Gabrilovich, Gein, Plotnikov, Zeebode, and "many others." It is not clear who this "Gabrilovich" was as no first initial or initial of his patronymic was provided. It would seem it was "G." (or perhaps "O. G.," discussed below. However, in other accounts of the meeting entitled "Protokoly" and cited here, two other Gabrilovich are named—M. L. Gabrilovich and L. G. Gabrilovich).

91. Osip Gustavovich's background and that of his prominent father, Gustav Osipovich, also a Master of Pharmacy and owner of pharmacies in Kovno and Minsk, are given in Ivan Sofronovich Tkeshelashvili, *Materialy istorii farmatsii v*

Rossii, Biograficheskii Slovar' farmatsevtov poluchivshchikh stepen' magistra farmatsii v Imperatorskikh russkikh Universitetakh i v Imperatorskoi Voenno-Meditsinskoi Akademii s 1845–1901 god (Moscow, 1901), pp. 20–21. For Gabrilovich's article on double-entry bookkeeping in the pharmacy see O. G. Gabrilovich, "Dvoinaia bukhgalteriia, primenenaia k aptechnomu delu," *Farmatsevt*, vol. 15, no. 6, 1907, pp. 173–176; ibid., nos. 11–12, pp. 301–302; ibid., no. 13, pp. 338–341.

For Gabrilovich in the early Soviet pharmacy administration see "Protokol No. 10 zasedaniia glavnago khimiko-farmatsevticheskoi promyshlennosti 'Farmatsentra' ot 5-go Noiabria 1918g.," Tsentral'nyi Gosudarstvennyi Arkhiv RSFSR (Moscow), fond 482, opis 5, delo 13, list 164; "Zhurnal No. 19 Plenarnogo Zasedaniia 'Farmatsentra,' 26 Noiabria 1918 goda," ibid., l. 161; "Plenarnogo Zasedaniia Farmatsentra 3 Dekabria 1918g.,".ibid., l. 159, and so on.

92. "Protokoly zasedanii," p. 563. Gabrilovich is merely designated as "G.," but it would seem "O. G." was more accurate in view of his writings cited below.

93. O. G. Gabrilovich, "'Predvaritel'noe soobshchenie' Vzaimnoe strakhovanie farmatsevtov s samovykupom aptek," *Farmatsevt*, vol. 14, nos. 7 and 8, 1906, pp. 197–202.

94. Ibid., pp. 197–199.

95. Ibid., p. 199.

96. Ibid., p. 201.

97. Ibid., p. 200.

98. Ibid., p. 201.

99. E. A. Al'tgauzen, commentary "Ot redaktsii" on Gabrilovich's proposal, *Farmatsevt*. vol. 14, nos. 7 and 8, 1906, pp. 202–204.

100. "Khronika," *Farmatsevt*, vol. 14, no. 9, 1906, p. 251.

101. "Khronika," *Farmatsevt*, vol. 14, no. 19, 1905, p. 559. The meeting was held May 5.

102. "Iz deiatel'nosti vseobshchago rossiiskago farmatsevticheskago s"ezda," *Farmatsevt*, vol. 14, no. 24, 1906, pp. 677–684.

103. "Khronika," *Farmatsevt*, vol. 14, no. 29, 1906, pp. 853–854.

104. Advertisement, *Farmatsevt*, vol. 14, nos. 7–8, 1906, p. 230. The editor was Val. Kozhevnikov. Contributors included Leonid Andreev.

105. "Khronika," *Farmatsevt*, vol. 14, nos. 7 and 8, 1906, p. 216. The owner, Pavel Shaskol'skii, denied the allegation. Ibid., no. 10, p. 285.

106. "Khronika," *Farmatsevt*, vol. 14, no. 10, 1906, p. 284.

107. "Khronika," *Farmatsevt*, vol. 14, no. 11, 1906, p. 319.

108. "Khronika," *Farmatsevt*, vol. 14, no. 28, 1906, p. 820.

109. "Khronika," *Farmatsevt*, vol. 14, no. 30, 1906, p. 882 describes demands at the Keler and Ostroumov factories.

110. "Khronika," *Farmatsevt*, vol. 14, no. 28, 1906, p. 821.

111. "Khronika," *Farmatsevt*, vol. 14, no. 30, 1906, p. 882.

112. "O bezrabotnykh farmatsevtakh," *Farmatsevt*, vol. 14, no. 24, 1906, p. 695.

113. A good example of these historians is Robert McKean. He blames the "secret police . . . repressions" under Stolypin for emasculation of labor organiza-

tions between 1907 and 1912. He laments the "rigid ban upon the publication of socialist newspapers" in St. Petersburg, which hampered both "proponents of the open labor movement and underground activists" although "some trade-union journals had respectable print runs." McKean, *St. Petersburg between the Revolutions,* pp. 66–67, 72.

114. "K voprosu o Vserossiiskom soiuze," *Farmatsevticheskii trud* [herafter cited *F. T.*], vol. 1, no. 3, 1907, p. 38.

115. "S Peterburgskoe professional'noe obshchestvo sluzhashchikh," *F. T.*, vol. 1, no. 27, 1907, p. 374, and I. B-ii, "Iz pis'ma v redaktsiiu," ibid., no. 32, p. 430.

116. "Khronika," *F.T.*, vol. 1, no. 28, 1907, p. 384.

117. "Iz provintsii," *F. T.*, vol. 1, no. 13, 1907, pp. 185–187.

118. Iu. Kuperman, "Zametki starogo farmatevta," *Khimiko-farmatsevticheskii zhurnal,* nos. 10–12 (13–15), 1924, pp. 2–4.

119. On his apprenticeship see Kuperman, "Zametki," *Khimiko-farmatsevticheskii zhurnal,* no. 7, 1924, pp. 2–5. On quotas for Jews see "Zametki," *Khimiko-farmatsevticheskii zhurnal,* nos. 10–12, p. 5. Kuperman took the Provizor examination at the University of Odessa, as was allowed. However, the chief examiner did not like to grant degrees to students from other universities. Additionally, Kuperman apparently became engrossed in political activities and, consequently, never received his Provizor degree. Ibid., p. 5.

120. O. Borisovskii, "Zabastovka farm. v Riazane," *F. T.*, vol. 1, no. 6, 1907, p. 86.

121. Ibid., pp. 86–87.

122. Ibid., pp. 87–88. Students' pay was to increase from 25 to 40 rubles, Assistant Pharmacists from 55 to 70 rubles, Provizors to 90 rubles.

123. "Provintsiia," *F. T.*, vol. 1, no. 25, 1907, p. 346.

124. Ia Serebriakov, "V kakom polozhenii zastaet Vserossiiskii s"ezd Tifliskikh tovarishchei," *F. T.*, vol. 1, no. 8, 1907, p. 115.

125. Editorial, *F. T.*, vol. 1, no. 1, 1907, p. 1.

126. "Professional'noe obshchestvo sluzhashchikh farmatsevtov Kievskoi gubernii," *F. T.*, vol. 1, no. 4, 1907, p. 61.

127. "Iz provintsii," *F. T.*, vol. 1, no. 13, 1907, p. 185.

128. "Ot pravleniia: Odesskago professional'nago soiuza sluzhashchikh farmatsevtov," *F. T.*, vol. 1, no. 5, 1907, p. 81.

129. "Iz Peterburga," *F. T.*, vol. 1, no. 20, 1907, p. 271. At the same time the journal *Sluzhashchii Farmatsevt* was suspended. Ibid., p. 272.

130. G. Gelibter, "Iz provintsii: Khar'kov," *F. T.*, vol. 1, no. 25, 1907, p. 346.

131. "Provintsiia," *F. T.*, vol. 1, no. 31, 1907, p. 417.

132. S. Aleksandrov, "Zapros 28 Oktiabria," *Zhizn' farmatsevta* [hereafter cited *Zh. F.*], vol. 1, no. 4, 1909, p. 2.

133. Zil'berg, *Professional'noe dvizhenie,* pp. 12–14, and *passim.*

134. This anticipated the later contest between Bolsheviks and Mensheviks over factory trade unions recounted by Robert B. McKean, *St Petersburg between the Revolutions,* p. 69.

135. Two short pieces, "Peterburgskie Men'sheviki" and "Peterburgskii Komitet

Sotsial demokraticheskoi partii," *F. T.*, vol. 1, no. 36, 1907, p. 483, described the clash between Bolsheviks and Mensheviks for allegiance of trade unions, noting that "the St. Petersburg Committee of the Social Democratic Party proposed to professional unions to coordinate their programs with the activity of the socialist parties, to reciprocally inform each other—in certain cases the professional unions were to be advised—and to elect representatives of socialist organizations to the administrative body (*pravlenie*) of local and regional unions." However, "one of the strongest professional unions" found it "unsuitable that representatives of the socialist parties enter the administrative body and regional professional unions" because this practice would bring into the union frictions which exist between various parties and fractions." The St. Petersburg Mensheviks then passed a resolution countering the proposal of the "Moscow Social Democrats." The latter were Bolsheviks, as the phraseology of the article made clear. "The St. Petersburg Mensheviks have undertaken a resolution on professional unions entirely opposed to the resolution of the Moscow S-D on that issue, namely, Mensheviks have recommended all forces to struggle for preservation of the wide and open character of professional organizations, in the case of closing of unions, not to regroup in small party cells but to transfer the unions to a semi-legal position."

136. "Organizatsiia bezrabotnykh," *F. T.*, vol. 1, no. 37, 1907, pp. 487–489.

137. *Farmatsevticheskii trud* claimed to be nonparty but it had a pronounced Marxist orientation. Editorial, *F. T.*, vol. 1, no. 1, 1907, p. 2. On p. 1 the journal stated that it was a "powerful new bell loudly proclaiming, 'Comrades—workers—pharmacists—unite!'"

138. "K izbiratel'noi kampanii," *F. T.*, vol. 1, no. 1, 1907, p. 13. The Soviet and journal rejected past support for the "Party of Popular Freedom."Ibid.

139. "Professional'noe obshchestvo sluzhashchikh farmatsevtov Kievskoi gubernii," p. 61. Four hundred pharmacists of all levels attended the founding meeting.

140. "Iz Provintsii: Kiev," *F. T.*, vol. 1, no. 13, 1907, pp. 185, 187.

141. "Provintsiia," *F. T.*, vol. 1, no. 31, 1907, p. 417.

142. Opening its meeting at 10 P.M., the Khar'kov Professional Society elected a presidium, an administrative body (*pravlenie*), a revision or auditing commission, including Libermann and Prokof'ev, and concluded at 2:30 A.M. Z. Gelibter, "Iz provintsii: Khar'kov," *F. T.*, vol. 1, no. 25, 1907, pp. 346–347.

143. "Artel'naia apteka," *F. T.*, vol. 1, no. 13, 1907, p. 191. The artel could hire nonpharmacists to make pharmaceutical preparations.

144. "Gde iskhod?," *F. T.*, vol. 1, no. 30, 1907, pp. 403–404.

145. "Gde iskhod?," *F. T.*, vol. 1, no. 30, 1907, p. 404.

146. "Professional'naia solidarnost' i natsional'naia rozn'," *F. T.*, vol. 2, no. 29, 1908, p. 476.

147. In Moscow, for example, in one pharmacy with a Provizor manager-owner, one male and one female Assistant, a *praktikant*, and a student, six night shifts were distributed among the manager, male Assistant and student; the monthly salary of the male Assistant was 80 rubles, that of the female, 50, and that of the student, 45; a second pharmacy had a double shift and a special night

shift *dezhurant* (a Provizor), who received 65 rubles, "relations between owner and staff were good." Another pharmacy had a double shift and the student received 30 rubles per month, the Assistant, 70 rubles! There were eight night shifts per month with a free day following. A fourth, fairly large pharmacy, employed a large number of "para-pharmacists"—perhaps because, with pharmacists on a double shift, they were cheaper to employ. The Provizor-manager and five Assistants had sizeable salaries: the Provizor received 135 rubles per month, the Assistants 70 to 85. To compensate there were two *praktikants*, two *mal'chiki* (or "boys"), and three "workers." The *praktikanty* received only 25 to 35 rubles per month; they did not have a double shift and were off one day per week and after eight-hour night duty; workers and *mal'chiki* were free after holidays. Assistants had six night shifts per month; workers, ten. The relationship between owner and staff pharmacists was "good." "Khronika: V Moskve" *F. T.*, vol. 2, no. 26, 1908, pp. 431–432. (No information was provided on the pharmacists' view of the *praktikanty*, generally regarded as undercutting pharmacists.)

The pharmacy of a Jewish hospital in Kiev had a nine-hour work day; the female Assistant made 50 rubles a month (although the male Assistant made only 30 and the student, only 15). "Khronika: Kiev," *F. T.*, vol. 2, no. 26, 1908, p. 432.

Pharmacists in Mogilev province had "done much in . . . improving our economic position . . . double shifts, salaries . . . three weeks' vacation. . . ." "Korrespondentsii: Mogilev gubernii," *F. T.*, vol. 2, no. 26, 1908, p. 435–436.

In St. Petersburg, six pharmacies were reviewed. In one, staff received *one month's vacation with two weeks' pay*, in another, the owner himself (who was truly "professional") did night duty. Relations between the owner and staff pharmacists were "good." In a third pharmacy, one Provizor made 100 rubles per month. "St. Petersburg," *F. T.*, vol. 2, no. 34, 1908, p. 556.

148. M. Tanin, "K organizatsionnomu voprosu," *F. T.*, vol. 2, no. 28, 1908, p. 457.

149. A. N., "K organizatsionnomu voprosu," *F. T.*, vol. 2, no. 28, 1908, pp. 459–460.

150. "Provintsiia: Kishinev," *F. T.*, vol. 2, no. 34, 1908, p. 551.

151. "Khronika: Nikolaev," *F. T.*, vol. 2, no. 26, 1908, p. 432.

152. "Professional'noe i rabochee dvizhenie," *F. T.*, vol. 2, no. 26, 1908, p. 434.

153. "Khronika: Kiev, Badamsk," *F. T.*, vol. 2, no. 26, 1908, p. 435.

154. "Khronika," *F. T.*, vol. 2, no. 26, 1908, p. 432.

155. "Korrespondentsii: Slaviansk, Khar'kov *guberniia*," *F. T.*, vol. 2, no. 26, 1908, p. 437.

156. "K organizatsii aptekarei," *F. T.*, vol. 2, no. 27, 1908, p. 443.

157. "Kherson," *F. T.*, vol. 2, no. 27, 1908, p. 451.

158. The radical press drummed on the notion of increasing the public institutions'—cities and zemstvos—role in pharmacy. The following chapter will recount in greater detail how thirty-four deputies to the Third Duma proposed replacing the "pharmacy monopoly" (government restrictions on founding pharmacies) with free trade, then, greater rights for public pharmacies. As a consequence, the Ministry of Internal Affairs drafted a proposal that did not abolish limitations on

establishing pharmacies but gave preference to municipalities and zemstvos over private individuals when conditions warranted new pharmacies.

159. "Otdel o III zasedanii Komissii Rossiiskago Farmatsevticheskago Obshchestva po aptechnoi reforme," *F. T.*, vol. 2, no. 30, 1908, p. 494.

160. "Diskussionnoi otdel: K voprosu ob unichtozhenii privilegii," *F. T.*, vol. 2, no. 26, 1908, p. 428.

161. "Otdel o III zasedanii Komissii Rossiiskago Farmatsevticheskago Obshchestva po aptechnoi reforme," *F. T.*, vol. 2, no. 30, 1908, p. 494.

162. "Otdel o III zasedanii Komissii Rossiiskago Farmatsevticheskago Obshchestva po aptechnoi reforme," p. 496.

163. "Protokol vtorogo zasedaniia organizovannoi pri Rossiiskoi Farmatsevticheskom Obshchestve Komissii dlia vyrabotki zakonoproekta reforma aptechnago stroia," *F. T.*, vol. 2, no. 29, 1908, p. 481.

164. "Otdel o III zasedanii Komissii Rossiiskago," p. 496.

165. "Protokol vtorogo zasedaniia," p. 480.

166. "Otdel o III zasedanii Komissii Rossiiskago farmatsevticheskago Obshchestva po aptechnoi reformi," *F. T.*, vol. 2, no. 30, 1908, p. 495.

167. "Otdel o III zasedanii Komissii Rossiiskago farmatsevticheskago Obshchestva po aptechnoi reformi," *F. T.*, vol. 2, no. 30, 1908, pp. 493, 496.

168. "Otdel o III zasedanii Komissii Rossiiskago farmatsevticheskago Obshchestva po aptechnoi reformi," p. 495.

169. See, for example, S. K. L., "Aptechnoe delo v khoziaistve Moskovskago Obshchestvennago Samoupravleniia," *Russkii farmatsevt*, vol. 1, no. 2, 1908, pp. 55–63; "Khronika zemskago i gorodskogo aptechnago dela," ibid., pp. 74–76; Mikh. Polumordvinov, "Obshchestvennyia uchrezhdeniia i vol'nyia apteki," ibid., pp. 51–54.

170. "Pervaia konferentsiia sluzhashchikh farmatsevtov Ekaterinoslavskoi gubernii," *F. T.*, vol. 2, no. 30, 1908, p. 498.

171. General Meeting of Kiev Union of Pharmacists," July 25, 1908, *F. T.*, vol. 2, no. 34, 1908, p. 549. These administrative changes would, in fact, be instituted in the Soviet period.

172. Editorial, *Zhizn' farmatsevta* (Kiev) [hereafter cited *Zh. F.*], vol. 1, no. 1 (September 10), 1909, p. 3.

173. Masthead, *Zh. F.*, vol. 1, no. 1, 1909, p. 1.

174. "Ot redaktsii," *Zh. F.* , vol. 1, no. 4, 1909, p. 17.

175. "Russkii farmatsevt," *Zh. F.*, vol. 1, no. 1, 1909, p. 7.

176. Editorial, *Zh. F.*, vol. 1, no. 1, 1909, pp. 3–4.

177. For example, "Za rubezhom" described a general strike in Sweden, *Zh. F.*, vol. 1, no. 1, 1909, p. 16.

178. "Voprosy soiuznoi praktiki," *Zh. F.*, vol. 1, no. 1, 1909, p. 4.

179. "Khronika," *Zh. F.*, vol. 1, no. 4, 1909, pp. 11–12.

180. V. Mikutskii, "Pis'ma iz Smolenska," *Zh. F.*, vol. 1, no. 5, 1909, p. 13.

181. Editorial, *Zh. F.*, vol. 1, no. 1, 1909, p. 3.

182. Ia. Serebriiakov, "Korrespondentsii: Tiflis," *Zh. F.*, vol. 1, no. 1, 1909, pp. 15–16.

183. "Korrespondentsii," *Zh. F.*, vol. 1, no. 3, 1909, p. 16.

184. "Pis'mo iz Gomelia," *Zh. F.*, vol. 1, no. 4, 1909, p. 10. Dues of 1 ruble for Assistant Pharmacists and 50 kopeks for student pharmacists were lowered to 50 and 25 kopeks, respectively. Publication of *Zhizn' farmatsevta* also sparked interest.

185. "Korrespondentsii" (Zhitomir), *Zh. F.*, vol. 1, no. 3, 1909, p. 16.

186. Editorial, *Zh. F.*, vol. 1, no. 1, 1909, p. 3. In Sumy, twelve staff pharmacists (*sluzhashchie*) from the eight students and eight Assistants employed in five local pharmacies were members of the union. All pharmacies had night-shift rooms, but in three pharmacies there was neither a double shift nor minimum wage. "Korrespondentsii," ibid., p. 15.

187. 'Korrespondentsii," *Zh. F.*, vol. 1, no. 4., 1909, p. 15. The literal term for a day off was "walked," i.e., pharmacists "walked in four or five."

188. Editorial, *Zh. F.*, vol. 1, no. 1, 1909, p. 3.

189. As for salaries, in one pharmacy student pharmacists earned 25–30 rubles per month and Assistant Pharmacists earned 60 rubles. At a second, pay was lower—two Assistant Pharmacists earned 35 to 40 rubles; the student pharmacist, with two years' practice earned only 10 rubles. At a third, pay for the Assistant Pharmacist was 40 rubles per month, that for the student, 20. Conditions in six other pharmacies were not detailed but, rather, listed as "no better." "Khar'kovskiia pis'ma," *Zh. F.*, vol. 1, no. 1, 1909, p. 10.

190. In one pharmacy, two Provizors received a hefty 100 and 140 rubles per month, respectively, eight "Assistants" earned between 65 and 75 rubles, and two student pharmacists, 25 and 40 rubles. Only five night shifts were required each month. In a second pharmacy with one Provizor, four Assistants, and five students there was a double shift, two hours for dinner, rest on holidays, and only seven night shifts per month. The Provizor's salary was 120 rubles per month, those of the Assistants and students were the norm established by the union—55 to 75 rubles for the first and 10 to 35 rubles for students. In a third pharmacy pay for the three Assistants was "normal" (*normal'noe*); that for students was a "little less than established." One *praktikant* also worked at this pharmacy. The fourth pharmacy, under the Society of Doctors, had one Provizor and three Assisitants; they worked two days in three. In the fifth pharmacy, with two students and one *praktikant*, work was "two days in three"; one student received 20 rubles per month, board and room, and 100 rubles' support while taking examinations; the second student received 18 rubles plus board and 100 rubles for exams. The *praktikant* received 20 rubles per month. There "sometimes was a double shift"; rest after night duty was from 8 A.M. to 11 A.M. after night duty. The sixth pharmacy also had a double shift; the one Provizor earned 90 rubles per month, the two students, 25 rubles. "Khronika," *Zh. F.*, vol. 1, no. 4, 1909, pp. 12–13.

191. Daichik, "Pis'mo iz Ekaterinoslava," *Zh. F.*, vol. 1, no. 1, 1909, pp. 11–12.

192. "V Ekaterinoslave," *Zh. F.*, vol. 1, no. 3, 1909, p. 12.

193. "Korrespondentsii," *Zh. F.*, vol. 1, no. 1, 1909, p. 15.

194. "V Sevastopole," *Zh. F.*, vol. 1, no. 1, 1909, p. 14.

195. In one Riga pharmacy a student pharmacist was paid only 12 rubles per

month but also received room and board. The Assistant Pharmacist received 50 rubles plus room and board. Additionally, annual dues of 10 rubles to the local Mutual Assistance Fund were deducted from his (600 rubles per year monetary) salary; in return, he received 25 to 100 rubles per semester to audit Provizor lectures at the university. Riga staff pharmacists received every other Sunday off. The student got half a rest day per week and a total (presumably counting holidays) of four rest days per month; the Assistant received one day off each week with a total of six days per month. Grigor'evskii, "Pis'mo iz Rigi," *Zh. F.*, vol. 1, no. 3, 1909, p. 10.

196. For example, in one laboratory a staff pharmacist was fired. His demand for two months' salary was satisfied through the court. In another case, pharmacy owner Rozenfel'd fired a staff pharmacist student "without cause"; the arbitration court satisfied the student's demand "half-way." "Khronika," *Zh. F.*, vol. 1, no. 3, 1909, p. 12.

197. "V guberniiakh—Polt. gub.," *Zh. F.*, vol. 1, no. 1, 1909, pp. 13–14.

198. "V Kremenchuge, Poltav. gub.," *Zh. F.*, vol. 1, no. 1, 1909, p. 14. The benificent owner was one Levin.

199. "Korrespondentsii," *Zh. F.*, vol. 1, no. 3, 1909, p. 15.

200. The Provizor manager of one pharmacy made 1,200 rubles per year with an apartment. The Assistant at that pharmacy received 600 rubles per year. (True, a student in another pharmacy made only 20 rubles per month.) Night duty was "obigatory" in nearly all pharmacies and nearly always was the responsibility of Assistants. The average number of nights on duty were fifteen per month with six or seven free days per month. Shatov admitted that conditions in the city pharmacy were better than in the districts. In the three private pharmacies salary for Assistants were 50 rubles plus room and board. The two students received 20 rubles per month plus room and board with one free day per week.

Salaries in the zemstvo pharmacy were high. The manager Provizor received 1,200 rubles per year base salary, extra for teaching at the feldsher school, and an apartment. The three Assistants received 70 rubles per month. One student received 20 rubles, the other 25. The work shift at the zemstvo was short—from 9 A.M. to 2 or 3 P.M. The one Assistant who stayed on for night duty received a meal and began work next day at 11 A.M. One wonders how well the public was served. At the railroad pharmacy the Assistant Pharmacist manager received 750 rubles per year plus twelve railway tickets and one year's pass. Six feldshers and 3 *akushery* assisted him. He worked in the pharmacy only from 9 A.M. to 1 P.M. each day. "Korrespondentsii," *Zh. F.*, vol. 1, no. 3, 1909, p. 15.

201. "Pis'ma iz Smolenska," *Zh. F.*, vol. 1, no. 5, 1909, p. 13.

202. "Korrespondentsii," Iv. Golub on Tashkent, *Zh. F.*, vol. 1, no. 4, pp. 14–15. Students started with 20 rubles per month for one year of practice, 20 to 30 rubles in the second year, and 30 to 50 rubles in the third year. Assistant Pharmacists received 75 rubles per month.

203. "Korrespondentsii," *Zh. F.*, vol. 1, no. 4, 1909, p. 15.

204. "Dnezhnyi otchet," *Zh. F.*, vol. 1, no. 4, 1909, p. 17. Those registered at the employment bureau were almost exclusively Assistant Pharmacists and phar-

macy students. For example, in October, fourteen Assistant Pharmacists from Kiev and eight from outside the city and seven student pharmacists from Kiev and ten from outside the city were registered compared with two local Provizors.

205. "Dnezhnyi otchet," *Zh. F.*, vol. 1, no. 1, 1909, pp. 17–18.

206. "Kievskii klub sluzhashchikh farmatsevtov," *Zh. F.*, vol. 1, no. 5, 1909, pp. 14–15.

207. "Khronika," ibid., p. 16.

208. Vas. Go-g, "Rabochii den' farmatsevta," ibid., pp. 5–9.

209. "Apotstol krasoty i svobody," ibid., p. 2.

210. "V Smolenske," *Zh. F.*, vol. 1, no. 1, 1909, p. 14.

211. "Khronika: V Iugo-Zapadnom Soiuze," *Zh. F.*, vol. 1, no. 1, 1909, pp. 11–12.

212. *Loc. cit.*

213. "Khronika," *F. T.* (Moscow, Malaia Lubianka—editor B. N. Saltykov), vol. 3, no. 2, 1909, p. 24.

214. E. Abramovich, "Moskovskiia pis'ma," *Zh. F.*, vol. 1, no. 5, 1909, pp. 11–12.

215. Abramovich, "Moskovskiia pis'ma," *Zh. F.*, vol. 1, no. 5, 1909, p. 12. The interconnection of the radical unions was illustrated by the request of the Turkestan Union of Staff Pharmacists to B. N. Saltykov and the Russian Pharmacy Society to return the money they had contributed the previous year for an All-Russian Congress, as the authorities had not given permission for the congress. "V Tashkente," *Zh. F.*, vol. 1, no. 3, 1909, p. 13.

216. For example, "Rabochee i profes. dvizhenie: V Peterburge," *F. T.*, vol. 3, no. 2, 1909, p. 27, and an account of a new artel of women in Nikolaev, ibid., p. 28. The journal was edited by B. N. Saltykov and headquartered on the Malaia Lubianka in Moscow.

217. *Farmatsevticheskii trud* also carried an article by A. Shatov on the "indifferentism" of the masses in Vologda. "Provintsiia," *F. T.*, vol. 3, no. 3, 1909, pp. 43–44. This article contained a few more details such as the fact that district towns were 700–800 versts from each other and from the capital city; nearly all were cut off during the autumn and spring "from the whole world." In nine districts of Vologda province, pharmacies belong exclusively to the zemstvo with private payment for dispensation. Staff Assistants received 50 rubles with rest one day per week. Students received 20 to 25 rubles per week and were free after 8 P.M. two times a week. Manager Provizors in zemstvo pharmacies received salaries of 1,300 rubles per year, Assistant Pharmacists received 840 (120 per month plus an apartment), students received 200 and 300 rubles. The workday was short—9 A.M. to 3 or 4 P.M. The one Assistant who did night duty did not come in until 11 A.M. the following day and received tea, dinner, and lunch.

218. "Provintsiia: Baku," *F. T.*, vol. 3, no. 2, 1909, pp. 28–29.

219. "Tiflis," *F. T.*, vol. 3, no. 3, 1909, p. 44.

220. Elshtein, "Diskussionnyi otdel. K voprosu o munitsipalizatsii aptechnago dela," *F. T.*, vol. 3, no. 4, 1909, p. 51.

221. Elshtein, "K voprosu,," *F. T.*, vol. 3, no. 4, 1909, p. 51.

222. Elshtein, "K voprosu," p. 53.
223. Elshtein, "K voprosu," p. 53.
224. "V obshchestve farmatsevtov-rabotnikov," *F. Zh.*, vol. 49, no. 38, 1910, pp. 415–416.
225. "Khronika: V Kieve," *Zh. F.*, vol. 3, no. 2, 1911, p. 9.
226. "Raznyia," *Zh. F.*, vol. 3, no. 2, 1911, p. 14.
227. "Khronika," *Zh. F.*, vol. 3, no. 1, 1911, p. 10.
228. "V farmatsevticheskom obshchestve," *F. Zh.*, vol. 49, no. 39, 1910, p. 425.
229. "Moskovskiia pis'ma," *Zh. F.*, vol. 3, no. 3, 1911, p. 11.
230. Editorial, *Zh. F.*, vol. 3, no. 1, 1911, p. 2. This reference was noted in chapter 12, "Professionalization," in this work.
231. *Loc. cit*—also noted in chapter 12, "Professionalization."
232. "Rabochaia khronika," *Zh. F.*, vol. 3, no. 1, 1911, p. 12.
233. "Moskovskiia pis'ma," *Zh. F.*, vol. 3, no. 3, 1911, p. 12.
234. "Likvidatsii del o-va Sluzh-Farmatsevtov," *F. Zh.*, vol. 49, no. 22, 1910, p. 286.
235. "Po Rossii," *Zh. F.* vol. 3, no. 3, 1911, p. 13.
236. "Odesskiia pis'ma," *Zh. F.*, vol. 3, no. 3, 1911, p. 12.
237. "Sobranie farmatsevtov," *F. Zh.*, vol. 49, no. 42, 1910, p. 458. Elected to the administration (*pravlenie*) were M. Semenov, M. Tuluevskii, S. Kusmarov, I. Krishtoponis, and L. Gurevich. Tuluevskii occupied the important position of secretary.
238. "Sredi farmatsevtov," *F. Zh.*, vol. 49, no. 32, 1910, p. 356.
239. "Obysk v Kievskom soiuze farmatsevtov," *F. Zh.*, vol. 49, no. 43, 1910, p. 468.
240. "Khronika: V Kieve," *Zh. F.*, vol. 3, no. 2, 1911, p. 9.
241. For example, in Rovno, Volynsk province, the double shift was abolished in one pharmacy; in Vinnitsa, there were "worsening conditions"—until recently there was one rest-day in three days and ten night shifts per month; now staff "walked" on the fourth day. The staff "categorically" rejected this change and all were fired. "Khronika," *Zh. F.*, vol. 3, no. 1, 1911, p. 10.

In Cherkassa, in the largest pharmacy in the district, there was a double shift only for the Assistant Pharmacists. This being laudable, the journal focused on the plight of *student* pharmacists. In summer, student pharmacists worked from 7 A.M. to 10 P.M. with only one hour for dinner; they were paid only 10 to 15 rubles per month. In Saratov, meanwhile, the pharmacy belonging to Shapiro paid salaries of 40 rubles plus board, a substantial wage. After one month there were raises of 5 rubles. "Korrespondentsii," *Zh. F.*, vol. 3, no. 1, 1911, p. 13.

242. This occurred in a Saratov pharmacy. "Po Rossii," *Zh. F.*, vol. 3, no. 3, 1911, p. 13.
243. *Loc. cit.*
244. Staff at the first pharmacy included three Assistant Pharmacists and two student pharmacists. Salaries of the Assistants ranged from 50 to 60 rubles; those of the students ranged from 30 to 35 rubles, with room. The personnel enjoyed a double shift with ten night shifts per week. The staff at the second pharmacy con-

sisted of a Provizor, two Assistants, and two students. Conditions were similar to those at the first pharmacy. The third pharmacy employed five staff pharmacists but had not been open long enough to make judgment. "Po Rossii," *Zh. F.*, vol. 3, no. 3, 1911, p. 14.

245. "K zabastovke v Lodze," *Zh. F.*, vol. 3, no. 2, 1911, p. 2.

246. Pharmacy workers were to be divided into two *six-hour* shifts, one from 8 or 8:30 in the morning to 2 or 2:30 in the afternoon and a second from 2 or 2:30 in the afternoon to 10 or 10:30 at night. Night duty was to last from 10 or 10:30 in the evening to 8 or 8:30 in the morning, with room and bedding available, and pay of 1 ruble, 25 kopeks when "the door was closed" and 2 rubles, 50 kopeks "when the door was open." Pharmacies were to open at 11 A.M.! Requested wages were high. Student pharmacists were to receive a minimum wage—25 rubles for the first half-year with a 5-ruble increase during the second half and 10-ruble raise after that. Assistant Pharmacists were to receive 75 rubles per month; Provizors, 100 rubles. Staff pharmacists were to receive two months' pay when sick, be covered by a substitute, and receive free medicine. Strikers demanded two days' vacation for each month worked or twenty-four days per year between April 27 and September 2. The owners was to contribute to an insurance fund for staff pharmacists (the contribution could not be higher than for the Pension Fund). Workers were to receive three months' notice before firing and were not to be fired until six months after the strike. Pharmacy owners were to pledge not to accept prescriptions from feldshers or *znakhari* (rural self-healers).

"K zabastovke farmatsevtov v Tsarstve Pol'skom," *Zh. F.*, vol. 3, no. 3, 1911, p. 10.

247. Masthead Page, *Zh. F.*, vol. 3, no. 1, 1911, p. 1. Levinshtein also was chair of the St. Petersburg Union in 1909. At that time he urged persons interested in opening higher pharmacy courses to write him at SPb, Raz'ezzhaia, 34, Kv. 19. "Gruppa peterburgskikh farmatsevtov," *Zh. F.*, vol. 1, no. 3, 1909, p. 13.

248. "V pravlenii Iugo-Zapadnago Soiuza farmatsevtov," *Zh. F.*, vol. 3, no. 2, 1911, p. 10.

In 1914, an S. Lapitskaia was elected secretary of the St. Petersburg Union of Staff Pharmacists. "Sredi sluzhashchikh farmatsevtov v Peterburge: V Pravlenii Peterburgskago soiuza," *Zhizn' farmatsevta* (St. Petersburg), vol. 1, no. 1, 1914, p. 12.

249. "V pravlenii Iugo-Zapadnago Soiuza farmatsevtov," *Zh. F.*, vol. 3, no. 2, 1911, p. 10.

250. "V Pravlenii Iugo-Zap. Soiuza farm.," *Zh. F.*, vol. 3, no. 2, 1911, p. 10.

251. "Raznyia," *Zh. F.*, vol. 3, no. 2, 1911, p. 14.

252. "Khronika: V SPb soiuze farmatsevtov," *F. Zh.*, vol. 53, no. 2, 1913, p. 20, and "V Obshchestve farmatsevtov sluzhashchikh," ibid., no. 5, p. 53.

253. "Iz istorii profdvizheniia aptechnykh rabotnikov," A. Aluf, "Oformlenie klassovykh organizatsii aptekorabotnikov," *Khimiko-farmatsevticheskii zhurnal*, vol. 6, no. 3, 1928, p. 5.

254. *Zh. F.* (St. Petersburg), vol. 1, no. 1, 1914, p. 15.

255. For Kuperman in 1914 see "Fond Zhurnala," *Zh. F.* (St. Petersburg), vol.

1, no. 1, 1914, p. 15, and "Sredi sluzhashchikh farmatsevtov," ibid., p. 12. Lapitskaia is mentioned ibid., p. 12. For Kuperman in 1918 see *Vestnik aptechnago truda* nos. 4 and 5, 1918, p. 2. He was elected representative from the St. Petersburg Union of Staff Pharmacists.

256. I. Levinshtein, RSFSR: Glavnyi Komitet Professional'no-Tekhnicheskogo Obrazovaniia, *Materialy po profess.-tekhnicheskomu obrazovaniiu. Farmatsevticheskoe obrazovanie* (Moscow, 1921) and I. Levinshtein, *Materialy po farmatsevticheskomu obrazovaniiu: programmy farmatsevticheskoi shkoly* (Moscow, 1922).

257. "V Petrogradskom Soiuze sluzhashchikh v aptekakh: Obshchee sobranie 31-go dekabria 1918 [1917?] goda," *Vestnik aptechnago truda* [hereafter cited *VAT*], vol. 5, no. 1, 1918, p. 12; "O kharaktere nashei revoliutsii," ibid., nos. 4 and 5, p. 3. Aluf was a Menshevik Internationalist. For more information on the Mensheviks in Russia at this time see Abraham Ascher, *Pavel Axelrod and the Development of Menshevism* (Cambridge, MA: Harvard University Press, 1972) pp. 310–315, and Ziva Galili, *The Menshevik Leaders in the Russian Revolution* (Princeton: Princeton University Press, 1989). The relationship of the prewar radical pharmacists with the new Bolshevik government will be discussed in later chapters.

258. A. Aluf, "Iz istorii profdvizheniia aptechnykh rabotnikov: oformlenie klassovykh organizatsii aptekorabotnikov," *Khimiko-farmatsevticheskii zhurnal*, vol. 6, no. 3, 1928 p. 5, and Iu. A. Kuperman, "Obshchaia Zabastovka v aptekakh Leningrada v oktiabre-noiabre 1917 g.," ibid., no. 5, pp. 15–16.

259. "Khronika: V SPb soiuze farmatsevtov," *F. Zh.*, vol. 52, no. 2, 1913, p. 20; "V obshchestve farmatsevtov sluzhashchikh," ibid., no. 5, p. 53; "Sobranie farmatsevtov," ibid., no. 12, p. 138.

260. Aluf, "Oformlenie klassovykh organizatsii aptekorabotnikov," p. 5.

Chapter 15

1. See Mary Schaeffer Conroy, *Peter Arkadevich Stolypin: Practical Politics in Late Tsarist Russia* (Boulder: Westview Press, 1976), pp. 152–177.

2. The State Council had operated as an appointed, consultative legislature from the early nineteenth century. In 1906 it was enlarged to form the upper chamber of the parliament. Ninety-eight, or half the members, of the State Council were appointed as before. The other half were elected by corporate groups. According to Peter A. Zaionchkovsky, the late nineteenth-century State Council, as lifetime appointees, had an independent cast of mind. For this earlier period see Zaionchkovsky, *The Russian Autocracy under Alexander III*, ed. and trans. David R. Jones (Gulf Breeze, FL: Academic International Press, 1976), pp. 52–55.

3. Reported in *Birzhevye vedomosti*, 1898, cited in "Khronika," *Farmatsevticheskii vestnik* [hereafter cited *F. V.*], vol. 2, no. 49, 1898, p. 795.

4. S. K. Lintser, "Bytovoi otdel: Aptechnaia Monopoliia," *F. V.*, vol. 7, no. 2, 1904, p. 21.

5. "Doklad aptechnoi sektsii VI s"ezda vrachei i predstavitelei zemstv Vologodskoi gubernii po peredannym na eia zakliuchenie zaprosam: 1) o proekte novago

aptechnago ustava i 2) ob obshche-gubernskoi vypiske medikamentov," *F. V.*, vol. 7, no. 45, 1904, p. 910, and "O proekte aptekarskago ustava" (Report of Yaroslavl' provincial zemstvo uprava), ibid., no. 48, p. 957. Zemstvos were invited to review the draft statute and present their conclusions before it was transferred to the State Council.

6. The new statute was discussed throughout the pages of pharmacy journals during 1904. For example, see "Neskol'ko zamechanii po povodu proekta aptechnago ustava," *F. V.*, vol. 7, no. 43, 1904, p. 680, and Gr. Grudinskii,"Po povodu novago aptechnago ustava," ibid., no. 40, p. 629. See also "Dumskii zakonoproekt izmenenii poriadka otkrytiia novykh aptek v Gosudarst. Sovet," *Farmatsevticheskii zhurnal* [hereafter cited *F. Zh.*], vol. 50, no. 22, 1911, p. 264.

7. "Raznyia izvestiia," *F. Zh.*, vol. 45 (28), no. 16, 1906, p. 318.

8. "Khronika," *Farmatsevticheskii trud* [hereafter cited *F. T.*], vol. 1, no. 14, 1907, p. 202.

9. "Proekt Ustava Aptekarskago razrabotannyi Vysochaishe utverzhd. S. Peterburgskim farmatsevticheskim obshchestvom po poruchenniiu s"ezda delegatov rossiiskikh farmatsevticheskikh obshchestv v S. Petersburge v Ianvare 1906 g.," *F. T.*, vol. 1, no. 24, 1907, pp. 330–331. It would seem that the St. Petersburg Pharmacy society was coerced into working out this clause.

10. "Khronika," *F. T.*, vol. 1, no. 14, 1907, p. 202.

11. "Iz zhurnalov Meditsinskago Soveta," *F. T.*, vol. 1, no. 30, 1907, p. 409.

12. "Ob izmenenii zakona ob otkrytii aptek," *Prilozheniia k stenograficheskim otchetam Gosudarstvennoi Dumy*, tretii sozyv, sessiia tret'ia, 1909–1910 g.g. (St. Petersburg, 1910), vol. 1, no. 89, pp. 4–5, and Dokladchik M. K. Safonov, "Doklad po peredannomu na osnovanii § 64 Nakaza Gosudarstvennoi Dumy zakonodatel'nomu zaiavleniiu ob izmenenii zakona ob otkrytii aptek," ibid., pp. 1–3. Also, Editorial, "Nyt'e ili bor'ba za budushchee," *F. Zh.*, vol. 49, no. 1, 1910, p. 1. The journal claimed that the debate on pharmacy reform had circulated for the past three years. Also, "Obzor pechati," ibid., p. 11.

13. "Obzor pechati," *F.Zh.*, vol. 49, no. 1, 1910, pp. 10–11.

14. "Pirogovskii S"ezd i reforma aptekarskago dela," *F. Zh.*, vol. 49, no. 3, 1910, pp. 25–26, and ibid., no. 4, pp. 37–38. The radical *pirogovtsy* usually favored the zemstvos. Additionally, the physician delegate cautioning against free establishment of pharmacies opined that such a system was acceptable in "cultured countries" but "competition had a commercial character" whereas the pharmacy was first and foremost a medical institution. Ibid., p. 25. Also "Nerazumenie ili nedorazumenie?" *F. Zh.*, vol. 49, no. 21, 1910, p. 235. On the Pirogov Society see John F. Hutchinson, *Politics and Public Health in Revolutionary Russia, 1890–1918* (Baltimore: Johns Hopkins University Press, 1990), pp. 52–53, 65.

15. "Obzor pechati," *F. Zh.*, vol. 49, no. 34, 1910, p. 374.

16. "Dumskii zakonoproekt izmenenii poriadka otkrytiia novykh aptek," *F. Zh.*, vol. 50, no. 22, 1911, p. 264. Serfdom was abolished in Russia in 1861.

17. "Khronika," *F. Zh.*, vol. 49, no. 3, 1910, pp. 34–35.

18. "Khronika," *F. Zh.*, vol. 50, no. 14, 1911, p. 168.

19. Tsentral'nyi Gosudarstvennyi Istoricheskii Arkhiv, St. Petersburg [hereafter

cited TsGIA], fond 1298, opis' 1, delo 1402, listy 4, 4 oborot, 5, 5 ob. [hereafter cited "f.," "op.," "d.," "l.," or "ll."].

20. TsGIA, f. 1298, op. 1, d. 1798, ll. 1, and ob., 2, 3, 6. Local authorities cited a long list of the zemstvo's hospital pharmacy contributions. It was under the immediate supervision of a physician; it never dispensed medicine on the side; it dispensed medicine free (*bezplatno*) only to patients with certification from the police and doctors as to their poverty; the district did not have its own clinic; the hospital had only a division for ill students under supervision of the zemstvo hospital doctor and zemstvo feldsher, which dispensed medicines free to the students in the hospital; the sick in the prison were managed by the zemstvo feldsher and medicines for them were dispensed in the same order as to the students.

21. "Khronika," *F. Zh.*, vol. 50, no. 14, 1911, p. 168.

22. In the latter crisis Stolypin passed the bill under the provisions of article 87 of the Fundamental laws of 1906, which permitted the government to temporarily implement measures when the Duma was not in session. For details of both crises and Stolypin's general relationship with the parliament see Conroy, *Peter Arkad'evich Stolypin*, pp. 165–171, 174–177.

23. The Medical Council did not agree with Malinovskii's proposal. Nevertheless, it was reported that in "the Capitals" and some large cities pharmacies had been established according to lower norms. "K proektu Farmatsevticheskago Ustava," *F. Zh.*, vol. 49, no. 14, 1910, pp. 158–159, and "Mnenie deputatov pri Meditsinskom Sovete ot Vysochaishe utverzhd. SPB Farmats. Obshchestva po voprosu umen'sheniia norm chisla zhitelei na kazhduiu apteku," ibid., pp. 159–160.

24. Dokladchik M. K. Safonov, "Doklad po zakonodatelnomu predpolozheniiu 'Ob izmenenii zakona ob otkrytii aptek'," *Prilozheniia k stenograficheskim otchetam Gosudarstvennoi Dumy*, tretii sozyv, sessiia 4, 1910–1911 g. g. (St. Petersburg, 1911), no. 360, pp. 1–3; section on drug stores, p. 2, bill on p. 3.

Also, "O nekotorykh izmeneniiakh v poriadke otkrytiia aptek," *F. Zh.*, vol. 50, no. 21, 1911, pp. 241–242, and "Doklad komissii po napravleniiu zakonodatel'nykh predpolozhenii po zakonodatel'nomu predpolozheniiu ob izmenenii zakona ob otkrytii aptek," ibid., pp. 242–244. Law of March 31 on p. 244.

25. List of thirty-four members, including five priests sponsoring the bill, "Ob"iasnitel'naia zapiska," *Prilozheniia k stenograficheskim otchetam Gosudarstvennoi Dumy*, tretii sozyv, sessiia 4, 1910–1911, p. 483. Report from the Ministry of Internal Affairs to the Governing Senate (Proekt, V Pravitel'stvuiushchii Senat, Ministerstvo Vnutrennikh Del, Raport), July 1912, TsGIA, f. 1298, op. 1, delo 1889, ll. 28–33. The contemporary press theorized that the purpose of the bill was to improve dispensing in cities and villages of the zemstvo provinces. *Loc. cit.*

26. "Otmena § 3 pravil 1873–1906 gg. ob otkrytii aptek," *F. Zh.*, vol. 49, no. 4, 1910, pp. 39–40; "Novyia pravila o poriadke otkrytiia aptek," ibid., no. 45, p. 483; "Farmatsevticheskii ustav: Proekt," ibid., p. 486 (article 23, chapter 3, of the draft statute).

27. "Obzor pechati," *F. Zh.*, vol. 49, no. 2, 1910, p. 22.

28. "Eshche izmenenie pravil 1873 goda," *F. Zh.*, vol. 49, no. 2, 1910, p. 13.

29. "O nekotorykh izmeneniiakh v poriadke otkrytiia aptek," *F. Zh.*, vol. 50, no. 22, 1911, p. 253.

30. "K proektu novago farmatsevticheskago ustava," *Zhizn' farmatsevta* (Kiev) [hereafter cited *Zh. F.*] vol. 3, no. 1, 1911, p. 7. The journal quoted this information from another journal, *Gigiena i Sanitariia*. Needless to say, *Zhizn' farmatsevta* was enthusiastic about Stolypin's proposal.

31. *Loc. cit.*

32. Masters of Pharmacy and Provizors could manage pharmacies of the first rank; Assistant Pharmacists could manage those of the second rank. All three were required to have a practicum of at least two years in a first-class pharmacy. *Loc cit.*

33. There were to be five categories of cities—those with population between of 200,000 or over were allowed one pharmacy for every 12,000 inhabitants; those with population between 100,000 and 200,000 were permitted to have one pharmacy for every 11,000 inhabitants; cities of between 50,000 and 100,000 inhabitants were permitted one pharmacy for every 10,000 inhabitants; towns of between 20,000 to 50,000 inhabitants were allowed one pharmacy for every 8,500 people; and finally, towns of less than 20,000 were allowed one pharmacy for every 7,000 people. *Loc. cit.*

34. The project also upgraded and streamlined pharmacy education. Males were to have finished five years of *gimnaziia* or real school (females seven years plus an examination in Latin). Apprentices were to study at special pharmacy schools to qualify them to sit for the examination for the title Assistant Pharmacist. The project envisioned the establishment of pharmacy schools of the "mixed type" for males and females—apparently analagous to feldsher schools. Initial apprenticeship was to be cut to one year. *Loc. cit.*

35. *Loc. cit.*

36. "Novyia pravila o poriadke otkrytiia aptek," *F. Zh.*, vol. 49, no. 45, 1910, p. 483.

37. For example, on May 23, 1911, the State Council sent the Duma bill back to committee. "O nekotorykh izmeneniiakh v poriadke otkrytiia aptek," *F. Zh.*, vol. 50, no. 22, 1911, p. 254.

38. "Dumskii zakonoproekt izmenenii poriadka otkrytiia novykh aptek v Gosudarst. Sovet," p. 264.

39. TsGIA, f. 1298, op. 1, d. 1889, l. 1 and ob.

40. TsGIA, f. 1298, op. 1, d. 1889, ll. 1, 2, 3, 4, 7, 8, 12. The correspondence from local authorities to the Chief Medical Inspector took place in March and April 1912.

41. TsGIA, f. 1298, op. 1, d. 1889, ll. 21, 22, 24, 26, 28.

42. Orenburg, Gubernator po Gubernskomu Pravleniiu, 28 June 1913, TsGIA, f. 1298, op. 1, d. 1889, ll. 100-100 ob.

43. Report to the Governing Senate, July 1912, TsGIA, f. 1298, op. 1, d. 1889, ll. 30-32. There also was confusion as to the limits of jurisdiction between the provincial zemstvo executive council, district zemstvo executive council, and city duma.

44. TsGIA, f. 1298, op. 1, d. 1889, l. 85.

45. TsGIA, f. 1298, op. 1, d. 1889, ll. 94 and 95.

46. "Protokoly Rossiiskago farmatsevticheskago S"ezda," *F. Zh.*, vol. 52, no. 22, 1913, p. 251.

47. TsGIA, f. 1298, op. 1, d. 1409, l. 5.

48. TsGIA, f. 1298, op. 1, d. 1409, l. 10. The first was 300 *sazhens* from the second–the third 100 *sazhens* from the boundaries of the city.

49. Report of E. K. Khrzhanovskii, "Protokol Rossiiskago farmatsevticheskago S"ezda," *F. Zh.*, vol. 52, no. 22, 1913, p. 251. In the *Osobye zhurnaly soveta ministrov* of the Stolypin years (1906–1911), Kokovtsov frequently came forth as a fiscal conservative. See also Conroy, *Peter Arkad'evich Stolypin*, p. 41, note 53.

50. "O dosuzhikh fantaziiakh i myl'nykh puzyriakh," *F. Zh.*, vol. 52, no. 10, 1913, p. 105 and "Protokol zasedaniia farmatsevticheskago Natsional'nago Komiteta 22-go Ianvaria 1913 goda," ibid., pp. 105–106. This became a part of the agenda for the Pharmacy Congress to be convened in May. "Ot Rasporiaditel'nago Komiteta Rossiiskago Farmatsevticheskago S"ezda," (A. S. Ginzberg was a member of this committee), ibid., no. 13, pp. 139–140. Also, "Pered s"ezdom," ibid., no. 14, p. 153.

51. The Swedish system was to be completed by 1920. "Protokol zasedaniia Natsional'nago Komiteta 28-go Fevralia 1913 goda," *F. Zh.*, vol. 52, no. 11, 1913, p. 117.

52. S. Zhitomirskii, "Pis'ma v redaktsiiu," *F. Zh.*, vol. 52, no. 15, 1913, pp. 172–174.

53. "Na temy dnia," *F. Zh.*, vol. 52, no 1, 1913, pp. 1–2; ibid., no. 17, 1913, pp. 189–190; ibid., no. 21, p. 235. In "K chitateliam," the editors alerted readers to the fact that "buying out and liquidating private pharmacy . . . at the moment have gained wide currency in Russia." Ibid., no. 6, 1913, pp. 57–58. The St. Petersburg Society organized a committee to study the system in Sweden. Ibid., no. 7, p. 68.

54. For example, S. Zhitomirskii, "Pis'mo v redaktsiiu," *F. Zh.*, vol. 52, no. 9, 1913, pp. 94–95. Zhitomirskii claimed the Don Society of Pharmacists had not been fully informed about *samovykup*–buying out private pharmacies.

55. "Rossiiskii farmatsevticheskii S"ezd," *F. Zh.*, vol. 52, no. 22, 1913, p. 249, and "Protokoly Rossiiskago farmatsevticheskago S'ezda," ibid., pp. 250–253.

56. Boris Puzis, "Samovykup," *F. Zh.*, vol. 52, no. 20, 1913, pp. 226–228. However, he distrusted payment in stocks and government bonds.

57. "Neskol'ko neozhidannoe izvestie," *F. Zh*, vol. 55, no. 3, 1916, pp. 21–23 and "Vol'nyia apteki," ibid., p. 29.

58. For more on the crisis see Conroy, *Peter Arkad'evich Stolypin*, pp. 174–178.

59. Upravlenie Glavnago Vrachebnago Inspektora, 2-e deloproizvodstvo, 28 Fevralia 1911, no. 363, TsGIA, f. 1298, op. 1, d. 1776, l. 20.

60. From the Minister of Finance to His Excellency P. A. Stolypin, 23 June 1911, TsGIA, f. 1298, op. 1, d. 1776, l. 24.

61. MVD, Upravlenie Glavnago Vrachebnago Inspektora, 2-e deloproizvodstvo, 28 Fevriala 1911, no. 363, TsGIA, f. 1298, op. 1, d. 1776, l. 20.

62. "K voprosam tekushchei praktiki" *F. Zh.*, vol. 50, no. 18, 1911, pp. 205–206.

63. Michael Robson, "The French Pharmaceutical Industry 1919-1939," *Pill Peddlers: Essays on the History of the Pharamceutical Industry*, eds., Jonathan Liebenau, Gregory Higby, and Elaine C. Stroud (Madison, WI: American Institute of the History of Pharmacy, 1990) p. 108.

64. Uchenyi sekretar Meditsinskago Soveta, MVD, 3 Maia 1911, TsGIA, f. 1298, op. 1, d. 1776, ll. 2 and 2 ob.

65. Excerpt from the journal of the Medical Council, 3 June 1911, TsGIA, f. 1298, op. 1, d. 1776, ll. 21-22.

66. TsGIA, f. 1298, op. 1, d. 1776, l. 24.

67. TsGIA, f. 1298, op. 1, d. 1776, ll. 26 and 26 ob.

68. TsGIA, f. 1298, op. 1, d. 1776, ll. 28-29.

69. Ministry of Justice, First department, Section of the Jurisconsult, 4 October 1911, TsGIA, f. 1298, op. 1, d. 1776, ll. 32-38.

70. "Spravka," 8 Dekabria 1912, TsGIA, f. 1298, op. 1, d. 1776, ll. 106 and 106 ob.

71. To the Governing Senate, 9 December 1911, TsGIA, f. 1298, op. 1, d. 1776, ll. 107-131.

72. TsGIA, f. 1298, op. 1, d. 1776, ll. 58-67.

73. "Meditsinskim Sovetom," *F. Zh.*, vol. 49, no. 40, 1910, p. 436 and "Obzor pechati: O farmatsevticheskoi promyshlennosti," *F. Zh.*, vol. 50, no. 20, 1911, p. 240.

74. "Farmatsevticheskii ustav: Proekt, articles 52 and 53," *F. Zh.*, vol. 49, no. 45, 1910, p. 489.

75. "Khronika: v Senate," *F. Zh.*, vol. 52, no. 6, 1913, p. 65. Apparently the Ministry of Internal Affairs had asked the Senate for clarification of article 386 of the Medical Statute on the importation of foreign medicaments.

76. "Khronika," *F. Zh.*, vol. 52, no. 12, 1913, p. 137.

77. Interdepartmental committee, TsGIA, f. 1298, op. 1, d. 2066, ll. 61, 62. This followed a request from Parke, Davis and Company for permission to import all its pharmaceutical wares without restriction.

78. A representative of the Keler firm recommended that tariffs on raw materials be lowered and tariffs on raw opium be eliminated. TsGIA, f. 1298, op. 1, d. 2066, ll. 40, 41. F. G. (A.) Ferrein demanded that imports of foreign galenicals be totally banned. TsGIA, f. 1298, op. 1, d. 2066, l. 72. The issue of Ferrein's patronymic is discussed in chapter 16 of this work, "Lekarstvennyi Golod," or Medicaments Crisis of World War I.

P. B. Shaskol'skii, representative of the Shaskol'skii Trading Firm and successful exporter of Russian mineral water, likewise contended that the Russian tariff encouraged imports of foreign mineral waters over domestic. Shaskol'skii report, "Mezhduvedomstvennago Komiteta," 1915, TsGIA, f. 1298, op. 1, d. 2066a, ll. 123, 123ob., 124, 126. B. P. Shaskol'skii participated in the Petrograd Committee on production of medicines of the fall of 1915.

79. D. Ia. Blumental', "Lekarstvennyi golod," *F. Zh*, vol. 55, no. 6, 1916, p. 55.

80. For devolution of government responsibility to the new zemstvos see, for example, Thomas S. Pearson, *Russian Officialdom in Crisis Autocracy and Self*

Government, 1861-1900 (Cambridge: Cambridge University Press, 1989), p. 9 and *passim.*

81. Meditsinskii Sovet: Proekt polozheniia o farmatsevticheskikh uchebnykh zavedeniiakh i utverzhenii okonchivshikh v ikh obuchenie lits v stepeni provizora i zvanii aptekarskago pomoshchnika, vnesennyi v Meditsinskii Sovet Glavnym Vrachebnym Inspektorom 4 Maia 1904 goda," TsGIA, f. 1298, op. 1, d. 1111, ll. 10, 10 ob, 11. The curriculum of the pharmacy "educational institutions"—no designation was made for lower or higher—included human anatomy, physiology, bacteriology, hygiene, first aid, pharmacognosy, pharmacy and pharmaceutical chemistry, prescriptions, pharmacology, botany, zoology, organic and inorganic chemistry, analytical chemistry, mineralogy, basic geology, legislation relating to pharmacy, accounting, and laboratory work involving chemistry, forensic-chemistry, physiology, and sanitation. Ibid.

82. MVD, Glavnyi Vrachebnyi Inspektor, 15 Ianvaria 1905, TsGIA, f. 1298, op. 1, d. 1111, ll. 22-30, and Zhurnal obshchago zasedaniia Meditsinskago Soveta, 8 Marta 1905, "O vysshem farmatsevticheskom obrazovanii," TsGIA, f. 1298, op. 1, d. 1111, ll. 34-39. The project or Polozhenie follows, ibid., ll. 55 e-55 zh.

83. Ministerstvo Vnutrennikh Del, upravlenie Glavnago Vrachebnago Inspektora, 2-e deloproizvodstvo, 1 aprelia 1906, "Po proekty Polozheniia o Nizshikh farmatsevticheskikh uchebnykh zavedeniiakh," V Gosudarstvennuiu Dumu, TsGIA, f. 1298, op. 1, d. 1111, ll. 55-55d.

84. TsGIA, f. 1298, op. 1, d. 1111, ll. 60-68.

85. Vypiska iz zhurnala Uchenago Komiteta Ministerstva Narodnago Prosveshcheniia 2 Ianvaria 1906 goda (No. 1719), TsGIA, f. 1298, op. 1, d. 1111, l. 88, 88 ob., 93. In l. 93 the St. Petersburg Pharmacy Society, "energetically protested against the proposed right [allowing] public institutions and private persons to open special pharmacy institutes."

86. "Reforma farmatsevticheskogo obrazovaniia," *F. V.*, vol. 7, no. 46, 1904, p. 930.

87. "At the present time the majority of pharmacies—if not all—do not give pharmacy students elementary familiarity with medicinal chemical substances and materials, nor sufficient practice on the preparation of various medicinal forms like plasters, oils, tablets, galenical preparations, syrups, extracts, and do not provide enough free time to practice dispensation and laboratory work. . . . Thirty years have passed . . . the pharmacy is still a school. . . ." Professor S. A. Przhibytek, as examiner of students for the degree Assistant Pharmacist, spoke about the absence of elementary knowledge of chemistry, botany, etc.: "too many pharmacies use the cheap labor of students—they learn little." TsGIA, f. 1298, op. 1, d. 1244, ll. 99, 100 and ob. The St. Petersburg Pharmacy Society collected information from pharmacy societies and pharmacy owners around the empire and presented it to the Chief Medical Inspector in January 1907.

88. "Zhurnaly zasedanii organizovannoi pri Rossiiskom farmatsevticheskom obshchestve komissii po razsmotrenniiu proekta aptekarskago ustava," *F. V.*, vol. 7, no. 32, 1904, p. 498-99. Also present at the meeting were those gadflies E.G. Basilaia, L. A. Zimin, and I. I. Kal'ning.

89. Ibid., pp. 498-499.

90. *Loc. cit.*

91. TsGIA, f. 1298, op. 1, d. 1244, ll. 94 ob, 95.

92. "Min. Narod. Prosveshchenie, Departamenta Narodnago Prosveshcheniia 5 Aprelia 1905 Gospodinu Ministru Vnutren. Del," TsGIA, f. 1298, op. 1, d. 1272, ll. 1 and ob. Abol' also wanted permission to open higher women's pharmacy courses in Moscow.

93. TsGIA, f. 1298, op. 1, d. 1300, ll. 1, 5 and ob., l. 23.

94. "Khronika," *F. V.*, vol. 7, no. 1, 1904, p. 11. He complained, however, that they were located far from pharmacies.

95. "Khronika," *F. V.*, vol. 7, no. 32, 1904, p. 508.

96. "Pervyi otchet po kafedre farmatsii i farmakognozii pri Imperatorskom Novorossiiskom universitete," *F. V.*, vol. 7, no. 41, 1904, p. 642-643. In a later article on the same subject the author recommended that pharmacist auditors and medical students take separate courses because the former needed additional courses, and for the latter pharmacy was not so important. Ibid., no. 42, pp. 662-663.

97. T. I. Lonachevskii-Petruniak, *Vopros ob obrazovanii russkikh farmatsevtov* (St. Petersburg, 1905), pp. 18-19.

98. "Ego Siiatel'stvu Gos. Min. Vnutrennikh Del ot Kazan. Farmatsevticheskago Obshchestva Proshenie," TsGIA, f. 1298, op. 1, d. 1111, ll. 20-21.

99. "Reforma vysshago obrazovaniia farmatsevtov," *Farmatsevt*, vol. 14, no. 9, 1906, pp. 246-248.

100. Ibid., p. 249.

101. Glenn Sonnedecker, *History of Pharmacy* (Philadelphia: J. B. Lippincott Company, 1976), pp. 226-236.

102. "Programma . . . ," *Ispytaniia na zvaniia i stepeni lekaria, zubnago vracha, povival'noi babki, provizora, aptekarskago pomoshchnika i aptekarskago uchenika* (ed.) N. Malinovskii (St. Petersburg, 1907), pp. 246-293.

103. "Po povodu novago aptekarskago ustava," *F. V.*, vol. 7, no. 34, 1904, p. 537.

104. TsGIA, f. 1298, op. 1, d. 1272, ll. 2-6.

105. TsGIA, f. 1298, op. 1, d. 1272, l. 8.

106. "Obshchee Sobranie chlenov S Peterburgskago farmatsevticheskago obshchestva," *F. T.*, vol. 1, no. 30, 1907, pp. 404-405. Originally the school was free; this seemed to indicate that tuition was being charged. Perhaps this change of policy was due to arrears in collecting the 1 ruble, 50 kopek payment per 1,000 prescriptions authorized in 1869 to pay for the school. At one point this fee was lowered to 1 ruble. *Loc. cit.*

107. "Storonnee Soobshchenie," pp. 410-411. Fifteen rubles was to be paid initially, the remainder after the tenth lesson. Special conditions were made for unemployed pharmacists. The wholesale drug firm was named "Provizor M. V. Polumordvinov."

108. See "Spravka," TsGIA, f. 1298, op. 1, d. 1111, ll. 56 and 56 ob.

109. TsGIA, f. 1298, op. 1, d. 1111, l. 77.

110. TsGIA, f. 1298, op. 1, d. 1111, ll. 75–76.

111. TsGIA, f. 1298, op. 1, d. 1111, l. 81.

112. TsGIA, f. 1298, op. 1, d. 1111, ll. 82–87.

113. "L. M. Gel'bukh, "K reforme farmatsevticheskago obrazovaniia," *Zh. F.*, vol. 1, no. 2, 1909, p. 6 and "Diskutsionnyi otdel: k reforme farmatsevticheskago obrazovaniia," ibid., p. 7.

114. TsGIA, f. 1298, op. 1, d. 1111, ll. 99 and 100.

115. TsGIA, f. 1298, op. 1, d. 1111, ll. 100, 100 ob, 101. A commission in the Medical Council recommended instituting of the degree, Doctor of Pharmacy. The Society of Military and Naval Pharmacists protested, claiming that this would worsen the position of pharmacists. They would lose the possibility of receiving the degree Master, which would be available only for graduates of higher natural science and medical faculties. The Military and Naval Pharmacists instead requested a three-year pharmacy program, such as that at Novorossiisk University, be instituted in all Russian universities to beef up pharmacy education.

116. "Khronika: Obrazovatelnoi tsenz dlia aptekarskikh uchenikov," *F. Zh.*, vol. 52, no. 11, 1913, p. 126.

117. "Zasedaniia natsional'nogo Komiteta 8-go Marta, 1913 and 20-go Marta," *F. Zh.*, vol. 52, nos. 12 and 14, 1913, pp. 131, 158–159.

118. Sidorkov, "Issledovanie organizatsionno-metodicheskikh printsipov razvitie farmatsevticheskogo uchenogo dela v SSSR," (Moscow, 1973), unpublished Ph.D. dissertation, p. 46 located in the Tsentral'naia Gosudarstvennaia Nauchnaia Meditsinskaia Biblioteka, Moscow.

119. For fairly recent discussion of the Progressive Bloc see Richard Abraham, *Alexander Kerensky: The First Love of The Revolution* (New York: Columbia University Press, 1987), pp. 99–100.

120. Boris Puzis, "Avtonomiia," *F. Zh.*, vol. 52, no. 13, 1913, pp. 149–150; Robert Idel'son, "K predstoiashchemy Vserossiiskomu s"ezdu," ibid., no. 5, p. 48; "Koe-chto ob upravlenii farmatsevticheskoi chast'iu," ibid., no. 13, p. 141.

Chapter 16

1. William Gleason, *Alexander Guchkov and the End of the Russian Empire* (Philadelphia: The American Philosophical Society, 1983), pp. 58–62.

2. "Ministerial leapfrog" has been discussed in numerous histories. Although he characterizes the Russian government in the following outlandish terms—"Viewed in its broader aspects, the imperial government on the eve of the war was a blend of medievalism and western democracy . . . ," Michael T. Florinsky, nevertheless, presents one of the clearest expositions of ministerial leapfrog in his venerable *Russia: A History and an Interpretation*, (New York: Macmillan, eighth printing 1963), vol. II, pp. 1363, 1365.

3. For more on Rein see John F. Hutchinson, "Who Killed Cock Robin?" *Health and Society in Revolutionary Russia*, eds., Susan Gross Soloman and John F. Hutchinson. (Bloomington: Indiana University Press, 1990), pp. 12–15.

4. "Zasedanie Meditsinskago Soveta po voprosu o vzdorozhanii medikamentov," *Farmatsevticheskii zhurnal* [hereafter cited *F. Zh.*], vol. 53, no. 32, 1914, p. 367. According to F. I. Kresling, representative to the Medical Council from the St. Petersburg Pharmacy Society, medicaments sold on list "A"—retail prices for the public—rose by about 10 percent. On the other hand, wholesale prices leapt geometrically—glass cost 20 percent or more. "Po povodu voprosa vzdorozhaniia medikamentov," *F. Zh.*, vol. 53, no. 34, 1914, p. 382.

5. "K vzdorozhaniiu aptekarskikh tovarov," *F. Zh.*, vol. 53, no. 33, 1914, p. 380.

Later, during the Civil War that followed the Bolshevik revolution in October 1917, Odessa benefited from German presence. In 1918, *Iuzhnyi vestnik aptechnago truda*, advertized on its back page that the Davidov warehouse in Odessa had stores of pharmaceutical wares from "all the best German firms"; the warehouse would "send out only with payment of half the cost of the order." *Iuzhnyi vestnik aptechnago truda*, 1918, no. 11, back page, half-page ad listing pharmaceuticals avaliable in the warehouse. Salvarsan was selling for 3 rubles, 50 kopeks a dose. This subject is discussed further in chapter 18 of this work.

6. "V farmatsevticheskom obshchestve," *F. Zh.*, vol. 53, no. 35, 1914, p. 399.

7. "Vzdorozhanie aptekarskikh tovarov," *F. Zh.*, vol. 53, no. 33, 1914, pp. 378–379.

8. V. Gadzhedlo, "Na farmatsevticheskom rynke," *F. Zh.*, vol. 54, no. 2, 1916, pp. 19–20. Salicylic "metal" had increased from 2 rubles, 60 kopeks to 80 rubles per kilogram.

9. "Sredi sluzhashchikh farmatsevtov, Petrograd sobranie, 15-go oktiabria 1914 g.," *Zhizn' Farmatsevta* (St. Petersburg/Petrograd) [hereafter cited *Zh. F.*], vol. 1, no. 6–7, 1914, p. 12–13. Kamenskii and Aluf planned to document the backwardness of the Russian chemico-pharmaceutical industry. Yet, interestingly and contradictorily, Kamenskii averred that Russian imports from Germany were not so large that loss of the Russian market would impact Germany economically.

Zhizn' farmatsevta also claimed that German firms were adulterating the patent medicines they exported. "Fal'sifikatsiia medikamentov i mery bor'by s neiu," *Zh. F.*, vol. 1, no. 8, 1914, p. 4.

10. Michael Robson, "The French Pharmaceutical Industry 1919–1939," *Pill Peddlers*, eds., Jonathan Libenau, Gregory J. Higby, and Elaine C. Stroud (Madison, WI: American Institute of the History of Pharmacy, 1990), pp. 109–110.

11. K. S. Sarkisov, "Kratkii obzor polozheniia khimiko-farmatsevticheskikh promyshlennosti i rynka v Rossii, a v chastnosti v Kavkaze v nastoiashchee vremia," *F. Zh.*, vol. 55, no. 7, 1916, p. 60.

12. Charles C. Mann and Mark L. Plummer, *The Aspirin Wars* (New York: Alfred A. Knopf, 1991), p. 67.

13. "Russkiia lechebnyia sredstva," *F. Zh.*, vol. 53, no. 35, 1914, pp. 398–99.

14. "The (American) establishments emerging after the Civil War first devoted themselves, as previously shown, to the manufacture of galenicals. In their further development until 1917 they concentrated on medicinal plant research and,

finally, on the production of biological products. The systematic synthesis and production of organic chemicals, particularly chemeotherapeutic agents, came later. The reason was that in the second half of the nineteenth century, or at least after Kolbe's synthesis of salicylic acid (1874) and Knorr's preparation of antipyrine (1883) the field of pharmaceutical chemistry was dominated by the Germans. Synthetic organic chemistry began to change a large sector of drug manufacturing and, ultimately, drug therapy. Exploiting these scientific and commercial weapons shrewdly, Germany kept much of the world, including America, heavily dependent upon her intermediate and finished medicinal chemicals. It required the exigencies of World War I to stimulate national pharmaceutical independence." Glenn Sonnedecker, *Kremers and Urdang's History of Pharmacy* (Philadelphia: Lippencott, 1976), p. 331.

15. *Schweig. Apoth. Zeitung* in "Zagranichnyia izvestiia: Vlyianie voiny na rynok lekarstvennykh sredstv," *F. Zh.*, vol. 55, no. 2, 1916, p. 13. The one exception was atropin sulfuric, which rose 308 percent in Germany and 370 percent in Switzerland.

16. F. A. Ferrein to the Interdepartmental Government Committee on the Needs of the Pharmaceutical Industry "Zhurnal mezhduvedomstvennago komiteta po delam farmatsevticheskoi promyshlennosti: Doklad F. A. Ferreina Mezhduvedomstvennomu Komitetu: 'O Nuzhdakh farmatsevticheskoi promyshlennosti'" 10 Aprelia 1915. Tsentral'nyi Gosudarstvennyi Istoricheskii Arkhiv, St. Petersburg [hereafter cited TsGIA], fond 1298, opis' 1, delo 2066, list 103 [hereafter cited "f.," "op.," "d.," "l.," or "ll."]

Strangely, on *list* 102 the author of this report is cited as *F. A.* Ferrein, initials of the Ferrein who was to become one of the leaders in nationalizing and managing the pharmaceutical sector in the early Soviet period. However, throughout the account of the Wartime Interdepartmental Committee on the Pharmaceutical Industry on preceding *listy* of this delo 2066, the member of the committee and author of the report is cited as *F. G.* Ferrein.

17. Sarkisov, "Kratkii obzor," *F. Zh.*, vol. 55, no. 7, 1916, p. 59. A factory was being built "in the north of Russia" to supply Bertoletov salts but had not been completed by late 1915. *Loc. cit.*

18. "Zasedanie Meditsinskago Soveta po voprosu o vzdorozhanii medikamentov," *F. Zh.*, vol. 53, no. 32, 1914, p. 367.

19. K. S. Sarkisov, "Kratkii obzor polozheniia khimiko-farmatsevticheskikh promyshlennosti i rynka v Rossii . . . ," *F. Zh.*, vol. 55, no. 6, 1916, pp. 49, 50.

20. An editorial, "O lekarstvennom golode," *Farmatsevticheskii zhurnal*, vol. 53, no. 36, September 6, 1914, p. 402, noted pharmaceutical enterprises "in Tsarist Poland in the depth of the theater of military activity" and particularly lamented the loss of the Pabiianitsak hygroscopic cotton and bandaging factory. However, wares from the Warsaw firm Motor were still advertised in 1915. *F. Zh.*, vol. 54, 1915, *passim*.

21. "Zasedanie Meditsinskago Soveta, p. 367. Parke, Davis promised to sell at its prewar price list but the Russian firms asked for an increase in the pharmacy

tax; "Vzdorozhanie aptekarskikh tovarov," *F. Zh.*, vol. 53, no. 33, 1914, p. 378. Kresling, "Po povodu voprosa vzdorozhaniia medikamentov," pp. 383-384.

22. Minister of Trade and Industry, Department of Trade to the Administration of the Chief Medical Inspector, 28 September 1915, TsGIA, f. 1298, op. 1, d. 2060, l. 29.

In December 1915, the Chief Medical Inspector protested the railroad administration's refusal to ship pharmaceutical wares from Vladivostok to Moscow and Petrograd, emphasizing pharmaceutical shortages and extreme expensiveness of pharmaceutical supplies on hand. Ibid., ll. 53 and 53 ob.

23. At the outset of the war, shipment of a railroad car of glass from the Riting factory to St. Petersburg cost 25-30 rubles; after railroads refused private shipments peasants took the glass wares in horse-drawn carts for 175 rubles. Kresling, "Po povodu voprosa vzdorozhaniia medikamentov," p. 383.

24. Sarkisov, "Kratkii obzor," p. 60.

25. For example, in June 1915 the Chief Medical Inspector informed Aleksandr Adamovich Shabunevich of the Society for Assistance in Developing the Chemical Industry and Trade that there were three wagons of filtered paper from the Ferrein firm on the Moscow-Kazan railroad waiting shipment "outside the regular order" to Perm. In July 1915, the governor of Arkhangel'sk forwarded a letter from the owner of a pharmacy in the city of Arkhangel'sk to the Chief Medical Inspector requesting help in quickly delivering to him 300 *puds* of medicaments and pharmaceutical supplies by railway from Moscow. In July 1915 the city of Iur'ev requested help from the Society for Assistance in Developing the Chemical Industry and Trade in getting two vacuum apparatus; there also was a request to ship 150 *puds* of chloroform from a factory in Perm for the Ferrein firm in Moscow. TsGIA, f. 1298, op. 1, d. 2060, ll. 1-2 ob.

(A *pud* is roughly equal to 36 pounds.) Additionally, letters, telegrams, and notes scribbled on small sheets of paper flew between the Chief Medical Inspector and the Society for Assistance in Developing the Chemical Industry and Trade regarding the dispatch of vaccuum tubes to the Merezhkovskii company in Petrograd, the request of the Ferrein firm for five long and five short wooden platforms, and the request of the firm Shering for help in getting supplies from Arkhangel'sk to Moscow. TsGIA, f. 1298, op. 1, d. 2060, ll. 4, 7-11, 13, 16.

Further examples for official help in unblocking shipments, ibid., ll, 30-40, involved a wagon of formalin for Shering, Merezhkovskii, Vogau and Co. and fifteen carloads of pharmacy wares for Ferrein from the ports of Vladivostok and Arkhangel'sk, August-October 1916; and twenty-six boxes or 226 *puds* of naftalan (or naftalin), sitting on the Caucasian railway for shipment to Ferrein, November 1915 (l. 39).

These requests provide information on purchasing practices of Russian pharmaceutical firms from foreign suppliers. In November 1915, Shtol' and Shmidt sent lading information from nine ships at the port of Arkhangel'sk, asking that cargoes, including palm oil, sublimate, bismuth, olive oil, aromatic water, medicinal herbs, and chloroform—in all 2,029 *puds,* 17 *funts*—be dispatched outside the regular order. Ibid., ll. 57 and 57 ob.

In December 1915, Shering requested help for four wagons of Chinese oak gall (*oreshka*), Ibid., l. 52.

26. TsGIA, f. 1298, op. 1, d. 2060, l. 29.

27. Telegram, Ministry of Ways and Communications, TsGIA, f. 1298, op. 1, d. 2060, l. 44.

28. See also TsGIA, f. 1298, op. 1, d. 2060, ll. 60–189; materials in this *delo* go through September 1917.

29. TsGIA, f. 1298, op. 1, d. 2060, l. 190.

30. Letter from Shtol' and Shmidt, cited in Kresling, "Po povodu voprosa vzdorozhaniia medikamentov," pp. 382–383.

31. "Vzdorozhanie aptekarskikh tovarov," *F. Zh.,* vol. 53, no. 33, 1914, pp. 378–379.

32. Ibid., p. 378.

33. "Vzdorozhanie medikamentov," *F. Zh.* , vol. 53, no. 33, 1914, p. 379; Yaroslavl' pharmacy owners contributed 500 rubles, "Pozhertvovaniia aptekarei," ibid., p. 380; Kiev pharmacy owners collected 434 rubles and 50 kopeks to help the city duma executive council get supplies for sick and wounded troops, "Soderzhateli i upravliaiushchie aptekami," ibid., p. 380; Taganrog pharmacy owners levied 2 kopeks from each prescription for war time use; the immediate sum totaled 200 rubles. "Vladel'tsy taganrogskikh aptek," *loc. cit.*

34. "Zagotovka medikamentov," *F. Zh.,* vol. 53, no. 35, 1914, p. 398. The Sanitary Commission met with the U. S. Department of Labor.

35. I. I. Diatroptov, of the medical union, requested the Vladivostok sanitary commission to purchase medicine from Japan; the mission left before the request arrived. "Medikamenty iz Iaponii," *F. Zh.,* vol. 53, no. 35, 1914, p. 398.

36. The St. Petersburg city duma elected a commission and attempted to send chief Dr. G. P. Oleinikov to Sweden but the Swedish envoy rejected the project on the grounds that the duma had no authority. Oleinikov then refused to go. "Vzdorozhanie medikamentov," *F. Zh.,* vol. 53, no. 33, 1914, p. 379.

37. "Iaponskii sal'varsan," *F. Zh.,* vol. 55, no. 11, 1916, p. 96.

38. Sarkisov, "Kratkii obzor," *F. Zh.,* vol. 55, no. 7, 1916, p. 60. He noted that "Among countries importing valuable products into Russia Japan quickly occupied an important place."

39. "Iaponskii sal'varsan," p. 96.

40. "Vneshniaia torgovlia cherez Vladivostok v 1915 g.," *F. Zh.,* vol. 55, no. 22, 1916, pp. 194–195. Specifically mentioned at this time were quinine, soda, and iodide soda.

41. Society for Assistance of the Growth of the Chemical Industry to the Administration of the Chief Medical Inspector, 27 September 1917, TsGIA, f. 1298, op. 1, d. 2060, l. 189 and 189 ob.

42. Sarkisov, "Kratkii obzor," p. 60.

43. Ferrein to the Department of Trade, Ministry of Trade and Industry, TsGIA, f. 1298, op. 1, d. 2060, l. 150.

44. This is contradicted by Mann and Plummer who relate that the English Pharmaceutical industry was able to produce salicylic acid only in laboratory quantities and in turn, of poor quality. *The Aspirin Wars*, p. 67.

45. Sarkisov, "Kratkii obzor," p. 60. Heretofore the substances had been called salvarsan and neosalvarsan and were produced only in Germany.

46. TsGIA, f. 1298, op. 1, d. 2060, l. 178.

47. TsGIA, f. 1298, op. 1, d. 2060, l. 160.

48. TsGIA, f. 1298, op. 1, d. 2060, l. 169. See also advertisements for Roche products such as that following *F. Zh.*, vol. 54, no. 42, 1915 (no pagination for ads).

49. TsGIA, f. 1298, op. 1, d. 2060 is replete with examples. The following few suffice:

In September 1915 the Ferrein firm asked the Ministry of Foreign affairs for help in prying loose pharmaceutical wares that were being held in Norway and Sweden. On May 7, 1916, the firm petitioned the Chief Medical Inspector to help in procuring medicaments from France, Holland, and England. (TsGIA, 1298, op. 1, d. 2060, ll. 22, 105, 106.) About two weeks later on May 24 the Ferrein firm sent a new list of pharmaceutical wares that it needed from England in order to supply pharmacies and clinics in Russia. On June 10 the Society for the Development of Chemical Industry and Trade asked the Chief Medical Inspector for assistance in getting ether oil and other medicaments that the Ferrein firm had ordered; the society further announced that it was sending a list of the necessary medicaments to the Russian-English Committee in London. (TsGIA, f. 1298, op. 1, d. 2060, ll. 105, 111.) In early June 1916, the Department for Foreign Trade in the Ministry of Trade and Industry noted that after the closure of the port of Arkhangel'sk, arsenic, which the Ferrein firm had ordered from New York, had been detoured to Narvik in Norway and was located with the French consul, S. Hammer. (TsGIA, f. 1298, op. 1, d. 2060, ll. 117-118.) In May, 1916, Shtol' and Shmidt in Petrograd requested assistance from the Chief Medical Inspector for getting mercury from the English firm Stedman, Crowther and Co,. "as this substance was particularly needed for pharmaceutical preparations and was lacking in the free market." (TsGIA, f. 1298, op. 1, d. 2060, l. 108.) In the same month, the Society for Assistance to Developing the Chemical Industry and Trade notified the Chief Medical Inspector that it needed amidopirin sent from the Swiss firm Bubeck and Dolder transferred from Basle to Arkhangel'sk for the needs of the War Ministry. (TsGIA, f. 1298, op. 1, d. 2060, l. 104.)

50. Sarkisov, "Kratkii obzor, p. 60.

51. When on August 12, 1914, the Medical Council drew up a list of the most crucial medicaments and disinfectants, it noted that thirty-nine of these were prepared in Russia and forty-eight were imported. "Zasedanie Meditsinskago Soveta," *F. Zh.*, vol. 53, no. 35, 1914, pp. 397-398. Further, according to a 1915 analysis, before the war some twenty Russian pharmaceutical factories produced wares

amounting to about 7 million rubles; Russia imported only 3 million rubles' worth of pharmaceutical wares. "Voina i sostoianie russkoi promyshlennosti," *F. Zh.*, vol. 54, no. 35, 1915, p. 341. Obviously, this figure excluded small enterprises described in chapter 8 on the pharmaceutical industry.

52. John F. Hutchinson, *Politics and Public Health in Revolutionary Russia, 1890–1918* (Baltimore: The Johns Hopkins University Press, 1990), p. 120.

53. "Zabota o lekarstvakh," *F. Zh.*, vol. 53, no. 35, 1914, p. 398. Also *Ustroistvo gorodskogo khimiko-farmatsevticheskago zavoda. Doklad komissii akademika N. S. Kurnakova soveshchaniiu o zagotovlenii gorodom lekarstve* (Petrograd, 1916), p. 49 [hereafter cited *Ustroistvo*].

54. "Zhurnal pervago zasedaniia Mezhduvedomstvennago Komiteta po delam farmatsevticheskoi promyshlennosti," TsGIA, f. 1298, op. 1, d. 2066a, l. 2.

Representatives from the Ministry of Internal Affairs included Privy Councillor Professor S. A. Przhibytek, Dr. P. N. Bulatov (for the Administration of the Chief Medical Inspector), Dr. N. Ia. Shmidt, and P. S. Kukuranov of the Chief Administration of the Affairs of the Local Economy. The representative from the Ministry of Trade and Industry was V. G. Varzar; those from the Ministry of Ways and Communications were M. G. fon-Byuting, D. M. Uspenskii, State Councillor A. A. Prokof'ev; M. G Tartakovskii represented the Chief Administration of Agriculture and Land Use. The representative from the Ministry of Foreign Affairs was Privy Councillor P. L. Vaksel; from the War Ministry, Privy Councillor P. M. Kravz-Tarnavskii; from the Naval Ministry, G. A. Makarov. Social organizations were represented by V. K. fon Anrep for the Russian Red Cross and Dr. P. N. Diatroptov from the All-Russian Zemstvo Union. Representatives from the pharmaceutical industry included V. I. Pokhitonov and F. G. Ferrein, of the Society for Assisting the Development of the Chemical Industry and Trade. The Interdepartmental Committee proposed a number of measures to alleviate the *lekarstvennyi golod*: collection of wild medicinal plants, cultivation of medicinal plants, search for minerals necessary in pharmaceutical production, lowering the tariff on necessary raw materials and raising the tariff to protect Russian-made medicaments; very important, were requests to eliminate "the strictures" of slow government approval for factory-produced medicaments and allow representatives from the pharmaceutical industry to sit in the Medical Council. "Doklad F. A. Ferreina," TsGIA, f. 1298, op. 1, d. 2066a, ll. 102–105 ob.

55. *Ustroistvo,* p. 50.

56. Natradze, *Ocherk,* p. 81.

57. *Ustroistvo,* pp. 51–52.

58. "Kul'tura lekarstvennykh rastenii," *F. Zh.*, vol. 54, no. 42, 1915, p. 416.

59. "Russkii iod," *F. Zh.*, vol. 55, no. 5, 1916, p. 44.

60. TsGIA, f. 1298, op. 1, d. 2066a, ll. 37–38, 40, 123–132 ob.

61. TsGIA, f. 1298, op. 1, d. 2066a, ll. 28–29, 79.

62. "Doklad F. A. Ferreina Mezhduvedomstvennomu Komitetu 'O Nuzhdakh farmatsevticheskoi promyshlennosti,' 10 aprelia 1915 goda," TsGIA, f. 1298, op. 1, d. 2066a, ll. 102–105 ob; ibid. l. 72.

63. "Doklad F. A. Ferreina, Mezhduvedomstvennomu Komitetu 'O Nuzhdakh farmatsevticheskoi promyshlennosti,' 10 aprelia 1915 goda," pp. 101-105, p. 102: TsGIA, f. 1298, op. 1, d. 2066a, ll. 102; 102-105 ob.

Unfortunately neither F. G. nor F. A. Ferrein's names and patronymics were recorded. If the patronymic began with "A," F. A. Ferrein could have been the son of Vladimir Karlovich's son Alexander. Alexander Karlovich had been born in 1864. He had studied in Berlin, received a Master of pharmacy degree and managed the Staraia Nikolskaia pharmacy (Tkeshelashvili, *Materialy dlya istorii farmatsii v Rossii*, p. 79) until his untimely death in 1906. (*Opyt istoricheskago ocherka vozniknoveniia i razvitiia vsego aptekarskago dela v Rossii, a v chastnosti Staroi Nikol'skoi apteki prinadlezhashchei nyne Tovarishchestvu "V. K. Ferrein"* [Moscow, 1911], p. 6.) Alexander Vladimirovich had children. "Pamiati Aleksandra Vladimirovicha Ferreina," *Farmatsevt*, vol. 14, no. 40, 1960, pp. 1151-1152, and "Nekrologi. Pokhorony A. V. Ferreina," *F. T.*, vol. 1, no. 18, 1907, p. 249. If he had had a son, born in 1887 when Alexander was 23, that son would have been 28 at the time of the Interdepartmental Committee and in his early thirties when pharmacies and factories were nationalized.

A second possibility is that F. A. was the son of Andrei Karlovich Ferrein, the older brother of Vladimir Karlovich. Neither F. G. nor F. A. Ferrein could have been the son of Karl Avgustovich Ferrein, owner of the "Novaia Polianka" pharmacy in *Serpukhovskaia ploshchad'*, because the patronymic was wrong. (The Novaia Polianka pharmacy was part of the Ferrein empire; it was mentioned in the brochure about the Ferrein Stock Association. *Opyt istoricheskago ocherka . . . Tovarishchestvu "V. K. Ferrein,"* p. 20. The pharmacy was cited as still under the ownership of Dvor ("The House of") K. A. Ferrein during the War. However, it was managed by Karl Avgustovich Lapin. *Rossiikii Meditsinskii Spisok* [Petrograd, 1916], p. 89.)

If the patronymic began with "G," F. G. Ferrein might have been the son of Genrikh Avgustovich Ferrein. Genrikh was born in 1843 in Arnfel'd, Prussia. He received his education in the third Moscow *gimnaziia*, then became an apprentice in the Staraia Nikol'skaia pharmacy of Karl Ivanovich, father of Vladimir Karlovich. He probably was a close relative of V. K. Ferrein. In any case, Genrikh took his Provizor examination at Moscow University and received his Master of Pharmacy degree there in 1872. From 1874 to 1897 he owned the Krasnovorotskaia pharmacy. However, he sold the pharmacy in 1897, continuing to live in Moscow. (Tkeshelashvili, *Materialy dlya istorii farmatsii v Rossii*, p. 79.) In the 1916 Medical Register the Krasnovorotskaia pharmacy was listed under the ownership of A. Kh. Braunshtein and managed by Provizor Braunshtein. *Rossiiskii Meditsinkii Spisok*, p. 88. By 1916 the main Ferrein pharmacy of Staraia Nikol'skaia, still flourishing with over two hundred employees, was under the management of an outsider, Robert Gerassimovovich Peter. *Loc. cit.*

64. Zhurnal No. 19 Plenarnogo Zasedaniia "Farmatsentra, 3 Dekabria 1918 g.," Tsentral'nyi Gosudarstvennyi Arkhiv RSFSR, Moscow [hereafter cited TsGA RSFSR], f. 482, op. 5, d. 13, l. 159.

Interestingly, in his April 10, 1915, report, F. A. Ferrein approvingly cited Aleksan. Semen. Ginzberg (mistakenly spelled Ginzburg)'s work on pharmaceutical education. Following the Bolshevik Revolution in October 1917, Ginzberg would become the head of the Pharmacy Institute in Petrograd-Leningrad, the former Women's Medical Institute.

65. For example, F. Ferrein, "Preparaty, izgotovlenie kotorykh mozhet byt' osushchestvleno vposledstviia," *Vestnik farmatsii,* nos. 8-9, 1924, p. 136, and F. A. Ferrein, "Farmatsevticheskaia promyshlennost': Tamozhnyi tarif 1927 goda," *Khimiko-farmatsevticheskii zhurnal,* vol. 5, no. 4, 1927, pp. 6-7, and F. Ferrein, "35-letie nauchnoi deiatel'nosti akademika V. N. Ignat'eva," ibid., no. 5.

66. Re: Chichibabin, see speech of Prince G. E. Lvov, cited in *F. Zh.*, vol. 55, no. 24, p. 213.

67. Article in *Kommersant,* cited in *F. Zh.*, vol. 55, no. 5, 1916, p. 44.

68. Anon., "Moskovskaia farmakopeinyia Soveshchaniia," *F. Zh.*, vol. 55, no. 23, 1916, p. 206.

69. Tat'iana Biriukova has done extensive research on the Ferrein family and is personally acquainted with one of the Ferrein descendents who currently resides in Germany. Conversation with Biriukova, June 1993.

A portion of her research on Ferrein is contained in "K devushke s tiul'panami," *Byloe,* vol. 1, no. 2, February, 1993, p. 15.

70. "Farmatsevticheskii komitet," *Zh. F.*, vol. 2, no. 2, 1915, p. 9.

71. See the previous chapter for details.

72. "Para litsemerov," *Zh. F.*, vol. 2, no. 3, 1915, pp. 3-4. Pharmacies stressed that these were not surrogates.

73. TsGIA, f. 1298, op. 1, d. 2062, ll. 1, 3; also f. 1298, op. 1, d. 2095, l. 1.

74. TsGIA, f. 1298, op. 1, d. 2095, l. 1-2.

75. TsGIA, f. 1298, op. 1, d. 2095, l. 15.

76. TsGIA, f. 1298, op. 1, d. 2095, l. 2 and 2 ob.

77. The Medical Council also published the recipes for all approved nostrums. For example, "Offitsialnyia izvestiia iz zhurnalov Meditsinskago Soveta," *F. Zh.*, vol. 55, no. 2, 1916, p. 16.

78. TsGIA, f. 1298, op. 1, d. 2095, l. 39. The remedy included Balsam Copaivae, *salol,* ether oil, Juniper oil, nitric acid.

79. TsGIA, f. 1298, op. 1, d. 2095, l. 71.

80. TsGIA, f. 1298, op. 1, d. 2095, l. 72.

81. TsGIA, f. 1298, op. 1, d. 2095, l. 42. The recipes of rejected remedies were not listed.

82. TsGIA, f. 1298, op. 1, d. 2095, l. 70. It also included oil of Santali, *salol,* and juniper oil.

83. TsGIA, f. 1298, op. 1, d. 2095, l. 111. The stationery still bore the stamp of the old MVD.

84. TsGIA, f. 1298, op. 1, d. 2095, l. 69. His remedy, sold in capsules, was similar to the foregoing.

85. TsGIA, f. 1298, op. 1, d. 2095, l. 68. The letterhead of the Ministry of

Internal Affairs Chancellery indicated the government continued to use old stationery after the February Revolution. Some letterheads included the term "Provisional Government"; this particular letter, as many others, did not.

86. TsGIA, f. 1298, op. 1, d. 2095, l. 59.

87. TsGIA, f. 1298, op. 1, d. 2095, l. 96.

88. TsGIA, f. 1298, op. 1, d. 2095, l. 106. The remedy was submitted May 1, 1917, and rejected May 10, 1917.

89. TsGIA, f. 1298, op. 1, d. 2095, l. 4.

90. TsGIA, f. 1298, op. 1, d. 2095, l. 6.

91. TsGIA, f. 1298, op. 1, d. 2095, l. 12–submitted in September 1916 and approved January 1917.

92. TsGIA, f. 1298, op. 1, d. 2095, l. 53. This substance was submitted for approval in mid-December 1916 and approved in early March 1917.

93. TsGIA, f. 1298, op. 1, d. 2095, l. 61.

94. TsGIA, f. 1298, op. 1, d. 2095, l. 107.

95. TsGIA, f. 1298, op. 1, d. 2095, l. 95.

96. TsGIA, f. 1298, op. 1, d. 2095, l. 51. The reducing tablets were named "Reduktsionnaia tabletka dlia lecheniia za porov i ozhireniia."

97. Editorial, "O lekarstvennom golode," *F. Zh.*, vol. 53, no. 36, 1914, p. 403.

98. *Ustroistvo*, p. 51. The exhibition was entitled "Guaranteeing the Independence of Russia from Foreigners in the Area of Practical Medicine."

99. Natradze, *Ocherk*, p. 80.

100. Advertisement for the "Preparaty Kievskago bakteriologicheskago instituta," *Zh. F.*, vol. 2, no. 1, 1915.

101. Sarkisov, "Kratkii obzor," *F. Zh.*, vol. 55, no. 6, 1916, p. 49.

102. V. Sadikov, "Voina i sostoianie," *F. Zh.*, vol. 54, no. 35, 1915, p. 341.

103. Sarkisov, "Kratkii obzor," *F. Zh.*, vol. 55, no. 6, 1916, p. 50.

104. Sarkisov, "Kratkii obzor," *F. Zh.*, vol. 55, no. 7, 1916, p. 60.

105. *Ustroistvo*, pp. 90, 104.

106. "Nesostoiavsheesiia zasedanie," *F. Zh.*, vol. 54, no. 39, 1915, p. 388.

107. Sadikov, "Voina i sostoianie," p. 342.

108. *Ustroistvo*, p. 93.

109. "Vystavka otechestvennoi promyshlennosti," *F. Zh.*, vol. 55, no. 15, 1916, p. 132.

110. "Novye Moskovskie Torgovye Doma," *F. Zh.*, vol. 54, no. 44, 1915, p. 434. The wife of a Provizor from Moscow University, P. M. Khopsaeva, and seven unnamed guarantors also established an association, or *tovarishchestvo*, to produce cinematographic film with capital of 35,000 rubles. *Loc. cit.*

111. "Urotropinnovyi zavod," *F. Zh.*, vol. 55, no. 16, 1916, p. 139.

The factory was under the supervision of the manager of the provincial excise department, F. E. Puzovskii; the builder of the factory was senior inspector of the excise administration, engineer N. A. Nemirovskii.

As stated above a *pud* equals about 36 pounds.

112. Mikhailo Gorgievich Ena, "Khimiko-farmatsevticheskaia promyshlen-

nost'," *Razvitie khimicheskoi tekhnologii na Ukraine,* vol. 2, eds., O. V. Avilov et al. (Kiev, 1976), pp. 264–265.

113. "Khronika: Zavod lekarstvennykh veshchestv," *F. Zh.*, vol. 55, no. 23, 1916, p. 206.

114. Sarkisov, "Kratkii obzor," *F. Zh.*, vol. 55, no. 7, 1916, p. 60.

115. "K delam Pabiianitskago Aktsionernago Obshchestva khimicheskoi promyshlennosti," *F. Zh.*, vol. 55, no. 28, 1916, p. 255.

116. TsGIA, f. 1298, op. 1, d. 2066, l. 28.

117. See note 54, above.

118. "Zhurnal zasedaniia nauchnoi sektsii pri aptechnoi komissii 29-go noiabria 1918 goda," TsGA RSFSR, f. 482, op. 5, d. 16, l. 46, and "Zhurnal . . . 20-go dekabria 1918 goda," ibid., ll. 47, 47 ob.

119. Natradze, *Ocherk*, p. 75.

120. M. I. Sosaar, "Po ankete 'chto sdelano nashei promyshlennost'iu za vremia voiny,'" *F. Zh.*, vol. 55, no. 29, 1916, p. 264.

121. TsGA RSFSR, f. 482, op. 5, d. 13, l. 174. Zhurnal no. 22, "Plenarnogo zasedaniia 'Farmatsentra,' 16/XII/18 g." F. A. Ferrein and O. G. Gabrilovich also were at this meeting, devoted to nationalizing wholesale firms trading in pharmaceutical supplies.

122. *Ustroistvo*, p. 51; TsGIA, f. 1298, op. 1, d. 2066, l. 28.

123. *Ustroistvo*, pp. 51–52.

124. Ena, "Khimiko-farmatsevticheskaia promyshlennost'," *Razvitie khimicheskoi tekhnologii na Ukraine*, p. 265.

125. *Ustroivstvo*, pp. 51–52.

126. "Farmatsevticheskie preparaty," *F. Zh.*, vol. 55, no. 2, 1916, p. 20.

127. Natradze,*Ocherk*, pp. 73–76.

128. D. D., "Rossiiskoe Farmatsevticheskoe Obshchestvo," *Zh. F.*, vol. 2, no. 3 (12), 1915, p. 3.

129. "Aptechnoe delo v Vologskom zemstve," *Zh. F.*, vol. 1, nos. 6–7, 1914, p. 12. During the war Vologda and a few other provinces did discuss establishing district warehouses.

130. *Ustroistvo* p. 13. The Petrograd Committee particularly singled out the Tver and Tomsk zemstvo warehouses for praise. The Tver zemstvo hospital had taken advantage of 6 to 8 percent fluctuation in market prices and realized turnover amounting to half a million rubles between 1912 and 1914. The Tomsk zemstvo warehouse was well-run.

131. "Zhurnal Mezhduvedomstvennago Komiteta po delam farmatsevticheskoi promyshlennosti," TsGIA, f. 1298, op. 1, d. 2066, l. 10: Dr. P. N. Diatroptov, representative from the All Zemstvo Union, advocated increasing government funds to Zemgor; l. 11: V. K. fon Anrep, representative from the Russian Red Cross, rejected requistioning; l. 12: V. G. Varzar, representative from the Ministry of Trade and Industry, stated that it was necessary either to reject or accept requisitioning and seconded giving government funds to zemstvos to acquire medicine; l. 13: M. G. fon Biuting, representative from the Ministry of Ways and Communi-

cations, reminded his colleagues that the Union of Zemstvos and Cities was only temporary.

132. "Zakupka medikamentov zagranitsei," *F. Zh.*, vol. 55, no. 41, 1916, p. 401.

133. "Udeshevlenie tovarov," *F. Zh.*, vol. 55, no. 35, 1916, p. 329.

134. "Torgovlia s Amerikoi," *F. Zh.*, vol. 55, no. 39, 1916, p. 376.

135. Natradze, *Ocherk*, p. 73.

136. *Ustroistvo*, p. 52.

137. Natradze, *Ocherk*, p. 73.

138. "Voina i sostoianie," p. 342.

139. V. D. Abramov, "Eksport leksyr'ia," *Khimiko-farmatsevticheskii zhurnal*, nos. 3–4 (6–7) 1924, pp. 2–3.

140. Natradze, *Ocherk razvitiia* (1967), p. 77.

141. R. Vaita, "Nauchnyi otdel," *F. Zh.*, vol. 55, no. 20, 1916, p. 169.

142. Natradze, *Ocherk*, p. 75.

143. TsGIA, f. 1298, op. 1, d. 2066, ll. 52–53.

144. *Ustroistvo*, p. 50.

145. TsGIA, f. 1298, op. 1, d. 2066, l. 28.

146. *Ustroistvo*, pp. 50–51.

147. Natradze, *Ocherk*, pp. 81–82. The firms were V. I. Vize, F. Gappikh, and the Association of the Northern Agricultural Society in Petrograd; V. Lisitsyn, Immer and Son, Vlasov and Laslov in Moscow; K. G. Vagner in Riga; Count F. A. Uvarov in the village of Perech'e in Moscow province; I. G. Karlson in Voronezh; L. A. Galakhov in Riazan province ; G. Bogdanov and A. Budakov in Khar'kov.

148. Natradze, ibid., pp. 73, 82.

149. "Khronika," *F. Zh.*, vol. 55, no. 2, 1916, p. 18.

150. Natradze, *Ocherk*, p. 84.

151. Sadikov, "Voina i sostoianie russkoi promyshlennosti," *F. Zh.*, vol. 54, no. 35, 1915, p. 342.

152. "Kul'tura lekarstvennykh rastenii v Krymu," *F. Zh.*, vol. 54, no. 42, 1915, p. 416.

153. Sadikov, "Voina i sostoianie," p. 342.

154. "Kul'tirovanie lekarstven. rastenii v Sibiri," *F. Zh.*, vol. 54, no. 39, 1915, p. 388. The Migration Station pharmacy realized 60,480 rubles from the mint oil, which completely satisfied the requirements of the pharmacopoeia.

155. Natradze, *Ocherk*, p. 81.

156. Sadikov, "Voina i sostoianie," pp. 341–342.

157. *Ustroistvo*, p. 52.

158. Sadikov, "Voina i sostoianie," p. 342.

159. "Kul'tura lekarstvennykh rastenii na Kavkaze," *F. Zh.*, vol. 55, no. 6, 1916, pp. 54–55.

160. E. Svirlovskii, "Osnovaniia sbora i sushki lekarstvennykh rastenii," *F. Zh.*, vol. 55, no. 28, 1916, pp. 253–354.

161. "Nemnozhno khimii," *F. Zh.*, vol. 55, no. 40, pp. 383–384 and "Khronika," ibid., no. 41, p. 401.

162. "Sbor lekarstvennykh rastenii," *F. Zh.*, vol. 55, no. 36, 1916, p. 340.

163. TsGIA, f. 1298, op. 1, d. 2066, l. 29.

164. Natradze, *Ocherk*, p. 84.

165. "Lekarstvennyia travy na Iuge," *F. Zh.*, vol. 55, no. 36, 1916, p. 340.

166. "Razvedenie lekarstvennykh trav," *F. Zh.*, vol. 55, no. 32, 1916, p. 297.

167. "Kursy instruktorov," *F. Zh.*, vol. 55, no. 32, 1916, pp. 297–298.

168. "Snabzhenie lekarstvennymi rasteniiami," *F. Zh.*, vol. 55, no. 19, 1916, p. 163. The applicants were instructed to show up with their birth certificates, education and military papers.

169. "K rabotam po lekarstvennym rasteniiam," *F. Zh.*, vol. 55, no. 1, 1916, p. 10.

170. "Snabzhenie lekarstvennymi rasteniiami," *F. Zh.*, vol. 55, no. 19, 1916, p. 163.

171. "Narodnoe zdravie," *F. Zh.*, vol. 55, no. 28, 1916, p. 255.

172. "Plakany o valeriane," *F. Zh.*, vol. 55, no. 32, 1916, p. 297.

173. Some sixty years later, and without citations, Soviet historian Natradze claimed that one of the first items successfully produced was salicylic acid. According to Natradze, in Moscow this item was produced in the "factories" of the Zemtvo Union, Sogor, the Red Cross, the "workshops" of the Medical Military Department, the joint-stock association, "ARS." In Petrograd the laboratory of the city duma was occupied with producing salicylic acid; in Kazan, this was done by the phenolo-salicylic factory of the Military Industrial Committee. In Kiev, Kazan, Khar'kov, Tiflis, and "other cities," according to Natradze, small enterprises were established and began to produce salicylic acids such as aspirin, methylene ether, salicylic natron (Natradze, *Ocherk*, p. 74) and V. P. Panteleev, member of the Russian Physico-Chemical Society together with V. I. Brashninym derived lysol and salicylic acid from technical carbolic acid in the chemical laboratories of the Moscow Industrial School. (Natradze, ibid., pp. 78–79) Natradze further asserted that small amounts of certain pharmaceuticals were produced, such as *salol* in the factory "Zemgor," protargol in the B. Merezhkovskii factory in St. Petersburg, phenacetin in the Ol'ginskii factory of P. Bekkel in Moscow. The factory of I. Balashev in the Crimea produced 33 t[ons] of bromine and 100–300 t[ons] of bromide soda per year. Veronal was produced in two factories by a method worked out by Academician A. E. Favorskii. From the seeds of *durmana* N. G. Patsukov began to obtain "*giostsiamine*." (Natradze, ibid., p. 74) In 1915, according to Natradze, Professors A. E. Chichibabin, V. M. Rodionov, and N. G. Patsukov began to make morphine and codeine in the laboratories of the Moscow higher technical School. (Natradze, ibid., p. 78) The factory "ARS" in 1917 began to produce morphine, dionin, and heroin (Natradze, ibid., p. 74). Natradze further claimed that at the beginning of the war the Physical-Chemical Society in the University of St. Vladimir in Kiev, under the direction of Professor S. N. Reformatsii, established laboratories in educational institutions that produced significant quantities of novocaine, aspirin, antifebrin, *salol*, benzolnaftol, camphor spirits, tiokol, antipyrine, codeine, caffeine salts, codein-benzoin soda, benzoinacid, mercury, salipirin, pira-

midon, chlorethyl, sublimate, and other medicines (Natradze, ibid., pp. 75-76). Natradze documented few of his claims. However, some of his information on wartime pharmaceutical production tally with information in the reports of the 1915 Interdepartmental Government Committee and the Petrograd City Committee of 1915-1916.

174. "Proizvodstvo russkikh termometrov," *F. Zh.*, vol. 54, no. 40, 1915, p. 397.

175. "O resul'tatakh laboratornago izgotovleniia nekotorykh khimiko-farmatsevticheskikh preparatov," *F. Zh.*, vol. 55, no. 36, 1916, p. 338.

176. "Est' i net," *F. Zh.*, vol. 55, no. 19, 1916, p. 163.

177. Sadikov, "Voina i sostoianie," *F. Zh.*, vol. 54, no. 35, 1915, p. 342. Russia also produced only 465 *puds* of organic dyes before the war, importing 94,000 *puds* of dyes and 40,000 *puds* of indigo. *Loc. cit.*

178. "Khimicheskaia promyshlennost'," *Kommersant*, reprinted in *F. Zh.*, vol. 55, no. 3, 1916, p. 30.

179. Sarkisov, "Kratkii obzor," p. 60.

180. "K postroike v Kazani gorodskogo fenol'no-salitsilovago zavoda," *F. Zh.*, vol. 55, no. 2, 1916, p. 20.

181. "Vystavka otechestvennoi promyshlennosti," *F. Zh.*, vol. 55, no. 15, 1916, p. 132.

182. "Khimicheskaia promyshlennost'," *Kommersant*, reprinted *F. Zh.*, vol. 55, no. 3, 1916, p. 30.

183. "Vystavka," *F. Zh.*, p. 132.

184. M. I. Sosaar, "Po ankete 'chto sdelano nashei promyshlennost'iu za vremia voiny,'" *F. Zh.*, vol. 55, no. 29, 1916, pp. 263-264.

185. "Khimicheskaia promyshlennost'," first published in *Kommersant*, reprinted in *F. Zh*, vol. 55, no. 3, 1916, p. 30.

It ought to be noted that similar developments occurred in the United States during the war as a result of America's effort to emancipate her pharmaceutical industry from dependency on Germany. Pharmaceutical giants like Parke, Davis and Company awed the Russians. TsGIA, f. 1298, op. 1, d. 2066, l. 64. Nevertheless, the United States was forced to hastily produce chemicals during World War I. At the outbreak of the war. America stepped up the mining of pyrites and thus increased her production of sulphuric acid. Stripping plants at city gas works increased production of benzol and toluol, both of which had been minimal before the war. Grinnell Jones, "War's Effect on Chemical Industries," *The Pharmaceutical Era*, October 1918, pp. 273-274.

186. "Razvedenie lekarstvennykh trav," *F. Zh.*, vol. 55, no. 15, 1916, p. 132.

187. "Sel'sko-khoziaistvennaia vystavka," *F. Zh.*, vol. 55, no. 36, 1916, p. 340.

188. Sarkisov, "Kratkii obzor," *F. Zh.*, vol. 55, no. 7, 1916, p. 59.

189. "Opytnaia stanstiia po dobyvaniiu ioda," *F. Zh.*, vol. 54, no. 44, 1915, p. 434; also Sadikov, "Voina i sostoianie russkoi promyshlennosti," *F. Zh.*, ibid., no 35, p. 341.

190. "Opytnaia stanstiia," p. 434.

191. N. D. Averkiev, "O dobyche ioda v USSR iz vodoroslei Chernogo moria

'Krasnaia fillofora,'" *Khimiko-farmatsevticheskii zhurnal,* vol. 6, no. 8 (56), 1928, p. 10.

192. "O dobychanii ioda na Murmane," *F. Zh.*, vol. 55, no. 28, 1916, pp. 251–252.

Also, *Ustroistvo,* pp. 51–52 and Natradze, *Ocherk,* p. 78. According to Natradze, iodine also was produced in Vladivostok.

For the Caspian area and Sea of Okhotsk, see Sadikov, "Voina i sostoianie," p. 342.

According to another source, at the end of 1916, preliminary figures showed production in Tomsk of 800 *puds* of iodine and 60,000 *puds* of potassium salts. "K razvitiiu otechestvennago proizvodstva lekarstvennykh materialov," *F. Zh.*, vol. 55, no. 41, 1916, pp. 401–402.

193. Natradze, *Ocherk razvitiia* (1967), p. 77.

194. Sarkisov, "Kratkii obzor," *F. Zh.*, vol. 55, no. 7, 1916, p. 59.

195. "K razvitiiu otechestvennogo proizvodstva lekarstvennykh materialov," *F. Zh*, vol. 55, no. 41, 1916, pp. 401–402.

196. "V lekarstevnn. organizatsii," *F. Zh.*, vol. 55, no. 39, 1916, pp. 375–376.

197. "Russkii atropin," *F. Zh.*, vol. 55, no. 37, 1916, p. 352. The leaves had been collected by the Central Caucasus Organization for the Collection, Cultivation, and Preparation of Medicinal Plants.

198. Ferrein, "Doklad mezhduvedomstvennomu Komitetu" 10 Aprelia 1915, TsGIA, f. 1298, op. 1, d. 2066, ll. 102ob and 103. The output of lanolin and cotton were increased as well.

199. Sadikov, "Voina i Sostoianie," pp. 341–342.

200. Sosaar, "Po ankete," p. 264.

201. *Ustroistvo*, p. 52.

202. *Ustroistvo*, pp. 18–19. Among the other needed inorganic preparations were hydrogen peroxide, and preparations of iodine, bromine, and mercury and as much of the raw materials of these substances that could be acquired. Among other organic prepartions needed were boric acid, chloral hydrate, antifebrin, veronal, theobromine, atropin, and novocaine.

203. The town councillors were N. N. Afanas'ev and A. E. Bari; V S Krivenko was a member of the Administrative Committee of the Red Cross; S. A. Gnozdev represented the St. Petersburg zemstvo executive council.

204. M. Ia. Breitman, A. D. Zotov, A. A. Kad'yan, N. M. Ivanov; M. A. Ignat'ev, Senior Doctor in the City Slaughterhouse; A. A. Nechaev, Chairman of the soviet of Chief Doctors; Chief Doctor N. A. Sokalskii; S. V. Posadskii, and A. Iu. Zuev, Chief Sanitary Inspector of the Navy. *Ustroistvo*, p. 15.

205. A. A. Bansheidt, Laborant in the Women's Medical Institute; N. E. Sum, Laborant in the Central Chemical Laboratory of the Ministry of Finance; Chief Laborant of the Pharmacy Society E. I. Svirlovskii; A. E. Efimov, Chairman of the Society of Military and Naval Pharmacists, V. M. Tol'stopiatov, Laborant at St Petersburg University. *Ustroistvo*, p. 15.

206. L. F. Il'in, N. D. Zelinskii, A. E. Makovetskii, A. Eporai-Koshits, Academi-

cian Professor S. A. Przhibytek, N. A. Prilezhaev; V. E. Tishchenko, A. E. Favorskii, P. I. Shestakov, L. A. Chugaev, and Director of the Mining Institute Professor I. F. Shreder. *Ustroistvo*, p. 15.

207. Engineer-Technologist P. G. Golovkov.

208. Chairman of the Hospital Commission F. M. Knipovich; V. P. Kuzmichev, Chairman of the Economic Committee of the Hospital Commission; V. M. Nalimov and N. M. Nizhegorodtsev, Members of the Hospital Commission, and Member of the Hospital Commission Georgii Sazonov. *Ustroistvo.*, p. 15.

209. *Ustroistvo*, p. 15. Three *deloproizvoditeli*, or clerks, completed the group.

210. It was estimated that remodeling the water treatment plant would cost about 240,000 rubles; the plant and warehouse was to be headed by a council, or *sovet*, of six. *Ustroistvo*, p. 25.

211. Natradze, *Ocherk*, p. 77.

212. Sarkisov, "Kratkii obzor," p. 49.

213. "V Sovete ministrov," *F. Zh.*, vol. 55, no. 11, p. 97.

214. "Zavod farm. preparatov," *F. Zh.*, vol. 55, no. 15, 1916, p. 131.

215. Sarkisov, 'Kratkii obzor," p. 50.

216. "Zemstvo i khimicheskie zavody," *F. Zh.*, vol. 55, no. 32, 1916, p. 297. This article claimed there were still shortages of wood alcohol products such as formalin.

217. "Russkii iod," *F. Zh.*, vol. 55, no. 32, 1916, p. 296.

218. "Otkrytie v krae zavoda dlia izgotovleniia aspirina," *F. Zh.*, vol. 55, no. 32, 1916, p. 296.

219. Sarkisov, "Kratkii obzor," p. 50.

220. "Gore boleiushchikh," *F. Zh.*, vol. 54, no. 40, 1915, pp. 397-398.

221. "Khimicheskaia promyshlennost'," *Kommersant*, republished in *F. Zh.*, vol. 55, no. 3, 1916, p. 30.

222. "Na farmatsevticheskom rynke," *F. Zh.*, vol. 54, no. 37, 1915, pp. 367-368. Phenacetin rose from 3 rubles 50 kopeks a kilo to 85 rubles; *salol*, which normally cost 3 rubles per kilo, cost 50 rubles. Mercury, formerly 90-95 rubles for 2 *puds*, 4 and 5/8 *funt* was now 300-400 rubles.

However, iodine, formerly 40 rubles per kilo, had fallen to 30-32 rubles.

223. "Khronika," *F. Zh.*, vol. 54, no. 39, 1915, p. 388.

224. Sarkisov, "Kratkii ocherk," *F. Zh.*, vol. 55, no. 7, 1916, pp. 60-61.

225. "Dokhodnost' aktsionernykh khimicheskikh predpriatii v 1913 i 1915 gg.," *F. Zh.*, vol. 55, no. 27, 1916, p. 255.

226. Anon., "Bol'nye i taksa," *F. Zh.*, vol. 55, no. 11, 1916, pp. 96-97.

227. "Nemnogo khimii," *F. Zh.*, vol. 55, no. 40, pp. 383-385. Wholesale prices per kilogram:

	Before War	*1916*
Aspirin	6 r.	120 r.
Boric Acid	7 r.	100 r.
Iodine	13 r.	45 r.
Carbolic Acid	1 r.	26 r.

	Before War	*1916*
Castor Oil	8 r.	50 r.
Salol	5 r.	170 r.
Phenacetin	5 r.	280 r.
Quinine	16 r.	100 r.
Chloroform	2 r. 50 k.	26 r.

228. "Khimicheskaia promyshlennost'," *Kommersant* reprinted in *F. Zh.*, vol. 55, no. 3, 1916, p. 30.

229. These were: Boric acid–3 rubles, 50 kopeks per kilo versus 2 rubles, 23 kopeks per kilo; aspirin–150 rubles per kilo vs 40 rubles, 20 kopeks per kilo (which was in line with the Pharmacy Tax); caffeine–12 rubles per hekto vs 1 ruble, 90 kopeks per hekto; yellow fish oil–4 rubles per kilo vs 2 rubles, 86 kopeks; white fish oil–4 rubles vs 2 rubles, 93 kopeks per kilo; phenacetin–12 rubles per kilo vs 4 rubles, 8 kopeks (in line with the Pharmacy Tax).

230. "K osveshcheniiu faktov," *F. Zh.*, vol. 55, no. 1, 1916, p. 10.

231. "Blizhaishiia perspektivy," *F. Zh.*, vol. 55, no. 31, 1916, p. 289; also "Peresmotr taksy," ibid., p. 297.

232. "Peresmotr taksy," p. 297.

233. "Blizhaishiia perspektivy," *F. Zh.*, vol. 55, no. 32, 1916, p. 289. *Farmatsevticheskii zhurnal* exulted that there had been "Significant improvement in the rate of exchange of our ruble."

234. "Udeshevlenie tovarov," *F. Zh.*, vol. 55, no. 35, 1916, p. 329.

235. "Zakupka medikamentov zagranitsei," *F. Zh.*, vol. 55, no. 41, 1916, p. 491.

236. "Medikamenty russkago proizvodstva," *F. Zh.*, vol. 55, no. 39, 1916, p. 375.

Chapter 17

1. See for example Tsuyoshi Hasegawa, *The February Revolution: Petrograd, 1917* (Seattle: University of Washington Press, 1981), p. 569 and *passim*.

2. A. Aluf, "Iz istorii profdvizheniia. aptechnykh rabotnikov. Oformlenie klassovykh organizatsii aptekorabotnikov," *Khimiko-farmatsevticheskii zhurnal*, vol. 6, no. 3 (51), 1928, p. 5. See also chapter 14 of this work.

3. "Ot Obshchestva Sluzhashchikh Farmatsevtov g. Peterburga," *Zhizn' farmatsevta* [hereafter cited *Zh. F.*], vol. 1, no. 1, 1914, pp. 1-2; Advertisement, ibid., p. 15. The publisher was Ia. L. Kanevskii. Aluf and Kuperman contributed. Annual subscription costs were to be 1 ruble until the end of 1914; after that 1 rubles, 50 kopeks. The journal was the mouthpiece of six groups: The Professional Society of Staff Pharmacists in St. Petersburg; the Russian Pharmacy Society in Moscow; the Society of Reciprocal Aid of Staff Pharmacists in Odessa; the South-Russian Union of Pharmacists, headquartered in Kiev; the Kiev Pharmacy Society of Reciprocal Aid; the Professional Society of Staff Pharmacists of Rostov-on-the-Don. Dates of 1914 and subsequent years for *Zh. F.* indicate St. Petersburg/ Petrograd as place of publication.

4. "Obzor professional'noi pechati," *F. Zh.*, vol. 53, no 32, 1914, pp. 365-366. The Russian language edition of *F. Zh.* dated from 1879.

5. "Den' rabochei pechati," *Zh. F.*, vol. 1, no. 1, 1914, pp. 6-7.

6. "Obshchee sobranie 23-go fevralia," *Zh. F.*, vol. 3, nos. 1-2, 1916, p. 13.

7. *Vestnik aptechnago truda*, vol. 1, no. 1, 1918, p. 12.

8. Ia. K-ii, "Munitsipal'nyia apteki," *Zh. F.*, vol. 1, no. 1, 1914, pp. 5-6; K. M., "Novyi farmatsevticheskii ustav," ibid., p. 4; Iu. A. Kuperman, "V Peterburge Obshchee sobranie S. P. B. farmatsevtov," ibid., no. 2, pp. 15-16.

9. "V gorodakh i zemstvakh," *Zh. F.*, vol. 1, no. 1, 1914, p. 3; "Otkrytie pervoi gorodskoi apteki v Kieve," ibid., p. 14 and "Gorodskaia apteka v Moskve" and "V Simferopole," *loc. cit.*, also "K otkrytiiu v Moskve gorodskoi apteki," *Zh. F.*, vol. 1, no. 3, 1914, p. 9.

The construction and outfitting of the Moscow pharmacy was to cost 23,000 rubles. It was scheduled to open January 1915. It would dispense medicine at a 25 percent reduction.

10. "V Orele," ibid. (nos. 4-5), p. 9.

11. "V Ekaterinodare," *Zh. F.*, vol. 1, no. 3, 1914, p. 9.

12. "Nizhni-Novgorod," ibid., nos. 4-5, p. 8.

13. "V Tomskoi gorodskoi apteke," *Zh. F.*, vol. 1, nos. 4-5, 1914, p. 8; "Bakinsk gorodskaia apteka," ibid., p. 8; "V Samarskoi Gorodskoi Apteke," ibid., p. 9.

14. "Zaregisterovannyia v Rossii professional'nyia obshchestva sluzhashchikh-farmatsevtov," *Zh. F.*, vol. 1, no. 1, 1914, p. 15.

15. "Pobochnyi zarabotok," *Zh. F.*, vol. 1, no. 1, 1914, p. 11.

16. "V Odesse: Sobranie farmatsevtov sluzhashchikh," *Zh. F.*, vol. 1, no. 1, 1914, p. 13.

17. "Fond zhurnala," *Zh. F.*, vol. 1, no. 1, 1914, p. 15; also pharmacists in Yelabuga, Viatka province, contributed. *Zh. F.*, vol. 2, no. 2, 1915, p. 15.

18. For example, in Kiev the police refused Jewish Assistant Pharmacists trade documents necessary to manage a pharmacy. "Eshche odno raz"iasnenie prav farmatsevtov-evreev," *Zh. F.*, vol. 1, no. 1, 1914, p. 12, and "Khronika," ibid., no. 2, p. 15.

19. For the *Peredvizhniki* see Elizabeth Valkenier, *Russian Realist Art: The State and Society: The Peredvizhniki and Their Tradition* (Ann Arbor: Ardis, 1977).

20. M. I.,"Sredi sluzhashchikh farmatsevtov v Peterburge: V Pravlenii Peterburgskago soiuza," *Zh. F.*, vol. 1, no. 1, p. 12, and "V Ob-va Sluzhashchikh farmatsevtov," ibid., no. 2, p. 17.

21. "Vydacha knig na l'gotnykh usloviakh" and "Literaturno-muzikal'nyi kruzhok," *Zh. F.*, vol. 1, no. 1, 1914, p. 13.

22. "V Odesskom Obshchestve Farmatsevtov," *Zh. F.*, vol. 1, no. 3, 1914, p. 11.

23. "Proekt novago farmatsevticheskago ustava i normal'nyi rabochii den' v apteke," *Zh. F.*, vol. 1, no. 3, 1914, pp. 2-3. No details were given.

24. "V peterburgskikh aptekakh," *Zh. F.*, vol. 1, no. 1, 1914, p. 10.

25. Ibid., "Kartiny aptechnoi zhizni," and "Proekt novago farmatsevticheskago ustava i normal'nyi rabochii den' v apteke," *Zh. F.*, vol. 1, no. 3, 1914, pp. 2-3;

"Po peterburgskim aptekam–Novo Ligovskaia apteka S. Morgena," *Zh. F.*, ibid., nos. 4-5, p. 5.

26. Student pharmacists in Berdichev received 5-10 rubles, Assistant Pharmacists, 25-35. "Korrespondentsii–Berdichev," *Zh. F.*, vol. 1, no. 1, 1914, pp. 14-15.

27. "Rabochee dvizhenie" and "1 maia v Rossii," *Zh. F.*, vol. 1, no. 2, 1914, p. 18.

28. "Sredi sluzhashchikh farmatsevtov," "V Peterburge," "Zabastovka v apteke," "Zaiavlenie ob iskliuchenii iz O-va farmatsevtov sluzhashchikh Ia. I. Lapidus za streikbrekherstvo," *Zh. F.*, vol. 1, no. 3, 1914, p. 9; "Konflikt v Triumfal'noi apteke," ibid., nos. 4-5, p. 4, and "Sredi sluzhashchikh farmatsevtov," p. 9.

29. "Sredi sluzhashchikh farmatsevtov," *Zh. F.*, vol. 1, no. 4-5, 1914, p. 9.

30. "Sredi sluzhashchikh farmatsevtov. V Peterburge. Zaiavlenie ob iskliuchenii iz O-va farmatsevtov sluzhashchikh Ia. I. Lapidus za streikbrekherstvo," vol. 1, no. 3, 1914, p. 9.

31. "V Rostovskom soiuze farmatsevtov," *Zh. F.*, vol. 1, no. 1, 1914, p. 13. The meeting of the Rostov professional society was held in February.

32. "Batum," *Zh. F.*, vol. 1, no. 1, 1914, p.1.

33. "V Odesskom Obshchestve Farmatsevtov," vol. 1, no. 3, 1914, p. 11. The job bureau found places for about forty unemployed, an insignificant number, given the "army of unemployed" in Odessa. An evening fund-raiser produced funds for the bureau.

34. "Odessa," *Zh. F.*, vol. 2, no. 2, 1915, p. 11. This report focused on the society's activities for the first half of 1914. The unemployed included four Provizors, fifty-five Assistant Pharmacists, and twenty-two students.

35. "Finansovaia komissiia," *Zh. F.*, vol. 1, no. 2, 1914, p. 17.

36. The St. Petersburg Society brought to court the case of the women pharmacist not allowed to visit the doctor. "V peterburgskikh aptekakh," 1914, p. 10. Staff pharmacists sued another pharmacy owner because he replaced the double shift with two rest days. The Justice-of-the-Peace court sided with the staff pharmacists. The case went to the appellate level. This court upheld the decision; the owner was to pay 25 rubles plus a percent of time the suit had taken and court costs. "Printsipal'noe delo," *Zh. F.*, vol. 1, no. 3, 1914, p. 12.

37. "Iuridicheskaia pomoshch'," *Zh. F.*, vol. 1, no. 1, 1914, p. 13.

38. "Novyi farmatsevticheskii ustav," *Zh. F.*, vol. 1, no. 1, 1914, pp. 3-4.

39. "Peterburg, 30 aprelia," *Zh. F.*, vol. 1, no. 1, 1914, p. 10.

40. "V Peterburge: Obshchee sobranie S. P. B. farmatsevtov," *Zh. F.*, vol. 1, no. 2, 1914, p. 16.

41. "Novoe obshchestvo," *Zh. F.*, vol. 1, no. 3, 1914, pp. 8-9.

42. "V Odesse: Obshchee sobranie odesskikh farmatsevtov," *Zh. F.*, vol. 1, no. 2, 1914, p. 17.

43. Ibid., p. 18.

44. "Strakhovanie meditsinskago personala na sluchai smerti," *Zh. F.*, vol. 1, no. 1, 1914, p. 14.

45. "V Khar'kove," *Zh. F.*, vol. 1, no. 2, 1914, p. 17.

46. "Sredi rostovskikh aptekarei," *Zh. F.*, vol. 1, no. 3, 1914, p. 9.

47. "Sredi sluzhashchikh farmatsevtov. V Peterburge," *Zh. F.*, vol. 1, nos. 6–7, p. 1. "Pomoshch' zhertvam voiny," ibid., p. 2.

48. Tsentral'nyi Gosudarstvennyi Istoricheskii Arkhiv, St. Petersburg [hereafter cited TsGIA], fond 1298, opis' 1, delo 2056, list 1, 2, 36, 236, listy 74–76, 185–186, 200–204, 205–210 [hereafter cited "f.," "op.," "d.," "l.," or "ll" for plural].

49. "Ot pravleniia Professional'nago Obshchestva sluzhashchikh farmatsevtov g. Petrograda," *Zh. F.*, vol. 2, nos. 8–9, 1915, p. 1.

50. "Sredi sluzhashchikh farmatsevtov," *Zh. F.*, vol. 2, no. 3, 1915, p. 10.

51. "Petrograd," *Zh. F.*, vol. 2, no. 3, 1915, p. 10. The Professional Society were informed that they should not mix their activities with the Union of Working Pharmacists. Ibid., p. 10.

52. "Iz Soiuznoi praktiki," *Zh. F.*, vol. 2, no. 3, 1915, p. 6. For example, when a pharmacist asked for a staff pharmacist at 60 to 65 rubles, the bureau secretary demanded "not less than 75." Additionally, pharmacists refused to work in pharmacies lacking double shifts. Ibid.

53. "Gosudarstvennoe strakhovanie farmatsevtov sluzhashchikh," *Zh. F.*, vol. 2, no. 1, 1915, p. 5.

54. Ia. K-skii, "V Petrogradskikh aptekakh," *Zh. F.*, vol. 2, no. 3, 1915, pp. 7–8.

55. V. K. Menskii, "Letnie otpuski v Petrogradskikh aptekakh," *Zh. F.*, vol. 2, no. 5, 1915, pp. 4–5, and "Sredi sluzhashchikh farmatsevtov," ibid., p. 9.

56. "Andreevskaia apteka T-va Pelia," *Zh. F.*, vol. 2, no. 5, 1915, p. 10.

57. "Po Petrogradskim aptekam," *Zh. F.*, vol. 2, no. 6, 1915, p. 14.

58. Ia. F-ch, "Voina i rabota v aptekakh," *Zh. F.*, vol. 2, no. 2 (February), 1915, pp. 1–2.

59. "Baku," *Zh. F.*, vol. 2, no. 5, 1915, pp. 13–14.

60. D. Akin, "Elizavetpol'," *Zh. F.*, vol. 2, no. 6, 1915, p. 17.

61. "Vil'na," *Zh. F.*, vol. 2, no. 5, 1915, p. 13.

62. "Pis'mo iz Khar'kova," *Zh. F.*, vol. 2, no. 5, 1915, p. 12.

63. "Samara," *Zh. F.*, vol. 2, no. 5, 1915, p. 14.

64. "Petrograd," *Zh. F.*, vol. 2, no. 5, 1915, pp. 10–11.

65. "Tsaritsyn," *Zh. F.*, vol. 2, no. 6, 1915, p. 18.

66. Iu. Minskii, "Askhabad," *Zh. F.*, vol. 2, no. 6, 1915, p. 18.

67. "Dva na tretii," *Zh. F.*, vol. 2, no. 5, 1915, p. 4.

68. "Ot Pravleniia Petrogradskago Professional'nago Obshchestva Farmatsevtov sluzhashchikh," *Zh. F.*, vol. 1, no. 9, 1914, p. 2.

69. V. K. Menskii, "Zemskaia farmatsiia," *Zh. F.*, vol. 1, no. 8, 1914, p. 2. The author reminded staff pharmacists that this was particularly necessary with the state and public institutions playing a larger role in production.

70. "Pis'mo iz Khar'kova," *Zh. F.*, vol. 2, no. 5, 1915, p. 12.

71. D. Akin, "Elizavetpol'," *Zh. F.*, vol. 2, no. 6, 1915, p. 17.

72. "Moskva," *Zh. F.*, vol. 2, no. 2, 1915, p. 13, and A. A., "Rossiiskoe farmatsevticheskoe obshchestvo," ibid., no. 3, p. 2.

73. "Tsaritsyn," *Zh. F.*, vol. 2, no. 6, 1915, p. 18.

74. G. N., "Tiflis," *Zh. F.*, vol. 2, no. 5, 1915, p. 5, and no. 6, p. 17.

75. "Odessa," *Zh. F.*, vol. 2, no. 5, 1915, p. 13.

Such negative reporting—which continued—may have been an Aesopian response to wartime censorship—parts of columns were blacked out or omitted. However, it was so consistent during the war and so paralleled reports prior to the war, as discussed in a previous chapter, that the idea that the negativism was just a ploy must be dismissed.

76. "Korrespondentsii: Baku," *Zh. F.*, vol. 2, no. 4, 1915, p. 13.

77. "Dnezhnyi otchet Professional'nago obshchestva sluzhashchikh farmatsevtov G. Petrograda," *Zh. F.*, vol. 2, no. 2, 1915, p. 15 and "Sostav chlenov Professional'nago farmatsevtov sluzhashchikh G. Petrograda i postuplenie chlenskikh vznosov," ibid., no. 4, p. 15.

78. "Ot pravleniia professional'nago obshchestva farmatsevtov sluzhashchikh," *Zh. F.*, vol. 2, no. 3, 1915, p. 1. and "Zhurnal i petrogradskie farmatsevty," ibid., pp. 1-2.

79. "Sredi sluzhashchikh farmatsevtov," *Zh. F.*, vol. 2, nos. 10-12, 1915, p. 13.

80. "Ot pravleniia Professional'nago Obshchestva sluzhashchikh farmatsevtov g. Petrograda," *Zh. F.*, vol. 2, nos. 8-9, 1915, pp. 1-2 and "K otchetu o deiatel'nosti Biuro Truda pri Professional'nom Obshchestve sluzhashchikh farmatsevtov g. Petrograda," ibid., pp. 7-8. The Minister of Internal affairs waived the refugee pharmacists' passport requirements. "O dokumentakh bezhentsev," ibid., p. 14.

81. "O farmatsevtakh bezhentsakh," *Zh. F.*, vol. 2, nos. 8-9, 1915, p. 14.

82. "Zametki," *Zh. F.*, vol. 2, no. 3, p. 5, and "Khronika: O Voennoi sluzhbe farmatsevtov evreev," ibid., pp. 8-9. Christian Assistant Pharmacists were called to sanitary military duty.

83. "Petrograd: Sobranie farmatsevtov sluzhashchikh po voprosu ob okazanii pomoshchi postradavshim ot voiny evreem," *Zh. F.*, vol. 2, nos. 10-12, 1915, pp. 13-14.

84. "Zasedanie revizionnoi Komissii," *Zh. F.*, vol. 2, no. 2, 1915, p. 11.

85. "Pis'mo iz Khar'kova," *Zh. F.*, vol. 2, no. 6, 1915, p. 16. Staff in other pharmacies also tried to get higher salaries; owners then tried to hire new workers who would accept less salary. However, in still another pharmacy staff finally agreed to accept a lower increase than their initial request. Thus there was compromise.

86. "Rostov n/Donu," *Zh. F.*, vol. 2, no. 2, 1915, pp. 12-13.

87. "Sredi sluzhashchikh farmatsevtov": "Obshchee sobranie," etc., *Zh. F.*, vol. 2, nos. 8-9, 1915, pp. 15-16.

88. "Sredi sluzhashchikh farmatsevtov," *Zh. F.*, vol. 2, nos. 10-12, 1915, pp. 11-13. Aluf was still on the administrative board. The War Industries Committees, under the leadership of Alexander Guchkov and uniting management and labor, operated in twenty-eight cities from 1915.

89. "Korrespondentsii," *Zh. F.*, vol. 2, nos. 10-12, 1915, pp. 16-17.

90. "Sredi sluzhashchikh farmatsevtov: Tiflis," vol. 2, nos. 10-12, 1915, p. 14.

91. D. D., "Gosudarstvennoe strakhovanie farmatsevtov—sluzhashchikh," *Zh. F.*, vol. 2, no. 1, 1915, pp. 5-7.

92. "O zhurnale," *Zh. F.*, vol. 2, no. 1, 1915, p. 4.

93. "Petrograd, 20 aprelia," *Zh. F.*, vol. 2, no. 4, 1915, p. 2.

94. "Svoim putem," *Zh. F.*, vol. 2, no. 5, 1915, pp. 3-4.

95. "Tavridskaia guberniia," *Zh. F.*, vol. 2, no. 6, 1915, pp. 9-10.

96. "Sredi sluzhashchikh farmatsevtov. Obshchee sobranie petrogradskago professional'nago obshchestva sluzhashchikh farmatsevtov," *Zh. F.*, vol. 3, nos 1-2 (3 February), 1916, p. 11.

97. "Stavki petrogradskikh aptekakh," *Zh. F.*, vol. 3, nos. 5-6, 1916, pp. 3-13.

98. "Apteka Pelia," *Zh. F.*, vol. 3, nos. 5-6, 1916, p. 7.

99. *Zhizn' farmatsevta*, vol. 3, 1916, *passim*.

100. S. Lapitskaia, "Zhenshchiny-Farmatsevtov," *Zh. F.*, vol. 3, nos. 1-2, 1916, pp. 4-5.

101. Miroslawa Pabis Braunstein, "The First Polish Women Pharmacists," *Pharmacy in History*, vol. 31, no. 1, 1989, p. 15.

102. Wojciech Roeske, *Antonina Lesniewska, 1866-1937* (Warsaw, 1970), p. 21.

103. "I-ia zhenskaia apteka Lesnevskoi," *Zh. F.*, vol. 3, nos. 5-6, 1916, p. 7.

104. Liza Ol'khoba, "Pis'mo v Redaktsiiu," *Zh. F.*, vol. 3, nos. 10-12, 1916, p. 20.

105. E. Kh., "Pis'mo iz Kieva," *Zh. F.*, vol. 3, nos. 1-2, 1916, p. 15.

106. I. D. K-skii, "Perspektivy budushchago," *Zh. F.*, vol. 3, nos. 7-8 (July-September), 1916, p. 1.

107. Antiani Kavnasieli, "Tiflis," *Zh. F.*, vol. 3, nos. 1-2, 1916, p. 15. Four large and two small pharmacies were specifically cited.

108. E. Kh. "Pis'mo iz Kieva," *Zh. F.*, vol. 3, nos. 1-2, 1916, p. 15.

109. "Odessa," *Zh. F.*, vol. 3, nos. 5-6, 1916, p. 19.

110. "Rostov na Donu," *Zh. F.*, vol. 3, nos. 5-6, 1916, p. 19.

111. Ia-k'ii, "Po Povodu," *Zh. F.*, vol. 3, nos. 3-4, 1916, p. 3.

112. "Sobranie farmatsevtov (7 April)," *F. Zh.*, vol. 55, no. 16, 1916, p. 140; E. I. Svirlovskii, "Godovoi otchet o deiatel'nosti Vysochaishe utverzhdennago Petrogradskago Farmatsevticheskago Obshchestva," ibid., no. 15, p. 125; "Sredi sluzhashchikh farmatsevtov," ibid., no. 36, pp. 339-340.

113. Svirlovskii, "Godovoi otchet," p. 125.

114. "Petrograd: Protokol obshchago sobraniia ot 3 iunia 1916," *Zh. F.*, vol. 3, nos. 5-6, 1916, p. 17.

115. "Protokol obshchago Sobraniia ot 18 Maia 1916 g. and 3 iunia," *Zh. F.*, vol. 3, nos. 5-6, 1916, pp. 15-17.

116. "Protokol," *Zh. F.*, vol. 3, nos. 5-6, 1916, p. 15.

117. "Obshchestvennyi indifferentizm farmatsevtov i zhurnal," *Zh. F.*, vol. 3, nos. 3-4, 1916, pp. 2-3.

118. "Obshchee sobranie petrogradskago professional'nago obshchestva (3 Feb)," *Zh. F.*, vol. 3, nos. 1-2, 1916, pp. 11-12.

119. "Protokol obshchago Sobraniia ot 18 Maia 1916 g." and "3 Iunia," *Zh. F.*, vol. 3, nos. 5-6, pp. 16-17.

120. "Protokol obshchago Sobraniia ot 18 Maia 1916 g.," *Zh. F.*, vol. 3, nos. 5-6, 1916, p. 16.

121. "Protokol 3 iunia," ibid., p. 17.

122. "Uchrezhdenoe sobranie Pol'tavskago obshchestva vzaimopomoshchi sluzhashchikh farmatsevtov," *Zh. F.*, vol. 3, nos. 1-2, 1916, p. 14.

123. "Korrespondentsii: O nashem zhurnale," *Zh. F.*, vol. 3, nos. 1-2, 1916, p. 15, and Antiani Kavnasieli, "Tiflis," ibid., pp. 15-16.

124. "Odessa," *Zh. F.*, vol. 3, nos. 5-6, 1916, pp. 18-19. The small pool of particpants in the Odessa Society is indicated by the fact that the same people stood as full and candidate members for election to the Administrative Board and Audit Commission. One prominent name was Kuperman.

125. "Pargolovskaia apteka," *Zh. F.*, vol. 3, nos. 7-8, 1916, p. 16.

126. "Odessa," ibid., p. 16.

127. "Odessa," *Zh. F.*, vol. 3, nos. 7-8, 1916, p. 19.

128. "Pis'mo iz Khar'kova," *Zh. F.*, vol. 3, nos. 7-8, 1916, p. 20.

129. *Loc. cit.*

130. "Rostov na Donu," *Zh. F.*, vol. 3, nos. 7-8, 1916, p. 17.

131. "Nizhni Novgorod," *Zh. F.*, vol. 3, nos. 7-8, 1916, pp. 17-18.

132. "Korrespondentsii: Moskva," *Zh. F.*, vol. 3, nos. 10-12, 1916, pp. 14-15, and ibid., nos. 7-8, p. 18.

133. "Baku," ibid., p. 20.

134. "Ekaterinburg," *Zh. F.*, vol. 3, nos. 7-8, 1916, p. 20.

135. "Zabytoe delo," *Zh. F.*, vol. 3, nos. 10-12, 1916, p. 18.

136. "Sredi sluzhashchikh farmatsevtov: Protokol . . . 10 sentiabria," *Zh. F.*, vol. 3, nos. 7-8, 1916, pp. 14-15.

137. Ibid., p. 15.

138. "Nasha tribuna," *Zh. F.*, vol. 3, nos. 10-12, 1916, p. 10.

139. "Otvet T. E-nu," *Zh. F.*, vol. 3, nos. 10-12, 1916, p. 11.

140. Sredi sluzhashchikh farmatsevtov," *Zh. F.*, vol. 3, nos. 10-12, 1916, p. 12.

141. "Primiritel'nyia kamery i organizatsii trudiashchikhsia," *Zh. F.*, vol. 3, nos. 10-12, 1916, p. 6.

142. "Sredi sluzhashchikh farmatsevtov. Obshchee sobranie chlenov professional'nago Ob-va sluzh. farm. g. Petr. i gub. ot 4-go noiabria 1916," *Zh. F.*, vol. 3, nos. 10-12, 1916, pp. 12-13. The vote of confidence in the editorial leadership was 43-23; the vote against self-taxation to help Jewish refugees was 48 vs 19.

143. Editorial, "O lekarstvennom golode," *F. Zh.*, vol. 53, no. 36, 1914, p. 401.

144. *Ustroistvo gorodskogo khimiko-farmatsevticheskago zavoda Doklad komissii akademika N. S. Kurnakova soveshchaniiu o zagotovlenii gorodom lekarstv* (Petrograd, 1916), pp. 17-18.

145. TsGIA, f. 1298, op. 1, d. 2066a, l. 105 oborot.

146. A. M. Sidorkov, "Issledovanie organizationno-metodicheskikh printsipov razvitiia farmatsevticheskogo uchenogo dela v SSSR," (Moscow, 1973) unpublished Ph.D. dissertation, pp. 49-50. Located in the Tsentral'naia Gosudarstvennaia Nauchnaia Meditsinskaia Biblioteka, Moscow.

147. "Khronika: Tsirkuliar Ministerstva Nar. Prosveshcheniia," *F. Zh.*, vol. 54, no. 36, 1915, pp. 356-357. Also, "Kursy dlia farmatsevtov," *Zh. F.*, vol. 2, nos. 8-9, 1915, p. 12. Nikolaevsk, Tomsk, and Saratov universities were specifically cited.

148. "Rasshirenie universiteta," *F. Zh.*, vol. 54, no. 40, 1915, p. 397.

149. "Farmatsevticheskie kursy," *F. Zh.*, vol. 54, no. 43, 1915, p. 426.

150. "Khronika: Tsirkuliar Ministra Narodnago Prosveshcheniia popechiteliam uchebnykh okrugov 25-go avgusta 1915, No. 38671," *F. Zh.*, vol. 54, no. 36, 1915, pp. 356–357, and "Kursy," ibid., no. 1, p. 12.

151. "Rasshirenie universiteta," *F. Zh.*, vol. 54, no. 40, 1915, p. 397.

152. "K voprosu o farmatsevticheskom obrazovanii," *Zh. F.*, vol. 2, nos. 8–9, 1915, pp. 4–6.

153. "Khronika: Deputatsii farmatsevtov u ministra nar. prosveshcheniia," *Zh. F.*, vol. 2, nos. 10–12, 1915, p. 8.

154. "Khimiko-farmatsevticheskoe otdelenie pri petrogradskom universitete," *Zh. F.*, vol. 2, nos. 8–9, 1915, p. 13.

155. Alexander Ginzberg, "O novykh napravleniiakh v voprose farmatsevticheskago obrazovaniia," *F. Zh.*, vol. 54, no. 42, 1915, p. 419.

156. Ginzberg, "O novykh," *F. Zh.*, vol. 54, no. 43, 1915, pp. 419–420. The program was as follows (per week):

1st year—34 hours: Inorganic chemistry, physics, general biology, geology and mineralogy, analytical chemistry, anatomy, elements of higher mathematics, general and experimental psychology (!), history of ancient philosophy (!), general history, history of Russian literature and art, logic, sociology, and religion (!).

2nd year—26 hours: Organic chemistry, analytical chemistry, zoology, botany, physiology, physics, pharmaceutical chemistry, history of philosophy (!), theory of law and government (!), political economy, and statistics (!).

3rd year—29 hours: Pharmaceutical chemistry, pharmacognosy, physiological chemistry, hygiene, pharmacology, bacteriology, physical chemistry, forensic chemical analysis, chemical technology, business, and "special additional courses."

157. "Khronika," *F. Zh.*, vol. 55, no. 20, 1916, p. 172.

158. "Khimiko-farmatsevticheskoe otdelenie zhenskikh kursov v Oddesse," *Zh. F.*, vol. 2, nos. 10–12, 1915, p. 9.

159. "Khimiko-farmatsevticheskie kursy pri Saratovskom universitete," *Zh. F.*, vol. 2, nos. 10–12, 1915, p. 10.

160. K uchrezhdeniiu khimiko-farmatsevticheskikh kursov v Tomske," *Zh. F.*, vol. 1, nos. 10–12, 1915, p. 9.

161. "Khodataistvo farmatsevtov," *F. Zh.*, vol. 55, no. 15, 1916, p. 131.

162. "Novaia farmatsevticheskaia shkola," *F. Zh.*, vol. 55, no. 12, 1916, p. 105. See also "Nachatoe i neokonchennoe," ibid., no. 14, p. 115–117.

163. "V Vysshikh uchebnykh zavedeniiakh: Moskva, Kiev, Odessa," *Zh. F.*, vol. 3, nos. 7–8, 1916, p. 12. "Kiev," *loc. cit.*

The first-year text for organic chemistry was that of A. Reformatskii, Sittin, edition of 1915; that for inorganic chemistry the *Konspekt* of lectures of professor Ia. N. Barzilovskii, edition 1912; that for physics: *Kontsentricheskii tekst* of physics by I. Ikosonogov, edition Br. Salaev 1914; Zoology: the Medical Zoology of A. M. Nikol'skii, editor A. S. Suvorin, 1916; Mineralogy: *Konspekt* of lectures on mineralogy taught by Prof. Armashevskii, edition Med. Students, 1912; Botany: *Kratkii uchebnik* of Botany by K. A. Purievich, edition 1913. In Odessa, Jews were to be admitted at 20 percent of the norm.

164. "Obrazovanie farmatsevtov," *F. Zh.*, vol. 55, no. 41, 1916, p. 402.

165. Sidorkov, "Issledovanie," p. 51.

166. "Novaia sensatsiia," *F. Zh.*, vol. 54, no. 40 (October 3), 1915, p. 393.

167. "Psikho-Nevrologicheskii Institut," *Zh. F.*, vol. 2, nos. 10–12, 1915, p. 14-15.

168. "Farmatsevticheskii s"ezd," *F. Zh.*, vol. 55, no. 21, 1916, p. 185 and "Nuzhdy farmatsevtov," *F. Zh.*, vol. 55, no. 35, 1916, p. 330. Saltykov had been a militant socialist in 1905, editor of defunct *Farmatsevticheskii vestnik,* and chair of the radical Russian Pharmacy Society in Moscow. From 1907 to 1909 he was editor of the journal *Farmatsevticheskii trud.*

169. "Farmatsevticheskii s"ezd," *F. Zh.*, vol. 55, no. 21, 1916, p. 185. At this time Ginzberg was also chair of Pharmaceutical chemistry at the Women's Medical Courses in St. Petersburg.

170. "Farmatsevticheskii s"ezd," *F. Zh.*, vol. 55, no. 21, 1916, p. 185. Valiashko continued to teach in Bolshevik Russia (Ukraine), organizing a chair of pharmaceutcial chemistry at Khar'kov University in 1924. M. G. Ena, "Khimiko-farmatsevticheskaia promyshlennost'," *Razvitie khimicheskoi tekhnologii na Ukraine,* eds. O. Avilov et al. (Kiev, 1976), p. 270.

171. "Nuzhdy farmatsevtov," *F. Zh.*, vol. 55, no. 35, p. 330.

172. "Godovoi otchet o deiatel'nosti Vysochaishe utverzhdennago Petrogradskogo Farmatsevticheskago Obshchestva," *F. Zh.*, vol. 55, no. 15, 1916, p. 125.

173. "Za nedeliu," *F. Zh.*, vol. 55, no. 21, 1916, p. 178.

174. "U farmatsevtov," *F. Zh.*, vol. 55, no. 20, 1916, p. 172.

175. A. N. Popovskii, *Obrazovanie farmatsevtov v sviazi s razvitiem khimiko-farmatsevticheskoi promyshlennosti i lekarstvennyi golod* (Petrograd, 1917), pp. 1-7.

Popovskii emphasized that before 1870 the French pharmaceutical industry was premier in the world. After the Franco-Prussian war of 1870, Germany "created a significant chemical-pharmaceutical industry." Pharmacists Shering, Merck, and Ridel established firms. Small pharmacies worked on an artisanal basis, to supply pharmaceutical products for larger firms. Russia had fallen behind in the creation of pharmaceutical chemists. Additionally, Popovskii insisted that the new Pharmacy Statute ignored special university pharmacy departments and thus contradicted the August 1915 Circular of the Minister of Public Enlightenment, which had proposed the creation of chemistry-pharmacy courses in the physics-mathematics faculties of universities.

176. "Nuzhdy farmatsevtov," *F. Zh.*, vol. 55, no. 35, 1916, p. 330.

177. After the Bolshevik revolution Alexander Semenovich Ginzberg became director of the Chemico-Medical Institute, which supplanted the Women's Medical Courses in 1919. He remained in that position for five years. He also occupied the chair of organic and pharmaceutical chemistry. Ginzberg died (he presumably was purged) in 1937. *Professory 1 Len. Med. In. za 50 let* (Moscow, 1947), p. 21,

and Trudy Leningradskogo Khimiko-farmatsevticheskogo instituta. vypusk X. *Istoriia farmatsevticheskogo dela v Peterburge-Petrograde-Leningrade* (Leningrad, 1960), pp. 134-137.

E. Ia Abol' was mentioned in the list of personnel in "Farmotdel." See, for example, "Rasporiazhenie narodnogo komissariata zdravo okhraneniia, 9 Fevralia 1920," Abol', E. Ia: Farmotdel: "post: Zan. Farm. Inst[itute]; salary: 2,600 rubles." Tsentral'nyi Gosudarstvennyi Arkhiv RSFSR [hereafter cited TsGA RSFSR], f. 482, op. 5, d. 79, l. 2.

O. G. Gabrilovich was listed in the administration of "Farmatsentr" in "zhurnal no. 19, 3 December 1918," TsGA RSFSR, f. 482, op. 5, d. 13, l. 159.

B. N. Saltykov editor of *Farmatsevticheskii vestnik* and *Farmatsevticheskii trud* also joined the Soviet pharmacy administration. See TsGA RSFSR, f. 482, op. 5, d. 12, l. 42 (1919).

178. "Zhurnal pervago zasedaniia Mezhduvedomstvennago Komiteta po delam farmatsevticheskoi promyshlennosti," TsGIA, f. 1298, op. 1, d. 2066a, l. 2.

179. *Ustroistvo*, p. 15.

180. *Ustroistvo*, p. 9.

181. Ibid., p. 13.

182. Ibid., pp. 13-14.

183. Ibid., pp. 76-77.

184. Ibid., p. 82.

185. Ibid., p. 83.

186. Ibid., p. 83. Lit: "*Prekratit' ili umerit' khimicheskuiu rabotu chastnykh predprinimatelei.*"

187. Ibid., pp. 85-86.

188. Ibid., pp. 77-78.

189. Ibid., p. 81.

190. Ibid., p. 88.

191. Ibid., p. 90.

192. Ibid., pp. 100-101. Lit: ". . . *budet pushcheno v khod germanskimi sindikatami*" and "*gibel'no dlia chastnykh predprinimatelei.*"

193. Ibid., p. 102.

194. Ibid., p. 101.

195. "Proekt munitsipalizatsii aptek," *F. Zh.*, vol. 54, no. 44, 1915, p. 433.

196. TsGIA, f. 1298, op. 1, d. 2060, ll. 75-75 ob.

197. "Blizhaishiia perspektivy," *F. Zh.*, vol. 55, no. 32, 1916, pp. 289-290. This report of the Petrograd Stock Exchange also noted falling prices on many pharmaceutical substances in the fall of 1916, a result of increased production as well as increased imports. See previous chapter.

198. "Likvidatsiia obshchestva," *F. Zh.*, vol. 55, no. 39, 1916, p. 376.

199. Similarly, John Hutchinson has emphasized the conflict which erupted between the government—most specifically G. E Rein—and public physicians before and during World War I. Hutchinson, *Politics and Public Health*, pp. 73-77, 104-107. He also has depicted the frustration on the part of public physicians

because of lack of government funding during the war and their hostility toward the authoritarian Prince Ol'denburg. Ibid., pp. 128-131, 134-136.

200. "Prikaz Verkhovnago Nachal'nika Sanitarnoi Evakuatsionnoi Chasti, 11 marta 1916, no. 134," *F. Zh.*, vol. 55, no. 13, 1916, pp. 113-114.

201. "Lekarstvennyi S"ezd," *F. Zh.*, vol. 55, no. 14, 1916, pp. 121-122.

202. "Ot Sanitarnago Otdela Tsentral'nogo Voenno-Promyshlennago Komiteta," and "Polozhenie o S"ezde po bor'be s lekarstevnnym golodom," *F. Zh.*, vol. 55, no. 31, 1916, pp. 279-280. Also "Polozhenie," ibid., no. 32, pp. 291-292.

203. "Otstrochka S"ezda,"*F. Zh.*, vol. 55, no. 33, 1916, p. 309.

204. Hasegawa, *The February Revolution*, pp. 572-573, 576-582.

205. Michael Melancon, "Who Wrote What and When? Proclamations of the February Revolution in Petrograd . . . ," *Soviet Studies*, vol. 40, no. 3, 1988, pp. 479-500.

206. "Moskva," *Zh. F.*, vol. 3, nos. 7-8, 1916, p. 18.

207. "Korrespondentsii: Moskva," *Zh. F.*, vol. 3, nos. 10-12, 1916, p. 14.

208. "Nashi blagodeteli," *Zh. F.*, vol. 3, nos. 10-12, 1916, p. 3.

209. "Voprosy dnia," *Zh. F.*, vol. 3, nos. 10-12, 1916, pp. 1-2.

Chapter 18

1. See Richard Abraham, *Alexander Kerensky: The First Love of the Revolution* (New York: Columbia University Press, 1987), pp. 114-145.

2. Abraham, ibid., pp. 146-246.

3. See chapter 16 on the medicaments crisis of World War I, in this work.

4. Tsentral'nyi Gosudarstvennyi Istoricheskii Arkhiv, St. Petersburg [hereafter cited TsGIA], fond. 1298, opis' 1, delo 2102a, listy 64-456 [hereafter cited "f.," "op.," "d.," "ll.," or "l." in singular]: "Registratsionnaia kartochka," March or early 1917 through December 1917. The cards came from settlements of Zabaikal Region (l. 64), Podolsk (l. 72), Taurida (l. 81), Fergana region (l. 89), Kherson (l. 96), Semirech'e region (l. 101), all from March 1917. April included cards from Penza and Simbirsk provinces (ll. 106, 114, 121). By June and July, (ll. 251-255) a number of pharmacies were closed, due to death of the Provizor, or leased or transferred in ownership. List 456 notes the selling of a normal pharmacy (*normal'naia apteka*) Vologda in September and the selling of another in October.

5. Vladmir Il'yich Lenin, "The Dual Power," *The Lenin Anthology*, ed., Robert C. Tucker (New York: W. W. Norton, 1975), pp. 301-306.

6. Donald Raleigh notes this point when discussing Saratov province and city. *Revolution on the Volga 1917 in Saratov* (Ithaca, NY: Cornell University Press, 1986), pp. 192-202, 210-224.

7. Lenin, "The Tasks of the Proletariat in the Present Revolution ('April Theses')," *The Lenin Anthology*, pp. 295-300. Also, "The State and Revolution," ibid., pp. 311-398.

8. See Alexander Rabinowitch, *Prelude to Revolution The Petrograd Bolsheviks and the July 1917 Uprising* (Bloomington, IN: Indiana University Press, 1968).

9. Esther Kingston-Mann, *Lenin and the Problem of Marxist Peasant Revolution* (Oxford, New York: Oxford University Press, 1985). Originally, Lenin preferred "large model farms." He switched on this point, condoning peasant take over of estates, inside or outside the peasant communes, when he realized collective farms were not popular with the peasantry who formed the bulk of the population.

10. See J. L. H. Keep, "The Countryside in Revolt," *The Russian Revolution: A Study in Mass Mobilization* (W. W. Norton, 1976), pp. 155-247, and Steve A. Smith, *Red Petrograd: Revolution in the Factories 1917-1918* (Cambridge: Cambridge University Press, 1983), pp. 168-170, 209.

11. See William G. Rosenberg, "Kadets and Kornilov," *The Russian Revolution and Bolshevik Victory*, eds., Ronald Suny and Arthur Adams (Lexington, MA: D. C. Heath and Company, 1990), pp. 306-307, excerpt from Rosenberg, *Liberals in the Russian Revolution: The Constitutional Democratic Party, 1917-1921* (Princeton: Princeton University Press, 1974), pp. 179-228.

12. For Saratov see Donald Raleigh, *Revolution on the Volga 1917 in Saratov*, pp. 232-234.

13. See N. N. Sukhanov, *The Russian Revolution*, vols. 1 and 2, edited, abridged, and translated by Joel Carmichael (Harper Torchbooks, 1962) or numerous other accounts of the October Revolution.

14. Richard Abraham, *Alexander Kerensky: The First Love of the Revolution*, full citation above, note 1.

15. Ziva Galili, *The Menshevik Leaders in the Russian Revolution Social Realities and Political Strategies* (Princeton: Princeton University Press, 1989).

16. For military and peasantry see Alexander Rabinowitch, Esther Kingston-Mann, and John H. L. Keep, respectively (full citations above.) On workers and Bolshevik relations with the workers, in addition to Steve A. Smith, see Diane P. Koenker and William G. Rosenberg, *Strikes and Revolution in Russia, 1917* (Princeton: Princeton University Press, 1989); and Mary McAuley, *Bread and Justice, State and Society in Petrograd, 1917-1922* (Oxford: Oxford University Press, 1991).

17. Raleigh, *Revolution on the Volga 1917 in Saratov* has been cited above. See also Rex A. Wade, "The Saratov Red Guards," *Politics and Society in Provincial Russia Saratov, 1590-1917*, eds., Rex A. Wade and Scott J. Seregny (Columbus, OH: Ohio State University Press, 1989), pp. 307-325; Russell E. Snow, *The Bolsheviks in Siberia, 1917-1918* (London: Associated University Presses, 1977).

18. John M. Thompson, *Revolutionary Russia, 1917* (New York: Charles Scribner's Sons, 1981).

19. Hans Rogger, *Russia in the Age of Modernization and Revolution, 1881-1917* (London, New York: Longman, eighth printing, 1990).

20. Tsuyoshi Hasegawa, *The February Revolution: Petrograd 1917* (University of Washington Press, 1981, pp. 569-586.

21. For easy access to this theory see Leopold H. Haimson, "Dual Polarization in Urban Russia, 1905-1917, *The Russian Revolution and Bolshevik Victory*, pp. 26-50.

22. Thompson, *Revolutionary Russia, 1917*, p. 71.

23. Galili, *The Menshevik Leaders in the Russian Revolution*, p. 42.

24. For a laudatory interpretation of the the Petrograd Soviet, particularly the Mensheviks' role in it, see Galili, *The Menshevik Leaders in the Russian Revolution, passim.*

25. Rogger, *Russia in the Age*, pp. 23–25.

26. Rogger, ibid., pp. 266–267.

27. Raleigh, *Revolution on the Volga*, pp. 205–210.

28. See Ronald Grigor Suny, *The Baku Commune 1917–1918* (Princeton: Princeton University Press, 1972), p. 125.

29. Koenker and Rosenberg, *Strikes and Revolution in Russia, 1917*, pp. 110–113, 151–178.

30. G. P., "27 fevralia v Petrograde, *Zhizn' farmatsevta* [hereafter cited *Zh. F.*], vol. 4, nos. 2–3, February–March, 1917, pp. 6–7.

31. The Mensheviks, erstwhile cousins of the Bolsheviks, had splintered into several camps during the first decades of the twentieth century and the War. Galili discusses the Menshevik Defensists, Liquidationists, and Internationalists in *The Menshevik Leaders in the Russian Revolution, passim.*

32. "Obshchee sobranie sluzhashchikh v Petrogradskikh aptekhakh," *Zh. F.*, vol. 4, Pribavlenie k no. 1, 1917, pp. 3–4.

33. "Petrograd, 10-go marta," *Zh. F.*, vol. 4, "Pribavlenie k no. 1," 1917, p. 1, and "Obshchee sobranie sluzhashchikh v Petrogradskikh aptekakh," ibid., pp. 3–4.

34. "K momentu, " *Zh. F.*, vol. 4, nos. 2–3, 1917, p. 4.

35. "Sredi sluzhashchikh-farmatsevtov: Petrograd," *Zh. F.*, vol. 4, no. 2–3, 1917, pp. 8–9.

36. "K momentu," *Zh. F.*, vol. 4, nos. 2–3, 1917, p. 4.

37. "Pravleniem prof. o-va sluzh. f-ov Petrograda i gub. i Redaktsieu Zhizn' Farmatsevta razoslano po organizatsiiam sluzhashch. f-ov nizhesleduiushchee pis'mo," *Zh. F.*, vol. 4, nos. 2–3, 1917, pp. 7–8.

38. "Pushkinskaia apteka," "Vvedenskaia apteka," "Nashi vragi," *Zh. F.*, vol. 4, nos. 2–3, 1917, pp. 11–12.

39. "Pribavlenie. Programma Rossiiskoi Sotsialdemokraticheskoi Rabochei Partii," *Zh. F.*, vol. 4, nos. 2–3, 1917, pp. 17–20 and "Pobeda," ibid., p. 20.

40. "Odessa," *Zh. F.*, vol. 4, nos. 2–3, 1917, p. 12.

41. "Odessa," *Zh. F.*, vol. 4, no. 4 (15 May), 1917, p. 6.

42. "Khar'kov," *Zh. F.*, vol. 4, nos. 2–3, 1917, pp. 12–14. Rodzianko had been president of the Fourth Duma. However, the chairman of the Provisional Government was Prince G. E. L'vov who had been head of the Union of Zemstvos.

43. A. G-n, "Pis'mo iz Saratova," *Zh. F.*, vol. 4, nos. 2–3, 1917, p. 14.

44. "Korrespondentsii: Yaroslavl'," *Zh. F.*, vol. 4, nos. 2–3, 1917, pp. 15–16.

45. "Tomsk," *Zh. F.*, vol. 4, no. 4, 1917, pp. 6–7.

46. Ia. Kanevskii, "Formy organizatsionnago stroitel'stva," *Zh. F.*, vol. 4, no. 4, 1917, pp. 1–2.

47. "Moskovskiia pis'ma," *Zh. F.*, vol. 4, no. 4, 1917, pp. 7–8.

48. "Korrespondentsii: Nizhni Novgorod, *Vestnik aptechnago truda* [hereafter

cited *VAT*; this title replaced *Zhizn' farmatsevta* after October 1918], vol. 5, nos. 6-7, 1918, p. 9.

49. Besha, "Pis'mo iz Ekaterinoslava," *Zh. F.*, vol. 4, no. 4, 1917, p. 8.

50. Ia. Kanevskii, "Formy organizatsionnago stroitel'stva," *Zh. F.*, vol. 4, no. 4 (May), 1917, pp. 1-2.

51. Shr-r,"Tula," *Zh. F.*, vol. 4, nos. 8-9, 1917, p. 15.

52. "Pobeda," *Zh. F.* , vol. 4, nos. 2-3, 1917, p. 20 and "Sredi sluzhashchikh farmatsevtov: Petrograd Sobranie Soveta aptekarskikh delegatov ot 21-go aprelia 1917 g. and Obshchee sobranie rabochikh Petrogradskikh aptek (23 marta)," *Zh. F.*, vol. 4, no. 4 (May), 1917, pp. 5-7.

53. "Kollektivnyi dogovor," *Zh. F.*, vol. 4, nos. 5-7, 1917, pp. 3-5.

54. "Konferentsiia predstaviltelei soiuzov sluzhashchikh v aptekakh," *Zh. F.*, vol. 4, no. 4 (May), 1917, p. 1 and "Postanovleniia konferentsii," *Zh. F.*, vol. 4, no. 6, 1917, p. 4.

55. Ia. Kanevskii, "Munitsipalizatsiia aptek," *Zh. F.*, vol. 4, no. 6 (15 June), 1917, pp. 2-4.

56. See Rabinowitch, *Prelude to Revolution*, pp. 135-205.

57. Michael T. Florinsky, *Russia: A History and an Interpretation*, (New York: Macmillan, 1963), vol. 2, pp. 1430-1432. This still is an excellent history of the period.

58. "Moskva," *Zh. F.*, vol. 4, nos. 8-9, 1917, p. 8.

59. G. Faingol'd, "Korrespondentsii: Moskovskiia pis'ma," *Zh. F.*, vol. 4, nos. 8-9, 1917, p. 13.

60. "Khar'kovskiia pis'ma," *VAT*, vol. 5, nos. 2-3, 1918, pp. 12-13.

61. "Khar'kov," *Zh. F.*, vol. 4, nos. 8-9, 1917, pp. 8-9.

62. "Ekaterinoslav," ibid., p. 9.

63. "O Ekaterinoslavskom s"ezde," ibid., pp. 14-15.

64. "Kostroma," ibid., pp. 9-10.

65. "Riazan," ibid., pp. 10-11.

66. "Kokand (Ferg. obl.)", ibid., pp. 11-12.

67. "Gomel," *Zh. F.*, vol. 4, nos. 8-9, 1917, p. 15.

68. "Ural'sk," *Zh. F.*, vol. 4, nos. 8-9, 1917, pp. 15-16.

69. "Kursk" and "Vitebsk," ibid., p. 12.

70. "Odessa," *Zh. F.*, vol. 4, nos. 8-9, 1917, pp. 13-14.

71. "Belaia-Tserkov'," *Zh. F.*, vol. 4, nos. 8-9, 1917, p. 16.

72. "N. Novgorod," *VAT*, vol. 5, nos. 2-3 (February), 1918, p. 14.

73. "Sredi sluzhashchikh farmatsevtov: Petrograd," *Zh. F.*, vol. 4, nos. 8-9 (August 15), 1917, pp. 6-7.

74. M. Epshtein, "Kul'turno-prosvetitel'naia rabota v professional'nykh soiuzakh," *VAT*, vol. 4, nos. 14-15, 1917, pp. 7-8.

75. "Resoliutsiia, priniataia 1 Maia 1917 g. v Obshchem Sobranii . . . Delagatov Farmatsevticheskikh obshchestv i organizatsii. Reforma farmatsevticheskago obrazovaniia," Tsentral'nyi Gosudarstvennyi Arkhiv RSFSR (Moscow) [hereafter cited TsGA RSFSR], f. 482, op. 5, d. 16, ll. 38, 38 ob, 39.

76. Professor A. S. Ginzberg, "O Reforme Farmatsevticheskago Obrazovaniia," TsGA RSFSR, f. 482, op. 5, d. 16, ll. 30–37.

77. "Komissiia po reforme vysshikh uchebnykh zavedenii pri Ministerstve Narodnago Prosveshcheniia," 1 Avgusta 1917, TsGA RSFSR, f. 482, op. 5, d. 16, ll. 44 and 44 ob. A. S. Ginzberg drafted the proposal. It petitioned the Minister of Public Enlightenment to ask university councils to address pharmacy education, to make women's pharmacy education equal to men's—again Ginzberg ignored Antonina Lesnevskaia's Women's Pharmacy School and the fact that her students finished secondary school—and proposed the establishment of a subcommittee in the Ministry of Public Enlightenment that would work on implementing the pharmacy departments in university physics-mathematics faculties. Among others the subcommittee was to include A. S. Ginzberg and socialists from the Petrograd Committee of the winter of 1915/1916 like academician N. S. Kurnakov, professors V. E. Tishchenko and L. A. Chugaev, N. A. Valiashko and so on.

78. "Polozheniia doklada: 'Obrazovanie farmatsevtov' E. O. Merukhes k s"ezdu sluzhashchikh farmatsevtov 25 avgusta 1917 goda," TsGA RSFSR, f. 482, op. 5, d. 16, l. 45. The learned title *Magistr* (Master) of Pharmacy was to be retained.

79. "V tsentral'nom sovete professional'nykh soiuzov sluzhashchikh v aptekakh," *VAT*, vol. 4, nos. 14–15, 1917, p. 11. The petition was dispatched September 17.

Representatives to the Pharmacy Soviet were to include members of many diverse bodies: the Central Executive Committee of the Petrograd Soviet of Workers and Soldiers Deputies, Peasants Soviet, city and zemstvo unions, All Russian Central Soviet of Professional Unions of Pharmacy Staff, Ministry of Internal Affairs, Ministry of Labor, State Comptroller, Ministry of Finance, Hospital Fund, Petrograd city duma, Petrograd Soviet of Workers and Soldiers' Deputies, Petrograd Union of Pharmacy Staff, and Professional Union of Workers in Pharmaceutical Enterprises.

80. "Moskva," *VAT*, vol. 4, nos. 14–15, 1917, p. 11, and "Korrespondentsii. Moskovskiia pis'ma: Zabastovka," ibid., p. 11.

81. "Sredi sluzhashchikh v aptekakh: Petrograd," *VAT*, vol. 4, nos. 14–15, 1917, p. 8.

82. E. B(ronshtein)., "Zabastovka v petrogradskikh aptekakh," *VAT*, vol. 4, nos. 14–15 (November 15), 1917, p. 4.

83. "Protokol obshchago sobraniia sluzhashchikh v aptekakh ot 1 oktiabriia 1917 g.," *VAT*, vol. 4, nos. 14–15, 1917, p. 9; "Protokol obshchago sobraniia ot 10-go oktiabria 1917 g.," ibid., p. 9.

84. Rosenberg, "Kadets and Kornilov," *The Russian Revolution and Bolshevik Victory*, p. 307.

85. Bronshtein, "Zabastovka," p. 5.

86. "Protokol obshchago sobraniia sluzhashchikh v aptekakh ot 1 oktiabria 1917 g.," *VAT*, vol. 4, nos. 14–15, 1917, p. 9.

87. Bronshtein, "Zabastovka," p. 4. Skobelev also tried to avert a strike in

Baku, informing workers that "the country was fast approaching a financial crisis, one of the causes of which was the drop in productivity of labor." Suny, *The Baku Commune*, pp. 126–128.

88. Ef. Bronshtein, "O prieme i uvol'nenii sluzhashchikh," *VAT*, vol. 4, nos. 14–15, 1917, p. 6.

89. Bronshtein, "Zabastovka," p. 4.

90. Bronshtein, "Zabastovka," p. 5.

91. "Protokol obshchago sobraniia ot 10-go oktiabria 1917 g.," *VAT*, vol. 4, nos. 14–15, 1917, pp. 9–10.

92. "Obshchee sobranie sluzhashchikh v aptekakh ot 17-go oktiabria 1917 goda," *VAT*, vol. 4, nos. 14–15, 1917, p. 10.

93. Af. B., "Zabastovka v Petrogradskikh aptekakh," *VAT*, vol. 4, nos. 16–17, pp. 7–8.

94. "Korrespondentsii: Nizhni-Novgorod," *VAT*, vol. 5, nos. 6–7, 1918, p. 9.

95. "Zabastovochnye fondy," *VAT* , vol. 4, nos. 16–17, 1917, p. 6.

96. "Vologda," *VAT*, vol. 5, no. 1, 1918, p. 14.

97. "Kremenchug," *VAT*, vol. 5, nos. 2–3, 1918, p. 14.

98. "Korrespondentsii: Odessa," *VAT*, vol. 5, no. 1, 1918, pp. 13–14.

99. "Arendatory," *VAT*, vol. 5, no. 1, 1918, pp. 6–7. Menshevik pharmacists of course condemned these senseless dreams.

100. "Zabastovka v petrogradskikh aptekakh," *VAT*, vol. 4, nos. 16–17, 1917, p. 8, and "Nekotoryia uroki," ibid., p. 9.

101. "Obshchee sobranie ot 7-go noiabria 1917 g.," *VAT*, vol. 4, nos. 16–17, 1917, pp. 10–11.

102. "Obshchee sobranie ot 7-go noiabria 1917 g.," *VAT*, vol. 4, nos. 16–17, 1917, p. 11.

103. "Obshchee sobranie ot 12-go noiabria." *VAT*, vol. 4, nos. 16–17, 1917, p. 11.

104. "Otkliki zabastovki," *VAT*, vol. 4, nos. 16–17, 1917, p. 11–12.

105. McAuley notes the strike of civil servants, bank employees, and school teachers in Petrograd in December 1917, *Bread and Justice*, p. 50.

106. "Pervyi Vserossiiskii S"ezd Professional'nykh soiuzov," *VAT*., vol. 4, nos. 16–17, 1917, p. 10.

107. "Otkliki zabastovki," *VAT*, vol. 4, nos. 16–17, p. 12.

108. "Iz deiatel'nosti pravleniia Slianie s soiuzom sluzhashchikh v aptekarskikh predpriatiiakh," *VAT*, vol. 5, no. 1, 1918, p. 12.

109. "Ditsiplina v professional'nykh soiuzakh," *VAT*, vol. 5, nos. 4–5, 1918, p. 2.

110. "V Tsentral'nom Sovete Professional'nykh Soiuzov sluzhashchikh v aptekakh: O bezrabotnykh," *VAT*, vol. 5, no. 1, 1918, p. 12 and "V Tsentr. Sovete professional'nykh soiuzov sluzhashchikh v aptekakh. (Demobilizatsiia i bezrabotnitsa," ibid., nos. 2–3, pp. 9.

111. "V Tsentr. Sovete professional'nykh soiuzov sluzhashchikh v aptekakh," *VAT*, vol. 5, nos. 2–3, 1918, pp. 9–11.

112. "Moskovskiia pis'ma 'Zheleznaia ditsiplina,'" *VAT*, vol. 4, nos. 16–17, 1917, pp. 13–14.

113. "Korrespondentsii, Baku, Simbirsk, Ekaterinburg, Ekaterinoslav, Gomel, Briansk, Sugul'ma," *VAT*, vol. 4, nos. 16–17, 1917, pp. 14–15.

114. "Briansk," *VAT*, vol. 5, no. 1, 1918, p. 15. Comrade Sverdlov made the report on unemployment. For two Russian stamps (one 1975, the other 1985) commemorating Ia. M. Sverdlov, revolutionary pharmacist (1885–1919), see George Griffenhagen, *Pharmacy in Philately Album* (Madison, WI: American Institute of the History of Pharmacy, 1989).

115. (No title on photocopy), *VAT*, vol. 5, no. 1, 1918, p. 9.

116. Iaroslav was here revealed to be a Bolshevik. "V Petrogradskom Soiuze sluzhashchikh v aptekakh," Obshchee Sobranie 31-dekabria 1918 goda [*sic*—the date must have been *1917* because the assembly discussed the Brest-Litovsk peace talks]. *VAT*, vol. 5, no. 1, 1918, p. 12.

117. "V Petrogradskom Soiuze sluzhashchikh v aptekakh: Obshchee sobranie 31-dekabria," *VAT*, vol. 5, no. 1, 1918, p. 12.

118. T. Paperin, "O kharaktere nashei revoliutsii," *VAT*, vol. 5, nos. 2–3, 1918, p. 3.

119. "Chemu nas uchit Marks," *VAT*, vol. 5, nos. 2–3, 1918, p. 3.

120. T. Paperin, "O kharaktere nashei revoliutsii," *VAT*, vol. 5, nos. 4–5, 1918, pp. 6–7.

Chapter 19

1. "Zabastovka v petrogradskikh aptekakh," *Vestnik aptechnago truda* [hereafter cited *VAT*], vol. 4, nos. 16–17, 1917, p. 7; Also "Natsionalizatsiia aptek v Petrograde, *Izvestiia aptechnoi komissii* [hereafter cited *IAK*], vol. 1, no. 1 (November), 1918, p. 3.

2. "Sredi sluzhashchikh v aptekakh: Petrograd," *VAT*, vol. 4, nos. 16–17, 1917 p. 9.

3. "Natsionalizatsiia aptek v Petrograde," *IAK*, vol. 1, no. 1, 1918, p. 3.

4. "K voprosu o munitsipalizatsii aptek," *VAT*, vol. 5, nos. 2–3, 1918, p. 2.

5. "V tsentr. Sovete professional'nykh soiuzov sluzhashchikh v aptekakh," *VAT*, vol. 5, nos. 2–3, 1918, p. 9.

6. "V tsentr. Sovete professional'nykh soiuzov sluzhashchikh v aptekakh," *VAT*, vol. 5, nos. 2–3, 1918, pp. 9–10.

7. "Postanovlenie Gorodskoi Dumy ot 24 ianv. 1918 g. o vospreshchenii vyvoza medikamentov iz aptek i ob obrazovanii komissii obshchestvennogo kontrolia nad aptekami," *IAK*, vol. 1, no. 1 (November), 1918, p. 6.

8. "Petrogradskaia Gorodskaia Duma 31-go ianvaria 1918 g. priniala sleduiushchee postanovlenie o munitsipalizatsii aptek v Petrograde," *VAT*, vol. 5, nos. 2–3, 1918, p. 10.

9. "Petrograd: munitsipalizatsii aptek," *VAT*, vol. 5, nos. 4–5, 1918, p. 7.

10. A. Aluf, *VAT*, vol. 5, nos. 6–7, 1918, p. 5.

11. "Instruktsiia po pereniatiiu aptek"; the form was entitled "ORDER." *IAK*, vol. 1, no. 2 (January), 1919, pp. 22-23.

12. "Munitsipalizatsiia aptek v Petrograde," *IAK*, vol. 1, no. 1 (November), 1918, pp. 3-6.

13. "Petrogradskaia Gorodskaia Duma 31-go ianvaria 1918 g. priniala sleduiushchee postanovlenie o munitsipalizatsii aptek v Petrograde," *VAT*, vol. 5, nos. 2-3, 1918, p. 10.

14. "Natsionalizatsiia aptek v Petrograde," *IAK*, vol. 1, no. 1 (November), 1918, p. 5.

15. Gosudarstvennyi Istoricheskii Arkhiv Peterburga [hereafter cited GIAP], fond 212, opis' 8, delo 127, list 229 [hereafter cited "f.," "op.," "d.," "l."]. Antonina informed authorities that the manager of her pharmacy was I. A. Poret, Provizor, and that the pharmacy employed "2 *retseptarshi*" [people who accepted prescriptions], 1 laborant, 2 controllers, 3—in dispensing prescriptions, 1 in over-the-counter sales, 1 *defektarizator*, or tester, 13 Assistant Pharmacists, 1 accountant—in all 36 persons [women] plus 14 called to the war."

16. GIAP, f. 212, op. 8, d. 127, l. 228.

17. GIAP, f. 212, op. 8, d. 127, l. 229.

18. "Sluzhashchie aptek i munitsipalizatsii," *VAT*, vol. 5, nos. 6-7, 1918, pp. 5-6.

19. "Obshchee Sobranie Soiuza sluzhashchikh v aptekakh ot 28 aprelia 1918 goda," *VAT*, vol. 5, nos. 6-7, 1918, p. 8.

20. "Khar'kovskie pis'ma," *VAT*, vol. 5, nos. 2-3, 1918, pp. 13-14.

21. The Perm *Farmpodotdel* used the term "nationalized" rather than "municipalized." Tsentral'nyi Gosudarstvennyi Arkhiv RSFSR (Moscow) [hereafter cited TsGA RSFSR], f. 482, op. 5, d. 26, ll. 2-5.

22. TsGA RSFSR, f. 482, op. 5, d. 26, l. 10.

23. TsGA RSFSR, f. 482, op. 5, d. 26, l. 15.

24. TsGA RSFSR, f. 482, op. 5, d. 26, l. 13.

25. Ibid., l. 14.

26. TsGA RSFSR, f. 482, op. 5, d. 26, l. 6.

27. TsGA RSFSR, f. 482, op. 5, d. 26, ll. 20, 24.

28. Ibid., l. 24.

29. "Kursk," *VAT*, vol. 5, nos. 8-9, 1918, p. 14.

30. "g. Kolomna," *VAT*, vol. 5, nos. 8-9, 1918, p. 14.

31. "Iz praktiki munitsipal'nykh aptek," *VAT*, vol. 5, nos. 8-9, 1918, p. 5.

32. "Petrograd: Obshchee sobranie sluzhashchikh aptek ot 2-go iunia 1918 g.," *VAT*, vol. 5, nos. 8-9, 1918, p. 14.

33. Soiuznaia khronika. Petrograd. Professional'nyi soiuz sluzhashchikh v aptekakh. Obshchee sobranie ot 10 iulia 1918 g.," *VAT*, vol. 5, nos. 10-11, 1918, p. 14.

34. TsGA RSFSR, f. 482, op. 5, d. 26, l. 6.

35. "Obshchee sobranie sluzhashchikh aptek ot 2-go Iunia 1918 g.," *VAT*, vol. 5, nos. 8-9, 1918, p. 13.

36. "Iz deiatel'nosti pravleniia Petrogradskago soiuza sluzhashchikh v aptekakh," *VAT*, vol. 5, nos. 6-7, 1918, p. 9.

37. *Loc. cit.*

38. "Bol'noe mesto," *VAT*, vol. 5, nos. 8-9, 1918, p. 6.

39. "Soiuznaia khronika. Petrograd. Professional'nyi soiuz sluzhashchikh v aptekakh. Obshchee Sobranie ot 10 iulia 1918 g.," *VAT*, vol. 5, nos. 10-11, 1918, p. 14.

40. "Iz deiatel'nosti pravleniia," *VAT*, vol. 5, nos. 8-9, 1918, p. 14. The Left SRs sided with the Bolsheviks until the Soviet government signed the Peace of Brest-Litovsk with Germany in March, 1918, taking Russia out of the war and transferring the periphery of the former empire to the central powers.

41. "V Narodnyi Komissariat Zdravookhraneniia," TsGA RSFSR, f. 482, op. 5, d. 12, l. 32.

42. "V Sovet Narodnykh Komissarov: dokladnaia zapiska o natsionalizatsii vsekh aptek Respubliki," TsGA RSFSR, f. 482, op. 5, d. 12, l. 10.

43. "V Narodnyi Komissariat Zdravookhraneniia," TsGA RSFSR, f. 482, op. 5, d., 12, l. 32.

44. M(ikhail). P(avlovich). Iroshnikov, *Predsedatel' Soveta Narodnykh Komissarov V. I. Ul'ianov (Lenin) Ocherki gosudarstvennoi deiatel'nosti v 1917-1918 gg.* (Leningrad, 1974), pp. 136-309, especially pp. 313-435. See also T. H. Rigby, *Lenin's Government Sovnarkom 1917-1922* (Cambridge University Press, 1979).

45. Helene Carriere d'Encausse makes this point in *Lenin: Revolution and Power* (London, New York: Longman, 1987 ed.), p. 197. The estimated 600,000 bureaucrats in the tsarist government rose to 4 million by 1928, before the government ran the entire economy.

Boris Pil'niak satirized the luxuriance of Bolshevik government bodies in his novel, titled in English, *The Naked Year*, trans., A. R. Tulloch (Ann Arbor, MI: Ardis, 1975), p. 31.

46. "Proekt: Polozhenie o farmatsevticheskom otdele narodnago komissariata zdravookhraneniia," TsGA RSFSR, f. 482, op. 5, d. 12, l. 29. The term subdepartment—"podotdel"—was not spelled uniformly. Different documents spelled the term differently.

47. "Vsem Gubotdelam Zdravookhraeniia (Farmatsevticheskim Pod'otdelam," Tsirkuliar No. 9, 25 marta 1919 g.: 'Dopolnitel'nye pravila o tovarnoi otchetnosti v aptekakh,'" *Tsirkuliary i rasporiazheniia Farmotdela N. K. Z. . . . Protokoly Kollegii farpoda Penzenskogo gubzdrava* (Penza: Tipografiia Gubsovnarkhoza No. 3, 1921), p. 8. In this work the term subdepartment—"podotdel" was spelled "pod'otdel."

48. TsGA RSFSR, f. 492, op. 5, d. 2, l. 1. VSNKh, or the National Council of Public Economy, was a special body attached to the Cabinet, the Council of People's Commissars.

See also TsGA RSFSR, f. 482, op. 5, d. 12, l. 13.

49. "Polozhenie o glavnom komitete khimiko-farmat. promyshlennosti,," no. 26276, TsGA RSFSR, f. 482, op. 5, d. 3, ll. 4-5.

50. "Protokol no. 1: I-go organizatsionnago zasedaniia 'Farmatsentra,' 20-go avgusta 1918." TsGA RSFSR, f. 482, op. 5, d. 13, l. 129. This first organizational meeting of Farmatsentr discussed the agency's budget, its tasks, and established a commission to work out a proposal to present to Narkomzdrav. Chichibabin, Ferrein, and I. P. Kornblium were among those elected to the commission. At the second meeting 2 September 1918 O. G. Gabrilovich, Ferrein, Chichibabin, and N. A. El'kind, workers' representative, were elected to the "Chief Committee on the Chemico-Pharmaceutical Industry." Unfortunately, *Farmatsentr* did not have a proper budget. Therefore, it requested 35,000 rubles for two months from the administration of the "State Chemico-Pharmaceutical Industry." Ibid., l. 130. El'kind was to form a housing committee and get a staff ready.

51. "Protokol zasedaniia Soveta Vrachebnik Kollegii ot 19-go Aprelia 1918 goda . . . Doklad d-ra Solov'eva ob obrazovanii pri farmatsevticheskom otdel Komissariata Vnutrennikh Del osoboi Komissii po uchetu i raspredeleniiu medikamentov i meditsinskikh sredstv." TsGA RSFSR, f. 482, op. 1, d. 1a, l. 29.

This Pharmacy Department was subordinate to a Medical College, its name hearkening back to the eighteenth century.

52. "Polozhenie o farmatsevticheskoi komissii pri farmatsevticheskom otdele narodnago komissariata zdravookhraneniia," TsGA RSFSR, f. 482, op. 5, d. 2, ll. 1–1 ob.

On the Scientific Chemico-Pharmaceutical Institute and Control-Educational Laboratory of Medicinal Preparations attached to the Pharmacy Deaprtment of the Commissariat of Health (*Nauchnoi khimiko-farmatsevticheskoi institut i kontrol'no-ispytatel'noi laboratorii lekarstvennykh preparatov pri Farmatsevticheskom otdele Narodnago komissariata Zdravookhraneniia*), see also TsGA RSFSR, f. 482, op. 5, d. 12, ll. 18 and 19.

The Medical College of the Commissariat of Internal Affairs, which included Lenin's longtime comrade, Dr. Bonch-Bruevich, discussed the organization of a "Pharmacy Commission" May 31, 1918, as point 5 of its 8-point agenda. TsGA RSFSR, f. 482, op. 1, d. 1a, ll. 55, 56.

It is unclear whether this was the Commission in the Commissariat of Health or another under the jurisdiction of the Commissariat of Internal Affairs, as the Internal Affairs Commission was labeled *farmatsevticheskaia komissiia* and the commission in the Commissariat of Health was called *Aptechnaia Komissiia* by November 1918. "Zhurnal zasedanii Soveta Vrachebnikh Kollegii ot 31 Maia 1918 goda," TsGA RSFSR, f. 482, op. 5, d. 16, l. 46.

53. "Iz deiatel'nosti Nauchnoi Sektsii. Zasedanie 17 avgusta 1918 goda," *IAK*, vol. 1, no. 1, 1918, p. 9. Aluf was in charge of the organizing department. Also, "Zhurnal Zasedaniia Nauchnoi Sektsii pri Aptechnoi Komissii 29-go Noiabria 1918 goda," TsGA RSFSR, f. 482, op. 5, d. 16, l. 46. For information on the Petrograd Commission see chapters 16 and 17 of the present work.

54. "Protokol zasedaniia Soveta Vrachebnikh Kollegii ot 19-go Aprelia 1918 goda," TsGA RSFSR, f. 482, op. 1, d. 1a, l. 29.

55. "Polozhenie o farmatsevticheskom otdele narodnago komissariata zdravookhraneniia," TsGA RSFSR, f. 482, op. 5, d. 2, l. 4. "Polozhenie o Narodnom Ko-

missariate Zdravookhraneniia, 20 iulia 1918," *VAT*, vol. 5, nos. 10–11, 1918, p. 18.

56. "Protokol No. 13. Zasedaniia 'Farmatsentr' 22-go oktiabria 1918 goda," TsGA RSFSR, f. 482, op. 5, d. 13, ll. 165, 165 ob.

57. George Leggett, *The Cheka: Lenin's Political Police* (Oxford: Clarendon Press, 1981), pp. xxxii–xxxv and *passim*.

58. Lenin, "The State and Revolution," *The Lenin Anthology*, ed., Robert C. Tucker (New York: W. W. Norton, 1975), pp. 311–398. Academics debate over whether Lenin meant "control" to consist of actual management or "kontrol" in the sense of supervision need not concern us here.

59. For a panoramic view of the Civil War see Evan Mawdsley, *The Russian Civil War* (Boston: Allen & Unwin, 1987). For a discussion of the economic aspects of War Communism see Alec Nove, *An Economic History of the USSR* (London, New York: Penguin Books, 1990), pp. 37–72.

60. "Polozheniia o glavnom komitete khimiko-farm. promyshlennosti," TsGA RSFSR, f. 482, op. 5, d. 3, ll. 2, 3. The other factories included Dongauer and Kaizer.

61. "V Narodnyi Komissariat Zdravookhraneniia," TsGA RSFSR, f. 482, op. 5, d. 2, l. 2.

62. "V Vserossiiskii tsentral'nyi ispolnitel'nyi komitet sovetov rabochikh, krest'ianskikh, kazach'ikh i krasnoarmeiskikh deputatov," 19 Aug 1918, " TsGA RSFSR, f. 482, op. 5, d. 2, l. 7, 7 ob.

(Duplicate in ibid., d. 12, l. 30.)

63. "Offitsialnyi otdel: Ob organizatsii Farmatsevticheskikh Podotdelov pri Mediko-Sanitarnykh otdelakh Sovdepov, 10 iulia 1918 g.," *VAT*, vol. 5, nos. 10–11, 1918, p. 18.

64. "Polozhenie o natsionalizirovannykh aptekakh . . . proekt," TsGA RSFSR, f. 482, op. 5, d. 12, l. 3

65. TsGA RSFSR f. 482, op. 5, d. 26, ll. 10–12.

66. TsGA RSFSR, f. 482, op. 5, d. 26, l. 14.

67. TsGA RSFSR, f. 482, op. 16, d. 2, l. 1; ll. 44 and 44 ob. (October 19, 1918).

68. For example, Fabrika "Sanagri," in TsGA RSFSR, f. 482, op. 16, d. 3, ll. 21 and 21 ob. This Moscow firm had been established in 1912. It itemized its basic capital at 120,000 rubles, stores at 80,000 rubles, 23 workers, and so on.

69. "Protokol No. 14," TsGA RSFSR, f. 482, op. 5. d. 13, ll. 165, 165 ob.

70. TsGA RSFSR, f. 482, op. 5, d. 13, ll. 159, 160.

71. "Iz Peterburga po telefony," and "O natsionalizatsii aptek," *Ekonomicheskaia zhizn'*, no. 31, Friday, December 13, 1918, p. 1.

72. "V vserossiiskii tsentral'nyi ispolnitel'nyi komitet sovetov rabochikh, krest'ianskikh, kazach'ikh i krasnoarmeiskikh deputatov," TsGA RSFSR, f. 482, op. 5, d. 2, l. 5, and "Postanovlenie o regulirovanii prodazhi i otpuska aptekarskikh tovarov, Moskva 27-go iulia 1918 g.," *VAT*, vol. 5, nos. 10–11, 1918, p. 18.

73. "Tsirkuliarno: Vsem mediko-sanitarnym otdelam sovdepov," TsGA RSFSR, f. 482, op. 5, d. 2, l. 3. Also, TsGA RSFSR, f. 482, op. 5, d. 12, l. 28.

74. "Polozhenie o farmatsevticheskom Biuro po uchetu i raspredeleniiu medikamentov, 6-avgusta," *VAT*, vol. 5, nos. 10–11, 1918, p. 19.

75. "Pravila deiatel'nosti Tsentro-Snabzheniia," *IAK*, vol. 1, no. 1 (November), 1918, p. 9.

76. "V Kommunal'nykh aptekakh: O takse . . . o zakrytykh aptekakh, o kozmeticheskikh sredstvakh," *IAK*, vol. 1, no. 1 (November 1), 1918, pp. 10–11, and "Polozhenii" on these topics in "Offitsial'nyi otdel," *IAK*, ibid., pp. 12–15.

77. "Zhurnal zasedaniia nauchnoi sektsii pri Aptechnoi Komissii 29-go noiabria 1918 goda," TsGA RSFSR, f. 482, op. 5, g. 16, l. 46.

78. "Preis-kurant Otdela Snabzheniia," *IAK*, vol. 1, no. 1, 1918, p. 9; "Iz deiatel'nosti Tsentro-Snabzheniia: "Uproshenie biurokraticheskoi formalistiki," *IAK*, vol. 1, no. 2, 1919, pp. 22–23. Debate on wholesale prices for items produced in Russia and prices for imported wares also in "Protokol no. 59 Ochered' Zasedaniia Kollegiia Nar. Kom. Zdravo 10-go dekabria 1918," TsGA RSFSR fond. 482, opis 16 delo 2 list 105.

79. Zhurnal No. 11, Zasedanie glavnogo komiteta khimiko-farmatsevticheskoi promyshlennosti, 15 oktiabria 1918," TsGA RSFSR, f. 482, op. 5, d. 13, ll. 167, 167 ob.

80. TsGA RSFSR, f. 482, op. 5, d. 13, ll. 161, 161 ob. 162, 162 ob., 164, 164 ob., 165 (October 22 to December 3, 1918).

81. TsGA RSFSR, f. 482, op. 16, d. 3, l. 17.

82. Letter of January 2, 1919, "V Narodnyi Komissariat Zdravookhraneniia," TsGA RSFSR, f. 482, op. 16, d. 3, ll. 14, 14 ob, 15. Luchich even put the stamps required by tsarist authorities on his letter.

83. TsGA RSFSR, f. 482, op. 16, d. 3, ll. 16, 16 ob.

84. "Grazhdaninu Vasiliiu Nikolaevichu Luchich," TsGA RSFSR, f. 482, op. 16, d. 3, l. 17.

85. TsGA RSFSR, f. 482, op. 16, d. 3, ll. 18, 18 ob.

86. Ia. Kamenskii, "O formakh upravleniia aptechnym delom," *IAK*, vol. 1, no. 2, 1919, pp. 18–19. Also, "V Kommunal'nykh aptekakh: O trudovoi ditsipline, O takse, Peremenovanie aptek, Zakrytie aptek, Snabzhenie aptek, Ob oblatakh, Tsentral'naia fasovochnaia, Natsionalizatsiia aptek v provintsii, reviziia aptek," *IAK*, vol. 1, no. 2, 1919, pp. 24–25; "Khronika: Ekonomiia medikamentov, Izgotovlenie tabletok, Subdebnye dela, Smeta bol'nichnykh aptek, ibid., pp. 25–26.

87. "V Kommunal'nykh aptekakh: O Dezhurstvakh," *IAK*, vol. 1, no. 1, 1918, pp. 10–11.

88. TsGA RSFSR, f. 482, op. 5, d. 9, 1. 1.

89. TsGA RSFSR, f. 482, op. 5, d. 9, l. 4.

90. TsGA RSFSR, f. 482, op. 5, d. 9, ll. 6 and 7.

91. TsGA RSFSR, f. 482, op. 4, d. 9, l. 10.

92. TsGA RSFSR, f. 482, op. 5, d. 9, l. 18.

93. TsGA RSFSR, f. 482, op. 5, d. 9, l. 26.

94. TsGA RSFSR, f. 482, op. 5, d. 26, ll. 10–12.

95. TsGA RSFSR, f. 482, op. 5, d. 26, l. 15.

96. See for example, "V Nauchnom Eksperimental'nom khimiko-farmatsevticheskom Institute," TsGA RSFSR, f. 482, op. 5, d. 16, ll. 23, 23 ob.

97. The staff union of the Kel(l)er Association was referred to at the November 5 meeting of *Farmatsentr.* TsGA RSFSR, f. 482, op. 5, d. 13, l. 164 ob.

98. "g. Kolomna," *VAT*, vol. 5, nos. 8-9, 1918, p. 8.

99. In the Russian: "*oni dolzhni prinimat' blizkoe i aktivnoe uchastie v pravil'noi organizatsii farmatsevticheskogo upravleniia.*" Rezoliutsiia ob upravlenii farmastevticheskim delom v Respublike po dokladu tov. Rapoporta," *VAT*, vol. 5, no. 12, 1918, p. 11.

100. "Petrograd: Profess. Soiuz sluzhashchikh v Aptekakh," *VAT*, vol. 5, no. 12, 1918, p. 13.

101. "Rezoliutsiia o tekushchem momente po dokladu tov. Alufa," *VAT*, vol. 5, no. 12, 1918, p. 10.

102. "Obshchee sobranie chlenov Petrogradskago soiuza sluzh. v aptekakh ot 3 noiabria 1918 g.," ibid., p. 14.

103. "Konferentsiia predstavitelei Farmatsevticheskikh Podotdelov i Mediko-Sanitarnykh Otdelov Sovdepov Petrogradskoi gub., 15 sentiabria 1918," *IAK*, vol. 1, no. 1, 1918, p. 12.

104. "Petrograd.-Delegatskie sobraniia," *VAT*, vol. 6, no. 2, 1919, p. 17.

105. "Priem raionnykh kontrolerov, adresa i No.No. telefonov raionnykh aptek," *IAK*, vol. 1, no. 1, 1918, p. 16.

106. Instruktsiia, TsGA RSFSR, f. 482, op. 5, d. 11, l. 27.

107. I. Levinshtein, *Materialy po profess.-tekhnicheskomu obrazovaniiu. Farmatsevticheskoe obrazovanie* (Moscow: Gosudarstvennoi Izdatel'stvo, 1921) and *Materialy po farmatsevticheskomu obrazovaniiu* (Moscow, 1922).

108. "O formakh upravleniia aptechnym delom," *IAK*, vol. 1, no. 2 (January), 1919, p. 18.

109. Sov Nar Kom: "Dekret o natsionalizatsii aptek," TsGA RSFSR, f. 482, op. 5, d. 12, l. 11.

110. "Spravochnyi otdel: dezhurnye voskresnye apteki dnem i noch'iu na 3-e i 10-e noiabria," *IAK*, vol. 1, no. 1, 1918, p. 15, and "Spravochnyi otdel. Spisok Kommunal'nykh aptek," *IAK*, vol. 1, no. 2 (January), 1919, pp. 29-31, *Pervaia zhenskaia (apteka)*, Nevskii Prospekt now called 25 October street, no. 32 (Phone: 4-05), listed ibid., p. 30.

111. TsGA RSFSR, f. 482, op. 5, d. 13, ll. 154, 155.

112. A. G. Natradze, *Ocherk razvitiia khimiko-farmatsevticheskoi promyshlennosti SSSR* (Moscow, 1967), pp. 93-94.

113. TsGA RSFSR, f. 482, op. 16, d. 3, ll. 23, 24, 24ob, 25.

114. "V Tverskoi gubernskii ispolnitel'nyi komitet sovetov rabochikh, krest'ianskikh i krasnoarmeiskikh deputatov," TsGA RSFSR, f. 482, op. 16 d. 3, ll. 28, 28 ob.

115. At the end of 1919, former owners were managing about eighty pharmacies—10 percent of the eight hundred pharmacies that had responded to a questionnaire from the still existing "All Russian Union of Pharmacy Workers." Twelve provincial organizations (*gubotdely*) reported that former managers existed among the managers of of local pharmacy organizations (*farpodotdely*) and five

district organizations reported that this was the case. In the twelve provinces there were twenty-two district pharmacy subdepartments where the managers were former pharmacy owners. In total, fifty-three managers on the provincial level were former pharmacy owners. Thirty district managers were pharmacy owners. "Byvshie aptekovladel'tsy sredi zaveduiushchikh farpodami i upravliaiushchikh aptekami," *VAT*, vol. 6, nos. 4–5 (December 5), 1919, pp. 4–5.

116. Terrible times ensued in St. Petersburg/Petrograd during 1918 and 1919, particularly for Poles and pharmacy owners. *Kurjer Polski*, 1918, 1919, *passim*.

117. Roeske, *Antonina Lesniewska*, p. 21. Also, p. 2 of typed copy of "Wspomneinie dzialalnosci spolecznej s. p. Antoniny Lesniewskiej," *Kurjer Poranny*, 1938, in Pharmacy Museum, Krakow, and pp. 3 and 4 of handwritten copy of "Wspomnienie dzialalnosci s. p. Antoniny Lesniewskiej," *Kurier Freimorgan*, 1938, in Pharmacy museum, Warsaw. Also, conversation with Dr. Jerzy Lesniewski, Antonina's nephew, Warsaw, March, 1990. Dr. Lesniewski was an infant at the time.

118. In Warsaw Lesnevskaia established a children's colony ("Nasza chata"). Roeske, *loc. cit.*; Lesniewski, *loc. cit.*. From 1933, Lesnevskaia again operated a pharmacy in Warsaw, at 72 Marzsalkowska Street, until her death in 1937. Notorized documents, Museum of Pharmacy, Warsaw, 72 Marzsalkowska St., Director Dr. Teodor Kikta.

119. TsGA RSFSR, f. 482, op. 5, d. 12, ll. 23, 23 ob., 24 and l. 12.

120. TsGA RSFSR, f. 482, op. 5, d. 26, l. 8.

121. TsGA RSFSR f. 482, op. 5, d. 12, l. 20.

122. TsGA RSFSR, f. 482, op. 5, d. 12, l. 47. A poorly stamped piece of 6x9-inch paper to Narkomzdrav or the Commissariat of Health, with this complaint was dated 29 October 1919.

123. "K. N. Z. Vyshevolotskago Ispolnitel'nago Komiteta, Soveta Krest'ianskikh i Rabochikh Deputatov: Otdel Mediko Sanitarnyi, 4 Sentiabria, 1918, V Narodnyi Komissariat Zdravookhraneniia," TsGA RSFSR, f. 482, op. 16, d. 3, l. 31.

124. "Ob"iasnitel'naia zapiska s finansovom polozhenii v Rossii," TsGA RSFSR, f. 482, op. 5, d. 12, ll. 1, 2.

125. "O zakrytykh aptekakh," *IAK*, vol. 1, no. 1 (November), 1918, p. 11.

126. I. G. Tsitron, (no title on xerox copy), *VAT*, vol. 5, no. 12, 1918, p. 7.

127. "g. Kolomna," *VAT*, vol. 5, nos. 8–9, 1918, p. 8.

128. See chapter following.

129. "Zhurnal No. 11, zasedaniia glavnago komiteta khimiko-farmatsevticheskoi promyshlennosti 15 Oktiabria 1918 goda," TsGA RSFSR, f. 482, op. 5, d. 13, ll. 167, 167 ob. Also ibid., l. 169.

130. "Protokol No. 12 zasedaniia 'Farmatsentra' 18 Oktiabria 1918 goda," TsGa RSFSR, f. 482, op. 5, d. 13, l. 166.

131. TsGA RSFSR f. 482, op. 5, d. 13, l. 168. Keler was spelled here as "Keller."

132. "Protokol No. 13 zasedaniia 'Farmatsentra' 22 Oktiabria 1918 goda," TsGA RSFSR f. 482, op. 5, d. 13, l. 165 ob.

133. "Zhurnal No. 19 plenarnogo zasedaniia 'Farmatsentra' 3 Dekabria 1918 g.," TsGA RSFSR f. 482, op. 5, d. 13, ll. 159, 159 ob. 160.

134. "Dokladnaia zapiska po povodu zakupki medikamentov na rynke Turke-

stana i sosednykh . . . gosudarstv instruktora iz NKZ proekta VtsIK Krasnyi Vostok," TsGA RSFSR, f. 482, op. 16, d. 3, l. 7.

135. TsGA RSFSR, f. 482, op. 16, d. 3, l. 29.

136. TsGA RSFSR, f. 482, op. 16, d. 3, l. 30.

137. TsGA RSFSR f. 482, op. 5, d. 26, l. 7.

138. "Rossiiskaia Federativnaia Sovetskaia Respublika, Komissariat Vnutrennikh Del, Sovet Moskovskoi Narodnoi Militsii, Komissar po grazhdanskoi chasti, gor. Moskvy," Maia 27 1918, TsGA RSFSR f. 482, op. 5, d. 1, l. 1, and "V Meditsinskuiu Kollegiiu Komissariata Vnutrennikh Del, Sovet Narodnykh Komissarov, g. Moskvy," Maia 8 1918, ibid., l. 2; ibid. l. 3 re: confiscating opium in Moscow region.

In August, 1918, the Council of People's Commissars reported on opium from Persia, diverted to Eastern Siberia and then China, whence it returned to Russia, and to speculation in opium. "Rossiiskaia Federativnaia Sotsialistichnaia Sovetskaia Respublika: Upravlenie delami Soveta Narodnykh Komissarov, Moskva, Kremel', 5 Avgusta 1918, no. 7420 : V Komissariat Zdravookhraneniia," TsGA RSFSR, f. 482, op. 5. d. 1, ll. 5, 5 ob.

Also, on opium see "V Komissariat Vnutrennikh Del, 8 Avgusta 1918," TsGA RSFSR, f. 482, op. 5, d. 1, ll. 7, 7 ob.

Re. cocaine, the Council of People's Commissars warned the Commissariat of Health in June on the spread of cocaine in Moscow. Not only dispensed from pharmacies it was freely sold in coffee houses, restaurants, tea houses, and other places. Speculation in cocaine was said to be widespread. "Rossiiskaia Federativnaia . . . upravlenie delami Soveta Narodnykh Komissarov, 31 Iunia, 1918: V Komissariat Zdravookhraneniia," TsGA RSFSR, f. 482, op. 5, d. 1, l. 6.

139. "V Vserossiiskuiu Chrezvychainuiu Komissiiu po bor'be s kont-revoliutsiei i spekuliatsiei pri Sovete Narodnykh Komissarov, Otdel bor'by so spekuliatsiei," TsGA RSFSR f. 482, op. 5 , d. 1, l. 8 and 8 ob.

Also "V vserossiiskii tsentral'nyi ispolnitel'nyi komitet sovetov rabochikh, krest'ianskikh, kazach'ikh i krasnoarmeiskikh deputatov, (August, 1918), TsGA RSFSR, f. 482, op. 5, d. 2, l. 7.

140. Dekret Soveta Narodnykh Komissarov o vospreshchenii vvoza, vyvoza, khraneniia i prodazhi opiia, morfiia i kokaina," n. d., TsGA RSFSR, f. 482, op. 5, d. 1, l. 10.

141. See Mary Schaeffer Conroy, "Abuse of Drugs other than Alcohol and Tobacco in the Soviet Union," *Soviet Studies*, vol. 42, no. 3, 1990, pp. 447–480.

142. "V. V. Ch. K. Soglasno zapros ot 29 1/21 Farmatsevticheskii Otdel N. K. Z. preprovozhdaet pri semsvedenii o sotrudnikakh i vysshenazvannogo otdela," TsGA RSFSR f. 482, op. 5, d. 79, ll. 5 and 5 ob.

143. "Proekt uchrezhdeniia Nauchnogo Eksperimental'nogo Khimiko-Farmatevticheskogo Instituta pri Farmatsevticheskom Otdele Narodnogo Komissariata Zdravookhraneniia," TsGA RSFSR, f. 482, op. 5, d. 16, l. 28.

144. "V Narodnyi Komissariat Prodovol'stviia/ Verkhnie Torgovye Riady 3-i etazh, 28 Iunia 1918, TsGA RSFSR, f. 482, op. 5, d. 8, l. 1.

145. TsGA RSFSR, f. 482, op. 5, d. 8, l. 2.

146. TsGA RSFSR, op. 16, d. 3, l. 36.

147. TsGA RSFSR, f. 482, op. 5, d. 26, l. 9.

148. For a discussion of the grandiose (and little fulfilled) plans for education in early Soviet Russia, see Larry E. Holmes, *The Kremlin and the Schoolhouse: Reforming Education in Soviet Russia, 1917–1931* (Bloomington: Indiana University Press), *passim*.

149. "V Narodnyi Komissariat Prosveshcheniia," TsGA RSFSR, f. 482, op. 5, d. 16, ll. 24, 24 ob.

150. "Rezoliutsiia farmatsevticheskoi kollegii k proektu vserossiiskogo soiuza farmatsevticheskikh obshchestv i organizatsii o kursakh dlia podgotovki farmatsevticheskikh inspektorov," TsGA RSFSR, f. 482, op. 5, d. 16, l. 43.

151. "Zhurnal zasedaniia nauchnoi sektsii pri Aptechnoi Komissii 29-go Noiabria 1918 goda," TsGA RSFSR, f. 482, op. 5, d. 16, l. 46–47 ob.

152. "Polozhenie o Farmatsevticheskom Obrazovanii prim . . . k skeme Prof. Tekhn. Obraz. NKZ," TsGA RSFSR f. 482, op. 5, d. 12, ll. 48 and 48 ob.

The "United Labor School" was the brainchild of the Commissariat of Enlightenment. The school was to combine academics and practical training in order to produce much-needed financial, administrative, and pedagogical specialists. Holmes, *The Kremlin*, pp. 88–89.

153. "V upravlenie delami Narkomzdrav," TsGA RSFSR f. 482, op. 5, d. 12, l. 38.

154. "Ob uskorennoi podgotovke assistentov praktikantov," TsGA RSFSR, f. 482, op. 5, d. 16, l. 48.

155. "Zhurnal Zasedaniia nauchnoi sektsii pri Aptechnoi Komissii 27-go Dekabria 1918 goda," TsGA RSFSR, f. 482, op. 5, d. 16, ll. 49, 49 ob.

156. Levinshtein, *Materialy po profess.-tekhnicheskomu obrazovaniiu. Farmatsevticheskoe obrazovanie*, p. 16.

157. Levinshtein, *Materialy po profess.-tekhnisheskomu obrazovaniiu*, pp. 16–19.

158. I. Levinshtein, *Materialy po farmatsevticheskomu obrazovaniiu Programmy farmastevticheskoi shkoly* (Moscow: Gosudarstvennoe izdatel'stvo, 1922), pp. 7–10.

159. "Ob"iasnitel'naia zapiska o finansovom polozhenii aptek v Rossii," TsGA RSFSR, f. 482, op. 5, d. 12, ll. 1, 1 ob, 2.

160. "Smeta po soderzhaniiu Farmatsevticheskago Otdela Narodnago Komissariata Zdravookhraneniia na 2-oe polugodnie 1918 g. s 1-go Iiulia 1918 g. po 1-oe Ianvaria 1919 g.," TsGA RSFSR, f. 482, op. 5, d. 12, ll. 15, 15 ob.

161. Smeta upravleniia natsionalizovanno soderzhaniiu Farmatsevticheskago Otdela Narodnago Komissariata Zdravookhraneniia," TsGA RSFSR, f. 482, op. 5, d. 12, ll. 15, 15 ob., 16, 16 ob., 17, 25, 26.

Also Spisok otdelov, pod'otdelov, sektsii, podsektsii i dolzhnostnykh lits Narodnago Komissariata Zdravookhraneniia, TsGA RSFSR f. 482, op. 5, d. 79, ll. 1 and 1 ob.

162. "Smeta po soderzhaniiu Farmatsevticheskago Otedela Narodnago Komis-

sariata Zdravookhraneniia na 2-oe polugodie 1918 g. s I-go Iiulia 1918 g. po I-oe Ianvaria 1919 g.," TsGA RSFSR, f. 482, op. 5, d. 12, ll. 15, 15 ob.

163. "Smeta farmatsevticheskogo [*sic*] otdela Narodnogo [*sic*] Komissariata Zdravookhraneniia na 2-iu polovinu 1918 goda. Lichnyi sostav," TsGA RSFSR, f. 482, op. 5, d. 12, ll. 16, 16 ob., 17.

164. "Kassovyi otchet Aptechnoi Komissii za noiabr 1918 goda," *IAK*, vol. 1, no. 2, (January), 1919, p. 32. Income neatly matched expenditure. Money on hand in former private pharmacies amounted to over 143,000 rubles; with their inventories nationalized pharmacies provided over 543,000 rubles. Hospital pharmacies provided another 17,000 rubles. The Nationalized State Bank provided 1,150,000 rubles.

165. TsGA RSFSR, f. 482, op. 5, d. 26, l. 4.

166. TsGA RSFSR, f. 482, op. 5, d. 26, l. 11.

167. TsGA RSFSR, f. 482, op. 5, d. 26, l. 23.

168. TsGA RSFSR, f. 482, op. 5, d. 26, ll. 8, 9.

Tambov authorities also asked for clarification of the rules under which they were to operate and acquire medicines.

169. TsGA RSFSR, f. 482, op. 16, d. 2, ll. 120–121.

170. TsGA RSFSR, f. 482, op. 16, d. 2, l. 123.

171. TsGA RSFSR, f. 482, op. 16, d. 2, l. 129.

172. TsGA RSFSR, f. 482, op. 5, d. 26, l. 35.

173. Ibid., l. 36.

174. TsGA RSFSR, f. 482, op. 5, d. 12, l. 5.

175. TsGA RSFSR, f. 482, op. 16, d. 2, l. 113 ob.

176. Ibid., l. 113 and 113 ob.

177. "Protokol no. 3, zasedaniia Kollegiia Narodnago Komissariata Zdravo 10-go ianvaria 1919," TsGA RSFSR f. 482, op. 16, d. 2, l. 133.

178. "Protokol no. 4, Zasedaniia Kollegiia 11 ianvaria 1919," TsGA RSFSR f. 482 op. 16 d. 2, l. 142.

179. TsGA RSFSR, f. 482, op. 5, d. 12, ll. 14–19.

180. For the situation in the Ukraine see W. E. D. Allen, *The Ukraine* (Cambridge: The University Press, 1940), Peter Kenez, *Civil War in South Russia* (Berkeley: University of California Press, 1971); Alex Motyl, *The Turn to the Right: Ukrainian Nationalism 1919–29* (East European Monographs, 1980).

181. "Normal'nyi rabochii den' i voskresnyi otdykh," *Iuzhnyi vestnik aptechnago truda* [hereafter cited *IuVAT*], vol. 1, no. 2, 1918, pp. 2–4.

182. "Zhizn' farmatsevtov-sluzhashchikh v odesskikh aptekakh," *IuVAT*, vol. 1, no. 2, 1918 (Odessa, 1 July), pp. 5–6.

183. "Taksa," *IuVAT*, vol. 1, no. 5, 1918, pp. 3–4.

184. Advertisements *IuVAT*, vol. 1, 1918, nos. 2, p. 12; no. 7, (November 1, 1918), pp. 10–12.

185. "Birzha: Tovarnyia tseny," *IuVAT*, vol. 1, no. 5, p. 10. The prices were those as of August 15, 1918. Quantities and prices for chief medicines and supplies were as follows. ASA or aceto-salicylic acid (which the Russians called aspi-

rin): 120 to 180 rubles per kilo; antipyrine: 160 to 180 rubles per kilo; phenacetin: 335 to 350 rubles per kilo. Codeine, cocaine, and morphia were higher at 4,500–5,000 rubles, 5,000–5,500 rubles, and 4,000 to 4,250 rubles per kilo repectively. Quinine went for 900 to 1,100 rubles a kilo.

186. "Khronika," *IuVAT*, vol. 1, no. 7, 1918, p. 8.

187. "Birzha: tovarnyia tseny," *IuVAT*, vol. 1, no. 7, 1918, p. 9.

188. Advertisement, *IuVAT*, vol. 1, no. 7, 1918, pp. 10–12.

189. "Ustav professional'nago Soiuza Sluzhashchikh Aptek g. Odessy," *IuVAT*, vol. 1, no. 5 (August), 1918, pp. 5–8; "Registratsiia bezrabotnykh farmatsevtov," ibid., p. 5; "Professional'naia zhizn': Komitet truda (Kiev), V Nikolaeve, V Khar'kove, V Krimu—Yalta and Sevastopol', ibid., pp. 8–9, and *passim*.

190. "Na Ukraine: na kremenchugskikh aptekakh," *IuVAT*, vol. 1, no. 2, 1918, pp. 8–9.

191. For example, "Offitsial'nyi otdel, including "Protokol Soveshchaniia u Vrachebnago Inspektora: Novyi kollektivnyi dogovor," *IuVAT*, vol. 1, no. 2, 1918, pp. 7–8.

192. Advertisements, *IuVAT*, passim.

193. "Khronika: 'Soiuz Iuga Rossii," *IuVAT*, vol. 1, no. 5, 1918, p. 9.

Chapter 20

1. *Tsirkuliary i rasporiazheniia farmotdela N. K. Z. Rasporiazheniia farpoda Penzenskogo gubzdrava. 2-i vserossiiskii s"ezd zavfarpodami. 2-i gubernskii s"ezd zavfarpodami Penzenskoi gubernii. Protokoly kollegii farpoda Penzenskogo gubzdrava* (Penza: Tipografiia Gubsovnarkhoza No. 3, 1921).

2. "Tsirkuliar No. 1: Vsem gubzdravootdelam, Farmatsevticheskim Pod'otdelam: O vvedenii dozirovannykh lekarstvennykh form," *Tsirkuliary i rasporiazheniia . . . Penzenskogo gubzdrava*, pp. 1–2.

3. "Tsirkuliar No. 16, 26-go iulia 1920 g.: O dal'neishem vvedenii dozirovannykh lekarstvennykh form," ibid., pp. 26–28.

4. "Tsirkuliar No. 4. . . : Ob izgotovlenii ol. kamforat. . . . ," ibid., p. 3.

5. "Tsirkuliar No. 21, 12 avgusta 1920 g. . . . : O dozirovannykh lekarstvennykh formakh," ibid., pp. 36–37.

6. "Vsem Gubernskim otdelam Zdravookhraneniia (Farmatsevticheskim Pod'otdelam.) Instruktsiia dlia Gubernskikh kontrolerov-instruktorov," [no date, no number] ibid., pp. 3–5.

7. "Tsirkuliar No. 31/137 . . . : O poriadke khraneniia iadovitykh i sil'nodeistvuiushchikh preparatov," ibid., pp. 52–53.

8. "Tsirkuliar No. 32 . . . : O spiske medikamentov, podlezhashchikh zagotovke v pervuiu ochered'," ibid., pp. 53–58.

9. "Tsirkuliar No. 33/116 . . . : O povtorom otpuske lekarstva," ibid., pp. 58–59.

10. "Tsirkuliar No. 6: Vsem Gubzdravotdelam (Farmatsevticheskom Pod'otdelam) [undated], ibid., p. 6.

11. "Tsirkuliar No. 14 . . . : Ob ogranichenii spiska tinktur," ibid., pp. 22–24.

12. Tsentral'nyi Gosudarstvennyi Arkhiv RSFSR (Moscow) [hereafter cited

TsGA RSFSR], fond 482, opis' 5, delo 11, list 33 [hereafter cited "f.," "op.," "d.," "l." or "ll." in plural].

13. "Tsirkuliar No. 11: O platnom i bezplatnom otpuske lekarstv iz aptek Respubliki," *Tsirkuliary i rasporiazheniia . . . Penzenskogo gubzdrava*, pp. 18–19.

14. "Tskuliar No. 27 . . . : Ob uluchshenii kachestva raboty v aptekakh," ibid., pp. 43–44.

15. "Tsirkuliar No. 9 . . . : Dopolnitel'nye pravila o tovarnoi otchetnosti v aptekakh," ibid., pp. 8–12.

16. "Tsirkuliar No. 10, 25-go Marta, 1920 g. . . : "O revizii aptek," ibid, p. 13, and "Instruktsiia po revizii aptek," ibid., pp. 13–18.

17. "Tsirkuliar No. 28, 15 sentiabria 1920 g. . . . : Ob organizatsii gubernskikh fasovochnykh," ibid., pp. 44–50.

18. "Tsirkuliar No. 5 [undated] . . . : Ob ispol'zovanii byvshego v upotreblenii aptechnogo stekla," ibid., pp. 5–6.

19. "Tsirkuliar No. 7 [undated] . . . : O raspredelenii medikamentov v predelakh gubernii," ibid., pp. 6–7.

20. "*Tsirkuliarno.* 8-go Marta 1920 g. No. 439 V Penzenskii Gubzdravotdel (Gubfarpod) [untitled], ibid., p. 76.

21. "Tsirkuliar No. 17 . . . : O zamene nekotorykh otsutstvuiushchikh preparatov," ibid., pp. 29–30. This circular also was undated, but, as it followed Circular No. 16, which spoke of the hope of increased factory production, it would appear to be later chronologically.

22. Tsirkuliar No. 13 . . . : "O razverstke medikamentov v predelakh gubernii," ibid., pp. 20–21.

23. "Tsirkuliar No. 20 . . . : O deiatel'nosti Gubernskikh aptechnykh skladov i uezdnykh raspredelitel'nykh punktov," ibid., p. 35.

24. "Tsirkuliar No. 25 . . . : O kul'ture i sbore lekarstvennykh rastenii," ibid., pp. 40–41.

25. "Tsirkuliar No. 30/136 . . . : O zamene destillirovannoi vody," ibid., pp. 51–52.

26. "Tsirkuliar No. 37, 24 noiabria 1920 g. . . . : Ob ogranichenii otpuska kamfory i ee preparatov," ibid., p. 69.

27. "Penzenskomu Gubernskomu Otdelu Zdravookhraneniia. (Farmatsevticheskomu Pod'otdelu), 24 fevralia 1920 g. No. 742," p. 72. A missive following (untitled, undated) discussed "normal staffs for pharmacies and warehouses," ibid., pp. 72–74.

28. "Tsirkuliar No. 19 . . . : O poriadke vozbuzhdeniia khodataistva ob otkomandirovanii mobilizuemykh farmatsevtov k mestu ikh nastoiashchei sluzhby," ibid., pp. 34–35.

29. Tsirkuliar No. 18, utv. 29 iulia 1920 g. izd. 16 avgusta . . . : "Polozhenie o normal'nykh aptechnykh shtatakh," ibid., pp. 31–34.

30. "Shtaty Farpodov na 1920 god." ibid., pp. 82–84.

31. "Tsirkuliar No. 12, 14 maia 1920 g. No. 2677 . . . : Ob uchete vsekh imeiushchikh muzeinoe znachenie, aptechnykh prinadlezhnostei," ibid., p. 19. (This interesting circular was signed by Aluf and Levinshtein, as were most others.)

32. "Tsirkuliar No. 24 . . . : O gomeopaticheskikh-aptekakh," ibid., pp. 39-40.
33. TsGA RSFSR, f. 482, op. 5, d. 13, l. 209.
34. Ibid., ll. 208, 208 ob.
35. "Zhurnal No. 23 Plenarnogo zasedaniia 'Farmatsentra' 20 XII 18," TsGA RSFSR, f. 482, op. 5. d. 13, ll. 173-173 ob.
36. "Zhurnal No. 24, Plenarnogo zasedaniia 'Farmatsentra,'" 22 dekabria 1918 goda.," TsGA RSFSR, f. 482, op. 5, d. 13, l. 174, 174 ob.
37. "Zhurnal No. 25 Zasedaniia 'Farmatsentra' 3 Ianvaria 1919 g.," TsGA RSFSR, f. 482, op. 5. d. 13, ll. 171 and 178.
38. Zhurnal No. 26 Zasedaniia 'Farmatsentra' 14-1-19 g.," TsGA RSFSR, f. 482, op. 5, d. 13, l. 179, 179 ob.
39. "Protokol No. 25, zasedaniia Biuro Farmatsentra," TsGA RSFSR, f. 482, op. 5, d. 13, l. 170.
40. "Protokol No. 27 Zasedaniia Plenuma 'Farmatsentra' ot 3-go fevralia 1919 g.," TsGA RSFSR, f.482, op. 5, d. 13, l. 181, 181 ob.
41. "Protokol No. 26 Zasedaniia Biuro 'Farmatsentra' ot 5-go fevralia 1919 g," TsGA RSFSR, f. 482, op. 5, d. 13, l. 177.
42. "Protokol No. 30 zasedaniia biuro 'Farmatsentra' ot 4-go marta 1919 g.," TsGA RSFSR, f. 482, op. 5, d. 13, l. 183, 183 ob.
43. "Protokol No. 33 Zasedaniia Biuro Farmatsentra," TsGA RSFSR, f. 482, op. 5, d. 13, l. 140.
44. "Ot Soveta Narod. Komissarov USSR, Dekret o natsionalizatsii aptechnogo dela," (13 V 1919), TsGA RSFSR, f. 482, op. 5, d. 11, ll. 6, 6 ob.
45. "Ot Narodnago Komissariata Zdravookhraneniia USSR, " 16 maia 1919, no. 63, TsGA RSFSR, f. 482, op. 5, d. 11, l. 11. The Commissar for Health was N. Kost; the Head of the Pharmacy section was Ia. Iaroslav.
46. "Tsirkuliar No. 6: USSR NKZ Farm Otdel vsem gubernskim farmatsevticheskim pod'otdelam, 16 maia 1919," TsGA RSFSR, f. 482, op. 5, d. 11, l. 14.
47. "Polozhenie k dekretu o natsionalizatsii aptechnago dela," TsGA RSFSR, f. 482, op. 5, d. 11, l. 7.
48. TsGA RSFSR, f. 482, op. 5, d. 11, ll. 17-25.
49. "Protokol zasedaniia aptech. sekt. Zvenigorod uezdnago sanitarnago soveta," 21 noiabria 1919, TsGA RSFSR, f. 482, op. 5, d. 11, l. 32.
50. Ibid., l. 35.
51. "Farmstevticheskomu podotdelu/VYPISKA iz protokola No. 165, Zasedaniia kollegiia Astrakhanskago otdela zdravookhraneniia, Gubispolkom 23 Dekabria 1918," TsGA RSFSR, f. 482, op. 5, d. 30, l. 1.
52. TsGA RSFSR, f. 482, op. 5, d. 30, l. 2.
53. Ibid., l. 3.
54. Ibid., l. 5.
55. Ibid., 5 ob.
56. *Loc. cit.*
57. TsGA RSFSR, f. 482, op. 5, d. 30, l. 6, 6 ob.
58. Ibid., l. 7.
59. Ibid., l. 16.

60. *Loc. cit.*
61. TsGA RSFSR, f. 482, op. 5, d. 28, ll. 2, 3, 5.
62. "Smeta Raskhodov po soderzhaniiu Arkhangel'skogo Gubernskogo Aptechnogo sklada na 2-iu polovinu 1919 goda," TsGA RSFSR, f. 482, op. 5, d. 28, ll. 18, 18 ob.
63. Ibid., l. 4.
64. Ibid., l. 13.
65. "Ob"iasnitel'naia Zapiska k smete na vtoroe polugodie po soderzhaniiu Arkhangel'skogo Gubernskogo Aptechnogo sklada i zakupi predmetov . . . ," TsGA RSFSR, f. 482, op. 5, d. 28, ll. 19, 19 ob.
66. "Zakliuchenie Farmotdela k smete Arkhangel'skogo Gubernskogo Aptechnogo Sklada, " TsGA RSFSR, f. 482, op. 5, d. 28, l. 23.
67. TsGA RSFSR, f. 482, op. 5, d. 28, l. 26.
68. Ibid., l. 27.
69. Ibid., l. 31.
70. "Smeta . . . ," TsGA RSFSR, f. 482, op. 5, d. 28, l. 18.
71. TsGA RSFSR, f. 482, op. 5, d. 20, l. 9.
72. Ibid., ll. 13, 25.
73. Ibid., ll. 11, 12.
74. TsGA RSFSR, f. 482, op. 5, d. 41, l. 3.
75. "V Tsentrospirt, 3 IV 1919, TsGA RSFSR, f. 482, op. 5, d. 34, ll. 1, 3, 4.
76. TsGA RSFSR, f. 482, op. 5, d. 34, l. 8.
77. Ibid., l. 9.
78. Ibid., l. 14.
79. Ibid., l. 44.
80. Ibid., l. 65.
81. TsGA RSFSR , f. 482, op. 5, d. 35, l. 5; "Smetnye predpolozheniia po organizatsii natsionalizatsii aptek v Vitebskoi Gubernii i po soderzhaniiu natsionalizirovannykh aptek na fevral' i mart mesiatsy 1919 goda," ibid., l. 6; "Poiasneniia i osnovaniia ischislenii," l. 7.
82. "*Vtorichno* [underlined in original] *V Finansovyi otdel NKZ Bukhgalteriia* [underlined in original] 30 June, 1919, TsGA RSFSR, f. 482, op. 5, d. 35, l. 56. The first request for this money was sent June 18, ibid., l. 53.
83. TsGA RSFSR, f. 482, op. 5, d. 40, l. 1.
84. "V Farm Otdel Narkomzdrav, 15 maia 1919," TsGA RSFSR, f. 482, op. 5, d. 40, l. 4.
85. "Gubernskii Farmatsev. Podotdel Gor. Voronezh" (July 1919), Ibid., l. 72.
86. "Komitet R and K, Mediko Sanitarn. otdel, farm pod'otdel, 7 iunia 1919 V Farm Otdel Narkomzdrav, Kratkii doklad," ibid., ll. 73–75.
87. RSFSR Gubern ispol kom otdel zdravo—farm pod'otdel Nachal'niku Sanitarnoi Chasti," (3 Jan 1920), ibid., l. 96.
88. "V Farmatsevticheskii otdel Narod Kom Zdravo," TsGA RSFSR, f. 482, op. 5, d. 45, l. 1.
89. Ibid., l. 2.
90. TsGA RSFSR, f. 482, op. 5, d. 46, l. 4–5.

91. "V Farm Otdel Narkomzdrav RSFSR NKZ [from] Ispolnitel'nyi komitet Kostromskogo Gubernskogo Soveta, Rab i Krest Dep/Gubernskii otdel zdravookhraneniia, 7 avgusta 1919," TsGA RSFSR, f. 482, op. 5, d. 46, ll. 7, 7 ob.

92. *Loc. cit.*

93. TsGA RSFSR, f. 482, op. 5, d. 46, ll. 29, 29 ob.

94. TsGA RSFSR, f. 482, op. 5, d. 46, l. 8.

95. TsGA RSFSR, f. 482, op. 5, d. 46, ll. 9–11 ob, (l. 9).

96. *Loc. cit.*

97. *Loc. cit.*

98. *Loc. cit.*

99. Ibid., l. 11 ob.

100. Ibid., ll. 25, 25 ob, 26.

101. TsGA RSFSR, f. 482, op. 5, d. 13, chast' 1, l. 3.

102. TsGA RSFSR, f. 482, op. 5, d. 13, chast' 1, ll. 4–11, 16, 35.

103. TsGA RSFSR, f. 482, op. 5, d. 27, Ekaterinburg: ll. 3-5, 6; Kursk: l. 26; Moscow and Penza: ll. 35-66; Samara: ll. 171, 185–197; Smolensk begins l. 177; information on districts in Tula begins, l. 231.

104. Ibid., l. 197.

105. TsGA RSFSR, f. 482, op. 5, d. 61, ll. 1, 2, 3, 5, 9, 15, 10, 18, 19.

106. Ibid, ll. 20, 21.

107. Ibid., l. 22.

108. Ibid., ll. 45, 46.

109. Ibid., l. 52.

110. TsGA RSFSR, f. 482, op. 5, d. 75, l. 1.

111. Ibid., l. 15.

112. Ibid., l. 7.

113. Ibid., l. 12.

114. Ibid, l. 13.

115. "Kollegiia mediko-sanitarnago otdela po upravleniiu aptekami," TsGA RSFSR, f. 482, op. 16, d. 3, ll. 20, 20 ob.

116. "V tsentral'nyi komitet vserossiiskogo soiuza aptechnykh rabotnikov/Doklad," TsGA RSFSR, f. 482, op. 5, d. 32, l 33.

117. Ibid., ll. 33, 33 ob.

118. TsGA RSFSR, f. 482, op. 5, d. 57, ll. 1, 2, 24, 27.

119. Ibid., l. 35.

120. Ibid., l. 43.

121. Ibid., l. 44.

122. *Loc. cit.*

123. TsGA RSFSR, f. 482, op. 5, d. 57, Zhurnal. no. 43, l. 45.

124. TsGA RSFSR, F. 482, op. 5, d. 57, l. 60.

125. See Mary NcAuley, *Bread and Justice: State and Society in Petrograd 1917–1922* (Oxford: Clarendon Press, 1991), *passim.*

126. TsGA RSFSR, f. 482, op. 5, d. 58, l. 46.

127. Ibid., l. 53.

128. Ibid., l. 54.

129. TsGA RSFSR, f. 482, op. 5, d. 57, l. 66.

130. Ibid., l. 105.

131. Ibid., l. 115 ob.

132. TsGA RSFSR, f. 482, op. 5, d. 11, l. 1.

133. TsGA RSFSR, f. 482, op. 16, d. 3, ll. 12, 12 ob.

134. "Smeta predpolagaemykh dokhodov i raskhodov farmatsevticheskogo otdela komissariata zdravookhraneniia za vremia s 1-go ianvaria po 30-oe iiunia 1919 g.; g. Petrograda," TsGA RSFSR, f. 482, op. 5, d. 58, ll. 1, 2, 2 ob; 3-26 (including oborot), 31, 31 ob, 32–in all 43 pages of budget documentation.

135. Ibid., l. 27.

136. Ibid., l. 43.

137. Ibid., l. 66.

138. Ibid., l. 67.

139. "Protokol soveshcheniia, sozvannago glavnym komitetom khimko-farmatsevticheskoi promyshlennosti vo voprosu o dezinfektiruiushchikh sredstvakh," TsGA RSFSR, f. 482, op. 5, d. 16, addendum, l. 1.

140. Aluf, "Tri mesiatsa bezdeistviia," *Vestnik aptechnogo truda,* [hereafter cited *VAT*], vol. 6, no. 2, 1919, pp. 3–4.

141. "Vypiska . . . 1 dekabria 1919 na zhurnala zasedaniia zakupuchnoi komissii pri otdele meditsinskago Snabzheniia Narkomzdrava, No. 21," TsGA RSFSR, f. 482, op. 16, d. 14, l. 1.

142. Levinshtein, "Normal'naia aptechnaia set'," *VAT,* vol. 6, no. 3, 1919, pp. 7–8.

143. "Organizatsiia i deiatel'nost' farpodov," *VAT,* vol. 6, nos. 4-5, 1919, p. 5. They noted that these local organization had begun in 1918 but played an "insignificant role" until the nationalization decree, when these organs were needed to manage nationalized institutions.

144. "Byvshie aptekovladel'tsy sredi zaveduiushchikh farpodami i upravliaiushchikh aptekami," *VAT,* ibid., pp. 6–7.

145. "Otvetstvennye rabotniki nashikh Soiuzov," *VAT,* ibid., pp. 12–13.

146. Epshtein (Petrogradskii), "Petrograd: 2-i gubernskii delagatskii s"ezd," *VAT,* ibid., pp. 20–21.

147. See "What We Are Fighting For" and "Where There is Authority There is No Freedom," *The Anarchists in the Russian Revolution,* ed., Paul Avrich (Ithaca: Cornell Paperbacks, 1973), pp. 159-163.

148. See *Khimiko-farmatsevticheskii zhurnal,* 1924-1930, *passim.*

Bibliography

I. Primary Sources

Archival Collections

TsGIA [SSSR] (Tsentral'nyi Gosudarstvennyi Istoricheskii Arkhiv: Central State Historical Archive, St. Petersburg):

Fond 565 Ministry of Finance

Fond 821 Polish Catholics in Russia

Fond 822 Polish Catholics in Russia

Fond 826 Department of Spiritual Affairs Archbishop Cheplowsk, Metropolit, Catholic Church, Polish Refugees, World War I

Fond 1297 Ministry of Internal Affairs, Medical Council, Medical Department, Chief Medical Inspector to 1880

Fond 1298 Ministry of Internal Affairs, Medical Council, Medical Department, Chief Medical Inspector, 1880-1917

GIA P (Gosudarstvennyi Istoricheskii Arkhiv Peterburga: State Historical Archive, City of St. Petersburg):

Fond 212 opis' 8, delo 127, O razreshenii uchredit' v S-Peterburge normal'nuiu apteku Antonine Lesnevskoi

TsGA RSFSR (Tsentral'nyi Gosudarstvennyi Arkhiv RSFSR: Central State Archive, Russian Soviet Federated Socialist Republic, Moscow:

Fond 482 Medical, Pharmaceutical Reports from Sovnarkom or Council of People's Commissars, Commissariat of Health, VSNKh or the Supreme Council of National Economy, and provinces and districts of Russia and the Ukraine after 1918

Farmatsevticheskii Musei (Pharmacy Museum), Moscow

(Includes pharmaceutical artifacts, as well as published materials)

Muzeum Farmacji (Pharmacy Museum), Krakow

(Includes pharmaceutical artifacts, photographs, correspondence, memoirs relating to Antonina Lesnevskaia

Muzeum Farmacji (Pharmacy Museum), Warsaw

(Includes correspondence and papers relating to Antonina Lesnevskaia)

Lesnevskii Family Papers and Photographs, Property of Dr. Jerzy Lesniewski, Warsaw; and Interviews and correspondence with Dr. Jerzy Lesniewski, 1990.

Published Laws, Government Regulations Available Outside Archives

Polnoe sobranie zakonov Rossiiskoi Imperii. Sobranie vtoroe., vol. XI, otdelenie 9494–9821 (St. Petersburg, 1837).

Sbornik Zakonopolozhenii dlia farmatsevtov, soderzhatelei aptek i drogistov, sostavil (ed.) P. N. Bulatov (St. Petersburg, 1897).

Ispytaniia na zvaniia i stepeni lekaria, zubnago vracha, povival'noi babki, provizora, aptekarskago pomoshchnika i aptekarskago uchenika, sostavil N. Malinovskii (St. Petersburg, 1907).

Tsirkuliary i rasporiazheniia Farmotdela N. K. Z. rasporiazheniia Farpoda Penzenskogo gubzdrava, 2-i Vserossiiskii s"ezd zavfarpodami. 2-i gubernskii s"ezd zavfarpodami Penzenskoi gubernii. Protokoly Kollegii Farpoda Penzenskogo gubzdrava (Penza, 1921).

Reference Works

Afanas'ev, N. I., *Sovremenniki. Al'bom biografii* vol. 1 (St. Petersburg, 1909), pp. 261–262 ("Lesnevskaia, Antonina Boleslavna").

"Akusherskie, fel'dsherskie, zubovrachebnye i farmatsevticheskie kursy—Zhenshchiny-Farmatsevty," in L. N. Ariian, *Pervyi zhenskii kalendar'* (St. Petersburg, 1889), p. 154.

Farmatsevticheskii Kalendar' (St. Petersburg, 1897, 1900, 1901).

Entsiklopedicheskii leksikon, vol. 2, 1835, p. 441.

Evreiskaia Entsiklopediia (St. Petersburg, n. d.).

Entsiklopedicheskii slovar', eds. Brokgauz-Efron (St. Petersburg, 1896, 1902).

Index Catalogue of the Library of the Surgeon General's Office [United States], Second Series.

Kikta, Teodor, *Nekropol Farmaceutyczny cmentarz powazkowski w Warsawie* (Warsaw, 1985).

Materialy dlia istorii farmatsii v Rossii. Biograficheskii slovar' farmatsevtov poluchivshikh stepen' magistra farmatsii v Imperatorskikh russkikh Universitetakh i v Imperatorskoi Voenno-Meditsinskoi Akademii s 1845–1901 god, ed. Magistr Farmatsii Ivan Sofronovich Tkeshelashvili (Moscow, 1901).

Prilozheniia k stenograficheskim otchetam Gosudarstvennoi Dumy. Tretii sozyv. Sessiia tret'ia. 1909–1910 g. g., Tom I (No No. 1–289). (St. Petersburg, 1910).

Prilozheniia k stenograficheskim otchetam Gosudarstvennoi Dumy. Tretii sozyv. Part 4, No. 4. 1910–1911 g. g. (St. Petersburg, 1911).

Professory I Len. Med. In. za 50 let (Moscow, 1947).

Rossiia. Entsiklopedicheskii slovar' (St. Petersburg, 1898; reprinted Lenizdat, 1991) ("Farmatsiia," p. 775).

Rossiiskii Meditsinkii Spisok (1916).

Journals, Newspapers

Russian:

Farmatsevticheskii zhurnal (1879-1916) (*F. Zh.*). The 1879 issue was listed as vol. 1; the 1916 issue as vol. 55. In 1901 vols. were cited from publication of the German-Russian language edition of the journal and given two volume numbers, i.e., in 1901: 40 (23).

Farmatsevticheskii vestnik (1897-1906) (*F. V.*)

Farmatsevt (1893-1907).

Farmatsevticheskii trud (1907-1909) (*F. T.*).

Russkii farmatsevt (1908).

Zhizn' farmatsevta (Kiev) (1909-1911) (*Zh. F.* (Kiev)).

Zhizn' farmatsevta (St. Petersburg, Petrograd) (1914-1917). *Zh. F.* (St. Petersburg, Petrograd).

Vestnik aptechnogo truda (1917-1919) (*VAT*).

Iuzhnyi vestnikh aptechnago truda (Kiev) (1918) (*IuVAT*).

Izvestiia aptechnoi komissii (1918, 1919) (*IAK*).

Vserossiiskii farmatsevticheskii vestnik (1923).

Vestnik farmatsii (1924).

Khimiko-farmatsevticheskii zhurnal (1924-1930).

Khimiko-farmatsevticheskii vestnik (1926).

Zubovrachebnyi vestnik, 1885, 1889, 1892.

Zhurnal Russkago Obshchestva okhraneniia narodnago zdraviia, 1902, 1903.

Dielo naroda, 1918-1919.

Ekonomicheskaia zhizn', 1918.

Polish:

Kraj (1905-1909).

Golos Warszawy, 1922.

Kurjer Polski, 1918, 1919.

Kurjer Warszawy, 1921.

Posiew, 1920.

Tygodnik Illustrowany, 1924, 1925.

English:

The Lancet, 1877, 1879, 1880, 1882, 1885, 1886, 1887, 1905, 1908, 1909.

Articles, Chapters

Only selected articles from the aforementioned journals are cited in this bibliography. In some cases, almost the entirety of the journal was cited. In other cases, hundreds of articles were used. In radical socialist journals the author frequently was designated by initials. In still other cases many important articles were anonymous, such as decisions of the Governing Senate, resolutions of the Medical

Council of the Ministry of Internal Affairs, accounts of pharmaceutical society meetings, and other important events. Therefore, this bibliography cites mainly articles authored by individuals who play important roles in the current work and selected anonymous articles under rubrics such as "Pharmacies, Pharmaceutical Practice," "Pharmaceutical Education," "Pharmacy Societies," "Government and Senate Rulings," and so on. For full citations of all articles see individual chapters.

Abramovich, E. "Moskovskiia pis'ma," *Zh. F.* (Kiev), vol. 1, no. 5, 1909, pp. 11-12.

Abramson, A. "K zashchite dissertatsii O. E. Gabrilovicha: Pis'mo v redaktsiiu," *Farmatsevt,* vol. 15, no. 1, 1907, pp. 9-12.

Aikin, D. "Elizavetpol'," *Zh. F.*, vol. 2, no. 6, 1915, p. 17.

Aizenshtadt. "Koe-chto o polozhenii zhenshchiny v apteke," *F. V.*, vol. 7, no. 44, 1904, 698-99.

Aleksandrov, Nik. A., "Obshchee vvedenie v kursy farmatstii i farmakognozii. Soderzhanie kursov. Tseli, metody i akademicheskoe prepodavanie farmatsii s farmakognoziei," *Izvestiia Imperatorskago Tomskago Universiteta,* vo. XIX, no. 4, 1902, pp. 1-18. (This article discusses the place of pharmacy in the curriculum. In Germany pharmacy was taught in the Philsophy Faculty. In Russia, pharmacy, pharmacology, and pharmacognosy were taught in the Medical Faculty. The teaching of pharmacy varied, however, from one Russian university to another. The author stressed that pharmaceutical chemistry–the aspects of chemistry related to pharmacy–was important for the pharmacy curriculum as was prescription writing.)

Al'tgauzen, E. As editor of *Farmatsevt* Al'tgauzen wrote scores of articles. Most are cited throughout the chapters of this work. A few samples on the Pharmacists' Pension Fund:

______. "Nepravy 'protest' i nespravedlivyi 'boikot'," *Farmatsevt,* vol. 14, no. 15, 1906, pp. 428-430.

______. "Obshchee godichnoe sobranie pensionno-vspomogatel'noi kassy farmatsevtov 1905 goda," *Farmatsevt,* vol. 13, no. 9, 1905, p. 269; ibid., no. 10, pp. 296-297.

Aluf, A. "Iz istorii profdvizheniia aptechnikh rabotnikov: Oformlenie klassovykh organizatsii aptekorabotnikov," *Khimiko-farmatsevticheskii zhurnal,* vol. 6, no. 2, 1928, pp. 3-5; ibid., no. 3, pp. 5-7.

______. "Tri mesiatsa bezdeistviia," *VAT,* vol. 6, no. 2, 1919, pp. 3-4.

About Aluf, A. Sh.: "Sredi sluzhashchikh farmatsevtov," *Zh. F.* (St. Petersburg), vol. 1, no. 1, 1914, p. 12.

Averkiev, N. D. "O dobyche ioda v USSR iz vodoroslei Chernogo moria 'krasnaia fillofora,'" *Khimiko-farmatsevticheskii zhurnal,* vol. 6, no. 8 (56), 1928, pp. 10-14.

Bakst, Vl. "O fiziologicheskom deistvii nekotorykh alkaloidov opiia i o terapevticheskom upotreblenii papaverina," *Meditsinskii vestnik,* vol. 8, no. 48, 1868, pp. 451-454; ibid., no. 50, pp. 470-477; ibid., no. 51, pp. 483-487; ibid., no. 52, pp. 491-495.

Basilaia, Evsevii [wrote scores of articles; a sample]:
______. "Neudachnaia vylazka," *Farmatsevt*, vol. 14, no. 27, 1906, pp. 787-790.
______. "Pis'ma v redaktsiiu," *Farmatsevt*, vol. 13, no. 8, 1905, p. 238.

Blumental', D. Ia. "Lekarstvennyi golod," *F. Zh.*, vol. 55, no. 6, 1916, pp. 55-56.

Borisovskii, O. "Zabastovka farm. v Riazane," *F. T.*, vol. 1, no. 6, 1907, pp. 86-87.

B(ronshtein), E. "Zabastovka v petrogradskikh aptekakh," *VAT*, vol. 4, nos. 14-15 (15 November), 1917, pp. 4-5.

B., R. "Die erste Frauen-Apotheke," *Apothekenbilder von Nah und Fern* III, ed. Hans Heger (Vienna, 1905). pt. 2, pp. 1-4.

______. "Die Staro-Nikolskaja-Apotheke des Wladimir Karlowitsch Ferrein in Mosco (Die grosste Apotheke der Erde)," Hans Heger, *Apothekenbilder*, I (Vienna, 1901), pp. 63-69.

Butkevich, K. "Mnenie po povodu predstoiashchago farmatsevticheskago s"ezda," *F. Zh.*, vol. 20, no. 42, 1898, pp. 600-601; ibid., no. 43, pp. 612-613; ibid., no. 45, pp. 640-641.

Chekhov, A. P. "Aptekarsha," in Chekhov, *Sobranie sochinenii*, Tom chetvertyi, *Rasskazy*, 1886 (Moscow, 1961), pp. 220-225.

______. "On the Injurious Effects of Tobacco," *Anton Chekhov's Plays*, trans., ed. Eugene K. Bristow (New York: W. W. Norton, 1977), pp. 251-255.

Chistovich, Ia. "Aptechnyi vopros v Rossii," *Meditsinskii vestnik*, vol. 4, 1864, pp. 236-248.

Claus, C. "History of Pharmacy in Russia," *American Journal of Pharmacy*, vol. 31, 1859, pp. 165-170.

Courgey, S. "La Femme pharmacien," *Le Correspondant Medical*, vol. 13, no. 271, 1906, pp. 13-15.

C, P. A. "Organization of Medicine and Pharmacy in Russia," *American Journal of Pharmacy*, vol. 12, 1840, pp. 343-346.

D., E. "Po povodu sobraniia zhenshchin farmatsevtov," *F. T.*, vol. 1, no. 20, 1907, p. 278.

Daichik, L. "Pis'mo iz Ekaterinoslava," *Zh. F.* (Kiev), vol. 1, no. 1, 1909, pp. 11-12.

Danilevskii, A. I., and N. P. Kravkov. "Doklad komissii po voprosu o vvoze opiia v Kvantunskuiu oblast'," *Voenno-meditsinskii zhurnal*, vol. 81, 1903, pp. 278-293.

Debogorii-Mokrievich, I. "Sluchai idiosinkrazii k morfiiu i opiiu," *Russkaia meditsina*, no. 26, 1893, pp. 430-431.

De-v. "Aptechnoe delo v Rossii po offitsial'nym statisticheskim dannym," *Russkii Farmatsevt*, vol. 1, no. 1, 1908, pp. 26-28.

Diatropov, I. I. "Medikamenty iz Iaponii," *F. Zh.*, vol. 53, no. 35, 1914, p. 398.

"Doklad po peredannomu na osnovanii § 64 Nakaza Gosudarstvennoi Dumy zakonodatel'nomy zaiavleniiu ob izmenenii zakona ob otkrytii aptek."

Dokladchik M. K. Safonov. No. 89 and "Ob izmenenii zakona ob otkrytii aptek," No. 89 (pp. 1-5), *Prilozheniia k stenograficheskim otchetam Gosudarstvennoi Dumy*, Tretii sozyv, sessiia tret'ia 1909-1910 (St. Petersburg, 1910), and Doklad po zakonodatel'nomu predpolozheniiu ob izmenenii zakona ob otkrytii aptek, no. 360, pp.1-3, *Prilozheniia* . . . pt. 4, No. 4, 1910-1911 (St. Petersburg, 1911).

Epshtein, M. "Kul'turno-prosvetitel'naia rabota v professional'nykh soiuzakh," *VAT,* vol. 4, nos. 14-15, 1917, pp. 7-8.

______. (Petrogradskii), "Petrograd: 2-i gubernskii delagatskii s"ezd," *VAT,* vol. 6, nos. 4-5, pp. 20-21.

El'shtein. "K voprosu o munitsipalizatsii aptechnago dela," *F. T.,* vol. 3, no. 4, 1909, pp. 51-53.

Ferrein, F. (A.) "Preparaty, izgotovlenie kotorykh mozhet byt' osushchestvleno vposledstviia," *Vestnik farmatsii* [no vol.], nos. 8-9, 1924, p. 136.

______. "Farmatsevticheskaia promyshlennost': Tamozhnyi tarif 1927 goda," *Khimiko-farmatsevtichekii zhurnal,* vol. 5, no. 4, 1927, pp. 6-7, and ibid., no. 6, pp. 9-10.

About Ferrein, Vladimir Karlovich: "Iubilei Vladimira Karlovicha Ferrein," *F. Zh.,* vol. 53, no. 18, 1914, pp. 201-202.

On Feldshers (*Fel'dshery*) (Anonymous Articles):

"Farmasevticheskii vopros na pervom fel'dsherskom s"ezde v Moskve," *F. T.,* vol. 1, no. 3, 1907, pp. 44-46.

"Aptechnoe delo i fel'dshery," ibid., no. 7, pp. 101-106.

Fletcher, Giles. *The Russe Commonwealth,* excerpt in "Russia at the End of the 16th Century," *Medieval Russia: A Source Book, 900-1700,* ed. Basil Dmytryshyn (Hinsdale, IL: The Dryden Press), pp. 239-255.

Gabrilovich, O. G. "Dvoinaia bukhgalteriia, primenennaia k aptechnomu delu," *Farmatsevt,* vol. 15, no. 6, 1907, pp. 173-176; ibid., nos. 11-12, pp. 301-302; ibid., no. 13, pp. 338-341.

______. "'Predvaritel'noe soobshchenie'. Vzaimnoe strakhovanie farmatsevtov s samovykupom aptek," *Farmatsevt,* vol. 14, nos. 7 and 8, 1906, pp. 197-202.

Garber, I. "Lekarstva, naibolee upotrebliaemye v narodnoi meditsine v derevniakh bliz Bogotola, Tomskoi gubernii," *Farmatsevt,* vol. 10, no. 8, 1902, pp. 232-234.

______. "Sel'skaia vrachebnaia pomoshch' v Eniseiskoi i Tomskoi guberniakh," ibid., pp. 400-402.

______. "Flora okrestnosti sela Bogotola, Tomskoi gub.," ibid., p. 1183.

Gadzhedlo, V. "Na farmatsevticheskom rynke," *F. Zh.,* 55, no. 2, 1916, pp. 19-20.

Geilig, G. A. "K delam pens.-vspom. kassy," *Farmatsevt,* vol. 14, no. 46, 1906, p. 1319.

Gelibter, Z. "Iz provintsii: Khar'kov," *F. T.,* vol. 1, no. 25, 1907, pp. 346-347.

"The German Congress of Internal Medicines: Alteration of the Arteries produced by Injections of Adrenalin," *The Lancet,* May 6, 1906, p. 1222.

Gershtein, I. A. "Soslovnyia dela: Chto nam delat' za zashchitu ot "praktikantov'," *F. Zh.,* vol. 6, no. 21, 1884, pp. 519-520.

Ginrikhson, A. K. "Kul'tura lekarstvennykh rastenii v Rossii do 62° s. sh.," *F. Zh.,* vol. 40 (23), no. 18, 1901. pp. 356-357; ibid., no. 19, pp. 376-377.

Ginzberg, A(leksandr). S(emenovich). "Ocherk razvitiia nauchnoi farmatsii v Rossii za 200-letnii period," *F. V.,* vol. 5, no. 16, 1902, pp. 185-187; ibid., no. 17, pp. 197-199; ibid., no. 18, pp. 209-211.

______. "O lekarstvennoi pomoshchi v Anglii i Severo-Amerikanskikh S. Shtatakh," *F. Zh.*, vol. 50, no. 20, 1911, pp. 230-232.

______. Aleksandr, "O novykh napravleniiakh v voprose farmarsevticheskago obrazovaniia," *F. Zh.*, vol. 42, 1915, pp. 419-420.

Ginzburg, Isaiah. "A Pharmacist in Tsarist Russia—A Reminiscence, 1892-1909," *Pharmacy in History*, vol. 27, no. 3, 1985, pp. 138-159.

Ginzburg, S(avelii). A(bramovich). "Khimiko-sanitarnoe izsledovanie prodazhnago moloka v gor. Iur'eve," *Zhurnal Russkago obshchestva okraneniia narodnago zdraviia*, vol. 7, no. 11, 1897, pp. 611-647.

Gol'dberg, El'mar. "O Russkom opii i kolichestvennom opredelenii morfina," *Farmatsevt*, vol. 9, no. 37, 1901, pp. 1161-1162; ibid., no. 38, p. 1200; ibid., no. 40, pp. 1261-1263.

Gordin, H. M. "Pharmacy in Russia," *Pharmaceutical Review*, November 1899, pp. 500-506.

Government and Senate Rulings (Anonymous articles):

"Meditsinskim sovetom Ministerstva vnutr. del razresheno, and Meditsinskim sovetam Ministerstva vnutr. del otkloneno khodataistvo," *F. V.*, vol. 4, no. 39, 1900, p. 693.

"Soslovnyia dela: Glavnyia polozheniia, izvlechennyia iz Ukaza 1-go departametna pravitel'stvuiushchago Senata 1 Marta 1889 g. vosposledovavshago v raz"iasneniia voprosa ob opredelenii prak. zemstv na bezplatnyi otpusk lekarst. iz aptechnykh zavedenii," *F. Zh.*, vol. 13, no. 2, 1891, pp. 28-29 and "Ukaz senata kasatel'no optuska lekarstv iz zemskikh aptek i zemskikh aptechnykh skladov," ibid., no. 47, p. 752.

Grich'ev, N. I. "Kokain pri vpravlenii vyvikhov," *Meditsinskoe obozrenie*, vol. 28, 1887, pp. 604-606.

Grudinskii, Gr., "Bytovoi otdel," *F. V.*, vol. 7, no. 38, 1904, p. 599.

______. "Po povodu novago aptekarskago ustava," ibid., no. 40. p. 629.

Heger, Hans. "Die grosste Apotheke der Erde (W. K. Ferrein in Moskau), 1901," *Apothekenbilder von Nah und Fern* II (Vienna, 1901) pp. 111-129.

Iakimov, V. M. "Fal'sifikatsiia pishchevikh veshchestv i bor'ba s neiu v zakone i zhizni," *Meditsinskaia beseda*, vol. 7, no. 7, 1893, pp. 169-177; ibid, no. 8, 1893, pp. 206-211.

Iakovlev, S. N. "Obzor naibolee vazhnykh uspekhov iz oblasti izsledovaniia pishchevykh veshchestv i otkrytii fal'sifikatsii ikh," *Vestnik obshchestvennoi gigieny, sudebnoi i prakticheskoi meditsiny*, vol. 6 (April-June), 2 sect., 1890, pp. 40-54.

Idel'son, Robert, "Kartiny s natury," *F. Zh.*, vol. 40 (23), no. 10, 1901, pp. 207-208.

______. "K predstoiashchemu Vserossiiskomu s"ezdu," *F. Zh.*, vol. 52, no. 5, 1913, p. 48.

Igumnov, S. "Zakonoproekt otnositel'no fal'sifikatsii pishchevykh produktov," *Obshchestvennyi Vrach. Zhurnal Obshchestva Russkikh vrachei v pamiat N. I. Pirogova. Izdavaemyi Pravleniem Obshchestva*, no. 9 (November), 1912, pp. 1-7.

Iordana, F. D. "Sharlatanstvo patentovannymi sekretnymi sredstvami," *F. Zh.*, vol. 1, no. 12, 1879, pp. 353-356.

Ivanov, N. P., and A. V. Pel'. "Obzor novykh vrachebnykh sredstv za poslednee trekhletie," *Zhurnal meditsinskoi khimii i farmatsii,* vol. I, 1892-93, pp. 378-395; 511-523. The authors discussed Pel"s new product, Spermine, on pp. 515-516.

James, Martha M. "That a Woman Makes as Good a Pharmacist as a Man, Providing They Have Equal Advantage," *Proceedings of the Wisconsin Pharmaceutical Association* (1898), p. 32-37.

Jones, Grinnell. "War's Effect on Chemical Industries," *The Pharmaceutical Era,* October 1918, pp. 273-274.

"K terapii otravleniia opiem i morfiem," *Novosti terapii,* vol. 1, nos. 1-6, 1896, p. 412.

Kagan, I. S. "Sluchai tiazhelogo geroinizma," *Nevrologiia i psikhiatriia: Trudy gosudarstvennogo meditsinskogo instituta v Moskve,* vol. 1, no. 1, 1923, pp. 257-265.

Kanevskii, Ia. F. "Aptechnye rabotniki Petrograda v 1917 g.," *Khimiko-farmatsevticheskii zhurnal,* vol. 6, no. 5, 1928, p. 15.

______. "Formy organizatsionnago stroitel'stva," *Zh. F.,* vol. 4, no. 4, 1917, pp. 1-2.

______. "Munitsipalizatsiia aptek," *Zh. F.*, vol. 4, no. 6, 1917, pp. 2-4.

______. "O formakh upravleniia aptechnym delom," *IAK*, vol. 1, no. 2, 1919, pp. 18-19.

About Kanevskii Ia. L.: "Sredi sluzhashchikh farmatsevtov," *Zh. F.* (St. Petersburg), vol. 1, no. 1, 1914, p. 12.

Kark, E. I. "K deistviiu margantsevo-kislago kaliia. Sluchai otravleniia opiumom, okonshivshiisia vyzdorovleniem. Otravlenie morfiem," *Voenno-meditsinskii zhurnal,* vol. 80, 1902, pp. 4625-4629.

About Keler, Roman Romanovich: [B. Saltykov, ed.?] "Nekrolog. R. R. Keler," *F. T.*, vol. 1, no. 15, 1907, pp. 214-215.

"Khimiko-bakteriologicheskie kursy pri institute doktora F. M. Bliumentalia," *F. T.*, vol. 1, no. 28, 1907, p. 385.

Kling, A. G. "Kul'tura i obrabotka lekarstvennykh i dushistykh rastenii," *F. Zh.*, vol. 20, no. 6, 1898, pp. 71-74.

Kovaleva, L. A. "Vliianie preparatov fosfora na protsessy okisleniia v zhivotnom organizme," *Arkhiv biologicheskikh nauk,* vol. 17, no. 3, 1912, pp. 293-320.

Kozlov, I. V. "Khimicheskie produkty," *Istoriko-statisticheskii obzor promyshlennosti Rossii,* vol. III, ed. D. A. Timiriazev (St. Petersburg, 1886), chapter VIII, pp. 1-101.

Kuperman, Iu. A. "Obshchaia zabastovka v aptekakh Leningrada v oktiabre-noiabre 1917 g.," *Khimiko-farmatsevticheskii zhurnal,* vol. 6, no. 5, 1928, pp. 15-16.

______. "Zametki starogo farmatsevta," *Khimiko-farmatsevticheskii zhurnal,* [no vol. listed], no. 7, 1924, pp. 2-5, and ibid., nos. 10-12 (13-15), pp. 2-5.

About Kuperman, Iu. A.: "Sredi sluzhashchikh farmatsevtov," *Zh. F.* (St. Petersburg), vol. 1, no. 1, 1914, p. 12, and "Fond zhurnala," ibid., p. 15.

Lapitskaia, S. (M.) "Voprosy bezrabotitsy Biuro truda," *Zh. F.* (St. Petersburg), vol. 1, no. 2, 1914, pp. 7-8.

______. "Zhenshchiny-Farmatsevty," *Zh. F.* (Petrograd), vol. 3, nos. 1-2, 1916, pp. 4-5.

About Lapitskaia, S. M.: "Sredi sluzhashikh farmatsevtov," *Zh. F.* (St. Petersburg), vol. 1, no. 1, 1914, p. 12.

Lavrova, L. "K reforme farmatsevticheskago obrazovaniia," *F. V.*, vol. 7, no. 49, 1904, p. 971.

______, L. N. "O deistvii ioda na patologicheskiia izmeneniia v sosudakh, obuslovlivaemyia vvedeniem zhivotnym adrenalina," *Arkhiv biologicheskikh nauk*, vol. 8, no. 3, 1908, pp. 205-236.

Lemberger, Joseph. "Laws Regulating the Sale of Poisons," *American Journal of Pharmacy*, September, 1902, pp. 428-437.

Lenin (Ul'ianov), Vladimir Il'yich. "The Dual Power," *The Lenin Anthology*, ed. Robert C. Tucker (New York: W. W. Norton, 1975), pp. 301-306.

______. "The State and Revolution," ibid., pp. 311-398.

______. "The Tasks of the Proletariat in the Present Revolution ('April Theses')," ibid., pp. 295-300.

Lesnevskaia, A. "Pis'ma v redaktsiiu," *F. Zh.*, vol. 20, no. 45, 1898, p. 643.

______. "Pis'ma v redaktsiiu," *F. V.*, vol. 4, no. 48, 1900, pp. 856-857 and "Pis'ma v redaktsiiu," ibid., no. 50, pp. 894-895.

______. "Pis'ma v redaktsiiu," *F. V.*, vol. 5, no. 3, 1901, p. 50 and ibid., no. 12, p. 192.

______. "Pis'mo v redaktsiiu," *Farmatsevt*, vol. 9, no. 5, 1901, p. 144.

______. "Pis'mo v redaktsiiu," *Farmatsevt*, vol. 10, no. 1, 1902, pp. 10-11.

______. "Pis'ma v redaktsiiu," *F. V.*, vol. 5, no. 1, 1902, p. 11 and "Pis'ma v redaktsiiu," ibid., no. 23, p. 278.

______. (speech to the 3rd All Russian Pharmaceutical Congress) "III Vserossiiskii farmatsevticheskii s"ezd," *Farmatsevt*, vol. 8, no. 3, 1900, p. 78.

______, A. B. "Bytovoi otdel. Doklad tret'emu s"ezdu Russkikh deiatelei po tekhnicheskomu i professional'nomu obrazovaniiu v Rossii, 'O farmatsevticheskom obrazovanii zhenshchin,'" *F. V.*, vol. 7, no. 4, 1904, pp. 55-59.

______, A. B. "Zhenshchiny-farmatsevty. Pervaia zhenskaia apteka. Zhenskaia farmatsevticheskaia shkola," I *Vserossiiskii zhenskii s"ezd. Trudy 10-16 Dek 1908 g.* (St. Petersburg, 1909) pp. 683-689.

About Lesnevskaia, Antonina Boleslavna, her pharmacy and her pharmacy school:

"Desiatiletie shkoly zhenshchin farmatsevtov," *F. Zh.*, vol. 52, no. 5, 1913, p. 53

"Kursy A. B. Lesnevskoi," *F. T.*, vol. 1, no. 27, 1907, p. 374.

"Otkrytie v S.-Peterburge pervoi zhenskoi apteki, *Farmatsevt*, vol. 9, no. 23, 1901, pp. 727-728.

"Prazdnik zhenshchin farmatsevtov," *F. Zh.*, vol. 52, no. 6, 1913, p. 65.

Sokolovskaia, A. "Pis'mo v redaktsiiu," *Farmatsevt*, vol. 13, no. 2, pp. 48-49 (this article praises Lesnevskaia's women's pharmacy school).

"Zhenskie farmatsevticheskie kursy," *F. Zh.*, vol. 55, no. 29, 1916, p. 263.

"I-ia zhenskaia apteka Lesnevskoi," *Zh. F.* (Petrograd), vol. 3, nos. 5-6, 1916, p. 7.

Lintser, S. [wrote scores of articles; a sampling]:

______. "Aptekarskii vopros," *F. V.*, vol. 2, no. 39, 1898, pp. 619-622.

______. "Aptechnaia monopoliia," *F. V.*, vol. 7, no. 2, 1904, pp. 21-26 and ibid., no. 3, pp. 40-42; ibid., no. 4, 59-61.

Marsden, Prosper H. "Pharmacy in Russia," *The Pharmaceutical Era*, February 16, 1905, pp. 197-199

______. "The Practice of Pharmacy in Russia," *American Druggist and Pharmaceutical Record*, 1905, pp. 94-97.

______. "The Laws Relating to the Practice of Pharmacy in Russia," *The Pharmaceutical Journal*, January 28, 1905, pp. 108-111.

About Mart'ianov, Nikolai Mikhailovich:

"Nauchnyi otdel—N. M. Mart'ianov," *Farmatsevt*, vol. 10, no. 8, 1902, pp. 225-228; ibid., no. 9, pp. 256-260; ibid., no. 10, pp. 293-295.

R. S. T., "Bytovoi otdel," *F. V.*, vol. 7, no. 30, 1904, p. 473 and Obituary of Mart'ianov, "N. M. Mart'ianov," ibid., no. 48, pp. 954-955.

"Medicine. Past and Present, in Russia. The Twelfth International Medical Congress. (Moscow, 1897.)" Supplement to *The Lancet*, August 7, 1897, pp. 343-374.

Menskii, V. K. "Letnye otpuski v Petrogradskikh aptekakh," *Zh. F.* (Petrograd), vol. 2, no. 5, 1915, pp. 4-6.

______. "Zemskaia farmatsiia," *Zh. F.*, vol. 1, no. 8, 1914, pp. 2-4.

Mikutskii, V. "Pis'ma iz Smolenska," *Zh. F.* (Kiev) vol. 1, no. 5, 1909, p. 13.

"Mrs. Anna B. Hummel, Pharmacist," *The New York Times*, June 22, 1896, p. 3, col. 3.

Mosal'skii, Vs. "Neskol'ko slov o zhenskom trude v aptekakh," *Farmatsevt*, vol. 9, no. 27, pp. 860-861, and ibid., no. 28, pp. 891-894; ibid., no. 29, pp. 920-921.

Mushchinskii, Ia. Ia. "O soderzhanii morfiia v opii, sobrannom v Iur'evskom botanicheskom sadu," *F. Zh.*, vol. 50, no. 21, 1911, pp. 246-247.

N(ensberg). "Ob ustroistve zemskikh aptek," *Moskovskaia meditsinskaia gazeta*, 1867, pp. 225-228.

Obukhov, N. "Solodokovyi koren', kak predmet eksporta," *Khimiko-farmatsevticheskii zhurnal*, vol. 6, no. 3 (51), 1928, pp. 10-11.

P., F. " Statisticheskiia svedeniia," *F. T.*, vol. 3, no. 2, 1909, p. 27.

Paperin, T. "O kharaktere nashei revoliutsii," *VAT*, vol. 5, nos. 2-3, 1918, p. 3; ibid., nos. 4-5, pp. 6-7.

Pharmacies (*Apteki*) both Private and Zemstvo and Pharmacy Practice (*Aptechnoe delo*) in Russia [See chapters 3 and 4; a few samples]:

"Apteki v Rossii," *F. Zh.*, vol. 1, no. 3, 1879, p. 86.

"Aptechnoe delo v zemstve i gorodskom khoziaistve," *F. V.*, vol. 7, no. 14, 1904, pp. 219-220.

"Doklad Kurskago gubernskago zemskago sobraniia," *F. V.*, vol. 7, no. 45, 1904, pp. 907-909.

"Khronika: Zemskoe sobranie," *F. Zh.*, vol. 49, no. 37, 1910, p. 404.

"Khronika zemskago i gorodskago aptechnago dela," *Russkii Farmatsevt*, vol. 1, no. 1, 1908, pp. 75-76.

"Odnym iz poslednykh zasedanii Moskovskago gubernskago zemstva," *F. Zh.*, vol. 19, no. 20, 1898, p. 279.
"Sessiia Permskago gubernskago zemstva," *F. Zh.*, vol. 52, no. 3, 1913, p. 32.
"Zemskiia dela," *F. Zh.*, vol. 19, no. 43, 1898, pp. 610-611.
"Zemskiia dela," *F. Zh.*, vol. 23, no. 3, 1901, p. 56.
"Zemskaia khronika," *F. V.*, vol. 7, no. 36, 1904, p. 571.

Pharmacies, Pharmacy Practice Abroad [a few samples]:
"Aptechnoe delo, aptekaria i sluzhashchie vo Frantsii," *F. T.*, vol. 1, no. 20, 1907, pp. 268-273.
"Aptechnoe delo za granitsei za 1912 g.," *F. Zh.*, vol. 52, no. 14, 1913, pp. 129-131, and "Na temu dnia," ibid., no. 11, p. 115 "Za rubezhom," *F. T.*, vol. 3, no. 2, 1909, pp. 29-30.

Pharmaceutical Education [See chapter 2; a few samples]:
"Farmatsevticheskoe obrazovanie," vol. 1, no. 1, 1879, pp. 4-7; "Soslovnyia dela: Farmatsevticheskoe obrazovanie," ibid., no. 2, pp. 53-58; "Obozrenie pravitel'stvennykh mer po delam farmatsevticheskago sosloviia: Slushanie lektsii farmatsevtami i mediko-khirurgicheskoi akademii," no. 5, ibid., pp. 149-152; "K voprosu o prepodavanii uchenikam," ibid., no. 22, pp. 696-700.
"Chego mozhno trebovat' ot farmatsevtov po voprosu ikh obrazovatel'nago tsenza," *F. Zh.*, vol. 20, no. 22, 1898, pp. 306-307.

Pharmacists' Pension Fund: [See chapters 12 and 13; a few samples]:
"Izvlechenie iz protokola revizii summ Vysochaishe utverzhdenoi Rossiiskoi pensionno-vspomogatel'noi kassy farmastevtov," *F. Zh.*, vol. 40 (23), no. 30, 1901, pp. 556-557; ibid., no. 39, 704-705.
"Obshchee sobranie Rossiiskoi Pensionno-Vspomogatel'noi kassy farmatsevtov, 28 fev. 1898," *F. Zh.*, vol. 20, no. 11, 1898, p. 152-153.
"O pensionnoi kasse," *F. Zh.*, vol. 49, no. 42, 1910, pp. 447-449.
"Pensionnaia Kassa," *F. T.*, vol. 1, no. 27, 1907, pp. 284-285 and ibid., no. 37, pp. 490-493.

Pharmacist Practitioners (*Praktikanty*) [one sample]:
"Khronika: Aptechnie praktikanty," *F. V.*, vol. 7, no. 32, 1904, p. 509.

Pharmaceutical Congresses [See appropriate chapters; for a few important meetings]:
"Iz deiatel'nosti vseobshchago Rossiiskago farmtevticheskago s"ezda," *Farmatsevt*, vol. 14, no. 24, 1906, pp. 677-684.

Pharmacy Societies [There are hundreds of articles discussing various societies. See chapters 12, 13, 14. For a few samples]:
"Iz deiatel'nosti S. Peterburgskago Farmatsevticheskago Obshchestva. Protokol sentiabr'skago zasedaniia," *F. Zh.*, vol. 49, no. 41, 1910, pp. 438-440.
"Otchet Vysochaishe utverzhdennago S. Peterburgskago farmatsevticheksago obshchestva za 1883 g.," *F. Zh.*, vol. 6, no. 11, 1884, p. 199.
"Otchet o III zasedanii Komissii Rossiiskago farmatsevticheskago Obshchestva po aptechnoi reforme," *F. T.*, vol. 2, no. 30, 1908, pp. 493-496
"Professional'noe obshchestvo sluzhashchikh farmatsevtov Kievskoi gubernii," *F. T.*, vol. 1, no. 4, 1907, p. 61.

"S. Petersburgskoe professional'noe obshchestvo sluzhashchikh," *F. T.*, vol. 1, no. 27, p. 374.

"Pharmacy in Russia," *The Druggists Circular and Chemical Gazette*, October, 1903, pp. 202–203.

Pharmacy Tax [There are scores of articles; one sample]:

"Soslovnyia dela: Aptekarskaia Taksa," *F. Zh.*, vol. 1, no. 1, 1879, pp. 21–24.

"Po povodu voprosa o vzdorozhanii medikamentov," *F. Zh.*, vol. 53, no. 33, 1914, p. 374–375.

Polumordvinov, Mikh., "Vol'nyia apteki v Imperii," *F. V.*, vol., 7, no. 2, 1904, pp. 26–28.

"The Prevention of Arterio-sclerosis following the Use of Adrenalin," *The Lancet*, vol. 22, November 28, 1908, p. 1641.

"Predpolozhenie ob ustroistve zemskoi apteki," *Meditsinskii vestnik*, vol. 8, no. 37, 1868, pp. 347–352.

Purve, A. "Ekzameny farmatsevtov v Amerike," *F. V.*, vol. 7, no. 10, 1904, pp. 153–156.

______, A. I. "Farmatsevticheskii institut," *Farmatsevt*, vol. 10, no. 12, 1902, pp. 376–378.

Puzis, Boris. "Memuary k istorii farmatsevticheskoi zabastovki v g. Kieve," *Farmatsevt*, vol. 13, no. 29, 1905, pp. 915–916.

______. "Avtonomiia," *F. Zh.*, vol. 52, no. 13, 1913, pp. 149–150.

______. "Samovykup, " *F. Zh.*, vol. 52, no. 20, 1913, pp. 226–228.

Reviews: of Germain. See, *Meditsinskoe obozrenie*, vol. 28, no. 13, 1887, p. 57; of Ball and Jennings, 'Lechenie morfinomanii,', ibid., no. 16, p. 366; of G. Pinchon, ibid., no. 20, p. 728; of Mattison, ibid., no. 22, pp. 914–915.

Rothmann, E. A. "The Removal of Erythma from the Face ('Red Nose') by the Prolonged Internal Administration of Adrenalin," *The Lancet*, Jan. 16, 1909, pp. 194–195.

Rubinshtein, I. "Nemnogo tsyfr," *F. V.*, vol. 5, no. 33, 1902, p. 391.

Ruffman, D. A. "Russian Pharmacy," *Bulletin of Pharmacy*, 1906, pp. 14–18.

"Russian, Danish, British, American Pharmacopoeias," *The British and Foreign Medical Review*, vol. 13, 1842, pp. 54–88.

Sadikov, V. "Voina i sostoianie russkoi promyshlennosti," *F. Zh.*, vol. 54, no. 35, 1915, pp. 341–343.

Sarkisov, K. S. "Kratkii obzor polozheniia khimiko-farmatsevticheskikh promyshlennosti i rynka v Rossii, a, v chastnosti v Zakavkaz'e v nastoiashchee vremia," *F. Zh.*, vol. 55, no. 6, 1916, pp. 49–50; ibid., no. 7, p. 59–60.

Schindelmeiser, J. "Nichtamtlicher Teil, Weibliche Pharmazeuten in Russland," *Apotheker-Zeitung*, no. 74, 1902, p. 636.

Serebriiakov, Ia. "Korrespondentsii: Tiflis," *Zh. F.* (Kiev), vol. 1, no. 1, 1909, pp. 15–16.

Shatov, A. "Provintsiia," *F. T.*, vol. 3, no. 3, 1909, pp. 43–44.

Shindel'meizer, I. "Persidskii opii," *Farmatsevt*, vol. 13, no. 3, 1905, pp. 65–68.

Semchenko, D. G. "Sluchai otravleniia rebenka opiem; primenenie atropina v kachestve fiziologicheskago protivoiadiia," *Vrach*, vol. 7, 29, 1886, pp. 529–530.

About Shaskol'skii, B. M.: [Obituary], Anon. "Chelovek dela: Posviashchaetsia pamiati B. M. Shaskol'skago," and "Nekrolog B. M. Shaskol'skii," *F. Zh.*, vol. 49, no. 39, 1910, pp. 417-418.

Shcherbakov, A. S. "Kratkiia besedy ob izsledovanii pishchevykh produktov," *Meditsinskaia beseda*, vol. 5, 1891, pp. 92-100, 127-134, 191-198, 270-274, 354-364, 503-506.

Sosaar, M. I. "Po ankete 'chto sdelano nashei promyshlennost'iu za vremia voiny'," *F. Zh.*, vol. 55, no. 29, 1916, pp. 263-264.

On Staff Pharmacists (*Sluzhashchie*):

"Khronika: Normirovki truda v Peterburgskikh aptekakh," *F. Zh.*, vol. 50, no. 1, 1911, p. 12.

"Khronika: Novyia normy dlia sluzhashchikh v aptekakh," *F. Zh.*, vol. 49, no. 40, 1910, p. 435.

"Kooperativ sluzhashchikh farmatsevtov," *Zh. F.* (Petrograd), vol. 3, nos. 1-2, 1916, p. 1.

Stavskii, I. V. "Obshchestvennye obshchesoslovnye interesy i sovremennaia aptechnaia privilegiia," *F. V.*, vol. 7, no. 3, 1904, pp. 39-40.

Svirlovskii, E. "Kul'tura maka i dobavlenie opiia v Semirech'i," *F. Zh.*, vol. 55, no. 37, 1916, pp. 350-351.

Taylor, Henry L. "Synopsis of the Pharmacy Practice Acts of the United States," *The Pharmaceutical Era*, vol. 45, no. 1 (January), 1912, p. 21. In ibid., (February), pp. 105-108, Taylor listed 73 colleges of pharmacy or departments of pharmacy in universities of the United States. Russian pedagogs of the era still believed Russian pharmaceutical education was superior.

Tsereteli, S. G. "Sobranie farmatsevtov sluzhashchikh po moskovskomu gorodskomu obshchestvennomu upravleniiu," *Farmatsevt*, vol. 13, no. 13, 1905, pp. 399-401.

"Torgovlyi otchet Russkago Obshchestva Torgovli Aptekarskimi Tovarami. S-Peterburg i Khar'kov.," *Zhurnal Meditsinskoi khimii i farmatsii*, vol. 1, 1892-93, pp. 396-401; 423-527. This article discussed price fluctuations in the international drug market. It emphasized that Russia exported as well as imported raw materials for medicines. It also indicated that the July 20, 1892, tariff with Germany and Austria Hungary would affect unfavorably pharmacy wares imported from these countries. However, Russia's currency was strong and Britain and Japan could also supply pharmacy wares lacking in Russia.

"Torgovyia i promyshlennyia svedeniia," *F. Zh.*, vol. 40 (23), no. 22, 1901, p. 434.

Toropov, D. I. "Dvizhenie i rost aptechnago dela v Imperii za poslednee desiatiletie (1901-1911 g. g.)," *Vestnik obshchestvennoi gigieny, sudebnoi i prakticheskoi meditsiny*, no. 9, 1911, pp. 1270-1306.

"Ukaz Pravitel'stvuiushchago Senata," *F. V.*, vol. 7, no. 41, pp. 645-647.

Uglow Woolcock. "Historical Sketch of the Pharmaceutical Society of Great Britain: XXI-Women Pharmacists; Examination Regulations," *The Pharmaceutical Journal*, vol. 75, no. 22, 1906, p. 634-635.

Uleveli, pharmacist. "Eshche o farmatsevticheskoi kasse i eia pravlenii," *F. V.*, vol. 5, no. 8, 1902, pp. 93-94.

"Uspekhi zhenshchin na vrachebnom i farmatsevticheskom poprishchakh," *F. V.*, vol. 4, no. 37, 1900, p. 664.

Vekhter, V. "Zhenshchiny v apteke," *F. V.*, vol. 4, no. 32, 1900, p. 580.

Wallace, Emma Gary. "Women in Pharmacy," *The Pharmaceutical Era*, vol. 45, no. 1 (January), 1912, pp. 17-20; ibid., no. 2 (February), pp. 101-104; no. 3 (March), pp. 181-184; no. 4 (April), pp. 265-268; no. 5 (May), pp. 328-332; no. 6 (June), pp. 397-400; no. 7 (July), pp. 402-464. The women Wallace described (with their photographs) were energetic and ambitious. American and Russian women pharmacists had similar characteristics and experiences but, because of space constraints, cannot be compared in the present work.

"Women in Pharmacy," *The Druggists Circular*, vol. 51, 1907, pp. 151-153.

Zaidman, Naum. "Soslovnyia dela: 'Aptekarskaia taksa,'" *F. Zh.* vol. 1, no. 8, 1879, pp. 243-244.

______, N. "Glavneishiia prichiny upadka u nas aptechnago dela," *F. Zh.*, vol. 40 (23), no. 16, 1901, p. 328.

______. "Russkiia apteki 50 let tomu nazad i teper'," *F. Zh.*, vol. 40 (23), no. 22, 1901, pp. 430-431; ibid., no. 26, p. 494; ibid., no. 28, p. 524; ibid., no. 29 p. 540.

Zeman, A. O. "Redkii sluchai otravleniia opiem," *Voenno-meditsinskii zhurnal*, vol. 72, 1894, pp. 77-82.

Zeskov, Z. "Po povodu aptechnago vorposa," *F. Zh.*, vol. 13, no. 38, 1891, pp. 606-607.

Zewalthoff, D. "The Origin and Progress of Pharmacy in Russia," *Pharmaceutical Record*, vol. 5, April 1, 1885, pp. 101-102.

"Zhenskie farmatsevticheskie kursy," *F. Zh.*, vol. 49, no. 38, 1910, p. 416, and "Zhenshchiny eksterny v universitete," ibid., no. 43, p. 468.

"Zhenskii den' v peterb. obshchestve farmastevtov," *Zh. F.* (St. Petersburg), vol. 1, no. 1, 1914, p. 9.

"Zhenskii vopros v apteke," *F. T.*, vol. 1, no. 24, 1907, pp. 327-329.

Zimin, L. Ia. [wrote scores of articles; a sample]:

"K polozheniiu del v Rossiiskoi Pensionno-Vspomogatel'noi Kasse Farmatsevtov," *Russkii Farmatsevt*, vol. 1, no. 4, 1908, p. 157, and "Pensionnaia kassa," ibid., no. 1, p. 31.

Pamphlets, Catalogs, Published Dissertations, Publications of Pharmacies, Pharmaceutical Houses, Pharmaceutical Warehouses

Apercu historique du developpement general de la Pharmacie en Russie, et en particulier de la "Pharmacie Ferrein," fondee sous le regne Pierre le Grand en 1901, par Daniel Gourtschin (Moscow, 1910).

Bereznitskii. M. I. *Lechenie gipnozom morfinistov, alkogolikov i kuril'shchikov* (St. Petersburg, 1905).

Bogoslovskii, V. S. *O prestoiashchei farmatsevticheskoi deiatel'nosti zhenshchin i neobkhodimosti ustroistva zhenskago farmatsevticheskago instituta* (Moscow, 1889).

Braunshtein, E. P. *K istorii zhenskogo meditsinskogo obrazovaniia* (Khar'kov, 1911).

Burkgart, R. *Morfinizm i ego lechenie*, trans. P. L. Leont'ev (St. Petersburg, 1900).

Danillo, S. N. *O vliianii nekotorykh iadov (spirt, opii, gasish) na soznanie u cheloveka* (St. Petersburg, 1894).

Doklad komissii, izbrannoi obshchestvom Odesskikh vrachei, po voprosu o snabzhenii zhitelei g. Odessy dobrokachestvennym molokom (Odessa, 1891).

Faerman, L. A. *Fal'sifikatsiia vazhneishikh pitatel'nykh produktov. Opisanie sposobov otkryvat porchu, poddelku i postoronniia primysi v vazhneishikih pitatel'nykh produktakh. Soderzhanie: moloko, maslo, syr, vino, pivo, vodka i likery, kakao, shokolad, kofe, chai, muka, i khleb* (Odessa, 1881).

Gabrilovich, O(l'ga) E. *Deishvuiushchee nachalo "p'ianago khleba" [Materialy dlia ustanovki sposoba vydeleniia ego iz muki i ego khimicheskikh svoistv] Dissertatsiia na stepen' magistra farmatsii* (St. Petersburg, 1906).

Ginzberg, A(lexander). S(emenovich). *K voprosu ob obshchem i spetsial'nom obrazovanii farmatsevtov* (St. Petersburg, 1913).

Gorianinov, Pavel. *Griby, pleseny i pyleviki v mediko-politseiskom i drugom otnosheniiakh* (St. Petersburg, 1848).

Iatsukovich, N. K. *Titrovanyi i kolorimetricheskii analyzy* (Khar'kov, 1878).

Iatsuta, K. Z. *Povtoritel'nyi kurs (conspekt) po farmatsii i farmakognozii* (St. Petersburg, 1899).

Ivanovskii, I. A. *Mnenie chlena komiteta po voprosu o tom, mogut li provizory schitat'sia litsami* (St. Petersburg, 1903).

Kagan, A. *"Ekspropriatsiia" (iz vospominanii farmatsevta.)* (Yakutsk, 1909). This booklet, which sold for 30 kopeks, was a scathing endictment of private pharmacies—the author claimed they were dirty, pharmacy owners reaped exorbitant profits, etc. His polemical allegations did not coincide with more objective reports.

Kamaev, A. L. *Anashizm* (Samara, 1931).

Keler, R(oman)., R(omanovich). *Pravda po odnomu obshchestvennomu voprosu* (Moscow, 1898).

Khimicheskaia fabrika i apteka E. Merk v Darmshtadt (Germaniia). *Otchet za 1897 god* (1898); *Otchet za 1898 god* (1899); *Otchet za 1899 god* (1900).

Kratkii ocherk deiatel'nost aptekarskago sklada Tverskogo gubernskago zemstva za istekshie 20 let ego sushchestvovaniia (1889–1909 g. g.). Sostavil M. E. Zaitsev (Tver, 1910).

Kratkii ocherk deiatel'nosti Obshchestva rasprotraneniia mezhdu obrazovanymi zhenshchinami prakticheskikh znanii (Moscow, 1912).

Lesnevskaia, Antonina. *Po neprotorennoi doroge* (St. Petersburg, 1901; reprinted 1914).

Lesniewska, A. *Nowa dziedzina pracy kobiet w zwiazku z reforma zawodu farmaceutycznego* (Warsaw, 1908).

Lesnevskaia, A. B. *K voprosu o reforme farmatsevticheskago obrazovaniia v Rossii* (St. Petersburg, 1912).

Levinshtein, I. *Istoriia farmatsii i organizatsiia farmatsevtichesogo dela* (Moscow, Leningrad, 1939).

______. *Materialy po profess.-tekhnicheskomu obrazovaniiu. Farmatsevticheskoe obrazovanie* (Moscow, 1921).

______. *Materialy po farmatsevticheskomu obrazovaniiu: programmy farmatsevticheskoi shkoly* (Moscow, 1922).

Levitov, Il'ia Semenovich. *Buzo-gashishnyi vopros na nashikh okrainakh* (St. Petersburg, 1909).

______. *O neobkhodimosti opiinoi reformy na Dal'nem Vostoke* (St. Petersburg, 1906)

Lonachevskii-Petruniak, T. I. *Vopros ob obrazovanii russkikh farmatsevtov* (St. Petersburg, 1905).

Mazing, I. F. *Khimiko-sanitarnoe izsledovanie prodazhavno khleba v gorode Iur'eve* (Iur'ev, 1901).

Mnenie chlenov komiteta I. A. Ivanovskogo (St. Petersburg, 1903).

Opyt istoricheskago ocherka vozniknoveniia i razvitiia vsego aptekarskago dela v Rossii, a v chastnosti Staroi Nikol'skoi apteki, prinadlezhashchei nyne Tovarishchestvu "V. K. Ferrein" i osnovannoi v 1701 godu, v tsarstvovanie Imperatora Petra Velikago, Daniilom Gurchinym (Moscow, 1911).

Optovyi Preis-Kurant za nalichnyi raschet sklada aptekarskikh tovarov Oskar Getling v Moskve (n. d.–late 19th, early 20th cent.).

Optovyi preis-kurant tovarov firmennoi zadelki Moskovskago tsentral'nago optovago sklada fabrichno-torgovago Tovarishchestva "R. Keler i Ko v Moskve" (Moscow, 1914).

Otchet o deiatelnosti Soiuza russkikh zhenshchin (St. Petersburg, 1912).

Otkrytie Vysshykh Zhenskikh meditsinskikh kursov v g. Odesse (Odessa, 1911).

Popovskii, A. N. *Obrazovanie farmatsevtov v sviazi s razvitiem khimiko-farmatsevticheskoi promyshlennosti i lekarstvennii golod* (Petrograd, 1917).

Pravila ob uchastii sluzhashchikh v Staroi Nikolskoi Apteke i Magazin aptekarskikh tovarov V. K. Ferreina, v pribyliakh predpriatiia (Moscow, 1881).

Rumiantsev, V. V. *Zhenskoe farmatsevticheskoe obrazovanie* (Moscow, 1912).

Russia: Ministry of Trade and Industry *Polozhenie o "Komitete po bor'be s fal'sifikatsiei pishchevykh produktov"* (St. Petersburg, 1909).

Semenov, A. M. *Zaslugu zhenshchin na vrachebno-farmatsevticheskom poprishche* (Moscow, 1892).

Smolenskii, P. O. *Ob oleomargarine i iskusstvennom korov'em masle. Sposoby ikh prigotovleniia, sanitarnoe znachenie, sposoby opredeleniia v natural'nom korov'em masle i vyzvannyia imi sanitarnyia i zakonodatel'nyia meropriiatiia zagranitsei i v Rossii* (St. Petersburg, 1898).

______. *Istoricheskii ocherk ucheniia o pitanii* (St. Petersburg, 1898).

Tomsk gor. komissiia. Vo vrachebno-sanitarnyi sovet. Doklad komissii po revizii 1-i gorodskoi vol'noi apteki (Tomsk, 1915).

Ustav Moskovskago Blagotvoritel'nago Obshchestva posledovatelei Gomeopatii (1894).

Ustroistvo gorodskogo-farmatsevticheskogo zavoda. Doklad komissii akademika N. S. Kurnakova soveshchaniiu o zagotovlenii gorodom lekarstv (Petrograd, 1916).

Books

Al'medingen, Aleksandr. *Domashnii opredelitel' poddelok pitatel'nykh, vkusovykh, i takzhe i drugikh veshchestv* (St. Petersburg, 1892).

Broido, Eva. *Memoirs of a Revolutionary*, trans., ed. Vera Broido (London: Oxford University Press, 1967).

Bogoliubov, M., ed. *Prakticheskaia farmakologiia po retseptam sovremennykh klinitsistov dlia vrachei i studentov* (Moscow, 1889).

Bukovskii, A. *Izsledovanie chaia i fal'sifikatsiia ego v Varshave* (Moscow, 1896)

Chirikov, Andrei. *Posobie pri prakticheskikh zaniatiakh po obshchei farmatsii* (Khar'kov, 1887).

Dobroslavin, A. *Ocherk osnov sanitarnoi deiatel'nosti* (St. Petersburg, 1874).

_______, A. P. *O zagranichnykh laboratoriiakh dlia izsledovaniia pishchevykh veshchestv* (St. Petersburg, 1887).

Durland, Kellogg. *The Red Reign in Russia* (New York: The Century Co., 1907).

Henderson, V. E. *A Text-Book of Materia Medica and Pharmacy for Medical Students* (University of Toronto Press, 1919).

Ioganson, F. A. *Dobavlenie k repetitorium po farmakologii. Sostavleno po noveishim istochnikam* (Kiev, 1889).

Isaev, A. S. *Kratkoe rukovodstvo po farmakologii* (Petersburg, Kiev, 1912).

Iur'ev, N. P. *K voprosu o materialnom polozhenii vrachei sluzhashchikh po vedomstvu Ministerstva Vnutrennikh Del v guberniiakh i oblastiakh Rossii* (St. Petersburg, 1904).

Kal'ning, I. *Kratkaia farmatsiia dlia studentov-medikov i farmatsevtov soglasno programme universitetskago kursa* (Moscow, 1899).

Kanonnikov, I. I. *Rukovodstvo k khimicheskomu izsledovaniiu pitatel'nykh i vkusovykh veshchestv* (St. Petersburg, 1891).

Kapustin, M. Ia. *Osnovnye voprosy zemskoi meditsiny* (St. Petersburg, 1889).

Khodnev, A. N. *Khimicheskaia chast' tovarovedeniia. izsledovanie s"estnykh pripasov i napitkov* (St. Petersburg, 1859).

Khrzhanovskii, E. K. *Polozhenie aptechnago dela v Rossii v osveshchenii tsifr i faktov* (St. Petersburg, 1913).

Korol'kov, I. I. *Farmatsevty Rossii* (Moscow, 1911).

Kourenoff, Paul M. *Russian Folk Medicine*, trans., ed., arranged by George St. George (London, New York: W. H. Allen and Co. Ltd., 1970).

Marvin, Charles. *The Region of the Eternal Fire: An Account of a Journey to the Petroleum Region of the Caspian Sea in 1883* (First ed. London, 1888; reprint Westport, CN: Hyperion, 1976).

Notkin, S. *Fal'sifikatsiia pishchevykh produktov i domashnie sposoby raspoznovaniia eia* (St. Petersburg, 1889).

Paleologue, Maurice. *An Ambassador's Memoirs,* trans. F. A. Holt (New York: George H. Doran Company, third edition), Vol. 3.

Pel', A. V. [published over 100 works. A few:]

______. *Fal'sifikatsii i mery bor'by s nimi* (St. Petersburg, 1899).

______. *Khimicheskiia i bakteriologicheskiia izsledovaniia po voprosam vodosnabzheniia i fil'trovaniia vody* (St. Petersburg, 1887).

______. *Khimicheskiia izsledovaniia po voprosu o gnienii rzhanoi muki i o deistvii sporini na muki dlia razzhizheniia ergotizma* (St. Petersburg, 1883).

______. *Sistematicheskii khode analiza rzhanago i pshenichnago zerna i muki* (St. Petersburg, 1873).

Piatnitskaia, I. N. *Klinicheskaia narkologiia* (Leningrad, 1975).

Pil'niak (Vogau) Boris. *The Naked Year,* trans. Tulloch, A. R. (Ann Arbor, MI : Ardis, 1975).

Podvysotskii, V. O. *Farmakologiia veshchestv organicheskoi khimii, rastitel'nykh i zhivotnykh. Po 3-mu izdan. lektsii farmakologii, byvsh. Prof. Kievsk. Univers. Dybkovskago* s pribavleniiami po sovremenomu sostoianiiu farmakologii do 1888 goda (Kiev, 1889).

Romanova, Tsaritsa Alexandra. *The Letters of the Tsaritsa to the Tsar 1914–1916* (London: Gerald Duckworth and Vo., Ltd., 1923; reprint, Stanford: Hoover Institution Press).

Shchepot'ev, N. *Uchebnik farmakologii dlia fel'dsherov i fel'dsherskikh uchenikov* (Kazan, 1886).

Smolenskii, P. O. *Prosteishie sposoby izsledovaniia i otsenki dobrokachestvennosti s"estnykh pripasov, napitkov, vozdukha, vody, zhilishch i proch.* (St. Petersburg, 1899).

Sukhanov, N. N. *The Russian Revolution,* 2 vols., ed., abridged, trans. Joel Carmichael (New York: Harper Torchbooks, 1962).

Toreia, E. A. *Sovremennyi vzgliad na russkuiu voennuiu i morskuiu farmakopei* (St. Petersburg, 1888).

Wallace, Sir Donald MacKenzie. *Russia* (reprint of 1877 edition, New York: AMS Press, 1970).

______. *Russia on the Eve of War and Revolution,* reprint, edited, and reproduced by Cyril Black, (New York: Vintage Books, 1961).

Zakharbekov, M. P. *K bakteriologii Peterburgskago moloka* (St. Petersburg, 1895).

Zil'berg, I. *Professional'noe dvizhenie sluzhashchikh-farmatsevtov* (Moscow, 1930).

Government, City Health Reports, Series

Russia:

Upravlenie glavnago vrachebnago inspektora MVD: *Otchet o sostoianii narodnago zdraviia i organizatsii vrachebnoi pomoshchi v Rossii za 1905 god* (St. Petersburg: Tipografiia Ministerstva Vnutrennikh Del, 1907).

______: *Otchet o sostoianii narodnago zdraviia i organizatsii vrachebnoi pomoshchi v Rossii za 1906 god* (St. Petersburg: Tipografiia Ministerstva Vnutrennikh Del, 1908).

Kiev:

Otchet Kievskoi gorodskoi ispolnitel'noi sanitarnoi komissii za 1893 god (Kiev, 1894).

Otchet Kievskoi gorodskoi . . . komissii za 1894 god (Kiev, 1895).

Otchet Kievskoi gorodskoi . . . komissii za 1895 god (Kiev, 1896).

Otchet Kievskoi gorodskoi . . . komissii za 1896 god (Kiev, 1897).

Moscow Sanitary Station:

Pervyi god: Otchet Moskovskoi gorodskoi sanitarnoi stantsii, ed. F. F. Erisman (Moscow, 1892).

Vtoroi godovoi otchet Moskovskoi gorodskoi sanitarnoi stantsii (May 1892–May 1893), ed. Erisman (Moscow, 1894).

Tretii godovoi otchet Moskovskoi gorodskoi sanitarnoi stantsii (May 1893–Jan. 1895), ed. Erisman (Moscow, 1895).

Chetvertyi godovoi otchet Moskovskoi sanitarnoi stantsii . . . za 1895 god (Moscow, 1897).

Piatyi godovoi otchet Moskovskoi gorodskoi sanitarnoi stansii . . . za 1896 god, ed. S. F. Bubnov (Moscow, 1897).

Shestoi godovoi otchet Moskovskoi gorodskoi sanitarnoi stantsii . . . za 1897 god, ed. Bubnov (Moscow, 1899).

Sed'moi godovoi otchet Moskovskoi gorodskoi sanitarnoi stantsii . . . za 1898 god, ed. Bubnov (Moscow, 1900).

Perm Sanitary Station:

Sbornik rabot permskoi sanitarnoi stantsii, I, ed. R. Rut (Perm, 1889).

St. Petersburg Sanitary Station:

Przhibytek, S. A. Otchet S.-Petersburgskoi gorodskoi laboratorii za 1896 god (St. Petersburg, 1897).

II. Secondary Works

Articles, Chapters in Books

Abramov, V. D. "Eksporty leksyr'ia," *Khimiko-farmatsevticheskii zhurnal,* [no vol. listed] nos., 3–4 (6–7), 1924, pp. 2–3.

Anon. "Wspomnienie dzialalnosci spolecznej s.p. Antoniny Lesniewskiej," *Kurjer Poranny,* 1938, three-page, typed copy in Pharmacy Museum, Krakow. No vol., no., or pagination.

Anon. "Wspomnienie dzialalnosci spolecznej s. p. Antoniny Lesniewskiej," *Kurier Freimorgan,* 1938, five-page handwritten copy located in Pharmacy Museum, Warsaw. No vol., no., or pagination.

Alexander, John T. "Medical Developments in Petrine Russia," *Canadian-American Slavic Studies,* vol. 8, no. 2, 1972, pp. 198–221.

______. "Medical Professionals and Public Health in 'Doldrums' Russia (1725-62)," *Canadian-American Slavic Studies*, vol. 12, no. 1, 1978, pp. 116-135.

Baicou, G. "Le XIIeme Congres international de medecine de Moscou (1897) et son importance pour le developpement des sciences pharmaceutiques," *Trudy XIII mezhdunarodnogo kongressa po istorii nauki*, (Moscow, 1974), sektsiia VIII, pp. 285-293.

Berman, Alex. "Early Russian Military and Naval Formularies 1765-1840," *American Journal of Hospital Pharmacy*, vol. 17, April, 1960, pp. 213-218.

Berridge, Virginia. "Professionalization and narcotics: the medical and pharmaceutical professions and British narcotic use 1868-1926," *Psychological Medicine*, no. 8, 1978, pp. 361-372.

______, and Nigel S. B. Rawson. "Opiate Use and Legislative Control: A Nineteenth Century Case Study," *Social Science and Medicine*, 13 A, 1979, pp. 351-363.

Biriukova, Tatiana. "K devushke s tiulipanami," *Byloe*, vol. 1, no. 2, February, 1993, p. 15.

Bonow, Eunice R. "The History of Professional Pharmaceutical Fraternities for Women," *American Journal of Pharmaceutical Education*, vol. 18, 1954, 409-412.

Bonow-Bardell, Eunice. "America's Only School of Pharmacy for Women," *Pharmacy in History*, vol. 26, no. 3, 1984, pp. 127-133.

Borisovskaia, S. Iu. "Iz istorii nauchnoi farmatsevticheskoi deialtel'nosti zhenshchin," *Farmatsiia*, no. 3, 1947, pp. 28-32.

Bychkov, I. "Problema syr'ia po piatiletnemu planu razvitiia farmatsevticheskoi promyshlennosti (1927/28-1931/31 g. g.)," *Khimiko-farmatsevticheskii zhurnal*, vol. 6, no. 2, 1928, pp. 8-10.

Ch., S. "Ot Kellerovskoi kulinarii k khimicheskomu i khim.-farm. proizvodstvu," *Khimiko-farmatsevticheskii zhurnal*, vol. 6, no. 11, 1928, pp. 7-9.

Conroy, Mary Schaeffer. "Abuse of Drugs other than Alcohol and Tobacco in the Soviet Union," *Soviet Studies*, vol. 42, no. 3, 1990, pp. 447-480.

______. "Education of the Blind, Deaf and Mentally retarded in Late Tsarist Russia," *Slavic and European Education Review* [now *East-West Education*], vol. 9, nos. 1-2 , 1985, pp. 29-49.

______. "Malaria in Late Tsarist Russia," *Bulletin of the History of Medicine*, vol. 56, no. 1, 1982, pp. 41-55.

______. "Pharmacy in Pre-Soviet Russia," *Pharmacy in History*, vol. 27, no. 3, 1985, pp. 115-137.

______. "School Hygiene in Late Tsarist Russia," *Slavic and European Education Review*, no. 2, 1981, pp. 17-26.

______. "Women Pharmacists in Russia before World War I: women's emancipation, feminism, professionalization, nationalism, and class conflict," *Women and society in Russia and the Soviet Union*, ed. Linda Edmondson (Cambridge: Cambridge University Press, 1992), pp. 48-76.

Cook, Harold J. "Policing the Health of London: the College of Physicians and the Early Stuart Monarchy," *Social History of Medicine*, vol. 2, no. 1, 1989, pp. 1-33.

Dagurov, V. G. Miazdrikova. "Stanovlenie farmakologii v Moskovskom universitete," *Farmakolgiia Toksikologiia*, vol. 44, no. 6, 1981, pp. 733-737.

Earles, P. M. "The Pharmacy Schools of the Nineteenth Century," *The Evolution of Pharmacy in History*, ed. F. N. L. Poynter (London, 1964), pp. 79-94.

Ena, M. G. "Khimiko-farmatsevticheskaia promyshlennost'," *Razvitie khimicheskoi tekhnologii na Ukraine*, eds. O. Avilov et al. (Kiev, 1976), vol. 2, pp. 257-321.

Fortunatov, S. P. "O rossiiskoi farmakopee 1866 g.," *Aptechnoe delo*, vol. 6, no. 1, 1957, pp. 53-58.

Frank, Allan Dodds. "Unwelcome side effects from peace in Afghanistan," *Forbes*, vol. 142, no. 3, 1988, pp. 34-36.

Gallagher, Theresa Catherine. "From Family Helpmeet to Independent Professional: Women in American Pharmacy. 1870-1940," *Pharmacy in History*, vol. 31, no. 2, 1989, pp. 60-77.

Gorovoi-Shaltan, V. A. "Morfinizm, ego rasprostranenie i profilaktika," *Voprosy narkologii*, no. 2, 1928, pp. 46-58.

Griffenhagen, George. "Russian (Zemstvo) Medicine Stamps," *The Congress Book 1972: Thirty-Eighth American Philatelic Congress* (Clearwater, Florida: The American Philatelic Congress, Inc., 1972), pp. 227-249.

Griffenhagen, George B., and James Harvey Young. "Old English Patent Medicines in America," *Pharmacy in History*, vol. 34, no. 4, 1992, pp. 200-229.

Gritskevich, V. P. "Iz istorii aptechnogo dela v Belorussii v period feodalizma," *Aptechnoe delo*, vol. 8, no. 6, 1959, pp. 57-60.

Haimson, Leopold. "Dual Polarization in Urban Russia, 1905-1917," *The Russian Revolution and Bolshevik Victory*, eds. Ronald Suny and Arthur Adams (Lexington, MA : W, C. Heath and Company, 1991), pp. 26-50.

Haimson, Leopold H., and Ronald Petrusha. "Two strike waves in Imperial Russia, 1905-1907, 1912-1914," *Strikes, Wars and Revolutions in an International Perspective*, eds. Haimson and Charles Tilly (Cambridge: Cambridge University Press, 1989), pp. 101-166.

Haller, John. "A Short History of the Quack's Materia Medica," *New York State Journal of Medicine*, vol. 89, no. 9, 1989, pp. 520-525.

______. "Opium Usage in Ninteenth-Century Therapeutics," *Bulletin of the New York Academy of Medicine*, vol. 65, no. 5, 1989, pp. 591-607.

Hamm, Michael. "The Breakdown of Urban Modernization: A Prelude to the Revolutions of 1917," *The City in Russian History*, ed. Michael F. Hamm (Lexington, KY: The University Press of Kentucky, 1976), pp. 182-200.

Hanchett. "Tsarist Statuatory Regulation of Municipal Government in the Nineteenth Century," *The City in Russian History*, ed. Hamm, pp. 91-114.

Hutchinson, John F. "Who Killed Cock Robin?" *Health and Society in Revolutionary Russia*, eds. Susan Gross Soloman and John F. Hutchinson (Bloomington, IN: Indiana University press, 1990).

Il'kiv, N. V., and M. I. Zomova. "Pervaia apteka Tomskoi gubernii," *Farmatsiia*, vol. 25, no. 4, 1976, pp. 86-87.

Khitrik, S. N. "Proizvodstvo alkaloidov v SSSR," *Khimiko-farmatsevticheskii zhurnal*, vol. 6, no. 7, 1928, pp. 5-8.

Kingston-Mann, Esther. "Peasant Communes and Economic Innovation: A Preliminary Inquiry," *Peasant Economy, Culture, and Politics of European Russia, 1800-1921*, eds. Esther Kingston-Mann and Timothy Mixter (Princeton: Princeton University Press, 1991), pp. 23-51.

Koenker, Diane E., and William G. Rosenburg. "Strikers in Revolution: Russia, 1917," *Strikes, Wars and Revolutions in an International Perspective*, eds. Haimson and Tilly (Cambridge: Cambridge University Press, 1989), pp.167-196.

Kondakov, I. L. "Kratkii istoricheskii ocherk razvitiia farmatsii i prichiny upadka farmatsevticheskoi shkoly," *Meditsina*, vol. 7, no. 10, 1895, p. 149.

Koroleva, M. "Moskovskie apteki v pervoi polovine XIX veka," *Aptechnoe delo*, vol. 9, no. 3, 1960, pp. 76-77.

Krilov, L. S., and E. L. Krilova. "Pro pershu zhinochu apteku v Rosii," *Farmatsevticheskii zhurnal* (Lviv), 1976, pp. 91-94.

Kutanin, M. P. "Narkomaniia," *Saratovskii Vestnik Zdravookhraneniia*, vol. 2, nos. 5-8, 1921, pp. 30-51.

Levinshtein, I. "Pervye zhenshchiny-farmatsevty v Rossii," *Farmatsiia*, vol. 5, no. 1-2, 1942, pp. 41-42.

Lurito, Pamela W. "The message was electric," *Institute of Electrical and Electronics Engineers Spectrum*, vol. 21, no. 9, 1984, pp. 2-6.

Matossian, Mary Kilbourne. "Climate, Crops, and Natural Increase in Rural Russia, 1861-1913," *Slavic Review*, vol. 45, no. 3, 1986, pp. 457-469.

Mazover, Ia. "Gosudarstvennyi salitsilovyi zavod," *Khimiko-farmatsevticheskii zhurnal*, vol. 6, no. 10, 1928, pp. 7-9.

McClelland, James. "Diversification in Russian-Soviet Education," *The Transformation of Higher Learning 1860-1930*, ed. Konrad H. Jarausch (Chicago: University of Chicago Press, 1983), pp. 180-195.

Melancon, Michael. "Who Wrote What and When? Proclamations of the February Revolution in Petrograd, 23 February-1 March 1917," *Soviet Studies*, vol. 40, no. 3, 1988, pp. 479-500.

Minor, L. S. "K voprosu o preduprezhdenii toksikomanii i lechenii toksikozov," *Vorposy narkologii* vol. 1, 1926, pp. 21-27.

Owen, Thomas C. "Entrepreneurship and the Structure of Enterprise in Russia, 1800-1880," *Entrepreneurship in Imperial Russia and the Soviet Union*, eds. Gregory Guroff and Fred V. Carstensen (Princeton: Princeton University Press, 1983), pp. 59-83.

Pabis-Braunstein, Miroslawa. "The First Polish Women Pharmacists," *Pharmacy in History*, vol. 31, no. 1, 1989, pp. 12-15.

Pintner, Walter M. "The Evolution of Civil Officialdom, 1755-1855," *Russian Officialdom*, eds. Pintner, Walter McKenzie, and Don Karl Rowney (Chapel Hill: University of North Carolina Press, 1980), pp. 190-220.

______. "Civil officialdom and the Nobility in the 1850s," Ibid., pp. 234-249.

Plavsic, Borovoj. "Seventeenth-Century Chanceries and Their Staffs," *Russian Officialdom*, eds. Pinter and Rowney, pp. 19-45.

Prozorov. L. "Narkotizm i bor'ba s nim," *Izvestiia narodnogo komissariata zdravookhraneniia*, nos. 2-3, 1924, pp. 21-28.

Ramer, Samuel C. "Who was the Russian Fel'dsher?" *Bulletin of the History of Medicine,* vol. 50, no. 2, 1976, pp. 213-225.

______. "Traditional Healers and Peasant Culture in Russia, 1861-1917," *Peasant Economy, Culture and Politics of European Russia, 1800-1921,* eds. Esther Kingston-Mann and Timothy Mixter (Princeton: Princeton University Press, 1991), pp. 207-232.

Riedel, Renate A. "A Brief History of the Pharmaceutical Industry in Basel," *Pill Pedlers,* eds. Gregory J. Higby and Elaine C. Stroud (Madison, WI: American Institue of the History of Pharmacy, 1990), pp. 50-58.

Robson, Michael. "The French Pharmaceutical Industry, 1919-1939," *Pill Pedlers,* eds. Higby and Stroud, pp. 108-110.

Rosenburg, William G. "Kadets and Kornilov," *The Russian Revolution and Bolshevik Victory,* eds. Suny and Adams, pp. 289-315.

Salo, V. M. "Akademik Rossiiskoi Akademii nauk Farmatsevt T. E. Lovits (k 250-letiiu Akademii nauk SSSR)," *Farmatsiia,* vol. 24, no. 1, 1975, pp. 36-39.

______. "Razvitie aptechnoi seti," *Farmatsiia,* vol. 25, no. 5, 1974, pp. 85-86.

______. "Perekhod aptechnogo khoziastva v gosudarstvennuiu sobstvennost'," *Farmatsiia,* vol. 27, no. 6, 1978, pp. 57-59.

______. "Ustroistvo i oborudovanie aptek pervoi poloviny XIX veka," *Farmatsiia,* vol. 23, no. 6, 1974, pp. 45-47.

______. "Vneaptechnaia torgovlia lekarstvennymi sredstvami v XVIII i XIX vekakh," *Farmatsiia,* vol. 34, no. 1, 1985, pp. 88-90.

______. "Vneaptechnaia torgovlia lekarstvennymi sredstvami vo vtoroi polovine XIX veka," *Farmatsiia,* vol. 24, no. 3, 1975, pp. 54-58.

______. "Vydaiushchiisia deiatel' otechestvennoi farmatsii A. P. Neliubin (k 130 letiiu so dnia smerti)," *Farmatsetiia,* vol. 37, no. 2, 1989, pp. 73-76.

______. Vydaiushchiisia deiatel' otechestvennoi farmatsii Georg Dragendorf," *Farmatsiia,* vol. 33, 1985, pp. 78-80.

Salo, V. M., and T. B. Grigor'eva. "Peterburgskoe farmatsevticheskoe obshchestvo," *Farmatsiia,* vol. 25, no. 2, 1976, pp. 78-80.

Sanders, Jonathan. "Drugs and Revolution: Moscow Pharmacists in the First Russian Revolution," *The Russian Review,* vol. 44, 1985, pp. 351-377.

Shuliatel, A. "Razvedenie miaty i dobyvanie miatnogo masla na Poltavshchine," *Khimiko-farmatsevticheskii zhurnal,* vol. 5, no. 9, 1927, p. 26.

Sidorkov, A. M. "Vozniknovenie i razvitie zhenskogo farmatsevticheskogo obrazovaniia v Rossii," *Aptechnoe delo,* vol. 6, no. 4, 1957, pp. 59-62.

Skinner, Frederick W. "Trends in Planning Practices: The Building of Odessa, 1794-1917," *The City in Russian History,* ed. Hamm, pp., 139-159.

Sonnedecker, Glenn. "Emergence of a Concept of Opiate Addiction," American Institute of the History of Pharmacy, reprinted from the *Journal mondial de pharmacie,* vol. 1, 1963, pp. 1-25.

______. "Women as Pharmacy Students in 19th-Century America," *Veroffentlichunger der Internationalen Gesselschaft fur Geshichte der Pharmazie,* vol 40 (Stuttgart, 1973), pp. 135-141.

Stieb, Ernest W. et al. "Women in Ontario Pharmacy, 1867-1927," *Pharmacy in History*, vol. 28, no. 3, 1986, pp. 125-134.

Tabagari, I. S. "Istoriia razvitiia aptechnogo dela v Gruzii posle prisoedineniia k Rossii," *Farmatsiia*, vol. 20, Jan.-Feb. 1971, pp. 56-59.

Timberlake, Charles E. "The Zemstvo and the Development of a Russian Middle Class," *Between Tsar and People*, eds. Edith W. Clowes, Samuel D. Kassow, and James D. West (Princeton: Princeton University Press, 1991), pp. 165-179.

Valuck, Robert J., Suzanne Poirier, and Robert G. Mrtek. "Patent Medicine Muckraking: Influences on American Pharmacy, Social Reform, and Foreign Authors," *Pharmacy in History*, vol. 34, no. 4, 1992, pp. 183-192.

Vinokurov, G. A. "Apteki Simbirskoi gubernii v XIX i nachale XX veka," *Farmatsiia*, no. 19, 1970, pp. 50-53.

Wade, Rex A. "The Saratov Red Guards," *Politics and Society in Provincial Russia Saratov, 1590-1917*, eds. Rex A. Wade and Scott J. Seregny (Columbus, OH: Ohio State University Press, 1989), pp. 307-325.

Weinburg, Robert. "The Politicization of Labor in 1905: The Case of the Odessa Salesclerks," *Slavic Review*, vol. 49, no. 3, 1990, pp. 427-445.

Wilbur, Elvira M. "A View from Russia's 'Impoverished Center' at the End of the Nineteenth Century," *Peasant Economy, Culture, and Politics of European Russia, 1800-1921*, eds. Kingston-Mann and Mixter, pp. 101-127.

White, Peter T. "The Poppy–for Good and Evil," *National Geographic*, vol. 167, no. 2, 1895, pp. 143-188.

Young, James Harvey. "The Pig that Fell into the Privy: Upton Sinclair's *The Jungle* and the Meat Inspection Amendments of 1906," *Bulletin of the History of Medicine*, vol. 59, no. 4, 1985, pp. 467-480.

Zinov'ev, P. M. "Sovremennoe sostoianie voprosa o toksikomaniiakh i bor'be s nimi," *Klinicheskaia meditsina*, vol. 2, no. 7, 1924, pp. 264-267.

Zmeev, L. F. "Pervyia apteki v Rossii," *Meditsinskoe obozrenie*, vol. 28, 1897, pp. 840-897.

Books

Abraham, Richard. *Alexander Kerensky: The First Love of the Revolution* (New York: Columbia University Press, 1987).

Alexander, John T. *Catherine The Great: Life and Legend* (New York: Oxford University Press, 1989).

Allen, W. E. D. *The Ukraine* (Cambridge: The University Press, 1940).

Alston, Patrick L. *Education and the State in Tsarist Russia* (Stanford, CT: Stanford University Press, 1969).

Ascher, Abraham. *Pavel Axelrod and the Development of Menshevism* (Cambridge, MA: Harvard University Press, 1972).

Avrich, Paul, ed. *The Anarchists in the Russian Revolution* (Ithaca, NY: Cornell University Press, 1973).

Bater, James H. *St. Petersburg: Industrialization and Change* (Montreal: McGill-Queen's University Press, 1976).

Belikov, V. G. *Farmatsevticheskaia khimiia* (Moscow, 1985).

Bonnell, Victoria E. *Roots of Revolution: Workers' Politics and Organizations in St. Petersburg and Moscow, 1900–1914* (Berkeley, CA: University of California Press, 1983).

Bradley, Joseph. *Muzhik and Muscovite: Urbanization in Late Imperial Russia* (Berkeley, CA: University of California Press, 1985).

Brooks, Jeffrey. *When Russia Learned to Read* (Princeton, NJ: Princeton University Press, 1985).

Conroy, Mary Schaeffer. *Peter Arkad'evich Stolypin: Practical Politics in Late Tsarist Russia* (Boulder, CO: Westview Press, 1976).

Courtwright, David T. *Dark Paradise: Opiate Addiction in America before 1940* (Cambridge, MA: Harvard University Press, 1982).

Cowen, David L., and William H. Helfand. *Pharmacy, An Illustrated History* (New York: Harry N. Abrams, 1990).

Crisp, Olga. *Studies in the Russian Economy before 1914* (London: Macmillan Press, 1976).

Crunden, Robert M. *Ministers of Reform: The Progressive Achievment in American Civilization, 1889–1920* (New York: Basic Books, 1982).

d'Encausse, Helene Carriere. *Lenin: Revolution and Power* (London, New York: Longman, 1987).

Edmondson, Linda Harriet. *Feminism in Russia,* 1900–1917 (London: Heinemann Educational Books Ltd., 1984).

Eklof, Ben. *Russian Peasant Schools* (Berkeley, CA: University of California Press, 1986).

Englestein, Laura. *Moscow, 1905* (Stanford, CA: Stanford University Press, 1982).

Florinsky, Michael T. *Russia: A History and an Interpretation* (New York: Macmillan, eighth printing, 1963).

Foust, Clifford M. *Rhubarb, the Wondrous Drug* (Princeton, NJ: Princeton University Press, 1992).

Friedgut, Theodore H. *Iuzovka and Revolution: Life and Work in Russia's Donbass, 1869–1924* (Princeton, NJ: Princeton University Press, 1989).

Frieden, Nancy Mandelker. *Russian Physicians in an Era of Reform and Revolution, 1856–1905* (Princeton, NJ: Princeton University Press, 1981).

Frumkin, Gregoire. *Archeology in Soviet Central Asia* (Leiden/Koln: E. J. Brill, 1970).

Galili, Ziva. *The Menshevik Leaders in the Russian Revolution* (Princeton, NJ: Princeton University Press, 1989).

Gantt, Horsley W. *Russian Medicine* (New York, 1937).

Gleason, William. *Alexander Guchkov and the End of the Russian Empire* (Philadelphia, PA: The American Philosophical Society, 1983).

Grabbe, Alexander. *The Private World of the Last Tsar,* ed. Paul and Beatrice Grabbe (Boston, MA: Little, Brown and Co., 1984)

Gregory, Paul R. *Russian National Income, 1885-1913* (Cambridge, MA: Cambridge University Press, 1982).

Grey, Ian. *Ivan III and the Unification of Russia* (Collier Books, 1964).

Griazov, Mikhail P. *Ancient Civilization of Southern Siberia* (Cowels Book Co., 1969).

Hardy, Deborah. *Petr Tkachev, the Critic as a Jacobin* (Seattle and London: Washington University Press, 1977).

Hasegawa, Tsuyoshi. *The February Revolution: Petrograd, 1917* (Seattle, WA: University of Washington Press, 1981).

Herlihey, Patricia. *Odessa: A History, 1794-1914* (Cambridge, MA: Harvard University Press, 1986).

Holmes, Larry E. *The Kremlin and the Schoolhouse: Reforming Education in Soviet Russia, 1917-1931* (Bloomington, IN: Indiana University Press, 1991).

Hough, Jerry F., and Merle Fainsod. *How the Soviet Union is Governed* (Cambridge, MA: Harvard University Press, 1979).

Hutchinson, John F. *Politics and Public Health in Revolutionary Russia, 1890-1918* (Baltimore, MD: Johns Hopkins University Press, 1990).

Iroshnikov, M(ikhail). P(avlovich). *Predsedatel' Soveta Narodnykh Komissarov V. I. Ul'ianov (Lenin). Ocherki gosudarstvennoi deiatel'nosti* v 1917-1918 gg. (Leningrad, 1974).

Istoriia farmatsevticheskogo dela v Peterburge-Petrograde-Leningrade, no eds. cited (Leningrad, 1960).

Jochelson, Waldemar. *Peoples of Asiatic Russia* (New York: American Museum of Natural History, 1928) (pp. 255-259: Russian bibliography on Minusinsk).

Kenez, Peter. *Civil War in South Russia* (Berkeley, CA: University of California Press, 1971).

Kikta, Teodor. *Przemysl farmaceutyczny w Polsce (1823-1939)* (Warsaw, 1972).

Kingston-Mann, Esther. *Lenin and the Problem of Marxist Peasant Revolution* (Oxford University Press, 1985).

Koenker, Diane P., and William G. Rosenburg. *Strikes and Revolution in Russia, 1917* (Princeton, NJ: Princeton University Press, 1989).

Leggett, George. *The Cheka: Lenin's Political Police* (Oxford: Clerendon Press, 1981).

Lincoln, W. Bruce. *In the Vanguard of Reform: Russia's Enlightened Bureaucrats 1825-1861* (DeKalb, IL: Northern Illionois University Press, 1982).

Lovejoy, Esther Pohl. *Women Doctors of the World* (New York, 1957).

Luk'ianov, P. M. *Istoriia khimicheskikh promyslov i khimicheskoi promyshlennosti Rossii do kontsa XIX veka* (Moscow-Leningrad, 1948).

Mann, Charles C., and Mark L. Plummer. *The Aspirin Wars: Money, Medicine, and 100 Years of Rampant Competition* (New York: Alfred A. Knopf, 1991).

Mawdsley, Evan. *The Russian Civil War* (Boston, MA: Allen and Unwin. 1987).

McAuley, Mary. *Bread and Justice, State and Society in Petrograd, 1917-1922* (Oxford: Oxford University Press, 1991).

McKean, Robert B. *St. Petersburg between the Revolutions* (New Haven, CT: Yale University Press, 1990).

McGrew, Roderick. *Russia and the Cholera, 1823–1932* (Madison, WI: University of Wisconsin Press, 1965).

Mehlinger, Howard D., and John M. Thompson. *Count Witte and the Tsarist Government in the 1905 Revolution* (Bloomington, IN: Indiana University Press, 1972).

Mosse, W. E. *Alexander II and the Modernization of Russia* (New York: Collier Books, 1962).

Motyl, Alex. *The Turn to the Right: Ukrainian Nationalism, 1919–29* (New York: Columbia, East European Monographs, 1980).

Natradze, A. G. *Ocherk razvitiia khimiko-farmatsevticheskoi promyshlennosti SSSR* (Moscow, 1967; 1977).

______. *Russkie i sovetskie farmakopei* (Moscow, 1978).

Nardova, V. A. *Gorodskoe samoupravlenie v Rossii v 60-x-nachale 90-x godov XIX* (Leningrad, 1984).

Nove, Alec. *An Economic History of the USSR* (London, New York: Penguin Books, 1990).

Orlovsky, Daniel T. *The Limits of Reform: The Ministry of Internal Affairs in Imperial Russia, 1802–1881* (Cambridge, MA: Harvard University Press, 1981).

Owen, Thomas C. *The Corporation under Russian Law, 1800–1917: A Study in Tsarist Economic Policy* (Cambridge: Cambridge University Press, 1991).

Parssinen, Terry M. *Secret Passions, Secret Remedies: Narcotic Drugs in British Society, 1820–1930* (Philadelphia: ISHI, 1983).

Pearson, Thomas S. *Russian Officialdom in Crisis: Autocracy and Local Self-Government, 1861–1900* (Cambridge: Cambridge University Press, 1989).

Rabinowitch, Alexander. *Prelude to Revolution: The Petrograd Bolsheviks and the July 1917 Uprising* (Bloomington, IN : Indiana University Press, 1968).

Raleigh, Donald. *Revolution on the Volga: 1917 in Saratov* (Ithaca, NY: Cornell University Press, 1986).

Rigby, T. H. *Lenin's Government: Sovnarkom 1917–1922* (Cambridge: Cambridge University Press, 1979).

Robbins, Richard G. *Famine in Russia, 1891–1892* (New York: Columbia University Press, 1975).

______. *The Tsar's Viceroys: Russian Provincial Governors in the Last Years of the Empire* (Ithaca, NY: Cornell University Press, 1987).

Rodionova, E. I. *Ocherki istorii professional'nogo dvizheniia meditsinskikh rabotnikov* (Moscow, 1962).

Roeske, Wojciech. *Antonina Lesniewska, 1866–1937* (Warsaw, 1970).

______. *Women of Polish Pharmacy* (Warsaw, 1976).

Ruckman, Jo Ann. *The Moscow Business Elite: A Social and Cultural Portrait of Two Generations, 1840–1905* (DeKalb, IL: Northern Illinois University Press, 1984).

Ruud, Charles A. *Russian Entrepreneur: Publisher Ivan Sytin of Moscow, 1851–1934* (Montreal: McGill-Queen's University Press, 1990).

Seregny, Scott J. *Russian Teachers and Peasant Revolution: The Politics of Education in 1905* (Bloomington, IN: Indiana University Press, 1989).

Skorokhodov, L. Ia. *Kratkii ocherk istorii russkoi meditsiny* (Leningrad, 1926).

Smith, R. E. F., and David Christian. *Bread and Salt: A social and economic history of food and drink in Russia* (Cambridge: Cambridge University Press, 1984).

Smith, Steve A. *Red Petrograd: Revolution in the Factories 1917–1918* (Cambridge: Cambridge University Press, 1983).

Snow, Russell E. *The Bolsheviks in Siberia, 1917-1918* (Associated University Press, 1977).

Sonnedecker, Glenn. *History of Pharmacy* (Philadelphia, PA: J. B. Lippincott Co., 3rd edition, 1963; 4th edition, 1976).

Stites, Richard. *The Women's Liberation Movement in Russia* (Princeton, NJ: Princeton University Press, 1961).

Suny, Ronald Grigor. *The Baku Commune 1917–1918* (Princeton, NJ: Princeton University Press, 1972).

Surh, Gerald D. *1905 in St. Petersburg: Labor, Society, and Revolution* (Stanford, CA: Stanford University Press, 1989).

Thompson, John M. *Revolutionary Russia, 1917* (New York: Charles Scribner's Sons, 1981).

Trease, George Edward. *Pharmacy in History* (London, 1964).

Turova, A. D., and E. N. Sapozhnikova. *Lekarstvennye rasteniia SSSR i ikh primenenie* (Moscow, 1984).

Tuve, Jeanette E. *The First Russian Women Physicians* (Newtonville, MA: Oriental Research Partners, 1984).

Valkenier, Elizabeth. *Russian Realist Art, The State and Society: The Peredvizhniki and Their Tradition* (Ann Arbor, MI.: Ardis, 1977).

Valt, L., ed. *Soviet Estonia: Land, People, Culture* (Tallinn, 1980).

Verner, Andrew M. *The Crisis of Russian Autocracy: Nicholas II and the 1905 Revolution* (Princeton, NJ: Princeton University Press, 1990).

Vucinich, Alexander. *Science in Russian Culture: A History to 1860* (Stanford, CA: Stanford University Press, 1963).

______. *Empire of Knowledge: The Academy of Sciences of the USSR (1917–1970)* (Berkeley, CA: University of California Press, 1984).

Wikler, Abraham. *Opiod Dependence* (New York, 1980).

Yaney, George L. *The Systematization of Russian Government* (Urbana: University of Illinois Press, 1973).

Youngblood, Denise J. *Movies for the Masses: Popular cinema and Soviet society in the 1920s* (Cambridge: Cambridge University Press, 1992).

Zaionchkovsky, Peter A. *The Russian Autocracy under Alexander III*, ed. and trans. David R. Jones (Gulf Breeze, Fl.: Academic International Press, 1976).

Dissertations

Sanders, Jonathan E. "The Union of Unions: Political, Economic, Civil, and Human Rights Organizations in the 1905 Russian Revolution," Columbia University, 1985.

Sidorkov, Andrei Mikhailovich. "Issledovanie organizatsionno-metodicheskikh printsipov razvitiia farmatsevticheskogo uchennogo dela v SSSR," Moscow, 1973, located in Tsentral'naia Gosudarstvennaia Nauchnaia Meditsinskaia Biblioteka, Moscow.

Manuscripts

Viktor Matveevich Salo. "Aptechnoe delo v Rossii v XIV-XVII vekakh," chapter I of Book-length MS, "Istoriia farmatsii v Rossii, XVI-pervaia polovina XIX v. v." (in author's possession).

______. On the Pharmacists' Pension Fund (in author's possession).

Index

About the Author

Mary Schaeffer Conroy is an Associate Professor in the Department of History, University of Colorado at Denver. She received her Ph.D. from Indiana University in 1964. She is the author of a book on P. A. Stolypin, Chairman of the Russian Council of Ministers and Minister of Internal Affairs, 1906–1911, and has written a number of articles on the history of medicine and the history of pharmacy.